THE OXFORD HANDBOOK OF

BUDDHIST ETHICS

THE OXFORD HANDBOOK OF BUDDHIST ETHICS

Edited by

DANIEL COZORT

and

JAMES MARK SHIELDS

OXFORD
UNIVERSITY PRESS

OXFORD
UNIVERSITY PRESS

Great Clarendon Street, Oxford, OX2 6DP,
United Kingdom

Oxford University Press is a department of the University of Oxford.
It furthers the University's objective of excellence in research, scholarship,
and education by publishing worldwide. Oxford is a registered trade mark of
Oxford University Press in the UK and in certain other countries

First Edition published in 2018

Impression: 5

Published in the United States of America by Oxford University Press
198 Madison Avenue, New York, NY 10016, United States of America

British Library Cataloguing in Publication Data
Data available

Library of Congress Control Number: 2017959073

ISBN 978–0–19–874614–0

Printed and bound by
CPI Group (UK) Ltd, Croydon, CR0 4YY

From Daniel Cozort

For Clara and Bethany, who bring light and happiness to me and everyone they know.

From James Mark Shields

For my sister, Marie, an early inspiration towards global citizenry.

Contents

List of Abbreviations xi
List of Contributors xiii

Introduction 1
Daniel Cozort and James Mark Shields

PART I FOUNDATIONS

1. Karma 7
Peter Harvey

2. The Bodhisattva Precepts 29
Paul Groner

3. Ethics, Meditation, and Wisdom 51
Justin S. Whitaker and Douglass Smith

PART II ETHICS AND BUDDHIST TRADITIONS

4. Moral Development in the *Jātaka*s, *Avadāna*s, and Pāli *Nikāya*s 77
Martin T. Adam

5. The *Vinaya* 96
Charles S. Prebish

6. *Bhikṣuṇī* Ordination 116
Bhikkhu Anālayo

7. The Changing Way of the Bodhisattva: Superheroes, Saints, and Social Workers 135
Barbra Clayton

8. Madhyamaka Ethics 162
Bronwyn Finnigan

9. Ethics in Pure Land Schools 184
MICHAEL CONWAY

10. A Perspective on Ethics in the *Lotus Sūtra* 205
GENE REEVES

11. Ethics in Zen 221
CHRISTOPHER IVES

12. Tantric Ethics 246
GARETH SPARHAM

13. Buddhist Ethics in South and Southeast Asia 260
JULIANA ESSEN

14. East Asian Buddhist Ethics 279
RICHARD MADSEN

15. Buddhist Ethics in Contemporary Tibet 293
HOLLY GAYLEY

PART III COMPARATIVE PERSPECTIVES

16. Buddhist Ethics Compared to Western Ethics 317
SĪLAVĀDIN MEYNARD VASEN

17. The Psychology of Moral Judgment and Perception in Indo-Tibetan Buddhist Ethics 335
EMILY MCRAE

18. Ethics without Norms? Buddhist Reductionism and the Logical Space of Reasons 359
DAN ARNOLD

PART IV BUDDHISM AND SOCIETY

19. The Buddhist Just Society 385
PETER HARVEY

20. Buddhist Economics: Problems and Possibilities 407
JAMES MARK SHIELDS

21. Buddhist Environmental Ethics: An Emergent and Contextual Approach 432
STEPHANIE KAZA

22. Buddhism, War, and Violence 453
MICHAEL JERRYSON

23. The Ethics of Engaged Buddhism in Asia 479
SALLIE B. KING

24. The Ethics of Engaged Buddhism in the West 501
CHRISTOPHER QUEEN

PART V CONTEMPORARY ISSUES

25. Human Rights 531
DAMIEN KEOWN

26. Buddhism and Women 552
ALICE COLLETT

27. Buddhism and Sexuality 567
AMY PARIS LANGENBERG

28. Buddhist Perspectives on Abortion and Reproduction 592
MICHAEL G. BARNHART

29. Euthanasia 611
DAMIEN KEOWN

30. Being and Its Other: Suicide in Buddhist Ethics 630
MARTIN KOVAN

31. Buddhism and Animal Rights 650
PAUL WALDAU

Index 675

List of Abbreviations

AKB	*Abhidharmakośa-bhāṣyam*
AN	*Aṅguttara Nikāya*
AN-a	*Aṅguttara Nikāya* commentary
Ap i	*Therāpadāna*
Asl	*Atthasālinī*
BCA	*Bodhicaryāvatāra*
CWS	*Collected Works of Shinran*
D	Derge edition
DĀ	*Dīrgha-āgama*
Dhp	*Dhammapada*
Dhs	*Dhammasaṅgaṇī*
Dīp	*Dīpavaṃsa*
DN	*Dīgha Nikāya*
DN-a	*Dīgha Nikāya* commentary
It	*Itivuttaka*
Jat	*Jātaka* and commentary
Khp	*Khuddakapāṭha*
Khp-a	*Khuddakapāṭha* commentary
KN	*Khuddaka Nikāya*
Kvu	*Kathāvatthu*
MECW	*Marx/Engels Collected Works*
Mhv	*Mahāvaṃsa*
Miln	*Milindapañha*
MMK	*Mūlamadhyamakakārikā*
MN	*Majjhima Nikāya*
MN-a	*Majjhima Nikāya* commentary
Ms	*Mahāyāna-saṃgraha*
Mvs	*Mahāvastu*

Pati	*Paṭisambhidāmagga*
Peṭ	*Peṭakopadesa*
PPMV	*Prasannapadā Madhyamakavṛtti*
PS	*Pramāṇasamuccaya*
Pv	*Petavatthu*
PV	*Pramāṇavārttika*
PVin	*Pramāṇaviniścaya*
Q	Peking edition
SN	*Saṃyutta Nikāya*
Sn	*Sutta-nipāta*
Sp	*Samantapāsādikā*
Ss	*Śikṣā-samuccaya*
T	*Taishō shinshū daizōkyō*
Thag	*Theragāthā*
Thig	*Therīgāthā*
TSN	*Trisvabhāvanirdeśa*
Ud	*Udāna*
Uss	*Upāsaka-śīla Sūtra*
Vibh	*Vibhaṅga*
Vibh-a	*Vibhaṅga* commentary
Vims	*Viṃśatikā-kārikā*
Vin	*Vinaya Piṭaka*
Vin-a	*Vinaya Piṭaka* commentary
Vism	*Visuddhimagga*
Vv	*Vimānavatthu*
Vv-a	*Vimānavatthu* commentary

List of Contributors

Contributors

Martin T. Adam (Ph.D., McGill) is Associate Professor of Religious Studies at the University of Victoria. He has published numerous essays and book chapters on Buddhist ethics, and is presently writing a stage play based on Tim Ward's *What the Buddha Never Taught* (2010).

Bhikkhu Anālayo is Professor at the Numata Center for Buddhist Studies, University of Hamburg. Ordained in Sri Lanka in 1995, in 2000 he completed a Ph.D. thesis at the University of Peradeniya and in 2007 a habilitation research at the University of Marburg. His main areas of research are early Buddhism, meditation, and women in Buddhism. He is the author of many articles and books, including *The Foundation History of the Nuns' Order* (2016).

Dan Arnold is Associate Professor of Philosophy of Religions at the University of Chicago Divinity School. He is the author of *Buddhists, Brahmins, and Belief: Epistemology in South Asian Philosophy of Religion* (2005), and *Brains, Buddhas, and Believing: The Problem of Intentionality in Classical Buddhist and Cognitive-Scientific Philosophy of Mind* (2012).

Michael G. Barnhart is Professor of Philosophy and Chair of the Department of History, Philosophy, and Political Science at Kingsborough Community College of the City University of New York. He has written widely on various subjects including the philosophical aspects of Buddhism, comparative ethics, international human rights, political liberalism, and the challenges of moral and epistemological relativism.

Barbra Clayton is Associate Professor of Religious Studies (Asian religions) at Mount Allison University in Canada. In addition to several articles and book chapters on Indian Mahāyāna morality as well as the Shambhala Buddhist community in Canada, she is author of *Moral Theory in Śāntideva's Śikṣāsamuccaya* (2006). Her recent work focuses on Bhutan's policy of Gross National Happiness.

Alice Collett (Ph.D., Cardiff) is Dean of the School of Buddhist Studies, Philosophy and Comparative Religion at Nālandā University, India. Her research has focused on women in early Indian Buddhism and she has published several books, articles, and book chapters on the topic. She is editor of *Women in Early Indian Buddhism: Comparative Textual Studies* (Oxford, 2013), and author of *Lives of Early Buddhist Nuns: Biographies as History* (Oxford University Press India, 2016). She is currently working on a funded project on women in early Buddhist inscriptions.

Michael Conway is Lecturer in the Shin Buddhist Studies Department at Otani University in Kyoto, Japan. His research interests span over much of the Shin doctrinal tradition, from its roots in China to its modern and contemporary iterations in Japan and elsewhere. He wrote his Ph.D. thesis on Daochuo, the fourth of the seven Shin patriarchs, and has published several articles on Shinran and the creation of the Shin tradition.

Daniel Cozort is Professor of Religion at Dickinson College (Carlisle, PA). A native of North Dakota, he earned a B.A. at Brown University and an M.A. and Ph.D. at the University of Virginia. His research has concerned facets of Highest Yoga Tantra (*annuttara-yoga-tantra*) and the Prāsaṅgika-Mādhyamaka philosophical school as understood in the Tibetan Gelukba tradition. He is the author of six books (including *Highest Yoga Tantra, Unique Tenets of the Middle Way Consequence School*, and *Buddhist Philosophy*), book chapters, journal articles, reviews, and a film about sand mandalas. He has been General Editor of the *Journal of Buddhist Ethics* since 2006.

Juliana Essen (Ph.D., University of Minnesota, Twin Cities) is Chief Impact Officer for the National Peace Corps Association. She was founder and Executive Director of the Global Well-Being Institute, and has taught at the Soka University of America. Her research interests are in Buddhist economic ethics, particularly in the context of Southeast Asia. She is author of *'Right Development': The Santi Asoke Buddhist Reform Movement of Thailand* (2005).

Bronwyn Finnigan is Lecturer in the School of Philosophy, RSSS, at the Australian National University. She works primarily in metaethics, moral psychology, and philosophy of mind in Western and Asian philosophical traditions. She is a member of the Cowherds that authored *Moonshadows: Conventional Truth in Buddhist Philosophy* (Oxford, 2010), and has published on Buddhist and Madhyamaka metaethics.

Holly Gayley is Associate Professor in the Department of Religious Studies at the University of Colorado Boulder. Her research examines the revitalization of Buddhism on the Tibetan plateau since the 1980s with a special interest in issues of gender, agency, ethics, and identity in contemporary writings by Buddhist masters and cleric-scholars. She is author of *Love Letters from Golok: A Tantric Couple in Modern Tibet* (2016).

Paul Groner (Ph.D., Yale) is professor emeritus at the University of Virginia. He is particularly interested in Japanese Tendai and the history of precepts and ordinations in Japan. Among his publications are *Saicho: The Establishment of the Japanese Tendai School* (2000) and *Ryogen and Mount Hiei: Japanese Tendai in the Tenth Century* (2002).

Peter Harvey is Emeritus Professor of Buddhist Studies at the University of Sunderland, UK. His research focuses on early Buddhist thought and practices, and Buddhist ethics. He edits *Buddhist Studies Review*, journal of the UK Association for Buddhist Studies, and is author of *An Introduction to Buddhism: Teachings, History and Practices* (1990; 2013), *The Selfless Mind: Personality, Consciousness and Nirvana in Early Buddhism* (1995) and *An Introduction to Buddhist Ethics: Foundations, Values and Practices* (2000).

Christopher Ives is a Professor of Religious Studies at Stonehill College. In his scholarship he focuses on ethics in Zen, and currently he is working on Zen approaches to nature and environmental issues. His publications include *Imperial-Way Zen: Ichikawa Hakugen's Critique and Lingering Questions for Buddhist Ethics* (2009) and *Zen Awakening and Society* (1992).

Michael Jerryson is Associate Professor of Religious Studies at Youngstown State University. His research interests pertain to religion and identity, particularly with regard to gender, race, and class. He is editor of *The Oxford Handbook of Contemporary Buddhism*, and author of *If You See the Buddha on the Road: Essays on Buddhism, Politics, and Violence* (Oxford, forthcoming).

Stephanie Kaza is professor emerita of Environmental Studies at the University of Vermont. Her books include *Dharma Rain: Sources of Buddhist Environmentalism* (2000) and *Hooked! Buddhist Writings on Greed, Desire, and the Urge to Consume* (2005). She is currently working on Buddhist approaches to food practice and climate change.

Damien Keown is Emeritus Professor of Buddhist Ethics at Goldsmiths College, University of London. His main research interests are theoretical and applied aspects of Buddhist ethics, with particular reference to contemporary issues. He is the author of many books and articles including *The Nature of Buddhist Ethics* (1992; 2001), *Buddhism and Bioethics* (2001), *Buddhism: A Very Short Introduction* (Oxford, 2000), *Buddhist Ethics: A Very Short Introduction* (Oxford, 2006), and the *Oxford Dictionary of Buddhism* (Oxford, 2003). In 1994 he co-founded *The Journal of Buddhist Ethics* with Charles S. Prebish, with whom he also co-founded the Routledge Critical Studies in Buddhism Series.

Sallie B. King is Professor Emerita of Philosophy and Religion at James Madison University and Affiliated Faculty, Professor of Buddhist Studies, Department of Theology, Georgetown University. She works in the areas of Buddhist philosophy and ethics; engaged Buddhism; Buddhist–Christian dialogue; and the cross-cultural philosophy of religion. She is the author of *Being Benevolence: The Social Ethics of Engaged Buddhism* (2005), and *Socially Engaged Buddhism* (2009).

Martin Kovan is completing doctoral research in philosophy at the University of Melbourne: a Buddhist-metaphysical account of intrahuman lethality, particularly in its state-sanctioned, religious, and terroristic forms. His published essays concern Buddhist violent and non-violent resistance, Tibetan Buddhist self-immolation, and theoretical issues between Buddhist political engagement and human rights, psychology and agency, and normative and metaethics.

Amy Paris Langenberg (Ph.D., Columbia) is Assistant Professor of Religious Studies at Eckerd College. A specialist in Indian Buddhism, her research interests include Buddhist legal traditions, Buddhist understandings of sexuality, gender, and body, and Buddhist medicine. In addition to numerous articles, she is author of *Birth in Buddhism: The Suffering Fetus and Female Freedom* (2017).

Richard Madsen is Distinguished Professor of Sociology Emeritus, adjunct professor of the Graduate School of Global Policy and Strategy, and Director of the UC-Fudan Center for Contemporary Chinese Studies at the University of California, San Diego. He is a co-author (with Robert Bellah et al.) of the *The Good Society* and *Habits of the Heart*, which received the Los Angeles Times Book Award and was jury nominated for the Pulitzer Prize. He has authored or co-authored seven books on China, including *Morality and Power in a Chinese Village* (1984) for which he received the C. Wright Mills Award; *China's Catholics: Tragedy and Hope in an Emerging Civil Society* (1998); and *China and the American Dream* (1995). His latest single-authored book is *Democracy's Dharma: Religious Renaissance and Political Development in Taiwan* (2007).

Emily McRae is Assistant Professor of Philosophy at the University of New Mexico. She specializes in Tibetan Buddhist philosophy, ethics, moral psychology, and feminism. Much of her work is in the philosophy of emotions. She has published articles on these topics in *American Philosophical Quarterly, Philosophy East and West, Journal of Religious Ethics*, and *History of Philosophy Quarterly*. Her translation (with Jay Garfield) of nineteenth-century Tibetan master Patrul Rinpoche's *Essential Jewel of Holy Practice* is forthcoming.

Charles S. Prebish is Professor Emeritus at both the Pennsylvania State University and Utah State University (where he held the Charles Redd Endowed Chair in Religious Studies). His books *Buddhist Monastic Discipline* (1975) and *Luminous Passage: The Practice and Study of Buddhism in America* (1999) are considered classic volumes in Buddhist Studies. In 1993 he held the Visiting Numata Chair in Buddhist Studies at the University of Calgary. In 2005 he was honoured with a Festschrift volume entitled *Buddhist Studies from India to America: Essays in Honor of Charles S. Prebish* (2005).

Christopher Queen is a lecturer on World Religions and Buddhist Studies in the Harvard University Division of Continuing Education, where he served as Dean of Students and Alumni Affairs for twenty years. His holds degrees in religion, theology, and the history and phenomenology of religion from Oberlin College, Union Theological Seminary, and Boston University. He co-edited and contributed to *Action Dharma: New Studies in Engaged Buddhism* (2003); *Engaged Buddhism in the West* (1995;

2000); *American Buddhism: Methods and Findings in Recent Scholarship* (1998); and *Engaged Buddhism: Buddhist Liberation Movements in Asia* (1996), and has published numerous articles, chapters, and reference entries on contemporary Buddhism in Asia and the West.

Gene Reeves has retired from Meadville Lombard Theological School at the University of Chicago, Tsukuba University in Japan, and Renmin University of China. He has been a scholar in residence at Rissho Kosei-kai in Tokyo for nearly thirty years and has lectured widely in East Asia, Europe, and the United States, primarily on the Lotus Sutra. He is translator of *The Lotus Sutra: A Contemporary Translation of a Buddhist Classic* (2008) and author of *The Stories of the Lotus Sutra* (2010).

James Mark Shields is Professor of Comparative Humanities and Asian Thought at Bucknell University (Lewisburg, PA). Educated at McGill University (Canada), the University of Cambridge (UK), and Kyoto University (Japan), he conducts research on modern Buddhist thought, Japanese philosophy, comparative ethics, and philosophy of religion. He has published numerous chapters, articles, and translations in peer-reviewed journals, including *Asian Philosophy, The Eastern Buddhist, Japan Review, Studies in Religion / Sciences religieuses, Japanese Journal of Religious Studies, Journal of Religion and Society, Kultura i Politkya*, and *Philosophy, Culture and Traditions*. He is author of *Critical Buddhism: Engaging with Modern Japanese Buddhist Thought* (Farnham, Surrey, 2011), and co-editor (with Victor Sōgen Hori and Richard P. Hayes) of *Teaching Buddhism in the West: From the Wheel to the Web* (London, 2003). He is the Associate Editor of the *Journal of Buddhist Ethics*. He is currently working on a book manuscript on progressivism and radicalism in modern Japanese Buddhism.

Douglass Smith (Ph.D., Wisconsin-Madison) is an independent scholar whose research interests include early Buddhism, secular Buddhism, and comparative philosophy.

Gareth Sparham has taught at the University of Michigan and University of California. He is the translator of Tsongkhapa's *Tantric Ethics: An Explanation of the Precepts for Buddhist Vajrayāna Practice* (2005). His recent publications include a series of translations of Indian and Tibetan Perfection of Wisdom (*prajñāpāramitā*) commentaries in eight volumes.

Sīlavādin Meynard Vasen studied philosophy in Holland and Belgium. His research interests are ethics, phenomenology, and analytical philosophy of mind, especially the area around subjectivity and selfhood. He is a member of the Triratna Buddhist Order.

Paul Waldau is Professor at Canisius College. An educator who works at the intersection of animal studies, law, ethics, religion, and cultural studies, he has been the senior faculty for the Master of Science graduate program in Anthrozoology since its founding in 2011. He has also taught at Harvard Law School and Tufts University School of Veterinary Medicine. He has completed five books, the most recent of which are *Animal*

Studies: An Introduction (Oxford, 2013) and *Animal Rights* (Oxford, 2011). He is also co-editor of the groundbreaking *A Communion of Subjects: Animals in Religion, Science, and Ethics* (2006).

Justin S. Whitaker (PhD, University of London) is an independent scholar whose research interests include early Buddhism, comparative philosophy, ethics, and mindfulness.

INTRODUCTION

DANIEL COZORT AND JAMES MARK SHIELDS

MANY forms of Buddhism, divergent in philosophy and style, emerged as Buddhism filtered out of India into other parts of Asia. But all of them embodied a moral or ethical core that was, and remains, remarkably consistent. Articulated by the historical Buddha in his first sermon, this moral core is founded on the concept of karma—that intentions and actions have future consequences for an individual—and is summarized as Right Speech, Right Action, and Right Livelihood, three of the eight elements of the Eightfold Path. Although they were later elaborated and interpreted in a multitude of ways, none of these core principles was ever abandoned. Inasmuch as the Buddhist ideal is one of human perfection—or perfectibility—ethics is an important, arguably central, concern. This is complicated, however, by the fact that the early texts also indicate that achievement of *nirvāṇa* involves a transformation or purification of consciousness, which links ethics closely to meditation, epistemology, and even metaphysics.

Ethical conduct is emphasized in Buddhism as in few other religions in part because it has historically been a tradition led by renunciants, the monks and nuns of the *saṅgha*. They operate under the guidance of an elaborate set of rules: 227 for fully ordained monks and 311 for nuns in the Theravāda tradition. The *saṅgha* collectively is Buddhism's moral exemplar. Ethics are also particularly important in Buddhism because its religious ideal is not submission or obedience to a particular deity, but rather the perfection of virtue and the attainment of insight. Hence, although in practice many Buddhists merely observe the Five Precepts (against misconduct) and support the *saṅgha*'s material needs, they admire and aspire to higher ethical standards. In the modern period, more explicit forms of 'lay Buddhism' have emerged in various parts of Asia and the West. Here too, ethics is considered a central aspect of living the *Dharma*, though in its encounter with the West Buddhist ethics often takes on new forms—or at least adopts new terms—including the discourse of 'rights' and 'social justice'.

The academic study of Buddhism has existed in the West for several centuries, and for much longer, perhaps up to two millennia, in the various regions of Asia in which Buddhism has flourished. The past forty years in particular have witnessed a flourishing of Buddhist scholarship within both Western and Asian academies. However, recognition of the importance of ethics within Buddhism has not, at least until recently, resulted in much critical, scholarly treatment. In the past twenty years, the sub-discipline of Buddhist ethics has expanded in terms of the breadth of methodological perspective and depth of inquiry.[1]

Scholars have used Buddhist resources to analyse a number of contemporary controversies, including human rights, women's rights, sexuality, war, terrorism, violence, social, economic, and retributive justice, as well as various issues of concern to biomedical and environmental ethics. One area that has seen significant development is the scientific study of the effects of meditation on the brain, which has been accompanied by a growth of studies connecting Buddhist thought and practice to psychotherapy and psychology more generally. Although this work is still very much ongoing, it has already produced some fascinating results, many of which have direct implications for ethics. Finally, beyond matters of philosophical and applied ethics, anthropologists and sociologists have studied the effect of Buddhism upon various cultures of Asia, an area of research that we feel should also be included in the broader field of Buddhist ethics.

Setting aside a number of non-academic works written from the standpoint of a particular sect or tradition such as Zen or Tibetan Buddhism, few books have attempted a cross-cultural and pan-sectarian analysis of ethics in Buddhist traditions. Two early English-language works on Buddhist ethics were Winston King's *In the Hope of Nibbana* (La Salle, 1964) and Sinhalese scholar-monk Hammalawa Saddhattissa's *Buddhist Ethics* (Boston, 1970; republished 1997). Yet the former is focused entirely on Theravāda (and specifically Burmese) tradition, while the latter, though more comprehensive than anything previously written, is primarily concerned with early Buddhism. Neither deal with contemporary issues or critical, historical scholarship.[2] Damien Keown's *The Nature of Buddhist Ethics* (Basingstoke, 1992; reprinted with minor revisions 2001) may be the best single introduction to Buddhist ethics from a philosophical perspective. But because its primary concern is elucidating the 'structure' of Buddhist ethics, it does not deal with contemporary moral and ethical issues. Among Keown's other works is *Buddhist Ethics: A Very Short Introduction* (Oxford, 2005), an excellent, but 'very brief' survey/guide.

[1] One important venue for this scholarship is the *Journal of Buddhist Ethics*, founded in 1994 by Charles Prebish and Damien Keown as the first journal entirely dedicated to the subject. The *JBE* has grown steadily and is now one of the largest journals in the field of Buddhist Studies. Both editors of this handbook have worked extensively with the *JBE*: Cozort as Editor-in-Chief since 2006 and Shields as Book Review Editor from 2002 to 2012 and Associate Editor from 2012.

[2] Four decades previously, Japanese scholar Tachibana Shundō (1877–1955), Professor of Pali and Primitive Buddhism at Komazawa University, penned what is very likely the first book to appear in English dedicated to Buddhist ethics: *The Ethics of Buddhism* (Oxford, 1926). In the Preface, Tachibana notes as precedents two works published in German: Paul Dahlke's *Buddhismus als Religion und Moral* (Breslau, 1914) and Wolfganag Bohn's *Die Psychologie und Ethik des Buddhismus* (Munich/Wiesbaden, 1921). Tachibana claims that only Pāli Buddhism takes 'morality' as wisdom (Mahāyāna, he notes, looks to philosophy, and roots its ethics in 'pantheism').

The standard in the field is Peter Harvey's *An Introduction to Buddhist Ethics* (Cambridge, 2000). It addresses many social, biomedical, and other ethical issues. However, it is, as its title suggests, an introduction and as such does not go deeply into the complexities of its subject. It is also now seventeen years old and hence is missing recent scholarship. Other notable recent books on Buddhist ethics are specialized to a particular subfield of ethics (*Buddhism and Bioethics; Buddhism and Human Rights; Zen Buddhism and Environmental Ethics*; etc.).

The *Oxford Handbook of Buddhist Ethics* differs from Harvey—as well as the other works mentioned above—in the following ways. First, it aspires to be comprehensive. With thirty-one essays in different areas, it covers most if not all of the important topics of Buddhist ethics. Among the topics not treated by Harvey, for instance, are 'Buddhism and the Psychology of Moral Judgments'; 'Buddhist Ethics and Cognitive Sciences'; and 'Tantric Ethics'. Second, its topics receive a much deeper treatment than was possible in an introductory text. Third, many topics are updated by more recent developments such as Asian movements for social justice and environmental protection, Tibetan self-immolations, and the revival of the order of *Bhikkhunīs* (fully ordained nuns). Fourth, it is organized not by Buddhist traditions but by major topic areas that can treat subjects across traditions and over time; the topic areas have been adapted from the successful model of the *Journal of Buddhist Ethics*. Finally, the *Handbook* is not the work of a single scholar attempting to master the entire Buddhist tradition; it is a collaboration of twenty-nine authors who are specialists in their assigned areas and who represent the finest standards of scholarship in Buddhist studies.

We hope that this volume will be of the greatest interest to those scholars around the globe working in the areas of Buddhist ethics and comparative moral philosophy. However, because of its scope it will also be of interest to anyone concerned with contemporary ethical problems and the social, psychological, economic, and political ramifications of religious doctrines. This volume could furnish the 'Buddhist perspective' for anyone interested in comparing the views of various religions on particular topics such as those of biomedical ethics. The *Oxford Handbook of Buddhist Ethics* is intended as a comprehensive overview of the state of the field of Buddhist ethics in the second decade of the twenty-first century.

PART I

FOUNDATIONS

CHAPTER 1

KARMA

PETER HARVEY

Introduction: The Central Place of the Ideas of Karma and Rebirth in Buddhist Thought

While beliefs in karma and rebirth were common in the Buddha's day, as part of Brahmanism and Jainism, they were not universal: Ājīvikas believed in rebirth driven by an impersonal force of destiny, rather than personal karma; materialists denied karma and rebirth; and sceptics saw no basis for either affirming or denying them.

Karma and rebirth beliefs are a central theme in Buddhism, but the Buddha is portrayed as having meditation-based personal knowledge of them, rather than simply having accepting them from his cultural environment. He is said to have awakened to them on the night of his enlightenment (MN I.247–249). From a state of great meditative calm, mindfulness, and sensitivity he developed the 'threefold knowledge': memory of many of his countless previous lives; seeing the rebirth of others according to their karma; and the destruction of the deep-seated spiritual taints which keep the mind unawakened and bound to repeated rebirths, so as to attain the Deathless, *nirvāṇa* (Pāli *nibbāna*).

The rebirth of beings according to the quality of their actions—good actions leading to relatively more pleasant rebirths, and bad ones leading to the more unpleasant ones—showed how beings moved within the many realms of sentient existence, experiencing ageing, sickness, death, and many other forms of *dukkha* (Pāli; Skt *duḥkha*): physical and mental pains, whether obvious or subtle, especially when one responds to them with grasping or aversion. While craving and ignorance determine *that* a person is reborn, *how* a person is reborn is seen to depend on their karma, their intentional actions. Whether good or bad, these *matter*, for they leave a trace on the psyche which shapes character, life-scenarios, and future rebirths.

For the Buddha, the epitome of the kind of right view that conduces to a good destiny in the round of rebirths, if not being pitched at the level of liberating wisdom, is:

> There is gift, there is offering, there is (self-)sacrifice [i.e., these are worthwhile]; there is a fruit and ripening of actions that are well done and ill done; there is this world, there is a world beyond [this world is not unreal, and one goes to another world after death]; there is mother and father [it is good to respect parents, who established one in the world]; there are spontaneously arising beings [there are also kinds of rebirth, such as in the heavens, in which beings arise without parents]; there are in this world renunciants and brahmins who are faring rightly, practising rightly, and who proclaim this world and a world beyond having realized them by their own higher-knowledge. (MN III.72)

To deny this is the epitome of wrong view (MN I.402), as expressed by the materialist Ajita Kesakambalī (DN I.55).

The Nature of Karma

In the Buddha's teaching, understanding and improving one's karma or action (Pāli *kamma*, Skt *karma*) help one to: (1) live more happily in the present life; (2) avoid a subhuman rebirth and attain a human or heavenly rebirth which is happier in itself and with more opportunities for spiritual development; and (3) develop the kind of wisdom-based mental actions that can cut off all rebirths.

In all of this, ethics is central. For the Buddha, the ethical quality of the impulse behind an action was the key to its being good or bad, rather than its conformity with ritual or class norms, as in Brahmanism (Gombrich 2006: 67–70; 2009: 19–44). Ritual is only helpful if it helps develop wholesome states of mind; hence things such as bowing and chanting Buddhist texts have a role. Moreover, in contrast with the Jains, the Buddha saw karma as essentially mental in nature. It is the volitional impulse or intention behind an act: 'It is volition (*cetanā*), O monks, that I call karma; willing, one acts through body, speech or mind' (AN III.415). Even thinking of doing some bad action is itself a bad (mental) karma, especially when one gives energy to such a thought, rather than just letting it pass. Deliberately letting go of such a thought is a good mental karma. The psychological impulse behind an action is 'karma', which then sets going a chain of causes culminating in a pleasant or unpleasant karmic result. Actions must be intentional if they are to generate karmic results: accidentally treading on an insect does not have such an effect, as Jains believe.

The Nature of *Cetanā*

Cetanā is variously translated as 'will', 'volition', and 'intention'. It is not 'will', though, as a factor that stands outside other conditioned mental states, totally 'free', but is itself a conditioned and conditioning state. As it is the impulse that immediately leads to action, *cetanā* is not 'intention' in the sense of a plan, a resolve to do something in the future, which may or may not actually be done (as in 'my intention was to visit him today, but something came up, so I could not'). That said, resolving to do an action in the future is itself a *present* mental action, which will have its own *cetanā*. Maria Heim (2014: 42) agrees it does not mean an intention to do a future action, but otherwise uses 'intention' as its translation. 'Volition' is a generally workable translation, with the related verb 'wills', to translate *ceteti*. 'Volition' may lack something of the full goal-directedness of 'intention', yet 'intention' is lacking in the impelling force of 'volition'.

The *Milindapañha* (61) says: 'Being willed/intended (*cetayita-*), sire, is the characteristic of *cetanā* and a characteristic is concocting (*abhisankharaṇa-*).' A simile then explains that just as someone might 'concoct' a poison or a delightful drink that would afflict or please those who drink it, so one who 'through volition, having willed (*cetanāya cetayitvā*)' an unwholesome or wholesome action, would be reborn in a hell or heavenly rebirth; and likewise for someone inspired to act in the same way. That is, *cetanā* brings together factors in an action that leads to future karmic results.

The Theravādin commentator Buddhaghosa defines *cetanā* thus:

> 'It wills' (*cetayatī ti*), thus it is *cetanā*; 'it puts together' (*abhisandahatī ti*) is the meaning. Its characteristic is the state of *cetanā*. Its function is directing towards (*āyūhana-*[1]). It is manifested as co-ordination (*saṃvidahana-*). It accomplishes its own and others' functions, as a senior pupil, a head carpenter etc. do. But it is evident when it occurs in the state of the instigation (*ussāhana-bhāvena*) of associated states in connection with urgent work, remembering and so on. (Vism. 463)

That is, *cetanā* gathers together and organizes various mental qualities and directs them towards a certain objective accomplished by an action (see Heim 2014: 41 n. 18). Heim summarizes, 'It is a dynamic activity of collecting and animating rather than a state, decision, choice or inclination' (2014: 105), that is:

> a matter of coordinating quite a large number of other mental factors ... [which] contribute to morally relevant thought and agency in complex ways not limited to either rational deliberation or various appetitive forces, but invoking sensibilities, motivational roots, faculties, aptitudes, energies, functions. Such a depiction stretches considerably beyond modern conceptions of intention construed as a combination of belief and desire and some kind of relation between them. (2014: 106)

[1] Pati. I.52 equates *āyuhanā* with the second of the links of Conditioned Co-arising, the *saṅkhāras*.

The Pāli *Nikāyas* define the fourth of the five *khandhas*, 'constructing activities' (*saṅkhārā*), in terms of *cetanā*, as: 'these six classes of *cetanā*: volition (*sañcetanā-*) regarding visual forms, sounds, smells, tastes, tangibles and mind-objects', these *cetanās* being (most immediately) conditioned by sensory contact (*phassa*) (SN III.63). In the Abhidhamma, though, the constructing activities (note the plural) are explained as *cetanā* along with a number of processes that initiate action or direct, mould, and give shape to character (e.g. Bodhi 1993: 91). Among these are processes which are ingredients of all mind states, such as sensory contact and attention, ones which intensify such states, such as energy, joy, or desire-to-do, ones which are ethically 'wholesome', such as mindfulness and a sense of moral integrity, and 'unwholesome' ones, such as greed, hatred, and delusion (e.g. Bodhi 1993: 76–91). A selection of these states are what *cetanā* brings together in carrying out an action, a karma.

Further, in the Theravāda (Bodhi 1993: 77–78) and Sarvāstivāda (AKB II.24) Abhidhammas, *cetanā* is a universal mental factor, thus occurring in every kind of mind state, including those of *arahants*, who generate no more karmic results, and ones that are the result of past karma and make no new karma. Thus while all *cetanā* is directed towards something—it is intentional—some forms of *cetanā* lack the factors of collecting and directing that generate karmic results. Asl. 111 explains:

> Its function is directing towards (*āyūhana-*); there is no *cetanā* in the four planes of existence [including actions of an *arahant*] that does not have the characteristic of being intended (*cetayita-*). All have the characteristic of being intended, but the state of the function of directing towards is only in regard to what is wholesome or unwholesome; once the role of directing (associated states) towards wholesome and unwholesome action is attained, there is only a partial role for the remaining associated states. But volition (*cetanā*) is exceedingly energetic; it makes a twofold instigation (*diguṇa-ussāhā-*), a twofold effort (*diguṇa-vāyāmā*).

This is explained to mean that *cetanā* is like a cultivator directing strong men at harvest time, or a coordinating chief disciple or general, who incites others by acting themselves (Asl. 111–112).

The Relation between the Karmic Results of an Action and Ethical Assessment of the Action

A bad action is seen to have bad, i.e. unpleasant, karmic results, but its having these results is not what makes it 'bad'. Hence there is talk (MN I.389–391, cf. DN I.163, SN V.104) of:

(1) 'Action that is dark and with a dark ripening (*kammaṃ kaṇhaṃ kaṇha-vipākaṃ*)': one 'generates an activity (*saṅkhāraṃ abhisaṅkharoti*)' of body speech or mind that is 'afflictive (*sabyābajjahaṃ*)' and hence is reborn in an 'afflictive' world such as hell, with afflictive contacts and afflictive, painful feelings. AN II.234 explains dark actions as killing, stealing, sexual misconduct, lying, and taking intoxicants.
(2) 'Action that is bright (*sukkaṃ*) with a bright ripening': generating unafflictive activities, so as to be reborn in an unafflictive world, such as a heaven. AN II.234 explains bright actions as abstention from killing etc.

This makes clear that while the nature of an action's karmic ripening corresponds to the nature of the action, it does not determine its nature. A 'dark' action is not to be counted as dark because it has a dark karmic result; rather, it has a dark result because it is itself dark: causing affliction here and now. Its having dark karmic results is a *sign* of its dark, afflictive, unwholesome nature, but not the *criterion* for its being unwholesome in the first place. Nevertheless, other passages hardly neglect to mention karmic results, in the form of pleasant or unpleasant experiences—perhaps as additional motivating or demotivating factors for the actions—and of course do concern themselves with the immediate (non-karmic) effects of actions on both others and oneself.

Wholesome and Unwholesome Actions and Their Roots

In Buddhism, one should avoid actions criticized by the wise (AN I.89) and a 'good' action is generally referred to as *kusala* (Pāli, Skt *kuśala*): informed by wisdom and thus 'skilful' in producing an uplifting mental state in the doer, or 'wholesome' in that it involves a healthy state of mind (Cousins 1996; Harvey 2000: 42–43). A 'bad' action is *akusala*: 'unwholesome/unskilful'. Key criteria for an action being 'unwholesome' is its conducing to the harm of oneself, of others, or of both (MN I.415–416), and its being 'destructive of intuitive wisdom, associated with distress, not conducive to *nirvāṇa*' (MN I.115). Correspondingly, a 'wholesome' action does not conduce to any such harm, but does conduce to the growth of wholesome states of mind (MN II.114). The 'harm' to oneself that is relevant here is spiritual harm, or material harm if this arises from self-hatred. In other respects, an act that benefits others at the expense of material harm to oneself is certainly not unwholesome. Thus one should avoid 'corrupt and harmful (*sandosa-vyāpatti*) actions of unwholesome volition (*akusala-sañcetanikā*) with painful consequences (*dukkhudrayā*), (karmically) ripening in suffering (*dukkha-vipākā*)', and do 'beneficial actions of wholesome volition, with happy consequences, ripening in happiness' (AN V.292–297).

In a detailed analytical survey that I conducted (Harvey 2011) of the factors related to an unwholesome/unskilful actions in the Pāli Canon, my summary was that they involved:

1. unwise attention, feeding
2. attachment/greed/covetousness, hatred/ill-will, delusion/ignorance, which are both 'the unwholesome' and are roots that sustain
3. 'the unwholesome': specified unwholesome actions of body, speech, or mind,
4. that are of unwholesome volition, and intentional,
5. that are dark, corrupt, with fault/blameable (*sāvajjaṃ*) (by the wise), as they
6. bring pain and injury to oneself or to others
7. in a way that is anticipated by correct perception of the immediate facts of the situation,
8. such that one should not inflict on another what one would not like inflicted on oneself
9. and are criticized by the wise,
10. as not to be done,
11. and that, as a karmic result, bring dark harm and pain in this and later lives to the agent, as well as
12. unwholesome character tendencies,
13. obscuring wisdom and moving one away from *nirvāṇa*.

Wholesome actions have the opposite qualities.

In the *Sammādiṭṭhi Sutta* is a passage (MN I.46–47) that identifies typical *akusala* and *kusala* actions and makes clear what lies at the root of such actions:

> When, friends, a noble-disciple understands the unwholesome (*akusalañ*) and the root of the unwholesome (*akusala-mūla-*), the wholesome and the root of the wholesome, in that way he is one of right view, whose view is straight, who has perfect confidence in the *Dhamma* and has arrived at this true *Dhamma*.
>
> And what is the unwholesome? ... Killing living beings is the unwholesome; taking what is not given is the unwholesome; misconduct in sensual pleasures is the unwholesome; false speech is the unwholesome; divisive speech is the unwholesome; harsh speech is the unwholesome; frivolous chatter is the unwholesome; covetousness is the unwholesome; ill-will is the unwholesome; wrong view is the unwholesome. This is called the unwholesome.
>
> And what is the root of the unwholesome? Greed is a root of the unwholesome; hatred is a root of the unwholesome; delusion is a root of the unwholesome. This is called the root of the unwholesome.
>
> And what is the wholesome? Abstention from ... [the above ten actions]. This is called the wholesome.
>
> And what is the root of the wholesome? Non-greed is a root of the wholesome; non-hate is a root of the wholesome; non-delusion is a root of the wholesome. This is called the root of the wholesome.

In this passage, 'the unwholesome' is explained as consisting of specific actions of body and speech that are widely recognized as harmful to others, plus mental states that are likely later to lead to such harmful actions. Greed, hatred, and delusion are presented here as the inner *causes* of 'the unwholesome', though not the *criteria* for labelling something as 'the unwholesome'. They are, though, themselves unwholesome (AN I.201).

As regards the nature of greed, hatred, and delusion: (1) greed (*lobha*) covers a range of states from mild longing up to full-blown lust, avarice, fame-seeking, and dogmatic clinging to ideas; (2) hatred (Pāli *dosa*, Skt *dveṣa*) covers mild irritation through to burning anger and resentment; and (3) delusion (*moha*) is expressed in stupidity, confusion, bewilderment, dull states of mind, ingrained misperception, specious doubt on moral and spiritual matters, and turning away from reality by veiling it from oneself. As to the opposites of these: (1) non-greed (*alobha*) covers states from small generous impulses through to a strong urge for renunciation of worldly pleasures; (2) non-hatred (*adosa*) covers friendliness through to forbearance in the face of great provocation, and deep loving-kindness and compassion for all beings; and (3) non-delusion (*amoha*) covers clarity of mind through to the deepest insight into reality. While phrased negatively, these three are more than the mere *lack* of their opposites. They are positive states in the form of anti-greed (generosity and renunciation), anti-hatred (loving-kindness and compassion), and anti-delusion (wisdom).[2]

Karmically Fruitful ('Meritorious') Actions

Good actions are said to be 'beautiful' (*kalyāṇa*) and to be, or have the quality of, *puñña* (Pāli, Skt *puṇya*), which term is either an adjective or noun. As an adjective, Lance Cousins sees it as the 'fortune-bringing or auspicious quality of an action' (1996: 153), while as a noun 'it is applied either to an act which brings good fortune or to the happy result in the future of such an act' (1996: 155). Thus we see:

> Monks, do not be afraid of *puñña*s; this, monks, is a designation for happiness, for what is pleasant, charming, dear and delightful, that is to say, *puñña*s. I myself know that the ripening of *puñña*s done for a long time are experienced for a long time as pleasant, charming, dear and delightful. (It. 14–15, cf. AN IV.88–89)

Puñña is usually, rather limply, translated as 'meritorious' (adjective) or 'merit' (noun). However, 'meritorious' implies being deserving of reward, praise, or gratitude, but *puñña* refers to something with a natural power of its own to produce happy results; it does not depend on anyone to give out what is due to the 'deserving'. In Christian

[2] As indicated by the fact that Dhs. 32–34 treats them as positive presences.

theology, 'merit' referred to a good deed seen to have a claim to a future reward from a graceful God, an idea that ill fits Buddhism. A *puñña* action is 'auspicious', 'fortunate', or 'fruitful', as it purifies the mind and thus leads to future good fortune (McDermott 1984: 31–58). The Sanskrit word *puṇya* may derive from the root *puṣ*, 'to thrive, flourish, prosper', or *pū*, 'to make clean or clear or pure or bright'; hence a Theravāda commentary explains '*puñña*' by saying 'it cleanses and purifies the life-continuity' (Vv-a. 10; Bodhi 1990, cf. AKB IV.46a–b). The effect of the translation 'merit' is to produce a flattened, dispirited image of this aspect of Buddhism, rather than conveying an uplifting and admirable action. Admittedly, *puñña* alone will not bring awakening, as wisdom is needed for this, but it does help prepare the ground for this.

As the noun *puñña* refers to the power of good actions as seeds for future happy fruits, an appropriate translation is '(an act of) karmic fruitfulness', with 'karmically fruitful' as the adjective. The *Saṅgha* is described as the best 'field of *puñña*', i.e. the best group of people to 'plant' a gift 'in' as regards good results of the gift, hence 'like fields are the *arahants*; the givers are like farmers. The gift is like the seed, (and) from this arises the fruit' (Pv. I.1). In defence of the above translation, while karmic results can be of either good *or* bad actions, and *puñña* relates only to good actions, the English word 'fruit' can also mean only edible, pleasant fruit such as apples, without referring to inedible, unpleasant ones. One might use the translation 'karmically beneficial', but this lacks a tone of inspiring uplift.

The opposite of *puñña* is *apuñña*, which one can accordingly see as meaning a '(act of) karmic harm' or 'karmically harmful', i.e. producing no pleasant fruits, but only bitter ones. A synonym for *apuñña* is *pāpa*, which, while often translated as 'evil' or 'bad', really means that which is 'infertile', 'barren', 'harmful' (Cousins 1996: 156) or 'bringing ill fortune'.

Buddhists are keen to perform 'karmically fruitful' actions; for *puñña* is an unlosable 'treasure', unlike physical goods (Khp. 7). The early texts refer to three 'bases for effecting karmic fruitfulness' (*puñña-kiriya-vatthus*): giving (*dāna*—especially by giving alms to monastics), ethical discipline (*sīla*), and meditative cultivation of wholesome qualities (DN II.218). Later texts add: showing respect, helpful activity, sharing karmic fruitfulness, rejoicing at the karmic fruitfulness of others, teaching *Dhamma*, listening to *Dhamma*, and straightening out one's views (DN-a III.999). Any act of giving is seen as karmically fruitful, even giving in the hope of some return, or giving purely to get the karmic result of giving. A purer motive, however, is seen as leading to a better karmic result. Thus it is particularly good to give from motives such as the appreciation of a gift as helping to support a holy way of life, or of the calm and joy that giving naturally brings (AN IV.60–63). While a large gift is generally seen as more auspicious than a small one, purity of mind can also make up for the smallness of a gift, for 'where there is a heart of calm and joyful faith (*citta-pasāde*), no gift is small' (Jat. II.85). Indeed, a person with nothing to give can act auspiciously by simply rejoicing at another person's giving. The same principle, of course, logically implies that if one verbally or mentally applauds someone else's unwholesome action, one is performing an unwholesome action oneself. For other aspects of karmic fruitfulness, see Harvey (2000: 17–23).

Degrees of Gravity of Good and Bad Actions

Acts of giving are perhaps the most typical ones seen to generate karmic fruitfulness, but the degree of this depends both on the purity of mind of the giver, and the virtue of the recipient (MN III.255–257). It is said that a gift to an animal yields a hundredfold, to an unvirtuous human a thousandfold, to an ordinary virtuous human a hundred thousandfold, and to a person of one of the Noble stages, it has an immeasurable fruit. The virtue and spiritual development of the recipient is seen to have this multiplying effect as giving to them makes an inspiring connection to an embodiment of wholesome states, which engenders much joy in the giver so as to have a powerful purifying effect. Mahāyāna texts add that it is particularly beneficial to give gifts to one's parents or the sick.[3]

Correspondingly, it is seen as worse, and generating more bad karmic results, to intentionally harm a more virtuous being.[4] It is also said to be more unwholesome to kill a larger insect, bird, or animal than a smaller one, as this requires more force of action and volition. It is worse to kill a human, and amongst humans, it is worse to kill a more virtuous person. In any case, the act is made worse by stronger defilements lying behind it. One can summarize this by saying that an unwholesome act is made worse according the strength or perversity of the volition of which it is a manifestation (Harvey 2000: 52).

The most heinous actions are to deliberately kill one's mother or father, or an *arahant*, to shed the blood of a Buddha, or cause a schism in the monastic *Saṅgha*. Such acts definitely lead to one's next rebirth being in hell for the remainder of an aeon.[5] This must be seen as because such acts harm those for whom one should have great respect.

Other aspects of a bad action affect its seriousness and karmic effect. It needs to be intentional (Harvey 1999, 2007a), and is worse if one is full control of oneself; it is less bad if one is unclear or mistaken about whether a living being is being harmed, and is worst when one fully knows the harmful effect of one's action but does not see anything wrong in it, so that one does not hold back on or regret the act (Harvey 2000: 52–58). Regretting a bad (or good) action, and resolving not to do it again, lessens its karmic result as it reduces the psychological impetus from the act (Harvey 2000: 26–28). However, while painful feelings at the thought of a past act may be part of its karmic result, entertaining heavy guilt feelings is seen as associated with (self-)hatred, and as an anguished state which is not conducive to calm, clarity, and thus spiritual improvement.

[3] *Mahāparinirvāṇa Sūtra*, T 12, 374, 38, 549b29–50b18.

[4] MN-a I.198, Khp-a 28–29, Asl. 97, Vibh-a 382–383, AKB IV.73a–b, Uss. 165.

[5] Vibh. 378, MN-a IV.109–110; Harvey 2000: 24–25.

The Sharing of Karmic Fruitfulness

All Buddhist traditions accept the idea that the beneficial effects of good actions—their karmic fruitfulness or 'merit'—can be shared with others. Typically this is done by sharing with a dead relative the karmic fruitfulness of acts of generosity to the monastic *Saṅgha*.

In Theravāda tradition, a karmically fruitful act may not only be performed by empathizing (*anumodanā*) with someone else's auspicious deed, but also by the auspicious quality of an act (*patti*, what has been gained) being transferred to or shared with another being. The Buddha was once asked by a brahmin if gifts given to a brahmin in the hope that they are transferred on to a deceased relative actually do benefit the dead. He replied that the dead will benefit only if reborn as departed ghostly beings known as *petas* (Pāli; Skt *pretas*), for these live either on the putrid food of their realm or on what is provided by gifts from relatives and friends (AN V.269–272, cf. Miln. 294). The *Petavatthu* accordingly describes a number of instances where a gift is given in the name of a suffering *peta*, so that they attain rebirth as a god due to the karmic fruitfulness of the giving. Theravāda rites for the dead therefore include the feeding of monks and the transference of the karmic fruitfulness to the deceased, or whatever other ancestors may be *petas*, in the hope that this will ease their lot as *petas* or help them to a better rebirth.

Another early text has the Buddha say that it is wise to support monks and to dedicate the gift to the local gods, so that they will look with favour on the donor (DN II.88). The gods are seen as having less opportunity to do auspicious deeds themselves, but can benefit from transferred karmic fruitfulness, which helps maintain them in their divine rebirth; in return, it is hoped that they will use whatever powers they have to aid and protect Buddhism and the person making the donation. A boy ordaining as a novice or full monk will also share the karmic fruitfulness of this act with his mother. Here, her karmic fruitfulness will come from both the act of 'giving up' her son to the monkhood, and her rejoicing at his auspicious act.

Given the Buddhist stress on the idea that someone can only generate karmic fruitfulness by their own deeds, the idea of 'transferring' it is potentially anomalous. To avoid such an anomaly, the Theravāda commentaries developed an orthodox interpretation, and Tibetan Buddhists have a similar idea. This is that no karmic fruitfulness is actually transferred, but that the food, etc. donated to monks is dedicated, by the performer of the auspicious donation, to an ancestor or god, so that the donation is done on their behalf, with their property. Provided that they assent to this donation-by-proxy by rejoicing at it, they themselves generate karmic fruitfulness. By a living being affirming someone else's action as good, particularly if it is done on their behalf, they directly perform a positive mental action of their own.

The idea of sharing karmic fruitfulness helps to modify any tendency in the karma doctrine to encouraging people to 'amass' karmic fruitfulness for themselves, like a kind of non-physical money in the bank. Karmic fruitfulness can and should be shared with others. Giving, for example, generates karmic fruitfulness; then when this is shared with others, there is another generous act which generates more karmic fruitfulness: the more karmic fruitfulness is shared, the more there is of it—unlike with money or material goods—and happiness increases in the world! Sharing karmic fruitfulness is a way of spreading the karmic benefits of good deeds to others, as a gesture of goodwill. This is expressed in the traditional simile to explain such sharing: lighting many lamps from one.

In Mahāyāna traditions, bodhisattvas on the first of the ten stages are urged to dedicate their good karma to the future buddhahood of themselves and others. Such transfer (*pariṇāmanā*) of karmic fruitfulness is seen as possible because karmic fruitfulness is 'empty' and does not inherently 'belong' to any particular 'being'. In the Mahāyāna, the aspiration is usually that karmic fruitfulness is shared with *all* beings, and typically to help them attain enlightenment. Humans should transfer it for the benefit of other humans, and beings in unfortunate rebirths. They should also transfer it to buddhas and bodhisattvas with a view to increasing their perfections and virtues (Ss. 205–206). In turn, though, bodhisattvas and buddhas are seen as transferring it to devotees who ask for such help in faith. Śāntideva praises the transfer of karmic fruitfulness in the final chapter (X) of his *Bodhicaryāvatāra*, aspiring that, by the good karma generated by his writing this poem, humans and other beings should be free from various afflictions and be endowed with morality, faith, wisdom, and compassion.

In verse 56 (cf. Ss. 256–257), he even prays that the sufferings of the world should ripen in him: that he should take on the bad karma of others, not just give them his karmic fruitfulness. How might this be possible? Perhaps by totally empathizing with a person who has acted badly, one becomes attuned to their actions and may generate some bad karma for oneself; and the experience of being empathized with and understood may help the other person reflect on their own past bad actions, regret them, and so lighten their karmic results.

The Mahāyāna idea of gaining rebirth in a Pure Land—a realm presided over by a buddha where the conditions for attaining enlightenment are ideal—also draws on the idea of the transfer of karmic fruitfulness. Pure Lands are seen as outside the normal system of rebirths, including heavenly ones, according to personal karma. To be reborn in one requires not only the dedication of one's own karmic fruitfulness to this end, but also a transfer of some of the huge stock of karmic fruitfulness of a land's presiding buddha, stimulated by devout prayer. This 'transfer' can perhaps be seen as brought about by a devotee's so rejoicing at the great virtues of the relevant buddha that this becomes a mental act of great karmic fruitfulness.

Is There Group Karma?

To what extent can karma relate to groups of people, rather than only to an individual? As volitional involvement is required to generate karmic results, then actions of other people can only bring an individual karmic results to the extent that that individual *approves* of such actions or is somehow involved in them (Payutto 1993: 68). This is because one kind of action is mental action. So, if one approves of a bad or good action carried out by someone else, this is a volitional action that generates corresponding karmic results—though probably not as strong as for those who physically do the action.

If one *orders* someone to do an action, one is as karmically involved as the person who does the action, if not more so. Again, if a group of people work together towards a common goal, e.g. robbing a bank, they share in the karmic results of this. That said, if someone is killed in the course of a robbery, only those who were aware of this as a possibility would get the karmic results of killing. This has implications for killing by an army. Vasubandhu, giving the Sarvāstivāda view, says that when an army kills, all the soldiers are as karmically involved as the ones who directly do the killing, for by sharing in a common goal (which here is bound to involve some killing) they mutually incite one another. Even someone forced to become a soldier is karmically involved, unless he has previously resolved, 'Even in order to save my life, I shall not kill a living being' (AKB IV.72cd). That said, defensive violence is not as bad as offensive violence, and if a killing is done against the rules of engagement, this aspect is only karmically relevant for those who do or approve of this kind of killing.

Also relevant is how an individual's actions are influenced by the actions of people with whom they associate (cf. AN II.158) or the actions of their society as a whole. To the extent that someone goes along with bad influences from others, they are likely to do a kind of bad action that is common within their social group.

The above has implications for whether there is such a thing as 'national karma'. For example, if someone approves of the past bad actions of his or her nation's army, then they will generate some bad karmic results for themselves. Also, of course, people who are reborn as humans *may* be rebirths of a member of a past generation from the same country.

Karmic 'Seeds' and When They Bring Their Results

The precise details of how actions bring karmic details are seen to be so complex as to be 'unthinkable' except to a buddha (AN IV.77), but certain general principles can be discussed. The Theravāda *Abhidhammattha-saṅgaha* and its commentary talks of: (a) 'weighty' karma, such as heinous bad actions or the strong wholesome actions such as attaining *jhāna*; (b) 'near' karma done or recalled near the time of death; (c) 'habitual' karma, which is done often, or is often dwelt on; (d) otherwise 'effective' karma. (a)–(d) is seen as the order of precedence as to which kind of karma ripens first after death. Also, some karma ripens in this life, some in the next, some at some later time, if it gets the opportunity, but some minor karma never gets the opportunity to ripen (Bodhi 1993: 203–205; Wijeratne and Gethin 2002: 174–177).

This implies that karma is not seen as just about habits, as habitual karma is only one kind of karma. Actions are more like seeds, which may be more or less potent, and take time to mature, when the conditions are right. Yet the analogy of a 'seed' has its limits, as seeds do not normally affect each other, while, at AN I.249–253, it is said that the same bad action done by a generally virtuous and an unvirtuous person will have a worse karmic effect on the latter, just as a pinch of salt in a cup of water has a bigger effect than in the Ganges. This suggests that good actions can 'dilute' the effect of bad actions, at least so as to make their 'seeds' less potent. For a detailed discussion of the Sarvāstivāda and Sautrāntika view of karma, which has had a variable influence on Mahāyāna traditions, see AKB IV.1–127.

The Range of Kinds of Rebirth

The cycle of rebirths is seen as involving innumerable lives over vast stretches of time. These lives can be in a variety of kinds of realm. A human rebirth is seen as relatively rare (AN I.35); while the human population has been increasing, there are still many more other creatures. Mahāyāna Buddhists talk of having attained a 'precious human rebirth' (Guenther 1971: 14–29; cf. DN III.263–264): a marvellous opportunity for spiritual growth that should be used wisely and respected in others. As it may be cut short at any time by death, it should not be frittered away. To be reborn as a human requires past good karma.

Animal rebirths include sentient creatures as simple as insects, along with fish, birds, and land animals. Plants are not included as a type of rebirth, though they are seen as having a very rudimentary consciousness in the form of sensitivity to touch (Vin.I.155–156).

Rebirth as a *peta* (Skt *preta*), literally the 'departed', is as a frustrated ghostly being who inhabits the fringes of the human world due to strong earthly attachments, not unlike the ghosts of Western literature. One type of *peta*, generally known as a 'hungry ghost', is portrayed as having a huge stomach, racked by hunger, and a tiny neck that allows little sustenance to pass.

The worst realm is hell (*niraya*), comprising a number of hellish rebirths. These are described as involving experiences of being burnt up, cut up, frozen, or eaten alive, yet being revived to re-experience these (e.g. MN III.183). They are, then, realms in which a tortured consciousness experiences abominable nightmares, where every object of the senses appears repulsive and ugly (SN IV.126). Some hells are worse than others, but all are seen as appropriate to the bad deeds that led to them. While life in the hells is measured in millions of years, *no* rebirth is eternal, so a being from hell will in time reach the human level again.

The animal, *peta*, and hell realms are the lower rebirths, where beings suffer more than humans. The Buddha is seen as compassionate in having warned people of the danger in actions that lead to such rebirths. The higher, more fortunate realms of rebirth are those of humans and *devas*, 'illustrious ones' or gods. Together all the above rebirths comprise the five realms. Sometimes this becomes six, by adding the *asuras*, the demi-gods, seen as proud, fierce, power-hungry divine beings (counted among the lower rebirths).

The gods are said to live in twenty-six heavens, which are grouped according to a threefold classification of rebirths. The lowest of these is the 'realm of sense-desire' (*kāma-dhātu*), which encompasses all the rebirths mentioned so far, including the six lowest heavens. In all of these realms, beings perceive sensory objects in such a way as to particularly notice their qualities of desirability or undesirability.

More subtle than and 'above' the realm of sense-desire is the 'realm of (pure, elemental) form' (*rūpa-dhātu*). Here dwell more refined gods, who are known in general as *brahmās*, in contrast to the *devas* proper of the six lower heavens. In the realm of form there are said to be sixteen heavens of a progressively more refined and calm nature. Beings at this level of existence are aware of objects in a pure way devoid of sensuous desire, and are without the senses of touch, taste, and smell. They suffer from other attachments and limitations, however.

More refined than the form realm is the 'formless realm' (*Pāli arūpa-dhātu*; Skt *ārūpya-dhātu*), which is comprised of the four most refined types of rebirth. They are purely mental 'spheres' (*āyatana*) completely devoid of anything having even subtle shape or form. They are named after the characteristic states of consciousness of the *brahmās* reborn 'there'. In the first, they have the experience of 'infinite space', i.e. contentless space in its limitless expanse; in the second, they dwell on the 'infinite consciousness' which can contemplate infinite space; in the third, they experience the apparent 'nothingness' (or no-thingness) of their level of existence; in the last, their resting state of consciousness is so subtle that their sphere is that of 'neither-perception-nor-non-perception'. This last rebirth, the 'summit of existence', is the highest and most subtle form of life in the cosmos, with a huge lifespan of 84,000 aeons; and yet even this eventually ends in death. All these rebirth realms parallel the kinds of human mental states and actions that are seen to lead to them; hence Buddhism has a kind of 'psycho-cosmology' (Gethin 1997; 1998: 112–132).

The Results of Karma in This and Other Lives

Living an ethical life is said to variously lead to: wealth, through diligence; a good reputation; self-confidence in all kinds of company, without fear of reproach or punishment; dying without anxiety; and rebirth in a good world (DN II.86). Unwholesome actions have the opposite kind of results. Virtue also gives a good basis for developing the meditative calm of *jhāna*, which then tends to rebirth in a corresponding heaven, as well as preparing the mind for insight. In order to attain *nirvāṇa*, a person must be able to perform a transcendental action, namely the attainment of deep insight into reality (AN II.230–232).

The movement of beings between rebirths is seen as governed by the principle that beings are 'heir' to their actions (MN III.203). It is said in the Tibetan tradition[6] that acts of hatred and violence tend to lead to rebirth in a hell, acts bound up with delusion and confusion tend to lead to rebirth as an animal, and acts of greed tend to lead to rebirth as a ghost.

A person's actions mould their consciousness, making them into a certain kind of person, so that when they die their outer form tends to correspond to the type of nature that has been developed. If bad actions are not serious enough to lead to a lower rebirth, or after having already done so, they affect the nature of a human rebirth: stinginess leads to being poor, injuring beings leads to frequent illnesses, and anger leads to being ugly—an extension of the process whereby an angry person gradually develops ugly features during their present life (MN III.203–206). Poor, ill, or ugly people are not to be presently blamed for their condition, however, for the actions of a past life are behind them, and the important thing is how they act and how others treat them now. But if bad karma can lead to being poor, that is not the same as saying that being poor cannot arise from other causes.

Is Everything Due to Karma?

Karma is seen as bringing about its effects partly through events in the world and the actions of other people. Does this mean that everything is due to karma? The answer, for the Theravāda tradition, is 'no': most things in the animate and inanimate world are seen as *not* due to karma, though they are conditioned in other ways.

At AN V.109–110, it is said that bodily afflictions include:

> ... illnesses (*ābādhā*) originating from bile, phlegm, wind, or a combination of these; illnesses produced by seasonal change (*utu-pariṇāma-jā*); illnesses produced by careless behaviour (*visama-parihāra-jā*); illnesses produced by exertion (*opakkamikā*[7]); or illnesses produced as a result of karma (*kamma-vipākāni-jā*) ...

SN IV.229–231 lists these as the various causes of (unpleasant) feelings (*vedayitāni*), such that it is incorrect to say, 'Whatever this person experiences, whether pleasant or painful or neither painful nor pleasant, all that is due to what was done earlier.'

[6] Gampopa's 'Jewel Ornament of Liberation' (Guenther 1971: 79), citing Nāgārjuna's *Ratnāvalī*.

[7] This may alternatively mean an effort of someone else, an assault, as at AN-a III.114 on AN II.87, though regarding an illness, it is more likely to mean a person's own exertion.

This passage is discussed at *Milindapañha* 134–138, where King Milinda is described as wrongly thinking 'all that is experienced is rooted in karma'. The monk Nāgasena points out the various causes of feelings, as above, and denies that karma underlies them all. Bodily winds, for example, can arise from a number of physical causes, though *some* do also arise due to past karma. On feelings in general, he says, 'small is what is born of the maturing of karma, greater is the remainder' (135). Of course, to suffer from human illnesses, one must be reborn a human, and have the karma for this, so in a general sense all illnesses have some karmic input. And genetic illnesses must be seen by a Buddhist as specifically due to karma, as one gets one's genes from one's parents but who one's parents are is a result of one's karma.

In Theravāda Abhidhamma, there is a view that is potentially at odds with the idea that there are many events in the world not due to karma. It is held that in any sense channel, e.g. the visual, there is a sense-consciousness rapidly followed by mind-consciousnesses that make sense of and respond to such an object. What is important, here, is that the initial eye-, ear-, nose-, tongue- and body-consciousness are all seen as results of past karma.[8] How can this be, if what they are conscious *of* is regarded as generally *not* due to past karma? A combination of three possible answers seems appropriate:

1. Karma determines what kind of being someone is reborn as, and as different kinds of beings have different kinds of sense organs, which are sensitive in different ways—e.g. human sight compared to that of a fly or eagle—then the form of a being's consciousness is influenced by karma.
2. A certain visual scene may not be due to past karma, but that a certain person is in a particular location so as to see it can be seen as possibly due to past karma.
3. Even if there are two people in the same place, they will notice different aspects of what is available to see, for example one will tend to notice pleasant aspects, and the other unpleasant. It is in this sense that their sense-consciousnesses can be seen as the result of past karma: it filters awareness of the surrounding environment so that only particular 'edited highlights' tend to be noticed.

The third explanation is not explicitly given in any text, but fits in well with other Buddhist ideas. It is supported by a passage at SN I.91–92, which recounts a tale of a man who is rich due to having given alms to a *pacceka-buddha* in a past life, but a miser unable to enjoy what wealth might buy due to later having regretted his generosity. Here, one can say, past karma entails that the man only notices unpleasant, unenticing aspects of the world. One's experienced world is shaped by one's karma-shaped character, as implied by SN I.62:

> It is in this fathom-long carcase, which has perception and mind, that, I declare, lies the world, and the arising of the world, and the cessation of the world, and the course that goes to the cessation of the world.

[8] Dhs. secs. 431 and 556, and see also Miln. 65, Vism. 488, and Harvey 1995: 151–152, 255.

That is, what one notices in the outer world, and how one labels and thinks about this—which all becomes 'the world' to one—is a construction shaped by the kind of person one is, which comes from one's cravings and attachments and karma.

In the Yogācāra, one of the schools of Mahāyāna philosophy, the question of whether everything is due to karma is set in a different context. This is because it holds—depending on how it is interpreted—either that (a) only mental phenomena exist, or that (b) all we ever have *access* to is the flow of experience, with any concept of a material world being a projected construct.

If a material world does not exist (interpretation a), then a physical body does not exist apart from the *experience* of 'body'. Hence there can be no physical causes in the body or environment that could be non-mental causes of feelings or illnesses. This makes it most plausible to see these as the result of past karma. In fact, the Yogācāra sees the flow of experiences as the ripening of karmic seeds generated by one's previous actions and stored in the *ālaya-vijñāṇa*—the 'storehouse consciousness' that is a background unconscious level of the mind—and matured by the subtle influence of *vāsanās* or perfuming 'impressions' generated by ingrained attachment to mental constructions.[9] Nevertheless, experiences that are part of *new* actions are not the result of past karma, and experiences can also arise from the actions of other mind-streams (Vims. vv.18–20), i.e. other beings. On interpretation b, we can know nothing of the body and illnesses other than the mental experience of them, which is greatly shaped by past karma. We cannot *know* of any causal sequences in 'the body itself' that could work independently of the mind in causing experienced illnesses, and it would seem that medical knowledge can only relate the *experienceable* features of 'medicines' and 'bodily processes'.

The Yogācāra does not hold that we all inhabit totally private worlds, though. The similarity in people's karmic 'seeds' means that our 'worlds' have much in common, though different types of being are seen as perceiving the 'same object' very differently: while humans see a river as a source of washing and drinking, for fish it is just their home environment, and for 'hungry ghosts' it is a stream of pus and excrement which cannot assuage their ravaging thirst (Ms. 2.4). This idea does imply that there is an extra-mental 'something' that is being perceived differently, which supports interpretation b.

Does Past Karma Remove Freedom of Action in the Present?

To what extent does Buddhism hold that past karma determines new karma in the present? As character often affects what actions one does, and character is largely seen as a product of past actions, does this limit freedom? A relevant passage here is MN III.169–171, where it is said that a being that is reborn in hell will take a very long time

[9] Harvey 2013: 127–138; Williams 2009: 97–100; Waldron 2003.

before regaining a human rebirth, for this is harder than a blind turtle putting its neck through ring floating on the ocean, when it only surfaces once a century. Even when a human rebirth *is* regained, the person will be poor, ugly, ill, or deformed *and* will behave badly, so as to return to hell! In contrast to this, MN III.177–178 says that a wise man who upholds the ethical precepts will be reborn in a heaven and only 'once in a very long while' will he be reborn as a human. When this does occur, he will be rich and handsome, etc., will behave virtuously, and so return to a heaven. In both cases, the effects of karma are seen as lasting a very long time, and even the patterns of good and bad actions, and thus the character traits which prompt these, are seen as similarly recurring: the form and directedness of character is seen as continuing over the ages.

Nevertheless a passage at SN I.93–96 has a different emphasis. It holds that one born as an outcaste, or as a hunter, or poor, ill-fed, ill-featured, diseased, or a cripple (due to relatively bad past karma), may do either evil *or* good actions, hence being reborn in a hell *or* heaven. Likewise for a person who is born as a Brahmin or as noble, rich, or good-looking. This implies that one is not stuck with carrying on in evil—or in good. Together, then, these passages imply that a past evildoer only *tends* to continue in evil. The pattern can be changed, perhaps by a bad person coming under the good influence of others (or vice versa), as with the murderous Aṅgulimāla (MN II.97–105) when he is confronted by the Buddha and goes on to become an *arahant*. It may also be changed by consistently acting in the best way one's current character tends to allow. One can think of a person's character as tending to be expressed in a characteristic spectrum of wholesome and unwholesome actions. Over time, the more a person acts towards the wholesome end of the spectrum, the more their character develops in a wholesome direction, so that their spectrum shifts its range to include more strongly wholesome actions and less strongly unwholesome actions. Focusing actions at the unwholesome end of the spectrum has the opposite effect. One becomes the kind of person one makes oneself, within one life, and from life to life.

An *arahant* is one who operates only with a wholesome spectrum, and has destroyed the roots that would have made a return to unwholesome actions possible. Indeed, Thig. 400–447 gives an account of a woman who had previously had a string of bad rebirths in hell or as an animal, but who becomes a Buddhist nun and then an *arahant*, a liberated person. There is a tendency to carry on in old character patterns set up by past actions, though one can also break out from these. If new karma was simply the result of past karma, this would entail that one would be condemned to eternally repeat the mistakes of the past, and would not be responsible for one's actions.

The Buddha in fact criticized any theories that undermined the idea of responsibility for action. These included:

1. Two forms of fatalism, which respectively saw all experiences (pleasant, unpleasant, or neutral) and associated actions as due either to past karma (*pubbe kata-hetu*) or the creation of a God (*Issara-nimmāna-hetu*).
2. A form of indeterminism, which saw all experiences as without any cause or condition (*ahetu-appaccayā*), being due to pure chance (AN I.173–175; cf. MN II.214).

The Buddha saw each of these views as implying that any action, e.g. being a murderer, is due to past karma (cf. Kvu. 545–546), a deity's action, or chance, presumably due to the feelings accompanying such acts being so based. He thus saw those who held such views as supporting 'inaction' (*akiriya*): if one is not responsible for one's actions, the will to act in a wholesome way, and not an unwholesome one, is paralysed. But one nearly always has some degree of choice.

Is it problematic, though, that Buddhism sees a person's karma as sometimes 'catching up' with them through the actions of other people (e.g. Thig 400–447, AN II.32)? A person's past karma might be the cause of their being murdered, injured, insulted, or offered poor or good alms food. So does this idea compromise the freedom, and thus responsibility, of the person who 'delivers' a person's bad karmic result: say of a murderer, if his victim's death is due to the victim's own bad karma? I think not. If person X is murdered by Y due to X's own karma, Y's freedom can be retained if:

a) X's character is the result of his past karma and is such as to provoke the easily irritated Y into murdering him, or
b) Due to his karma, X unconsciously puts himself into a position where Y feels that it is advantageous to murder him: note that Moggallāna's murder is seen as having been ordered by ascetics jealous of his success in gaining converts (Jat. V.126), or
c) Y is intent on killing an unspecified person(s) (e.g. due to madness, war, or terrorism), and X's karma determines that it is *X* who is killed.

In all three cases, Y's self-chosen action (unless mad) fulfils, as it happens, X's karma, without Y being a passive, blameless agent of X's karma coming to fruition. So, there is no good reason to see one's actions as sometimes determined by *other* people's past karma.

For Buddhism, karmic results of a particular action are actually seen to vary, so past karma does not inflexibly determine a fixed result, produced in a mechanical-like way. Only intentional actions bring karmic results, and even then, the result may vary according to the nature of the person that does the act, the results being worse for a morally and spiritually undeveloped person (AN I.249–253; *Mahā-parinirvāṇa Sūtra*, T 12, 374, 38, 549b29–50b18): in this case, the bad action 'reverberates' so to speak, with other such actions, undiluted by many good actions. Without this flexibility, it is held that there would be 'no living of the holy life, no opportunity for the utter destruction of suffering' (AN I.249). Not only does regret reduce the karmic effect of a (bad or good) past action, but when a person attains 'stream-entry', the first glimpse of *nirvāṇa*, they are free of any rebirths at less than a human level (SN V.357). While this must be partly due to the fact that they, from now on, always act morally, it must also imply that any previous bad karma that might have led to a bad rebirth can now no longer do so. So karmic results are not inflexibly determined by past karma alone, but also need cooperating conditions to foster their arising, and these may modify the form and timing of their arising (Thanissaro 1996: Part I, B, cf. Vism 601–602).

The Question of Free Will

As for the broader issue of whether Buddhism accepts 'free will' in the context of it seeing all mental states, including volition, as arising from conditions, there is not space here to fully discuss it. Suffice it to say that if there were a will or self that was *un*conditioned, it would be permanent and unchanging, and hence not capable of *doing* anything, as the arising of an impulse to action is a change. But a conditioned being can have a degree of self-direction, and this quality can grow as mindfulness increases and helps the undermining of limiting mental defilements (Harvey 2007b, 2016).

Karma and *Nirvāṇa*

While Buddhists aim to avoid bad actions and do good actions, even good actions have their limitations, in that the good rebirths that they lead to are still within the conditioned realm of existences that entail suffering and death. *Nirvāṇa*, though, is a state beyond birth, death, rebirth, and suffering. So the ideal karma is not even 'bright', good karma/action. Hence MN I.390 says that beyond actions that are bright, dark, or mixed is 'action that is neither dark nor bright with neither-dark-nor-bright ripening, action that leads to the destruction of action': the 'volition for abandoning' the latter three kinds of action. AN II.236 explains this kind of action as the factors of the Noble Eightfold Path, and AN I.263 sees actions born of non-greed, non-hatred, and non-delusion as leading to the cessation of (rebirth-fuelling) actions. AN III.384–385 sees *nirvāṇa* as neither dark nor bright, in the sense of neither a bad nor a good rebirth. Thus while wholesome actions generally lead to more pleasant rebirths, some have the potential to lead beyond all rebirths and their diverse forms of suffering.

Works Cited

Bodhi, Bhikkhu (1990) Merit and spiritual growth. In: *Nourishing the roots: essays on Buddhist ethics*. Kandy: Buddhist Publication Society, 13–17. Available from: http://www.bps.lk/olib/wh/wh259.pdf

Bodhi, Bhikkhu (ed.) (1993) *A comprehensive manual and Abhidhamma: the Abhidhammattha Sangaha: Pali text, translation and explanatory guide*. Kandy: Buddhist Publication Society.

Cousins, L. S. (1996) Good or skilful? *kusala* in canon and commentary. *Journal of Buddhist ethics*, 3, 136–164.

Gethin, R. (1997) Cosmology and meditation: from the *Aggañña Sutta* to the Mahāyāna. *History of religions*, 36, 183–219.

Gethin, R. (1998) *The foundations of Buddhism*. Oxford and New York: Oxford University Press.

Gombrich, R. F. (2006) *Theravāda Buddhism*, second edition. London and New York: Routledge.

Gombrich, R. F. (2009) *What the Buddha thought*. London: Equinox.

Guenther, H. V. (1971) *The jewel ornament of liberation*. Berkeley: Shambhala.

Harvey, P. (1995) *The selfless mind: personality, consciousness and nirvana in early Buddhism*. London: Curzon Press.

Harvey, P. (1999) *Vinaya* principles for assigning degrees of culpability. *Journal of Buddhist ethics*, 6, 271–291.

Harvey, P. (2000) *An introduction to Buddhist ethics: foundations, values and issues*. Cambridge: Cambridge University Press.

Harvey, P. (2007a) Avoiding unintended harm to the environment and the Buddhist ethic of intention. *Journal of Buddhist ethics*, 14, 1–34.

Harvey, P. (2007b) 'Freedom of the will' in the light of Theravāda Buddhist teachings. *Journal of Buddhist ethics*, 14, 35–98.

Harvey, P. (2011) An analysis of factors related to the *kusala/akusala* quality of actions in the Pali tradition. *Journal of the International Society of Buddhist Studies*, 33, 175–210.

Harvey, P. (2013) *Introduction to Buddhism: teachings, history and practices*, second edition. Cambridge: Cambridge University Press.

Harvey, P. (2016) Psychological versus metaphysical agents: a Theravāda Buddhist view of free will and moral responsibility. In: R. Repetti (ed.), *Buddhist perspectives on free will: agentless agency?* London and New York: Routledge, 158–169.

Heim, M. (2014) *The forerunner of all things: Buddhaghosa on mind, intention and agency*. Oxford: Oxford University Press.

McDermott, J. P. (1984) *Development in the early Buddhist concept of kamma/karma*. Delhi: Motilal Banarsidass.

Payutto, P. A. (1993) *Good, evil and beyond: kamma in the Buddha's teaching*. Bangkok: Buddhadhamma Foundation Publications. Available from: http://www.buddhanet.net/pdf_file/good_evil_beyond.pdf

Thanissaro (1996) *The wings to awakening: an anthology from the Pali Canon*. Barre, MA: Barre Center for Buddhist Studies.

Waldron, W. S. (2003) *The Buddhist unconscious: the ālaya-vijñāna in the context of Indian Buddhist thought*. London and New York: RoutledgeCurzon.

Wijeratne, R. P., and Gethin, R. (2002) *Summary of the topics of Abhidhamma and exposition of the topics of Abhidhamma*. Oxford: Pali Text Society.

Williams, P. (2009) *Mahāyāna Buddhism: the doctrinal foundations*, second edition. London and New York: Routledge.

Suggested Reading

Cousins, L. S. (1996) Good or skilful? *kusala* in canon and commentary. *Journal of Buddhist ethics*, 3, 136–164.

Gethin, R. (1998) *The foundations of Buddhism*. Oxford and New York: Oxford University Press, esp. 112–132, 140–146, 215–218.

Harvey, P. (2000) *An introduction to Buddhist ethics: foundations, values and issues*. Cambridge: Cambridge University Press, esp. 8–66.

Harvey, P. (2011) An analysis of factors related to the *kusala/akusala* quality of actions in the Pali tradition. *Journal of the International Society of Buddhist Studies*, 33, 175–210.

Heim, M. (2014) *The forerunner of all things: Buddhaghosa on mind, intention and agency.* Oxford: Oxford University Press.

Nagapriya (2004) *Exploring karma and rebirth.* Birmingham: Windhorse.

Payutto, P. A. (1993) *Good, evil and beyond: kamma in the Buddha's teaching.* Bangkok: Buddhadhamma Foundation Publications. Available from: http://www.buddhanet.net/pdf_file/good_evil_beyond.pdf.

CHAPTER 2

THE BODHISATTVA PRECEPTS

PAUL GRONER

Introduction

THE precepts of the *Vinaya* have remained relatively unchanged through Buddhist history, but their practice has evolved, sometimes through ignoring or emphasizing practices delineated in them. One of the main ways in which practice evolved was through the development of bodhisattva precepts, which were found in Mahāyāna scriptures attributed to the Buddha. Terms such as 'Mahāyāna precepts', 'the perfection of morality', 'sudden-perfect precepts', and the 'bodhisattva precepts' refer to the rules and attitudes that motivated Mahāyāna practitioners or bodhisattvas. A great variety of these rules appear in Mahāyāna texts, some simply as vague rubrics and others with considerable detail. Descriptions and analyses of the wide variety of these rules and their primary sources that were included in the Chinese canon are found in a comprehensive study by Ōno Hōdō, *Daijō kaikyō no kenkyū* (Studies of Mahāyāna *prātimokṣa*).

In all of these cases, however, one must be aware of the difference between interpreting these as *prescriptions* of behaviour and *descriptions* of how people actually behaved. Although in the case of India, we usually do not know how broadly these precepts were applied or how influential a text was at a particular time or place, the situation becomes clearer in China and Japan; as a result, this essay will focus on how these precepts were interpreted in China and Japan. The study is divided into two parts: a survey of a variety of sets of bodhisattva precepts with an emphasis on sets found in Indian Yogācāra texts and apocryphal texts (compiled in China, but passed off as Indian). The second part concerns some of the ethical issues that the interpretation of the bodhisattva precepts presented, with particular emphasis on the Tendai school of Japan. I focus on Tendai because it represents the greatest challenge to traditional Buddhist views of the precepts, with Tendai monks violating many of the most basic precepts. Even as they violated the precepts, some of the more serious Tendai monks were concerned with how their actions could be justified, leaving us with some penetrating analyses of Buddhist ethics.

A Survey of Bodhisattva Precepts

Yogācāra texts—such as the *Yogācāra-bhūmi śāstra*, the *Bodhisattva-bhūmi*, and the *Upāsaka-śīla sūtra*—sometimes clearly distinguished between the bodhisattva precepts for lay and monastic practitioners. In contrast, some important apocryphal texts, such as the *Brahma's Net Sūtra* (*Fanwang jing*) and *The Book of Original Acts that Adorn the Bodhisattva* (*Pusa yingluo benye jing*, hereafter referred to as *Original Acts*), mixed lay and monastic precepts together. These differences affected how these precepts were used and spread in East Asia. Several other sources should be briefly mentioned to give the reader a full sense of the bodhisattva precepts. One of the earliest sets of bodhisattva precepts are the 'ten good precepts' (discussed below). The Mahāyāna *Nirvāṇa Sūtra* relates stories of killing the enemies of Buddhism without incurring karmic consequences. The *Lotus Sūtra*, discussed by Gene Reeves elsewhere in this volume, identifies the precepts with behaviour extrapolated from the stories in the text, an approach used in preaching by both modern and earlier exponents of the text. For a focus on how the text was used in medieval Tendai, see Groner 2014.

The friction between Mahāyāna and so-called 'Hīnayāna' attitudes on the precepts appears in some of these texts. The requirement that Mahāyāna practitioners make offerings of flowers and music to images of the Buddha conflicted with rules in the *Vinaya* for monks. Some Mahāyāna texts suggested that it would be better to drop into hell than to aspire to Hīnayāna goals. A rule in the *Brahma's Net Sūtra* states that one should never turn away from Mahāyāna to the two vehicles (T 24: 1005c05–7). To cite an extreme interpretation of this precept, the Tendai exegete Annen (b. 841) cites a Mahāyāna text to argue that people might ignore the *Vinaya* to follow the bodhisattva precepts.

> According to the *Great Perfection of Wisdom*, 'If a bodhisattva over kalpas as numerous as the sands of the Ganges receives the desires of the five senses, in the bodhisattva precepts, it is not called a violation. If one were to have even an instant of thought of the two vehicles, then it would be termed a violation.'[1]

The *Nirvāṇa Sūtra* justifies killing by laymen to protect Buddhism. It identifies some groups of Hīnayānists as being *icchantikas*[2] and seems to suggest that they might even be

[1] *Futsū jubosatsukai kōshaku*, T 74: 778a05–9. This passage is found in both the commentaries by Taehyon and Fazang on the *Fanwang jing* (T 40: 701a02–4; T 40: 638b15–17).

[2] The term *icchantika* has been defined in various ways, but usually has the sense of deluded greedy beings who can never realize enlightenment. However, the *Nirvāṇa Sūtra* was the focus of an intense debate over whether the *icchantika* could realize *nirvāṇa* or not. In addition, some East Asian

killed as being enemies of the Dharma. It particularly criticizes the use of Buddhism to collect riches, such as fields, servants, animals, vehicles, jewels, silver, gold, and luxury items. Despite the vitriol found in such passages, as will be discussed below, Mahāyāna practitioners later used the Vinaya precepts and followed them with bodhisattva precepts.

Thus the bodhisattva precepts played an important role in establishing Mahāyāna's identity. The role of the precepts in the rise of Mahāyāna has been emphasized by some modern scholars such as Hirakawa Akira, who suggested that groups of quasi-lay practitioners at stupas who followed sets of precepts might have been crucial to establishing an independent Mahāyāna tradition (1990: 302–308). He argued that as time passed, ways to harmoniously combine the *Vinaya* and the bodhisattva precepts emerged. Although Hirakawa's hypothesis has been harshly criticized by many Japanese and Western scholars, his use of the bodhisattva precepts in discussing the social background of Mahāyāna has continued to be influential, even as scholars such as Jan Nattier and Paul Harrison have refined our understanding of early Mahāyāna. Below, I survey several of the most influential sets of bodhisattva precepts in East Asia.

The Ten Good Precepts

This list had its origins in the *Āgamas* as ten virtuous actions (Skt. *daśa-kuśala-karma-patha*) that would result in gaining the karma that would enable one to have a good rebirth and thus was applicable to both monastic and lay Buddhists (for example, see *Zhong ahan jing*, T 1: 440a–c). However, in early Mahāyāna texts, particularly in the Perfection of Wisdom literature, they were sometimes referred to as the ten good precepts (rather than virtuous actions) and interpreted as an intrinsic part of bodhisattva practice of perfections by emphasizing that they did not apply only to one's own cultivation, but to efforts to benefit others. They were sometimes said to correspond to the perfection of morality (for example, see *Mohe boruo boluomi jing*, T 8: 250a13–16). The list of ten good precepts or actions consisted of prohibitions on: (1) killing; (2) stealing; (3) sexual misconduct; (4) lying; (5) speaking divisively; (6); harsh speech; (7) engaging in frivolous prattle; (8) being covetous; (9) being angry; (10) having wrong views. In some texts, such as the *Ugraparipṛcchā*, which Jan Nattier (2005) has argued was influential in the establishment of Mahāyāna, the ten precepts were combined with the five lay precepts with which they overlapped for the most part, resulting in a list of eleven lay precepts, consisting of the ten with the prohibition on alcohol added.

A comparison of the ten good precepts with those from the *Vinaya* reveals a number of characteristics of many Mahāyāna precepts. First, the three precepts at the beginning of the list are concerned with physical actions, the next four with verbal actions, and

scholars from the Yogācāra Hossō school argued that bodhisattvas could be called *icchantikas* of great compassion because they postponed their *nirvāṇa* until everyone else had realized enlightenment.

the last three with mental acts. The inclusion of mental states as precepts deepened the ethical dimension of the precepts. In contrast, the *Vinaya* was primarily concerned with physical and verbal acts, which could be objectively observed and judged. Thought was a concern of intention and meditative practice, which were emphasized more than they had been in the precepts of the *Vinaya*.

Second, a distinction was traditionally made in the *Vinaya* between precepts that were intrinsically ethical and those that were based on cultural norms, but were not intrinsically ethical even though they might lead to ethical transgressions. Examples of the first are killing and stealing; the second might include alcohol or excessive numbers of robes. Sexual behaviour also might fit in this category because the restrictions depended on one's status, with sexual intercourse being allowed for married couples. Restraints on the cultural aspects of Buddhism, such as dress, lodging, and the performance of rituals, do not play an important role in the ten good precepts. The ethical sense of the ten precepts led to their interpretation as much more than simple prohibitions of an act. Besides refraining from wrong actions, one was expected to do good and to benefit others; these three types of action were referred to as the three collections of pure precepts and are discussed below.

Third, the ten good precepts are excessively broad. For example, any killing, stealing, or lying would seem to be prohibited, even though differences between the gravity of offences, such as killing a human and killing an animal or insect, would seem to differ. Examples of when such activities might be permissible are usually not discussed along with the prohibitions, though they are sometimes raised in other contexts. For example, the differences between killing insects and animals, humans, and sages, as well as non-believers, are discussed in the *Nirvāṇa Sūtra*. The ambiguous or broad aspects of the bodhisattva precepts was evident when they were said to be general rubrics, such as doing good, that encompassed all other precepts, as opposed to the distinct and more specifically formulated precepts found in the *Vinaya*.

Fourth, the ten good precepts had little or no institutional basis for enforcing them. For example, little distinction was made between lay and monastic behaviour. No specific penalties such as expulsion or suspension from an order are specified. Although terms such as lay bodhisattvas and monastic bodhisattvas appear in the beginnings of some Mahāyāna scriptures in descriptions of the audience, the connection with the ten good precepts is vague at best, reflecting little about institutions for the practitioners. How were ordinations to be conducted? How were penalties for violations to be levied? For the most part, any penalty was karmic, and some texts identify particular observances or transgressions with specific rebirths.

The Three Collections of Pure Precepts

This concept in an inchoate form probably first appeared in the *Avataṃsaka Sūtra* (*Dafangguangfo huayan jing*, T 9: 513ab), but was clarified in early commentaries (*Shidi jinglun* [attributed to Vasubandhu] T 26: 145c15–16). It was particularly developed in the literature of the Yogācāra tradition in texts such as the *Bodhisattva-bhūmi* and the *Yogācāra-bhūmi*. The three collections are: (1) precepts that prevent wrongdoing; (2) precepts that result in the accumulation of wholesome or good qualities; and (3) precepts that benefit sentient beings (*Pusa dichi jing* [*Bodhisattva-bhūmi*], T 30: 9120b–c). These can be interpreted in various ways, either as separate collections or as separate aspects of the same precepts.

Although a full formulation was initially found in Yogācāra texts, it was used in many Mahāyāna texts. According to the *Bodhisattva-bhūmi*, the precepts that prevent wrongdoing are identical with the precepts in the *Vinaya*, including the precepts for both lay and monastic practitioners; these are called the 'Bodhisattva-*Vinaya*', indicating that the precepts of the *Vinaya* could be considered as Mahāyāna (*Pusa shanjie jing* [Guṇavarman's translation of the *Bodhisattva-bhūmi*], T 30: 982c–983a). This formulation led to the harmonious combination of the *Vinaya* with the bodhisattva precepts in much of East Asia. The most authoritative Chinese scholar on the *Vinaya*, Daoxuan (596–667), argued that the meaning of the *Dharmaguptaka-Vinaya* (Ch. *Sifen lü*) was harmonious with the Mahāyāna (*Si-fenlu xingshi chao*, T 40: 26b6–10; *Sifenlu suichi jiemo shu, Shinsan Zokuzōkyō* 41: 261a), a position summarized by many *Vinaya* scholars as the partial Mahāyāna quality of the *Dharmaguptaka-Vinaya* (*fentong Dasheng* or *yi dang Dasheng*). Daoxuan also identified the *Vinaya* precepts with the collection of precepts preventing wrongdoing (*Sifenlu xingshi chao*, T 40: 149b8). Yijing (635–713), the translator who went to India in search of the Mūlasarvāstivādin *Vinaya* and then translated it, noted in a travel diary that both Hīnayāna and Mahāyāna practitioners used the *Vinaya* (T 54: 205c10–11). Today, many East Asian monks undergo a series of ordinations, similar to climbing a multi-storied building; one might begin with the lay precepts, then progress to the precepts for novices, the full precepts for a monastic, and conclude with the bodhisattva precepts (Welch 1967: 285–301). If one attempted to go straight to the highest precepts, it would be like trying to leap to a higher floor without first traversing the lower floors (*Pusa shanjie jing*, T 30: 1013c–14a).

The second collection of pure precepts concerns all of the good actions done to gain enlightenment, including everyday actions such as greeting a superior and asking questions, meditation paying obeisance, making offerings, nursing the sick, dedicating one's merits to all beings, making offerings to the Three Jewels, and never allowing any negligence to enter his actions. One of the emphases in this collection and the third collection is the focus on benefiting other beings. While the *Vinaya* mostly focuses on one's own cultivation, for the bodhisattva practice helping others is identical to self-cultivation. One must not only prevent wrongdoing, but must establish circumstances so that others will not be tempted into wrongdoing.

The third collection concerns benefiting sentient beings, including such acts as helping those who suffer from illness and natural disasters; protecting those who fear dangerous animals demons, kings, and bandits; preaching using various expedients to lead people to the Buddhist path. One knows one's benefactors and repays their favours. One comforts those who meet with disaster, lose loved ones, or are impoverished. One gives to the poor. When one hears the Dharma, one praises it and is joyous. Criticisms are met with forbearance. One associates with those who seriously practise and study. One praises those who do good, but compassionately criticizes those do wrong. These practices served as the basis for some of the social welfare activities of East Asian monks. In some cases, such as the Japanese monk Gyōki (668–749), who led groups around Japan and who constructed bridges, levees, irrigation ditches, dams, docks, ponds, and temples, the local populace called him a 'bodhisattva', and he was seen as exemplifying the bodhisattva precepts. Because he was active when monks were aware that an orthodox ordination tradition had not yet been transmitted to Japan, his followers probably received some form of bodhisattva precepts.

Besides these general categories, the *Bodhisattva-bhūmi* also included a number of more specific precepts for monastic bodhisattvas. The number of these varies with translation; the earliest Chinese translation, the *Dichi jing*, mentions four major precepts—(1) not to praise oneself and disparage others; (2) not to be stingy with the Dharma or wealth; (3) not to be angry, resentful, and refuse to accept another's apology; and (4) not to slander the bodhisattva scriptures (T 30: 913b1–12); these are followed by forty-two minor ones (T 30: 913c–916c) (or forty-three in later translations). A slightly later translation of the *Bodhisattva-bhūmi* by Guṇavarman, the *Shanjie jing*, had eight major (adding the four *pārājika* from the *Vinaya* to the four found in the *Dichi jing*) and forty-two minor precepts (T 30: 1015a3–18) (later expanded to forty-eight in Xuanzang's translation of the *Yogācāra-bhūmi*). A related text only for lay bodhisattvas, the *Youposai jie jing*, was translated by Dharmakṣema in 426. It listed six major precepts (refraining from [1] killing, [2] stealing, [3] lying, [4] engaging in illicit sexual misconduct, [5] speaking ill of a Buddhist, [6], selling alcohol) and twenty-eight minor precepts (also called the precepts concerning negligence, including drinking alcohol, failing to go and listen to the Dharma, making offerings to parents and teachers, failing to visit the sick, serving leftovers to monastics, staying overnight at a nunnery) (*Youposai jie jing*, T 24: 1049a–1050b; Shih 1994: 78–83). The text was a guide to practice for lay Buddhists and did not have their eventual ordination as monastics as a goal. The ordination laid out in the text required twenty correctly ordained lay practitioners, a number greater than traditional monastic ordinations (T 24: 1049a4–5).

The relation between these sets of precepts and the three collections of pure precepts is usually not clearly spelled out. A variety of sets of bodhisattva precepts could be used by lay practitioners, including those discussed in the next section. Bodhisattva ordinations enabled lay practitioners to identify with a Buddhist organization (Getz 2005; Haar 2001; Meeks 2009). In some groups, people might even keep track of their good and bad deeds in books. The bodhisattva precepts were particularly popular among women in premodern East Asia (Yan 2012).

Apocryphal Texts

Because we know little about the social history of the bodhisattva precepts in India, its early history in China is instructive for understanding their social impact. Chinese monks had to wait several centuries before they acquired a translation of the full *Vinaya*. Kumārajīva (344–413) translated Mahāyāna texts and the complete Sarvāstivāda *Vinaya*, all of which would have a decisive influence on China.

The issue of how the 'Hīnayānist' *Vinaya* was to be combined with Mahāyāna teachings was a major concern for monastics (Funayama 2004; Heirman 2008). During the first half of the fifth century, four translations of full *Vinaya*s had been completed. Around the same time, the *Bodhisattva-bhūmi* was translated by both Dharmakṣema (385–433) and Guṇavarman (367–431); later the text was included in the *Yogācāra-bhūmi* translated by Xuanzang (602–664).

Several apocryphal texts were composed around this same time; the most influential of these was the *Brahmā's Net Sūtra*, a text that Kumārajīva was said to have translated from Sanskrit, but which most modern scholars believe was compiled in China several decades after his death. Although it is regarded as an apocryphal text today, it exhibits considerable influence from Indian scriptures. It enumerated ten major precepts, refraining from: (1) killing, (2) stealing; (3) improper sexual activities; (4) lying; (5) selling alcohol; (6) finding fault with others; (7) praising oneself and denigrating others; (8) stinginess with one's own possessions and providing Buddhist instruction; (9) becoming angry; and (10) libelling the Three Jewels. These were followed by forty-eight minor precepts, several of which had major impacts on East Asian Buddhism, including prohibitions on eating meat and the five pungent herbs; encouraging the release of animals; and a prohibition on storing weapons. Several significant aspects of this text deserve mention. Precepts applicable to both lay and monastic practitioners were combined in the text. Compassion and filial piety, the latter a quintessential Chinese virtue, were stressed.

The precepts of the *Brahmā's Net Sūtra* were said to have originated with the primordial Vairocana Buddha and to have been passed down to the historical Buddha Śākyamuni and then to bodhisattvas and worldlings. Thus its recipients were said to hold the precepts of the Buddha, which reflected his enlightened mind; they thus were fundamentally different from the *Vinaya*, which is said to have arisen as the early Buddhist order encountered problems and the historical Buddha formulated rules for his order. The receipt of the bodhisattva precepts was said to confer an exalted state on the recipient and thus differed from ordinations as initiation into an order; the text claimed, 'When sentient beings receive the precepts of the Buddha, they enter the ranks of the Buddhas; their rank is the same as the great enlightened [ones]; they are truly children of the Buddha' (T 24: 1004a20–21). The exalted state of those who received the bodhisattva precepts led to their conferral on kings and ministers by eminent monks (Janousch 1999). In the Japanese Tendai school, ordination was frequently identified with the realization of Buddhahood with this very body (Jp. *sokushin jōbutsu*), a status that did not necessarily mean full enlightenment, but was still believed to be more exalted than the ordination with the precepts of the *Vinaya* (Groner 1990: 266–268).

The *Original Acts Sūtra*, also an apocryphal text, advanced a significantly different view of the three collections of pure precepts than that found in texts such as the *Bodhisattva-bhūmi*. The precepts that prevent wrongdoing are identified with the ten *pārājika* (T 24: 1021a), a term that is often associated with the ten major precepts of the *Brahma's Net Sūtra*. The precepts promoting good are identified with the 84,000 Buddhist teachings, and the precepts that benefited sentient beings are described as loving-kindness, compassion, empathetic joy, and equanimity (sometimes called the four divine abidings or boundless states (T 24: 1020b29–c3). The social aspect of the precepts of benefiting sentient beings reflects the Mahāyāna concern with compassion. According to this formulation, the precepts of the *Vinaya* play no part in the bodhisattva precepts. This was used by the Japanese Tendai school to reject the *Vinaya* and to develop a unique interpretation of morality.

The significance of whether the *Vinaya* was considered to be part of the three collections of pure precepts must be emphasized. Both Chinese and Japanese monks conducted ordinations using the precepts of the *Brahma's Net Sūtra*, but interpreted them in vastly different ways. The Chinese usually conferred the bodhisattva precepts after a person had received the precepts specified in the *Vinaya*. The bodhisattva precepts were thus seen as giving a Mahāyāna sense to the precepts of the *Vinaya*. The *Brahma's Net Sūtra* did not contravene the *Vinaya* even though it contained a precept prohibiting contact with Hīnayāna.

In contrast, Japanese Tendai and many of the schools of Kamakura Buddhism simply used the precepts of the *Brahma's Net Sūtra* to ordain both monks and lay believers, rejecting the *Vinaya*. The result was frequently a lax attitude towards traditional Buddhist monastic discipline. Eventually, even the precepts of the *Brahma's Net Sūtra* came to be seen as expedients that could be ignored when necessary. Consequently Japanese monks sometimes engaged in such activities as drinking alcohol, eating meat, and sexual intercourse. Modern Japanese temples are frequently handed down from father to son (or occasionally a daughter, adopted son, or other relative).

Bodhisattva Ordinations

When people received the bodhisattva precepts ordination in Japan, many but not all referred to themselves as 'bodhisattva precepts disciples' or 'bodhisattva monks'. At times lay believers received Dharma names. A brief consideration of the first bodhisattva ordination in China suggests the impact of the translation and compilation of texts on the bodhisattva precepts. Daojin (d. 444) wished to receive the bodhisattva precepts from Dharmakṣema (385–433), the translator of the *Bodhisattvabhūmi*. Dharmakṣema refused, saying Daojin was not ready. After three years of confession and meditation, Daojin received a sign from the Buddha and went to tell Dharmakṣema. Before he even spoke, Dharmakṣema exclaimed that Daojin had received the precepts and then proceeded to explain their contents. The story is important because the precepts came directly from the Buddha, not from an order of Buddhist practitioners. The danger with such an ordination was that various practitioners might keep altering the precepts. The following passage from the *Brahma's Net Sūtra* sums up the procedures and issues:

O children of the Buddha. If after the Buddha's death, you have a mind to do good and desire to take the bodhisattva precepts, you may confer the precepts upon yourself by taking vows in front of an image of a Buddha or bodhisattva. For seven days, you should confess in front of the Buddha [image]; if you experience a sign from the Buddha, then you have acquired the precepts. If you do not see a sign, you should [practise] for two weeks, three weeks, or even a year; during that time you surely should receive a sign. After receiving a sign, you acquire the precepts in front of an image of a Buddha or bodhisattva. If you have not received a sign, then even if you take the precepts, you have not actually acquired them.

If you acquire the precepts directly from a teacher who has, in turn, [properly] acquired the precepts, then it is not necessary to receive a sign. Why? Because the precepts have already been transmitted through a succession of teachers, a sign is not necessary. You should be solemn and obtain the precepts.

If no teacher capable of granting the precepts can be found within one thousand *li*, you should go before an image of the Buddha or bodhisattva to acquire the precepts. You must receive a sign [from the Buddha in this case]. (T 24: 1006c)

Daojin subsequently ordained many with the bodhisattva precepts as a qualified teacher (Jp. *juta jukai*). This type of ordination was preferred over self-ordinations because it provided a lineage of practitioners and an institutional basis for practice. In fact, Indian texts and almost all Chinese texts limited self-ordinations to the bodhisattva precepts when one could not find a qualified teacher; Indian texts did not allow one to become a monk or nun with a self-ordination (for example, see the Chinese translation of the *Yogācāra-bhūmi, Yuqielun*, T 30: 589c22–28). However, one apocryphal text, the *Scripture of Divining the Requital of Good and Evil Actions* (*Zhancha shan'e yebao jing*), allowed full ordinations of *bhikṣu* and *bhikṣuṇī* through self-ordinations if a qualified teacher could not be found (T 17: 904c5–a3). This text served as one of the authorities by which Japanese monks occasionally established or re-established broken monastic lineages. For example, the text is cited by Japanese monks prior to Ganjin (688–763), who brought orthodox ordinations to Japan, as an authority guaranteeing the full ordinations of monks even though no orthodox monastic lineage existed. At times, Tendai monks would cite it to argue that their ordination lineages had an orthodox beginning.

An ordination from a qualified teacher was obviously easier than one in which one would meditate and confess until a sign from the Buddha had been received, a period that might be years. In fact, the *Original Acts Sūtra* suggested that an ordination from a qualified teacher was to be preferred over a self-ordination (T 24: 1020c04–13). One of the rationales behind this position was probably fear of the possibility that self-ordained people could claim that the Buddha had directly given them new precepts. For example, in Japan, Eison, the founder of the Shingon Ritsu tradition, used a self-ordination to establish a new lineage for full ordinations from the *Vinaya*, but closed off this possibility for others to use self-ordinations as soon as he was qualified by seniority to conduct traditional full ordinations (Groner 2005).

A number of ordination manuals were produced in China during the Six Dynasties period that relied on a variety of texts, but the *Brahma's Net Sūtra* and *Bodhisattva-bhūmi* were the most important. By the Tang dynasty, a twelve-step ordination ritual conferring the *Brahma's Net* precepts formulated by the Tiantai patriarch Zhanran (711–782) was the most influential. It was then adopted by the founder of the Japanese Tendai school, Saichō (767–822). This ritual was used by qualified teachers to confer the bodhisattva precepts on others, but contained elements from self-ordinations, such as inviting Śākyamuni, Mañjuśrī, and Maitreya to preside over it and having a section devoted to experiencing a sign from the Buddha. These elements came from the *Sūtra on the Procedures for Visualizing Samantabhadra* (*Guan Puxian pusa xingfa jing*), a text considered to be the sequel of the *Lotus Sūtra*. Because the Buddha and advanced bodhisattvas were not visible to the ordinary practitioner, the visible person who *transmitted* the precepts was distinct from the Buddha who *conferred* the precepts. Although the *Original Acts Sūtra* allowed lay practitioners to transmit the precepts (T 24: 1021b), the *Brahma's Net Sūtra* specified that it be an ordained bodhisattva.

According to the ordination manuals by such figures as Zhanran and Saichō, the contents of the conferral of the precepts were the three collections of pure precepts, but later in the ceremony the ten major precepts of the *Brahma's Net Sūtra* were explained and the ordinee was asked if he or she could observe each of them. Elements such as asking about obstacles to ordination were taken from the procedures for full ordinations in the *Vinaya* even though only heinous wrongdoing (according to the *Brahma's Net Sūtra*: matricide, patricide, killing an *arhat*, shedding the blood of the Buddha, breaking the harmony of the order, killing a preceptor, killing a teacher) would prevent one from receiving the bodhisattva precepts. Later, Annen, extrapolating from comments in Korean commentaries on the *Brahma's Net Sūtra*, would suggest that the recitation of certain *dhāraṇī* could vanquish the bad karma from heinous sins and allow people to receive the bodhisattva precepts (T 74: 759b).

An ordination based on the *Vinaya* only extended until the end of one's current lifetime, when one violated a *pārājika*, or abandoned the precepts, but bodhisattva ordinations were often said to last over many lifetimes until one finally realized supreme enlightenment. Such ordinations were said to be based on Buddha-nature or Suchness. The bodhisattva precepts in the *Brahma's Net Sūtra* were said to have an essence that could be identified with Buddha-nature (Jp. *busshōkai*) or to be adamantine (Jp. *kongōhōkai*). In some texts, there is a tension between interpreting the precepts as being based on an unchanging essence and as a set of prescriptive practices that were transmitted and cultivated. For example, Annen (b. 841), the author of an authoritative commentary on Japanese Tendai ordinations, argues that three types of precepts exist: (1) those that are transmitted by a teacher; (2) those that are called forth from a practitioner through the correct ceremony; and (3) those that are innate in everyone (*Futsūju bosatsukai kōshaku*, T 74: 767a16–19). His views contributed to a lax observance of the precepts when he argued that the precepts were expedients that differed according to one's religious abilities. He cited a number of canonical examples in which killing and sexual misconduct were used as expedient means in propagating Buddhism; these included Devadatta, Aṅgulimāla, and Ajātaśatru, figures that were portrayed as murderous villains in some Buddhist texts, but were also described as becoming good Buddhists in some Mahāyāna texts. A courtesan, Vasumitrā, was described as leading men to Buddhism through her sexual wiles (T 74: 765c–766a; paraphrasing Zhiyi's *Mohe zhiguan*, Donner and Stevenson 1993: 308–309).

The relation of the ordination and precepts with Buddha-nature also led Annen and later Tendai monks to link the ordination with the attainment of various stages on the path, integrating it with the realization of Buddhahood with this very body, in a formula that did not mean that one was fully enlightened with his ordination, but that he had realized his fundamental nature or identification with Buddhahood to some degree. By the Kamakura period, an advanced re-ordination—distinguished from an initial bodhisattva ordination that marked entry into the order—culminated a long retreat on Mount Hiei; the 'consecrated ordination' (*kai kanjō*) was used by the Kurodani lineage on Mount Hiei, but was not accepted by other branches of Tendai. In this ordination, the student and teacher sat side by side on a platform with a canopy over their heads, re-enacting Śākyamuni's sitting next to Prabhūtratna Buddha in a stupa as it was portrayed in the *Lotus Sūtra*. In this ritual, which included the student and teacher performing a gasshō (placing the hands together in a gesture of supplication) with their hands intertwined, the soles of their feet and foreheads touching, and an exchange of robes, the student gained the assurance or faith that he too was a Buddha (Groner 2009). Variations of such ordinations led to the use of ordinations in Sōtō Zen transmissions of the Dharma (Licha).

Expiation of Transgressions

Violations of the precepts of the *Vinaya* for monastics were subject to the order's determination of sanctions that included expulsion, suspension, confession before certain numbers of monks, or reflection by oneself. Penalties were imposed with an institutional basis; the *Vinaya* describes a number of procedures for determining whether offences have been committed. Detailed descriptions of exactly what constitutes an offence are included in the precepts. Such issues as the role of intent when an offence was committed are considered in detail, as are definitions of the terms used in the rules.

In contrast, violations of the bodhisattva precepts were usually subject to karmic recompense rather than the determination of a monastic order. In some texts, such as the *Bodhisattva-bhūmi* and the *Brahmā's Net Sūtra*, violations of the bodhisattva precepts were usually expiated with confession, but no order of monks determined this. Instead, the fear of bad karma led the practitioner to expiate wrongdoing. In many cases, the bodhisattva precepts were divided into major and minor categories, much vaguer categories than those found in the *Vinaya*. A minor precept might be expiated by confession to another person. Major precepts were sometimes referred to as *pārājika*, a term borrowed from the *Vinaya*, where violation would have entailed life-long expulsion from the order of monks or nuns. However, recent research by Shayne Clarke has shown that in many orders violations of the precept on sexual intercourse may have been dealt with by depriving the violator of his status as a monk, but not expelling him from the order (Clarke 2000). According to the *Brahma's Net Sūtra*, violating a major precept entailed losing the precepts, but meditation and confession in front of an image of the Buddha might lead to restoration of the precepts if one received a supernatural sign from the Buddha. If one did not receive a sign, then one did not regain the precepts. However, the *Brahma's Net Sūtra* left the possibility of being re-ordained open as a means of regaining the precepts (T 24: 1008c18); even so, violation of the seven heinous sins would result in permanent loss of the precepts for that lifetime, but the Japanese Tendai exegete Annen argued that recitation of *dhāraṇī* could vanquish the bad karma from such acts and restore the precepts.

At one extreme of the spectrum of positions on the bodhisattva precepts, the *Original Acts Sūtra* declares that the bodhisattva precepts could be violated but could never be lost, could be received but never abandoned by stating that one no longer observed them (T 24: 1021b07). Moreover, unlike the precepts of the *Vinaya* that ceased to be effective when one died, the bodhisattva precepts were said to continue from lifetime to lifetime (T 24: 1021b2). It was better to receive the precepts and break them than to have not received them but follow their dictates. In the first case, one was still a Buddhist, but in the second one was heterodox. In such cases, the bodhisattva precepts were identified with Buddha-nature, a quality that was said to endure virtually forever. When such a position was taken, although the contents of the bodhisattva precepts could be said to be ethical, they really were more closely connected with affirming one's spiritual potential than one's ethical behaviour.

Ethical Issues in the Bodhisattva Precepts

A sense of how the bodhisattva precepts might be used in ethical arguments can be gained from a consideration of the first major precept in the *Brahma's Net Sūtra*, the precept against killing:

> O Children of the Buddha. If you yourself kill, teach others to kill, prepare the necessities for killing, praise killing, take pleasure in witnessing killing, and so forth even down to killing through spells, these are the causes, conditions, the ways, and the acts of killing. One may not purposely kill any living thing. A bodhisattva should give rise to eternally abiding compassion, be filial and obedient, and use all means to protect the living. Conversely, if he kills out of greed or anger, this is a *pārājika* for the bodhisattva.[3] (T 24: 1004b16–20)

[3] I have followed the commentary attributed to the Tiantai patriarch Zhiyi, the *Pusajie yishu*, in my interpretation of this precept.

The precept is clearly idealistic, but also impractical because of the very high standards it sets without including substantial institutional support. Among the questions that immediately arise is whether killing an insect or animal is equivalent to killing a human being. One of the earliest commentaries on the text, the *Pusajie yishu*, attributed to the founder of the Tiantai school, Zhiyi (538–597), divided violations of the precept into three categories. The gravest was killing a buddha, sage, parent, or monastic teacher, violations that were included in heinous sins (*Fanwang jing*, T 24: 1008c1–3; *Pusajie yishu*, T 40: 571c). A middling level of violation is taking the life of a god or human, and the lowest level is killing any being in the four lowest levels of rebirth (hell, hungry ghosts, animals, and titans). This categorization followed passages found in the Mahāyāna *Nirvāṇa Sūtra* (T 12: 460b11–13), and was typical of the way in which commentaries utilized other scriptures to augment the interpretation of the terse provisions of the bodhisattva precepts. Such considerations raise the issue of asking what a term such as 'major precept' actually means if it can be divided into such categories. Certainly, it is different from the use of *pārājika* in the *Vinaya*.

Another issue is whether there were any circumstances in which killing might be justifiable, such as protecting others. The precept in the *Brahma's Net Sūtra* certainly does not include any exceptions or explanation of the precept, but specifically prohibits killing out of greed or anger. What if compassion motivated one to kill? In a discussion of this, the author of the *Pusajie yishu* concludes that if one considers the religious abilities or salvific impetus of a sentient being, then killing might be permissible (T 40: 571b22). The phrase 'looking at religious abilities', referring to a person's religious sensibilities that are the result of both his or her practices over a lifetime and innate qualities, occurs several times in the *Pusajie yishu* and opens the possibility of more nuanced interpretations of the bodhisattva precepts. Among the precepts in which it is mentioned are the major precepts on killing (1) and stealing (2) and the minor precepts on drinking alcohol (2), teaching non-Mahāyāna doctrines (15), accepting separate invitations to eat (27). One can easily think of occasions when these rules might be violated in order to benefit others. For example, the exception to the prohibition on drinking alcohol gives a sense of how this might be interpreted. The story of Mallikā, the wife of Prasenajit, is cited. When Prasenajit became angry at his cook and wished to have him put to death, Mallikā encouraged her husband to drink with her until his anger had dissipated, thereby saving the life of the cook. When Mallikā later went to talk to the Buddha about whether she had violated the rule against drinking alcohol, the Buddha said she had not done so.[4]

Several decades after Zhiyi died, Xuanzang went to India and brought back major Yogācāra texts and translated them. A passage in the *Yogācārabhūmi-śāstra* set forth the basic problem with the precept on killing:

[4] I follow Zhuhong's explanation of the short mention in the *Pusajie yishu*. See *Fanwangjing xindipin pusajie yishu fayin Shinsan Zokuzōkyō* 38: 181a6–10. Zhuhong, perhaps following the *Vinaya*, also notes the use of alcohol in medicine is permitted. The Tang dynasty encyclopedist and *Vinaya* specialist Daoshi (d. 683) suggested that Mallikā's actions were good, but impure, but meant to help others in their religious practice (*Fayuan zhulin*, T 53: 971b–c).

> This is like a bodhisattva who sees a robber and brigand who out of his desire for wealth wishes to kill many. The robber may wish to harm elders, *śrāvakas*, *pratyekabuddhas*, and bodhisattvas. Or he may wish to commit a [wrongdoing that results in] inexpiable and immediate retribution. When the bodhisattva realizes this, he thinks, 'If I cut off his evil [intent to end] sentient beings' lives, [I] will drop into hell. If I do not cut it off, the karma of inexpiable retribution will be incurred and he will receive great suffering. I should kill him and drop into hell myself so that he will not incur inexpiable retribution ... Thus this bodhisattva ... knows this situation and understands that in the future he must develop deep remorse and with a profound sense of compassion end [the brigand's] life. In such a case, the bodhisattva has not transgressed the precepts and will produce many merits. (*Yuqie shidi lun*, T 30: 517b6–17)

This led to a number of questions by the Japanese Tendai exegete Jitsudō Ninkū (1309–1388), one of the leading exegetes of the Tendai school and the Seizan branch of the Pure Land school. Ninkū wrote the most extensive subcommentary on Zhiyi's commentary on the *Brahma's Net Sūtra*. Among the questions he raised was whether it was only an advanced practitioner who could perform such an action and whether a worldling could perform it. Ninkū strove to interpret the bodhisattva precepts as applying to ordinary people in a conflicted world. While violations of the precepts might be permissible under extraordinary circumstances, he warned against being too permissive. As the abbot of several important monasteries, he wrote several sets of monastery rules strengthening the rules. Ninkū and other exegetes asked whether violations as serious as killing were to be limited to lay bodhisattvas or whether monastic bodhisattvas might also commit them. Most limited violations to laymen. An interesting case study from the Mahāyāna *Nirvāṇa Sūtra* was sometimes cited in these discussions.

> At that time there were many evil monks who, when they heard the teaching [that monks should not have slaves, oxen or sheep] developed evil intentions, took up swords and threatened the Dharma-preacher. At that time, there was a king named Bhavadatta, who having heard of these events went to the Dharma-preachers and helped them by fighting with the evil monks, enabling the Dharma-preachers to escape harm, but the king received numerous wounds. At that time, the monk Buddhadatta praised the king, saying, 'Excellent! Excellent! The king is truly a protector of the Dharma. His body will be a vessel for innumerable implementation of the Dharma.' When the king heard this, he was overjoyed. He then died and was reborn in Akṣobhya Buddha's land, where he became the Buddha's foremost disciple. The king's people, retainers, and warriors were all joyful, none backslid from the aspiration to enlightenment. When they died, they were reborn in Akṣobhya Buddha's land. When Buddhadatta died, he too was reborn in Akṣobhya Buddha's land, where he became that Buddha's second-ranking *śrāvaka* disciple ... Kāśyapa, I was that king and you were the Dharma-teacher monk. (T 12: 623c–624a)

The *Nirvāṇa Sūtra* justified killing to protect the Dharma and protect the true teaching, even if that violence was directed against other monks. In this text, *icchantika*, a class of people that were incorrigible, could be killed; the Buddha in a past life had done such deeds as a layman and been rewarded for it. Violence to protect Buddhism is mentioned in a text by Zhiyi's teacher Huisi (515–577) concerning the *Lotus Sūtra*'s Course of Ease and Bliss, another version of bodhisattva precepts (Stevenson 2006: 298). However, the violent episodes from the *Nirvāṇa Sūtra* were not cited frequently in Buddhist writings, perhaps because they were so violent.

A number of Mahāyāna doctrines contributed to a more nuanced interpretation than would have been permitted under strict rules of the *Vinaya*. If the three collections of pure precepts were invoked, then the requirement that a bodhisattva perform good actions and benefit sentient beings might require killing in some circumstances. Killing one person or a small number might be necessary to save many. Such explanations were based on a hierarchy of the three collections of pure precepts and an evaluation of which should take precedence.

Another approach applied the metaphor of Indra's net, an image in which the stars are like jewels suspended from the god Indra's net with each jewel reflecting every other jewel. While each element has its own distinct identity, they reinforce each other through their reflections. Ninkū suggested that if one were to break a precept for the right reason, then all other phenomena might help to repair any damage because all is connected by cause and effect; the wrong could be outweighed by all of the good it did for a variety of beings.

> If a *śrāvaka* violates [a major rule in the *Vinaya*], he permanently loses his status as a monk. In the bodhisattva precepts, one does not lose the precepts from lifetime to lifetime. But this does not mean that the *śrāvaka* [precepts] are heavy and the bodhisattva precepts are light. If we discuss the great power of the bodhisattva precepts, when the precept against killing is upheld, then one obtains the merit of not killing the sentient beings in the whole *Dharma*-realm. If one were to kill one or two people or even a hundred or a thousand, this would only be like a drop in the ocean. The radiant virtue of the precept for the rest of the sentient beings would be pure without a flaw. In other words, the merit of holding the precepts is great and the losses from violating them small. Needless to say, the ten major precepts are identical to the ten inexhaustible precepts. . . . A single precept contains inexhaustible precepts; the observance of unbounded precepts is contained in a single precept. Though one major precept is violated, the others complete it, helping each other just like Indra's net. In contrast, the *śrāvaka* precepts are each separate. If one breaks a precept, the other precepts do not have the power to assist it. If one kills a person, then the virtue of not killing all the remaining people is ineffective. (Tendai shūten kankōkai 15:240a)

Arguments like this one were also used by exegetes who questioned how a figure like Prince Shōtoku (574–622), credited with establishing Buddhism in Japan, could have killed someone. Depending on which biography is considered, Prince Shōtoku as a young man either performed rituals to defeat Buddhism's enemy, Mononobe no Moriya (d. 587), or actually shot the arrow that killed Moriya. Because Shōtoku is considered to be an incarnation of Kannon, the bodhisattva of compassion, or a buddha, the question is raised of how could killing by such a holy figure be justified or explained. In the *Jōgū taishi shūi ki*, compiled by the monk Hōkū around 1314, a number of explanations for Shōtoku's act of killing are suggested, indicating that the issue was probably discussed by monks. Many of the rationales are similar to those discussed above, but several others are suggested, such as killing is only an expedient means to teach, but does not actually occur: 'Another theory says that although sentient beings are made to see killing, yet truly no one kills, nor is anyone killed. The expedient means of the buddhas and bodhisattvas are all like this' (Suzuki gakujutsu zaidan 1972: 71, 212a).

Perfection of Wisdom teachings were sometimes applied to the precepts. Because good and evil could be seen as empty, an advanced bodhisattva might not have to observe the precepts. Such teachings sometimes led to lax or virtually non-existent restraints on behaviour. At other times they could be used to free a person from paralysing guilt over wrongdoing. When Shōtoku's killing was considered, Hōkū suggested:

> Another explanation is that these very defilements are enlightenment; thus bad karma and defilements need not be discarded. Samsara is identical to *nirvāṇa* means there is no buddhahood to be sought. Thus the layman Vimalakīrti's salvation was found in the sixty-two [wrong] views. The youth Sudhana's comrades are within samsara. Vasumitrā is lascivious and yet chaste; Aṅgulimāla kills and is compassionate. Isn't this the profound expression of great compassion, the actions of remarkable bodhisattvas? (Suzuki gakujutsu zaidan 1972: 71, 212b)

Such passages probably relied on Zhiyi's neither walking nor sitting *samādhi*, which could be practised among evil *dharmas* (Donner and Stevenson 1993: 305–318). In this ritual for advanced practitioners, one focused on realizing that actions and karma were empty. Although such passages were not used to justify all killing, they were important for a tradition that depended on state support to build temples and support monks. Rulers went to great lengths to portray themselves as pious Buddhists. In return, Buddhist monks promised their support and freedom from the bad karma that actions might have incurred. At the same time, many Mahāyāna Buddhists were acutely aware that Buddhism did not sanction killing.

General Exceptions to the Precepts

The Japanese Tendai school is well known for a lax attitude towards other precepts and morality; monks married, ate meat, and drank alcohol, all actions that both the *Vinaya* and bodhisattva precepts prohibited. Although such activities were recognized by the government during the Meiji period, many examples of these activities can be found in earlier periods (Jaffe 2010). Many of these issues are summed up in an influential commentary on the Tendai ordination by Annen. Near the end of the text, he discusses ten rationales for observance of the precepts. The first is to observe all precepts, a rubric that would include the precepts of the *Vinaya*, but the rest are considerations of the circumstances when violations might be justified. In many of these cases, Annen is quoting passages from a Korean exegete Taehyŏn (fl. mid-eighth century) and the Huayan scholar Fazang (643–712), indicating that these justifications may have occasionally been used throughout East Asia. However, Chinese and Korean monks usually combined the bodhisattva precepts with the *Vinaya*; many in Japan did not. Several of these rationales deserve comment.

The precepts can be seen as expedients designed to bring people to Buddhism, but if they are interpreted too strictly, people may abandon Buddhism. Annen states, 'For example, in fishing, when the fish is strong, but the hook is weak, one will lose both the fish and the hook. If one loosens the hook and line, he will catch the fish' (T 74: 777c18–19; paraphrasing Zhiyi's *Mohe zhiguan*, Donner and Stevenson 1993: 311–312). Thus the precepts should not be enforced strictly because Buddhism would lose its adherents.

A practitioner should be in accord with what is superior. In terms of potential conflicts between strict observance of the precepts and the pursuit of wisdom, Annen cites a passage from the *Nirvāṇa Sūtra* that claims wisdom takes precedence over strict adherence to the precepts. In Tendai discussions, the person who observed the precepts to the detriment of wisdom would be a Hīnayānist. In contrast, Vimalakīrti would be an example of someone who would emphasize wisdom over the strict observance of the precepts. Another example would be a passage from the *Lotus Sūtra* that emphasizes that holding the *Sūtra* (that is, memorizing, reciting, and propagating it) is equivalent to observing the precepts (T 9: 34b15–17). Eventually, Sonshun (1451–1514), a Tendai exegete, would suggest that Tendai had no ordination other than holding the *Lotus Sūtra* (Tendai shūten kankōkai 1973: 9, 225a). Other positions would elevate doctrines such as Suchness and compassion over the literal adherence to the precepts.

The tenth and final rationale considers the precepts in terms of realization of Suchness. When the bodhisattva realizes the true aspect of everything, the distinction between observance and violation is transcended. After citing a number of scriptures, primarily from the Perfection of Wisdom literature, Annen concludes,

> You should know that for the bodhisattva of the Perfect vehicle, all the *dharmas* are the characteristic of Suchness. There is no male or female, no perception of self or other, no observance or violation of the precepts. This is called truly observing the precepts. (T 74: 778a18–20)

Annen did not emphasize the *Brahma's Net Sūtra* precepts; in fact, he described them as elementary when viewed from the perspective of esoteric Buddhist texts (*Futsū jubosatsukai kōshaku*, T 74: 764b9; citing T 39: 808a22). His major work on the precepts stresses ordinations and makes very little mention of actual precepts. Were there precepts that were important for him? Annen argues that both the *Vinaya* and the *Brahma's Net Sūtra* precepts all emerged from the esoteric *samaya* precepts.

He cites a passage from the *Vajraśekhara Sūtra* in which Śākyamuni tries but is unable to realize Buddhahood until various Buddhas come and bestow Esoteric practices and teachings on him (Geibel 2001, 23–25). For Annen, this is identified with the esoteric *samaya* precepts.

> Long ago Śākyamuni bodhisattva practised for six years and then sat in the place of enlightenment, but did not realize supreme enlightenment. All of the buddhas came and conferred the samaya precepts on him. Then going through the five stages of realization of Buddhahood (*gosō jōbutsu*), the World Honoured One with the direct path [to buddhahood] suddenly entered the Buddha realm. (T 74: 764b12–15)

The Tendai ordinee repeats this process in his own ordination. For Annen, this is the essence of the Tendai ordination, and supports his claim that the ordination is a form of realization of Buddhahood with this very body. Although the *Vajraśekhara* does not specify that the *samaya* precepts were received at that time, Annen may have interpreted the vague 'five stages of realization of Buddhahood' as being the five aspects of the Buddha's body, the first of which is the precepts. This is a formula found in the *Vajraśekhara*.

The esoteric precepts are mentioned in another esoteric scripture valued by Tendai, the *Mahāvairocana Sūtra*. In the eighteenth chapter, 'Receiving the Code of Training with Expedient Means', the four *pārājika*s and ten good precepts are listed, but in each case exceptions to the rule are mentioned. Typical is the precept prohibiting taking life:

> Lord of Mysteries, those bodhisattvas keep the precept of not taking life for as long as they live. They should forsake the sword and the rod, be free from murderous intent, and guard the life of another as if it were their own. There is [also] another expedient means: in order to liberate some kinds of beings from retribution for evil deeds in accordance with their deeds, [the taking of life] is [on occasion] carried out, but without thoughts of enmity or animosity. (Geibel 2005: 166–167)

The *Vinaya* precepts, and according to Annen, the ten good precepts and *Brahma's Net* precepts are all expedients derived from the esoteric precepts. Annen notes: 'The precepts of the bodhisattva-piṭaka refer to the samaya precepts of all the Buddhas. In full, they include the four pārājikas, the ten major precepts, the four grave wrongdoings, and the ten expedient studies' (T 74: 764b10–12). The repetition of the numbers four and ten refer to the manner in which the four *pārājikas* and ten good precepts are reinterpreted as expedients in the *Mahāvairocana Sūtra*. Various definitions of the *samaya* precepts exist, and Annen does not define them in the *Futsū kōshaku*, but generally they focus on not abandoning the mind of enlightenment, a somewhat vague rubric from which more detailed precepts emerge.

Space constraints prevent an investigation of how the bodhisattva precepts were treated in the Pure Land and Nichiren schools, but the power of the Buddha and the depiction of the current age as one of decline led to a de-emphasis or rejection of monastic discipline.

Conclusion

Because relatively little has been written about many aspects of the bodhisattva precepts in Western languages, I had two goals in writing this chapter. The first was to introduce some of the variety of collections of precepts found in Mahāyāna texts and the ways in which they interacted with the *Vinaya*. The number of Mahāyāna scriptures mentioning precepts suggests that the need to give the rules of the *Vinaya* a more nuanced interpretation was felt by many Mahāyāna practitioners in India and China. At the same time, the bodhisattva precepts in India must be viewed as a prescribed way to act rather than an actual description of practice because we know little about the actual practice of the majority of Mahāyāna practitioners. Moreover, we do not know whether many of the texts mentioned in this essay were widely used in India and at what time periods they might have been popular. The situation is clearer in China and Japan, and thus these areas have been the focus of this paper.

Among some of the key issues that emerge in the bodhisattva precepts are a more nuanced understanding of how the precepts were to be observed. Among the issues that preoccupied some of the compilers of these texts were whether and how Buddhism might be defended against its enemies, and whether killing by Buddhists was ever justified. Precepts could be modified so that performing ethically good acts and benefiting others might transcend the literal meaning of the *Vinaya*. The intention of the practitioner is stressed. Some of the practices that served as major markers of Buddhists in East Asia, most notably vegetarianism, were based on the Mahāyāna emphasis on compassion, and differed from the precepts in the *Vinaya*. An increased focus on confession practices as obviating violations of the precepts is striking, as is the sense that the precepts are often seen as giving one a direct connection with the Buddha. Finally, apocrypha such as the *Brahma's Net Sutra* played important roles in the conversion of East Asia to Mahāyāna Buddhism. The bodhisattva precepts gave lay practitioners a focus for their practice, and bodhisattva ordinations often provided a sense of identity with a larger group.

The second part of this chapter focused on some of the ways in which the bodhisattva precepts enabled practitioners to have a more nuanced view of ethical issues. I focused on Japanese Tendai because it represented one of the more extreme and interesting forms of Buddhist practice, and was also the tradition with which I was most familiar. If the chapter had focused on Chinese or Korean Buddhism or other schools of Japanese Buddhism, it might have been significantly different. In addition, the use of the bodhisattva precepts changed over time, sometimes being emphasized and at other times declining as the importance of the *Vinaya* was emphasized. Buddhism's encounters with demands of a modernizing world continue to influence views of ethics and karma. Tracing these changes requires the examination of specific texts; this has begun with the translation and studies of commentaries, but much remains to be done (Muller 2012; Park 2003).

Some of the most important rubrics that the bodhisattva precepts contributed to the interpretation of Buddhist ethics can be found in the three collections of pure precepts. Benefiting others and performing good actions were emphasized more than refraining from evil actions. The precepts of the *Vinaya* could be viewed as expedients that could be followed when appropriate, but violated when circumstances demanded a more liberal interpretation. The need to defend Buddhist temples, sometimes against competing Buddhist institutions, led to the need to store arms and occasionally use them. The application of doctrines such as emptiness suggested to some that precepts and ethical rubrics were nothing more than conventional concepts without lasting import. In contrast, arguments that the precepts were based on Buddha-nature and therefore were held over many lifetimes no matter what a person did sometimes led to a lax interpretation of monastic discipline. Defining the parameters of confession, the recitation of *dhāraṇī* and the chanting of the Buddha's name (*nenbutsu*) and their power to vanquish bad karma also significantly impacted observance of the precepts. At the same time, serious monks strove to define what it meant to be a Buddhist monk and to delineate Buddhist practice with more precision.

Works Cited

Clarke, S. (2000) The existence of the supposedly non-existent Śikṣādattā-śramaṇerī: a new perspective of parajika penance. *Bukkyō kenkyū*, 29, 149–176.

Donner, N., and Stevenson, D. (1993) *The great calming and contemplation: a study and annotated translation of the first chapter of Chih-i's mo-ho chih-kuan*. Honolulu: University of Hawai'i Press.

Funayama T. (2004) The acceptance of Buddhist precepts by the Chinese in the fifth century. *Journal of Asian history*, 38, 97–120.

Geibel, R. (trans.) (2001) *Two esoteric sūtras*. Berkeley: Numata Center for Buddhist Translation and Research.

Geibel, R. (trans.) (2005) *The Vairocanābhisaṃbodhi Sūtra*. Berkeley: Numata Center for Buddhist Translation and Research.

Getz, D. (2005) Popular religion and pure land in Song-dynasty Tiantai bodhisattva precept ordination ceremonies. In: W. Bodiford (ed.), *Going forth: visions of Buddhist vinaya*. Honolulu: University of Hawai'i Press, 161–184.

Groner, P. (1990) The *Fan-wang ching* and monastic discipline in Japanese Tendai: a study of Annen's *Futsū jubosatsukai kōshaku*. In: R. Buswell (ed.). *Buddhist apocryphal literature*. Honolulu: University of Hawai'i Press, 251–290.

Groner, P. (2005) Tradition and innovation: Eison, Kakujō, and the re-establishment of orders of monks and nuns during the Kamakura period. In: W. Bodiford (ed.), *Going forth: visions of Buddhist vinaya*. Honolulu: University of Hawai'i Press, 210–235.

Groner, P. (2009) Kōen and the 'consecrated ordination' within Japanese Tendai. In: J. A. Benn, L. R. Meeks, and J. Robson (eds), *Buddhist monasticism in east Asia: places of practice*. New York: Routledge, 178–207.

Groner, P. (2014) The *Lotus Sutra* and the perfect-sudden precepts. *Japanese journal of religious studies*, 41 (1), 103–132.

Haar, B. T. (2001) Buddhist-inspired options: aspects of lay religious life in the lower Yangzi from 1100 until 1340. *T'oung pao*, 87 (1–3), 92–152.
Heirman, A. (2008) Indian disciplinary rules and their early Chinese adepts: a Buddhist reality. *Journal of the American Oriental Society*, 128 (2), 257–272.
Hirakawa A. (1990) *A history of Indian Buddhism from Śākyamuni to early Mahāyāna*. Honolulu: University of Hawai'i Press.
Jaffe, R. (2010) *Neither monk nor layman: clerical marriage in modern Japanese Buddhism*. Honolulu: University of Hawai'i Press.
Janousch, A. (1999) The emperor as bodhisattva: the bodhisattva ordination and ritual assemblies of emperor Wu of the Liang Dynasty. In: J. P. Mcdermott (ed.), *State and court ritual in China*. Cambridge: Cambridge University Press, 112–149.
Licha, S. K. (forthcoming) Dharma transmission rituals in Sōtō Zen Buddhism. *Journal of the International Association of Buddhist Studies*.
Meeks, L. (2009) Vows for the masses: Eison and the popular expansion of precept-conferral ceremonies in premodern Japan. *Numen*, 56, 1–43.
Muller, A. C. (2012) *Exposition of the sutra of Brahma's net*. Seoul: Jogye Order of Korean Buddhism.
Nattier, J. (2005) *A few good men: the bodhisattva path according to the Inquiry of Ugra (Ugrapariprccha)*. Honolulu: University of Hawai'i Press.
Ōno H. (1954) *Daijō kaikyō no kenkyū*. Tokyo: Risōsha.
Park, J.-Y. (2003) Wŏnhyo's writings on bodhisattva precepts and the philosophical ground of Mahayana Buddhist ethics. *International journal of Buddhist thought and culture*, 2, 147–170.
Shih H.-C. (trans.) (1994) *The Sutra of Upāsaka Precepts*. Berkeley: Numata Center for Buddhist Translation and Research.
Shinsan zokuzōkyō (Xuzangjing). In: CBETA Chinese electronic tripitaka collection version 2014. Taibei: Zhonghua dianzi fodian xiehui.
Stevenson, D. B., and Kanno H. (2006) *The meaning of the Lotus Sūtra's course of ease and bliss: an annotated study of Nanyue Huisi's Fahua jing anlexing yi*. Tokyo: International Research Institute for Advanced Buddhology.
Suzuki gakujutsu zaidan (ed.) (1972) *Dainihon Bukkyō zensho*. Tokyo: Suzuki gakujutsu zaidan.
Tendai shūten kankōkai (ed.) (1973) *Tendaishū zensho*. Tokyo: Daiichi shobō.
Welch, H. (1967) *The practice of Chinese Buddhism: 1900–1950*. Cambridge, MA: Harvard University Press.
Yan Y. (2012) Buddhist discipline and the family life of Tang women. *Chinese studies in history*, 45 (4), 24–42.

Suggested Reading

Groner, P. (1990) The *Fan-wang ching* and monastic discipline in Japanese Tendai: a study of Annen's *Futsū jubosatsukai kōshaku*. In: R. Buswell (ed.), *Buddhist apocryphal literature*. Honolulu: University of Hawai'i Press, 251–290.
Groner, P. (2017) Medieval Japanese Tendai views of the precepts. In: Susan Andrews, Jinhua Chen, and Cuilan Liu (eds), *Rules of engagement: medieval traditions of Buddhist monastic regulation*. Hamburg: Hamburg University Press, 137–162.
Schlütter, M. (2017) The transformation of the formless precepts in the *Platform Sūtra (Liuzu tanjing)*. In: Susan Andrews, Jinhua Chen, and Cuilan Liu (eds), *Rules of*

engagement: medieval traditions of Buddhist monastic regulation. Hamburg: Hamburg University Press, 411–450.

Taehyeon (2012) *Exposition of the Sutra of Brahma's Net*, edited and translated by Charles A. Muller. Seoul, Korea: Jogye Order of Korean Buddhism.

Yamabe, N. (2005) Visionary repentance and visionary ordination in the *Brahmā net sūtra*. In: William M. Bodiford (ed.), *Going forth: visions of Buddhist Vinaya: essays presented in honor of Professor Stanley Weinstein*. Honolulu: University of Hawai'i Press, 17–39.

Shih, Heng-ching (1994) *The Sutra on Upāsaka precepts*. Berkeley, CA: Numata Center for Buddhist Translation and Research.

CHAPTER 3

ETHICS, MEDITATION, AND WISDOM

JUSTIN S. WHITAKER AND DOUGLASS SMITH

Introduction

The teachings of the Buddha are not merely a philosophical system to be understood or accepted, but rather are a soteriological path (*magga*) to be undertaken and completed. One common and early formulation of this path is the trio of ethics (*sīla*), meditation (*samādhi*), and wisdom (*paññā*). Another common formulation is the Eightfold Path (see Chapter 4 in this volume). Although these two formulations overlap substantially, they emerge from slightly different viewpoints.

The Eightfold Path has the pride of place of being set forth in what is accepted as the Buddha's first teaching, the *Dhammacakkappavattana Sutta* (SN V.420). However, when asked by the layperson Visākha about the priority of these two formulations, the nun Dhammadinā, with approval of the Buddha, replied, 'the three categories are not arranged in accordance with the Noble Eightfold Path, but the Noble Eightfold Path is arranged in accordance with the three categories' (MN I.299; Keown 2001: 38). Keown suggests that from this we might surmise that it is the Three Trainings rather than the eightfold enumeration that is of primary importance.

As Keown (2001) has demonstrated, reference to the Three Trainings is inconsistent in the early suttas, with variations on the terms used for each of the three as well as several versions that omit meditation altogether. An example of the latter is in the *Soṇadaṇḍa Sutta* (DN I.111) wherein ethics and wisdom alone are discussed as the defining features of a great person. In the *Ambaṭṭha Sutta* (DN I.87), conduct (*caraṇa*) and higher knowledge (*vijjā*) are the dual factors to be perfected.

However, the combination of ethics, meditation, and wisdom appears numerous times in the Pāli suttas (DN I.47, AN II.1, AN IV.100, It 50, Thag 65, Ap i 302, Peṭ para 100). This threefold formulation also appears in the Abhidhamma and in commentaries on both the *Vinaya* and the suttas. Furthermore, it is part of the very structure of

Buddhaghosa's *Path of Purification* (*Visuddhimagga*), the most influential commentary in Theravāda Buddhism. We should therefore keep in mind that a variety of formulations were employed in the early texts in different contexts and for different purposes while we concern ourselves with this version of the path.

The formulation of ethics, meditation, and wisdom is also expanded in numerous ways, as in the *Ambaṭṭha Sutta* (DN I.110), where it is further broken down as a 'gradual instruction' (*anupubbikathā*), beginning with generosity (*dāna*), on ethics (*sīla*), and on heaven (*sagga*), followed by teachings focused on meditation, namely the disadvantages of sensuality (*kāma*) and the advantages of renunciation (*nekkhamma*), and finally the particular Buddhist wisdom of dependent origination (*paticcasamuppāda*).

The *Sikkhā Suttas* (AN I.231–235, also AN I.236–239, AN III.444, DN III.219, MN I.324, and variously in the KN) put forth the same three-part structure as above, replacing meditation (*samādhi*) with mind (*citta*). Here they are taught as 'higher training in ethics' (*adhisīlasikkhā*), 'higher training in mind' (*adhicittasikkhā*), and 'higher training in wisdom' (*adhipaññāsikkhā*). The higher training in ethics, aimed at monks and nuns, includes living in accordance with the monastic rules of discipline (*pāṭimokkha*). The higher training in mind continues to advise on withdrawal from sensuality, following with a description of the states of meditative absorption (*jhāna*) culminating at equanimity (*upekkhā*) and mindfulness (*sati*). Finally, the higher training in wisdom is composed of discerning suffering as it really is (*dukkhanti yathābhūtaṃ pajānāti*); similarly recognizing the arising of suffering, the cessation, and the path leading to that cessation as they truly are. That is, the higher training in wisdom comprises a complete understanding of the Four Noble Truths as they truly are.

Anyone following the path will begin at their own starting point, and it will lead them towards the destination. The destination is awakening (*bodhi*), an experiential knowing that fulfils certain canonical criteria but defies complete description. As for the starting point, because it will be unique to each traveller, it is similarly difficult to pin down. Although the directions along the path will vary to some extent from person to person, the Buddha provides broad categories to describe the unawakened, as well as generalized descriptions of the path. Indeed, this threefold formulation is just such a generalization of what in practice is a complex and always entirely personal journey.

Given that we have a starting point, the state of being unawakened, a path of Three Trainings, and a goal of awakening, where shall we begin? One obvious place to start is right where we are, as unawakened beings. What did the Buddha teach about such beings?

The Path Begins: The Worldling (*Puthujjana*)

The path begins with a very important binary: the lineage of ordinary worldlings (*puthujjana-gotta*) and the lineage of the noble ones (*ariya-gotta*), those who have reached any of the four stages of awakening. An ordinary worldling can be either a monastic or a layperson. He or she may be completely inexperienced or may have undergone a great deal of practice but have not reached the first stage of awakening, called stream-entry (*sotāpanna*), wherein one has overcome the first three of the ten fetters (*saṃyojana*) that bind one to the cycles of rebirth. The fetters are commonly listed as: (1) self-identity views (*sakkāya-diṭṭhi*); (2) doubt (*vicikiccha*); (3) attachment to rules and rituals (*sīlabbata-parāmāsa*); (4) sensual desire (*kāma-rāga*); (5) ill-will (*vyāpāda*); (6) desire for material existence (*rūpa-rāga*); (7) desire for immaterial existence (*arūpa-rāga*); (8) conceit (*māna*); (9) restlessness (*uddhacca*); and (10) ignorance (*avijjā*). As one progresses in the Buddhist path, the fetters are overcome in a roughly linear sequence.

The worldling's experience, bound by these fetters, is driven by ignorance (*avijjā*), the first step on the wheel of dependent origination, making this an obvious topic to be addressed by the Buddha. In a teaching on 'the ignorant' (*assutavā*), the Buddha notes that a being, ignorant and ordinary (*assutavato puthujjana*), might grow weary and detached from the body, recognizing it as not the self (*attā*) (SN II.94). This is because the body is a relatively easy object in which to see the rise and fall of the elements or constituents. It is easy to see that we are not our bodies, in that food and water enter and pass through us, in that individual parts of us die and are replaced in an ongoing succession such that the physical 'us' of today may be made up of no part of the 'us' of a few years ago. However, notes the Buddha, the ordinary person seems unable to notice this same nature in the mind, thought, or consciousness (*citta, mano, viññāṇa*), even though the mind changes with much more rapidity than the body (SN II.94–95). Thus in the ignorant and ordinary person the mind, thought, or consciousness are often clung to as 'This is mine, I am this, this is my self' (*etaṃ mama, esohamasmi, eso me attā*). This is the state we find ourselves in as worldlings before entering upon the Buddhist path.

For the ordinary worldling, the path of overcoming clinging begins in generosity (*dāna, cāga*). While generosity may be considered *de facto* part of the traditional 'gradual training' (*anupubbasikkhā*) exemplified in texts such as the *Sāmaññaphala Sutta* (DN I.47), it is not explicitly mentioned as such. This is perhaps because accounts of the gradual training are aimed at the monastic context: training begins when the worldling gains faith in the Buddha and goes forth into homelessness. Generosity on the other hand is a practice confined to the lay context, since (the gift of *Dhamma* aside) only laypeople have possessions to give. Therefore, *in practice*, generosity is usually considered separate from the standard training in ethics (*sīla*) that one finds in the gradual training.

An illustration of the importance of generosity can be found in the *Sīha Sutta* (AN III.38). There, the layman Sīha visits the Buddha over the protests of his teacher, Mahāvīra, the head of the Jains (known in the Pāli Canon as Nigaṇṭha Nātaputta). Sīha quickly converts to Buddhism, but the Buddha accepts him on the condition that he will continue to support the Jains as he had previously. Thus, the sutta extols the benefits of generosity that are visible in the here and now (*sandiṭṭhikaṃ*). These benefits included being dear and charming to people, being admired by good people, having a good reputation spread far and wide, having a presence in society free from embarrassment, and obtaining a future rebirth in heaven.

The benefits of generosity also redound to oneself in the present life. One of generous mind is 'free from the stain of miserliness' (AN II.66); one has begun work towards lessening the greed of clinging to possessions. One also has begun work towards lessening hatred through gladdening the mind. Indeed, 'When a noble disciple recollects his generosity, on that occasion his mind is not obsessed by lust, hatred, or delusion' (AN III.286). In this way, generosity is the proper base for practice, one that also not incidentally materially supports the *saṅgha* of monastics with food, clothing, and shelter, without which the *saṅgha* would not be possible.

From the development of generosity, one is directed to next develop *sīla*, or a broader ethical relationship with the world. This begins the gradual training, 'gradual' since it is expected to be slow and steady rather than immediate, although there are some exceptions to that rule (e.g. Ud 48).

There is both an ordinary (*lokiya*) and a transcendent (*lokuttara*) or noble (*arya*) version of the path. The difference between them involves the character of right view (*sammā diṭṭhi*) one grasps at that stage of the path. The worldling will usually begin her ethical development at the ordinary level of understanding. She begins with a general, conceptual understanding of right view: that there is merit and demerit (*puñña, apuñña*) in terms of body, speech, and mind; that there are skilful and unskilful (*kusala, akusala*) ways of behaving; that skilful acts create kammic merit that ripens in future benefit; and that unskilful acts create kammic demerit that ripen in future sorrow. These make up the background of ethical conduct.

On the transcendent level, right view refers to 'transformative direct insight' into the Noble Truths, and at least first glimpses of *nibbāna* (MN I.48; Harvey 2013: 82–83). This insight is transformative in that it results in a relinquishing of the bonds of attachment. That is, a distinctive shift is made away from the particular content of views and towards *how* views are to be held by the agent, namely without clinging (Fuller 2005; Collins 1982: 85–144).

Ethics (*sīla*)

We have thus far been translating the Pāli term *sīla* as simply 'ethics'. This is a useful and accurate definition in most contexts. However, a fuller etymology and defence of this translation is in order. An early and influential etymology of the term comes from Buddhaghosa's *Visuddhimagga*, wherein it is said that 'the meaning of *sīla* is the meaning "head" (*siras*), the meaning of *sīla* is the meaning of "cool" (*sītala*)' (Vism 1.19, quoted and translated in Keown 2001: 49). Thus one cultivating virtue or ethics literally cultivates a cool head. This points to a transcultural experience associated with the human physiology of anger versus opposite states of mind (Kövecses 1986: 11–38; cf. Lakoff and Johnson 1999). Vasubandhu likewise describes the Sanskrit *śīla* as coming from the root *śī* in the sense of 'refreshing' or having a cooling effect (Keown 2001: 49). The importance of cool temperature resonates with the metaphor famously described in the Fire Sermon (SN IV.19) that the Buddhist goal of *nibbāna* is a 'putting out' of the fires of greed, hatred, and delusion.

In this sense *sīla* should be seen as describing ethics in a manner similar to Western philosophy, primarily in terms of the inner mental states or intentions of the agent. Note that 'ethics' stems from the Greek *ethikos* and *ethos*, meaning 'moral character; habitual character and disposition'. This is the same internal state described by *sīla* that nonetheless shapes outward actions. As the first verse of the *Dhammapada* states:

> All experience is preceded by mind,
> Led by mind,
> Made by mind.
> Speak or act with a corrupted mind,
> And suffering follows
> As the wagon wheel follows the hoof of the ox.
> (Fronsdal 2005: 1)

In this regard, a person who has mastered *sīla* might rightly be called a virtuous person. In common usage, indeed even in specialized philosophical discussion, virtues are very often understood as a particular discrete set of enumerable traits (Honderich 1995: 900), but it is not entirely clear that there is any one such set in Buddhism. Dreyfus (1995: 44) suggests that the 'five faculties' (*indriya*) in the Abhidhamma could serve as Buddhist virtues, e.g. faith, energy, mindfulness, concentration, and wisdom. However, as he points out, there are other, similar lists one could choose from.

Sīla's importance in the Buddhist path is emphasized in many canonical and commentarial sources that describe it as a foundation for all of one's successes in life. Buddhaghosa describes *sīla* as the 'root of all success' of which *nibbāna* is the 'fruit' (Keown 2001: 50). It provides an absence of regret (*avippaṭisāra*), since it is regret that clouds the mind (AN V.312). In the *Milindapañha*, *sīla* is called the 'basis and mark of all good things', including the path (*magga*) itself and *satipaṭṭhāna*, the very presence of or attention with mindfulness (see Anālayo 2006: 236 for a discussion of the etymology of *satipaṭṭhāna*). Furthermore, *sīla* is not always considered just the basis for more important work. As Buddhaghosa remarks: 'Where can such another stair be found that climbs, as *sīla* does, to heaven? Or yet another gate that gives one the city of nibbāna?' (Keown 2001: 53). For Buddhaghosa, *sīla* is not simply a stage to be passed along the way but is constitutive of the 'holy life to be lived'. Thus the Buddha says of himself, 'it is I who am the foremost in the highest morality (*adhisīla*)' (DN I.174).

Sīla is highly valuable even if it is not cultivated for the attainment of *nibbāna*. It leads to worldly goods in this life as well as guaranteeing heavenly rebirth. According to the Buddha, the first benefit of earnestness in *sīla* for the layperson is 'much wealth' (*bhogakkhandhaṃ*) (DN II.86, DN III.236; see also Vism I.23, Keown 2001: 45). Presumably this is because honesty and righteousness are good business. But honesty and righteousness are their own wealth as well: *sīla* is also listed along with the two key mental qualities of moral shame (*hiri*) and moral dread (*ottappa*) as three of the seven kinds of wealth (AN IV.5). In practice, *sīla* requires moral shame and moral dread as 'two bright qualities that protect the world' (AN I.51), and without which moral restraint would be impossible.

The Buddha provides several lists of the elements of *sīla*. The most widely known are the five (lay) precepts and their monastic counterparts in the 'gradual training': to avoid killing, stealing, sexual misconduct, false speech, and intoxicants. One is also to avoid livelihoods that involve harm, such as trading in weapons, living beings, meat, intoxicants, or poison (AN III.208). But occasionally the Buddha gives a broader picture. For example (AN IV.281), when asked by the layman Dīghajāṇu to teach the *Dhamma* 'in a way that will lead to our welfare and happiness in this present life and in future lives' the Buddha elaborates upon eight actions for the layperson, four that will lead to welfare and happiness in this life and four that will ensure better future lives. For this life one is to be skilful and diligent in earning a living, to guard one's wealth assiduously, to associate with good people, and to balance one's expenditures to one's income. For one's future lives, one is to place trust in the Buddha as an awakened being, to behave in accordance with the five precepts, to be generous and charitable, and to pursue wisdom.

Because accomplishment in wisdom eventually leads to the awakened state associated with the end of *dukkha, sīla* can be seen to encompass the entire practice, not becoming perfected until one becomes an *arahant*. Until that point, the practice of *sīla* is a training that one undertakes conceptually, with effort (e.g. MN I.446).

The Buddha also recommended an expanded list of eight precepts for the laity on Uposatha days, including abstaining from sexual intercourse, eating only one meal a day, and eschewing entertainments and high beds (AN IV.248–251). This is an expanded practice of renunciation, giving lay followers a taste of monastic living. It might, therefore, function as the thin end of a wedge for attracting some to monastic life. This would be for the best, for lay life, according to the Buddha, is ethically difficult. It is 'a path of dust … It is not easy for one dwelling at home to lead the perfectly complete, perfectly purified holy life, bright as a polished conch' (DN I.63).

The monk in training also follows rules, but they are part of a 'higher training in ethics' (*adhisīlasikkhā*) according to the stricter and more complex Pāṭimokkha rules. These involve the abandoning of certain activities of lay life, most famously sexual activity and handling money, but also dancing, attending shows, playing games, enjoying luxurious beds and fancy clothes, using makeup, telling fortunes, and so on (DN I.63–69; Bodhi 1989: 13). In addition 'higher training' involves sense restraint in which one guards one's actions by withdrawing oneself from situations that might promote 'evil unwholesome states such as covetousness and grief' (DN I.70). That is to say, such rules, indeed all ethical rules one finds in Buddhist practice, are aimed at minimizing harm and thus *dukkha* on a gross social level.

Although rules form a central part of ethical training, there is a danger that one can become dogmatically attached to them (Anālayo 2003: 220 n. 12). Believing that rules are the essence of training is just as extreme as claiming that there is no harm in sensual desires (Ud 71). The fetter of 'grasping to rules and rituals' (*sīlabbata-parāmāsa*) is exemplified by those who aspire to higher rebirth through ethical conduct (MN I.102) or by those who undertake ritual ascetic practices such as the dog- or ox-duty, whereby renunciants would behave as dogs or oxen to gain liberation (MN I.387ff.).

MEDITATION (*SAMĀDHI*)

The second training is variously referred to as meditation or concentration (*samādhi*), mind (*citta*), or cultivation (*bhāvanā*). These Pāli terms are tied together by the late Bhikkhu Buddhadasa (1989: 26): 'constraining the mind to remain in the condition most conducive to success'. This points to the nature of meditation in early Buddhism as a mental training that bridges the trainings in ethics and wisdom. This placement has allowed some scholars (notably Keown 2001: 38) to explain the Buddhist soteriology in terms of a 'binary model' of ethics (*sīla*) and wisdom ('insight', *paññā*), apparently leaving meditation to one side. However, Keown relies on the *Soṇadaṇḍa Sutta*, which explicitly links the development of *paññā* to states of absorption (*jhāna*) and meditative insight (DN I.124ff.). In that text, the Buddha tries to bring a brahmin around to an understanding of the *Dhamma*. Hence the Buddha's agreement that ethics and wisdom alone comprise 'the highest thing in the world' should be seen in the context of introductory pedagogy and not as a definitive description of the relative worth of meditation as compared to the other two limbs of this triad.

Others (Dreyfus 1995; Mills 2004) see meditation as playing a crucial role in the Buddhist path, even though the relative importance of various types of meditation continues to be debated (Anālayo 2016b, see below); canonical texts use several terms for the types of meditation that may be undertaken as well as for the states of absorption (*jhāna*) that might thereby be achieved. Here, however, we will discuss only a few of the terms most salient to the 'Three Trainings' model, beginning with *samādhi*.

Meditation and Ethics

How does ethics affect meditation? *Sīla* aims at non-harming, one benefit of which is that it prevents regret, which can become a hindrance to successful meditation practice. Lack of regret (*avippaṭisāra*) (AN V.312) is critical to the development of open, clear, and focused mindfulness. It is also essential for right concentration, since achievement of *jhāna* requires that we overcome the five hindrances of sense desire, ill will, restlessness, sloth, and doubt (AN III.428–429). In particular, behaving in a way that harms others will tend to increase one's restlessness, both because moral shame (*hiri*) will disturb one's mind and because moral dread (*ottappa*) will make one worried about the consequences of unethical actions. A mind that is restless and worried is not conducive to concentration, hence not conducive to *jhāna*.

In the *Bāhiya Sutta* (SN V.165–166), ethics and upright or clear view form the basis of wholesome states. These, when taken into the practice of mindfulness meditation, lead the ascetic Bāhiya to awakening: 'What is the start of wholesome states (*kusala dhamma*)? Ethics thoroughly purified, and upright view.' In the discourse, Bāhiya is instructed to then practise the four 'attendings with mindfulness' (*satipaṭṭhāna*) and, having done so, gains complete awakening, thus becoming an *arahant*.

How, in turn, does meditation affect ethics? Keown (2001: 77–78) considers that calming meditation (*samatha-bhāvanā*) 'cultivates moral virtue' by suppressing sense desire and ill will. Of course, calming meditation requires a modicum of ethical awareness, for without it, calm would prove inaccessible, but at the same time concentration practice makes one less prone to becoming snared by sense desire and ill will into acting unethically. Mills (2004) argues that calming meditation cultivates ethical concern through practice of the divine abodes (*brahmavihāras*) in particular. That is, Mills suggests it may be the calming practices of loving-kindness (*mettā*), compassion (*karuṇā*), sympathetic joy (*muditā*), and equanimity (*upekkha*) that work to rid the mind of unskilful and unethical mind states related to harming oneself and others rather than the calming states of *jhāna*.

Similarly, focusing on *mettā*, Gombrich argues that the Buddha taught that *brahmavihāras* have the power to bring about liberation in the practitioner (see discussion of Lance Cousins and Anālayo on *jhāna* [section 'Absorption (*jhāna*)']). As Gombrich puts it, 'the Buddha saw love and compassion as means to salvation—in his terms, to the attainment of nirvana' (2009: 76). Gombrich has made this argument in previous works, based on analysis of early Buddhist texts as well as *Upaniṣads* (the *Bṛhad-āraṇyaka* and *Chāndogya*) with which the Buddha was likely familiar and to which he was therefore likely responding (1996: 58–64; 1998). Gethin has termed this interpretation 'something of a puzzle' (2012). It is contradicted by several canonical passages that put attainment of the *brahmavihāras* below that of liberation (e.g. MN I.38, MN I.351, AN I.180–185), and has therefore been criticized for diverging from the Theravādin Buddhist tradition (Bodhi 1997).

Effort (*vāyama*)

In general, effort belongs to the meditation division of the path because it is a practice of active cultivation (*bhāvanā*) of wholesome states and avoidance of unwholesome states, but effort and meditation, like ethics and meditation, have a reciprocal relationship. Effort is also related to ethics. The *Vibhaṅga Sutta* (SN V.8ff.) offers four aspects of right effort: (1) generating desire (*chanda*), and so on, for the sake of the non-arising of evil (*pāpakā*) and unskilful qualities (*akusalā dhammā*); (2) generating desire, and so on, for the abandonment of evil and unskilful qualities; (3) generating desire, and so on, for the sake of the arising of skilful qualities; and (4) generating desire, and so on, for the maintaining of non-confusion and cultivation (*bhāvanā*) of skilful qualities that have arisen. In this sense, right effort is as much a matter of ethics as it is of meditation. Without a developed sense of right and wrong, of skilful and unskilful, right effort will be misdirected or ineffective at achieving its proper end of producing wisdom and awakening.

A second discourse on right effort brings the topic of meditation to the forefront. In the *Soṇa Sutta* (AN III.374), the monk Soṇa is having trouble with striving in his secluded meditation (*paṭisallīna*). The Buddha comes to him with an analogy, pointing out that a lute is not 'well tuned and easy to play' either if its strings are too loose or too tight.

> In the same way, Soṇa, overly exerted effort leads to restlessness, overly loose effort leads to idleness. Therefore you, Soṇa, should determine the correct effort and, having comprehended thus, attune the [five] faculties, and there take hold of the object [of meditation].

Here the Buddha links right effort and the meditative hindrances, in particular the hindrances of restlessness (*uddhacca-kukkucca*) and sloth-and-torpor (*thīna-middha*). All effort, but particularly that in *jhāni*c meditation, requires one to overcome these hindrances in order to achieve a mind that is clear, unified, and focused enough to enter absorption. (Indeed, the former of these hindrances, restlessness, is not abandoned completely until full awakening.) Gauging one's intensity of effort therefore is a critical aspect of progress along the path.

Meditation also enhances effort. Certain mind states that are beneficial for formal meditation are also beneficial for right effort generally. The practice of mindfulness meditation (*sati*) includes making an effort to act in full awareness 'when going forward and returning; ... looking ahead and looking away; ... eating, drinking ... defecating and urinating ... walking, standing, sitting, falling asleep, waking up, talking, and keeping silent (etc.)' (MN I.57). That is, one is to make the effort to cultivate the skilful quality of mindful attention essentially at all times during one's life. Thus one should understand right effort as being ideally continuous and constant, even when occurring in a practice usually considered that of formal meditation, i.e. mindfulness.

Meditative effort or cultivation (*bhāvanā*) extends beyond the cultivation of concentration or mindfulness. Cousins (1996: 41) makes the point that 'such monastic activities as studying or teaching the *dhamma* as well as chanting *sutta*s or repetition of *gāthā* may equally be forms of *bhāvanā*'. Similarly, Gethin (2004: 215) points to chanting and recollection practices as canonical examples of meditative cultivation. Thus, lay participation in meditation may have been more widespread than some scholars assume, since traditional categories of *bhāvanā* were quite accommodating.

In summation, in both the case of formal mindfulness meditation and in wider social practices such as studying, chanting, or recollecting we see that right effort is a field of practice wider than ordinarily assumed. In the case of the monastic engaged in right mindfulness, effort should ideally be unstinting. In the case of the lay practitioner it may involve practices of ethical restraint such as the five or eight precepts, but also meditative practices with a more devotional flavour. In recent times, with the advent of the *vipassanā* movement begun by Ledi Sayadaw in modern Burma (Braun 2013), right effort for the layperson has expanded to encompass most of traditional mindfulness practice.

Absorption (*jhāna*)

The Buddha's first recorded experience with meditation was as a young boy under a rose-apple tree. There he says he entered the first *jhāna*, an experience of 'pleasure that has nothing to do with sensual pleasures and unwholesome states' (MN I.246–247). Later on in his days of wandering and experimentation before the attainment of awakening the Buddha says he learned techniques of deep meditative absorption from two masters, Āḷāra Kālāma and Uddaka Rāmaputta. There is scholarly disagreement over whether these masters taught Jain (Bronkhorst 2009: 49–56) or Brahminical (Wynne 2007) techniques, but it is sufficient to say that the Buddha did not consider them liberative. In any case, these historical vignettes demonstrate that techniques of meditative concentration were not uncommon in a pre-Buddhist milieu; they may even have been considered essential aspects of the Indian renunciant's path.

The Buddha taught meditative absorption as the 'four *jhānas*' or 'four form (*rūpa*) *jhānas*' (SN V.10). These constitute a process of absorption into progressively calmer, subtler, and more pleasant states of mind that retain a subtle experience of form, unlike the techniques of meditative absorption canonically known as the 'formless spheres' (*āyatanas*) he had learned earlier from his two teachers as a *bodhisatta*. While these 'formless spheres' became known also as states of *jhāna* in later tradition, they are always treated separately from *jhāna* in the canonical texts, and therefore should not be run together in the early tradition (e.g. Norman 1997: 31; Gethin 2001: 347). Indeed, there is scholarly disagreement as to whether formless sphere meditation was practised by the historical Buddha (e.g. Gethin 2001, Wynne 2007) or whether it is a later interpolation (Bronkhorst 1985; Vetter 1988: xxii).

Each state of absorption is considered a 'superhuman state (*uttari manussa dhammā*), a distinction in knowledge and vision worthy of the noble ones' (MN I.207ff.), in that it involves wholesome pleasures. In the *Sāmaññaphala Sutta* (DN I.47ff.) the Buddha's awakening is said to have taken place soon after exiting the fourth *rūpa jhāna*, which is absorption into equanimity. Here as elsewhere the fourth *jhāna* is said to provide the mental power necessary to provide mundane (*lokiya*) powers such as the ability to disappear or walk through walls, the ability to hear things not normally heard, the ability to read minds, to remember past lives, and to see the effects of kammic reward (Ñāṇamoli and Bodhi 2009: 37). More importantly, achievement of the fourth *jhāna* often precedes the supramundane (*lokuttara*) power of knowing the extinction of the defilements (*āsavas*) that correspond to *nibbāna*.

There is some question as to whether or to what extent achievements in *jhāna* are actually necessary to attain awakening (Vism I.6, Gunaratana 1980: 17, Anālayo 2015: 13, Cousins 1984, 1996). For example in the *Mahāmālunkya Sutta* (MN I.435) the Buddha describes a process of awakening that seems only to require attainment of the first *jhāna*. The *Susima Sutta* (SN II.119ff.) seems to support this because it presents a number of *arahant* bhikkhus who are without the mundane powers typically said to result from attainment of the fourth *jhāna*. When asked how this could be, they reply that they are 'liberated by wisdom' (*paññavimuttā*). While this does not establish that they entirely lacked the experience of *jhāna*, it suggests that *jhāna* was not the focus of their efforts, and that perhaps they had not perfected their way to the fourth *jhāna* in particular. This would be a path of so-called 'dry insight', or awakening without the perfection of at least certain of the *jhānas*. However, as Anālayo points out, none of the versions of the *Susima Sutta* 'supports the assumption that a purely intellectual approach could lead to full awakening, without having cultivated a level of tranquillity that at least borders on absorption attainment' (2015: 13).

Anālayo also notes that *jhāna* is not without its 'potential drawbacks' (2016: 45). One's attachment to the pleasures of *jhāna* can divert one from the path. One can also mistake *jhānic* states for states of awakening. These constitute two of the 'doctrines of *nibbāna* here and now' (*diṭṭhadhammanibbānavāda*) mentioned as wrong views in the *Brahmajāla Sutta*.

Mindfulness (*sati*)

Mindfulness is perhaps the most famous of the Buddha's suggested practices. It is best seen as a large suite of practices oriented around breath meditation. These are sketched out in the *Ānāpānasati* (MN III.78), *Satipaṭṭhāna* (MN I.55), and *Mahāsatipaṭṭhāna* (DN II.290) suttas, in four general categories.

The first of these is mindfulness of the body. This refers to breath following and being aware of one's body and bodily position, posture, motion, and indeed all of one's daily activities. It even includes awareness of the parts of the body, including the internal organs, awareness of the four elements in the body, and nine various charnel ground contemplations of dead bodies and bodily remains. Notably, although mindfulness is often characterized as a practice of non-conceptual awareness of the present moment, several of these body-oriented practices involve active, even creative contemplation. To meditate upon one's kidneys and intestines, or upon the solid and gaseous parts of one's body, or upon the fact that one's body will end up a bloated corpse, is to engage in an active, conceptually mediated process of analysing one's body into physical and temporal parts.

The second category of mindfulness practice is that of feeling (*vedanā*). Here one is to become aware of feelings as being pleasant, painful, or neutral. In the schema of dependent origination, feeling precedes craving (*taṇhā*), which in turn is the proximate cause of *dukkha*. Since one key aim of practice is to break the link between feelings and the craving they produce, awareness of feelings as they occur is key to developing skilful habits.

The third category of mindfulness practice is that of mind. That is, one is to become aware of the character of one's mind: is it filled with greed, lust, hatred, or confusion? Is it free of these characteristics? Here we can think of the verses from the *Dhammapada* cited above that suffering follows from speaking or acting with a corrupted mind whereas happiness follows from speaking or acting with a peaceful mind. In order to make use of such advice, one must practise attending to one's own mental state: if one does not know the character of one's own mind, one will be without the capacity to mitigate its ill effects.

The last category of mindfulness practice involves mindfulness of *dhammas*, which Ñāṇamoli and Bodhi (2009) translate 'mind-objects', Gethin (1998: 195) 'physical and mental processes', and Anālayo (2006) leaves untranslated. This is a broad basket of practices (enlarged somewhat in DN II.290ff.) that essentially involve training oneself to view phenomena according to Buddhist categories. As Anālayo (2006: 186) says,

> contemplation of *dhammas* skillfully applies *dhammas* (classificatory categories) as taught in the *Dhamma* (the teaching of the Buddha) during contemplation in order to bring about an understanding of the *dhamma* (principle) of conditionality and lead to the realization of the highest of all *dhammas* (phenomena): Nibbāna.

In particular, when practising mindfulness of *dhammas* one trains oneself to be aware of the five mental hindrances to meditation practice, i.e. to be aware of when they are present or when they are absent. By right effort one can work to eliminate them and keep them from returning. Similarly, one trains oneself to be aware of the five aggregates and their arising and passing; of the six sense bases and the fetters that they create, attaching one to objects of desire; of the factors that accompany awakening; and of the Four Noble Truths themselves. It is again notable that in this type of mindfulness one is not merely being aware of the present moment. There is a strong conceptual overlay at work, analysing and categorizing phenomena in categories relevant to awakening.

The practices of the four mindfulness categories are described with an accompanying refrain: one is to contemplate the matter at hand internally, externally, and both internally and externally. One is to contemplate its arising, passing, and arising and passing. One is to be aware of it 'to the extent necessary for bare knowledge and continuous mindfulness' (*ñaṇamattāya paṭissatimattāya*). One is to do all of this 'abiding independent, not clinging to anything in the world' (*anissito ca viharati, na ca kiñci loke upādiyati*). All of these directions suggest that one should take an objective attitude to the practices, seeing them as revelatory of the universal character of experience in the world. One is also to take an objective attitude towards the practices in the sense that one does not allow oneself to be carried off by proliferations of thought nor by dependencies of clinging.

Mindfulness and Insight (*vipassanā*)

In the early texts meditative practices are most generally described in terms of mindfulness or absorption. Beginning in the late nineteenth century, Ledi Sayadaw, a Burmese

Theravāda monk, began a revitalization of insight (*vipassanā*) meditation (Braun 2013). Although the early texts do at times speak of meditation in terms of insight, Ledi's goal was to make insight practice the focus of effort. This subtle shift in emphasis occurred in the context of Western colonialism. To compete with Christian proselytization, Ledi aimed to promote a path tailored to a broad audience of laypeople as well as monastics. To this end he deemphasized *jhāna* in favour of direct awareness of the changing, unsatisfactory, and selfless nature of reality. He also made a number of other subtle innovations in emphasis that revitalized Buddhism, such as translating the teachings into vernacular languages and bringing about a modest levelling of the lay/monastic distinction (Braun 2013: ch. 3). Nevertheless, as Braun notes (139), Ledi's approach to Buddhist meditation had canonical grounding. Essentially, he was supporting the practice of 'dry insight', i.e. to pursue awakening without benefit of (or at least with less emphasis upon) the *jhānas*.

A few early texts describe insight. For example, in the sutta of the Kiṃsuka Tree (SN IV.191ff.) the Buddha gives a parable comparing the person to a walled city with six gates that correspond to the senses. The gatekeeper is mindfulness (*sati*), recognizing who should and should not be allowed into the city. The gatekeeper admits two messengers from outside, serenity (*samatha*) and insight (*vipassanā*), who provide information to the lord of the city, consciousness (*viññāṇa*). We may assume that 'serenity' refers to the concentration practice of *jhāna*, and 'insight' to the wisdom gained through mindfulness practice (see, e.g., Cousins 1984: 58). If so, these messengers can also be seen as corresponding to meditation (*samādhi*) and wisdom (*paññā*). The route the messengers take is the Eightfold Path, and the message provided by the messengers is awakening itself.

This parable suggests a tight interrelation between serenity and insight and between these both and mindfulness: mindfulness allows for the development of serenity as well as insight, and serenity and insight arrive by the same route. So for example we find the pair 'serenity (*samatha*) and insight (*vipassanā*)' listed as the 'things to be developed by direct knowledge (*abhiññā*)' (SN V.52, AN II.247). In this sense, in the early texts insight should not be seen a practice so much as the result of practice. So if mindfulness is the practice, insight is its goal, a goal that can be seen as essentially identical to wisdom (*paññā*) itself. While Ledi's so-called 'insight practice' was canonical in its details, its name has something of an oxymoronic flavour. Nevertheless his aim was towards practices he saw as most directly aimed at promoting wisdom, that is practices (themselves recommended in the canonical texts) of attending to the changing, unsatisfactory, and selfless nature of phenomena, rather than (e.g.) *jhāna*ic practices *per se*.

WISDOM (*PAÑÑĀ*)

The Buddha uses many metaphors to illustrate the key importance of wisdom to the path. 'Just as, bhikkhus, among animals the lion is declared to be their chief, so too, among the states conducive to enlightenment the faculty of wisdom is declared to be their chief, that is, for the attainment of enlightenment' (SN V.228). 'Just as, bhikkhus, the footprints of all living beings that walk fit into the footprint of the elephant ... so too ... the faculty of wisdom is declared to be their chief' (SN V.231). So too heartwood (SN V.231). So too various trees chief in their realms (SN V.237–239).

If wisdom is a mental faculty in early Buddhism, it is also a suite of practices aimed at strengthening or reinforcing that faculty. Among these are the so-called 'insight' practices recommended in the *Satipaṭṭhāna Sutta* such as the contemplation of the arising and passing of phenomena in experiences that were highlighted by Ledi Sayadaw. One comes to be wise by such practices, which lead to full understanding of the truth of the Noble Truths by immediate experience: by seeing and understanding not only that suffering exists, but that its cause is craving, and that craving and hence suffering can be extinguished by proper development along the path. This seeing and understanding cannot merely be conceptual; it must be transformative.

When asked the purpose of wisdom, Sāriputta responds that its purpose 'is direct knowledge (*abhiññā*), its purpose is full understanding (*pariññā*), its purpose is abandoning (*pahāna*)' (MN I.293). On the standard pericope, wisdom is a faculty (*indriya*) 'directed to arising and passing away, which is noble and penetrative, leading to the complete destruction of suffering' (e.g. SN V.197). This is full understanding of each of the Four Noble Truths 'as it really is' (*yathābhūtaṃ*) (SN V.199). These descriptions jointly imply that wisdom cannot merely be a form of propositional knowledge, although it is compatible with the possession of such knowledge. Instead, wisdom is essentially liberative: one who is truly wise abandons craving. In so doing, the wise one destroys suffering.

Wisdom is a faculty of perceiving the world 'as it really is' whereas (ordinary) perception (*saññā*) is distorted by ignorance born of kammic residue (Bausch 2015: 166, 170). Wisdom pierces through the four inversions or distortions of perception: perceiving the impermanent to be permanent, the suffering to be pleasurable, the non-self to be self, and the unattractive to be attractive. Rather, wisdom, 'by the acquisition of right view' (*sammādiṭṭhisamādānā*), perceives the world as it really is: that all conditioned things are impermanent, suffering, non-self, and unattractive. People who see the world in this way are considered wise (*sappaññā*) (AN II.52).

Wisdom also is a form of supramundane right view, i.e. one that encompasses propositional forms of right view such as that all conditioned things are impermanent without thereby clinging to such views. In the *Mahācattārīsaka Sutta* (MN III.72) wisdom is described as 'right view that is noble, taintless, supramundane, a factor of the path' (*sammādiṭṭhi ariyā anāsavā lokuttarā maggaṅgā*). That is, wisdom is a kind of right view that in Paul Fuller's (2005) sense transcends all views by relinquishing attachment to them. Wisdom can be seen as that faculty that sees through all attachments and relinquishes them as unskilful and productive of suffering. One who really sees directly that all conditioned things are impermanent will cease clinging to them, since (at least in the Buddha's view) all beings wish to avoid suffering (cf. SN I.75).

Wisdom and Ethics

As we have mentioned, the uninstructed worldling's first glimmers of wisdom (*paññā*) consist in so-called mundane right view (MN III.72; Ñāṇamoli 1991: 47): that actions have kammic consequences that can lead one to better or worse future outcomes. Mundane right view is an understanding that rejects the 'nihilist' or 'annihilationist' views of thinkers such as Ajita Kesakambalī (MN I.402, DN I.55) that there is no such thing as ethical action. The contrasting view of ethical efficacy then becomes one of the supports for correct action in the world. These first glimmers of mundane wisdom become the early foundations of ethical behaviour.

Conversely, behaving ethically lays the groundwork for wisdom. Ethical behaviour is claimed to have beneficial kammic results that may include rebirth into a condition where awareness of the *Dhamma* becomes possible. Indeed, human birth is considered surpassingly rare and special (SN II.263, SN V.456–457), so the kamma required to achieve it must be substantial. Even more so must be the kamma required to put one into contact with the Buddha *Dhamma*, and to achieve success in practice within this very life.

In the *Sammādiṭṭhi Sutta*, Sāriputta identifies one of right view as 'a noble disciple who understands the unwholesome, the root of the unwholesome, the wholesome, and the root of the wholesome' (MN I.46). One who fully understands these ethical dualities and the unwholesome roots of greed, hatred, and delusion also understands that those roots must completely be abandoned through ongoing effort to cultivate the wholesome (MN I.47). In that abandonment lies wisdom, since one abandons greed and hatred through an abandonment of self-directed conceit and through a complete penetration of the Noble Truths that leads eventually to an abandonment of clinging in all its forms.

Wisdom and Meditation

The various practices of mental cultivation (*bhāvanā*) also prepare the mind for wisdom. In this process, effort (*vāyama*), mindfulness (*sati*), and concentration (*samādhi*) are necessary. Given a base of ethical behaviour, the practice of concentration becomes tenable, since the various hindrances to such meditation can be overcome.

The practice of concentration and eventually absorption (*jhāna*) calms and focuses the mind, a process aimed at making it 'purified, unblemished, rid of imperfection, malleable, wieldy, steady, and attained to imperturbability' (MN I.22). Having a mind thus perfected makes mindfulness practice clearer, easier, more precise, and more effective. While this description implies a perfection of concentrative attainment, perfection is only the ultimate goal. A process of training will always begin and persist while perfection remains well out of reach.

With a mind made malleable, wieldy, and steady by such practice, one can mindfully turn to observe and investigate the world as presented in sense experience. When one confronts this experience one becomes aware of its instability, of its continual arising and passing, of the lack of any permanent or controlling self. Further, one becomes aware of the role of craving and clinging in producing *dukkha*. This combined awareness of impermanence, non-self, and the source and production of *dukkha* constitutes insight (*vipassanā*), and lays the groundwork for eventual breakthrough into awakening. However, as Keown (2001: 80) notes, the wisdom thus gained cannot be glossed simply as a knowledge of facts. Instead it must essentially involve ethical transformation, a process whereby one has become trained to see and act in the world skilfully through the practice of mental cultivation.

Turning the matter around, the attainment of wisdom (*ariyañāṇa*) is said also to progressively stabilize mindfulness (*sati*) and concentration (*samādhi*) (SN V.228). In this formulation, however, wisdom is probably intended to be more akin to wise propositional knowledge: if one knows intellectually that all things change, or that *dukkha* arises from clinging, one will be better equipped to confront the phenomena of meditative practice.

Unity or Disunity of Practice?

Western scholars disagree as to whether the forms of practice in early Buddhism comprise a unified path or whether there are in effect two competing paths: that of absorptive concentration (*jhāna*) and that of intellectual insight (*paññā*). The claim that there are two competing paths in the old texts apparently goes back to de La Vallée Poussin (Anālayo 2016b: 39); however, this claim has been more recently supported by Schmithausen (1981), Vetter (1988), and Polak (2016) among others. Bronkhorst (1986: 77) has argued, following Schmithausen (1981: 204), that in the 'old discourses' (Bronkhorst 2009: 130; also Norman 1997: 29) liberation occurs in the fourth *jhāna*. This raises the possibility that originally *jhāna* meditation may have been understood more as access to some 'mystical dimension' (Bronkhorst 2009: 55) than as a method of concentrative meditation *per se*. If this is correct, it may then be that descriptions of the content of liberating insight, e.g. as an understanding of the Four Noble Truths, as an understanding of dependent origination, or as confirming the unstable, unsatisfactory, and selfless character of lived reality, are later interpolations (Bronkhorst 2009: 36). Originally liberation might have been thinly described or undescribed: 'simpler, non-intellectual' (Wynne 2007: 124). The content of liberating knowledge might then have been formulated at a later date, even after the Buddha's demise, perhaps in response to competing philosophico-religious ideologies' own theories regarding such knowledge (Bronkhorst 2009: 36, 43 n. 81, 57). In that case, the complex theoretical edifice of articulated Buddhist *paññā* might in fact have played no essential role in the Buddha's own awakening, and could be seen even to amount to a species of otiose, *ex post facto* rationalization.

In contrast, Swearer (1972: 369), Gethin (2004: 209), Cousins (2009), and Anālayo (2015, 2016b), among others, argue that the path of meditative practice encompassed by the concentrative techniques of *jhāna* and the insight techniques of mindfulness practice are essentially unified. Both appear to be necessary for the attainment of awakening. Without some degree of concentration (although the precise degree remains a point of contention) one cannot effectively do the investigative work necessary to bring insight wisdom to fruition. Anālayo (2016: 41) traces concerns over disunity of practice back to 'an erroneous projection of the Western contrast between the thinker and the mystic', a contrast which did not exist as such in ancient India. It may also be that the threefold distinction of ethics, meditation, and wisdom hardened into a more rigid difference of practice during later Buddhist history, where some monastics saw themselves as specializing in one or another aspect of the path (Anālayo 2016a: 18; Cousins 2009).

If this picture of the unity of practice in early Buddhism is correct, then as we have noted the insight gained from such practice cannot be understood as mere intellectual acceptance of certain propositions (Anālayo 2003: 90). While awakening may indeed result in the acceptance of propositions, those should be understood as 'retrospective descriptions' of the state of awakening, in Anālayo's (2016: 44) terms, rather than as intellectual discoveries that constitute that state of awakening. This leaves open the possibility that early descriptions of the Buddha's awakening might indeed have been thin and non-intellectual without that necessarily having any bearing on the truth or falsity of later descriptions thereof. Indeed, it is not difficult to imagine that a system as complex and profound as that of early Buddhism might have required many years to fully describe, irrespective of the precise character of the Buddha's original experience of awakening.

The Path Ends: The Worthy One (*Arahant*)

The culmination of the Three Trainings constitutes awakening. In the Pāli Canon, four levels of awaking are given: the stream-enterer (*sotāpanna*), once-returner (*sakadāgami*), non-returner (*anāgāmi*), and *arahant*. All who have achieved one of these levels qualify as members of the noble (*ariya*) *saṅgha*. The levels are sequential and, as mentioned above in the section on the *puthujjana*, involve abandoning a series of five lower and five higher fetters en route to awakening (*bodhi*) or *nibbāna*, which is the state of the *arahant*.

Regarding the initial attainment of wisdom, the practices leading to stream-entry are fourfold:

> Association with superior persons ... is a factor for stream-entry. Hearing the true Dhamma is a factor for stream-entry. Careful attention is a factor for stream-entry. Practice in accordance with the Dhamma is a factor for stream-entry. (SN V.347)

At stream entry one is said to obtain the 'eye' or 'vision' of the *Dhamma* (*dhammacakkhupaṭilābha*) (SN II.134). This vision of *nibbāna* makes clear the efficacy of the path and thus erases doubt. It also is said to erase the other two lower fetters of 'self-identity views' and 'attachment to rules and rituals'. In short, to be a member of the *ariya saṅgha* one must have abandoned any doubt about the validity of the path, one must have abandoned all views of there being a substantial self, and one must have abandoned any notion that awakening comes from rule-following or ritual observance.

The once-returner will additionally have substantially reduced sensual desire, ill will, and ignorance. The non-returner will have abandoned sensual desire and ill will, while further reducing ignorance (DN I.156). (Thus, the non-returner has abandoned the five lower fetters and has attenuated ignorance, which is one of the five higher fetters.) Finally, the *arahant* will have entirely abandoned the remaining five higher fetters of desire for material existence (*rūparāgo*), desire for immaterial existence (*arūparāgo*), conceit (*māna*), restlessness (*uddhacca*), and ignorance (*avijjā*).

While it is instructive to consider this progress from the bottom up, as it were, it is also illuminating to consider it from the top down. For example, all members of the noble *saṅgha* who are not yet fully awakened may still display conceit, restlessness, and desire for some form of rebirth. Additionally, stream-enterers and once-returners may display sensual desire and ill will. This underlines the gradual nature of the path in early Buddhism: one should expect even relatively advanced members of the noble *saṅgha* to have unskilful mental states and display unskilful verbal and bodily behaviour.

The final stage of this progression is that of the *arahant*, exemplified by the Buddha himself. Indeed, the first stage of the gradual training involves the arising of just such an awakened Buddha, described thus:

> [H]ere a Tathāgata appears in the world, accomplished, fully enlightened, perfect in true knowledge and conduct, sublime, knower of worlds, incomparable leader of persons to be tamed, teacher of gods and humans, enlightened, blessed. He declares this world with its gods, its Māras, and its Brahmās, this generation with its recluses and brahmins, its princes and its people, which he has himself realised with direct knowledge. He teaches the Dhamma good in the beginning, good in the middle, and good in the end, with the right meaning and phrasing, and he reveals a holy life that is utterly perfect and pure. (MN I.179)

To what extent has one who has mastered the path either abandoned a sense of agency or transcended ethics entirely (see Finnigan 2011, Garfield 2011)? Several sutta passages suggest an end to agency for those who have attained awakening. Passages in two suttas say that 'no new action is done' (*navañca kammaṃ na karoti*) by one who is awakened (AN I.221, AN II.198). However, these suttas involve the Buddha or his disciples speaking with Jains; indeed, Bronkhorst (2009: 48–49) believes that both may have been interpolated at a later date by Buddhist followers under Jain influence. A similar passage can be found in the *Aṭṭhakavagga* (Sn 953):

> For one who knows, who has no agitation,
> There is no accumulation.
> Abstaining from activity,
> One sees safety everywhere. (Adapted from Fronsdal 2016)

The traditional interpretation of these passages is that an awakened being *does* act, i.e. *has* agency, but without laying down kammic accumulations. Thus, Bodhi translates *navañca kammaṃ na karoti* as 'he does not create any new kamma', and Fronsdal interpolates 'karmic' in front of 'accumulation' and 'activity'. Presumably this is because such accumulations depend upon the actions being accompanied by delusional volitional formations related to some subtle conceit or desire for existence. Once delusion has been uprooted by wisdom, and all subtle conceit has been extirpated, action is no longer kammically efficacious, and hence kamma ceases to accumulate with action.

If this is correct, such passages do not imply that an awakened person lacks agency or has transcended ethics. Indeed, such a position would run contrary to the example of the Buddha in the canonical texts, who is plainly one who acts carefully, decisively, and ethically. His actions are moral not out of any calculated adherence to rules or ideals, but 'spontaneously virtuous' (Anālayo 2003: 258). In the *Bhaddāli Sutta* (MN I.437) the Buddha clarifies this with the simile of a thoroughbred colt. The colt's trainer begins by placing a bit in the thoroughbred's mouth. This is uncomfortable at first, but eventually the colt calms and accepts it peacefully. Then the trainer introduces a harness. Again, the colt displays some discomfort, but comes to accept it. Finally, the trainer leads the colt through a series of developmental steps until he becomes 'worthy of the king'. At no time does the colt transcend or abandon the bit or harness. In the same way a bhikkhu is trained towards awakening, with ethical rules as bit and harness. 'Hence the *summum bonum* of the Buddha's path entails not an escape from ethics, but rather its lived perfection' (Smith and Whitaker 2016: 529). Such an embodiment of ethics is taken up at length in Keown (2001: 83–105). There, Keown quotes Winston King as proposing an interpretation similar to his own:

> One cannot say that Sila is first perfected and then left behind when one reaches Samadhi and Paññā stages—even though there is talk of rising above mere morality as one progresses in the meditative life. For even the meditating saint remains moral in his actions. Indeed his saintliness, at least in part, is the perfection of his morality, the turning from mere observance of external standards to the spontaneous exercise of inward virtues. So it is that morality is never left behind (1964a: 188). (Keown 2001: 90)

Keown continues, 'in the condition of *kilesa-parinibbāna* the Buddha remains a moral subject and member of the moral community' (91). Keown notes that 'it was through [his contemporaries'] interaction with him as a moral agent that the foundation of Buddhist ethics was laid' (91). For instance, the Buddha scolds wayward monks for wrong view (e.g. MN I.130ff.).

Notwithstanding his role as ethical exemplar, the Buddha exhibits recognizably human traits in the early texts. He undergoes strong physical pain (DN II.127–128). He is visited by Mara, the Buddhist personification of doubt and other negative emotions (DN II.104). He also at one point dismisses a group of monastics because of the noise they are making (MN I.457). Although the Buddha's action should be understood as exemplifying a species of ethical perfection, the early texts nevertheless depict him as human rather than a kind of idealized theoretical placeholder or automaton.

Conclusion

In this chapter we have focused on the Pāli material from early Buddhism and Theravāda in order to illuminate the nature of the Three Trainings (*tisikkhā*) of ethics, meditation, and wisdom. These trainings are found in other schools of Buddhism as well, however those lie outside the scope of this work.

The Three Trainings comprise a complete and concise statement of the Buddhist path. Ethics forms the foundation, necessary for the development of meditation and wisdom, and meditation constitutes a complex suite of mental practices aimed at inculcating wisdom, but any of the three can be cultivated at any time as one traverses the path. The three together form and inform the character of the individual, much as virtues do in Western forms of virtue ethics. Thus, we might think of them as constitutive of the holy life (*brahmacarya*) according to the early Buddhist texts. Any one may be emphasized or separately developed, but none can be left out in a successful pursuit of the good life.

A passage in the *Mahāparinibbāna Sutta* (DN II.81) suggests that progression along the Three Trainings from ethics to meditation to wisdom (*sīla, samādhi, paññā*) is linear:

> This is ethics, this is meditation, this is wisdom. Meditation, when cultivated with ethics, brings great fruit and profit. Wisdom, when cultivated with meditation, brings great fruit and profit. The mind, cultivated with wisdom becomes completely free of the mental influxes, that is, from the influx of sensuality, of becoming, and of false views and ignorance.

The ethics developed in the early portion of the path may appear to be merely rule based, but such rules when practised regularly become part of the character of the individual. Ethics are also cultivated in meditation, as when one cultivates states conducive to ethical conduct such as the *brahmavihāra*s, wherein one promotes positive mental states aimed at all sentient beings and thereby changes one's emotional responses and behaviour towards them. As one achieves higher stages of wisdom one likewise expands one's sphere of ethical development, until the final liberative insight that includes the realization of non-self and resulting connection (to greater or lesser extents) to all beings in the world. Buddhaghosa wrote of this as 'the breaking down of the barriers (between oneself and others)' as a result of successful meditation on loving-kindness (Vism 9.40–43). He cites the *Kakacūpama Sutta* (MN I.122), wherein the Buddha tells his monks that should they be assailed by bandits demanding a sacrifice of one of their lives, they should be unable to choose any among their group, including themselves, to be sacrificed. In this way, meditation on loving-kindness links the ethical goals of non-harm and the philosophical wisdom of non-self. We might say, following the metaphor given by the brahmin Soṇadaṇḍa, that ethics, meditation, and wisdom are like three hands washing each other, and that this combination is 'the highest thing in the world'. While we can separate them out analytically and definitionally, they come together in complex ways in the lives of practitioners.

Works Cited

Anālayo, Bhikkhu (2003) *Satipaṭṭhāna: the direct path to realization*. Cambridge: Windhorse.

Anālayo, Bhikkhu (2006) Mindfulness in the Pali nikayas. In: D. K. Nauriya, M. S. Drummond, and Y. B. Lal (eds), *Buddhist thought in applied psychological research*. New York: Routledge, 229–249.

Anālayo, Bhikkhu (2015) Brahmavihāra and awakening, a study of the *Dīrgha-āgama* parallel to the *Tevijja-sutta*. *Asian literature and translation*, 3 (4), 1–27.

Anālayo, Bhikkhu (2016a) The gradual path of training in the *Dīrgha-agama*, from sense-restraint to imperturbability. *Indian international journal of Buddhist studies*, 17, 1–24.

Anālayo, Bhikkhu (2016b) A brief criticism of the 'two paths to liberation' theory. *Journal of the Oxford Centre for Buddhist Studies*, 11, 38–51.

Bausch, L. (2015) *Kosalan philosophy in the Kāṇva Śatapatha Brāhmaṇa and the Suttanipāta*. PhD, University of California, Berkeley.

Bodhi, Bhikkhu (1989) *The discourse on the fruits of recluseship*. Kandy: Buddhist Publication Society.

Bodhi, Bhikkhu (1997) Review: How Buddhism began. *Journal of Buddhist ethics*, 4, 293–296.

Bodhi, Bhikkhu (2000) *The connected discourses of the Buddha*. Boston: Wisdom Publications. [SN]

Bodhi, Bhikkhu (2012) *The numerical discourses of the Buddha*. Boston: Wisdom Publications. [AN]

Braun, E. (2013) *The birth of insight*. Chicago: University of Chicago Press.

Bronkhorst, J. (1985) Dharma and Abhidharma. *Bulletin of the School of Oriental and African Studies*, 48 (2), 305–320.

Bronkhorst, J. (1986) *The two traditions of meditation in ancient India*. Stuttgart: Steiner Verlag.

Bronkhorst, J. (2009) *Buddhist teaching in India*. Boston: Wisdom.

Buddhadasa, Bhikkhu (1989) *Me and mine: selected essays of Bhikkhu Buddhadasa*. Albany: SUNY Press.

Collins, S. (1982) *Selfless persons: imagery and thought in Theravāda Buddhism*. Cambridge: Cambridge University Press.

Cousins, L. S. (1984) Samatha-yāna and Vipassanā-yāna. In: G. Dharmapala, R. Gombrich, and K. R. Norman (eds), *Buddhist studies in honour of Hammalava Saddhātissa*. Nugegoda, Sri Lanka: Hammalava Saddhātissa Felicitation Volume Committee, 56–68.

Cousins, L. S. (1996) The origin of insight meditation. *The Buddhist forum*, 4, 35–58.

Cousins, L. S. (2009) Scholar monks and meditator monks revisited. In: J. Powers and C. S. Prebish (eds), *Destroying Māra forever: Buddhist ethics essays in honor of Damien Keown*. New York: Snow Lion, 31–46.
Dreyfus, G. (1995) Meditation as ethical activity. *Journal of Buddhist ethics*, 2, 28–54.
Finnigan, B. (2011) How can a Buddha come to act? The possibility of a Buddhist account of ethical age. *Philosophy east and west*, 61 (1), 134–160.
Fronsdal, G. (2005) *The dhammapada*. Boston: Shambhala.
Fronsdal, G. (2016) *The Buddha before Buddhism*. Boulder, CO: Shambhala.
Fuller, P. (2005) *The notion of diṭṭhi in Theravāda Buddhism: the point of view*. New York: RoutledgeCurzon.
Garfield, J. (2011) Hey, Buddha! Don't think! Just act!—a response to Bronwyn Finnigan. *Philosophy east and west*, 61 (1), 174–183.
Gethin, R. M. L. (1998) *Foundations of Buddhism*. Oxford: Oxford University Press.
Gethin, R. M. L. (2001) *The Buddhist path to awakening*. Oxford: Oneworld Publications.
Gethin, R. M. L. (2004) On the practice of Buddhist meditation. *Buddhismus in Geschichte und Gegenwart*, 9, 201–221.
Gethin, R. M. L. (2012) Review of Richard F. Gombrich, *What the Buddha thought. H-Buddhism, H-Net Reviews*. January.
Gombrich, R. (1996) *How Buddhism began: the conditioned genesis of the early teachings*. London: The Athlone Press.
Gombrich, R. (1998) *Kindness and compassion as means to Nirvana*. Available from: http://ocbs.org/wp-content/uploads/2015/09/gonda.pdf.
Gombrich, R. (2009) *What the Buddha thought*. Sheffield, UK: Equinox.
Gunaratana, H. (1980) *A critical analysis of the jhanas*. PhD, The American University.
Harvey, P. (2013) *An introduction to Buddhism: teachings, history and practices*. Second edition. Cambridge: Cambridge University Press.
Honderich, T. (ed.) (1995) *The Oxford companion to philosophy*. New York: Oxford University Press.
Keown, D. (2001) *The nature of Buddhist ethics*. London: Palgrave.
Kövecses, Z. (1986) *Metaphors of anger, pride, and love: a lexical approach to the structure of concepts*. Philadelphia: John Benjamins Publishing Company.
Lakoff, G., and Johnson, M. (1999) *Philosophy in the flesh: the embodied mind and its challenge to western thought*. New York: Basic Books.
Mills, E. (2004) Cultivation of moral concern in Theravāda Buddhism. *Journal of Buddhist ethics*, 11, 21–45.
Ñāṇamoli, Bhikkhu (1991) *The discourse on right view*. Revised edition. Kandy, Sri Lanka: Buddhist Publication Society.
Ñāṇamoli, Bhikkhu, and Bodhi, Bhikkhu (2009) *The middle length discourses of the* Buddha. Fourth edition. Boston: Wisdom. [MN]
Norman, K.R. (1997) *A philological approach to Buddhism*. London: University of London School of Oriental and African Studies.
Polak, G. (2016) How was liberating insight related to the development of the four jhānas in early Buddhism? A new perspective through an interdisciplinary approach. *Journal of the Oxford Centre for Buddhist Studies*, 10 (5), 85–112.
Schmithausen, L. (1981) On some aspects of descriptions or theories of 'liberating insight' and 'enlightenment' in early Buddhism. In: K. Bruhn and A. Wezler (eds), *Studien zum Jainismus und Buddhismus: Gedenkschrift für Ludwig Alsdorf*. Wiesbaden: Franz Steiner Verlag, 199–250.

Smith, D., and Whitaker, J. (2016) Reading the Buddha as a philosopher. *Philosophy east and west*, 66 (2), 515–538.
Swearer, D. (1972) Two types of saving knowledge in the Pāli suttas. *Philosophy east and west*, 22 (4), 355–371.
Vetter, T. (1988) *The ideas and meditative practices of early Buddhism*. Leiden: Brill.
Walshe, M. (1995) *The long discourses of the Buddha*. Boston: Wisdom. [DN]
Wynne, A. (2007) *The origin of Buddhist meditation*. London: Routledge.

Suggested Reading

Anālayo, Bhikkhu (2016a) The gradual path of training in the *Dīrgha-agama*, from sense-restraint to imperturbability. *Indian international journal of Buddhist studies*, 17, 1–24.
Bodhi, Bhikkhu (1984) The noble eightfold path. *Wheel publication*, 308/311. Kandy: Buddhist Publication Society.
Gethin, R. M. L. (1998) *Foundations of Buddhism*. Oxford: Oxford University Press, especially ch. 7.
Gethin, R. M. L. (2001) *The Buddhist path to awakening*. Oxford: Oneworld Publications.
Gombrich, R. (2009) *What the Buddha thought*. Sheffield, UK: Equinox, especially pp. 60–160.
Goodman, C. (2009) *Consequences of compassion*. New York: Oxford University Press, especially chs 3 and 6.
Keown, D. (2001) *The nature of Buddhist ethics*. London: Palgrave.

PART II

ETHICS AND BUDDHIST TRADITIONS

CHAPTER 4

MORAL DEVELOPMENT IN THE *JĀTAKAS*, *AVADĀNAS*, AND PĀLI *NIKĀYAS*

MARTIN T. ADAM

INTRODUCTION

If one understands the term *morality* to refer to the personal quality of being in accord with a system of values or code of conduct, then the idea of *moral development* can be understood as referring to the development of the individual's *capacity* to live by that system or code. In this chapter we will examine the manner in which the Buddhist tradition conceives individual moral development, specifically as it is represented in three overlapping classifications of early Buddhist literature: *jātaka*s, *avadāna*s, and the Pāli *Nikāya*s. How do Buddhists understand the growth of the individual's capacity to live morally? To what extent and in what senses is this capability perfectible? On what basis? To what degree is it under one's control?

This chapter takes its cue from Ohnuma, who has suggested that *jatāka*s and *avadāna*s can be helpfully viewed as representing the first two of the three kinds of knowledge (*tivijjā*/*trividyā*) attained by the Buddha over the three watches of the night of this awakening (2003: 36–39). In the first watch, the Exalted One is said to have recalled many of his own myriad past lives, struggling and questing through repeated births and deaths. During the second, he is said to have seen the operations of karma more generally—in a cosmic vision of *saṃsāra*, with beings everywhere dying and being reborn according to their deeds. Given these correspondences, it only seems natural to complete the final third of Ohnuma's thought by associating the *Nikāya*s' non-narrative, systematic discourses with the third watch of the night, in which the Buddha directly realized the Four Noble Truths and thereby achieved his long-sought goal. If the *jātaka*s and *avadāna*s demonstrate the Buddha's unparalleled psychic prowess, the *Nikāya*s' systematic discourses demonstrate his awakening.

The discussion is divided into three parts. The first aims to provide an overview of the manner in which Buddhists themselves understand moral development as represented in these categories of text. In the second part the goal is to offer a deeper analysis of the framework of concepts underlying the doctrines of moral development discussed. We conclude with a brief characterization of the end of moral development: the figure of the *arahant*, the religious ideal. In all three sections the terms of explanation are drawn from the texts themselves.

Throughout this chapter we will view our material through a very particular lens, one that thematizes the *progressive* nature of the Buddhist path (*magga/mārga*) with a continuous eye towards the notion of *hierarchy* on that path. We will indicate those aspects of the material that imply an idea of hierarchy—whether this be in reference to various categories of spiritual actor, the stages of accomplishment along the path to the goal, fields of merit, or any other morally relevant sense. Hierarchy is an important feature of early Buddhist thought that has not, perhaps, received the attention it deserves. Many have rightly pointed out the radical egalitarian implications of the Buddha's teachings (*Dhamma/Dharma*) relative to the value system of his day—with regard to social class and gender issues, for example (Gombrich 2009: 195; also see Adam 2013). At the same time, we would do well to identify those respects in which the Buddha's teachings continue to assume a hierarchical structure and outlook.

Overview: Moral Development in the *Jātakas*, *Avadānas*, and *Nikāyas*

Background

Early Buddhist ideas of morality need to be understood as part of a practical system of personal liberation that aims for the release of the individual from the rounds of rebirth (*saṃsāra*) and suffering (*dukkha/duḥkha*). As is the case with other ancient Indian systems (e.g. those of Jainism and the *Upaniṣads*), cyclical existence is understood to be relentlessly driven on by the individual's own actions (*kamma/karma*), which have the effect of planting the seeds of future experiences, both in this life and in lives to come. Final freedom (*mokkha/mokṣa*) is possible only through the realization or knowledge (*ñāṇa/jñāna*) of a liberating truth. The attainment of such knowledge is thought to require purity of character and conduct, and hence a moral component. This idea of morality as a prerequisite of knowledge may not be intuitively obvious—at least to a Western mindset in which moral and epistemic achievements are viewed as independent. Indian systems tend to regard morality and knowledge as intertwined, a perspective that is particularly clear in the case of Buddhism (see DN 4 *The Qualities of a True Brahmin*; Walshe 1995: 131). This thought should remind us of our hermeneutical imperative to identify bedrock cultural assumptions in the material under study, and in ourselves.

In spite of sharing a certain common conceptual basis with other Indian systems, the Buddhist understanding of the content of liberating knowledge is unique in at least one key respect. Rather than positing the existence of a hidden Self, knowledge of which leads to liberation, precisely the opposite is maintained. It is the very belief in such an entity that is said to lie at the root of rebirth and suffering. The deluded imputation of a Self enables the arising of self-centred craving, and thereby causes individuals to become attached, suffer, and be reborn. Buddhist practice, including the development of morality, is thus conceived of as a kind of personal training and mental purification, enhancing one's self-control, and ultimately leading to the realization of liberating knowledge. The object of this knowledge is usually articulated in terms of either the Four Noble Truths or the very causal chain through which rebirth and suffering are thought to occur: dependent origination (*paṭiccasamuppāda/pratītyasamutpāda*). Our focus here is on how Buddhism understands the role of morality in breaking this chain.

Sīla (Not to Do Any Evil)

The term that most closely corresponds to *morality* in the Buddhist lexicon is *sīla* (*śīla*). *Sīla* can also be translated as moral conduct, virtue, good habit, moral training, ethics, and so on. Throughout the *Nikāyas* the word appears as a category heading in a number of lists of positively valued behaviours whose practice is thought to facilitate the attainment of liberating knowledge, while at the same time benefiting other living beings. If we follow the well-known Indian division of action into bodily, vocal, and mental acts, *sīla* in the technical sense is understood to refer to moral actions of the body and speech. In Buddhism, however, the very notion of action is understood as entailing an underlying mental intention or volition (*cetanā*). As the Buddha famously put it, 'It is volition, Bhikkhus, that I call kamma. For having willed, one acts by body, speech, or mind' (AN 6.63 *Penetrative*, Bodhi 2012: 963). Thus all action, whether bodily, vocal, or mental, is to be understood in terms of the agent's underlying intentional state. It follows that *sīla* includes a deeper, mental component.

Most employments of the term *sīla* share in the idea of a disciplined restraint of activity, an ongoing effort of will *not to act* (as opposed to an impulse *to act*) in certain specific ways—usually through the following of a rule or precept. There is a further implication that *sīla* involves a *deliberate effort*, as opposed to a spontaneous impulse, not to act in particular ways. The behaviour enjoined is described in terms of *restraints* of various kinds on one's conduct, aiding to bring it, and the mind of craving on which it rests, *under control*. There exist a number of important sets of such restraints for practitioners at different levels of attainment; these vary in terms of complexity, difficulty, and the specific number of injunctions to be observed. Most famous among these are the lay precepts or *pañcasīla*, a set of five moral principles governing daily activities. They are expressed as commitments or vows:

1. I undertake the precept to abstain from the taking of life
2. I undertake the precept not to take that which is not given

3. I undertake the precept to abstain from misconduct in sensual actions
4. I undertake the precept to abstain from false speech
5. I undertake the precept to abstain from intoxicants that cause heedlessness

Similar lists of basic moral principles can be found in other Indian traditions contemporary with early Buddhism, notably the five-fold formulae of Jainism and the Yoga school (*yamas*). Aside from being viewed as enabling the emergence of a clear mindset and thus spiritual insight, the very act of formally committing to a set of moral principles is regarded as a profoundly beneficial karmic act in and of itself. It is precisely such an act that allows one to get started, and stay on, a spiritual path.

In the Buddhist tradition the recitation of the *pañcasīla* occurs on formal, ritual occasions, usually following the rehearsal of another formula in which one marks one's faith in the tradition by 'going for refuge' (*saraṇagamana*) to the Three Jewels: the Buddha, the *Dharma*, and the *Saṅgha*.

> *Buddhaṃ saraṇaṃ gacchāmi* (I go for refuge to the Buddha)
> *Dhammaṃ saraṇaṃ gacchāmi* (I go for refuge to the *Dharma*)
> *Saṅghaṃ saraṇaṃ gacchāmi* (I go for refuge to the *Saṅgha*)
> (see AN 8:39 *Streams*, wherein the three jewels and five precepts are collectively referred to as the 'eight streams of merit' [Bodhi 2012: 1173–1174])

For Buddhists, the act of taking the triple refuge is the single most highly esteemed symbolic gesture that an individual can make; it has clear implications for a person's moral development—representing as it does the deliberate, self-conscious decision to follow the Buddhist path. Although Buddhist teachings do not deny that non-Buddhists develop morally, for a Buddhist the initial act of taking refuge signals the individual's recognition that a serious break from habitual negative tendencies and patterns of life has become necessary. It also signals a willingness to place one's faith or confidence (*saddhā/śraddhā*) in the Buddha, his teachings, and the community of monks and nuns who uphold those teachings. The communal recital of the triple refuge formula, along with that of the *pañcasīla*, serves to reinforce one's dedication to the path. (A similar function can be seen in the public performance of other sets of precepts, such as the *saṅgha*'s recitation of the *pātimokkha* formula during the *uposatha* ceremony). When we consider the idea of moral development, then, we need to take account of beginnings, and for the Buddhist the starting point is marked by an act of commitment to the path taught by the Buddha.

The Path (To Develop What Is Skilful)

The fact that such acts of commitment are viewed as meritorious and praiseworthy in and of themselves points to a deeper scale of values at play in the Buddhist scriptures, one that is not captured in lists of external conduct such as the *pañcasīla*. In Indian thought generally, any action that leads one to a better rebirth qualifies as good. Such acts are said to be *puñña* (*puṇya*): 'meritorious, karmically fruitful' or, understood as a noun, 'merit 'or 'karmic fruitfulness'. Throughout the *Nikāyas* such praiseworthy actions are also referred to as 'skilful' or 'wholesome' (*kusala*), indicating that they lead one in the direction of the highest good, liberation (*nibbāna*). As we shall see below, this is because their underlying volitions are based in a mindset that is free from the so-called three roots of the unwholesome: greed, hatred, and delusion (*lobha, dosa, moha*). They are based on the opposite wholesome roots of non-attachment, love, and wisdom (*alobha, adosa/metta, paññā*).

The idea of a path leading to the highest good, composed of skilful, karmically fruitful elements, is represented by a number of schemas in which the term *sīla* figures as one component. Among the earliest of these schemas referred to in the *Nikāyas* are the three 'bases of making merit' (*puñña-kiriya-vatthus*): giving (*dāna*), morality (*sīla*), and meditation (*bhāvanā*) (DN 33 *The Chanting Together*, Walshe 1995: 485). Here *dāna* and *sīla* appear as separate items; this implies, once again, that the term *sīla* does not share the same semantic range as the English word *morality*—since giving, as a practice, is clearly encompassed by the latter. The fact that Buddhists also unreservedly think of giving as a morally praiseworthy action clearly indicates that there are at least two senses of morality at play in the texts: a narrower sense associated with the term *sīla* and a wider sense encompassing praiseworthy acts more generally (*puñña, kusala*). While the former is associated with outer conduct, the latter points to morality as an inner state.

The three bases of merit can be viewed as a progression beginning with the practice of giving, proceeding through the disciplined morality of *sīla*, and then advancing to meditation. Gethin sums up the rationale for this order:

> In order to see the four truths, the mind must be clear and still; in order to be still, the mind must be content; in order to be content, the mind must be free from remorse and guilt; in order to be free from guilt, one needs a clear conscience; the bases of a clear conscience are generosity and good conduct. (1998: 83)

The Noble Eightfold Path (*ariyāṭṭhangikamagga*)

Two of the better known early path schemas that incorporate *sīla* are the Noble Eightfold Path leading to arahantship, found throughout the *Nikāyas*, and the bodhisatta path leading to Buddhahood, which we find represented in the *jātakas*. The most famous formulation of the Buddhist path is that of the Eightfold Path, the fourth of the Four Noble Truths taught by the Buddha (DN 22 *The Greater Discourse on the Foundations of Mindfulness*, Walshe 1995: 348–349). The Eightfold Path is the complete set of factors whose cultivation is said to lead away from a self-centred, worldly orientation and place one on a clear and irreversible trajectory toward the final goal, *nibbāna* (Table 4.1).

The eight factors are called 'right' (*sammā*) in the pragmatic sense of being appropriate, fitting responses to the way things actually are. This is to say that they are regarded

Table 4.1 The Noble Eightfold Path

1. Right view (*sammā-diṭṭhi*)	Understanding the reality of karma and rebirth. Seeing the Four Noble Truths.
2. Right resolve (*sammā-sankappa*)	Desirelessness. Friendliness. Nonharmfulness.
3. Right speech (*samma-vāca*)	Refraining from false speech. Refraining from divisive speech. Refraining from hurtful speech. Refraining from idle chatter.
4. Right action (*sammā-kammanta*)	Refraining from harming living beings. Refraining from taking what is not given. Refraining from sexual misconduct.
5. Right livelihood (*sammā-ājiva*)	Refraining from harmful forms of earning a living.
6. Right effort (*sammā-vāyama*)	To discourage unarisen unwholesome states of mind. To abandon arisen unwholesome states of mind. To develop unarisen wholesome states of mind. To encourage arisen wholesome states of mind.
7. Right mindfulness (*sammā-sati*)	Contemplation of body. Contemplation of feelings. Contemplation of mind. Contemplation of mental contents.
8. Right concentration (*sammā-samādhi*)	Practice of the four *jhānas*.

as *effective* in bringing about the end of rebirth and suffering. Contrary to the view that would ascribe any kind moral relativism to early Buddhist ethics, the Buddha's teachings maintain that there is an objective moral law (*Dharma*) governing the manner in which events unfold, and more specifically how rebirth and suffering arise and cease. If one wants to bring suffering to a final end, one must first bring one's body, speech, and mind under control. In order to accomplish this most difficult of tasks some kinds of practice work, while others simply do not. In general, extreme behaviours are to be avoided. The Eightfold Path is thus also known as the Middle Path (*majjhima-paṭipadā*), an epithet indicating the unprofitability of two extreme and opposite ways of living, namely, a self-indulgent life of the senses (associated with normal worldly existence), or a severe life of ascetic self-denial (associated with other renunciate traditions). Practising the middle way eventually has the effect of bringing one's will into alignment with the *Dharma*, allowing one to make progress (SN 1.1 *Crossing the Flood*, Bodhi 2012: 89–90).

Thus, all eight factors can be considered skilful and wholesome in that their practice brings about the insight and moral purity that lead to liberation. A common analysis of the path divides its eight elements into three groups of trainings (*sikkhā*), with those comprising *sīla* (3–5) placed at the beginning, followed by *samādhi* or meditation (6–8), and *paññā* or wisdom (1–2) (DN 10 *Subha Sutta*, Walshe 1995: 171–174). The reason for placing the *sīla* components first in this constellation parallels that of the three bases of making merit: one cannot progress in meditation and wisdom if one has not first restrained one's outer behaviour, thereby allowing the mind to gain some immediate freedom from distractions and disturbances. Through *sīla* the mind is provided the opportunity to become self-aware and focused. On this basis, insight can emerge. In this way, *sīla* can be viewed as the foundation of the entire path. Amongst noble persons (*ariya-puggala*; discussed below) *sīla*, *samādhi*, and *paññā* are respectively perfected by the stream-enterer, non-returner, and *arahant* (see AN I.231–232, Harvey 2013: 61).

Even so, it has also been widely noted that there is a good reason for the placement of right view and right intention *before* the *sīla* components in the eightfold formula: *sīla* cannot properly take root unless one possesses a correct understanding of the necessity of making an effort in the first place. It is only by understanding the reality of being subject to karma and rebirth that one forms the appropriate resolve to free oneself from worldly entanglement through the practices of *sīla* and *samādhi*. To this extent it is possible to discern a kind of progressive logic to the ordering of the Eightfold Path, with each limb understood as having a special dependence on the one that precedes it (see DN 18 *About Janavasabha* [Walshe 1995: 299]). This being said, the most widely held understanding of the path is that each of the eight elements is regarded as conditioning and aiding the others. They are not regarded as individual steps or stages of a sequential practice, but rather as mutually reinforcing components of an integrated system designed to gradually enhance one's morality, self-awareness, and understanding. They are to be cultivated together.

There is an important sense, however, in which this cultivation of the path can *itself* be considered as possessing an initial stage of practice. To understand this, we need to take account of an important distinction. The development of the Eightfold Path is said to eventually give rise to a pivotal transformative moment of spiritual insight. The content of this life-changing event is described in different terms in different contexts; but for our purposes can best be identified as the direct initial experience of the Four Noble Truths, an experience that is also identified as the arising of 'noble right view' (in contradistinction to 'mundane right view', which contains only a conceptual understanding of the four truths rather than an experiential one; see AN 5.57 *Themes*, Bodhi 2012: 686–688; and Bodhi 1995: 1184). This instant marks the beginning of the *Noble* Eightfold Path proper. This noble path is also referred to as the supramundane path (*lokuttara-magga*), in contrast to the worldly path (*lokiya-magga*) practised initially (see Bodhi 1999: 105). Upon entering the supramundane path, the practitioner himself also receives the designation 'noble' (*ariya*)—indicating that a fundamental spiritual transformation has occurred. Formerly deemed an ordinary person (*puthujjana*), the follower of the path is now designated a noble person (*ariya-puggala*), or noble disciple (*ariya-sāvaka*). More precisely yet, he is referred to as a disciple in higher training (trainee, learner; *sekha*).

Upon achieving this advanced stage the practitioner is said to glimpse the reality of *nibbāna* for the first time. Despite the fact that effort is still required, one has entered the stream that will inevitably lead one to the final goal; it is no longer possible to be reborn in one of the lower realms. It is difficult to overestimate the impact of this moment upon the psyche of the practitioner, and therefore upon his subsequent moral development. At this juncture one's faith in the Three Jewels becomes unshakable owing to the disappearance of doubt (*vicikicchā*). This is due to the direct experience of the Four Noble Truths, which experience, it must be noted, also allows one to definitively see through the illusion of self (*sakkāya-diṭṭhi*) for the first time. This moment thus signifies the opening of a completely different way of being in the world—establishing a foundation for genuine altruism. Interestingly, it is at this stage that one's attachment to rules and rituals (*sīlabbata-parāmāssa*) is said to fall away. This is notable, as it is also said that that one's outer *sīla* is perfect from this point on. In spite of this, some residual mental defilements do remain—including the residual vague sense of 'I am' (*māna*). This feeling, and other subtle mental fetters (*samyojana*), will not entirely disappear until one has completely purified the mind, thereby becoming a liberated being or *arahant*.

Buddhist Narrative Literature

Thus, for ordinary persons walking the mundane Eightfold Path, moral development can be understood as a gradual process of enhancing control over the different dimensions of one's life: bodily, vocal, and mental. It occurs over vast numbers of lifetimes as one finds one's way to the Noble Eightfold Path, which leads directly out of *saṃsāra*. For most sentient beings, however, the vicissitudes of cyclical existence are unending; one wanders deluded, with a mind out of control, through the six realms of existence, perpetually dying and being reborn according to one's deeds. Morally good actions (*puñña*) result in heavenly or human birth; morally bad actions (*apuñña, pāpa*) lead to lower realms. Even the gods eventually exhaust their good karma and fall from their elevated positions. It is extremely rare for an individual to find the path that leads away from and out of the repetitive patterns of samsāric existence. In general, the Buddhist tradition maintains that such an achievement requires exposure to the Buddha's teachings—ideally in the form of an encounter with a Buddha, who either through explicit instruction or sheer presence inspires one to practice. Without such practice, moral progress is possible but limited in its effects to temporarily attain a higher rebirth.

In the Buddhist narrative genres known as *jātaka*s (birth stories) and *avadāna*s (glorious deeds) we find the idea of moral development over many lifetimes illustrated in colourful detail. *Jātaka*s concern deeds remembered by the Buddha to have taken place during his own past lives, when he was yet a being aspiring for awakening: a bodhisatta/bodhisattva. In the *jātaka*s, narrated by the Buddha himself, present events and circumstances are traced back to actions performed during one of those earlier lives. At least one of the characters, usually the hero, is the bodhisattva. *Avadāna*s, on the other hand, mainly concern the praiseworthy acts of the Buddha's disciples and devotees. (Although there are some that are centred on the actions of the Buddha-to-be as well. Technically these also qualify as *jātakas*.) A general point of contrast between these two genres can be drawn in terms of the respective goals of their heroes. In the *jātakas* the bodhisattva is aiming to become a fully awakened buddha (*sammā-sambuddha*); in the *avadānas* the protagonist is striving for arahantship. In this, the *avadānas* share the same ideal as the systematic treatises of the *Nikāyas*, albeit with a focus on faith and generosity directed at noble beings.

Thus both genres of literature are concerned to illustrate morally significant actions and their fruits. As moral exhortations, the stories they contain can be understood as serving to reinforce acceptance of the reality of karma and rebirth, which is to say, mundane right view. They offer moral examples, inspiration, and entertainment to their audiences—in contrast to the kind of systematic explanation and practical instruction that characterizes so much of the *Nikāyas*. There is clearly a strong association between these stories and Buddhist lay culture. Some of the Buddhist *jātaka* stories, for example, circulated as popular Indian folktales before being modified and incorporated into the Buddhist Canon (Ohnuma 2003: 37). It is likely that many of these stories were composed with the express purpose of attracting lay support for the *saṅgha*; this seems especially true of the *avadānas*, which regularly extol the merits of devotion to the *saṅgha*.

Jātakas

As told in the *Nidānakathā*, the Buddha's career as a bodhisattva begins with the story of the brahmin ascetic Sumedha, who encounters a previous Buddha named Dīpaṅkara passing through the city of Ramma (Rhys Davids 1878: 91–97). Inspired by faith, the young seeker lays himself down upon a muddy road for the Exalted One to walk upon, vowing that one day he too will become a buddha. Dīpaṅkara then makes a prediction of his future success. The moment of Sumedha's aspiration (*abhinīhāra*) marks the starting point of his journey to Buddhahood. Thus the *jātakas* record only those of Gotama's former lives that occur after this fateful commitment—a vast number, in any case (Ohnuma 2003: 46; Appleton 2014: 108). The *jātaka* collection of the *Khuddaka Nikāya* alone contains 547 such stories.

The Bodhisattva takes on myriad forms and interacts with beings in every realm on his cosmic journey, from hell-beings to gods. It should be noted that while the Bodhisattva is often depicted as *interacting with* beings in lower realms, some commentaries assert that he is excluded from taking on certain lower rebirths himself (Appleton 2010: 93–97). A number of possible structural parallels with the path of the disciple in higher training might be noted here. The moment of the arising of the bodhisattva path leading to Buddhahood and the moment of arising of the supramundane path leading to arahantship are both understood as having the effect of forever eliminating the possibility of particular kinds of lower rebirth. Additionally, the disciple in higher training and the Bodhisattva both share the certainty of attaining their respective goals, in the latter case on account of Dīpaṅkara's prediction. There are, of course, some differences. The certainty associated with the moment of the achievement of the supramundane path is characterized as one based on insight; the certainty of the Bodhisattva, on the other hand, is based on his extraordinary resolve and faith in the Buddha's truthfulness (Rhys Davids 1878: 100). In addition, the disciple in higher training, as a stream-enterer, is traditionally said to be assured of achieving his goal in no more than seven lives—for the Bodhisattva no such number is specified; it is clear that his path is much, much longer.

In stories too numerous to count, the Bodhisattva takes on a huge variety of human roles and vocations: teacher, acrobat, merchant, lumberjack, prince. Often he appears in spirit form, whether as a highly placed god or a humble tree fairy. In other tales yet, he appears as an animal—a deer, a lion, a monkey, a parrot—or as we find demonstrated in the following story, a fish.

> '*They twain in fisher's net.*'—This story was told by the Master while at Jetavana, about two aged Elders. After a rainy-season spent in a forest in the country they resolved to seek out the Master, and got together provisions for their journey. But they kept putting off their departure day by day, till a month flew by. Then they provided a fresh supply of provisions, and procrastinated till a second month was gone, and a third. When their indolence and sluggishness had lost them three months, they set out and came to Jetavana. Laying aside their bowls and robes in the common-room, they came into the Master's presence. The Brethren remarked on the length of the time since the two had visited the Master, and asked the reason. Then they told their story and all the Brotherhood came to know of the laziness of these indolent Brethren.
>
> Assembling in the Hall of Truth the Brethren talked together of this thing. And the Master entered and was told what they were discussing. Being asked whether they were really so indolent, those Brethren admitted their short-coming. 'Brethren,' said he, 'in former times, no less than now, they were indolent and loth to leave their abode.' So saying, he told this story of the past.
>
> Once on a time when Brahmadatta was reigning in Benares, there lived in the river of Benares three fishes, named Over-thoughtful, Thoughtful, and Thoughtless. And they came down-stream from the wild country to where men dwelt. Hereupon Thoughtful said to the other two, 'This is a dangerous and perilous neighbourhood, where fishermen catch fish with nets, basket-traps, and such like tackle. Let us be off to the wild country again.' But so lazy were the other two fishes, and so greedy, that they kept putting off their going from day to day, until they had let three months slip by. Now fishermen cast their nets into the river; and Over-thoughtful and Thoughtless were swimming on ahead in quest of food when in their folly they blindly rushed into the net. Thoughtful, who was behind, observed the net, and saw the fate of the other two.
>
> 'I must save these lazy fools from death,' thought he. So first he dodged round the net, and splashed in the water in front of it like a fish that has broken through and gone up stream; and then doubling back, he splashed about behind it, like a fish that has broken through and gone down stream. Seeing this, the fishermen thought the fish had broken the net and all got away; so they pulled it in by one corner and the two fishes escaped from the net into the open water again. In this way they owed their lives to Thoughtful.
>
> His story told, the Master, as Buddha, recited this stanza:
>
> They twain in fisher's nets are ta'en;
> Them Thoughtful saves and frees again.
>
> His lesson ended, and the Four Truths expounded (at the close whereof the aged Brethren gained fruition of the First Path), the Master identified the Birth

by saying: 'These two Brethren were then Over-thoughtful and Thoughtless, and I Thoughtful.'

Mitacinti-Jātaka (Jat 114; Chalmers 1895)

In this short *jātaka* we can discern a number of features typical of the genre. At end of the story the Buddha identifies himself as one of its characters. This is essential. In addition, other present-day personages are also identified (this element, however, is not found in all *jātakas*). The karmic impact of hearing the story, or a subsequent *Dharma* discourse (usually on the four truths), upon members of the assembled audience, is also stated. Again, this is standard. In many, but not all, cases the effects of hearing the Buddha's words are described in terms of attaining a higher spiritual status, often on the supramundane path. (This motif is common at the end of suttas throughout the *Nikāyas*.)

Throughout the *jātakas*, we find the Buddha-to-be planting karmic seeds through his actions and cultivating the personal qualities that will eventually reach their perfection in his awakening as Gotama Buddha. The Theravāda tradition identifies these qualities as a set of ten specific virtues known as the *pāramitās* or *pāramīs*: giving (*dāna*), morality (*sīla*), renunciation (*nekkhamma*), wisdom (*paññā*), energy (*viriya*), patience (*khanti*), truthfulness (*sacca*), determination (*adhiṭṭhāna*), loving-kindness (*mettā*), and equanimity (*upekkhā*). Owing to the fact that the quality being illustrated is not usually named in the *jātaka* itself, it is not always clear which, if any, of the ten qualities is being demonstrated. Appleton has convincingly argued that the elaborate rubric of ten specific virtues is a late commentarial preoccupation. While we are not concerned with the historical development of this schema here, it seems clear enough that its emergence may be related to developments in the early stages of the Mahāyāna (Appleton 2010: 98f.).

As skilful character traits, each *pāramitā* is seen as a repository or accumulation of morally beneficial karma (*puñña*) to be developed and perfected over many lifetimes. The ten *pāramitās* are clearly among the most distinctive values promulgated in the *jātakas*, and were used as an organizing principle by the texts' compilers. Indeed, they can be viewed as framing the entire *jātaka* section of the *Khuddaka Nikāya*. In the *Buddhavaṃsa* the story of Sumedha *qua* bodhisattva commences with a series of successive resolutions to fulfil each of the ten *pāramitās* in turn, beginning with giving (Rhys Davids 1878: 101–108), while the last ten stories of the *jātaka* collection (Jat 538–547) demonstrate the ten once again, culminating where it all began, with the perfection of giving (in what is arguably the most popular and incredible story of them all, the *Vessantara Jātaka*) (see Ohnuma 2007).

Aside from the *pāramitās* other values are promulgated in various *jātakas*, notably compassion (*Jātakamālā* 1 The Tigress) and non-harm; the latter is particularly notable in tales showing the folly of animal sacrifice, associated with the brahmanical tradition (Jat 18 *Matakabhatta Jātaka*). Worldly virtues such as wiliness are also sometimes in evidence (Jat 318 *Kanavera Jātaka*). In some cases the Bodhisattva is depicted in ways that are hard to square with Buddhist values. Indeed, as Appleton points out, there are even some *jātaka*s that openly show the Bodhisattva acting immorally (2010: 26–28). Such stories of bad karma are used to explain negative events in the life of the historical Buddha—for example, personal injuries and ailments (see Dhammajoti 2012).

Avadānas

One of the basic differences between *jātaka*s and *avadāna*s is the marked presence in the latter of what has been called a devotional ethos. Scholars have noted that the *pāramitā*s themselves are not the focus of the *avadāna*s; what we find being celebrated instead are the merits of devotional acts directed towards the Buddha and the *Saṅgha*:

> [W]e might say that *jātaka*s illustrate the bodhisattva's arduous cultivation of certain moral perfections, whereas *avadāna*s take place in Buddhist devotional context and involve the performance of devotional acts by disciples and lay followers. In short, we might say that *jātaka*s are about 'perfections' whereas *avadāna*s are about 'devotions' . . . (Ohnuma 2003: 41)

As Ohnuma is quick to point out, however, there are notable exceptions to this generalization. As a *jātaka* with a strong devotional ethos, the story of Sumedha and Dīpaṅkara itself demonstrates this. Nevertheless the devotional flavour of the *avadāna* genre is manifest and this is clearly connected to the presence of a Buddha in the world, a state of affairs that is presupposed in stories of this genre. With this circumstance a whole new range of praiseworthy actions becomes possible in the form of devotional acts, donations to the *saṅgha* and so on. All such acts are, of course, karmically meritorious, and so remain moral in the wide Buddhist sense being considered here.

The following past life story narrated by the elder Sopāka demonstrates many of these features. Having taken birth as an ascetic, Sopāka encounters and honours a buddha of the remote past, named Siddhattha, who then proceeds to instruct him.

> While cleaning my cave in the highest mountain in a forest, the blessed one named Siddhattha came into my vicinity. Seeing the Buddha arrived, I arranged a mat for the venerable one, supreme in the world, [and] gave him a seat of flowers. Having sat down on the seat of flowers and understanding my disposition, Siddhattha, leader of the world, declared impermanence:
>
> > The formations are indeed impermanent, subject to arising and decay. Having arisen, they cease. Their quiescence is joyful.
>
> Having said this, the all-knowing one—supreme in the world, bull among men, hero—rose into the air like a king of geese in the sky. Abandoning my own view, I developed the perception of impermanence. Having developed it for one day, I died there. After experiencing the two fortunate state[s of being a god or a human], impelled by a pure foundation, when my final rebirth had been reached I entered the womb of an outcaste.
>
> Having departed from the house, I went forth to the houseless state. While seven years old, I attained arahatship. Putting forth energy, resolute, well concentrated upon the virtuous practices, pleasing the great man, I obtained full ordination.

> Ninety-four aeons ago I performed the deed at that time. I am not aware of [having been reborn in] a bad destination [since]. This is the fruit of giving [a seat of] flowers. Ninety-four aeons ago I developed the perception [of impermanence] at that time. Developing that perception [of impermanence] I attained the annihilation of the taints. The four analytical insights and also the eight liberations and the six supernormal knowledges have been realised. The Buddha's teaching has been accomplished.
>
> In this way the venerable elder Sopāka ('Outcaste') spoke these verses. The *apadāna* of the elder Sopāka is concluded.
>
> *Sopāka* (trans. Clark 2015: 232–233; reformatted)

In the story of Sopāka we find the simple act of honouring the Buddha with a seat of flowers bearing the fruit of higher rebirths. At the same time, it should be noted that it is the perception of impermanence that leads to the final destruction of taints, the condition of the *arahant*. The fruitfulness of karma remains the central theme in this story and of the *avadāna*s in general, as well as the *jātaka*s. The basic lesson is clear: 'Actions do not disappear even after a hundred aeons. When they have reached completion and it is time, they fruit for living beings' (*Avadānaśataka* 15, 16, 18–20 in Appleton 2013). As Speyer observes:

> [I]t is not without importance that the conclusion of half of the hundred texts out of which the *Avadānaśataka* is made up and several parts of the *Divyāvadāna* is the standing phrase that black actions bear black fruits, white actions white fruits, and mixed ones mixed fruits, with the exhortation to strive only after white actions, shunning or letting alone the other two … (Speyer 1909: 1)

Underview: Towards an Experiential Account of the Path

Our discussion thus far has aimed to provide an objective general overview of the manner in which the path of moral development is portrayed in the *Pāli Nikāya*s, *jātaka*s, and *avadāna*s. In pointing to the importance of the concept of volition (or intention, *cetanā*) we have already alluded to the *subjective* dimension of the path; we have not, however, explored this aspect in detail. Here, then, we will offer a deeper analysis of the conceptual framework underlying this general account, one that focuses on moral development *as it is experienced* by different kinds of spiritual agent. In previous writings (Adam 2005, 2008) I have argued that the hierarchy of three categories of agent provides a critically important key for interpreting Buddhist moral discourse in general. These have been introduced above as the ordinary person (*puthujjana*), the disciple in higher training (*sekha*), and the liberated being (*arahant*) (see Bodhi 1992: 14–15). In this section we will draw a distinction between the ordinary person's experiences of moral development upon the worldly path, and the disciple in higher training's experiences of moral development, *qua* mental purification, upon the supramundane path. We will conclude with a brief discussion of the distinctive moral experience of the *arahant*—a task fraught with conceptual difficulties, in part because any further moral 'development' at this stage is technically impossible.

That moral development in early Buddhist thought should be appropriately interpreted in terms of the inner experience of the agent of moral conduct is clear enough when one considers the emphasis that the tradition places on volition. As noted above, the Buddha's identification of karma with volition had radical implications for the notion of moral conduct in ancient Indian thought and civilization. Not only did it pull the carpet out from under the feet of a culture of ritual animal sacrifice, it also had the effect of undermining the conceptual basis of the Indian fourfold class (*varṇa*) system, in which nobility, or purity, is based on birth. The Buddha's teachings redefined this concept in terms of wisdom and morality rather than occupational inheritance.

It is nevertheless important to recognize that the idea of nobility does persist in the Buddha's teachings—we have already noted many applications of the concept: to the path walked, the person walking, the view experienced, and indeed the very truths realized. As with so many other concepts afloat in the air of his times, it is apparent that a pernicious idea was here subverted and put to good use by the historical Buddha, who seems to have had a special talent for this kind of skilful transmutation of existing ideas (see esp. Gombrich 2009).

Thus the 'noble person' is situated in a hierarchy, not based on social class or occupation but on insight and moral purity. The social–spiritual hierarchy of the *varṇa* system comes to be displaced, on the one hand by a spiritual hierarchy based on inner character, and on the other by a new social division based around the partition of lay and monastic. We will not discuss the latter division in any detail here, nor its relationship with the hierarchy of spiritual agents. While it is clear that there is a significant overlap between the two schemas, it would be an obvious mistake to equate monastics and laity respectively with noble persons and ordinary persons. The texts often depict some monks as ordinary persons and some lay people as noble ones.

To understand the differences between the experiences of moral development of ordinary persons and disciples in higher training, we need make use of a conceptual schema employed by the Buddha himself in order to explain the nature of karma. In the *Kukkuravatika Sutta* (MN 57 *The Dog-duty Ascetic*) the Buddha provides an outline of the four basic kinds of action:

1. Dark with dark result.
2. Bright with bright result.
3. Both dark and bright with dark and bright result.
4. Neither dark nor bright, neither dark nor bright in result, the action that leads to the destruction of actions (see Bodhi 1995: 495).

The first three categories of action are precisely the same as those observed by Speyer in the *Avadānaśataka* (see above). It seems clear that they were employed in that context to encourage their intended audiences to aim for higher rebirths in *saṃsāra*. As such, the terms would seem be referring to karmically meritorious and unmeritorious actions (*puñña* and *apuñña*). But what are we to make of the fourth category, included in the sutta but not in the passage from the *avadāna*s? With its reference to the 'destruction of actions' it would seem to be referring to actions that lead to *nibbāna*, and hence skilful actions (*kusala*) *par excellence*. Why would this category be absent from the exhortation noted by Speyer? To whose actions does it refer?

Elsewhere I have argued that this fourth kind of action belongs to none other than the disciple in higher training (Adam 2005, 2008). To see this how this is so, one needs to give proper weight to the consideration that it is the state of mind characterizing a person's volition (*cetanā*) that is deemed the key factor determining the moral quality of any action. Importantly, the positive and negative terms translated here as 'bright' and 'dark' (*sukka* and *kaṇha* / *śukla* and *kṛṣṇa*) have strong epistemic connotations as well as the more obvious moral ones: bright and dark, white and black, pure and impure, good and evil.

Dark actions are those that are based upon afflictive, unskilful mental formations (i.e. those conditioned by the three roots of the unwholesome: greed, hatred, and delusion). As such, they prevent insight into the Four Noble Truths. Actions that are not dark are those based on skilful mental formations (those arising from non-greed, non-hatred, and non-delusion). They do not block or darken such insight. For an ordinary person such actions are deemed 'bright'; as such, they clearly do not fit the description of the fourth category: 'neither bright nor dark, with neither dark nor bright result . . .'. On the other hand, the conduct of the *arahant* does not quite fit the description of the fourth category of action either. His conduct cannot accurately be characterized as 'action that *leads to* the destruction of actions'; as a liberated being, the *arahant* has *already achieved* the destruction of actions.

Thus, by necessity, actions of the fourth category need to belong to someone in an intermediate position—a person who has not yet achieved the final freedom of *nibbāna*. This person is the disciple in higher training (Adam 2005; Ñāṇamoli and Bodhi 1995: 1258; Payutto 1999: 76). As discussed above, the supramundane path walked by the disciple in higher training leads directly to *nibbāna*; it is the embodiment of skilful action. With this understanding, the reason the fourth category is missing from the *avadāna* passage discussed by Speyer becomes apparent: the exhortation it contains is directed towards ordinary persons, those still practising on the worldly path. This interpretation helps to sharpen our earlier observations regarding the intended audience of Buddhist narrative literature, which can now be understood as directed towards ordinary persons, including monks, on the mundane path—rather than simply the laity (see Appleton 2010: 11–12).

Ordinary persons are motivated by a concern marked by the delusion of a permanent self; moral action is performed under the deluded desire to benefit such a self (i.e. with a higher rebirth, the prospect of pleasure, and so on). The agent's mentality is samsāric. But once a person enters the supramundane path, his or her actions are indelibly marked by the intimation of *nibbāna*; efforts are thereafter undertaken in the light of an unwavering recognition of the final goal. The mistaken belief in a Self has been penetrated by an ever-deepening experiential insight into the reality of the Four Noble Truths. This agent's mentality is nirvanic.

In terms of moral development, the experiential quality of moral conduct for the two classes of agent is entirely different. They display radically different intentional structures in relation to the binary poles of *saṃsāra* and *nibbāna*. For a person with a samsāric orientation, actions can be viewed as positively and negatively 'charged' with attachment—in the sense that they are undertaken with positive or negative results in mind. They are either bright or dark (or both). For a person with a nirvanic orientation, actions are neither positively nor negatively charged with attachment to results. They are neither bright nor dark. They have been emptied of such 'charge' in virtue of the absence of a false view of self to become attached to. The agent feels inescapably drawn towards *nibbāna*, but, paradoxically, is not motivated by the goal of attaining it for a falsely imagined 'self'. While the agent's actions continue to have unintended effects on their rebirths, this prospect does not form part of their motivation.

Similar considerations apply to the disciple in higher training's experiences of *free agency* on the way to the final goal (Adam 2010). Different degrees of the feeling of freedom can be associated with each of the various subdivisions of *disciple in higher training*. Unlike the ordinary person's experience, which is punctuated by a recurring sense of not being in control over one's life and fate, the disciple in higher training's experience is free from such oppressive feelings. Being irreversibly oriented away from suffering and its causes, such a person can be characterized as more consistently having the desires she wants to have. An internal harmony is being progressively established in such a person; we can say that her will is being brought into alignment with the *Dharma*. Interestingly, from a Western philosophical perspective, such an agent feels that she *cannot do otherwise* than act in ways that are consistent with her eventual attainment of *nibbāna*. Outwardly, her *sīla* is perfect; inwardly, she is progressively purifying her mind. As with the disciple in higher training's experiences of attachment and freedom, we can also recognize a parallel when it comes to feelings of *effort*. As one ascends along the supramundane path, one's inner struggles become fewer and the effort needed to act virtuously less burdensome and more natural. One happily does what one has to do. When one finally reaches the end of the path, effort is no longer required. One has become a moral virtuoso.

No More View, No More Path

The above considerations suggest that the Buddhist tradition recognizes fundamental differences between the inner moral lives of the ordinary person and the disciple in higher training. Thus far, however, we have said very little concerning the third and final class of agent—the liberated being or *arahant*. If a vast distance exists between the mentality and outer conduct of a disciple in higher training and those of an ordinary person, this is even more the case when it comes to those who have actually attained the final goal. In fact, the systematic *Nikāyas* seem to recognize that the inner lives of the *arahant* and those who are still on the path must differ in fundamental ways. Indeed, because the *arahant* is precisely one who will no longer be reborn, the very language of karma *cannot* be applicable to her. The fourfold schema of action laid out in the *Kukkuravatika Sutta* is meant to be exhaustive, and in it there is no place for the conduct of the *arahant*.

So it is that the texts describe the *arahant*'s conduct and consciousness (*kiriya-citta*) as 'adhering to the moral, but not "full of" morality' (that is, *sīlavā* but not *sīlamaya*; alternative translation below). The implication is that it is completely empty of attachment, and hence beyond both merit (*puñña*) and evil actions (*pāpa*). Clearly, a tension exists within the texts on the matter of how best to characterize the inner reality lying behind the *arahant*'s conduct. On the one hand the *arahant* represents inner perfection, the religious ideal, the living example of all that is worth striving for. As such, she is the embodiment of the positive qualities developed on the path. On the other hand, she also represents the realization of *nibbāna*, a value that lies beyond all dualistic predication. As such, the consciousness associated with the *arahant*'s conduct is said to be indeterminate (*avyākata*).

> And where do these wholesome habits (*kusala sīla*) cease without remainder? Their cessation is stated: here a bhikkhu is virtuous (*sīlavā*) but he does not identify with his virtue (*no ca sīlamaya*) and he understands as it actually is that deliverance of mind and deliverance by wisdom where these wholesome habits cease without remainder. (MN 2.27; trans. Ñāṇamoli and Bodhi 1995: 651)

In spite of the difficulties involved in providing a literal description of the *arahant*'s paradoxical condition, we can see that this figure personifies the perfection of the inner qualities we find developing on the paths taught by the Buddha: knowledge, moral purity, non-attachment, freedom. In the inner world behind the *arahant*'s selfless conduct lies a pure, unified state of stillness born from the realization of the highest good.

Works Cited

Adam, M. T. (2005) Groundwork for a metaphysic of Buddhist morals: a new analysis of *puñña* and *kusala*, in light of *sukka*. *Journal of Buddhist ethics*, 12: 62–85.

Adam, M. T. (2008) Classes of agent and the moral logic of the Pali canon. *Argumentation: special volume: Buddhist logic and argumentation*, 22: 115–124.

Adam, M. T. (2010) No self, no free will, no problem: implications of the *Anattalakkhaṇa sutta* for a perennial philosophical issue. In: M. T. Adam (ed.), *Indian Buddhist metaethics*. Panel proceedings from the 2008 IABS Meeting. *Journal of the international association of Buddhist studies*, 33: 239–265.

Adam, M. T. (2013) Buddhism, equality, rights. *Journal of Buddhist ethics*, 20: 422–443.

Appleton, N. (2010) *Jātaka stories in Theravāda Buddhism*. Farnham, UK: Ashgate Publishing.

Appleton, N. (2013) The second decade of the *Avadānaśataka*. *Asian literature and translation*, 1 (7): 1–36.

Appleton, N. (2014) *Narrating karma and rebirth: Buddhist and Jain multi-life stories*. Cambridge: Cambridge University Press.

Bodhi, Bhikkhu (1992) *The discourse on the root of existence: the Mūlapariyāya sutta and its commentaries*. Kandy: Buddhist Publication Society.

Bodhi, Bhikkhu (1999) *The noble eightfold path: the way to the end of suffering*. Available from: www.buddhanet.net/pdf_file/noble8path6.pdf [accessed 1 April 2016].

Bodhi, Bhikkhu (trans.) (2000) *The connected discourses of the Buddha: a new translation of Saṃyutta nikāya*, 2 volumes. Boston: Wisdom Publications [SN].

Bodhi, Bhikkhu (trans.) (2012) *The numerical discourses of the Buddha: a translation of the Aṅguttara nikāya*. Boston: Wisdom Publications [AN].

Chalmers, Robert (trans.) (1895) Mitacinti-Jātaka. In *The Jataka: or stories of the Buddha's former births*. Cambridge: C. J. Clay and Sons, 256.

Clark, C. (2015) *A study of the Apadāna, including an edition and annotated translation of the second, third and fourth chapters*. PhD, University of Sydney. Available from: ses.library.usyd.edu.au//bitstream/2123/13438/1/Clark_C_thesis.pdf [accessed 1 April 2016].

Dhammajoti, Bhikkhu (trans.) (2012) *Pubbakammapilotika-buddhāpadānaṁ: the traditions about the Buddha (known as) the connection with previous deeds, or why the Buddha suffered*. Available from: www.ancient-buddhist-texts.net/Texts-and-Translations/Connection-with-Previous-Deeds/index.htm [accessed 1 April 2016].

Gethin, R. (1998) *The foundations of Buddhism*. Oxford: Oxford University Press.

Gombrich, R. (2009) *What the Buddha thought*. Sheffield, UK: Equinox.

Harvey, P. (2013) The saṅgha of noble sāvakas, with particular reference to their trainee member, the person 'practising for the realization of the stream-entry-fruit'. *Buddhist studies review*, 30 (1): 3–70.

Ñāṇamoli, Bhikkhu, and Bodhi, Bhikkhu (trans.) (1995) *The middle-length discourses of the Buddha: a new translation of the Majjhima nikāya*. Boston: Wisdom Publications.

Ohnuma, R. (2003) *Head, eyes, flesh, and blood: giving away the body in Indian Buddhist literature*. New York: Columbia University Press.

Payutto, P. A. (1999) *Good, evil and beyond: kamma in the Buddha's teachings*. Bangkok: Buddhadhamma Foundation.

Rhys Davids, T. W. (1878) *Buddhist birth-stories (Jataka tales): the commentarial introduction entitled Nidāna-kathā, the story of the lineage*. London: George Routledge & Sons. Available from: archive.org/stream/buddhistbirthoodaviuoft#page/n15/mode/2up [accessed 1 April 2016].

Speyer, J. S. (1909) *Avadānaśataka: a century of edifying tales*. Available from: https://archive.org/details/avadanacatakacenooavaduoft [accessed 1 April 2016].

Walshe, M. (trans.) (1995) *The long discourses of the Buddha: a translation of the Dīgha nikāya*. Boston: Wisdom Publications.

Suggested Reading

Appleton, N. (2014) *Narrating karma and rebirth: Buddhist and Jain multi-life stories*. Cambridge: Cambridge University Press.

Ohnuma, R. (2003) *Head, eyes, flesh, and blood: giving away the body in Indian Buddhist literature*. New York: Columbia University Press.

Rotman, A. (2008). *Divine stories: Divyāvadāna part I*. Boston: Wisdom Publications.

Shaw, S. (2006) *The Jātakas: birth-stories of the bodhisatta*. New Delhi: Penguin.

Strong, J. (2012) Explicating the Buddha's final illness in the context of his other ailments: the making and unmaking of some Jātaka tales. *Buddhist studies review*, 29: 17–33.

Tatelman, J. (2004) Avadāna. *Encyclopedia of Buddhism*, 36–37.

CHAPTER 5

THE *VINAYA*

CHARLES S. PREBISH

INTRODUCTION

MODERN Buddhological studies have been enhanced in recent years by the fruitful researches of the many scholars who have focused their attention on the primary literature of Buddhism. To be sure, one of the most promising endeavours in understanding the historical, religious, philosophical, and social dimensions of Buddhism has been the textual approach in which 'the texts are allowed to speak for themselves'. Nevertheless, with so many differing aspects to examine, in the various Buddhist countries and languages, the organization of this overwhelming corpus of literature has proved to be the researcher's dilemma and the bibliographer's nightmare.

It is my contention that this form of enterprise in Buddhist Studies must necessarily begin with basics, and in this regard, no aspect of Buddhist literature is more essential than the *Tripiṭaka*. Within the *Tripiṭaka*, in the *nikāya* Buddhist tradition, the first collection of texts comprises the *Vinaya Piṭaka* or the rules of training and discipline for the monks and nuns on the individual level and the guidelines for monastic regulation on the institutional level. Charles Hallisey notes, 'The *Vinaya Piṭaka*, as a canonical collection, survives in the versions of five different schools of the Nikāya Buddhist tradition, in addition to those found in the Theravāda tradition: Mahāsāṃghika, Sarvāstivāda, Mūlasarvāstivāda, Dharmaguptaka, and Mahīśāsaka' (2007: 810). To summarize all the problematics inherent in *Vinaya* study, historically, comparatively, and with a view towards its position in the Indian Buddhist sectarian movement is not germane here, and has been clearly stated elsewhere. Buddhist scholar Michael Carrithers is quoted to have said, 'No Buddhism without the Sangha and no Sangha without the Discipline' (1984: 133). In other words, in order to effect the highest level of ethical conduct from the monastic and lay communities, disciplinary codes for each unit were enacted. For the monastic community, this took the form of a portion of the canon known as the *Vinaya Piṭaka*. No doubt the heart of *Vinaya* literature is in the canon itself, including editions of texts, translations, and in a secondary sense, textual studies. The canon, however, did not emerge in a vacuum, and thus it is essential to include an examination of the formative root texts which served as canonical precursors and prototypes. Further, once the canons of the various *nikāyas* were closed, an active commentarial tradition proliferated in Buddhism, and to some extent at least, it is still active today.

Properly speaking, the *Vinaya Piṭaka*, or that portion of the Buddhist canon regulating the monastic life of the monks and nuns, is composed of three parts: (1) *Sūtravibhaṅga*, (2) *Skandhaka*, and (3) Appendices. However, a consideration of Buddhist monastic discipline must be taken in broad perspective, focusing not only on that portion of monastic law which was canonized, but on *Vinaya* literature in general, thus affording us an opportunity to view the developmental process going on within the early Indian Buddhist community in the first few centuries following Buddha's death. Consequently, we can include the *Prātimokṣa* and the *Karmavācanās*, although not considered to be canonical in the strictest sense, under the heading of Paracanonical *Vinaya* Literature, and the commentaries and miscellaneous texts under the heading of Non-Canonical *Vinaya* Literature. Thus we arrive at the following arrangement:

- Paracanonical *Vinaya* Literature
  - *Prātimokṣa*
  - *Karmavācanā*
- Canonical *Vinaya* Literature
  - *Sūtravibhaṅga*
  - *Skandhaka*
  - Appendices
- Non-Canonical *Vinaya* Literature
  - Commentaries
  - Miscellaneous Texts

We can now proceed to an examination of these categories.

Paracanonical *Vinaya* Literature

Prātimokṣa

The *Prātimokṣa* is an inventory of offences that govern the conduct of the *Bhikṣus* and *Bhikṣuṇīs*. Many scholars have attempted to explicate the etymological meaning of the term *Prātimokṣa*, but these pursuits remain, for the most part, speculative. The *Prātimokṣa* was recited at each *Poṣadha* day, and regarding its function, Miss Horner candidly states,

> This recitation served the double purpose of keeping the rules fresh in the minds of the monks and nuns, and of giving each member of the monastic community the

> opportunity, while the rules were being repeated or recited, to avow any offences that he or she had committed. (1938–1966: I, xii)

For each breach of the rules, appropriate punitive measures are indicated. Since the *Prātimokṣa* concerns both monks and nuns, it is twofold (i.e. *Bhikṣu Prātimokṣa* and *Bhikṣuṇī Prātimokṣa*). The monks' *Prātimokṣa* contains eight categories of offences, classified according to the degree of gravity. The nuns' *Prātimokṣa* covers the same categories with the third (or *Aniyata* offences) being omitted. The eight categories of offences can now be listed and explained (with reference to the monks' text).

Pārājika-dharmas

These four offences are the most serious which can be committed by the monks. They include (1) sexual intercourse, (2) theft, (3) deprivation of life (of a human), and (4) false proclamation of superhuman faculties. Mention of these four offences is not distinct to the *Prātimokṣa* or *Sūtravibhaṅga*, as we find them, for example, elsewhere in the Pāli *Vinaya*. Violation of any one of the *pārājika-dharmas* results in permanent expulsion from the *saṃgha*. It should be noted that the term *pārājika* remains a puzzle. Miss Horner renders it 'defeat', following Rhys Davids and Oldenberg. E. J. Thomas notes that, 'Buddhaghosa interprets *pārājika* as "suffering defeat," and the Mūlasarvāstivādins do the same ...' (1963: 16 n. 2). More recently, however, Gustav Roth has thrown some light on the subject by interestingly re-examining Sylvain Lévi's suggestion of an earlier form of the term: *pārācika* (1968: 341–343).

Saṃghāvaśeṣa-dharmas

These thirteen offences represent, following the *pārājika-dharmas*, the most severe breach of monastic discipline. Five offences deal with sexual transgressions, two with dwelling places, two with false accusation, two with schisms, one with a monk who is difficult to speak to, and one with monks who corrupt families. The first nine of these become offences at once, while the final four do not become offences until the third admonition of the monk involved. The section of the *saṃghāvaśeṣa-dharmas* is unique in that it represents the only class of *Prātimokṣa* offences that contains specific provisions for disciplinary action. When a monk is culpable of a *saṃghāvaśeṣa* offence, he is subjected to a probationary period (*parivāsa*) for as many days as the offence was concealed. If the offence was confessed at once, the *parivāsa* period is reduced to nil. When the *parivāsa* is completed, a further period called *mānatva* must also be spent. It is interesting that an entire *vastu* (i.e. chapter) in the *Skandhaka* portion of the *Vinaya*, the *Pārivāsikavastu*, is devoted to these issues. The term *saṃghāvaśeṣa*, like *pārājika*, is problematic. No etymological rendering of the term seems to make much sense. However, a careful discussion of the term, stressing the plausibility of the variant *saṃghātiśeṣa* (as found in the Sanskrit version of the Mahāsāṃghika-Lokottaravādin text), is presented by Gustav Roth (1968: 343–345) and also by Sylvain Lévi (1912: 503–504). Regarding this class of offences, Miss Horner perceptively notes,

> It is not impossible that originally the various *Saṅghas*, which were really sub-divisions of the whole *Saṅgha*, exercised their jurisdiction over each individual member only in the case of the *Saṃghādisesa* offences, only coming later to exercise such jurisdiction in the case of all classes of offence. If this is so, we do well, I think, to underline the formalities which the *Saṅghādisesa* offences entailed, and were very likely alone in so doing at first. For by this means some early feature of the Order's history may be kept in mind. (1938–1966: I, xxxii)

Aniyata-dharmas

These two offences include cases whereby a monk may be accused by a trustworthy female lay follower, and dealt with according to her dictate. In case 1, if a monk should sit together with a woman in a secret place convenient for sexual intercourse, he may be charged either with a *pārājika, saṃghāvaśeṣa*, or *pāyantika* (discussed below) offence, according to what actually transpired. In case 2, if a monk should sit together with a woman in a place unfit for indulging in sexual intercourse, but suitable for speaking to her in lewd words, he may be charged with a *saṃghāvaśeṣa* or *pāyantika* offence, the *pārājika* offence of unchastity having been ruled out. Due to the manner in which the monk may be charged, expressing the variety of monastic offences open to him, this category is referred to as 'undetermined (i.e. *aniyata*) offences'. The two offences in this category reflect an outstanding and somewhat surprising degree of trust in the female lay follower.

Niḥsargika-Pāyantika-dharmas

There are thirty offences in this class, violation of which require expiation and forfeiture, as can be seen from the class title. Horner notes, 'From internal evidence, *pācittiya* [Skt. *pāyantika*] is a (minor) offence to be confessed, *āpatti desetabbā* [Skt. *āpatti deśayitavyā*], a state common to all the *Nissagiyas* [Skt. *Niḥsargikas*]' (1938–1966: II, vii). The *niḥsargika-pāyantika-dharmas* are arranged in three *vargas*, or sections, of ten rules each. Using the description of E. J. Thomas (1963: 19):

a. Ten rules concerning robes
   These refer to the length of time during which an extra robe might be kept, to repair and exchange of robes, and to receiving them as alms. He might not ask a lay person for a robe unless he had lost his own, nor might he suggest the kind he was to receive.
b. Ten rules for rugs and the use of money
   The material of which the rug was made was prescribed, and it had to be used for six years. The monk might accept the material for it under certain conditions. Gold and silver must not be accepted or used in transactions, and buying and selling were forbidden.
c. Ten rules concerning, bowl, medicine, and robes
   A monk might not keep an extra bowl beyond ten days, nor exchange his bowl if it was broken in less than five places. Medicine (ghee, butter, oil, honey, raw sugar) must not be stored for more than seven days. There are special rules for robes in the rainy

season and for having them woven. Nothing intended to be given to the order was to be applied by the monk to his own use.

If we tabulate the offences, we discover that sixteen refer to robes, five to rugs, four to money and appropriating *saṃgha* property, two to sheep's wool, two to bowls, and one to medicines. This is the first class of offences in the *Prātimokṣa* in which the numbering system employed by the various *nikāyas* becomes widely divergent. In commenting on the nature of the forfeiture and confession, and on the general value of this form of punishment, Miss Horner remarks,

> As a general rule, the *Padabhājaniya* [Old Commentary] states that forfeiture and confession were to be made to an Order, that is to any part of the whole Order, five monks or more, living within a boundary, *sīmā*, or within one residence, *āvāsa*; or to a group, *gaṇa*, of monks, that is to a group of from two to four monks; or to an individual monk. When the article has been forfeited and the offence confessed, the offence was to be acknowledged, in the first two stances, by "an experienced, competent monk;" in the third by the monk to whom the forfeiture and confession had been made. The forfeited article was then to be given back to the monk who, having acquired it wrongly, had forfeited it.
>
> The value of the *nissaggiya pācittiya* [Skt. *Niḥsargika-pāyantika*] type of penalty was, I think, in the eyes of the framer or framers of the *Pātimokkha* [*Prātimokṣa*] rules, its deterrent effect on the commission of further similar offences, and its redemptive power for each particular offender. It was apparently held that an offence whose penalty was of this nature was annulled by confessing it and having it acknowledged, combined with this hardly more than symbolic act of forfeiting the article wrongly acquired. This involved some formality, but evidently the offence was not considered bad enough to warrant the offender's permanent loss of the goods he had obtained improperly. (1938–1966: II, xii; the brackets are mine)

Regarding the terms *niḥsargika* and *pāyantika*, several of the alternate readings should be pointed out. For *niḥsargika*, we find, for the most part: *nissargika*, *naissargika*, *naisargika*, and *naiḥsargika*. For *pāyantika*, we also find: *pāyattikāḥ*, *papattikā*, *pāpantikā*, *pācittiyakā*, *pātayantika*, *prāyaścittikā*, *pācittiya*, *payti*, *pāyacchitika*, *pācchita*, and *pācattika*.

*Pāyantika-dharma*s

There are ninety offences in this category, violation of which require expiation.[1] Although the number pattern in this class of rules is widely divergent in the various *nikāya*s, an examination of the contents of the rules yields surprising results. The vast majority of rules (seventy-four) may be grouped under five major headings:[2]

[1] The Pāli and Chinese Mahāsāṃghika texts each have ninety-two rules, while the Chinese Mahīśāsaka version has ninety-one rules. The Sanskrit Mahāsāṃghika and Mūlasarvāstivādin texts have ninety-two and ninety rules respectively.

[2] These headings have been outlined by Thomas, but I deviate considerably from his placement of the rules into various categories.

a. Moral rules: 23 rules
b. Conduct with women: 14 rules
c. Food and drink: 16 rules
d. *Dharma, Vinaya*, and their application: 11 rules
e. Use of requisites: 10 rules

The remaining rules (sixteen) may be grouped under three further rubrics, each containing a lesser number of items:

a. Behaviour in the *vihāra*: 6 rules
b. Travel regulations: 5 rules
c. Various types of destruction: 5 rules

The placement of the rules into these categories is necessarily somewhat arbitrary, and several of the rules are more accurately co-terminus. The various *Prātimokṣa* texts generally group the rules numerically in divisions of ten rules. Some texts supply *uddānas* or summaries at the end of each section of ten rules, presumably as a memory aid for the monk, and one text (the Sanskrit Mahāsāṃghika-Lokottaravādin version) even provides a summary of the *vargas* at the end of the entire section. E. J. Thomas, primarily because of the use of the term *vihāra* and the denotation of furniture common to the *saṃgha*, is of the opinion that,

> Several rules in this section show a more developed communal life than that implied in the *Saṅghādisesa* rules, and the whole section has probably been collected or put into shape at a later period than the previous rules. (1963: 20)

*Pratideśanīya-dharma*s

The *Pratideśanīya* section contains four straightforward offences that are to be confessed. They include (1) partaking of food obtained through the intervention of a nun, (2) not reproving a nun for giving orders (pertaining to a meal) while a meal is being served, (3) accepting food from a family which is undergoing training, and (4) obtaining food while living in a dangerous setting, without having announced it being so beforehand (unless the monk is ill).

*Śaikṣa-dharma*s

This group of rules is the most disparate in the entire *Prātimokṣa*. The number of *Śaikṣa-dharma*s varies in number from 66 in the Chinese Mahāsāṃghika version to 113 in the Chinese Sarvāstivādin version. Dr. Pachow describes the section in the following manner:

> The nature of these rules is essentially concerned with the daily conduct and decorum of the *Bhikṣus* such as: walking, moving to and fro, looking, dressing, contracting, and stretching and so forth. They do not come under any penal section inasmuch as there will not be any sanction or punishment for their breaches of violations. The violation of any of them by a *Bhikṣu* is not considered to be a criminal act but simply bad manners. (1954: IV, 2, 69)

This section of the *Prātimokṣa* is perhaps the most revealing with regard to delineating the particular customs of individual Buddhist sects in the earliest sectarian movement.

Adhikaraṇa-Śamatha-dharmas

These seven rules represent a system by which offences may be resolved. The first, *saṃmukhavinaya*, literally means: in the presence of. The *Samathakkhandhaka* of the Pāli *Vinaya* explains this by the presence of the individual, the *Saṃgha*, the *Dharma*, and the *Vinaya*. The second, *smṛtivinaya*, literally means: verdict based on recollection. However, the *Samathakkhandhaka* makes it clear that it is a verdict of innocence and outlines five requirements for such a decision: (1) that the monk is pure and faultless, (2) that he is accused, (3) that he asks for dismissal of the charge, (4) that the *saṃgha* gives the *smṛtivinaya* decision, and (5) that the *saṃgha* is complete. The third, *amūḍhavinaya*, literally means: verdict of past insanity. The *Samathakkhandhaka* notes three criteria for granting such a verdict: (1) the offence was not remembered, (2) the offence was remembered and confessed, and (3) the monk remains insane. The fourth, *yadbhūyaṣikīya*, literally means: decision of the majority. The *Samathakkhandhaka*, however, states that when a decision of the majority is not reached, monks at another *āvāsa* may be consulted. The fifth, *tatsvabhāvaiṣīya*, literally means: special nature (of the accused monk). The *Samathakkhandhaka* notes three occasions for carrying out this act against a monk: if he (1) is a maker of fights, (2) is a maker of quarrels, or (3) is a maker of disputes. The sixth, *tṛṇaprastāraka*, literally means: cover (as) with grass. The *Samathakkhandhaka* explains that when monks are engaged in dispute, many unbecoming things may be said. Monks should gather together under the direction of an experienced monk, confess their collective fault, and unless it is a grave act (*sthūlavadya*) or connected with the laity (*gṛhapatisaṃyukta*), enact this procedure. The seventh, *pratijñākāraka*, literally means: verdict that effects confession. The *Samathakkhandhaka* advises that acts must not be carried out against a monk without his acknowledgement. The *adhikaraṇa-Śamatha-dharmas* are discussed at length in Sukumar Dutt's volume *Early Buddhist Monachism* (1960: 113–145). Strangely enough, we also find an explanation of this class of rules in the *Sāmagāma-sutta* of the *Majjhima Nikāya* (*Sutta* No. 104).

These eight classes of rules comprise the monks' *Prātimokṣa-sūtra*. The texts are preceded by a series of verses praising the disciplined life, and also by a ritual formulary. A series of verses, often concurring with similar verses in the *Dhammapada* or *Udānavarga*, also follow the text proper, uniformly mentioning the six buddhas immediately antecedent to Śākyamuni Gautama and Gautama himself.

The nuns' *Prātimokṣa-sūtra* consists of the same classes of rules as the monks' text, but with the omission of the *aniyata-dharmas* as noted above. The number of rules in the nuns' *Prātimokṣa-sūtra* is considerably larger than in the monks' version, many rules having been inserted specifically for females. A comparative study of the nuns' *Prātimokṣa-sūtra*, quite similar in structure and format to Pachow's study of the monks' text, was published by Chatsumarn Kabilsingh in 1984. Kabilsingh's volume presents a number of extremely useful charts and tables as well as a helpful bibliography.

Karmavācanā

All the transactions pertaining to the communal life of a *saṃgha* were settled by acts referred to as *Saṃghakarmas*. *Saṃghakarmas* could arise in either of two ways (Dutt 1960: 225):

1. By a general requisition
2. By a dispute

Regarding the *Karmavācanā*, Dr B. Jinananda notes,

> A formula, styled *karmavācanā* (Pāli: *kammavācā*) was resorted to for performing *saṃghakarmas*. There are two forms of arriving at a resolution (i) a summary decision (*Jñaptidvitīyakarma*) in which a resolution is arrived at by the first reading and (ii) a decision by the third reading (*Jñapticaturthakarma*). (1961: 3)

Herbert Härtel finds the earliest evidence for *Karmavācanā* in several portions of the Pāli Canon. He then quotes Herman Oldenberg:

> While, however, in the case of *suttavibhaṅga* the liturgy on which it has been founded (*pātimokkha*) has been preserved in a separate shape, the formularies in the *Khandhakas* [Skt *Skandhakas*] have not as yet, except in some instances, been found in existence apart from the *Khandhakas*. The principal exception is the *Upasampadā-kammavācā*, which recurs in its entirety in the first *Khandhaka* of the *Mahāvagga*. (1956: 16; the brackets are mine)

Since the book that Härtel is quoting from was published in 1881, he is careful to point out that there are several newer examples of independent *Karmavācanās*, not only in Pāli, but also in Sanskrit and Chinese. Both Härtel and Jinananda cite fourteen *Karmavācanās* (Jinananda 1961: 3; Härtel 1956: 8):

1. Admission into the order (*pravrajyā*)
2. Ordination of monks (*upasaṃpadā*)
3. Holding the confession ceremony (*poṣadha*)
4. Holding the ceremony of invitation (*pravāraṇā*)
5. Residence obligation during the rainy season (*varṣopagamana*)
6. Use of leather objects (*carman*)
7. Use and preparation of medicines (*bhaiṣajya*)
8. Robe-giving ceremony (*kaṭhina*)
9. Discipline
10. Daily life of monks
11. Beds and seats, i.e. dwellings (*śayanāsana*)
12. Schisms in the order (*saṃghabheda*)

13. Duties of a student and teacher to one another
14. Rules for nuns

In commenting on the *Karmavācanā*, Jinananda observes,

> The importance of this formula for the history of community life of Buddhism is very great. It permits us to have a peep into the Buddhist church organisation which did not have any supreme head. The whole organisation is imbued with a democratic spirit and follows the parliamentary method. (1961: 3)

As the *Saṃghakarma* is so significant to the lawful functioning of the monastic community, it must be explained more fully, with a particular emphasis on its application to the *Vinaya*. A valid *Saṃghakarma* consists of the following requisites (Dutt 1960: 125):

1. The presence of the proper number of competent monks
2. The conveyance of all absentee ballots (*chanda*)
3. The motion (*jñapti*) being proposed
4. The proper proclamation of *karmavācanā*

Sukumar Dutt, in *Early Buddhist Monachism* (1960: 125–142), provides an excellent account of the proceeding of a *Saṃghakarma*. It is summarized here, replacing the Pāli terms with their now more familiar Sanskrit equivalents (and supplying page references wherever appropriate). Dr Dutt treats both disputatious and disciplinary *Saṃghakarmas*, and we shall examine the former first.

Disputes (*adhikaraṇas*) are of four classes (pp. 126–127):

1. *Vivādādhikaraṇa*: disputes concerning *Dharma, Vinaya*, matters concerning the *Tathāgata*, and the nature of monastic offences
2. *Anuvādādhikaraṇa*: disputes concerning a monks general deportment
3. *Āpattyadhikaraṇa*: disputes concerning *pārājika, saṃghāvaśeṣa, pāyantika, pratideśanīya, duṣkṛta, sthūlātyaya*, and *durbhāṣita* offences of which a monk is accused
4. *Kṛtyādhikaraṇa*: disputes concerning *Saṃghakarma* procedure of or *saṃgha* responsibilities

The following stages are outlined (pp. 125–126):

1. The Dispute (preliminary)
   a. Accusation and denial, or
   b. Confession, or
   c. Difference of opinion
2. The Procedure
   a. Proposal of the *jñapti*

b. Proclamation of *Karmavācanā*
c. Rules of *Adhikaraṇa-Śamatha*
3. The *Saṃgha's* Decision

The *saṃgha*'s decision must be in terms of the original *jñapti* or motion. If the *jñapti* was for acquittal or discharge, the matter was dismissed. If the *jñapti* was for conviction, a disciplinary *Saṃghakarma* was required, and this leads to an examination of this second type of *Saṃghakarma*.

When a monk is charged with an offence, six pleas are open to him (pp. 136–138):

1. Past insanity
2. Not remembering committing the offense
3. Refusal to make confession
4. Confession
5. Hedging (retraction of a plea)
6. Confession of a different offence than that with which charged

If the first plea is taken, and the *saṃgha* is satisfied with it, request for *amūḍhavinaya* is made by the accused, and transacted according to the *Saṃghakarma* rules outlined above. If the *saṃgha* is not satisfied, the monk may be suspended for non-confession of a fault or sentenced to the *parivāsa* and *manātva* penalties. The second plea may be accepted only from one whose memory is trusted, and the process is as above. In the third case the monk may be suspended for non-confession of a fault or sentenced in other appropriate but lawful ways. In no wise is the accused to be discharged or absolved. For the fourth plea the monk must confess his offence and request the *mānatva* discipline. A *jñapti* is then set out and the *Karmavācanā* employed, after which the monk is officially sentenced. In the fifth plea the monk should ask for punishment suited to his obstinate nature. With regard to the sixth plea, the monk's confession cannot be accepted. He can only be tried for the offence with which he is charged. Dr Dutt seems to feel that the most prudent course would be to change to the second plea, remaining open, of course, to later accusation for the originally confessed offence.

The following penalties are to be administered for the various offences (pp. 138–142):

1. *Parivāsa*

The *parivāsa* penalty is enforced for the violation of a *saṃghāvaśeṣa-dharma*. It involves a probationary period with some of the monk's rights, such as attending the *Poṣadha* ceremony or living with the *saṃgha*, suspended. The *parivāsa* period is determined in one of four ways:

a. *Apraticchanna*: when the offence is immediately confessed (in which case *parivāsa* is reduced to nil)
b. *Praticchanna*: when the offence may be concealed, *parivāsa* is imposed for as many days as the offence was concealed (from the time of sentence)

c. *Śuddhāntika*: when it is impossible to determine the date on which the offence was committed, the *parivāsa* period is counted from the date of the monk's ordination to the date of the sentence
d. *Samodana*: when a new offence is committed by a monk while serving *parivāsa*, a new *parivāsa* period begins (and the longer period, i.e. for the first or second offence, is served)

2. *Mānatva*

The *mānatva* period is imposed with the *parivāsa* and served immediately following the conclusion of *parivāsa*. The difference between *parivāsa* and *mānatva* is that the latter has a fixed period: six days.

3. *Tarjanīyakarma*

This penalty was imposed for any offence excepting a *pārājika-dharma* or a *saṃghāvaśeṣa-dharma*. Disabilities were imposed on the monk, continuing until the monk asked for and was granted reinstatement.

4. *Nigarhaṇīyakarma*

This penalty subjects a monk to careful observation, being imposed on one who repeatedly committed *saṃghāvaśeṣa* offences.

5. *Pravāsanīyakarma*

This penalty, consisting of banishment, was inflicted on a monk creating scandals.

6. *Pratisaṃharaṇīyakarma*

This measure was inflicted on a monk who offended a householder, and required his obtaining a pardon from the offended party. If pardon was not granted, attempts could be made by a companion, the *saṃgha*, and again by the monk, humbly confessing his guilt in the presence of the householder.

7. *Utkṣepaṇīyakarma*

This penalty was assessed for not confessing a fault, not expiating a fault, or not renouncing an improper doctrine. The penalty involves suspension.

8. *Brahmadaṇḍa*

This penalty resulted in social (but not religious) excommunication.

Having recounted the structure of the Paracanonical *Vinaya* literature, and having examined the administration of the *Vinaya* system of monastic discipline, we can consider the structure and contents of the Canonical *Vinaya* Literature.

CANONICAL *VINAYA* LITERATURE

Sūtravibhaṅga

The term *Sūtravibhaṅga* is literally translated as 'analysis of a sutra'. Thus, the *Sūtravibhaṅga* is a detailed analysis concerning the offences recorded in the *Prātimokṣa-sūtra*. As we should expect, the *Sūtravibhaṅga* has the same eight sections as the *Prātimokṣa-sūtra*. Regarding each of the *Prātimokṣa* rules, the *Sūtravibhaṅga* has a fourfold structure:

1. A story (or stories) explaining the circumstances under which the rule was pronounced
2. The actual *Prātimokṣa* rule
3. A word for word commentary on the rule
4. Stories indicating mitigating circumstances in which exceptions to the rule or deviations in punishment might be made

In addition to the *Prātimokṣa* offences, several new disciplinary terms are found in the text of the *Sūtravibhaṅga*. These include: *duṣkṛta* (light offence), *sthūlātyaya* (grave offence), and *durbhāṣita* (offence of improper speech). Miss Horner describes the nature of these offences:

> One or other of these offences is said to be incurred if behaviour has approximated to that particular *Pātimokkha* rule has been designated to restrain, but which is, so far as can be judged, not so grave in nature as a breach of the rule itself, because of certain differences in its execution, or because of certain extenuating circumstances. (1938–1966: I, xxxv)

In explaining why these new terms were used, instead of simply including new offences under the standard headings, Oldenberg declares,

> Now the circle of offences which constitute a *Pācittiya* [Skt *Pāyantika*], etc., appeared in later times as completed; if a punishment was to be inflicted for a transgression not specified in the *Pātimokkha*, they avoided using the expression *Pācittiya*, because, in doing this, they would have made an unauthorized addition of new matter to the ordinances of the *Pātimokkha* as fixed of old, which was considered inadmissible. Hence any offence of this kind, if it was a slight one, was termed *Dukkaṭa* [Skt *Duṣkṛta*]; if grievous, *Thullaccaya* [Skt *Sthūlātyaya*]. (1964: I, xx; the brackets are mine)

Like the *Prātimokṣa*, there is both a *Bhikṣu Sūtravibhaṅga* (referred to as the *Mahāvibhaṅga*) and a *Bhikṣuṇī Sūtravibhaṅga*.

Skandhaka

The *Skandhaka* contains the regulations pertaining to the organization of the *saṃgha*. The *Skandhaka* functions on the basis of the acts and ceremonies dictated by the *Karmavācanās*. Two statements can be made in the way of analogy:

1. The *Skandhaka* represents to the *saṃgha* what the *Sūtravibhaṅga* represents to the individual monk or nun
2. The *Karmavācanās* are to the *Skandhaka* what the *Prātimokṣa* is to the *Sūtravibhaṅga*

There are twenty chapters in the *Skandhaka*, each referred to as a *vastu*, which shall now be listed with a brief summary of the main features of each.[3]

Chapter 1 Pravrajyāvastu

This *vastu* discusses, at length, admission into the order (*pravrajyā*), ordination to full monkhood (*upasaṃpadā*), admission of novices (*śrāmaṇeras*), regulations regarding behaviour of a monk towards his master (*upadhyāya*) or teacher (*ācārya*), and a résumé of the cases disqualifying one from admission into the order.

Chapter 2 Poṣadhavastu

The *Poṣadhavastu* discusses the monthly confession ceremony from its inception to its final form, and also outlines the rules connected with the *Poṣadha* ceremony. The *Poṣadha* ceremony is instituted on King Bimbisāra's suggestion, based on his observation of other, non-Buddhist, sects. At first, the ceremony was held on the eighth, fourteenth, and fifteenth of every fortnight, but later, observance on the eighth was eliminated, and Buddha declared that the *Prātimokṣa-sūtra* should be recited at the *Poṣadha* ceremony. Finally, many rules follow, discussing how the confession ceremony is to be announced and the monks called together, how the *Prātimokṣa* recitation should begin, how the *Poṣadha* is to be kept up, various kinds of confession ceremonies, the procedure itself, atonement of offences, how to handle monks arriving while the ceremony is going on, and arrangements for avoiding any interruptions of the ceremony.

Chapter 3 Varṣāvastu

The third *vastu* sets forth the rules for the observance of the rainy season. The *Varṣāvastu* begins with an account of the events leading up to the Buddha's decision to have the monks spend the rainy season in fixed residence. The period for rainy season residence is fixed at three months, and a discussion of when to enter the rain residence, acceptable

[3] These summaries are taken, in part, from Frauwallner 1956: 68–129.

and forbidden dwellings, and room and furniture distribution follows next. Conditions under which the rainy season residence may be abandoned are carefully explained. Finally, the offences and non-offences are outlined in the case of a monk abandoning a rainy season residence which the monk had promised a layman to inhabit for the duration of the rainy season.

Chapter 4 Pravāraṇāvastu

This chapter treats the invitation (*Pravāraṇā*) ceremony that comes at the end of the rainy season. The ceremony is designed to prevent disharmony in the monastic community, and involves each monk inviting other monks to state whether there is anything for which he should be reproved, being prepared, of course, to make the proper reparation. Precise procedural rules for the ceremony are given, defining the preparations for the ceremony, how the ceremony is begun, etc. Provisions are outlined for various kinds of *Pravāraṇā* ceremonies, and how to carry out an abbreviated ceremony in case of danger. It is noted that unauthorized persons are excluded from the ceremony. The method for making amends is outlined, emphasizing that a monk may not participate in the ceremony without having done so. Finally, some exceptional cases are discussed.

Chapter 5 Carmavastu

The *Carmavastu* deals with the usage of leather (and shoes in particular). The *vastu* begins with a story concerning Śroṇa Koṭīviṃśa. Following this account, the subject of the chapter title is discussed in detail. The chapter concludes with a second legendary story, that of Śroṇa Koṭīkarṇa.

Chapter 6 Bhaiṣajyavastu

This chapter discusses the rules concerning foods and medicines allowed to the monks. Several stories are utilized to outline a definition of medicinal drugs and an explanation of how and when they are to be used. With regard to food, the rules are severe, stating which alms food may be accepted, how an invitation should be dealt with, how alms foods are to be prepared, and how the storeroom (*kalpikaśālā*) is to be used. Relaxation of these rules is allowed in hard times. Several legends conclude the *vastu*.

Chapter 7 Cīvaravastu

The *Cīvaravastu* treats the rules regarding monks' clothing. The legend of the physician Jīvaka is recounted, at length, culminating with the Buddha allowing monks to accept robes from the laity. Rules concerning which robes may and may not be worn, the cutting and sewing of robes, the disfiguring of robes, and the number of robes are set forth. Many rules regarding the distribution of clothing are outlined. The distribution of a deceased monk's requisites is also treated at length.

Chapter 8 Kaṭhinavastu

This *vastu* sets forth rules concerning the manufacture and distribution of robes for the monks, initiated because of the poor condition of the clothing of the monks after the period of rainy season residence. The actual procedure is considered, followed by an explanation of when the *kaṭhina* procedure is or is not properly conducted. Cases in which a monk's *kaṭhina* privileges are suspended are also set forth, with subdivisions of these cases.

Chapter 9 Kośāmbakavastu

The *Kośāmbakavastu* is a short chapter relating a dispute that develops between two groups of monks in Kauśāmbī concerning the expulsion of a monk. At first, the Buddha makes a vain attempt to settle the quarrel. Alms offerings by the laymen of Kauśāmbī are withdrawn, whereby the monks travel to Śrāvastī. Elaborate instructions on proper conduct are given to the community by the Buddha. Finally, the excluded monk confessed his guilt, is readmitted, and harmony is restored.

Chapter 10 Karmavastu

This chapter discusses acts carried out by the monastic community, emphasizing the various sorts of assemblies in the *saṃgha* and in which acts they are competent to function. Valid and invalid procedures are also outlined.

Chapter 11 Pāṇḍulohitakavastu

This *vastu* outlines monastic disciplinary measures. Five cases are mentioned, the first two of which refer to the individuals for whom the chapter is named:

a. For their argumentative natures, Pāṇḍuka and Lohitaka are sentenced to the *tarjanīyakarma*
b. For continuous offences, Śreyaka is sentenced to the *nigarhaṇīyakarma*
c. For scandalous conduct, Aśvaka and Punarvasuka are sentenced to the *pravāsanīyakarma*
d. For offences to a layman, Uttara is sentenced to the *pratisaṃharaṇīyakarma*
e. For not recognizing an offence, and for refusing to make reparation, Chanda is sentenced to the *utkṣepaṇīyakarma,* as is Ariṣṭa, for not giving up false doctrines

Chapter 12 Pudgalavastu

The *Pudgalavastu* discusses the treatment of *Saṃghāvaśeṣa* offences, precipitated by the conduct of a monk named Udāyī. The *parivāsa* and *mānatva* probations are outlined, in detail, as well as formal enactment of the reinstatement ceremony (*āvarhaṇa*).

Chapter 13 Pārivāsikavastu

This chapter discusses the standards of behaviour to be observed during the *parivāsa* and *mānatva* periods.

Chapter 14 Poṣadhasthāpanavastu

This chapter discusses the prohibiting of a monk from participating in the *Poṣadha* ceremony. The chapter commences with the Buddha refusing to recite the *Prātimokṣa*, despite Ānanda's several requests, because there is an impure monk in the assemblage. When the monk is removed, the Buddha announces that in the future the *saṃgha* itself (and not the Buddha) must hold *Poṣadha* and recite the *Prātimokṣa*. Moreover, monks guilty of offences are excluded from the ceremony.

Chapter 15 Śamathavastu

The *Śamathavastu* is divided into two parts, the first of which outlines the procedures for the resolution of legal questions (*adhikaraṇas*). The seven *adhikaraṇa-ṣamatha-dharmas* are discussed, as well as the four classes of disputes. The second part is concerned with motives for the various conciliation procedures.

Chapter 16 Saṃghabhedavastu

This chapter discusses schisms in the *saṃgha*. The Devadatta legend occupies a large portion of the *vastu*, emphasizing the following points:

a. Devadatta obtains great powers and gains the support of Prince Ajataśatru
b. Maudgalyāyana is informed of Devadatta's plans (to usurp Buddha's control of the *saṃgha*) and tells the Buddha
c. Devadatta enjoins Buddha to leave the *saṃgha* under his direction after the Buddha's death
d. After being denied, Devadatta tries to found his own community
e. Devadatta asks Ajātaśatru to help replace Bimbisāra as king and exterminate the Buddha
f. Ajātaśatru complies, setting himself up as king in the place of his father Bimbisāra
g. Devadatta sends men to murder the Buddha, but the Buddha converts them
h. Devadatta attempts to kill the Buddha with a rock, but only wounds him
i. Devadatta sends a mad elephant against the Buddha, but Buddha tames it
j. Devadatta lures 500 monks away from the Buddha, actually founding a new *saṃgha*
k. Śāriputra and Maudgalyāyana lead the 500 monks back to the Buddha; Devadatta dies

Following the Devadatta legend, there is a general discussion of schisms in the *saṃgha*.

Chapter 17 Śayanāsanavastu

The *Śayanāsanavastu* concerns the dwellings of the *saṃgha*. After an introductory story relating the building of dwellings for the *saṃgha* by a householder in Rājagṛha, the legend of Anāthapiṇḍada, a wealthy merchant in Śrāvastī who presents Jetavana to the *saṃgha*, is recounted. Various abuses lead the Buddha to allow a monk to be put in charge of assigning dwellings and furniture to the other monks. Other monks are given administrative roles such as superintendent of buildings or distributor of clothes. Provisions are also made to avoid the decay of donated buildings by having a monk dwell in each constantly.

Chapter 18 Ācāravastu

This chapter is a miscellany concerning rules of conduct. Behaviour with regard to alms begging, meals among the laity, attitudes towards newly arrived monks and forest-dwelling monks are also issues of discussion.

Chapter 19 Kṣudrakavastu

The *Kṣudrakavastu* is an inventory of rules that are of minor importance, and by their nature, could not be appropriately placed elsewhere. Such topics as toothpicks and bathroom furniture are discussed.

Chapter 20 Bhikṣuṇīvastu

As is obvious from the title, this chapter treats rules designed specifically for nuns. At the beginning of the *vastu*, the story leading up to the admission of women into the *saṃgha* is related. The nuns' admission, confession, and invitation ceremonies are discussed, as well as rules for conduct towards the male *saṃgha* members. Minor regulations conclude the chapter.

In addition to the twenty *vastus* in the *Skandhaka*, there is an introductory section discussing the Buddha's genealogy, birth, and life history up to the conversion of Śāriputra and Maudgalyāyana, and also a concluding section covering the Buddha's death, the council of Rājagṛha, the history of the patriarchs, and the council of Vaiśālī. We may thus outline the following schema for the structure of the *Skandhaka*:[4]

a. Introduction: Buddha's early life and career
b. Buddhist monastic institutions (chapters 1–4)
c. Daily needs of the monks (chapters 5–8)
d. Monastic law (chapters 9–10)
e. Disciplinary proceedings (chapters 11–13)
f. Miscellaneous (chapters 14–20)
g. Conclusion: the Buddha's death and afterwards

Appendices

Appendices are attached to several *Vinayas* as a supplement. They serve two basic functions (Lamotte 1976: 183):

[4] The suggestions for groupings b, c, d, and e may be found in Frauwallner (1956: 70, 89, 104, 107). I have added a, f, and g, so as to set forth a reasonable outline (which Frauwallner does *not* provide).

1. Providing summaries of the rules found in the *Sūtravibhaṅga* and *Skandhaka*
2. Providing interesting bits of monastic history

Non-Canonical *Vinaya* Literature

Commentaries

Fortunately, a wide variety of *Vinaya* commentaries have been preserved, and their importance for the student of *Vinaya* literature need not be stressed here. The most complete commentarial traditions have been preserved in the Theravādin and Mūlasarvāstivādin *nikāyas* (in Pāli and Tibetan, respectively). We also possess Chinese translations for *Vinaya* commentaries in many of the Indian Buddhist *nikāyas*, lacking only modern texts.

Miscellaneous Texts

In this category, we can place two types of texts. First, we must list those texts, existing only in translation, which can no longer be identified with a particular *nikāya*. Second, we have a rather amorphous groups of texts which, although not being classified as *Vinaya* literature in the strictest sense, are clearly *Vinaya*-related and which influence the *Vinaya* traditions of several *nikāyas*.

Having now examined the structure, contents, and application of the *Vinaya*, we are now in a position to proceed to our survey, focusing on the citation of the vast majority of *Vinaya* literature published since 1800. The most compelling summary of the nature and importance of *Vinaya* literature remains Miss Horner's assessment, published in the Preface to the first volume of her translation of the Pāli version of the *Vinaya Piṭaka*:

> Yet, as in any others, the *Vinaya* shows that there were in Gotama's Orders indolent, lax, greedy monks and nuns, those who were lovers of luxury, seekers after pleasure, makers of discord. We should, however, be greatly mistaken if we insisted upon regarding the Order as riddled by scandal, by abuses and by minor forms of wrongdoing. There is no doubt that these existed; but there is no justification, simply because they happen to be recorded, for exaggerating their frequency, or for minimizing the probity and spiritual devotion of many men who, in Gotama's days, were monks. Records of these are to be found in the *Nikāyas*, in the *Thera-therī-gāthā*; and, too much overlooked, there are in the Vinaya, the virtuous, moderate monks who, vexed and ashamed, complain of the misdemeanours of their fellows.
>
> As historians, we must be grateful to these inevitable backsliders, for theirs is the legacy of the *Pātimokkha* rules. Had the Order contained merely upright, scrupulous monks and nuns—those who were steadfastly set on the goal of the Brahma-life,

> and those who had, in the circumstances, to voice their annoyance with the wrong-doers—in all likelihood the *Vinaya*, the Discipline, the *Pātimokkha* rules would not have come into being, and much of the early history of the Order would now be known to us solely through the indirect and fragmentary way of the *Sutta-Piṭaka* (1938–1966: I, xviii).

Conclusion

Having now surveyed the entire corpus on *Vinaya* literature, several observations which are at once both obvious and predictable can be made. The period up to 1900 seems to have been one of preliminary preparation. Almost all of the publications furnished either editions or translations of texts, or both, and roughly three fourths of these dealt with the Theravādin tradition. As there was a great emphasis in Europe on the exploration of the Theravādin *nikāya*, primarily promoted by such scholars as Thomas W. Rhys Davids, Hermann Oldenberg, and Robert Childers, this focus was certainly not unexpected.

During the period from 1900 to 1930, nearly as many *Vinaya* works were published as in the preceding hundred years, but the emphasis was changing in two ways: first, we find almost as many secondary studies (primarily articles) as textual editions and translations, and second, interest began to shift away from the Theravādin tradition, which now merited only about one third of the total publications. Largely through the research of scholars like Sylvain Lévi, Louis Finot, and Louis de La Vallée Poussin, study of the Sarvāstivādin tradition began to emerge as an independent enterprise. Of course the added discovery of Sanskrit *Vinaya* manuscripts in the various emerging collections afforded added momentum to this movement. The years from 1930 to 1950 produced only slightly more *Vinaya* works than the years immediately preceding, again revealing about one third of these studies devoted to the Theravādin *nikāya* and an equal emphasis on secondary and primary studies. Articles rather than books still occupied the overwhelming majority of the secondary studies as well. We might say that this period represented an interval of consolidation and further definition of *Vinaya* problematics, foreshadowing the boom that was to emerge in the 1950s and 1960s. The manuscript discoveries at Gilgit and in Tibet were a driving force in promoting new, active interest in *Vinaya*, and we are still experiencing it today.

From 1950 on, *Vinaya* study has exhibited a remarkable growth spurt. Theravāda *Vinaya* study, once the giant, seems to have fallen out of vogue, perhaps coinciding with the general state of affairs in Buddhist Studies generally, and now finds itself receiving only about one sixth of the market. During this period the Mahāsāṃghika-Lokottaravādin and Mūlasarvāstivādin *nikāya*s have merited the vast majority of scholarly studies. Full length *Vinaya* studies now compete with articles on an equal footing, and the character of both forms of publication becomes general and interpretive rather than specific and simply informative. It is only now that we can say with any assurance that *Vinaya* study has come of age.

Works Cited

Carrithers, M. B. (1984) 'They will be lords upon the island': Buddhism in Sri Lanka. In: H. Bechert and R. Gombrich (eds), *The world of Buddhism: Buddhist monks and nuns in society and culture*. New York: Facts on File, 133–146.

Dutt, S. (1960) *Early Buddhist monachism*. Revised edition. Bombay: Asian Publishing House.

Frauwallner, E. (1956) *The earliest vinaya and the beginnings of Buddhist literature*. Serie Orientale Roma 8. Rome: Instituto Italiano per il Medio ed Estremo Oriente.

Hallisey, C. (2007) Vinayas. In: D. Keown and C. Prebish (eds), *Encyclopedia of Buddhism*. London: Routledge, 807–810.

Härtel, H. (ed. and trans.) (1956) *Karmavācanā*. Berlin: Deutsche Akademie der Wissenschaften zu Berlin, Institut für Orientforschung.

Horner, I. B. (trans.) (1938–1966) *The book of discipline*. 6 vols. London: Luzac.

Jinananda, B. (ed.) (1961) *Upasaṃpadājñaptiḥ*. Tibetan Sanskrit Works 6. Patna, India: Kashi Prasad Jayaswal Research Institute.

Journal of the Gaṅgānāth jhā Research Institute 10 (1–4): Appendix, 1–48.

Kabilsingh, C. (1984) *A comparative study of the bhikkunī pātimokkha*. Varanasi: Chaukambha Orientalia.

Lamotte, É. (1976) *Histoire du Bouddhisme indien*. Louvain, Belgium: Institut Orientaliste.

Lévi, S. (1912) Sur une langue précanonique du Bouddhisme. *Journal asiatique*. Série X Tome XX (Nov.–Déc.): 505–506.

Roth, G. (1968) Terminologisches aus dem Vinaya der Mahāsāṃghika-Lokottaravādin. *Zeitschrift der deutschen morgenländischen Gesellschaft*, 118: 334–348.

Thomas, E. J. (1963) *The history of Buddhist thought*. 2nd edition, reprint. London: Routledge and Kegan Paul.

Suggested Reading

Dutt, S. (1957) *The Buddha and five after centuries*. London: Luzac & Company.

Frauwallner, E. (1956) *The earliest vinaya and the beginnings of Buddhist literature*. Serie Orientale Roma 8. Rome: Instituto Italiano per il Medio ed Estremo Oriente.

Holt, J. C. (1981) *Discipline: the canonical Buddhism of the Vinayapiṭaka*. Delhi: Motilal Banarsidass.

Kabilsingh, C. (1984) *A comparative study of the bhikkunī pātimokkha*. Varanasi: Chaukambha Orientalia.

Pachow, W. (2000) *A comparative study of the prātimokṣa (on the basis of Chinese, Tibetan, Sanskrit and Pali versions)*. Revised edition. Delhi: Motilal Banarsidas.

Prebish, C. S. (1994) *A survey of Vinaya literature*. Taipei, Taiwan: Jin Luen.

CHAPTER 6

BHIKṢUṆĪ ORDINATION

BHIKKHU ANĀLAYO

INTRODUCTION

A Buddhist community consists in principle of four 'assemblies', which are monastic and lay, each of which can have male or female members. Two of the three monastic traditions still alive today—the Mūlasarvāstivāda in the Himālayan areas and the Theravāda in South and Southeast Asia—do not have an order of *bhikṣuṇīs*/*bhikkhunīs*, fully ordained female monastics, and thus are reduced to only three assemblies. Only in the Dharmaguptaka *Vinaya* tradition in East Asia does an order of *bhikṣuṇīs* still exist.

The question of reviving such an order is controversial, involving a conflict between the pressing need to improve the situation of women in these Buddhist traditions by enabling them to participate fully in the monastic life, similar to their male brethren, and the imperative to respect the basic legal principles of a monastic tradition.

In order to shed light on the complexity of the legal problem and possible solutions, I begin with the account of the foundation of the *bhikṣuṇī* order in the way this is found in the Dharmaguptaka, Mūlasarvāstivāda, and Theravāda *Vinayas*. These three *Vinayas* agree in reporting that the acceptance of eight *gurudharmas*, 'principles to be respected', formed the ordination of Mahāprajāpatī Gautamī, who thereby became the first *bhikṣuṇī* in the Buddhist tradition. Next I survey the legal parameters that emerge from one of these *gurudharmas*, which concerns *bhikṣuṇī* ordination, and how according to these three *Vinayas* subsequent ordinations were carried out. Then I turn to the transmission of the *bhikṣuṇī* ordination lineage until modern times to set the frame for appreciating the present situation.

The topics to be covered in the course of my study are:

- Mahāprajāpatī's ordination
- The eight *gurudharmas*
- The *gurudharma* on *bhikṣuṇī* ordination

- The procedure for *bhikṣuṇī* ordination
- The transmission of *bhikṣuṇī* ordination to Sri Lanka
- The transmission of *bhikṣuṇī* ordination to China
- Legal requirements for a valid ordination
- The revival of *bhikṣuṇī* ordination

Mahāprajāpatī's Ordination

The events leading up to the ordination of Mahāprajāpatī Gautamī and thereby to the founding of the *bhikṣuṇī* order are recorded in a range of texts (Anālayo 2011: 269–272 and 2016a). In what follows I take up three of these texts only, namely the *Vinaya*s of the three monastic traditions still alive in modern days.

The *Vinaya*s of the Dharmaguptaka, Mūlasarvāstivāda, and Theravāda traditions report that Mahāprajāpatī Gautamī approached the Buddha with the request to allow the going forth of women in his dispensation. The three *Vinaya*s agree that the Buddha refused to grant this request.

This refusal stands in contrast to a statement made in another text extant in these same traditions. The statement is found in versions of the *Mahāparinirvāṇa-sūtra* preserved in the Dharmaguptaka *Dīrgha-āgama*, Sanskrit fragments of the Mūlasarvāstivāda tradition, and the Theravāda *Dīgha-nikāya*. The three versions agree that, soon after his awakening, the Buddha had announced his plan to have four assemblies, namely *bhikṣus*, *bhikṣuṇīs*, male lay disciples, and female lay disciples (DĀ 2 at T I.15c2, Waldschmidt 1951: 208,15; §16.8, and DN 16 at DN II.104,18).

Once discourses of these three traditions report that the Buddha from the outset wanted to have these four assemblies of disciples, it is not easy to understand why according to *Vinaya*s of the same three traditions he should be refusing to found an order of *bhikṣuṇīs*. Because at that juncture in time the other three assemblies had already come into existence, complying with Mahāprajāpatī Gautamī's request would have resulted in bringing into existence the fourth and up to that point missing assembly of *bhikṣuṇīs*.

In the Sanskrit fragment version of the Mūlasarvāstivāda *Vinaya*, the Buddha's reply to Mahāprajāpatī Gautamī's request takes the following form (Schmidt 1993: 242,5; §3a2): 'In this way, Gautamī, with head shaven and putting on a monastic outer robe (*saṃghāṭī*), for your whole life practice the holy life that is totally complete, pure and perfect.'

This is the second instance of this exchange between the Buddha and Mahāprajāpatī Gautamī; the first has not been preserved in the fragment. The Chinese version of this second instance reads (T 1451 at T XXIV.350b27): 'Mahāprajāpatī, you should shave off your hair and wear plain patchwork robes and for your whole life firmly cultivate the holy life in single and complete purity, without blemish.'

The Tibetan version of this second instance reads (D 6 *da* 101a6 or Q 1035 *ne* 98b1): 'In this way for your whole life, Gautamī, with head shaven and putting on a patchwork robe, practise the holy life that is completely perfect and completely pure for your whole life.'

In the case of the first instance of this permission, the Chinese and Tibetan versions speak of wearing white robes instead of monastic robes (T 1451 at T XXIV.350b15 and D 6 *da* 100b2 or Q 1035 *ne* 97b4). Since in the other versions the same permission is given throughout, this appears to be a later change of formulation.

Indications similar to the Mūlasarvāstivāda *Vinaya* can be found in two discourse versions of how the order of *bhikṣuṇīs* came into existence (MĀ 116 at T I.605a17 and T 60 at T I.856a14), and in the Mahīśāsaka *Vinaya*, with the additional specification that the shaving of the head and wearing of robes should be done while 'staying at home' (T 1421 at T XXII.185b28).

This suggests the refusal of the Buddha to have been more specifically concerned with the going forth of women into a life of wandering around freely in ancient India. In view of the frequent occurrence of rape and other abuses of *bhikṣuṇīs* reported elsewhere in *Vinaya* literature, the Buddha's reply in the Mūlasarvāstivāda *Vinaya*, as well in as some other versions, appears to offer women an alternative and less risky option, namely living a life of renunciation in the more protected environment at home.

Although the Dharmaguptaka and Theravāda *Vinayas* do not report such a permission by the Buddha, according to both versions Mahāprajāpatī Gautamī and a group of followers did indeed shave off their hair and put on robes (T 1428 at T XXII.922c18 and Vin II.253,22 = AN 8.51 at AN IV.274,30).

If these texts are considered on their own, this reads almost like an act of open defiance. Instead, some permission along the lines of the above translated passage from the Mūlasarvāstivāda *Vinaya* must stand in the background of the events described in the Dharmaguptaka and Theravāda *Vinayas* as well (Anālayo 2011 and 2016a). On this assumption, for Mahāprajāpatī Gautamī and her group of followers to shave off their hair and put on robes is only natural.

The alternative perspective on the Buddha's reply to Mahāprajāpatī Gautamī's request that emerges in this way is more in line with the discourse literature of these three monastic traditions, in that the Buddha from the outset planned to have an order of *bhikṣuṇīs*. Instead of a flat refusal of granting the going forth to women in his dispensation, he rather offers them the option of living an alternative life of renunciation in a more protected environment.

The Eight *Gurudharmas*

The actual ordination of Mahāprajāpatī Gautamī reportedly took place through her acceptance of eight principles to be respected (*gurudharmas*). Perhaps the most famous of these *gurudharmas* concerns paying homage. The version of this *gurudharma* in the

Dharmaguptaka *Vinaya* reads as follows (T 1428 at T XXII.923a28): 'On seeing a newly ordained *bhikṣu*, even a *bhikṣuṇī* of a hundred years' [standing] should rise up to welcome him, pay homage, prepare a clean seat, and invite him to sit on it.'

The Mūlasarvāstivāda and Theravāda *Vinayas* have a similar *gurudharma*/*garudhamma* (Schmidt 1993: 246,8; § 6a1, T 1451 at T XXIV.351a16, D 6 *da* 103a3 or Q 1035 *ne* 100a4, and Vin II 255,6 = AN 8.51 at AN IV.276,22). For appreciating the implication of this *gurudharma*, it needs to be mentioned that among monastics in general the paying of homage is usually done according to seniority of ordination.

The Theravāda *Vinaya* reports that, once ordained, Mahāpajāpatī Gotamī requested the Buddha to allow the paying of respect according to seniority across the gender divide. In reply, the Buddha is shown to refuse to do this with the explanation that other monastic traditions also did not permit the paying of homage to women (Vin II.258,2). In fact later Jain sources expect the same type of behaviour from their female monastics. Jaini (1991: 168) quotes from the *Upadeśamālā*: 'Even if a nun were initiated for a hundred years and a monk were initiated just this day, he is still worthy of being worshipped by her through such acts of respect as going forward in reverential greetings, salutation, and bowing down.'

This suggests that to expect such submissive behaviour reflects social norms current in the ancient Indian setting.

The *gurudharma* on behavioural etiquette is not the only 'principle to be respected' that involves a clear element of discrimination. Other *gurudharmas* stipulate that a *bhikṣuṇī* is not permitted to criticize or scold a *bhikṣu*, whereas a *bhikṣu* is allowed to criticize a *bhikṣuṇī*.

Other *gurudharmas* concern the carrying out of various communal transactions. Thus *bhikṣuṇīs* should spend the period of the rainy season in a place where *bhikṣus* are also present (no such requirement exists for *bhikṣus*). At the end of the rainy season they should perform the invitation, *pravāraṇā*, a formal request to be pointed out one's shortcomings, in front of both communities (*bhikṣus* only have to perform the invitation in front of the community of *bhikṣus*). A *bhikṣuṇī* who has committed a serious offence has to undergo penance, *mānatva*, in front of both communities (*bhikṣus* only have to do this in front of the community of *bhikṣus*). The *bhikṣuṇīs* should every fortnight request instructions from the *bhikṣus* (no such requirement exists for *bhikṣus*). Another *gurudharma* regulates ordination, which I will study in more detail in the next part of this chapter.

In sum, it is unmistakably clear that with these eight *gurudharmas* the *bhikṣuṇīs* are placed in a hierarchically lower position and made dependent on *bhikṣus*. Such placing in a hierarchically lower position is not characteristic of the *gurudharmas* alone, but pervades the regulations in the *Vinaya* in general.

The rules on defeat, *pārājika*, provide an illustrative example. Whereas *bhikṣus* have four such rules, *bhikṣuṇīs* have eight *pārājika* rules. A *bhikṣuṇī* can incur a *pārājika* simply by allowing, out of lustful feelings, her torso be touched by a male. This *pārājika* rule appears to be common to the different *Vinayas* (Kabilsingh 1984: 55). In contrast a *bhikṣu* only incurs the less serious *saṃghāvaśeṣa* offence for lustful bodily contact with a woman. This *saṃghāvaśeṣa* rule is common to the different *Vinayas* (Pachow 1955: 79f.).

In this way, what for a woman is a *pārājika* offence, leading to an irrevocable loss of the condition of being a fully ordained monastic (Anālayo 2016b *pace* Clarke 2009), for a male is a *saṃghāvaśeṣa* offence, resulting only in his temporary suspension. This is just one of several such instances which show that, even without taking into account the *gurudharmas*, becoming a *bhikṣuṇī* in any of these three *Vinaya* traditions does not result in full gender equality.

Nevertheless, it needs to be mentioned that there are also instances where the *bhikṣus* are at a disadvantage when compared to the *bhikṣuṇīs*, and several rules are aimed at preventing *bhikṣus* from taking advantage of *bhikṣuṇīs*.

The *Gurudharma* on *Bhikṣuṇī* Ordination

One of the eight *gurudharmas* concerns the ordination of *bhikṣuṇīs*. In the three *Vinaya* traditions under study, this takes the following form:

> Dharmaguptaka *Vinaya* (T 1428 at T XXII.923b8): 'A probationer (*śikṣamāṇā*) who has trained in the precepts should request the higher ordination from the community of *bhikṣus*.'
>
> Mūlasarvāstivāda *Vinaya* (Schmidt 1993: 244,21; §4b5): 'A woman should expect in the presence of the *bhikṣus* the going forth and the higher ordination, the becoming of a *bhikṣuṇī*.'
>
> Theravāda *Vinaya* (Vin II.255,19 = AN 8.51 at AN IV.277,9): 'A probationer who has trained for two years in six principles should seek for higher ordination from both communities.'

A noteworthy difference between these three *gurudharma* formulations is that the Dharmaguptaka and Theravāda versions additionally mention the need for a probationary training as a *śikṣamāṇā*. The need for such training is recognized elsewhere in the Mūlasarvāstivāda *Vinaya*, where the successful completion of two years of probationary training is one of the conditions to be ascertained when higher ordination is to be given (Schmidt 1993: 253,26; §16b4). In the Mūlasarvāstivāda monastic tradition, such ascertaining that all required conditions have been fulfilled results in a formal expression of approval of the candidate for higher ordination, the *brahmacaryopasthānasaṃvṛti* (Kishino 2015). However, the probationary training is not mentioned in the Mūlasarvāstivāda version of the *gurudharma* on ordination.

The two *Vinayas* that do mention the probationary training in their respective *gurudharmas* also report a ruling given at a time when a *bhikṣuṇī* order was already in existence.

This ruling takes its occasion from the repercussions caused when a pregnant woman was ordained. The same two *Vinayas* report that one of the requirements of the probationary training is the observance of celibacy for a period of two years (T 1428 at T XXII.924b7 and Vin IV.319,26). Yet it would have been impossible to complete the probationary training successfully and still be pregnant. This makes it less probable that the probationary training had been instituted already at the time when the order of *bhikṣuṇīs* was founded.

Even if one were to imagine that the ordaining of a pregnant candidate happened due to lax observance of the probationary training stipulated in the *gurudharma*, the logical response in such a case would have been the promulgation of a ruling that prevents such lax observance, thereby covering also breaches of celibacy that do not result in pregnancy. Instead, the Dharmaguptaka and Theravāda *Vinaya* report a ruling to stop *bhikṣuṇīs* from giving the higher ordination to a pregnant woman (T 1421 at T XXII.92b3 and Vin IV.317,20). This in turn suggests that the reference to the probationer in the two *gurudharmas* versions translated above is with great probability a case of later addition.

The identifying of such a later addition reflects the fact that the *gurudharmas* in the form they have come down by tradition are of course the final result of a process of textual formation, rather than verbatim records of what happened when the order of *bhikṣuṇīs* came into existence.

Alongside this historical-critical perspective, however, it needs to be kept in mind that for monastics ordained in a particular *Vinaya* tradition the finalized text is relevant for legal purposes. The version of a rule, in the way it is found now in the canonical records, forms the legal basis for ordination and other legal acts carried out by monastics, not what might seem historically plausible from an academic perspective.

It is important to keep this difference between a legal reading and a historical-critical reading in mind, especially when examining the complexity of the legal situation of *bhikṣuṇī* ordination. In the debate surrounding the revival of *bhikṣuṇī* ordination, these two modes of reading are easily conflated. Traditionalists opposed to *bhikṣuṇī* ordination often take it as their point of departure that the particular *Vinaya* they follow accurately reflects what happened at the Buddha's time. Supporters of *bhikṣuṇī* ordination often tend to assume that historical-critical readings of a particular ruling and its coming into existence can be made the basis for legal decisions. Both types of conflation involve the same basic problem and in combination result in a situation where two ideological constructs clash with each other and attempts at dialogue easily become talking at cross-purposes, with neither side able to appreciate what underpins the position taken by the other.

The Procedure for *Bhikṣuṇī* Ordination

Following the ordination of Mahāprajāpatī Gautamī through acceptance of the *gurudharmas*, the next stages in the evolution of *bhikṣuṇī* ordination reported in the *Vinayas* concern her followers and other candidates.

In the Dharmaguptaka *Vinaya* the same act of acceptance of the eight *gurudharmas* also serves for ordaining a group of five hundred women followers of Mahāprajāpatī Gautamī. The Dharmaguptaka *Vinaya* continues by reporting the Buddha's promulgation of the procedure for ordaining other female candidates. According to its presentation, *bhikṣuṇīs* bringing female candidates for ordination to the *bhikṣus* had been assaulted by robbers along the way they had to travel (T 1428 at T XXII.923c13). In response to this, the Buddha promulgated that a candidate (who has earlier received the novice and probationary ordination and completed the probationary training) should first receive higher ordination from an order of *bhikṣuṇīs* and then approach an order of *bhikṣus* for completing the ordination.

It is perhaps worthy of note that the ensuing procedure does not avoid the problem, because the female candidate(s) still has (have) to approach the order of *bhikṣus*. At a later juncture, the *Vinaya* reports that *bhikṣuṇīs* were violated by robbers, in reply to which the Buddha reportedly promulgated the alternative procedure of receiving ordination via a messenger (T 1428 at T XXII.926b8). This procedure would help avoid such problems, whereas the standard procedure described previously does not really solve the problem of potential assault by robbers. The problem of potential assault also motivates the rule on ordination by messenger in the Theravāda *Vinaya* (Vin II.277,3). The Mūlasarvāstivāda *Vinaya* has a different narration in relation to this procedure (Yao 2015).

The Mūlasarvāstivāda *Vinaya* agrees that the acceptance of the eight *gurudharmas* served not only for Mahāprajāpatī Gautamī's ordination, but also for that of her followers (Schmidt 1993: 248,6; §9a1, T 1451 at T XXIV.351c1, and D 6 *da* 105a1 or Q 1035 *ne* 102a4.). The Chinese version of the Mūlasarvāstivāda *Vinaya* continues by reporting that, in reply to the question how other female candidates should be ordained, the Buddha promulgated the proper procedure (T 1451 at T XXIV.351c5). This proper procedure, described in detail in the Sanskrit fragment as well as in the Tibetan version of the Mūlasarvāstivāda *Vinaya*, requires the higher ordination to be granted by an order of *bhikṣus* together with an order of *bhikṣuṇīs* (Schmidt 1993: 256,8; §18b5 and D 6 *da* 111a2 or Q 1035 *ne* 107a8).

In this way, whereas in the Dharmaguptaka *Vinaya* there are two separate legal acts, first higher ordination granted by an order of *bhikṣuṇīs*, followed by a second higher ordination conferred by an order of *bhikṣus*, in the Mūlasarvāstivāda *Vinaya* both orders come together and conduct the higher ordination conjointly (Kieffer-Pülz 2010: 223).

In the Theravāda *Vinaya* already the *gurudharma/garudhamma* differs. The Theravāda *garudhamma* stipulates that the higher ordination of female candidates should be carried out in both communities, that is, the community of *bhikkhus* and the community of *bhikkhunīs*. The other two versions had only mentioned the need for the involvement of the community of *bhikkhus*.

Another difference is that in the Theravāda *Vinaya* the acceptance of the eight *garudhammas* only serves for the ordination of Mahāpajāpatī Gotamī, not for her followers. This results in the situation that Mahāpajāpatī Gotamī has been asked by the Buddha to accept a *garudhamma* regulation that she was unable to fulfil. As a single *bhikkhunī* she was not able to form the quorum required for constituting a 'community of *bhikkhunīs*' that, according to the *garudhamma* stipulation, could cooperate with the community of *bhikkhus* in giving ordination.

The Theravāda *Vinaya* continues by reporting that she inquired from the Buddha how she should proceed in relation to her followers. In reply, the Buddha made the following statement: 'I authorize the giving of the higher ordination of *bhikkhunīs* by *bhikkhus*' (Vin II.257,7). This regulation is of considerable importance, because it shows the Buddha permitting the ordination of *bhikkhunīs* by *bhikkhus* alone in a situation where a *bhikkhunī* order is not in existence. It is this ruling, and the narrative context depicting the rationale for its promulgation, that enable a legally valid reviving of the *bhikkhunī* order in the Theravāda tradition, a topic to which I will return below.

The Theravāda *Vinaya* continues by reporting that female candidates for ordination felt ashamed on being interrogated by *bhikkhus* regarding their suitability for higher ordination. Such interrogation requires answering several questions, some of which are of a rather personal nature. On being informed of the embarrassment of the candidates, the Buddha promulgated a procedure according to which the female candidate will first receive ordination by the *bhikkhunīs*, who conduct the interrogation, and afterwards by the *bhikkhus* (Vin II.271,34): 'I authorize the higher ordination in the community of *bhikkhus* for one who has been higher ordained on one side and has cleared herself in the community of *bhikkhunīs*.' This resembles the procedure in the Dharmaguptaka *Vinaya*.

The Theravāda *Vinaya* has a specific term for a female candidate who has already received ordination by the *bhikkhunīs*, but not yet by the *bhikkhus*. She is reckoned 'ordained on one side', *ekato-upasamapannā*, which other passages in the same *Vinaya* show to involve a lesser monastic status, not being on a par with a fully ordained *bhikkhunī*.

For example, a monk getting his robe washed by an unrelated *ekato-upasamapannā* incurs only a *dukkaṭa*, but for getting an unrelated *bhikkhunī* to do the same, a *pācittiya* (Vin III.207,23). The same pattern obtains for accepting a robe (Vin III.210,14). Another example is unauthorized exhortation of those who are *ekato-upasamapannā* being only a *dukkatā*, but in the case of *bhikkhunīs* a *pācittiya* (Vin IV.52,4). The same holds for exhorting after sunset (Vin IV.55,18). These passages leave no doubt that the *ekato-upasamapannā* falls short of being considered a fully ordained *bhikkhunī*.

In sum, according to the finalized procedure for *bhikṣuṇī* ordination in the Dharmaguptaka and Theravāda *Vinayas*, a female candidate first receives ordination from an order of *bhikṣuṇīs* and afterwards is brought to the presence of an order of *bhikṣus* for completing the higher ordination. In the Mūlasarvāstivāda *Vinaya*, the two orders instead come together to confer the higher ordination.

A key element common to the three *Vinaya* versions is that the ordination of a *bhikṣuṇī* depends on the collaboration of *bhikṣus*. In fact only the order of *bhikṣus* is mentioned in the Dharmaguptaka and Mūlasarvāstivāda *Vinaya* version of the *gurudharma* on ordination. The possibility of receiving ordination from an order of *bhikkhus* alone is explicitly recognized in the Theravāda *Vinaya* as a regulation promulgated by the Buddha in a situation when no *bhikkhunī* order capable of giving ordination was in existence. These are the basic parameters to be kept in mind when evaluating how *bhikṣuṇī* ordination can be carried out according to these three monastic traditions.

The Transmission of *Bhikṣuṇī* Ordination to Sri Lanka

The Ceylonese chronicle *Dīpavaṃsa* reports that the recently converted king of Sri Lanka requested *bhikkhu* Mahinda, the son of King Asoka, to confer ordination on Queen Anulā and her followers. Mahinda's reply to this request takes the following form: 'Great King, it is not proper for a *bhikkhu* to confer the going forth on a woman' (Dīp 15.76, Oldenberg 1879: 84,19). Although in the Theravāda *Vinaya* the conferring on a woman of the going forth to become a novice is done by *bhikkhunīs*, the same text does not explicitly rule out that a *bhikkhu* might do the same. An explicit prohibition only makes its appearance in the commentary (Sp V.967,21).

It is possible that the statement by Mahinda, taken out of its context, led to this commentarial gloss. Yet this statement needs to be read within its context. It is not a blanket statement that a *bhikkhu* cannot confer the going forth on a woman at all. Instead, it reflects the circumstance that, at the time the king made this request, a flourishing order of *bhikkhunīs* was in existence back in India. Therefore, the proper way to effect the transmission of *bhikkhunī* ordination to Sri Lanka was to bring *bhikkhunīs* from India who could confer ordination and give training to the female candidates. According to the *Dīpavaṃsa* this is indeed what happened, as Mahinda's sister, *bhikkhunī* Saṅghamittā, came together with a group of *bhikkhunīs* from India to Sri Lanka for this purpose.

The Sri Lankan *bhikkhunī* lineage initiated in this way seems to have disappeared in the eleventh century during a period of warfare and political turmoil that had decimated the entire monastic community on the island (Skilling 1993: 34). By that time the *bhikkhunī* order in India appears to have been extinct as well. According to our present state of knowledge, at that time a legally instituted order of *bhikkhunīs* was not in existence in other Theravāda countries of Southeast Asia. Tsomo (2014: 345) sums up that 'there is no conclusive evidence that the lineage of full ordination for women was established in Burma, Cambodia, Laos, Mongolia, Thailand, or Tibet'.

The unavailability in Theravāda countries of the option to receive full ordination has led to the coming into existence of a renunciate type of life for women located somewhere in between the lay and the monastic sphere. This usually involves the taking of eight or ten precepts, shaving off the hair, and wearing distinct type of clothing. White clothes are worn by women who wish to renounce lay life in Cambodia, Laos, as well as by the *mae chi* of Thailand; pink clothes are mostly used by the *thila shin*s of Myanmar; and monastic colours of the type also used by *bhikkhu*s are worn by the *dasasil mātā*s of Sri Lanka. The different orders of women renunciants that have come into existence in

Theravāda countries share being disadvantaged in several respects, compared to males who are able to receive full ordination (Anālayo 2013: 162–169).

The Transmission of *Bhikṣuṇī* Ordination to China

Turning from South and Southeast Asia to China, in the early fifth century CE a group of *bhikkhunī*s travelled from Sri Lanka to China (T 2063 at T L.939c12; see also Guang Xing 2013). By that time different *Vinaya* traditions for *bhikṣu*s had reached China (Funayama 2004). The *bhikṣuṇī* ordination lineage had apparently not yet reached China, and local *bhikṣuṇī*s had received ordination from *bhikṣu*s only. The group of Sri Lankan *bhikkhunī*s had apparently been decimated during their journey, leaving those who arrived short of the required number for forming the full quorum to conduct ordination. Four years later another group of *bhikkhunī*s arrived from Sri Lanka. Together with those who had arrived earlier and had learned Chinese in the meantime, the Sri Lankan *bhikkhunī*s gave ordination to a great number of Chinese *bhikṣuṇī*s.

By the eighth century the Dharmaguptaka *Vinaya* was apparently imposed on all monastics in China by imperial decree (T 2061 at T L.793c26; see Heirman 2002: 414). Thus from then onwards this *Vinaya* was followed when giving ordination and carrying out other legal acts.

For evaluating this act of transmission from a legal perspective, it is significant that Guṇavarman, a *Vinaya* expert, affirmed the legality of the *bhikṣuṇī* ordinations done in China earlier, even though, due to the lack of both communities, ordination of female candidates had been conferred by the community of *bhikṣu*s only. The relevant passage reports: 'Guṇavarman said: "The country did not have both communities, therefore the ordination was [to be] received from the great community [of *bhikṣu*s]"' (T 2063 at T L.941a18). Another passage records Guṇavarman's approval of an explanation given by the Chinese *bhikṣuṇī*s that, in taking ordination from *bhikṣu*s only, they had followed the precedent set by Mahāprajāpatī Gautamī (T 2063 at T L.939c17). In reply to inquiries by the Sri Lankan *bhikkhunī*s, the Chinese *bhikṣuṇī*s explained that they had taken ordination just from the community of *bhikṣu*s 'because this is just as Mahāprajāpatī [through] the eight *gurudharma*s obtained her precepts, and in relation to the five hundred Śākyan women [Mahā]prajāpatī was most senior. This is our lofty precedent.'

Guṇavarman agreed with this understanding (T 2063 at T L.939c19). Whereas the first part of this statement points to the *gurudharma*s, the remainder seems to imply that Mahāprajāpatī, even though she had not received ordination from both communities, was considered the most senior *bhikṣuṇī* and thus clearly as being properly ordained. Thus this is probably best understood to point to the *gurudharma*s themselves as the legal basis, in particular to the *gurudharma* according to which a female candidate should receive higher ordination from the community of *bhikṣu*s (discussed above).

Alternatively, the same approval can be taken to imply that the precedent for ordination in China was rather the act of acceptance of all eight *gurudharmas* by Mahāprajāpatī Gautamī, which according to the *Vinaya* accounts formed her ordination. Yet one would not expect a *Vinaya* master like Guṇavarman to agree to such a proposition, as ordination by way of accepting the *gurudharmas* could only be administered by the Buddha himself and was no longer a legal option after his passing away. Therefore, it seems more probable that the *gurudharmas* themselves, in particular the stipulation that *bhikṣuṇīs* should be ordained by *bhikṣus*, should be considered as forming the legal basis for ordinations carried out in China before the arrival of the Sri Lankan *bhikkhunīs*.

Guṇavarman is on record for translating a Dharmaguptaka *Vinaya* text for *bhikṣuṇīs* into Chinese (T 1434 at T XXII.1065b16; see also T 2059 at T L.341a26). This makes it probable that he was ordained in the Dharmaguptaka tradition himself, in which case he would have been speaking from the perspective of its legal parameters. Another *Vinaya* expert, Daoxuan, in a commentary on the Dharmaguptaka *Vinaya*, also concludes that for the first Chinese *bhikṣuṇīs* to receive ordination from the community of *bhikṣus* only had been a valid procedure (T 1804 at T XL.51c15; see also Shih 2000: 524 and on Daoxuan's attitude towards nuns in general Heirman 2015).

Even though Guṇavarman considered the ordinations done previously as valid, he approved of the Chinese *bhikṣuṇīs* taking ordination again from the Sri Lankan *bhikkhunīs* (T 2063 at T L.939c21): 'receiving it again is beneficial and fine'.

This seems to have had a function similar to a procedure known in the Theravāda commentarial tradition as *daḷhīkamma*, literally 'an act of strengthening' (Kieffer-Pülz 2010: 223f.). In the present case, the ordination by the Sri Lankan *bhikkhunīs* strengthened the appeal to legal validity of the Chinese *bhikṣuṇīs*. Heirman (2010: 65) notes that the conducting by the Sri Lankan *bhikkhunīs* of an 'ordination ceremony for Chinese nuns seems to have put an end to widespread discussion on the validity of the Chinese nuns' ordination'; although according to Adamek (2009: 9), 'controversy as to whether or not the Chinese nuns' Saṅgha is legitimate still reverberates to this day'.

Regarding the ordination conferred by the Sri Lankan *bhikkhunīs*, no further information is available about the actual procedure adopted at that time. It has been assumed that the Sri Lankan *bhikkhunīs* based themselves on the Dharmaguptaka *Vinaya* (Lévi and Chavannes 1916: 46 and Heirman 2001: 297). An evaluation of this suggestion requires a closer look at the motivation of the Sri Lankan *bhikkhunīs*.

The arrival of the first group of Sri Lankan *bhikkhunīs* in China might well have been inspired by the wish to transmit the *bhikkhunī* lineage. Just a few years earlier the Chinese pilgrim Fǎxiǎn had visited Sri Lanka (T 2085 at T LI.864c10). This visit was part of a longer pilgrimage whose main purpose had been to procure *Vinaya* texts (T 2085 at T LI.857a8). During Fǎxiǎn's stay in Sri Lanka, information about the situation in China for female monastics would have spread, making it highly probable that the wish to transmit the *bhikkhunī* ordination lineage motivated the first group of Sri Lankan *bhikkhunīs* to set out on what in those days was a long and dangerous journey. In fact, according to Guang Xing (2013: 116), 'Gunavarman came to China with the first group of nuns' from Sri Lanka. This would make it even more probable that the motivation for their voyage was to transmit the *bhikkhunī* ordination lineage to China. The same must have been the case for the second group, whose arrival served to complete the required quorum for ordinations to be given in China.

In view of this it seems improbable that, after undertaking such a risky journey to transmit the lineage of *bhikkhunī* ordination, the Sri Lankan *bhikkhunī*s would confer ordination in a way that openly conflicts with Theravāda monastic law. The early fifth century is the time of Buddhaghosa's redaction of the Theravāda commentaries. The basic ideas about the validity of an ordination, in the form in which these are recorded in the Pāli commentary on the *Vinaya*, must have come into existence earlier than that.

According to the Theravāda *Vinaya* commentary, a mispronunciation of the Pāli formula to be used for ordination invalidates the legal act (Sp VII.1399,3; von Hinüber 1994), let alone using a language different from Pāli. With subsequent developments this concern with correct formulation of Pāli eventually went so far that the taking of refuge as part of the going forth had to be done twice, using two different ways of pronouncing the same words, just to make sure that the act of going forth carries its full legal validity (Bizot 1988: 49 and Kieffer-Pülz 2013: 1715–1718). In view of these requirements it is difficult to conceive that the Sri Lankan *bhikkhunī*s would have conducted an ordination in Chinese, and that moreover based on a different *Vinaya*.

Yet even teaching the Chinese candidates how to perform the ordination ritual in Pāli would not have resulted in a full transmission of the Theravāda ordination lineage, because for that the cooperation of Theravāda *bhikkhus* would have been required. Thus the ordination conferred by the Sri Lankan *bhikkhunī*s at that time could anyway not have fulfilled Theravāda legal requirements.

The problem of fulfilling legal requirements is not merely a question of the situation in China in the past, but is of considerable relevance for the current setting. It is precisely the question of the legal feasibility of receiving or granting ordination in a way that involves different *Vinaya* traditions that renders the revival of orders of *bhikṣuṇī*s in the Mūlasarvāstivāda and Theravāda traditions so challenging.

Legal Requirements for a Valid Ordination

Buddhist monastic legal procedures are based on laws believed to have been promulgated by the Buddha. From the *Vinaya* viewpoint, only the Buddha himself had legislative authority. According to an episode reported in the different *Vinaya*s, the Buddha had given explicit permission that the minor rules could be abrogated after his passing away (Anālayo 2015b). This did not happen, because the assembled *bhikṣus* found themselves unable to come to an agreement regarding which rules in the *prātimokṣa* should be considered minor and therefore can be abolished.

The failure to act, due to a lack of agreement, reflects the basic need to do legal acts 'in harmony', that is, with the consensus of all who are present. In addition, the same episode also exemplifies a central characteristic of Buddhist monastic law up to modern times, namely its basic inalterability. A pervasive legal conservatism is an almost inevitable result of the attitudes enshrined in this episode.

When it comes to conferring higher ordination, an essential ingredient for legal validity is considered to be the correct demarcation of the area within which the fully ordained monastics converge to hold the ordination ceremony. The boundary of this area, the *sīmā*, needs to be established with the type of markers that the respective *Vinaya* prescribes. These markers need be determined through the correct performance of the demarcation ritual. A fault in regard to correct performance of the ritual or use of wrong markers is held to invalidate a legal act performed within this *sīmā*. A general principle to be kept in mind with such ritual requirements is succinctly formulated by Hüsken and Kieffer-Pülz (2012: 266) as follows: 'legal acts and ritual performances ... in the case of the Buddhist monastic discipline they are two sides of the same coin'.

The Dharmaguptaka, Mūlasarvāstivāda, and Theravāda *Vinaya*s differ on the markers they recognize as valid for demarcation; they also have different textual formulas, *karmavācanā*s, for the demarcation ritual (Chung and Kieffer-Pülz 1997). Practically speaking this means that a legal act performed according to one of these *Vinaya*s does not carry validity from the viewpoint of another of these *Vinaya*s.

Within a correctly established *sīmā*, fully ordained monastics who belong to the same community, *samānasaṃvāsa*, need to congregate to perform a legal act. The notion of belonging to the same community stands in contrast to being of a different community, *nānasaṃvāsa*, or else not being in communion, *asaṃvāsa*. A monastic who has committed a *pārājika* offence, the most severe breach of conduct recognized in the *Vinaya*, is no longer in communion, *asaṃvāsa* (Anālayo 2016b). One who is no longer in communion is disqualified from full participation in legal acts carried out by the community. The other alternative of belonging to a different community, *nānasaṃvāsa*, comes into being when a monastic has been suspended by the community, or else when a monastic disagrees with the community on whether a particular act constitutes an offence and then carries out legal acts with his followers apart from the community.

The canonical *Vinaya*s do not explicitly recognize the existence of different *Vinaya*s and the problems that result from this situation. However, in view of the fact that the *prātimokṣa*s for *bhikṣu*s and for *bhikṣuṇī*s differ from one *Vinaya* to another (Pachow 1955 and Kabilsingh 1984), the resultant situation corresponds to what the *Vinaya*s recognize under the header of being of a different community, *nānasaṃvāsa*. From a strictly legal perspective, those who are from different communities cannot perform a legal act together that can later successfully claim recognition as valid from all members of their respective monastic traditions.

The invalidity of legal acts done in reliance on the participation of someone who is of a different community is explicitly stated in the Mūlasarvāstivāda and Theravāda *Vinayas*. The *Karmavastu* of the Mūlasarvāstivāda *Vinayavastvāgama* lists a legal act done in this way as contrary to *Dharma* and *Vinaya* (Dutt 1984: 204,10; see also Tsering

2010: 167f.). In addition, one of the questions regarding possible impediments to eligibility for higher ordination, which are to be asked during the procedure for *bhikṣuṇī* ordination, is whether the candidate is of a different community (Schmidt 1993: 253,21; §16b2; the same holds in the case of *bhikṣus*; see Härtel 1956: 79,13 §22).

Although being of a different community is not one of the impediments to be investigated as part of the ordination procedure in the Theravāda *Vinaya*, this monastic code also considers a legal act done in reliance on the participation of someone who is of a different community as lacking validity (Vin I.320,15).

It is against these legal problems that attempts to revive the *bhikṣuṇī* order in the Theravāda and Mūlasarvāstivāda traditions need be evaluated.

The Revival of *Bhikṣuṇī* Ordination

Attempts to revive *bhikkhunī* ordination in the Theravāda tradition have a long history. One such attempt in Thailand led to the promulgation of a Saṅgha Act in 1928, still in effect today, which prohibits Thai *bhikkhus* from participating in any ordination of *bhikkhunīs*, as well as from giving novice or probationer ordination to female candidates (Seeger 2006/2008: 159f.).

In Myanmar, the situation has come to a stalemate when controversy surrounding the return home of a Burmese *bhikkhunī*, ordained in Sri Lanka, eventually culminated in a ban on further discussions of *bhikkhunī* ordination in 2004 (Kawanami 2007: 233f.).

In Sri Lanka the turning point seems to have come following an ordination conducted with the help of Dharmaguptaka *bhikṣuṇīs* in 1998 at Bodhgayā (Li 2000); earlier attempts are an ordination in the USA in 1988, when Ayyā Khemā was ordained, and at Sārnāth in 1996, when *bhikkhunī* Kusumā received ordination. After completing the ordination in 1998 at Bodhgayā, the new *bhikkhunīs* underwent a second ordination at which only Theravāda *bhikkhus* officiated. This combination of a dual ordination with the assistance of *bhikṣuṇīs* from the Dharmaguptaka tradition with another ordination done solely by Theravāda *bhikkhus* seems to have been successful in resolving the legal problem from the viewpoint of the Theravāda *Vinaya* (Anālayo 2013, 2014, 2015a, and 2017).

The candidates had done their best to receive ordination from both communities in a dual ordination. If this ordination is considered valid, then the subsequent ordination by the Theravāda *bhikkhus* served as a *daḷhīkamma*, an 'act of strengthening', mentioned earlier. Through such a formal act a monastic who has received ordination elsewhere can gain the recognition of a particular community of which s/he wishes to be part.

If the dual ordination carried out at Bodhgayā is considered invalid, due to not fulfilling one or more of the various legal requirements for valid ordination according to the Theravāda tradition, then this implies that at present there is no *bhikkhunī* order in existence that can give valid Theravāda ordination to female candidates. This in turn implies that the regulation given according to the Theravāda *Vinaya* by the Buddha for such an occasion holds: 'I authorize the giving of the higher ordination of *bhikkhunīs* by *bhikkhus*.' It follows that the single ordination given by Theravāda *bhikkhus* subsequent to the dual ordination at Bodhgayā was successful in instituting an order of *bhikkhunīs*.

The order of *bhikkhunīs* in Sri Lanka has steadily grown since then and won the approval of the laity (Mrozik 2014). Although the Saṅgha Act of 1928 is still in effect in Thailand, by taking ordination abroad several *bhikkhunī* communities have come into existence and are also successful in winning public approval (Itoh 2013 and Delia 2014).

Turning to the Tibetan tradition, from a legal perspective ordination given by *bhikṣus* only, when an order of *bhikṣuṇīs* is not in existence, similarly can claim validity. In the case of the Mūlasarvāstivāda *Vinaya* this principle is enshrined in its version of the *gurudharma* on *bhikṣuṇī* ordination, which stipulates that 'a woman should expect from the *bhikṣus* the going forth and the higher ordination, the becoming of a *bhikṣuṇī*'.

The suggestion that the *gurudharma* on *bhikṣuṇī* ordination in the Mūlasarvāstivāda *Vinaya* can be relied upon as a legal basis for reviving an order of *bhikṣuṇī* in the Tibetan tradition gathers additional strength from the circumstance that this *gurudharma* is repeated in the Tibetan version of the Mūlasarvāstivāda *Vinaya*. This repetition occurs at the end of the description of how *bhikṣuṇī* ordination should be carried out. The ordination being completed, the new *bhikṣuṇī*(s) are to be taught some essential aspects of moral conduct and etiquette, and it is in the context of these teachings that the eight *gurudharmas* should be repeated (D 6 *da* 118b7 or Q 1035 *ne* 114b2; Tsedroen and Anālayo 2013). From a legal perspective, the circumstance that the *gurudharma* on ordination is found at this juncture makes it part of the latest procedure on ordination, instead of being a regulation that has been rescinded by the promulgation of ordination to be given by both communities.

In this way a procedure similar to the one adopted by the Sri Lankan Theravāda candidates at the Bodhgayā ordination in 1998 would also provide a legally acceptable solution for the Tibetan tradition, namely an ordination done in collaboration with Dharmaguptaka *bhikṣuṇīs* combined with another ordination given by Mūlasarvāstivāda *bhikṣus* only.

The Dalai Lama has for a long time been trying to promote *bhikṣuṇī* ordination, but his efforts have so far met with resistance from within the tradition. At a conference on the theme of *bhikṣuṇī* ordination in 2007 at the University of Hamburg, he explained (Dalai Lama 2010: 268 and 277):

> As for re-establishing the ordination ceremony ... although I may wish for this to happen, it requires the consensus of the senior monks. Some of them have offered strong resistance. There is no unanimous agreement and that is the problem. ... When it comes to re-establishing the Mūlasarvāstivāda bhikṣuṇī ordination, it is extremely important that we avoid a split in the saṅgha. We need a broad consensus within the Tibetan saṅgha as a whole, and we need to address not only bhikṣuṇī ordination but subsequent issues as well.

In January 2015, the Karmapa announced plans to re-establish the *bhikṣuṇī* order in the Tibetan tradition (Tsedroen 2016).

Conclusion

The legal complexity surrounding ordination in the Buddhist monastic traditions makes it perhaps understandable that attempts to revive the *bhikṣuṇī* order in the Mūlasarvāstivāda and Theravāda traditions are not simply a matter of overcoming resistance by *bhikṣus* who are unwilling to grant women their proper place, although such attitudes of course have an impact on the situation. Yet, in view of the nature of monastic law, resistance to procedures that challenge the foundation of monastic legal observances is to some degree only to be expected.

Here the *gurudharma* regulations, often seen as emblematic of gender discrimination, turn out to provide a legal solution to the impasse. The *gurudharma* on ordination in the Dharmaguptaka *Vinaya* seems to have provided the legal foundation for the first ordinations of *bhikṣuṇīs* in China. This holds even on the (in my view less probable) alternative interpretation suggested above, according to which the acceptance of the eight *gurudharmas* would have provided the legal basis, in which case it is still the very promulgation of the *gurudharmas* that serves as the legal precedent.

The same *gurudharma* in the Tibetan Mūlasarvāstivāda *Vinaya* offers a possibility to revive the order of *bhikṣuṇīs* in the Tibetan tradition. In the case of the already successful revival of the Theravāda *bhikkhunī* order, it is again this *garudhamma*, in combination with a subsequent ruling resulting from the way this *garudhamma* is formulated, that has provided the required legal basis.

In this way the dependence of the *bhikṣuṇīs* on the *bhikṣus* in the legal monastic texts, which implies a hierarchically inferior position of ordained women vis-à-vis ordained men, is at the same time what enables a revival of an extinct *bhikṣuṇī* order. In contrast, an extinct order of *bhikṣu* cannot be revived in a comparable manner.

This complements a recurrent emphasis in academic and popular writings on the discriminating nature of the *gurudharmas*. Without intending to deny that the *gurudharmas* are discriminatory (as are other *Vinaya* regulations), let alone approving of such discrimination, it remains worthy of note that the very dependence on male monastics, enshrined in the *gurudharmas*, appears to offer the legal basis for *bhikṣuṇī* lineages in the three monastic traditions still in existence today.

Acknowledgement

I am indebted to Alice Collett, *bhikkhunī* Dhammadinnā, Ann Heirman, and Amy Langenberg for commenting on a draft version of this chapter.

Works Cited

Adamek, W. L. (2009) A niche of their own: the power of convention in two inscriptions for medieval Chinese Buddhist nuns. *History of religions*, 49 (1), 1–26.

Anālayo (2011) Mahāpajāpatī's going forth in the *Madhyama-āgama*. *Journal of Buddhist ethics*, 18, 268–317.

Anālayo (2013) The revival of the bhikkhunī order and the decline of the sāsana. *Journal of Buddhist ethics*, 20, 110–193.

Anālayo (2014) On the bhikkhunī ordination controversy. *Sri Lanka international journal of Buddhist studies*, 3, 1–20.

Anālayo (2015a) The *Cullavagga* on bhikkhunī ordination. *Journal of Buddhist ethics*, 22, 401–448.

Anālayo (2015b) The first *saṅgīti* and Theravāda monasticism. *Sri Lanka international journal of Buddhist studies*, 4, 1–17.

Anālayo (2016a) *The foundation history of the nuns' order*. Bochum: Projektverlag.

Anālayo (2016b) The legal consequences of pārājika. *Sri Lanka international journal of Buddhist studies*, 5, 1–22.

Anālayo (2017) The validity of bhikkhunī ordination by bhikkhus only, according to the Pāli Vinaya. *Journal of the Oxford Centre for Buddhist Studies*, 12, 9–25.

Bizot, F. (1988) *Les traditions de la pabbajjā en Asie du sud-est, recherches sur le bouddhisme khmer, IV*. Göttingen: Vandenhoeck & Ruprecht.

Chung, J., and Kieffer-Pülz, P. (1997) The karmavācanās for the determination of sīmā and ticīvareṇa avippavāsa. In: T. Dhammaratana and Pāsādika (eds), *Dharmadūta: mélanges offerts au vénérable Thích Huyên-Vi à l'occasion de son soixante-dixième anniversaire*. Paris: Édition You-Feng, 13–55.

Clarke, S. (2009) When and where is a monk no longer a monk? On communion and communities in Indian Buddhist monastic law codes. *Indo-Iranian journal*, 52, 115–141.

Dalai Lama XIV (2010) Human rights and the status of women in Buddhism. In: T. Mohr and J. Tsedroen (eds), *Dignity and discipline, reviving full ordination for Buddhist nuns*. Boston: Wisdom, 253–279.

Delia, N. (2014) Mediating between gendered images of 'defilement' and 'purity', continuity, transition and access to spiritual power in a northern Thai Buddhist monastic community for women. MA dissertation, University of Hamburg.

Dutt, N. (1984) *Gilgit manuscripts, Mūlasarvāstivāda vinayavastu*. Volume III, part 2. Delhi: Sri Satguru.

Funayama, T. (2004) The acceptance of Buddhist precepts by the Chinese in the fifth century. *Journal of Asian history*, 38 (2), 97–120.

Guang X. (2013) Maritime transmission of the monastic order of nuns to China. In: S. Amatayakul (ed.), *The emergence and heritage of Asian women intellectuals*. Bangkok: Institute of Thai Studies and Institute of Asian Studies, Chulalongkorn University, 111–120.

Härtel, H. (1956) *Karmavācanā: formulare für den Gebrauch im buddhistischen Gemeindeleben aus ostturkestanischen Sanskrit-Handschriften*. Berlin: Akademie Verlag.

Heirman, A. (2001) Chinese nuns and their ordination in fifth century China. *Journal of the International Association of Buddhist Studies*, 24 (2), 275–304.

Heirman, A. (2002) Can we trace the early dharmaguptakas? *T'oung pao*, 88, 396–429.

Heirman, A. (2010) Fifth century Chinese nuns: an exemplary case. *Buddhist studies review*, 27 (1), 61–76.

Heirman, A. (2015) Buddhist nuns through the eyes of leading early Tang masters. *The Chinese historical review*, 22 (1), 31–56.

Hüsken, U., and Kieffer-Pülz, P. (2012) Buddhist ordination as initiation ritual and legal procedure. In: U. Hüsken and F. Neubert (eds), *Negotiating rites*. Oxford: Oxford University Press, 255–276.

Itoh A. (2013) The emergence of the bhikkhunī-saṅgha in Thailand: contexts, strategies and challenges. PhD dissertation, École Pratique des Hautes Études.

Jaini, P. (1991) *Gender and salvation: Jaina debates on the spiritual liberation of women*. Berkeley: University of California Press.

Kabilsingh, C. (1984) *A comparative study of bhikkhunī pāṭimokkha*. Delhi: Chaukhambha Orientalia.

Kawanami H. (2007) The bhikkhunī ordination debate: global aspirations, local concerns, with special emphasis on the views of the monastic community in Burma. *Buddhist studies review*, 24 (2), 226–244.

Kieffer-Pülz, P. (2010) Presuppositions for a valid ordination with respect to the restoration of the bhikṣuṇī ordination in the Mūlasarvāstivāda tradition. In: T. Mohr and J. Tsedroen (eds), *Dignity and discipline, reviving full ordination for Buddhist nuns*. Boston: Wisdom, 217–226.

Kieffer-Pülz, P. (2013) *Verlorene Gaṇṭhipadas zum buddhistischen Ordensrecht, Untersuchungen zu den in der Vajirabuddhiṭīkā zitierten Kommentaren Dhammasiris und Vajirabuddhis*. Wiesbaden: Harrassowitz Verlag.

Kishino R. (2015) The concept of sdom pa in the Mūlasarvāstivāda-vinaya: on possible misunderstandings of the Brahmacaryopasthāna-saṃvṛti. *The bulletin of the Association of Buddhist Studies, Bukkyo University*, 20, 147–192.

Lévi, S., and Chavannes, É. (1916) Les seize arhat protecteurs de la loi. *Journal asiatique*, 11 (8), 5–50 and 189–304.

Li Y. (2000) Ordination, legitimacy and sisterhood: the international full ordination ceremony in Bodhgaya. In: K. L. Tsomo (ed.), *Innovative Buddhist women: swimming against the stream*. Richmond, UK: Curzon, 168–198.

Mrozik, S. (2014) 'We love our nuns': affective dimensions of the Sri Lankan bhikkhunī revival. *Journal of Buddhist ethics*, 21, 57–95.

Oldenberg, H. (1879) *The Dīpavaṃsa, an ancient Buddhist historical record, edited and translated*. London: Williams and Norgate.

Pachow, W. (1955) *A comparative study of the prātimokṣa, on the basis of its Chinese, Tibetan, Sanskrit and Pali versions*. Santiniketan: Sino-Indian Cultural Society.

Schmidt, M. (1993) Bhikṣuṇī-Karmavācanā, Die Handschrift Sansk. c.25(R) der Bodleian Library Oxford. In: M. Hahn (ed.), *Studien zur Indologie und Buddhismuskunde: Festgabe des Seminars für Indologie und Buddhismuskunde für Professor Dr. Heinz Bechert zum 60. Geburtstag am 26. Juni 1992*. Bonn: Indica et Tibetica, 239–288.

Seeger, M. (2006 [2008]) The bhikkhunī ordination controversy in Thailand. *Journal of the International Association of Buddhist Studies*, 29 (1), 155–183.

Shih, H.-C. (2000) Lineage and transmission: integrating the Chinese and Tibetan orders of Buddhist nuns. *Chung-Hwa Buddhist journal*, 13 (2), 503–548.

Skilling, P. (1993) A note on the history of the bhikkhunī-saṅgha (II): the order of nuns after the parinirvāṇa. *The World Fellowship of Buddhists review*, 30 (4) and 31 (1), 29–49.

Tsedroen, J. (2016) Buddhist Nuns' ordination in the Mūlasarvāstivāda tradition: two possible approaches. *Journal of Buddhist ethics*, 23, 165–246.

Tsedroen, J., and Anālayo (2013) The Gurudharma on bhikṣuṇī ordination in the Mūlasarvāstivāda tradition. *Journal of Buddhist ethics*, 20, 743–774.

Tsering, T. (2010) A lamp of vinaya statements, a concise summary of bhikṣuṇī ordination. In: T. Mohr and J. Tsedroen (eds), *Dignity and discipline, reviving full ordination for Buddhist nuns*. Boston: Wisdom, 161–181.

Tsomo, K. L. (2014) Karma, monastic law, and gender justice. In: R. R. French and M. A. Nathan (eds), *Buddhism and law, an introduction*. New York: Cambridge University Press, 334–349.

von Hinüber, O. (1994) Buddhist law and the phonetics of Pāli, a passage from the Samantapāsādikā on avoiding mispronunciation in kammavācās. In: O. von Hinüber (ed.), *Selected papers on Pāli studies*. Oxford: Pali Text Society, 198–232; first published in German in 1987.

Waldschmidt, E. (1951) *Das Mahāparinirvāṇasūtra, Text in Sanskrit und tibetisch, Verglichen mit dem Pāli nebst einer Übersetzung der chinesischen Entsprechung im Vinaya der Mūlasarvāstivādins*, vol. 2. Berlin: Akademie Verlag.

Yao F. (2015) The story of Dharmadinnā, ordination by messenger in the Mūlasarvāstivāda vinaya. *Indo-Iranian journal*, 58, 216–253.

Suggested Reading

Anālayo (2013) The revival of the bhikkhunī order and the decline of the sāsana. *Journal of Buddhist ethics*, 20, 110–193.

Anālayo (2016a) *The foundation history of the nuns' order*. Bochum: Projektverlag.

Heirman, A. (2001) Chinese nuns and their ordination in fifth century China. *Journal of the International Association of Buddhist Studies*, 24 (2), 275–304.

Hüsken, U., and Kieffer-Pülz, P. (2012) Buddhist ordination as initiation ritual and legal procedure. In: U. Hüsken and F. Neubert (eds), *Negotiating rites*. Oxford: Oxford University Press, 255–276.

Kieffer-Pülz, P. (2010) Presuppositions for a valid ordination with respect to the restoration of the bhikṣuṇī ordination in the Mūlasarvāstivāda tradition. In: T. Mohr and J. Tsedroen (eds), *Dignity and discipline, reviving full ordination for Buddhist nuns*. Boston: Wisdom, 217–226.

Tsedroen, J., and Anālayo (2013) The Gurudharma on bhikṣuṇī ordination in the Mūlasarvāstivāda tradition. *Journal of Buddhist ethics*, 20, 743–774.

CHAPTER 7

THE CHANGING WAY OF THE BODHISATTVA

Superheroes, Saints, and Social Workers

BARBRA CLAYTON

Introduction

The term *bodhisattva* means literally a 'being for awakening' or an 'enlightenment being', and while the etymology is uncertain, it may originally stem from the word *bodhisakta*, one 'bound for' or 'devoted to' awakening (Harvey 2007: 58; Apte s.v. '*sakta*': 1600).[1] It refers to one who aims to achieve the supreme, perfect awakening (*anuttarā-samyaksaṃbodhi)* of a buddha. Such a being discovers the *Dharma* without benefit of a teacher and introduces it into a world where it has been lost. Though considered an optional path in the Theravāda tradition, as well as in some earlier texts propounding the 'great vehicle' of the Mahāyāna (Nattier 2003: 176), in later Mahāyāna texts this is upheld as the goal for all practitioners. Indeed, in this literature the term *mahāyāna* is equated with the *bodhisattva-yāna,* the 'vehicle of the bodhisattvas', or those whose goal is full Buddhahood. This is contrasted with both the 'vehicle of the disciples' (*śrāvaka-yāna*), intended for those who use the teachings of a buddha to gain the liberation and the more limited knowledge of an *arhat*, and the vehicle of the solitary buddhas (*pratyeka-yāna*), for beings who become liberated on their own, without the benefit of a buddha's teachings.

There are many variations in the nature of the bodhisattva path (*mārga*) and its duration, but in general it was understood to require an immense number of lifetimes and to entail the cultivation of various virtues or perfections (*pāramitā*s), the accomplishment

[1] I would like to thank Deborah Wills for comments on an early draft of this article, and in particular Steven Jenkins for his extensive and thoughtful critique. The limitations and errors that remain are my own.

of which is often associated with different stages (*bhūmis*) of the path. Also called the conduct (*bodhisattva-cārika*) or course of conduct of the bodhisattva (*bhadracarya*) (Edgerton, s.v. '*bhadracarya*'), this path includes vows (*praṇidhāna, praṇidhi, pratijñā*, or *saṃvara*), precepts (*śīla*), virtues or perfections (*pāramitās*), and devotional practices, though not all descriptions of the bodhisattva path include all elements. While some of the earlier bodhisattva literature seems not to have done so (Nattier 2003: 145–149) many bodhisattva texts emphasize the importance of the 'mind of awakening' or *bodhicitta*, the altruistic motivation to liberate all beings from suffering, as the foundation for this demanding spiritual career. This points to what became in later Indian Mahāyāna, and now the Mahāyāna tradition more broadly, the central association between the bodhisattva ideal and universal compassion. Such compassion is articulated in the characteristic resolve of the bodhisattva to liberate all beings from suffering. This is perhaps most eloquently expressed in a well-known verse by Śāntideva:

> As long as space abides and as long as the world abides,
> so long may I abide, destroying the sufferings of the world
>
> (BCA 10:55)

The Question: Engaged Buddhism and the Bodhisattva Path

In contemporary Buddhism, the altruism of the bodhisattva has been taken to entail active participation in the social and political world. Such 'socially engaged Buddhism' is identified as one of the notable features of modern Buddhism (McMahon 2008: 14), particularly beginning in the mid-twentieth century (King 2009; King 2005; Queen 1996). Thich Nhat Hanh coined the term 'Engaged Buddhism' in 1954 to articulate his understanding of 'the role of Buddhism in the realms of education, economics, politics, and so on' (Nhat Hanh 2008: 30).

While the precise definition of 'engaged Buddhism' is still under debate, the term generally is associated with a modern form of Buddhism that recognizes and responds to the collective causes of suffering: the social, political, and economic conditions that give rise to human ills. As Christopher Queen suggests, Engaged Buddhism recognizes that 'suffering and its quenching are not the sole responsibility of the sufferer' (Queen 2013: 328). In addressing the systemic and not just individual causes of suffering, Engaged Buddhism is characterized by activism to effect social change. (See Chapters 23 and 24 in this volume.)

Given these developments, this chapter explores the relationship between the altruism advocated and nurtured on the bodhisattva path and modern social engagement. In 'Do Bodhisattvas Alleviate Poverty?' (2003), Stephen Jenkins draws on a number of Indian Mahāyāna sutras (as well as mainstream sources) to persuasively argue that this literature does support an Engaged Buddhist agenda, at least with regard to the alleviation of poverty. A rejoinder by Amod Lele, however, uses evidence from the works of Śāntideva to argue that bodhisattvas are not directed to address the material causes of suffering (2013). I would like to extend this debate and offer a refined understanding of the question being addressed by taking into account recent critiques of the ways Engaged Buddhism has been defined and categorized. I will argue that it is legitimate to ask what kinds of social engagement are advocated in premodern texts, but that it may be anachronistic to seek for Engaged Buddhism in such literature, depending on how 'Engaged Buddhism' is understood.

The question being posed in this debate could easily be interpreted as a version of the question, 'Does Engaged Buddhism reflect the contemporary expression of inherited Buddhist traditions, or is it best understood as an innovative development?' Is it a 'new vehicle' (*navayāna*), as B. R. Ambedkar called a Buddhism concerned with collective suffering and goals (Queen 2003: 23), or has Buddhism always been engaged, as the American scholar-practitioner David Loy, referencing Thich Nhat Hanh, claims (Loy 2003: 17, cited in Temprano 2013: 264)?

The question of whether Engaged Buddhism is 'old' or 'new' echoes the debate over whether Engaged Buddhism is 'traditional' or 'modern'. This dichotomy is reflected in Thomas Freeman Yarnall's categorization of scholars of Engaged Buddhism as 'traditionist' or 'modernist' (2003: 286f.). 'Traditionists', according to Yarnall, are those who view the social engagement of contemporary Buddhists as being in continuity with Buddhist traditions, whereas 'modernists' stress the discontinuity with prior traditions (Yarnall 2003: 287).

Commenting on this debate, Jessica Main and Rongdao Lai (2013: 10f.) point out that the label 'Engaged Buddhism' has been problematically used as a normative rather than an explanatory category, and they critique the implicit, positive valuation assumed in many descriptions of Engaged Buddhism. They further caution that questions over whether socially engaged Buddhism is traditional or modern tend to reflect normative concerns about legitimacy, and are part of the need for contemporary Engaged Buddhist groups to establish their identity as Buddhist. They argue that Engaged Buddhist groups will want to claim that their innovative approach to practice—one which claims that social and political actions are themselves expressions of Buddhist practice—are not, in fact, novel or innovative but true to 'original' Buddhism. This suggests that arguments about the traditional or modern nature of Engaged Buddhism can be implicated in a normative agenda to approve or discredit the authenticity of a given Buddhist practice or group.

Focusing on academic discussions of Engaged Buddhism, Temprano (2013) similarly highlights the normative implications of defining Engaged Buddhism, and argues that scholar-practitioners like the Dalai Lama and Thich Nhat Hanh tend to be 'traditionists' who have reason to highlight the continuity of contemporary engagement with past practices. But Temprano is particularly concerned to show how certain 'modernist' scholars and scholar-practitioners within the Western academy deviate from the academic project of *describing* Buddhist beliefs and practices and fall into an Orientalist perspective that both authorizes modernized and Westernized expressions of Buddhism as legitimate, while disenfranchising Asian Buddhist practices and perspectives (see also Quli 2009).

It is important to clarify, then, that in exploring the nature of engagement in Indian bodhisattva texts I am neither seeking to legitimate nor undermine contemporary Engaged Buddhist movements or activities: I do not aim to proclaim Engaged Buddhism as either old or new, traditional or modern. Nor, while I am certainly sympathetic to many of the contemporary efforts of Engaged Buddhists, do I assume that Engaged Buddhism is necessarily *good*, while 'disengaged' Buddhism—Buddhist practices or ideas that do not entail or assume social involvement—is necessarily *bad*. What I *am* doing is investigating the continuities and differences between premodern views of the bodhisattva path and contemporary engaged beliefs about it (cf. Temprano 2013: 272).

In attempting to construct 'Engaged Buddhism' as an analytic category, Main and Lai further suggest that Engaged Buddhism involves a logic and religious vision that is the product of modernity (2013: 8). They make a clear distinction between Buddhist altruistic action as broadly understood and 'Engaged Buddhism': while both might involved the same concrete actions, such as providing food and shelter to the poor, Engaged Buddhism sees 'social action within the secular sphere as an indispensible form of religious practice' as part of its resistance to secularism, and the sense that religion should be relegated to the private realm (8). On this view, Engaged Buddhism is by definition a reaction to modernity and secularization. However, Main and Lai's definition contrasts with Christopher Queen's assertion that the term 'Engaged Buddhism' is best understood to include *both* altruistic service, such as giving to the poor, *and* political activism to effect systemic change, which he agrees is a contemporary development (Queen 2003: 22).

As such, the guiding question here is in what sense might we see the bodhisattvas of Indian Mahāyāna literature as Engaged Buddhists? What kind of involvement with the social world do the values and virtues of the bodhisattva path imply? Are bodhisattvas required or expected to express their altruism in pragmatic ways? Do they consider and address collective, social causes of suffering? What is the connection between the virtues espoused in Mahāyāna bodhisattva literature and social action espoused by contemporary Buddhists? How is this literature interpreted by contemporary practitioners of Engaged Buddhism?

Approach

In approaching Mahāyāna literature it is important to keep in mind the great diversity reflected in these texts. As Nattier suggests, Mahāyāna literature presents a 'kaleidoscopic assortment' of features that together we associate with the Mahāyāna, not all of which will be present in any one text. Hence, not all texts associated with the Mahāyāna treat the bodhisattva path, and not all that treat the bodhisattva path will have the same components (Nattier: 192; Williams 1989: 204). As it would be impossible to adequately represent all of these versions, this chapter focuses on two significant canonical presentations of the bodhisattva's career and one contemporary exposition. The canonical texts to be discussed are the *Ugraparipṛcchā-sūtra* and the works of Śāntideva, and the contemporary commentary on Śāntideva is by Pema Chödrön, a prominent Western Buddhist teacher and writer.

The *Ugraparipṛcchā*, 'The Inquiry of Ugra' (hereafter *Ugra*), represents one of earliest Mahāyāna sutras, perhaps dating from the first century CE. It is considered to be an important work in the formative period of Mahāyāna (Nattier 2003: 45). It was widely cited and commented upon and was very influential in India and China. My analysis is based on Nattier's study and translation of the Chinese, Tibetan, and Mongolian versions of the text.

The *Ugra* comprises a dialogue about the bodhisattva path between the Buddha and the Bodhisattva Ugra, who is a *gṛhapati* ('lord of the house'), i.e. a layperson of high standing (24). The overall message of the text is that although a layman may perform the preliminary parts of the bodhisattva path, because he must become a monk in order to obtain the final goal of Buddhahood he should seek ordination as soon as possible.[2] As a monk, he should emulate the Buddha Śākyamuni's life and spend large amounts of time performing ascetic practices in the wilderness. The *Ugra* presents a simple though arduous path of practice based largely on traditional Buddhist teachings, but with the overriding Mahāyāna goal of full Buddhahood (Nattier 2003: ch. 7). As I hope to show, the path outlined in the *Ugra* holds interesting parallels but also differences from the path presented by the great Indian master Śāntideva.

While little about Śāntideva is historically verifiable,[3] traditional hagiographies claim that he was a late seventh- or early eighth-century scholar and monk associated with the great monastic University of Nālandā. The texts attributed to him—the *Bodhicaryāvatāra* and the *Śikṣāsamuccaya*—express a mature stage of Mahāyāna thought in India, and were highly influential in Tibet, particularly in the Bka 'gdams tradition. The nature of the bodhisattva path is the focus of both of these works.

The *Bodhicaryāvatāra* or 'Entrance to the Way of Awakening' (hereafter BCA) is a long poem treating the subject of the bodhisattva path. Regarded as a masterful work of religious poetry, it elicited numerous commentaries in India and Tibet, including one extant in Sanskrit, by the Indian commentator Prajñākaramati (950–1030), and ten in Tibetan (Harrison 2007: 215). Its influence has persisted into the modern period, during which it has been translated numerous times, and it continues to be the subject of interest to both scholars and contemporary Buddhist practitioners (e.g. Batchelor 1979,

[2] Because of the androcentric focus of this text as well as those of Śāntideva, I have opted to use the masculine pronoun when discussing the bodhisattva in these premodern texts.

[3] See Garfield, Jenkins, and Priest (2016) for a discussion of the difficulties in ascribing a single author to these texts.

Crosby and Skilton 1996, Padmakara Translation Group 1997, Wallace and Wallace 1997). It is a favourite text of the fourteenth Dalai Lama, who frequently cites it and has published five commentaries on the work in English (Gyatso 1988, 1994, 1999, 2005, 2009). It has even been made into an illustrated children's book (Townsend 2015). The standard edition of the BCA exists in ten chapters and 913 verses, and is thought to have been composed after the other work attributed to Śāntideva, the *Śikṣāsamuccaya* (Harrison 2007: 224–227). This chapter relies on the Sanskrit edition published by Vaidya (1960) and the translation by Crosby and Skilton (1996).

The *Śikṣāsamuccaya* (hereafter Śikṣ) is an anthology of passages of primarily Mahāyāna sutras, organized around twenty-seven *mūla-kārikā*s or root verses, on the topic of the training (*śikṣā)* of a bodhisattva. Until relatively recently, the text was thought to consist overwhelmingly of quotations from other works and to reflect very little original material. However, Harrison (2007) discovered that a number of verses were misattributed to other texts, and proposes that an additional 133 verses in the *Śikṣāsamuccaya* were authored by Śāntideva, indicating that a revised understanding of the text is in order. A new translation by Charles Goodman (2016) provides a welcome update to the 1922 translation by Bendall and Rouse. This chapter relies on the Sanskrit edition by Bendall (for the reader's convenience I have also included references to the English translation by Bendall and Rouse, but the reader should be cautioned that this version is notoriously problematic; see Harrison 2007: 216).

Together these texts provide a useful window onto the bodhisattva's career because they share similar Mahāyāna elements: first and foremost, a central focus on the bodhisattva path, which includes vows, precepts, and the cultivation of key virtues (*pāramitā*s).

Furthermore, the *Ugra* reflects an understanding of the bodhisattva path from very early Mahāyāna period (Nattier 2003: 191), while Śāntideva's works represent the fully developed Indian Mahāyāna tradition. Both the *Ugra* and Śāntideva were influential in the Indian and Tibetan Buddhist traditions, and the *Ugra* became significant in East Asia. Because the ancient communities that used these texts would have had multiple texts with various interpretations and emphases, we should be cautious about assuming that these texts represent whole stages in the development of the bodhisattva path. However, by focusing on these texts we can gain insight into two significant perspectives on the bodhisattva path and have some indication of the early and late Mahāyāna period in India, as well as a range of views on key doctrines.

The Bodhisattva Path According to the *Ugra*

Departing from the more typical Mahāyāna idea that all Buddhists are or should be on the bodhisattva path, the *Ugra* assumes that the career of a bodhisattva is only one spiritual option, reserved for the few, uniquely ambitious practitioners who are willing to take on the heroic task of becoming fully enlightened buddhas. The other option is the path of the *śrāvaka* leading to arhatship, which is a worthy, though less admirable, spiritual goal.

Since the practices of the *śrāvaka* overlap in many ways with those of the bodhisattva, this lesser option presents a kind of spiritual hazard for the bodhisattva, as there is the possibility that the bodhisattva might 'fall' into the *śrāvaka*'s goal of arhatship. The path of the bodhisattva requires an unimaginable number of lifetimes to complete because it demands the acquisition of both the superior insight and the vast quantities of merit characteristic of a buddha. Such merit is needed in order to achieve not only the virtues of a buddha but also the physical manifestation of those virtues in the distinctive marks (*lakṣaṇa*) of a 'great man'(*mahāpuruṣa*) and the wondrous body of a buddha (see Powers 2009 and Mrozik 2007 on the relationship between morality and the body in Indian Buddhism). Because arhatship entails no further rebirth, it would mean the goal of Buddhahood is out of reach for the bodhisattva. As such, the *śrāvaka* path presented a danger of pre-empting the bodhisattva's long journey to Buddhahood (Nattier 2003: 140–141). That this was the case is evident in the *Ugra*'s idea of *pariṇāmanā*. This term is normally translated as 'transferring' and is associated with the common Mahāyāna practice of dedicating the results of one's good deeds to the benefit of others. In the *Ugra*, however, merit is not transferred to another but redirected away from its normal fruition in material rewards or a better rebirth, and towards the attainment of the supreme perfect enlightenment or Buddhahood (Nattier 2003: 114f.; see also Kajiyama 1989).

The immense number of lifetimes required of the bodhisattva to complete the path is suggestive of the self-sacrificing motivation needed to undertake it. The *Ugra* stresses that the bodhisattva is willing to take on the great burden of living in *saṃsāra* for an infinite number of lifetimes, just as Śākyamuni did. The image of a bodhisattva as one who mimics the *Jātaka*s' accounts of Śākyamuni's self-sacrifices, and who willingly 'carries the burden' (*bhārahārin*) of the *skandha*s (the mental and physical aggregates that make up the human form) and prolonged existence in the world of rebirth is a common theme in Mahāyāna texts (Nattier 213 n. 36; Ohnuma 2007 chs 1, 2).

However, Nattier argues that in the *Ugra*, the core motivation for the bodhisattva's self-sacrifice is the desire to become the most superior being in existence, a buddha, more than the compassionate motive to save all beings, found in later treatments such as that of Śāntideva. On the path advocated in the *Ugra*, compassion is to be cultivated but it is directed towards beings who are deficient in some way: they lack nobility, are slow to learn the *Dharma*, have broken precepts, or fail to give alms (*Ugra* 5D, 8B, 17A, 24B; references are to sections in Nattier's translation of the *Ugra*). This is called 'great compassion' (*mahākaruṇā*) but it is not the universal compassion directed to all beings that comes to be associated with the bodhisattva.

The inception of the bodhisattva's career is often marked by the adoption of particular vows. In the *Ugra*, four vows are associated with the beginning of the path. Using the common synonym for the vows as 'armour' (*saṁnāha*), the bodhisattva is described as one who girds himself with the following:

> The unrescued I will rescue.
> The unliberated I will liberate.
> The uncomforted I will comfort.
> Those who have not yet reached final nirvāṇa (*parinirvāṇa*)
> I will cause to attain final nirvāṇa.
>
> (*Ugra* 2C)

These vows, which occur in other texts as well (e.g. the *Aṣṭasahasrikaprajñāpāramitā* and the *Saddharmapuṇḍarīka sūtra*) likely originated in a description of a buddha's behaviour (Kagawa 1989, cited in Nattier 2003: 149 n. 27; Nattier 2003: 151). The presence of such vows in the *Ugra* suggest that a concern to relieve the suffering of all beings was still assumed to be the central motive of a bodhisattva, even if cultivating compassion or *bodhicitta* was not a main focus of the bodhisattva's practice.

The text divides the practices of the bodhisattva into two: those of the lay and the monastic bodhisattva. These are treated as two 'levels' (*bhūmi*) of practice, with the level of the monastic as distinctly higher and more desirable than that of the layman.

The practices of lay bodhisattva are of three types: ritual actions, moral precepts, and cultivating detachment. Ritual actions include taking refuge and conducting the *triskandhaka*, a 'three part' liturgy comprising elements which may vary, but principally include: (1) confession and repentance of past misdeeds; (2) rejoicing in the merit of others, in the marks of the Buddha, and in the turning of the *Dharma* wheel; and (3) requesting the teachings (Nattier 2003: 162–168).

The ethical precepts involve a list of eleven 'training rules' (*śikṣāpada*), which combines the traditional five precepts (*pañcaśīla*) and the 'ten good deeds' (*daśa-kuśala-karmapatha*), to create a list of eleven. The precepts enjoin the bodhisattva to refrain from (1) harming life; (2) taking what is not given; (3) sexual misconduct; (4) lying; (5) taking intoxicants; (6) slander; (7) harsh speech; (8) idle chatter; (9) covetousness; (10) malice; and (11) wrong views, including reverence to gods other than the Buddha (*Ugra* 7A). Among these, the greatest attention is paid to sexual misconduct. The married layman is encouraged to avoid all sexual contact, even with his wife, whom he is enjoined to regard as an impermanent, impure, hag—indeed, as the source of all harm and misdeeds (*Ugra* 13; see Wilson 1996 on the connection between asceticism and misogyny in Indian Buddhism).

The practices of the monastic bodhisattva focus on his dwelling in the wilderness and avoiding contact with others, as well as the four 'noble traditions' (*āryavaṁśa*) of cultivating contentment with his limited possessions (i.e. robes, alms, lodgings, and medicine), and maintaining humility with regard to his lofty ambitions (Nattier 2003: 127–136). The wilderness is advanced as the ideal place to master the various requisite practices, including the Eightfold Path, paranormal powers (*ṛddhi*) (see Dayal 1932: 106–121), the six kinds of mindfulness (*Ugra* 25B–C), as well as understanding the truth of no-self (25H) and maintaining *bodhicitta* and the roots of goodness (*kuśala-mūla*) (25K). Moreover, the isolation of the wilderness facilitates the cultivation of the key virtues (*pāramitās*) of the bodhisattva: giving (*dāna*), moral discipline (*śīla*), patience (*kṣānti*), courage (*vīrya*), meditative absorption (*dhyāna*) and wisdom (*prajñā*) (25L). In the *Ugra*, skilful means (*upāya-kauśalya*) is not listed as one of the *pāramitās*; it refers not to the skilfulness in teaching the *Dharma* but to the ability to maintain states of meditative absorption (especially the four *dhyānas*) while avoiding their usual karmic result of higher rebirth in one of the heavens, or the enlightenment of arhatship. Life in the wilderness facilitates this important meditative ability (25B).

In the *Ugra*, most of the perfections except giving are treated in a somewhat cursory manner. Moreover, giving in this text is a focus of practice more for lay than monastic bodhisattvas (163). Compared to earlier treatments of giving, which focus on the monastic community as the recipient, the *Ugra* is distinct in not identifying the recipient at all, or in focusing on giving to (non-monastic) beggars (Nattier 2003: 112; *Ugra* 11). So rather than emphasizing giving to the *saṅgha* as a way to earn merit, the emphasis in the *Ugra* is on giving as a way to practise and learn renunciation (*tyāga*) (Nattier 2003: 163–166). Similarly, the monastic bodhisattva can perfect the virtue of giving by abandoning regard for his body and life—the ultimate form of renunciation (25L).

Overall, the *Ugra*'s understanding of the bodhisattva path reflects the two overriding themes of renunciation of worldly life and detachment from the people and objects in it. The primary practices that comprise this path are social withdrawal, meditation, moral restraints, and ritual devotion. Nattier suggests that the mentality needed to undertake this prolonged and difficult journey can be compared to that of an elite Olympic athlete or Marine Corps recruit—one of the very few to earn the praise of the buddhas and esteem of noble beings (Nattier 2003: 147). However, given that the goal is to become the greatest being in the universe, we might take this a step further and liken this mentality to that of someone who wants to become a superhero, with the glorious, supramundane body of a 'great man' (*mahāpuruṣa*) and the powers of the perfected virtues.

The Bodhisattva Path According to Śāntideva

If we compare the two works of Śāntideva we can see clear parallels in the structure of the bodhisattva path (Clayton 2006: 144 n. 8). For Śāntideva, the career of the bodhisattva begins with the generation of *bodhicitta* and the adoption of the bodhisattva vows (*Śikṣ*: ch. 1; BCA: chs 1–4). This is followed by the cultivation of the perfections in the BCA (chs 5–9), which correspond to process of guarding (*rakṣa*) and purifying (*śuddhi*) one's self, possessions, and merit in the *Śikṣāsamuccaya* (chs 2–15). The path culminates in the cultivation and dedication of merit to benefit of all beings (*pariṇāmanā*) (*Śikṣ*: chs 16–19; BCA: ch. 10; see also Crosby and Skilton 1996: xxxiv). Since the BCA is thought to likely represent the most mature expression of Śāntideva's thought, and the *Śikṣāsamuccaya* is primarily an anthology of scriptures likely meant to be used in conjunction with the BCA, the latter is the focus of the following summary.

The BCA serves as a guidebook for the aspiring bodhisattva. It emphasizes that the motivation for this journey is the altruistic wish to liberate all beings from suffering, and that the perfection of the virtues needed to realize this goal rests on understanding the empty nature of all phenomenon. Thus, it stresses the ideas of *bodhicitta* and the perfection of wisdom.

The first three chapters are comprised of elements of a liturgy sometimes called the Supreme Worship (*anuttara-pūja*), a widespread Mahāyāna ritual that predates Śāntideva (Crosby and Skilton 1996: 8–11). Its flexible sevenfold structure is related to the *triskandhaka* ritual cited in the *Ugra*. This ritual can be seen both as a rite of passage that marks the bodhisattva's adoption of the bodhisattva vow and as a means of reaffirming this vow and cultivating the bodhisattva mindset (Gómez 1995: 183f.; cf. *Śikṣ*[4] K. 25; 289.12; 290.1; 316.14, 15; Clayton 2006: 61).

While the elements of the ritual may vary, the first part is usually praise, and indeed the BCA opens with a chapter on the 'Praise of the Awakening Mind'. This establishes that for Śāntideva, *bodhicitta*, or the altruistic intention to 'relieve creatures of their sorrows' (BCA 1.7) and liberate them from *saṃsāra*, is the foundation of the bodhisattva's journey. Śāntideva memorably compares the first instance of the idea of seeking Buddhahood for the sake of others to a 'flash of lightning in the dark of night' (BCA 1.5). This first arising of *bodhicitta* must be treasured and nurtured as the 'seed of pure happiness' and as the 'remedy for the suffering of the world' (1.26).

Chapters 2 and 3 include the other elements of the liturgy, such as worship of the buddhas and bodhisattvas, going for refuge, the confession of faults, rejoicing in merit, requesting the teaching, and begging the buddhas not to abandon beings. Śāntideva expresses the final element, the dedication of merit (*pariṇāmanā*), in a series of profound aspirations (BCA 3.6–21): 'With the good acquired by doing all this that is described, may I allay all the suffering of every living being. I am medicine for the sick. May I be both the doctor and their nurse, until the sickness does not recur ... may I be an inexhaustible treasure for impoverished beings' (BCA 3.6–7). Chapter 3 concludes with a section on arousing the awakening mind (*bodhicittotpāda*), and chapter 4, 'Vigilance regarding the Awakening Mind', focuses on strengthening the bodhisattva's resolve to 'generate the Awakening Mind for the welfare of the world' (BCA 3.23). The first four chapters, then, are concerned with ritually arousing and consolidating the bodhisattva's altruistic intention to save all beings.

Chapters 5 to 9 describe how the bodhisattva should cultivate the six perfections—the key virtuous qualities of the bodhisattva that must be mastered progressively in the

4 References to the *Śikṣ* are to the verses (*kārikās*) (K.) or pages and line numbers in Bendall's Sanskrit edition. References to the English translation are to pages in Bendall and Rouse's 1922 edition, abbreviated BR. References to the BCA indicate chapters and verses. The Sanskrit edition of the BCA by Shastri (1988) was consulted, with reference to the English translation by Crosby and Skilton (1996).

traditional order (generosity, moral discipline, patience, enthusiasm, meditation, wisdom). Pointing to Śāntideva's overall focus on mental transformation as the crux of the bodhisattva path, giving (*dāna*) and morality or moral discipline (*śīla*) are treated summarily in two verses and are defined in terms of mental qualities rather than outward actions. Perfect generosity arises through the 'mental attitude of relinquishing all that one has to all people, together with the fruits of the act' (BCA 5.10). Similarly, moral discipline or morality (*śīla*) is perfected when 'the mind of renunciation' is obtained (BCA 5.11). While morality does entail disciplined actions of body and speech, and is reflected by following the etiquette and moral rules of monastic discipline (*prātimokṣa*), the foundation of this discipline lies in taming the mind, since 'rutting elephants roaming wild do not cause as much devastation in this world' as an untamed mind (BCA 5.2; see also 5.85, 88–98; cf. BR 1922: 125). Consequently, the remainder of the chapter focuses on the mental disciplines of mindfulness (*smṛti*, the ability to recall one's mental and physical states and overall purpose) and awareness (*samprajanya*, the immediate awareness of one's body, mind, and situation) (Crosby and Skilton 1996: 31). Such mental discipline is essential to maintaining the bodhisattva's compassionate intentions, since a distracted mind is vulnerable to the defilements (*kleśa*s) that cause suffering in the self and others. The priority of compassion is reflected in Śāntideva's understanding that a bodhisattva may contravene moral rules if the motivation is compassion and the deed will be beneficial (5.84) (see Jenkins 2010, Clayton 2006: 102–109, and Harvey 2000: 135–138).

The perfection of patience (*kṣānti*), vigour (*vīrya*), meditative absorption (*dhyāna*), and wisdom (*prajñā*) are the topics of chapters 6 to 9 respectively. Patience or forbearance is conceived as the antidote to hatred (*dveṣa*), one of the root defilements (*kleśa*) and a much greater fault for the bodhisattva than attachment or lust (*rāga*), since hatred leads to the abandonment of beings and is a fault that cuts at the root (*mūlac-cheda-doṣa*) of his aspiration to aid others (*Śikṣ* 164.14–15). Śāntideva instructs the bodhisattva to cultivate patience in the face of physical suffering as well as the injuries and insults inflicted by others. He makes reference to the doctrine of dependent origination to validate patience, arguing for an impersonal view of the objects and conditions that make one angry. Since there is no such thing as a self-caused, independent agent, the bodhisattva should view the poor behaviour of others as the consequence of defilements, which are themselves the result of a complex of causes and conditions (BCA 6.22–33). Not only is anger therefore unjustified; the bodhisattva should view the suffering and obstacles encountered on the path as opportunities to overcome attachment and practise patience. Hence, even one's enemies should be honoured as a treasured source of virtue (BCA 6.99–107).

Based on the perfection of patience, one is in a position to develop *vīrya*: 'vigour', 'courage', 'energy', or 'enthusiasm'. Synonymous with 'exertion' (*utsāha*), energy is essential for the bodhisattva to cultivate any benefits or virtues whatsoever: just as there is no movement without wind, the bodhisattva makes no progress without courage and energy. Śāntideva first explains the qualities that oppose vigour (sloth, clinging to what is vile, despondency, and self-contempt), and then explains how to resist them (6.2–29). For instance, one of the causes of sloth is 'apathy about the sufferings of cyclic existence' (6.3), which Śāntideva counters with a reminder about the preciousness of human rebirth (6.14) and with graphic images of the inevitability and unpredictability of one's death, when there is no escape from the hellish consequences of one's evil actions (*pāpa*). By contrast, to accomplish the perfection of vigour one should cultivate desire for the *Dharma*, have a healthy pride in being capable of the bodhisattva's task, be constantly mindful and diligent with regard to lethargy and lapses, and delight in one's deeds as a bodhisattva.

The need for mental discipline is a theme repeated throughout the text, but in chapter 8 the perfection of meditative absorption, *dhyāna*, is the focus. The term *dhyāna* is a technical one used in the early Buddhist tradition to refer to the higher levels of consciousness attained through the practice of calming (*śamathā*) meditation, and for Śāntideva a stable, tranquil mind is a prerequisite for the insight the bodhisattva will need to be free of the 'fangs of the defilements' (8.1). Rather than focusing on the techniques to develop meditative absorption per se, Śāntideva emphasizes the value of renouncing worldly and social life, and 'sequestering' the self in solitude, echoing the value placed on forest-dwelling found in the *Ugra*. Indeed, the *Śikṣ* cites passages from the *Ugra* on the virtues of forest-dwelling (e.g. *Ugra* [25F] at *Śikṣ* 198.6–19). Meditative absorption is described as *viveka-ja*, 'born of isolation', both of the body (8.5–38), through physical isolation in the forest, and of the mind (8.39–89). This requires above all overcoming attachment to women, which can be achieved through meditating on the foulness of the body (*aśubha-bhāvanā*) (8.41–69).

Having described how to calm the mind, Śāntideva turns to the cultivation of *bodhicitta*, for which he advocates two practices that have become particularly important in the Tibetan tradition. These are the 'equality of self and other' (BCA 8.90–119) and the 'exchange of self and other' (BCA 8.120–173; see Garfield, Jenkins, and Priest 2016; The Cowherds 2016; Lele 2015). The practice of the 'equality' or 'sameness' of self and other (*parātma-samatā*), is also found, with some variation, in a section of the final chapter of the *Śiks* that was originally thought to be derived from the *Tathāgatagūhya sūtra*, but has now shown to be original to Śāntideva (Harrison 2007: 220, 242, 243). This practice demonstrates what Śāntideva sees to be the connection between wisdom and compassion, the two fundamental components of the bodhisattva path. The practice is based on contemplating the true nature of the self and seeing the universal nature of suffering. When one sees that self and other exist only relatively, like two banks of a river, and that the self is, like all things, conditioned and impermanent, one will see the truth about the self (*ātma-tattva*). With this insight one will realize that all suffering stems from clinging to an illusory self and one will also be able to see that others are just as much the 'self' as one's own impermanent and conditioned body-mind complex. Through seeing the emptiness of the self, one will see that other's suffering and welfare is as important as one's own: 'all equally experience suffering and happiness. I should look after them as I do myself' (BCA 8.90). Because there is no essential self, there is no moral ground for privileging one's own suffering. 'When fear and suffering are disliked by me and others equally what is so special about me that I protect myself and not others?' (BCA

8.94). Caring for others is in fact *more* important than protecting the self, for, 'When the world is burning with the fire of *duḥkha*, what pleasure can there be in one's own happiness? If one's whole body is on fire, what is the pleasure of one unburned nail?' (*Śikṣ* 361.15–16; Clayton 2006: 65, 93). This recognition that there is no happiness while others suffer is the basis of the bodhisattva's vow to remain in *saṃsāra* for the benefit of all beings.

The idea that compassion rests on an understanding of the lack of an essential self is reinforced in Śāntideva's view of wisdom (*prajñā*), which for Śāntideva is equated with understanding emptiness (*śūnyatā*)—the idea that all phenomena are dependently originated and therefore lack inherent existence. Chapter 9, which treats this topic, is a notoriously dense presentation of the Madhyamaka view of emptiness, and includes many abbreviated arguments critiquing other Buddhist and non-Buddhist positions, relying on the Prāsaṅgika method of *reductio ad absurdum*. The emptiness of phenomena must not only be understood intellectually, but also grasped directly, in order to counter the fundamental delusion that grounds attachment and aversion to things and people. Only through insight into emptiness can one cut the root causes of suffering, the defilements (*kleśas*), and finally achieve the full perfection of the other virtues (*Śikṣ* 242.1–6; BR 225). Thus, the essence of giving (*dāna*) is compassion (*karuṇā*) and emptiness (*śūnyatā*) (*Śikṣ* K.23). To achieve full awakening, then, the bodhisattva must realize great or universal compassion as well as have direct insight into the emptiness of all phenomena.

In the final chapter, the merit of the bodhisattva's practices are dedicated to the benefit of all beings.

Comparison of the *Ugra* and Śāntideva

As we have seen, the key values represented in the *Ugra* are renunciation and detachment. While the *Ugra* advocates compassion and the 'cognate' emotion, loving kindness (*maitri*), to a degree (e.g. Nattier 2003: 116, 304, 306), there is not the clear and central focus on compassion that we find in Śāntideva, who stresses the essential need for *bodhicitta*, understood as the altruistic aspiration to attain full enlightenment. For him, the two defining characteristics of Buddhahood are great or universal compassion (*mahākaruṇā*) and wisdom, which ultimately depends on seeing emptiness. There is also a contrast in understanding of merit transfer (*pariṇāmanā*): in the *Ugra* it is the meditative skill of transforming the benefit of one's good deeds away from the goal of worldly benefits and arhatship, and towards the supreme perfect enlightenment of Buddhahood. For Śāntideva, it has the sense more typically associated with the Mahāyāna of transferring the merit of one's actions from benefits to oneself to the benefit of others. In his strong emphasis on altruism and overcoming one's own shortcomings and attaining Buddhahood for the sake of all others, and in his focus on cultivating the perfections or virtues, Śāntideva's vision resembles more that of a saintly figure than that of the *Ugra*'s superhero.

Contemporary Reading of the BCA

Pema Chödrön (b. 1936) is a prominent teacher in the Shambhala Buddhist tradition, a Westernized form of Tibetan Buddhism associated with the teachings of Chögyam Trungpa Rinpoche (1939–1987). One of the first Western women to become a fully ordained Buddhist nun (in 1981) and the principal teacher at Gampo Abbey (the first Tibetan monastery in North America), Chödrön is perhaps the most influential teacher in the lineage of Chögyam Trungpa, himself one of the most significant figures in Western Buddhism. She has published over fifteen books, and through these as well as magazine interviews, public lectures, and online teachings, her understanding of the Buddhist tradition reaches a broad Western audience. In 2007, she published *No Time to Lose: A Timely Guide to the Way of the Bodhisattva*, a commentary on the BCA based particularly on the commentary by the nineteenth-century Tibetan yogi Patrul Rinpoche. As Chödrön's understanding of the nature and structure of the bodhisattva path follows that reflected in the BCA as already discussed, I will focus my discussion on what is novel in her interpretation.

In contrast to the canonical texts, Chödrön assumes that the practitioners of the bodhisattva path will be lay people. While the *Ugra* may be addressed to lay practitioners of the path—and in fact the entire text is framed as a response to a question about how a layman should practise—the *Ugra*'s response is that although a layman can perform the preliminary parts of the path, he must become a monk in order to attain Buddhahood, and indeed that no lay bodhisattva has attained Buddhahood. Similarly, while Śāntideva's audience at Nālandā University would likely have included some laymen, he primarily seems to have had a monastic audience in mind, and the legendary first recitation of the BCA was a teaching given to monks (de Jong 1975). But Chödrön's modern reading of Śāntideva is addressed to 'ordinary' (presumably non-monastic) people (x), assumes either implicitly or explicitly that the audience consists of laypeople, and that these lay people are or could be the bodhisattvas described.

While Chödrön's reading of the BCA does not always explicitly interpret Śāntideva as advocating social involvement (e.g. 108f.), her commentary as a whole is clearly framed in terms of social engagement. The introduction to the text is titled 'People Like Us Can Make a Difference', reflecting Chödrön's understanding that the BCA can help people to address 'the state of the world today' (xvii) and that it provides answers to contemporary social problems (xiv). She clearly views a bodhisattva as a being who can 'change the world', for she states that through Śāntideva's teachings 'ordinary people like us can make a difference in a world desperately in need of help' (x). In the conclusion to her commentary, Chödrön reiterates that the BCA can 'help us realize our full potential and support us in becoming peacemakers: effective, responsible, and compassionate citizens in a turbulent world' (360). *Bodhicitta* is described as the longing for all beings to be healed, and as the kind of 'big heart' that can make a 'positive difference this is world', a mindset she compares to that of Martin Luther King Jr (xiv).

This framing of the BCA in terms of social engagement surfaces in numerous instances in the commentary. For example, when explaining the bodhisattva's vast intention to free all beings, she considers the objection that it is pragmatically impossible to relieve the suffering of each and every being. As a response, Chödrön offers the example of Bernard Glassman Roshi, a well-known Engaged Buddhist who works to alleviate poverty and homelessness in New York. 'He knew there was no way to end homelessness,' Chödrön states, 'yet he would devote his life to trying. Similarly, this is the aspiration of the bodhisattva' (15). To give an example of a 'remedial action' for faults, she cites Thich Nhat Hanh's advice to an American Vietnam veteran who was overwhelmed by guilt over his actions in the war. His advice was for the veteran to return to Vietnam and work 'to help alleviate people in distress' (38). For Chödrön, such social engagement exemplifies the bodhisattva's intentions and activities.

Chödrön in Context

This is not to suggest that all contemporary readings of the bodhisattva path reflect this socially engaged slant. The Dalai Lama's commentaries on Śāntideva, for example, focus on the bodhisattva's cultivation of altruism and wisdom as virtuous individual traits, more in line with the 'bodhisattva as saint' understanding of the path (e.g. Gyatso 2009). Nonetheless I would argue that the assumption that the bodhisattva is 'engaged' and works for social change is widespread in contemporary Buddhism. In the picture-book adaptation of the BCA, for example, rather than emphasizing the idea of generosity as a mental trait as we saw in the BCA, the bodhisattva is depicted as a king wanting to alleviate the suffering of his subjects (Townsend 2015: 20; see discussion of BCA 5.13, 14 below). This 'engaged' reading of the bodhisattva is also evident elsewhere: in David Loy's notion of a 'New Buddhist Path' wherein the bodhisattva seeks a form of personal transformation that is interwoven with socio-ecological transformation (2015); in Thich Nhat Hanh's Order of Interbeing, where practitioners adopt fourteen precepts based in traditional Buddhist moral principles, but oriented to broad awareness of and action to address social and environmental issues (Nhat Hanh 2005), and in Alan Senauke's work, where the contemporary bodhisattva is presumed to 'embrace' and alleviate social and political ills (2010).

Engagement, Canonical and Contemporary

We can now return to the question with which we began: what kind of engagement with the social world do the Indian Mahāyāna texts imply, and what is the relationship between this and how social engagement has been interpreted in contemporary Buddhist social movements and commentaries on the bodhisattva path?

In order to examine this, we can look more closely at the two *pāramitās* most closely aligned with social concern: generosity and moral discipline. Śāntideva summarizes the perfection of generosity and morality in a few verses with the analogy of the sandals (BCA 5.9–14). He considers the following questions: How can there be buddhas who have perfected generosity, when poverty is endemic? Where can creatures go where they will not be killed, or where I will have no enemies? He answers: 'The earth is covered over merely with the leather of my sandals. In the same way, since I cannot control external events, I will control my own mind' (BCA 5.13, 14). Just as you cover your feet with leather and not the whole surface of the earth in order to walk comfortably, the bodhisattva restrains his mind, not the external world (BCA 5.14). Generosity is therefore defined as the 'mental attitude of relinquishing all that one has to all people' (BCA 5.10). Similarly, morality is 'the mental attitude of abstaining from worldly actions' (BCA 5.11). The remaining virtues—patience, enthusiasm, meditative absorption, and wisdom—are by nature states of mind. Therefore, for Śāntideva the virtues that comprise the focus of the bodhisattva's path are defined in terms of mental transformations and qualities of mind, not primarily transformations in the world. The final verse of the *Śikṣ* is indeed a reminder that all aspects of the path rely on the various forms of mental discipline (K.27; 356 8–9; BR 313).

Similarly, Nattier suggests that in the *Ugra* the bodhisattva's compassion is not meant to be expressed in practical terms (Nattier 2003: 135). The *Ugra* strongly advocates that the bodhisattva conduct his practice in the wilderness and seems aware of the potential problem of reconciling the compassion the bodhisattva represents with the social isolation the path demands. However, the text argues that the bodhisattva is 'not indifferent to the maturing of beings, but devotes himself to amassing the roots of goodness' (*Ugra* 25L). The ideal is social withdrawal rather than involvement. The bodhisattva should be isolated because that way he will bring forth the roots of goodness 'for all beings, not just for one being' (25E).

Thus, the assumption of these texts is that while the bodhisattva is still on the way to full enlightenment and while he is still 'in training' he is not in a position to truly help beings. Rather, it seems the bodhisattva is meant to express compassion towards others in concrete, practical terms, primarily in the far distant future, once the highest stages of the path have been reached (Nattier 2003: 135). When that time comes, the bodhisattva should return to society to help beings—in particular by preaching the *Dharma* (25M). Until then, the bodhisattva must focus on his own cultivation and the accumulation of merit, in order to later become the greatest source of benefit to all beings through the realization of Buddhahood.

In effect, both the early bodhisattva sutra (e.g. *Ugra*) and the later, mature Indian Mahāyāna treatise (BCA) agree that the bodhisattva *qua* bodhisattva on the path should be primarily concerned with his own spiritual cultivation rather than actively helping others and relieving material suffering. The best thing he can do for others is to follow the path to full Buddhahood, and this ideally entails a considerable period of social withdrawal and disengagement.

However, if these texts are not concerned with social engagement or change, one might ask why the *Ugra* emphasizes that lay bodhisattvas should practise giving to beggars. Recall that in the *Ugra*, giving is a practice more for lay bodhisattvas than for monastic bodhisattvas (Nattier 2003: 163). The householder bodhisattva *should* give to beggars, when asked, and if he baulks, he should apologize to the beggar that he is only a beginner in the Great Vehicle, and that he is still subject to 'not giving', i.e. that he is still attached to his material wealth (15B). So evidently lay bodhisattvas *should* be generous to those in need. However, Nattier points out that in the majority of cases, the identity of the recipient is not given, and there is no concern with the object of giving as a 'field of merit' as is evident in other texts. This suggests that the emphasis is on the practice of giving in itself, not on the target of giving: 'giving up' something verses 'giving to' a particular being (163), and thus is really about the lay person's need to learn renunciation (*tyāga*). Moreover, the rationale for this practice is described in terms of the benefits of generosity *to the bodhisattva*, not to the beggar: through giving the bodhisattva will 'extract the substance' from his wealth—i.e. develop liberality or generosity (6B). Even the gift of alcohol, though normally prohibited, is permitted if it helps achieve the bodhisattva's perfection of giving (7A). Thus, Nattier sees the representation of generosity in the *Ugra* as a focus of practice not because of concern for those who might need material offerings, but as a spiritual practice to cultivate the attitude of renunciation, which is especially important for those who have not yet renounced.

Śāntideva seems to share a similar perspective on the value of generosity as primarily lying not in how it can help the recipient in practical ways, but in what it does for the spiritual cultivation of the bodhisattva and the recipient. For Śāntideva, the practice of giving helps the bodhisattva learn renunciation and non-attachment, which as we have seen is the way Śāntideva defines the perfection of generosity. However, it is also one of the means to attract beings to the *Dharma* (*saṃgrahavastu*), which is, after all, the greatest gift the bodhisattva can give. One may even violate the prohibition on giving anything that would be harmful—even such things as alcohol, sexual favours, or weapons—if it will 'win over' beings and attract them to the bodhisattva (Lele 2013). Such attraction will help 'develop' (*paripāka*) or transform beings in some way, such as by inducing mindfulness and awareness, or create the recipient's 'root of good' (*kuśala-mūla*)—the foundation of spiritual progress (Lele 2013: 716). Thus if there is concern for the recipient, it is principally a spiritual concern, rather than a concern for material welfare.

The overall picture of social engagement in the canonical texts we have examined would appear to be this: *saṃsāra* as a whole is irredeemable (the 'poor will always be with us', to borrow a Christian phrase). No one can forever eliminate poverty, crime, war, or injustice, as such ills are endemic to the realm of rebirth where sentient beings are limitless. Therefore, the best way to help beings is to help them deal with the unsatisfactory nature of conditioned existence, and the best way to do that, and the way to reach the most beings, is to become a buddha. A bodhisattva who is on his way to becoming a buddha needs first and foremost to concentrate on cultivating and perfecting the characteristics of a buddha. This may sometimes involve helping other beings in practical ways, but such active assistance to suffering beings will only form part of the bodhisattva path insofar as it contributes to the bodhisattva's perfection of the virtues and other qualities needed to reach Buddhahood, or if it is a way that the bodhisattva can attract beings to the *Dharma*.

This is not to say that the bodhisattva is never instructed to alleviate poverty or to address other forms of material suffering. Both the *Ugra* and Śāntideva do indeed describe the bodhisattva as giving food to the hungry, possessions to the poor, and medicine to the sick, but this is often alongside the aim to provide whatever fulfils the desires of sentient beings. As Lele points out, such gifts can include garlands, sandalwood balm, and ornaments, suggesting that giving to the poor is but one type of giving among many (*Śikṣ* 325f.; BR 251f.; BCA X.20, 22; Lele 2015: 721). It is notable that these expressions of the wish to alleviate poverty occur alongside the wish that animals be free of the risk of being eaten and that hungry ghosts be fed (BCA 10.17–18). This suggests that the concern is with satisfying the wants and needs of individual beings, not changing the structures that cause distress. That the bodhisattva should want to give the poor what they need is no more a call to eliminate poverty than the wish that animals not be eaten is a call to end predation.

Furthermore, in Śāntideva these examples of giving to the poor occur in sections (in chapters 3 and 10 of the BCA) that are focused on the dedication of merit: on the bodhisattva's attitude of giving away good karma and all of his resources to benefit all beings. In these contexts, Śāntideva is articulating the attitude or intention that the bodhisattva should cultivate rather than prescribing actions *per se*. That is, to nourish the desire to provide for the material and practical needs of sentient beings is part of cultivating the bodhisattva's genuine wish to satisfy beings in all ways—to be the 'magical tree that grants every wish' (BCA 3.19). Although actual actions and material offerings that follow on such intentions are also endorsed (see Jenkins 2003: 42), there is no indication here of an awareness of or concern to change the structural causes of suffering in *saṃsāra*. In this light, it is important to recall Śāntideva's reminder that no material offering can bring the 'superior satisfaction' of Buddhahood (*Śikṣ* K.22; 273.12). In the *Ugra*, too, the lay bodhisattva is encouraged to give away all of his possessions, but all such offerings are surpassed by the 'mere thought of becoming a renunciant', since anyone—from kings to rogues—can give material gifts, but renunciant bodhisattvas trade their material wealth for the truly 'substantial' qualities of morality, learning, and pure conduct (20A).

It would appear that the pragmatic relief of ordinary suffering is generally viewed positively, but as primarily palliative. That is, it is important inasmuch as it eases the pain of beings in *saṃsāra*, but since it does not free them from it, it does not reflect the ultimate aim of the bodhisattva. As Birnbaum points out, based on his reading of Chinese Mahāyāna sutras, the vows of a bodhisattva often include the resolution to aid beings in very practical ways, such as providing food, shelter, and medicine and protection from harm, but the overriding goal is to liberate beings from suffering by helping them achieve complete awakening (Birnbaum 2009: 34). '[B]odhisattva vows do not focus simply on helping others to get on with life and be more comfortable with things. After all, that getting comfortable with things in a sense may be principally a skillful adaptation to circumstances that are fundamentally flawed' (Birnbaum 2009: 34). He further notes that such adaptations might be problematic if they serve to reinforce deluded views about the nature of samsaric life. The bodhisattva's aim is not simply to acclimatize beings to the realm of *saṃsāra*, but to liberate them from it.

This ultimate goal, and the bodhisattva's own immediate goal of becoming a buddha, sets important parameters on the nature of the bodhisattva's social involvement. The texts examined here would suggest that the answer to the question posed by Jenkins (2003), 'Does the bodhisattva relieve poverty?', is not an unqualified yes or no, but that it depends on where the bodhisattva is on the path, which virtue is being cultivated, what effect it will have on the bodhisattva and the recipient, and whether it will attract the recipient to the *Dharma*. Consequently, while the bodhisattva path does entail alleviating the suffering of poor individuals and attending to their material needs, it does not appear to focus on the elimination of poverty *per se*, or any other form of social suffering.

Such a conditional answer to the question of whether the bodhisattva is socially engaged helps shed light on Lele's and Jenkins's disparate views. While Jenkins (2003) argues that a concern for poverty alleviation and the satisfaction of material needs is evident in a wide range of Indian Buddhist sources, both mainstream and Mahāyāna, and in fact is a *prerequisite* for spiritual development, Lele argues that there is little evidence in these texts for the idea (2013: 720–725). These two positions can be reconciled if we consider that Jenkins provides an assessment of the view of poverty (and by implication social engagement) in Buddhist traditions more broadly, whereas Lele focuses on Śāntideva and the requirements of bodhisattva path in particular. That is, Jenkins shows that there is a general sense in Indian Buddhist materials that poverty is a social ill that can hinder spiritual progress, whereas Lele holds that for Śāntideva poverty is not a hindrance and can in fact be a positive factor in spiritual growth. The difference here, I believe, is that Śāntideva's advice is directed at the bodhisattva who needs to cultivate such qualities as non-attachment, generosity, and endurance, for whom material wealth could be a barrier to spiritual progress, and by extension, poverty—meaning living a simple life with limited material wealth—could be an asset. By contrast, I believe Jenkins's sources are reflecting a more general recognition in Indian Buddhism that poverty in the sense of not being able to satisfy basic material needs is for most people[5] an obstacle to their interest in and ability to pursue the *Dharma*. This recognition is perhaps most clearly reflected in Buddhist advice to kings to prevent poverty in order to avoid the social and moral degeneration that poverty incurs (Jenkins 2003: 43–45). It is in such sources that we are more likely to find ideas about the societal and state causes of suffering—the kind of institutional sources of *duḥkha* with which contemporary Engaged Buddhists are concerned. On the other hand, to address social ills is not a priority for bodhisattvas who are in the course of their training, and hence the lack of focus on such matters in the *Ugra* and BCA.

[5] Note there are different meanings of poverty likely at play here that would require further research to tease out. Thanks to James Mark Shields for pointing this out.

'Engagement' in Everyday Life

Does this indicate that the bodhisattva is essentially 'disengaged' from society while on the bodhisattva path? The idea that perfection of virtues such as giving and morality are fundamentally mental attitudes cultivated in monastic isolation would suggest so, and might also seem to be reflected in the ubiquitous Mahāyāna practice of dedicating merit to the benefit of all beings. That is, one might be tempted to interpret this practice as simply an imaginary offering without much practical import.

Birnbaum (2009), however, argues that this type of resolution 'lies at the heart of Mahayana practice' and implies that one dedicates *all* of one's talents, resources, and abilities to the benefit of others, and that this actually means that the social engagement of the bodhisattva is far more wide-reaching than what is entailed by 'socially engaged Buddhism' (32f.). We see this kind of far-reaching engagement advocated by Śāntideva, who says that the bodhisattva must think of the welfare of other beings in all circumstances: when he sits, he should wish that all beings sit in wisdom; when he bathes or brushes his teeth, he should wish that beings be cleansed of defilements (*Śikṣ* K.26; 348.17). This parallels what Thich Nhat Hanh's calls the 'first meaning' of Engaged Buddhism, which he describes as 'the kind of Buddhism that is present in every moment of our daily life. While you brush your teeth, Buddhism should be there. While you drive your car, Buddhism should be there. While you are walking in the supermarket, Buddhism should be there' (Nhat Hanh 2008: 31).

The canonical texts we have examined do support this broadest sense of engagement—a sense which is all the more demanding because it must be grounded in in an understanding of the emptiness of self and other (2009: 36). But they do not indicate the second type of engagement Thich Nhat Hanh describes: actions to address issues in the social world such as climate change, war, and social conflict that are more commonly associated with 'engaged Buddhism'. It is important to clarify that when Thich Nhat Hanh said that 'all Buddhism is engaged', he was referring to this first meaning of engagement—the relevance of Buddhist ideals and attitudes to all acts of daily life, and not the second type, of actions to alter social structures (cf. Temprano 2013: n. 3).

The Spectrum of Engagement

It might be helpful, then, to think of a spectrum of what is meant by 'engagement' in Buddhist traditions. On one end of the spectrum there is the engagement of everyday life: Thich Nhat Hahn's 'first meaning' of engagement, whereby all daily actions are infused with altruistic intentions. This form of engagement *is* presented part of the bodhisattva path, but insofar as it could be done by the bodhisattva in complete isolation from others—by the bodhisattva practising in the forest, for example—it is not truly a form of 'socially' Engaged Buddhism *per se*, although certainly the altruistic attitudes it inculcates should have implications for the bodhisattva in society.

Somewhere in the middle of this spectrum we can place what we might call Buddhist altruistic service: selfless actions that aim to satisfy the needs and desires of other beings. Engagement of this kind is presented mostly in aspirational form in Śāntideva, but is clearly endorsed and presented as actively practised by the lay bodhisattva in the *Ugra*. In both sources, altruistic service is enjoined not only as a way to satisfy the wants and wishes of beings, but also to benefit them spiritually by attracting them to the *Dharma*, and as way for the bodhisattva to perfect certain virtues. Although such service by necessity entails some degree of social interaction, or at least interaction with other sentient beings, because it is associated with addressing individual needs and desires we might not consider it socially engaged Buddhism, which we would find at the other end of the spectrum of engagement.

'Socially Engaged Buddhism' would correspond to Thich Nhat Hahn's second type of engagement and involves actions to address collective suffering and its social causes. As with the other two forms of engagement, such actions themselves would constitute Buddhist spiritual practice. This is the type of engagement with structural and institutional suffering that is associated with many contemporary Buddhist traditions and is reflected in Chödrön's understanding of the BCA and her assumption of the activist role of the bodhisattva. The importance of this in the contemporary period presumably reflects a heightened understanding of the significance of systemic and institutional sources of suffering in modernity. However, we might also see this kind of social engagement in premodern Buddhist texts that provide advice to kings. Although this would not conform to Main and Lai's understanding of social engagement, since for them Engaged Buddhism by definition entails a response to modernity, it might be fruitful for future studies to look more closely at this literature for premodern Buddhist ideas about social and institutional *duḥkha* (e.g. see Jamspal 2010: esp ch. 6).

The Bodhisattva Path in One Lifetime

Aside from increased awareness of the significance of collective causes of suffering, another factor that may help explain the contemporary understanding of the bodhisattva as socially engaged is the rejection of or tendency to diminish the idea of rebirth, and a corresponding idea that bodhisattvas are not meant to wait to express their compassion once they have perfected themselves. In the canonical, premodern texts, the assumption is that the goal will take multiple aeons and virtually infinite numbers of rebirths to complete, and the willingness to take on such an epic journey is part of what makes the bodhisattva heroic. From this multi-life perspective, the bodhisattva needs to focus on his own cultivation in order to become a buddha as quickly as possible.

In the contemporary reading, that far-reaching vision of the bodhisattva's journey has been reduced to one lifespan, with the focus on how the bodhisattva can best live up to all the ideals and virtues of the bodhisattva path within this life, with a diminished or perhaps blurred vision of the goal of Buddhahood. Thus, whereas Śāntideva stresses faith in transmigration, and in the ripening of the consequences of actions, i.e. the doctrine of karma (BR 283; Clayton 2006: 61), Chödrön offers a demythologized and psychologized understanding of karma. For example, when Śāntideva (BCA 4.5–4.6) warns that reneging on the bodhisattva vow will lead to rebirth in one of the lower realms (viz. the realm of animals, hungry ghosts, or a hell-realm), Chödrön interprets this to mean that wavering on one's commitment will 'lead to sorrow' (2007: 79). She explains the hungry ghost realm as a 'poverty mentality ... of insatiable neediness and "never enough"' (79). The 'pains, bondage, wounds and lacerations' of the lower realms are equated with the 'uneasiness' of attachment to habitual reactions to discomfort, and falling into a lower realm (BCA 4.12) is explained as becoming 'more set in our ways' (83f.). So Chödrön—who is often following Chögyam Trungpa in this—interprets karma in terms of the cause and effect of habitual behaviours on one's psyche within this lifetime, and the realms of rebirth as psychological states within it. We can see this tendency to downplay or elide the idea of past and future lives and the impulse to 'naturalize' karma as the result of secularization and the need to demythologize the Buddhist teachings in order to comply with a secular-scientific worldview (see McMahon 2008: ch. 1).

To help understand the difference between the canonical and the contemporary, secularized perspectives on the bodhisattva path, we might use an analogy of the bodhisattva as an astronaut. The bodhisattva of the premodern texts is like someone who has been told that all life on earth is suffering from a disease that can only be cured by a rare mineral found on Mars. The bodhisattva's overall concern is with the welfare of all beings, but in order to truly help them he has to become an astronaut first. The most important thing the bodhisattva can do is to fully focus on the training that will allow him to become the type of being best able to help. Although he might occasionally minister to the sick beings around him, and although the fuel in his rocket will be the vast stores of merit he has gained in his past lives,[6] for now he must primarily focus on developing the various qualities and expertise of an astronaut.

By contrast, from the contemporary perspective the bodhisattva is an astronaut-in-training who finds herself in possession of some of the curative mineral, and who has to distribute it to all beings on earth as soon as possible before all beings perish. As such, the bodhisattva is concerned with handing out the mineral to those beings directly around her, but she also must distribute the cure around the globe, which requires her to deal with mass communication and transportation systems. The contemporary bodhisattva is aware of all the systemic and institutional barriers to equal distribution of the cure around the world, and must focus on addressing those barriers as well, and she may have no clear sense that her goal is achievable—much less the goal of becoming an astronaut and reaching Mars. She must just do what she can in the present. Hence while the

[6] This merit, of course, would have been gained from helping other beings. Thanks to Steve Jenkins for this reminder and the analogy of merit to fuel.

canonical, premodern bodhisattva is in a long-term, multi-lifetime, elite training programme, the contemporary bodhisattva must be a social worker and activist right now.

Conclusion

The texts examined here suggest that the bodhisattva path may have evolved from being focused on the highly elite goal of becoming a buddha—the most rare, awesome, and perfect of beings—to being centred on the altruistic motive and unsurpassed wisdom that characterize such a being. The superhero ethic of the *Ugra* is not without altruism, of course, but the practice for the bodhisattva on the path is directed to cultivating the qualities of a buddha, rather than actively expressing the altruism of a buddha. As the *Ugra* states, 'the renunciant bodhisattva who lives in the wilderness fully acquiring the perfection of concentration, is not indifferent to the maturing of beings, but devotes himself to the amassing the roots-of-goodness' (25L). After the bodhisattva has perfected these virtuous qualities, he should re-enter society in order to preach the *Dharma* (25M), but his main role in society is as a religious teacher, not one who works for social change.

By contrast, in his strong emphasis on altruism and attaining Buddhahood for the sake of all others, and his focus on cultivating the virtues, Śāntideva paints a vision that resembles more a saintly figure than that of a superhero. In fact, the self-sacrificing altruism reflected in Śāntideva's ideal has inspired some to compare the bodhisattva to a Christ figure (Nhat Hanh 2007; Lopez and Rockefeller 1987). Śāntideva's assertion that the bodhisattva resolves to 'abide in each single state of misfortune through numberless future ages ... for the salvation of all creatures ... because it is better indeed that I alone be in pain, than that all those creatures fall in to the place of misfortune' is indicative of this altruism (*Śikṣ* 181.1–4; BR 256). Śāntideva's view is that to become a being who embodies this compassionate resolve, a buddha, one must focus on first cultivating this intention through ritual practice, and then perfect the virtuous qualities that characterize a buddha, with the path culminating in the offer of all of one's talents and resources to the benefit of other beings.

In Chödrön's contemporary understanding of the bodhisattva path, there is the assumption that ordinary laypeople, not monastics, will be the practitioners, and that these bodhisattvas are consistently involved in the social world in a compassionate way, both in terms of altruistic service and social engagement. Implicit in Chödrön's reading of Śāntideva is what is explicit in many contemporary Engaged Buddhist thinkers, namely that a bodhisattva will confront the structural and systemic causes of suffering as well as the individual, psychological ones. As Chödrön's comparisons to figures such as Mahatma Gandhi and Martin Luther King reveal, the bodhisattva is envisioned more as the ideal social activist than as a superhero or saint.

We can track the differences in the bodhisattva path in the text we have examined through the concept of merit transfer. In the *Ugra*, merit transfer means transforming the fruit of one's practice from worldly benefits and/or arhatship to the more difficult and long-term goal of Buddhahood. Here, merit transfer is equated with a meditative skill, which we might count as one of the skills or powers of the superhero bodhisattva. In Śāntideva, merit transfer means the willingness and wish to offer completely all of one's talents, abilities, and resources to the welfare of others, and so it reflects the altruistic non-attachment of the saint. Chödrön's understanding is in line with Śāntideva's in that transferring or dedicating merit is interpreted as a practice intended to overcome self-absorption and possessiveness (Chödrön 2007: 58). However, she takes this idea a step further in suggesting that this method of 'softening the heart' is the most significant step towards world peace (342), thus giving this saintly practice a significance for broad social change.

I identified a range of forms of 'engagement': from the infusion of every daily act with the intention to benefit others, to altruistic service to meet the needs and desires of sentient beings, to the effort to tackle the underlying causes of social ills. I suggested that in some measure the first two forms of engagement were evident in the bodhisattva path of the *Ugra* and Śāntideva. While a clear awareness of the need to address systemic suffering was lacking, it would seem that there is precedent in premodern Buddhism to address structural causes of suffering in texts that offer advice to kings. If we are looking for textual sources for Engaged Buddhism in this sense we might look to those that treat statecraft, rather than those whose primary interest is in the bodhisattva path.

Works Cited

Batchelor, S. (trans.) (1979) *A guide to the bodhisattva's way of life*. Dharamsala: Library of Tibetan Works and Archives.

Bendall, C., and Rouse, W. H. D. (1922) *Śikshā-samuccaya: a compendium of Buddhist doctrine*. Reprint, Delhi: Motilal Banarsidass, 1990.

Birnbaum, R. (2009) In search of an authentic engaged Buddhism. *Religion east and west*, 9 (October), 25–39.

Chödrön, P. (2007) *No time to lose: a timely guide to the way of the bodhisattva*. Edited by Helen Berliner. Boston: Shambhala.

Clayton, B. (2006) *Moral theory in Śāntideva's Śikṣāsamuccaya: cultivating the fruits of virtue*. London: Routledge.

Cowherds (2016) *Moonpaths: ethics and emptiness*. Oxford: Oxford University Press.

Crosby, K., and Skilton, A. (trans.) (1996) *Śāntideva: the Bodhicāryāvatara*. Oxford: Oxford University Press.

Dayal, H. (1932) *The bodhisattva doctrine in Buddhist Sanskrit literature*. Reprint, Delhi: Motilal Banarsidass, 1999.

De Jong, J. W. (1975) La légende de Śāntideva. *Indo-Iranian journal*, 16 (3), 161–182.

Garfield, J. L., Jenkins, S., and Priest, G. (2016) The Śāntideva passage *Bodhicaryāvatāra* VIII. 90–103. In: Cowherds, *Moonpaths: Ethics and Emptiness*. Oxford: Oxford University Press, 55–76.

Gómez, L. (1995) A Mahāyāna liturgy. In: D. Lopez, Jr (ed.), *Buddhism in Practice*, Princeton, NJ: Princeton University Press, 183–196.

Goodman, C. (2016) *A training anthology of Śāntideva: a translation of the Śikṣāsamuccaya*. Oxford: Oxford University Press.

Gyatso, T., the 14th Dalai Lama (1988) *Transcendent wisdom: a commentary on the ninth chapter of Shantideva's guide to the bodhisattva way of life*. Reprint: Ithaca, NY: Snow Lion, 2009.

Gyatso, T., the 14th Dalai Lama (1994) *A flash of lightning in the dark of night*. Boston: Shambhala.

Gyatso, T., the 14th Dalai Lama (1999) *Healing anger*. Ithaca, NY: Snow Lion Publications.

Gyatso, T., the 14th Dalai Lama (2009) *For the benefit of all beings: a commentary on the Way of the Bodhisattva*. Translated by the Padmakara Translation Group. Revised edition. Boston: Shambhala.

Gyatso, T., the 14th Dalai Lama, and Jinpa, T. (2005) *Practising wisdom: the perfection of Shantideva's bodhisattva way*. Edited by T. Jinpa. Boston: Wisdom.

Harrison, P. (2007) The case of the vanishing poet: new light on Śāntideva and the *Śikṣāsamuccaya*. In: K. Klaus and J.-W. Hartman (eds), *Indica et Tibetica: Festschrift für Michael Hahn: Zum 65. Geburtstag Von Freunden und Schülern Überreicht*. Vienna: Arbeitskreis für Tibetische und Buddhistische Studien, 215–248.

Harvey, P. (2000) *An introduction to Buddhist ethics*. Cambridge: Cambridge University Press.

Harvey, P. (2007) The bodhisattva career in the Theravāda. In: C. Prebish and D. Keown (eds), *Encyclopedia of Buddhism*. London: Routledge.

Jamspal, Lozang (trans.) (2010) *The range of the Bodhisattva, A Mahāyāna sūtra (Ārabodhisattva-gocara): The teachings of the Nirgrantha Satyaka*. Paul G. Hackett (ed), Treasury of the Buddhist Sciences Tengyur Translation Initiative Associated Texts CK 164 (Tōh. 146). New York: The American Institute of Buddhist Studies, Columbia University Center for Buddhist Studies, Tibet House.

Jenkins, S. (2003) Do bodhisattvas relieve poverty? In: C. Queen, C. Prebish, and D. Keown (eds), *Action dharma: new studies in engaged Buddhism*. London and New York: RoutledgeCurzon, 38–49.

Jenkins, S. (2010) On the auspiciousness of compassionate violence. *Journal of the International Association of Buddhist Studies*, 33 (1–2), 299–331.

Kagawa T. (1989) Shi guzeigan no genryū [The origins of the universal vow]. *Indogaku bukkyō kenkyū*, 30 (1), 294–302.

Kajiyama Y. (1989) Transfer and transformation of merits in relation to emptiness. In: M. Katsumi (ed.), *Studies in Buddhist philosophy*. Kyoto: Rinsen Book Company, 1–20.

King, S. B. (2005) *Being benevolence: the social ethics of engaged Buddhism*. Honolulu: University of Hawai'i Press.

King, S. B. (2009) *Socially engaged Buddhism*. Honolulu: University of Hawai'i Press.

Lele, A. (2013) The compassionate gift of vice: Śāntideva on gifts, altruism, and poverty. *Journal of Buddhist ethics*, 20, 702–734.

Lele, A. (2015) The metaphysical basis of Śāntideva's ethics. *Journal of Buddhist ethics* 22, 249–283.

Lopez, D. S., Jr, and Rockefeller, Steven C. (eds) (1987) *The christ and the bodhisattva*. Albany: SUNY.

Loy, D. R. (2003) *The great awakening: a Buddhist social theory*. Boston: Wisdom.

Loy, D. R. (2015) *A new Buddhist path: enlightenment, evolution and ethics in the modern world*. Boston: Wisdom.

Main, J., and Lai, R. (2013) Introduction: reformulating 'socially engaged Buddhism' as an analytical category. *The eastern Buddhist*, 44 (2), 1–34.

Mrozik, S. (2007) *Virtuous bodies: the physical dimension of morality in Buddhist ethics.* Oxford: Oxford University Press.

Nattier, J. (2003) *A few good men: the Bodhisattva path according to the Inquiry of Ugra (Ugraparipṛcchā).* Honolulu: University of Hawai'i Press.

Nhat Hanh, T. (2005) *Interbeing: fourteen guidelines for engaged Buddhism.* 2nd revised edition. Berkeley, CA: Parallax Press.

Nhat Hanh, T. (2007) *Living Buddha, living Christ.* 20th anniversary edition. New York: Riverhead Books.

Nhat Hanh, T. (2008) History of engaged Buddhism: a dharma talk by Thich Nhat Hanh—Hanoi, Vietnam, May 6–7, 2008. *Human architecture: journal of the sociology of self-knowledge*, 6 (3), 29–36.

Ohnuma, R. (2007) *Head, eyes, flesh, and blood: giving away the body in Indian Buddhist literature.* New York: Columbia University Press.

Padmakara Translation Group (trans.) (1997) *The way of the bodhisattva.* Boston: Shambhala.

Powers, J. (2009) *A bull of a man: images of masculinity, sex, and the body in Indian Buddhism.* Cambridge, MA: Harvard University Press.

Queen, C. S. (1996) Introduction: the shapes and sources of engaged Buddhism. In: C. S. Queen and S. B. King (eds), *Engaged Buddhism: Buddhist liberation movements in Asia.* Albany: State University of New York Press, 1–44.

Queen, C. S. (2003) Introduction: from altruism to activism. In: C. S. Queen, C. Prebish, and D. Keown (eds), *Action dharma: new studies in engaged Buddhism.* London and New York: RoutledgeCurzon, 1–35.

Queen, C. S. (2013) Socially engaged Buddhism: emerging patterns of theory and practice. In: S. M. Emmanuel (ed.), *A companion to Buddhist philosophy.* Chichester, UK: John Wiley and Sons, 524–535.

Quli, N. E. (2009) Western self, Asian other: modernity, authenticity and nostalgia for 'tradition' in Buddhist Studies. *Journal of Buddhist ethics*, 16, 1–38.

Shastri, D. D. (ed.) (1988) *Bodhicāryāvatara of Śāntideva with the commentary Pañjikā of Prajñākaramati.* Bauddha Bharati 21. Varanasi: Bauddha Bharati.

Temprano, V. (2013) Defining engaged Buddhism: traditionists, modernists, and scholastic power. *Buddhist studies review*, 30 (2), 261–274.

Townsend, D. (2015) *Shantideva: how to wake up a hero.* Boston: Wisdom.

Senauke, A. (2010) *The bodhisattva's embrace: dispatches from engaged Buddhism's front lines.* Berkeley: Clear View Press.

Vaidya, P. L. (ed.) (1960) *Bodhicaryāvatāra of Śāntideva with the commentary Pañjikā of Prajñākaramati.* Buddhist Sanskrit Texts XII. Darbhanga, India: Mithila Institute.

Wallace, V., and Wallace, B. A. (trans.) (1997) *A guide to the bodhisattva way of life by Śāntideva.* Ithaca, NY: Snow Lion.

Williams, P. (1989) *Mahāyāna Buddhism: the doctrinal foundations.* Abingdon, UK: Routledge.

Wilson, L. (1996) *Charming cadavers: horrific figurations of the feminine in Indian Buddhist hagiographic literature.* Chicago: University of Chicago Press.

Yarnall, T. F. (2003) Engaged Buddhism: new and improved? Made in the USA of Asian materials. In: C. S. Queen, C. Prebish, and D. Keown (eds), *Action dharma: new studies in engaged Buddhism.* London and New York: RoutledgeCurzon, 286–344.

Suggested Reading

Chödrön, P. (2007) *No time to lose: a timely guide to the way of the bodhisattva.* Edited by Helen Berliner. Boston: Shambhala.

Crosby, K., and Skilton, A. (trans.) (1996) *Śāntideva: the Bodhicāryāvatara.* Oxford: Oxford University Press.

Goodman, C. (2016) *A training anthology of Śāntideva: a translation of the Śikṣāsamuccaya.* Oxford: Oxford University Press.

Gyatso, T., the 14th Dalai Lama (2009) *For the benefit of all beings: a commentary on the Way of the Bodhisattva.* Translated by the Padmakara Translation Group. Revised edition. Boston: Shambhala.

Jenkins, S. (2003) Do bodhisattvas relieve poverty? In C. Queen, C. Prebish, and D. Keown (eds), *Action dharma: new studies in engaged Buddhism.* London and New York: RoutledgeCurzon, 38–49.

King, S. B. (2005) *Being benevolence: the social ethics of engaged Buddhism.* Honolulu: University of Hawai'i Press.

King, S. B., and Queen, C. S. (eds) (1996) *Engaged Buddhism: Buddhist liberation movements in Asia.* Albany: State University of New York Press.

Lele, A. (2013) The compassionate gift of vice: Śāntideva on gifts, altruism, and poverty. *Journal of Buddhist ethics*, 20, 702–734.

Main, J., and Lai, R. (2013) Introduction: reformulating 'socially engaged Buddhism' as an analytical category. *The eastern Buddhist*, 44 (2), 1–34.

Nattier, J. (2003) *A few good men: the Bodhisattva path according to the Inquiry of Ugra (Ugraparipṛcchā).* Honolulu: University of Hawai'i Press.

CHAPTER 8

MADHYAMAKA ETHICS

BRONWYN FINNIGAN

Introduction

Madhyamaka is one of two major philosophical schools of Mahāyāna Buddhism, alongside Yogācāra.[1] It is best known for its philosophy of emptiness (*śūnyavāda*) as articulated by Nāgārjuna in his *Mūlamadhyamakakārikā* and has an illustrious lineage of eminent exponents in India, Tibet, and China. While Mādhyamikas are primarily concerned with metaphysical and semantic issues, central figures also address ethical matters. Śāntideva's *Bodhicaryāvatāra* (BCA), in particular, provides the most extensive treatment of ethics within the Madhyamaka tradition. So influential is this text that the current Dalai Lama represents it as the epitome of Buddhist ethical thought (Gyatso 2004, 2009).

There is a growing body of philosophical literature focused on critically examining how the Madhyamaka analysis of emptiness (*śūnyatā*) bears on the ethical claims and commitments that were held and asserted by historical Mādhyamikas. There are two main loci of contemporary debate. The first concerns the general issue of whether Madhyamaka emptiness is consistent with a commitment to systematic ethical distinctions. The second queries whether the metaphysical analysis of no-self (*anātman*) presented by Śāntideva in BCA entails or provides good reasons for the compassion or altruism of a bodhisattva. This second issue was galvanized by Paul Williams (1998), who powerfully argued that these ontological considerations not only fail to provide a rational basis for altruism but that Śāntideva's argument for this claim, if followed to its logical conclusion, actually undermined the bodhisattva path. Given the importance placed on this text within the Buddhist tradition, Williams's argument has unsurprisingly provoked a growing body of literature aimed at rationally reconstructing a positive

[1] Many thanks to Sara McClintock, Tom Tillemans, and the editors of this collection for helpful comments on a previous draft of this chapter.

account of Śāntideva's views and, thereby, a positive account of the relationship between a Madhyamaka metaphysical analysis and the Mahāyāna bodhisattva ideal of acting out of great compassion for the suffering of all sentient beings.

While many aim to rationally reconstruct Madhyamaka ethics in positive terms, there is considerable disagreement about what this should be. This chapter will critically examine this literature and will demonstrate that much disagreement turns on competing interpretations of the doctrine of the two truths from the perspective of Madhyamaka: in particular, competing accounts of conventional truth or reality (*saṃvṛtisatya*) as well as the forms of reasoning admissible for differentiating conventional truth from falsity and conventional good from bad. To draw this out, this chapter will begin by providing a general introduction to Madhyamaka *śūnyavāda* and outlining a range of positions on the nature of conventional reality that have been advanced and disputed by historical Madhyamaka thinkers in India and Tibet. It will then use these different conceptions to navigate the above two loci of contemporary debate.

Preliminary Background

Nāgārjuna's *Mūlamadhyamakakārikā* (MMK) is the foundational text of Madhyamaka (English translations and commentaries can be found in Garfield 1995, Westerhoff 2009, and Siderits and Katsura 2013). It seeks to establish that all things are empty (*śūnya*) of an essence or intrinsic nature (*svabhāva*).

The notion of *svabhāva* is rooted in early Buddhist attempts to explain the Buddha's doctrine of no-self (*anātman*). Abhidharma literature (the earliest scholastic literature of Indian Buddhism) proposed a two-tier mereological ontology whereby conceptually constructed wholes (universals, genera, kinds, and types) were considered to be reducible to ontologically simple, impartite entities (called *dharmas*). The reducible level was designated 'conventional reality' (*saṃvṛtisat*) as entities at this level are considered to be constructed, in part, in dependence on social and linguistic conventions. The reduced level was designated 'ultimate reality' (*paramārthasat*) and was considered to have mind-independent reality. To the extent that persons are complexes that are analysable into more primitive (psycho-physical) elements, they are conventionally but not ultimately real. It is also now commonplace to attribute to Ābhidharmikas the semantic principle that truth is a matter of what exists (Tanaka 2014, Cowherds 2011). More specifically, a conventional truth is (a statement about) what conventionally exists and an ultimate truth is (a statement about) what ultimately exists, i.e. simple, impartite entities. Thus, while it may be conventionally true that a person exists at a certain time and location, this (statement) is ultimately false.

For this metaphysical and semantic analysis to be plausible, some criterion is needed to differentiate the reducible and the reduced levels of analysis. According to Ābhidharmikas, the criterion of ultimate reality is possession of an essence or *svabhāva*. There is some controversy about precisely how this notion is to be understood. In particular, there is historical and contemporary dispute about whether Ābhidharmikas maintained that *svabhāva* secures the independent existence of an object (Robinson 1972, Hayes 1994, Westerhoff 2009, Siderits 2007, Tanaka 2014, Tillemans 2016). It would seem that, on Nāgārjuna's understanding, to say that an object has *svabhāva* is to say that it has an essential property which is intrinsic to the object and that accounts for its independent existence. This essential property thus secures the numerical identity of the object and accounts for a genuine plurality of ultimately real entities. This essential property is also thought to withstand analysis in the sense of neither being further reducible (it is the bedrock of analysis) nor dissolving into contradictions under analysis.

In MMK, Nāgārjuna provides a series of reductio (*prasaṅga*) arguments aimed at showing that this notion of *svabhāva* is inconsistent with another central Buddhist teaching, the doctrine of dependent origination (*pratītyasamutpāda*). Nāgārjuna argues that it is not possible, on pain of contradiction, for an object to both possess *svabhāva* and causally depend on other things for its existence. Since everything that exists is dependently originated, it follows that everything must be empty of *svabhāva* (MMK 24.19). If possessing *svabhāva* is the criterion of ultimate reality, it also follows that nothing ultimately exists. Moreover, if ultimate truth is (grounded in or corresponds to or is about) ultimate reality, it then follows that there is no ultimate truth. These entailments raise difficult questions. Do they imply, for instance, that nothing exists at all? What would secure the truth of these claims given that they seem to be statements about ultimate reality and thus of ultimate truth? Moreover, does this not remove the semantic underpinnings for the truth of the Buddha's teachings? Nāgārjuna insists that the key to avoiding these problematic implications lies in a proper understanding of the distinction between conventional and ultimate truth (MMK 24.8).

How best to understand Nāgārjuna's views on these two truths is enormously controversial and has been the subject matter of considerable commentarial dispute in India and Tibet. At least one interpretive issue bears on contemporary debates about the nature of Madhyamaka ethics. The issue concerns whether Nāgārjuna's reasoning does or does not establish a positive thesis as the result of a valid argument. The view that it does, defended by Bhāvaviveka, has come to be known as 'Svātantrika Madhyamaka' and the view that it does not, defended by Candrakīrti, is known as 'Prāsaṅgika Madhyamaka'. Later Tibetan Mādhyamika commentators bitterly divide over how this distinction is best understood (Dreyfus and McClintock 2003). While some consider it to be insubstantial, reflecting a mere difference in rhetorical style (e.g. Bu ston rin chen grub [1290–1364] in Dreyfus and McClintock 2003, and Gorampa [1429–1489] in Tillemans 2003), others maintain that it has substantive philosophical import. Tsongkhapa (1357–1419), for instance, influentially argues that the distinction turns on different accounts of the nature of conventional truth (Tsongkhapa 2002, Tillemans 2003).

While contemporary debates about Madhyamaka ethics all refer to the notion of conventional truth, here also there are subtle differences in what this is taken to mean. As a result, it is not always obvious whether a disagreement is substantive or an equivocation in assumed accounts. To help navigate this terrain, I will individuate three distinct philosophical positions on the nature of conventional truth and the possibilities of its rational and epistemic analysis that have been attributed to Madhyamaka thinkers. In particular, I will follow Tom Tillemans (2016) in distinguishing two distinct philosophical positions that have been attributed to Prāsaṅgika Madhyamaka and which he respectively labels 'typical Prāsaṅgika' and 'atypical Prāsaṅgika'. I will contrast these positions to that of Svātantrika Madhyamaka, which I will interpret in the sense ascribed to Bhāvaviveka by Tsongkhapa. It is not my intention to establish that these philosophical positions are the best deservers for the labels Prāsaṅgika and Svātantrika nor establish that they accurately reflect the viewpoint of any particular historical Mādhyamika thinker. My aim is simply to highlight a spectrum of philosophical positions on the nature of conventional truth and demonstrate how they respectively inform current debates about Madhyamaka ethics.

At one end of the spectrum lies what Tillemans calls the 'typical Prāsaṅgika', which, in his view, is the 'common, traditional Indian and Tibetan interpretation of Candrakīrti' (2016: 5). According to this view, it is impossible for Mādhyamikas to accept a positive thesis about ultimate reality as the result of a valid argument because this would presuppose the semantic underpinning which MMK has shown to be internally inconsistent (see Westerhoff 2009: 183, Tillemans 2016: 3, Ruegg 1981: 78). Mādhyamikas are thus methodologically constrained to using reductio arguments against their opponents' theses but without having a thesis of their own (Huntington 2003). This is not thought to foreclose *holding* views about *conventional* reality. Nevertheless, it does methodologically constrain the typical Prāsaṅgika to simply accept what 'the world acknowledges' to be the case (*lokaprasiddha*) without subjecting it to rational or epistemic analysis (Candrakīrti PPMV 18.8, in Tillemans 2011: 151, Ruegg 1981). Typical Prāsaṅgikas accept and practise according to the widely accepted standards and language of ordinary, everyday folk but do not engage in deeper philosophical questions about justificatory status or grounds.

This approach to conventional truth was heavily criticized by philosophers that have come to be classified as Svātantrika Mādhyamikas. Kamalaśīla (fl. 740–795), for instance, complained that it absurdly entailed that every belief would be true simply because its content was acknowledged to be the case, including the 'mistaken' views that the Buddha claimed to be at the root of suffering (Tillemans 2011, 2016). This approach flattens out conventional truth to mere belief without offering any intelligent means of adjudicating competing beliefs. According to Svātantrikas, for Madhyamaka to count as providing a plausible characterization of the Buddha's teachings, it needs to provide some rational way of differentiating conventional truth from falsity.

There are a variety of ways in which the philosophers who have been identified as Svātantrika respond to this challenge. These differences are not often considered in Madhyamaka ethics literature. When Svātantrika is referred to in this literature, it is often understood in terms of the position ascribed to Bhāvaviveka by Tsongkhapa (Tillemans 2003). In this chapter, I shall use the term Svātantrika to pick out this philosophical position. On Tsongkhapa's interpretation, adherents of Svātantrika respond to the above challenge by reintroducing a two-tier reductive ontology but classifying both as distinct modes of conventional reality. A claim about conventional reality is thus conventionally true if it can be established by a legitimate epistemic means (*pramāṇa*, e.g. perception or a valid inference). However, according to Tsongkhapa's interpretation, the ontological grounds of these epistemic means were considered to be a more fundamental conventional reality of entities differentiated by possession of *conventional svabhāva*. Svātantrika thus appear to overcome the problem of flattening out truth to mere belief but at the cost of reintroducing the notion of *svabhāva* that was so thoroughly undermined by Nāgārjuna in MMK.

As Tillemans helpfully draws out, between the extremes of the 'typical Prāsaṅgika' and Svātantrika are a range of Mādhyamikas who seek to preserve the possibility of rationally analysing conventional truth without reintroducing the notion of *svabhāva*. Tillemans calls this group of philosophers the 'atypical Prāsaṅgikas' and identifies Tsongkhapa as their principal representative. There are several rational norms that are potentially acceptable to a Prāsaṅgika for the analysis of claims about conventional reality. Here are at least two.

(1) Logical or conceptual coherence and consistency are two obvious candidates given that they were adhered to by Nāgārjuna to refute his opponent's theses. A claim about conventional reality might thus be falsified if, for instance, it is inconsistent or contradicts other widely accepted beliefs.
(2) An appeal to 'widely accepted epistemic standards' might also be consistent with a commitment to *lokaprasiddha*. Candrakīrti considered at least four epistemic means to be widely accepted by the 'people of the world' for establishing the truth of ontological claims; namely, empirical observation (*pratyakṣa*), inference (*anumāna*), reliable testimony recorded in scriptures (*āgama*) and/or analogical similarity (*upamāna*; Ruegg 1981). A claim about conventional reality might thus be falsified if it cannot be verified by at least one of these epistemic means.

There is much more that can be said about these different Madhyamaka approaches to the nature and analysis of conventional truth. This much should suffice, however, for us to now consider how they bear on contemporary debates about Madhyamaka ethics.

Emptiness and Systematic Ethical Distinctions

One locus of contemporary debate about the nature and possibilities of Madhyamaka ethics concerns whether a commitment to *śūnyavāda* is consistent with accepting and promoting systematic ethical distinctions between good and bad, right and wrong, virtue and vice. Madhyamaka is a school in the Mahāyāna Buddhist tradition. The principal Indian Madhyamaka philosophers each wrote treatises promoting Mahāyāna ethical values (some examples include Āryadeva's *Catuḥśataka*, Nāgārjuna's *Ratnāvalī*, and Candrakīrti's *Catuḥśatakaṭīkā*). Central to these values is the bodhisattva ideal. A bodhisattva is one who, motivated by compassion (*karuṇā*) towards the suffering of others, has both committed to remaining in the realm of cyclic rebirth (*saṃsāra*) in order to relieve all suffering (i.e. they have perfected *bodhicitta*) and has cultivated those moral virtues or perfections (*pāramitā*) which enable them to enact this commitment.

Historical Indian Mādhyamika thinkers do not merely accept and promote specifically Mahāyāna values. They also accept unchallenged the Buddhist monastic rules (*Vinaya*); the typical Abhidharma lists of virtuous and non-virtuous mental factors (*caitta*); and the role of karma and its consequences as a ground for both evaluating and motivating action. It would thus seem that historical Mādhyamika thinkers did not consider *śūnyavāda* to have any significant impact on ethics or ethical reasoning. Indeed, they insisted that *śūnyavāda* does not entail moral nihilism (*ucchedavāda*). But were they correct in this view? What argument could be offered to support this conclusion? And how could Mādhyamikas justify their assumed ethical distinctions?

Mādhyamikas cannot consistently argue that certain actions, qualities, and mental factors are *ultimately* good or bad in virtue of possessing an essential property. They nevertheless could (and often did) insist that ethical distinctions are a *conventional* matter, where holding views about conventional reality is consistent with *śūnyavāda*. While this might warrant the *holding* of ethical views, in general and as such, it does not yet provide reasons for the specific ethical distinctions that Mādhyamikas endorse. What reason can a Mādhyamika offer for why certain conventional actions, qualities, and mental factors (e.g. compassion, generosity, refraining from murder) are to be considered conventionally good while certain others (e.g. selfishness, envy, murder) are to be considered conventionally bad?

According to Tillemans (2010–2011), Prāsaṅgikas can justify these distinctions by appeal to *lokaprasiddha*, treating the 'the world's fundamental moral intuitions' (364) as justificatory grounds for moral claims. This argument is offered as a response to that presented in Finnigan and Tanaka (2011). Finnigan (2015) takes the referent of this remark to be the typical Prāsaṅgika and gives reasons to think that, on a range of interpretations, this response is unsatisfactory. For instance, it is argued that if by 'the world's moral intuitions' is meant 'the set of moral intuitions shared by every intuiting individual', the fact of widespread intra-cultural and cross-cultural moral disagreement gives reason to think that there is no such agreed set (771). If, instead, one contextualized this claim to some group of intuiting individuals with some set of beliefs and values (e.g. the conventional beliefs and intuitions of Buddhists rather than those of 'the entire world'), this would problematically imply a conservatism that undermines the possibility of critiquing the views of others and revising one's own (772–773).

Perhaps the most plausible interpretation is one that grounds ethical distinctions in the widely held moral intuition that suffering is bad and to be prevented. While there might be widespread moral disagreement about a range of values, norms, and rules, few would argue that pain and suffering are intrinsically and non-instrumentally good and to be promoted. The intuition that suffering is bad also seems to be in keeping with the Buddha's teaching of the Four Noble Truths, the first of which states the fact of suffering and the remaining three (diagnosing its cause, inferring the possibility of its cessation, and proposing a way to achieve this goal) presuppose its undesirability. However, this view has its limitations. The ground for the truth of these claims, according to the *lokaprasiddha* of the typical Prāsaṅgika, is their widespread acceptance. The typical Prāsaṅgika does not engage in rational or epistemic analysis of what is commonly accepted by ordinary folk. Belief is thus the condition for truth rather than truth being a standard for the assessment of belief. It follows that the Buddha's teachings would only be true to the extent that they replicate the beliefs of the majority rather than providing a corrective to widespread delusion. This not only undermines the universality and stability of the Buddha's realizations and insights but also deprives these concepts of sense. Insight, realization, and wisdom are all flattened out to mere majority opinion. This is an unsatisfactory outcome.

These arguments target the *lokaprasiddha* of the typical Prāsaṅgika. We know, however, that not all Mādhyamikas are typical Prāsaṅgikas and *lokaprasiddha* need not be interpreted as passive acquiescence to the majority view without positive analysis. A more liberal approach might admit the rational assessment of conventional claims by worldly epistemic standards. This is one of the positions we have attributed to the atypical Prāsaṅgika. From this perspective, it could be argued that the Buddha correctly diagnosed a psychological problem faced by all sentient beings; that they are prone to various forms of suffering (*duḥkha*). On the Buddha's analysis, the most prominent human form of suffering arises from a tension between:

1. A deep-seated desire (*tṛṣṇā*) for, attachment (*rāga*) to, and belief in the persistence of oneself and what one owns and loves, and
2. The fact that everything is causally conditioned (*pratītyasamutpāda*) and thus impermanent (*anitya*).

The majority of the world's citizens might not agree with this psychological analysis of the human condition but it might nevertheless be verified by accepted epistemic means, such as empirical observation, inductive and analogical reasoning, and/or reliable testimony.

A problem remains, however. These epistemic means may well warrant descriptive claims about matters of (psychological) fact. However, they do not seem adequate for ascertaining moral properties (of good, bad, right, wrong). How then does the atypical Prāsaṅgika justify their specifically evaluative distinctions beyond mere acceptance of the majority view?

One possibility is to argue that they are evaluated relative to a goal; namely, *nirvāṇa*. There are several ways of characterizing *nirvāṇa* and thus several ways of conceiving this evaluative relation. If *nirvāṇa* is understood as the bare cessation of suffering, for instance, one might argue that actions, qualities, and mental factors are good or right to the extent that they are instrumental to this goal (or cause it as a consequence). If *nirvāṇa* is understood as a lived state of well-being, one might alternatively argue that actions (and so on) are good or right to the extent that they are constitutive of this way of living. These distinct conceptions of the goal of Buddhist practice need not be exclusive but may be nested or variously related (Finnigan 2014, 2017a).

There may also be several ways of grounding the normative force of evaluative claims relative to these distinct goals. For instance, normative force might be grounded in desire, such that if you do not desire to attain *nirvāṇa*, evaluative claims about actions or qualities that are instrumental or constitutive of this goal have no normative appeal for you. Alternatively, normative force might be grounded in an innate tendency, according to which we all, in fact, strive for *nirvāṇa* (whether the cessation of suffering or a lived state of well-being), as evident in our reactions and emotional responses. On either account, an atypical Prāsaṅgika could argue that while evaluative distinctions are themselves not evaluated using ordinary epistemic means, the desired or innately aspired for goal, relative to which they are normatively grounded, *is* a matter of empirically verifiable descriptive psychology.

This might seem to be a plausible rendering of Madhyamaka ethics from the perspective of the atypical Mādhyamika. It is consistent with both *śūnyavāda* and an epistemically constrained conception of *lokaprasiddha*. Nevertheless, it has two major implications that are potentially problematic for Buddhists, in general, as well as the Mādhyamika Śāntideva, in particular.

First, the above account would seem to rule out appeal to karmic consequences as a way of justifying evaluative claims because the operations of karma are not considered to be verifiable using ordinary epistemic means. Some philosophers argue that this is all for the best (Batchelor 2011, 2015, Tillemans 2010–2011, 2016). It has significant implications, however. Historical Mādhyamikas not only refer to karma, they frequently appeal to the notion of karmic merit (*puṇya*) as a central means by which bodhisattvas alleviate the suffering of other sentient beings (Keown 2001, Velez de Cea 2004, Adam 2005). Śāntideva's *Bodhicaryāvatāra* and *Śikṣāsamuccaya* both emphasize the role of bodhisattva's benefiting other sentient beings by accumulating and sharing their karmic merit rather than offering direct physical or material assistance (Clayton 2006, Goodman 2009). These claims and assumptions may need to be radically revised to be consistent with the evaluative standards of the atypical Prāsaṅgika.

Second, the account offered above suggests that evaluative claims either take the form of desire-dependent hypothetical imperatives or are normatively grounded in goals that implicitly inform our behaviour. However, some read Śāntideva as arguing that a particular evaluative position (i.e. great compassion, often taken to mean altruism or impartial benevolence) is *entailed* by a proper understanding of reality. That is, if one has a right understanding of ontology, one will not only have a reason to remove the suffering of all other sentient beings but one will also be *obliged* to act in this way (Harris 2015). Williams (1998) provides a highly influential argument that attempts to establish that this argument fails. Since Williams's analysis of Śāntideva is at the heart of much contemporary dispute about the nature of Madhyamaka ethics, it is worth considering it in some detail. As in the previous section, competing views on the nature of conventional truth will function as an organizing principle when considering the various positions advanced in current literature.

Does Emptiness of Self Give Good Reasons for Altruism?

In BCA 8.101–103, Śāntideva appears to argue from the fact that we are empty of self (*ātman*) to the conclusion that we should exercise impartial benevolence.[2] He writes:

> The continuum of consciousness, like a queue, and the combination of constituents, like an army, are not real. The person who experiences suffering does not exist. To whom will that suffering belong? (101)
>
> Without exception, no sufferings belong to anyone. They must be warded off simply because they are suffering. Why is any limitation put on this? (102)
>
> If one asks why suffering should be prevented, no one disputes that! If it must be prevented, then all of it must be. If not, then this goes for oneself as for anyone. (103)

One way to reconstruct these verses is as the following argument:

(1) There is no self (*ātman*); 'we' are just composites of psycho-physical elements, and composites are not real;
(2) Given (1), there is no basis for distinguishing my pain from yours; pains are ownerless;
(3) Pain is bad and to be prevented;
(4) Given (2) and (3), either all pain is to be prevented (we should act altruistically without partiality) or no pain is to be prevented (we should be apathetic without partiality);
(5) All pain is to be prevented (we should act altruistically without partiality).

According to Williams, this argument turns on removing the ontological grounds of egoism. Since there is no self, there are no grounds for distinguishing my suffering from yours. It follows that egoistic self-interest in preventing one's own suffering is irrational and thus, for reasons of rational consistency, one should be impartially benevolent. Williams contends, however, that there are two possible ways of interpreting the first premise of this argument, both of which fail to secure this conclusion:

1(a) Śāntideva denies the ultimate reality of a self (*ātman*, understood as a persistent, unchanging, essence of persons) but allows that persons are conventionally real.

According to Williams, if *this* is what Śāntideva meant then his argument fails because it does not remove the grounds for egoistic self-interest. One can still privilege the interests of a conventional self.

[2] English translations of this text can be found in Batchelor (1998), Crosby and Skilton (1996), Wallace and Wallace (1997), Padmakara Translation Group (2006). Citations come from Crosby and Skilton.

1(b) Śāntideva denies both the ultimate and conventional reality of selves. All that exist are psycho-physical elements in causal relations.

This interpretation removes all possible ontological grounds for egoistic self-interest, and is, in Williams's view, the only way Śāntideva's argument will work. However, as Williams argues, this interpretation has dire consequences for ordinary ethical transactions. By removing the distinction between 'self' and 'other', it makes nonsense of a bodhisattva's commitment to sacrifice their 'own' karmic merit for the sake of 'others'. Since there are no 'others' there is no object of a bodhisattva's compassion or altruistic concern. By removing the notion of an agent, there can also be no actions of a bodhisattva that could be evaluated and accrue merit—and thus no act of 'committing' oneself to removing the suffering of others. Williams not only thinks this view has dire ethical implications, he also thinks it presupposes mistaken views on the metaphysics of personality. He insists, for instance, that the reductive analysis of persons as collectives of elements *presupposes* the concept of a person (i.e. parts are identified in relation to the whole rather than the whole derived from an otherwise random collection of parts). Williams concludes that Śāntideva faces a dilemma, neither horn of which is acceptable. As a result, Śāntideva not only fails to provide a rational basis for altruism but, according to Williams, if you follow his argument to its logical conclusion, it destroys the bodhisattva path.

Most contemporary responses to Williams's argument deny that Śāntideva intended interpretation 1(b). These responses typically emerge from reflections on a puzzle concerning premise (1). This premise is most straightforwardly read as a statement of ultimate truth from the perspective of Abhidharma ontology, according to which only causally related psycho-physical elements are real and persons are unreal. But Śāntideva is a Mādhyamika. Why would a Mādhyamika argue from an Ābhidharmika ontological position? Some offer a methodological explanation of this apparent fact (Siderits 2000, 2015). Others deny that this is the best way to read premise (1), offering instead an alternative interpretation that is more in keeping with Madhyamaka. I will discuss three alternative interpretations below. Whichever way one goes, it would seem that neither an Ābhidharmika nor a Mādhyamika would accept 1(b). Not only do Mādhyamikas accept the conventional reality of persons, so too do Ābhidharmikas. It has also been noted that Śāntideva writes elsewhere as if there are conventional selves (Clayton 2001, 2006, Harris 2015). Moreover, some argue that since the implications of 1(b) are so disastrous for ethics, it would be more charitable *not* to attribute this interpretation to Śāntideva (Harris 2015).

While rejecting interpretation 1(b) might avoid one horn of Williams's dilemma, it does not thereby successfully navigate the other. Interpreting premise (1) in terms of 1(a) is also problematic, for several reasons.

First, how are we to understand premise (2) and its entailment from 1(a)? As above, these premises seem to be most straightforwardly read as claims about ultimate reality from an Abhidharma perspective. On this view, pain (a kind of *vedanā*) is a proper constituent of ultimate reality, an element of the psycho-physical aggregate to which persons are reducible. Since persons, subjects, and agents are not ultimately real, pain does not ultimately occur in or for anyone; it just occurs. It is not obvious that a Mādhyamika can accept this premise. Certainly not if construed as a statement about ultimate reality since, as we know, Mādhyamikas typically deny that anything ultimately exists (in the sense given to this notion by Ābhidharmikas). It might be possible for a Svātantrika Mādhyamika to rationally accept these premises if construed as claims about (a judiciously revised) conventional reality. From the perspective of the typical Prāsaṅgika, however, persons and instances of pain have the same ontological standing; namely, as constituents of the conventional reality as accepted by most ordinary people (*lokaprasiddha*). From this perspective, (2) is false. Common sense distinguishes between the pains of distinct subjects.

What about the atypical Prāsaṅgika? The answer to this question might depend on how we understand the idea of 'ownerless pain'. There seem to be at least two ways to understand this claim. First, as the claim that pains are not mental events that are possessed by persons (where this assumes a possession-relation between two entities; a pain event and a person). Second, as a claim that pains just occur without being felt or experienced by a subject. Williams takes the latter to be the sense required by Śāntideva's argument and insists that it does not make sense. For Williams, conscious mental states necessarily involve an element of subjectivity; phenomenal content always appears to or for a subject. Clayton (2001) responds that to reject the idea of ownerless pains is to 'effectively dismiss all of Buddhism: the heart of Buddhist insight is the mystery of experience without subject' (86). This is not necessarily true. Prominent Yogācāra and Pramānavāda thinkers maintained that ordinary conscious experiences necessarily involve both phenomenal content and the subjective experiencing thereof.[3] A version of this idea is accepted and defended by several prominent Yogācāra Svātantrika Mādhyamikas (e.g. Śāntarakṣita and Kamalaśīla), although it does not seem in keeping with the form of Svātantrika that we have been discussing in this chapter. To the extent that it reflects a common intuition about the nature of consciousness, it might nevertheless be consistent with the *lokaprasiddha* of typical Prāsaṅgikas. The case of the atypical Prāsaṅgika is more challenging. A prominent analysis of this thesis (subjectivity analysed as *svasaṃvedana*) was rejected by Tsongkhapa, although there is reason to think that his arguments against this view would not vindicate the notion of ownerless pain at the level of conventional truth (Garfield 2006, Williams 2013). For these reasons, it would thus seem that premise (2) is problematic from a range of Madhyamaka perspectives.

We might also query the status of premise (3), the claim that pain is bad and to be prevented. If (3) is understood as a statement of ultimate reality, then it is unacceptable to a Mādhyamika. Could it be accepted as a conventional truth? To the extent that it is a common moral intuition that is accepted by most ordinary people, it is acceptable to

[3] This idea is captured in the notion of ordinary experiences having 'subject–object duality'. See Vasubandhu in TSN, Dignāga in PS, and Dharmakīrti in PV and PVin. For a brief overview of these ideas and references to relevant secondary literature, see Finnigan (2017b).

the typical Prāsaṅgika. Indeed, this might be one way to read Śāntideva's qualification that 'no one disputes that!' (BCA 8.103). Could it be accepted by the atypical Prāsaṅgika? It might seem that their response would be much the same as the typical Prāsaṅgika. However, this might depend on whether the atypical Prāsaṅgika thinks that conventional claims must be verified to be held as true or merely unfalsified by rational and epistemic analysis. Perhaps the rational norm of consistency might verify the truth of (3) (as more consistent with other widely accepted moral intuitions than its denial) but it is not clear that it can be verified by epistemic norms, which are concerned with matters of descriptive fact rather than normative evaluation. If, however, the position is that conventional claims need merely be *unfalsified* by these epistemic means, then (3) might be reasonably held as conventionally true.

The case of Svātantrika is interesting. We have been presenting it as rationally analysing conventional claims in terms that assume a reductive ontology (albeit one that holds within the scope of conventional reality). In the Abhidharma context, reductive analysis eliminates social, linguistic, and conceptual construction to expose a mind-independent reality. Interestingly, this reduction is not thought to eliminate evaluative considerations. Abhidharma thinkers assumed that the mental elements that constitute ultimate reality are fundamentally valenced (positive, negative, or neutral). Pain is thus ultimately bad, not because we judge pain to be bad but because its ultimate valence is negative, a fact that is bodily registered and evident in our aversive reactions. This is a fascinating idea but highly controversial. It is also not clear that it is equivalent to the claim that pain is bad and to be removed. Svātantrikas, unlike Ābdhidharmikas, can avoid some of these problems, however, given that they clearly maintain that their reduction occurs in the sphere of the conventional. There is thus no question, for them, of reducing away all social, linguistic, conceptual construction from the reduced level of conventional reality.

While premise (3) seems to be acceptable to all Mādhyamikas, we might still question the entailment from (4) to the conclusion. Premise (4) is a disjunction between removing all pain and removing none. The conclusion affirms one of these disjuncts. What reason is there for this affirmation? Why should a proper understanding of the nature of persons lead us to extend our (otherwise egoistic) concern to the removal of all pain rather than, for instance, ceasing to care at all about its occurrence (Harris 2011)? It could be argued that premise (3) supplies the necessary reason; it is because pain is bad and to be removed which, as we have already suggested, is acceptable as a conventional truth by all Mādhyamikas.

Even if we grant the entailment between (4) and the conclusion, Williams argues that the overall argument has a structural flaw; namely, it attempts to infer certain prescriptive claims about how we 'ought' to behave from certain descriptive facts about what 'is' the case. The attempt to derive an ought-from-is is a fallacy that was famously diagnosed by Hume. It might seem, however, that premise (3) inserts the requisite normative element to avoid this charge. That is, the normative claim that pain is bad and to be removed seems to be doing the normative work with respect to the conclusion and not the descriptive claim about the emptiness of persons.

Finally, even if the 'is–ought' issue can be resolved, the argument still faces Williams's fundamental concern with 1(a); namely, if we opt for this interpretation, how does it avoid reinstating self-interested egoism and thereby undermining Śāntideva's argument?

While Mādhyamikas may be able to accept some of the premises in the argument reconstructed from BCA 8.101–103, it would thus seem that they cannot accept them all. Does this mean that Williams is right and Śāntideva's argument fails? Not necessarily. We might still query whether the idea contained in these verses is best reconstructed as an argument consisting of these premises or even whether there is a better argument to be found in Śāntideva's thought. We might also query whether his verses are best understood as presenting arguments at all. This chapter shall conclude by considering three alternative reconstructions of Śāntideva's thought that have been advanced in recent literature and shall assess whether they offer a more plausible account of the relationships between a Madhyamaka understanding of emptiness, conventional truth, compassion, and impartial benevolence.

The 'We Are All One' Conventional Self Argument

The first alternative draws on additional verses contained in BCA 8 to justify modifying Williams's reconstructed argument in a way that would consistently allow a moderate sense of egoistic self-interest. According to this alternative, the sense of conventional persons that is reinstated in 1(a) is not the unrevised, common-sense notion that 'we' are all distinct persons. Rather, it is a revised, 'enlightened' view that 'we' are just aspects of one, whole, unified, integrated conventional self. A version of this idea is defended by Wetleson 2002 (see Priest 2015 for a different argument to a similar conclusion). Wetleson derives evidence for this revised conventional self from an 'organismic analogy' (2002: 64) he finds in the following verses:

> If you think that it is for the person who has pain to guard against it, a pain in the foot is not of the hand, so why is the one protected by the other? (BCA 8.99)
>
> In the same way that the hands and other limbs are loved because they form part of the body, why are embodied creatures not likewise loved because they form part of the universe? (BCA 8.114)

According to Wetleson, this organismic analogy extends to relations between persons, which are thereby to be understood as aspects of a more comprehensive organism—a unified but multi-aspected conventional self. The clear advantage of this suggestion is that it is consistent with egoistic self-interest and thus avoids Williams's main challenge to Śāntideva. Since we are all part of the same self, interest in one's own welfare includes an interest in that of others *as part of* one's own welfare (2002: 52). The conclusion of this argument is no longer that we should be *impartially* benevolent but, rather, we should be *partially* benevolent, where the revised scope of this partiality encompasses all sentient beings.

Despite overcoming Williams's major objection to Śāntideva's argument, this account has several problems from the perspective of Madhyamaka. First, it implies a radical revision to Williams's premise (2). It is no longer the case that all pains are similar in being ownerless but, rather, all pains are similar in being *mine* (Williams 1998). To say that a pain is mine is typically taken to mean that it is experienced by me. However, it is highly counter-intuitive to say that I experience *all* pain. Not only is it widely assumed that we do not and cannot literally experience the pain that is experienced by another, this (conventional) fact informs our attitudes, reactions, and conduct. This revision to premise (2) is clearly unacceptable to the typical Prāsaṅgika, who only agrees with what is widely accepted by the world.

It would also seem that, for this very same reason, the typical Prāsaṅgika would also reject Wetleson's revised notion of the 'one' conventional self. It is much more widely believed that persons are separate and distinct than that they are all aspects of a single, integrated being. It is also not clear that this idea is acceptable to Svātantrika, who grounds conventional claims in a reduced conventional ontology, which is methodologically antithetical to increased unification.

What about atypical Prāsaṅgikas? Could they accept the conventional reality of a unified self? The answer will depend on the assumed criteria for conventional existence. According to Wetleson, conventional claims are determined on the basis of pragmatic considerations which are validated by consensus (2002: 43) and linguistic use (48). The criterion for conventional reality thus seems to be a matter of collectively agreed social construction. There are two problems with this view, however. For the 'one' self to count as conventionally real, according to this criterion, it must either be a construction about which there is collective agreement (*lokaprasiddha* in the sense accepted by the typical Prāsaṅgika) or one about which there *should be* consensus. We have already argued that it does not satisfy the former. This criterion also does not seem robust enough to satisfy the atypical Prāsaṅgika who, as we have characterized the view, takes widely accepted epistemic norms as standards for truth. Further argument is needed to show that the notion of a single, integrated self can satisfy such standards as empirical observation and inductive inference and thus should be accepted.

THE 'NO RELEVANT DIFFERENCE' OR 'RATIONALITY' ARGUMENT

A second alternative to Williams's reconstruction of the argument contained in BCA 8.101–103 draws on verses 90–98 to reconstruct a more minimal and seemingly more plausible argument from Śāntideva's thought. Versions of this argument can be found in Williams (1998: ch. 2), Pettit (1999), Clayton (2001), Wetleson (2002), and Garfield, Jenkins, and Priest (2015). The argument turns on the idea that there is no relevant difference between you and me to justify prioritizing the prevention of my pain over yours. We might reconstruct this argument as follows:

(1) Egoistic self-interest assumes that there is something relevantly distinctive about oneself that justifies prioritizing one's own interest over that of others;
(2) (1) is false. There is nothing relevantly distinctive about oneself that justifies prioritizing one's own interest over that of others;
(3) Pain is bad and to be prevented;
(4) Given (2) and (3), there is no good reason to privilege preventing my pain over yours;
(C) (Given 4), self-interest is irrational and so, for reasons of rational consistency, one should prevent pain without partiality.

As Clayton (2001) points out, this has the same structure as anti-discrimination arguments. Since I am not special in any morally relevant sense, my suffering should not count as more important than yours and so I should treat your suffering as just as important as mine. An advantage of this argument is that it does not presuppose the idea of ownerless pains, which we have argued is questionable from a Madhyamaka perspective. It also tackles Williams's problem of egoism head on and appears to shift the burden of proof onto the egoist rather than providing an independent proof for impartial benevolence (Pettit 2000, Garfield, Jenkins, and Priest 2015). Its plausibility, however, hangs on the truth of (2). What reasons are there to accept this premise and do they require taking a perspective on conventional reality that is unacceptable to Madhyamaka?

In BCA 8.94–98, Śāntideva seems to offer two reasons for thinking that (conventional) persons are relevantly similar to justify equal consideration with respect to the prevention of pain. The first reason is contained in BCA verses 94–96:

> I should dispel the suffering of others because it is suffering like my own suffering. I should help others too because of their nature as beings, which is like my own being. (BCA 8.94)
>
> When happiness is liked by me and others equally, what is so special about me that I strive after happiness only for myself? (BCA 8.95)
>
> When fear and suffering are disliked by me and others equally, what is so special about me that I protect myself and not the other? (BCA 8.96)

The intended answer to these rhetorical questions is: 'Nothing'. There is nothing special about me to warrant privileging the prevention of my pain over yours. Why? Because we are relevantly similar in our nature as sentient beings who desire happiness and seek to avoid suffering. Whether or not we think this is a sufficient reason for the conclusion, it would seem to be a reason that all Mādhyamikas could accept if construed as a conventional truth that is either accepted on the basis of rational reflection, epistemic analysis, or a common intuition that is widely accepted by most ordinary people. Moreover, it would seem to be a reason all Mādhyamikas would *want* to accept given that it is a central presupposition of the Buddha's Four Noble Truths and all Mādhyamikas seek to be consistent with the Buddha's teachings.

This is not the only reason offered by Śāntideva, however. The following verse offers a slightly different one: 'If I give them no protection because their suffering does not afflict me, why do I protect my body against the future suffering when it does not afflict me?' (BCA 8.97). Here, Śāntideva seems to be pointing out that egoistic self-interest is future oriented. The pain we seek to prevent is not pain we are currently experiencing; it is pain that will occur in the future. However, Śāntideva appears to suggest that a future self is similar to contemporary others in (having the property of) being non-identical to our present self. And he infers from this fact that there is thus no good reason to privilege preventing pain to a future self over that of a contemporary other since in neither case is the pain experienced by me. Moreover, he insists that it is no good saying 'but the future self will be *me*' because this, he claims, is a 'false construction' (BCA 8.98).

It is not obvious that Mādhyamikas can accept this second reason. First, it seems to be most straightforwardly read as a claim about ultimate reality from an Abhidharma perspective. According to Abhidharma, 'we' are just continua of psycho-physical elements with momentarily fleeting existence. It follows that none of the ultimate constituents of (what is conventionally called) 'me' now will be the same as the ultimate constituents of (what is conventionally called) 'me' at any future time and so, quite literally, the term 'me' does not pick out the same person from one moment to the next. Given this ontology, one can straightforwardly infer analogical similarity in 'non-identity' between (a) current-me and future-me to (b) current-me and current-you.

As we know, Mādhyamikas deny that there is an ultimate reality, so construed, and thus cannot accept this reason as a statement of ultimate truth. If construed as a rationally revised claim about conventional reality, it *might* be acceptable to a Svātantrika Mādhyamika. It would be inconsistent with the *lokaprasiddha* of the typical Prāsaṅgika, however. While most people may not believe that they have a soul or essence (*ātman*) that exists permanently and unchanging through time and across lives, it is ordinarily assumed that the embodied being that is ourselves now will be (despite inevitable changes) continuous in several important respects (e.g. memory, body) with our embodied being in the future in a way that it is not continuous with the embodied being of others.

It is also not clear that this second reason is consistent with the *lokaprasiddha* of the atypical Prāsaṅgika, given that it has implications that are not only in tension with norms of rationality but might also undermine our rational capacities. A belief in a (conventionally) enduring self not only informs much of our ordinary conduct (e.g. we brush our own teeth, rather than the teeth of others, to prevent the decay that we would otherwise experience in future; Williams 1998), but to suppose otherwise would seem to undermine our capacity to plan as forms of instrumental reasoning that concern ourselves (Wetleson 2002).

Moreover, as Harris (2015) points out, just as we have moral intuitions to take care of others, we also have moral intuitions that admit a moderate amount of egoism. A certain amount of self-care is often considered to be morally praiseworthy. We commend those who, for instance, quit smoking to prevent cancer, exercise to prevent obesity-related illnesses, refrain from drinking over the legal limit before driving. While these actions might benefit both the agent in the future as well as others, we typically would not blame or criticize the agent for performing these preventative actions if done purely for the sake of their own future well-being. It would thus seem that, with respect to some moral intuitions, the fact that the 'future self will be me' *does* count as a good reason for performing certain forms of action. Harris takes this as grounds for shifting the burden of proof back to Śāntideva. While emphasizing the similarity of (conventional) persons might support certain moral intuitions, emphasizing their differences supports others. A new argument is needed to show why the latter are irrational and the former not.

A final issue with this argument is that the textual support for this reconstruction is drawn from verses other than 101–103. It thus seems to avoid the problems Williams raises for verses 101–103 by reconstructing a different argument for impartial benevolence from a different set of verses that are concerned with the same issue. While this alternative argument is perhaps more plausible (particularly if one focuses only on the first reason offered to justify (2), as do Garfield, Jenkins, and Priest 2015), this is in part due to the fact that it omits the problematic elements that Williams finds so objectionable in 101–103.

A Meditational Technique Aimed at Psychological Transformation

The third alternative this chapter will consider (but by no means the only remaining possibility) denies that BCA 8.101–103 provides an argument aimed at proving that we should be impartially beneficent. Rather, according to this alternative, these verses are best read as raising considerations that, in the context of meditation, will help undermine the attachment to self, or self-grasping, that underpins many of our negative emotions. The objective of these verses is thus not to establish the rationality of impartial beneficence but, rather, to assist in actually generating a compassionate concern for others when incorporated into meditative practice.

A version of this suggestion was initially proposed by Pettit (1999), who identifies prominent Tibetan Gelug Madhyamaka thinkers, Tsongkhapa in particular, as differentiating two problematic senses of 'self' that need to be eliminated. The first is *ātman*, the philosophical view that there is an enduring substance, wholly present from moment to moment, that exists separate from and as the owner of events in conscious awareness. The second, however, is an innate and largely unconscious sense of self-grasping that Gelugpas think underlie our negative emotions and can be exposed when subjects are placed in situations of emotional duress. Pettit calls this sense of self-grasping an 'innate misconception of self' (1999: 132) or an 'emotionally conflicted self' (132). From this perspective, ordinary, conventional life is to be understood as a mixture of an ordinary, innocent sense of persons (useful for practical and ethical transactions) and a problematic misconceived sense of self that informs our negative emotions.

If we grant this distinction, Śāntideva's thought might then be read as merely providing suggestions that, in the context of meditative practice, help undermine the 'innate misconceived self' and contribute to positive changes in one's moral psychology. For instance, if one recognizes a habitual selfish tendency in oneself (or its emergence in a particular instance), reflecting on the idea that we are empty of selves might help undermine the self-grasping that is constitutive of this emotional state and thereby help transform it to another psychological state, such as unselfishness or compassionate concern for others. According to Westerhoff (2015), merely reflecting on (or believing the truth of) this idea is insufficient for bringing about this transformation. What is required is a 'meditational realization' of the truth of this claim. This is claimed to result not in a belief about what one *should* do but, rather, a change in what one *actually* does, given an understanding of emotions as behavioural tendencies that habitually implicate how we react. Such transformation is also thought to change how one experiences the world given the assumption that emotions implicate our phenomenology.

There are several advantages of this alternative reading of Śāntideva's verses. First, it avoids Williams's charge that Śāntideva fallaciously infers a normative conclusion from descriptive facts. On this account, one psychological state (i.e. realizing the truth of a claim) helps produce another psychological state with behavioural implications, both of which are matters of descriptive fact (Harris 2011, Westerhoff 2015). Second, it avoids Williams's charge that the argument fails to prove its conclusion because it fails to remove the grounds of egoism. This is because it is no longer conceived as an argument aimed at proving a conclusion. Third, this way of understanding 101–103 avoids some of the problems that arise for the idea of 'ownerless pains' and the Abhidharma-style reduction it implies because it does not require Mādhyamikas to *accept* these ideas. Rather, it could be argued that Mādhyamikas merely *utilize* these ideas as a matter of skilful means (*upāya*) aimed at psychological transformation rather than endorsing them as positive theses. Fourth, this reading might explain why these verses are contained in a chapter titled 'The Perfection of Meditative Absorption'. Finally, this reading suggests broader Buddhist themes concerning the role of self-conception and self-grasping in moral psychology, thereby promising to complement a more extensive body of Buddhist literature.

As with the previous alternatives, this reading of BCA 8.101–103 is not unproblematic. One issue concerns whether it can be considered an accurate reconstruction of the idea contained in Śāntideva's verses. As pointed out by Williams (1999), Pettit explicitly attributes this distinction between (a) a belief in a philosophical *ātman* and (b) an innate sense of self implicated by our negative emotions to later Tibetan Gelug Mādhyamikas writing between the fourteenth and sixteenth centuries. It is not obvious that the seventh-century Śāntideva himself had this distinction in mind when writing these verses.

This reconstruction also seems to imply a more sophisticated analysis of emotions than that presupposed by Śāntideva's verses. In 101–103, pain seems to be conceived as a simple and unstructured mental occurrence. This analysis of psychological transformation, however, requires an analysis of emotions as behavioural dispositions that are constituted by certain intentional attitudes and beliefs. There thus seems to be a mismatch in presuppositions about the nature of mental states.

One might also query whether there is a genuine distinction to be drawn between (a) and (b). For instance, (b) is sometimes characterized as a latent tendency to reify the self, a grasping at permanence and self-essence. However, this is also how the notion of *ātman* is sometimes conceived. There might thus seem to be no substantive difference between the two. If this is right, one might use this fact to resist the previous objection. That is, one could argue that both are implicated by the denial of self, and thus one does not need the later Tibetan distinction to draw the latter sense out of Śāntideva's thought.

One might nevertheless wonder whether the denial of self in the sense of both (a) and (b) could allow for an innocent and acceptable notion of conventional self. As reconstructed by Pettit, (b) is a sense of self constitutive of negative emotions. Williams (1999) expresses doubt that one could differentiate this from a sense of self implicated by positive emotions or even one that is emotionally neutral but necessary for ordinary, practical transactions (149). If there is no clear difference, one might then worry whether eliminating (b) would result in eliminating *all* conventional notions of self (including the notions of subject, agent, and the distinction between self and other). One way to avoid this implication might be to argue that the difference between (b) and an innocent, acceptable notion of conventional self lies not in a distinct *sense* of conventional self but in a distinct attitude towards it (i.e. one of attachment or grasping). Thus, in removing (a) one removes (b) understood as the attitude of *attachment* to or grasping at self rather than the conventional notion of there *being* a self. Alternatively, it could be argued that since (b) is a form of (a), it has properties that are inconsistent with the broader set of our conventional beliefs unlike an innocent, acceptable notion of conventional self as subject and agent (Westerhoff 2015). It would thus be open to an atypical Mādhyamika to reject conventional conceptions of self that are inconsistent with rational norms of consistency and coherence but retain those that are consistent.

Finally, it would seem that much more would need to be said to explain how exactly a 'meditational realization' that we are empty of selves functions to transform various psychological attitudes and behaviour. The idea is intriguing; there does seem to be a substantive difference between believing something and *understanding* it and *realizing* its truth. However, further explanation is needed for how these distinct notions are implicated by various forms of psychological attitudes and behavioural response. This might not be a problem if the claim is simply that an event of realization merely provides meditative *assistance* for the removal of selfishness and production of compassion. The need for explanation becomes more pressing, however, if the claim is that it is a sufficient cause of this transformation.

Works Cited

Adam, M. T. (2005) Groundwork for a metaphysic of Buddhist morals: a new analysis of *puñña* and *kusala*, in light of *sukka*. *Journal of Buddhist ethics*, 22, 61–85.

Batchelor, S. (1998) *Guide to the Bodhisattva's way of life*. 6th edition. Dharamsala: Library of Tibetan Works and Archives.

Batchelor, S. (2011) *Confession of a Buddhist atheist*. New York: Spiegel & Grau.

Batchelor, S. (2015) *After Buddhism: rethinking the dharma for a secular age*. Princeton, NJ: Yale University Press.

Clayton, B. (2001) Compassion as a matter of fact: the argument from no-self to selflessness in Śāntideva's *Śikṣāsamuccaya*. *Contemporary Buddhism*, 2 (1), 83–97.

Clayton, B. (2006) *Moral theory in Śāntideva's Śikṣāsamuccaya: cultivating the fruits of virtue*. New York: Routledge.

Cowherds (2011) *Moonshadows: conventional truth in Buddhist philosophy*. New York: Oxford University Press.

Crosby, K., and Skilton, A. (1996) Translator's introduction. In: K. Crosby and A. Skilton (trans.), *The Bodhicaryāvatāra*. Oxford: Oxford University Press, xxvii–xlii.

Dreyfus, G., and McClintock, S. L. (2003), *The Svātantrika-Prāsaṅgika distinction*. Boston: Wisdom.

Finnigan, B., and Tanaka, K. (2011) Ethics for Mādhyamikas. In: Cowherds, *Moonshadows: conventional truth in Buddhist philosophy*. New York: Oxford University Press.

Finnigan, B. (2014) Examining the bodhisattva's brain. *Zygon*, 49 (1), 231–241.

Finnigan, B. (2015) Madhyamaka Buddhist meta-ethics: the justificatory grounds of moral judgments. *Philosophy east and west*, 65 (3), 765–785.

Finnigan, B. (2017a) The nature of a Buddhist path. In: J. H. Davis (ed.), *A mirror is for reflection: understanding Buddhist ethics*. New York: Oxford University Press, 33–52.

Finnigan, B. (2017b) Buddhist idealism. In: K. Pearce and T. Goldschmidt (eds), *Idealism: new essays in metaphysics*. New York: Oxford University Press, 178–199.

Garfield, J. L. (1995) *The fundamental wisdom of the middle way: Nāgārjuna's Mūlamadhyamakakārikā*. New York: Oxford University Press.

Garfield, J. L. (2006) The conventional status of reflexive awareness: what's at stake in the Tibetan debate. *Philosophy east and west*, 56, 201–228.

Garfield, J. L., Jenkins, S., and Priest, G. (2015) The Śāntideva passage: *Bodhicāryāvatāra* VIII.90–103. In: Cowherds, *Moonpaths: ethics and emptiness*. New York: Oxford University Press, 55–76.

Goodman, C. (2009) *Consequences of compassion: an interpretation and defense of Buddhist ethics*. New York: Oxford University Press.

Gyatso, Tenzin (XIV Dalai Lama) (2004) *Practising wisdom: the perfection of Shantideva's bodhisattva way*. Boston: Wisdom.

Gyatso, Tenzin (XIV Dalai Lama) (2009) *For the benefit of all beings*. Boston and London: Shambhala.

Harris, S. (2011) Does anātman rationally entail altruism? On *Bodhicaryāvatāra* 8: 101–103. *Journal of Buddhist ethics*, 18, 92–123.

Harris, S. (2015) Demandingness, well-being and the bodhisattva path. *Sophia*, 54, 201–216.

Hayes, R. P. (1994) Nāgārjuna's appeal. *Journal of Indian philosophy*, 22, 299–378.

Huntington, C. W., Jr (2003) Was Candrakīrti a prāsaṅgika? In: G. Dreyfus and S. McClintock (eds), *The Svātantrika-Prāsaṅgika distinction*. Boston: Wisdom, 67–92.

Keown, D. (2001) *The nature of Buddhist ethics*. Hampshire, UK: Palgrave.

Pettit, J. (1999) Review of *Altruism and Reality*. *Journal of Buddhist ethics*, 6, 120–137.

Priest, G. (2015) Compassion and the net of Indra. In: Cowherds, *Moonpaths: ethics and emptiness*. New York: Oxford University Press, 221–240.

Robinson, R. H. (1972) Did Nāgārjuna really refute all philosophical views? *Philosophy east and west*, 22, 325–331.

Ruegg, D. S. (1981) *The literature of the Madhyamaka school of philosophy in India*. Wiesbaden: Otto Harrassowitz.

Siderits, M. (2000) The reality of altruism: reconstructing Śāntideva. *Philosophy east and west*, 50 (3), 412–424.

Siderits, M. (2007) *Buddhism as philosophy: an introduction*. Aldershot, UK: Ashgate.

Siderits, M., and Katsura Shōryū (2013) *Nāgārjuna's middle way: Mūlamadhyamakakārikā*. Boston: Wisdom.

Siderits, M. (2015) Does Buddhist ethics exist? In: Cowherds, *Moonpaths: ethics and emptiness*. New York: Oxford University Press, 119–140.

Tanaka, K. (2014) In search of the semantics of emptiness. In: J. Liu and D. Berger (eds), *Nothingness in Asian philosophy*. London: Routledge, 55–63.

Tillemans, T. J. F. (2003) Metaphysics for Mādhyamikas. In: G. Dreyfus and S. L. McClintock (eds), *The Svātantrika-Prāsaṅgika distinction*. Boston: Wisdom, 93–124.

Tillemans, T. J. F. (2010–2011) Madhyamaka Buddhist ethics. *Journal of the International Association of Buddhist Studies*, 33 (1–2), 359–381.

Tillemans, T. J. F. (2011) How far can a Mādhyamika Buddhist reform conventional truth? Dismal relativism, fictionalism, easy-easy Truth, and the alternatives. In: Cowherds, *Moonshadows: conventional truth in Buddhist philosophy*. New York: Oxford University Press, 151–166.

Tillemans, T. J. F. (2016) *How do Mādhyamikas think?* Boston: Wisdom.

Tsong-ka-pa (2002) *The great treatise on the stages of the path to enlightenment*. Vol. 3. Translated by Lamrim Chenmo Translation Committee. Edited by G. Newland. Ithaca, NY: Snow Lion.

Velez de Cea, A. (2004) The criteria of goodness in the Pāli nikāyas and the nature of Buddhist ethics. *Journal of Buddhist ethics*, 11, 123–142.

Westerhoff, J. (2009) *Nāgārjuna's Madhyamaka: a philosophical introduction*. Oxford: Oxford University Press.

Westerhoff, J. (2015) The connection between ontology and ethics in Madhyamaka thought. In: Cowherds, *Moonpaths: ethics and emptiness*. New York: Oxford University Press, 203–220.

Wetleson, J. (2002) Did Śāntideva destroy the bodhisattva path? *Journal of Buddhist ethics*, 9, 1–30.

Williams, P. (1998) *Studies in the philosophy of the Bodhicaryāvatāra: altruism and reality*. Delhi: Motilal Banarsidass.

Williams, P. (1999) Reply to John Pettit. *Journal of Buddhist studies*, 6, 138–153.

Williams, P. (2013) *The reflexive nature of awareness: a Tibetan Madhyamaka defence*. London: Routledge.

Suggested Reading

Arnold, D. (2015) Madhyamaka Buddhist philosophy. In: *The internet encyclopedia of philosophy*. Available from: http://www.iep.utm.edu/b-madhya [Accessed 28 December 2015].

Candrakīrti (2003) *Catuḥśatakaṭīkā*. In: *Four illusions: Candrakīrti's advice to travelers on the bodhisattva path*. New York: Oxford University Press, 109–208.

Cowherds (2015) *Moonpaths: ethics and emptiness*. New York: Oxford University Press.

Nāgārjuna (1975) *Ratnāvalī*. Translated by J. Hopkins, L. Rinpoche, and A. Klein. In: *The precious garland and the song of the four mindfulnesses*. New York: Harper and Row.

Shantideva (1996) *The Bodhicaryavatara*. Translated by K. Crosby and A. Skilton. Oxford: Oxford University Press.

Tillemans, T. J. F. (2016) *How do Mādhyamikas think?* Boston: Wisdom.

Williams, P. (1998) *Studies in the philosophy of the Bodhicaryāvatāra: altruism and reality*. Delhi: Motilal Banarsidass.

CHAPTER 9

ETHICS IN PURE LAND SCHOOLS

MICHAEL CONWAY

INTRODUCTION

PURE Land Buddhism, one of the most popular and widely practised forms of Buddhist devotion in East Asia, poses a variety of complex, interesting problems when considering the issue of Buddhist ethics because its foundational sutras deny the necessity for moral action or ethical behaviour as a prerequisite to enlightenment. The *Wuliangshoujing* states that hearing the name of Amitābha and wishing sincerely to be born in that buddha's Pure Land are sufficient conditions to bring about enlightenment in that realm (these statements appear in the eighteenth vow and its fulfilment passage [T 360, 12:268a26–28 and 12:272b11–13]). The *Guanwuliangshoujing* suggests that enlightenment is available even to those who have committed the gravest evils throughout their lives provided they simply chant the name of Amitābha ten times on their deathbed (T 365, 12:346a16–26). The *Amituojing* holds that just a day or week of sustained chanting is enough to assure one of Buddhahood in the next life (T 366, 12:347b10–15) and disparages engaging in other lesser goods, stating that they are ineffectual for attaining the goal of birth in Amitābha's Pure Land (T 366, 12:347b9–10). These passages not only call into question some of the fundamental assumptions about Buddhism which much English-language discourse about Buddhist ethics takes for granted (such as the functioning of karmic retribution for immoral acts and the central role of keeping moral precepts [*śīla*] in Buddhist practice), but have also historically led Pure Land devotees to make a variety of highly nuanced answers to the central ethical question of 'How should one live in this world?'

In spite of the importance and pervasiveness of Pure Land devotion throughout East Asia and in spite of the variety of answers to this question presented by various Pure Land thinkers throughout history, relatively little scholarship exists in English on ethics in Pure Land Buddhism. Most of the scholarship that does exist focuses on Shinran (1173–1262) and his Jōdo Shinshū (Shin sect), an iteration of Pure Land Buddhism that particularly stresses the ineffectuality of human attempts to bring about one's own enlightenment, thus relegating the issue of ethical action to a different status than found in more traditional types of Buddhism. Much of that work has been written by Shin clergy or believers attempting to engage with the Jōdo Shinshū tradition to find answers to ethical questions, or to propose a unique Shin ethics somehow relevant to contemporary concerns.[1] Scholars of religion and religious thought have also made forays into the issue of ethics in Shin Buddhism (e.g. Pye 1989, Kasulis 2001, and Lewis and Amstutz 1997), the most significant of which is Ugo Dessì's *Ethics and Society in Contemporary Shin Buddhism* (Dessì 2007), which broadly outlines the contours of the discourse on ethical issues within contemporary Shin doctrinal studies and introduces the major points of social engagement by Shin followers in Japan. Some scholars have addressed Shin Buddhist responses to modernity, mostly focusing on the role of ethics in the thought of Kiyozawa Manshi (1863–1903), a Shin reformer (see Blum 1988, Johnston 1991, Unno 1998, Main 2012).

The works that address Pure Land ethics outside the Shin tradition are few and far between. Charles Jones has a short article that considers how Chinese Pure Land Buddhists after the Song dynasty (960–1279) interpreted the implications of the passages introduced above, but covering over nine centuries in less than fifteen pages, it is barely a start at considering how the tradition developed in China, let alone the ideas about ethics of the various Pure Land thinkers there (Jones 2003). The ethical implications of the thought of Shinran's teacher, Hōnen (1133–1212), and the different schools of thought that grew up among his many disciples have yet to be explored in detail. Although Fabio Rambelli discusses the radical, almost revolutionary, nature of some of Hōnen's disciples who were criticized for taking the statement that the evil will be saved on saying the name as a licence to do wrong (2004), the significance of the reincorporation of the precepts as a critical element for salvation within the thought of some of Hōnen's successors, as well as Hōnen's practice of bestowing precepts on lay followers well after writing that keeping the precepts was not an essential practice for birth in the Pure Land, has not been addressed in English. As such, there is much fertile ground for considering the significance of Pure Land Buddhism and what the tradition might have to say to our understanding of Buddhist ethics as a whole. While Shinran's thought is certainly rich in insight and complex enough to engage even the most supple mind, it is not the only form of Pure Land devotion

[1] *The Pure Land*, the journal of the International Association for Shin Buddhist Studies, has many contributions of this type in its pages, such as Ishihara 1987, Tanaka 1989, Zotz 1989, and Taniguchi 1999. More authoritative voices from within the Hongwanji-ha (one of the two major branches of Jōdo Shinshū in Japan today) have appeared in *Pacific World*, especially Shigaraki 2001, 2009, and Tokunaga and Bloom 2000. Ama Toshimaro, a representative of the Ōtani-ha (the other major branch), has also presented his formulation of Shin ethics (2001, 2002). The contributions by Kenneth Tanaka, Gregory Gibbs, and Shigeki Sugiyama in *Engaged Pure Land Buddhism* (1998) fall into this category as well.

nor have his conclusions had a monolithic authority within the Shin institution in its 750-year history.

This chapter aims to point out that a variety of answers have been posed to ethical problems in light of Pure Land scripture in hopes of opening up some room for dialogue between Pure Land thought and scholars engaged in the project of clarifying Buddhist ethics in the West. What is most striking about the majority of the scholarship introduced thus far is that it fails to engage (whether critically or constructively) with the broader Western academic discipline devoted to discussions of Buddhist ethics or moral philosophy. Conversely, most scholars addressing the topic of Buddhist ethics give little or no attention to Pure Land thought. There appears to be a failure of communication to the extent that it is difficult to imagine that both sides are actually talking about the same Buddhism. Part of the responsibility for this failure surely lies in the presentations by the Shin side. Scholars of Buddhist ethics, eager to answer the question of what Buddhism tells us about how we should live, must certainly be frustrated with declarations like 'The Jōdo Shinshū conception of salvation through the power of the original vow of Amida leaves no room for reliance on works' (Pye 1989: 165), or that Shinran's thought has an 'inherent reluctance to formulate a code of ethics' (Dessì 2007: 51), or 'Basically, Shin Buddhist social ethics is not anything that can be expressed through general plans or slogans, but rather something that those who have attained *shinjin* will undertake, based on their own decisions in accordance with the particular circumstances in which they find themselves' (Ama 2001: 49), or yet again, that Shin 'was associated with a kind of distinctive personal character [but] . . . the nature of this Shin character is a matter of post hoc anthropological observation rather than doctrinal or programmatic stipulation' (Lewis and Amstutz 1997: 150). The Shin expositors, for their part, are alienated by the persistent assumption that precepts play a central role in Buddhist practice, because they believe that that is an issue that Shinran faced and resolved convincingly 800 years ago.

The aim of this chapter is to reframe the discussion so that these two sides can at least get to the same table. First, I hope to show that there has been a plurality of ethical thought in the broader Pure Land tradition throughout history and within the Shin tradition itself, in order to get some breathing room between the two claims that *śīla* is essential to Buddhism and that it is not to Pure Land Buddhism. Shinran is making highly original conclusions in his rejection of traditional forms of Buddhist practice, and by showing how that differs from those Pure Land Buddhists before and after him, I hope to point out some possible avenues of future investigation that might lead to fruitful discussion. Second, I will point out that the vocabulary that Shinran uses to set forth his unique view of the Pure Land teachings is very much a Buddhist vocabulary that resonates with the concerns of scholars of Buddhist ethics. Even though Shinran refuses to create a code for moral behaviour, he is still deeply concerned with issues of karmic consequence, virtue (*kudoku*, *guna*, or *punna*), and wisdom as guides to action—all central issues in discussions of Buddhist ethics in English. These considerations are aimed at laying a foundation for a discussion that seems to me is long overdue.

Tension within the Pure Land Tradition: Amitābha's Working and Human Endeavour

The Pure Land tradition takes the larger *Sūtra of Immeasurable Life* (often referred to as the *Larger Sukhāvatīvyūha Sūtra* in English scholarship) as foundational. This sutra tells the story of a perfect bodhisattva, Dharmākara, who gives rise to a series of vows wherein he promises to effect universal liberation, that is, to realize the Mahāyāna ideal of compassion. The sutra then explains that Dharmākara fulfilled these vows in the distant past, becoming a buddha by the name of Amitābha (meaning 'immeasurable light') and Amitāyus (meaning 'immeasurable life'). It also describes in detail how the various vows made by Dharmākara were fulfilled (later commentators came to refer to these portions of the sutra as 'fulfilment passages').

This sutra, by positing a figure external to sentient beings who is able to intervene in their karma and change its course based on the power of his vows, set up a tension in the relationship between Amitābha's liberative power and the acts of human beings. What do sentient beings need to do to access that liberative power? If sentient beings once access that power, what do they need to do to ensure it will function all the way to the goal of Buddhahood? Is there a danger that some human action might disqualify one from the benefits of that power? Discussions within the Pure Land tradition about ethical issues revolve around problems like these that arise out of this tension. The exegete's view of the relative relationship between the power of the vows and human action in bringing about liberation informs and determines the answers to those ethical questions (see Jones 2003). This section will show that the weight given to the power of the vows was not necessarily consistent even during the development of the Pure Land tradition in India.

The *Wuliangshoujing* referenced at the outset of this chapter is only one of five extant Chinese translations of the *Sūtra of Immeasurable Life*. The earliest of these five translations was likely completed in the middle of the third century while the latest was completed during the Song dynasty (960–1279). The different recensions provide us with a snapshot of the sutra at the time of its translation. They differ considerably in terms of overall content (for instance, two have twenty-four vows for Dharmākara, two have forty-eight, and one has thirty-six) and in terms of the thrust of the message presented. For our purposes here, it is particularly significant that the earliest translation, the *Daamituojing*, clearly holds ethical action to be a necessary prerequisite to receiving the salvific working of the power of the vows, whereas those requirements are repositioned such that faith becomes the deciding factor of liberation in the translation that became foundational for Hōnen, Shinran, and their Chinese forerunners.

Of the twenty-four vows by Dharmākara presented in the *Daamituojing*, five are related to beings who will be born in Amitābha's Pure Land. The fourth vow holds that those who hear the name of Amitābha as praised by the myriad buddhas in the ten directions and rejoice will give rise to a mind of loving-kindness (*ci*) and be caused to be born in his land (T 12:301b8–13). The twenty-fourth states that those who encounter Amitābha's light (a symbol of the Buddha's wisdom) will 'all be caused to perform good acts with a mind of loving-kindness' (T 12:302b13) and ultimately be brought to the Pure Land. (The full vow appears at T 12:302b9–14.) These two vows clearly emphasize the power of Amitābha, working in the form of the name and light, to bring about a change within the practitioner both in the present life and in the life in the Pure Land. We should note that this working is said to bring about ethical action (*zuoshan*) in the lives of those who encounter it.

Although this emphasis on the liberative and morally efficacious power of Amitābha is present even at this early stage of the development of Pure Land thought, the other three vows instead emphasize the importance human action for bringing about birth in the Pure Land. In all three vows, aspirants to birth in the Pure Land are told to perform different levels of good, based on their varied karmic capacity. In the fifth of Dharmākara's vows, those who have done evil acts in the past are told to 'govern themselves well, repent of their wrongdoings, do good for the sake of enlightenment, and uphold the precepts and the sutras' (T 12:301b16–17). It is vowed that such a person will never again return to the three evil realms of existence (hells, animals, and hungry ghosts; T 12:301b18–19). In the sixth vow, 'good men and women' are encouraged to 'do even more good by using me [Dharmākara]' (T 12:301b23) and perform the good acts expected of a householder such as making offerings at stupas, financially supporting the *saṅgha*, and uprooting desire (T 12:301b23–25). Dharmākara vows that such devout householders will become bodhisattvas upon birth in the Pure Land (T 12:301b25). The seventh vow is directed at 'good men and women' who are instructed to 'walk the bodhisattva path, practise the six *pāramitās*, become renunciants, not slander the sutras and precepts, and purely uphold the rules on abstention' (T 12:301b28–c1). Such a person will, upon birth in the Pure Land, become a bodhisattva in the stage of non-retrogression, that is, one who is assured to attain Buddhahood.

These three vows set a variety of conditions upon practitioners who aim for birth in Amitābha's land, based essentially on their karmic capacity to perform different levels of good: abstaining from further evil for evildoers, acting as good householders for those lay followers who can, and choosing a monastic life for those situated to do so. The highest fruit, attainment of assurance of Buddhahood, is only open to those who lead a monastic lifestyle and practise the six *pāramitās*. The lesser practitioners, although they receive some benefits through the working of these vows, are only helped along the way in their long endeavour to Buddhahood.

This prioritization of doing good, in particular the good of monastic bodhisattvas, in the *Amituojing* is even more evident when we turn our attention to the fulfilment passages that correspond to the vows introduced above. First, there is no passage that might be read as the fulfilment of the fourth vow, the only vow that promises birth for those who simply hear Amitābha's name. Second, the fulfilment passages for the fifth and sixth of Dharmākara's vows close by stating that those who are born in the Pure

Land based on lesser goods than the six *pāramitās* all 'think to themselves, "I regret that I did not know that I should uphold the rules on abstention and do good even more than I have"' (T 12:310b4 and 12:310c21–22).

Clearly, from the perspective of the *Daamituojing*, doing good is an essential element for attaining Buddhahood. The power of the vows is supplemental, and the degree to which the vows are effective is dependent on the degree to which the practitioner engages in Buddhist practice. This stance, which encourages doing good and discourages doing evil, is particularly evident in the last section of the sutra, which describes in vivid detail the negative karmic results that arise from engaging in five types of evil acts based on the three poisons of greed, anger, and ignorance and strongly encourages pursuing the excellent karmic fruits of five good acts (T 12:313b26– 316b22).

This understanding of the relative efficacy of doing good and the power of the vows apparently changed considerably in India over the next two hundred years. By the beginning of the fifth century, when the *Wuliangshoujing* was translated, the decisive role of the vows in bringing human beings to Buddhahood had been brought to the fore and the performance of good acts by human beings took on a secondary role. The forty-eight vows of Dharmākara in that sutra do contain many of the elements present in those of the *Daamituojing*, but they have been reordered and reorganized. The distinctions between the grades of practitioners are played down and the benefits that they are accorded are equalized. That is to say, in the three vows regarding those who will be brought into the Pure Land (the eighteenth, nineteenth, and twentieth; T 12:268a26–b5; Inagaki 1995: 34; Gómez 1996: 167–168) there is no clear distinction between evildoer, householder, and monastic. The practices laid out are far less detailed. The eighteenth vow simply calls for sincere faith and wishing to be born in the Pure Land as many as ten times (T 12:268a26–27). The nineteenth says that those who 'practise various forms of virtue' will be met by Amitābha on their death (T 12:268a29–b2). The twentieth states that those who 'plant roots of virtue' will ultimately attain birth and the goal of Buddhahood (T 12:268b3–5). Further, all those who are born in the Pure Land are assured of entering the stage of non-retrogression based on the eleventh vow in this translation, not just those who have practised the six *pāramitās*. Speaking colloquially, we might say that the vows in this version of the sutra offer more bang for much less buck. The eighteenth vow just requires faith, while the eleventh insures that those who have that faith become assured of attaining Buddhahood on birth in the Pure Land.

The fulfilment passages in the *Wuliangshoujing* are also considerably different. Hearing the name as preached by the myriad buddhas is presented as the central element that brings about birth (T 12:272b9–13; Inagaki 1995: 54; Gómez 1996: 186–187). There are few other conditions put on the practitioner in the fulfilment passage, simply that they 'rejoice in faith and for but one thought moment sincerely direct their virtue to realize their aspiration to be born in that land' (T 12:272b11–13). We should note, however, that this passage, as well as the eighteenth vow, includes the caveat that 'those who commit the five grave offences and slander the right dharma are excepted' (T 12:272b13–14), which shows that in spite of the broadening of the realm of efficacy of the vows, practitioners were still expected to remain within certain ethical limits, and some sins were seen as being weightier than the power of the vow.

Although the passages about three grades of practitioners are still present in the *Wuliangshoujing* (T 12:272b15–c10; Inagaki 1995: 54–55; Gómez 1996: 187–188), they do not play the central role that they did in the *Daamituojing*. The passages themselves have been significantly simplified and there is no mention of regret at having not done more good in one's previous life after birth in the Pure Land. All are born, albeit with different levels of attainment, but here the eleventh vow, which promises all ultimate enlightenment, serves to cancel out the significance of those distinctions. The section on the karmic recompense for the five evils is still present in the *Wuliangshoujing*, but its absence in the *Wuliangshourulaihui*, which was translated around the turn of the eighth century, indicates that it ultimately ceased to be seen as pertinent to the theme of the sutra.

All of these changes show that the *Sūtra of Immeasurable Life* gradually came to emphasize the power of Amitābha's working to bring about Buddhahood within sentient beings, while also de-emphasizing the role that human action played in effecting enlightenment.[2] This shift of focus, however, did not utterly resolve the tension created by the addition of the concept of 'vow power' to the myriad conditions leading to Buddhahood, but it did provide opportunities for reflection on the efficacy and necessity of moral action by Buddhist practitioners, especially in Tang dynasty (618–907) China and Kamakura era (1185–1333) Japan, where the message about the supreme efficacy of the vows in the *Wuliangshoujing*, in conjunction with the promise of birth and ultimate Buddhahood for the gravest of sinners in the *Guanwuliangshoujing*, led some thinkers to radically reject the idea that human beings are capable of bridging the gap to enlightenment at all, save for the intervention of Amitābha within karmic circumstance. In the next section, we will consider the ideas of one such thinker, Shandao (613–681).

Reflections on the Limitations of Human Good: Shandao and 'Good Tainted with Poison'

The emphasis laid on the power of Amitābha's vow in the *Wuliangshoujing* was noticed and commented upon by a small group of Pure Land devotees who were active in present-day Shanxi province in the sixth and seventh centuries. During this time, throughout China, there was a growing interest in Pure Land Buddhism and a growing devotion to Amitābha, but among the works from this period that are extant today, those by Tanluan, Daochuo, and Shandao are the primary ones that make significant

[2] The vows in the *Wuliangqingjingpingdengjuejing* (T. 12:281a–c, esp. 281c2–9) are also of interest in documenting this shift, but space concerns do not allow me to introduce them here.

reference to Amitābha's vows and consider their implications.[3] Shandao, in particular, notes both the effectiveness of Amitābha's vows in bringing about liberation and the difficulties facing human beings who attempt to bring it about themselves, but he too remains caught up within the tension between the agency of Amitābha and the agency of the human being that we saw in the previous section. In fact, some passages in his *Guanwuliangshoujingshu* sound much like the admonitions of the *Daamituojing* to 'do good and cease evil'. Shandao's response to this tension and his movement within it is most apparent in his comment on the three aspects of faith that Śākyamuni says are essential to birth in the Pure Land toward the end of the *Guanmuliangshoujing*. This section will explore his commentary there with an eye to the insights that discussion might hold for future considerations of Buddhist ethics.

Shandao's discussion of the three aspects of faith (a mind of sincerity, a mind of profound understanding, and a mind that directs virtue with an aspiration for birth) contains several intense exhortations to behave according to the prescriptions set forth by the Buddha. Although he does not use the word 'precept', he very much encourages doing good and avoiding evil. In his comment on the mind of sincerity, for instance, he writes,

> There are two types of truly benefiting oneself: First, within the true mind one should prevent and discard all of the various evils of self and other, defiled lands, etc., and think 'Just as all the bodhisattvas prevent and discard all the various evils, so too will I'. . . . One should necessarily discard non-good in the three types of action [bodily, verbal, mental] within the mind of truth. Also, when one does good, one should necessarily do it within the mind of truth. (T 1753, 37:271a10–25)

Here, Shandao is saying very clearly that faith in Amitābha (the 'true mind' discussed above) entails a strong ethical commitment to strive ceaselessly to realize the bodhisattva ideal, to do good oneself, and to encourage others to do good as well. A passage from his comment on the mind of profound understanding states,

> Profound understanding means respectfully wishing that all practitioners and others will singlemindedly trust in the Buddha's words, and, decisively without concern for their own welfare, through practice renounce what the Buddha makes them renounce, practise what the Buddha makes them practise, and leave behind what the Buddha makes them leave behind. This is called following the Buddha's teachings and following the Buddha's intention. It is called following the Buddha's vow. Such a person is called a true disciple of the Buddha. (T 37:271b6–10)

[3] There are commentaries on both the *Wuliangshoujing* and the *Guanwuliangshoujing* by Jingyingsi Huiyuan (523–592, T 1745 and 1749, respectively) and Jiaxiangsi Jizang (549–623, T 1744 and 1752), two major exegetes of this period, but they both essentially overlook the significance of Dharmākara's vows. Tiantai Zhiyi (538–597) and his disciples also comment on Amitābha (for instance, T 1750) and incorporated meditations focused on him into their regimen of practice (in his *Mohe zhiguan*, e.g. T 1911, 46:12a19–13a23), but discussions of the vows are relatively sparse.

Shandao again holds that faith in Amitābha includes a stringent desire to live in accord with the words of the Buddha, to do exactly as they instruct—to perform the actions they encourage and avoid the actions they prohibit. This seems to include a willingness to strive continually to put into practice all of the teachings of the Buddha, including maintaining moral standards and engaging in meditation.

On the other hand, on these same pages, literally lines apart from these bold declarations, we find passages where Shandao voices deep scepticism about the capacity for ethical behaviour on the part of the practitioner to effect liberation or serve as a cause for birth in Amitābha's Pure Land. He writes,

> Do not pretend outwardly to be intelligent and rigorously engaged in good when one is inwardly false and empty. Greed, anger, wicked falsehood, malignant deception arise constantly and it is difficult to cease one's evil nature. It is just like snakes and scorpions. Although one gives rise to the three types of action [bodily, verbal, mental], they are all to be called 'good tainted with poison', or 'false, empty practices'. They cannot be called 'true action'. When one has this sort of faith and engages in this sort of practice, even if one were to endeavour strenuously in body and mind, running all through the day and night, working frantically as if one were trying to extinguish a fire on one's head, all such action is called 'good tainted with poison'. If one were to direct this good tainted with poison and seek to be born in that Buddha's land, this is necessarily impossible. (T 37:270c29–271a7)

The thrust of Shandao's criticism here is against disingenuous action on the part of human beings. That is to say, Shandao is discussing the problem of behaving morally while being inwardly motivated by other, less than noble drives. The poison that he is referring to is human beings' selfish, covetous, self-centred nature. We could call it the poison of the standard Buddhist formula of the three poisons: greed, anger, and ignorance. The image of snakes and scorpions, which lash out at anything that comes within their reach, is a metaphor for the reactive nature of the ignorant human mind that responds with either desire or revulsion at the various stimuli that appear before it. From Shandao's perspective, the good actions that humans undertake are consistently tainted by ignorant, self-centred motives that disqualify them from being considered genuinely good, either morally or in terms of being fruitful in the quest for liberation. Shandao's position here seems to offer a point of communication in the discussion of the human potential for altruism in the broader discourse on ethics.

His rather pessimistic view is informed by his understanding of the nature of the power of Amitābha's vows, another stance of Shandao's that might add something to the discussion of the role of karma in Buddhist ethics. His poor estimation of the human capacity to genuinely act selflessly and compassionately arises because he contrasts that human action with the compassionate, pure action of Dharmākara, who is the perfection of the bodhisattva ideal and has 'never once given rise to a thought of greed, anger, or hostility' (T 12:269c11). Shandao continues the above passage with:

> Why is this the case? For truly when Amitābha was engaged in bodhisattva practises in his causal stage, all of the three types of actions he performed were for each thought-moment, every instant, performed within the true mind. (T 37:271a7–9)

Based on the *Wuliangshoujing*, Shandao presents Dharmākara as the perfect bodhisattva who had from the start of his practice already overcome karmic bondage and defilement. His vows and the virtues that he perfected through his practice are said to be of a completely different karmic status from those of human beings who are possessed of greed, anger, and ignorance. From Shandao's perspective, only such good—performed based on perfect wisdom and free of the taint of the poisons of human passions—can truly be called pure or good and only such pure good can lead to entry into the pure realm of Amitābha and ultimately to complete enlightenment. This good has a karmic status that is fundamentally, substantively different from the goods carried out by human beings possessed of the three poisons. While Dharmākara acts are pure and undefiled, the acts of ordinary human beings are defiled and tainted by the very fact that they are carried out by human beings with passions. This position forces us to question whether the bodhisattva ideal of compassionate, selfless action is genuinely practicable in our ordinary state of mind or our present existence, conditioned as it is by a variety of results of unskilful karma and unwholesome mental states.

Shandao's own answer to that question is neither simple nor clear. On the one hand, he writes that we should aim to practise within the 'true mind' in which Dharmākara himself practised. This answer, introduced in part above, calls the practitioner to overcome karmic bondage and emulate the ideal set forth by Dharmākara through sincere striving in Buddhist practice. Shandao's own moral fastidiousness indicates that he did indeed attempt to do just that (see Nogami 1970: 160). Many of Shandao's followers in China and some of Hōnen's disciples in Japan took Shandao's exhortations to moral rectitude just as they were written, believing that the true expression of faith in Amitābha was to live as an expression of the 'true mind'—striving to act truly selflessly and compassionately and in direct accord with the Buddha's teachings on living a moral life. That is to say, for this group of followers, the faith called for in the eighteenth vow was seen to be an extremely high bar, an almost superhuman will to attempt to overcome one's own ignorance and selfish desires. This strand of Pure Land thought, which takes moral behaviour and human striving to break through the bonds of karmic conditioning to be a condition for faith, is present in some of the Pure Land schools in contemporary Japan that follow in Hōnen's lineage. For them, the *nenbutsu* or verbal chanting of Amitābha's name is an easy practice, but developing a true and genuine faith in accord with Dharmākara's 'true mind' is 'the most difficult of difficulties among all difficulties' (T 12:279a17).

On the other hand, however, there are elements in Shandao's presentation that indicate that only the power of Amitābha's vow is capable of breaking through our evil natures and bringing about a truly pure cause within us. Although he exhorts practitioners to do good in accord with the Buddha's words and in 'the true mind', he also appears to take a stance that such pure good is genuinely impossible for human beings.

The passage on 'good tainted with poison' certainly seems to take that position, in that anything a human being possessed of ignorance, desire, and hatred might do is necessarily informed and shaped by that ignorance, desire, and hatred. Further, in his comment on the profound understanding that Śākyamuni holds is the centrepiece of faith in Amitābha, Shandao writes,

> There are two types [of profound understanding]. First one decisively and profoundly recognizes that one is an evil, ordinary being of birth and death who has for innumerable *kalpas* constantly been submerged, constantly transmigrating, entirely without a karmic condition leading to liberation. Second, one decisively and profoundly recognizes that the forty-eight vows of Amitābha embrace sentient beings so that when one without doubt or hesitation gives oneself over to the power of the vows, one will assuredly attain birth. (T 37:271a27–b2)

The first element of understanding presented here is that there is absolutely no karmic cause that one might create that would have the weight and the power to overcome the effects of the unwholesome karma piled up over the course of incalculable past lifetimes. From this passage, it seems that for Shandao simply acting in line with the moral standards laid out by Śākyamuni is not nearly enough to cancel out the effects of the karma created since time immemorial. The sheer weight of karmic circumstance is left virtually unaffected by such behaviour, and it is only something that is substantively different—the karmic purity realized in Amitābha's aeons of bodhisattva practice—that can affect it. Shandao here holds up the vows as the only effective counterweight to that karmic burden, which he presents as the sole avenue for escape from the bondage of karma.

We should note here that Shandao does not describe the necessity to rely on the vows as being the result of some sort of personal frailty or deficiency, that is, as an issue that would not be problematic for more advanced or skilled practitioners. The problem as he sees it lies in the very fabric of karmic bondage, the nature of the universe, and the nature of the human being within it. The use of the term 'karmic condition' rather than 'capacity' in the above passage indicates that clearly. When taken together with the passage on 'good tainted with poison' introduced above, Shandao seems to be intimating the complete ineffectuality of human action to bridge the karmic gap between the defiled and the pure, 'good tainted with poison' and the truly good, ignorant self-centredness and selfless, compassionate action. The second element of profound understanding indicates, however, that that gap does not need to be bridged by human action at all and that instead the working of Amitābha (particularly in the form of the name as chanted) serves to overcome it.

Although complicated by the introduction of the figure of Amitābha, structurally, the problem that Shandao is facing is extremely similar to the problem of the relationship between karmically conditioned action and unconditioned *nirvāṇa* that has come up in discussions of Buddhist ethics in recent years. The issue of whether karmic causes sown by human beings can really add up to *nirvāṇa*, which is said to be transcendent of karmic conditions, is a problem that cuts to the heart of any theory of praxis in Buddhism.

Shandao and other Pure Land thinkers have engaged with that question and offered answers that might be of interest for contemporary theorists of Buddhist ethics who are facing a similar problem now. Shandao's answer that although it is impossible for tainted human action to lead to genuine purity, the compassionate nature of the Tathāgata itself bridges that apparently unbridgeable gap, may also be of interest as one of the many solutions that Buddhists have traditionally offered as a solution to this problem.

The presentation of the Pure Land as a solution to the problem of karmic bondage neither starts nor ends with Shandao. Tanluan and Daochuo both devote considerable attention to it as well as to the criticisms of the idea raised by their contemporaries (e.g. T 1957, 47:10b12–12b1; see Inagaki 2014: 55–66 for an English translation). Their discussions, as well, might have something to contribute to the current debates. The above is far from an exhaustive presentation of the ideas that have some bearing on the issue of ethics in Chinese Pure Land Buddhism. Not only does it entirely ignore the Pure Land devotion that was incorporated within Chinese Buddhist schools that kept to the traditional views of practice, it only manages to point out one of many issues that relate to ethics within the exclusivist strand itself. The issue of the exclusion clause in the eighteenth vow and its interpretation by Chinese thinkers in particular deserves mention here. Tanluan takes up the problem (T 1819, 40:833c20–834c26), as does Shandao (T 1753, 37:277a22–277b11), each offering answers that stress the broad, non-discriminating nature of the vow itself while also seeing it as an admonition to maintain certain ethical norms and standards. These are all issues that could contribute to the field of Buddhist ethics that I sincerely hope might be explored in future scholarship.

As I stated at the outset of this section, Shandao does not resolve the tension between the requirements for ethical action as a prerequisite to liberation (in this case, as an element or expression of faith in Amitābha) and the liberative working of Amitābha's vows. Although the latter two passages introduced above indicate that he stretched that tension to its breaking point, he continued his exhortations for practitioners to engage sincerely in practice, including keeping precepts and certain ethical norms. These are not necessarily presented as essential for accessing the power of Amitābha's vows, but they are not disregarded entirely. Thus, some later Pure Land devotees, focusing on the message contained in passages like those presented in the first part of this section, took sustained engagement in moral improvement to be one of many elements of the Pure Land path, while others, such as Hōnen and especially Shinran, focused on the implications of the passages presented in the latter half, concluding that moral action was in no way a condition for coming into contact with the power of the vows and, given the self-centred and egoistic nature of human beings, could even serve as a hindrance to genuine liberation.[4] In the next section, we will consider how Shinran took hints from

[4] See Nasu (2006) for a description of how Shinran rewrites some of the passages introduced above by making creative translations of Shandao's Chinese into Japanese to indicate that Dharmākara's 'true mind' is bestowed on human beings through the working of Amitābha. Nasu's discussion shows how Shinran collapsed the tension between human action and attitudes and the working of Amitābha in Shandao's works by reading these passages as an expression of a pure faith that arises based on the other power of Amitābha.

Shandao to reconsider the way that the vow functions in this world, as well as the implications that his argument holds for scholars considering problems of Buddhist ethics.

Internalizing the Tension: Received Virtue, Non-Volitional Compassion, and Transformative Wisdom in Shinran's Thought

The ethical implications of Shinran's thought have, as I stated in the introduction, received the greatest amount of scholarly attention up to this point. The first and second chapters of Ugo Dessì's book provide a good overview of the various doctrinal issues and the primary source texts for the standpoints taken by contemporary advocates, as well as some insight into the shifts in ethical thinking that have occurred within the Shin institution throughout its history. Kenneth Tanaka's chapter in *Engaged Pure Land Buddhism* discusses in great detail the concept of 'constantly practising great compassion' and its relationship to 'repaying one's debt of gratitude', two benefits that, according to Shinran, accrue to the person who has attained faith. As these two concepts form the core of Shinran's answer to the question of how we should live in the world and have especially informed the Shin Buddhist social ethic through most of the history of the school, any attempt to grasp Shinran's ideas on ethics should begin with a reading of that piece.

The discussion of ethics in Shinran's thought has been complicated by the relative accessibility and widespread popularity of the *Tannishō*, a short tract written by Shinran's disciple Yuien that attributes some bold and very memorable statements to Shinran. To give but a few: 'I, Shinran, have not even a single disciple' (T 2661, 83:729b1–2). 'Since I am incapable of any religious practice, hell is my only home' (T 83:728c3–4). 'If even the good person is born in the Pure Land, how much more so the evil one' (T 83:728c16–17). 'We will do anything that karmic conditions prompt us to' (T 83:731c28–29).

These striking declarations have immense implications in the sphere of ethics and have captivated many of those who have presented aspects of Shinran's ethical viewpoint. Because of their very forcefulness and power as declarations, however, they have the tendency to shut off the possibility for discussion and mask some of Shinran's subtlety as a Buddhist thinker. Faced with these words, those who think they have some capacity for religious practice or performing good deeds are completely barred from the conversation.

Shinran's *Kyōgyōshinshō* is, in that sense, far more approachable, although not nearly as accessible and easy to read as the *Tannishō*. Since it is directed at a monastic audience, mainly members of other schools of Buddhism (unlike the *Tannishō*, which was written as a text to be read by lay and ordained followers within the Shin school), it is written with the conventions of Buddhist scholarship and discourse among schools in mind.

Therefore, when seeking for points of congruence and conversation with the broader discipline of Buddhist ethics, it seems advisable to focus on Shinran's thought as it is presented there (rather than the 'sound bites' that Yuien provides in the *Tannishō*).

In the *Kyōgyōshinshō*, Shinran collapses the tension between human action and the working of Dharmākara's vows by arguing that:

> Be it practice or faith, taken together, there is absolutely nothing that is not brought about by the fulfilment of the directing of virtue of the pure mind of the vow of Amida Tathāgata. There is no cause [for enlightenment] other than this cause. (T 2646, 83:603c27–29; CWS, vol. 1:93)

That is, Shinran holds that everything in human experience that leads to the attainment of enlightenment is the result of the working of Amitābha, and not of causes created by human endeavour. The bulk of the *Kyōgyōshinshō* is devoted to describing the way in which Amitābha's 'directing of virtue' serves to bring those who have received it to the realization of complete *nirvāṇa* at the instant before their death (T 83:609b18; CWS, vol. 1:123).

Put very simply, in this work Shinran is describing the transformative power of religious language—the teachings about Amitābha—to effect a change in the perspective and way of life of the person who listens to it at a profound level different from the conscious level of normal human volition and discursive thinking. He bases the crux of that argument on the fulfilment passages for the seventeenth and eighteenth vows that appear at the start of the second fascicle of the *Wuliangshoujing* which state that those who hear of the virtues of Amitābha and are moved to faith and joy by those teachings will immediately attain birth in the Pure Land and enter into the stage of non-retrogression (T 12:272b9–13; Inagaki 1995: 54; Gómez 1996: 187). Based on this passage, Shinran argues that the teachings about Amitābha's virtues (expressed most succinctly in the name) are the result of the working of the seventeenth vow in the world, while the faith that arises within human beings who hear those teachings is the result of the working of the eighteenth vow. This process of hearing and being moved (and changed) is what he calls 'the fulfilment of the directing of virtue of the pure mind of the vow' (T 83:603c28).

In order to make this argument and completely remove human volition (with its self-centred, poisoned nature and resultant incapacity to create something truly pure) from the equation for the realization of faith—for Shinran the 'true cause of realizing great *nirvāṇa*'—he radically reinterprets the basic Buddhist concept of directing of virtue (*ekō*; Skt *pariṇāma*), holding that human beings benefit from the virtues directed to them through the working of Amitābha. That directing of virtue primarily takes two forms: the teachings that describe Amitābha's virtues and the profound reaction that hearing those teachings brings forth in those who hear them (the internal arising of 'the mind of the vow' as the faith of human beings). We all understand how listening to someone speak or reading someone's work can profoundly affect the way that we look at the world and also, I think, how those recognitions and changes take place at a level more immediate than volition or discursive thinking.

In discussing the arising of faith as the result of the working of Amitābha, Shinran is pointing out this non-volitional element of having an insight and thereby removes human volition (tainted by self-centred greed) and human discursive thinking (tainted by ignorance) as a condition for attaining enlightenment. In doing so, however, Shinran moves the tension that we have seen from that between the works of human beings and the power of the vow apparent in the *Daiamituojing* and Shandao's works and sets it up as a tension between 'the mind of the vow' and the human beings' ordinary, 'poisoned' consciousness, in a sense internalizing it.

The Shin commentators I quoted in the introduction focus primarily on Shinran's denial of the efficacy of human volition and discursive thinking, but that seems to have squelched any further discussion of its ethical implications. Therefore, here I would like to point out that Shinran employs the idea of directing of virtue to make this argument. This term 'virtue', it seems to me, is quite pregnant with significance for the discussion of ethical issues, because it refers to the positive moral or spiritual qualities that are endowed to a person by merit of their practices. Strictly speaking, the Japanese *kudoku* corresponds to the Sanskrit *guṇa*, but is semantically broad enough to cover the Sanskrit *puṇya*, as well, such that it is often used as a translation for it (although the term *fukutoku* corresponds more closely with the latter). This concept of virtue appears to often be conceived as some sort of mystical spiritual capital housed in some great karmic bank account, such that 'directing of virtue' (or 'merit transference', as *ekō* is sometimes translated) is envisioned as a sort of bank transfer from one account to another. In Shinran's formulation, at least, *kudoku* has a far more concrete meaning than this sort of ephemeral karmic wealth, referring instead to the change in the character and capacities of the person who hears Amitābha's name.

In the chapter on faith in the *Kyōgyōshinshō*, Shinran lists ten benefits that are received by the person who has attained this faith that is brought about by the working of Amitābha's vows.[5] These ten benefits, and the exposition on the true disciple of the Buddha where Shinran fleshes them out based on a variety of scriptural passages (T 83:608b4–609c10), are Shinran's description of how the person of faith lives in this world. Because of Shinran's understanding of human volition and reason as necessarily poisoned by greed and ignorance, he would object to the framing of the question, 'How should we live in this world?'—arguing that any response we gave would be tainted by our limited perspectives and thus insufficient. However, in this portion of the *Kyōgyōshinshō*, he answers the question 'How does the person who has attained faith live in this world?' in great detail, providing many scriptural references that show how the non-volitional experience of insight that he calls faith transforms the life of the practitioner. These passages have traditionally served as a point of reference for answering that question and thus I will touch on a few of them in the following.

[5] They are: (1) to be protected by unseen powers, (2) to be endowed with supreme virtues, (3) to have evil transformed into good, (4) to be protected by all buddhas, (5) to be praised by all buddhas, (6) to be protected by the light of Amitābha's mind, (7) to have great joy, (8) to know one's debt of gratitude and repay the virtue received, (9) to constantly practise great compassion, (10) to enter the stage of definite assurance. T. 83:607b21–26; see CWS, vol. 1:112.

The second benefit that he lists is 'to be endowed with supreme virtues' (T 83:607b22). For Shinran, the insights brought about from listening to the teachings about Amitābha's virtues bring about those same virtues within the practitioner. The Pure Land scriptures are filled with praise of the various positive spiritual qualities that Amitābha and his Pure Land possess. The implication of this benefit and Shinran's use of the term 'directing of virtue' to describe Amitābha's working in this world in general is that those positive spiritual qualities (loving-kindness, compassion, non-discrimination, human fellowship, and so on) are expressed in people who have attained faith. They do not become operative on the level of volition and self-awareness, which would 'poison' them with self-centred ignorance, but instead function at a more fundamental level, closer to that of character traits and attitude towards the world.

That is, listening to the teachings about Amitābha and his Pure Land and what is truly good and valuable there, leads to a (less-than-volitional) reorganization of values within practitioners that informs their behaviour in this world. By hearing and being moved by the teachings about Amitābha and the ideal bodhisattva Dharmākara, listeners come to take those values for their own, as something to be sought after and cherished, not so much at the level of conscious striving, but more as a set of presuppositions about what is good that informs and permeates their actions. The 'distinctive personal character' that Lewis and Amstutz discovered in their 'anthropological observation' in fact is firmly rooted within Shinran's doctrinal system, in this concept of being endowed with virtue. When framed in the terms in which Shinran frames it, however, it can at least be seen as existing on the same general plane as other discussions of karma and virtue in Buddhist ethics. A consideration of the points of intersection and disconnect between those sets of ideas would certainly be welcome.

Among the ten benefits of attaining faith, Shinran also lists 'constantly practising great compassion' (*jōgyō daihi*, T 83:607b25; CWS, vol. 1:112) and 'knowing one's debt of gratitude and repaying the virtue received' (*chion hōtoku*, T 83:607b24–25; CWS, vol. 1:112). Kenneth Tanaka has already discussed these two, and their sources in the works of Daochuo and Shandao that Shinran quotes in the *Kyōgyōshinshō*, so I will not consider them at length here. Suffice it to say that the person with faith is said to live in such a way as to express a sort of non-volitional compassion in their every act.

While this may be difficult to imagine, Shinran, quoting Daochuo, describes it concretely saying, 'Those who encourage each other, one after the next, to say the *nenbutsu* are all called people who practise great compassion' (T 83:608c21–22; CWS, vol. 1:119). That is, those who constantly praise the name of Amitābha and his various virtues, encouraging others to do the same, function as agents of great compassion. Shinran further defines 'repaying one's debt of gratitude' to be causing that 'great compassion to transform others universally', by presenting a creative interpretation of a passage by Shandao (T 83:609a1–2; CWS, vol. 1:120). The other point to note here is the use of the term *hōtoku*. It indicates that the person who has received the virtues of Amitābha responds in kind, repaying the debt incurred with virtues, or virtuous action.

Yet we must also keep in mind that Shinran presents all of these as benefits of faith. That is, he says that they are natural outgrowths of the experience of listening to and being moved by the teachings. They are not at all conditions of faith, but instead are the consequences of it which arise not based on human volition, but through the pure working of Amitābha's virtues within the human being.

The new form of tension between Amitābha's working and human action that is set up in Shinran's works creates a very delicate situation where Shinran calls the person of faith 'equal to Maitreya' on one page (T 83:609b17–19) of the *Kyōgyōshinshō* and literally two pages later laments,

> How sad I, foolish, stubble-headed Shinran, am! Drowning in the vast ocean of lust, lost in the great mountain of seeking fame and profit, I take no joy in having entered the company of the rightly settled, am not pleased by approaching the realization of true enlightenment. (T 83:609c11–13; see CWS, vol. 1:125)

From the perspective of having received the virtues of Amitābha and the working of the vow, Shinran can be said to be an agent of great compassion and Maitreya's equal, assured of attaining complete *nirvāṇa* at the moment of death, but on the level of his self-awareness, his self as it appears to his ordinary, daily consciousness (his discursive mind, if you will) is consumed with self-centred greed and desire.

This duality and the tension created by it are key elements of Shinran's thought. Although they greatly complicate any discussion of ethical issues in the Shin tradition, they also create the possibility for a process of dynamic, self-reflective spiritual growth and development that continues throughout the life of the practitioner. Neither the 'mind of the vow' nor 'the ordinary, defiled mind' completely takes precedence. Instead Amitābha's virtues gradually and gently reshape the ordinary mind and orient it towards the values expressed there.

Lastly, I would like introduce another one of the benefits of faith that seems to have great importance for the issue of Buddhist ethics but has not yet been touched upon in previous scholarship: 'the benefit of transforming evil into good' (*ten'aku jōzen no yaku*, T 83:607b22–23; CWS, vol. 1:112). In the preface of the *Kyōgyōshinshō*, Shinran writes, 'The wonderful name endowed perfectly with ultimate virtues is the true wisdom that transforms evil into virtue' (T 83: 589a9–10). Again, in the chapter on practice, he quotes *Lebangwenlei* saying, 'As one grain of an alchemist's potion will change iron and make it gold, a single word of truth will transform evil karma and turn it into good karma.'

In both of these passages, Shinran writes that Amitābha's name and the wisdom expressed therein has the power to reassign karmic value from negative to positive (for a discussion of Shinran's view of the transformative power of wisdom, see Conway 2015). This indicates that Shinran was far from rigidly deterministic about the value assigned to specific acts, but instead took a much more fluid view of the nature of good and evil. When seen in the light of Amitābha's wisdom, the significance of specific acts can be transformed, such that there is no definitely 'evil act' that will necessarily bring about an 'evil result'. The perspective afforded by the Buddha's wisdom (a wisdom of non-discrimination that sees there is no inherent nature in anything) can turn actions that seemed decidedly evil into something with positive karmic significance.

Shinran's attention to the story of Prince Ajātaśatru, who killed his father and plotted to depose Śākyamuni from his role as head of the Buddhist community (two of the five heinous acts prohibited in the eighteenth vow), is of particular interest in this regard. Shinran quotes at length the portion of the *Nirvāṇa Sūtra* that describes how Ajātaśatru is transformed from trembling in fear at falling into hell as the result of his sins to declaring that he would gladly go to hell to save the beings stuck there upon listening to Śākyamuni's sermon (T 83:609c23–614c9; he expresses his willingness to go to hell at T 83:613a26–27). Through Ajātaśatru's encounter with the Buddha's wisdom, the evil deed of killing his father is transformed from a source of pain and fear in the present over the promise of *kalpa*s of agony in the most horrific of hells, and into an opportunity for compassionate action. Shinran's view of this transformative power of the Buddha's wisdom is grounded firmly in the Mahāyāna understanding of the nature of wisdom and so seems to have implications for the broader field of Buddhist ethics as a whole, particularly in discussions of karma, because it forces us to question if, from the perspective of the wisdom of emptiness, one can really determine anything to be definitively and definitely 'bad karma' or 'evil action'.

In sum, Shinran's thought has much potential to speak to the current discussions of Buddhist ethics, although that potential has barely begun to be explored. Shinran is very much concerned with issues of good and evil, right and wrong, and has offered one response to those issues that is steeped in Buddhist thought and tradition. As the field of Buddhist ethics as a normative, reflective enterprise in the West develops towards maturity, it could be much benefited by engagement with the ideas of a thinker like Shinran, who has devoted considerable attention to careful reflection into matters such as karma, virtue, and the transformative power of the Buddha's wisdom.

Conclusion

As we have seen, the Pure Land tradition is marked by a tension between the liberative power of Amitābha and the human being who receives that power. This tension complicates and colours the consideration of ethical issues within the tradition in a variety of ways. In a sense, the complicating factor of Amitābha adds a richness to the reflections on issues of ethics and human responsibility made by representatives of the tradition. In particular, it allows them to consider with an unflinching gaze the human capacity for genuinely realizing the bodhisattva ideal of compassion in the face of the burdens of karma.

As I have said, the above is only a small sampling of ideas from just one portion of what is a very broad tradition. My treatment in this limited space fails to do justice even to Shandao or Shinran, let alone the rest of the tradition. The development of ethical thought within the Shin tradition after Shinran's passing is an important issue that has been addressed to a degree in previous scholarship, but the position on ethical issues of figures like Rennyo (1415–1499), a descendent of Shinran whose thought was of almost equal importance through much of Shin history, and Kiyozawa Manshi, a Shin modern thinker whose ideas set the tone for doctrinal studies in the Ōtani-ha especially after World War II (see Rogers and Rogers 1996; Blum and Rhodes 2011: 77–91; Haneda 2014: 33–39), has yet to be addressed adequately. The ideas of Soga Ryōjin (1875–1971), a disciple of Kiyozawa's, about the nature and function of past karma and its relationship to human responsibility are yet another subject that could add something to the general discussion on Buddhist ethics (see Blum and Rhodes 2011: 139–156).

This chapter has ended up a laundry list of possible subjects for future research, for, as I stated at the outset, the conversation between Pure Land ideas and the broader discipline of Buddhist ethics is just beginning. Since, like our contemporary Buddhist ethicists, the thinkers in the Pure Land tradition struggled intensely with the implications of Indian Buddhist concepts for their lives and proffered what seemed to them to be genuinely Buddhist solutions, their ideas may help in thinking through some of the problems facing the field today. Although the texts are quite challenging—almost baroque in complexity—thanks to the efforts of scholars like Inagaki Hisao and Dennis Hirota, most of them are available in English translation. I hope that scholars with an interest in such problems will turn to them as a resource. Although they do not have a simple list of dos and don'ts, they clearly have something to offer those willing to grapple with them—and with the complexity of human experience.

Works Cited

Ama Toshimaro (2001) Towards a Shin Buddhist social ethics. *The Eastern Buddhist*, 33 (2), 35–51.

Ama Toshimaro (2002) Shin Buddhism and economic ethics. *The Eastern Buddhist*, 34 (2), 25–50.

Blum, M. L. (1988) Kiyozawa Manshi and the meaning of Buddhist ethics. *The Eastern Buddhist*, 21 (1), 61–81.

Blum, M. L., and Rhodes, R. F. (2011) *Cultivating spirituality: a modern Shin Buddhist anthology*. Albany: State University of New York Press.

Conway, M. J. (2015) Medicinal metaphors in a soteriology of transformation: Shinran's view of the power of the *nenbutsu*. *Ōtani daigaku Shinshū sōgō kenkyūjo kiyō*, 33, 13–25.

Dessì, U. (2007) *Ethics and society in contemporary Shin Buddhism*. Berlin: Lit Verlag.

Gibbs, G. (1998) Existentializing and radicalizing Shinran's vision by repositioning it at the center of Mahayana tradition. In: K. K. Tanaka and E. Nasu (eds), *Engaged Pure Land Buddhism: essays in honor of Professor Alfred Bloom*. Berkeley: WisdomOcean Publications, 267–315.

Gómez, L. O. (1996) *The land of bliss: the paradise of the Buddha of measureless light*. Honolulu: University of Hawai'i Press.

Haneda, N. (trans.) (2014) *December fan: the Buddhist essays of Manshi Kiyozawa*. Second edition. Los Angeles: Shinshu Center of America.

Inagaki, Z. H. (trans.) (2014) *Collection of passages on the land of peace and bliss: AN LE CHI by Tao-ch'o*. Singapore: Horai Association International.

Ishihara, J. S. (1987) A Shin Buddhist social ethics. *The Pure Land*, 3, 14–33.
Jones, C. B. (2003) Foundations of ethics and practice in Chinese Pure Land Buddhism. *Journal of Buddhist ethics*, 10, 1–20.
Johnston, G. L. (1991) Morality versus religion in late Meiji society: Kiyozawa Manshi. *Japanese religions*, 16, 4, 32–48.
Kasulis, T. P. (2001) Shin Buddhist ethics in our postmodern age of *mappō*. *The Eastern Buddhist*, 33, 1, 16–17.
Lewis, S. J., and Amstutz, G. (1997) Teleologized 'virtue' or mere religious 'character'? A critique of Buddhist ethics from the Shin Buddhist point of view. *Journal of Buddhist ethics*, 4, 138–159.
Main, J. L. (2012) 'Only Shinran will not betray us': Takeuchi Ryō'on (1891–1967), the Ōtani-ha administration, and burakumin. PhD dissertation, McGill University.
Nasu, E. (2006) 'Rely on the meaning, not on the words': Shinran's methodology and strategy for reading scriptures and writing the *Kyōgyōshinshō*. In: R. K. Payne and T. D. Leighton (eds), *Discourse and ideology in medieval Japanese Buddhism*, 240–258. New York: Routledge.
Nogami S. (1970) *Chūgoku jōdo sanso den*. Kyoto: Bun'eidō.
Pye, M. (1989) The source and direction of ethical requirements in Shin Buddhism. *The Pure Land*, 6, 165–177.
Rambelli, F. (2004) 'Just behave as you like; prohibitions and impurities are not a problem': radical Amida cults and popular religiosity in premodern Japan. In: R. K. Payne and K. K. Tanaka (eds), *Approaching the land of bliss: religious praxis in the cult of Amitābha*. Honolulu: University of Hawai'i Press, 169–201.
Rogers, A. T., and. Rogers, M. L. (1996) *Rennyo shōnin ofumi: the letters of Rennyo*. Berkeley: Numata Center of Buddhist Translation and Research.
Shigaraki, T. (2001) The problem of the true and the false in contemporary Shin Buddhist studies: true Shin Buddhism and false Shin Buddhism. *Pacific world*, 3, 27–52.
Shigaraki, T. (2009) *Shinjin* and social praxis in Shinran's thought. *Pacific world*, 11, 193–217.
Sugiyama, S. J. (1998) The essence of Shinran's teaching: understanding to praxis. In: K. K. Tanaka and E. Nasu (eds), *Engaged Pure Land Buddhism: essays in honor of Professor Alfred Bloom*. Berkeley: WisdomOcean Publications, 285–315.
Tanaka, K. K. (1989) Ethics in American Jodo-Shinshū: trans-ethical responsibility. *The Pure Land*, 6, 91–116.
Tanaka, K. K. (1998) Concern for others in Pure Land soteriological and ethical considerations: a case study of *Jōgyō daihi* in Jōdo Shinshū Buddhism. In: K. K. Tanaka and E. Nasu (eds), *Engaged Pure Land Buddhism: essays in honor of Professor Alfred Bloom*. Berkeley: WisdomOcean Publications, 88–110.
Taniguchi, S. M. (1999) Examination of the meaning of ethics and practice in Jodo Shinshū: a critical and practical examination from the Nikaya textual point of view. *The Pure Land*, 16, 147–171.
Tokunaga, M., and Bloom, A. (2000) Toward a pro-active engaged Shin Buddhism: a reconsideration of the teaching of the two truths (*shinzoku-nitai*). *Pacific world*, 2, 191–206.
Unno, M. T. (1998) Shin Buddhist social thought in modern Japan. In: K. K. Tanaka and E. Nasu (eds), *Engaged Pure Land Buddhism: essays in honor of Professor Alfred Bloom*. Berkeley: WisdomOcean Publications, 67–87.
Zotz, V. (1989) Shin Buddhism and the search for new ethics in the West. *The Pure Land*, 6, 117–126.

Suggested Reading

Ama Toshimaro (2001) Towards a Shin Buddhist social ethics. *The Eastern Buddhist*, 33 (2), 35–51.

Blum, Mark L. (1988) Kiyozawa Manshi and the meaning of Buddhist ethics. *The Eastern Buddhist*, 21 (1), 61–81.

Dessì, Ugo. (2007) *Ethics and society in contemporary Shin Buddhism*. Berlin: Lit Verlag.

Kasulis, Thomas P. (2001) Shin Buddhist ethics in our postmodern age of *mappō*. *The Eastern Buddhist*, 33 (1), 16–17.

Lewis, Stephen J., and Amstutz, G. (1997) Teleologized 'virtue' or mere religious 'character'? A critique of Buddhist ethics from the Shin Buddhist point of view. *Journal of Buddhist ethics*, 4, 138–159.

Pye, M. (1989) The source and direction of ethical requirements in Shin Buddhism. *The Pure Land*, 6, 165–177.

Tanaka, Kenneth K., and E. Nasu, eds (1998) *Engaged Pure Land Buddhism: essays in honor of Professor Alfred Bloom*. Berkeley: WisdomOcean Publications.

CHAPTER 10

A PERSPECTIVE ON ETHICS IN THE *LOTUS SŪTRA*

GENE REEVES

Introduction

The *Lotus Sūtra* has been central to East Asian Buddhism from the very beginning of the reception of Buddhist teachings in China, Korea, and Japan. It is a tradition whose historical and contemporary importance is so great that to claim to have an understanding of Buddhism without taking it into account is to make extremely light of the empirical realities of Buddhism—of what Buddhism actually is. The *Lotus Sūtra* perspective is only a perspective, but it is an extremely important, even essential, one for understanding Buddhism as a whole. Though usually called 'The Lotus Sutra' in English, this text never calls itself that, nor is that term used in Chinese or Japanese to refer to the sutra. The full name, in the most widely used Chinese version, word for word, is 'Wonderful Dharma Lotus Flower Sutra', *Miao-fa-lian-hua jing*, pronounced in Japanese *Myō-hō-ren-ge-kyō*. The shortened version of the title most often used in the text is *Fa-hua jing*, *Hō-ke-kyō* in Japanese. In English this is 'Dharma Flower Sutra'.

In my view at least, the *Lotus Sūtra* is primarily a storybook. Though it certainly makes doctrinal claims from time to time, and cannot avoid making philosophical, even metaphysical, assumptions, it is not its purpose to provide a systematic view of anything. Although it is a very ethical book, one that it is driven by ethical concerns, it contains nothing even approximating a systematic ethics. This means that its perspective is not easily pinned down. Though vitally concerned about ethical behaviour, its views of ethics is not captured by traditional Western philosophical categorizations of ethical theories in part because it utilizes more than one perspective.

The *Lotus Sūtra* is primarily soteriological. By this I mean simply that its primary concern is neither understanding nor obedience, but salvation. Running through the text like a red thread, holding it all together and making it whole, is the conviction that anyone can become a buddha, the highest possible attainment. Especially by those who tend to love abstractions, this is often expressed as a doctrine of universal buddha nature. But what the *Lotus Sūtra* really cares about is not an abstract notion about 'everybody'; it is concerned about the realization of the buddha nature in each of us. Anyone, it says, can be a buddha, especially you.

Here, buddha nature should not be thought to be some sort of homunculus or being within us. In the *Lotus Sūtra* what is affirmed is the possibility of becoming a buddha. Given enough lifetimes, that possibility, like any other, can be seen as an inevitability. Another thing that is important to know about the *Lotus Sūtra* is that it does not shy away from being highly unconventional. Since the *Lotus Sūtra* has been very popular in East Asian Buddhism and is associated with Mahāyāna teachings, it is easy to forget how unconventional some of its teachings actually are, or at least were.

In chapter 11, the Buddha Abundant Treasures suddenly arises in his great stupa to praise Śākyamuni Buddha for preaching the *Lotus Sūtra*, and before long the two are sitting together in Abundant Treasures Buddha's stupa. This story is used in part to persuade people that a deceased, even extinct, buddha from the past can be very much alive in the present. And thus, Śākyamuni Buddha, though having entered into final *nirvāṇa*, can be alive in the present. To make this point, the *Sūtra* simply ignores the tradition that says that two buddhas cannot be alive and present in the same place at the same time.

In chapter 12, a young girl, a dragon at that, proves that a girl can become a buddha quickly by doing so in the face of conventional objections by the leading *śrāvaka* and a prominent bodhisattva, thus denying the conventional Buddhist wisdom that women are not eligible to become buddhas. Also in chapter 12, Devadatta, the cousin of Śākyamuni Buddha and known throughout the Buddhist world as an epitome of evil, is told by the Buddha that he, too, is to become a buddha, thus rejecting or ignoring conventional teachings about the existence of beings who are evil beyond redemption.

Everyone knows that credentials are very important in Buddhism and Buddhist organizations. In Theravāda Buddhism, in Buddhism based on Chinese texts, in Tibetan style Buddhism, even in new forms of Japanese Buddhism, one has to be credentialed in order to be recognized as any kind of leader, even to be a proper *Dharma* teacher. But in chapter 10 of the *Lotus Sūtra*, it is said very clearly that anyone can be teacher of buddha *Dharma*, including, equally clearly, women. Though now not terribly surprising, this teaching was very unconventional when it first appeared in this sutra, and has largely been ignored since.

There are many other cases in which the *Lotus Sūtra* either ignores or makes light of traditional Buddhist teachings. Everyone knows, for example, that buddhas and bodhisattvas are distinct and different, that a bodhisattva is, like Maitreya in his Tuṣita Heaven, waiting to be a buddha or at least is not yet a buddha. Yet, the *Lotus Sūtra* does not hesitate to say that both Wonderful Voice (Skt Gadgadasvara; Ch. 妙音) and Guanyin[1] bodhisattvas manifest themselves as buddhas, in an important way making

[1] Avalokiteśvara (Ch. 觀世音), Regarder of the Cries of the World. In Chinese this name is often shortened to Guanyin or Kuanyin and in Japanese to Kannon. While the exact meaning of Avalokiteśvara is controversial, the Chinese/Japanese name literally means 'perceiver of the world's sounds'. The name is

light of the distinction. If a bodhisattva can appear as a buddha, or a buddha as a bodhisattva, what is left of the distinction beyond a formal difference?

It has been thought that when the *Lotus Sūtra* ignores or makes very light of a traditional teaching it does so only because it assumes such teachings. So, for example, it has been widely assumed that traditional Buddhist ethics is deontological, based exclusively or at least largely on precepts. It can be argued that if the *Lotus Sūtra* pays little attention to precepts, it is only because it assumes their efficacy and appropriateness. Thus, it can be claimed that the *Lotus Sūtra*, like the sutras that preceded it, indeed like all Buddhist ethics, is deontological and precept based. Thus we can find scholars claiming that the *Lotus Sūtra* teaches what it does not say. It is hard to argue definitively against such views, but I think that to understand what the *Lotus Sūtra* has to say about ethics, we had better look at what the *Sūtra* itself says, and particularly at what the parables and other stories in the *Lotus Sūtra* have to say about ethical behaviour.

I say 'ethical behaviour' because I think that ultimately that is what ethics has to be concerned with. Ethics consists primarily of teachings about how human beings should behave. It is not primarily about theories, about whether behaviour should be based on deontological or utilitarian or virtue assumptions or theories. Accordingly, the ethics of the *Lotus Sūtra* does not offer a theory about how to be good. It has, rather, some ideas and recommendations about how to be good, ideas and recommendations that are not always well integrated in a single theory or even perspective. It can, for example, advocate the utility of traditional precepts, without having such precepts be fundamental to its perspective.

The Ethical Perspectives of the *Lotus Sūtra*

It can be said that the ethics of the *Lotus Sūtra* is patriarchal; that is, that it is an ethics of father knows best. There is good reason for this. In the *Sūtra* there are parables of a father and his children, or a father and his son, or a father-like king. They begin with what is probably the most famous of the parables of the *Lotus Sūtra*, the story of the father who draws his children from a burning house with the promise of vehicles. They include the Parable of the Rich Father and His Poor Son, which comprises chapter 4, the Parable of the Good Physician, and perhaps to some extent the Parable of the Jewel in the Topknot. In these stories, a father figure, usually an actual father, is the one who knows best and in his wisdom finds ways, generally skilful means, to have the child or children follow his way and benefit from it. In none of these stories is there a wife or mother or even a hint of a woman of any kind.

also translated as World-Voice-Perceiver, Perceiver of the World's Sounds, He Who Observes the Sounds of the World, and so on.

These are parables of course, and in them the father figure is always also the Buddha. Here, father knows best is also Buddha knows best. Even when the protagonist is not a father per se, there are stories in the *Sūtra* in which one figure plays a fatherly, authoritative role, such as the story of the fantastic castle-city in which a group of exhausted pilgrims are basically rescued by an enlightened guide. Even the story of Devadatta has an element of this, as the Buddha knows what Devadatta does not. As is the case so often in stories of the Buddha's former lives, this story portrays a king who benefits greatly from the wisdom of a seer who would later become Devadatta. Having great wisdom, the Buddha can proclaim, despite what anyone else may think, that Devadatta will become a buddha.

The ethics throughout these stories is decidedly patriarchal. Accordingly, to do good is to follow the Buddha's teachings. This would be the ethics of the *Lotus Sūtra* if these stories were the whole story. Clearly, they are not.

King Wonderfully Adorned

To begin with, we have the interesting but largely ignored story of King Wonderfully Adorned and his family, in chapter 27, almost at the end of the *Lotus Sūtra*. In this story, the king, which makes him in part a buddha figure, is led by his two sons to follow the buddha of his time and place, leading him to declare much later to the Buddha that his two sons are his good friends because he has learned much from them. These two sons persuade both the king and his wife that they should all leave home and follow the Buddha. Thus, this story is the very opposite of patriarchal. The sons teach their father and persuade their father and mother to follow the Buddha. Moreover, the mother, Queen Pure Virtue, plays a very important role in this story. It is she who persuades the sons to respectfully impress and persuade their father. It is she who is a kind of linchpin of this family and plays a central, even quietly authoritative role among the men.

We might conclude that this story just does not fit in with the previous ones. And it is true that at least with respect to patriarchy it does not. But another, perhaps more useful, perspective would see this story as a sort of capping story, one that puts the stories of the *Lotus Sūtra* as a whole into a different perspective, a perspective which is non-patriarchal and perhaps even anti-patriarchal.

The Dragon Princess

From one of the least noticed stories in the *Lotus Sūtra* we turn to what is probably the most popular story in the *Sūtra*, the story of the dragon princess who becomes a buddha very quickly. In the *Sūtra*'s current configuration, this story appears in chapter 12, the

Devadatta chapter. There are complications and differences in its interpretation, but the main story line and the purpose of the story are reasonably clear.

The main character is a young girl. She is a dragon princess, but both in the story and outside of it, no one has been much concerned either about her being a princess or about her being a non-human dragon. And in East Asian Buddhist art, so far as I know, she is always portrayed as a human. What is of concern, both in the story and in its interpretations, is that she is young and inexperienced, and therefore incapable of becoming a buddha quickly, and especially that she is a girl, a female, and therefore incapable of becoming a buddha at all. The clear purpose of including this story in the *Lotus Sūtra*, possibly as a relatively late addition, is to teach that even women can become buddhas.

But for our purposes there is another very interesting aspect of the story. In the story, two men, the Bodhisattva Accumulated Wisdom and the *Śrāvaka* Śāriputra, are portrayed as representatives of bodhisattvas and *śrāvaka*s, that is, of monks, and, probably by extension, of men in general. They are highly regarded senior monks, albeit of different kinds. At the climax of the story, the young girl hands a valuable jewel to the Buddha and he readily accepts it. She then turns to these two male elders and asks them whether the Buddha has accepted the jewel quickly or not. And when they answer in the affirmative, she instructs them to use their special eyes and watch her become a buddha even more quickly. They do—and are amazed.

An important point here is that this young girl teaches these two senior men. She teaches them not merely in the sense of saying something to them, but actually transforms their understanding by showing them that a young girl can become a buddha and can do so quickly.

What has become of patriarchal ethics here? While we certainly can say that some of the stories in the *Lotus Sūtra* display a patriarchal ethics, it is clear that this is not true of the whole *Sūtra*, nor, one can easily think, of the *Sūtra* as a whole.

Other Examples

There are other stories and passages in the *Lotus Sūtra* where good behaviour cannot be interpreted either as being based on precepts or rules or as patriarchal. One that comes immediately to mind is the long popular story of Never Disrespectful Bodhisattva found in chapter 20. This monk, we are told, did not devote himself to reading or reciting sutras, but simply went around telling everyone he met that he would never, ever, disrespect them, and that they too would become buddhas. And, the story insists, Never Disrespectful Bodhisattva was not only respectful towards other men, and other monks, and seniors, and superiors; he was equally respectful to everyone that he met. No patriarchy here.

Another example of where patriarchal ethics is impossible might be found in the Dharma Teachers chapter. Here the Buddha points to the vast assembly before him, an assembly that includes monks and nuns, men and women, as well as others, and he tells Medicine King Bodhisattva that if any of them rejoices for even a single moment from hearing even a single verse of the *Sūtra*, they will become buddhas. Throughout this chapter, great care has been taken to use language that includes both men and women.

Finally, there are the stories late in the *Sūtra* of Wonderful Voice Bodhisattva and Guanyin Bodhisattva. These stories are basically about where we can encounter these bodhisattvas. The story and character of Wonderful Voice has not been very important historically, but Guanyin, and this chapter of the *Sūtra*, have played an enormously significant role in the history and development of East Asian Buddhism, and even in current developments of American Buddhism (for an excellent account of the influence of Guanyin on East Asian, especially Chinese, Buddhism, see Yü 2001). Though it is not uncommon for devotees to treat Guanyin as a kind of god who answers the prayers of those in trouble, I believe that the more important purpose of this story is to teach us where we can encounter or see Guanyin. And included in the places where Guanyin can be embodied and seen are the bodies and persons of women and girls of several kinds. Since we are told that Guanyin can also be the Buddha, and we know that for many people she has been, and still today is, the Buddha, we should understand that we, or anyone, can encounter the Buddha in our grandmother or in the little girl across the aisle.

Here too the authors of the text seem to have taken some care to ensure that we understand that the Buddha can be found in female as well as male forms. It should come as no surprise that that the most common figure in Chinese Buddhist art is a female Guanyin. Here too, then, we are a long way from any kind of patriarchal ethics.

We might also want to take note of the fact that in none of these stories, all of which are about ethical behaviour, is anyone admonished to follow Buddhist precepts. So, while parts of the *Lotus Sūtra* definitely are patriarchal, there are parts that definitely are not. So, if the ethics of the *Lotus Sūtra* is neither deontological nor patriarchal, what is it?

The Bodhisattva Way

Climbing the stairway to the Great Sacred Hall of Risshō Kōsei-kai in Tokyo, glancing up you can see magnificent paintings of three of the most familiar Mahāyāna bodhisattvas. On the right, riding on his lion and symbolizing wisdom, is Mañjuśrī. On the left, mounted on a cow and symbolizing compassion, is Maitreya. And in the centre, riding his white elephant with six tusks, is Universal Sage Bodhisattva,[2] symbolizing the embodiment of wisdom and compassion in everyday life.

The wisdom of Mañjuśrī is not to be understood as something highly esoteric and abstract, but rather as something closer to intelligence. It includes practical knowledge, knowledge of how to do things that can be helpful to others, including highly developed

[2] Samantabhadra (Ch. Puxian), also translated as Universal Worthy, Universally Worthy, Universal Virtue, and so on.

skills such as brain surgery or psychological insight into the behaviour and motivation of others. The wisdom of a bodhisattva, in other words, is useful, practical wisdom.

But a bodhisattva needs to be more than just wise. One could be wise sitting in a cave somewhere, not utilizing wisdom at all. A bodhisattva is moved by compassion for others. Bodhisattva wisdom is not cold and detached, but driven by a genuine, deeply felt desire to help others that is rooted in a profound sense of togetherness with others. Still, if intelligence and compassion are not embodied in some concrete ways, they do not amount to much. Universal Sage can be called a 'sage' because he is both wise and good. He represents the ideal of making the bodhisattva way alive in everyday actions and relationships.

There are, of course, many ways to symbolize such things. If you go around or through the Great Sacred Hall and enter the great hall of the Horinkaku, the Dharma-wheel Hall, you will be in the presence of still another of the great Mahāyāna bodhisattvas: Guanyin, the Regarder of the Cries of the World.

This magnificent statue of Guanyin, a so-called 'Guanyin of a Thousand Hands', was introduced to me on my first visit to Tokyo by the founder of Risshō Kōsei-kai, Nikkyō Niwano. Each of the thousand hands, here as usual represented by forty-two hands, holds a tool or symbol of some skill or special ability. Sometimes Guanyin is treated by the devout as a kind of god, and the powers she holds in her hands are understood to be powers with which she can help those in trouble. But, Niwano told me, a bodhisattva should not be treated as a god who can do favours for us; rather a bodhisattva should be seen as a model of what we can be. If Guanyin has a thousand different skills with which people can be helped, he said, this means that we should develop a thousand skills for helping other people!

Like Mañjuśrī, Maitreya, and Universal Sage in the front of the Great Sacred Hall, Guanyin is understood to have deep compassion and intelligent wisdom. And, since this statue is standing, it symbolizes the embodiment, the putting to work, of intelligence and compassion in our everyday lives.

Risshō Kōsei-kai's 'Members' Vow' says, 'We pledge ourselves to follow the bodhisattva way, to bring peace to our families, communities, and countries, and to the world'. Thus the ethics of the *Lotus Sūtra* is understood, at least in Risshō Kōsei-kai, as an ethics of compassionate action to bring peace to individuals, families, communities, and, finally, to the world. Thus, the ethics of the *Sūtra* is taken to be teleological, with the highest good understood to be world peace.

Helping Others

In the West it is often said that a bodhisattva is someone who is able to enter the bliss of *nirvāṇa* but postpones his own happiness in order to return to the world to help others selflessly. Such an idea of postponing *nirvāṇa* is definitely not found in the *Lotus Sūtra*, nor in any other sutra of which I am aware. In the *Lotus Sūtra*, a bodhisattva is one who is wise enough to know that he or she cannot be saved unless everyone is. A bodhisattva, in other words, is well aware of the interconnectedness and interdependence of all things. He or she is not completely selfless, but is intelligent and compassionate, and, therefore, continues to work in the world to help others.

Helping others, however, should not be taken to be only a matter of helping individuals with their personal problems, though that is very important. The *Lotus Sūtra* repeatedly speaks of bodhisattva practice as two things: transforming individuals and purifying lands. In other words, we should recognize that people are profoundly affected by their social and natural environments. This, I believe, is one important reason why Founder Niwano gave so much importance to working for world peace, becoming among other things a founder of Religions for Peace and leading other Japanese religious leaders into interfaith organizations.

Nowadays, thanks to Thich Nhat Hanh, Sulak Sivaraksa, and others, there is an international Engaged Buddhism movement in which Buddhist teachings and practices are related not only to individual issues but as well to issue of common or social or political import. From the perspective of the *Lotus Sūtra* this is as it should be, but we should not assume from it that we can first have a Buddhism that is not socially engaged and then add social engagement as a kind of secondary or tertiary matter. From the perspective of the *Lotus Sūtra*, Buddhism is necessarily socially engaged.

It is not the case, however, that the *Lotus Sūtra* was seen as having social and political import only in the modern period. In much of premodern China from time to time there were groups who rebelled against the established order, often going by such titles as 'White Lotus Teachings'. But such movements were led by illiterate peasants and virtually all that we know of them was written by literate monks and laymen who despised and denigrated them.

In Japan as well, especially towards the end of the Tokugawa era, there were 'pilgrimages of thanksgiving' that embodied passive resistance to the feudal regime and sometimes turned into riots and outright rebellions against social and political authority. Marked by ecstatic religious frenzy, such movements or uprisings were highly disorganized, but were clearly related to Nichiren, and thereby to the *Lotus Sūtra*. To some degree such passion for social reform carried over into new religious movements such as Risshō Kōsei-kai, which is heavily influenced both by Tendai and Nichiren Buddhism, and takes the *Lotus Sūtra* as its foundational text.

Buddhist Practice

Somewhere along the way—I do not know where and how—for many people, Buddhist 'practice' came to be closely associated with meditation, or even defined as meditation. Meditation is one of India's great gifts to humanity. It can do wonders for all sorts of human conditions. Probably most people could benefit from practising it. And because it was during meditation that the Buddha became awakened, it has special importance for Buddhists. But there is nothing peculiarly Buddhist about meditation. And the vast majority of people who regard themselves as Buddhist never meditate. For them, Buddhist practice may be many things, but it is not primarily meditation.

Meditation and concentration are important in the *Lotus Sūtra*, but they are not given special prominence. It is also said there that even a million aeons of meditating does not produce as much merit as hearing about and accepting, even for a moment, the everlasting life of the Buddha—which means embodying the Buddha in one's own life.

But, if meditation is not the primary Buddhist practice in the *Lotus Sūtra*, what is? Many practices are recommended, especially receiving and embracing the *Sūtra*, chanting it from memory, copying it, teaching and explaining it, and living in accord with its teachings. But pre-eminent among the practices advocated by the *Lotus Sūtra* is the way of behaving towards others generally termed 'the bodhisattva way'. This bodhisattva way is the *Lotus Sūtra*'s encompassing vision of Buddhist practice.

A Way of Action

In a key passage in the *Sūtra* we find:

> Distinguishing the real Dharma,
> The way of action of bodhisattvas,
> [The Buddha] taught this Dharma Flower Sutra
> In verses as numerous as the sands of the Ganges. (Reeves 2008: 202)

We see here that the bodhisattva way is a way of doing, of action. What kind of action? Basically it is whatever action works to save or liberate or even help living beings.

For the *Sūtra*, the most important way of serving others is by leading them to embrace the *Lotus Sūtra* itself. In the text, the Buddha says:

> Medicine King, though there are many people, both lay people and monks, who walk in the bodhisattva way, if they are not able to see, hear, read, recite, copy, embrace, and make offerings to this Dharma Flower Sutra, you should know that they are not yet walking well in the bodhisattva way. But if any of them hear this sutra, then they will be able to walk well in the bodhisattva way. If any living beings who seek after the Buddha way either see or hear this Dharma Flower Sutra, and after hearing it believe, understand, and embrace it, then you should know that they are nearer to supreme awakening. (Reeves 2008: 230)

Yet it would be a mistake to understand this *Sūtra* as teaching that leading people to itself in any narrow sense is the only way to save others. The *Lotus Sūtra* is replete with parables, used in part to illustrate the use of appropriate means in practising the bodhisattva way. A father gets his children out of a burning house by promising them a reward. Another father gets his kids to take an antidote for poison by pretending to be dead. Still another father guides his unambitious son towards greater and greater responsibility. A tour guide conjures up a city in order to give people a needed resting place during a hard journey. A man sews a valuable jewel into the garment of his poor friend. A very powerful king holds back an extraordinarily precious and unique jewel that he keeps in the topknot of his hair until he sees a soldier of great merit. In none of these stories, or in any others in the *Lotus Sūtra*, is there any mention of the *Lotus Sūtra* itself.

A Way of Appropriate Action

What the stories illustrate is practical, appropriate action for helping others. What we are told over and over again in the *Sūtra* is that these acts need to be skilful, appropriate to the condition of the hearers. It is because people are different and their situations are different that, just as the rain nourishes a great variety of plants according to their different needs, the buddhas give the *Dharma* to people according to what is needed.

What is it that makes an action appropriate? In the Parable of the Burning House a father manages to get his kids out of a burning house by promising to give them carriages, but actually rewards them with a much more luxurious model than he had promised. At the end of the story, the Buddha asks Śāriputra whether the father has lied or not, and Śāriputra responds that the father had not lied, and would not have been lying had he given the children even very tiny carriages. Why? Simply because the strategy worked. It got the kids out of the burning house in time to save their lives.

Two things are relevant here: the action worked, and it worked to save lives. Some people apparently think that Buddhist ethics is primarily a matter of what is inside oneself, i.e. that being ethical or good is primarily a matter of internal consciousness, mindfulness, and/or compassion. But there is hardly a hint of this in the *Lotus Sūtra*. The ideal in the *Lotus Sūtra*, too, is a combination of wisdom or insight, compassion, and practice. But, in contemporary jargon, this sutra is also very results oriented. Of course it is important that the fathers or parents in the *Lotus Sūtra*'s stories are concerned about their children and want to save them, but it is more important that they are smart enough to figure out ways to be successful at doing so. Ethical action is skilful, appropriate action, and skilful, appropriate action is always effective action.

Indeed, while there are many, many examples of skilful means in the *Lotus Sūtra*, there are none at all of skilful means that are unsuccessful. Accordingly, it is probably the case that for the *Lotus Sūtra* the very notion of skilful means includes being successful at what is being attempted.

The story of Devadatta found in chapter 12 of the *Sūtra* is very instructive. According to this story, even our enemies, regardless of their intentions, can be bodhisattvas for us if we regard them as such. Devadatta, the embodiment of evil in so much Buddhist literature, in this sutra is thanked by the Buddha for being helpful. 'Thanks to my good friend Devadatta', the Buddha says, 'I was able to become fully developed in the six transcendental practices, in kindness, compassion, joy, and impartiality' and so on (Reeves

2008: 249). The Buddha, we are told, learned from his experiences with Devadatta, making Devadatta a bodhisattva, but it is not suggested that this was in any way a function of what Devadatta himself intended. Good intentions may be good in their own right, but they may not always be what is most important. Often what is more important is effectiveness, effectiveness in helping, or saving, others.

Buddhism as Skilful and Appropriate Means

There is much ambiguity in the *Lotus Sūtra* about the nature of salvation. We are told that the Buddha has vowed to save all the living. But the nature of that state, variously termed becoming a buddha, supreme awakening, and so on, is not unambiguously clear. Having said that, if we look at the stories in the text the matter is not, or at least not always, so complicated. Lives are saved. Sometimes they are saved from fire or poison, literally from death. In other cases, they are saved from a mean existence, from poverty and from an attitude that is complacent about poverty. In all cases, what is involved is overcoming a failure to achieve one's potential to become a bodhisattva and buddha.

Basically, in the *Lotus Sūtra* being a bodhisattva means using appropriate skilful means to help others. And that, finally, is what Buddhism itself is: an enormous variety of means developed to help people live more fulfilling lives, which can be understood as lives lived in the light of their interdependence. This is what most of the stories are about: someone—a father figure, or a friend, even a son, or a guide—helping someone else gain more responsibility for their own lives. 'Even if you search in all directions', the *Sūtra* says, 'you will find no other vehicles—except the skilful means of the Buddha' (Reeves 2008: 128).

As Founder Niwano puts it, 'The Fundamental spirit of the bodhisattva practice is [unity] between oneself and others' (Niwano 1976: 330). Though the unity is never perfect, there are times when the mind of a bodhisattva is not one of compassionate giving but rather one of spontaneous empathy. Though disputes and quarrels arise because people do not realize that even though we seem to be independent of one another, at a basic level there is unity of all human beings, and a unity of all living beings.

Thus, bodhisattva practice through appropriate skilful means is at once both a description of what Buddhism is, or of what Buddhist practice primarily is, and a prescription for what our lives should become, a teaching about how we should behave in order to contribute to the good. It is prescriptive not in the sense of being a precept or commandment, but in the sense of urging us, for the sake both of our own salvation and that of others, to be intelligent, imaginative, even clever, in finding ways to be helpful. The *Lotus Sūtra*, accordingly, is a prescription of a medicine or a kind of religious method for us—and is, therefore, extremely practical.

As I understand the *Lotus Sūtra*, it would be a serious mistake to think that skilful means are lesser teachings that can be replaced by some higher teaching or truth. Never in the *Lotus Sūtra* is the term 'skilful means' used except to reference something that is to be welcomed, applauded, even celebrated. There are no 'mere' skilful means in the *Lotus Sūtra*. There is, of course, a larger purpose that they serve. They are, after all, means not ends. But the encompassing purpose or truth that they serve is not another teaching. It is a *Dharma* that can only be found embodied in concrete teachings, including actions that are instructive, just as the Buddha can only be found embodied—in Śākyamuni, and in people just like you and me.

World-Affirming Practice

This teaching of bodhisattva practice is radically world-affirming. By this I mean simply that it is this *sahā* world where suffering has to be endured, and can be, that is Śākyamuni Buddha's world. It is in this world that he is a bodhisattva and encourages us to be bodhisattvas. This world is our home, and it is the home of Śākyamuni Buddha, precisely because he is embodied in it, not only as the historical Buddha but as the Buddha in all things. Thus, things, ordinary things, including ourselves and our neighbours and the trees that are our neighbours, are not primarily to be seen as empty, though they are; not primarily to be seen as phenomenal, though they are; not primarily to be seen as illusions, though in one sense they are; not primarily to be seen as evil even though they may be in part. It is only in things, in 'conventional' existence, that the *Dharma* exists at all. It is in transient, changing things that the Buddha lives. This whole world, therefore, is to be treated with insight and compassion and respect.

It is something of an irony that a sutra that affirms a cosmic Śākyamuni Buddha, one who is in every world and every time, does so, not to reject the historical Śākyamuni or the temporal world, but precisely to affirm their supreme importance, as Nichiren saw so clearly (see Nichiren 1985, 79ff.). And their importance is nothing more or less than that this world is where we, having been taught by the historical Buddha, are called to embody the life of the Buddha in our own actions and lives. This is why a part of the everyday liturgy of Risshō Kōsei-kai is the so-called *dōjō-kan (*Contemplating the Place of the Way): 'You should understand that this place is the place of the Way. This is where the Buddhas attain supreme awakening. This is where the Buddhas turn the *Dharma*-wheel. This is where the Buddhas reach complete *nirvāṇa*' (Kyoden 2009). And here, 'this place' means any place.

It is relevant in this connection to notice that there is very little use of the notion of emptiness in the *Lotus Sūtra*. Of course all things are empty of independent existence. But it is because they are empty that there is space, so to speak, for the development of their potential to be a buddha. If things were substantial, they could not truly grow or change. But because they are without substantiality, they can be influenced by and have influence on others. Emphasis on emptiness is not found in this Mahāyāna sutra because such an emphasis can easily become a kind of nihilism in which nothing matters, while in the *Lotus Sūtra* everything matters. The Buddha works to save all beings. Even poor Never Disrespectful Bodhisattva, going around telling everyone that they are to become buddhas, though initially not very successful, eventually 'transformed a multitude of tens of millions of billions, enabling them to live in the state of supreme awakening' (Reeves 2008: 339). And this is to say nothing of the account that he later became the Buddha Śākyamuni!

Hoza

Followers of the *Lotus Sūtra* believe that they should practise the bodhisattva way all the time. Being kind and helpful to others should become a habit. But the practice of *hoza*[3] is a special, and especially intentional, application of the ideal of the bodhisattva in religious practice. In *hoza*, Risshō Kōsei-kai members and guests sit in relatively small circles and try to apply Buddhist teachings in order to help one another with very ordinary but very important issues and problems of everyday life, often of an interpersonal nature such as one's relationship with one's mother-in-law, or with one's boss, or with one's spouse. Whatever the issue brought to the *hoza*, people in the group, as they are able, become bodhisattvas for each other, with genuine caring and practical help.

So, from the perspective of the *Lotus Sūtra*, full Buddhist practice is necessarily action-oriented and social. Everything else—e.g. chanting, ceremonies, preaching, meditation, institutions—is instrumental to saving others and to creating a kind of peaceful and beautiful world in which all are buddhas.

Bodhisattva as Becoming a Buddha

Sometimes the term 'bodhisattva' is understood to be a kind of position or rank, the rank just below that of a buddha. And very often in the *Lotus Sūtra* and elsewhere, a bodhisattva is an attendant of a buddha. These uses of 'bodhisattva' can be useful, but it is more important, I think, to see that being a bodhisattva is much more a kind of activity, a way of being and acting, than it is an achieved status. Just as a teacher is not really a teacher unless he or she teaches and someone is actually taught, a bodhisattva is not really a bodhisattva unless he or she is actually practising the bodhisattva way by helping others. Being a bodhisattva, in other words, involves a reciprocal relationship; it is a relational activity, something done only with others.

[3] The term *hoza* is composed of two Chinese characters (法座) literally meaning '*Dharma* sitting'. I think the term originated in another Japanese lay Buddhist organization, Reiyūkai, from which Risshō Kōsei-kai and many other lay Buddhist organizations split off.

When Śāriputra is assured by the Buddha that in a distant time he is to become a buddha with his own buddha-land and era, Śāriputra realizes for the first time that he is not merely a *śrāvaka* but also a bodhisattva (Reeves 2008: 101–110). Here 'bodhisattva' is not a rank, but a way of being and living indicating that one is on the way to becoming a buddha. Thus the *Lotus Sūtra* often uses the term 'buddha way' as an equivalent alternative to 'bodhisattva way'.

> What you are practicing
> [the Buddha says to his disciple Kāśyapa]
> Is the bodhisattva way.
> As you gradually practice and learn,
> Every one of you should become a buddha. (Reeves 2008: 168)

This is entirely consistent with the earliest uses of 'bodhisattva', where it meant Śākyamuni Buddha before he became a buddha. But in the *Lotus Sūtra* the Buddha says that he has lived in this world for innumerable countless aeons, from the beginning practising the bodhisattva way (Reeves 2008: 193).

It is absolutely central to the *Lotus Sūtra* that Śākyamuni Buddha is, first of all, a bodhisattva, i.e. one who has been doing bodhisattva practice, helping and leading others for innumerable aeons. Whenever the enormously long life of the Buddha is described in the *Sūtra*, it is not meditation that he has been doing, at least not primarily, but teaching and leading others, thus transforming them into bodhisattvas, followers of the bodhisattva way. This is the ethical ideal of the *Lotus Sūtra*.

Never Disrespectful Bodhisattva

Practice of the bodhisattva way certainly is not limited to buddhas or even to bodhisattvas in the conventional sense. Six of the last chapters of the *Lotus Sūtra*, generally believed to have been added late in the process of the compilation of the *Sūtra* as a kind of appendix, are fairly self-contained accounts of individual bodhisattvas, including Guanyin. In a sense, these bodhisattvas, though not exactly models for us, are understood to be suggestive of what we can be as bodhisattvas ourselves.

Among them is one not well known outside of the *Lotus Sūtra*, a monk named 'Never Disrespectful'.[4] Why was he named Never Disrespectful? That monk bowed humbly before everybody he met and praised them saying, 'I deeply respect you. I would never

[4] The name of this bodhisattva is a curious matter. In the Sanskrit versions of the *Lotus Sūtra* that we have now he is called Sadāparibhūta, which means 'always held in contempt' or perhaps 'always despised'. But in the Chinese translation he is called Chang Buching, meaning 'never treated lightly'. By itself this name could be taken to mean 'never despising', which is why his name has been translated into English as Never Despise. But few people despise one another, and the clear intention of the chapter itself is to teach that we should never disrespect others, never put them down or make light of them.

dare to be disrespectful or arrogant toward you. Why? Because all of you are practising the bodhisattva way and surely will become buddhas' (Reeves 2008: 338).

Here, then, everyone is, to some degree, practising the bodhisattva way. Thus *śrāvakas* are also bodhisattvas. Most, of course, do not know they are bodhisattvas, but they are nonetheless. And, of course, most importantly, every reader of the *Lotus Sūtra* is a bodhisattva. No matter how trivial our understanding or merit, no matter how trivial our practice, we are, to some extent, perhaps tiny, already bodhisattvas. And we are called to grow in our practice of the bodhisattva way by leading others to realize that potential in themselves. Finally, since being a bodhisattva is a matter of activity in relation to others rather than a rank or status, there is no requirement that a bodhisattva be a monk or even a Buddhist. Just as anyone can be a *Dharma* teacher, anyone can be a bodhisattva, even without ever having heard the term 'bodhisattva'. In a sense, in this kind of Buddhism, 'bodhisattva' has the meaning of 'doing good' or being ethical.

The Buddha Way

Thus the bodhisattva way is the buddha way in at least two senses: it is both the way in which one becomes a buddha and it is the practice of the buddhas. These two senses, however, are two in appearance only. That is, in the *Lotus Sūtra* the Buddha is understood to be always at work, in every time and place, seeking to fulfil his 'original' or 'primordial' vow to save all living beings. But how he is at work in the world is not through supernatural intervention, but rather by being embodied in the concrete actions of bodhisattvas.

Being respectful to others, not merely in the rather superficial way of Never Disrespectful Bodhisattva but in ways that are more effective, involves genuine listening to others and attending to both their sorrows and their opportunities, helping them in whatever ways are appropriate to develop their buddha nature, but equally importantly, learning from them, being open to their being a bodhisattva for us.

In chapter 25 of the *Lotus Sūtra*, Guanyin Bodhisattva is said to be able to take on many forms according to what is needed to help others. For example, if someone needs someone in the body of a buddha in order to be saved, Guanyin appears to them in the form of a buddha and teaches them. Likewise, Guanyin may appear as a king or general of heaven, as the Indian gods Indra or Īśvara, as a rich old man or the wife of a rich old man, as an ordinary citizen, government official, priest, monk, nun, layman or laywoman, boy or girl, or heavenly being of any kind.

This means, not only that we have to adapt our approach to those we want to help, but, just as importantly, that anyone can be a bodhisattva for us—if we have the eyes to see. If we can, even for a moment, put on the eyes of a buddha, we will see bodhisattvas everywhere, we will see that the world is full of bodhisattvas, beings from whom we can learn, who can help us in countless ways. Thus, we can understand the bodhisattva way as both helping others and being open to being helped by others.

In the *Lotus Sūtra* the Buddha does many things, but perhaps most important among them is his ability to see the Buddha in others. When the Buddha assures someone, such as Śāriputra or Devadattta, that they are to become a buddha with such and such a name, in a certain buddha land, with a realm of pure *Dharma* for so many aeons, what he is doing is not making a 'prediction' in the way that we might predict rain in the evening, what the Buddha is doing is assuring someone that at the core of their being there is the ever-present possibility of being the Buddha for someone through bodhisattva practice. Thus, the buddha way is not only a matter of being a bodhisattva for others, it is to recognize the bodhisattva in each one we encounter.

This, for the *Lotus Sūtra*, is what it means to be ethical—to practise the bodhisattva way, thus bringing peace to ourselves and to those around us, with an ultimate goal of a peaceful world.

Works Cited

Kyoden: sutra readings (2009) Tokyo: International Buddhist Congregation.

Nichiren (1985) The selection of the time. In: *The major writings of Nichiren daishonin*, volume 3. Tokyo: Nichiren Shoshu International Center.

Niwano N. (1976) *Buddhism for today: a modern interpretation of the Lotus Sutra*. Tokyo: Kosei Publishing Company.

Reeves, G. (trans.) (2008) *The Lotus Sutra: a contemporary translation of a Buddhist classic.* Boston: Wisdom.

Suggested Reading

Niwano N. (1976) *Buddhism for today: a modern interpretation of the Lotus Sutra*. Tokyo: Kosei Publishing Company.

Reeves, G. (ed.) (2002) *A Buddhist kaleidoscope: essays on the Lotus Sutra*. Tokyo: Kosei Publishing Company.

Reeves, G. (trans.) (2008) *The Lotus Sutra: a contemporary translation of a Buddhist classic.* Boston: Wisdom.

Tamura Y. (2014) *The Lotus Sutra: truth • life • practice*. Trans. G. Reeves and M. Shinozaki. Boston: Wisdom.

Teiser, S. F., and Stone, J. I. (eds) (2009) *Readings of the Lotus Sutra*. New York: Columbia University Press.

ter Haar, B. J. (1999) *White lotus teachings in Chinese religious history*. Honolulu: University of Hawai'i Press.

Yü Chün-fang (2001) *Kuan-yin: the Chinese transformation of Avalokiteśvara*. New York: Columbia University Press.

CHAPTER 11

ETHICS IN ZEN

CHRISTOPHER IVES

Introduction

ZEN master Dōgen (1200–1253) once instructed his disciples, 'Although the precepts and the eating regulations should be maintained, you must not make the mistake of establishing them as of primary importance and basing your practice on them; nor should they be considered a means to awakening' (Masunaga 1978: 6; adapted).[1] He also told them that 'strictly obeying the precepts is simply to practice concentrated meditation, as did the Zen masters of old. When doing meditation, what precepts are not upheld, what merits not produced?' (Masunaga 1978: 7). He even said, 'Setting everything aside, think of neither good nor evil, right nor wrong' (Yokoi and Victoria 1976: 46).

We might interpret these statements as indicating that Zen, unlike most other forms of Buddhism, rejects ethics as part of the path to awakening, refuses to consider what might be good or evil, and chooses simply to focus on meditation. Coupled with popular images of eccentric monks snubbing their noses at convention, these statements might lead us to think that Zen somehow negates ethics or exists 'beyond' ethics in some sense. Indeed, we often hear such claims.

Historically, however, Zen leaders have usually valued such core components of Buddhist ethics as precepts, compassion, and the bodhisattva ideal, though they often do so in unique ways. In the case of Japan, which is the main focus of this overview, the ethical stances of such thinkers as Dōgen and Eisai (1141–1215) have been shaped by the overall Zen approach, Confucianism, and other factors. As a result, such constructs as the Five Precepts have played roles in traditional Japanese Zen that in certain respects differ from how they have functioned in other strands of Buddhism. Recently, in response to violence, gender discrimination, and environmental degradation, Zen

[1] The author thanks the editors of the *Journal of Buddhist Ethics* for permission to incorporate into this chapter sections of 'What's compassion got to do with it? Determinants of Zen social ethics in Japan' (*Journal of Buddhist Ethics* 12 [2005]) and Steve Heine for providing feedback on a draft of this chapter.

Buddhists, especially in the West, have been reinterpreting precepts and other components of Buddhist ethics, often in ways that diverge from traditional Zen.

Precepts in Early and Theravāda Buddhism

When Dōgen argues that precepts should not be seen as leading instrumentally to awakening and that to follow them one should simply engage in concentrated meditation without any thoughts of good and evil, he is diverging from many other Buddhist views of precepts. Not surprisingly, like other multi-strand religious traditions, Buddhism is not monolithic, and its core components—such as ethics, meditation, rituals, and awakening—have been interpreted and practised in a variety of ways. In the case of ethics, Buddhism includes various sets of precepts and various views of their role.

At the risk of oversimplification, we can say that in early and Theravāda Buddhism, precepts function as an ethic of restraint (de Silva 1990: 15). For example, the first five precepts are often framed with the expression, 'I undertake to refrain myself from', which is followed by five actions: harming living beings; taking that which has not been given; sexual misconduct; false speech; and use of intoxicants that cause heedlessness. When someone joins a monastic order as a novice, he (usually he, not she) undertakes an additional five precepts, which consist of refraining from 6) eating at the wrong time (after noon), 7) attending entertainments, 8) wearing jewellery and using perfume, 9) sleeping on high or luxurious beds, and 10) handling gold or silver. When he becomes a fully ordained monk (Pāli *bhikkhu*) in a monastic community he will follow the Theravāda *pātimokkha* (Skt *prātimokṣa*), a set of 227 guidelines that constitutes the core part of the monastic code or *Vinaya*. Twice a month on days termed *uposatha* (Skt *poṣadha*), he will gather with the other monks to recite the *pātimokkha*, confess transgressions from an attitude of repentance, and, as appropriate, receive punishments.

In early and Theravāda Buddhism the precepts function to restrain external 'unwholesome' (or 'unskilful') actions. The practitioner undertakes these restraints while monitoring the unwholesome mental states that lead to those actions and cultivating their opposites, the wholesome mental states that conduce to liberation from suffering; for example, the practitioner will attempt to eliminate the 'three poisons' of greed, ill will, and ignorance and replace them with the wholesome mental states of generosity, loving-kindness, and wisdom. This ethic of restraint contributes to the purification of the mind, as flagged by the oft-cited verse in the *Dhammapada*:

> To refrain from the unwholesome,
> to cultivate the wholesome,
> to purify the mind—
> this is the teaching of all of the awakened ones (buddhas).

Rupert Gethin, a scholar of Theravāda Buddhism, writes,

> The goal of the Buddhist path is to eradicate the unwholesome motivations that cause harmful behaviour. To achieve this the mind needs to be "trained" [purified]. Part of the training involves the undertaking of various precepts, literally principles or bases of training ([Skt] *śikṣāpada*/[Pāli]*sikkhāpada*), in order to try to restrain the mind and draw it back from the grosser kinds of unwholesome behaviour. (2005: 170)

More simply put, practitioners 'abide by the precepts as rules of training in order to curb the grosser forms of bad conduct' (2005: 172).

As indicated by his statements, Dōgen took a different approach to the precepts, and we can attribute this divergence in large part to the doctrinal milieu from which Zen emerged in sixth-century China. As we will see, however, his is not the only Zen approach to the precepts.

Doctrinal Milieu in China

Chan (Jp. Zen) Buddhism emerged in the early sixth century, and it did so in a rich doctrinal milieu, influenced by Daoism, Confucianism, and other elements of Chinese culture. One cluster of doctrines shaping early Chan and other forms of Buddhism at that time in China consisted of Mahāyāna theories of emptiness, two truths, and non-dualism, each of which carried ethical ramifications. The doctrine of emptiness, which claimed that all things are 'empty' of any unchanging essence or soul, indicated to many Chinese and Japanese Buddhists that unwholesome mental states (*kleśa*) are 'nonsubstantial and empty', and that '[i]nstead of trying to obliterate essentially non-existent defilements, which reifies them even more, one is simply to put the mind at rest and let it return to a pristine state of purity' (Poceski 2006: 30). The doctrine of two truths makes a distinction between conventional truth and the absolute truth of emptiness. In this scheme, while ethical categories like purity and impurity, good and evil, *nirvāṇa* and *saṃsāra* may obtain at the conventional level, they do not at the absolute level, where the emptiness of all categories and non-dualism reign supreme. Consequently, 'since all things, including sins and karmic transgressions, are empty of own-being (Skt: *svabhāva*) in the realm of principle or the absolute beyond concrete phenomena, the need to repent for actual misdeeds is vitiated' (Heine 2008: 161); and in terms of non-dualism, 'Mahāyāna precepts were influenced by the notion that "defilements are awakening, *saṃsāra* is no different from *nirvāṇa*"' (Faure 1998: 89). The philosophical and ethical issue that emerges here, of course, is how to take ethical categories and distinctions seriously at the conventional level, at the level of living in society as opposed to dwelling in a rarefied religious experience.

Further complicating Buddhist ethics from the emergence of Chan in the sixth century through its introduction to Japan in the twelfth and thirteenth centuries was a cluster of overlapping doctrines: buddha nature, original awakening, and the *tathāgata-garbha* (the embryo or womb of buddha). Though each of these doctrines lends itself to multiple interpretations and debates, in broad strokes they make the claim that all sentient beings are fundamentally awakened and hence religious practice should be done not to purify or transform one's unawakened mind into an awakened mind but to realize and give expression to the pure, awakened mind that one possesses from the start. This realization takes place through a reorientation, from seeking awakening in the future to confirming one's innate awakening here and now. To use a visual metaphor, rather than looking horizontally out across years of sustained practice and gradual change to the far horizon of awakening, one does an abrupt about-face or, we might say, an abrupt down-face, and looks vertically within oneself to realize innate awakening. This radical shift in orientation is referred to as 'sudden awakening' (Ch. *dunwu*, Jp. *ton'go*) and much of early Chan intellectual history centred on debates about sudden versus gradual awakening (as well as debates about the exact connotation of *dun*, 'sudden' or, as the term is sometimes translated, 'abrupt') (see Gregory 1987).

Dōgen

It is in light of these doctrines circulating in East Asia that we can understand Dōgen's stance on the precepts, 700 years after the founding of Chan/Zen. When he returned from China and established the Japanese Sōtō Zen school in thirteenth-century Japan, Dōgen had several sets of precepts from which to choose. His options included the five precepts observed by all Buddhists; the initial ten precepts received by novice monks in Theravāda Buddhism; and the ten major and forty-eight minor precepts in the *Fanwang-jing* (Jp. *Bonmō-kyō*; Brahma's Net Sūtra), which constitute a set of 'bodhisattva precepts' aimed not just at monastics but at the laity as well. To set up monasteries he could also draw from the 227 guidelines in the Theravāda *pātimokkha*, or the 250 guidelines in the *prātimokṣa* of the *Dharmaguptaka Vinaya* (Jp. *Shibunritsu*; Four-Part *Vinaya*), the main monastic code followed in East Asian Mahāyāna Buddhism.

Dōgen championed a set of sixteen precepts (*jūroku-jōkai*) that he compiled as the 'Bodhisattva Precepts That Have Been Correctly Transmitted by Buddhas and Ancestors' (*Busso shōden bosatsu kai*). The first three are the three refuges in the three jewels or treasures (taking refuge in the Buddha, *Dharma*, and *Saṅgha*). The next subset—the three pure precepts (*sanju-shōjō-kai*)—follows the lifting up of compassion in the Mahāyāna reworking of the above verse in the *Dhammapada* and consists of the observance of all rules that eradicate evils (*shōritsugi kai*), the commission of all things that are good (*shōzenbō kai*), and the liberation of all sentient beings (*shōshujō kai*). Dōgen rounded his list with the ten major Mahāyāna precepts in the *Fanwang-jing*, the first five of which are the same as in the Theravāda and the last five of which consist of refraining from 6) discussing the faults of others, 7) praising oneself and slandering others, 8) being stingy with the *Dharma* assets, 9) giving way to anger and resentments, and 10) slandering the three jewels.

Dōgen viewed precepts through the lens of what he termed *shushō-ittō*, the unity of practice (*shu*) and realization or confirmation (*shō*). In this approach, he construed the practice of *zazen*—seated meditation—not as a means to awakening in the future but as the optimal way to realize and express one's innate awakening or buddha nature here and now, that is to say, to bring about the sudden awakening discussed above. More exactly put, when we exert (*gūjin*) ourselves in zazen, this act of meditation is awakening, and the typical means–end relationship between practice and realization does not hold. Insofar as it is the most direct and effective way to confirm innate awakening, seated meditation takes precedence over other parts of the Buddhist path, including the practice of precepts.

This priority of meditation over following the precepts finds expression in Dōgen's *Zuimonki* (Record of Things Heard): 'Chanting the *Precept Sutra* [the *Fanwang-jing*] night and day and strictly obeying the precepts is simply to practice concentrated zazen, as did the Zen Masters of old. When doing zazen, what precepts are not upheld, what merits not produced?' (Yokoi and Victoria 1976: 7). Along these lines Dōgen also writes, 'Just do zazen. You will then naturally improve' (8). William Bodiford comments, 'Dōgen repeatedly stressed that all three aspects of Buddhist learning (i.e. precepts, meditation, and wisdom) are found simultaneously within the act of Zen meditation' (1993: 169). It is for this reason that an expression circulating in early Japanese Zen, *zenkai-itchi*, should be read in Dōgen's case not as 'the unity of Zen and the precepts' but as 'the unity of *zazen* and the precepts'.

This does not mean, however, that Dōgen rejected precepts. Just as *zazen* confirms the awakened buddha nature within us, following the precepts authenticates and manifests it in everyday action. That is to say, the precepts indicate how an awakened being (buddha) acts, and when one acts that way one is expressing one's buddha nature, acting as a buddha does, being a buddha, being awakened. To support his disciples in this endeavour, Dōgen directed them to emulate fully awakened people, people who were buddhas ('awakened ones') and acted accordingly. In the *Zuimonki*, for example, he emphasizes 'trusting in the actions of the old Masters' (Yokoi and Victoria 1976: 7) and he elaborates on what this entails: 'Just focus your mind on one thing, absorb the old examples, study the actions of former Zen masters, and penetrate deeply into a single form of practice' (8).

This exhortation applies not only to moral precepts but also to the other guidelines found in monastic codes, which in general should be seen as pertaining less to ethics in a strict sense than to harmonious monastic life. While honouring the main Chan monastic code in China, the *Chanyuan qinggui* (Regulations for Pure Conduct in Zen Monasteries), Dōgen wrote a number of essays about monastic life, six of which were later compiled as his monastic code, the *Eihei shingi*; he also discussed proper monastic behaviour in many of the fascicles of his magnum opus, the *Shōbōgenzō*. From his perspective, guidelines about the minutiae of monastic life—how to chant, bow, serve tea, prepare meals, do chores, entertain distinguished guests, brush one's teeth, take a bath, and defecate—function not to control the monks but to show them how an awakened person performs such actions. When acting in these ways monastics are expressing their innate awakened nature, they are being/acting awakened. As Dan Taigen Leighton, Zen teacher and translator of the *Eihei shingi* puts it, 'The purpose of Zen community... [is] to embody fully the reality of buddha nature' (1995: 5). Leighton also comments that 'Dōgen asserts that just to maintain dignified demeanor while in accord with the daily community activities is exactly the practice of full awakening' (9) and insofar as this awakening is most powerfully confirmed in *zazen*, the monastic code delineates a 'harmonious lifestyle based on and emerging from the experience of zazen' (16). As William Bodiford has pointed out, Dōgen even went so far as to regard 'the implementation of the Zen monastic codes as being more important than the precepts. ... [T]he true expression of the precepts could be realized only through the routines of monastic life' (1993: 170).

In his rigour around following the precepts and the forms that orchestrate monastic life, Dōgen was, in key respects, ritualizing morality. Hee-Jin Kim writes that in the case of Dōgen, 'Scrupulous instructions, exhortations, and admonitions with respect to the rules, manners, virtues, and behaviour, are not codes that bind the monastics' outward movements, but are ritualized expressions and activities of Buddha-nature and absolute emptiness' (1987: 173). This ritualization of morality was happening in East Asia at a time when morality was also getting interiorized. As Dōgen scholar Steven Heine points out,

> the *Prātimokṣa* was designed to regulate the outer behaviour of monks in training, whereas in the Tendai and early Ch'an view this concern was relegated to the level of ordinary or relative truth. From the standpoint of absolute or ultimate truth, there is a full realization of the precepts, which altogether vitiates the need for external guidelines expressed in the *Prātimokṣa* or allows them to be seen merely as a kind of metaphorical reflection of what is essentially an interior state of mind. (2005: 18)

In short, Dōgen was rigorous in his prescription of sixteen precepts and an array of other ways of acting around the monastery and thus set the bar high for behaviour, but he was not advocating these guidelines primarily as a means of restraining oneself as the first step of a process of self-purification leading to a future state of awakening. Rather, to uphold guidelines is to express the buddha nature one already has or, more exactly, is.

Another way to summarize Dōgen's approach is to say that based on the doctrines of buddha nature (Jp. *busshō*), original awakening (*hongaku*), and the unity of practice and realization (*shushō-ittō*), he was setting forth an approach to the precepts that is not (simply) prescriptive but descriptive—describing how an awakened person acts: not harming but being compassionate, not stealing but being generous, not lying but being truthful. His approach is also performative, in that when one acts in accord with the precepts, one is expressing or performing one's buddha nature.

In setting forth his approach to the precepts, Dōgen also discussed ordination. In the *Jukai* ('receiving the precepts' or 'ordination') fascicle of the *Shōbōgenzō*, he makes a comment about awakened people and Zen patriarchs before him: 'They received the precepts either directly from the Buddha himself or one of his disciples. In either case they have all inherited the essence of the Way' (Yokoi and Victoria 1976: 85). In Dōgen's version of the ritual of conferring and receiving the precepts, the preceptor says, 'Since you have discarded wrong and taken refuge in good, the Buddhist precepts are already fulfilled' (86). From this perspective, the precepts are fulfilled upon receiving them or, more dramatically put, the ordination ritual transmits 'the essence of the Way' by conferring awakening. William Bodiford comments, 'Individual precepts do not govern behaviour or actions, but describe the spiritual characteristics of the Buddha nature. Thus ordination signifies not the beginning of the Buddhist path, but its final culmination' (2005: 206).

It is important to note that Dōgen was not alone in taking such an approach. As Bodiford has noted, several beliefs about the precepts were shared across Japanese Buddhism, including the beliefs that

> the Buddha proclaiming the precepts is the ultimate Buddha . . . ; each precept of the ultimate Buddha expresses the same unified, all-embracing reality that is Buddha nature (*busshō*); and thus the goal of the ordination ceremony is the proper ritual confirmation of this Buddha nature . . . (2005: 186)

In this approach, 'Precepts are the vehicle of salvation' (*kaijō-itchi*) (187).

As a result, Sōtō Zen Buddhists since Dōgen have focused more on the reception of the precepts, seen as conferring enlightenment, than on the actual observance or application of the precepts. We see this emphasis in rituals for conferring the precepts, whether on large groups of laypeople in what amounts to mass ordination ceremonies (*jukai'e*), on local spirits who need placation, or on the dead, who through the conferral in funerals are ritually turned into buddhas, which by extension ensures that the deceased will not become dangerous unmourned spirits, will not be reborn again, and will, as buddhas, listen to the prayers of remaining family members and grant boons (see Bodiford 1993: 185–208). At the same time, debates have taken place in Sōtō circles about the precepts. Menzan Zuihō (1683–1769), for example, argued that monks need to follow the precepts, not simply receive them (Riggs 2015: 198).

Eisai

Dōgen's approach to precepts has coloured how Sōtō Zen Buddhists have viewed precepts in Japan, but we see a different stance in the case of Myōan Eisai (or Yōsai), the Japanese monk who introduced the Rinzai strand of Zen from China several decades before Dōgen's trip to China. Eisai's approach harks back in key respects to early (and Theravāda) Buddhist views of precepts. In his *Kōzen-gokoku-ron* (Treatise on Propagating Zen to Protect the Realm), he writes that 'the Zen School considers keeping precepts to be what precedes everything else' (Eisai 2005: 121), and then quotes the

Chanyuan qinggui: 'For the practice of Zen and investigation of the Way, precepts and monastic codes (*Vinaya*) come first (*kairitsu-isen*).' But which set of precepts and which monastic code did he recommend? Did he, like Dōgen, come up with his own set of precepts? And what did he see as their role?

Although Eisai started his training as an acolyte in the Tendai school of Japanese Buddhism, which at that time was emphasizing the *Fanwang-jing* precepts, he came to advocate that Zen monks follow both the 250 guidelines in the *Dharmaguptaka Vinaya* and fifty-eight precepts in the *Fanwang-jing*. With this stance he argued for the importance of both restraining and disciplining oneself through the guidelines in the *Vinaya* and compassionately responding to others as guided by the bodhisattva precepts in the *Fanwang-jing*: 'externally practicing the precepts of restraint to prevent wrongs while internally benefitting others out of compassion—this is called the principle of the Zen school; it is called the Buddha-Dharma' (Eisai 2005: 115–116). In this way, unlike Dōgen, Eisai followed the *Chanyuan qinggui*'s advocacy of following both sets of guidelines.

Taking this stance, Eisai referred to his brand of Zen as '*Vinaya*-supporting Zen' (*furitsu zen*). In response to the Tendai Buddhist use of only the *Fanwang-jing* precepts, he claimed that his '*Vinaya*-supporting Zen' is something that had been lost by Tendai and that he is engaging in a reformation or revival of Buddhism (Bodiford 2005: 196).

Following the tripartite organization of the Eightfold Path in terms of morality, meditation, and wisdom, Eisai saw the precepts as the foundation for meditation and wisdom. The line in the *Chanyuan qinggui* that he quoted, 'For the practice of Zen and investigation of the Way, precepts and monastic codes come first', is followed by the question, 'Without taking leave of offenses and avoiding prohibited actions, how can one become a buddha and act like the patriarchs?' In accord with this view, Eisai writes, 'If you want to attain deep meditative states (*dhyāna*), you must depend on practicing morality' (2005: 149; adapted). To support his stance, Eisai quotes a Tendai text, *Great Calming and Insight*: 'The destruction of evil depends on the purification of wisdom. The purification of wisdom depends on the purification of meditation. The purification of meditation depends on the purification of the monastic precepts' (Welter 2006: 99; see Eisai 2005: 110). He also quotes the *Sūtra on Perfect Enlightenment*: 'All unobstructed pure wisdom arises from Zen meditation (*zenjō*). . . . If one wants to realize [the power of] meditation, one must carry out the practice of the *Vinaya* [precepts]' (cited by Welter 2006: 95). In short, Eisai believed that monks must not simply 'receive the precepts' (*jukai*, a term that can also mean ordination) but 'protect' or 'guard' the precepts (*gokai*), in other words, follow them (Welter 2006: 105). We might add that when Eisai was making this argument about following both sets of precepts, the doctrine of the 'end of the *Dharma*' (*mappō*) was prevalent in Japanese religious perspectives and leading other reformers to declare that following the precepts was impossible at such a time of decline.

In his advocacy of following the precepts, Eisai was not simply trying to revive the precepts as the necessary foundation for cultivating meditative states and wisdom. He was also concerned about the moral laxity of his fellow Buddhists. As Albert Welter writes, 'In Eisai's view, Zen represented a remedy for the degenerate state into which Buddhist moral discipline had fallen in Japan' (1999: 64). This degeneration had ramifications beyond the monks' progress on the religious path and the moral health of the *Saṅgha*. Like other Buddhists at his time, Eisai believed that the well-being of the society and the safety of the nation depended upon an upright Buddhist clergy, for if the monks were not morally sound, their rituals and actions would not be effective in prompting deities to protect Japan. He writes that 'insofar as there are people within the land who keep precepts for moral conduct, deities will protect the state' (2005: 79). Welter explains:

> Buddhist as well as native Japanese deities served to protect and defend Buddhist countries from disaster. These deities were summoned through rituals and prayers conducted by members of the Buddhist clergy. The willingness of deities to intervene on a country's behalf was believed to be determined by the moral character of those who summoned them. (Welter 1999: 65)

It was in this context that Eisai advocated that his variety of Zen offered the best way to protect the country. As flagged by the title of his main work, *Treatise on Propagating Zen to Protect the Realm*, he argued that Japan would flourish and be a model Buddhist country if the rulers were to patronize Zen and moral Zen leaders in turn were to perform rituals that would protect the country. Along these lines Eisai prescribed a set of rituals aimed at promoting the emperor's rule, repaying debt to the emperor, and securing protection by local deities, who, again, would look approvingly on moral monks performing rituals properly (Welter 2008: 113–138).

Eisai also believed that by following the precepts, monks were sustaining not only the state but Buddhism: 'Moral precepts (*kai*) and monastic codes (*ritsu*) are what causes the Buddha's teachings to abide long. Now, the Zen school regards precepts and monastic codes as its principles. Therefore, it has the meaning of causing the Buddha's teachings to abide long' (2005: 109–110).

For the above reasons Eisai was strict in his advocacy of following the precepts (2005: 166). At one point he writes, 'There should be no association with those who break precepts.' And in monastic life, 'on the occasion of *poṣadha* assemblies for recitation of the *Vinaya* rules every half-month, one should open oneself to the other practitioners. Violators of morality should be dismissed, like corpses in the great ocean, which does not allow them to remain on the bottom' (Eisai 2005: 169).

Although Eisai advocates not just receiving the precepts but 'protecting' or observing them strictly, he does not discuss how they should be applied to specific situations or to social issues outside the monastery, except to say that upholding them will make rulers and the country secure.

In Rinzai Zen since Eisai the precepts have generally received less treatment than they have in the Sōtō tradition, as reflected by the fact that precepts are rarely mentioned by recent Japanese Zen thinkers who operate largely within a Rinzai framework, whether D. T. Suzuki (1870–1966), Hisamatsu Shin'ichi (1889–1980), or Abe Masao (1915–2006). And when Rinzai figures over the centuries did discuss the precepts, they often sounded more like Dōgen than Eisai. Rinzai priest Kokan Shiren (1278–1346) argued in his *Zenkaiki* that Mahāyāna precepts embody awakening as opposed to regulating behaviour, and, as William Bodiford summarizes Kokan's stance, 'The purpose of ordination is not to instill morality but to confirm the inherent awakening naturally possessed by all beings' (2005: 200).

In Japanese Rinzai Zen monastic life at present, precepts play little role. Monks in training do not study the precepts or monastic codes; and though the ten precepts appear toward the end of the *kōan* curriculum, they are worked with as *kōans*, not as ethical constructs. And despite what Eisai wrote about *poṣadha* assemblies, no such ritual is currently performed for reciting the precepts or confessing transgressions. Moreover, there is no formal practice of repentance, even though the 'Verse of Repentance' (*Sange mon*) is frequently chanted in monasteries:

> All evil actions ever committed by me since long ago,
> on account of my beginningless greed, ill will, and ignorance,
> born of my body, mouth, and mind—
> now I repent for all of them.

What we often encounter instead are claims about how *zazen* and the insights it fosters are ethically transformative. Hakuin (1686–1768) wrote in his 'Hymn in Praise of Zazen', 'Observing the precepts, repentance, and giving, the countless good deeds, and the way of right living all come from zazen. Thus one true samadhi extinguishes evils; it purifies karma, dissolving obstructions' (Low 1988: 89). More recently, Abe Masao, from his largely Rinzai framework, portrayed *zazen* as directed towards a satori experience in the form of an awakening to emptiness (*śūnyatā*), which bestows wisdom and compassion on the awakened person, who then automatically functions to liberate others through vows (Skt *praṇidhāna*) and effective action (*carita*) or skilful means (Abe 1991: 58).

As a general rule, while Japanese Zen Buddhists for centuries have received the sixteen bodhisattva precepts arranged by Dōgen or the larger sets advocated by Eisai, they have rarely written about how they might put specific precepts into practice in their personal or interpersonal lives. Nor, historically, have they applied the precepts to their socio-political situations in any systematic and critical manner.

Ethics in Zen, however, is not exhausted by the precepts and the possible fruits of *zazen*.

Compassion

Insofar as Zen is a form of Mahāyāna Buddhism, the tradition is replete with references to compassion. Monastic practice includes frequent chanting of the *Shigu seigan* (Fourfold Great Vow), which begins with a commitment 'to liberate sentient beings, however innumerable'. Despite Zen rhetoric of not relying on anyone outside oneself (as conveyed by the line in the *Lin-ji-lu* (Jp. *Rinzai-roku*) about killing buddhas and patriarchs), veneration of and reliance on the compassionate bodhisattva Kannon (Skt

Avalokiteśvara) is ubiquitous in Zen chanting: Kannon compassionately hears the travails of suffering human beings at the beginning of the *Heart Sūtra*, appears as a 'great compassionate bodhisattva' in the *Jūbutsu-myō* (The Names of the Ten Buddhas), and is celebrated in the *Enmei jikku kannon-gyō* (The Life-Extending Kannon Ten-Phrase Sūtra), in the *Kannon wasan* (Hymn in Praise of Kannon), and, especially, in the 'sutra' dedicated to Kannon, the *Kannnon-gyō* (ch. 25 of the *Lotus Sūtra*), which includes the passage:

> He of the true gaze, the pure gaze,
> the gaze of great and encompassing wisdom,
> the gaze of pity, the gaze of compassion—
> constantly we implore him, constantly we look up in reverence. (Watson 1993: 305)

In *Banmin-tokuyō* (Virtuous Action for All People), Suzuki Shōsan (1579–1655) lifts up both precepts and compassion when he writes that 'Buddhist practice is to observe the precepts strictly, never opposing the teaching of the Buddha and of the patriarchs; to banish the mind warped and twisted, and to become of good mind; ... and to lead all people, uprightly and with compassion, to enlightenment' (Tyler 1977: 56–57).

Several factors, however, complicate compassion as an ethical resource for Zen. Mahāyāna texts allow for violation of precepts if the actor's intent is compassionate, which has resulted in the notion of compassionate violence if not killing. For example, in the *Mahāparinirvāna-sūtra*, the historical Buddha states that in an earlier life he killed several brahmins for slandering the *Dharma* and thereby spared them the retribution that would follow from their actions (cited by Williams 1989: 161). Presumably it was compassion that was being expressed in Zen *kōans* when Nanquan (Jp. Nansen *c.*749–835) cut a cat in half and Juzhi (Jp. Gutei *c.*ninth century) cut off an acolyte's finger. During the Second World War Zen figures deployed rhetoric about compassionate killing to justify actions by the Japanese military (see Ives 2009b: ch. 1, and Victoria 2006). What is operating here may be akin to Kierkegaard's 'teleological suspension of the ethical', in which one must make a leap of faith to get from the realm of morality to the realm of religion, as Abraham was commanded to do when God told him to sacrifice his son Isaac (Gen. 22:1–19).

One might argue along these lines that awakening others as the telos of the functioning of compassion is Zen's *summum bonum*, but even if awakening is the supreme good, does that necessarily mean that compassion in and of itself is something 'moral' (as opposed to being a non-moral instrument to a religious good)? Granted, insofar as compassion pertains to one's motivation, to one's intention to help or liberate others, it carries moral weight, but Kant would most likely interject here with an admonition to consider not only the motive but also the act.

There is at least one other complicating factor. Apart from issuing a broad call to recognize the suffering of others and ameliorate it, the doctrine of compassion in Zen comes with little specificity. In this respect it is what Christian ethicists term a theological virtue, like love, which needs to be coupled with considerations of justice.

Moreover, cases where people have done harmful things in the guise of helping or saving others are not uncommon. For this reason, compassion needs something else to guide the actions motivated by it, and traditionally Zen and other Mahāyāna Buddhists have looked to wisdom (Skt *prajñā*) in this regard.

This is especially important when we move from the individual ethics of a Zen master working with a disciple to the social ethics of a person responding to complex issues in society. One needs some sort of guidance about, for example, what the best interests of others (or the environment) might be, what actions would promote those interests, and whether immoral means can be used to pursue moral and religious ends. In short, compassionate intentions are admirable, but when it comes to analysing existing problems, conceptualizing solutions, and figuring out which actions might be most expected to lead to those solutions, something else is needed. One possibility is a knowledgeable and informed 'wisdom' that builds upon and goes beyond the wisdom (*prajñā*) that accompanies compassion in traditional formulations (see, e.g., Ives 1992).

Some of these issues have come into play in relation to images of and actions by Zen masters. Traditionally, especially in Rinzai Zen, masters have been seen as fully awakened, which grants them charisma and authority. The assumption has often been that insofar far as they are fully awakened, they do not need to restrain or purify themselves and their actions express their awakening. And insofar as they have come to embody the compassion and wisdom believed to accompany a full realization of awakening, they act with compassionate intent and wise savvy and hence may violate precepts as part of their bodhisattva functioning.

This representation of Zen needs careful scrutiny in light of the fact that Zen masters have done things that seem to be unethical and lacking in wisdom. For example, how do we understand Zen justifications of Japanese militarism and the killing and destruction it entailed during the Second World War? How might we come to terms with ostensibly enlightened Zen masters sexually abusing their students? One option is to say that they are not fully awakened, for if they were awakened they would not do such things. Another option is to let go of rhetoric about how doing *zazen* and realizing awakening equips the person morally and simply argue that *zazen* and that realization, while *existentially liberating*, are not necessarily *ethically transformative*.

Needless to say, the portrayal of awakened Zen masters as wise and compassionate can also create problems in a Zen community after the master does an action that is deemed unethical. This portrayal can be used by the teacher to avoid responsibility by justifying his actions as wise and compassionate functioning—as a form of skilful means (*upāya*)—that should not be expected to square with the precepts. Or it can lead students to accept what the master is doing, leaving them unwilling and unable to question or challenge the master, thereby rendering them enablers.

With the lack of reflection on the social application of precepts and the lack of specificity in compassion, the de facto formulations of social ethics by historical Japanese Zen figures and the actual socio-political stances of Zen in Japanese history have been determined by a range of other factors, which, depending on how one construes compassion, can be viewed as having augmented, muted, refracted, or even contravened this ostensible cardinal virtue in Mahāyāna Buddhism.

Actual Values

To understand the *actual* as opposed to *ideal* ethics functioning in Zen over the centuries in Japan, one must take stock of values and practices that may have played a possibly greater role than precepts, *zazen*, and compassion have in shaping practitioners ethically. An inventory of Rinzai Zen, for example, reveals that monastic life conveys and reinforces a set of values with moral ramifications:

1. Restraint, cultivated by letting go of personal desires and giving oneself to the monastic regimen;
2. Simplicity, insofar as in the traditional pattern supplicant monks arrive at the training hall (*sōdō*) gate with only robes, bowls, a razor, straw sandals, a straw hat, and several other possessions;
3. Thrift, the commitment to wasting nothing, to using things at one's disposal as much as possible without throwing them away, as seen in the strict limitation of water for brushing teeth and washing faces, the ideal of scavenging scraps to make robes, and *oryōki* meals (ritualized meals with participants using three bowls each), in which monks eat all the food they receive from servers and then wash their bowls with tea, which they drink;
4. Manual labour, done as work practice (*samu* or *fushin*);
5. Doing tasks thoroughly and in an aesthetically pleasing manner;
6. Diligence in personal application to practice, as reinforced, for example, by the chanting of the *Daitō-kokushi yuikai* (Daitō Kokushi's Last Admonition), which closes with the refrain, 'Be diligent, be diligent' (*bensen bensen*);
7. Perseverance, as conveyed by frequent exhortations by the *rōshi* (Zen master) or *jikijitsu* (leader of *zazen*) to push through pain in retreats (*sesshin*), rhetoric about sitting *zazen* even if one dies while doing so (*shinu kakugo de zazen o kumu*), and advocacy of solitary 'night sitting' (*yaza*);
8. Humility, as embodied, for example, in ritualized bowing;
9. Penitent self-criticism, as conveyed by the 'verse of repentance';
10. Deference and obedience, as monks submit to the strict and often challenging directives of the *jikijitsu*, the *rōshi*, the *kanchō* (abbot), and administrators in denominational head temples;
11. Respect, expressed through honourific forms of addressing those superiors;
12. Physical closeness to nature and appreciation of the beauty of nature (though the nature that is close by is often the tamed, miniaturized, and stylized nature of, for example, flower arrangements, bonsai trees, and rock gardens; see Ives 2005a).

Looming large here is one additional value, *on*, the blessings one has received from others and the resultant indebtedness incurred because of those blessings. Buddhist texts usually treat *on* in terms of four types (*shi'on*): blessings from and indebtedness to 1) the ruler, 2) one's parents, 3) all sentient beings, and 4) the three jewels (Buddha, *Dharma, Saṅgha*). In *Mōanjō* (A Staff for the Blind), Suzuki Shōsan substitutes one's teachers and 'heaven and earth' (*tenchi*) for sentient beings and the three jewels (Tyler 1977: 37–38). In actual Zen practice, indebtedness and gratitude are expressed to Bodhidharma (on the *Daruma-ki* held every 5 October), the founder of the temple (commemorated on the *Kaisan-ki*), one's parents, those whose labours produced the food that supports monastic practice, and the current emperor or a patron emperor. In *Reirōshū* (Clear Sound of Jewels), Takuan (1573–1645) calls attention to indebtedness to one's feudal lord (*daimyō*):

> In regard to this, from the time one has been taken into a lord's service, of the clothes on his back, the sword he wears at his side, his footgear, his palanquin, his horse and all of his materiel, there is no single item that is not due to the favor (on) of his lord. (Wilson 1986: 49; adapted)

Hakuin writes in *Orategama* (Embossed Tea Kettle):

> To be an ordinary human living as a subject means that you eat the lord's food, wear clothes obtained from him, tie a sash he has given to you, and wear a sword obtained from him. You do not have to fetch water from a faraway place. The food you eat you do not grow yourself; the clothes you wear you do not weave for yourself. In fact, your whole body in all its parts is dependent on blessings from your lord (*kun'on*). (Yampolsky 1971: 53)

In *Mōanjō* (Peaceful Staff for the Blind), Suzuki Shōsan writes, 'Know well that it is to your lord's generosity that you owe your very life, and serve him by giving your body' (Tyler 1977: 32). Pronouncements by Zen figures leading up to and during the Second World War are peppered with references to one's indebtedness to the emperor and the need to repay that debt through military service.

In actual practice, the reinforced sense that one carries a burden of debt for various blessings, ought to feel gratitude for those blessings, and, more importantly, ought to seek ways to repay that debt (*hō'on*) can, of course, compete with what may justifiably be seen as broader demands of the precepts and compassion.

Confucianism in Zen

The value that Zen places on humility, obedience, and indebtedness bears traces of Confucianism, arguably the main determinant of Zen social ethics over the centuries in Japan. Zen monks of the Kamakura (1185–1333) and Muromachi (1333–1573) periods introduced Song Neo-Confucianism, made their monasteries centres of Confucian learning, and disseminated Confucian thought through their writings and lectures to warrior rulers and emperors (Araki 1993). In the Tokugawa period (1600–1867), leading Zen masters conveyed Confucian values to the laity through popular talks (*kana hōgo*) and to political leaders through letters and treatises. For example, organizing his *Banmin-tokuyō* along the lines of the four-tiered Confucian social hierarchy, Suzuki Shōsan configures Confucian values into different sets of guidelines for warriors, farmers, craftspeople, and merchants (*shi-nō-kō-shō*). In *Fudōchi shinmyō roku* (The Mysterious Record of Immovable Wisdom) and *Reirōshū*, Takuan champions core Confucian values of loyalty, filial piety, benevolence, and righteousness as part of his overall discourse on the unity of Confucianism and Buddhism (*Jubutsu-itchi*). In the Meiji period Imakita Kōsen (1816–1892) argues for such a unity in his *Zenkai ichiran* (One Wave on the Zen Sea) (Morinaga 1987). During the Second World War, Zen figures applauded and helped disseminate the largely Confucian imperial ideology.

With these values and social stances, Zen has been, contrary to popular images, not a radical or subversive player in Japanese history but a 'conservative' one. We see evidence of this conservative character in Zen's treatment of karma, the 'doctrine of the law of cause and effect across the three worlds [of past, present, and future]' (*sanze-inga-setsu*).

Karma

Some Buddhists have claimed that karma offers a Buddhist formulation of justice, at least in the sense of retributive and compensatory justice, with people getting what they deserve, negatively or positively. When looking at socio-economic differences, Zen figures have usually interpreted karma in this way. As Zen priest, professor, and ethicist Ichikawa Hakugen (1902–1986) and others have noted, Zen ethical thought has deployed the doctrine of karma in conjunction with notions of equality and difference. Zen thinkers have located equality in the doctrine of shared buddha nature: people are equal in that they all possess (or, as Dōgen might prefer, *are*) buddha nature. They have located difference in variations of wealth, power, status, health, and gender. As Ichikawa puts it, the tradition maintains that 'human beings are equal only in that we all possess buddha-nature and hence have the potentiality of becoming buddhas. Differing social positions, abilities, and circumstances are the retributive fruits of good and bad actions (karma) in previous existences' (Ichikawa 1970: 16–17, adapted). In short, historical Zen thinkers have explained, accepted, and justified societal differences in terms of karma.

Ichikawa singles out Hakuin as a prime example of a Zen thinker who affirms equality at the fundamental level of buddha nature (the first line of *Zazen Wasan* [Song in Praise of Zazen] reads, 'sentient beings are fundamentally buddhas') while accepting the notion that karma determines social standing. For example, in *Segyō-uta* (Song about the Practice of Giving), Hakuin valorizes inequality:

> Those who have riches and honours in this world are reaping the fruits of seeds that they planted in previous lifetimes. ... This life depends on the seeds from previous lifetimes, and the future depends on seeds from this lifetime. The amount of wealth and honour depends on the amount of seeds sown. In this lifetime there is not much for us to sow, so select good seeds and sow them. ... People who have to go and scavenge food that has been thrown away by others did not sow sufficient seeds in their previous existence, so now they are beggars. (Shaw 1963: 179, 181; adapted)

Hakuin is not alone in thinking this way. In *Muchū-mondō* (Zen Exchanges in Dreams), Musō Soseki (1275–1351) offers a karmic justification of poverty: 'Being poor in this lifetime is karmic retribution for greed in a previous life' (Ichikawa 1993: 1:495). And in *Banmin-tokuyō,* Suzuki Shōsan writes, 'Distinctions between noble and humble, high and low, rich and poor, gain and loss, and long life and short life are all due to karma from past lives' (Tyler 1977: 71; adapted). The accompanying message is for Japanese to 'know their rightful station in life' (Tyler 1977: 35).

To mitigate the tension between socio-economic differences and the underlying equality of shared buddha nature, Zen and other Buddhist thinkers have deployed the notion that 'differences are none other than equality' (*sabetsu soku byōdō*). Ichikawa claims that with this construct they have prompted their audience to accept the differences and discrimination permeating social, political, and economic life and view them as secondary to a deeper religious equality. Some Buddhists have brandished the notion of 'evil equality' (*aku-byōdō*) to attack those who would seek to remedy inequalities in the secular realm, as if the attempt to ameliorate discrimination were a violation of the natural law of karma and a misplaced search for equality at the social level that ignorantly overlooks the deeper religious equality of shared buddha nature.

Symbiosis with Those in Power

The conservative character of Japanese Zen's de facto social ethic is also evident in Zen's relationship with ruling powers in Japan. In exchange for protection and patronage, Zen leaders have performed rituals to secure such benefits for rulers as good health, success in battle, law and order across the land, and national security. This feature of Japanese Zen started with Eisai, who, as we saw, advocated Zen as the best way to ensure the security of the realm. Eisai was later joined by other prominent Zen leaders in offering support for the government. Dōgen reportedly submitted to Emperor Go-Saga a treatise titled 'Principles of the True Dharma [Buddhist teachings] for the Protection of the Realm' (*Gokoku-shōbōgi*; no longer extant). In the next century, Musō Soseki worked with the Ashikaga military government to erect sixty-six regional 'temples for the protection of the realm' (*ankokuji*); although these temples ostensibly functioned to memorialize those who had died in the war that had brought the Ashikagas to power, they also served as fortifications that enabled the Ashikaga warrior-leaders to defend distant reaches of their territory and keep an eye on the populace.

It is important to note, however, that this historical pattern in Japan is not limited to Zen institutions. Unlike strands of political philosophy that advocate the separation of 'church' and state, from the time Buddhism was introduced to Japan in the sixth century the religion has generally been intertwined with the government. Buddhist leaders have, almost without exception, actively supported Japanese rulers and their endeavours, and more often than not they have viewed this support as their duty. This on-going symbiosis between Buddhism and the ruling powers has been encapsulated in such expressions as 'the interdependence of the sovereign's law and the Buddha's law' (*ōbō-buppō sōi*), with 'Buddha's law' referring to the *Dharma* or the teachings of the Buddha. A term for Buddhism collaborating in this way is 'Buddhism that protects the realm' (*gokoku-bukkyō*).

In the case of Zen, this symbiosis has been exacerbated by what Ichikawa Hakugen has termed 'accommodationism' (*junnō-shugi*), the act of according with the situation in which one finds oneself. He traces this to the supposed founder of Chan/Zen, Bodhidharma, and his notion of *suiyuan-xing* (Jp. *zuien-gyō*), the practice of according with circumstances. In *Anxin-famen* (Jp. *Anjin hōmon*; Method for Pacifying the Mind) Bodhidharma purportedly states:

> The wise entrust themselves to things, not to the self. For this reason, there is no grasping or rejecting, no opposing or obeying. The ignorant entrust themselves to the self and do not accord with things. For this reason, there is grasping and rejecting, opposing and obeying. (Broughton 1999: 79; adapted)

Three centuries later, in his characterization of the 'true person of the Way', Linji (Jp. Rinzai d. 866), puts it this way: 'Merely according with circumstances, he uses up his past karma; entrusting himself to things as they come (*nin'nun*), he puts on his clothes; when he wants to walk he walks, when he wants to sit he sits' (Sasaki 1975: 9–10; adapted). We see a modern instance of this symbiosis and 'accommodationism' during the Second World War in Japan, when Zen leaders, through their writings, statements, and other actions, supported Japanese militarism and imperialism (Ives 2009b, Victoria 2003, 2006).

In the postwar period, however, Zen thinkers have criticized this ethical pitfall and started conceptualizing what a more critical Zen social ethic might entail. Lay Zen master and Kyoto University professor Hisamatsu Shin'ichi advocated freeing Zen from its symbiosis with the Japanese nation state and re-establishing Zen in the three-dimensional framework of F, A, and S:

> Awakening to the Formless Self,
> the dimension of depth, the Self as the ground of human existence;
> Standing on the standpoint of All Humankind,
> the dimension of width, human being in its entirety;
> Creating history Suprahistorically,
> the dimension of length, awakened human history. (Abe 1981: 143)

Ichikawa Hakugen pulled from Christian ethics, Western philosophy, and Marxist thought to criticize historical Zen's social stances and its collaboration with the imperialism and warfare of the early Shōwa period (1926–1945). He called for a reformation of Zen that would free it from the 'accommodationism' mentioned above and give it critical rigor (Ives 2009b).

In recent decades Sōtō scholars Hakamaya Noriaki and Matsumoto Shirō have offered another criticism of Zen's accommodation of the status quo (see Shields 2011 and Hubbard and Swanson 1997). They lift up 'critical Buddhism' (*hihan Bukkyō*) with its doctrines of dependent origination and no-soul and its use of reason and language to discriminate and analyse the ways things are. They contrast this early Buddhist stance with later 'topical Buddhism', which through doctrines like buddha nature (Skt *buddha-dhatu*) and the *tathāgata-garbha* posits a unified topos or ground that exists beneath and prior to phenomenal reality and can be intuited in a purportedly translinguistic, ineffable experience. This approach, 'by forsaking critical discrimination in favor of a precritical unity or harmony … tends to downplay or even deny the reality of actual historical differences, thus allowing for an affirmation of the status quo and negating the need for social criticism' (Hubbard 1997: 98). Hakamaya and Matsumoto argue that with this 'topical' character Zen and other forms of Japanese Buddhism have celebrated 'tolerance' and 'harmony' (Shields 2011: 54) at the expense of criticism and dissent and thus enabled if not promoted authoritarianism during the Second World War and other times in Japanese history.

The challenge for Hisamatsu, Ichikawa, Hakamaya, Matsumoto, and other Japanese Zen ethicists is the fact that their Zen historically has been an embedded *Japanese* religion embracing *conventional* norms, and hence it has never systematically and rigorously formulated its ethical and political stances on the basis of the *universal* resources in the Mahāyāna tradition of which it is part, on the basis of Buddhist values that can function as norms *transcendent* of conventional and at times parochial Japanese morality, that is to say, as norms that provide a basis for critiquing prevailing moral stances and socio-political arrangements. In key respects, such a (re)formulation characterizes much of what see in contemporary Zen ethics, especially in the West. (That being said, just as Japanese Zen ethics was coloured by Confucianism, much of Western Zen ethics has been coloured by non-Buddhist ethical traditions and resources such as philosophical ethics (including virtue ethics, deontology, and utilitarianism), theories of social justice, human rights theory, environmentalism, and feminist and womanist theories.)

Contemporary Zen Ethics in the West

Early American and European interest in Zen was permeated with images of Zen that suggested an antinomian character: trickster hermits rejecting society and enlightened masters acting iconoclastically relative to conventional morality. As Zen sank roots in Western soil this image faded, and serious practitioners tapped ethical resources as they set up new types of Zen institutions and responded to issues in the world around them.

In general, Zen leaders in the West have taken the precepts seriously. Some Zen teachers have followed the approach of Dōgen. Richard Baker, former Zen master at the San Francisco Zen Center, has written, 'The precepts are a manifestation and expression of an enlightened mind' (1993: 162). John Daidō Loori (1931–2009), founder of Zen Mountain Monastery in the Catskills, wrote: 'In essence, the Precepts are a definition of the life of a Buddha, of how a Buddha functions in the world. They are how enlightened beings live their lives, relate to other human beings, make moral and ethical decisions, manifest wisdom and compassion in everyday life' (2002: 133–134).

Zen teachers have also echoed Eisai in giving the precepts a more instrumentalist reading. Vietnamese Zen master Thich Nhat Hanh (b. 1926) has written, 'Practicing the precepts ... helps us be more calm and concentrated and brings more insight and enlightenment' (1993: 8). According to Baker, 'The precepts are the starting point for us personally, for society, for the planet, because they are the necessary and essential foundation for developing practical wisdom and effective [skilful] compassion' (1993: 158).

What is most distinctive about contemporary approaches to the precepts in the West, however, is the application of precepts to social issues. As one part of what Thich Nhat Hanh termed 'Engaged Buddhism', Zen Buddhists have been working with the precepts and other components of Buddhist ethics—and in some cases reinterpreting both their content and their function—in response to war, challenges faced by women, environmental problems, and other issues.

War

Over the centuries Zen figures supported Japanese warriors in various ways and advocated Zen practice as helpful on the battlefield. Famous in this regard are Chinese master Wuxue Zuyuan (1226–1286), who counselled military ruler Hōjō Tokimune (1251–1284) in the face of a Mongol invasion; Japanese master Takuan, who expounded on Zen mental states as no-mind, no-thought, non-abiding, and immovable wisdom to master swordsman Yagyū Munemori (1571–1646); and modern Zen masters who made claims about the martial fruits of Zen in their nationalist discourse leading up to and during the Second World War. The close Zen connection to the samurai and their swordsmanship has been termed 'the unity of Zen and the sword' (*kenzen-ichinyo*).

Zen outside of Japan has in recent years diverged from the Japanese pattern of symbiosis with warrior rulers. In the middle of the Vietnam War, Thich Nhat Hanh and other monks started the Order of Inter-being, which has expanded the Five Precepts into fourteen 'mindfulness trainings', most of which aim at reducing conflict and war. These precepts admonish against attachment to one's political views, intolerance, forcing one's views on others, fanaticism, acting on anger, saying things that cause division, and turning one's eyes from suffering. The twelfth reads:

> Aware that much suffering is caused by war and conflict, we are determined to cultivate nonviolence, understanding, and compassion in our daily lives, to promote peace education, mindful mediation, and reconciliation within families, communities, nations, and in the world. We are determined not to kill and not to let others kill. We will diligently practice deep looking with our Sangha [Buddhist community] to discover better ways to protect life and prevent war. (Nhat Hanh 1998: 21)

Zen teachers Robert Aitken (1917–2010) and Nelson Foster (b. 1951) were instrumental in the founding of the Buddhist Peace Fellowship in 1978. Zen teacher Bernie Glassman (b. 1939) founded the Zen Peacemaker Order, which has engaged in 'bearing witness' at sites of violence (including Auschwitz), orchestrated projects to foster peaceful coexistence between Palestinians and Israelis, and offered nonviolence trainings. Glassman has augmented the precepts with Four Commitments: 'I commit to 1. a reverence for life; 2. a sustainable and just economy; 3. equal rights for all; 4. stewardship of the Earth' (ZPO Rule).

Challenges Faced by Women

Influenced by dominant Confucian views of women and other factors in East Asia, Zen has generally denigrated and subordinated women. In a colloquial sermon Rinzai master Bankei (1622–1693) preaches, 'Women tend to anger easily and stir up delusions, even over quite trivial things' (Haskel 1984: 55). In *Mōanjō*, Suzuki Shōsan writes:

> Women ... stick to other women. Their clinging to self is deep, and they are spiteful and jealous. ... A woman's nature, now, is twisted deep down. Her greed is enormous, her egotism profound, and she is drawn to bewilderment until she knows no right or wrong. Her words are crafty and her mind is shallow. What you do when you yield to her turns to karma for rebirth; when you oppose her she is your sworn enemy. Know, at any rate, that she is pitifully ignorant. (Tyler 1977: 46–47)

Many Sōtō Zen thinkers viewed women as polluted and polluting because of the blood of menstruation and childbirth, and karmically destined to fall into the Blood Pool Hell unless Zen priests ritually intervene (Williams 2005: 50–53).

The Zen view of women has shifted in the West. Many prominent Zen teachers are women. Recently women in North America created a new lineage chart with female Zen figures of the past; this document has been used when female practitioners receive the precepts (*jukai*) (Fowles 2014). Over the past decade, instances of sexual harassment and abuse in Zen institutions have received the attention and response they deserve. Temples and meditation centres have been formulating guidelines about proper behaviour of teachers and procedures for dealing with complaints. In response to reports of mistreatment of women in one Zen community, a group of Zen teachers formed a Witness Council in November 2012, heard testimony from those involved, and issued a summative report. In January 2015 a group of ninety-two Zen teachers in North America signed an 'open letter confronting abuse'.

Environmental Issues

Western Zen Buddhists have responded in various ways to climate change and other environmental problems. For over fifty years Gary Snyder (b. 1930) has been on the vanguard of this concern about environmental issues. Such Zen institutions as San Francisco Zen Center's Green Gulch Farm, Zen Mountain Monastery in the Catskills, and Zen Mountain Center in southern California have taken steps to make themselves into green communities. At Zen Mountain Monastery, John Daidō Loori started a Zen Environmental Studies Institute. Zen Buddhists have also crafted new practices, including the 'earth relief ceremony' performed by the Zen Center of Rochester, backpacking retreats ('mountains and rivers sesshins') led by Nelson Foster of the Ring of Bone Zendo, a ritual memorializing plants and animals that have died in the gardens of Green Gulch Farm, and retreats led by Thich Nhat Hanh for environmentalists (Kraft 1994).

In May of 2015 a number Zen teachers participated in the first Buddhist delegation to the White House, and the group presented a 'Buddhist Declaration on Climate Change' that had been crafted by Zen thinker David Loy (a teacher in the Sanbō Kyōdan strand of Japanese Zen) and others involved in a new group, Ecological Buddhism. In the months leading up to the 2015 climate conference in Paris, followers of Thich Nhat Hanh played a major role in getting Buddhist leaders to sign the 'Buddhist Climate Change Statement to World Leaders'.

Zen Buddhists have also moved the precepts in an ecological direction, as evidenced by the eco-precepts formulated by Christopher Reed (Reed 1990: 235) and the Tiep Hien Order's 'mindfulness trainings', which include such guidelines as the eleventh, '*Aware that great violence and injustice have been done to our environment and society*, we are committed not to live with a vocation that is harmful to humans and nature', and the thirteenth, '*Aware of the suffering caused be exploitation, social injustice, stealing, and oppression*, we are committed to cultivating loving kindness and learning ways to work for the well-being of people, animals, plants, and minerals' (Nhat Hanh 1998: 20–21). Thich Nhat Hanh has crafted 'earth gathas', one of which reads,

> In this plate of food,
> I see the entire universe
> supporting my existence. (1990b: 195)

In monographs, anthologies, and articles in journals and popular Buddhist publications, Zen Buddhists have also been writing extensively about environmental problems.

In this 'greening' of Zen, they have tapped an array of sources: texts, doctrines, ethical values, and ritual practices. For example, Zen thinkers often celebrate how meditative practice generates non-dual ways of experiencing that connect people more deeply to nature and, by extension, lead them to value and protect it more. Doug Codiga writes, 'A skillful Zen student will strive to be awakened to an identity with all phenomena' (108), and Thich Nhat Hanh argues, 'We should be able to be our true self. That means we should be able to be the river, we should be able to be the forest. ... That is the non-dualistic way of seeing' (1990a: 68–69). Zen environmentalists often tap several fascicles of Dōgen's *Shōbōgenzō: Sansuikyō* (The Mountains and Waters Sutra) and *Keisei-sanshoku* (The Voice of the Valley [Stream], the Form of the Mountain). They also turn for inspiration to Chinese poet-hermit Hanshan (ninth century) and Japanese poet-hermit Ryōkan (1758–1831).

Their analyses and arguments, however, are not without controversy. Critics have claimed, for example, that historical Buddhist doctrines and practices are not as ecological as these Zen writers have made them out to be, that these writers are engaging in acts of eisegesis by looking selectively in Buddhist sources to support the environmental ethic they brought to their practice of Zen in the first place, or simply that they are distorting those sources as they apply them to problems like the climate crisis (Ives 2009a and 2016).

Engaged Zen Buddhists have also been addressing poverty, racism, corporate power (Loy 2003: ch. 4, and Ives 2005b), and other issues, and it remains to be seen whether the largely progressive Zen ethical approach to these issues holds sway in coming decades. Like all traditions, Zen has changed over the centuries and from culture to culture, and in all likelihood Zen thinkers will continue to articulate new ethical stances in the centuries to come.

Works Cited

Abe M. (1981) Hisamatsu Shin'ichi, 1889–1980. *The Eastern Buddhist*, 14 (1), 142–149.

Abe M. (1991) Kenotic God and dynamic sunyata. In: J. B. Cobb, Jr and C. Ives (eds), *The emptying God: a Buddhist-Jewish-Christian conversation*. Maryknoll, NY: Orbis Books, 3–65.

Araki K. (1993) *Bukkyō to jukyō* (Buddhism and Confucianism). Tokyo: Kenbun Shuppan.

Baker, R. (1993) Notes on the practice and territory of the precepts. In: T. Nhat Hanh (ed.), *For a future to be possible: commentaries on the five wonderful precepts*. Berkeley: Parallax Press.

Bodiford, W. M. (1993) *Sōtō Zen in medieval Japan*. Honolulu: University of Hawai'i Press.

Bodiford, W. M. (2005) Bodhidharma's precepts in Japan. In: W. M. Bodiford (ed.), *Going forth: visions of Buddhist vinaya*. Honolulu: University of Hawai'i Press, 185–209.

Broughton, J. (1999) *The Bodhidharma anthology: the earliest records of Zen*. Berkeley: University of California Press.

De Silva, P. (1990) Buddhist environmental ethics. In: A. H. Badiner (ed.), *Dharma Gaia: a harvest of essays in Buddhism and ecology*. Berkeley: Parallax Press, 14–19.

Eisai (2005) A treatise on letting Zen flourish to protect the state. Translated by G. Tokiwa. In: J. R. McRae et al. (eds). *Zen texts*. Berkeley: Numata Center for Buddhist Translation and Research, 45–240.

Faure, B. (1998) *The red thread: Buddhist approaches to sexuality*. Princeton: Princeton University Press.

Fowles, M. (2014) Roused from a dream: restoring Zen's female lineage. *Tricycle* (Summer), n.p. Available from: https://tricycle.org/magazine/roused-dream/ [accessed 18 January 2016].

Gregory, P. N. (ed.) (1987) *Sudden and gradual: approaches to enlightenment in Chinese thought*. Honolulu: University of Hawai'i Press.

Haskel, P. (trans.) (1984) *Bankei Zen: translations from the record of Bankei*. New York: Grove Press.

Heine, S. (2005) Dōgen and the precepts, revisited. In: D. Keown (ed.), *Buddhist studies from India to America: essays in honor of Charles S, Prebish*. London: RoutledgeCurzon, 11–31.

Heine, S. (2008) *Zen skin, Zen marrow: will the real Zen Buddhism please stand up?* New York: Oxford University Press.

Hubbard, J. (1997) Topophobia. In: J. Hubbard and P. L. Swanson (eds.), *Pruning the bodhi tree: the storm over Critical Buddhism*. Honolulu: University of Hawai'i Press, 81–112.

Hubbard, J., and Swanson, P. L. (eds) (1997) *Pruning the bodhi tree: the storm over Critical Buddhism*. Honolulu: University of Hawai'i Press.

Ichikawa H. (1970) The problem of Buddhist socialism in Japan. *Japanese religions*, 6 (3) (August), 15–37.

Ichikawa H. (1993) *Ichikawa Hakugen chosaku-shū* (The collected works of Ichikawa Hakugen). 4 volumes. Kyoto: Hōzōkan.

Ives, C. (1992) *Zen awakening and society*. London and Honolulu: Macmillan/University of Hawai'i Press.

Ives, C. (1992) (2005a) Japanese love of nature. In: B. R. Taylor (ed.), *The encyclopedia of religion and nature*, volume 1. New York: Thoemmes Continuum, 899–900.

Ives, C. (2005b) Liberation from economic dukkha: a Buddhist critique of the gospels of growth and globalization in dialogue with John Cobb. In: C. Cornille and G. Willis (eds), *The world market and interreligious dialogue*. Eugene, OR: Cascade Books, 107–127.

Ives, C. (2009a) In search of a green dharma: philosophical issues in Buddhist environmental ethics. In: C. Prebish and J. Powers (eds), *Destroying Mara forever: Buddhist ethics essays in honor of Damien Keown*. Ithaca, NY: Snow Lion Publications, 165–186.

Ives, C. (2009b) *Imperial-way Zen: Ichikawa Hakugen's critique and lingering questions for Buddhist ethics*. Honolulu: University of Hawai'i Press.

Ives, C. (2016) A mixed dharmic bag: current debates about Buddhism and ecology. In: W. Jenkins and M. E. Tucker (eds), *Routledge handbook of religion and ecology*. New York: Routledge, 43–51.

Kim, H.-J. (1987) *Dōgen Kigen, mystical realist*. Tucson, AZ: University of Arizona Press.

Kraft, K. (1994) The greening of Buddhist practice. *Crosscurrents* 44 (2), 163–179.

Leighton, T. D. (trans.) (1995) *Dōgen's pure standards for the Zen community: a translation of Eihei Shingi*. Albany, NY: State University of New York Press.

Loori, J. D. (2002) *The eight gates of Zen: a program of Zen training*. Boston: Shambhala.

Low, A. (1988) Master Hakuin's gateway to freedom. In: K. Kraft (ed.), *Zen: tradition and transition*. New York: Grove Press, 88–104.

Loy, D. R. (2003) *The great awakening: a Buddhist social theory*. Boston: Wisdom.

Masunaga R. (trans.) (1978) *A primer of Sōtō Zen: a translation of Dōgen's Shōbōgenzō Zuimonki*. Honolulu: University of Hawai'i Press.

Morinaga S. (ed.) (1987) *Zenkai ichiran* (One wave on the Zen sea). Tokyo: Hakujusha.

Nhat Hanh, T. (1990a) *Being peace*. Berkeley: Parallax Press.

Nhat Hanh, T. (1990b) Earth gathas. In: A. H. Badiner (ed.), *Dharma Gaia: a harvest of essays in Buddhism and ecology*. Berkeley: Parallax Press, 195–196.
Nhat Hanh, T. (1993) Introduction. In: T. Nhat Hanh (ed.), *For a future to be possible: commentaries on the five wonderful precepts*. Berkeley: Parallax Press, 1–4.
Nhat Hanh, T. (1998) *Interbeing: fourteen guidelines for engaged Buddhism*. 3rd edition. Berkeley: Parallax Press.
Poceski, M. (2006) *Guishan jingce* (*Guishan's admonitions*) and the ethical foundations of Chan practice. In: S. Heine and D. S. Wright (eds), *Zen classics: formative texts in the history of Zen Buddhism*. New York: Oxford University Press, 15–42.
Reed, C. (1990) Down to earth. In: A. H. Badiner (ed.), *Dharma Gaia: a harvest of essays in Buddhism and ecology*. Berkeley: Parallax Press, 233–235.
Sasaki, R. F. (trans.) (1975) *The record of Lin-chi*. Kyoto: Institute for Zen Studies.
Shaw, R. D. M. (trans.) (1963) *The embossed tea kettle: Orate Gama and other works of Hakuin Zenji, the Zen reformer of the eighteenth century in Japan*. London: George Allen & Allen.
Shields, J. M. (2011) *Critical Buddhism: engaging with modern Japanese Buddhist thought*. Richmond, UK: Ashgate.
Tyler, R. (trans.) (1977) *Selected writings of Suzuki Shōsan*. Cornell University East Asia Papers, 13. Ithaca, NY: Cornell China-Japan Program.
Victoria, B. (2003) *Zen war stories*. New York: RoutledgeCurzon.
Victoria, B. (2006) *Zen at war*. 2nd edition. Lanham, MD: Rowman & Littlefield.
Watson, B. (trans.) (1993 *The Lotus Sutra*. New York: Columbia University Press.
Welter, A. (1999) Eisai's promotion of Zen for the protection of the country. In: G. J. Tanabe, Jr (ed.), *Religions of Japan in practice*. Princeton: Princeton University Press, 63–70.
Welter, A. (2006) Zen Buddhism as the ideology of the Japanese state: Eisai and the *Kōzen gokokuron*. In: S. Heine and D. S. Wright (eds), *Zen classics: formative texts in the history of Zen Buddhism*. New York: Oxford University Press, 65–112.
Welter, A. (2008) Buddhist rituals for protecting the country in medieval Japan: Myōan Eisai's 'Regulations of the Zen School'. In: S. Heine and D. S. Wright (eds), *Zen ritual: studies of Zen Buddhist theory in practice*. New York: Oxford University Press, 113–138.
Williams, D. (2005) *The other side of Zen: a social history of Sōtō Zen Buddhism in Tokugawa Japan*. Princeton: Princeton University Press.
Williams, P. (1989) *Mahāyāna Buddhism: the doctrinal foundations*. New York: Routledge.
Wilson, W. S. (trans.) (1986) *The unfettered mind: writing of the Zen master to the sword master*. New York: Kodansha International.
Yokoi Y., and Victoria, D. (trans.) (1976) *Zen master Dōgen: an introduction with selected writings*. New York: Weatherhill.
Yampolsky, P. B. (trans.) (1971) *The Zen master Hakuin: selected writings*. New York: Columbia University Press.
ZPO Rule (n.d.) Available from: http://zenpeacemakers.org/zpo-rule/ [accessed 30 December 2015].

Suggested Reading

Bodiford, W. M. (2005) Bodhidharma's precepts in Japan. In: W. M. Bodiford (ed.), *Going forth: visions of Buddhist vinaya*. Honolulu: University of Hawai'i Press, 185–209.
Bodiford, W. M. (1993) *Sōtō Zen in medieval Japan*. Honolulu: University of Hawai'i Press.

Heine, S. (2005) Dōgen and the precepts, revisited. In: D. Keown (ed.), *Buddhist studies from India to America: essays in honor of Charles S. Prebish*. London: RoutledgeCurzon, 11–31.

Heine, S. (2008) *Zen skin, Zen marrow: will the real Zen Buddhism please stand up?* New York: Oxford University Press.

Ives, C. (2009) *Imperial-way Zen: Ichikawa Hakugen's critique and lingering questions for Buddhist ethics*. Honolulu: University of Hawai'i Press.

Leighton, T. D. (trans.) (1995) *Dōgen's pure standards for the Zen community: a translation of Eihei Shingi*. Albany, NY: State University of New York Press.

Nhat Hanh, T. (ed.) (1993) *For a future to be possible: commentaries on the five wonderful precepts*. Berkeley: Parallax Press, 1–4.

Welter, A. (2006) Zen Buddhism as the ideology of the Japanese state: Eisai and the *Kōzen gokokuron*. In: S. Heine and D. S. Wright (eds), *Zen classics: formative texts in the history of Zen Buddhism*. New York: Oxford University Press, 65–112.

CHAPTER 12

TANTRIC ETHICS

GARETH SPARHAM

What is Buddhist Tantric Morality?

A discussion of Buddhist Tantric morality requires at the outset an identification of sources. As a generalized system, in the sense of Christian morality, Confucian morality, or Islamic morality, it is to be discovered, if indeed it can be found, primarily in Indian Buddhist Tantric literature of the late tenth and early eleventh centuries. It is true that there is valuable knowledge to be gained from researching the mores or practices of living communities of Indians, Bhutanese, Nepalese, or Tibetans who profess Tantric Buddhist beliefs, and much knowledge to be gained from sifting the residue of living communities of the past, their gravestones, architecture, and so on. However, although such investigations are necessary, as Max Nihom (1994: 9) has pointed out, somewhat acerbically, when it comes to the study of Tantra, in particular, it is illusory to think that a theoretically privileged (read, more scientific) knowledge can be derived from carefully sifting 'realia', in contrast to a somehow less rigorous knowledge gleaned from high-status texts.

> The current interest in realia, Buddhist or Hindu, is but a high-status reflex of the academic study of pop-culture. … Things of universal import are by any definition parcel of high, or elitist culture, while the import of realia is only recognizable after cognizance of the universalia to which they refer.

The Indian and Tibetan Buddhist Tantric texts of the late tenth and early eleventh centuries that systematize a distinct Tantric morality comprise a set of instructions on how to govern personal conduct (i.e. what you do, how you speak, and how you think) as the axle around which ordinary and extraordinary *siddhis* (achievements) turn. The rim that binds the *siddhis* is *samādhi* (a deep yogic state of mental absorption). The spokes are nonconceptual knowledge, Mahāyāna altruism (*bodhicitta*), and special feelings of bliss. The ordinary *siddhis* include activities of use to people such as kings (such as magical spells to defeat 'enemies of the *Dharma*' or to pacify superhuman creatures who might be blocking timely rains or causing epidemics). All the ordinary *siddhis* are included in the extraordinary *siddhi*—enlightenment or awakening (*bodhi*)—an exalted personal status that serves as the best possible vehicle to benefit others, primarily by teaching them Buddhist doctrines of liberation.

Buddhist Tantric moral codes are not timeless laws, and although they are in accord with nature, as explained below, to break them is not to go against the will or the word of a creator god. Rather, Buddhist Tantric moral codes describe a psychology of morals, similar to the Greek morality Michel Foucault discovers in classical (Greek and Latin) literature. Foucault's observation that the ancient Greeks were concerned with the construction of an ethical self holds equally true for Buddhist Tantra.

> The sexual austerity that was prematurely recommended by Greek philosophy is not rooted in the timelessness of a law that would take the historically diverse forms of repression, one after the other. It belongs to a history that is more decisive for comprehending the transformations of moral experience than the history of codes: a history of 'ethics', understood as the elaboration of a form of relation to self that enables an individual to fashion himself into a subject of ethical conduct. (1986: 251)

Buddhist Tantric morality, then, is premised on the need for a person to refashion him or herself continually in the service of an ever-higher conduct: a noblesse oblige of the spiritual elite. What is forgiven in the masses is the proper object of contempt in the ruler or the spiritual elite. It is a morality 'meant for elite practitioners alone' (Wedemeyer 2013: 152).

Systematic Buddhist Tantric Morality

The primary source for later commentaries setting out a systematic Buddhist Tantric morality is the *Vajraśekharatantra* (*rgyud rdo rje rtse mo*).[1] According to Steven Weinberger (2003: 96–98, 102, 204) it is a single work made up of two separate texts from amongst a group of eighteen texts called the **Vajroṣṇiṣa* (*jīngāng dǐng*) associated with Amoghavajra (705–774), an important figure in the spread of Tantric Buddhism in China. The date the two texts, or early versions of them, were compiled into the *Vajraśekhara* as we have it today is not clear but was possibly as early as the latter half of the eighth century. Weinberger (2003: 205) writes:

> ... the Vajraśekhara Tantra represents a significant landmark in the development of Indian Buddhist tantra because it contains an extensive presentation of tantric vows

[1] In the Sde dge edition of the Bka' 'gyur (D 482) the work is named *gsang ba rnal byor chen po'i rgyud rdo rje rtse mo* (*vajraśekharamāhaguhyayogatantra*).

> and pledges ... [its] presentation is significant not only for its depth but also because its elucidation of the required and prohibited activities for each of the Buddha families individually is likely the first of its kind found in a Buddhist tantra itself.

A passage probably taken from the *Vajraśekhara* in the *Saṃpuṭa* (composed in the middle of the tenth century; Szántó 2012: 50), extant in a Sanskrit manuscript,[2] establishes a set of commitments (*samaya*) for each of the five buddhas who represent the five transformed (buddhified) *skandhas* of the practitioner. A similar passage is also found in the *Sarvadurgatipariśodhana Tantra*.

The set of five *samayas*, related to the transformed *skandhas*, are commitments to remain true to transforming ordinary body, speech, and thoughts into those of the deities of the different *maṇḍalas* in the *Tattvasaṃgrahatantra* (the *Vajraśekhara*'s root Tantra). The *samayas* taken together form a proto-systematic morality that transcends being simply rules for a specific practice of deity yoga.

The relevant passage from the *Vajraśekharatantra* found in the *Saṃpuṭa* (there is no extant Sanskrit version of the *Vajraśekharatantra* itself) initially says it is a *sādhana* (i.e. a means of accomplishment). Christian Wedemeyer (2013: 174), following Yael Bentor, observes that 'the structure of the *sādhana* constitutes the ritual template' for all Tantric rituals, including rites for ordination. They 'are not only based upon but actually nested within the overarching and primary ritual pattern of the *sādhana*'. Thomas Yarnall (2013: 78–84, 201) shows where the rite occurs in a *sādhana* according to an early fifteenth-century Tibetan work by Tsongkhapa.

Here is a summary and translation of the relevant passage from the *Saṃpuṭa*. The Tantric practitioner (*mantrin*), having first entered into the deity's residence, visualizes a letter A, from that a moon, and on top of that a five-spoked *vajra*. Then, having made worship and a prostration, the practitioner says in a ritual manner (*vidhinā*) to the buddhas and bodhisattvas, 'Please pay attention to me' (*samanvāharantu mām*). The supplicant then states his or her name and says, 'Just as the buddhas (*nātha*) of the three times were unwavering (*krtaniścayāḥ*) in their concern for beings, I too will cultivate the *bodhicitta* motivation (*utpādayāmi paramaṃ bodhicittam uttamam*) until I reach enlightenment (*yāvad ā bodhimaṇḍaniṣadanā[t]*).'

Following this the *sādhaka* (the Tantric practitioner) makes commitments (*samaya*) specific to each of the five buddha families. These families represent the transformations of the five *skandhas* of an ordinary person. The first commitment is to the physical transformation born of the practice of the Buddha [Vairocana] (*samvaraṃ buddhayogajam*). The practitioner articulates the first set of commitments (i.e. the *samaya*) associated with Vairocana Buddha by saying, 'I will keep the bodhisattva's threefold practice of morality (*trividhāṃ śīlaśikṣāṃ*). I will firmly hold the three jewels--Buddha, *Dharma*, Saṃgha as supreme.' This constitutes a pledge of allegiance to Buddhism in general

[2] Available online from the University of Tokyo, numbered New 427, Old 324 at http://picservice.ioc.u-tokyo.ac.jp/03_150219~UT-library_sanskrit_ms/MF14_52_003~ MF14_52_003/?pageId=001, accessed January 2016.

(Szántó 2012: 33), after which the *sādhaka* commits to the *Bodhisattvabhūmi*'s three categories of morality (explained in more detail below).

The Great Buddha Family [Akṣobhya] (*mahābuddhakūlodbhave*) is the transformation of the consciousness *skandha*. The practitioner articulates the second set of commitments (i.e. the *samaya*) associated with Akṣobhya Buddha by saying, 'I will firmly keep the *vajra*, bell, and *mudrā*.' The *vajra* is the symbol of *upāya* (means) and the bell of *prajñā* (wisdom). The unity of these two is the *mudrā* ('seal', 'consort'). A second meaning of *mudrā* references the great bliss born simultaneously with the unity.

The Great Ratna[sambhava] Family is the transformation of the feeling *skandha*. The commitment is to 'giving the four gifts six times each day'. The four are of material things, freedom from danger, Buddhist teaching, and giving free from the conception of a giver, gift, and recipient.

The Great Lotus Family of Amitābha is the transformation of the *saṃjñā* ('perception', 'naming') *skandha*. The commitment is to the *Dharma*. This may be an open-ended revelation, or may end with the myriad Tantras. It means to keep (in the sense of believe in) outer (non-Buddhist, or at least non-Tantric) *Dharma* secret (Buddhist Tantra), and the three vehicles (*bāhyaguḍkatriyānika*). The three vehicles in the *Prajñāpāramitā* literature are of the *śrāvaka*s, the *pratyekabuddha*s, and the bodhisattvas. This is non-Tantric Mahāyāna's appropriation of foundational, or older Buddhist, scriptures through a hermeneutics of *abhisamdhi* and *abhipraya* (that is, categorizing scriptures for particular persons, times, or situations, with the actual intention of the speaker hidden behind words that may or may not be taken at their face value), and *neyārtha* and *nitārtha* (that which requires interpretation and that which is explicit).

Here I leave aside a fuller discussion of docetism as a principle informing Tantra. In the context of Buddhist Tantra such a discussion would not be about whether the sufferings of the Son of God are actually real sufferings or apparitional demonstrations for the benefit of the beholders, but whether or not the apparitional bodies (*kāya*) of a buddha are real. Suffice it to say that the *samaya* of Amitābha in the *Vajraśekhara* (in essence governing speech), as a commitment to hold all the diverse Buddhist teaching (and perhaps even non-Buddhist teaching) as sacred and equally important, presupposes a doctrine of teaching and meanings that convey no truth on their own, but are merely appearances in an altruistic world tailored to, and for the benefit of, those who behold or hear them.

The fifth Great Action [Amoghasiddhi Buddha] Family is the transformation of the *saṃskāra* ('volition') *skandha*. It is conceived as the generality where the other four families are the particulars, insofar as all of the other families incorporate action in one form or the other. The commitment here is to keeping the entire code (*samvaraṃ sarvasayuktaṃ*). In addition, the practitioner commits to perform the worship (*pūjā*) as much as possible, this being in particular the worship involved in the specific *sādhana* of the individual *devatā* (Tib. *yi dam*), that is, oneself in the form of the god (buddha) one will become. Thus the final *samaya* is the commitment to deity yoga.

Bodhisattva Morality

The texts propounding a systematic Buddhist Tantric morality written towards the end of the tenth century find a moral code in the *Vajraśekharatantra* beyond the moral codes set forth in the *Vinaya* and *Bodhisattvabhūmi*. Still, in essence it is the morality set forth in the *Bodhisattvabhūmi* together with the commitment to deity yoga explained below. This is what is meant by the incorporation of the bodhisattva's morality as three of the six *samaya*s of the buddha Vairocana (the six together constituting the first of the five sets of *samayas*).

In regard to a bodhisattva's morality, as I have explained elsewhere (Sparham 2005), first the bodhisattva has to have a psychologically active moral standard (akin to Foucault's construction of an ethical self). This standard is in operation where he or she has ideals embodied in others who are admired. It presupposes the restraining or activating mental force (*caitta*) of *vyapatrāpya* (Tib. *khrel yod*) operating when experiencing the positive emotion of embarrassment. The social ritual of ordination (*parataḥ samādāna*) is the necessary complex for cultivating such a mental force: to wit, being accepted by, and entering into association with, those whose ideals are admired. The restraining or activating mental force called *hrī* (Tib. *ngo tshar*) is in operation when there is the experience of something like the emotion of shame. It requires that the moral standard is one's own, embodying one's purest aspiration (*suviśudhāśaya*).

This alone does not constitute the full psychology of a vowed morality. It constitutes the moving enlightenment experience (the so-called Mahāyāna attitude) no doubt, but does not explain the effective operation of a vowed morality in all the sites and situations where training (*śikṣāpada*) occurs. That requires the impulse to continually 'make correction' (*pratyāpatti*) after failure, and an admiration (*ādara*) for the ethical self accompanied by mindfulness (*smṛti*) to avoid failure in all and every situation. Both admiration and mindfulness are restraining or activating mental forces and the complex of all four mental forces constitutes moral behaviour.

The Morality Chapter of the *Bodhisattvabhūmi* breaks this general explanation of morality into three categories: *saṃvaraśīla* ('vowed morality'), *kuśaladharmasaṃgrāhakaśīla* ('morality involved in accumulating the wholesome [buddha]dharmas'), and *sattvārthakriyāśīla* ('morality involved in doing what helps beings'). These are the three *samaya*s (together with the three commitments to Buddha, *Dharma*, and *Saṅgha*) of Vairocana.

The first category is the morality detailed in earlier Buddhism, namely the codifications of conduct (the *Vinaya*) for the four branches of the community (*saṅgha*)—the monks (*bhikṣu*) and nuns (*bhikṣuṇī*), and the male (*upāsaka*) and female householders (*upāsikā*). These can be further expanded into seven or even eight branches. It is a vowed morality codified in sets of rules or laws to govern personal behaviour, particularly restraint from the unbridled, shameless, gratification of the senses. In bodhisattva morality this basic morality is re-envisioned as part of a larger, altruistic moral project.

The second category includes rules for the development of the physical and mental qualities (*dharma*) that make up a perfectly awakened being. The physical is not restricted to a single language or to a single physical body but comprises: infinite bodies, in infinite forms, in line with the dispositions of those who are there to benefit from them; and perfect speech in all languages for those with an inclination to listen. The mental qualities are, similarly, infinite knowledge, kindness, and skill in means. All are a means to an end (the welfare of beings). They do not partake of an absolute and have no purpose beyond the welfare of beings dictated by the altruistic principle—*bodhicitta* ('the thought of enlightenment'). This category of bodhisattva morality clearly anticipates, or provides room for, a specifically Buddhist Tantric morality.

The third category (*contra* Zimmermann 2013) codifies ordinary altruism, and reflects the insight that altruistic behaviour is not restricted to endeavours of altruistic persons to develop or 'educate' themselves, but necessarily includes simply doing for others what they want, just because they want it, with the thought that they may become receptive. Asaṅga's *Bodhisattvabhūmi* says it is for the purpose of 'maturing beings', that is, making them receptive to Buddhist teachings about morality and practice. It is incorrect to take this third category as the codification of all altruistic acts. The three moralities together describe altruistic morality in its entirety. It is also incorrect to interpret the first of the three categories fleshing out Mahāyāna morality as a vowed morality and the other two moralities as pious aspiration.

Additionally, there is a code of eighteen major and forty-six minor infractions. Bodhisattvas take vows in a detailed ordination ritual, as in the older *Vinaya*, and major infractions entail exclusion from the bodhisattva community. Unlike in the older *Vinaya*, however, the exclusion does not take place in the ordinary social sphere, but happens in the more rarefied realm of truth (*dharmatā*) where the offender is no longer counted a member of the bodhisattva *saṅgha*.

The Buddhist Tantric Moral Code

The (*Summary of) Vajrayāna Root Downfalls* (*vajrayānamūlāpattisaṃgraha*) attributed in Tibetan translation to Rta dbyangs (an Aśvaghoṣa) or Bha bi lha (Bhavideva), extant in Sanskrit (Lévi 1929: 266) and in two Tibetan translations, sets forth a systematic Buddhist Tantric morality. It gives a fourteen-point code framed negatively as *āpatti*s ('downfalls'):

> Having bowed down with complete respect to the lotus feet of my guru I shall explain the fourteen root downfalls spoken of in tantra. Vajradhāra said *siddhi*s flow from the masters, so the first root downfall is said to be disparaging them. The second downfall is said to be overstepping the command of the Sugatas. The Jinas say the third is displaying cruelty to vajra relatives out of anger, the fourth is giving up love for beings. The fifth is giving up *bodhicitta*, the root of dharmas. The sixth is criticizing

> the doctrine of your own or another tenet system, the seventh is speaking publicly about secrets to immature beings, the eighth is treating with contempt the *skandhas* that are in essence the five buddhas, and the ninth is to question the essential purity of dharmas. The tenth is held to be persisting in showing affection to the wicked,[3] eleventh is the false imagination of dharmas without names and so on, twelfth is said to be spoiling the minds of living beings who have faith. Thirteenth is not resorting to pledges as they are found, and fourteenth is despising women whose essence is wisdom.

Besides the fourteen major downfalls there is also a list of eight minor infractions (*sthūlāpatti*). The short Indian commentaries on the code are only extant in Tibetan translation and though they add little of substance to the short lists, they demonstrate the acceptance, in some circles at least, in India of a Tantric Buddhist moral code not specific to a particular deity yoga.

These codes were first formulated in north-east India towards the second half of the tenth century, and it may well be that contact with Tibetans acted as the catalyst for their formulation. It is well known that Dīpaṃkaraśrījñāna Atiśa (b. 980 in north-east India, d. 1054 in Tibet, and to whom one of the commentaries on the root downfalls is attributed) wrote his *Lamp for the Path* (*bodhipathapradīpa*) and *Commentary* (Sherburne 2000) in order to demonstrate to Tibetans that although the Tantric code was necessarily in harmony with the two lower Buddhist moral codes, antinomian-type behaviour was reserved for an elite, and amongst the elite only the laity (Sherburne 2000: 283–306). He explicitly says monks and nuns should not be given the last two—the secrets (*guhya*) and knowledge (*jñāna*)—of the four consecrations (*abhiṣeka*) (essentially achieved together with sexual contact) because it will lead to a degeneration of Buddhism.

Deity Yoga and Morality in the Nature of Things

It has been said there are as many gods in South Asia as there are people (Smart 1977), and for each of them there are rules—ascetic observances (*vrata*). These observances include fasting, abstaining from sexual contact, wearing particular clothes, making a pilgrimage and worshipping at a particular religious site, taking a ritual bath, and so on, observances that may be associated with a particular day in the religious calendar, with longer periods of time, with an attempt to gain a boon (for example a child), or with an attempt to ward off sickness or financial hardship. In addition to these observances

[3] This renders sde dge Zi179b2 *gdug pa rtag tu byams ldan pa* (snar thang Ru127b7–128a1 *gdug la rtag tu byams sems ldan*) / *byed pa de ni bcu par 'dod*. The Sanskrit version (*duṣṭamaitrī sadātyājyā daśamī tatkṛtau matā*) perhaps says, 'Those whose kindness is destroyed not always being those to be rejected. The tenth is accepted to have done that.'

there are also rules codified in the Dharmaśāstra literature governing the ritual purity of groups relative to other groups in Hindu society, and there are strict rules that govern the behaviour of orthodox Brahmin priests, especially when they are involved in Vedic fire rituals. In each case, the rules governing these activities do not attain to the status of a systematic Tantric moral code because they are time-bound, or bound by a particular person or situation.

In Buddhist Tantra, deity yoga is the practice of imaginatively transforming the five *skandhas* (understood as the unity of wisdom and method) into a Buddhist Tantric deity of choice. The pledges (*samaya*) the *sādhaka* makes to effect this transformation, to 'become' the deity (at least in his or her vivid imagination) are listed in the Buddhist Tantras. These *samayas* are initially not systematic, but they become the basis of the later systematic Buddhist Tantric moral code.

Alexis Sanderson (2009: 165–166), talking about the origins of Tantric antinomian behaviour in general within Brahmanical orthodoxy, writes:

> Orthodox sources rule that one who is guilty of this crime [killing a Brahmin] may free himself from his sin only if he removes himself from society for twelve years, living in a cremation ground and begging for his food, carrying a skull-staff and skull-bowl when he does so.

Sanderson and his students trace the evolution of this particular ascetic practice (*vrata*) from its early role as a rite of purification for a 'brahmin-slayer' to its role as 'an *ātmasamskāraḥ*, a rite that bestows or prepares the soul for liberation' (191). Judit Törzsök, explaining the *mahāvrata* ('great ascetic observance', also called *kapālavrata* or *paśuvrata*) of the Kāpālakas (an early Śaivite sect), says of an ascetic that 'he will possess all the qualities that the supreme and transcendental (*tattvātīta*) lord [Śiva] has' (2014: 360).

The function of specific Buddhist *samayas* ('commitments', 'rules') that are promises to 'practise' fully (in body, speech, mind, and actions, essentially imitate) a particular chosen Buddhist deity are functionally similar to the Śaivite *mahāvrata*—the commitment of the *sādhaka* to be the same (*sāmyam*) as Śiva. To the extent they are both a commitment to a particular deity (a deity yoga) the Buddhist observance and the Śaivite observance function in a similar manner (but see Wedemeyer 2011: 354–360; 2013, who argues there is a difference between the ascetic observance in Śaivite texts and Buddhist *caryāvrata* or *vratacaryā*).

This should not be taken as a view unique to modern scholarship, as it is found earlier in Tibetan Buddhist commentarial literature, where the difference between Buddhist Tantra and Hindu (*phyi rol pa*) Tantra is articulated in terms of wisdom and means, not in terms of deity yoga. The absence or presence of deity yoga, it is said, is the mark distinguishing non-Tantric from Tantric Mahāyāna Buddhism, not the mark distinguishing Buddhist and non-Buddhist Tantra (see, e.g., Hopkins 1987: 115).

It may well be that the Hindu *mahāvrata* as the commitment of the *sādhaka* to be the same (*sāmyam*) as Śiva, a *vrata* (ascetic practice) that functions like the developed

Buddhist *samayas* that are promises to practise fully (in body, speech, mind, and actions) a particular chosen deity, is a systematized Tantric moral code in the sense I have been using it here. Certainly in later Śaivism, with the ultimate nature of Śiva a central concern, it may be that such a *mahāvrata* is rooted in the natural way of things, at the deepest level, not just, as in its origins, specific to a particular time or practice. As the twentieth-century Indian Buddhist writer Khunu Rinpoche (1999: 137), in his praise of *bodhicitta*, says,

> Those who are proclaimed as the greatest
> gods in existence—Brahmā, Viṣṇu,
> and Indra—do they have *bodhicitta*,
> the source of all benefit and happiness? (verse 317)

He means if they do, they would be equally 'Buddhist' gods for the benefit of others.

The systematic Buddhist Tantric moral code set forth above, with its rules to engage in antinomian behaviour, is presented by its authors as a natural code, in the sense of embedded in the basic nature of things.

Buddhist *Vinaya*, the Bodhisattva code, and Buddhist Tantric codes include two kinds of restraint (*saṃvara*, Tib. *sdom*): (1) from natural (in the sense of base) immorality (*prakṛtisāvadya*; Tib. *rang bzhin gyi kha na ma tho ba*)—for example, killing; and (2) from immorality that depends upon breaking a personal commitment to a particular social mores (*pratikṣepaṇasāvadya*; Tib. *bcas pa'i kha na ma tho ba*)—for example, when a fully ordained Buddhist monk (*bhikṣu*) eats a meal after twelve noon.

In Buddhist Tantra, ascetic observances differ from systematized morality in the same way that a *prakṛtisāvadya* (natural) differs from a *pratikṣepaṇasāvadya* (socially ordained) immorality. Even though both, given the axiom of *śūnyatā* ('emptiness'), are equally arbitrary and have no final basis in reality, whereas the latter are the outcome of laws governing behaviour in an institution, in a country, or as the member of a particular society (bounded), the former are natural (unbounded).

Systematic Buddhist Tantric morality, in the sense of a supreme regimen of discipline, constitutes itself as a 'natural' discipline. A wild horse runs wild in nature, but all discipline is not, on that account, unnatural. Whatever the romantic view of wild horses running free over the plains, while the 'nature' in 'in nature' is, to continue the metaphor, 'red in tooth and claw', antinomian-type behaviour included as rules for persons governed by codes of conduct in systematic Buddhist Tantric morality (e.g. destroying towns, sex outside the bounds of accepted convention, and so on) is natural behaviour in a different sense.

Buddhist Tantra characterizes the nature in 'it is in the nature of things', that is, basic reality, as *nirvikalpika*, 'free from *vikalpa*', and *advaya*, 'non-dual'. The word *vikalpa* means to divide, to form ideas. The word *advaya* (from *dvi* cognate with the English word 'two') means the total collapse of subject/object bifurcation. This natural state, a state of abandonment, a state of freedom, running free like water, finding its own way without the inner subject/object duality, is a natural state characterized by spontaneity (*anābhoga*).

Generally speaking, the unity of wisdom (emptiness and the mind that knows it) and means (a universal altruistic principle) set forth in Buddhist Tantras is not found in orthodox (Hindu) texts. The orthodox (*āstika*) Indian thinker Śaṅkarācārya, whose views on ultimate reality are considered closest to those propounded in Buddha Tantras, still characterizes the Buddhist understanding of wisdom as nihilism and says (*Brahmasūtrabhāṣya* 2.2.31),

> I do not dignify with a refutation the position of the [Buddhist] Propounders of Emptiness and so on, though, because it is prohibited by every standard (*śūnyavādipakṣas tu sarvapramāṇavipratiśiddha iti tan nirākaraṇāya nādaraḥ kriyate*).

If all moral or immoral behaviour, from the smallest to the greatest good, from the most base to the faintest evil, is equally without any basis, if things have no intrinsic nature that makes them what they are, if everything is fabricated, then there is no absolute basis for morality or immorality. This, for Śaṅkarācārya is nihilism.

For the formulators of the systematic morality set forth above, however, this wisdom or emptiness is balanced by *upāya* ('means') in the sense of a means to an end. The fourth to sixth rules in the systematic moral code attributed to Aśvaghoṣa or Bhavideva set forth above make this abundantly clear: 'the fourth is giving up love for beings, the fifth is giving up *bodhicitta*, the root of dharmas, the sixth is criticizing the doctrine of your own or another tenet system'. The *upāya*, skilful means not separate from an ultimate that skirts nihilism, is intimately connected with the ultimate through the doctrine of dependent origination (*pratyītyasamutpāda*). Together they provide the description of the nature of things; even though the means do not partake of any absolute good or bad, they are ultimately arbitrary, though not on that account less important than the ultimate reality that underpins them.

The essential point in systematic Buddhist Tantric morality is just how arbitrary, but necessary, the means are as a complement to the absence of their having an absolute basis. Ultimately, there are no beings, there is no suffering, and there is no altruism. All this is fabricated like a magical apparition conjured up by a magician. Accordingly, there is no absolute right and wrong and no absolute prohibitions when it comes to what can and cannot be employed as a means to the end. The means vary according to what is of benefit to those beholding such appearance. Reality does not dictate it because, ultimately, there is no true reality. It is just done as a means to an end because others' well-being is privileged.

In Buddhist Tantra the view is represented by or embodied in the bell (*ghaṇṭā*) and is associated with the female. Skilful means are represented by or embodied in a *vajra* (a sphere with two sets of five prongs meeting at their tips extending out in both directions) and is associated with the male. The unity of the bell and *vajra* (wisdom non-dual with emptiness and the means) is the focus at the start of a Buddhist Tantric *sādhana* and ritual consecration (*abhiṣeka*). The master directs the supplicant to visualize a *vajra* on a moon disk (the symbol for emptiness) and meditate on the unity of wisdom and means in that form. All beneficial Tantric appearances arise from that.

The Three Codes in Tibet

By the time of the Indian master Atiśa's stay in Tibet, Tibetans were already writing seminal works on Tantric ethics. Rongzom (Rong zom chos kyi bzang po, a.k.a. Dharmabhadra, 1012–1088) in his *Pledges in Brief and at Length* (*dam tshig mdo rgyas*) anticipates the 'Three Codes' (*sdom gsum*) genre that developed more fully in the early thirteenth century. Rongzom (1999: 248–249) says, 'Those who have Bodhisattva vows must take shared *prātimokṣa* vows. Those who have Tantric vows must take both shared bodhisattva and *prātimokṣa* vows. … This is not only in Action (*kriyā*) Tantra, but is the same in Yoga Tantra too.' After citing the *Vajraśekhara* in Tibetan translation he continues,

> Therefore the general vows from the traditions are construed as those vows from the earlier tradition that those in the later tradition share. The particular vows from the traditions are (1) those shared vows as a morality (*spyod pa*, *caryā*) informed by method and wisdom as well as (2) the particular morality of unshared profound and vast vows.

The defining Three Codes text in Tibet is *A Clear Differentiation of the Three Codes* (*sdom gsum rab dbye*; Rhoton 2002) by Sakya Pandita (sa skya paṇḍita kun dga' rgyal mtshan, 1182–1251). It expands on a shorter explanation of Mahāyāna and Tantric moral codes by his uncle Drakpa Gyaltsen (grags pa rgyal mtshan, 1147–1216; Tatz 1986). *A Clear Differentiation of the Three Codes* defends Drakpa Gyaltsen's views against criticism by Vibhūticandra (fl. *c.* 1200) who wrote a short but influential work—*sdom gsum 'od kyi phreng ba, trisamvaraprabhamala* (sde dge rgyud) Tshu54v–56v—while staying at Drikung ('bri gung) monastery, a seat of opposition to Drakpa Gyaltsen's Sakya sect (Stearns 1996; Sobisch 2002). The Sakya works, together with Vibhūticandra's text, mark the establishment of Three Codes as a definable Tibetan genre discussing the relationship between the *Vinaya*, Mahāyāna, and Tantric Buddhist moral codes.

Vibhūticandra explains how *prātimokṣa*, bodhisattva, and Tantric (*rig 'dzin*) vows (*sdom pa*) are taken, kept, and broken, and how it is feasible for somebody to be governed by two or three codes at the same time. The codes are to be understood as codes for one person, not three separate types of person. He says the supreme vessel for the Tantric code is a fully ordained monk, and then argues against the Sakya position that each lower code transforms (*gnas 'gyur*) into the higher one while remaining a single entity (*ngo bo gcig*), and that when you break a higher vow you also break a lower one. Vibhūticandra says the lower codes (understood as restraint patterns informing mental states) remain as potencies on the *ālayavijñāna* (the eighth, storehouse consciousness), eclipsed as it were, as is the light of lesser heavenly bodies, by the light of the sun. They are there, but do not operate for as long as the higher code is in operation. He also says they do not relate to each other as a watered ground and a seedling do, citing Aśvaghoṣa and Lalitavajra as corroboration that they relate as 'pervaded and pervader' (*khyab bya khyab byed*).[4]

Tsongkhapa wrote three texts on morality. He accepts a Tantric moral code as a given, but as I have argued elsewhere (Sparham 2005), he separates the works on the three codes into separate volumes to ensure basic *Vinaya* morality is not compromised. In this he is similar to Atiśa in his *Lamp for the Path*. He follows Vibhūticandra, however, in saying the supreme vessel for the Tantric moral code is a fully ordained monk, but reserves the status of supreme vessel for a theoretical elite, perhaps suggesting implicitly thereby that transgressive behaviour is only to be acted out in the vivid imagination of the meditator.

Beginning in the fifteenth century, works that use the Three Codes as a vehicle to explain the entire Buddhist path became textbooks (*yig cha*) for conveying small but important differences in the views of different Tibetan sects. Amongst these, Gorampa's two commentaries on Sakya Pandita's *A Clear Differentiation of the Three Codes* are of great importance (Sobisch 2002). In the Nyingma (*rnying ma*) sect, Minling Lochen (smin gling lo chen) Dharmaśrī's (1654–1717) long commentary on Ngari Panchen's (mnga' ris paṇ chen padma dbang rgyal, 1487–1542) *Ascertaining the Three Vows* (Ngari Panchen 1996) has great importance. Finally, the section on morality in Jamgön Kongtrül Lodrö Tayé's (byams dgon kong sprul blo gros mtha' yas, 1813–1899) *Treasury of Knowledge* (*shes bya kun khyab*) has been made available in an English translation (Jamgön 2003). Noteworthy is Kongtrül's statement (2003: 227) that 'the vows are fully assumed at the conclusion of the initiation and not before', exemplifying how in later Tibetan commentarial literature the focus is not on whether or not there is a systematic Tantric morality, but on the details of ordination and so on.

Works Cited

Foucault, M. (1986) *The use of pleasure: the history of sexuality*, volume 2. Translated by R. Hurley. New York: Vintage.

Hopkins, J. (1987) *Deity yoga in action and performance tantra*. Ithaca: Snow Lion.

Jamgön Kongtrul Lodrö Tayé (byams dgon kong sprul blo gros mtha' yas) (2003) *The treasury of knowledge*, book 5: *Buddhist ethics*. Translated by K. Rinpoché Translation Group. Ithaca, NY, and Boulder: Snow Lion.

Khunu Rinpoche (1999) *Vast as the heavens, deep as the sea*. Somerville, MA: Wisdom.

Lévi, S. (1929) Autour d'Aśvaghoṣa. *Journal asiatique* (Oct.–Dec.), 266–267.

[4] Sobisch (2002) provides a detailed explanation of the exchange between Vibhūticandra and the Sakya hierarchs based on the views of later writers, especially Gorampa (go rams pa bsod nams seng ge, 1429–1489).

Ngari Panchen Pema Wangyi Gyalpo (1996) *Perfect conduct: ascertaining the three vows.* Commentary by His Holiness Dudjom Rinpoche. Translated by Khenpo Gyurme Samdrub and Sangye Khandro. Boston: Wisdom.

Nihom, M. (1994) *The Kuñjarakarṇadharmakathana and the Yogatantra.* Publications of the De Nobili Research Library. Volume 21. Vienna: De Nobili Research Library.

Rhoton, J. D. (trans.) (2002) *A clear differentiation of the three codes. Essential distinctions among the individual liberation, great vehicle and tantric systems. The sDom gsum rab dbye and six letters.* Albany: State University of New York Press.

Sanderson, A. (2009) The Śaiva age: the rise and dominance of Śaivism during the early medieval period. In: S. Einoo (ed.), *Genesis and development of tantrism.* Tokyo: University of Tokyo, Institute of Oriental Culture, 41–349.

Sherburne, R. (ed.) (2000) *The complete works of Atiśa.* New Delhi: Aditya Prakashan.

Smart, N. (1977) *The long search.* Boston: Little, Brown.

Sobisch, J.-U. (2002) *Three-vow theories in Tibetan Buddhism.* Wiesbaden: Dr Ludwig Reichert.

Sparham, G. (trans.) (2005) *Tsongkhapa, Tantric ethics: an explanation of the precepts for Buddhist Vajrayāna practice.* Boston: Wisdom.

Stearns, C. (1996) The life and Tibetan legacy of the Indian Mahāpaṇḍita Vibhūticandra. *Journal of the International Association of Buddhist Studies,* 19 (1), 127–168.

Szántó, P.-D. (2012) Selected chapters from the *Catuṣpīṭhatantra.* D.Phil. thesis, Oxford University.

Tatz, M. (trans.) (1986) *Asanga's chapter on ethics, with the commentary of Tsong-kha-pa, the basic path to awakening, the complete bodhisattva.* Studies in Asian Thought and Religion, volume 4. Lewiston/Queenston: The Edwin Mellen Press.

Törzsök, J. (2014) Kāpālikas. In: K. A. Jacobsen, H. Basu, and A. Malinar (eds), *Brill's encyclopedia of Hinduism,* volume 3. Leiden: Brill, 355–361.

Wedemeyer, C. K. (2013) *Making sense of tantric Buddhism.* New York: Columbia University Press.

Weinberger, S. N. (2003) The significance of yoga tantra and the compendium of principles (tattvasaṃgraha tantra) within tantric Buddhism in India and Tibet. PhD dissertation, University of Virginia.

Yarnall, T. E. (2013) *Great treatise on the stages of mantra (sngags rim chen mo). Critical elucidation of the key instructions in all the secret stages of the path of the victorious universal lord, great Vajradhara. Chapters XI--XII: the creation stage by Tsong Khapa Losang Drakpa. Introduction and translation.* New York: American Institute of Buddhist Studies, Columbia University.

Zimmermann, M. (2013) The chapter on right conduct in the Bodhisattvabhūmi. In: U. T. Kragh (ed.), *The foundation for yoga practitioners: the Buddhist Yogācārabhūmi treatise and its adaptation in India, East Asia, and Tibet.* Harvard Oriental Series, volume 75. Cambridge, MA and London: Harvard University Press, 872–883.

Suggested Reading

Cozort, D. (1986). *Highest Yoga Tantra.* Ithaca, NY: Snow Lion.

Dorje, G. (2012) The rNying-ma interpretation of commitment and vow. In: T. Skorupski (ed.), *The Buddhist forum, volume 2: seminar papers 1988–90.* Tring, UK: The Institute of Buddhist Studies, 71–96.

George, C. S. (ed. and trans.) (1974) *Candramahāroṣaṇa tantra. Chapters I–VIII: a critical edition and English translation*. New Haven: American Oriental Series Monographs, 56.

Lessing, F. D., and Wayman, A. (eds and trans) (1968) *Mkhas grub rje's Fundamentals of the Buddhist Tantras*. Indo-Iranian Monographs, volume 8. The Hague: Mouton.

Pinte, K. (2011) Shingon Risshū: esoteric Buddhism and vinaya. In: C. Orzech, H. Sørensen, and R. Payne (eds), *Esoteric Buddhism and the tantras in east Asia*. Leiden: Brill, 845–853.

Snellgrove, D. (1987) *Indo-Tibetan Buddhism*. Boston: Shambala.

Steinkellner, E. (1978) Remarks on tantristic hermeneutics. In: L. Ligeti (ed.), *Proceedings of the Csoma de Korös memorial symposium*. Bibliotheca Orientalis Hungarica, volume 23. Budapest: Akadémiai Kiadó, 445–458.

Törzsök, J. (1999) The doctrine of magic female spirits: a critical edition of selected chapters of the *Siddhayogeśvarīmata* (tantra) with annotated translation and analysis. D.Phil. thesis, Oxford University.

Törzsök, J. (2014) Nondualism in early Śākta tantras: transgressive rites and their ontological justification in a historical perspective. *Journal of Indian philosophy*, 42 (1), 195–223.

Tsong-ka-pa (1977) *Tantra in Tibet: the great exposition of secret mantra*, volume 1. Translated and edited by J. Hopkins. London: George Allen and Unwin.

Tsong-ka-pa (1981) *The yoga of Tibet: the great exposition of secret mantra*, volumes 2 and 3. Translated and edited by J. Hopkins. London: George Allen and Unwin.

Wedemeyer, C. K. (2011) Locating tantric antinomianism. *Journal of the International Association of Buddhist Studies*, 34 (1–2), 349–419.

CHAPTER 13

BUDDHIST ETHICS IN SOUTH AND SOUTHEAST ASIA

JULIANA ESSEN

INTRODUCTION

THE anthropological literature dealing with Buddhist ethics in the Theravāda countries of South and Southeast Asia may be divided into five categories, whereby ethics is defined as guidelines for right action oriented towards a particular goal: (1) ethics of statehood or political ethics; (2) ethics of salvation or monastic ethics; (3) ethics of engagement including both social and environmental ethics; (4) karmic ethics for the laity; and (5) ethics of worldly benefit, as emphasized by some modern urban Buddhist movements. These categories highlight debates that have historically occupied anthropological scholarship, countering claims that Buddhism is an apolitical, purely individualistic or asocial, world-renouncing religion that is divisible into 'big' and 'little' traditions. This review, covering both theory and rich ethnographic evidence from Thailand, demonstrates the plurality and complexity of ethical Buddhist practice in the region.

ETHICS OF STATEHOOD (POLITICAL ETHICS)

Much anthropological literature on Buddhism in South and Southeast Asia deals with the relationship between Buddhism and the state, primarily to counter Max Weber's view of Buddhism as a 'specifically unpolitical and anti-political' religion (1958: 206). According to S. J. Tambiah's extensive historical and ethnographic research, 'The strain to identify the Buddhist religion with the polity, and the Buddhist polity in turn with the society were deep structural tendencies in the Buddhist kingdoms of Southeast Asia' (1978: 112). In his classic work *World Conqueror and World Renouncer*, Tambiah demonstrates that contrary to the position of Weber and others, early Buddhism was not merely a salvation quest for the virtuosi but also had a developed view of the world process (1976: 515). Aśoka's illustrious reign during the third century BCE is seen as a realization of this world image and a charter for all succeeding Theravāda kingdoms.

In the traditional relation between the *saṅgha* and the polity, it is the king's duty to protect religion from external invasion and internal disorder. The *saṅgha* in return upholds the legitimacy of the ruler. Peter Jackson explains:

> Fundamental to the legitimatory function of Thai Buddhism, both in the past and in the present, is the belief that the welfare of the country is intimately related to the welfare of the *dharma*, the teaching and practice of the Buddha's message of salvation. (1989: 12–13)

Histories of Thai kingship commonly begin with King Taksin, who took the throne in 1767 after his army recaptured the capital of Ayuttaya from the invading Burmese. King Taksin re-established the capital in Thonburi (across the river from the present capital of Bangkok) and turned his attention to rehabilitating the monastic order. According to Tambiah, 'Fostering Buddhist education and scholarship and the purification of the Sangha were traditional expressions of a king's religious piety and devotion; for that very reason they represented effective means of legitimating royal power' (1978: 38).

The most important religious reformer in Thailand's history was King Mongkut (1851–1868), Rama IV. His rule was influenced by his experience as a monk for twenty-seven years and by the heightening of Western cultural and political impact on Thailand. His study of the Pāli Canon led him to perceive discrepancies between Buddhist scriptures and actual practice in Thailand, while his exposure to Mon monastic practice convinced him that this discipline was closer to original Buddhist practice. Due to his rejection of superstition and his strong interest in Western scientific knowledge, Rama IV worked to rationalize Buddhist thought and practice and demythologize its world view. According to Kirsch:

> The available evidence indicates Mongkut was not simply reacting to existing social strains in Thai society, nor was he seeking to harmonize Buddhism with an impinging modern world. The primary impetus for his reforms seems clearly to have been purely religious. (1978: 62–63)

Mongkut was succeeded by his son Chulalongkorn, Rama V (1868–1910), who is credited with consolidating the absolute monarchy in response to the economic and political pressures of European colonialism. Buddhism played an important role in amplifying the monarchy's presence up-country. Chulalongkorn's Sangha Act of 1902, which unified the *saṅgha* for the first time into a single nationwide organization, developed the Thammayut Order (established by Mongkut in the 1830s) into an administrative elite within the *saṅgha*. The Thammayut Order functioned to extend the monarchy's control over Buddhism in the provinces similar to the Bangkok bureaucracy's ascendancy over secular provincial life. Rama V reasoned that a national *saṅgha* controlled from the capital and encompassing the provinces would be conducive to national politico-cultural integration. It was intended to incorporate regional varieties of Buddhism and monastic organization into one national standardized form.

This is not to say that such exercise of Buddhist political ethics was universally accepted. In this regard, Kamala (1997) asks an important question: How did provincial monks react to Bangkok's assertion of authority? Local resistance to Bangkok's religious control was sometimes open and violent. In the first half of the twentieth century, there were a number of uprisings in the north-east led by *phu mi bun* ('men with merit' or holy men), all of which were crushed by the military. Other resistance was subtler—monks in outlying areas simply continued with their traditional ways and ignored the dictates of Bangkok. Some regional monks accepted the Bangkok monastic system, taking the standardized Pāli exams while pursuing their involvement with local matters (e.g. construction work, herbal medicine, village arbitration, blessings). Still other monks who wanted to devote more time to meditation withdrew into the wilderness. Kamala suggests that the Bangkok elite acted like a colonial power, imposing its own rules and language over local customs and languages in the name of 'modern education' (44).

Scholarly interest has more recently shifted from classical or historical studies of Buddhist statehood to Buddhist state approaches to social progress. There are at least two contemporary cases that illustrate such Buddhist moral governance in practice. The most well known is Bhutan's alternative to the Gross National Product, the most widely used measure of social progress expressed in monetary terms. In 1972, Bhutan's King Jigme Singye Wangchuck instituted the Gross National Happiness approach, declaring the Buddhist nation's value of factors beyond finances as the true indicators of well-being. In particular, GNH promotes equal distribution of economic prosperity while maintaining cultural traditions, a healthy environment, and a responsive government. The GNH model has received accolades in Buddhist circles and beyond (e.g. Sivaraksa 2009) and has otherwise generated much discussion among scholars, practitioners, and activists as to how to operationalize happiness as a measure of social progress (e.g. Braun 2009). To be sure, the Gross National Happiness approach has its critics as well. Bhutan's own prime minister, Tshering Tobgay, has argued that happiness is a distraction from pressing issues such as the ballooning national debt and rising youth unemployment (Kelly 2012). Nevertheless, GNH exemplifies how national policy may be shaped by Buddhist ethics.

A lesser-known Buddhist-inspired approach to modern moral governance is Sufficiency Economy. The King of Thailand first publicly introduced his 'New Theory', later known as Sufficiency Economy, in his annual birthday address to the nation on 4 December 1997, following the onset of the global economic crisis (which originated in Thailand). To speed recovery from such a blow after decades of seemingly unstoppable growth, the King advised a change in mindset: 'To be a tiger is not important,' he declared to those who aspired to attain recognition as the 'Fifth Tiger' among the East Asian miracle economies. 'The important thing for us is to have a self-supporting economy. A self-supporting economy means to have enough to survive' (cited in Senanarong 2004: 4).

The King's 'New Theory' was in fact not new but rather the culmination of decades of observation and experimentation. Beginning in the early days of his over-sixty-year reign, he regularly toured the Thai Kingdom to see first hand how his people were living. From the 1960s onwards, the King noted that small farmers, rather than benefiting from the modernization spreading rapidly through the country, were bearing a heavier burden of the economic, social, and environmental costs. In response to the suffering he witnessed, the King formulated an alternative development approach and set up centres to experiment with agricultural techniques that would cultivate a comfortable existence for the rural population. As the surplus of individual holdings grew, the farmers were encouraged to set up networks to produce and exchange their goods more efficiently (ORDPB 2004; UNDP 2007). Although the King's New Theory for Agriculture managed to germinate in the poorest region, Isan, it failed to proliferate.

In the aftermath of the economic crisis, however, Thais across the country were re-evaluating their nation's development path and considering alternatives—particularly Buddhist-inspired ones. Thus after the King's 1997 birthday address, governmental working groups, most notably the National Economic and Social Development Board (2000), immediately set to explicating and codifying the King's ideas into a workable policy framework. What emerged was a set of decision-making guidelines to advance mindful human development first at the individual and company level, and then when stable, branching out into networks or communities of specialized production and distribution units and other relevant entities such as savings cooperatives and seed banks. At the same time, the newly articulated Sufficiency Economy approach was sufficiently broad to be applied to nations and the global economy as well. These guidelines, simultaneously Buddhist and pragmatic, include three components—moderation, reasonableness and self-immunity—with wisdom and integrity as necessary conditions. Sufficiency Economy finds its strength in its compatibility with capitalism; that is, an individual, firm, or nation could adopt this model of ethical activity regardless of religious or philosophical beliefs and still perform comprehensibly within the context of global capitalism. At this point, the Sufficiency Economy approach is being implemented by individuals, associations, and villages in scattered locales across Thailand but has yet to be rolled out as a concrete national economic plan. This case underscores the reality of present-day social organization, in which the political and economic, as well as the local and the global, are inextricably intertwined, calling for ethics of moral governance that are equally flexible.

Ethics of Salvation (Monastic Ethics)

Although anthropologists have historically been more interested in socio-political organization, they have also made meaningful contributions to the scholarly discussion of monastic ethical practice. Most importantly, ethnographic studies provide a more complete understanding of Buddhist ethics oriented towards salvation by distinguishing between forest-, town-, and village-dwelling monks.

One notable difference is vocational: scholarship versus meditation (Tambiah 1984). Ideally, the way to enlightenment combines intellectual understanding or wisdom (Pāli: *paññā*), morality (*sīla*), and meditation (*samādhi*); however, disagreements are common as to which is more effective. In Sri Lanka, in the first century BCE, a debate took place among several hundred monks assembled to decide whether the basis of Buddhism was study or practise. Study was declared to be both necessary and sufficient for the perpetuation of the religion. However, those who did not agree with the verdict continued with their contemplative pursuits, and monastic life separated into divergent paths. Kamala Tiyavanich (1997) discusses the role of meditation in the lives of forest monks in twentieth-century Thailand. The word 'recollection' in her book's title is the English equivalent of a Buddhist term in Pāli (*anussati*) that refers to the act of remembering or contemplating an important religious theme, such as the Buddha, his teachings, monkhood, or the ethical life. *Anussati* and the related term *sati* (mindfulness) are integral parts of the forest monks' religious practice (Tiyavanich 1997: 12).

Regarding morality, both forest and town monks are similarly bound to abide the 227 precepts set out in the canonical *Vinaya* code, though forest monks lean more towards asceticism. These rules forbid thoughts and actions which would lead to greed, hatred, and delusion, thus hindering the monk's salvation quest: possession of goods except seven necessary items, economic transactions, slanderous speech, sexual activity, enjoying food, sleeping on a high bed, consuming sense-altering substances, and so on. The moral code also suggests practices to help monks overcome their negative cravings. According to Jim Taylor (1993), the hallmark of the forest monk is that he follows more of the ascetic practices that are optional in the *Vinaya* code than the urban scholastic monk. One such custom is wearing robes made of rags, as opposed to the silk worn by many influential *saṅgha* administrators. Wandering, another optional practice, has been a crucial feature of the forest monk tradition and a symbol of asceticism. Forest monks wander in order to cultivate patience, endurance, and fortitude, to find a quiet place to meditate, to overcome desires and to seek detachment, or to visit remote pilgrimage sites or other meditation masters (1993: 165–166). Taylor, following Tambiah, holds up the forest monk practice as the ideal:

> Regardless of the exteriority of forest monks to the establishment and their marginality to ecclesiastical and government centers (which accounts for their individuated charisma won through the austere renunciant quest), in the doctrinal traditions of Buddhism they are its 'greatest achievers'. (1993: 11)

As an aside, the existence of an ethical code does not ensure ethical action. In Thailand, escalating instances of moral defilement and materialism in the *saṅgha* continue to weaken its credibility. Stories of 'lust-tainted corruption' within the *saṅgha* appear regularly in the national and international press. These cases range from the disregard of basic vows to illegal activity: (1) a raid on one monk's secret love pad where police found women's underwear, pornographic magazines, and flasks of whisky (*Associated Press*, 27 October 2000); (2) the astounding exploits of two monks carousing in karaoke bars, wearing wigs to hide their shaven heads (*Associated Press*, 27 October 2000); and (3) the arrest of the abbot of a large temple near Bangkok who was charged with sexually assaulting young hill tribe girls (*The Times*, 21 June 1998). Materialism and commercialism in Thai Buddhist temples are also rising. Donations are often mismanaged or squandered on elaborate and ornate temple facilities. Moreover, it is common in even the remotest temples to find air conditioners, refrigerators, televisions, and other modern conveniences that violate monastic vows of poverty. Like sex scandals, money-related scandals are splashed across the media. For instance, at Wat Lat Phrao, a temple in the prosperous eastern suburbs of Bangkok, street vendors seeking funeral rites for a family member were turned away because they could not meet the monk's high fee (*The Times*, 21 June 1998).

Returning to the distinction between forest- and town-dwelling monks, a third significant difference is an active laity-oriented life versus a reclusive one (Tambiah 1984). At the same debate in Sri Lanka mentioned above, an issue arose regarding whether a monk should concern himself with humanitarian service, or only his personal salvation. Rahula (1956) relates a story brought into the discussion about the monk Cullapindatiya Tissa who did not sympathize with a female devotee when her house burnt down. He simply showed up the next morning as usual to receive alms (cited in Tambiah 1970: 67). This story illustrates one of the fundamental paradoxes of practical Buddhism: the rules designed to remove monks from secular society cannot be effective because monks are entirely dependent upon the laity for material support (Obeyesekere 1968). Although Rahula states that the contending monks' opinions were divided, the historical ideal became *gramavasi* (residing in towns and villages and engaging themselves in study and community and religious activities) rather than *vanavasi* (residing in the forest and engaging in meditation with no obligations to the laity). In Thailand, the established view is that monks have at least a ritual and spiritual obligation to the laity, and may have social obligations as well (Somboon 1976).

Although the distinction is generally made between forest- and town-dwelling monks, the latter of which typically emphasize scholarship, village monks deserve a category of their own. By nature of their embedded position within a community, village monks can neither devote themselves to a reclusive meditative lifestyle nor to a purely intellectual one; instead, they must attend to the needs of their community. Traditionally, village monks have been active in lay life in a number of ways: as educators (before the modern school system), arbitrators in minor disputes, counsellors in domestic affairs, practitioners of traditional medicine, technicians in architecture, sculpture, and well-digging, fortune tellers, and astrologists. With the expansion of government social services, many of these secular functions have greatly diminished in importance (Mulder 1996: 118). However, the temple is still central in village social life as the site of both secular and religious events such as New Year's celebrations, cremations, *kratin* festivals to make collective donations to monks, and many others. It is unclear whether such activities are doctrinally derived ethical actions oriented towards salvation or stem from a humanistic concern for others.

Ethics of Engagement

Regardless of the motivation, this ethical concern for others is now pervasive enough to have earned a name: Engaged or socially engaged Buddhism. Some Buddhist scholars question the legitimacy of engagement for a world-renouncing religion. Anthropologists in particular counter Max Weber's contention that 'universal compassion is merely one of the stages sensitivity passes when seeing through the nonsense of the struggle for existence of all individuals in the wheel of life, a sign of progressive enlightenment, not however, an expression of active brotherliness' (1958: 213). In response, Engaged Buddhists themselves counter that the 'principles and even some of the techniques of an Engaged Buddhism have been latent in the tradition since the time of its founder' (Eppsteiner 1988: xiii). Take the *gramavasi* ideal, for example. Yet even if these ethics of engagement are not doctrinally derived, a growing number of Buddhists are motivated to action by their everyday experiences of environmental degradation, economic struggle, and shifts in social values. As Buddhists have done since the Buddha's time, they adapt their religious interpretations and practices to fit a changing socio-economic and natural environment.

Engaged Buddhism has a rich history in Thailand, inspired largely by the teachings of Buddhadasa Bhikkhu (Swearer 1989; Santikaro 1996). Buddhadasa did not perceive the quest for personal enlightenment as one of isolated individuals pursuing their own greatest good. Moreover, individuals do not merely live in shared environments; they are an integral part of communities embedded in the natural order of things. Consequently, the good of individual parts is predicated on the good of the whole and vice versa (Swearer 1989). At the very least, conditions of material reality force engagement, as demonstrated by Cullapindatiya Tissa's failure to collect alms from a burnt-out house. Alternately, engagement may follow from compassion that arises from true understanding about the interdependence of all things (*paṭicca-samuppāda*). Tambiah summarizes Buddhadasa's intellectual career into a central aim: 'What Buddhadasa tries forcefully to refute and deny is the fatalism, the suspension of action because of the unreality of the world, and therefore the apathy attributed to Buddhism by certain stereotype commenters' (Tambiah 1978: 130). While Buddhadasa remained a thinker and not a doer, his political importance lies in the actions of individuals inspired by his ideas, such as prominent Thai social critic and activist Sulak Sivaraksa, founder of the International Network of Engaged Buddhists.

Socially engaged Buddhism in Thailand is best exemplified by the work of development monks operating outside governmental purview. During the late 1970s many monks in rural villages realized that after years of living under the government's national economic development plans, villagers were worse off than before. As they searched for alternative development models based on local Buddhist tradition, economic improvement was not their only objective. They also hoped to preserve village culture and to promote communal values as an alternative to what they regarded as growing materialism, moral degradation, and the deterioration of rural institutions (Seri 1988). In 1984, Somboon (1988) conducted a study of seventy-two development monks, who offered the following reasons for their activities: (1) involvement in development activities is consistent with the *saṅgha*'s responsibility to serve society; (2) the prosperity of the religion and the *saṅgha* depends on the prosperity of society; and (3) because secular development has proceeded too rapidly and people have become excessively materialistic, people neglect religion.

Adding more detail, Thai journalist Sanitsuda Ekachai writes about the experiences of one particular development monk:

> Abbot Nan Sutasilo of Samakkhii Temple used to think development meant a road and electricity for his village. He quickly found out how wrong he was. Determined to combat poverty and backwardness, he convinced reluctant villagers to give up their land to build a new road that would link their home to the city. 'Development' quickly streamed in. Motorcycles started roaring into the village. TV antennas quickly followed electric poles. ... Electric rice cookers, jeans, lipstick, shampoo, fragrant soap and other consumer goods advertised on television established themselves as an integral part of the villagers' lives. ... And the villagers plunged deeper into debt. (1994: 202–203)

When the abbot finally understood that the 'real enemy' was a person's own cravings (just as the Buddha taught), he changed his approach to build 'spiritual immunity' against the onslaught of consumerism.

More recently, some Thai monks have focused specifically on environmental concerns. Susan Darlington (1998) suggests that 'ecology monks' emerged from the development monk phenomenon. The first time Thai monks concerned about development incorporated specifically environmental concerns in their actions was in response to the 1985 proposal to build a cable car up Doi Suthep mountain in Chiang Mai to promote tourism and economic development at one of the most important pilgrimage sites in Thailand. Although there is a ongoing international scholarly debate as to the relationship between Buddhism and ecology, Sponsel and Natadecha-Sponsel (1992) feel that Buddhism is indeed relevant for coping with the environmental crisis in Thailand. Susan Darlington (1998; 2012) contends that most studies denying such a connection have not examined the conscious efforts of Buddhists to become actively engaged in dealing with the environmental crisis.

To Darlington's point, examples abound depicting Thai monks working to protect the environment. Ajaan Pongsak was the abbot of a temple near Chiang Mai where he worked with villagers to reforest and irrigate their rapidly desertifying land and ran an environmental education programme for villagers, government officials, and other monks from a permanent nature centre. There are now scores of monks around the country following Pongsak's example in their own communities (Brown 1992).

Elsewhere, Phra Somkit collects alms in his village for the forest, maintains a model natural integrated farm on land belonging to the temple, and regularly takes children on ecology meditation walks (Sanitsuda 1994). Taylor (1998) discusses the similar work of Phra Prajak, Luang Phor Naan, and Luang Phor Khamkian. Phrakhru Pitak uses his NGO 'We Love Nan Province' to reach an audience beyond his local community. Although Pitak's conservation programme involves a number of activities, his and other monks' use of the 'tree ordination' ceremony has made it a popular act of protest to protect threatened forests. In this ceremony, trees are wrapped with monks' saffron robes and a modified ordination ritual is performed. Thais will view cutting this tree as a form of religious demerit likened to killing a monk; hence, the ceremony is used symbolically to remind Thais that nature should be respected as much as humans (Darlington 1998).

A number of forest monks have become environmentalists out of necessity as their tradition quickly recedes with the nation's forests. Wat Paa Sukhato in Chaiyaphum is a typical example of forest monastery that has the only remaining forest in the area. One abbot at a forest temple near Bangkok muses that people do not go to him for *Dharma* advice, as he envisioned. They go to him to learn how to plant trees (Sanitsuda 1988). In a volume on environmentalism in Thailand, Taylor (1998) discusses the work of Phra Baen Thanaakaro and Phra Wan Uttamo, two other conservation-oriented forest monks in the north-east. Forest monks tend to have a more instrumentalist perspective of nature. The forest is a conduit of *Dharma* for a person on an internal spiritual journey. Going further, Buddhadasa Bhikkhu identifies *Dharma* with nature and being attuned with the lessons of nature as tantamount to at-one-ment with the *Dharma*. In fact, the Thai word for nature (*thammachat*) has *Dharma* (*thamma*) as its root. From Buddhadasa's standpoint, then, the destruction of nature is the destruction of *Dharma* itself (Santikaro 1996).

These examples of monastic engagement provide strong evidence for the existence of Buddhist social and environmental ethics; yet even stronger evidence may come from lay engagement. The ethical beliefs and practices of the Santi Asoke Buddhist Reform Movement of Thailand, a predominantly lay organization, were documented in a year-long ethnographic study at one community, Srisa Asoke (Essen 2005). At the core of the Asoke group's philosophy is biting critique of capitalism—particularly the prevalence of greed, competition, and exploitation—as the root of Thai society's problems. In their view, modern 'social preferences' influenced by the global flow of Western culture and capitalism exacerbate human suffering and the ruin of nature. To counter these forces, the Asoke movement proposes meritism or *bun-niyom*, Asoke's unique development model based on Buddhist and Thai ethics and values. The fact that the seven Asoke communities thrived throughout the 1997 economic crisis and continue to do so is a testament to meritism's success.

The principles of meritism are expressed in the slogan 'Consume Little, Work Hard, and Give the Rest to Society'. This slogan is not empty rhetoric but is enacted daily by Asoke residents in countless ways. First, residents limit consumption by adhering to the Buddhist precepts (at least the five basic householder precepts but often up to ten), sharing communal resources (for example by cooking, eating, and watching television together in the Common Hall), and following a Western environmental edict, 'The Four Rs': recycle, reuse, repair, reject. As for the slogan's second component, Asoke residents work hard most obviously because they must support themselves in their rural community. Many do so through the meritism version of right livelihood, the 'Three Professions to Save the Nation'. These professions—natural agriculture, chemical-free fertilizer, and waste management—form a circuit in which organic waste is composted as fertilizer for the crops, which people then eat, the remains becoming fertilizer again. The third component, 'Giving the Rest to Society', is training in selflessness or non-self, the pillar of Buddhism. By giving away their surplus time, energy, and resources, the Asoke movement aids material and spiritual development in Thai society in many ways. For example, they run vegetarian restaurants and non-profit markets that provide the Thai public with healthy food and useful goods at low cost while promoting the concepts of meritism. The most time-, energy-, and resource-intensive, outwardly oriented activities are free trainings in the Asoke way of life. The seminars, called 'Dharma Builds People; People Build the Nation', teach ordinary Thais specific knowledge and skills in the area of (Asoke) Buddhist morality and occupation, particularly the Three Professions.

By consuming little, working hard, and giving the rest to society, the Asoke movement exemplifies an explicit environmental and social ethic informed by both formal and substantive rationality. The 'Three Professions to Save the Nation' demonstrates a pragmatic ethic to preserve the environment on which they depend directly for their material existence through chemical-free agriculture. Their adoption of the Western environmental edict, 'The Four Rs', also reflects an instrumental ethic because these practices help them minimize consumption, a means to achieve *anattā*. Yet their appreciation for nature's inherent value also suggests a substantive ethic. One monk at Srisa Asoke explained their complex outlook, referring to the forest residents planted years ago:

> Asoke people try to construct and develop the environment to give rise to abundance and wholeness, in order to bring about thriving soil, sincerity, wooded shade, soft breezes, beautiful views, richness in goodwill, energy to work, joyfulness in *dhamma*, [a sense of] the profoundness of *kamma* and bad deeds, the five *khandhas* [form, feeling, perception, volitional impulses, and consciousness], doing what is natural. (personal communication)

Such sentiments, emerging through not just need but also mindful reflection, give rise to a more profound ethic that endures regardless of nature's immediate use or exchange value.

The Asoke group similarly manifests a social ethic that is simultaneously instrumental and substantive. The group's emphasis on giving refutes Weber's assertion that Buddhism evokes no social responsibility, yet the motivation for this ethic requires further analysis. At first glance, Asoke members' eagerness to help others could be explained by compassion or *karuṇā*, one of the Sublime States and a universally recognized Buddhist ethic valued for its own sake. However, during months of conversations with Asoke residents, *karuṇā* was referenced infrequently, whereas *bun* (merit) or *tombun* (merit-making) came up several times a day. Because the accumulation of merit buys a better rebirth and ultimately enlightenment, their impetus to give is more likely instrumentalist. Nevertheless, efforts to propagate the Asoke way of life through training seminars, boarding schools, and markets for the public, while merit-making activities, are also inspired by a genuine desire to improve people's lives. From this perspective, Asoke members are indeed motivated by the ethic of compassion even if they don't label their actions so.

Karmic Ethics (for Laity)

The case study on the Santi Asoke Buddhist Reform Movement serves as a good reminder that monks are but a small minority of the Buddhist populace. Few individuals make a lifelong commitment to religious pursuits, and of those that do, many were sent to the temple as young boys by their impoverished families in order to be fed, clothed, and educated. More commonly, young Thai men may become monks following the custom to ordain for one Lenten period as a rite of passage between adolescence and marriage. It is hoped that young men will improve their characters through higher training in Buddhist wisdom, morality, and meditation. It is also the custom for eldest sons to ordain for a short time as an act of filial piety, to make merit for their mothers. This last point hints at the power of karmic ethics over those oriented towards salvation.

So if the majority of Buddhist practice occurs outside the *saṅgha*, what does it mean to be a lay Buddhist? Anthropologist Niels Mulder observes, 'To conventional believers, who constitute the vast majority, Buddhism is a way of life, an identity, and the key to primordial "Thai-ness"' (1996: 129). Given the centrality of Buddhism in Thai culture and social life, a central question in the anthropological literature historically concerned 'how a lay public rooted in this world can adhere to a religion committed to the renunciation of the world' (Tambiah 1968: 41). In thinking about lay practice of Buddhism, Tambiah makes one insightful suggestion:

> [I]f we bear in mind that there is some dialectic between religious ideas and mundane interests, we shall better appreciate the two intriguing aspects of religious conduct—what existential anxieties generate the 'ethical', and why the 'ethical', formulated in a certain way, is viewed by the actors as falling within their human capacity. (Tambiah 1968: 45)

Max Weber's (1958) solution to this paradox is a 'religion of the masses' that develops alongside the official doctrine. Gananath Obeyesekere, following Weber, asserts:

> In orthodox doctrine the prescriptions for the layman are very inadequate so that under pressure of mass needs there has developed a peasant (little) tradition of Buddhism, some elements of which have no doctrinal justification. These elements have continued to flourish partly, at least, because the orthodox (great) tradition was not centrally interested in lay soteriology. (1968: 26)

Here, Obeyesekere refers to the theory of great and little traditions popularized by Redfield:

> In a civilization there is a great tradition of the reflective few, and there is a little tradition of the largely unreflective many. The great tradition is cultivated in schools or temples; the little tradition works itself out and keeps itself going in the lives of the unlettered in their village communities. (1956: 70)

Both Weber and Obeyesekere maintain that in Buddhism salvation is only available to those follow the path of monkhood; however, Obeyesekere allows that salvation is eventually possible for the individual who accumulates good karma and is reborn into a better life (as a monk). Alternatively, Obeyesekere states that in practical (as opposed to doctrinal) Buddhism, an individual can limit the effects of bad karma by using magic or appealing to the appropriate deities. And thus begins the big debate about the little tradition: although other anthropologists respect much of Obeyesekere's work, they argue that this particular theory is inaccurate and oversimplifies reality.

S. J. Tambiah, who conducted extensive ethnographic research in Thailand, contends that the 'spirit cult' is more complicated than this 'little tradition' characterization might suggest:

> It is a phenomenon which some writers have called 'animism' and which with pseudo-historical conjecture they have identified as pre-Buddhist. Moreover, they have variously treated it both as incompatible with, and as combining with, Buddhism. In actual fact its relationship to Buddhism is not simple but complex, involving opposition, complementarity, linkage, and hierarchy. (1970: 263)

Anthropologist Charles Keyes (1983a) further argues that Obeyesekere's theory is inaccurate because South and Southeast Asians call upon magic and spirits to solve mundane—not karmic—problems. 'Spirit houses' for local spirits are ubiquitous in Thailand, protecting homes and businesses alike. Similarly, every city has a shrine to the local guardian spirit where citizens may give offerings and ask for material wealth and well-being. In addition, festivals may be held to honour such spirits, such as the Pii Ta Khon festival in Loei Province. Amulets of certain saintly forest monks are also quite popular, even among educated urbanites. These amulets are thought be imbued with supernatural power that will make the wearer safe, wealthy, virile, or clever (Tambiah 1984). Lastly, monks are often called upon to perform ritual blessings—to sprinkle holy water, draw symbols over the door of a new house or car, or tie a white string around the wrist—as protection from malevolent spirits that bring sickness or peril. In short, although ideas about spirit cults and karma may commingle in the minds of some, such practices do not relate to intentional ethical (or unethical) action.

Returning to the issue of practice options available to the laity, Charles Keyes (1983a) agrees with Obeyesekere that Buddhism's moral code for lay life (*sīla*) is vague and 'humanly impossible to fulfill ... "to the letter" ' (Obeyesekere 1968: 27). However, both Keyes and Tambiah (1968) argue that this is not the only doctrinally derived option available for lay practice. Although nothing can change past karma—neither magic nor spirits—an individual may balance the negative effects of past karma by improving future karma through meritorious actions. Karma is not an exclusively Buddhist concept; nevertheless, Buddhism holds that the laws of causal dependence governing nature encompass human behaviour, such that 'good deeds bring good results; bad deeds bring bad results' (Payutto 1995: 7). Keyes explains that good karma or merit 'is conceived almost as a substance that can be possessed in variable quantities and that can be translated into this-worldly virtue or power as well as stored up to be used at death to ensure a good rebirth' (Keyes 1983b: 270).

Thais conceptualize karma as a relationship between *wibaaggaam*—the consequences of past evil deeds—and *bun*—merit that may be accumulated through good deeds to improve one's lot in this life or the next. During ethnographic research on the Santi Asoke Buddhist Reform Movement of Thailand (Essen 2005), one Asoke monk shared his unsettling experience with the law of karma:

> I was traveling [to Srisa Asoke] from Bangkok, and when I got to Surin Province, there was an accident. The vehicle had a bad axle and it fell to the middle of the road. I almost didn't escape with my life. Part of my skull caved in, my molars came loose and were bleeding, the eye on this side popped out. I can't see with this eye. I was lucky [he laughs]. So I believed in *wibaaggaam*. When I was a child at home, I used to kill animals.... When the cutting [of the chicken's neck] was finished, the chicken was not yet dead. It would wriggle and writhe. We would grab its legs and hit it hard with a pole. Its head would break, the eyes would pop out, red blood would flow from the mouth. We did it a lot because the farmers helped each other harvest rice, so we made food following the custom of *long khaek* [feeding guest workers].... I had the feeling that I had killed so much that *wibaaggaam* would come. But when? I was afraid one day I would meet with an accident, and it would surely be like this.... So I felt, it was urgent to make good, to sacrifice, to help others. Because I read a book [about karma], and I felt I have made karma, and I must certainly receive karma—karma will surely come. Slow or fast, this life or next, it depends. When I had this accident—Bap! It was the same image as of the chickens we killed.... Just like that, I thought, 'Oh ho! This is *wibaaggaam*'. (personal communication)

Than Din Thaam believes that ordaining as a monk a few years before this accident may have saved his life. Thus, the urgency 'to make good' to lessen future suffering caused by karma can be a force so powerful that laypeople take the leap into monkhood.

As a phenomenon ordinary people experience in their everyday lives, karma may provide a stronger motivation to be 'a good Buddhist' via merit-making than the elusory notion of enlightenment. As such, making merit (*thombun*) is central to most Thais' understanding of practising Buddhism. A typical ranking of merit-making activities in Thailand might include completely financing the construction of a temple, becoming a monk, having a son become a monk, contributing money to repair a temple, giving food daily to monks, observing every Buddhist Sabbath, and strictly observing the Five Precepts (Tambiah 1968: 69). Most laypeople tend to rank morality and meditation low as merit-making activities because they perceive these practices as beyond their capabilities—or simply because they have other priorities.

Susan Darlington's (1990) study of morality and change in a Buddhist development project in northern Thailand demonstrates how priorities compete when ethical schemas are considered within the context of social life. The villagers who participated in this development project respected and upheld as an ideal the principles of the 'great' tradition of doctrinal Buddhism espoused by the abbot who ran the project. However, conflict arose in the way the elements of their shared moral system were prioritized and acted upon in daily practice. The abbot stressed individual efforts of intention and behaviour; yet for the rural northerners, the social was paramount. Darlington explains:

> In practice, this means that the villagers, while recognizing and even striving for the ideal standard of individual behavior represented in Buddhism, give priority to social obligations and relations over personal concerns. They feel a stronger moral need to fulfill their responsibilities of hospitality and cooperation than to uphold the precepts all Buddhists are expected to follow. (1990: 8)

Returning to possible merit-making activities, given the social embeddedness of most Buddhists, acts of giving deserve special attention. According to Phra Rajavaramuni (1990), an esteemed Thai scholar monk, lay training in Theravāda countries emphasizes religious giving or charity (*dāna*), in addition to morality (*sīla*) and mental development (*bhāvana*) as the three bases of meritorious action (rather than higher monastic training in *sīla, samādhi*, and *paññā*). Phra Rajavaramuni suggests the stress on giving has to do with lay concern for good social relationships, as revealed in Darlington's study. Other scholars (e.g. Gutschow 2004) point to the necessarily reciprocal relationship between monasteries and households: material support flowing in one direction (i.e. donations to temples) and spiritual support flowing the other, which creates the optimal conditions for salvation.

This second perspective serves as a reminder that Buddhism is concerned with *individual* salvation. Thus, acts of giving may simply be the easiest way for an individual layperson to earn merit—the currency of spiritual wealth, which he or she may invest for a better future in this lifetime or the next. To maximize spiritual wealth, givers must choose among 'fields of merit' for the best return. According to the hierarchical concept of *dāna*, the more noble and accomplished the recipient, the higher the field of merit. And, of course, the more one donates, the greater the merit, such that funding the construction of a new temple ranks higher than giving daily alms to monks, as mentioned above (Tambiah 1968).

Interestingly, Keyes has identified a practice that bridges the individualism of Buddhism and the sociality of lay life. He explains that popular Theravādin traditions of South and Southeast Asia incorporate practices believed to transfer merit from one party to another (1983b). For example, in Thailand, a man who ordains as a monk transfers merit to his mother; an elderly woman may go to the temple on holy days to *tombun* (make merit) for the entire family; and a company may donate money to a temple in the name of all of its employees (a Buddhist alternative to stock options, perhaps). Keyes proposes that these practices make it possible for people who prioritize social obligations—i.e. who have not renounced the world—to adhere to the Buddhist theory of karma. Keyes explains:

> Ideas of karmic transference are clearly counter to those of a fully ethicized karmic theory predicated upon the assumption that each person is solely responsible for his or her own actions and their consequences. ... The idea of moral responsibility for one's present actions has been adapted to other notions deriving from what I call the social imperative, that is, the imperative to commit oneself to the demands of a social order. (1983a, 19–20)

Acts of merit transfer thus debunk Weber's limited view of Buddhism as 'a solely personal act of the single individual' (1958: 206), 'an absolutely personal performance of the self-reliant individual [in which] no one and particularly no social community can help him' (213). This may be a specific example of adaptation, but it underscores the relevance of Buddhism for lay life.

Ethics of Worldly Benefit

Some might question whether the practices addressed in this final category should be labelled as ethical, but they are included here for two reasons: (1) with the rise of the urban middle class, some Buddhists seek a more worldly spin on Buddhism that fits their lifestyle and world view, so to them, they are indeed guided by right action towards a particular goal; and (2) a handful of social scientists have taken an interest in what they call 'modern urban Buddhist movements', and thus at least brief mention of this literature should be included in this review.

An example of a public figure exhibiting worldly Buddhist ethics is former Bangkok governor Chamlong Srimuang (historically associated with the Asoke movement), who earned the nickname 'Mr Clean' by employing Buddhist principles in his governance. His biography suggests that his personal spiritual development contributed directly to his and his wife's careers. According to Duncan McCargo (1997), when Chamlong first met his wife, she was a devout Buddhist who adhered to the Five Precepts. Chamlong decided he would do the same:

> I stopped smoking, drinking, and chewing gums and lozenges. We made a vow that we would not seek to be out together seeing movies or indulging in other forms of entertainment which wasted our time. In this way we helped each other and she also did very well in her studies. (79)

In his detailed study of Chamlong, McCargo points out that by curtailing activities deemed frivolous by Buddhist standards, the couple attained academic and political success.

The Dhammakāya movement of Thailand is perhaps the most extreme case of worldly Buddhism. Every Sunday, 50,000 laypeople are bussed in from all over Bangkok to this mammoth modern temple where they partake in highly orchestrated rituals and practise meditation on the expansive green lawn. According to Wat Thammakai (as the movement is known in Thailand), meditation helps people become more productive and efficient and thus achieve more successful lives (Taylor 1989; 1990). In the Wat Thammakai approach, Donald Swearer (2010) identifies several characteristics of new mass religious movements, most notably 'an emphasis on direct religious experience; a simple but specific form of practice and teaching; ... a materialistic orientation; [and] a desire to be modern' (139). Wat Thammakai does indeed seem to be palatable to modern Buddhists: it is the fastest growing religious movement in Thailand, with twenty-eight centres throughout the country, helped by backing from the military and political leaders as well as patronage from the royal family. Spreading further, the first international centre was established in the United States in 1992, and now there are thirty-eight worldwide.

Criticism of this movement as excessively worldly abounds. Swearer points out: 'With millions of dollars in assets, its aggressive recruiting methods, and a commercial approach to evangelism, the religion has been characterized as "religious consumerism"' (2010: 140). According to Theodore Mayer (1996), this upwardly mobile, urban, middle-class movement sees no contradiction between striving for spiritual growth and accumulating material wealth. Scholars of Buddhist economics (e.g. Essen 2009) might counter that accumulating wealth is not such an issue for Buddhist ethics as what a person does with that wealth. Yet the fact that in 1999 the abbot of Wat Thammakai was charged with embezzling funds (959.3 million baht to be exact) as well as distorting Theravāda Buddhist teachings suggests that this movement is not an exemplar in ethical Buddhist action. The case of Wat Thammakai stands as a caution for the potential of manipulating Buddhist thought and practice to achieve non-Buddhist goals.

Conclusion

This review surveyed literature from anthropology as well as other social sciences, including both theory and ethnographic evidence, exploring the practice of Buddhist ethics in South and Southeast Asia, especially Thailand. By no means exhaustive, it identified five meaningful categories of ethics, defined as guidelines for right action oriented toward a particular goal: (1) ethics of statehood or political ethics; (2) ethics of salvation or monastic ethics; (3) ethics of engagement, including both social and environmental ethics; (4) karmic ethics for the laity; and (5) ethics of worldly benefit, as emphasized by some modern urban Buddhist movements. The discussion countered claims that Buddhism is an apolitical, purely individualistic or asocial, world-renouncing religion that is divisible into 'big' and 'little' traditions; and it further demonstrated the plurality and complexity of ethical Buddhist practice in the region. As modern pressures of consumerism and deep-seated social and environmental problems continue to mount, contemporary Buddhists will have even greater need for ethical guidance that fulfils the spirit (if not the letter) of the Buddha's teachings.

Works Cited

Braun, A. A. (2009) Gross national happiness in Bhutan: a living example of an alternative approach to progress. *Social impact research experience journal (SIRE)*, 1–137. Available from: http://repository.upenn.edu/cgi/viewcontent.cgi?article=1003&context=sire [Accessed 2 December 2015].

Brown, K. (1992) In the water there were fish and the fields were full of rice: reawakening the lost harmony of Thailand. In: M. Batchelor and K. Brown (eds), *Buddhism and ecology*. London: Cassell, 87–99.

Darlington, S. (1990) Buddhism, morality, and change: the local response to development in northern Thailand. PhD diss., University of Michigan.

Darlington, S. (1998) The ordination of a tree: the Buddhist ecology movement in Thailand. *Ethnology*, 37 (1), 1–15.

Darlington, S. (2012) *The ordination of a tree: the Thai Buddhist environmental movement*. New York: State University of New York Press.

Eppsteiner, P. (1988) Foreword. In: S. Sivaraksa, *A socially engaged Buddhism*. Bangkok: Thai Inter-Religious Commission for Development.

Essen, J. (2005) *'Right development': the Santi Asoke Buddhist reform movement of Thailand*. Lanham, MD: Lexington.

Essen, J. (2009) Buddhist economics. In: J. Peil and I. Van Staveren (eds), *Handbook of economics and ethics*. Cheltenham, UK: Edward Elgar Publishers, 31–38.

Gutschow, K. (2004) *Being a Buddhist nun: the struggle for enlightenment in the Himalayas*. Cambridge, MA: Harvard University Press.

Kelly, A. (2012) Gross national happiness in Bhutan: the big idea from a tiny state that could change the world. *The Guardian*, 1 December.

Keyes, C. (1983a) Introduction: the study of popular ideas of karma. In: C. Keyes and E. V. Daniel (eds), *Karma: an anthropological inquiry*. Berkeley: University of California Press, 1–26.

Keyes, C. (1983b) Merit transference in the kammic theory of popular Theravada Buddhism. In: C. Keyes and E. V. Daniel (eds), *Karma: an anthropological inquiry*. Berkeley: University of California Press, 261–286.

McCargo, D. (1997) *Chamlong Srimuang and the new Thai politics*. London: C. Hurst & Co.

Mayer, T. (1996) Thailand's new Buddhist movements in historical and political context. In: B. Hunsaker (ed.), *Loggers, monks, students, and entrepreneurs*. Dekalb, IL: CSEAS, Northern Illinois University, 33–66.

Mulder, N. (1996) *Inside Thai society: interpretations of everyday life*. Amsterdam: The Pepin Press.

National Economic and Social Development Board (2000) An introductory note: sufficiency economy. Paper presented at the 10th UNCTAD Conference, Bangkok, Thailand.

Obeyesekere, G. (1968) Theodicy, sin, and salvation in a sociology of Buddhism. In: E. Leach (ed.), *Dialectic in practical religion*. Cambridge, UK: Cambridge University Press, 12–18.

Office of the Royal Development Projects Board (ORDPB) (2004) The royal development study centres and the philosophy of sufficiency economy. Paper presented at The Ministerial Conference on Alternative Development: Sufficiency Economy, Bangkok, Thailand.

Payutto, P. (1995) *Good, evil, and beyond: kamma in the Buddha's teaching*. Bangkok: Buddhadamma Foundation.

Rahula, W. (1956) *History of Buddhism in Ceylon*. Columbo, Sri Lanka: M. D. Gunasena & Co.

Rajavaramuni, P. (1990) Introduction. In: R. F. Sizemore and D. K. Swearer (eds), *Ethics, wealth, and salvation: a study in Buddhist social ethics*. Columbia, SC: University of South Carolina Press, 1–11.

Redfield, R. (1956) *Peasant society and culture*. Chicago: University of Chicago Press.

Sanitsuda E. (1994) *Seeds of hope: local initiatives in Thailand*. Bangkok: Thai Development Support Committee.

Santikaro B. (1996) Buddhadasa Bhikkhu: life and society through the natural eyes of voidness. In: C. Queen and S. King (eds), *Engaged Buddhism: Buddhist liberation movements in Asia*. New York: State University of New York Press, 147–194.

Senanarong, A. (2004) His majesty's philosophy of sufficiency economy and the Royal Development Study Centres. Paper presented at The Ministerial Conference on Alternative Development: Sufficiency Economy, Bangkok, Thailand.

Seri P. (1988) *Religion in a changing society: Buddhism, reform, and the role of monks in community development in Thailand*. Hong Kong: Arena Press.

Sivaraksa, S. (2009) *The wisdom of sustainability: Buddhist economics for the 21st century*. Kihei, HI: Koa Books.

Somboon S. (1976) *Political Buddhism in southeast Asia: the role of the sangha in the modernization of Thailand*. New York: St. Martin's Press.

Somboon S. (1988) A Buddhist approach to development: the case of 'development monks' in Thailand. In: L. T. Ghee (ed.), *Reflections of development in southeast Asia*. Singapore: ASEAN Economic Research Unit, Institute of Southeast Asian Studies.

Sponsel, L., and Natadecha-Sponsel, P. (1992) A theoretical analysis of the potential contribution of the monastic community in promoting a green society in Thailand. In: M. Batchelor and K. Brown (eds), *Buddhism and ecology*. London: Cassell, 45–68.

Swearer, D. (1989) Introduction. In: Bhikku Buddhadasa, *Me and mine: selected essays of Bhikkhu Buddhadasa*. New York: SUNY Press.

Swearer, D. (2010) *The Buddhist world of southeast Asia*. Second edition. New York: SUNY Press.

Tambiah, S. J. (1968) The ideology of merit and the social correlates of Buddhism in a Thai village. In: E. Leach (ed.), *Dialectic in practical religion*. Cambridge, UK: Cambridge University Press, 41–121.

Tambiah, S. J. (1970) *Buddhism and the spirit cult in northeast Thailand*. Cambridge, UK: Cambridge University Press.

Tambiah, S. J. (1976) *World conqueror and world renouncer: a study of Buddhism and polity in Thailand against a political background.* Cambridge, UK: Cambridge University Press.

Tambiah, S. J. (1978) Sangha and polity in modern Thailand: an overview. In: B. Smith (ed.), *Religion and legitimation of power in Thailand, Laos, and Burma.* Chambersburg, PA: ANIMA Books, 111–133.

Tambiah, S. J. (1984) *The Buddhist saints of the forest and the cult of amulets: a study of charisma, hagiography, sectarianism, and millennial Buddhism.* Cambridge, UK: Cambridge University Press.

Taylor, J. (1989) Contemporary urban Buddhist 'cults' and the socio-political order in Thailand. *Mankind,* 19 (2), 112–185.

Taylor, J. (1990) New Buddhist movements in Thailand: an 'individualistic revolution', reform, and political dissonance. *Journal of southeast Asian studies,* 21 (1), 135–154.

Taylor, J. (1993) *Forest monks and the nation-state: an anthropological and historical study in northeastern Thailand.* Singapore: Institute of Southeast Asian Studies.

Taylor, J. (1998) Thamma-chaat: activist monks and competing discourses of nature and nation in northeastern Thailand. In: P. Hirsch (ed.), *Seeing forests for trees: environment and environmentalism in Thailand.* Chiang Mai, Thailand: Silkworm Books, 37–52.

Tiyavanich, K. (1997) *Forest recollections: wandering monks in twentieth century Thailand.* Honolulu: University of Hawai'i Press.

United Nations Development Programme (2007) Thailand human development report 2007: sufficiency economy and human development. Bangkok, Thailand: UNDP.

Weber, M. (1958) *The religion of India: the sociology of Hinduism and Buddhism.* Glencoe, IL: Free Press.

Suggested Reading

Darlington, S. (2012) *The ordination of a tree: the Thai Buddhist environmental movement.* New York: State University of New York Press.

Keyes, C., and Daniel, E. V. (eds) (1983) *Karma: an anthropological inquiry.* Berkeley: University of California Press.

Queen, C., and King, S. (eds) (1996) *Engaged Buddhism: Buddhist liberation movements in Asia.* New York: State University of New York Press.

Sivaraksa, S. (1988) *A socially engaged Buddhism.* Bangkok: Thai Inter-Religious Commission for Development.

Swearer, D. (2010) *The Buddhist world of southeast Asia.* Second edition. New York: SUNY Press.

Weber, M. (1958) *The religion of India: the sociology of Hinduism and Buddhism.* Glencoe, IL: Free Press.

CHAPTER 14

EAST ASIAN BUDDHIST ETHICS

RICHARD MADSEN

Historical Background and Modern Transformation

East Asian Buddhism, predominant in Han China, Japan, Korea, and Taiwan as well as the Chinese diaspora around the world, belongs to the Mahāyāna tradition.[1] A chief characteristic of this is its embrace of the bodhisattva ideal, a commitment to achieve enlightenment for all living beings rather than just for oneself. Transmitted to China at the beginning of the first millennium CE, Mahāyāna Buddhism became the state religion during the Tang dynasty (618–905 CE) and although losing that position in subsequent dynasties it has remained a major part of the Chinese cultural landscape. In the Song dynasty (960–1278 CE), it helped to shape what came to be called the neo-Confucian tradition and it also was commonly practised in syncretism with Confucianism and Daoism. Its major monasteries enjoyed the patronage of the state and generally supported imperial rule. In so doing, they adopted the ethical system of the politically hegemonic Confucian tradition. There were, however, 'unorthodox' Buddhist sects, usually led by laypeople, which defied some orthodox social conventions and sometimes inspired social movements through an expectation of the imminent coming of Maitreya Buddha (Overmyer 1976). The Han Chinese Buddhist tradition produced many different lineages and schools, predominant among which were the Pure Land and Chan.

During the Tang dynasty, these lineages and schools were transmitted to Japan and Korea, and later also to Vietnam, where they became important parts of these nation's cultures. Buddhism became deeply embedded—'diffused', as sociologist C. K. Yang put

[1] The author would like to thank Jake Lory and Payton Carrol for their research assistance.

it—into daily life (Yang 1961). Buddhist concepts like reincarnation and karma were a part of ordinary vocabulary. Images of buddhas and bodhisattvas stood in the temples found in every village and neighbourhood. But the images shared space with Daoist immortals, Confucian sages, and the deified heroes of folk tradition. Buddhism had only a weak presence as an institutionally separate religion.

There were monasteries, of course, but these were usually seen as refuges for life's losers. Monks were called upon to offer specific services, especially to chant sutras at funeral ceremonies. Lay people normally did not take refuge in temples. There was no membership requirement for seeking the services of Buddhist monks or nuns at any given temple, and rituals were hired on a simple fee for service basis. Laypeople worshipped different deities in different temples on different occasions. A person might pray to Guanyin (Avalokiteśvara) in hope for a male heir but then to a Daoist deity for healing of an illness. 'Selection of a temple was guided not by faithful attachment to a single religious faith but by the reputed magical efficacy of a certain god for a certain purpose' (Yang 1961: 328).

Buddhist ethical ideas were diffused throughout life. People generally knew the content of the Five Precepts. They kept ledgers of merit to gauge how they might fare in the afterlife. The images of fearsome door gods and depictions of the torments of Buddhist hells conveyed cautionary lessons to avoid evil. But outside the monastic *Vinaya* there was no organized Buddhist authority to guide laypeople through moral dilemmas. And the life of monastics was no role model. By the end of the nineteenth century in China, the popular image of monks was that they were ignorant and corrupt. As Peter Van der Veer summarizes, Buddhist clerics 'were described not only as ignorant buffoons, but also as criminals, drunkards, gluttons, and, foremost, as sexually debauched' (Van der Veer 2011: 148).

From the mid-nineteenth century, in the crucible of imperialist aggression, political upheaval, war, and revolution, Buddhist monks and lay followers were challenged to reform their traditions to meet the unprecedented ethical challenges of modernity. In the twentieth century, reformers like the Chinese monk Taixu (1890–1947) and his followers propagated new visions of Buddhism in the 'human realm' (Ch. *renjian*). This modernized Buddhism takes different forms and goes by different names in different parts of Asia. Thich Nhat Hanh called it 'Engaged Buddhism', but in English writings referring to Taiwan and Hong Kong is usually called 'Humanistic Buddhism', while in Korea it might be called 'Buddhism of the masses'. By whatever name, it aims to guide Buddhists beyond the capitalistic greed, technological delusions, militarized anger, and ethnic hatreds of the modern world.

Modern reformers struggled to make Buddhism relevant to national modernization and national salvation by reinterpreting Buddhist doctrines, reforming Buddhist education, and reorganizing the *Saṅgha* (Pittman 2001). This was for the sake of preserving Buddhism, but also for contributing to secular nationalism. The project was engulfed by war and revolution. Hatred and class struggle ruled the day. But in the latter half of the twentieth century, especially in Taiwan, this vision of 'humanistic Buddhism' was expanded into a genuinely universalistic, global vision, and it began to have great appeal to emerging middle classes in developing parts of East Asia. By the end of the twentieth century, modern East Asian Buddhist leaders had developed systematic training programmes for their monastics and established large lay organizations with their own resources for Buddhist education and systematic practice. They had also created universities, primary, and secondary schools to develop and propagate Buddhist ideas and values (Madsen 2007). Most of these East Asian Buddhist organizations stayed out of direct engagement with politics, although in Japan the Sōka Gakkai movement created its own political party. Their leaders made wide use of modern media to propagate their messages.

Meanwhile, in rural villages throughout East Asia, farmers continued to practise Buddhism as part of a socially embedded syncretistic polytheism, with new deities being regularly added to the mix. The author recently saw, for instance, a medallion with an image of the Bodhisattva Guanyin on the one side and Mao Zedong on the other: compassionate radicalism!

The polytheistic syncretism of East Asian rural life took on a more sophisticated, expansive form in the 'redemptive societies' that flourished in urban areas in the early twentieth century. These combined Buddhist doctrine and ethical teachings with Confucian, Daoist, and even Christian traditions. They often used shamanistic divination to develop doctrines and attracted millions of lay followers. Some of these have left descendants that still exist in the form of the influential 'Unity Way' founded in China but now active especially in Taiwan and throughout Southeast Asia, and the 'New Religions' of Japan. Buddhist influences are also obviously present in *qigong* groups like the Falungong (wheel of *Dharma* practice), which have been persecuted in China as 'evil cults' but continue to have a worldwide presence (Goossaert and Palmer 2011: 91–121; 306–313). Although Buddhist teachings are an important component of all these forms of syncretistic religious practice, it is difficult to isolate this component and assess the actual extent of its influence. It is also difficult to extract from them a distinctively Buddhist answer to the particular dilemmas of modern and postmodern industrial societies.

For the rest of this chapter, therefore, while showing areas of continuities and change with older traditions, we will focus on the East Asian Buddhist ethics that emerged in the late twentieth century from modern Buddhist organizations, which have developed articulate responses that have shaped the moral lives of millions of lay followers. The predominant ethic in the diffused folk Buddhism might be termed a 'fortune-bringing' ethic: one should do good and avoid evil so as to gain the good consequences of a favourable rebirth; and if one cannot avoid evil, one can at least gain compensatory merit by paying monks and others to carry out rituals on one's behalf. But based on modernist interpretations of classical teachings, the ethic propagated by twentieth-century Buddhist reformers is more akin to what Western philosophers call a virtue ethic: one should steadily expand one's capacities to discern and to practise the good so that one can fulfil the potential of the buddha nature buried within oneself and reach the goal of being a bodhisattva—one who can help lift the whole world to a better state.

There do not exist systematic treatises on such Buddhist ethics. My account is gleaned from the *Dharma* talks of Buddhist leaders and especially the responses of practitioners to challenges of realizing the bodhisattva ideal in modern East Asia. Although there is no pope of modern East Asian Buddhism—no single authority to determine correct teaching—and there are variations in the teachings of many Buddhist masters, one can discern common themes.

Buddhism and the Family

Having appropriated much of the Confucian ethic, the starting point for East Asian ethical discourse is family relations, and the modern challenge is how to sustain such relations in face of the social breakdown brought about by urbanization and industrialization. But modern East Asian Buddhists then move beyond the family to confront challenges to the wider community, including the national community, and finally the globe and the fate of all sentient beings threatened by advanced warfare and ecological destruction.

Buddhists have not developed a body of rules for dealing with such challenges. They simply seek to practise the Five Precepts and through various skilful means to cultivate deepening awareness of the fundamental interconnectedness of reality—to follow a path of cultivating virtues that would enable them to respond to novel situations with Great Compassion and True Wisdom. The predominant ethic, at least as promoted by the teachers who shape common Buddhist consciousness in East Asia, is a virtue ethic, not the application of complicated moral rules but the cultivation of expansive moral selves which can be properly motivated and wisely guided to bring healing and enlightenment to suffering beings everywhere.

Although renunciation of the family through entering monastic life remains an ideal, modern East Asian Buddhist movements want to mobilize and organize large numbers of lay followers. They emphasize that to be a good family member—a caring spouse or a filial child—is also an excellent karmic seed and lay people have as much agency as monks to propagate the *Dharma*.

In line with Confucian ethical teaching, the teaching of Buddhist masters is that familial relationships are determined not by contracts but by a primordial system of interdependent roles: parent/child, husband/wife, senior/junior siblings. The ethical challenge for a good Buddhist is to play these roles well: to be a benevolent parent, a loyal spouse, and a responsible sibling so that the family will be harmonious. When asked for advice by a woman whose husband is having an affair with a mistress, the Ven. Cheng-yen of the Still Thoughts Abode (and head of the Tzu-chi charitable foundation) in Taiwan answers that she should be patient and still loyal to her husband and learn to love the one that he loves (Rebirth 1997: 148).

Such challenges are raised to a new level by modern social conditions. Modern urban industrial societies do not provide strong support for a harmonious interlocking of familial roles. Children move far away in search of education and jobs; wives take on professional careers that give them an increasing measure of independence; divergent economic and political opportunities push siblings even further apart than they might have become in a simpler agrarian society. When faced with such challenges, Buddhist teachers counsel family members to continue to play their roles but to re-imagine how to play them through the lens of great compassion. For example, children who live far away from their parents should continue to be filial but (aside from being in regular phone contact with their parents) they should find ways to help the parents through social service agencies, especially those run by compassionate Buddhists. Husbands and wives should develop a relationship not based on patriarchal authority but on mutual respect and support. This is done through cultivating virtues such as filial piety, but doing so in a very dynamic way so that, while following a bodhisattva path of great compassion for all, one develops a moral character able to respond with wisdom to new challenges.

What is not provided in advice to lay people is a clear set of rules, like the monastic *Vinaya* rules, for what one must *not* do. Exhortations are much more a matter of positive encouragement than negative warnings. The idea of 'skilful means' is used to refrain from censuring wrong behaviour. The effort is to encourage the practitioner to follow a path towards ever greater benevolence and the wisdom to respond properly to unforeseeable challenges.

Expanding Family Ethics into the Public Sphere

The key feature in Mahāyāna Buddhist ethics is the intention to extend compassion to all. So East Asian Buddhists encourage practitioners to offer love and care outside the confines of one's immediate family. Yet the language for how to do this mirrors the language of fulfilling role responsibilities in the family. The moral logic is not one of leaving behind family relationships but of extending those relations to encompass the whole world—treating the world as one's big family. As Ven. Hsing Yun, the founder of the Buddha's Light Mountain monestary in Taiwan, says: 'In order to fully understand the value of life, we must perceive the universe as our parents and every form of existence as our brothers and sisters' (Hsing 2003: 19). Just as a family ethic is based on each family member fulfilling their particular roles, so one must work to fulfil all the other roles placed upon one or chosen by one in the wider world.

> Different people have different missions in life ... Parents take educating their children as their mission and are willing to work hard toward that end. Some spouses make sacrifices in order to help their partners succeed. Soldiers in battle are prepared to die for their country. Teachers spend their lives teaching and lecturing in class. Medical professionals work around the clock to save lives and alleviate suffering. Religious leaders live a life of simplicity so as to spread the truth and liberate all

> sentient beings. In addition, truckers and drivers transport people and goods day and night; journalists and reporters risk their lives in order to get to the truth; and actors laugh and cry in performances in order to entertain their audiences. They all have missions in life. (Hsing 2003: 45)

Though in continuity with older visions of engaging with the world, this vision is challenged in the present day by the sheer number and complexity of the various interdependent roles that constitute modern society. A 'mission' to be a physician, for example, involves a degree of specialization, research, and scientific training well beyond what a premodern healer would have had. Being a good doctor also often involves a greater detachment from other life spheres—a greater degree of tension for example between work and family. Finally, although devoted to the karmically good work of healing the sick, it can involve karmically bad actions like killing animals in the course of medical research. The most popular modern Asian Buddhists, however, do not want to give up the benefits of scientific medicine. Their leaders thus quietly approve the sacrifice of animals in medical experiments, as long as the experiments are necessary for medical progress and the animals are treated as humanely as possible (Madsen 2007: 40). Similar compromises with the first Buddhist precept, of course, come with the role of the modern soldier. The principle here seems to be that the good actions involved in fulfilling a modern professional role would outweigh the bad actions that are incidental to the role. Once again the Buddhist ethic is framed not as a set of limits on what can be done but a set of exhortations to fulfil in the best way possible one's professional role in benefiting the human community. The goal is not to establish rules but to promote virtues, to develop capacities for building a harmonious society composed of compassionate individuals exercising mutually interlocking roles that work to the benefit of all.

The stated aim of recent movements to develop a modern Buddhism is to 'enter the world to leave the world' (Ch. *rushi wei chushi*), that is to so reform the world that it can transcend its suffering-filled existence and itself become a Pure Land. The hope for a good reincarnation is not to be reborn into a Pure Land in the Western heavens but to be reborn on earth, in a world made better, more loving, and more cooperative by the virtuous actions of multitudes following the bodhisattva path.

But does such Buddhism have a social ethic that can solve the problems of modern political conflict, total war, structural economic inequality, changing understandings of sexuality, ethnic discrimination, and environmental degradation?

Politics and War

Unlike 'Engaged Buddhisms' (some Mahāyāna, but mostly Theravāda) in Southeast Asia, modern East Asian Buddhisms for the most part attempt to stay out of direct political action. The Tzu-chi Buddhist Compassionate Relief Association in Taiwan, for example, adds five additional precepts, one of which is to stay out of partisan politics.

This means that the organization will not endorse any candidate in an election, even as it encourages members to take part in civic life by voting according to their consciences. Its many educational programmes, however, are intended to help members develop a compassionate heart and a global awareness that should lead to an informed, compassionate political conscience. Politicians of all parties seeking election visit the Ven. Cheng-yen, the organization's founder (along with other major Buddhist leaders in Taiwan), to discuss the moral issues facing their country. With Cheng-yen, as with most of the other Buddhist leaders, they get an exhortation to moral uplift rather than to restrictive conflict. For example, the author was present at a dialogue between Ven. Cheng-yen and Annette Lu, who at the time was running for vice-president on the Democratic Progressive Party ticket. Lu, a strong feminist and assertive politician, decried the practice of Betel Nut Beauties—scantily clad young women selling Betel Nut around Taiwan. The vice-presidential candidate seemed to be suggesting the need for legislation banning the practice. But the Ven. Cheng-yen answered that the young women did this because there were not better jobs available and it would be better if the government provided more wholesome opportunities (author's field notes 1999).

Some Buddhist groups, however, do become actively involved in politics, even to the point of becoming co-opted to an extent that seem difficult to reconcile with any ideals of the Buddhist tradition. In the early twentieth century, both Japanese Zen and Pure Land Buddhists supported Japanese military aggressions. Buddhist sects officially contributed to the 'spiritual mobilization' for the war against China beginning in 1937. The Zen resolve in the face of death was drawn upon in the training of kamikaze pilots at the end of the Second World War. With the idea that death was preferable to the dishonour of surrender, it played its part in the ill treatment of prisoners of war, as well as the mass suicides of captured Japanese soldiers (Harvey 2000: 270).

On the other hand, in post-war Japan, many Buddhist-inspired New Religions have played an active role in peace movements. One of the most important, the Sōka Gakkai (which was founded in the 1930s and unlike most other Buddhist groups resisted the war), has founded its own political party (the Kōmeitō Party, which usually forms a coalition with the Liberal Democratic Party), which strongly opposes nuclear weapons, promotes international human rights and cross-cultural understanding, and carries out a wide variety of peace education programmes (Seager 2006).

Economic Inequality

The highest ideal for East Asian Buddhists is to 'leave the family' and join a monastery, where goods are owned in common. Yet such institutions always rely on the generosity of lay benefactors for support—especially wealthy benefactors who can gain great merit by generous support of the monastics. Buddhists are not against wealth, as long as it is used in the right spirit, which is to avoid attachment to one's wealth and to use it generously to help those in need. What people need is to be relieved of the sufferings of extreme poverty, which is not good because it can block the poor from seeking enlightenment.

Insofar as East Asian Buddhists want to create large lay organizations, they tend to emphasize even more than Buddhists at other times and places the karmic value of the lay condition. This includes especially an appreciation of the need to provide well for one's family. East Asian Buddhist leaders do not challenge the capitalist system of property ownership. As we have seen, they refrain from political critiques that would challenge the structures of wealth and poverty in the economy.

The challenges of inequality are to be dealt with by following the bodhisattva path and cultivating the virtue of compassion. One cultivates this virtue through the practice of giving. One should be grateful for the opportunity to give, for it helps one develop virtue and gain merit. A motto of the Tzu-chi organization is 'give with gratitude, receive with joy'.

Filtered through the Confucian lens of Chinese culture, the East Asian way for a layperson to cultivate the bodhisattva virtue of great compassion is to expand one's notion of what constitutes the boundaries of one's family to ideally encompass the whole globe—where 'all men are brothers'. Organizations like Tzu-chi and the Buddha's Light International Association run extremely effective and generous programmes that alleviate suffering caused by poverty and natural disaster around the globe. The practice of imagining the world of needy people through the lens of a family writ large leads to a personalistic style of generosity. Buddhist volunteers in these organizations give out their aid directly to individuals, if possible face to face, rather than simply contributing money to fund bureaucratically defined categories of needy people.

If such practices were followed by everyone there would be a significant redistribution of wealth and a narrowing of the gap between rich and poor. But absent such universal cultivation of Buddhist virtue, the root causes of inequality within a globalized capitalist system will not be addressed. A more comprehensive critique of the modern economy is the Buddhist critique of consumerism. Insofar as the engine of this economy depends on ceaseless competition for symbols of status driven by advertising that stimulates insatiable desires, the economy is the very embodiment of the forms of suffering which Buddhism seeks to relieve. East Asian Buddhist leaders constantly warn their followers of the dangers of embracing consumerism. At the same time, they advocate a middle way of simple but gracious living, in which rooms are adorned with beautiful flowers, people build relationships through delicious vegetarian meals and elegant tea ceremonies, and comport themselves with comfortable dignity. Poverty is seen as the inability to live this way, and poverty should be alleviated through grateful giving.

Sexuality and Reproductive Ethics

The third Buddhist precept, officially embraced in the ceremony of 'taking refuge', forbids 'unorthodox sex', which includes any sex outside of monogamous marriage. Sex is dangerous because it arouses desires that must be extinguished if one is to receive enlightenment. The moral ideal is a life of complete celibacy, lived within a monastic community.

In East Asian Buddhism, this negative view of sexuality is modified through the encounter with Chinese culture. The precepts are paths to perfection and the approach of Buddhist leaders is not to condemn imperfect people but to encourage them to better themselves through cultivation under guidance from the Buddhist community. In Chinese culture, marriage and family are very highly valued; they can produce almost as much good karma as the monastic vocation. The Chinese cultural tradition does not have an equivalent of Western puritanism. In both Confucianism and Daoism, sex is seen as something natural, to be fully enjoyed and if possible perfected through Daoist arts of the bedchamber. When Buddhist masters warn their followers about extramarital sex it is often in terms of the jealousy and conflict—and associated negative emotions—aroused by the practice rather than something intrinsically wrong about the sex act itself. Buddhist leaders in East Asia have not engaged in moral crusades to eliminate prostitution, which in fact flourishes in countries with a strong Buddhist influence. Brothels sometimes display statues of the Maitreya Buddha or various bodhisattvas. Although Buddhist leaders see prostitution as an unhealthy aspect of society, they usually try to address the problem by advocating healthy alternatives to the profession, such as better jobs. This accords with the skilful means of encouraging the good rather than condemning the bad.

Homosexual sex acts would fall into the category of 'unorthodox sex' based on the Mahāyāna tradition of defining such orthodoxy in terms of 'person, place, and orifice'. However, contemporary humanistic Buddhist leaders are much more focused on the ethic of compassion than on prescriptions and some at least acknowledge proscriptions against homosexual sex as based on outdated cultural understandings rather than original Buddhist scriptures. They emphasize preaching tolerance to all persons. Hsing Yun, the founder of Buddha's Light Temple writes:

> Marriage is an institution that reflects the values of the society that supports it. If the people of a society no longer believe that it is important to be married, then there is no reason why they cannot change the institution of marriage.
>
> Marriage is a custom. Customs can always be changed. We can find the same core point in this question as we have in others—the ultimate truth of the matter is that individuals can and should decide for themselves what is right. As long as they are not violating others or breaking the laws of the society in which they are living, then they are free to do what they believe is right. It is not for me or anyone else to tell them that they must get married if they want to live together. That is their choice and their choice alone.
>
> The same analysis can be applied to homosexuality. People often ask me what I think about homosexuality. They wonder, is it right, is it wrong? The answer is, it is neither right or wrong. It is just something that people do. If people are not harming each other, their private lives are their own business; we should be tolerant of them and not reject them.

> However, it will still take some time for the world to fully accept homosexuality. All of us must learn to tolerate the behavior of others. Just as we hope to expand our minds to include all of the universe, so we should seek also to expand our minds to include all of the many forms of human behavior.
>
> Tolerance is a form of generosity and it is a form of wisdom. There is nothing anywhere in the Dharma that should ever lead anyone to become intolerant. Our goal as Buddhists is to learn to accept all kinds of people and to help all kinds of people discover the wisdom of the teachings of Shakyamuni Buddha. (Hsing 2001: 137–138)

The first wedding between two gay Buddhists in Taiwan was presided over by a Buddhist master with a Buddhist ritual in 2012.

For East Asian Buddhists, there is not much concern about contraception, but abortion is seen as problematic. The foetus is seen as a living, sentient being, which it is prohibited to kill. It is worse to kill a more fully developed foetus than an early term one. The intention of the persons engaged in the abortion make the act more or less severe. Yet applied to modern circumstances, the doctrine of 'skilful means' leads to a casuistry in which sometimes even killing might be necessary for the greater good of relieving maternal or familial suffering. The director of the Buddhist Tzu-chi Hospital in Taiwan says that even though they do not approve of abortion they would not interfere with the therapeutic decision of one of their physicians to provide it (Madsen 2007: 81). Also, in keeping with their reluctance to engage in politics, most East Asian Buddhists are unwilling to force changes in civil laws allowing abortion.

One response they do make, especially in Japan, is to carry out memorial service rituals for 'foetus ghosts'. These are ways for mothers to assuage guilt by apologizing to their aborted foetus and to transfer merit to the foetus so that he or she might quickly have a happy rebirth. (If an unhappy foetus were to return to the womb of the woman who had the abortion, it might grow up to be a very unruly child.) In Japan there are temples with tens of thousands of statues of Jizō, a bodhisattva who looks after dead children, each put up by a woman who has had an abortion. There are similar large temples in Taiwan as well. The practice was begun in Japan in the mid-1970s and is aimed not at legitimating abortion but at compassionately alleviating the suffering of those who have performed an illegitimate deed (LaFleur 1992; Moskowitz 2001).

As for genetic engineering, East Asian Buddhist intellectuals are just beginning to explore the ethical consequences of this new technology. No clear-cut consensus has yet emerged. The general attitude seems to be that just because technology makes such procedures possible, it does not necessarily follow that it should be done. As Sheng Yen, the founder of the Dharma Drum Mountain Monastery in Taiwan, put it during a dialogue on the subject with the head of the Academia Sinica:

> Let's look at things from a religious perspective ... The negative side of technology is that it has hurt many innocent people. In the 20th century, 30 million people died from the instruments of war. ... The achievement of genetic engineering poses problems. It would be an insult to human dignity if wealthy people were allowed

> to determine what kind of baby they wanted to have. The Earth would become a machine where ethics were no longer valued. (Fang 2000)

The emphasis here is less on intrinsic characteristics of the technology itself (although if the genetic engineering requires the destruction of human embryos, it raises the same questions as abortion for Buddhists), but on the social effects of the technology. Does it create happiness for the few and misery for many others, with resultant temptations for hatred and conflict?

Environmental Ethics

According to Damien Keown, classical 'Buddhist attitudes toward the natural world are complex and sometimes contradictory' (Keown 2005: 50). On the one hand, kindness towards all sentient beings is central to all Buddhist doctrines, enshrined in the first precept against killing and expressed in rituals of saving life by releasing captive animals. On the other hand, Buddhism is anthropomorphic: 'value belongs to humans alone and nature is to be protected for their sake and no other'. But 'virtues such as loving-kindness, compassion, non-violence, and wisdom promote ecological concern by their very nature' (Keown 2005: 51). In any case, even when Buddhism held sway in East Asia in imperial times, environmental degradation continued.

However, modern East Asian Buddhism draws on the tradition of the virtues—especially compassion for all things—interpreted in the light of scientific understandings of global ecology in such a way as to produce an environmental ethic that is by no means contradictory. Insofar as humanistic Buddhists are devoted to creating a 'Pure Land on earth', they are devoted not to escaping the world but to making this world a better place. They have to overcome the destruction of the earth about which environmental scientists are warning. According to Hsing Yun:

> Nowadays, people often mention the end of the world.... However, there is no need to be overly worried, because the so-called 'age of the end of Dharma', commonly known as the end of the world, if calculated according to the Buddhist perspective of time, is still many thousands of years away.... Furthermore, while the First, Second, and Third Meditation Heavens will be destroyed by the Three Disasters, there is still a Fourth Heaven, which is free from disasters.... Therefore, as long as we have the right conditions and merits, we will be among those who are fortunate enough to live within the Fourth Meditation Heaven. Thus there is no need to be afraid or worried. Instead of that, it is better to accrue merits. As long as we love and cherish our blessings, keep accumulating merits and virtue, and look after the earth, then we will give it a longer life. Nevertheless, the future of the earth still depends on human behaviors, because everything in the world follows the law of cause and effect. (Hsing 2010)

Hsing Yun and other contemporary humanistic Buddhist masters reinforce this commitment to environmentalism with an interpretation (not shared by all traditional Buddhists) of the classic teaching that all beings have buddha nature, even non-animate ones. 'Both the sentient and insentient possess the potential to attain Buddhahood... The Buddhist doctrine of equality views all beings as equals, and advocates that not only humans and animals deserve love and care, mountains, rivers, and the great earth also need to be protected' (Hsing 2010). Contemporary Buddhist leaders also invoke the doctrine of dependent origination to further the environmental cause. As Hsing Yun puts it:

> Everything in this world has a life, thus, we cannot just cherish our own life but also that of others. Without other lives in this world, there will not be causes and conditions that allow our existence. 'I' will not exist. Therefore, in order to survive, we must love and cherish our causes and conditions and 'be one' and 'coexist' with all things. Only mutual respect, assistance, and support can enable all beings to coexist on earth. (Hsing 2010)

Such theory becomes the justification for a great deal of environmental practice. Environmental protection seems to have been made into a distinguishing marker of the Buddhist 'brand' in Asian societies. It is, for example, a major mission of the Taiwan-based Tzu-chi foundation, which mobilizes millions of volunteers throughout Asia and indeed around the world in efforts to recycle trash, replant trees, and clean up water sources. Especially impressive is a programme to turn plastic bottles into all manner of household items, including warm blankets.

Typical of the Buddhist approach to environmental protection in most of Asia, however, is a reluctance to address the problems though political means. The Buddhist approach is to save the natural environment by cultivating a good spiritual environment, that is, by cultivating virtues like compassion and care, and striving to overcome greed and delusion. Vegetarianism is promoted not simply because classic Mahāyāna Buddhism is opposed to the killing of animals but because eating meat consumes far more resources and leads to the production of far more greenhouse gases than following a vegetarian diet.

In the Buddhist analysis, the major ecological problem of our time is not caused by population growth or by technology in itself, but by the growth of insatiable desires provided by modern consumerism. As Master Sheng Yen says:

> The wasteful consumption of natural resources and destruction of ecology are caused by humankind's psychological craving for convenience and wealth. If we can practice the Buddha's teaching of 'leading a contented life with few desires' and 'being satisfied and therefore always happy', and if we are willing to use our intelligence to deal with problems and engage diligently in productive work, then, without having to contend with one another or fight with nature, we can lead very happy lives. (Sheng Yen 2000)

A spiritual salvation is therefore key to salvation of the material environment. But the practice of saving the planet can itself be a form of cultivation that leads to higher spiritual awareness. According to Sheng Yen:

> The environmental tasks of general people are mostly restricted to the material aspects. . . . The environmental tasks we carry out have to go deeper from the material level to the spiritual level of society and thinking. Environmental protection must be combined with our respective religious beliefs and philosophical thinking into an earnest mission, so that environmentalism will not become mere slogans. So, strictly speaking, the purification of humankind's mind is free from evil intentions and is not polluted by us. However, for ordinary people, it is advisable to set out by cultivating the habit of protecting the material environment, and go deeper step by step until at last they can cultivate environmentalism on the spiritual level. (Sheng Yen 2000)

Conclusion

East Asian Buddhism built upon the Mahāyāna tradition, became deeply embedded in Han Chinese society, and spread from there to other parts of East Asia. It became intertwined with Confucian and Daoist teaching and practices and constituted the local custom of agrarian communities. The monastic *saṅgha* stood apart from this customary life and was used by laypeople to provide ritual services, but did not exercise a great deal of moral influence, especially in the few centuries leading up to the modern era. Under pressure from Western imperialism and modernization, East Asian Buddhism was pulled out of its embedding in local custom and reformed institutionally and intellectually so as to provide an independent and distinctive approach to modern problems. The modern Buddhist organizations emerging from this process have attracted large followings among the urban middle classes and exercised considerable moral influence. In general, they do not articulate a body of clear-cut moral rules, but rather promote a virtue ethic that cultivates compassion so as to follow the bodhisattva path in confronting the ambiguous moral dilemmas of modernity.

Works Cited

Buddhist Compassion Relief Tzu Chi Foundation (1997) *Rebirth: transformations in Tzu Chi*. Taipei: Still Thoughts Cultural Mission. Available from: http://www.tuvienquangduc.com.au/English/rebirth/25transformations-rebirth.html.

Fang, R. (2000) Keeping the integrity of man intact. *Taiwan info*, 26 May (n.p.).

Goossaert, V., and Palmer, D. (2011) *The religious question in modern China*. Chicago: University of Chicago Press.

Harvey, P. (2000) *An introduction to Buddhist ethics*. Cambridge: Cambridge University Press.

Hsing Y. (2001) *Buddhism pure and simple*. Translated by T. Graham. Trumbull, CT: Weatherhill.

Hsing Y. (2003) *A moment, a lifetime: between ignorance and enlightenment III*. Translated by Ven. Miao Hsi and C. Lai. Hacienda Heights, CA: Buddha's Light Publishing.

Hsing Y. (2010) Environmental and spiritual preservation. Keynote speech at BLIA General Conference, Foguangshan, Taiwan, 2–7 October, n.p. Available from: http://www.bliango.org/2011/06/20/2010-keynote-speech-by-venerable-master-hsing-yun/.

Keown, D. (2005) *Buddhist ethics: a very short introduction*. Oxford: Oxford University Press.

LaFleur, W. R. (1992) *Liquid life: abortion and Buddhism in Japan*. Princeton, NJ: Princeton University Press.

Madsen, R. (2007) *Democracy's dharma: religious renaissance and political development in Taiwan*. Berkeley: University of California Press.

Moskowitz, M. L. (2001) *The haunting fetus: abortion, sexuality, and the spirit world in Taiwan*. Honolulu: University of Hawai'i Press.

Overmyer, D. (1976) *Folk Buddhist religion: dissenting sects in late traditional China*. Cambridge, MA: Harvard University Press.

Pittman, D. A. (2001) *Toward a modern Chinese Buddhism: Taixu's reforms*. Honolulu: University of Hawai'i Press.

Seager, R. H. (2006) *Encountering the dharma: Daisaku Ikeda, Soka Gakkai, and the globalization of Buddhist humanism*. Berkeley: University of California Press.

Sheng Yen (2000) Environmental protection. Speech given at the Waldorf Astoria, New York, 30 August 2000, as part of United Nations World Peace Summit, n.p. Available from: http://ddmba.org/pages/about-us/founder/speeches/environmental-protection.php.

Van der Veer, P. (2011) Smash temples, build schools: comparing secularism in India and China. In: M. Jurgensmeyer, C. Calhoun, and J. Van Antwerpen (eds), *Rethinking secularism*. Oxford: Oxford University Press, 270–281.

Yang, C. K. (1961) *Religion in Chinese society*. Berkeley: University of California Press.

Suggested Reading

Chandler, S. (2004) *Establishing a pure land on earth: the Foguang Buddhist perspective on modernization and globalization*. Honolulu: University of Hawai'i Press.

Harvey, P. (2000) *An introduction to Buddhist ethics*. Cambridge: Cambridge University Press.

Keown, D. (2001) *The nature of Buddhist ethics*. Basingstoke, UK: Palgrave.

Madsen, R. (2007) *Democracy's dharma: religious renaissance and political development in Taiwan*. Berkeley: University of California Press.

Pittman, D. A. (2001) *Toward a modern Chinese Buddhism: Taixu's reforms*. Honolulu: University of Hawai'i Press.

Seager, R. H. (2006) *Encountering the dharma: Daisaku Ikeda, Soka Gakkai, and the globalization of Buddhist humanism*. Berkeley: University of California Press.

CHAPTER 15

BUDDHIST ETHICS IN CONTEMPORARY TIBET

HOLLY GAYLEY

INTRODUCTION

TODAY Buddhist ethics are becoming intertwined with Tibetan identity. In an ethical reform movement currently underway in nomadic regions of eastern Tibet, cleric-scholars are calling on ordinary Tibetans to live up to their Buddhist civilizational heritage and cultivate a 'lifestyle in accord with the *Dharma*' (*chos dang mthun pa'i 'tsho ba*). This is not simply a reassertion of tradition, since it requires a dramatic shift in customary practices related to dress, diet, and livelihood. Vows are being taken en masse to adhere to a newly formulated set of ten Buddhist virtues, with prohibitions against selling livestock for slaughter, smoking, drinking alcohol, gambling, visiting prostitutes, fighting with weapons, and more. The new ten virtues (*dge bcu*), first promulgated in 2008 by Larung Buddhist Academy in Serta, have spread to neighbouring areas in Kandzé Prefecture, Sichuan Province, and beyond since at least 2010.

The new ten virtues are part of a broader effort by cleric-scholars at Larung Buddhist Academy, the largest and most influential monastic institution on the Tibetan plateau,[1] to address current social issues, including fighting over the grasslands, the threat of AIDS, and the effects of state marketization policies such as the Develop the West campaign launched in the early 2000s. Unlike current Buddhist monastic mobilizations in Southeast Asia, in which a rhetoric of 'endangered identities' is linked to xenophobia and religious intolerance (Gravers 2015), for Tibetans under Chinese rule, there is a renewed commitment to nonviolence despite state repression following the 2008 Olympic-year

[1] As this chapter was being finalized for publication, Larung Buddhist Academy (also known as Larung Gar) was facing demolitions and a dramatic reduction of its resident population of monks and nuns by state order. See www.rfa.org/english/news/tibet/demolition-07212016110342.html, posted 21 July 2016.

protests and even as the tragic wave of self-immolations calls into question the very boundary between violence and nonviolence (Buffetrille 2012; Makley 2015).

This chapter explores how Buddhist ethical principles are being marshalled in novel ways as a means to unify Tibetans and articulate a vision of ethnic identity and progress in line with Buddhist values. Rather than turn to canonical sources to envision Buddhist applications to contemporary moral issues (e.g. Harvey 2000; Keown 2000), I am interested in how Buddhists themselves are responding to social change in line with previous studies on Buddhists ethics in modernizing Asia and engaged Buddhist movements (Queen and King 1996; Hansen 2007; Stewart 2016). I think of Buddhist ethics not in terms of static doctrine or theories of ethical action, but rather as a fluid and shifting process of negotiation between competing discourses and practices that coexist in Tibetan areas of China and also flow across Himalayan borders. In doing so, I pay close attention to how specific facets of Buddhism come into 'central visibility' in an ongoing process of contestation and change (Abeysekara 2008: 29).

The role of Buddhist ethics in Tibetan lives and identity is being promoted and contested in speeches and writings by cleric-scholars, posters and flyers in public spaces, photos and videos circulating on social media, debates in the Tibetan-language blogosphere, and literary and artistic works, including pop music videos. These various types of media have played a role in initiating trends, sparking debate, eliciting affect, and instantiating collective memory with respect to the fur burnings in 2006, the pre-Olympic demonstrations of 2008, the wave of self-immolations starting in 2009, and the spread of the new ten virtues in eastern Tibet since at least 2010.

In what follows, I trace several strands of ethical mobilization among Tibetans over the past two decades with a keen interest in the process of forming ethical Buddhist subjects. Within this context, I consider the self-reflexive ethical project of fashioning oneself into a certain kind of person and the related issue of the exercise of freedom, as engaged in recent scholarship on moral anthropology (Laidlaw 2002; Zigon 2009; Faubion 2001). Note that such a project does not imply the 'free will' of a presumed autonomous subject nor the process of liberation in a political sense. Rather the exercise of freedom, as situated within social and cultural parameters and severely constrained in contexts of colonial or inter-ethnic domination, is integral to 'technologies of the self' in Foucault's sense. These are practices by individuals on their own or in conjunction with others that involve 'operations on their own bodies and souls, thoughts, conduct, and way of being, so as to transform themselves' (Foucault 1994: 225).

While Buddhist cleric-scholars have campaigned for ethical reform through persuasive speeches, writings, posters, and videos as a way to maintain and reform specific aspects of Tibetan culture and temper the effects of state modernization initiatives, their efforts have met with intense criticism by secular intellectuals in the Tibetan blogosphere (Gayley 2016). The issue of freedom is significant in online critiques that invoke the international discourse on human rights and regard monastic efforts as coercive intrusions into secular affairs that impede the ability of ordinary Tibetans to choose their own lifestyle and seek their own economic advantage in line with neoliberal state policies.

To illustrate the range of contemporary ethical mobilizations, I contrast monastic-driven reform—which I discuss primarily in relation to the emergence and spread of the new ten virtues in eastern Tibet—with more dispersed efforts, such as the Lhakar or 'White Wednesday' movement underway since 2009. Spanning the plateau and the diaspora, Lhakar champions voluntaristic acts of resistance, such as boycotts, and cultural empowerment in the form of personal pledges that relate to upholding Tibetan culture and Buddhist values. I also consider a distinct articulation of nonviolence that emerged with the introduction of the 'amulet for peace' (*zhi bde rtags ma*) in 2012 to a crowd of thousands gathered at Larung Buddhist Academy (Gayley and Padma 'tsho 2016). The accompanying speech, by Khenpo Rigdzin Dargyé, called for Tibetan unity and an end to internal fighting, articulating a heroic masculinity in Buddhist terms. Finally, I touch on the political, ritual, and ethical dimensions of self-immolations and their memorialization in poetry and song. In surveying these movements, I illustrate the diverse ways that Tibetans today are actively engaging in an ethical project of forming themselves into loyal subjects of Tibetan culture and Buddhist values.

Exhortations to Virtue

Moral exhortations have been part of broader efforts to revitalize Buddhism and Tibetan culture after the devastating years leading up to and including the Cultural Revolution. In the 1980s, Buddhist teachers who survived the Maoist period began to transmit esoteric teachings once again and to reinstate vows for monastics and lay practitioners. Ritual occasions such as public empowerments were opportunities to deliver 'exhortations to virtue' (*dge ba'i bskul ma*), encouraging ordinary Tibetans to observe basic devotional practices, like paying homage to the Three Jewels and making daily offerings on the family shrine. They also exhorted Tibetans to renounce 'behaviour discordant with *Dharma*' (*chos dang mi mthun pa bya spyod*), such as smoking and drinking alcohol.

These types of exhortations can also be found in texts of advice to the laity, such as 'heart advice' (*snying gtam*), 'appeals' (*zhu yig*), and simply 'teachings' (*bka' slob, slob gso*). The broad category of advice literature (*gdams ngag*) consists of 'directives for practice, whether in the general conduct of life or in some specialized field such as medicine, astronomy, politics, yoga or meditation', which Matthew Kapstein has referred to as 'Tibetan technologies of the self' (1996: 275). In terms set forth by James Laidlaw, also based on Foucault's conception of ethics, we might think of such works as 'invitations and injunctions to make oneself into a certain kind of person' (2002: 321–322). In the contemporary context, in which articulations of Buddhist ethics and Tibetan identity overlap, we might amend Laidlaw's phrase and consider the project of making oneself into a certain kind of Tibetan, one who is loyal to Tibetan culture and Buddhist values.

This conception of an ethical project both subsumes and goes beyond the moral codes involved in proper conduct or discipline (Skt *śīla*, Tib. *tshul khrims*) normally associated with Buddhist ethics. Indeed, for Foucault, ethics has more to do with the Greek understanding of *ethos* as a 'way of being and of behaviour' (1994: 286), including dress and comportment. This broad conception aligns with a key Tibetan expression for ethical discernment, namely 'what to accept and what to reject' (*blang dor*), to the extent that it invites self-cultivation in crafting a 'lifestyle in accord with the *Dharma*'. Notably, works of advice by contemporary Buddhist teachers surveyed here address issues beyond the domain of moral conduct in emphasizing the importance of cultural preservation in terms of language, dress, and customs as well as secular education.

A landmark work of this nature is *Heart Advice to Tibetans for the 21st Century* (*Dus rabs nyer gcig pa'i gangs can pa rnams la phul ba'i snying gtam*), composed in 1995 by Khenpo Jigmé Phuntsok (1933–2004), the founder of Larung Buddhist Academy. The great Khenpo was a pivotal figure in revitalizing Buddhist monasticism in eastern Tibet while also serving as a champion of Nyingma esoteric teachings and an early advocate of Buddhist modernism (Germano 1998; Gayley 2011). In his work of advice, Jigmé Phuntsok crystalized the connection between Buddhist ethics and Tibetan identity by emphasizing a shared history, cultural heritage, and nobility of character among Tibetans, anchored in Buddhist values.

Expressing a sense of 'endangered identity', given the violence of the Maoist period and the post-Mao encroachment of market capitalism, he states: 'In the midst of such transformation, we Tibetan people should maintain the worthy traditions of our forefathers so that they do not vanish, including the beneficial aspects of our values, our distinctive system of erudition, and local customs and habits' ('Jigs med phun tshogs 1995: 3–4). Later, in the same work, he characterizes Tibet's language, civilizational inheritance, and customs as the as the 'life force' (*srog*) of the Tibetan people. Thus, in contrast to Chinese Communist Party (CCP) rhetoric which depicts Tibetans as backward (Ch. *luohou*, Tib. *rjes lus*),[2] Jigmé Phuntsok boldly asserts that 'we as a people with a magnificent history can benefit the entire world with our distinctive tradition of learning' (1995: 4). Tibetans are thereby invited to take pride in their past and to fashion themselves as stewards of their own cultural heritage.

Moreover, he depicts Buddhist values such as compassion as integral to the Tibetan character, citing a common saying that Tibetans learn to say '*ama*' (mother) and '*maṇi*' at the same age, where *maṇi* refers to the mantra *Oṃ Maṇi Padme Hūṃ*, invoking the bodhisattva of compassion Avalokiteśvara. Without upholding such values as part of the 'worthy traditions of our forefathers', in his estimation, Tibetans will become nothing more than an imitation of other ethnicities. In expressing the threat of assimilation, Jigmé Phuntsok accords a prominent place to Buddhist values in Tibetan cultural heritage, deemed the legacy from the past and the foundation for the 'path forward' (*mdun lam*) into the twenty-first century.

[2] For example, Tibet prior to 1950 is routinely characterized as a 'feudal serfdom under theocracy' during the rule of Dalai Lamas. See, for example, the Chinese Government White Paper on 'Development and Progress in Tibet'. <www.china.org.cn/government/whitepaper/2013-10/22/content_30367925.htm>, posted 22 October 2013.

Reforming Tibetan Customs

Jigmé Phuntsok's influence is evident in the writings and speeches of Khenpo Tsultrim Lodrö, a leading figure at Larung Buddhist Academy today and the architect of the new ten virtues. Like his predecessor, Tsultrim Lodrö frames his ethical advice as maintaining Tibetan traditions in continuity with the past, while reforming specific customs to align with Buddhist values. Indeed, he anchors Tibetan unity to a shared history dating back to the imperial period (seventh to ninth centuries) when Buddhism first entered Tibet. Despite the later fragmentation of empire, in his 2004 work, *Timely Advice: The Mirror that Illuminates the Two Systems* (*Dus su bab pa'i gtam lugs gnyis gsal ba'i me long*), Tsultrim Lodrö asserts that Tibetans have maintained—in an uninterrupted fashion until the present—their own identity, distinct culture, and way of life.

Nonetheless, the pristine social body of Tibet is now threatened due to the intermingling (*'dres*) of ethnicities (*mi rigs*) and their respective cultures (*rig gnas*):

> From now onwards into the immediate future, the various ethnicities and cultures of the world are intermingling. Over time, there is a danger of transforming into a mottled mass. There are already early signs of this now. At this time, some cultures belonging to discrete ethnicities are disappearing into thin air, and some are becoming adulterated in various ways [due to the influence of] other [cultures]. [Many] are crossing the borders of their people and land and spreading to other places. There is no doubt that a variety of transformations are taking place. For this reason, one will certainly encounter other cultures and their myriad faulty behaviours. In the midst of such changes, we must protect the pure culture that was established by our ancestors. We should prevent against the faulty views and conduct of others while drawing out the good [in them]. This timely action is very important and valuable, and we should exert ourselves in it. (Tshul khrims blo gros 2003–2004: 259–260)

In this passage, note the concern with border crossings and maintaining the integrity of the Tibetan social body against polluting infiltration. What is needed, in Tsultrim Lodrö's view, is a prophylactic against such a threat, a preventative mechanism to keep at bay the faulty (and potentially infectious) view and conduct of other ethnicities, while still being open to the positive aspects of such an encounter. Though left unstated, his concern with 'intermingling' likely refers to Tibetan identity being absorbed into the dominant (implicitly Han) culture of China.

Tsultrim Lodrö proposes Buddhist ethics as the preventative safeguard to forestall this. In *Timely Advice*, he provides advice to the laity on an array of topics including food, dress, hygiene, education, and cultural preservation (Gayley 2013). A number of features of the new ten virtues are already evident in this work, such as injunctions not to fight with weapons, not to wear fur, and not to drink alcohol, while other issues are discrete, including his advocacy of vegetarianism, promotion of the Tibetan language, and emphasis on the importance of secular education. In proposing reforms to certain customs, Tsultrim Lodrö positions Buddhism, as Tibetans have long held, as a civilizing force rather than Han modernity as CCP rhetoric would have it.

A prime example is Tsultrim Lodrö's discussion of the faults of wearing fur on the trim of traditional Tibetan coats. Although there is considerable debate over how traditional this practice is, during the late 1990s and early 2000s, due to state promotion of cultural tourism among other factors, Tibetans were encouraged to wear larger sized pelts and more jewellery during horse festivals and other public occasions (Yeh 2012a). Countering this trend, Tsultrim Lodrö describes how wearing fur may seem beautiful to Tibetans but appears cruel to other nationalities. Moreover, it goes against Buddhist values, such as compassion to all living creatures who have been one's mother in the infinite web of rebirths, and secular ones, including the enormous economic cost of purchasing pelts and environmentalist concerns over the extinction of endangered species. In *Timely Advice*, Tsultrim Lodrö attempts to synthesize religious and secular values as a persuasive means to encourage the reform of certain Tibetan customs.

Fur-Burning Incidents

While there had been local efforts to effect a change in Tibetan usage of pelts, it was not until a speech by the Fourteenth Dalai Lama at the 2006 Kālacakra in south India, which many Tibetans from the plateau attended, that the movement spread and dramatically changed Tibetan sartorial practices. Emily Yeh has traced events before and after the impactful statements by the Dalai Lama, demonstrating the pressures on him by diverse environmentalist groups, particularly the international tiger campaign, once it was discovered that Tibetans had become a major demand for its illegal trade (2012a, 2013). The Dalai Lama's responsiveness to appeals by environmentalist groups had much to do with the contemporary Buddhist embrace of environmentalism and his own advocacy since the 1980s.

In his remarks, the Dalai Lama stated that he felt ashamed after viewing images of Tibetans on the plateau wearing large pelts and excessive amounts of jewellery, so much so that he regarded such a display to be a threat to the reputation of Tibetans around the world, and it made him wonder whether or not it would be worthwhile to continue to reincarnate. As Yeh points out, 'no reference to or explanation of the ethical-religious reasons for not killing animals' was given; instead, 'the speech was primarily concerned with the issue of shame, disgrace and the reputations of Tibetans as a nation, and how they compare to other peoples' (2012a: 415). Nonetheless, his remarks could be regarded as an injunction to his audience to make themselves into a certain kind of Tibetan.

Loyalty to the Dalai Lama was dramatically performed in fur-burning incidents that spread across the Tibetan plateau in 2006. These were hastily organized events that involved the display of lavish pelts, often by young men, followed by their sacrifice into the fire. Images and news of these events circulated by phone, word of mouth, and the Internet, emboldening others to follow suit. Yeh estimates that pelts worth several millions of US dollars were burned in acts of 'spectacular decommodification' (2013: 339). Since then, it is rare to find Tibetans wearing fur-trimmed coats with a few exceptions. For example, in an ironic twist, the Chinese state required its Tibetan news broadcasters and performance troupes to continue to wear pelts despite their illegality according to its own environmental laws.

Ad Hoc Pledges

In the fur burnings and other movements charted in this chapter, loyalty to Buddhist teachers as preeminent representatives of Tibetan culture and to Buddhist institutions is expressed through specific vows or pledges (*dam bca', khas len*). The taking of ethical vows and pledges represents a significant articulation of Tibetanness in Buddhist terms. At the Kālacakra, Tibetans availed themselves of booths set up by environmentalist groups where pledges could be taken to stop wearing fur (Yeh 2012a), and similar voluntaristic pledges have been a feature of ethical exhortations in contemporary Tibet altogether.

Video recordings of Jigmé Phuntsok's speeches in the 1990s and early 2000s show him as an impassioned orator exhorting Tibetans to virtue and, in response, nomads can be seen raising their hands amongst the listening crowd in ad hoc fashion to pledge to uphold one or another ethical precept. In a speech delivered at Larung Buddhist Academy in 2000, which circulated widely on video compact disc (VCD) titled simply 'Liberate Lives' (*Tshe thar* 2001), the Khenpo asked Tibetans to give up selling their livestock for slaughter, a formative moment in launching what Gaerrang (Kabzung) calls the 'slaughter renunciation movement' (2015). In his speech, Jigmé Phuntsok described in vivid terms the suffering of livestock on their way to slaughter in Chinese cities and the gruesome conditions of mechanized slaughterhouses. And on the VCD, his speech was accompanied by footage from a Hui slaughterhouse, showing yaks slowly dying in pools of their own blood.

Persuasive appeals like this by Buddhist teachers and the taking of ad hoc pledges constitute an important aspect of contemporary ethical mobilization among Tibetans. Whether in speeches or writings, such 'exhortations to virtue' invite their audience into the ethical project of self-reflection and discernment about their own way of life and behaviour. Pledges taken in voluntaristic fashion, by raising hands in a crowd or signing up at a booth, differ in approach to the monastic-driven implementation of the new ten virtues. This is because the new ten virtues have been spread through vows taken en masse by whole villages and clans with monastic oversight and regulation. In the view of its critics, this approach has curtailed the freedom of ordinary Tibetans and their ability to choose their own lifestyle.

Mobilizing Consent

As efforts at ethical reform by leaders at Larung Buddhist Academy gained momentum, ad hoc gestures of taking vows gave way to a more deliberate process involving the collaboration of cleric-scholars and village or clan (*sde ba, tsho ba*) leaders. This shift took place following the death of Jigmé Phuntsok and under the leadership of his successors, particularly Tsultrim Lodrö. In his ethnographic study of slaughter renunciation in Wakhor village, Gaerrang charts the 'entangled cultural knot' of development in which village leaders find their loyalties divided as 'key implementers' of state development projects and protectors of the 'moral and ethical needs of the traditional tribe' (2015: 940).

This dilemma is particularly keen in the slaughter renunciation movement given the intensification of market forces since the Develop the West campaign and pressures to increase livestock sales. When cleric-scholars arranged to have Tsultrim Lodrö visit Wakhor to give religious teachings, village leaders mobilized the consent of households to take vows to refrain from selling their livestock for slaughter for a period of three years, between 2006 and 2009, alongside not smoking, drinking alcohol, and gambling. Tsultrim Lodrö used the occasion to emphasize the importance of economic development in line with Buddhist values and the causal operations of karma across lifetimes for those who harm animals. In his zeal, he characterized the traditional occupation of herding as more shameful than jobs ordinarily consider dirty like shoe shining (Gaerrang 2015: 937–938).

Elsewhere, in speeches collected in *Healing Medicine for Our Times* (*Dus rabs kyi gsos sman*), Tsultrim Lodrö has encouraged Tibetans in nomadic areas to diversify their household income by finding other means of livelihood, whether in road construction, business, traditional crafts, or harvesting medicinal herbs, while maintaining herds for dairy and wool products. In his view, the path forward for Tibetans is to engage the market economy in ways aligned with the *Dharma*. In particular, he has censured those who 'just rest at home without doing work' (*las ka mi byed nas rang gar khyim na nyal*), selling a yak or sheep whenever they need money, especially if funds are put to immoral use, such as gambling or purchasing weapons (Tshul khrims blo gros *c.*2012: 85–87). At play in his views and their potential resonances for contemporary audiences may be state development discourse and initiatives that help shape minority subjectivities, such as tropes of indolence and the value-laden concept of 'quality' (Ch. *suzhi*) in persons (Anagnost 2004; Yeh 2007).

The New Ten Virtues

The formalization of ethical reform by leaders at Larung Buddhist Academy into a set of new ten virtues can be regarded as a constructive response to rapid social change in order to address a range of social issues, such as fighting over the grasslands. Tsultrim Lodrö has been on the forefront of several related campaigns, including AIDS prevention, advocacy for animal welfare, and the preservation of Tibetan language. This constructive approach offers a significant alternative to modes of resistance, such as the protests that swept across the Tibetan plateau in 2008, the same year that the new ten virtues were introduced.

The new ten virtues, as promulgated by Larung Buddhist Academy, are presented as a code or customary system (*lugs srol*) placed in a series of exhortative statements as follows:

The Code of Ten Virtues Promulgated by Serta Larung

1. Not to sell for slaughter: One should not sell horses, cattle, sheep, or dogs to be butchered.
2. Not to steal or rob: One should not steal secretly inside or outside [the home] or rob by force.
3. Not to fight with weapons: One should not fight using knives or guns.
4. Not to consort with prostitutes: One should not consort with prostitutes, Chinese or otherwise, due to the current danger in Tibetan areas of many dreadful diseases arising from this.
5. Not to sell guns or opium [i.e. drugs]: One should not buy guns of various sizes from other places and sell them within Tibet, and one should not buy or sell opium.
6. Not to smoke opium or cigarettes: One should not smoke any type of opium or tobacco.
7. Not to drink: One should not drink any type of liquor.
8. Not to gamble: One should not play games based on wagers of a lot of money or valuables.
9. Not to hunt: One should not kill by various means any wild animals, predator or prey.
10. Not to wear animal fur: One should not wear the skin of wild animals such as leopard, otter, or fox.

Please cast off these ten—selling for slaughter, etc.—in this life and in future lives.

Through these ten, such as the vows to not sell [livestock] for slaughter, one experiences well-being and benefits in both this life and the next. And that's not all: one secures the welfare of [every being] including animals.

Faithful people, this is very important. Please be diligent in this system of ethics.[3]

The language of the 'The Code of Ten Virtues' is exhortative, calling for moral improvement among Tibetans. Combining injunctions for temperance and nonviolence, it

[3] This handout, *Gser ljongs bla ma rung gis gtan la phab pa'i dge bcu'i lugs srol*, was circulated by Larung Buddhist Academy, and the translation here is reproduced from from my article, 'Reimagining Buddhist Ethics on the Tibetan Plateau' (2013). Thanks to Gaerrang (Kabzung) for sharing the handout and explanatory text of the same name with me.

invites Tibetans to help safeguard social welfare, including concern for both humans and animals. Yet it also delineates a discrete set of precepts for lay Tibetans to follow, and their binding nature is reinforced by vows made under the aegis of local monasteries.

Part of the debate over ethical reform concerns whether this code is based on tradition (*srol rgyun*) or constitutes a newly imposed law or set of rules (*khrims*) by cleric-scholars. Presenting it as tradition, Tsultrim Lodrö cites antecedents such as the sixteen human mores (*mi chos*) of the seventh-century Tibetan emperor Songtsen Gampo, the traditional ten Buddhist virtues (*lha chos dge ba bcu*), and state law (*chab srid khrims*) (interview, May 2011).[4] While its name and authority derives from the ten Buddhist virtues, this new formulation emphasizes physical acts, largely in the public domain, as opposed to the traditional organization of precepts into body (not killing, stealing, engaging in sexual misconduct), speech (not lying, slandering, using harsh speech or idle chatter), and mind (not harbouring malice, covetousness, or wrong views).

According to Tulku Tendzin Dargyé who founded the Monastic Association (Dge 'dun mthun tshogs) in Serta in 2010, which now oversees the implementation of ethical reform, the new ten virtues are a simplification of the traditional ones due to the difficulty in upholding precepts of mind and speech (interview, July 2014). This also means that for the first time the observance of the ten virtues can be regulated.

The Issue of Free Choice

While Buddhist teachers, both reincarnate lamas (*sprul sku*) and cleric-scholars (*mkhan po*), tend to use moral persuasion and exhortative language in their speeches and writings of advice, the implementation of the new ten virtues has been criticized as coercive. This reflects a gap in the conception and implementation of ethical reform, whereby the new ten virtues were promulgated by leaders at Larung Buddhist Academy but local monasteries are the ones to organize and regulate adherence in their local communities, issuing punishments for those who transgress their vows.

Reports of fines exacted for violations, forcible confessions, and the denial of religious services have circulated in the Tibetan-language blogosphere, garnering widespread attention among urban Tibetans in cities like Xining and Lhasa, at a far remove from the areas in which the new ten virtues are spreading. Given the relatively unregulated space of the Tibetan blogosphere, where censorship occurs by removing controversial posts already in circulation, secular critics have had the opportunity to question the role

[4] Further antecedents can be found in the the *upāsaka* (*dge bsnyen*) vow for devout lay practitioners, namely to uphold one or more of the following precepts—refraining from killing, stealing, lying, sexual misconduct, and consuming intoxicants—and Buddhist scriptures delineating lay conduct, such as the *Sigālovāda Sūtta* with injunctions against drinking, gambling, adultery, and so on.

of religion in the public sphere, going so far as to label cleric-scholars as 'religious dictators' (*chos lugs pa'i sger gcod*) and pointing to the potential damage of their reform efforts to the nomadic way of life. Elsewhere, I have discussed the contours of online debate in detail (Gayley 2016); here let me provide just a few highlights.

Overall, the main objections to the new ten virtues and their implementation, as posed by secular intellectuals and bloggers, include the economic toll on nomads who refrain from selling their livestock for slaughter, the detrimental effects to the environment and nomadic way of life as a result, the harshness of punishments for violators, and the perceived lack of free choice. Raising the issue of freedom, the former monastic Notreng (Rno sbreng 2013) objects to the new ten virtues as 'severe rules' (*drag khrims*) that fail to 'respect free choice among the nomadic people' (*'brog pa mang tshogs kyi rang dbang gi gdam gses la brtsi bkur*). Here freedom has the sense of empowerment or control over oneself (*rang dbang*), different in connotation than the standard term for political independence (*rang btsan*).

The most heated year of debate followed a post in November 2012 by Xining-based intellectual and feminist writer Jamyang Kyi (her pen name is Smin drug) who recounted a series of incidents involving punishments, including one where the '*Dharma* door' (*chos sgo*) was shut on the family member of someone who had transgressed his vows. It describes a father who had sold his herd of yaks for slaughter and later, when his son died of illness, had to throw the corpse in a river because no monastics would perform a funeral (Smin drug 2012a). In a second post, later the same month, she condemned the new ten virtues as 'the oppression of rigid traditions and strict religious rules that hinder [ordinary people's] desires and aspirations and curtail [freedom of] speech' (Smin drug 2012b). Her posts were viewed by more than 10,000 readers and followed by more than a dozen posts on the new ten virtues within a year.

The issue of punishments came to the fore again in August 2013 after a series of photographs circulated of young men in a monastery courtyard with placards dangling from their necks, saying 'gambler' (*rgyal 'jog*) and 'thief' (*rkun ma*). The photos were hauntingly reminiscent of struggle sessions, and bloggers like Notreng hastily associated them with Tsultrim Lodrö and the new ten virtues, decrying the punishments:

> In general, whether or not someone liberates their livestock or whether or not they give up eating meat is their own individual affair. This [right] should not be plundered by a dharma association or other authority. However, you speak of love and compassion and at the same time covertly establish taxes. If we don't call something like this 'dictatorship', what do we call it? If it's not the spirit of the Cultural Revolution, what is it? (Rno sbreng 2013)

There are a few inaccuracies to his claim, showing how easily misinformation circulates online. It turned out that the photos had no connection to the new ten virtues promulgated by Larung Buddhist Academy and came instead from Kirti Monastery in Ngawa, which has its own version of moral precepts and system of dealing with violators. Also, as previously mentioned, vegetarianism is not part of the new ten virtues. Alongside misinformation, mudslinging is common in the contentious atmosphere of online debate, with cleric-scholars labelled duplicitous and corrupt, secular critics accused of being Red Guards seeking to 'destroy the old' (*rnying gtor*), and ordinary Tibetans characterized as gullible and susceptible to blind faith (*rmongs dad*), the term also used for superstition.

Yet Notreng's point remains: that ethics should be a matter of 'free choice', especially when the economic viability and well-being of nomadic households is at stake. Interestingly, Tsultrim Lodrö acknowledges this point in his promotion of vegetarianism among monastics, asking the laity only to give up meat on special religious holidays (Tshul khrims blo gros 2012a). His reasons for this include the variability of access to vegetables in diverse geographic areas on the plateau and differences in individual constitutions in terms of what provides a healthy diet (interview, May 2011). For this reason, and also due an appeal for vegetarianism by the Seventeenth Karmapa, monastics are more inclined to become vegetarian than the laity, and many Nyingma and Kagyu monasteries in eastern Tibet no longer prepare and serve meat from the monastery kitchen.

In defence of the new ten virtues, Tsultrim Lodrö points out that households can and do opt out of taking the vows and that fines for violations are designated for social service projects benefiting the laity and not the ongoing operations of the monastery (interview, June 2014). While it is true that a small percentage of households decide not to take the vows, the social cost is enormous, no less than participation in the moral community centred on the monastery. Given the connection between a village or clan and its monastery over generations, reinstated for the most part after the nearly twenty-year hiatus in public religious activities during the Maoist period, Tibetans cannot so easily switch affiliation. Unlike ad hoc pledges, the social cost for nonconformity calls into question the scope of free choice in vowing to uphold the new ten virtues.

The Lhakar Movement

Concurrent with the emergence of the new ten virtues is a more loosely coordinated and voluntaristic movement, called Lhakar or 'White Wednesday' (*lhag dkar*), where white connotes virtue and Wednesday refers to the so-called 'soul day' of the Fourteenth Dalai Lama (Buffetrille 2012: 3 n. 13). Its beginnings are traced to several boycotts in the winter of 2009 around the anniversary of the 2008 demonstrations, including the refusal of Tibetans in some agricultural areas to till their land and the cancellation of celebrations for the Tibetan new year. But it soon morphed from collective boycotts into a more personalized expressions combining Tibetan identity and Buddhist values.

This aspect of the movement was formally articulated in June 2010 in a Tibetan-language blog post, the 'Lhakar Pledge' (*Lhag dkar dam bca'*) on Tibet123.com, inviting Tibetans to take a pledge to speak Tibetan, wear Tibetan clothes, and eat vegetarian food on Wednesdays.[5] The post gestured to the kinds of grassroots efforts that were happening around this time in Tibetan areas of China, such as the decision of a group of Lhasa elders to eat vegetarian food on Wednesdays (Novick 2013) and a donation box in Dzachukha into which Tibetans could offer 1 yuan at the local monastery if they mixed Chinese words into Tibetan speech (Phayul 2010).

The invitation on the 'Lhakar Pledge' post epitomizes an opt-in style of expression typical of social media. As such, Lhakar differs from the new ten virtues in being decentralized, based largely on grassroots actions and personalized pledges. In contrast to monastic-driven reform, Lhakar is an attempt on the part of ordinary Tibetans to devise discrete practices affirming Tibetan identity and Buddhist values.

The online presence of the movement shifted to the exile-based website Lhakar.org after Tibet123.com was shut down. (While the new site is bilingual in English and Tibetan, the pledges are only accessible via Facebook, which precludes users based in China.) On Lhakar.org, the pledges have been reframed in Gandhian terms as acts of nonviolent resistance, non-cooperation, and self-reliance (see lhakar.org/about). Along similar lines, in a January 2013 post on *The Tibetan Political Review*, Tenzin Dorjee characterizes the Lhakar movement as an 'undercurrent of resistance [that] is transforming the landscape of Tibetan activism'. He states:

> Emphasizing individual acts of resistance rather than public acts of protest, Lhakar has decentralized the resistance. By treating their homes, workplaces, and computers as battlefields of resistance, Tibetans are wielding their limited personal choices and daily activities as a wedge to pry open more social, political and economic space. A Lhakar practitioner does not expect freedom to come from a tweak in policy or a change of heart in Beijing, but from his or her own daily thoughts, decisions and actions fostering a parallel world of freedom that will outgrow China's superstructure of repression. (Tenzin Dorjee 2013)

This statement highlights the Lhakar movement as an exercise of freedom, however limited, in personal choices of dress, diet, and lifestyle.

Notably, Tenzin Dorjee articulates everyday acts of affirming Tibetan identity with respect to two divergent configurations of power: as resistance to domination and as empowerment in creating a 'parallel world of freedom'.[6] The former enables the identification of Lhakar in continuity with previous demonstrations and boycotts, while the latter emphasizes personal pledges as a form of cultural empowerment. Rebecca Novick has cautioned against the politicization of Lhakar as 'resistance' and 'non-cooperation', given the risk that it entails for Tibetans in China, arguing instead that 'the nature of the Lhakar movement is closer to Gandhi's swadeshi village self-reliance movement than it

[5] The original post, *Lhag dkar dam bca'*, is no longer online. For a translation, see <highpeakspureearth.com/2011/white-wednesday-the-lhakar-pledge>.

[6] My thanks to Emily Yeh for drawing out this distinction and for her comments on an early version of this chapter.

is to satyagraha'. Or as she succinctly encapsulates the distinction, 'The power of Lhakar lies in its "yes" more than in its "no"' (2013).

In line with her observation, it may be more accurate to characterize Lhakar pledges as a cultural empowerment movement that entails the public performance of Tibetanness within a politics of belonging (Lokyitsang 2014). It is unclear how widespread the movement remains on the plateau, given that Tibetans under Chinese rule cannot readily publicize their actions as Lhakar without fear of being targeted. Yet it is thriving in the diaspora with pledges offered via Facebook and a blog called Lhakar Diaries (lhakardiaries.com) with ongoing reflections on Tibetan culture.

'I Am Tibetan'

The assertion of Tibetan identity can also be seen in literary and artistic forms, including pop music videos. With the emergence of VCD technology among Tibetans in China during the late 1990s and early 2000s, pop music videos have celebrated Tibetan identity and sometimes mirrored cleric-scholars' calls for a unified 'path forward' for Tibetans in Buddhist terms. Exemplary in this regard is the 2004 song 'The Path Forward for Tibetan Youth' (*Gangs phrug gi mdun lam*) in which pop star Kunga calls for Tibetan unity and loyalty to the 'snowy mountains' (*gangs ljongs*, an epithet for Tibet), including studying the traditional domains of knowledge associated with the monastic curriculum. Better known is the song 'Mentally Return' (*Sems kyi log phebs*), performed by Yadung, Kunga, and others at 2006 Rebkong Music Festival, staking out bravery and nonviolence as integral to the Tibetan character and calling on Tibetans to unite. The assertion of ethnic identity in this way is permissible under the Chinese state conception of nationalities (Ch. *minzu*, Tib. *mi rigs*) so long as it is done in cultural rather than political terms.

This trend has continued and intensified. After 2008, there was a spate of 'I am Tibetan' (*Nga ni bod yin*) themed videos and poetry tracked by *High Peaks, Pure Earth*,[7] in which Novick notes the tenor of identity assertion changed from 'marginalized and oppressed' to 'empowered and ready for anything' (2013). Later, in proximity to the 2010 student protests over the threat to Tibetan-medium instruction in primary and secondary schools, music videos on the importance of preserving Tibetan language came to the fore. Within a year, the rising pop star Shertan dedicated a VCD set to the issue of the Tibetan language and another to concerns over environmental and cultural preservation.[8] On the lighter side, in 2012, the Lhakar Dairies featured the latest song on

[7] See highpeakspureearth.com/2010/i-am-tibetan, posted on 4 February 2010 and www.scribd.com/doc/45000460/I-am-Tibetan-Poetry-Booklet, accessed 1 May 2016. Also notable in this regard, released in 2011, is 'Made in Tibet' by Karma Emchi (Shapaley), available at sociosound.wordpress.com/2011/11/27/spotlight-on-karma-emchi.

[8] Songs from these VCDs, *Pha skad la bcings ba'i brtse sems* and *Ma yum rtsa thang gi 'bod skul*, can be found on *High Peaks, Pure Earth*: highpeakspureearth.com/2010/two-songs-about-tibetan-unity-

Tibetan food, 'Tsampa' (*Rtsam pa*), by exile rap artist Karma Emchi, known by Shapaley, celebrating dietary markers of Tibetan identity, here the staple food of roasted barley (Shapaley 2012).

These efforts at cultural empowerment are part and parcel of the project of making oneself into a certain kind of Tibetan, espousing Buddhist values, exhibiting identity markers such as language and diet, and oriented towards a common 'path forward'. A poster from 2011 at Larung Buddhist Academy illustrates this well by dramatizing the importance of maintaining purity in the Tibetan language. Purity in this case means not mixing Chinese terms into Tibetan speech, and to facilitate this project, Tsultrim Lodrö worked with secular intellectuals to develop a dictionary of Tibetan neologisms for a host of modern terms from tractors to shampoo (*Rgya bod dbyin* 2007). While educational posters pairing images and their neologisms can be found in Tibetan homes, this one deploys characters from the popular television rendition of *Journey to the West*, a Chinese literary classic with Buddhist themes that plays repeatedly on television. In it, the pig character (looking rather befuddled) says, 'I'm pig-headed. I speak a combined language,' and the monkey retorts 'You're a pig-man who lacks self-determination.'

The key word here is *rangtsuk* (*rang tshugs*) meaning self-determination, a term coined by Jigmé Phuntsok in his widely circulating slogan 'Don't lose self-determination. Don't agitate the minds of others' (*rang tshugs ma shor/ gzhan sems ma dkrugs*; for a commentary on this slogan, see Rig 'dzin dar rgyas *c.*2004). This slogan—found in pool halls, tea houses, and outside schools in the years following his passing in 2004—asks Tibetans not to lose their moral integrity or distinctive culture (first half of the slogan) while upholding inter-ethnic harmony (Ch. *minzu tuanjie*), a key term in state discourse (second half of the slogan). If the integrity of Tibetan culture is lost or diluted, as depicted in the poster, what results is an aberration, no longer one thing or another, but a monstrous hybrid: half human and half beast. A choice is posed to Tibetans in terms of what sort of person to become: a steward of their language and culture with self-determination or someone compromised and confused, no longer fully Tibetan—or fully human for that matter.

What Makes a Tibetan Hero

If ethics involves a self-reflexive project to fashion oneself into a certain kind of person, then we need to think beyond the declarative online statements of 'I am Tibetan' and probe: what sort of Tibetan, especially when that identity is articulated in Buddhist terms? As discussed so far, ethical subject formation among contemporary Tibetans is bound up with exhibiting loyalty (*la rgya*) to Tibetan culture and Buddhist values.

mentally-return-and-the-sound-of-unity, posted on 31 August 2010, and highpeakspureearth.com/2013/music-video-the-call-by-sherten, posted on 6 November 2013.

While the Lhakar movement emphasizes pledges to maintain Tibetan culture in terms of dress, diet, and language, and Tibetan pop music reinforces Buddhist values, an initiative that emerged in 2012 at Larung Buddhist Academy invokes the ideal of nonviolence and articulates a new kind of Tibetan hero.

In a 2012 speech to 13,000 gathered at Larung Buddhist Academy for their annual 'Great Accomplishment Practice for the Land of Bliss' (*Bde chen zhing sgrub chen mo*) prayer festival, Khenpo Rigdzin Dargyé reconfigured the Buddhist principle of nonviolence from its previous expressions in peaceful demonstrations and boycotts into an impassioned call for the end of 'internal fighting' (*nang dme*) among Tibetans (Gayley and Padma 'tsho 2016). At the end of the speech, reportedly 98 per cent of the audience took a pledge to stop participating in internal fighting and to develop unity at the local, regional, and pan-Tibetan level (including central Tibet, Kham, and Amdo).

As a token of their pledge, men over the age of fifteen were given an 'amulet for peace' (*zhi bde rtags ma*) to be worn around the neck, featuring an image of the Tenth Paṇchen Lama on one side and a globe with a dove flying above it on the other. Combining global and Buddhist symbols for peace, the dove carries a bodhi leaf with a *Hriḥ* emblazoned on it, and a peace sign dangles from its claw. Although not fighting with weapons was already included in the new ten virtues, leaders at Larung Buddhist Academy decided that a more explicit pledge and physical reminder in the amulet of peace would be beneficial.

In his 2012 speech, as transcribed in *A Discourse on Harmonious Relations* (*Mthun 'brel gyi slob gso*), Rigdzin Dargyé envisions a certain kind of Tibetan. Employing the language of loyalty to one's nationality or ethnicity, he defines what makes a 'national hero' (*mi rigs kyi dpa' bo*). Central to his definition is a nonviolent masculinity that runs counter to the ferocity and independence associated historically with the clans of Golok in the region surrounding Serta (Pirie 2005). Rigdzin Dargyé connects a 'national hero' with Tibetan erudition by choosing the progressive early twentieth-century monk Gendun Chöphel as a role model based on his literary contributions to Tibetan culture. In moralistic terms, Rigdzin Dargyé presents erudition and nonviolence as elevated (*ya rabs*) pursuits that help to promote unity and progress, while associating violence, especially internal fighting, with degraded (*ma rabs*) behaviour. Considering the reputation of Tibetans as a people, he states that when Tibetans wear swords around their waists or tote guns, they appear foolish and backward to other ethnicities (Rig 'dzin dar gyas 2013).

In his speech, Buddhism is marshalled as a civilizing influence on Tibetans with cleric-scholars providing both a role model and source for moral guidance. Throughout the speech, Rigdzin Dargyé delineates a heroic masculinity in which individuals sacrifice their own advantage achieved through conflict, such as fighting over grazing rights, and instead work for the greater good. In the process, he redefines the purpose of a 'precious human birth' (*mi lus rin po che*) from the pursuit of enlightenment to working for the welfare and advancement of Tibetans as a people. Here loyalty to Tibetans as a collective is expressed through the Buddhist ideal of nonviolence and the promised outcome of ethnic unity. While promoted by cleric-scholars, the 'amulet for peace' returns to a voluntaristic model of ad hoc pledges. Meanwhile, its explanation by Rigdzin Dargyé invites ordinary Tibetans into self-reflection on what it means to be heroic and civilized in Buddhist terms.

Self-Immolation as Sacrifice

Although not referenced in that speech, the term 'hero' (*dpa' bo, dpa' mo*) has been used in poetry and song to memorialize self-immolators and is sometimes translated as 'martyr' in that context. A poignant example is 'Patriotic Martyrs' (*Rgyal gces dpa' bo dpa' mo*), performed by Jamphel, which expresses gratitude for the courage of such heroes in 'a world ablaze with the massive flames of loyalty' (*la rgya'i me dpung 'bar ba'i 'jig rten*).[9] Self-immolation involves the ultimate sacrifice, the 'gift of the body' (*lus sbyin*) in one of the competing Tibetan terms to characterize it with Buddhist resonances (Benn 2012; Woeser 2014). Unlike the constructive heroism outlined by Rigdzin Dargyé, characterizing the person who works for the welfare of Tibetans, self-immolation is a multivalent form of resistance and sacrifice.

Self-immolation has political, ritual, and ethical dimensions without being reducible to any one of them. Scholars have emphasized the political character of self-immolations as a novel form of protest among Tibetans, initially occurring in exile in 1998 and performed on the Tibetan plateau for the first time in 2009, in which the body is sacrificed for the nation (Shakya 2012). With respect to the issue of freedom, Yeh points out that 'self-immolation is a reclamation of sovereignty over one's own self within a state of siege' (2012b). Although exile lamas like the Seventeenth Karmapa have asked Tibetans to abandon the practice, since March 2011 there have been more than 150 self-immolations among Tibetans, most of them occurring on the Tibetan plateau.[10]

A ritual and devotional frame is also salient in emergent understandings of self-immolation as an offering. A number of self-immolators have expressed political sentiments in a devotional tenor by shouting 'Long live the Dalai Lama' and calling for his return alongside more overt cries for independence (Woeser 2016: 34–42). Ritual idioms are also invoked through coded references in Tibetan poems to self-immolators as 'butter lamps' (*mar me*) usually made as offerings before Buddha images, but here referencing the spectacle of a body enveloped in flames (Robin 2012, Woeser 2014).

Exemplary in this regard is the taped message left behind by Lama Sobha, who articulated his self-immolation as a 'long life offering' to the Dalai Lama as well as an 'offering of light to clear away the darkness' with the aim to free all living beings from suffering

[9] For a translation, see highpeakspureearth.com/2013/music-video-patriotic-martyrs-by-jampel, posted on 17 July 2013. Here I use the translated title from *High Peaks, Pure* Earth; the Tibetan literally means 'heroes and heroines who cherish their country'.

[10] See www.savetibet.org/resources/fact-sheets/self-immolations-by-tibetans for ongoing tracking of self-immolations among Tibetans.

and especially guide the consciousness of other self-immolators who may have died in angst (International Campaign for Tibet 2012). Amid prayers for the Dalai Lama's long life, he eulogized those Tibetans who have given their lives as courageous heroes and invoked the 'gift of the body' in *jātaka* tales of the Buddha's past lives as a model of self-sacrifice, where such tales exemplify the perfection of generosity (Ohnuma 2006). In line with other Buddhist leaders, Lama Sobha called on Tibetans to preserve their culture, practise Buddhist principles, and forge unity by giving up fighting amongst themselves.

Tenzin Mingyur Paldron reads Lama Sobha's act—and self-immolation more generally—as an offering that seeks to intervene in suffering. Here an ethical understanding comes to the fore, even as the boundary between nonviolence and violence is blurred in ways that 'exceeds our moral and political categories' and the 'secular liberal practices of applauding or delegitimizing various social and political struggles' (2012; see also Makley 2015). As a mode of resistance and sacrifice, self-immolation stands in stark contrast to constructive approaches to ethical mobilization that seek to synthesize Buddhist ethics and cultural preservation in crafting a 'path forward' for Tibetans as a people. Nonetheless, it offers a distinct (however worrisome) ideal of Tibetan heroism and ethical engagement.

Conclusion

This chapter has surveyed several strands of contemporary ethical mobilization and identity assertion among Tibetans on the plateau and in the diaspora. These include the new ten virtues promulgated by Larung Buddhist Academy and debated in the Tibetan blogosphere, the Lhakar movement which spans the plateau and diaspora in the form of grassroots initiatives and individual pledges, literary and artistic trends of promoting ethnic identity and cultural preservation, and the 'amulet for peace' that redefines the Buddhist value of nonviolence in an attempt to galvanize unity and reshape Tibetan masculinity. Each of these are constructive approaches to preserving Tibetan culture and forming ethical Buddhist subjects, and as such can be distinguished from modes of political protest, such as demonstrations and self-immolations.

The constructive approaches surveyed in this chapter attempt to carve out a Tibetan ethos or 'way of being and of behaviour' that seeks continuity with the past and promotes nonviolence as a core Buddhist value. Yet a key difference among these approaches is the extent to which 'maintaining' Tibetan customs of dress, diet, and language actually entails reform—by creating neologisms, promoting vegetarianism, or relinquishing fur trims on coats. Advocating reform has generally been the work of Buddhist leaders, highlighting a notable variant in these mobilizations, ranging from monastic-driven and collective in nature to individual pledges and actions by ordinary Tibetans. Only the latter has spread widely in the diaspora.

As part of a broader effort to maintain and reform Tibetan culture, contemporary ethical mobilization is forging a certain kind of Tibetan, one with renewed loyalty to the integrity of Tibetan culture and an invigorated commitment to Buddhist values, such as nonviolence. This loyalty is bound up in a devotional impulse to rally around charismatic Buddhist leaders, who are capable of galvanizing collective action and constituting a moral community across a broad domain. Yet it remains an open question whether all of such mobilizations are 'technologies of the self' that ordinary Tibetans voluntarily adopt in order to transform self and society or whether monastic-driven reform, in certain ways, further constricts their freedom.

Works Cited

Abeysekara, A. (2008) *Colors of the robe: religion, identity, and difference.* Columbia, SC: University of South Carolina Press.

Anagnost, A. (2004) The corporeal politics of quality (*suzhi*). *Public culture*, 16 (22), 189–208.

Benn, J. (2012) Multiple meanings of Buddhist self-immolation in China—a historical perspective. *Revue d'études tibétaines*, 25, 203–212.

Buffetrille, K. (2012) Self-immolation in Tibet: some reflections on an unfolding history. *Revue d'études tibétaines*, 25, 1–17.

Faubion, J. (2001) Toward an anthropology of ethics: Foucault and the pedagogies of autopoiesis. *Representations*, 74 (1), 83–104.

Foucault, M. (1994) *Ethics: subjectivity and truth.* Translated by R. Hurley. New York: The New York Press.

Gaerrang (Kabzung) (2015) Development as entangled knot: the case of the slaughter renunciation movement in Tibet, China. *The journal of Asian studies*, 74 (4), 927–951.

Gayley, H. (2011) The ethics of cultural survival: a Buddhist vision of progress in Mkhan po 'Jigs phun's *Heart advice to Tibetans for the 21st century*. In: G. Tuttle (ed.), *Mapping the modern in Tibet*. Sankt Augustin, Germany: International Institute for Tibetan and Buddhist Studies, 435–502.

Gayley, H. (2013) Reimagining Buddhist ethics on the Tibetan plateau. *Journal of Buddhist ethics*, 20, 247–286.

Gayley, H. (2016) Controversy over Buddhist ethical reform: a secular critique of clerical authority in the Tibetan blogosphere. *Himalaya journal*, 36 (1), 22–43.

Gayley, H., and Padma 'tsho (2016) Non-violence as a shifting signifier on the Tibetan plateau. *Contemporary Buddhism*, 17 (1), 62–80.

Germano, D. (1998) Re-membering the dismembered body of Tibet: contemporary Tibetan visionary movements in the People's Republic of China. In: M. Goldstein and M. Kapstein (eds), *Buddhism in contemporary Tibet: religious revival and cultural identity.* Berkeley: University of California Press, 53–94.

Gravers, M. (2015) Anti-Muslim Buddhist nationalism in Burma and Sri Lanka: religious violence and globalized imaginaries of endangered identities. *Contemporary Buddhism*, 16 (1), 1–27.

Hansen, A. R. (2007) *How to behave: Buddhism and modernity in colonial Cambodia, 1860–1930*. Honolulu: University of Hawai'i Press.

Harvey, P. (2000) *An introduction to Buddhist ethics.* Cambridge: Cambridge University Press.

International Campaign for Tibet (2012) Harrowing images and last message from Tibet of first lama to self-immolate. Available from: www.savetibet.org/harrowing-images-and-last-message-from-tibet-of-first-lama-to-self-immolate, posted 1 February.

'Jigs med phun tshogs, Mkhan po (*c.*1995) *Dus rabs nyer gcig pa'i gangs can pa rnams la phul ba'i snying gtam sprin gyi rol mo*. Serta: Larung Buddhist Academy.

Kapstein, M. (1996) '*gDams ngag*: Tibetan technologies of the self. In: J. Cabezón and R. Jackson (eds), *Tibetan literature: studies in genre*. Ithaca, NY: Snow Lion, 275–289.

Keown, D. (ed.) (2000) *Contemporary Buddhist ethics*. Richmond, UK: Curzon Press.

Laidlaw, J. (2002) For an anthropology of ethics and freedom. *The journal of the Royal Anthropological Institute*, 8 (2), 311–332.

Lokyitsang, D. (2014) 'Speak Tibetan, stupid': concepts of pure Tibetan and the politics of belonging'. *Lhakar Diaries*. Available from: lhakardiaries.com/2014/04/30/speak-tibetan-stupid-concepts-of-pure-tibetan-the-politics-of-belonging, posted 30 April.

Makley, C. (2015) The sociopolitical lives of dead bodies: Tibetan self-immolation protest as mass media. *Cultural anthropology*, 30 (3), 448–476.

Novick, R. (2013) Why Lhakar matters: a response. *Tibet political review*. Available from: www.tibetanpoliticalreview.com/articles/whylhakarmattersaresponsedom, posted 14 January.

Ohnuma, R. (2006) *Head, eyes, flesh, and blood: giving away the body in Indian Buddhist literature*. New York: Columbia University Press.

Phayul (2010) Tibetans protest in Zachukha over spoken language. Available from: http://www.phayul.com/news/article.aspx?id=28518, posted 9 November.

Pirie, F. (2005) *Feuding mediation and the negotiation of authority among the nomads of eastern Tibet*. Halle/Saale: Max Planck Institute for Social Anthropology.

Queen, C., and King, S. (eds) (1996) *Engaged Buddhism: Buddhist liberation movements in Asia*. Albany, NY: State University of New York Press.

Rgya bod dbyin gsum gsar byung rgyun bkol ris 'grel ming mdzod (2007). Chengdu: Sichuan Nationalities Publishing House.

Rig 'dzin dar rgyas, Mkhan po (*c.*2004) *Chos rje dam pa 'jigs med phun tshogs 'byung gnas dpal bzang po mchog gi mjug mtha'i zhal gdams rang tshugs ma shor/ gzhan sems ma dkrugs zhes pa'i 'grel ba Lugs gnyis blang dor gsal ba'i sgron me*. Serta: Larung Buddhist Academy.

Rig 'dzin dar rgyas, Mkhan po (2013) *Mthun 'brel gyi slob gso*. Serta: Larung Buddhist Academy.

Rno sbreng (2013) Rig gsar kyi me ro gso mkhan de su red. *New youth network*. Available from: www.tbnewyouth.com/article/show-5/201308299927.html, posted 29 August (later removed).

Robin, F. (2012) Fire, flames and ashes: how Tibetan poets talk about self-immolations without talking about them. *Revue d'études tibétaines*, 25, 123–131.

Shakya, T. (2012) Transforming the language of protest. *Hot spots, cultural cnthropology*. Available from: culanth.org/fieldsights/94-transforming-the-language-of-protest, posted 8 April.

Shapaley (2012) Tsampa. Available from: https://www.youtube.com/watch?v=lZE6DHzZUFg, posted 24 October.

Smin drug (2012a) Dge bcu'i khrims dang 'brel ba'i dngos tshul. *Sangdhor*. Available from: www.sangdhor.com/blog_c.asp?id=9290&a=menzhu>, posted 4 November (website now defunct).

Smin drug (2012b) Dge bcu'i khrims kyi shugs rkyen. *Sangdhor*. Available from: www.sangdhor.com/blog_c.asp?id=9547&a=menzhu>, posted 27 November (website now defunct).

Stewart, J. (2016) *Vegetarianism and animal ethics in contemporary Buddhism*. New York: Routledge.
Tenzin Dorjee (2013) Why Lhakar matters: the elements of Tibetan freedom. *Tibet political review*. Available from: www.tibetanpoliticalreview.com/articles/whylhakarmattersthee lementsoftibetanfreedom, posted 10 January.
Tenzin Mingyur Paldron (2012) Virtue and the remaking of suffering. *Hot spots, cultural anthropology*. Available from: culanth.org/fieldsights/98-virtue-and-the-remaking-of-suffering, posted April 8.
Tshe thar srog blu byed rogs (2001) VCD produced by Larung Buddhist Academy, ISRC CN-G04-01-417 00/V.J6. Chengdu: Chengdu Yinxiang Chubanshe.
Tshul khrims blo gros, Mkhan po (2003–2004) *Dus su bab pa'i gtam lugs gnyis gsal ba'i me long*. In: *Yang dag lam gyi 'jug sgo blo gsar yid kyi dga' ston*, volume 2. Hong Kong: Fojiao cihui fuwu zhongxin, 258–349.
Tshul khrims blo gros, Mkhan po (*c.*2012) *Dus rabs kyi gsos sman*. Serta: Larung Buddhist Academy.
Woeser, T. (2014) Self-immolations are a kind of political resistance. *High peaks, pure earth*. Available from: highpeakspureearth.com/2014/self-immolations-are-a-kind-of-political-resistance-by-woeser, posted 26 September.
Woeser, T. (2016) *Tibet on fire: self-immolations against Chinese rule*. Translated by K. Carrico. London: Verso.
Yeh, E. (2007) Tropes of indolence and the cultural politics of development in Lhasa, Tibet. *Annals of the Association of American Geographers*, 97 (3), 593–612.
Yeh, E. (2012a) Transnational environmentalism and entanglements of sovereignty: the tiger campaign across Himalaya. *Political geography*, 31, 408–418.
Yeh, E. (2012b) On 'Terrorism' and the politics of naming. *Hot spots, cultural anthropology*. Available from: culanth.org/fieldsights/102-on-terrorism-and-the-politics-of-naming, posted 8 April.
Yeh, E. (2013) Blazing pelts and burning passions: nationalism, cultural politics and spectacular decommodification in Tibet. *Journal of Asian studies*, 72 (2), 319–344.
Zigon, J. (2009) Within a range of possibilities: morality and ethics in social life. *Ethnos: journal of anthropology*, 74 (2), 251–276.

Suggested Reading

Gayley, H. (2013) Reimagining Buddhist ethics on the Tibetan plateau. *Journal of Buddhist ethics*, 20, 247–286.
Goldstein, M., and Kapstein, M. (eds) (1998) *Buddhism in contemporary Tibet: religious revival and cultural identity*. Berkeley: University of California Press.
Gyatso, T., Dalai Lama XIV (1999) *Ethics for the new millennium*. New York: Riverhead Books.
Klieger, C. (ed.) (2002) *Tibet, self, and the Tibetan diaspora: voices of difference, PIATS 2000, Tibetan studies: proceedings of the ninth seminar of the International Association for Tibetan Studies, Leiden 2000*. Leiden: Brill.
Kolås, Å., and Thowsen, M. (2005) *On the margins of Tibet: cultural survival on the Sino-Tibetan frontier*. Seattle: University of Washington.
McMahan, D. (2008) *The making of Buddhist modernism*. Oxford: Oxford University Press.

PART III

COMPARATIVE PERSPECTIVES

CHAPTER 16

BUDDHIST ETHICS COMPARED TO WESTERN ETHICS

SĪLAVĀDIN MEYNARD VASEN

INTRODUCTION

IN this chapter, I will compare Buddhist ethics with Western ethics by placing it in the context of the three main theories of normative ethics in Western philosophy: deontological, consequentialist, and virtue ethics—or, rather, the three families of theories, because each of these has many forms that are connected by family resemblance.[1] My starting point is that it cannot be proven that Buddhist ethics belongs to one or the other family, as if it were a matter of fact, but that one or another interpretation can be more or less fruitful.

By 'fruitful' I mean in two main respects: first in the sense that most, if not all, aspects of Buddhist ethics can be integrated into a coherent whole, so that it increases our understanding of it; and second in the sense that it is motivating to actually *live* according to that vision. My thesis will be that Buddhist ethics can best be seen as a form of neo-Aristotelian virtue ethics, a thesis that has been put forward by Keown (1992), and that has been accepted by many, though not all. I will further deepen and broaden this thesis and also consider other views.

What are the differences between the three families of theories? The most essential differences are those between the formal features, which can be summarized in three keywords: *results, norms,* and *excellences.* To *consequentialist* views the *result* of an act is what determines the rightness of it.[2] An act is instrumental in respect to the result,

[1] With thanks to Ruth Rudd, Thomas Dhivan Jones, Damien Keown, and the community members of Vajraloka Meditation Centre.

[2] When I say 'act' I imply that the same holds for a rule, in rule-consequentialism, a character, in character-consequentialism, and so forth.

and thus is not right or wrong in itself. If a result is good, then the act is right. One result points to a further one, and the ultimate good result is generally described as the maximum welfare for as many people (or beings) as possible.

Opposed to this are the *deontological* views, which in principle disconnect the results of an act from its rightness, and hold that acts are right in themselves if they conform to a norm. The norm could be the word of God, the *Dharma* (in the sense of law), Kant's categorical imperative, or something else. The crucial point is that there is a principle of rightness that stands apart from the results of an act, and the norm in question expresses that principle.

The central notion of *virtue ethics* is excellence or virtue (which I will take to be synonymous). An act is right if it is an excellent act, i.e. an act that is an expression of a human being at its best. A further question is, of course, how 'at its best' will be specified, to which I will return. What matters here is that there is, as in the consequentialist views, a relation of an act with its goal, but the crucial difference is that in virtue ethics it is an *internal* rather than an external goal. To put it differently: the goal of an act, excellence, is not achieved *through*, but *in* the act. That is, virtue ethics is teleological; the goal of an act is constituted by the means to achieve it, and the goal cannot be described without reference to the means.[3]

The three theories can be applied in a weak sense, i.e. as merely *using* the respective notions of results, norms, and excellences. In this weaker sense they don't exclude each other, as norms can very well have a role in virtue ethics theories and *mutatis mutandis* for the other notions. But I will use a stronger definition of the three theories, where the notions in question are *decisive*. A character virtue, for example, can be important for a consequentialist, but it has, ultimately, to lead to better results in order to be considered as right, and is therefore for a consequentialist of secondary importance. For a virtue ethicist the results of an act will carry weight to determine whether an act is excellent or not, but will not be decisive, and so forth. In the stronger definition the theories can sit alongside each other for a while, but eventually they exclude each other, and therefore the stronger definition is more informative.

Buddhist ethics is usually considered in the context of the moral rules of conduct (*śīla*). I believe this way of looking at ethics is too restricted; moral rules of conduct are only *an aspect* of the answer to the ethical question 'How should one live?' which, I will argue below, is the most fundamental ethical question. If I ask myself what living the best life would be, it is relevant to include things such as enjoyment, health, taking part in communal life, cultural activities, and so on, as well as moral matters such as keeping promises and taking the interests of others to heart. In this way the whole of the Buddhist path, not just right conduct, can be regarded as the area of Buddhist ethics. In other words, I differentiate between ethics and morality. Ethics is the discourse that

[3] I take teleology to mean a relation of the means with the goal in which they imply each other; this is contrasted with consequentialist reasoning, in which the means are merely instrumental in achieving the goal. See Arius: 'A *skopos* is a target to be hit, like a shield for archers; a goal (*telos*) is the hitting of the target' (quoted in Annas 1993: 34).

comes into being as an answer to the question of how to live; whereas morality is the aspect of ethics that relates to social norms and conduct (cf. Williams 1985: ch. 10).

Hermeneutical Questions

The first question that arises when comparing Buddhist ethics and Western ethics is: *why*? As Hayes put it: 'Many Buddhists ... may well wonder why it matters at all whether Buddhism subscribes to virtue ethics ... or one of the flavours of consequentialism. ... [W]hat is gained by putting Western philosophical labels on the long tradition of Buddhism?' (2011: 394). Connected with this is the question of the legitimacy of a comparison. Is Buddhism, with its cultural and historical roots in Asia, not put into a Procrustean bed by forcing it into a Western framework?

As Clayton (2006: 11–16) shows, this question can present itself as a dilemma. One horn of the dilemma is to see the 'otherness' of Buddhism as making it impossible to compare with Western forms of thinking, therefore to suspend all judgments, and to confine oneself to description of it in terms as neutral as possible. This might resemble respect, or scientific restraint, but we also avoid a dialogue, and run the risk of disregarding significant Buddhist insights with the result of making it appear irrelevant. The other horn of the dilemma is the attitude that seeks Western analogies for Buddhism. This runs the risk of overlooking or undervaluing differences, and thus missing important aspects of Buddhism simply because there is no Western analogy. The 'otherness' of Buddhism is violated by forcing it into the framework of familiar concepts. In this way it seems we are caught in a choice between neglecting its importance on the one hand, and deformation of its character on the other. If this is the choice, says Clayton, she would rather risk the danger of deformation. 'We must put things "in our own words" if we are to understand them, and in doing so we may get some things wrong. But as an interpreter I would rather be wrong than completely ignorant, and as the object of interpretation I would rather be misunderstood than ignored' (16).

I would agree with her, if we had to choose between the two horns. But I think the matter can be taken further, and the dichotomy of neglect and deformation be transcended. Gadamer in his hermeneutics gives us tools for doing that. In *Truth and Method* he discusses the dynamics of the hermeneutical process as a conversation (1989: 181). In a conversation there is generally a tendency either to overpower the other, or to be overpowered, he says. This polarity can only be transcended if one sees that the goal of a conversation is not so much getting to know the other, as to *bring up a subject matter*. The other is important in this process because of his point of view, and the formal right of his opinion, and not because of his person.

In the same manner, studying a 'strange' world view with the goal of getting to know it is only a starting point. Learning about a world view as a religious, historical, or sociological phenomenon can be interesting and helpful, but it is not the same as engaging in a conversation. A conversation is essentially about the subject matter that is brought up. The tradition that the world view in question has built up in the course of its history is the partner that helps us to reach understanding and insight into the subject matter. In this way we can engage in conversation with a 'strange' world view as with a partner that has their own world with their own horizon. We bring our own world with our horizon with us into the conversation, not either to enforce or relinquish it, but to bring it into play, and thus to 'risk' it, just as the other brings their own horizon into play and risks that. The goal is not to get to know each other, or to see the resemblances and differences (although that can be helpful), but to clarify the subject matter that is brought up.

What is the subject matter that is brought up in Buddhist ethics? I believe it is the same question *How should one live?* that forms the basis of Western ethics. As Williams (1985: 4) argued, this question is more basic to ethics than 'what is the good', 'what are our moral duties', or even 'how may we be happy', which seem to be derived from the basic question (cf. Annas 1993: 27). Socrates and the Buddha asked this question at around the same time in ancient Greece and Northern India, respectively. The Buddha's answer to the question was to follow the Eightfold Path, which was the beginning of the Buddhist tradition. The answer of Socrates was to live a life that led to the development of the excellences; this became one of the starting points of Western ethics.

If we ask this same question of Buddhism, from our contemporary Western horizon—one that has been shaped by Christianity, the European Enlightenment, the industrialization, the twentieth-century wars and so on—we inevitably do that from within our horizon's network of images and concepts. In other words, the question is posed from within our prejudgments, in the neutral sense of the term that Gadamer has proposed (1989: 273). Gadamer wanted to reinstate the value of prejudgments, because he saw how it is inevitable, when interpreting something, that we start with a particular conception or opinion, as otherwise there is no question of beginning at all. If something were radically new we would not even recognize it. These prejudgments arise from the tradition we live in, which forms an important part of our horizon. In the course of the hermeneutical process we bring these prejudgments into play, and give them up or confirm them.

The Buddhist tradition answers the question of how to live in ways that do not directly fit into a network of Western images and concepts. This makes the Western mind aware both of the 'otherness' of this tradition and its own prejudgments. But, on the other hand, because we look at the Buddhist tradition from within our Western tradition, we can also ask questions of it that were never asked before, and in that way bring new aspects of Buddhism to the fore. The Buddhist perspective, in its turn, may come with answers, and new questions, that cast our prejudgments in a new light. The hermeneutical conversation moving back and forth puts our prejudgments into play and at equal risk—nothing on either side is held to be 'sacred' in the sense of unquestionable. There is no need to force Buddhist ethics into a framework, or to enshrine it in a gilded frame. Attention is wholly directed towards the subject matter, not towards either of the partners in the conversation. One point of view does not take precedence over the other;

of importance is what the conversation itself can contribute towards answering the central question: *How should one live?*

Buddhist Ethics as Virtue Ethics

From the time of ancient Greece in the fifth century BCE until the rise of utilitarianism in the eighteenth century, thinking in terms of virtues was standard in Western ethics, even though it was often strongly blended with deontological notions. As MacIntyre argues in *After Virtue*, modern ethical discourse is fragmented, but under this fragmentation virtue ethics is still a common-sense way of thinking. Therefore he thinks it is important to develop a contemporary form of virtue ethics, and he describes the contours of it, based on the notions of practices, narratives, and traditions. These notions are expanding hermeneutical circles; an excellence or virtue is best understood in the context of a practice, a practice in the context of a narrative, and a narrative in the context of a tradition. I believe this is, supplemented with a naturalistic perspective, a very fruitful theoretical perspective for Buddhist ethics. It mirrors the prejudgments of Western ethical thinking, while at the same time it seems to give enough space for other forms of thinking.

Practices

Buddhism knows many practices.[4] As an example I may take the practice of Right Speech (*samyag-vāc*), the third branch of the Eightfold Path. When someone takes on this practice, she tries to realize the qualities of this practice in her communication, such as honesty, truthfulness, kindness, and harmony, and therefore tries to abstain from telling lies, speaking superficially, speaking harshly, gossiping, and suchlike. By doing this in a progressive way, she realizes more and more the goods of this practice, such as openness, reasonability, profoundness, and harmony in communication with others. These goods are valuable in themselves regardless of results outside themselves they may have, such as approval or appreciation from other people. They typically do have these good external results, but sometimes, in unfavourable circumstances, they do not. Whatever the external results, however, the goal of a practice, i.e. achieving the mentioned goods, is valuable, and that goal can only be achieved by developing the qualities of this practice.

MacIntyre defines a practice as a 'human activity through which goods internal to that form of activity are realized in the course of trying to achieve those standards

[4] The following paragraphs have been adapted, with revisions, from my previous publication (2014).

of excellence that are appropriate to, and partially definitive of, that form of activity' (1984: 187). A practice in this sense is thus teleological: the goal is realized by developing the excellences that constitute the goal. A practice is also autarkic, not in the sense of being independent of external circumstances, but in the sense that it needs nothing outside the practice itself to make it a *meaningful* activity. In that respect it resembles playing a game, or artistic activity. A game too is characterized by an internal goal, and the meaning of it is in the playing itself. Playing a game can sometimes have external goals, such as earning money, or learning skills that can be used in the pursuit of something else, but someone who is playing only for that kind of purpose is not playing in the proper sense. A third characteristic of both a practice and playing a game is that the person who is engaged in it is in a cognitive mode in which she believes things that do not hold outside of the game (Gadamer 1989: 103). Someone who is watching a theatrical play knows that what she sees it is not 'really' true, and yet in a way believes it, and the question as to the reality of it is irrelevant. The same goes for the artist, for the 'sacred play' of a ritual, for the 'romantic nonsense' of lovers, and, of course, for children at play. The 'real' world is bracketed out for the duration of the game. And a fourth characteristic, I would note, is that it is of secondary importance who is doing the playing; the subjectivity of playing is not the one who is playing, but the playing of the game itself. The game plays itself through the players; the players are, in a manner of speaking, the means of the game to play itself (101). In this way playing a game, as well as being engaged in a practice, has an impersonal character. This is a theme to which I will return.

It is not only Right Speech and the other branches of the Eightfold Path that have the formal structure of a practice, but also other activities that traditionally belong to the Buddhist path of development, such as the development of the *brahmavihāra*s and *kalyāṇa-mitratā* in early Buddhism, the *pāramitā*s in Mahāyāna, the art of calligraphy in Zen, and many others.

Acting in the context of a practice was called *prattein* (from which the word *praxis* is derived) by Aristotle, and was contrasted with what he called *poiein*: acting in the sense of producing. In producing, the goal of an act points to a good independent of the act itself, and the act is instrumental with respect to that goal. This goal may point to further goals, but it ultimately ends at an act in the sense of a practice. For example, someone may build a house for the sake of having a family life, but having a family life is not done for the sake of a further goal, it is a practice (*praxis*) with its own internal end, i.e. to flourish as a family. A family life could of course also be a *poiesis*; for example, one could seek a family in order to improve one's career; in that case the career is the further goal, and the practice in this case is to have a flourishing career. In this way a practice is embedded in a network of producing acts, while at the same time being independent of it, just as a game is embedded in a world of considerations of utility, and at the same time is lifted up from it. A game or a practice has its own constituent rules and its own goal, which consists of the flourishing of itself. This is achieved by nothing else than developing the qualities of the practice in question. A Buddhist practice like Right Speech, as well as other practices, in this way has dynamics that, as it were, lifts it up from the world of external goals.

Narratives

A man like Gauguin found himself faced with the dilemma whether he should pursue the practice of his family life or that of his artistic development (cf. Williams 1981: 20–25). A Buddhist variant of this problem could be someone who needs to choose between his or her family life and a life of intensive meditation. These are only two examples of how practices may conflict, and it raises the question of how different practices can cohere. A related question is how a particular practice can be criticized. Activities such as hunting, or amassing vast amounts of wealth, can take on the described formal structure of a practice. A practice can by definition not be evaluated on the basis of external results, as we have seen. So how can it be evaluated?

The narrative of the path to awakening provides coherence for the diversity of Buddhist practices. As a story this is the well-known tale of how Gautama left his parental home, went into the wilderness, awakened to Buddhahood, and wandered around as a teacher; this is a tale that has all the elements of a quest, and has many variations in the life stories of other Buddhist saints. In conceptual shape the most classic formulation of the central Buddhist narrative is that of the Eightfold Path, but it is also described as the path of the bodhisattva in the Mahāyāna, and in different ways in other forms of Buddhism. The essential thing is that there is the notion of a unity in life, connected to the notion of a goal, and a path that leads to this goal.

MacIntyre also describes the unity of a human life as a narrative. Human beings are storytelling animals, he says. We are not born as a blank slate, as Locke argued, and we are more than a context-independent individual who chooses on the basis of what he believes will bring most happiness. On the contrary, from our birth onward we find ourselves in a society with stories, and it is in finding our place within these stories that we shape ourselves. We are embedded in the stories that tell us what is good, and it is on these stories that we base our choices. A basic theme within these stories is the story of a life which, according to MacIntyre, resembles a quest. A quest is characterized by being aimed towards an end, which is increasingly understood as it is approached, and also by being unpredictable, involving all kinds of inner and outer hindrances (1984: 215). Through this overarching practice of a life's quest towards the *summum bonum*, we are able to evaluate individual practices: a given practice can be a hindrance or helpful on the overall quest. And *vice versa*, a narrative can bring, or fail to bring, unity to the multitude of practices of a life. The narrative of a life has the same teleological and autarkic structure as a practice, with the same characteristics that I described above, but it has an organizational function, and should be seen as an overarching, or second-order, practice.

MacIntyre argues that the notions of a character, and of personal identity, can be understood as abstractions of a narrative (1984: 217). The narratives are primary; we find ourselves in life playing the parts in the narratives of our family and society and shaping our identity according to these roles. This dependence of personal identity on narratives can be the starting point for a critique of the existence of an inherent self, an important theme in Buddhism. It corresponds with what I have called above the impersonal character of a practice, and to which I will return below.

In ancient Greece, the unity of a life was seen as something in which rationality (*logos*) plays an important part. As an infant or otherwise immature person I strive towards different goals, which I think will bring me pleasure or fulfilment, but through the development of rationality I can see that all these different goals are often counteracting each other, and that they are therefore unlikely to bring fulfilment. Higher-order goals appear, which bring coherence to the first-order goals, and that results in the notions of the unity of a life, and a goal of life, which the ancient Greeks called *eudaimonia*. That can be translated as 'happiness', if that is understood to be a higher-order concept, and not happiness in the sense of subjective enjoyable experiences. *Eudaimonia* is a thin concept that was fleshed out differently by the various philosophical schools (cf. Annas 1993: 27–47). It is important to note that rationality in this vision does not have an exclusively cognitive meaning as opposed to the alleged irrationality of the emotions, as it is often viewed in modernity. Rationality in ancient Greece and Rome did not exclude the qualities of the heart, such as a mature emotionality and imaginative qualities, as is understood when we call a person 'reasonable' as opposed to 'rational'.

In Aristotle's ethics, rationality and the emotions are clearly connected. The quality of practical wisdom (*phronesis*) plays a crucial part in the development of the emotions and character virtues; it is the cognitive aspect of the character qualities, and directs a particular emotional ability, so that it is used in the right way—i.e. directed at *eudaimonia*. The ability to withstand dangers and to take risks, for example, can turn into recklessness if used at the wrong moment or at the wrong place. But when directed by practical wisdom it can become courageousness. The practical wise person, or *phronimos*, is a person who, typically, has much life experience, who has developed the relevant emotions, and has brought them as an integrated unity to excellence. Therefore he can be an example or advisor, and serve as a standard for excellence. Progress towards *eudaimonia* in Aristotle's vision is a matter of developing both the cognitive and character virtues: *eudaimonia* supervenes on the excellence of both in mutual coherence.

This view on the realization of *eudaimonia* shares structural features with the Buddhist path to awakening, as Keown has shown (1992). *Nirvāṇa* is also a second-order end that supervenes on the excellence of both cognitive and character qualities, which balance each other out. Sometimes the Buddhist path is described as if developing morality (*śīla*) is a preliminary stage for the development of wisdom (*prajñā*), but Keown shows that this view is based on a misunderstanding, and that both aspects are equally important. The Buddhist path is a path of development, or, more imaginatively, a quest, and is aimed at the internal goal of *nirvāṇa*, which at the same time is the excellence of life itself. Just as in a practice, this is not a goal that can be 'reached' in the way that the finishing line of a trip can be reached, whereby the trip was merely instrumental and best forgotten as soon as one has arrived. It is rather like the goal in a road movie, in which the perceived end changes and evolves while travelling, and the characters typically realize on arrival that the journey itself was really the goal.

In some forms of Zen and Tibetan Buddhism it is denied that there is a path with a goal (cf. Williams 2009: 119–122), which seems to contradict the classic descriptions of the path, as they appear in, for example, the Pāli scriptures. To my mind this apparent contradiction can be dissolved by looking at it from this point of view of an internal goal of a life's narrative as a second-order practice. There is no goal in the sense of an external result, but, for example, meditating, helping a neighbour, or performing a music piece can in themselves be purposeful while at the same time they can be directed towards the realization of *nirvāṇa*.

Tradition and Naturalism

Just as a practice like Right Speech, or other Buddhist practices, needs the context of the narrative of the path to be understood and evaluated, a Buddhist narrative needs the context of a Buddhist tradition. Traditions as intended here have a resemblance to Wittgensteinian *forms of life* or the *grand narratives* of Lyotard.

It is clear that Buddhism is a varied family of traditions, with different shapes in the various historical periods and social contexts. The North Indian *śrāmaṇa* tradition from which it originated was very different from later Mahāyāna forms in East Asian cultures, and the (post) modern Western culture in which it has been growing for the last sixty years is again radically different. What was held 'sacred' in one context was thrown overboard in another, and *vice versa*. The notion of *nirvāṇa* has similarly had many formulations, from the more negative ones in early Buddhism, to positive and very imaginative ones in Mahāyāna and Vajrayāna Buddhism. But despite all its different expressions, every Buddhist tradition has—in the language of stories, images, philosophies, social institutions, and so forth—pointed to the Buddhist path as the development of cognitive, emotional, and social qualities towards their excellence. In early Buddhism the classic formulation was the Eightfold Path; a description of how eight areas of life can be developed completely (*samyak*), and *nirvāṇa* emerges as the fruition of the whole. In Mahāyāna Buddhism it is described as the path of the bodhisattva, and emphasis is put on the altruistic aspect that was more implicit in early Buddhism. The path of the six transcendent excellences (*pāramitās*) of the bodhisattva is a reformulation of the Eightfold Path, as is clear from the fact that they share three aspects (*śīla, samādhi,* and *prajñā*). Even when it is said in Buddha-nature (*tathāgatagarbha*) doctrines that Buddhist practice is only an expression of our original perfection, and that we do not have to 'do' anything, is it still thought of as a development to fully recognize and realize this (Williams 2009: 112–122). Despite the diversity in the family of Buddhist traditions, each of them is the background for the narrative of the quest to *nirvāṇa*.

A living tradition, according to MacIntyre, is 'an historically extended, socially embodied argument ... about the goods which constitute that tradition' (1984: 222). A tradition is important as the background of a narrative because it is an illusion that we undertake our life quest on our own, independent of others, or that we are the sole authors of our life stories. But, above all, a tradition is important because it is a socially embedded form of rationality; a lived argument about what is important, what the ultimate good is, what the end of a human life is, and therefore also what the excellences are that correspond with the ultimate good. Each tradition has another conception of the ultimate good, and another list of virtues. For a man like Aristotle, the 'good' had to do with personal flourishing and greatness in the context of the *polis*, and hence humility was seen as a weakness, while for a medieval Christian monk, the 'good' would include obedience to God, and humility was seen as a virtue. Both are part of a different form of life, and have a view on the good and a list of virtues that are determined by that.

It is impossible to defend a particular conception of the good in a tradition against a radical sceptic from outside that tradition. This raises the question of the circularity of a conception of the good. A conception of the good is based on a tradition, and the tradition is shaped in an important way by its conception of the good. Is every conception of the good then nothing more than an expression of a given tradition, and every tradition merely a rationalization of that conception? To put it differently: how can a given conception of the good be criticized? It looks as if this way of looking is very vulnerable to the objection of relativity.

Naturalism in ethics is a response to that objection. It can be a basis for a tradition, while at the same time accommodate the fact that different cultures and traditions have different conceptions of the good and emphasize different values—an observation which impresses the relativist. Naturalism can give grounds for the phenomenon that there are similarities across cultures that are more striking than the differences. According to ethical naturalism one can determine what is good for a human being by looking at what is good for them as a natural being. The basic idea is that every being possesses certain potentialities, and that to bring these out and make them flourish is the good. This implies that naturalism denies the fact/value gap that has dominated Western ethical discourse since Hume. According to Hume, there is a fundamental logical gap between facts and values, and it is impossible to derive values from natural facts. An upshot of this is non-cognitivism in ethics, which says that it is principally impossible to say anything true or false about ethical values, thus paving the way for ethical theories such as emotivism. Naturalism, on the contrary, implies a cognitivist position, and holds that one can make true or false statements about 'good' and 'bad'.

Aristotle was the first to articulate a form of ethical naturalism in Western philosophy, and since then many other forms have been developed, such as the *physis* doctrine of the Stoics and the Natural Law of Aquinas. It has been discredited since the European Enlightenment by the criticisms of Hume, Moore, and others, but since the 1950s thinkers like Foot, McDowell, Hursthouse, and others have formulated answers to these criticisms, and developed contemporary forms of naturalism.

McDowell (1995) differentiates between a 'first' and a 'second' nature in a person. He performs the thought-experiment of a wolf that acquires *logos*, i.e. consciousness and rationality, and in that way is not only *capable* of distancing himself from his needs and instincts, but inevitably *must* do so. The wolf is condemned to make choices, to paraphrase Sartre, because he cannot escape consciousness. This rational wolf can decide to pull his full weight in hunting with the pack, as his first nature with its instincts tell him to, and as he would have done before, or to be a free-rider and just join in for appearances, so that he can share in the booty without making too much effort. What he *cannot* do without harming himself is to leave the pack, or to stop eating. With the choices he makes, and which gradually become habits, he develops a second nature. When it occurs collectively (in a society or social group), this development of a second nature becomes a culture.

We are limited by our first nature. As members of the human species we strive for the survival of ourselves, as individuals and as a species, we avoid pain and seek pleasure, and we live, just as bees, elephants, and apes, in groups (Hursthouse 1999: 197–205). We cannot neglect goals connected to this without doing harm. But our second nature is in an essential way free of these limits. When I have self-consciousness and reason, I can neglect the demands of my first nature (although, as said, not without harm) or conform to them, but even this conforming is necessarily free in two ways. First I always have an interpretation of my first nature and its demands, and second I can conform to those demands in different ways. However, most of these decisions are made based on habits from my upbringing and culture rather than on conscious considerations. These decisions reflect the narratives of my culture, the cumulative reason of my tradition. It is my second *nature*; it appears to be naturally given to me and not to involve many direct choices. It is, however, because it is rational in origin, fundamentally open to reflection, and can therefore renew itself. This takes place according to the Neurathian procedure, that is, as a sailing ship that can only be repaired in open sea by having its components replaced one at the time. There is no haven, i.e. no neutral vantage point possible—outside a tradition—from which a tradition can be evaluated, because a form of life can not be put on hold to observe it from the outside. Of course one can place oneself outside a particular tradition, but then one would inevitably find oneself inside another tradition, and therefore a neutral point of view is not available. However, components of a tradition can be criticized and changed from within, so that, over time, the whole of a second nature can be transformed.

From this it follows that there are many possible ways to form a second nature on the basis of the 'facts' of our first nature. In other words, the second nature is underdetermined by the first nature. It is not possible to construct a second nature (a culture, a character, a form of life) positively on the basis of the facts of the first nature. In this way there is a fact/value gap, although not as Hume meant it. There is, however, a negative control of the first nature over the second, because first nature can say when its demands are *not* met. Although many forms of life are possible, there are minimum demands that must be met, if a life is to be called a good life. Just as one can call a bee 'good' qua bee if it can dance in such a way as to let other bees know when it has found a source of nectar, and so forth (cf. Foot: 2001: 16), one can call the proverbial bad guy, the mafioso drug baron, 'not good' qua human being because he is—by definition—dishonest, reckless, unjust, and so forth. With these qualities he hinders the flourishing of himself and others. To put it differently, we might say that human beings are 'excellent' when they develop optimally the qualities of both their second *and* first natures. If we completely unfold our physical, psychological, social, and spiritual qualities, we have an excellent life.

Within this framework of ethical naturalism, many forms of virtue ethics can exist. They have different conceptions of the *summum bonum*, expressed in a different list of virtues. Yet all of them can be seen as forms of virtue ethics, and the conceptions of the good life can be understood by looking at how their cultural traditions view human nature.

In Buddhism, similar naturalistic arguments for ethics can be found. The fundamental principle of dependent co-arising (*pratītya-samutpāda*) implies that everything is impermanent. Another given for Buddhism is that all human beings by nature possess a desire (*tṛṣṇā*) for continuity. These two principles collide, and in this way our existence is characterized by a continuous state of dissatisfaction (*duḥkha*), which we cause ourselves. These are the first and second Noble Truths, according to which the human condition is fundamentally conflicted. The third Noble Truth, however, points to another aspect of human nature, i.e. that we can develop in such ways as to stop thirsting after continuity. Thus in the first three Noble Truths it is made clear that it is no more than rational, given the natural state we find ourselves in, to try to realize awakening. Then, in the fourth Noble Truth, follows the description of how to do that, or, in other words, the Buddhist answer to the question of how to live. In later forms of Buddhism, for example in the doctrine of Buddha-nature (*tathāgatagarbha*), this is expressed even more explicitly. It states that every person has, by nature, a buddha in him- or herself, but this is covered by the defilements (*kleśa*). The ultimate good is to uncover this Buddha-nature, the discovery that is at the same time the fruition of Buddha-nature.

One might object that an appeal to human nature, and especially Buddha-nature, postulates an essence, and is therefore in contradiction with the doctrines of no-self, emptiness, and dependent co-arising. However, the *tathāgatagarbha* tradition is clear that Buddha-nature is not meant in this way, but rather as an expression of the very principle of emptiness and dependent co-arising, or, in other words, 'suchness' (*tathatā*). Nagao describes the 'nature' of emptiness beautifully:

> Beings that exist in emptiness exist just as they are. ... Because of emptiness, the existence of beings together with their causes is ineffable (*avācya*) and inconceivable (*acintya*). In truth, the phenomenal world is first and foremost a beautiful world and phenomenal being is a being wondrous and enjoyable beyond description. (1992: 18–19, cf. King 1991: ch. 4)

In this way, Buddhism can be seen as a tradition based on a naturalistic vision: human nature (and in some forms of Buddhism nature in its broadest sense) is such that the potentiality of awakening is present in everyone (or everything), and the realizing of this potentiality is the *summum bonum* of life.

Buddhist Ethics and Consequentialism

A different view on Buddhist ethics is expressed by Goodman (2009). He points to the contemporary utilitarian/consequentialist Peter Singer, who argues (e.g. 2016) that there is never any justification whatsoever for one person having a higher level of welfare than another. It is morally just always to share everything one has with an arbitrary other person, until both are on the same level of welfare. In this way, people in the affluent West are morally obligated to share everything they have with other people, until they are on the same level as the very poorest. His altruism goes even further, because he involves all living beings in it, and says we also have a moral obligation towards animals (Singer 1995).

Singer finds a metaphysical foundation for this view in the critique on the self and personal identity as it is developed in Western philosophy by Hume, Parfit, and others. According to this critique, the self on which we rely in daily life, and very often in ethics, does not really exist, and is nothing more than an illusion based on a psychological habit and a social convention (Goodman 2009: 109–115). When one takes this critique seriously, according to Singer, one does not have a reason to take oneself more seriously than any other person. It also implies the attitude of agent-neutrality in ethics; whether my child, a complete stranger, or myself is affected by an act is morally speaking not relevant. In this way, a Singerian consequentialist finds himself in a position of radical altruism. Agent-neutrality is an especially high demand of consequentialism, as it seems to be counter-intuitive, and to assign little ethical value to the emotions. Williams (1981: 16), for example, imagines a man in a lifeboat who has to choose whether to save the life of his wife or a complete stranger. It seems intuitively right, or at least permitted, for him to choose his wife. If he needs to think about his choice, according to Williams, he has 'one thought too many'.

Goodman rightly points to the resemblance of Singer's view to the bodhisattva-ideal in Mahāyāna Buddhism (2009: 89–95). As the Mahāyāna author Śāntideva says: 'See, I give up without regret my bodies, my pleasures, and my good acquired in all three times, to accomplish good for every being' (1995: 20). According to Goodman, a bodhisattva also takes on the high demands of agent-neutrality to renounce one's own point of view. Moreover, it is, ultimately, not decisive what she actually does to achieve more welfare for as many beings as possible. A bodhisattva can lie, steal, kill, and so on, as long as the net results are more benefits than harm for as many beings as possible. The only reason lying, killing, and so forth, are not permitted is that in the long run these actions will produce less well-being overall, not because they are unjust acts in themselves. In this, Goodman sees a correspondence with the Mahāyāna doctrine of skilful means (*upāya-kauśalya*), according to which it is permitted for a bodhisattva in special circumstances to act apparently immorally if that actually results, ultimately, in a better outcome.

All these characteristics—the strong emphasis on altruism, the possibility of breaking moral codes for the sake of better outcomes, agent-neutrality, and the underlying critique on the notion of a self—are, according to Goodman, reasons to see the ethics of Mahāyāna Buddhism as a form of utilitarianism/consequentialism.

Nonetheless, I believe he is wrong. Without doubt, a bodhisattva would agree with the ideals of Singer and other consequentialists. I doubt, however, if he would try to realize these ideals in this way, i.e. by passing over the intrinsic value of an act, and the personal standpoint with its emotions. One of the defining qualities of a bodhisattva is his or her measureless loving-kindness (Pāli *mettā*) towards all living beings. The *Karaṇīyamettā sutta*, which, although it is not a Mahāyāna scripture, is the classical description of this ideal of all-encompassing love, speaks of *mettā* for all beings 'as the love of a mother for her only child' (Sn 1.8). It is, in other words, a passionate and personal love that expands to immeasurable proportions and eventually encompasses all beings. The personal, agent-relative, point of view is not passed over, or renounced, but taken as a starting point. The compassion of an awakened being is characterized by the quality of equanimity (Pāli *upekkhā*), the highest level of *mettā*, which might be described as the synthesis of strong personal love and neutral impartiality. Thus it still has the warmth of agent-relative love, only that the word 'agent' will have lost its ordinary meaning. The abundant hyperboles of many Mahāyāna texts, in which a bodhisattva bears humiliations, sacrifices herself to feed other beings, and so on, should in my opinion be seen as so many exercises in altruistic intentions. They are meant as bending backward our ingrained self-centredness, rather than statements about the greater value of others as opposed to oneself.

Altruism is not about trying to renounce the self-centred side of the apparent dichotomy of self and other, and in a radical move switch to being other-centred. This interpretation of altruism is still dependent on the opposition of self and other, and in this way only reinforces it. Better than declaring self-centredness as unwanted is to take personal love as a starting point, and the non-difference of self and other as an end to be realized. The path of the bodhisattva, then, is the gradual incarnation of that end in the present (cf. Keown 1992: 194). And that is precisely what is teleology, the central notion of virtue ethics.

As is, I hope, clear, a critique on the notion of an independent self is implied therein. This responds to the often-heard objection against virtue ethics that it is self-centred, because it is overly concerned with the flourishing of oneself, at the expense of being concerned with the welfare of others. But even in Aristotle's ethics it is already clear that the communal good was of higher value than the merely individual. He says one should strive for the good of the community rather than for oneself 'because it is nobler (*kalon*) and more godlike' (2002: 1094b10). In other words: virtue is lifted to another level when directed from the individual to the community. He stopped at the borders of the community, but there is nothing inherent in virtue ethics that stops us from expanding it even further until it encompasses all living beings. In this way, virtue ethics can accommodate a fundamental and fruitful critique on the notion of an independent self, one that should start with the impersonal character of a (first- and second-order) practice, as discussed above. In this critique it can be argued that the self that we experience in daily life is merely a provisional way of looking, and can gradually be transcended. That topic, however, exceeds the scope of this chapter.

It could be objected that the Buddha described the *Dharma* as a raft that should be left behind when one has reached 'the other shore' of *nirvāṇa*, and that this is a clear example of consequentialist reasoning. However, as Keown has made clear, the parable of the raft should not be interpreted to mean that the *Dharma* is transcended and left behind upon the realization of awakening (1992: 92–105). The *Dharma* is indeed a means to awakening, but awakening is the fulfilment of the *Dharma* rather than the 'outcome' of it. The parable of the raft is better interpreted to mean that one should not be too attached to specific views and doctrines.

Buddhist Ethics and Deontology

As mentioned, deontological ethics are concerned about the principal 'rightness' of a norm. At first sight, they may seem to resemble Buddhist ethics. Buddhist ethics are often summarized as the following of the Five (or sometimes Eight, or Ten) Precepts, which do appear to have the status of moral norms. But what kinds of norms do the precepts of Buddhist ethics imply? The original Pāli term that is usually translated as 'precepts' is *sikkhāpada*. That has the component *sikkhā*, which means something like 'the desire to do something well', and *pada*, which can mean 'path'. *Sikkhāpada* can therefore be translated as 'the path one follows out of the desire to do something well'. It is of course handy to summarize that in one word, but to choose the word 'precept' is, I believe, over-reliant on the preconception that ethics should be based on norms. 'Rules of training' or 'principles of training' would conform more closely to the original meaning. This is confirmed by the fact that in the standard formula (Pāli *veramaṇī-sikkhāpadaṃ samādiyāmi*), what is said is not 'I may not' or 'I shall not', but, rather, 'I undertake to refrain from', after which the observances in question are stated: taking life, taking the not-given, sexual misconduct, using untruthful speech, and using intoxicants.

Translated this way it is clear that they are principles by which to retrain behaviour, to practise intentions and conduct in order to realize the end of awakening, and separated from that end they lose their meaning. In other words there is a *conditional* obligation and not an absolute one. Even the obligation of a bodhisattva to bring all living being to awakening is only an obligation by the force of his vow. Initially it can be useful to follow a code of ethics that has been prescribed from outside, perhaps by parents, society, or even by oneself (as if from outside), and it is primarily obedience and discipline to the code that is asked for. In this phase it can be useful, provisionally, to experience the rules of training as absolutes. But when the path is followed further, this external compulsory force should be replaced by insight into what in a given situation will lead to a more awakened state, for oneself as well as for others.

What guidance, then, *does* Buddhist ethics provide? The Mahāyāna doctrine of skilful means (*upāya-kauśalya*) expresses an essential uncodifiability in ethics, and is, I believe, intended as a correction of a too rigid conception of the rules of training and morality. In other words, the right way of acting in a given situation cannot be formulated or fixed in advance. It depends on a range of conditions, and often there are several ways of acting in the 'right' way, depending on the person and the situation. Although the 'precepts' are, as well as rules of training, also very suitable as rules of thumb to be applied in making everyday decisions, and will in most cases deliver the right course, there is no guarantee in this. In fact *absolute* values would contradict the central Buddhist doctrine of dependent co-arising (*pratītya-samutpāda*), which implies that everything, including ethical norms, exists only in relation to something else, and that therefore there can be no absolutes.

A guidance for acting is what in a given situation leads to a more awakened state, or, put differently, expresses such an awakened state in the given situation. This cannot be tied to a particular decision-making procedure, as is the case in deontology and consequentialism, but is an ability that must be learned. Education, *Bildung*, and other forms of ethical training are therefore of crucial importance. The example of those who have completed the path, or at least have developed to such a degree that they can be an example, can serve as guidance. The Buddha himself, of course, but also others, such as the *arhant*s, the bodhisattvas, and other Buddhist saints, can fulfil the role of ethical exemplar. They are the 'ethical experts' of Buddhism, and fulfil the role that the practical wise person (*phronimos*) plays in Aristotelian virtue ethics.

However, the dependent character of the 'good' in Buddhism, and in virtue ethics in general, should not be overstated (cf. McDowell 1998). Actions committed from greed, hatred, and delusion are bad regardless of context, and the precepts work as rules of training precisely because they express what is *in fact* the right thing to do or not to do. Therefore, they are universally valid, regardless of cultures or different conceptions of the good, or whether one has taken the precepts. What I contend here is that in Buddhist ethics there is a dependence of the precepts on the notion of *nirvāṇa*, which is the flourishing life for Buddhists. An act of cruelty, for example, is 'not right' because it leads one away rather than towards *nirvāṇa*. Thus, there is a place for the notion of duty and obligation in Buddhist ethics as virtue ethics, or, if one wishes, a deontological element, but only in the weak sense of the term that I described above.

Conclusion

The framework of virtue ethics as it is described first by Aristotle, and developed further in contemporary philosophical ethics, appears to be a good context in which to understand Buddhist ethics. In my opinion it avoids the Scylla and Charybdis of interpretation—i.e. the dangers of distortion and neglect. It does justice to all important aspects of Buddhism. The doctrines of dependent co-arising, the Four Noble Truths, no-self, the middle way, can all have their place in a non-artificial way, just as the ethical value of emotions and intentions, of ethical training, and the role of the wise. Consequentialist and deontological notions, such as results and external goals, duties and norms, also have their places, as I have shown, but, at least in Buddhist ethics, these notions are more appropriately placed in a virtue ethics context.

Do we gain something by placing Buddhist ethics in this framework? I believe we do.[5] First, such placing creates an appropriate context for the idea that Buddhist ethics concern the development of potential. Virtue ethics has a *motivational force* that is inherent in the pursuit of the development of qualities. Developing and growing is intrinsically motivating, in contrast to the idea that some things are mandatory, or not allowed (as when precepts are being taken to be absolute norms), or that demands are made that you can never fully meet (as is the case with the utilitarian view on the bodhisattva-ideal). The Buddhist path of training is essentially about developing the potential of awakening, and the virtue ethics perspective brings this out clearly.

Second, by setting Buddhist ethics in the context of the notion of a practice, we *better understand the dynamics of practising the Buddhist path*, what is traditionally expressed as 'going for refuge to the *Buddha, Dharma*, and *Saṅgha*'. When one practises meditation, or moral conduct in the sense of *śīla*, or any other Buddhist practice, one does it the way one plays the piano, or plays a football game with friends. It is essentially about playing the game itself, training and refining your skills, and reaping the rewards that are inherent in the game. External outcomes are (sometimes welcome) side effects, but if those gain the upper hand the game is no longer being played in the proper sense. Buddhist practice is not the same as playing the piano, of course; 'going for refuge' is more existentially charged, which makes it another sort of 'game'. However, the dynamics are the same. Both are places of refuge in the world of external goals, and both have a lightness and momentum characteristic of playing games.

Thirdly, the virtue ethics perspective *clarifies the place of norms and precepts in Buddhist ethics.* Norms and precepts have a derived rather than an absolute meaning. This was already clear to those who translated the original Pāli terms for 'precepts' in the right way, as I have shown in my discussion of them above. In virtue ethics the *good* is dependent on context and cannot be fixed in the formulation of laws or rules; the framework of virtue ethics helps show that this is also the case in Buddhist ethics. The Buddhist precepts are important as rules of training, and as rules of thumb in daily life decision-making procedures, but they do not have an absolute existence.

Fourthly, the virtue ethics perspective enables us to see how *practices other than the traditional Buddhist ones*—for example, family life, marriage, the arts, and the sciences—can also be fruitful on the Buddhist path. The virtue ethics perspective shows it is very possible that through these practices one may develop qualities that fit well into the Buddhist path, although the reverse is of course also possible.

Finally, the virtue ethics perspective shows that *Buddhist ethics can cohere with the ethical perspective of Western thinking.* The virtue ethics point of view can be a framework through which many differences and resemblances fall into place, and can offer conceptual tools for Buddhists to employ when partaking in debates and discussions with Western philosophers.

[5] The following paragraphs have been adapted, with revisions, from my previous publication (2014).

Works Cited

Annas, J. (1993) *The morality of happiness.* New York and Oxford: Oxford University Press.
Aristotle (2002) *Nicomachean ethics.* Translated by C. Rowe. New York and Oxford: Oxford University Press.
Clayton, B. (2006) *Moral theory in Śāntideva's Śikṣāsamuccaya: cultivating the fruits of virtue.* London and New York: Routledge Curzon.
Foot, P. (2001) *Natural goodness.* New York and Oxford: Oxford University Press.
Gadamer, H.-G. (1989) *Truth and method.* Second edition. London: Sheed and Ward.
Goodman, C. (2009) *Consequences of compassion: an interpretation and defense of Buddhist ethics.* Oxford: Oxford University Press.
Hayes, R. P. (2011) Review of *Consequences of compassion: an interpretation and defense of Buddhist ethics. Journal of Buddhist ethics*, 18, 288–395.
Hursthouse, R. (1999) *On virtue ethics.* New York and Oxford: Oxford University Press.
Keown, D. (1992) *The nature of Buddhist ethics.* Basingstoke, UK: Palgrave Macmillan.
King, S. (1991) *Buddha nature.* Delhi: Sri Satguru Publications.
McDowell, J. (1995) Two sorts of naturalism. In: R. Hursthouse, G. Lawrence, and W. Quinn (eds), *Virtues and reasons: Philippa Foot and moral theory.* Oxford: Clarendon Press, 149–179.
McDowell, J. (1998) Are moral requirements hypothetical imperatives? In: *Mind, value and reality.* Cambridge, MA: Harvard University Press, 77–94.
MacIntyre, A. (1984) *After virtue: a study in moral theory.* Second edition. London: Duckworth.
Nagao, G. (1992) *The foundational standpoint of Mādhyamika philosophy.* Delhi: Sri Satguru Publications.
Śāntideva (1995) *Bodhicaryāvatāra.* Translated by K. Crosby and A. Skilton. New York and Oxford: Oxford University Press.
Singer, P. (2009) *Animal liberation: a new ethics for our treatment of animals.* New York: HarperCollins Publishers.
Singer, P. (2016) *Famine, affluence, and morality.* New York: Oxford University Press.
Williams, B. (1981) *Moral luck.* Cambridge: Cambridge University Press.
Williams, B. (1985) *Ethics and the limits of philosophy.* Cambridge, MA: Harvard University Press.
Williams, P. (2009) *Mahāyāna Buddhism: the doctrinal foundations.* Second edition. London and New York: Routledge.

Suggested Reading

Foot, P. (2001) *Natural goodness.* New York and Oxford: Oxford University Press.
Gadamer, H.-G. (1986) *The relevance of the beautiful and other essays.* Cambridge: Cambridge University Press.
Keown, D. (1992) *The nature of Buddhist ethics.* Basingstoke, UK: Palgrave Macmillan.
MacIntyre, A. (1984) *After virtue: a study in moral theory.* Second edition. London: Duckworth.
Sangharakshita (2010) *The ten pillars of Buddhism.* Cambridge: Windhorse.
Williams, P. (2009) *Mahāyāna Buddhism: the doctrinal foundations.* Second edition. London and New York: Routledge.
Zahavi, D. (2008) *Subjectivity and selfhood: investigating the first-person perspective.* Cambridge, MA: MIT Press.

CHAPTER 17

THE PSYCHOLOGY OF MORAL JUDGMENT AND PERCEPTION IN INDO-TIBETAN BUDDHIST ETHICS

EMILY MCRAE

INTRODUCTION

IN Western principle-based ethics, moral judgment is the ability to put moral principles (or rules) into action—to apply an abstract moral principle to a concrete, particular situation. (Moral principles, as opposed to rules, admit of no exceptions; see Blum 1991). Helpfully, it connects principle to action. I may understand the moral rule that one should help others, for example, but I cannot actually help others unless I can judge that *this* particular person needs help and that *I* am in the position to give it.

If we think of moral judgment in these terms—'the ability to bring principle to bear on particular situations' (Blum 1991: 710)—then, other than discussions of the monastic code (*Vinaya*) and its application, Indo-Tibetan Buddhist ethical texts have little to say about it. This may not be surprising for those of us who do not categorize Buddhist ethics as rule-based (see, e.g., Hallisey 1996). But neither do we find in Buddhist ethics, as we do in Western virtue ethics, theoretical models of practical reasoning that attempt to explain moral judgment and how moral action issues from some combination of abstract and particular knowledge.

There are so few examples in Buddhist ethics of individuals deliberating about which is the right action in a given situation that we might wonder if Buddhist ethicists simply ignore the standard problem of moral agency in Western ethics: What should I do? The *Jātaka* tales—stories of Buddha's moral and spiritual achievements in previous lives before he became enlightened—abound with examples of how the bodhisattva responded to difficult moral situations, yet they rarely include accounts of him wondering what he, morally, ought to do (perhaps because his moral wisdom is already perfected). In the *Mahosadha Jātaka* the bodhisattva adjudicates a conflict between two women who both claim to be the mother of an infant. In a moral decision strikingly similar to that of King Solomon (1 Kings 3:16–28), the bodhisattva draws a line, lays the infant across it, and tells the women that whoever pulls the child to her side can keep him. The real mother, of course, lets go of the baby to avoid hurting him, and the bodhisattva rightfully awards the baby to her (for a historical account of these stories, see Brewster 1962). Unlike the biblical version, which emphasizes King Solomon's *judgment*, the Buddhist version emphasizes the bodhisattva's *skill* and the tenderness of maternal *love*.

On the other hand, if we think of the capacity for moral judgment not in terms of applying abstract rules to concrete particular situations but in the broadest sense as the ability to discern, evaluate, appraise, and in general make meaning in the moral context, Indo-Tibetan Buddhist ethics is a rich resource for our investigation. What we find among Indo-Tibetan Buddhist ethicists are sophisticated moral psychologies that prioritize the exploration of emotionality, desire, ignorance, perception, attention, and imagination, and tend to leave the concept of moral judgment in the strict (Western philosophical) sense on the periphery of their analyses. More pressing in Buddhist ethics than the question 'What should I do?' is 'How can I become the kind of person who can do it?' This interest is related to, but ultimately distinct from, the guiding question of Western virtue ethics—What is the virtuous person like?—because, in Buddhist ethics, the focus is not only on presenting a general description of what the morally and spiritually developed person is like but also on how the ordinary person (or, at least, ordinary monastic), with all of her flaws, fixations, negativities, and delusions, can develop morally and spiritually.[1]

This chapter argues for two general claims about moral psychology in Indo-Tibetan Buddhist ethics. First, although Buddhist moral psychology shares some interests with Western moral psychology, such as a general interest in moral motivation and the psychological aspects of moral success and failure, Buddhist moral psychology is centrally interested in the psychology of moral improvement: How do I become the kind of person who can respond in the best possible way to the moral needs of myself and others? It is, centrally, a psychology of moral development. This approach differs from typical Western inquiries in moral psychology, which does not typically prioritize inquiries into the psychology of moral self-cultivation. (One exception to this general trend is the moral psychology of the Stoic philosophers, particularly in the works of Seneca and Epictetus; see Nussbaum 1994; Hadot 1995; McRae 2015).

Second, and related, I argue that the skills of moral perception and attention are central to Buddhist moral psychology. It is deeply interested in the question of how we perceive and attend morally, how we fail to perceive and attend, and how we can learn to

[1] This is not to imply that there is no discussion of the sensibilities of morally accomplished beings, such as bodhisattvas and buddhas. But the more central project in Buddhist ethics, I suggest, is how an imperfect, afflicted being can improve morally and spiritually.

perceive and attend differently. Moral philosophical arguments, I argue, are generally offered in the context of self-cultivation exercises and not, as they often are in Western ethics, as models of moral deliberation. I focus on two Buddhist moral psychological categories: the *brahmavihāras* (the Four Boundless Qualities), which are the main moral affective states in Buddhist ethics, and the *kleśas*, or the afflictive mental states. In addition to being foundational categories of Buddhist moral psychology, our examination of the Boundless Qualities and the afflictions also illustrate the general orientation towards self-cultivation and the primacy of perception and attention in Buddhist ethics.

In my analysis of the Boundless Qualities and the afflictions, several sub-themes emerge, including: (1) a view of the human mind as having literally boundless potential; (2) the emphasis on psychological freedom and the exercise of choice in our cognitive and affective states; and (3) the relevance of personal relationships for moral self-cultivation projects. The following story illustrates the themes of self-cultivation, moral perception, and moral attention, as well as the sub-themes listed above, in Indo-Tibetan Buddhist ethics.

An Illustration: The Story of Asaṅga

In his classic treatise *The Words of My Perfect Teacher*, the nineteenth-century Tibetan Buddhist master Patrul Rinpoche (1808–1887) tells the story of the fourth-century Indian scholar and saint Asaṅga, who retreated to Kukkatapāda Mountain to practise love and compassion meditation in hopes of having a vision of Maitreya Buddha (Maitreya is the buddha associated with love and compassion; he is the buddha of the future era). Twelve years passed, and 'although he meditated hard he did not have as much as a single auspicious dream'. Having become increasingly discouraged by his lack of progress, Asaṅga gave up and started walking down the mountain. At the side of the road, he saw a dog with crippled hind legs and covered with maggots. 'Swept by deep, unbearable compassion', he felt a great urge to help her, and, realizing that he would kill the maggots if he picked them off with his fingers, decided to lick them off with his tongue. But, 'whenever he looked at the whole of the creature's body, so rotten and full of pus, he could not bring himself to do it. So he shut his eyes and stretched out his tongue . . .'. But his tongue did not touch the dog; instead, it touched the ground. When Asaṅga opened his eyes in surprise, he saw that dog had disappeared and in its place was Maitreya. In response to Asaṅga's protests that it was unfair of Maitreya to not show himself sooner, despite twelve years of intense and dedicated practice, Maitreya says:

> It is not that I have not shown myself. You and I have never been separate. But your own negative actions and obscurations were too intense for you to be able to see me (*khod sdig sgrib che bas ma mthong ba yin*). Because your twelve years of practice have diminished them a little, you were able to see the dog. Just now, because of your great compassion, your obscurations have been completely purified and you can see

> me with your own eyes (*nga rang rngus mthong ba yin*). If you do not believe me, carry me on your shoulder and show me to everyone around.

So Asaṅga carried Maitreya on his shoulder and went to the market. No one there saw anything on his shoulder, except for one older woman 'whose perception was slightly less clouded by habitual tendencies' (literally 'an old woman whose habitual tendencies were "thinned out"' [*bag chags srab ba'i rgun mo*]). She said, 'You are carrying the rotting corpse of a dog' (Patrul 1994: 212).

Asaṅga's tale illustrates some core themes in Indo-Tibetan Buddhist moral psychology explored in this chapter: the boundless potential of the human mind to cultivate love and compassion through practice, the ways that negative emotionality and ignorance warp moral perception, the fact that moral perception comes in degrees, and the power of positive emotionality to clarify and make accurate our moral perception. In the first part of this chapter, I unpack the concepts of boundless love and compassion ('The Four Boundless Qualities [*Brahmavihāras*]') and negative mental states ('The Afflictions [*Kleśas*]'). The second part of the chapter investigates the role of moral perception, attention, and moral philosophical argument in Buddhist moral psychology, particularly in relation to the *brahmavihāras* and the *kleśas*.

The Four Boundless Qualities (*Brahmavihāras*)

The four *brahmavihāras*, literally the Abodes of Brahmā (often translated as 'Divine Abidings' or 'Sublime Abidings'), are the central virtuous affective experiences in Buddhist ethics: love (*mettā, maitri, byams pa*), compassion (*karuṇa, snying rje*), sympathetic joy (*mudita, dga' ba*), and equanimity (*upekka, btang snyoms*). The *brahmavihāras* are also referred to as the four boundless or immeasurable qualities (Tib. *tsad med gzhi*) because, with proper training, they can be extended boundlessly to eventually include all sentient beings and be felt with increasing depth and sincerity (McRae 2013). As the twentieth-century Tibetan philosopher Khenpo Ngawang Pelzang put it, 'They are called boundless qualities because the object on which they focus is boundless, the form they take in the mind is boundless, and their result is boundless' (2004: 136).

The Boundless Qualities refer originally and most basically to kinds of meditative concentrations, or 'absorptions' (Heim 2017). This is why Buddhaghosa, the fifth-century Buddhist scholar of the Pāli Canon, begins his discussion of the four *brahmavihāras* by advising that one should be well digested and 'should seat himself comfortably on a well-prepared seat in a secluded place' (1956: IX.1.295). The Boundless Qualities are perfected cognitive-affective states that are cultivated and experienced through meditation practice. Each Boundless Quality, as we will see, has associated practices designed to elicit, cultivate, and strengthen, including introspective meditation practice that can be done alone and social practices done in relationship with others. To some degree, love, compassion, sympathetic joy, and equanimity are everyday mental states that we have all experienced. But our experience of these states is usually warped or truncated by our biases; we may be overwhelmed with compassion for a dying pet, for example, and feel little for refugees displaced by war or famine. One of the main functions of the practices associated with the Boundless Qualities is to correct for the limitations and expand the scope of our everyday experience of love, compassion, sympathetic joy, and equanimity, that is, make them boundless.[2]

Love

Love, or loving-kindness, is the earnest, heartfelt desire for the happiness of another. Buddhaghosa (1956) describes it as 'promoting the aspect of welfare' which is 'manifested as the removal of annoyance'. Love, he argues, is caused by 'seeing lovableness in beings'. Successful love diminishes and eventually eliminates ill will; love fails 'when it produces (selfish) affection' (IX.93). It is what allows us to 'see virtues' in others (IX.98). Buddhaghosa distinguishes it from its 'far enemy' or opposite, which is ill will and resentment, and from its 'near enemy' of greedy attachment. To love another, then, is to genuinely desire the other's happiness without becoming attached in a self-serving way (for an excellent overview of love in Buddhaghosa's work, see Heim 2017).

Love, like the other Boundless Qualities, is not simply a feeling, although it includes feelings: it is a complex experience that includes physical actions and habits of speaking and thinking. Patrul Rinpoche advises that one cultivating love should look at others with a pleasant expression rather than an aggressive glare, and take special care with the vulnerable, such as people who work for you and older people. A loving person is able to live up to the difficult standard of 'mak[ing] every single word [she] says pleasant and true'. He warns of the more subtle traps of self-centredness when cultivating love: 'Do not be a hypocrite and try to make other people see you as a Bodhisattva because of your kind words and actions. Simply wish for others' happiness from the bottom of your heart and only consider what would be most beneficial for them' (Patrul 1994: 199).

Patrul Rinpoche compares love to the attitude of parents of young children. Parents 'ignore all their children's ingratitude and all the difficulties involved, devoting their every thought, word, and deed entirely to making their little ones happy, comfortable, and cozy' (198). Metaphors of parenting—especially mothering—are common in

[2] In what follows, I use the terms *brahmavihāras* and Boundless Qualities interchangeably, as is typical in Buddhist ethics. The only thinker I have found who differentiates the two is Khenpo Ngawang Pelzang who claims that the *brahmavihāras* are not synonymous with the Boundless Qualities, since the former lack *bodhicitta* and are not taken on 'the path of omniscience' (2004: 135–136).

descriptions of the Boundless Qualities. Although sublime, these qualities have their roots in the everyday, yet profoundly deep, orientation of care expressed by parents towards their children. We are encouraged to see other beings both as our children and as our own mothers.

But many Buddhist texts, including the *Words of My Perfect Teacher*, also emphasize the limitation of mother love (or parental love), especially when compared to the Boundless Qualities. In *The Ornament of the Great Vehicle Sutras*, Asaṅga (dictating the words of Maitreya) writes that the great love of a bodhisattva 'is unlike what any sentient being could possibly have toward a precious, only child' (XVII.28). The Tibetan master Mipham Rinpoche (1846–1912) comments on this verse: 'No father or mother could possibly give rise to this type of love toward their only child, no matter how gifted, adorable, and in need of help it might be' (600). This suggests that parental love is an affective and cognitive door into accessing the Boundless Qualities, but since such love is unacceptably partial in its application, cannot capture the full scope of boundless love (see Ohnuma 2012, and Powers and Curtin 1994).

Compassion

Compassion is the affective and cognitive response to suffering. It is the state that recognizes the badness of suffering and desires to alleviate it. Compassion, according to Buddhaghosa, is triggered by 'see[ing] helplessness of those overwhelmed by suffering'. Proper compassion 'makes cruelty subside' and allows us to fully register and respond to the moral urgency of another's suffering. Because compassion is a response to such a core moral need—the suffering of beings—it is considered central to cultivating the main moral orientation in Mahāyāna Buddhist ethics, *bodhicitta*, the radically altruistic attitude to perfect oneself as a moral agent in order to benefit all beings (Garfield 2011).

The centrality of compassion in Buddhist ethics, though, poses an immediate problem for Buddhist moral psychology: if compassion is, in some sense, suffering with another, then how is it compatible with the general Buddhist project of liberation from suffering? Or, put differently, if we are motivated by the desire to be free from suffering, as Buddhist thinkers affirm, what would motivate compassion? One response is to differentiate the compassion of the *brahmavihāras*, which is liberating, from suffering-producing states such as grief or depression. Buddhaghosa (1956) argues that, if, when encountering another's suffering, we instead feel sorrow or grief, then our attempts to generate compassion have failed (IX.94). On his view, compassion has a different phenomenological profile than sorrow or grief (compassion's 'near enemy'). This provides the conceptual space to claim that compassion, unlike sorrow or grief, does not cause suffering and thus is not in tension with liberation.

This view, however, is not shared by all Indo-Tibetan Buddhist ethicists. In fact, some Tibetan thinkers emphasize and even exploit the tension between compassion and liberation that Buddhaghosa's model could relieve. Patrul Rinpoche (1994: 212–213), for example, gives this heart-wrenching imagery to describe compassion meditation:

> The image given for meditating on compassion is that of a mother with no arms, whose child is being swept away by a river. How unbearable the anguish of such a mother would be. Her love for her child is so intense, but as she cannot use her arms she cannot catch hold of him.
>
> 'What can I do now? What can I do?' she asks herself. Her only thought is to find some means of saving him. Her heart breaking, she runs after him weeping.

Patrul Rinpoche describes compassion as 'unbearable' and capable of 'filling your eyes with tears'. Compassion, on this account, hurts (Frakes 2007).

The connection between compassion for others and one's own pain, though, is complicated. In his *Great Treatise on the Stages of the Path to Enlightenment* (*Lam rim chen mo*), the fifteenth-century Tibetan philosopher Tsongkhapa lists five good qualities of suffering, a somewhat surprising project in the context of the project of attaining liberation from suffering (see Cozort 2009). One of the good qualities of suffering is that of 'producing compassion for those who wander in cyclic existence. This is because after you have assessed your own situation, you think, "Other beings suffer like this"' (2000: 174). We also see this idea in Śāntideva: 'The virtue of suffering has no rival, since, from the shock it causes, intoxication falls away and there arises compassion for those in cyclic existence, fear of evil, and a longing for the Conqueror' (2009: VI.21). For at least some Buddhist ethicists, then, compassion can cause personal suffering, and personal suffering can cause compassion.

The *Ornament of the Great Vehicle Sutras* discusses the case of 'those who, due to compassion, are brought to suffer because of suffering'.

> A bodhisattva free from suffering
> Experiences suffering because of love;
> First there is fear, but upon contact
> There follows utterly intense joy. (XVIII.46)

'Suffering because of suffering' on this view is simply part of the experience of compassion, even for the bodhisattva, who is 'free from suffering'. Patrul Rinpoche tells the story of four brothers who are all highly accomplished *Dharma* practitioners: one brother gives *Dharma* lectures to hundreds, another is skilled at religious art, and a third is a meditation master, meditating all day and night. But it is only the fourth brother—who spends his days weeping for beings who are suffering—that earns the highest praise: 'That is really practicing the Dharma!' (1994: 210).

However, the line between feeling compassion and being paralysed by it is not easy to locate. Clearly, for compassion to be an aid—and not an obstacle—to liberation the first 'suffering' in the 'suffering because of suffering' cannot be afflictive but must have some liberatory potential. The verse quoted above suggests the difference between regular suffering and the 'suffering because of suffering' that is part of the experience of compassion is explained by the bodhisattva's absence of fear. To be fearless in the face of the suffering of self and other, to approach it with courage and wisdom, is itself liberating and can, perhaps, explain the 'intense joy' of the one who 'suffers because of suffering'.

Sympathetic Joy

There it is no word in English for *mudita* (Skt; Tib. *dga' ba*), usually translated effectively but somewhat inelegantly as 'sympathetic joy'. *Mudita* is the genuine joy one takes in another's success, virtue, and happiness. Buddhaghosa describes it as analogous to the attitude a mother takes towards her successful son: she is genuinely happy about his success and wishes for him to have more of it. It is joy taken in the success of others that is not mediated by self-interest—what another's success means about you—which when properly cultivated can extend to all sentient beings. It is, according to Patrul Rinpoche, a state completely free of envy (1994: 213).

Buddhist ethicists often suggest beginning one's cultivation of sympathetic joy by focusing on someone whose success is easy and natural to wish for. Buddhaghosa advises focusing first on the 'boon companion', for he is constantly glad: he laughs first and speaks afterword' (IX.84). Patrul Rinpoche and Khenpo Ngawang Pelzang suggest starting one's meditation by bringing to mind a very dear person, such as a close relative. As with the other Boundless Qualities, once one's meditation becomes established in this easiest case, then one tries to extend it to others, including strangers and enemies. The ultimate goal is the ability to feel joy for the success and happiness of any sentient being.

The reason that we are advised to begin our mediation on sympathetic joy by bringing to mind a very dear person is because these are people towards whom we are the least likely to feel envy. In a sense, envy and sympathetic joy share an object (the good of another); the difference lies in the attitude one has about that good. Buddhist ethicists are unusually perceptive in their acknowledgement that envy can creep into many relationships, even those with friends. For the untrained, there may be only a few people for whom contemplating their continued success does not provoke envy. Khenpo Ngawang Pelzang instructed, when in doubt, begin the meditation with one's own mother: 'Meditate on sympathetic joy. With regard to your attitude, we are all mother and child; it is impossible for a child to be jealous of its mother being happy, so rejoice' (2004: 172).

Equanimity

Equanimity (*upekkhā*, Tib. *btang snyoms*), the final Boundless Quality, is the freedom from habits of craving and aversion that create morally problematic partiality. It is also sometimes translated as 'impartiality', but I resist this translation since it connotes an intellectual perspective that one can take on (and off). Equanimity, like the other Boundless Qualities, is a way of being in the world that one cultivates over time and to which one habituates oneself. Like love, compassion, and sympathetic joy it has affective, cognitive, and connative aspects.

Buddhaghosa describes equanimity as a 'neutral' attitude towards all beings and claims that the function of equanimity is 'to see equality in all beings', which 'is manifested by quieting resentment and approval' (IX.96). The philosopher Vasubandhu's fourth-century commentary to the *Mahāyānasūtrālamkāra* (The Universal Vehicle Discourse Literature) defines equanimity as being 'free from addictions in the midst of (pleasant and unpleasant) experiences' (Thurman et al. 2004: 228). The ninth-century Indian scholar Kamalaśīla, whose work was very influential in Tibet, describes equanimity as simply 'eliminating attachment and hatred' (2001: 48). Tsongkhapa offers a similar definition: equanimity is 'an even-minded attitude, eliminating the bias which comes from attachment to some living beings and hostility to others' (2000: 36). The underlying theme of these definitions is a basic freedom with regard to one's own craving and aversion. Unlike the other Boundless Qualities, which have other sentient beings as their objects, the object of equanimity is oneself, or, more precisely, 'the attachment and aversion in one's own mind' (Pelzang 2004: 137; McRae 2013).

Many Buddhist ethicists insist that having equanimity does not mean being indifferent or uncaring towards others. According to Buddhaghosa, 'the equanimity of unknowing'—the dull ease one feels when one is ignorant of danger or the consequences of one's actions—is the 'near enemy' of equanimity (IX.101) and should be guarded against (Heim 2017). Patrul Rinpoche and Khenpo Ngawang Pelzang encourage a 'levelling up' approach to equanimity: by eliminating bias, equanimity is what allows one to have the 'same love for them [innumerable beings] as you do for your present parents' (Pelzang 2004: 198; McRae 2013). Pelzang claims that equanimity must be infused with love and compassion in order to be proper equanimity. An orientation towards love and compassion prevents one's equanimity from becoming what he and Patrul Rinpoche call 'mindless equanimity'—'just think[ing] of everybody, friends and enemies, as the same, without any particular feelings of compassion, hatred or whatever'—which brings no benefit (Patrul 1994: 198).

What Is the Relationship between the Boundless Qualities?

Although the Boundless Qualities are always presented as a set, it is not immediately obvious that they are mutually supportive or even compatible. Love, compassion, and sympathetic joy seem to require an emotional investment in particular others; equanimity seems to require an emotional detachment from them. Christopher Gowans has suggested that the *brahmavihāras*, with their inclusion of equanimity, are an explicit challenge to the ethical importance of personal relationships (see Gowans 2015: 193).

Although interpersonal relationships—and the assumptions and ways of thinking that usually go along with them—are often treated with considerable scepticism in South Asian Buddhism, this interpretation cannot accommodate the repeated warnings not to confuse equanimity with indifference and a lack or caring. Recall Patrul Rinpoche's warning of cultivating 'mindless' equanimity or Buddhaghosa's assertion that the near enemy of equanimity is indifference. These thinkers suggest that love, compassion, sympathetic joy, and equanimity are mutually supportive states.

One way in which equanimity and the other Boundless Qualities could be mutually supportive is suggested by Patrul Rinpoche's idea of equanimity as 'levelling up'. Equanimity, on this view, does not make us feel more detached from love ones, it makes us feel more invested in strangers and enemies; ideally, everyone is raised up to the level of the emotional investment that one has for one's family. Equanimity supports love, compassion, and joy by making them impartial, that is, not subject to the partiality that arises when we fail to monitor our craving and aversion. This is why Patrul Rinpoche suggests that we practise equanimity first, otherwise, he warns, our love, compassion, and sympathetic joy will be biased (and not, therefore, truly boundless) (Pelzang 2004: 195). Love, compassion, and joy support equanimity by preventing one's equanimity from becoming 'mindless', or turning into indifference.

To summarize, the four Boundless Qualities of love, compassion, sympathetic joy, and equanimity are complex moral psychological experiences with affective, cognitive, and connative components. They are deeply integrated and mutually supportive. Each is, in some form, a commonplace experience—as the metaphors of parenting imply—yet each can be expanded, through practice, to become boundless. Such practices often focus on overcoming the affective and cognitive obstacles to experiencing the Boundless Qualities. As we will see in the next section, the details of such practices reveal a nuanced and sophisticated understanding of human emotion and desire.

The Afflictions (*Kleśas*)

As is perhaps clear by now, one of the functions of the Boundless Qualities is to correct for and eventually help eliminate certain negative mental states. They are often defined in terms of the absence of these negative states, as, for example, in Patrul Rinpoche's definition of sympathetic joy as freedom from envy and equanimity as freedom from craving and aversion. Buddhaghosa sometimes treats the Boundless Qualities as antidotes for negative mental states: 'lovingkindness is the way to purity for one who has much ill will, compassion is that for one who has much cruelty, gladness is that for one who has much aversion (boredom), and equanimity is that for one who has much greed' (IX.108). These negative qualities of ill will, cruelty, boredom, and greed are examples of a class of mental states known as *kleśas* in Indo-Tibetan moral psychology.

The *kleśas* (Tib. *nyon smyongs*) are the negative mental states that cause suffering for ourselves and others. Sometimes translated as 'afflictions' or 'disturbing emotions', the *Great Tibetan Dictionary* (*bod kyi tshig mdzod chen mo*) defines them as: 'mental state[s] that afflict the body and mind with difficulty and fatigue and [make] one's being extremely ill at ease by inciting one to unwholesome actions'. Afflictions, then, have the following characteristics: (1) they afflict, that is, they are experienced as compelling negative states that we would not, in our better moments, choose; (2) they have physical and mental aspects; (3) they produce bad effects for self, such as fatigue and feeling ill at ease; and (4) they harm others by inciting unwholesome acts.

The afflictions are enumerated in several different ways in Buddhist moral psychology. The three core afflictions—also called the three root poisons—are attachment (*'dod chag*), hatred (*zhe stang*), and ignorance (*gti mug*). Tibetan Buddhist thinkers often refer to five central afflictions, which adds pride (*nga rgyal*) and envy (*phrag dog*) to the three poisons. The Abhidharma lists six main afflictions: the three root poisons plus pride, doubt, and wrong belief. It also contains a list of the more minor, subsidiary afflictions, of which there are twenty (including rage, resentment, spite, envy, laziness, distraction, forgetfulness, lethargy, and others). It is sometimes claimed that there are 84,000 different afflictive mental states!

The Causes of Affliction

The Abhidharma lists three causes of afflictive mental states. Vasubandhu, in his *Abhidharmakośa Bhāṣyam*, writes, 'Kleśas [with complete causes] arise from the non-abandoning of the latent tendencies (*anusayas, phra rgyas*), from the presence of their object, and from erroneous judgment' (V.34). Tsongkhapa, who uses a slightly different taxonomy of the causes of affliction, discusses Vasubandhu's first cause under the category of the 'basis' (*gzhi*) of an afflictive mental state, which he refers to as 'seeds left by afflictions to which [one] is previously habituated' (2000: 161).[3] Afflictions can, and usually do, become habit, and the psychological momentum of those habits provoke more afflictive experience. If afflictive response becomes very familiar, we may even seek out reasons to be afflicted, for example when one has a 'chip on his shoulder' and is looking for someone to knock it off. The basis of an afflictive experience is similar to what contemporary philosopher of emotion Amelie Rorty has called the 'magnetizing disposition', or the 'disposition to gravitate toward and to create conditions that spring other dispositions'. Like Tsongkhapa, she sees this as one of the main organizing forces in emotional life (1980: 106).

The second cause of the afflictive mental state is the 'object' (*yul*) of the affliction. Vasubandhu defines it as 'coming into contact with a provocative object (*nyon mongs skye ba'i yul nye bar gnas pa*)'. This is perhaps the clearest cause of afflictive experience, at least to the one who experiences it. Śāntideva points out that anger, for example, can

[3] Instead of discussing the object, the latent tendencies, and the unhelpful thinking, Tsongkhapa uses the categories of object, basis, and subject. There is, however, considerable overlap between Vasubhandu's causes and Tsongkhapa's.

be provoked by physical objects, such as physical assault (VI.43), and mental objects, such as humiliation (VI.52–54). Like other Buddhist ethicists, he tends to downplay this cause, not because it is less important than the others in terms of explaining the causal chain that led to afflictive experience, but because, as we will see in the next section, it is not helpful for the project of liberation from affliction to fixate on the object of our afflictive experience, as we usually do.

The third cause of afflictions is 'incorrect thinking or an unhelpful attitude (*tshul bzhin ma yin pa'i yid la byed pa*)'. Patrul Rinpoche tells the story of a beggar whose incorrect ways of thinking blossomed into a murderous (and ill-fated) envy:

> There was once a beggar who, as he was lying in the gateway of the royal palace, was thinking, 'I wish that the king would have his head cut off and I could take his place!'
> This thought was continually going round in his mind all night long. Towards the morning he fell asleep and while he was sleeping the king drove out in his carriage. One of the wheels rolled over the beggar's neck and cut off his head.

If we are not careful, Patrul Rinpoche warns, similarly ridiculous and violent thoughts can become objects of our own obsessive ruminations. 'Unless you remember the purpose of your quest for Dharma with mindfulness and vigilance, and watch your mind all the time, violent feelings of attachment and hatred can easily lead to the accumulation of very serious negative effects' (1994: 216). Quoting Geshe Shawopa, he warns, 'Do not rule over imaginary kingdoms of endlessly proliferating possibilities!' (216).

The focus on the intentionality of emotions in the Western philosophy of emotion has highlighted the ways the object can serve as a cause for that emotion but has also tended to obscure the roles of other causes. In Buddhist philosophy, however, the object is only one of three types of causes and not necessarily the primary one (McRae 2012a: 348–350). It is interestingly absent in the story about the beggar; the object of his envy, the king, is hardly mentioned and assumed not to be more than a trivial trigger of the beggar's envy. Yet the object is the cause that is usually the most obvious to the person who feels the affliction—for example, when I think 'I'm angry at you because you lied to me'. Here, your lying (the object of my anger) is assumed to be the sole cause of my anger. But the Buddhist analyses point out that afflictions such as anger have other causes; my anger at your lying is not only caused by your lying, but also by my tendency towards anger and, on the Buddhist view, my unhelpful and wrong-headed attitude about our situation. (Vasubhandu, and Tsongkhapa [2000: 160–161], imply that all three causes are present in the afflictive experience.)

Transformative Practices: Dealing with Affliction

There are myriad ways to deal with afflictive responses in Buddhist ethics. Buddhaghosa's discussion of love offers at least eleven ways to overcome resentment (a main obstacle to love), including finding a loveable quality of the resented one (IX.16–20), and giving him a thoughtful gift (IX.39). The Tibetan Buddhist tradition has an entire genre of texts and practices called *lo jong* (*blo sbyong*), or 'mind-trainings', that detail hundreds of specific practices for overcoming afflictive mental states. These practices often fall into one (or more) of the following categories of general approaches: (1) abandoning or preventing affliction by changing one's habits of thought; (2) exchanging them for (or transforming them into) positive mental states, particularly compassion; or (3) transforming them by 'taking them as the path' of moral-spiritual development.[4] In what follows I will give a brief example of each approach.

One method for abandoning afflictive emotions is to examine critically the assumptions that trigger the affliction and come to see these assumptions as unjustified or irrational. This approach intervenes in the third cause of affliction, incorrect thinking, and resembles some contemporary cognitive therapies. When dealing with hatred or anger, for example, we can reflect on the fact that we do not know all the conditions that caused another to act in the way that has provoked our anger or hatred. We may even come to see the other as lacking self-control over her harmful actions. Śāntideva, for example, writes:

> I feel no anger towards bile and the like, even though they cause intense suffering. What am I angry at the sentient? They too have reasons for their anger.
>
> As this sharp pain wells up, though unsought for, so, though unsought for, wrath wells up against one's will.
>
> A person does not get angry at will, having decided 'I shall get angry', nor does anger well up after deciding 'I shall well up'. (VI. 22–24)

In his commentary on this passage, Tsongkhapa writes, 'when bodhisattvas are hurt by others, they think "They do this because the demons of the afflictions have eliminated their ability to control themselves"' (2000: 161).[5] This radical shift in the way one cognizes one's situation helps reduce and eventually eliminate one's afflictive reaction. (The fact that anger subsides when we see it as unjustified has been noted by Western philosophers of emotion; see, e.g., Frye 1983.)

The second main approach to dealing with affliction is to exchange it for a positive mental state, especially if one is not able to abandon the affliction through reasoning and philosophical analysis. This practice draws on the idea, discussed above, that the Boundless Qualities are antidotes for the afflictions, not just in a general way, but rather in the sense that specific positive qualities act as correctives for specific afflictions. The Tibetan philosopher, physician, and yogin Gampopa (1070–1153)

[4] Some therapies for afflictive experience do not neatly fall into one of these categories, an example being Buddhaghosa's recommendation to give a gift to the one towards whom we feel resentment (IX.39). Other therapies may combine more than one approach listed above (see McRae 2015a).

[5] These passages introduce the interesting question of how it is that those who harm us through their anger are 'slaves' to their afflictions, yet we (readers of Śāntideva and Tsongkhapa) are expected to manage and even abandon our own afflictions, which implies that we have the freedom to do so. I have explored this puzzle elsewhere (McRae 2012b).

suggests the following antidotes for the afflictive mental states: ugliness, especially of the human body, as an antidote to attachment (especially lust); love as an antidote to hatred; meditation on the causally dependent nature of phenomena as an antidote to confusion or ignorance; equalization of self and other as an antidote to envy; and the practice of exchanging self and other as an antidote to pride (1998: 224–229). In Tsongkhapa's discussion of anger, he suggests cultivating compassion for those who wrong you since they are obviously mired in the suffering caused by their own affliction (2000: 166).

The third approach to dealing with afflictive mental states is by 'taking them as the path'. This approach includes many kinds of practices, but the underlying theme is using one's afflictive experience for one's moral and spiritual development: rather than trying to abandon it through analysis or exchange it for a more wholesome affective experience, one harnesses the power of the afflictive experience and uses it for good. The tenth-century Indian Buddhist philosopher Dharmarakṣita compares the bodhisattva who can transform afflictive experience by taking it as the path of enlightenment to the peacock who, unlike the other forest animals, can eat poisonous plants and not just survives, but thrives on them (Sopa 2001: 195; see McRae 2015b).

In an influential Tibetan mind-training text entitled *Seven-Point Mind Training*, the twelfth-century master Chekawa Yeshe Dorje presents sixty-four pithy therapeutic slogans that together offer a practical path of moral and spiritual development. In an explanation of one of the points entitled 'Taking Adverse Conditions onto the Path of Enlightenment', Se Chilbu Chokyi Gyaltsen (1121–1189) explains how we can use even afflictive experience for moral and spiritual growth:[6]

> Reflect, 'Since beginningless time I have failed to distinguish between enemies and friends, and as a result I have failed to recognize what is to be relinquished and what is to be adopted. I have erred, because whatever spiritual practices I may have pursued have all been endeavors of self- grasping ... Today I shall therefore differentiate enemies from friends ... Now my own self is the enemy, and sentient beings are the friends'. (Jinpa 2006: 98)

Here, Gyaltsen is suggesting that we use the enmity that typically have towards enemies and apply it to the real enemy—one's own clinging to self. We harness the energy and motivation of our enmity but apply it in such a way as to foster moral and spiritual development. Feeling frustrated? Apply that to your self-clinging rather than directing it towards others, Gyaltsen argues, since self-clinging is actually a more pernicious enemy than any other being could be.

All three approaches to afflictive experience are designed to fundamentally change our ways of thinking and feeling. But how effective are they? Psychologists have

[6] The original slogan by Dorje reads: 'When the world and its inhabitants boil with negativity, transform adverse conditions into the path of enlightenment. Banish all blames to the single source. Toward all beings contemplate their great kindness' (Jinpa 2006: 83).

recently become interested in testing whether various meditation practices, including some of the ones mentioned above, really have the transformative effects that Buddhist thinkers have claimed. The conclusions of these studies are mixed, as we might expect given that there are hundreds of Buddhist meditation practices.[7] Some studies of Buddhist compassion meditations suggest that they do increase one's capacity for compassion and one's ability to empathize (measured by face-reading), even when done for a short period of time (see Klimecki et al. 2013; Kristeller et al. 2005; see summary in Trautwein et al. 2013. For the face-reading studies see Mascaro et al. 2013 and Flanagan 2011: 43–49). It is not clear from these studies, though, whether there is a natural limit to our ability to feel compassion or if, with enough practice, the ability could be cultivated without limit, as Buddhist moral philosophers claim. Other studies suggest that some Buddhist contemplative practices, such as the contemplations on no-self, may actually increase the fear of death, the opposite response from the one such practices are designed to elicit (see Garfield et al. 2015). Clearly more research is needed to adequately access the psychological feasibility of various Buddhist self-cultivation practices.

Moral Perception, Imagination, and Attention

In summary, the theories of the Boundless Qualities and afflictions present a moral psychology that takes seriously emotional experience and its motivational, developmental, and epistemic significance. Two claims in particular stand out, not least because of the contrast they make with Western moral psychology: (1) we have choice in our emotional life—positive emotions and attitudes can be cultivated, negative ones can be abandoned, exchanged, or transformed; and (2) human beings have a boundless capacity for positive emotionality and mental states, which can be cultivated through intensive practice.

In the remainder of this chapter I explore another theme that emerges from this analysis: that Boundless Qualities enhance one's moral perception and afflictions obscure it. It follows as a corollary to these claims that one can, through practice, enhance one's moral perception.

Most basically, as an analogy to sense perception, moral perception refers to the direct and immediate recognition of moral facts or features. (The analogy with sense is perhaps especially apt in the Buddhist moral psychological tradition, according to which there are six senses, the usual five and a mental sense.) It is sometimes used to

[7] To complicate matters further, it is not always clear from the description or name of the meditation practice used in the studies what, if any, traditional meditation practice it is supposed to correspond to. See Lutz 2007.

refer to the ability to immediately recognize an act as wrong or right prior to or even in the absence of reasons. (This is what philosopher Charles Starkey [2006: 78] calls 'normative moral perception'.) Following Iris Murdoch, Lawrence Blum, and others, I will use moral perception in a broader sense as the ability to directly and immediately perceive the moral contours of one's situation, that is, what features of one's situation are morally salient, what moral weight they have, what are the obvious and subtle moral effects of one's thoughts or actions in this situation, and even the ability to see a situation as *moral*.

There is no lack of perception metaphors evoked in discussions of moral phenomena in Buddhist ethical texts. Just within the texts already quoted in this chapter, we have seen references to Asaṅga 'seeing' (or failing to see) Maitreya and the old woman 'seeing' the rotting corpse of a dog; Buddhaghosa's claim that love is what 'sees virtues', compassion 'sees helplessness of those overwhelmed by suffering', and equanimity is about 'seeing equality in beings'; and Patrul Rinpoche's advice to 'see all infinite beings as your own parents and children' (1994: 197–198) and his warning that a mind tainted with jealousy no longer sees the good in others (213). Many Buddhist moral meditation practices emphasize one's capacity to alter one's moral vision. As we have seen in the practices quoted in this chapter, it is not uncommon to be encouraged to imagine another being as one's own mother or child, to imagine the helplessness of an enemy, or to imagine one's own future suffering or happiness. These are commands to see other moral possibilities—that your enemy is actually suffering or your enemy is not actually out to get you, for example—and often rely on cultivating visual imagery, for instance trying to form a mental image of your enemy suffering.

These are not surprising observations; even introductions to Buddhist thought describe the Buddhist project as fundamentally about seeing things the way they really are (for examples, see Harvey 2011, Heim 2008, and Rahula 1959). It would not be surprising, then, that the Buddhist ethical project is centrally concerned with seeing the moral world as it really is. However, despite the ubiquity of perception metaphors and visual imagery in Buddhist ethical texts, little has been said about the role of moral perception in Buddhist ethics.

Indo-Tibetan Buddhist ethicists are deeply interested in the ways we see, or fail to see, morally. This is certainly true in the story of Asaṅga, which opened this chapter. It is clear that Asaṅga perceives the dog with maggots as worthy of moral concern and her suffering as having moral salience. His training in the Boundless Qualities gives him a moral sensitivity that most others lack, which causes him not only to act more altruistically but also to see the world differently and, as implied by the story, more accurately.

Asaṅga has perfected what Charles Starkey has called 'sympathetic moral perception'. Borrowing the concept from Iris Murdoch, sympathetic moral perception is seeing others not only accurately but 'justly and lovingly' (2006: 81). Murdoch argues that love just is an activity of attention, and, in general, much of moral life is about how and to what we choose to attend. 'Where virtue is concerned', she writes, 'we often apprehend more than we clearly understand and *grow by looking*' (1971: 30). Asaṅga, we could imagine Murdoch arguing, has a vision of Maitreya because he attends in a different way than the market-goers, or the old women; he attends lovingly and justly. He grew by looking. The Boundless Qualities can be understood just as a kind of moral attention, in the sense Murdoch has used: 'the idea of a just and loving gaze directed upon an individual reality'. This captures Buddhaghosa's notion that the four Boundless Qualities are 'four kinds of attention to beings' (*Atthasālinī* 195, Heim's translation [Heim 2017: 9 n. 60]). As the story of Asaṅga and the dog illustrates, this kind of charitable attention is, in Murdoch's words, 'the characteristic and proper mark of the active moral agent' and not at odds with accurate moral vision; on the contrary, it enhances it (1971: 33).

Murdoch, like many Buddhist ethicists, links the loving gaze to moral knowledge; 'Love', she writes, 'is the knowledge of the individual' (1971: 27). This is clearly one of the main points of Patrul Rinpoche's rendering of the story of Asaṅga and the dog: through his love and compassion for the dog, Asaṅga was able to clearly see the moral contours of his situation and gain moral knowledge, even wisdom. This moral knowledge fundamentally changes him—it is not a flash insight that soon disappears—and, it is implied, indicates a major spiritual transformation.

But how do love and compassion clarify our moral perception and lead to moral insight and spiritual transformation? As John Makransky has noted in his discussion of the *Ornament of the Mahāyāna Scriptures*, without boundless love, we are highly susceptible to opposing, deluded tendencies such as malice, jealousy, violence, and prejudice (2005). According to this text, 'boundless love destroys deluded tendencies ... It unravels the mind-made knot of deluded emotions' (17.19). The point here is not only that the Boundless Qualities leave no emotional space for destructive and delusional emotions. These qualities also can break those habits of thinking and feeling (that is, 'unravel the mind-made knots') that create, and cement, delusions. It is in this way that love and compassion can contain great insight. The Boundless Qualities help structure how we pay attention and what we pay attention to. They make us wise, at least in part, because of what they bring to our attention.

One of the most important things that the Boundless Qualities bring to our attention is the basic moral equality of members of the moral community. By moral equality, I simply mean the idea that we are all moral equals in the sense that we are equally deserving of basic respect and care. Moral equality is clearly at the heart of Buddhist conceptions of equanimity, which, in Buddhaghosa's words, involves 'see[ing] equality between beings'. But is also central to the other Boundless Qualities: love, compassion, and joy see the happiness, suffering, and success of others (respectively) as deserving as much attention as one's own happiness, suffering, and success.[8] To love someone or feel compassion when she suffers is to affirm her worth. It is to recognize her well-being as an end worth pursuing for its own sake. It directs attention away from 'me and my' to

8 For Patrul Rinpoche (and many other influential thinkers in the Tibetan traditions, such as Kamalaśīla and Tsongkhapa), the moral equality of beings is based on the equality in fundamental motivation (the desire for happiness and the wish to avoid suffering). See, for example, Patrul 1994: 196.

'you, us and ours'. By attending to another's well-being in this way, we can experience—on cognitive and affective levels—the moral equality of all members of the moral community. Our understanding of equality should not be just intellectual or 'merely conceptual', as Patrul Rinpoche would say; it must be integrated into all aspects of our psychology, including our affective responses. This is not to downplay the importance of rational reflection on the moral equality of others (as discussed in the next section), but rather to point to the significance of the *direct experience* of moral equality. By orienting our attention in certain ways, the Boundless Qualities make possible a direct, visceral experience of the moral equality of beings.

On the other hand, the so-called afflictive emotions, such as resentment, hatred, and envy, do not recognize the moral equality of others but habituate us to assuming a fundamental inequality between beings, which is one reason why they are morally dangerous. They often involve seeing ourselves as fundamentally more important, more real, or more deserving than others. When we feel envy, for example, we are not properly appreciating another's desire for happiness as fundamentally equal to our own. Feeling envy is also a sure sign that we are not paying attention to the complexities of human life, since the object of our envy has, most likely, a past largely unknown to us, and a completely unknown future. This uncertainty makes the ferocity and venom of envy seem extreme and unjustified. Other afflicted emotions, such as despondency, may undervalue (rather than overvalue) one's own well-being. Even spite may involve an undervaluing of oneself, as when a person 'cuts off her nose to spite her face'. Afflictions, then, prevent our recognition of moral equality by habituating us to an obsession with the self, experienced either as self-aggrandizement or self-neglect.

Buddhist ethics, then, can explain the psychology of moral failure in terms of failures of perception and attention: failing to see other beings as moral equals and failing to attend to their suffering and happiness. We can, for example, imagine some counter stories in which Asaṅga fails to see morally. Perhaps (1) Asaṅga walks by the dog and does not notice her because he is so absorbed in his own thoughts about his failure to have a vision of Maitreya. Or, (2) Asaṅga walks by the dog but does not feel compassion because he is overcome with fear and disgust. We could imagine, too, that (3) Asaṅga walks by the dog but does not feel compassion because of his belief that 'it is just a dog'.

In the first case, Asaṅga lacks moral perception in a basic way—he literally does not see the dog. This phenomenon is recorded in the Good Samaritan experiments in which it seemed that at least some of the participants failed to literally see the person in need, even as they stepped over the needy person to rush to their lecture (Darley and Bateson 1973). In the second case, Asaṅga does not fail to literally see the dog, but the dog's suffering fails to register because he is overwhelmed by his own fear and disgust. (Note that, in the original story, Asaṅga does feel disgust, but is not overwhelmed by it.) In the third case, Asaṅga both sees the dog and registers its suffering, but fails to see the suffering as having moral significance. All three failures, on the Buddhist view, are caused by afflictive mental states. All three are failures of moral perception and attention.

The Role of Philosophical Argument in Buddhist Moral Psychology

The focus on the moral perception and attention does not imply that moral reasoning or philosophical argument is of little importance in Indo-Tibetan Buddhist moral psychology. But it does suggest that Indo-Tibetan Buddhist ethicists have different ways of understanding the function of moral reasoning. What we do not see emphasized in Indo-Tibetan Buddhist ethics is a certain way of applying moral reasoning and philosophical argument that is typical of Western moral psychology: one is presented with a moral problem, which means one must decide what one ought to do; one thinks through the reasons for (or against) various actions by applying a principle (such as the Principle of Utility) or a test (such as the Categorical Imperative); and, if one has reasoned correctly, one comes to a correct judgment and (ideally) acts accordingly. This model of moral deliberation is certainly not universal among Western moral philosophers—David Hume and Adam Smith famously challenged it—but it is nevertheless influential in Western moral psychology, if only as a foil.

In Buddhist ethics moral philosophical reasoning is not typically offered as the standard model of deliberation from which one can make objective moral judgments. This is not because Indo-Tibetan ethicists explicitly reject the idea of moral deliberation, and it is not due to anti-rationalism or an anti-philosophy position in Indo-Tibetan Buddhist ethics. (They are not, as I see it, engaged in a kind of Humean project regarding moral judgment.) Rather, Buddhist ethicists tend to prioritize other moral problems, such as the problem of moral self-cultivation (how do I become a person who can act morally?) discussed above. Because of this self-cultivation orientation, moral philosophical arguments are typically employed to (1) counteract strong afflictive experience or (2) habituate oneself to hard-to-integrate moral realities.

When one is caught by a strong afflictive experience, such as anger or despondency, philosophical arguments are rehearsed as a method for freeing oneself from that affliction, as we saw in the example of Śāntideva's arguments against anger quoted previously. Many Buddhist moral philosophical arguments share with Hellenistic philosophers a tendency to offer therapeutic arguments, arguments that, in addition to being sound, need to actually reduce suffering to be considered successful (see Nussbaum 1994: ch. 1; McRae 2015a; and Burton 2010). These arguments, although morally significant, are not usually presented as ways to determine which action, among several possibilities, is the right one. They are offered as a way to reclaim the psychological freedom (from affliction) required to act morally.

Moral philosophical arguments are also used to habituate one to important moral positions that are difficult to integrate. They are offered as practices to be routinely employed to root out deeply held yet hard-to-pin-down wrong beliefs, such as the subtle ways we unfairly prioritize our own interests or assumptions about our own permanence or autonomy. Consider, for example, Śāntideva's argument for the equality of self and other (VIII.90–103):

> I should dispel the suffering others because it is suffering like my own suffering. I should help others too because of their nature as beings, which is like my own being. (VIII.94)
>
> When happiness is liked by me and others equally, what is so special about me that I strive after happiness only for myself? (95)
>
> When fear and suffering are disliked by me and others equally, what is so special about me that I protect myself and not the other? (96)

The argument from which these verses are excerpted forms a substantial part of Śāntideva's chapter on meditation. The argument is presented as a practice; it is not offered as a model for making a particular moral decision or even formulating a general rule of action (except, perhaps, for the general commitment to care about others' suffering). Rather, it is presented as a tool to gradually correct the warp in one's moral vision caused by conscious and subconscious wrong beliefs, most notably the belief that my happiness and suffering are more worthy of attention than the happiness and suffering of others.

One meditation practice in Buddhaghosa's *Path of Purification*—the practice of internalizing of equality of self and other, which he calls 'breaking down the barriers'—illustrates the difference between understanding the equality of beings as a spiritual or ethical practice and understanding it as a model of deliberation for determining right action.

> Suppose this person [who has broken down the barriers] is sitting in a place with a dear, a neutral, and a hostile person, himself being the fourth; then bandits come to him and say, 'Venerable sir, give us a bhikkhu [a monk]', and on being asked why, they answer, 'So that we may kill him and use the blood of his throat as an offering'; then if that bhikkhu thinks, 'Let him take this one, or this one', he has not broken down the barriers [between beings]. And also if he thinks, 'Let them take me but not these three', he has not broken down the barriers either. Why? Because he seeks the harm of him whom he wishes to be taken and seeks the welfare of the others only. But it is when he does not see a single one among the four people to be given to the bandits and he directs his mind impartially towards himself and towards those three people that he has broken down the barriers. (1956: 299)

What is interestingly absent, from the perspective of mainstream Western ethics, is the answer to the question: What *should* the bhikkhu do, then? This is the obvious question that arises if we think of equality practices as ways to model deliberation for right action. But, for Buddhaghosa, the thought experiment is not offered as an exercise in difficult moral deliberation, as such similarly structured thought experiments often are in Western ethics, but rather as a test to gauge the thoroughness of one's practice. He discusses this thought experiment in the context of developing a 'sign' indicating the level of one's meditation practice (IX.40, 43). In the context of the *Path of Purification*, contemplating the difficult situation of the bhikkhu is more useful in assessing the progress of one's own meditation practice than in answering the question, 'how ought one, morally, to act in this situation?'

Moral philosophical arguments are an important part of Buddhist ethics, but there is also an acknowledgement of the limitations of such arguments to make real and lasting change in one's habits of thinking, feeling, or acting. There is a recognition that one can genuinely assent to the conclusions of the argument without that conclusion being fully integrated into they way one feels, attends, imagines, and perceives. We can, according to this moral psychology, genuinely accept and profess the basic moral equality of self and other, for example, yet fail to express this 'commitment' in many of our actions, feelings, and desires. This anticipates (by over a thousand years) contemporary concerns about un-integrated ethical commitments and implicit bias, for example the cases of self-described egalitarians who demonstrate racist or sexist implicit bias when performing various tasks (Kelly and Roedder 2008). According to Indo-Tibetan moral psychology, moral failure and moral success is not only or even primarily dependent upon reasoning about moral concepts; the roles of emotional attunement, attention, perception, and imagination cannot be underestimated. Moral philosophical argument, then, works in service of the cultivation of the Boundless Qualities and the elimination of the afflictions.

Concluding Remarks

As I hope is now clear, Buddhist ethical texts are rich in moral psychological insights, too many to do justice to in this chapter. I located what I take to be two central categories of Buddhist moral psychology, the Boundless Qualities (*brahmavihāras*) and the afflictive mental states (*kleśas*). Taken together, the *brahmavihāra*s and *kleśa*s present a moral psychology that takes seriously the power and potential of positive and negative emotionality and encourages psychological freedom with regard with our mental states, including our emotions. Mental states, on this view, are cultivated, abandoned, transformed, and even exchanged for better ones. The *brahmavihāra*s and *kleśa*s are not only *not* categories of Western moral psychology, but they defy categorization into the Western moral psychological dichotomies of reason and emotion, cognitive and affective, body and mind, or agent and patient.

I have argued that one main motivating question of Buddhist moral psychology is 'How can I be the kind of person who can do and be good?' This orientation is remarkable because (from a Western perspective) it shifts the lines of moral inquiry in such a way as to make the question 'which action is the right one?' peripheral. The moral self-cultivation orientation in Buddhist ethics explains why moral philosophical argument is generally offered as a tool for that self-cultivation (either as ways to abandon afflictive experience or to habituate one to difficult moral truths) rather than as a model of moral deliberation.

Finally, I have presented Buddhist ethics as prioritizing the skills of moral perception and attention to explain both moral success and moral failure. Becoming a 'good person', the kind who can lovingly, justly, and genuinely respond to suffering, means becoming a person who can 'see' and attend to one's moral situation, particularly the (hard-to-integrate) fact of moral equality among members of the moral community. Afflictions, on the Buddhist view, are what obscure that perception and distract or dull that attention. Moral perception and attention is itself a trainable skill, as the practices for the cultivation of the *brahmavihāras* and the transformation of the *kleśas* show.

Works Cited

Batson, C. M., and Darley, J. D. (1973) 'From Jerusalem to Jericho': a study of situational and dispositional variables in helping behavior. *Journal of personality and social psychology*, 27, 100–108.

Blum, L. (1991) Moral perception and particularity. *Ethics*, 101 (4), 701–725.

Brewster, P. (1962) Solomon's judgment, Mahosadha, and the Hoei-kan-li. *Folklore studies*, 21, 236–240.

Buddhaghosa (1956) *The path of purification*. Translated by Bhikkhu Ñānamoli. Colombo: R. Semage.

Burton, D. (2010) Curing diseases of belief and desire: Buddhist philosophical therapy. In: J. Ganeri and C. Carlisle (eds), *Philosophy as therapeia*. Royal Institute of Philosophy supplement, 66. Cambridge: Cambridge University Press, 187–217.

Cozort, D. (2009) Suffering made sufferable: Śāntideva, Dzongkaba, and modern therapeutic approaches on suffering's silver lining. In: C. Prebish and J. Powers (eds), *Destroying Mara forever: Buddhist ethics essays in honor of Damien Keown*. Ithaca, NY: Snow Lion, 207–220.

Curtin, D., and Powers, J. (1994) Mothering: moral cultivation and feminist ethics. *Philosophy east & west*, 44 (1), 1–18.

Flanagan, O. (2011) *The bodhisattva's brain: Buddhism naturalized*. Cambridge, MA: MIT Press.

Frakes, C. (2007) Do the compassionate flourish? *Journal of Buddhist ethics*, 14, 99–122.

Frye, M. (1983) *The politics of reality*. Berkeley: The Crossing Press.

Gampopa (1998) *The jewel ornament of liberation*. Edited by A. K. Trinley Chodron. Translated by K. K. Gyaltsen Rinpoche. Ithaca, NY: Snow Lion.

Garfield, J. (2011) What is it like to be a bodhisattva? Moral phenomenology in Śāntideva's *Bodhicaryāvatāra*. Available from: http://www.smith.edu/philosophy/docs/garfield_bodhisattva.pdf [Accessed 20 October 2014].

Garfield, J. L., et al. (2015). Ego, egoism and the impact of religion on ethical experience: What a paradoxical consequence of Buddhist culture tells us about moral psychology. *Journal of ethics*, 19 (3), 293–304.

Gowans, C. (2015) *Buddhist moral philosophy: an introduction*. New York: Routledge.

Hadot, P. (1995) *Philosophy as a way of life*. Edited by A. Davidson. Translated by M. Chase. Malden, MA: Blackwell Publishing.

Hallisey, C. (1996) Ethical particularism in Theravada Buddhism. *Journal of Buddhist ethics*, 3, 32–43.

Harvey, P. (2011) An analysis of factors related to the *kusala/akusala* quality of actions in the Pali tradition. *Journal of the International Association of Buddhist Studies*, 33 (1–2), 175–209.

Heim, M. (2008) Buddhism on the emotions. In: J. Corrigan (ed.), *Oxford handbook of religion and emotion*. New York: Oxford University Press, 17–35.

Heim, M. (2017) Buddhaghosa on the phenomenology of love and compassion. In: J. Ganeri (ed.), *Oxford handbook of Indian philosophy*. New York: Oxford University Press.

Jinpa, T. (2006) *Mind training: the great collection*. Boston: Wisdom.

Kelly, D., and Roedder, E. (2008) Racial cognition and the ethics of implicit bias. *Philosophy compass*, 3 (3), 522–540.

Klimecki, O. M., et al. (2013) Functional neural plasticity and associated charges in positive affect after compassion training. *Cerebral cortex*, 23 (7), 1552–1561.

Kristeller, J. L., et al. (2005) Cultivating loving-kindness: a two stage model of the effects of meditation on empathy, compassion, and altruism. *Zygon*, 40 (2), 381–408.

Lutz, A., Dunne, J., and Davidson, R. (2007) Meditation and the neuroscience of consciousness: an introduction. In: P. D. Zelazo, M. Moscovitch, and E. Thompson (eds), *Cambridge handbook of consciousness*. Cambridge: Cambridge University Press, 499–551.

Maitreyanātha, and Āryāsaṅga (2004) *The universal vehicle discourse literature (Mahāyānasūtrālaṁkāra)*. Translated by R. Thurman. New York: Columbia University Press.

Makransky, J. (2005) No real protection without love and compassion. *Journal of Buddhist ethics*, 12, 25–36.

Mascaro J. S., et al. (2013) Compassion meditation enhances empathic accuracy and related neural activity. *Social cognitive affective neuroscience*, 8 (1), 48–55.

McRae, E. (2012a) Emotions, ethics and choice: lessons from Tsongkhapa. *Journal of Buddhist ethics*, 19, 344–369.

McRae, E. (2012b) A passionate Buddhist life. *Journal of religious ethics*, 40 (1), 99–121.

McRae, E. (2013) Equanimity and intimacy: a Buddhist-feminist approach to the elimination of bias. *Sophia*, 52 (3), 447–462.

McRae, E. (2015a) Buddhist therapies of the emotions and the psychology of moral improvement. *History of philosophy quarterly*, 32 (1), 101–122.

McRae, E. (2015b) Metabolizing anger: a tantric Buddhist solution to the problem of moral anger. *Philosophy east & west*, 65 (2), 466–484.

Murdoch, I. (1971) *The sovereignty of good*. New York: Routledge.

Nussbaum, M. (1994) *Therapy of desire: theory and practice in Hellenistic ethics*. Princeton, NJ: Princeton University Press.

Ohnuma, R. (2012) *Ties that bind: maternal imagery and discourse in Indian Buddhism*. New York: Oxford University Press.

Patrul (1994) *The words of my perfect teacher*. Translated by Padmakara Translation Group. San Francisco: Harper Collins.

Pelzang, K. N. (2004) *A guide to the words of my teacher*. Translated by Padmakara Translation Group. Boston: Shambhala.

Rahula, W. (1959) *What the Buddha taught*. New York: Grove Press.

Sopa, G. L. (2001) *Peacock in the poison grove: two Buddhist texts on training the mind*. Boston: Wisdom Publications.

Starkey, C. (2006) On the category of moral perception. *Social theory and practice*, 32 (1), 75–96.

Trautwein, F.-M., Naranjo, J. R., and Schmidt, S. (2013) Meditation effects in the social domain: self-other connectedness as a general mechanism? In: S. Schmidt and H.

Walsh (eds), *Meditation: neuroscientific approaches and philosophical implications.* New York: Springer, 175–198.
Tsongkhapa (2000) *The great treatise of the stages of the path to enlightenment.* Ithaca, NY: Snow Lion.

Suggested Reading

Flanagan, O. (2011) *The bodhisattva's brain: Buddhism naturalized.* Cambridge, MA: MIT Press.
Frakes, C. (2007) Do the compassionate flourish? *Journal of Buddhist ethics*, 14, 99–122.
Garfield, J. (2012) Mindfulness and ethics: attention, virtue and perfection. *Thai international journal of Buddhist studies*, 3, 1–24.
Gowans, C. (2015) *Buddhist moral philosophy: an introduction.* New York: Routledge.
Heim, M. (2008) Buddhism on the emotions. In: J. Corrigan (ed.), *Oxford handbook of religion and emotion.* New York: Oxford University Press, 17–35.
Murdoch, I. (1971) *The sovereignty of good.* New York: Routledge.

CHAPTER 18

ETHICS WITHOUT NORMS?

Buddhist Reductionism and the Logical Space of Reasons

DAN ARNOLD

Introduction: The Problem of Ethics without Selves

Buddhist thought has long resisted characterization in terms drawn from the modern Western discourse of ethics. This is, no doubt, largely because Buddhist philosophers are constitutively concerned to deny the reality of something that might reasonably be thought integral to the very idea of ethics; pretty much all of the positions taken by Indian Buddhist philosophers arguably follow from the doctrine that persons are 'without selves' (*anātmavāda*)—and it is reasonable to wonder whether there can be any robust conception of ethics if it is thought that the agents of ethically evaluable actions are not finally real.

Buddhists themselves well understood that this worry naturally arises given their characteristic refutation of the kind of *selves* that would seem to be necessary for making sense of such ethical ideas as (perhaps especially) justice. Buddhist philosophers significantly affirmed, in this regard, that their approach uniquely achieved a desirable 'middle way' that they took to circumvent this kind of worry. They affirmed that the Buddhist position eschews not only the extreme of *eternalism* (*śāśvatavāda*)—the view that there is something essentially unchanging that represents what persons 'really' are (which extreme it is clearly the point of the no-self doctrine to refute)—but also the extreme of *nihilism* or *eliminativism* (*ucchedavāda*). Significantly, the Buddhist concern to avoid the latter extreme seems invariably to find expression as a clearly *ethical* concern—as a concern, in particular, to retain and make sense of the doctrine (which Buddhists shared with most other Indian philosophers) that *action* (*karma*) invariably has ethical consequences in the form, especially, of the kind of life into which one is born. The Buddhist concern to avoid nihilism thus shows up as the concern that the no-self doctrine might entail the unintelligibility of the doctrines of *karma* and rebirth; it is particularly *ethical* nihilism that thus concerned Buddhists.

This concern comes through clearly in a quasi-canonical text that has long been favoured as a way to introduce the basic no-self doctrine: the Pāli *Milindapañha* ('Questions of Milinda'). This text famously stages a dialogue between the Bactrian Greek king Milinda (a historical figure the Greek form of whose name was Menander), and a Buddhist monk named Nāgasena. Nāgasena's teaching of the no-self doctrine is immediately launched by his introduction of himself to the king; for having told Milinda that his name is Nāgasena, the monk proceeds to say there is no real referent of the name 'Nāgasena', which term, he emphasizes, is 'only a generally understood term, a designation in common use. For there is no permanent individuality (no soul) involved in the matter' (Rhys Davids 1890: 41; see also Siderits 2007: 51). Thus introduced to the counter-intuitive claim of central concern to Buddhist philosophers, Milinda immediately raises what can only be characterized as *ethical* objections:

> If, most reverend Nāgasena, there be no permanent individuality (no soul) involved in the matter, who is it, pray, who gives to you members of the Order your robes and food and lodging and necessaries for the sick? Who is it who enjoys such things when given? Who is it who lives a life of righteousness? Who is it who devotes himself to meditation? Who is it who attains to the goal of the noble way, to an arhat's nirvāṇa? And who is it who destroys living creatures? who is it who takes what is not his own? who is it who lives an evil life of worldly lusts, who speaks lies, who drinks strong drink, who (in a word) commits any one of the five sins which work out their bitter fruit even in this life? If that be so there is neither merit nor demerit; there is neither doer nor causer of good or evil deeds; there is neither fruit nor result of good or evil karma. (Rhys Davids 1890: 41, slightly modified)

Milinda thus raises just the worries that make the very idea of Buddhist ethics seem counter-intuitive—and it is clear that in elaborating the cardinal Buddhist doctrine that persons are without selves (*anātma*), the figure of Nāgasena is chiefly concerned to show why the doctrine does not entail these ethically problematic consequences, which he clearly joins Milinda in thinking objectionable.

The Buddhist tradition well recognized, then, that its cardinal doctrine would be supposed by many to fly in the face of ordinary ethical intuitions, and was concerned from the start to argue that this kind of objection was misguided. Pretty much all Buddhist philosophers shared the conviction that their characteristic refutation of selves steered clear of the nihilism so vividly imagined by Milinda, and were confident that the intelligibility of ordinary ethical intuitions could be explained simply with reference to causal continuity. While it is true, they would thus argue, that there is a sense in which the person who committed some heinous crime on one occasion is not just the same person who stands trial for it a year later, it is also true, Buddhist philosophers characteristically emphasized, that the two person-stages are not altogether *different*, either; rather, there obtains a degree of causal continuity that makes it possible to maintain something like the basically *forensic* idea that the philosopher John Locke took to be most salient for the category 'persons'. (See Locke 1975: Book 2, ch. 27, sect. 26. The category of the 'person' is a vexed one in the Buddhist tradition, which almost unanimously condemned a 'personalist' [*pudgalavādin*] school of thought that affirmed the reality of 'persons' [*pudgala*] while accepting the tradition's orthodox refutation of the 'self' [*ātma*]. Nonetheless, I would argue that Nāgārjuna's Madhyamaka in fact has *pudgalavādin* tendencies.)

It is possible, Buddhist philosophers would thus urge, to be a reductionist with regard to selves and at the same time to think that human actions are ethically significant. That is why the Indian Buddhist philosopher Dharmakīrti, writing many hundreds of years after the literary dialogue between Milinda and Nāgasena, could argue that the main reason for epistemic confidence in the truths taught by the Buddhist tradition is that the Buddha exemplified a degree of compassion (*karuṇā*) so astonishing that it could only be based on his having seen how things really are (see Franco 1997; Arnold 2008; Taber 2003). Surely a tradition thus dedicated not only to maintaining our ordinary ethical intuitions, but also to venerating the singular compassion of a being taken to have acted with concern for the welfare of all sentient beings, is nothing if not an *ethical* tradition. What is the problem in making sense of that?

Causal Explanation and the Problem of Normativity

Among the problems in making sense of Buddhist ethics, I suggest, is the problem of *normativity*. While Buddhist philosophers had much to say, then, about how causal continuity can suffice to preserve typical ethical intuitions, I want to bring into view a rather different set of concerns relevant to the characterization of Buddhist ethics—a set of concerns that follows, to be sure, from the Buddhists' orienting commitment to the no-self doctrine, but that represents a different angle on the problem of Buddhist ethics than does the question of personal identity we have so far scouted. I have in mind, in particular, the question of whether Buddhists are in any position to make sense of the very idea of *reasons*—the question, in perhaps the predominant contemporary idiom, of whether Buddhist philosophers can account for *normativity*, which is surely an idea that figures centrally in the discourse of ethics.

That normativity presents something of a problem for Buddhist philosophers is a function of the particular significance, for most Buddhist philosophical projects, of *causal* explanation. Causation figures centrally in the 'deep grammar' of Buddhist thought; the flip side of the no-self doctrine is the doctrine of *dependent origination* (*pratītyasamutpāda*), which represents the Buddhist tradition's most general formulation of the kind of causal continuity that figures (we have noted) in explaining the apparent continuity of persons. Thus, the reason it makes sense for Buddhists to deny the reality of *selves* is that every moment of experience (of feeling, sensing, thinking, being) turns out upon analysis to depend upon a host of impersonal factors, none of which makes sense as what the event in question 'really' is. Much like philosopher David Hume, Buddhists thus typically held that 'when I enter most intimately into what I call myself, I always stumble on some particular perception or other'—without, that is, ever finding anything like my *self*. All that really exists, we ought therefore to conclude, is a 'bundle or collection of different perceptions, which succeed each other with an inconceivable rapidity, and are in a perpetual flux and movement' (Hume 1978: 252). And this is to say that every moment of experience depends, as Buddhists are wont to put it, on *causes and conditions*. Indeed, one famous statement of this idea came to figure across the Buddhist world as a *mantra*, an intrinsically powerful epitome of the whole Buddhist teaching: 'The Tathāgata explained the cause of those existents whose origination is due to causes, as well as that which is their cessation—the great renunciant is one whose doctrine is thus' (on this *mantra*, see Boucher 1991).

The characteristically Buddhist emphasis on reductionist, causal explanations is surely among the considerations that have led many contemporary philosophers and cognitive scientists to recognize Buddhists as philosophical fellow travellers; for many contemporary thinkers, too, have been strongly critical of all the vestiges of *essentialism* in Western philosophy, arguing in various ways that there is no really existent 'essence' of a human being—no real soul or Cartesian ego, only a series of momentary, sub-personal events (chiefly, for contemporary thinkers, *brain* events) that have productively yielded to the increasingly fine-grained analyses of cognitive scientists (of neurologists, psychologists, evolutionary biologists, and so on). There is, to be sure, a crucial difference between Buddhist reductionism and the varieties of reductionism that hold sway nowadays: reductionism is taken by many (if not most) contemporary thinkers to vindicate some kind of *physicalism* (some kind of view, that is, according to which everything there is to being a person must finally be explicable in terms of physical goings-on in a body and central nervous system); Buddhist reductionists, though, strenuously resisted physicalism, holding instead that mental events are distinct in kind from physical events and that moments of mind therefore cannot be causally dependent on the latter. (That mental events are irreducible to physical events is, indeed, the main point of Dharmakīrti's argument for rebirth. On the centrality of this difference from contemporary thinkers, considered in the context of more attention to the history of the 'Buddhism and science' meme, see Lopez 2012.)

Nevertheless, it is not wrong to see Buddhist reductionism as having significant affinities with some predominant trends in contemporary philosophy. Indeed, notwithstanding their own rejection of physicalism, Buddhist thinkers faced some of the same philosophical challenges that bedevil many contemporary philosophical projects. Many of these contemporary projects are commonly characterized as aiming to 'naturalize' the mind—as aiming, that is, to explain mental phenomena in the kinds of *causal* terms that are taken to be the hallmark of scientific explanation. And chief among the difficulties that persistently beset this kind of approach is to make sense of the eminently *normative* character of thinking (see De Caro and Macarthur 2010).

The normative character of thought consists in the fact that we recognize, of any belief or claim, that we could be wrong—that there is, in other words, a truth of the matter that is independent of whatever we happen to think, and that deliberative thinking thus aims at getting things right. This is the idea, as Kant emphasized, that in any particular case, there's some way we *ought* to think or act, often quite independent of how in fact we *do* think or act. And the problem this idea presents for proponents of exhaustively causal explanations is that it's hard to see how any considerations regarding what *ought* to be the case can figure as causes; what *causes* our behaviours, it seems, is just what *does* happen, not what ought to happen. As Kant put it, the problem is thus 'how the *ought*, which has never yet happened, can determine the activity of this being and can be the cause of actions whose effect is an appearance in the sensible world' (1997: 96). Making sense of this is a philosophical challenge that bedevils Buddhist reductionists and contemporary physicalists alike, insofar as proponents of both approaches are committed to reducing the normative character of thought to something essentially *non*-normative (such as the psychological dispositions or neurophysiological states that cause us to behave as we do). Such a reduction, I am suggesting, threatens to make some of our most basic ethical intuitions unintelligible—and an appreciation of this can give us some purchase on why Buddhist thought has persistently resisted characterization in terms of Western traditions of philosophical ethics. Before developing that point, though, it will be worthwhile to entertain a brief excursus on the problem of normativity as that was framed by Immanuel Kant; among other things, this will bring more sharply into focus the extent to which the issues we have so far scouted have everything to do with ethics.

Excursus: Kant's 'Moral Law' as Responsiveness to Reasons

The entire philosophical project of Immanuel Kant most basically concerned the question, *how is freedom possible?* What, that is, are the conditions of the possibility (of the *intelligibility*) of our experience of ourselves as reasonably held responsible for the lives we live? A good deal of what Kant says about this is in the highfalutin idiom of 'the moral law', and we are typically taught to associate Kant with *deontological* ethics—with a conception of ethics, that is, as centrally a matter of *duty*. (This way of framing things not coincidentally fits particularly well with theistic traditions of religious ethics.) This way of expressing Kant's ideas can, though, be helpfully demystified somewhat by saying that what Kant means by 'freedom' is really just the fact that we are *responsive to reasons as such*. (This framing of Kantian concerns figures prominently in McDowell 1996.) The fact that we are free, that is, consists in the distinctively human capacity to step back from the immediate perceptual present and ask, of any action or decision that has been or might be undertaken, whether it is as one *ought* to have done or to do.

This capacity is most basically evident whenever persons recognize demands for justification. When we are asked to *justify* any action or decision, we generally understand what is asked of us—we understand, that is, that what is demanded is not a causal explanation ('I did it because events in my central nervous system caused certain movements of my body'), but rather, *reasons* for thinking it right (or wrong) for having done as we did or as we aim to do. Over and above all of the various causal considerations relevant to human action, then, there are always logically distinct questions of how one *takes* oneself to have acted, and of whether that is as one *ought* to have done—questions essentially irreducible to questions of psychological or neurophysiological disposition. As long as such additional questions remain so much as intelligible, it can be said that we have in view a distinctively *human* phenomenon, which can, as such, be described in terms of freedom.

It remained for Kant an intractable question just how we are to reconcile the description of human persons as free in this way with also plausible descriptions of persons as consisting in material bodies subject to (among other things) the laws of physics. Kant could only conclude his *Critique of Pure Reason* by affirming that it is at least *coherently thinkable* that there is—as he put it in an unfortunate phrase that attests to the extent of his own enduring thralldom to the idea of causation—'causation through freedom'. We cannot, he supposed, ever explain just how it is that having a belief or a reason could, among other things, cause various movements of the body and so forth; we must be content with appreciating only that there is no contradiction entailed in nevertheless thinking ourselves free.

Kant did have, though, a stronger argument (albeit, a deceptively simple one) for thinking that the limits of our understanding of this cannot coherently be taken to count against the fact of freedom. What Kant adds to the conclusion he allows himself in the *Critique of Pure Reason*—adds, that is, to the conclusion that even though we may not understand how it works, we can without contradiction think that we are free—is the central argument of the *Critique of Practical Reason*, wherein he most basically argues just that reason *is* 'practical', which is to say that it is among the 'determining grounds of the will'. (As I would put it, this is the point that any complete account of human persons must include some reference to them as responsive to reasons.) Kant argues that anyone who would *deny* that reason is 'practical' in this sense—who would argue, say, that our responsiveness to reasons can finally be shown to be an epiphenomenal by-product of our neuro-evolutionary history (or in any other way explained away)—can make sense of anyone (even herself) as entertaining the truth of her proposal only by *arguing* for it. But that means, of course, that one must use *reasoning* to show that reason is not really practical; our responsiveness to reasons is necessarily exhibited, then, even by anyone who would deny its reality. To that extent, it cannot coherently be denied that reasoning has an ineliminable role to play in human behaviour. As Kant puts the point, 'if as pure reason it is really practical, it proves its reality and that of its concepts by what it does, and all subtle reasoning against the possibility of its being practical is futile' (1997: 3).

Moreover, as we most basically find ourselves responsive to reasons simply insofar as we understand questions about what we *ought* to do (or to have done), it makes sense for

Kant to have held that it is particularly as *moral* beings that we discover our capacities for reasoning. That it is, as Kant says, '*practical reason* which first poses to speculative reason' the possibility of our freedom—that practical reason has 'come in and forced this concept upon us'—can, then, very aptly be expressed as the claim that 'morality first discloses to us the concept of freedom' (1997: 27). We do not, in other words, have the idea of freedom because theoretical reason shows its possibility; indeed, the idea that we are free emerges only as eminently *problematic* from the perspective of theoretical reason. (That is why it has been possible for generations of philosophers to debate the question of whether we really are 'free', or whether instead some kind of deterministic picture must finally be right.) Rather, we always already find ourselves responsive to reasons just insofar as we understand the idea that there may be some way one *ought* to decide. And the idea that anything is as one *ought* to do surely has significant ethical implications—which is why Kant could reasonably say, of the fact that we are inexorably responsive to reasons regardless of the difficulty of theoretically *explaining* that, that 'the moral law thus determines that which speculative philosophy had to leave undetermined' (1997: 42).

The inexorable fact of our responsiveness to reasons as such means that regardless of what it seems our best theories recommend in this regard, if there is any conflict between our best theories and what it is that we manifestly *do* in entertaining (thinking about, arguing for, knowing the truth of) them, it is the latter—the incontrovertibly manifest fact that reason is 'practical'—to which we must defer. (As Kant puts the point, 'one cannot require pure practical reason to be subordinate to speculative reason and so reverse the order, since all interest is ultimately practical and even that of speculative reason is only conditional and is complete in practical use alone' [1997: 102].) If our theoretical reasoning seems to make that problematic—if, e.g., a theoretical perspective we are entertaining recommends the conclusion that we are *not* 'really' responsive to reasons, and that some causal explanation can account for everything about the illusion that we are—the conflict should be taken to count *against that theory*. It cannot coherently be thought that theoretical reason is to be privileged over practical reason, just insofar as it can only be *by practically engaging in reasoning* that any theoretical claim could in the first place be considered.

Dharmakīrti's Reduction of the 'Logical Space of Reasons'

The foregoing line of argument suggests what is reasonably thought problematic about such recently fashionable projects as 'neuroethics' (and neurotheology, neuroethics, and so on). Cognitive scientific research regarding characteristically ethical activity—research, for example, that shows altruistic behaviour to generate beneficial or pleasurable neurophysiological developments (see, e.g., Davis 2011)—may very well yield interesting and important knowledge about the biological beings we are; insofar, however, as such research can give us no purchase on questions of why or whether we *ought* to act in such ways, it cannot be *as* ethical activity that anything is in view in such studies. Rather, it is arguably just insofar as ethically significant activity will admit of characterization in essentially normative terms that it so much as counts *as ethical activity* in the first place—and that characterization drops out altogether when the angle of inquiry is exclusively empirical. (As Elizabeth Anscombe puts this, the idea of acting *intentionally* 'would not exist if our question "Why?" did not. It is not that certain things, namely the movements of humans, are for some undiscovered reason subject to the question "Why?"' Rather, she elaborates, 'the description of something as a human action could not occur prior to the existence of the question "Why?", simply as a kind of utterance by which we were *then* obscurely prompted to address the question' [2000: 83]. For a sophisticated attempt, though, to think through ethics in light of empirical work in the cognitive sciences, see Flanagan 2007.)

I have suggested that some Buddhist philosophers face the same problems in dealing with the normative character of thought that beset some contemporary reductionist approaches; it is now time to make good on that claim, which I will do with reference to perhaps the most influential of all Indian Buddhist philosophers: Dharmakīrti (*c.* 600–660 CE), whose works are studied to this day in most Tibetan monastic curricula. Dharmakīrti exemplified the kind of empiricist intuitions that privilege a supposedly immediate, nonconceptual kind of awareness—that privilege, in particular, *perception*, understood by Dharmakīrti as by many empiricists as just 'giving' us something whose reality is quite independent of our conceptions thereof, and thus as putting us in touch with something uniquely real. To that extent, some contemporary scholars have regarded him as vulnerable to the same line of critique that philosopher Wilfrid Sellars influentially levelled against what he called the 'myth of the given'. (On Dharmakīrti vis-à-vis Sellars, see Tillemans 2003: 97. The idea that Dharmakīrti is vulnerable to Sellars's critique is resisted in Dreyfus 1996, 2007.)

Among the problems with a view such as Dharmakīrti's, as Sellars influentially argued, is that bare, uninterpreted 'sensings' are not the kinds of things that figure in what Sellars called the 'logical space of reasons'. As Sellars explains, 'in characterizing an episode or a state as that of *knowing*, we are not giving an empirical description of that episode or state; we are placing it in the logical space of reasons, of justifying and being able to justify what one says' (1997: 76). To characterize someone as *knowing* anything is thus to characterize her not only as rightly *taking* things as thus-and-so, but as *responsible for* so taking things—and when anyone is called on to justify her so taking things, we understand that what is demanded is not an account of how she happens to have come to believe, but *reasons* for so believing. Given the empiricist's understanding of it, however, it seems that *perception* cannot give us any 'reasons' at all—which is just to say that perception cannot, on such an account, be thought to make any contribution to our knowledge.

Dharmakīrti faces just this problem because of the radically sharp distinction he draws between perception and conception. The gap between these bedevils

Dharmakīrti's entire project, and his attempt to bridge it, I now want to show, is among the points of his development of the famously elusive *apoha* ('exclusion') doctrine—the innovative version of nominalism that represents the Buddhist tradition's signal contribution to the philosophy of language. Against the many Brahmanical thinkers for whom *language* represents a realm of ultimately real things that are integral to the possibility of thought, Buddhists were commonly concerned to argue that linguistic items are fundamentally relative to varying and episodic human interests; for Buddhists, the linguistic order was generally to be understood as a product of psychology, rather than (as for many Brahmanical thinkers) the other way round. The Buddhist concern in this regard reflects, as well, the overriding preoccupation of Buddhist philosophers with the cardinal *no-self* doctrine; Buddhists can be said to have recognized that the kinds of abstractions that figure in the analysis of language are conceptually similar to the abstraction (of governing importance for Buddhists) that is a 'self'. Linguistic universals therefore should not be allowed into a final ontology for the same kinds of reasons that reference to *selves* does not belong in an ultimately true account of what there is. (On the recurrence of some Buddhist argument strategies in this regard, see Hayes 1988: 20–24.)

The point of the *apoha* doctrine, then, was to show how it is that language can work, even given that linguistic items are conceptual fictions that do not track any ultimately real features of the world. In its most basic form, the *apoha* doctrine affirms that the referents of words are not real universals (the word *cow* does not denote any really existent property such as *being a cow*, nor any really existent extension like *the set of all cows*); rather, the referent of a word like *cow* is finally to be understood simply by 'excluding' all *non*-cows. There is much to be said about how the specifics of this work, and about whether it can avoid the circularity that's evident in the foregoing thumbnail sketch; it is, among other things, reasonable to think that our excluding all *non*-cows makes sense only insofar as we already know what *cows* are. (On circularity objections to *apoha*, see Hugon 2011; on *apoha* more generally, see Siderits et al. 2011.) We will consider something of what Dharmakīrti says in this regard, but I want to stress that what is most important for our purposes is that the *apoha* doctrine can aptly be taken as showing that we are *not*, in fact, 'responsive to reasons as such'; rather, Dharmakīrti's view is that it is only under an altogether different description that what we think of as our 'reasons' for acting really have any explanatory significance. We can, in other words, understand Dharmakīrti's development of the famously elusive *apoha* doctrine as effectively denying (what Kant affirms) *that reason really is practical.*

Getting clear on this requires saying a bit about Dharmakīrti's characteristic understanding of the quintessentially Buddhist idea that there are two essentially different levels of 'truth': the world of *conventional* truth (in which our ordinary reference to things like 'selves' and 'persons' has a place), and the radically alternative, *ultimately* true description of reality as finally including no such things. In the Abhidharma traditions of Buddhist philosophy to which Dharmakīrti was heir, an ultimately true description of reality would involve reference only to the fleetingly existent events (called *dharma*s in this tradition) that alone are reckoned as *ultimately existent* (*paramārthasat*). (The difference, then, between a conventionally true description and the kind of redescription proposed by the Abhidharma traditions is roughly analogous to the difference between what Sellars referred to as the 'manifest image' of common sense, and scientific redescriptions thereof.) What is most significant about Dharmakīrti's appropriation of this idea is that he supposes that it is possible to specify just what kinds of things are *ultimately real*, and thus to affirm an ultimately true account of the world that differs fundamentally from the naïve picture affirmed as conventionally true. (It is, I will note in concluding, just this understanding of the two truths that proponents of the Madhyamaka school of thought reject.)

Dharmakīrti's basically empiricist orientation provides intuitively plausible support for this kind of picture. On Dharmakīrti's understanding of the two truths, *reasoning itself* is among the things to be characterized as just 'conventionally' real. This is as pretty much all Buddhists are apt to affirm, and it is so because the kinds of things (*conceptual* things) that figure in the logical space of reasons are, by Dharmakīrti's lights, paradigmatic of things that do not ultimately exist. There are no really existent properties like *being a cow* (or *being a mammal* or *being an animal*) over and above any of the particular critters that can be brought under such concepts—such abstractions do not 'exist' any more than there are real *selves* over and above the countless factors that constitute experience. What distinguishes Dharmakīrti's understanding of the two truths is his view that such things must therefore be finally explicable with reference only to ultimately real existents; the kinds of abstractions that figure in our ordinary practices of giving and asking for reasons are not really real, but it *is* possible, Dharmakīrti affirms, to specify something essentially more real that explains these things. (As we will see in concluding, though, for proponents of Madhyamaka the conventional status of reasoning does not amount to its having a deficient status.)

The essentially unreal kinds of things that figure in the content of our reasoning, then, are explained in terms of causally describable psychological processes that are themselves affirmed as *ultimately real*. Among the salient points about this is that it is thus only under a different, ultimately true description that our conventionally true 'reasons' really turn out to do anything—which is to say that the *content* of our reasoning need not finally figure in a total account of our acting, only the momentary mental states that 'have' this content. For Dharmakīrti, a philosophically motivated redescription of reasoning explains what that *really* consists in—which is what it means to say that for Dharmakīrti, we are not, at the end of the day, responsive to reasons *as such*.

Now, the fact that the kinds of things that figure in our ordinary practices of reasoning have a deficient sort of reality relative to the really existent mental events that explain them follows from Dharmakīrti's characteristic emphasis on *causal efficacy* as the criterion of the real. This is among the intuitively plausible ideas at the heart of empiricism; surely it makes sense to say that an abstraction like *being a tree* is not really real in anything like the way that *a particular tree* is, and that the difference is that in the latter case alone one can actually *do* something with the thing in question. (One can chop down a particular tree and use it for firewood or for building; one cannot interact with the concept *being a tree* in anything like the same way.) In our sensory perception of concrete particulars, that is, we actually come up against something in the world itself, something that impinges upon our sense faculties and directly *causes* us to be aware of it. When, in contrast, we entertain the idea that what thus impinges upon us can be understood as this or that (as suitable for a fire, or for building, or whatever), our own explanatory interests have become part of the mix. That there are innumerable ways in which we can find it convenient to *take* what is given in perception is evidence that our thought now floats free of the world in a way that the perceptually given particular did not.

So, Dharmakīrti held that the *perceptible* is to be understood as whatever can actually *cause* some appearing to awareness (it is not up to us just how some particular ruminant appears to us, but a function, rather, of objective conditions of lighting, proximity, and so on). In contrast, the kinds of things that figure in *conceptual* awareness are characterized, as Dharmakīrti says, by their 'lacking the capacity for projecting their nature directly into thought'. (I here cite Dharmakīrti's *Pramāṇaviniścaya*, as quoted and discussed in Arnold 2012: 25–26.) This prima facie plausible empiricist intuition about the difference between *perceptual* awareness and *conceptual* thought then provides the basis for an ontological claim—the claim, in particular, that 'ultimately existent' (*paramārthasat*) things are just those that can causally interact with other particulars (and that can, therefore, *produce* perceptual cognitions), whereas 'anything general, because of its being without suitability for causal efficacy, is not a real thing'. (I here cite Dharma-kīrti's *Pramāṇavārttika*, as quoted and discussed in Arnold 2012: 117.)

Owing, however, to the peculiar sharpness with which he thus distinguishes perceptual from conceptual awareness, Dharmakīrti is ever at pains to bridge the gap between these; the doctrine of *apoha*, as he elaborates it, can be understood as meant precisely to accomplish this task. Dharmakīrti elaborates the *apoha* doctrine to show how the kinds of things that figure in Sellars's 'logical space of reasons' can be explained given only the resources of an ontology according to which causally efficacious particulars alone are finally real. In terms of my guiding concerns, Dharmakīrti's point is thus to explain the *normativity* that characterizes reasons in terms of a finally non-normative, causal level of description. And the way he links these fundamentally different 'logical spaces' is by arguing that there is something intermediate between our initial, causal contact with the world and the conceptual judgments we are here trying to explain. In particular, perceptual contact with the world produces *mental representations* (akin to the 'sense data' posited by the classical British empiricists); and while these do not yet involve fully formed judgments—rather, these representations are *caused* by whatever impinges upon our senses, and they are, to that extent, themselves causally efficacious particulars—they are taken as the basis for the 'exclusions' (*apoha*) that Dharmakīrti takes to explain the construction of conceptual content. The strategy, in other words, is to argue that while the abstractions that figure in our practices of reasoning are not really real—things like *the truth of a claim* cannot explain anything just because such abstractions cannot *cause* anything—it can nevertheless be affirmed that it is 'the *things* ("mental states") that *have* these true or false contents that do the explaining' (Schueler 2003: 58).

The appeal to particular mental states or brain states as what *has* conceptual content represents, then, one way to argue that we are not responsive to reasons *as such*, and that reasons instead represent 'a determining ground of the will only as empirically conditioned'. On this sort of view, the conceptual content that is 'had' by any of these mental states turns out to be epiphenomenal; it is only *the mental states themselves* that are doing any explaining. Dharmakīrti makes just this move in emphasizing that (as Georges Dreyfus puts it) 'concepts as real mental events are to be distinguished from concepts as content' (2011: 217). Thus, while the conceptual content of our reasons is essentially unreal, the particular mental states that 'have' this content really do occur. That is why Dharmakīrti can suppose that mental representations—which he variously refers to as 'aspects' (*ākāra*), 'reflections' (*pratibimba*), and 'appearances' (*pratibhāsa*)—provide the necessary link between perceptual and conceptual content. These mental representations are themselves *particular* states or events that are causally produced by contact with perceptibles—and insofar as they are produced by perceptual encounters, these representations are themselves real, and must to that extent be distinguished from whatever semantic content they might be said to 'bear'. As Dharmakīrti's commentator Manorathanandin explains, 'Even a universal is admitted as being a particular insofar as it is the aspect (*ākāra*) of a cognition' (quoted in Arnold 2012: 135). The semantic content of concepts can only be available, that is, insofar as it shows up as the 'aspect' or content of some cognition—and as really occurrent, these mental aspects must themselves be causally describable particulars. That such representations seem to their subjects to be *about* something is a further, strictly *phenomenal* fact; only the occurrence of the particular representations really counts as real.

Insofar, however, as mental representations themselves thus count as particulars, we are still owed an account of how these can explain the normative, *conceptual* content that figures in the logical space of reasons; if, in other words, mental representations are genuinely perceptual, it remains to be seen how these get us any closer to the *conceptual* thought that we want to understand as somehow related to perception. This is the point of departure for Dharmakīrti's elaboration of the *apoha* doctrine. His idea is that while mental representations are not themselves concepts, they are the bases of the 'exclusions' (*apoha*) by means of which concepts are constructed; it is, then, as the bases of a conceptual process of 'exclusion' that mental representations are meant to bridge the gap. On one characteristically elliptical expression of the account he proposes, Dharmakīrti says that 'even though it is without basis for distinguishing the capacity of an external object, verbal expression (*śruti*) of what we perceive is connected to conceptual reflections (*vikalpa-pratibimba*) that are themselves based on that external object' (quoted in Arnold 2012: 136). That is, the names by which we refer to particulars are not themselves among the things produced by the 'capacity' (*śakti*)—that is, the causal efficacy—of the real objects supposedly referred to thereby (when one sees a stand of trees, those particular objects cause a mental representation, but they do not cause one to call them 'trees'); nevertheless, words are associated with 'conceptual reflections' that *are* themselves so produced.

The mental representations produced by our perceptions, Dharmakīrti thus argues, serve as links to universals insofar as the cognitions produced by objects—reckoned by Dharmakīrti as among the *effects* thereof—appear to a subject as similar to one another. To that extent, reference particularly to the 'object that appears in cognition' (*jñānapratibhāsiny arthe*) represents the point at which Dharmakīrti brings in the kind of 'sameness' in virtue of which (say) lots of distinct, particular ruminants can commonly be referred to as *cows*. While the particulars that are represented in cognition are in fact irreducibly unique, Dharmakīrti thus allows that there is at least *phenomenal* similarity in the mental representations thereof.

Dharmakīrti holds, though, that the strictly phenomenal similarity he thus allows is itself to be described in causal terms; in particular, what is 'excluded' from the range of things to which any concept refers is *all those particulars that do not produce the same effect*. As Dharmakīrti puts this, it is 'by virtue of having the same effects and causes' (*ekasādhyasādhanatayā*)—and by virtue, as well, of the latent dispositions (*vāsanā*) we have to imagine and exploit useful cognitive regularities—that distinct existents can and do fruitfully appear to cognition as exemplifying *kinds* of things. As Manorathanandin says to similar effect, 'There is not *really* any being the same, i.e., being one; rather, there is the similarity of being a single effect (*ekakāryatāsādṛśyam*).' (Dharmakīrti and Manorathanandin are both quoted here as cited and discussed in Arnold 2012: 137.)

Thus, what is *excluded* as not coming under any concept is all the particulars that do not produce the effect which is a *cognition* of the expected sort. To be sure, this appeal to the sameness of causal capacity may be thought tantamount to appeal to an alternative sort of *universal*; after all, one might rejoin that insofar as Dharmakīrti appeals to the idea that various particulars might commonly have the capacity to cause the same kind of cognition, *that causal capacity* counts as the shared property in virtue of which it makes sense to say there is some really existent *type*, after all. Anticipating this objection, Dharmakīrti stresses that the only 'sameness' that characterizes the concepts thus constructed attaches to the *judgments* that are caused by what is perceptually encountered in the course of using the concept; there is nothing really or 'ultimately' the same about the supposed referents of our concepts. This means, to be sure, that there is after all something invariant across uses of a concept; however, the relevant sameness is really not a property *of real things in the world*, but only of the perceptual judgments produced thereby. Dharmakīrti thus means to argue not only that the construction of *kinds* is relative to our explanatory or practical interests (what we exclude, when conceiving a *cow*, will vary depending on whether it is milk that is wanted, or manure for fuel), but also that the 'sameness' that constitutes the 'kinds' in question exists only (as it were) in our heads. There are, then, no real, mind-independent similarities that could warrant the idea that our concepts correspond to natural kinds; rather, there are only *phenomenal* similarities that guide our attention to particulars, facilitating our sorting of things in one way or another depending on our interests.

Dharmakīrti's Denial that We Are Responsive to Reasons

The foregoing sketch of one of Dharmakīrti's major philosophical contributions shows that there is a case to be made for thinking that Dharmakīrti is committed to denying that we really are responsive to reasons as such. He holds, rather, that everything of the sort that figures in Sellars's 'logical space of reasons' must be finally reducible to (or otherwise explained in terms of) the kinds of perceptible, causally efficacious particulars that alone count as ultimately real for Dharmakīrti. It is, then, only under a philosophically motivated redescription that what we think of as our 'reasons' really have any explanatory significance; all that is really *real* is the occurrence of particular, momentary mental events, which are misleadingly (if often usefully) taken by their subjects as representing a world populated not only by irreducibly unique particulars, but also by natural kinds (cows, mammals, animals, and so on).

What figures in our practical reasoning will, then, for Dharmakīrti admit of an altogether different description, one that he proposes as *ultimately true*. Insofar, though, as an ultimately true description makes reference, on Dharmakīrti's view, only to ultimately real existents—to, that is, unique particulars that are distinguished as such by their causal efficacy—that means that the only real *causation* that is happening here (the only real *explaining*) involves just the mental representations that Dharmakīrti posits to bridge the gap between the perceptual and the conceptual. That means, however, that the conceptual content that is 'had' by any of these mental states turns out to be epiphenomenal; it is only *the mental states themselves* that are doing any explaining, and the way these figure in what Dharmakīrti proposes as an ultimately true description is not at all the way in which they seem to us to work. This is what I mean in saying that Dharmakīrti denies (what Kant affirms) that reason really is 'practical': responsiveness to reasons need not, on an account such as Dharmakīrti's, finally figure in an exhaustive account of what there is and what we're like—it is, rather, only 'as empirically conditioned' (as occurring in a particular mental state) that anything to do with 'reasons' makes any difference.

That is just to deny, however, that we are responsive to reasons *as such*, and to affirm instead that this feature of human beings will admit of an altogether different description. And that, *pace* Kant, just is to deny that we are *free* in the way Kant thinks is necessarily presupposed by our ordinary ethical intuitions. (Note that my characterization in terms of 'responsiveness to reasons' represents a different way of talking about *freedom* than is in view when one invokes a criterion such as 'could have done otherwise'; attention to the latter criterion figures importantly in Meyers 2010, an excellent study of Indian Buddhist thought vis-à-vis contemporary discussions of free will.) To that extent, the commitments that find expression in Dharmakīrti's development of the *apoha* doctrine turn out, I suggest, to be eminently relevant to attempts at characterizing Buddhist ethics.

Recall, then, Kant's argument to the effect that 'morality first discloses to us the concept of freedom'—which is an argument, I said, to the effect that our responsiveness to reasons is inexorably exhibited just insofar as we understand what is asked of us whenever we are asked whether anything we have done or claimed is as we *ought* to have done or claimed. To say that 'morality first discloses to us the concept of freedom', then, is just to say that it is '*practical reason* which first poses to speculative reason' the possibility of our freedom, and that practical reason has thus 'come in and forced this concept upon us'. And if that is right, then for Dharmakīrti to deny that reason really *is* 'practical'—for him to argue, instead, that the conceptual items that figure in our ordinary practices of giving and asking for reasons will admit of being reduced to causally describable psychological processes—is effectively for him to deny that we have the idea of Kant's 'moral law'. It is to say, in other words, that the kinds of reason-exchanging practices that alone make ethical activity intelligible as such do not finally belong in a complete account of what is real.

And that, I am suggesting, is among the reasons why it makes sense that Buddhist thought might particularly resist characterization in terms of the categories of Western ethics. While there are, of course, many attested alternatives to the kind of deontological ethics typically associated with Kant, there is a case to be made for thinking Kant was nevertheless right to argue that most if not all other meta-ethics necessarily presuppose that we are responsive to reasons in the sense he aimed to characterize. This, I would argue, is why it is misleading to suppose (as many do) that a Kantian approach to ethics is antithetical to, say, neo-Aristotelian virtue ethics. Among the intuitions behind *virtue ethics*, I take it, is that human beings are so epistemically and psychologically complex that confidence in our rational capacities is misplaced; in the kinds of ethically challenging situations where real decision is called for, we are compellingly unlikely to respond only to the deliverances of reasoned deliberation. What matters most, therefore, is having cultivated the kinds of virtues (courage, generosity, honesty) that are apt to have *habituated* one to responding in ethically appropriate ways. Indeed, I would join those who argue that Buddhist ethics has particular affinities with virtue ethics, insofar as Buddhists, too, characteristically emphasize that spiritual progress consists in the 'cultivation' or 'actualization' (*bhāvanā*) of the truths taught by the tradition (see, e.g., Dreyfus 1995; Mrozik 2007).

The Kantian ethicist can, however, acknowledge this; indeed, Kant himself emphasized that we can never *know* even of ourselves whether we have acted ethically (whether, as he puts it, we have acted only in virtue of reasons or 'maxims' or whether instead we are to some extent under the influence of the heteronomous force of this or that psychological disposition). This concession can be taken to count against a Kantian approach only if one supposes that Kant is offering us an ethical *programme*—if, that is, what he says about the demands of the moral law is proposed as an exhortation to act in empirically achievable kinds of ways. On the reading I have sketched, though, that is the wrong way to think about what he is up to; rather than offering ethical instruction, the Kantian approach aims only to *characterize*, in strictly formal terms, the responsiveness to reasons (the *freedom*) that is necessarily integral to the very idea of ethics. His characterization of this, moreover, does not require that we can know whether we ever realize the freedom in question, or that we can ever be altogether free of all of the countless causal factors under which we are invariably constrained to act; the point, rather, is just that responsiveness to reasons is among the considerations that must figure in any complete account of human action—and indeed, that it is *the* one among these in virtue of which we can so much as have the idea of ethics in the first place.

Therefore, there is plenty of room for Kantian ethicists to attend to the important considerations that virtue ethicists emphasize. Conversely, there is much to be said for the view that many if not most alternative approaches to ethics inevitably presuppose something like the Kantian account I have sketched—for the view, that is, that it is only given responsiveness to reasons that anything at all could count *as* 'ethical' in the first place. (How, after all, is the neo-Aristotelian ethicist to decide *which* virtues it is most important to cultivate? While it may well be that only those who have habituated themselves to the appropriate virtues are apt to act ethically, surely it is only by *reasoning* that we can in the first place assess any claims about which virtues are most desirable, and why.) To the extent that it is thus right to suppose that many contemporary ethical theorists harbour something like the Kantian intuitions I have tried to develop, it is as we should expect that the very idea of 'Buddhist ethics' might seem strange—for there is reason to think that the very idea of *ethically* evaluable action is rendered unintelligible by any account, such as Dharmakīrti's, that denies that reason really *is* 'practical'.

Madhyamaka's Rejection of Causal Realism and the Recuperation of Reasons

Buddhist reductionists, I hope to have shown, face some of the same philosophical difficulties in accounting for normativity as do contemporary physicalists—and that, I have suggested, gives us some handle on the question of why the Buddhist tradition has proven resistant to characterization in terms of contemporary ethics. Central to most (if not all) conceptions of ethics is the idea of *reasons*; it is, as Kant put it, because we understand what is asked of us when we're asked *why* we have done as we have that 'morality first discloses to us the concept of freedom'—and it is arguably just because we have this idea that the very idea of ethical action is intelligible. But on a view such as Dharmakīrti's, this whole picture fails to correspond to anything real; everything about the space of reasons can, rather, be redescribed and explained with reference only to habituated psychological processes. The predominance of this idea in the Buddhist tradition gives us one angle on the question of why it has proven difficult to characterize Buddhist ethics.

I want to conclude, though, by emphasizing that Dharmakīrti's reductionism does not represent the only way to make philosophical sense of the Buddhist tradition's cardinal doctrine of no-self. Indeed, according to most Tibetan traditions of Buddhist thought, it is Madhyamaka that represents the definitive elaboration of the tradition's guiding insights—and Madhyamaka is to be understood chiefly as challenging precisely the kinds of philosophical intuitions that find such clear expression in Dharmakīrti. While Dharmakīrti follows his Ābhidharmika predecessors in affirming that it is possible to specify and characterize what is *ultimately existent*, Madhyamaka's guiding conviction is that this approach badly compromises the Buddhist tradition's most important idea; the ultimate truth, as Madhyamaka's main idea is often put, is rather that *there is no ultimate truth*. The upshot of this is to effect a dramatic recuperation of conventional truth; if it doesn't make sense to say there is anything essentially 'more real' than the world as conventionally described, then the latter is all we're left with. And one way to think about this recuperation of the conventional, I want to suggest in concluding, is as making room for a recovery of the idea of responsiveness to reasons. (For fuller elaborations of my reading of Madhyamaka, see Arnold 2005, 2010, 2012. On Madhyamaka specifically vis-à-vis ethics, see especially the essays in The Cowherds 2015, most of which focus on the specific case of the Mādhyamika thinker Śāntideva—on whom, see, as well, Bronwyn Finnigan in the present volume.)

The Madhyamaka tradition that begins with the philosophical works of Nāgārjuna directly challenges the characteristically Ābhidharmika view of the two truths that Dharmakīrti inherits. On a view like Dharmakīrti's, the world of ordinary common sense is credited with a deficient existential status—as finally superseded, that is, by an ultimately true description. The no-self doctrine, on such a view, is thus to be understood as affirming that we can specify what *really* exists in place of the kinds of things we typically take ourselves to be; there are no *selves*, but we can say that causally continuous series of momentary events really do exist.

The guiding conviction of Madhyamaka is that this picture does violence to the central insight of the Buddhist tradition—the insight, in particular, that all existents are dependently originated. One could suppose that the dependently originated, illusory sense of self is really *explained* by ultimately real existents only if the latter do not themselves admit of the same analysis—only, that is, if ultimately real existents are not themselves dependently originated. But the whole point was supposed to be that there *is* no exception to the rule that everything is so; the same analysis that shows *selves* not to be ultimately real should be taken to show, as well, that the kinds of things to which persons are reducible are not ultimately real, either. For Madhyamaka, there *is* no ontological bedrock, no point at which it makes sense to think that one has finally arrived at the real, mind-independent truth of the matter.

Chief among the reasons for this is that anything one could posit as ultimately existent will turn out, on analysis, to be intelligible only relative to the very phenomena it was posited to explain; nothing can coherently be conceived as being what it is quite independent of everything else. Supporting this intuition, the arguments advanced by Nāgārjuna invariably show, of all manner of categories that might be posited as explanatorily basic, that they turn out to make sense only relative to something else. The upshot of the consequent understanding of the two truths is to effect a recuperation of conventional truth; for chief among the ways in which explanatory categories are themselves relative is that they invariably turn out to make sense only relative to the very phenomena they were supposed to explain.

This can be briefly illustrated by considering a Mādhyamika treatment of *causation*, which is surely the most basic explanatory category for Buddhists. We have seen that causal efficacy, for Dharmakīrti, is the criterion of the ultimately real, and that everything about the common-sense picture of the world must therefore be reducible to causal transactions among momentary particulars. Madhyamaka's countervailing insight can be brought into view by considering a worry that Dharmakīrti himself anticipates with regard to causal explanation: How can one suppose that a causal redescription of one's ordinary perspective represents the real truth of the matter, when it is only *from* one's ordinary perspective that causal explanations can so much as be entertained? How, to put it another way, can it be supposed that causal explanations involve only ultimately real particulars when causation itself is accessible to us *only conceptually*? We cannot, as Hume famously argued, ever *perceive* 'the causation' that supposedly occurs in cases of causal relations; indeed, insofar as causal relations are constitutively sequential, reference to *memory* is necessarily involved in inferring these. Insofar, however, as reference to memory is, by Dharmakīrti's own lights, chief among the things that distinguish conceptual awareness from perceptual—perceiving something *as* a tree involves remembering past experience of the use of the word 'tree'—Dharmakīrti's own account of the privileged status of perception turns out, it seems, to depend upon precisely such epistemically deficient procedures as perception is supposedly privileged to lack.

Dharmakīrti is unfazed by the worry he thus anticipates, and he responds by blithely conceding the point; even though causation itself is only intelligible from the conventionally true perspective we are constrained to occupy, he thinks there is no problem in nevertheless invoking causal relations to explain that very perspective. Against this, Madhyamaka's guiding thought can be expressed as the insight that *Dharmakīrti cannot coherently concede this*. One cannot, in particular, grant that causation is only conventionally intelligible without also allowing all of the other things that are conventionally said about causation—which means allowing that causal relations obtain not only (as on Dharmakīrti's view) among unique, uninterpreted particulars, but rather, among the kinds of ordinary events that can be individuated only relative to the explanatory interests of persons. Insofar, though, as the explanatory interests of persons thus necessarily remain in play, it cannot coherently be thought that causal transactions represent something essentially *more real* than persons. Some reference to a *personal* level of description is necessarily evident, then, even in the arguments of someone who (like Dharmakīrti) would explain that level away. (On this problem, see Siderits 2009. Siderits is sanguine about the prospect of circumventing this difficulty, but the Mādhyamika conviction, I think, is that this problem counts decisively against reductionist accounts.)

The Mādhyamika's point in arguing this is not, however, to affirm (against the Buddhist tradition) that *selves* are, after all, real; the point, rather, is just that the conventional—which is to say contingent, relative, dependent—existence exhibited by the things of the common-sense view represents the only kind of 'existence' that anything *could* have. That persons are just *conventionally* real does not, if we take Madhyamaka's claims seriously, mean they enjoy an essentially deficient status relative to what 'really' exists. This point is nicely captured by Jay Garfield, who notes that the worry regarding specifically Mādhyamika ethics would seem to be the problem of whether 'ethical truths or injunctions can be binding on us if they are "only" conventionally true'. I concur with Garfield's sense of the right way to address this worry: 'Adding "conventionally" to any [of our ethical] claims appears to weaken their force and to render ethics insufficiently important. And of course, for any non-Mādhyamika, for whom there is a substantial *difference* between conventional and ultimate truth, this *would* be a weakener. On the other hand... for a Mādhyamika, for whom these truths are in an important sense *identical*, it is not' (2015: 77–78).

The Mādhyamika can still claim, then, that selves do not ultimately exist; it's just that this line of thought further emphasizes that that conclusion does not entail that there's something else that *does* so exist. While Madhyamaka thus affirms, with all Buddhists, that the conventionally experienced world does not exist the way we habitually think it does, this tradition of thought crucially adds that there is nothing it could look like to say is 'more real', i.e. that *does* exist that way. On the understanding I take Madhyamaka to advance, the theoretical positing of new kinds of *things* can never coherently be thought to tell us what we really are, for the finally simple reason that there *is*—indeed, that there *can be*—no such thing as 'what we really are'. It is possible, then, to be committed to the no-self doctrine, and yet to deny that this makes it necessary to explain what there really is instead of the selves we had thought there to be. Indeed, it is reasonable to think the Buddhist tradition had all along held that insistence on answering the question *what am I really?* is just the problem to be overcome by Buddhist practice.

Among the most dramatic ways in which Nāgārjuna clarifies the idea he is advancing is in the twenty-fourth chapter of his magnum opus, the *Mūlamadhyamakakārikā* (MMK). Having by that point in his text shown the failure of all manner of explanatory categories to withstand scrutiny—having shown, in his characteristic idiom, that they are all 'empty' (*śūnya*) of any essence (*svabhāva*)—he here anticipates what for him as a Buddhist would be the most important objection of all: If, his imagined interlocutor says, all these things are empty, it follows that the Four Noble Truths cannot obtain. Like nearly all the objections Nāgārjuna entertains, this worry mistakenly presupposes that for Nāgārjuna to have shown that everything is *empty* is to have shown that everything is *non-existent*—and clearly, if nothing at all *exists*, then the Four Noble Truths do not exist. Clarifying (as he recurrently does) that 'empty' does not mean 'non-existent', Nāgārjuna offers a compelling rejoinder: It is only *because* everything is empty that the Four Noble Truths make sense. This is so because for everything to exist *essentially*, Nāgārjuna emphasizes, would be for everything to be *unchanging*. It can, then, only be *because* nothing is individuated by an ultimately real essence—because nothing is what it is independently of everything else—that change is possible, and that anything at all can *happen*. And it is because change is possible that suffering, having arisen as a contingent phenomenon, can be ameliorated.

Everything about a Buddhist world view makes sense, Nāgārjuna thus argues, only insofar as absolutely everything is dependently originated—only insofar, that is, as everything exhibits the same contingent, relative status as the conventionally experienced world. Thus having shown that it cannot coherently be thought that there is anything essentially 'more real' than conventional truth, Nāgārjuna effects a profound recuperation of the whole level of description at which ordinary ethical intuitions make sense. While persons do not have enduring essences (do not have *selves*), persons remain as real as anything *can* be—remain, that is, contingently, relatively, *conventionally* real. (Here it should be noted that my expression of this point specifically vis-à-vis 'persons' is controversial; for my defence of a quasi-*pudgalavādin* reading of Madhyamaka, see Arnold [forthcoming].)

Chief among the reasons why Nāgārjuna could find it important thus to recuperate the world of conventional truth is that the ethical intuitions most central to Mahāyāna Buddhism—such as that the suffering of all sentient beings warrants compassionate attention—make sense only at the level of conventional truth. It is not causally continuous series of momentary *dharma*s that are the subjects and objects of compassion, it is *persons* that are. This is why it makes sense that proponents of this tradition characteristically affirmed that Madhyamaka can be rightly understood only by those who remain thoroughly grounded in compassion—a point that is emphasized in a great many Mādhyamika texts (see, e.g. the beginning of chapter 6 of Candrakīrti's *Madhyamakāvatāra*, in Huntington 1989: 157). Far from representing token deference to a standardly Mahāyāna commitment, this emphasis is meant to preclude the possibility of a nihilist understanding of Madhyamaka—meant to preclude, that is, just the worries that King Milinda raised in his dialogue with the monk Nāgasena. Proponents of Madhyamaka well understood that it would be shocking to hear that all *dharma*s are empty of any essence, and that there are therefore no ultimately existent phenomena. (The shock value of such expressions was surely part of the point, and was arguably meant to invite just the kinds of objections that gave Nāgārjuna the occasion to clarify his intent in MMK 24.) That this is not a nihilistic claim is clear, however, if one takes the truth of this claim as not just compatible with, but indeed as a *condition of the possibility of*, compassion. With compassion always in view, then, it becomes easier to see that Madhyamaka's claim is not that *nothing at all exists*, but rather that *there is nothing essentially more real than the conventionally experienced world*—given which, there is no other world than this for the exercise of a bodhisattva's compassion.

The characteristically Mādhyamika recuperation of the conventional, I want to suggest in concluding, can be understood as restoring a place for responsiveness to reasons. While Mādhyamikas do not put it this way themselves, it seems to me it would be a consistently Mādhyamika position to affirm, against Buddhists like Dharmakīrti, that while our practices of giving and asking for reasons are not, of course, ultimately real, that does not mean there must be something essentially more real that explains these practices. A Mādhyamika can consistently affirm, rather, that our ordinary ethical intuitions and all that they presuppose—persons who are the subjects and objects of compassion, reasons for preferring this course of action to that one—are, as contingently and relatively real, just as 'real' as anything can be.

If, then, consideration of a reductionist approach like Dharmakīrti's helps us see why Buddhist thought may represent an uneasy fit with Western ethical theories—helps us see, in particular, that some mainstream Buddhist philosophers were committed to denying that we really are responsive to reasons at all—consideration of Madhyamaka can help us see that the Buddhist tradition has alternative resources for making sense of ethical intuitions that are arguably threatened by Dharmakīrti's approach. As Buddhists, Mādhyamikas are just as committed to the no-self doctrine as Dharmakīrti, but the implications of that doctrine for ethics look totally different, I think, when it is understood (as Mādhyamikas urge) that the doctrine commits us only to denying that we are really *selves*, and not to affirming additionally that there is something else that we really are instead. Given such an understanding, the subject matter of ethical discourse remains untouched by the Buddhist tradition's self-denial, and it remains open to us to think there are distinctively ethical reasons for such things as practising compassion.

Works Cited

Anscombe, G. E. M. (2000) *Intention*. Second edition. Cambridge, MA: Harvard University Press.

Arnold, D. (2005) *Buddhists, brahmins, and belief: epistemology in south Asian philosophy of religion*. New York: Columbia University Press.

Arnold, D. (2008) Dharmakīrti's dualism: critical reflections on a Buddhist proof of rebirth. *Philosophy compass*, 3 (5), 1079–1096. DOI: 10.1111/j.1747-9991.2008.00175.x.

Arnold, D. (2010) Nāgārjuna's 'Middle Way': a non-eliminative understanding of selflessness. *Revue internationale de philosophie*, 64, 253 (3), 367–395.

Arnold, D. (2012) *Brains, buddhas, and believing: the problem of intentionality in classical Buddhist and cognitive-scientific philosophy of mind*. New York: Columbia University Press.

Arnold, D. (forthcoming) The sense Madhyamaka makes as a Buddhist position: reflections on a 'performativist account of the language of self'.

Boucher, D. (1991) The *Pratītyasamutpādagāthā* and its role in the medieval cult of the relics. *Journal of the International Association of Buddhist Studies*, 14, 1–27.

Carpenter, A. (2015) Persons keeping their *karma* together: the reasons for the *Pudgalavāda* in early Buddhism. In: K. Tanaka et al. (eds), *The moon points back*. New York: Oxford University Press, 1–44.

The Cowherds (2015) *Moonpaths: ethics and emptiness*. New York: Oxford University Press.

Davis, J. (2011) What feels right about right action? *Insight journal*. Available from: www.bcbs-dharma.org/article/what-feels-right-about-right-action/.

De Caro, M., and Macarthur, D. (eds) (2010) *Naturalism and normativity*. New York: Columbia University Press.

Dreyfus, G. (1995) Meditation as ethical activity. *Journal of Buddhist ethics*, 2, 28–54.

Dreyfus, G. (1996) Can the fool lead the blind? Perception and the given in Dharmakīrti's thought. *Journal of Indian philosophy*, 24, 209–229.

Dreyfus, G. (2007) Is perception intentional? In: B. Kellner et al. (eds), *Pramāṇakīrti: papers dedicated to Ernst Steinkellner on the occasion of his seventieth birthday*, Part I. Vienna: Arbeitskreis für tibetische und buddhistische Studien, Universität Wien, 95–113.

Dreyfus, G. (2011) Apoha as a naturalized account of concept formation. In: M. Siderits, T. J. F. Tillemans, and A. Chakrabarti (eds), *Apoha: Buddhist nominalism and human cognition*. New York: Columbia University Press, 207–227.

Flanagan, O. (2007) *The really hard problem: meaning in a material world*. Cambridge: The MIT Press.

Franco, E. (1997) *Dharmakīrti on compassion and rebirth*. Vienna: Arbeitskreis für tibetische und buddhistische Studien Universität Wien.

Garfield, J. (2015) Buddhist ethics in the context of conventional truth: path and transformation. In: The Cowherds, *Moonpaths: ethics and emptiness*. New York: Oxford University Press, 77–96.

Hayes, R. (1988) Principled atheism in the Buddhist scholastic tradition. *Journal of Indian philosophy*, 16, 5–28.

Hugon, P. (2011) Dharmakīrti's discussion of circularity. In: M. Siderits, T. J. F. Tillemans, and A. Chakrabarti (eds), *Apoha: Buddhist nominalism and human cognition*. New York: Columbia University Press, 109–124.

Hume, D. (1978) *A treatise of human nature*. Edited by L. A. Selby-Bigge. Second edition. Oxford: Clarendon Press.

Huntington, C. W., with Geshe Namgyal Wangchen (1989) *The emptiness of emptiness: an introduction to early Indian Mādhyamika*. Honolulu: University of Hawai'i Press.

Kant, I. (1997) *Critique of practical reason*. Translated by M. Gregor. Cambridge: Cambridge University Press.

Locke, J. (1975) *An essay concerning human understanding*. Edited by P. H. Nidditch. Oxford: Clarendon Press.

Lopez, D. S., Jr (2012) *The scientific Buddha: his short and happy life*. New Haven: Yale University Press.

McDowell, J. (1996) *Mind and world: with a new introduction*. Cambridge, MA: Harvard University Press.

Meyers, K. (2010) Freedom and self-control: free will in south Asian Buddhism. PhD diss., University of Chicago.

Mrozik, S. (2007) *Virtuous bodies: the physical dimensions of morality in Buddhist ethics*. New York: Oxford University Press.

Rhys Davids, T. W. (1890) *The questions of King Milinda*. Oxford: Clarendon Press.

Schueler, G. F. (2003) *Reasons and purposes: human rationality and the teleological explanation of action*. Oxford: Clarendon Press.

Sellars, W. (1997) *Empiricism and the philosophy of mind: with an introduction by Richard Rorty and a study guide by Robert Brandom*. Cambridge, MA: Harvard University Press.

Siderits, M. (2007) *Buddhism as philosophy: an introduction*. Indianapolis: Hackett.

Siderits, M. (2009) Is reductionism expressible? In: M. D'Amato (ed.), *Pointing at the moon: Buddhism, logic, analytic philosophy*. Oxford: Oxford University Press, 57–69.

Siderits, M., Tillemans, T., and Chakrabarti, A. (eds) (2011) *Apoha: Buddhist nominalism and human cognition*. New York: Columbia University Press.

Taber, J. (2003) Dharmakīrti against physicalism. *Journal of Indian philosophy*, 31, 479–502.

Tillemans, T. (2003) Metaphysics for Mādhyamikas. In: G. Dreyfus and S. McClintock (eds), *The Svātantrika-Prāsaṅgika distinction: what difference does a difference make?* Boston: Wisdom, 93–123.

Suggested Reading

Anscombe, G. E. M. (2000) *Intention*. Second edition. Cambridge, MA: Harvard University Press.

Arnold, D. (2010) Nāgārjuna's 'Middle Way': a non-eliminative understanding of selflessness. *Revue internationale de philosophie*, 64, 253 (3), 367–395.

The Cowherds (2015) *Moonpaths: ethics and emptiness*. New York: Oxford University Press.

Flanagan, O. (2011) *The Bodhisattva's brain: Buddhism naturalized*. Cambridge, MA: MIT Press.

Garfield, J. (2015) Ethics. Chapter 9 in *Engaging Buddhism: why it matters to philosophy*. New York: Oxford University Press, 278–317.

Heim, M. (2013) *The forerunner of all things: Buddhaghosa on mind, intention, and agency*. New York: Oxford University Press.

Kant, I. (1997) *Critique of practical reason*. Translated by M. Gregor. Cambridge: Cambridge University Press.

Siderits, M. (2007) Buddhist ethics. In *Buddhism as philosophy*. Indianapolis: Hackett, 69–84.

PART IV

BUDDHISM AND SOCIETY

CHAPTER 19

THE BUDDHIST JUST SOCIETY

PETER HARVEY

Introduction

The idea of a 'just' society is of one in which there is 'justice' in the distribution of resources and treatment of people. A key aspect of this is the idea of 'fairness' and a respect for individuals. While I know of no direct equivalent to the word 'justice' in Pāli or Sanskrit, it can be seen as one aspect of the meaning of *Dhamma/Dharma* in its sense of compassionate ethical norms that should guide the conduct of individuals and rulers.

Buddhism posits a basic equality of sentient beings as faced with suffering and in need of liberation. It also regards humans in particular as having a precious kind of rebirth with great potential for liberation in spite of their different karmic backgrounds. Respect for others is seen in the reflection, 'For a state that is not pleasing or delightful to me, how could I inflict that on another?' (SN V.353–354; Harvey 2000: 33–34). This is given as a reason for not inflicting wrong action or wrong speech on others. Other aspects of respect are discussed in Harvey 2000: 36–37.

The Justice of Economic Distribution

Russell Sizemore and Donald Swearer make the point that in Buddhism there is more concern with the mode of acquisition and use of wealth—that should respectively be ethical and generous (Harvey 2000: 187–192)—than on the question of the justice of its distribution (1990: 2). In Buddhism, moral virtue is seen to lead to wealth, and Sizemore and Swearer hold that wealth is seen as a result, and proof, of previous generosity (3–4).

Nevertheless, to help the poor is seen to generate good karma, and the receipt of such help will also be karmically deserved (12). Thus,

> when the doctrine of kammatic [i.e. based on karma] retribution is understood as an exceptionless moral explanation and justification for the present distribution of wealth and poverty in society, it undercuts moral criticism of the distribution per se. Consequently, Buddhists concerned with how to make their present society more just appeal not to a distribution of wealth corresponding more adequately to moral desert, but to the principles of non-attachment and virtues such as compassion and generosity. (12; see Ornatowski 1996)

Thus, 'There are norms for redistributing wealth and visions of the well-ordered society which serve as guides in criticizing existing social arrangements. These norms have primarily to do with the practice of giving, or *dāna*, and the appeal to the higher principle of non-attachment' (19).

While the above is in the main true to how many Buddhists think, it includes some unwarranted assumptions, at least as regards how true such readings are to the texts of early Buddhism. While those texts certainly hold that generosity leads to wealth as a karmic result, and stinginess leads to being poor (DN II.86, MN III.170–171, MN III.205), it is not said anywhere that these are the *only* causes of wealth or poverty. Indeed, the fact that it is said that karmic causes are only *one* among a variety of possible causes for illnesses (see pp. 21–22 in this volume) suggests that such a view would *not* be warranted in these texts. Thus while a person's wealth and poverty *may* be due to past karma, this is only one possibility. Thus, it is not right to assume that all poverty and wealth are karmically deserved. To assume that karma is an 'exceptionless moral explanation' is, indeed, to come close to karmic fatalism, which is not true to the original Buddhist vision. Thus, while appeals to generosity, non-attachment, and compassion certainly *are* key persuaders for Buddhists in working for a more just society, this need not be at odds with an appeal to justice per se. Mavis Fenn has pointed out that when the *Cakkavatti-sīhanāda Sutta* (see 'Political Ideals' section in this chapter) talks of the duty of a good ruler to prevent poverty, there is no reference to poverty being karmically deserved (1996: 102, 121; also, see Fenn 1991), and that a king reacting to poverty with sporadic personal giving is seen as ineffective: he must act more systematically and effectively by preventing poverty becoming systemic (Fenn 1996: 107). Moreover, this and the *Kūṭadanta Sutta* (see 'Duties of a Government Regarding the Economy and Welfare' section in this chapter) express 'views that correspond to simple notions of social justice—everyone should have sufficient resources to care for themselves and others, and to make religious life possible—and the notion that these values should be incorporated into the political system' (Fenn 1996: 108).

Nevertheless, ideas of distributive justice may be muted by the idea that at least some poverty and wealth is a result of karma. Moreover, at least in Theravāda lands, those who seek to persuade others of the legitimacy of their wealth do so by reference to some or all of: (a) the idea that it is due to their past karmically fruitful (or 'meritorious') actions; (b) that it was ethically made; and (c) that it is not the result of self-indulgent craving, by demonstrating present generosity (Reynolds 1990: 73). In fact, a rich person is seen as having a greater opportunity to do karmically fruitful actions by giving liberally to the *Saṅgha* and the community. As Phra Rājavaramuni, a noted Thai scholar-monk who is also known as Phra Payutto, says, 'A wealthy man can do much more either for the better or for the worse of the social good than a poor man ... acquiring wealth is acceptable if, at the same time, it promotes the well-being of a community or society' (1990: 45).

The philanthropy of the wealthy is thus an admired and encouraged quality in Buddhism. Nevertheless, Rājavaramuni holds that as long as wealth is used for the well-being of all members of society, 'it does not matter to whom it belongs, whether the individual, community or society' (1990: 53). Indeed, in modern times we see Buddhist ideas being drawn on to support socialism in Burma, capitalism in Thailand, and communism in China and Laos. Thus, while Buddhism has no central drive towards economic equality per se: (a) rulers have an obligation to seek to avoid poverty among their people, and (b) the well-off have an obligation to be generous to other members of the community.

While the *Saṅgha*'s relationship to the state has been typically one of 'cooperation and an amelioratory approach to social change, along with support for the status quo distribution of wealth' (Ornatowski 1996: 213), monasteries have themselves traditionally had a redistributive effect (Harvey 2000: 194–195, 204–206).

Also relevant are various 'Engaged Buddhism' movements, as discussed in this volume. These include: the Sarvōdaya Śramadāna village development movement in Sri Lanka (Harvey 2000: 225–234); the Santi Asoke movement in Thailand, which emphasizes a simple life, organic agriculture, and clear and low profit margins (Harvey 2013: 391–394); the social critic Sulak Sivaraksa in Thailand (Harvey 2000: 218–227); the Vietnamese Tiep Hien (Order of Interbeing) of Thich Nhat Hanh (Harvey 2013: 411–412); and the Sōka Gakkai offshoot of Japanese Nichiren Buddhism (Harvey 2013: 404–406).

Social Equality and Cohesion

The Buddha was no social revolutionary advocating the abolishment of all social divisions, but while he saw a person's class at birth as determined by past karma, he saw no obligation to stay within the limitations of this class if talent and energy lead elsewhere. He was critical of Brahmanical claims associated with the system of four supposedly divinely ordained social classes—the *varṇa*s of the so-called 'caste system'—that certain people were superior or inferior by birth (e.g. at DN I.119; DN III.81; MN II.83–90, 125–133, 147–157, 178–196; see Krishan 1986 for further discussion). He taught, 'Not by birth does one become an outcaste, not by birth does one become a brahmin. By (one's) action one becomes an outcaste, by (one's) action one becomes a brahmin' (Sn 136), appropriating the term 'brahmin' and changing its meaning to refer to a truly noble spiritual person, an *arahant*. He argued that the human race was one species, not four (Sn 594–656; MN II.196–197), that the social classes observable in society were not eternal, but had gradually evolved (DN III.93–95; Sn 648). A person is designated as a farmer, trader, thief, Brahmanical priestly celebrant, or king by the kind of work he does (Sn 612–619), people of different classes are equally capable of good and bad action, and gifts to a virtuous monk are of great fruit, no matter what class he comes from (SN I.98–99).

Admittedly, in Sri Lanka, due to Hindu influence, a sort of mild caste system developed. This mainly concerns who a person can eat with or marry, but it also, unfortunately, led to different monastic fraternities recruiting from different castes (Gombrich 1971: 294–317). It has also been the case that, in a number of Buddhist societies, such people as slaughterers, and, sometimes, fishermen, have been treated as social outcastes, due to their unwholesome way of life. Thailand has had a class of royalty and nobility, but of small proportions, due to a uniquely Thai feature: in each generation, the offspring of nobility are reduced in rank by one grade. For nineteenth-century Burma, Fielding Hall remarks, 'There was, and is, absolutely no aristocracy of any kind at all. The Burmese are a community of equals, in a sense that has probably never been known elsewhere' (1902: 54).

Buddhism greatly values social harmony and cohesion, as seen in the value placed on the four 'foundations of social unity' (Pāli *saṅgaha-vatthu*; Skt *sagraha-vastu*), as found in the *Sigālovāda Sutta*: giving (*dāna*); kindly speech (Pāli *piya-vācā*; Skt *priyavākya*); helpful action (Pāli *attha-cariyā* Skt *tathārthacaryā*); impartial treatment and equal participation (Pāli *samānattatā*; Skt *samānārthatā*), or even-mindedness to pleasure and pain (Skt *samāna-sukha-duḥkhatā*) (DN III.152, 232; AN II.32, 248; AN IV.218, 363; Mvs II.395; see Rājavaramuni, 1990: 36, 40 and Payutto 1993: 69–71).

The good of self and others is seen as inter-twined: 'How, monks, guarding oneself, does one guard others? By the pursuit, development and cultivation [of mindfulness]. . . . And how, monks, guarding others, does one guard oneself? By patience, harmlessness, a mind of lovingkindness, and sympathy' (SN V.169). The ideal is to treat all in a friendly way (Rājavaramuni 1990: 36), but close associations and friendships are best cultivated with good, rather than bad, people, so as to receive good influences, as well as being supported rather than exploited (Sn 259, DN II.185–187).

Right Action, Speech, and Livelihood

The Noble Eightfold Path includes three factors relating to ethical discipline (Pāli *sīla*, Skt *śīla*): right speech, right action, and right livelihood (MN I.301). Right action is defined as keeping three of the five lay precepts: avoiding intentional killing of any sentient being, stealing by theft or deception, and sexual misconduct. Right speech concerns not only the avoiding of lying, as in the fourth of the precepts, but also other aspects of harmful speech.

Speech is a powerful way of affecting other people's state of mind and well-being, as well as one's own, sending ripples through family, work context, and community and setting the tone for how people interact. MN III.48–49 gives four aspects of right speech, the first of which is truthful speech: 'Abandoning lying speech, he is one who abstains from lying speech, a truth-seeker, a bondsman to truth, trustworthy, dependable, no deceiver of the world.' Yet truth needs to be delivered sensitively, so that unblameworthy speech is 'spoken at the right time, in accordance with truth, gentle, purposeful, and with a friendly heart' (AN III.243–244). Hence the Buddha declared he only spoke what was timely, true, and spiritually beneficial—even if it was sometimes disagreeable to his hearers (MN I.395).

The second aspect of right speech is explained as follows:

> Abandoning divisive speech, he is one who abstains from divisive speech. Having heard something here, he is not one for repeating it elsewhere so as to divide people there from those here; or having heard something elsewhere, he is not one to repeat it here so as to divide people here from those there. In this way he is a reconciler of those who are divided, and a promoter of friendship. Harmony is his pleasure, harmony is his delight, harmony is his joy, harmony is the motive of his speech.

The third aspect of right speech is explained as:

> Abandoning harsh speech, he is one who abstains from harsh speech. Whatever speech is gentle, pleasing to the ear, and loveable, as goes to the heart, is courteous, desired by many, and agreeable to many: such speech does he utter.

Angry speech has the most obvious bad impact on others. Even hearing it directed at someone other than oneself tends to generate tension. If one gets angry when raising a problem with someone, their barriers will tend to go up so that they stop listening properly. One who slanders and uses harsh speech is said (Sn 657) to have a tongue like an axe: by its use, he causes himself much future suffering. Amongst other things, speech which is not harsh should be unhurried, otherwise 'the body tires and the thought suffers and the sound suffers and the throat is affected; the speech of one in a hurry is not clear and comprehensible' (MN III.234).

Finally, the fourth aspect of right speech is explained as:

> Abandoning frivolous chatter, he is one who abstains from frivolous chatter. He is a speaker at a right time, a speaker of fact, a purposeful speaker, a speaker on the *Dhamma*, a speaker on ethical discipline, he speaks words that are worth treasuring, with similes at the right time that are discriminating, purposeful.

Frivolous chatter is sometimes explained (SN V.355) as problematic due to its boring people. Indulging in it also makes it more difficult to calm the mind in meditation, as the mind tends to keep talking to itself. Hence this aspect of right speech is most important on a meditation retreat.

Right livelihood is one that is not dishonest or otherwise causing of suffering. Wrong livelihood is trade in: weapons (being an arms salesman), living beings (raising animals for slaughter),[1] meat (being a slaughterer, meat salesman, hunter, or fisherman), alcoholic drink, or poison (AN III.208). It is also seen as any mode of livelihood that is based on trickery, pressure tactics, or greed (MN III.75); hence it is said that in his past lives as a bodhisattva, the Buddha: 'earned his living by right livelihood: he was one who abstained from crooked ways such as cheating with weights, false metal and measure, taking bribes, deceiving and fraud and from such acts of violence as maiming, beating, binding, mugging and looting' (DN III.176). To have an eye on how to increase one's wealth is fine, but to be blind to ethical considerations, so as to do so 'with tricks, fraud and lies: worldly, purse-proud', is to be 'one-eyed' (AN I.129–130).

The Mahāyāna *Upāsaka-śīla Sūtra* adds that one should also avoid making nets or traps, dying silk, and tanning leather (T 24, 1488, 1048c02–08). The *Mahā-ratnakūṭa Sūtra* (T 11, 310, 312a29–b06) adds that:

> 10. A son of the Buddha should not horde swords, sticks, bows, or arrows, or do business with people who cheat others using false scales or measurements. He should not abuse a position of authority to appropriate others' property, nor restrict and sabotage others' success out of jealousy. Neither should he raise cats, foxes, pigs, or dogs. A bodhisattva who does so disgraces himself by committing a secondary offence.

In the modern context, a Buddhist might add others forms of wrong livelihood to the list (Whitmyer 1994). For example: doing experiments on animals; developing pesticides; working in the arms industry; and perhaps even working in advertising, to the extent that this is seen as encouraging greed, hatred, and delusion, or perverting the truth (Saddhatissa 1971: 52; Aitken 1984: 52).

The *Maṅgala Sutta* holds that a great blessing is 'work which is free from upset (*anākulā*)' (Sn 262), which of course can often arise from conflict amongst employees or between employees and employer. The *Sigālovāda Sutta* says that a person should look after servants and employees 'by arranging their work according to their strengths, by supplying them with food and wages, by looking after them when they are ill, by sharing delicacies with them and by letting them off work at the right time' (DN III.191). In response, they should be diligent, honest, and uphold their employer's reputation. The *Ārya-bodhisattva-gocara*, an early Mahāyāna text,[2] says that a good ruler should censure those: 'who do not properly share with their wife, children, servants, maids or workers; or who make the livelihood of others difficult through overworking them or asking them to perform degrading work', as this is 'wrong livelihood' (Jamspal 107b).

[1] Ven. Payutto sees this as including controlling prostitutes (1993: 61).

[2] Full title, *Bodhisattva gocara-upāya-viṣaya vikurvaṇa-nirdeśa Sūtra*, also known as the *Ārya-satyaka-parivarta*. Jamspal holds that it was composed some time between the second century BCE and the first century CE. References are to the Tibetan pagination as indicated in the translation.

Political Ideals

Several texts outline an ideal for a Buddhist ruler to follow so as to ensure a peaceful and harmonious society (cf. Saddhatissa 1970: 149–164). The Buddha had an admiration for some of the tribal republics of his day. At one time, he said that the Vajjian republic would flourish if the people continued to:

> hold regular and frequent assemblies ... meet in harmony, break up in harmony, and carry out business in harmony ... not authorise what has not been authorised, but proceed according to what has been authorised by their ancient tradition ... honour, respect, revere and salute the elders among them, and consider them worth listening to ... not forcibly abduct others' wives and daughters and compel them to live with them ... honour, respect, revere and salute the Vajjian shrines at home and abroad, not withdrawing the proper support made and given before ... make proper provision for the safety of *Arahants*, so that such *Arahants* may come in future to live there, and those already there may dwell in comfort. (DN II.73–75)

One can see these as the principles of respecting collective decision-making, concord, tradition, elders, women, religion, and holy men and women. The importance of these social principles was such that the Buddha saw them, or adapted versions of them, as ensuring the flourishing of the monastic *Saṅgha*. Nevertheless, he could see that the days of the tribal republics were numbered, as they were gradually being swallowed up by new, expanding kingdoms. Indeed, he saw the falling away from the above principles as the thing that would allow their being overwhelmed by these kingdoms.

The Buddha also had views on kingship: the role of a king was to serve his people by ensuring order and prosperity for them. The *Aggañña Sutta* (DN II.80–98; Collins 1998: 448–451) describes the origins of human society as part of a process of moral decline from relatively ideal conditions at the start of a cycle of world evolution (Fenn 1996: 111–117). Here, the first king is said to have been chosen by his people—as the most handsome, pleasant, and capable—to punish wrongdoers, in return for a share of the people's rice (DN III.92). This can be seen as a kind of 'social contract' theory of kingship. Opposing the Hindu idea of divine kingship, Candrakīrti later argued: 'The first king was created by his own action and the people, not by the Almighty One. A king is the same as a common person in lineage and in nature' (*Ṭīkā* [Derge Tengyur fol.75a] on Āryadeva's *Bodhisattva-yogācāra-catuḥśātaka*, cited by Jamspal at xxxi).

The Buddha's advice on how best to run society was often couched in terms of ideal legendary rulers known as *Cakkavatti* (Pāli; Skt *Cakravartin*), or 'Wheel Turning' kings, whose ethical, compassionate rule is said to have caused a divine wheel to appear in the sky. In the *Cakkavatti-sīhanāda Sutta* (DN III.58–79),[3] the duties of such a ruler are that

[3] See: Saddhatissa 1970: 154–157, 159–160; Collins 1998: 480–496; Fenn 1996: 100–108; Reynolds and Reynolds 1982: 135–72 gives a developed Theravāda view on *Cakkavatti*s.

he should revere *Dhamma* and rule only in accordance with it. He should: look after all his people, and also animals and birds; prevent crime and give to those in need; and consult monks and brahmins regarding what are wholesome or unwholesome actions (DN III.61; Rājavaramuni 1990: 38–39). B. G. Gokhale says that the key contribution of Buddhism to Indian political theory was 'the acceptance of a higher morality as the guiding spirit behind the state'.[4]

In the *Jātaka* stories, the Bodhisattva teaches the ten duties of a true king (*rāja-dhammas*): generosity, ethical discipline, self-sacrifice, honesty and integrity, gentleness, self-control, non-anger, non-injury, forbearance, and non-opposition/uprightness (e.g. Jat III.274 and Jat V.378). In the *Mahāvastu* (I.274–277), a Lokottaravāda text, advice to a king includes: do not fall under the power of anger; be impartial in arbitrating disputes; do not be indulgent in sensual pleasures; admit large bodies of immigrants; favour the poor and protect the rich; cultivate ties of friendship with neighbouring kings; act ethically; and be circumspect, and diligent in the care of the treasury and granary.

It is said that when kings act unethically (*adhammika*), this bad example spreads through the various groups of their people. Hence the seasons go awry, and gods are annoyed so as to bring about bad weather, crops are poor, and the humans who live on them are weak and short-lived (AN II.74–76; see Reynolds and Reynolds 1982, 153 and Jamspal 111a–b). That is, a king is seen to have a responsibility to maintain, through his actions and influence, the moral fabric of society and nature (cf. Payutto 1993: 63–68). Stanley Tambiah refers to this as the 'multiplier-effect' of kingship on the conduct of the rest of society (1976: 50), such that it is acceptable to unseat an unworthy king. In one *Jātaka* story (Jat III.502–514), a king who is a thief is overthrown.

In Buddhist history, the Indian emperor Aśoka (*c.*268–239 BCE) is particularly revered as a great example of a Buddhist ruler who sought to live up to the *Cakkavatti* ideal, though he never actually claimed to be one himself.[5] The Magadhan empire, which he inherited, was the largest India was to see until its conquest by the British, and included most of modern India except the far south. An important source of knowledge on Aśoka are the many edicts which he had published by having them carved on rocks and stone pillars (see Nikam and McKeon 1959; Dhammika 1993; and Gurugé 1993). In the Sixth Rock Edict, he expressed his aspiration thus: 'No task is more important to me than promoting the well-being of all the people. Such work as I accomplish contributes to discharging the debt I owe to all living creatures to make them happy in this world and to help them attain heaven in the next' (Nikam and McKeon 1959: 38). Aśoka inaugurated various public works: wells, rest houses, and trees for both shade and fruit for travellers; and medical herbs and roots for humans and animals. Such measures were also fostered

[4] Gokhale 1996: 22. See Tambiah 1976: 9–53 on early Buddhist ideas of kingship; 39–53 on the *Cakkavatti* ideal. On the latter, see also Obeyesekere and Reynolds 1972, which also deals with ideas of kingship and social order in Sri Lanka.

[5] He came to be seen as a *Cakkavatti*, however (*Divyāvadāna*, Vaidya edition, 1958: 239). On Aśoka, see: Ling, 1973: 151–174; Basham 1982; Swearer 1995: 64–66. For the later Theravāda view of Aśoka, see Reynolds and Reynolds 1982: 172–189.

in Indian regions beyond his actual empire, by what must have been early 'foreign aid' measures (Nikam and McKeon 1959: 64–65). He exhorted his people to live by moral norms, particularly nonviolence, himself abandoning his forebears' custom of violent expansion of their realm. He also gave up hunting, gradually became vegetarian, and passed various animal welfare laws. Though he was personally a Buddhist, and ruled in accordance with Buddhist ethics, he did not make Buddhism the state religion, and urged mutual religious tolerance and respect. He not only supported Buddhist monks and nuns, but also brahmin priests, Jain monks and nuns, and ascetics of other religious sects. His Twelfth Rock Edict says:

> King Priyadarśī honors men of all faiths, members of religious orders and laymen alike, with gifts and various marks of esteem. Yet he does not value either gifts or honors as much as growth in the qualities essential to religion in men of all faiths.
>
> This growth may take many forms, but its root is in guarding one's speech to avoid extolling one's own faith and disparaging the faith of others improperly or, when the occasion is appropriate, immoderately.
>
> The faiths of others all deserve to be honored for one reason or another. By honoring them, one exalts one's own faith and at the same time performs a service to the faith of others. By acting otherwise, one injures one's own faith and also does disservice to that of others. For if a man extols his own faith and disparages another because of devotion to his own and because he wants to glorify it, he seriously injures his own faith.
>
> Therefore concord alone is commendable, for through concord men may learn and respect the conception of Dharma accepted by others.
>
> King Priyadarśī desires men of all faiths to know each other's doctrines and to acquire sound doctrines. (Nikam and McKeon 1959: 51–52)

The spirit of the above is in tune with modern emphases on respect for diversity, and multiculturalism.

To varying extents, many Buddhist rulers have sought to follow such ideals and examples, though sometimes they only went in for a 'self-serving proclamation' to this effect (Tambiah 1976: 226). In Sri Lanka, the king came to be seen, from at least the tenth century, as the lay head of Buddhism, its protector, and as a bodhisattva, with the idea that 'The king is a *bodhisattva* on whom the sangha bestows kingship in order that he may defend the bowl and robe' (Tambiah 1976: 97). Kings of the Pagan period (1084–1167) in Burma came to see themselves as *Cakkavatti*s and bodhisattvas (Tambiah 1976: 81). In Thailand too, in Sukhothai and Ayutthaya times (fourteenth–eighteenth centuries), and into the nineteenth century, kings were seen in these terms and sometimes identified themselves with the Bodhisattva Metteyya, who will be the next buddha on earth (Tambiah 1976: 96–97). They have also been expected to follow the above ten duties of a king and the twelve duties of the *Cakkavatti*. Nevertheless, as elsewhere: 'The heads of kings rolled frequently because succession rules were vague, rebellions endemic, the overall political scaffolding fragile, and the territorial limits expanding and contracting with the military fortunes of the ruler, his subordinate chiefs, and his rivals' (Tambiah

1976: 482). On the other hand, one of the advantages that Chinese emperors saw in Buddhism was that its nonviolent emphasis discouraged rebellions.

Where Buddhism has been the dominant religion:

> Kingship as the crux of order in society provides the conditions and the context for the survival of the *sasana* (religion). They need each other: religion in being supported by an ordered and prosperous society is able to act as a 'field of merit [karmic fruitfulness]' in which merit making can be enacted and its fruits enjoyed, while the king as the foremost merit maker needs the sangha to make and realize his merit and fulfil his kingship. (Tambiah 1976: 41)

While monks are generally expected to keep aloof from overt political activity, this is not always the case. In modern times, in Tibet, monks and nuns have been active in demonstrations against the Chinese Communist colonization of the country. In Burma, monks have sometimes led the populace in demonstrations against the corrupt military regime that has only recently been open to democratic reforms; some monks have, though, also encouraged repressive measures against the Muslim Rohingya minority. In Sri Lanka, monks have publicly voiced their allegiance to particular political parties—though the laity often see this as inappropriate for them.

Attitudes to Democracy

Many of the above ideals can also be applied to rule by an elected government, and Buddhist values are open to democratic rule. Indeed, within the monastic *Saṅgha*, there is provision for voting on matters where a consensus cannot be reached (MN II.247; Vin II.93–100, Vin IV.206; Collins 1998: 436–448). That said, there is an expectation that those who govern should be an ethical example to others, along with a realistic acceptance that this has often not been the case. It is notable that a wise person is said to protect their wealth from various threats, including it being taken by 'kings and thieves' (AN IV.282).

As to whether rule based on majority voting will produce good laws, well, if one focuses on the Buddha-nature, or luminous mind (AN I.10), and that people need to have had good karma to have been reborn as humans, one will have more confidence in majority rule. But if one focuses on the greed, hatred, and delusion that often feed human actions, one will be less confident. Politicians pandering to greed and prejudice to gain votes are a danger.

Press alertness to corrupt politicians and ethical dangers in policies can be a safeguard, but this needs to be done in a discerning and fair way; Buddhist texts value criticism given by the wise, though not criticism from 'foolish and ignorant people who speak without having investigated and evaluated' (MN II.114). Having a judiciary that is separate from law makers is in line with the Buddhist idea that even a ruler is subject to ethical norms, albeit that the law and morality are not the same.

In Myanmar/Burma, reputedly devout Buddhist Aung San Suu Kyi has been a focus for bringing democracy back to the country (it existed there previously from 1948 to 1962), and in Japan the third largest party in parliament is the Kōmeitō, which originated as the political wing of the Sōka Gakkai and remains influenced by it.

Duties of a Government Regarding the Economy and Welfare

In the *Cakkavatti-sīhanāda Sutta* (see 'Political Ideals' section in this chapter) it is said that a new *Cakkavatti* once followed all the duties of such a ruler *except* giving to the needy, resulting in poverty arising for the first time in ages. Consequently, stealing arises. When a thief is caught and is brought before the emperor, he explains that he stole as he was poor: so the emperor gives him some goods with which to support himself and his family, carry on a business, and make gifts to renunciants and brahmins. When others hear of this, though, stealing only increases. The emperor therefore makes an example of the next thief by executing him. This then leads to thieves arming themselves and killing those that they rob, so that there are no witnesses (DN III.64–68). The Buddha sums this up as follows:

> Thus, from the not giving of property to the needy, poverty became rife, from the growth of poverty, the taking of what was not given increased, from the increase of theft, the use of weapons increased, from the increased use of weapons, the taking of life increased—and from the taking of life, people's life-span decreased, their beauty decreased. (DN III.68)

Thus, a government that allows poverty to develop is sowing the seeds of crime and social conflict. Systemic poverty threatens law and order and thus inhibits both social cohesion and personal morality (Fenn 1996: 107). Of course, all those who are poor do not commit crimes, but poverty makes crime, especially theft (and perhaps also rebellion) more likely, and in certain cases relatively more excusable. It is interesting that the sutta contains what might be called both left-wing and right-wing emphases, respectively: look after the poor, harsh punishments breed more violence in society; if welfare provision is too easy to attain, this encourages unjustified claims on it.

Related themes are found in the *Kūṭadanta Sutta* (DN I.134–136; Collins 1998: 476–480). Here, the Buddha tells of a rich and powerful king of the past who wanted to offer a lavish sacrifice to secure his own future welfare, in accordance with Brahmanical practices. He therefore asks his brahmin adviser, the Buddha in a past life, how to go about this. In reply, the brahmin points out that the kingdom was being ravaged by thieves and brigands. This situation would not be solved by executions, imprisonments, or other repressive measures, for those who survived such measures would continue to cause problems (as often happens in anti-guerrilla measures today). He then gives an alternative plan to 'completely eliminate the plague', which involves granting grain and fodder to those who cultivate crops and raise cattle; granting capital to traders; and giving proper living wages to those in government service:

> Then those people, being intent on their own occupations, will not harm the kingdom. Your Majesty's revenues will be great, the land will be tranquil and not beset by thieves, and the people, with joy in their hearts, will play with their children and dwell in open houses. (DN I.136)

The king then carries out this advice and, in line with further counsel, conducts a great sacrifice, but one in which only such things as butter and oil were offered, not the lives of animals, no trees were cut down, and no one was forced to help (DN I.141). While Gombrich (2006: 85) comments that this passage was meant mainly as a critique of Brahmanical sacrifice, and that he knows of no Indian king who did such things as grant capital to businessmen, the spirit of the passage still expresses a Buddhist ideal—and one which has often been cited by a number of Buddhists in recent times. Moreover, in his *Traibhūmi-kathā*, the fourteenth-century Thai prince Phya Lithai has a *Cakkavatti* advise other kings to lend capital, at no interest, to subjects in need of it for trading (Reynolds and Reynolds 1982: 151–152).

A key message of both the above texts is that if a government allows poverty to develop, this will lead to social strife, such that it is its responsibility to avoid this by looking after the poor, and even investing in various sectors of the economy.

The Mahāyāna philosopher Nāgārjuna (*c.*150–250 CE), in his *Rāja-parikathā-ratnamālā* (RPR), advised King Udayi that he should support doctors, set up hostels and rest houses, supply water at arid roadsides, and:

> Cause the blind, the sick, the lowly,
> The protectorless, the wretched
> And the crippled equally to attain
> Food and drink without interruption. (v. 320)
>
> Always care compassionately for
> The sick, the unprotected, those stricken
> With suffering, the lowly and the poor
> And take special care to nourish them. (v. 243)
>
> Provide extensive care
> For the persecuted, the victims (of disasters),
> The stricken and diseased,
> And for worldly beings in conquered areas. (v. 251)
>
> Provide stricken farmers
> With seeds and sustenance,
> Eliminate high taxes
> By reducing their rate. (v. 252)

Eliminate thieves and robbers
In your own and others' countries.
Please set prices fairly and keep
Profits level (when things are scarce). (v. 254)

The *Ārya-bodhisattva-gocara*, which Lozang Jamspal says was the favourite handbook of many teachers in Tibet, such as Tsong kha pa, particularly in their advice to rulers (Jamspal xv and xxvii), says that a ruler should not tax people in a way that harms the poor, such as when crops fail or during a famine, but give them aid (Jamspal 104b). Those who refuse to pay taxes are not exactly *stealing* but are doing 'an acutely nonvirtuous act brought about by miserliness' (Jamspal 108b).

Buddhist kings have varied considerably in the extent to which they have lived up to the above high ideals, but in Sri Lanka, people regard medieval kings as having presided over a period of agricultural abundance based on extensive irrigation works, religious flourishing, and charity. In the *Cūḷavaṃsa* chronicle (Geiger 1929), it is said of King Upatissa I (362–409) that 'For cripples, women in travail, for the blind and sick he erected great nursing shelters and alms-halls' (ch. 37, vv. 182–183), and of Mahinda IV (956–972 or 1026–1042):

> In all the hospitals he distributed medicine and beds, and he had food given regularly to criminals in prison. To apes, the wild boar, the gazelles and to dogs he, a fount of pity, had rice and cakes distributed as much as they would. In the four vihāras [monasteries] the king had raw rice laid down in heaps with the injunction that the poor should take of it as much as they wanted. (ch. 54, vv. 30–33)

In Cambodia, King Jayavarman VII (1182–1218) built a chain of 102 hospitals open to all and ordered the gathering of herbs, minerals, and animal parts to supply these, each of which had a shrine to the buddha of healing, Bhaiṣajyaguru.

Duties and Rights of Citizens

The above implies that citizens have a duty to pay taxes, as a support for various public benefits provided through the government, provided their administration and the rate is not oppressive. They also have an interest in a lawful society, and a duty to obey laws that have a basis in ethics and fairness.

They have a right not to be oppressed by their government, though: in the social contract model of kingship implied by the *Aggañña Sutta* (see 'Political Ideals' section in this chapter), the very basis of a ruler's legitimacy is that he should protect the welfare of those he rules.

With its emphasis on non-harming, Buddhism has strong support for rights to freedom from oppression. When it comes to the rights to positive benefits, its emphasis is somewhat less strong, seeing such things less as *entitlements* and more as something that it is good for others to choose to provide. Nevertheless, its political ideals, as outlined above, clearly see governments as having key responsibilities to look after their people.

Punishments

A ruler should not only seek to prevent crime by preventing poverty, but also to deal with crime appropriately to prevent its increase. The *Aggañña Sutta* describes the first king as chosen by his people to punish wrongdoers. In return for being supported by his people, he should 'show displeasure (*khīyeyya*) at that which one should rightly show displeasure, censure (*garaheyya*) that which should rightly be censured, and banish (*pabbājeyya*) those who should rightly be banished' (DN III.92). The duties of a *Cakkavatti* include that he should 'let no crime (*adhamma-kāro*) prevail' (DN III.61).

In the Buddha's day, some kings used gruesome forms of executions (MN I.87; MN III.164), but the *Mūga-pakkha Jātaka* (no. 538) says that a king is reborn in hell through harshly punishing robbers by having them hit with a whip barbed with thorns, chained up, speared, or impaled (Jat VI.3–4).[6] Steven Collins (1998: 419–459) discusses this *jātaka* as a typical example of what he calls '*Mode 2* Dhamma' in which 'the assessment of violence is context-independent and non-negotiable, and punishment, as a species of violence, is itself a crime'. This contrasts to other Pāli material in '*Mode 1* Dhamma', in which 'the assessment of violence is context-dependent and negotiable. Buddhist advice to kings in Mode 1 tells them not to pass judgment in haste or anger, but appropriately, so that the punishment fits the crime' (420).

The *Janasandha Jātaka* (no. 448) has the bodhisattva as a king who ended executions and even opened the doors of prisons (Jat IV.176). In the *Petavatthu* (Book IV, story 1), a ghost appeals to a king not to execute his former friend for trading in stolen goods: the friend will be reborn in hell if this happens, whereas if freed, he can do good deeds and not experience the results of his crime in hell. The king then goes with the criminal to a monk, who advises that the man is released and should concentrate on good actions.

The present Dalai Lama echoes such ideas:

> every one of us has the potential to commit crimes, because we are all subject to negative disturbing emotions and negative mental qualities. And we will not overcome these by executing other people. … My overriding belief is that it is always possible for criminals to improve and that by its very finality the death penalty contradicts this. … I believe … that the deeper nature of mind is something pure. Human beings

[6] Andrew Huxley discusses the influence of this text on certain traditional legal texts in Southeast Asia (1991: 345).

> become violent because of negative thoughts which arise as a result of their environment and circumstances. (Dalai Lama 1998)

Here a story from Ajahn Brahm (an English monk based in Australia) is relevant. He had taught prisoners and a prison officer told him, 'All the prisoners who attended your classes never returned to jail once they were released.' Ajahn Brahm, on reflection, thought that this was because:

> In all my years teaching in prisons, I had never once seen a criminal. I have seen many people who had committed murder, but I have never seen a murderer. ... I saw the person more than the crime. It is irrational to define people by one, two, or even several, horrible acts that they have done. It denies the existence of all other deeds that they have performed, the many noble acts. I recognized those other deeds. I saw people who had done a crime, not criminals. When I saw the people not the crimes, they also saw the good part of themselves. They began to have self-respect, without denying the crime. Their self-respect grew. When they left the jail, they left for good. (Brahm 2014: 24–25)

Emperor Aśoka set up a 'Ministry of *Dhamma*', through which he sought to prevent wrongful imprisonment and punishment, to free prisoners when appropriate, and to aid prisoners' families if they were in need (Nikam and McKeon 1959: 58–63). Nikam and McKeon's translation (60–61) of his Pillar Edict IV has a reference to his use of the death penalty, although K. R. Norman's more recent translation sees no such reference (1975: 21). Richard Gombrich (n.d.) comments:

> K. R. Norman showed ... the word which had been taken to refer to execution refers only to flogging. So Aśoka was the first [known] ruler in history recorded to have abolished the death penalty. Make no mistake: the state that uses the death penalty is to that extent corrupting its citizens and going against the Buddha's teaching.

In Gupta times (320–540 CE) in India, the mainly Hindu kings, probably due to Buddhist influence, abolished the death penalty in their empire, with fines being the most usual punishment, and only serious revolts leading to the amputation of a hand. Later the Buddhist Harṣa (606–647) also abolished the death penalty and replaced it with life imprisonment (Basham 1967: 120). The Korean monk Hye Ch'o (eighth century) reported that Buddhist kings of central India only used fines as punishment. However, in Tang China, the legal code included capital punishment (Ch'en 1973: 96). In Japan, Damien Horigan (1996: 285–286) reports that: 'In 724 AD, Emperor Shomu (r. 724–749), a devout Buddhist ... forbade the use of the death penalty. This was during the end of the Nara Period (715–794). Likewise, there were very few executions during the Heian Period (794–1185).' However, executions resumed in the more turbulent Kamakura period (1192–1336).

The *Milindapañha*, a Theravāda text dating from perhaps the first century CE, says that acts done by those who are mentally disturbed should not be punished (Miln 221).

The monk Nāgasena, when asked about punishments, ignores King Milinda's reference to maiming, torture, and beating but admits that thieves should be 'rebuked, fined, banished, imprisoned ... or executed (*ghātetabbo*)'. This was not because this execution is 'approved of (*anumata*)' by buddhas, but because of their own wrong actions (Miln 184–188).

Among Mahāyāna texts, the *Ārya-bodhisattva-gocara* says:

> When a ruler believes that punishment [of the wicked] will not be effected through mere obloquy, then, concentrating on love and compassion and without resort to either killing, damaging of sense organs, or cutting off of limbs, he should try warning, scolding, rebuking or beating them, or confiscating their property, exiling them from the state, tying them up, or imprisonment.[7] A ruler should be tough, but not in any heavier way than these. (Jamspal 105a)

Nāgārjuna, in his *Rāja-parikathā-ratnamālā*, advised King Udayi to banish murderers rather than executing them (RPR 337). Moreover:

> Especially generate compassion
> For those murderers, whose sins are horrible;
> Those of fallen nature are receptacles
> Of compassion from those whose nature is great. (v. 332)
>
> Free the weaker prisoners
> After a day or five days
> Do not think the others
> Are never to be freed. (v. 333)
>
> As long as the prisoners are not freed,
> They should be made comfortable
> With barbers, baths, food, drink,
> Medicine and clothing. (v. 335)
>
> Just as unworthy sons are punished
> Out of a wish to make them worthy,
> So punishment should be enforced with compassion
> And not through hatred or desire for wealth. (v. 336)

Yet for many crimes, it is no real 'compassion' to let people get away with their actions: this both threatens the peace and order of society and allows people to persist in ways which are morally harmful to themselves: 'If a ruler ... is too compassionate, he will not chastise the wicked people of his kingdom, which will lead to lawlessness and, as a result, the king will be unable to remove the harm done by robbers and thieves' (Jamspal 115a–b). The *Suvarṇa-bhāsottama Sūtra* also says a king 'must not knowingly

[7] Though Stephen Jenkins (2014: 435–436) suggests a harsher reading of the list of acceptable punishments.

without examination overlook a lawless act. No other destruction in his region is so terrible' (Emmerick 141–142, cf. 135–137).

In the *Ārya-bodhisattva-gocara*, the aim of punishment is that criminals 'might become good persons again' (Jamspal 108a) who do not neglect their obligations (Jamspal 105a). David Loy claims that a common feature of judicial systems in countries where Buddhism has been the predominant religion is that 'the only acceptable reason for punishment is education and reform' (2000: 149). On Tibetan practice, he cites (159) Rebecca French, 'The goal of a legal proceeding was to calm the minds and relieve the anger of the disputants and then—through catharsis, expiation, restitution and appeasement—to rebalance the natural order' (1995: 74), while Virginia Hancock says that 'Buddhist punishment is arguably specific to the character of the individual (rather than being driven by principles or facts) and the affected community, and is oriented to future practice and rehabilitation' (2008: 121).

Karma brings appropriate results for crime—what some might see as retributive punishments, but Buddhism sees as unfortunate natural results—such that 'the Buddhist theory of crime is first and foremost a theory of reconciliation and rehabilitation' (Hancock 2008: 127). The important thing is not to exact revenge on a person for an act expressing an indelibly evil nature, but to help them change in a better direction. Indeed, there is evidence that teaching Vipassanā meditation to prisoners reduced reoffending rates by helping prisoners to accept their wrongdoing and seek to change their ways (Harvey 2009: 59–60).

The idea of the Buddha-nature, or the earlier idea that 'this mind is luminous, but it is defiled by defilements which arrive' (AN I.10), points to a potential for good deep in everyone, no matter how it is covered by negative mental states. This can be seen to represent a potential for reform in all. A famous case of rehabilitation is that of Aṅguḷimāla (MN II.97–105), who used to kill and collect the fingers of his victims (cf. Loy 2000: 149–151). Tamed by the Buddha, he gave up his way of life and ordained. King Pasenadi accepts that as a precept-keeping monk, he would respect him, rather than seek to drive him from his kingdom (M II.101); Aṅguḷimāla later became an *arahant*. In the United Kingdom, the Buddhist prison-visiting organization is called the Angulimala Trust (http://www.angulimala.org.uk).

While there are clearly Buddhist arguments against the use of the death penalty, and these have been acted on to varying extents, there are still states with majority Buddhist populations that make some use of capital punishments. It is used in Japan, though criminals are executed only after they have confessed and repented, so they can be on death row for many years. It is outlawed in Cambodia (1989) and Bhutan (2004), its use is de facto banned in Sri Lanka (1976), Burma (1993), South Korea (1997), Mongolia (2012), and Laos, and it is permitted in Thailand, but in recent years the king has been commuting most death penalties (Horigan 1996: 287). It is used in Taiwan, Vietnam, and Singapore, which has the highest rate per population in the world.[8]

[8] Harvey 2009: 60–61; Infoplease: The Death Penalty Worldwide https://www.infoplease.com/world/political-statistics/death-penalty-worldwide; http://www.deathpenaltyworldwide.org/.

The Relationship between Morality and Law

The extent to which any country encodes the ethics of its people in law is a variable matter (see Harvey 2000: 342–350). Aśoka, while placing some legal restrictions on the killing of animals, felt that careful reflection and meditation were better means to moral improvement than legal compulsion (Nikam and McKeon 1959: 40, see 33–34). In Buddhist countries, while there have been and are certain legal restrictions on the killing of animals, which clearly breaks the first precept, these are limited. Butchers are not sent to prison. Likewise, though selling alcohol offends against the principle of 'right livelihood', doing so is not banned in any Buddhist country. That said, while all Burmese kings used the rhetoric of enforcing Buddhist morality, few went to the lengths of Alaungpaya (*c.*1755) and Badon (*c.*1790), who outlawed the slaughter of animals, and it seems that Badon even imposed the death sentence for alcohol or opium use.

Passages cited above suggest that for Buddhism, the job of a ruler or government is to prevent immorality descending into social disorder and to encourage morality, if not rigidly enforce it. The *Ārya-bodhisattva-gocara* (Jamspal 106a–b) says that 'slaughterers, bird killers, and pork sellers' should be punished, but only by being chastised and warned. It also sees the king as having a role in improving the morality of his people: 'Rulers ... are called 'pleasing ones' [*rāja*] in that they [are responsible for] maintaining the happiness of people, causing them [the people] to be good' (Jamspal 102b). The *Suvarṇa-bhāsottama Sūtra* says: 'For the sake of suppressing what is unlawful, a destroyer of evil deeds, he would establish beings in good activity in order to send them to the abode of the gods' (Emmerick 135).

What do we find when we look at Buddhist-influenced premodern law? Of all Buddhist countries, Burma has had a traditional legal literature most strongly influenced by Buddhist norms (Huxley 1995: 49–50). In Sri Lanka, no traditional law texts survive, and caste was the basis of dispute settlement and social organization. In Thai and Khmer traditions, the king was seen as the primary source of law. In China, Buddhism could only marginally influence the existing legal tradition. Surprisingly, Tibet's laws were much less influenced by Buddhist ideas than in Burma, perhaps because it took its law from Central Asian states to its north (Huxley 1995: 55).[9] In Burma, as elsewhere in Southeast Asia, the main types of law texts were:

1. *Rājathat*: the less ephemeral of a king's commands (Huxley 1995: 48), which included general guidance to the judges in the royal courts (Huxley 1997: 75).
2. *Dhammathat*: 'customary law' (Huxley 1995: 52), which gives guidance on unofficial dispute settlement, especially at village level (Huxley 1997: 74). In the form of

[9] Though French reports that Buddhist ideas affected the way the law was applied (1995: 114).

digests of law for popular consumption, their rules 'should be obeyed because they are as old as human society, or because they are universally acknowledged as correct because they are implicit in the Buddha's dhamma' (Huxley 1997: 73). Indeed, they were seen as 'editions of the age-old law text which is written on the walls at the boundary of the universe' (Huxley 1995: 52).

3. *Pyatton: Jātaka*-type stories of clever judges, or reports of cases (Huxley 1995: 49) which give 'helpful legal information' in the form of non-binding precedents (Huxley 1997: 78).

The *dhammathat* texts were often composed by monks (Huxley 1995: 48), especially those expert in monastic discipline (53), and indeed, the *Vinaya* is often quoted in Southeast Asian legal literature, as well as its reasoning style being influential on law (Huxley 1997: 70–71). Both in Burma and elsewhere in Southeast Asia, it is notable that 'no sharp distinction was made between law, morality and good behaviour. Law texts [of any of the above three types] are often bound together with Jatakas and other works on ethics and *politesse*' (Huxley 1997: 81).

In spite of the strong Buddhist influence on traditional Burmese law, Andrew Huxley, an expert in this field, can find no ruling on abortion in it,[10] even though Buddhist texts see abortion as a serious act of killing a human (Vin III.73; Harvey 2000: 313–326). He speculates that this may be because abortion did not 'threaten the king's peace … nor does it lead to a claim for compensation to be mediated at village or suburb level', and so came under the remit of neither *rājathat* nor *dhammathat*.

In Thailand, one 1978 study found that the majority of people saw abortion as immoral, yet also held that the abortion law should be liberalized to allow it on socio-economic grounds and for a broader range of medical grounds (Florida 1998: 24). In 1981, when Parliament was debating liberalization of the law, a poll of monks found that 75 per cent held that the bill was immoral, yet 40 per cent felt it should pass, with only 40 per cent opposing this (the figures for nuns were 12 per cent and 78 per cent) (*World Fellowship of Buddhists Review* 1981: 30). While such a mismatch of views might seem surprising, there is a logic to it. On the one hand, Buddhism is clear that abortion is an unwholesome action; it also holds that to deny that an unwholesome action is unwholesome is itself a potently unwholesome action. On the other hand, Buddhists may be concerned about the suffering of women undergoing botched illegal abortions, which threaten their health, with only the wealthy being able to afford safe abortions. Thus, while a Buddhist would expect the karmic results of abortion to arise in the future, she may see less need for legal punishment to follow from the act. Thus the support for liberalizing the law, or the lax enforcing of the existing law, as occurs in some countries.

[10] Personal communication.

Works Cited

Aitken, R. (1984) *The mind of clover: essays in Zen Buddhist ethics.* San Francisco: North Point Press.

Basham, A. L. (1967) *The wonder that was India.* London: Sidgwick and Jackson.

Basham, A. L. (1982) Asoka and Buddhism: a re-examination. *Journal of the International Association of Buddhist Studies*, 5 (1), 131–143.

Brahm, A. (2014) *Don't worry, be grumpy: inspiring stories for making the most of each moment.* Boston: Wisdom.

Ch'en, K. K. S. (1973) *The Chinese transformation of Buddhism.* Princeton: Princeton University Press.

Collins, S. (1998) *Nirvana and other Buddhist felicities.* Cambridge: Cambridge University Press.

Dhammika, S. (1993) *The edicts of King Asoka.* Wheel pamphlet nos 386–387. Kandy: Buddhist Publication Society. Available from: http://www.accesstoinsight.org/lib/authors/dhammika/wheel386.html.

Emmerick R. E. (trans.) (1970) *The Sūtra of Golden Light.* London: Luzac and Co. Ltd. Reference to Sanskrit pagination, as indicated in the translation.

Fenn, M. L. (1991) Unjustified poverty and karma (Pali kamma). *Religious studies and theology*, 11 (1), 20–26.

Fenn, M. L. (1996) Two notions of poverty in the Pāli canon. *Journal of Buddhist ethics* 3, 98–125.

Florida, R. E. (1998) Abortion in Buddhist Thailand. In: D. Keown (ed.), *Buddhism and abortion.* London: Macmillan, 11–30.

French, R. R. (1995) *The golden yoke: the legal cosmology of Buddhist Tibet.* Ithaca, NY: Cornell University Press.

Geiger, W. (1929) *Cūḷavamsa, parts I and II.* London: Pali Text Society.

Gokhale, B. G. (1966) Early Buddhist kingship. *The journal of Asian studies*, 26 (1), 15–22.

Gombrich, R. F. (1971) *Precept and practice: traditional Buddhism in the rural highlands of Ceylon.* Oxford: Clarendon Press.

Gombrich, R. F. (2006) *Theravāda Buddhism: a social history from ancient Benares to modern Colombo.* Second edition. London and New York: Routledge and Kegan Paul.

Gombrich, R. F. (n.d.) Buddhism and non-violence. Available from: http://www.vesakday.net/vesak50/article/pdf_file/08_Buddhism_and_Non.pdf [Accessed 23 December 2008].

Gurugé, A. W. P. (1993) *Asoka: a definitive biography.* Colombo, Sri Lanka: Ministry of Cultural Affairs and Communication.

Gyatso, Tenzin, Dalai Lama XIV (1998) Message supporting the moratorium on the death penalty. Available from: http://www.engaged-zen.org/HHDLMSG [accessed 4 February 2016].

Hall, F. (1902) *The soul of a people.* London: Macmillan.

Hancock, V. (2008) 'No-self' at trial: how to reconcile punishing the Khmer Rouge for crimes against humanity with Cambodian Buddhist principles. *Wisconsin international law journal*, 26 (1), 87–129.

Harvey, P. (2000) *An introduction to Buddhist ethics: foundations, values and issues.* Cambridge: Cambridge University Press.

Harvey, P. (2009) Buddhist perspectives on crime and punishment. In: J. Powers and C. S. Prebish (eds), *Destroying Māra forever: Buddhist ethics essays in honor of Damien Keown.* Ithaca, NY: Snow Lion, 47–66.

Harvey, P. (2013) *An introduction to Buddhism: teachings, history, practice.* 2nd edition. Cambridge: Cambridge University Press.

Horigan, D. P. (1996) A Buddhist perspective on the death penalty: of compassion and capital punishment. *The American journal of jurisprudence*, 41, 271–288.

Huxley, A. (1995) Buddhism and law: the view from Mandalay. *Journal of the International Association of Buddhist Studies*, 18 (1), 47–95.

Huxley, A. (1997) Studying Theravāda legal literature. *Journal of the International Association of Buddhist Studies*, 20 (1), 63–91.

Jamspal, Lozang (trans.) (2010) *The Range of the Bodhisattva, A Mahāyāna Sūtra: Ārya-bodhisattva-gocara, Introduction and Translation*. New York: American Institute of Buddhist Studies, Columbia University Center for Buddhist Studies, and Tibet House US. Reference to Tibetan pagination, as indicated in the translation.

Jenkins, S. L. (2014) A review of *The range of the bodhisattva: a Mahāyāna sutra*. *Journal of Buddhist ethics*, 21, 431–441.

Krishan, Y. (1986) Buddhism and the caste system. *Journal of the International Association of Buddhist Studies*, 9 (1), 71–83.

Ling, T. (1973) *The Buddha: Buddhist civilization in India and Ceylon*. London: Temple Smith.

Loy, D. (2000) How to reform a serial killer: the Buddhist approach to restorative justice. *Journal of Buddhist ethics*, 7, 145–168.

Nāgārjuna and the Seventh Dalai Lama (1975) *The Precious Garland and the Song of the Four Mindfulnesses (translation of Rāja-parikathā-ratnamālā* by J. Hopkins and L. Rinpoche), London: George Allen and Unwin.

Nikam, N. A., and McKeon, R. (1959) *The edicts of Asoka*. Chicago and London: University of Chicago Press.

Norman, K. R. (1975) Aśoka and capital punishment. *Journal of the Royal Asiatic Society*, Part I, 16–24.

Obeyesekere, G., and Reynolds, F. (1972) *The two wheels of dhamma: essays on the Theravada tradition in India and Ceylon*. Chambersburg, PA: American Academy of Religion.

Ornatowski, G. K. (1996) Continuity and change in the economic ethics of Buddhism: evidence from the history of Buddhism in India, China and Japan. *Journal of Buddhist ethics* 3, 198–240.

Payutto, P. A. (1993) *Good, evil and beyond: kamma in the Buddha's teaching*. Bangkok: Buddhadhamma Foundation Publications. Available from: http://www.buddhanet.net/pdf_file/good_evil_beyond.pdf.

Rājavaramuni, Phra (1990) Foundations of Buddhist social ethics. In: R. Sizemore and D. Swearer (eds), *Ethics, wealth and salvation: a study in Buddhist social ethics*. Columbia, SC: University of South Carolina Press, 35–43.

Reynolds, F. E. (1990) Ethics and wealth in Theravāda Buddhism. In: R. Sizemore and D. Swearer (eds), *Ethics, wealth and salvation: a study in Buddhist social ethics*. Columbia, SC: University of South Carolina Press, 59–76.

Reynolds, F. E., and Mani, B. (1982) *Three worlds according to King Ruang: a Thai Buddhist cosmology*. Berkeley: Asian Humanities Press.

Saddhatissa, H. (1970) *Buddhist ethics: essence of Buddhism*. London: George Allen and Unwin.

Saddhatissa, H. (1971) *The Buddha's way*. London: George Allen and Unwin.

Sizemore, R. F., and Swearer, D. K. (eds) (1990) *Ethics, wealth and salvation: a study in Buddhist social ethics*. Columbia, SC: University of South Carolina Press.

Swearer, D. K. (1995) *The Buddhist world of southeast Asia*. Albany, NY: State University of New York Press.

Tambiah, S. J. (1976) *World conqueror and world renouncer: a study of Buddhism and polity in Thailand against a historical background*. Cambridge: Cambridge University Press.

Whitmyer, C. (ed.) (1994) *Mindfulness and meaningful work: explorations of right livelihood.* Berkeley: Parallax Press.

Suggested Reading

Harvey, P. (2000) *An introduction to Buddhist ethics: foundations, values and issues.* Cambridge: Cambridge University Press.

Harvey, P. (2009) Buddhist perspectives on crime and punishment. In: J. Powers and C. S. Prebish (eds), *Destroying Māra forever: Buddhist ethics essays in honor of Damien Keown.* Ithaca, NY: Snow Lion, 47–66.

Nikam, N. A., and McKeon, R. (1959) *The edicts of Asoka.* Chicago and London: University of Chicago Press.

Ornatowski, G. K. (1996) Continuity and change in the economic ethics of Buddhism: evidence from the history of Buddhism in India, China and Japan. *Journal of Buddhist ethics* 3, 198–240.

Payutto, P. A. (1993) *Good, evil and beyond: kamma in the Buddha's teaching.* Bangkok: Buddhadhamma Foundation Publications. Available from: http://www.buddhanet.net/pdf_file/good_evil_beyond.pdf.

Saddhatissa, H. (1970) *Buddhist ethics: essence of Buddhism.* London: George Allen and Unwin.

Sizemore, R. F., and Swearer, D. K. (eds) (1990) *Ethics, wealth and salvation: a study in Buddhist social ethics.* Columbia, SC: University of South Carolina Press, especially ch. 1, by Phra Rājavaramuni.

CHAPTER 20

BUDDHIST ECONOMICS

Problems and Possibilities

JAMES MARK SHIELDS

INTRODUCTION

ECONOMICS is an umbrella concept that like *religion* or *ethics* contains a vast array of elements, not all of them easily compatible. Like ethics, economics is often conceived as an academic 'discipline', but like religion, it also delimits a particular realm or sphere of everyday human activity—albeit one that is normally understood as being profoundly, perhaps dangerously, *profane*. As is well known, the linguistic roots of 'economics' are in the Greek *oikonomikè*, roughly, 'private' or 'domestic management' (from *oikos*, household). For Aristotle, 'economics' in this sense dealt with immediate needs; it was thus subordinate to 'politics', an active and engaged life with others in the *polis*, the only sphere in which human beings could fulfil the 'good life' (see Crespo 2009). Thus, arguably for Aristotle 'economics' and 'ethics' are incompatible—or perhaps economics, however valuable, is ultimately only a prelude towards ethics/politics, supplying the necessary but not sufficient conditions for the achievement of *eudamonia* (see, e.g., *Politics* I, 4, 1253b, 23–25; cf. Payutto 1992: 88, for a Buddhist parallel). At any rate, today it is generally agreed that 'economics' extends well beyond the domestic realm, and that, in fact, it verges into what Aristotle would surely have called 'political life'. (This was certainly Marx's conception, and is arguably a Buddhist one as well.)

One of the problems in trying to clarify the significance of economics in relation to ethics and religion, including the specific tradition commonly known as 'Buddhism', is that the inherent multivalence of each term is multiplied further, so that one is tempted to throw up one's hands in despair. And yet, the very breadth of possibilities opened up by combining several such large and ambiguous terms can also be a source of liberation—a nudge towards experimenting with creative combinations that may serve to highlight hitherto unexpected aspects of Buddhism and economics, singularly and in combination. In that spirit, this chapter provides both an overview of some historical, sociological, and doctrinal connections between Buddhism and economics as well as a critical and constructive analysis of more recent attempts to delimit something called 'Buddhist economics'. It is not intended to be comprehensive, but rather to highlight some key, intriguing features of the relationship between Buddhism and the theory and practice of economics. The chapter concludes with five theses on which to build a progressive 'Buddhist economics' in the context of twenty-first-century global capitalism.

Buddhism and 'Economics Ethics'

As Peter Harvey writes:

> Economic ethics covers a wide range of issues: types of work or business practices, the approach to work in general and entrepreneurship in particular, the use to which income is put, attitudes to wealth, the distribution of wealth, critiques of politico-economic systems such as capitalism and Communism, and the offering of alternatives to these in both theory and practice. (Harvey 2000: 187)[1]

Scanning this list, which is inevitably incomplete, one begins to see that what Harvey calls 'economic ethics' might be simply *the reflective or critical evaluation of economic ideas, theories and/or practices*. In other words, it does not seem that there is anything specifically 'economic' about economic ethics other than as a descriptor of the *object* of certain ethical insights. Perhaps this is true for other subfields of ethics, at least those that are tied to a social scientific category or discipline. Extending this further, it would appear that the sphere of 'economics' as described by Harvey covers a significant amount of human social activity—to the extent that it could be plausibly redescribed as 'relationality' or perhaps 'intersubjectivity'. Labour, production, exchange, the distribution of wealth and property, consumption—one need not be a doctrinaire Marxist to recognize how deeply embedded these things are in human social existence, and not merely in the modern, industrial, or post-industrial context.

And yet, on one important level, the classical Buddhist ideal appears to run counter to a 'materialist' conception of human social existence, as exemplified by the life of the (generally male) 'householder'. (As Essen 2009: 31 puts it: '"Buddhist economics"—isn't that an oxymoron?'; see Daniels 2005: 246.) The monastic ideal inculcated within and represented by the *saṅgha* or monastic community has been understood as a radical rejection of the forms of life that are conditioned by economic activity: labour, exchange,

[1] As with many topics discussed in this *Handbook*, Harvey's *Introduction to Buddhist Ethics* is an excellent resource for understanding economic ethics in relation to Buddhist textual as well as cultural traditions. While very much indebted to Harvey's work, my intentions here are more philosophical and 'critical-constructive'—if not quite prescriptive—in nature. For a list of scholarly works in English on the issue of Buddhism and economics, see the Works Cited as well as Suggested Reading.

wages, surplus, distribution, and so on. But we must be cautious of the temptation to render the historical *saṅgha* (or *saṅgha*s, given the eventual diversity of monastic practices across cultures and traditions) and Buddhist monastic ideal as 'an-economic'—just as, as I have argued elsewhere, we should be hesitant to see these as 'apolitical' (see Shields 2016). This for at least three reasons: (1) research on the social context(s) out of which Buddhism emerged and developed appears to show that the *saṅgha* was especially attractive to members of the merchant classes (see, e.g., Reynolds 1990; Pryor 2001: 156); (2) as Schopen's work (e.g. 2004) has shown, the monastic communities were themselves deeply enmeshed in 'secular' economic activities; (3) even in ideal terms, the tradition (or traditions) inaugurated by the Buddha and his immediate followers was not intended to *reject* the world of everyday affairs, but rather, we might say, to *supplement* this world by providing an alternative avenue for select men (and eventually, women), whose activities could in fact support the life of the majority, i.e. the 'householders'. It is this last point, in particular, that calls for further exploration and elucidation.

In short, employing one of the tradition's own tropes, the Buddhist perspective on economics may be fruitfully conceived as a 'middle way' between full acceptance of 'economic life' and a blanket rejection of such.[2] Of course, this still leaves us with a lot of room. I hope to show in what follows that, rather than the standard conception of this middle path as a form of 'moderation'—understood here as accepting the basic premises and practices of prevailing economic systems, particularly late industrial global capitalism, while providing cautionary provisions against their excesses—Buddhist 'divergence' may be more fruitfully interpreted along progressive and even 'radical' lines of critique. (Here I follow the lead of Simon Zadek [1997], though my approach is grounded in comparative thought.)

Classical Buddhist Economics

A primary trope of classical Buddhism—at least as expressed in ideal terms, i.e. within the textual tradition—is simplicity in lifestyle, which is intrinsically connected to the virtue, attitude, or psychological/affective state of *contentment* (Pāli *santuṭṭhi, appichatā*) (see Tachibana 1992: 124–130). The *Dhammapada* is often considered a locus classicus for this theme (e.g. *D.* 15; 205, *D.* 25; 365), but it is a teaching that resonates with the universally accepted Buddhist soteriology of awakening understood as liberation

[2] Essen (2009: 31) argues that because Buddhism's 'ontology and objective differ from those of capitalism, the economic means and ends resulting from each ideology logically differ, as does the currency valued: money versus *kamma* or merit'. While on one level this is unobjectionable, it is a statement heavily weighted towards Theravādin traditions, and, perhaps more important, begs the questions not only of Buddhist 'ontology' but also its 'objective'. I argue that the 'objective' of human flourishing (i.e. in communities, with minimized suffering) is crucial to Buddhism in many of its forms, and that this implies a 'Buddhist economics' that is not merely 'spiritual' but material—i.e. economic.

from suffering through renunciation of craving (Pāli *taṇhā*; Skt *tṛṣṇā*). Indeed, the very terms for monk and nun—*bhikkhu* and *bhikkhunī*—explicitly denote a person who has committed him or herself to renouncing commonplace domestic, social, economic, and political forms, i.e. both the *productive* and *reproductive* aspects of the ordinary social order (see Fenn 1996: 100).

And yet, as noted above, the early textual tradition also takes pains to distinguish the Buddhist ideal from that of other homeless wanderers and, especially, the more extreme ascetic renunciants of the day. As the *Dhammapada* puts it: 'That one I call a brahmin whose wants are few, who is detached from householders and homeless mendicants alike' (26; 404). Monks were allowed a few personal possessions, such as robes, a bowl, razor, needle, in addition to other 'useful' items such as a bag, umbrella, clock, and books. The justification is simple, and, as is frequently the case in Buddhism, connected to psychological rather than 'religious' reasoning: without many possessions, one is less likely to worry about them being lost or stolen, and one will presumably be less prone to want more things, and to suffer accordingly (*M.* I.85–87). It also makes for ease of travel (despite the fact that monks and nuns were *not* 'homeless mendicants'). The emphasis is clearly on the 'use value' of goods—though *use* here does not necessarily mean *convenience*, a leitmotif of the contemporary capitalist economy.

The monastic ideal, then, was a simple (moderately) self-sufficient lifestyle, in which monks and nuns could dedicate most of their time to 'spiritual' tasks, supported largely or entirely by lay donations. This last aspect alludes to what we has been called a 'structural tension' within the Buddhist monastic framework: on one hand the *saṅgha* by its very existence denies the hegemonic economic and political structures surrounding it, while on the other it has always been dependent for its very survival on donations from those invested in these economic and political institutions—particularly those who have gained the most 'success' in worldly terms of wealth and power. (See Collins 2013, who argues on this basis for a fundamental distinction between Christian and Buddhist monastic traditions vis-à-vis social theory and 'utopia'.) Indeed, as Harvey puts it, formulaically: 'monastic simplicity attracts lay donations' (2000: 204). The better monks are at opting out of the ordinary cycles of production and reproduction, the more they stand to gain from the 'surplus value' of these very cycles (i.e. via donations and new recruits) from laypeople who seek to gain 'merit' from this exchange. (Citing the anthropological work of Tambiah 1976 and Bunnag 1973, Harvey [2000: 204–205] suggests that the potential problem of corruption is resolved in practice by an equitable distribution of the 'wealth' donated to certain esteemed monks throughout the monastic community, but this does not resolve the more fundamental structural tension alluded to above.) In some countries, such as Sri Lanka, China, and Japan, monasteries and monastic institutions became through this process wealthy landowners and, partly as a result, economic and political playmakers. Despite the occasional critic (more often, at least in the case of Japan) from outside the *saṅgha* or from rival institutions, there was generally little resistance to the notion of monastic wealth and power in and of itself.

When it comes to the laity, it is also clear that their economic activities were expected to follow certain guidelines, ostensibly set forth by the Buddha himself (e.g. *AN* III.45, IV.281; *DN* III.188). These are, on the whole (and bereft of the cosmological and soteriological superstructure in which they are embedded) rather commonsensical instructions, such as would not be out of place in, say, Victorian England: *wealth should be made without causing violence; products should be shared with others rather than hoarded for oneself; greed is bad*, and so on. In short,

> in his or her work, a Buddhist should be energetic, industrious, diligent, skillful, proficient, and prudent. People should protect their earnings, keep good company, and live within their means. Wealth, he taught, provided that it is lawfully obtained, brings four kinds of happiness: economic security; having enough to spend generously on oneself and others; the peace of mind that accompanies freedom from debt; and the leading of a blameless life. (Batchelor 2001: 65)

As reasonable as this may sound at first glance, I contend that there is very little to be gleaned from such blandishments to upright wealth generation for lay Buddhists, not least because they assume a relatively simple economic system, one that barely extends beyond the individual and her immediate environs, and—as a natural consequence—are focused entirely upon individual decision-making (and karma) rather than social or systemic issues, i.e. with the mode of acquisition and use of wealth rather than the justice of its distribution (see Sizemore and Swearer 1990: 2, 13, and Harvey 2000: 202; also Fenn 1996: 107 for a critique of this view on the basis of at least some early texts such as the *Cakkavatti-sīhanāda Sutta.*) Rather, we would do well to look elsewhere to find Buddhist resources for contemporary economic ethics, extrapolating from more general teachings and ideas, including, perhaps most centrally, the notion of 'Right Livelihood' (see Daniels 2004: 246). I will return to this below, after discussing several contemporary attempts to develop a theory of 'Buddhist economics' as a middle path between capitalism and communism.

'Buddhist Economics' from Schumacher to Payutto

The first serious attempt by a Western scholar to bring together Buddhism and economics was E. F. Schumacher's classic essay entitled 'Buddhist Economics,' initially published in 1966 but reprinted as a chapter in his bestselling 1973 book *Small is Beautiful* (rather snarkily subtitled *Economics as if People Mattered*). Here Schumacher, a German-born economist and long-time Chief Economic Advisor to the UK Coal Board, presents a sweeping critique of Western development models—both capitalist and Marxist—calling for new form of life rooted in a 'Middle Way between materialist heedlessness and traditionalist immobility' (1973: 56).

Although Schumacher's argument is developed in the short chapter on 'Buddhist Economics', the foundations for his thesis appear throughout *Small is Beautiful.* In a chapter entitled 'Peace and Permanence', for instance, he introduces the argument that human flourishing—understood in terms of both external and internal 'peace'—cannot be achieved through material 'prosperity', since such prosperity, 'if attainable at all, is attainable only by cultivating such drives of human nature as greed and envy, which destroy intelligence, happiness, serenity, and thereby the peacefulness of man' (1973: 30). By the logic of the current global capitalist economic system, the lure of prosperity requires the (endless) 'cultivation and expansion of needs'—and yet, 'every increase of needs tends to increase one's dependence on outside forces over which one cannot have control, and therefore increases existential fear' (31). Here as elsewhere Schumacher prefigures the so-called 'capability approach' to economics, as developed by thinkers such as Amartya Sen and Martha Nussbaum since the 1980s. Like Schumacher's Buddhist economics, Sen and Nussbaum criticize the over-simplified *homo economicus* of the neo-liberal model, expanding the definition of 'needs' to include 'capabilities' and questioning 'rational choice' (and an exclusive appeal to 'mental states') as the standard for making decisions about economic matters (see, e.g., Robeyns 2009; Sen 1985; Nussbaum 2000).

This is a point that has undeniable resonance with classical Buddhist conceptions of simplicity and moderation—as well as, I will argue below, with the work of 'second-order materialists' from Epicurus to Spinoza and Marx. And yet, here, as elsewhere, Schumacher might be accused of overplaying his hand with dichotomies, and thereby simplifying some important nuances. For instance, he persistently pushes the conventional but overly simplistic distinction between 'material' and 'spiritual' pursuits, as well as 'external' knowledge—or 'cleverness'—and 'internal' wisdom. This higher wisdom, which Schumacher says follows upon 'liberation',

> enable[s] us to see the hollowness and unsatisfactoriness of a life devoted primarily to the pursuit of material ends, to the neglect of the spiritual . . . man's needs are infinite and infinitude can be achieved only in the spiritual realm, never in the material. Man assuredly needs to rise above this humdrum 'world' . . .[3]

Here, I suggest, Schumacher has introduced several vague and moralistic distinctions that distract from the insight about the relationship between needs and 'control', and liberation. I will return to this below.

In another chapter entitled 'The Role of Economics', Schumacher cites John Stuart Mill's expansive conception of economics—or at least 'political economy'—as 'a branch of social philosophy, so interlinked with all the other branches that its conclusions, even in its own peculiar province, are only true conditionally, subject to interference

[3] Cf. Pryor (1990, 1991), who uses the *Cakkavatti-Sihanada Sutta* (*DN*. 26) to argue that it is the role of the state to promote 'spiritual improvement' of the population by reducing or eliminating poverty as a key inhibitor to spiritual growth (and morality).

and counteraction from causes not directly within its scope' (1973: 39). This broader understanding opens up the possibility of a 'Buddhist economics', since Buddhism—as any significant religious tradition or ideology—provides a foundation of ideas, values, beliefs, and habits that are expected to transform one's behaviour with regard to all facets of life.

It is important to note that Schumacher is not making claims to a form of economics that is somehow necessary or 'essential' to Buddhism, but rather that the 'logic'—or perhaps, to borrow Steven Collins's term, 'imaginaire'—of classical Buddhism may provide a *better* foundation for economic theory and practice in the contemporary period ('better' here understood in relation to human flourishing, broadly conceived). 'Buddhist economics', Schumacher argues, is founded primarily on the Eightfold Path's injunction of 'Right Livelihood'. Whatever else it may imply, Right Livelihood clearly entails relating to others in some form of social system, which in turn entails some measure of labour, production and distribution of goods, as well as a medium of exchange.

On this basis, Schumacher goes on to make an insightful, if broad-stroked, case for a 'Buddhist theory of labour', based on the principle that human labour is or can be a *liberating* process, if and when it: (1) utilizes and develops all human faculties (physical and mental); (2) promotes a bonding with others in a common project, which subverts or softens egoism; (3) leads to the production of 'useful' goods—i.e. goods that provide 'value' to human individual and/or social existence. These three overlapping requirements for labour are very much in line with Marx's critique of 'alienation' under the capitalist system of wage labour (Kołakowski 2008: 182; see Pryor 2001: 155), though the second and third points hearken to certain streams of classical anarchism as well as the more 'romantic' or 'aesthetic' socialism of William Morris.

A key feature to this argument, and one that continues to bear relevance, I believe, is that under the current socioeconomic system 'work' is abstracted from, and even opposed to, 'leisure'—with the consequence that labour is a necessary evil that one has to perform in order to: (a) materially survive; and (b) be able to enjoy one's 'free time' (should one be fortunate enough to have any!). Schumacher suggests that under a 'Buddhist theory of labour' things would be different, since,

> to strive for leisure as an alternative to work would be considered a complete misunderstanding of one of the basic truths of human existence, namely that work and leisure are complementary parts of the same process and cannot be separated without destroying the joy of work and the bliss of nature. (1973: 52)[4]

[4] It bears noting that Schumacher's ideal Buddhist society is one that is—like most actual Buddhist societies—irredeemably sexist; e.g., while 'full employment' is a goal, that would only be for men, since '[w]omen, on the whole, do not need an 'outside' job ... In particular, to let mothers of young children run wild would be as uneconomic in the eyes of a Buddhist economist as the employment of a skilled worker as a soldier in the eyes of a modern economist' (1973: 53–54).

Of course, given the nature of much labour under our current system, this would seem to imply *either* a radical transformation of labour (and thus, of the economic system itself) *or* a fundamental shift in our individual and collective capacity to endure activities that do not have obvious 'value' (other than, of course, the economic 'value' they create as part of the system). Of these two options, most modern Buddhists who have seen this as a problem have opted for the latter as the more properly Buddhist option. And in this they are not entirely unjustified, given canonical and traditional precedents. Still, I would like to push for the possibility of the alternative as plausibly Buddhist.

Here it may be worth summarizing Marx's labour theory of value, as developed in the first three chapters of *Capital*. While Schumacher clearly borrows from Marx's most significant economic insight—recognized even by many non-Marxists as a key to understanding modern, capitalist economics—he does not seem to acknowledge the depth (and thus the provocation) embedded in Marx's thinking on labour in relation to commodification, alienation, and the destruction of community. The labour theory of value is rooted in the distinction between 'use-value' and 'exchange-value': 'As use-values, commodities are, above all, of different quantities, and consequently do not contain an atom of use-value' (Marx 1993: 5). Moreover, while different use-values have different *qualities*, different exchange-values have different *quantities*. Thus, the shift, as it were, from an economic rooted in 'use' to one rooted in 'exchange' implies a turn from qualitative to quantitative considerations—one step forward on the slippery slope to 'materialism' (understood as 'commodity fetishism'). And once money (and credit) is introduced into the economic equation, a necessary step from a barter economy to a 'capitalist' one, then at least in theory *anything* can be exchanged for anything else, and thus *everything* becomes a commodity, including, importantly for Marx, labour and—by extension—workers themselves. Although *real* (i.e. human) value comes from labour power, this gets lost as money replaces 'things' as the central element of exchange.

According to this thesis, prior to the money system that has now become ubiquitous, basic economic—and thus *social*—relations were different, because the efforts, needs, and desires of others were not only more evident, but also had to be taken into account for successful exchange. Now, under this system, human social relations are themselves quantified on the basis of monetary 'worth'. In Marx's wonderful phrase: 'We have material relations between persons and social relations between things.' That is to say, mute objects become not only objects of desire but also objects of value, *in themselves*; they are fetishized (this, again, is the beginning of 'materialism'). At the same time, social relations are 'materialized' as human beings—especially but by no means exclusively the producing classes—are 'reduced' to their 'occupations'. In short, any real meaning of 'community' disappears (Luxemburg 2014: 225). Each person's share of social labour comes to be dictated by the 'market', and the erstwhile solidity of the social unit 'melts into air' (which, it should be noted, was not an unalloyed negative for Marx). While Marx takes this as the basis for material inequality, more important, I think, is the harm that this system does to human social relations and, arguably, 'human nature' itself.

Rosa Luxemburg nicely sums up this idea in words that parallel Schumacher's. Under the current system, she writes, over time, much or all of humanity will 'groan …

> with frightful suffering under the yoke of a blind social power, capital, that it has itself unconsciously created. The underlying purpose of every form of social production, the maintenance of society by labor, the satisfaction of its needs, is placed here completely on its head, with production not being for the sake of people, but production for the sake of profit becoming the law all over the earth, with the under-consumption, constant insecurity of consumption, and sometimes non-consumption of the immense majority of people becoming the rule. (2014: 297)

Here we have a penetrating (and prophetic) critique of neo-classical economics as a system that is not only economically disastrous for the many, but, perhaps more importantly, destructive of both human possibility and communal identity for all. And while it aligns well with Schumacher's 'Buddhist economics', it goes rather further in developing the systemic and social aspects of the critique. Moreover, within the Marxian conception of labour lies the fundamental assertion that human productive activity not only shapes nature, it shapes *human* nature (see, e.g., *Capital I*; Marx 1993: 83; also *MECW* 6: 192). In other words, just as there is great possibility for harm, so too is there, in labour-as-production, the promise of 'liberation' in the sense of a radically transformed way of being as a 'self' in the world, with others and nature. (See Geras 2016: 89–90 for a penetrating analysis of this idea in relation to materialism, idealism, and human nature.)

As noted above, Schumacher attempts to situate his Buddhist economics *between* capitalist and socialist alternatives—though it would seem that the difference is more of underlying assumptions and priorities than of some compromise between these two systems, as he understands them. According to Schumacher, *both* modern capitalism and socialism fall prey to the Siren song of 'materialism', which places goods before people, profit before happiness, and the individual before the community. In both systems, in practice if not theory, the production, ownership, and consumption of goods become ends in themselves, whereas in Buddhist economics all of this activity is a means to the much more significant end of (a particular 'Dharmic' conception of) human flourishing. In short, 'Buddhist economics is the systematic study of how to attain given ends with the minimum means' (1973: 55). When it comes to economics, the 'moderate' aspect of Buddhism boils down to the traditional understanding of *Dharma* as promoting a mode of life that avoids both rigid asceticism and hedonism.

> While the materialist is mainly interested in goods, the Buddhist is mainly interested in liberation. But Buddhism is 'The Middle Way' and therefore in no way antagonistic to physical well-being. It is not wealth that stands in the way of liberation but the attachment to wealth; not the enjoyment of pleasurable things but the craving for them. (1973: 54)

As such, the problem with the primary twentieth-century alternative to global industrial capitalism, socialism, is not that it is too 'extreme' in its opposition to capitalism, but rather that at least in an important respect *it does not go far enough*. Schumacher clearly recognizes the value of certain socialist ideas, but, ironically, only when they are divested of their actual 'economic' aspects. In the end, socialism 'is of interest solely for its non-economic values and the possibility it creates for the overcoming of the religion of economics' (1973: 239). Large-scale socialist economic proposals such as the nationalization of industry are doomed to failure, since their purpose is more often than not to compete with capitalism at its own game, i.e. the achievement of faster economic growth (measured in meaningless abstractions such as GDP), greater efficiency, and superior planning. Greed once again wins out—albeit framed in the socialist system in a more explicitly 'public' sense. In short, what is at stake in Buddhist economics is less economics (as normally conceived) than 'culture'—*not the standard of living but the quality of life* (Schumacher 1973: 245; Schumacher's text reads 'equality of life', but I can only assume that is a typo).

Buddhist Economics as *Habitus*

What we are dealing with here, then, is less an alternative economic programme than a proposal for a change in *subjectivity*, or, to invoke Bourdieu, *habitus*; a transformation in priorities and—it would seem—basic assumptions about the self, society, and world. Habitus is created through a social, rather than individual, process leading to patterns that are enduring and transferable from one context to another, but that also shift in relation to specific contexts and over time. Habitus 'is not fixed or permanent, and can be changed under unexpected situations or over a long historical period' (Navarro 2006: 16). And how might this 'revolutionary' change come about? Schumacher argues for a perspective that aligns with virtue ethics: adopting and practising fundamental, classical Buddhist virtues such as humility, simplicity, moderation, commitment to non-harm, and awareness of consequences of one's actions—all encapsulated under the directive to Right Livelihood—will lead to increasingly altered perception and behaviour. But here too we see, not for the last time, a distinct emphasis on *autonomy* and *will* over structure and social construction; a preference, we might say, for *subjectivity* over *habitus*.

Padmasiri de Silva notes Schumacher's distinction between *forward stampeders* and *homecomers*. The former preach relentless striving; every problem has a concrete solution, involving new laws, technologies, or institutional practices—and generally accepts the 'logic' of capitalist economic growth: 'If there are problems about natural resources, we shall turn to synthetics... and so on' (de Silva 1975: 5). Contrariwise, *homecomers* are those who:

> attempt to get out of this vicious circle. They feel that what is important is not accelerating the set patterns of development, but re-directing them.... [He or she] examines afresh the purpose of economic activity and raises the question, 'economic activity for whose sake?' (5)

The term *homecomer* is provocative, given the classical Buddhism emphasis of 'home-leaving'—the very definition of what is required to join the *saṅgha*. (De Silva comments that '[t]he term "homecomer" has a religious connotation and implies that one should get back to the basic truths about man and the world' (6)—such as those found in the classical religious texts of the world's religions. But this sidesteps several issues, I think; most significantly, the world- [and 'home-']renouncing aspect of at least several of these traditions.) Clearly, Schumacher's contrast here is meant to reinforce the importance of scale and simplicity; hence it may be that 'opting out' of contemporary capitalist culture *is* in fact a way of 'coming home' to a more sustainable *habitus*, just as the traditional monastery may have played this role (among others).

Along similar lines, in the 'Epilogue' to *Small is Beautiful*, Schumacher invokes the four Christian Cardinal Virtues—*prudentia, justicia, fortitudo*, and *temperantia*—as a bulwark against 'the philosophy of materialism' (1973: 277–280). Of these, he singles out *prudentia*, the 'mother' of all virtues, which 'signifies the opposite of a small, mean, calculating attitude to life, which refuses to see and value anything that fails to produce an immediate utilitarian advantage' (280). This term provides substance to thinking of Right Livelihood as a 'virtue', not least because it squarely connects ethics with knowledge or contextual awareness. We might also relate 'prudence' to the (admittedly overused) Buddhist trope of 'mindfulness'—or, more specifically, the virtue of *appamāda*, which can be glossed as 'heedfulness, diligence, and earnestness', 'a combination of mindfulness and effort, energy or exertion' (*viriya*), or even 'a responsibility for the good' (Rājavaramuni 1990: 51). According to Joseph Pieper:

> The pre-eminence of prudence means that realisation of the good presupposes knowledge of reality. He alone can do good who know what things are like and what their situation is ... so-called 'good intentions' and so-called 'meaning well' by no means suffice. Realisation of the good presupposes that our actions are appropriate to the real situation, that is to the concrete realities which form the 'environment' of a concrete human action; and that we therefore take this concrete reality seriously, with clear-eyed objectivity. (quoted in Schumacher 1973: 280)

Without, perhaps, being fully aware of it, Schumacher's invocation of prudence here lets in the spectre of 'materialism', at least as understood in the philosophical tradition associated with a line of thinkers such as Epicurus, Lucretius, Giordano Bruno, and Spinoza. Prudence was the first of the Epicurean virtues (see Stewart 2014: 285). If prudence implies nothing less than 'a transformation of the knowledge of truth into decisions corresponding to reality', then there is nothing more significant than sustained attention to the world as it is, without the disrupting (or soporific) effects of non-empirically verifiable religious beliefs (Stewart 2014: 257–258). Of course, this is also the tradition that would inspire most of the progressive and radical economic theories of the nineteenth century, which called for massive transformation of social, political, and economic systems that have distorted our view of 'reality' on both an individual and collective level.

In fact, Theodore Roszak situates Schumacher's work within the anarchist tradition of Kropotkin, Gustav Landauer, Tolstoy, William Morris, Gandhi, Mumford, Alex Comfort, Paul Goodman, and Murray Bookchin. The logic behind this connection is primarily Schumacher's emphasis on *scale*—but also, I suggest, the recognition of the deep and abiding interplay between economic activities and personal growth and development. Despite its stereotypical representation as a promoter of bomb-throwing chaos, classical anarchism distinguished from both orthodox socialism and capitalism 'by insisting that the *scale* of organization must be treated as an independent and primary problem'.

> The [anarchist] tradition, while closely affiliated with socialist values, nonetheless prefers mixed to 'pure' economic systems. It is therefore hospitable to many forms of free enterprise and private ownership, provided always that the size of free enterprise and private ownership is not so large as to divorce ownership from personal involvement, which, of course, is now the rule in most of the world's administered capitalisms. Bigness is the nemesis of anarchism. (Roszak 1973: 4)

And yet, despite this fundamental connection to a tradition of collective 'revolt' against commonplace understandings, Schumacher's arguments, like those of Thich Nhat Hanh, seem to get stuck in (moral) appeals to 'inner', 'spiritual transformation':

> Everywhere people ask: 'What can I actually *do*?' The answer is as simple as it is disconcerting: we can, each of us, work to put our own inner house in order. The guidance we need for this work cannot be found in science or technology, the value of which utterly depends on the ends they serve; but it can still be found in the traditional wisdom of mankind. (Schumacher 1973: 281)

In other words, for all his genuine insights into the nature of the problem, Schumacher's critique fails to question the fundamental framework of the capitalist economic system itself, instead relying on some form of Buddhist moral/spiritual wisdom as a balm to the dehumanizing tendencies of that system. It scratches the surface of the problem but does not dig far enough down to its roots—to the *radical*, which is the *human*.

Other attempts to work out a 'Buddhist economics' fall prey to the sort of idealism, moralism, and residual dualism that one finds in Schumacher. For instance, H. N. S. Karunatilake's analysis in *This Confused Society* (1976) looks back wistfully to the age of the Mauryan emperor Aśoka as a model, painting an idyllic picture of a co-operative and harmonious agrarian community (see Harvey 2000: 216–217). More recent forays into the same theme tend to focus on a Buddhist critique of *consumerism* rather than capitalism per se, and thus, although undoubtedly of use, move further away from the possibility of a more systematic, structural critique. Thus, both Thai monk-scholar P. A. Payutto (b. 1938), author of the 1992 work *Buddhist Economics: A Middle Way for the Market Place*, and Buddhadasa Bhikkhu (1906–1993), who espoused a form of Dhammic socialism, focus their critique on the 'worldly' character of both capitalist and communist systems, upholding an idealized Buddhist tradition as the moral exemplar.[5]

Although more nuanced in his appreciation of the complexities of Marxist thought, B. R. A. Ambedkar (1891–1956), too, shares with these later critics a tendency towards a reading of Marxism on the basis of its most problematic 'fruits', while giving historical Buddhism a pass in favour of a highly idealized *Dharma* (see, e.g., Ambedkar 2011). Even Sulak Sivaraksa (b. 1933), who after Ambedkar has advocated the closest thing to a 'radical' form of Engaged Buddhism in South and Southeast Asia, and who in an essay entitled 'Alternatives to Consumerism' provides a withering critique of the many problems of capitalism—in particular the destruction of real community and the fomenting of rampant alienation—allows his analysis to fall back from the structural and systemic to the individual and psychic, concluding that, 'At the most profound level, consumerism owes its vitality to the delusion of the autonomous individual self; self that exists independently of social relations and of human relations with nature' (Sivaraksa 2001: 135–136; for Marx, this is a *consequence* of the capitalist system, not a *cause*).

Most of these writers follow Payutto in highlighting the Buddhist approach to wealth and poverty as (inevitable) conditions of human being, rather than as products of a particular, contingent, and plausibly flawed and 'un-Buddhist' economic system. Payutto argues that 'poverty' is entirely a matter of one's perception (an 'inappropriate attitude' rooted in greed and craving). As such, Buddhism preaches 'contentment' with what one has. This is certainly true, to a degree, but it easily slides into a justification for economic disparity and an attitude of 'the poor will always be with us'. However much it might be justified by citations from classical sources, there seems to be something fundamentally wrong with the notion that, as far as Buddhism is concerned, extreme scarcity will be bad if and only if 'it stimulates greed and provokes acts of crime' (Swearer and Sizemore 1990: 2). More significantly, it denies that material conditions can and do 'shape' our consciousness, and our desires, relying instead on what can only be called an Enlightenment view of autonomy and free will. Everything revolves around one's 'attitude'; systems (and communities) are ultimately meaningless, both as causes of suffering (alienation) and as vehicles for release. In addition, the focus is turned from issues of labour and distribution of wealth (again, the 'social' aspects of economics) to 'appropriate acquisition and use' (the individual or personal aspects) (Swearer and Sizemore 1990: 5).

Payutto argues that Buddhist social ethics can be thought of in terms of an interconnection between *Dharma*, understood as 'natural law' (from which flow Buddhist doctrines) and *Vinaya*, understood as an 'artificial', 'human law' whose purpose is to allow for the integration and expression of *Dharma*. Whereas 'in the *dhamma* the individual has responsibility for his or her own development...

[5] Payutto has published under various names; the Works Cited to this chapter includes one essay he published under the name Rājavaramuni.

> through the *vinaya* the community or society offers sanctions or rules to regulate the actions of individuals. With the *vinaya* the Buddha puts people into reciprocal or interdependent relationships ... with the *dhamma* the individual's internal independence and freedom are to be attained and retained ... (Rājavaramuni 1990: 52)

For Payutto, as for many scholars of Buddhist ethics, individual perfection and the social good are 'interdependent and inseparable'. And yet, as I have been arguing, this 'inseparability' is burdened by residual, dualistic assumptions regarding a) 'self' (or 'no self') versus 'society', and b) 'spiritual' versus 'worldly' affairs (see Essen 2009: 33, following Payutto 1992). As a result, despite paying homage to 'inseparability', Buddhist ethicists more often than not leave the matter on a superficial level of mutual advantage; e.g., the *saṅgha* relies on society for material support, and 'pay back'—via the *Dharma*—the security and peace that is necessary for society to continue and flourish (see, e.g., Reynolds 1990: 64). While this is certainly historically accurate, it provides little for further ethical thinking or development. What if there is more to this? What if we were to consider the relation between *Dharma* and *Vinaya* as more fundamentally integrative?

In short, the basic thesis of much of what has passed as 'Buddhist economics' amounts to the following: an idealized and often dehistoricized 'Buddhism' becomes the new 'middle way' (or even 'third way') between the two dominant socio-economic systems of the twentieth century: capitalism and communism or state socialism. There are problems with this picture. First, as noted, 'Buddhism' is here often abstracted from its actual historical effects within particular states and societies. Second, now that actual state socialism has largely gone the way of the dodo, the pressing need to bridge the imagined divide also withers away. This, I believe, gives us an opportunity to rethink not only Buddhism in its relation to socio-economic forms but also to reconsider alternative perspectives associated with anarchism, socialism, and communism—particularly their understanding of and commitment to philosophical materialism.[6] We might say that contemporary Buddhist or Buddhist-inspired critiques of economics tend to espouse individual, moral transformation rather than structural change, and thus focus less on materialism as a philosophical stance than as a synonym for consumerist acquisition (or 'commodity fetishism'). They also often present an idealized vision of Buddhist tradition, which is contrasted favourably to a Western tradition or traditions ostensibly rooted in greed, selfishness, and individualism. As such, they fail to examine problems rooted within Buddhism, such as the tendency towards forms of idealism and transcendence—or what the Japanese Critical Buddhists have called *topicalism*.[7]

[6] In addition to the early twentieth-century experiments of East Asian 'radical Buddhists' such as Uchiyama Gudō (1874–1911), Senoo Girō (1889–1961), Ichikawa Hakugen (1902–1986), and Taixu (1890–1947), I am inspired here in part by a recent series of writings by mainly European thinkers under the lead of Alain Badou and Slavoj Žižek regarding the potential rebirth of what Badou calls 'the communist hypothesis'.

[7] See Shields 2011. Along these lines, as I have argued elsewhere (2013), there may be room for a 'Buddhist criticism' that takes seriously the 'ruthless criticism' advocated by Marx—as, it has been argued, the *ne plus ultra* of his thought—one that serves as a 'universal solvent' on all preconceptions and dogmas.

Rethinking Buddhist Materialism

I suggest that part of the problem here rests with the term 'materialism'—which, as we have seen, is bandied about by Buddhist authors and scholars as a representation of what Buddhism strives *against*—and what plagues Western society most. Yet there are important distinctions to be made between (1) 'materialism' as the thirst for objects and possessions (i.e. consumerism, though often conflated with 'economics' per se), (2) materialism as a philosophical premise and perspective (one that emphasizes the significance of the material world and downplays or denies the existence of the non-material), and (3) the more specific thesis of 'historical materialism' as developed by Marx. (I deliberately avoid a fourth possibility, so-called 'dialectical materialism', as I concur with Kołakowski [2008] that it is an inchoate concept of little to no real significance.)

The first meaning, which happens to be the way most people today use the term, is obviously problematic for Buddhists of all stripes and traditions. It goes without saying that a life predicated on or dedicated to the desire to possess and consume material goods (or anything, for that matter) is impossible to reconcile with Buddhist teachings. And yet, this blanket rejection of this form of materialism does not need to bleed into a rejection of the two other forms of materialism. In fact, I suggest that Buddhists would gain from at least considering these other forms, allowing for the possibility that they may not only be true but useful to Buddhist thought and practice, particularly when it comes to questions of politics and economics. I have discussed this issue in detail elsewhere (Shields 2013), so will just present a brief summary here.

For Marx overcoming alienation—and dehumanization—involves nothing less than a recovery, via proletarian revolution, of humanity's 'species-being' (alternatively called 'social being'). At one level, to make this claim is to assume that humanity has some sort of 'essence', and that Marx, or the proletariat, knows what that is. And yet, as Kołakowski persuasively argues, human nature or the 'self' for Marx is *not* conceived as 'a set of features which may be empirically ascertained', but rather as 'a set of requirements that must be fulfilled in order to make human beings genuinely human'.[8] In other words, while Marx does indeed presuppose a non-historical norm of humanity, this is 'not a collection of permanent, unchanging qualities belonging to some arbitrary ideal, but a conception of the conditions of development enabling men to display their creative powers to the full, untrammelled by material needs' (Kołakowski 2008: 217–218). Human fulfilment, then, is not a matter of attaining some sort of utopian state of

[8] It should be noted that this does *not* exclude a concept of human nature, which seems necessary to any ideology that posits a vision of human flourishing (see Geras 2016). Buddhism, too, I would suggest, includes a sense of 'human nature' (perhaps: 'Buddha-nature') that is *not* essentialist. Though the connection between the Buddhist conception of self/mind and that of Hume is often noted, I suggest that the Marxian 'self' is actually closer, in that it, too, is very much a 'work in process'. This connections bears further analysis.

perfection, but rather of liberating humanity from the conditions that make us the slaves of our own works.

One counter to the argument that Buddhism can contribute meaningfully to the discussion of a revised materialism is the common conception that Buddhism—to some extent *qua* religion, but even more so by virtue of it *ascetic* qualities—is simply incompatible with materialism. Certainly there are ascetic roots to Indian Buddhist monasticism; a simple, abstemious life was and remains for the most part a non-negotiable requirement for membership in the *saṅgha*. Again, no one would dispute that 'materialism' in the ('consumerist') sense of 'fulfilment of life via the pursuit and attainment of material possessions' is unacceptable by any Buddhist standard. And yet, this is surely true of most or all normatively inclined thought traditions—including Marxism. After all, alienation in Marx's thought is nothing less than the subjugation of humanity by its own works, i.e. through 'reification' (Lukács) or 'commodity fetishism' (Marx), which might be summarized as 'the inability of human beings to see their own products for what they are, and their unwilling consent to be enslaved by human power instead of wielding it' (Kołakowski 2008: 227).

Even a 'hedonistic' form of materialism is more complex than a simple thirst for 'things'. A focus on the *world-as-it-is* may in fact amount to a valorization of the simple, the mundane, and the everyday—one thinks here of the humble and potentially Buddhistic 'hedonism' of the Epicurean tradition up to Thoreau's *Walden*. Perhaps the strongest case to be made for a Buddhism that embraces a limited hedonistic materialism (i.e. of the Thoreauian sort) would be the Chan/Zen traditions that emerged out of a medieval and early modern Sino-Japanese cultural context.

Moving further among types of materialism, we come to the philosophical materialism generally accepted by Marxists and anarchists, following upon classical and Enlightenment thinkers such as Epicurus, Democritus, Lucretius, Bruno, and (arguably) Spinoza—but also including the Indian Cārvāka (or Lokāyata) school and certain Chinese thinkers such as Xunzi. Here the emphasis is less on *pleasure* than on an acceptance of the *conditioning power of material relations*. And yet, even here there is some dispute within Marxist theory. While Engels and Lenin, along with most orthodox Marxists, followed the materialist emphasis on *matter* as the foundation of meaning and value, Marx himself clearly understood materialism less as a theory about reality—an ontology or metaphysic—than a 'warning' against the tendency to privilege ideals and totalities at the expense of particularity and contingency, and the 'human'.

In short, at the heart of Marxian materialism is a fundamental element of *critique*, one that points towards causal factors that may otherwise go unnoticed in our attempts to discern—and ultimately address—our existential situatedness. This is the foundation of 'historical materialism', a position that, I contend, has been largely ignored by Buddhists and Buddhist scholars alike, but which may prove amenable in thinking through Buddhist ethics in the twenty-first century. Moreover, Marx's broader thesis of historical materialism has roots in his fundamental conception of economics as understood principally through the lens of the value and effects of labour and the mode of production, which 'must not be considered:

> simply as being the reproduction of the physical existence of the individuals. Rather it is a definite form of activity of these individuals, a definite form of expressing their life, a definite *mode of life* on their part. What they are, therefore, coincides with their production, both with *what* they produce and with *how* they produce. Hence what individuals are depends on the material conditions of their production. (*MECW* 5: 31–32; see Geras 2016: 64–65)

In what follows, and with a nod to future work, I propose we take this (Marxian if not Marxist) holistic approach to human labour and production as a challenge to any and all attempts to develop a 'Buddhist economics' for the twenty-first century. I begin this task by bringing a historical materialist critique to several more recent proposals for Buddhist economic ethics.

Mindfulness in the Marketplace

A 2001 compilation of essays edited by Allen Hunt Badiner, entitled *Mindfulness in the Marketplace*, provides both a glimpse at the possibilities in rethinking Buddhist economics and the limits to many of the approaches developed on the heels of critics like Schumacher and Payutto. In the Introduction to the volume, Badiner cites Schumacher's definition of Buddhist economics: 'The ownership and the consumption of goods... is a means to an end, and Buddhist economics is the systematic study of how to attain given ends with the minimum means' (2001: xiii). While Badiner adds that Buddhist economics should also be concerned with attaining goods by causing 'minimal damage', one cannot help feel that this definition *assumes* a certain utilitarian and even consumerist paradigm for economic activity that may fit only uncomfortably with some aspects of Buddhist ethics. Later, Badiner writes: 'Buddhism is all about changing consciousness in order to affect changes in behavior' (xv). Again, while there is undeniably truth to this statement, I wonder if this is not indeed a *limiting* factor to Buddhist perspectives on economics (as well, for that matter, politics). *What if, as most radical thinkers have long asserted, changing behaviour is part and parcel of changing consciousness?*

A more provocative take on the matter is provided by Riane Eisler, who in 'A Systems View of Overconsumption' rejects the lazy dichotomy of 'capitalism vs. communism, industrial vs. pre- or postindustrial, hi-tech vs. technologically undeveloped'—and, we might add, 'material vs. spiritual'. As Eisler rightly notes, economic and technological systems 'are inextricably interconnected with the larger cultural system in which they operate'. Thus, it is imperative that we closely examine 'the underlying cultural models that inform the construction of economics' (2001: 41). In other words, we must go beyond the purely psychologistic (and ultimately individualistic) perspective that colours most contemporary Buddhist analyses of economics. Eisler goes on to distinguish two fundamentally different models for constructing human cultures: 'the *partnership* model and the *domination* model' and argues that '[t]he degree to which a culture orients to one of the other ... moulds all our relationships ... [and] profoundly affects how we structure all our institutions, from the family, and education, to economics, and politics' (41). Though the contrast is still somewhat oversimplified, Eisler's general point is well taken and can be used as a basis for further philosophical-ethical investigation.

Right Livelihood as Foundation

As noted above, at first glance, Buddhist traditions might be conceived as *an*-economic, since the monastic community, the *saṅgha*, is set up as an explicit rejection of 'worldly' systems of exchange of goods (both production and reproduction) (Swearer and Sizemore 1990: xi). And yet, beyond the 'tension' of having to rely on lay support, we find in some monastic traditions also the more positive aspect of the valuation of work or *labour*, which is at least as fundamental to economics as the exchange or consumption of goods—perhaps more so. 'The Buddhist view of work is that it is an integral part of life. The Buddha recognized this by highlighting 'livelihood' as one of the components of his eightfold path of practice' (Inoue 2001: 57).[9]

'Livelihood' clearly indicates a realm that is both personal *and* political, and seems ineluctably intertwined with a sense of human flourishing in community, i.e. akin to Aristotle's *eudaemonia* (Critchley 1995: 1). Indeed, right livelihood—connected to Buddhist concepts of interdependence, no-self, and so on—suggest that the personal is inexorably 'social' (and vice versa, of course). We might further develop this by going back to the work of P. A. Payutto. In an essay entitled 'Buddhist Perspectives on Economic Concepts', Payutto parses the classical Buddhist distinction between two types of desire: *taṇhā* and *chanda* (see also Rājavaramuni 1990: 51). Whereas the former, he argues, is directed towards the fulfilment of 'self-interested' pleasure, the latter is concerned with a broader sense of flourishing or 'well-being'—which appears to imply both an altruistic or at least interdependent aspect as well as a focus on long-term as opposed to short-term benefits. Payutto goes on to connect these to two opposing types of consumption, one good and one bad:

> [R]ight consumption always contributes to well being and forms a basis for the further development of human potentialities. This is an important point often overlooked by economists. Consumption guided by *chanda* does much more than satisfy one's desire; it contributes to well-being and spiritual development. This is also true

[9] See Reynolds's (1990: 71) claim that the commitment to diligence and frugality indicates the 'unmistakably bourgeois' character of Theravādin economic ethics, allowing comparison with the Puritan work ethic as described by Weber (2010). Little (2001: 83–84) demurs, arguing that, unlike the Puritans, Theravāda Buddhists emphasize *giving* (especially religious giving) rather than *saving* (as a sign of God's grace). He is right, and as such, this fundamental Buddhist impulse may align with Bataille's (1988) concept of the 'general economy' typified by the 'accursed share' (following Mauss's [2000] insights, which David Graeber [2004] associates with anarchism).

> on a global scale. If all economic activity were guided by *chanda*, the result would be much more than just a healthy economy and material progress—such activities would contribute to the whole of human development and enable humanity to lead a nobler life and enjoy a more mature kind of happiness. (Payutto 2001: 77–79)

As with my above critique of Payutto, once again I have problems with his fundamental premise, i.e. with the assumption that if only we could change our minds (or attitudes, desires), then we would be able to participate fruitfully in the economic system *as it is*. In other words, by this understanding the problem is simply the *spirit* in which we undertake consumption—not consumption itself, nor the industrial capitalist system that promotes and sustains the habits that we so readily (and literally) buy into. Perhaps—as 'radical Buddhists' such as Senoō Girō (1889–1967) would argue—the only alternative is revolution; or at least a radical restructuring of prevailing economic and political systems (see Shields 2017, ch. 5). But my main point is to suggest that the current ideas of Buddhist economics are unable to imagine *real* alternatives to contemporary industrial capitalism.

And yet, as with Schumacher, there is in Payutto material to work with in re-envisioning Buddhist economics along more radical lines. If we take the distinction between *taṇhā* and *chanda* out of the purely psychologistic realm—that is, as names indicating types of desire—and reframe them as distinctive 'habits' or 'ways of being' which are deeply implicated in social, political, and economic structures, then we may avoid the pitfalls of Payutto's residual idealism, and come closer to a 'moderate materialism'. Moreover, in giving legitimate place for 'desire'—and by extension, the fulfilling of 'human needs'—as a motivation for not only consumption but production, Payutto allows us to turn back, again, to the alternative tradition of Western thinkers like Epicurus and Spinoza, for whom 'desire' was foundational to human flourishing, but understood in a significantly modified form than in the 'common' or conventional understanding. Marx, as well, made a clear distinction between unenlightened ('bourgeois') and enlightened ('proletarian' or, perhaps more suitable for our purposes here, 'radical') ways of being, and in fact framed the distinction in terms almost identical to that of Payutto: whereas the 'bourgeois' (an ideal type, not necessarily a particular person or class) is intent on maintaining their own wealth, power, and status by exploiting others (and nature), the 'revolutionary' (again, an ideal type) is anyone who rejects the relentless quest for power and control, and who dedicates herself to the construction of a new society in which the 'well-being' of humanity (and nature) becomes the only goal. The difference between this distinction and that of Payutto is that Payutto's 'Buddhist' perspective is still very much caught within the assumptions of liberal individualism (even if dressed in classical Buddhist guise).

As an extension of his exploration of 'right livelihood', Payutto engages in a sustained critique of the modern, Western understanding of 'the pursuit of happiness' as the relentless pursuit of self-interested pleasure. In contrast, he uplifts the First Noble Truth's recognition of suffering as a bulwark against the naive and misleading search for 'happiness' as *satisfaction of desire*. He contrasts this with two alternative, Buddhist-inspired forms of 'happiness': (1) arguably the more 'classical'—and, in Payutto's view, higher and more exalted, he calls 'independent happiness ... the happiness that arises from within a mind that has been trained and has attained some degree of inner peace'; and (2) to me, the much more valuable and interesting option: 'harmonious happiness':

> a happiness that is altruistically based, directed toward well-being, and motivated by goodwill and compassion. Through personal development, people can appreciate this truer kind of happiness—the desire to bring happiness to others (which in Buddhism we call *metta*). With this kind of happiness, we can experience joy at the happiness of others, just as parents fell glad at the happiness of their children. (2001: 92)

Payutto's second option, which is more directly rooted in community, seems to come close once again to a decidedly 'worldly' and even 'radical' conception of human flourishing, as well as the possibility of a 'Buddhist economics' that enhances happiness at this level. The basic premise here is that 'work' or 'labour', rightly conceived and properly executed, is a form of (simultaneously) fashioning both 'self' and 'community' (see Stewart 2014: 296).

And yet, as a necessary corrective to this rather sunny view of economics as proverbial Amish barn raising, we must bear in mind the Marxian insight that labour can and frequently is a source—perhaps *the* source—of alienation and dehumanization (beyond the more obvious problems of poverty and injustice). In this regard, despite being labelled a 'materialist', Marx described his own perspective as being something closer to a 'naturalism' or 'humanism' that 'differs equally from idealism and materialism, being the truth which unites them both' (quoted in Kołakowski 2008: 113; see Senoō 1975: 359). As such:

> Human consciousness is merely the expression in thought of a social relationship to nature, and must be considered as a product of the collective effort of the species. Accordingly, deformations of consciousness are not to be explained as due to the aberrations or imperfections of consciousness itself: their sources are to be looked for in more original processes, and particularly in the alienation of labour. (Kołakowski 2008: 114)

If we take this insight seriously, it opens up some potentially fertile avenues of extension of 'Buddhist economics', since it draws an explicit connection between ordinary 'deformations of consciousness' (ignorance or delusions), suffering (as alienation or dissatisfaction), and labour both as a cause of these fundamental Buddhist concerns *and* as a potential vehicle for their amelioration if not release (see Kolakowski 2008: 113–114).

Another contemporary writer has, like Schumacher, argued for a reintroduction of both 'scale' and 'home' to contemporary economics theory and practice. Rather than 'prudence', however, poet and cultural critic Wendell Berry (2001) introduces the old-fashioned—and somewhat more Asian-sounding—term *propriety* to describe a form of resistance against contemporary habits of mind:

> Its value is in its reference to the fact that we are not alone. The idea of propriety makes an issue of the fittingness of our conduct to our place and circumstances, even to our hopes. It acknowledges the always-pressing realities of context and of influence; we cannot speak or act or live out of context. Our life inescapably affects other lives, which inescapably affect our life. We are being measured, in other words, by a standard that we did not make and cannot destroy. It is by that standard, and only by that standard, that we know we are in a crisis in our relationship to nature. (2001: 13)

In this sense, 'propriety' may be a more appropriate foundation for Buddhist economics than either 'prudence' or 'responsibility', since, as Berry indicates, it pushes towards context and sociability rather than the locus of the individual. As a *habitus* rather than simply a virtue or mindset, one that Berry considers the 'antithesis of individualism', propriety might serve as a bulwark against simple-minded encomiums to 'the pursuit of happiness', which to a large degree structure and justify our current economic system, in which the 'individual's wish is the ultimate measure of the world' (Stewart 2014: 290).

Conclusion

In an essay in *Mindfulness in the Marketplace*, Stephen Batchelor, a British Buddhist and scholar who advocates an atheistic, demythologized, and naturalized form of Buddhist practice, makes the following remark with regard to Buddhism and economics:

> One view is that mainstream economic theory is in itself 'value free' and able to incorporate and reflect any system of values, including a Buddhist one. An alternative view is that mainstream economic theory is inherently unable to reflect adequately the Buddhist 'practice of generosity,' for instance, as part of economic activity. (2001: 65)

On one level, this is undeniably true, although I suggest that, given the hegemony of the neo-liberal (or 'neo-classical') economic paradigm, the number of Buddhists in the former far outweighs those in the latter camp.[10] Indeed, as we have seen in this chapter, most liberal or progressive writers on Buddhist economics—Asian and Western alike—tend to assume that Buddhism is compatible with global capitalism, but can (and should) serve as a kind of moral buttress to the excesses of such. In so doing, as noted

10 'Because Buddhism adapts easily to new contexts, it may be tailored to a modern Buddhist nation's economic plan' (Essen 2009: 36; cf. Pryor 1991: 22). Though perhaps more innocuous, this reminds me of D. T. Suzuki's (1959: 63) infamous remark regarding Zen, i.e. that it 'is extremely flexible in adapting itself to almost any philosophy and moral doctrine as long as its intuitive teaching is not interfered with . . . [thus it] may be found wedded to anarchism or fascism, communism or democracy, atheism or idealism, or any political or economic dogmatism.'

above, they are rather too hastily accepting the principle of separation between religion/ethics and the 'secular' realms of politics and economics.

Schumacher, Ambedkar, Sulak Sivaraksa, and a few others have been more critical, inclining towards the latter view, where there is something fundamentally incompatible between certain, perhaps non-negotiable Buddhist values and contemporary global capitalism. Even here, though, the emphasis quickly becomes personalized and moralized, such that 'Buddhist economics' is largely a matter of internal transformation towards 'compassion' and 'charity', under the assumption that this transformation will manifest in a new and different economic system.

This chapter is intended as an opening gambit in a much larger project, which I intend to pursue over the following years. (I only hope that I have not sacrificed too many pawns in the process of my attack on the Queen!) As noted at the outset, I envision this as a collaborative, critical-constructive project carried out under the auspices of cross-cultural philosophy. Much of the above has been critical; here I conclude with a schematic overview of the most salient starting points of a 'radical' Buddhist economics (or economic ethics).

Thesis 1: Buddhist ethics, and in particular Buddhist economic ethics, must take progressive and radical theory seriously; this includes (1) a deeper reflection on the tendency to separate (conceptually and in practice) the spheres politics and economics from 'religion'; and (2) greater recognition of the place and significance of 'labour' in social life and the path towards 'liberation of suffering'.

Thesis 2: Historical and philosophical materialism, particularly as developed in the work of Marx and the classical anarchist thinkers but with earlier precedents in both Western and Asian thought traditions, provides a fertile locus for Buddhist ethical reflection on labour, production, and community.

Thesis 3: Schumacher's thesis on the significance of 'scale' (rooted in classical Buddhist monastic virtues) is crucial to Buddhist economics, as is the similar anarchist critique of hierarchies and power structures, including the state.

Thesis 4: Mahāyāna Buddhist reflections on the mutual interpenetration of self and society, such as one finds in the Japanese Nichiren tradition, are of great value in pushing beyond individualist conceptions of liberation, which often recapitulate and reinforce neo-liberal assumptions.

Thesis 5: The traditional Asian virtue of 'propriety'—combined with contemporary ideas regarding *habitus* (Bourdieu) and *home* (Schumacher; Berry)—help to consolidate the *critical* with the *communal* elements of a truly progressive or radical Buddhist economics.

Along lines of the criticism developed in this chapter, I suggest that a 'radical' perspective—one that cuts deep within and challenges Buddhist conceptions of 'self', 'community', and 'human nature'—is a more effective approach to reconsidering Buddhist economics in the twenty-first century, in the midst of continuing market turmoil and rampant ecological devastation. Buddhism is, or at any rate *can be*, a significant social force challenging the alienated relationships—between self, other, and nature—brought on by the dynamics of late capitalist culture.

Works Cited

Ambedkar, B. R. A. (2011) *The Buddha and his Dhamma: a critical edition*. New Delhi: Oxford University Press.

Aristotle (1984) *Politics*. In J. Barnes (ed.), *The complete works of Aristotle*, Volume 2. Sixth edition. Princeton: Princeton University Press, 1986–2129.

Bataille, G. (1988) *The accursed share: an essay on general economy*. New York: Zone Books.

Batchelor, S. (2001) The practice of generosity. In A. H. Badiner (ed.), *Mindfulness in the marketplace*. Berkeley: Parallax Press, 59–66.

Berry, W. (2001) *Life is a miracle: an essay against modern superstition*. Berkeley: Counterpoint Press.

Bunnag, J. (1973) *Buddhist monk, Buddhist layman: a study of urban monastic organization in central Thailand*. Cambridge: Cambridge University Press.

Collins, S. (2013) *Self and society: essays on Pali literature and social theory, 1988–2010*. Chiang Mai: Silkworm Books.

Crespo, R. (2009) Aristotle. In J. Peil and I. van Staveren (eds), *Handbook of economics and ethics*. Cheltenham, UK: Edward Elgar, 14–20.

Critchley, P. (1995) *Aristotle and the public good*. Available from: www.academia.edu/705315/Aristotle_and_the_Public_Good [accessed 25 February 2016].

Daniels, P. (2005) Economic systems and the Buddhist world view: the 21st-century nexus. *The journal of socio-economics*, 34, 245–268.

De Silva, P. (1975) The search for Buddhist economics. *Bodhi leaves*, 69. BPS online edition. Available from: www.bps.lk/olib/bl/bl069.pdf [accessed 15 January 2016].

Essen, J. (2009) Buddhist economics. In J. Peil and I. van Staveren (eds), *Handbook of economics and ethics*. Cheltenham, UK: Edward Elgar, 31–38.

Fenn, M. L. (1996) Two notions of poverty in the Pāli canon. *Journal of Buddhist ethics*, 3, 98–125.

Geras, N. (2016) *Marx and human nature: refutation of a legend*. London: Verso.

Graeber, D. (2004) *Fragments of an anarchist anthropology*. Chicago: Prickly Paradigm Press.

Harvey, P. (2000) *An introduction to Buddhist ethics*. London and New York: Oxford University Press.

Inoue S. (2001) A new economics to save the earth: a Buddhist perspective. In A. H. Badiner (ed.), *Mindfulness in the marketplace*. Berkeley: Parallax Press, 49–58.

Kołakowski, L. (2008) *Main currents of Marxism: the founders, the golden age, the breakdown*. 3 volumes. New York: W. W. Norton.

Little, D. (2001) Ethical analysis and wealth in Theravāda Buddhism: a response to Frank Reynolds. In: R. Sizemore and D. Swearer (eds), *Ethics, wealth and salvation: a study in Buddhist social ethics*. Columbia, SC: University of South Carolina Press, 77–86.

Luxemburg, R. (2014) Introduction to political economy. In P. Hudis (ed.), *The complete works of Rosa Luxemburg*, Volume 1. London: Verso, 89–300.

Marx, K. (1993) *Marx's Capital, a student edition*. Edited by C. J. Arthur. London: Lawrence and Wishart.

Mauss, M. (2000) *The gift: the form and reason for exchange in archaic societies*. New York: W. W. Norton.

Navarro, Z. (2006) In search of cultural interpretation of power. *IDS bulletin*, 37 (6), 11–22.

Nussbaum, M. (2000) *Women and human development: the capabilities approach*. Cambridge: Cambridge University Press.

Payutto, P. A. (1992) *Buddhist economics: a middle way for the marketplace.* Bangkok: Buddhadhamma Foundation.

Payutto, P. A. (2001) Buddhist perspectives on economic concepts. In: A. H. Badiner (ed.), *Mindfulness in the marketplace.* Berkeley: Parallax Press, 77–92.

Pryor, F. L. (1990) A Buddhist economic system in principle. *American journal of economics & sociology*, 49 (3), 339–351.

Pryor, F. L. (1991) A Buddhist economic system in practice. *American journal of economics & sociology*, 50 (1), 17–33.

Pryor, F. L. (2001) Buddhist economic systems. In A. H. Badiner (ed.), *Mindfulness in the marketplace.* Berkeley: Parallax Press, 155–160.

Rājavaramuni, P. [P. A. Payutto] (1990) Foundations of Buddhist social ethics. In: R. Sizemore and D. Swearer (eds), *Ethics, wealth and salvation: a study in Buddhist social ethics.* Columbia, SC: University of South Carolina Press, 29–53.

Reynolds, F. E. (1990) Ethics and wealth in Theravāda Buddhism: a study in comparative religious ethics. In: R. Sizemore and D. Swearer (eds), *Ethics, wealth and salvation: a study in Buddhist social ethics.* Columbia, SC: University of South Carolina Press, 59–66.

Robeyns, I. (2009) Capability approach. In: J. Peil and I. van Staveren (eds), *Handbook of economics and ethics.* Cheltenham, UK: Edward Elgar, 39–46.

Roszak, T. (1973). Introduction to: E. F. Schumacher, *Small is beautiful: economics as if people mattered.* New York: Harper & Row, 1–9.

Schumacher, E. F. (1973) *Small is beautiful: economics as if people mattered.* New York: Harper & Row.

Sen, A. (1985) *Commodities and capabilities.* Amsterdam: North Holland Press.

Schopen, G. (2004) *Buddhist monks and business matters: still more papers on monastic Buddhism in India.* Honolulu: University of Hawai'i Press.

Seno'o G. (1975) Shinkō bukkyō e no tenshin (Converting to revitalized Buddhism). *Shinkō bukkyō no hata no shita ni*, 1. Reprinted in: *Seno'o Girō shūkyō ronshū* (The religious thought of Seno'o Girō). Tokyo: Daizō shuppan, 260–301.

Shields, J. M. (2011) *Critical Buddhism: engaging with modern Japanese Buddhist thought.* Richmond, UK: Ashgate Press.

Shields, J. M. (2013) Rethinking Buddhist materialism. *Journal of Buddhist ethics*, 20, 461–499.

Shields, J. M. (2016) Opium eaters: Buddhism as revolutionary politics. In: H. Kawanami (ed.), *Buddhism and the political process.* London: Palgrave Macmillan, 213–234.

Shields, J. M. (2017) *Against harmony: progressive and radical Buddhism in modern Japan.* Oxford: Oxford University Press.

Sivaraksa, S. (2001) Alternatives to consumerism. In: A. H. Badiner (ed.), *Mindfulness in the marketplace.* Berkeley: Parallax Press, 135–142.

Stewart, M. (2014) *Nature's god: the heretical origins of the American republic.* London: Norton.

Suzuki, D. T. (1959) *Zen and Japanese culture.* London: Routledge.

Sizemore, R F., and Swearer, D. K. (eds) (1990) *Ethics, wealth and salvation: a study in Buddhist social ethics.* Columbia, SC: University of South Carolina Press.

Tachibana S. (1992) *Ethics of Buddhism.* Richmond, UK: Curzon Press.

Tambiah, S. J. (1976) *World conqueror and world renouncer: a study of Buddhism in Thailand against a historical background.* Cambridge: Cambridge University Press.

Weber, M. (2010) *The Protestant ethic and the spirit of capitalism.* Revised 1920 edition. Oxford: Oxford University Press.

Zadek, S. (1997) Towards a progressive Buddhist economics? Another view. In: J. Watts, A. Senauke, and S. Bhikku (eds), *Entering the realm of reality: towards dhammic societies.* Bangkok: INEB, 241–273.

Suggested Reading

Alexandrin, G. (1993) Elements of Buddhist economics. *International journal of social economics*, 20 (2), 3–11.

Daniels, P. (2005) Economic systems and the Buddhist world view: the 21st-century nexus. *The journal of socio-economics*, 34, 245–268.

Payutto, P. A. (1992) *Buddhist economics: a middle way for the marketplace.* Bangkok: Buddhadhamma Foundation.

Pryor, F. L. (1990) A Buddhist economic system in principle. *American journal of economics & sociology*, 49 (3), 339–351.

Pryor, F. (1991) A Buddhist economic system in practice. *American journal of economics & sociology*, 50 (1), 17–33.

Schumacher, E. F. (1973) *Small is beautiful: economics as if people mattered.* New York: Harper & Row.

Zadek, S. (1993) The practice of Buddhist economics? Another view. *American journal of economics & sociology*, 52 (4), 433–445.

CHAPTER 21

BUDDHIST ENVIRONMENTAL ETHICS

An Emergent and Contextual Approach

STEPHANIE KAZA

Introduction

GLOBAL pressures on human–environment systems are higher than ever before in human history, generating broad ethical engagement from many quarters. With human population and consumption soaring, biodiversity plunging, and inequity across race, class, and gender only increasing, the scope of environmental concerns has become increasingly complex and beyond any single solution. Citizen calls for moral response from world religious and political leaders have grown more urgent as pressures mount. Rising levels of greenhouse gases are expected to cause massive systemic climate change with potentially devastating consequences for people and all beings everywhere. The pain, grief, anxiety, and sense of impending loss are galvanizing much ethical soul searching around the world, with high motivation to correct the human course in the cosmos.

Buddhist philosophy and religious teachings contain a wealth of instruction and moral guidance regarding human–environment relations, offering a promising avenue for ethical response. Early Buddhist environmental ethics urged followers to protect clean water and sacred trees and to make food choices that minimize harm (such as vegetarianism). *Jātaka* tales and other texts call for compassion towards animals through minimizing cruelty and acknowledging animal suffering. Chinese and Japanese Zen sources emphasize the dynamic flow of energy through beings and ecosystems and support an aesthetic harmony with nature. Some Western thinkers have posited that Buddhism is the most eco-friendly of the world's religions. Others have challenged this claim as overly influenced by the recent wave of interest in religious engagement with environmental concerns. A number of anthologies have laid the groundwork for

Buddhist environmental ethics with classical Buddhist texts and commentaries on ethics, practices, and current issues (Callicott and Ames 1989; Hunt-Badiner 1990 and 2002; Batchelor and Brown 1992; Chapple 1993; Tucker and Williams 1997; Kaza and Kraft 2000).

These conversations are all relatively new within scholarly Buddhist studies and also new to the academic field of religion and ecology. To lay some groundwork, I begin by acknowledging some of the most well-known thinkers and the issues they have engaged to date through a Buddhist lens. Among environmental concerns, global economic development is taking an enormous toll on the earth's ecosystems due to rising population levels and rampant consumerism. Buddhist scholar Rita Gross (1998) drew on Buddhist analysis to expose pro-natalist cultural and religious attitudes that drive high population rates in many countries, pointing out that this is not supported in Buddhist philosophy. Loy (2008) examined the three poisons teaching in the context of global drivers of greed, avarice, and delusion, showing how consumerism has penetrated almost every modern culture to toxic levels. Sivaraksa (2001), through his work with International Network of Engaged Buddhists, has taken up the widespread poverty and inequity associated with development and its environmental costs. And I have explored how the cycles of greed, desire, and consumption are driven through the powerful links of dependent origination; a range of Buddhist approaches to reducing overconsumption are addressed in *Hooked!* (Kaza 2005b).

Western Buddhists have shown great interest in food ethics, often regarding this as an environmental choice. Oregon Zen teacher Jan Chozen Bays (2009) has developed a mindfulness approach to eating that includes environmental awareness, and Vietnamese teacher Thich Nhat Hanh (2008) has used food awareness to invite understanding of the co-arising of human and planetary health and well-being. In earlier work, I reviewed Buddhist motivations for vegetarianism and eating practices that support ethical awareness (Kaza 2005a). To address food gaps and mass hunger, Bhikkhu Bodhi's Global Relief organization brings a compassionate and systemic approach to address the need for adequate nutrition in many places.

Concepts of well-being and resilience as keys to sustainability have been broadly addressed by the Gross National Happiness programme in the small Buddhist nation of Bhutan, based on Buddhist goals of personal and social contentment. Similar goals are promoted by the Western mindfulness movement, with marked success in reducing anxiety, aggression, pain, and insecurity in settings as varied as hospitals, prisons, and schools. To date, these trainings have been minimally applied to environmental contexts, but they may prove effective in future environmental disasters such as flooding, heat waves, and drought. Climate sustainability is the greatest challenge of modern times, with significant implications for agriculture, energy choices, health, and biodiversity. Stanley et al. (2009) have urged Buddhist religious leaders to participate in ethical calls for global climate action. Related issues of environmental justice and intersectionality have been taken up by the Buddhist Peace Fellowship through online seminars and activist trainings.

Buddhist environmental ethics can be helpful in addressing these and other environmental issues at both the personal and systemic level, offering a thoughtful and much needed contribution to the global ethics dialogue. Much of the writing to date has built on Western approaches to ethics which emphasize three types of guidelines for moral actions: (1) virtue ethics, (2) consequentialist or utilitarian ethics, and (3) deontological ethics. Western environmental ethicists have built a substantial literature using these approaches to address complex aspects of environmental wrongdoing. Traditionalist ethics scholars have been challenged by radical environmental philosophers in the fields of deep ecology, ecofeminism, social ecology, and environmental justice to go beyond individual culpability and engage systems drivers shaping environmental actions. They contend that today's planetary crises reflect complex economic, political, biological, sociological, and cultural contexts that reinforce destructive behaviours. Buddhist scholars have generally drawn on the three traditional Western frames for their explorations into potential frameworks for Buddhist environmental ethics, with much of the work supporting a *virtue ethics* orientation to environmental concerns. They propose that an ethically reflective Buddhist practitioner will cause less harm to the earth through personal cultivation of Buddhist virtues such as modesty, frugality, non-harming, and compassion. Others have argued for a consequentialist orientation, pointing to the law of karma as a strong moral motivation for cautious choices.

In this chapter I review Buddhist environmental ethics work to date and propose a role for Buddhist social ethics to complement Buddhist individual ethics regarding the environment. I take a constructivist approach, informed by Western radical environmental philosophers, systems thinkers, and Buddhist scholars and activists. It is my sense that the virtue ethics ideal of 'the good life' reflects a privileged position that may be seen as elitist in some of the contexts of environmental choice-making. Instead, I argue for Buddhist environmental ethics that are contextual, responsive, and emergent. Such ethics would reflect specific geographic and cultural contexts, would respond to ethical dilemmas as they arise, and would be receptive to solutions that emerge out of existing conditions. I believe this offers the greatest opportunity for engaging Buddhists across cultural and religious differences of different lineages, biogeographies, and cultural norms. It also offers the greatest range of meeting points with partners in dialogue from other faith traditions, academic, or civil perspectives. Developing principles for a Buddhist environmental ethic can be an honourable part of the global efforts to move forward in a thoughtful way, in spite of all the damage that has already been done.

Buddhist Approaches to Environmental Ethics

The literature on Buddhist environmental ethics is wide-ranging and exploratory in the relatively recent development of this field of scholarly inquiry. Ives (2013) provides a preliminary framework of key topics often considered in philosophical claims regarding the environment and human–nature relations. This offers a foundation for his assessment of relevant Buddhist textual resources and concepts that can address these claims. I recap these here to affirm the scope of this discussion and lay out a potential scaffolding for future scholarly work in Buddhist environmental ethics. They are:

1. The nature of human beings.
2. The nature of reality.
3. How we should view/know reality.
4. How to value non-human relations.
5. Principles and guidelines for making decisions and taking action.

Buddhist writings describe the nature of human beings as impermanent (like all things), marked by suffering (due to the physical, mental, and emotional dilemmas presented by impermanence), and absent an identifiable separate self. Efforts to inflate, solidify, or cling to any idea of an individual autonomous self reinforce a fundamental delusion. In a Buddhist world view, the so-called 'self' is made up of elements (the five *skandhas*) that are constantly changing, thereby undermining and refuting any possibility of a permanent identity. The self is seen as more of a loose container with permeable boundaries through which endless streams of sensations, perceptions, feelings, thoughts, and consciousness flows. Such a dynamic view of the self is well aligned with the Chinese understanding of *qi*, the dynamic flow of energetic presence through infinite forms and expressions in the vast universe. From a Buddhist perspective, an assertion of the existence of an autonomous self is deeply flawed and cannot be justified either experientially or philosophically. Misunderstanding the true nature of human beings (in this Buddhist view) can explain a number of modern era behaviours and attitudes that seem environmentally short-sighted and highly damaging. Modern industrial societies are well known for high rates of consumption, much of it oriented around self-identity and self-affirmation. The massive global production of cars, clothes, and confections, to name a few, requires enormous environmental resources and generates enormous waste in its relentless pursuit of a false goal. The preference for private fossil fuel based transit contributes significant carbon pollution and climate change to an already overloaded atmosphere.

This Buddhist view of the self is reflected in a view of reality as an infinitely complex set of actors and processes, none of which is permanent or identifiable as an autonomous self. Two foundational laws underlie the nature of these processes, according to Buddhist thought. The first is the law of interdependence, or co-arising of all phenomena, an understanding that all beings and events are co-determined, co-created, co-produced by multiple factors, causes, and conditions. This view aligns well with an ecological view of interdependence but goes beyond the physical and biological agents and interactions to include the energetic role of thoughts, ideas, emotions, cultures, and psychic intangibles. The second law is the law of karma, or consequences arising from actions. The law describes the sum total of action spinoffs resulting from a single action and understands the origin of a single action in terms of multiple previous actions. These two laws have been central to modern Buddhist environmental thought, as they readily offer a natural and systemic way to understand the scope of environmental impacts, whether from reductionist views of nature or industrial extraction. The web of interdependence, Indra's Net, is emphasized in Chinese Mahāyāna teachings of the Huayan School and highlighted in environmental commentaries by Thich Nhat Hanh and Joanna Macy, among others. The law of consequences, Kraft has suggested, can include 'eco-karma', a category of environmental consequences resulting from human and other influences (1997: 277). Such eco-karma may be accrued by individuals or collective entities such as states and nations.

The nature of knowing, i.e. how humans construct their modes of making sense of their world, has been studied in depth by Buddhist philosophy and psychology. These processes are relevant to a Buddhist environmental ethic because how humans know 'nature' (or the biogeophysical world) influences how they behave towards 'nature'. Knowing may include a wide range of modes, from scientific hypothesis-testing to experiential sensory input to energetic field alignment. The Buddhist emphasis on multi-causal complexity allows room for many modes of reality construction without insisting on a single approach. Regarding ethical choice-making, the Eightfold Path laid out in the teaching of the Four Noble Truths considers 'right view' a key prerequisite for 'right action', with 'right view' helping to determine ethically appropriate environmental actions. Right view refers to the laws of interdependence and karma, i.e. a systemic, mutually co-creating understanding of agent and action. Such a view can be a resounding antidote to the shortsighted environmental behaviours common in the modern industrial era. Right view calls for close reflection on short- *and* long-term consequences of one's actions, such as dependence on fossil fuels for personal mobility, shipping goods, producing plastics, and so on. Practising with right view may draw on any mode of knowing; those engaged with environmental concerns have actively expanded the range of creative and ethically helpful ways of knowing.

An important subset of interdependent coexistence relevant to environmental ethics is the realm of relations with non-humans, or 'other-than-humans' (Abram 1997). To date the primary Western emphasis has been on relations with animals, especially vertebrates, through moral principles developed for animal welfare policies and animal rights concerns. Trees and plants, invertebrates, fungi, single-celled organisms have received far less attention. Non-species entities such as mountains and rivers often only merit ethical attention if they are sacred to a specific culture. Buddhist attitudes towards animals have ranged widely across historical periods, social cultures, food practices, and economic geographies as well as specific Buddhist schools of thought (addressed by Waldau in Chapter 31 of this volume). Attitudes towards plants, especially their degree of sentience, is a matter of debate between Buddhist schools. While cultural norms vary on these points, the foundations of Buddhist philosophy allow room for granting moral standing to a wide range of subjects.

Two approaches can be broadly applied in exploring ethical dimensions to animal relations as well as plant, microbe, and bioregional relations. These are compassionate action and skilful means. Compassionate action is rooted in a 'right view' understanding of interdependence and no separate self, leading one to view the 'other' as related and even part of one's field of co-arising conditions. From this derives the ethical guideline to treat others (of all scales and varieties) with a sense of kind regard and a desire to relieve suffering. This includes the many varieties of environmental suffering, from clearcutting to toxic pollution. The teaching of skilful means encourages a broadly thoughtful and creative approach to relieving suffering, using whatever tools are available and effective.

Finally, an environmental ethic must include specific principles and guidelines for making decisions and taking action. A Buddhist environmental ethic would draw on Buddhist foundations for moral behaviour such as those identified in the vows of monks and laypeople, i.e. the primary precepts. Nhat Hanh (2008), Loori (1999), Aiken (1984), and others have considered environmental contexts for the Five Precepts of not killing, not stealing, not lying, not abusing intimate relations, and not giving or taking mind-altering substances. Each guideline provides opportunities for considering abusive actions at all levels, from harming an individual being to harming a socio-ecological system. These guidelines are complemented by a number of potentially ecologically positive virtues and practices. Ives (2013) and Keown (2005) point to: (1) the four *Brahmaviharas* of loving-kindness, compassion, sympathetic joy, equanimity; (2) contentment, modesty, non-greed, and non-covetousness in everyday life; and (3) mindfulness and skilful means in cultivating responsiveness to environmental relations. James (2004) and Sahni (2007) emphasize insight, awareness, and awakening as natural results of virtue practice, arguing for a Buddhist virtue environmental ethic as a path to enlightenment. Through virtuous practice, the awakened Buddhist thus naturally undertakes environmental right action.

A Range of Scholarly Approaches

The field of Buddhist environmental thought as a whole is very recent and can be traced academically to the 1996 Harvard conference on Buddhism and Ecology, organized by Mary Evelyn Tucker and John Grim. This was one of the first in a series of a dozen conferences that helped to establish and legitimize the academic dialogue around religion and ecology. Exploratory papers at the conference included reflections by Buddhist monks, teachers, activists, and lay practitioners as well as Buddhist scholars (Tucker and Williams 1997). Approaches to environmental ethics at that time drew on an assortment of relevant Buddhist principles in response to other religious perspectives, highlighting the best of Theravāda, Zen, and Tibetan offerings. In the past twenty years serious critiques and in-depth philosophical positions have broadened the field of inquiry, building a more thoughtful basis for a Buddhist environmental ethic.

Ian Harris, British Theravāda scholar, for example, has looked closely at the early Pāli teachings and challenged a number of claims positing Buddhism as an eco-friendly religion (Harris 2002). He points out the problematic relationship with animals, who are understood to represent a lower rebirth realm and are therefore an indication of human shortcoming or unfortunate behaviour in an earlier life. He argues that although the *Jātaka* tales offer teachings on compassion, they do not necessarily make a statement on the status of animals in human culture. Harris also challenges Joanna Macy and other Buddhist environmental scholars (such as Barnhill 2001) for their overdependence on the Huayan metaphor of the jewelled net of Indra, an emphasis not shared across all traditions and schools of Buddhist thought. Based on his exhaustive review of early Buddhist sutras, he supports Schmithausen (1991) in concluding there is no arguable basis in Buddhist thought for an environmental ethic.

David Loy, Zen Buddhist scholar and practitioner, works closely with the Buddhist penetration of the delusion of a separate self and all the dualisms that arise from this flawed misunderstanding. He presents this as a sense of 'lack' or dissatisfaction that drives almost all human behaviour, including such environmental problems as resource extraction, pollution, and consumerism (2008). He argues that this foundational delusion of self as separate from others (as in nature) is the suffering that calls for liberation through a Buddhist path of understanding. Loy has built on this core theme in interpreting the Five Precepts of non-harming in environmental terms, with pioneering work on application of the precepts to a social critique of systems drivers causing environmental damage.

Loy's work aligns well with Joanna Macy's comparison of Buddhist philosophy with principles of systems thinking (1991). Macy's scholarly understanding of systems is central to her analysis of environmental issues emphasizing the complexity of interdependence throughout space and time. Her activist training exercises draw on Mahāyāna themes and world views to provide a broad context for engagement. She works closely with Buddhist psychology to help environmentalists transform debilitating emotions into effective motivation. Macy's orientation to a Buddhist environmental ethic is pragmatic (using skilful means) and applied (often issue specific), using awareness practices to sustain 'eco-bodhisattvas' across endless challenges. She reinforces insights that generate 'greening of the self', a dynamic understanding of self as conditioned by and co-created with nature. Her work has been particularly helpful for climate action groups undertaking radical systems change to break free from fossil fuel dependence.

Several Buddhist scholars have argued that Buddhism is most suited to support an environmental ethic based in the cultivation of personal virtue. Damien Keown (2005) places his argument in the context of philosophical thought with parallel domains such as sexuality and abortion. Simon James (2004) works this same approach within Zen Buddhism specifically, showing how the path to enlightenment is based on personal ethics. He argues that the environmentally concerned person would choose actions that reflect ethical practices such as frugality, equanimity, and non-harming. Pragati Sahni (2007) takes up environmental virtues in the Pāli texts, particularly the *Jātaka* tales, making the case for the foundation of a Buddhist environmental ethic in the earliest teachings.

Two other approaches seem relevant to mention here, though they are not specific to Buddhist thought but rather to environmental ethics generally. Philosopher Anthony

Weston (1999) makes a strong claim that *all* environmental ethics are emergent ethics, far from fully shaped and still evolving. He places environmental thinking in its very short time frame relative to both Western and Asian traditions of philosophy, as well as indigenous ethics that evolved through intimate relations with the lands of their cultures. He suggests an exploratory orientation is more appropriate than rigorously tested arguments in this still emerging conversation. This seems more open and fruitful to me in the rapidly changing context of environmental values today. One example of this sort of dialogue is *Moral Ground*, a collection of perspectives built on arguments for 'why we should care' about the environment. Editors K. D. Moore and Michael P. Nelson (2010) include a number of voices organized around fourteen stated reasons: for our children, for the sake of the earth itself, for the sake of all life forms, because we love the world, and so on. The sum total of the commentaries opens many thoughtful reflections, and provides a broader view than any single perspective could offer alone. A parallel Buddhist volume might develop arguments based on the Buddha-nature of all beings and the social need for enlightened human–nature relations.

Areas of Tension

Environmental ethics as a field of study has generally built its arguments and philosophies with a focus on *individual* ethical responsibility, i.e. how best a person should act to reduce environmental harm, live in harmony with nature, and enjoy a fulfilling quality of life while embodying environmental virtue. This follows the dominant approach of most ethical systems, whether based in religious or philosophical principles, and is also somewhat true to date for Buddhist environmental ethics. I would argue that *social* ethics are equally and possibly more important in relation to environmental concerns, since almost every environmental problem must be addressed at a systemic level across multiple governance, geographic, and cultural units. Individual actions such as recycling and reducing energy use may generate a sense of personally virtuous satisfaction but, in the end, make only a modest contribution to environmental health and stability. It has been argued that the sum of individual actions is what generates broad scale social change, but this is only partially true. The greatest crises threatening the planet's life systems, such as loss of biodiversity, water and air pollution, habitat destruction, and rising carbon emissions, cannot be solved through individual ethical choices. They require a social ethic that can inform policy and regulation, planning and zoning, best practices protocols, and coordinated global change.

Zen scholar Thomas Kasulis suggests that Eastern thought traditions such as Buddhism are well suited to a socially based approach to ethics (2006). He contrasts Western ethics based on responsibility to rules and principles with Eastern ethics based on situational responsiveness (both cognitive and affective). Western thinking assumes that relationships between parties must be constructed through relational interaction and that ethical guidelines can help build these relationships. Eastern thinking emphasizes already existing links of interdependence, generating the recognition that acting for the other is acting for one's self (2006). Responsive ethics arise situationally and are guided by the desire to respond to the other as already related to one's self. Ethical work drawing on these principles is fundamental to the socially engaged Buddhist movement. Organizations such as Buddhist Peace Fellowship, International Network of Engaged Buddhists, and Buddhist Global Relief promote a relational Buddhist social ethic based on interdependence of self and other to address systemic injustice, poverty, and privilege in specific cultural and political situations.

Across the last century, environmental concerns have only become more complex and multi-causal, as is perhaps best illustrated by global climate change. Population and consumption pressures along with weather irregularities and disasters make for an uncertain world, where ethical guidelines may not be well thought out or clearly reinforced by cultural norms. Evangelical environmentalism has produced its own backlash, revealing class differences in priorities and communication styles. A Buddhist contribution to environmental ethics may only be a small part of a rapidly evolving response to ever-increasing moral dilemmas. Here I argue for a range of ethical responses that are inspired by the dynamic nature of what is unfolding. As climate philosopher Dale Jamieson writes, 'We will have to abandon the Promethean dream of a certain decisive solution and instead engage with the messy world of temporary victories and local solutions while a new world comes into focus' (2014: 10). A Buddhist environmental ethic might best be based on this creative co-arising itself, a direct response to the situation at hand.

One of the greatest sources of tension in environmental problem-solving is the Western habit of dualistic thinking that reinforces oppositional frames such as jobs versus environment, short-term versus long-term, rural versus urban, conservation versus preservation, and so on. The most basic of these is 'man' versus nature, the view that humans are above, apart, separate from the natural world, which is then seen as 'other'. (An extensive literature exists on these dualisms, particularly well developed by ecofeminist philosophers.) A Buddhist perspective challenges the oversimplification of dualistic thinking and supports a karmic interdependent systems view across all aspects of environmental concern. This would be a significant and useful contribution, particularly where conversations are blocked or stuck. Non-dualistic thinking is already a part of sustainability frameworks, mediation approaches, and ecosystems management; this is a natural opportunity to draw on Buddhist views to support these more inclusive approaches to environmental work.

Another area of tension is sorting out exactly what falls within the domain of moral evaluation in difficult environmental issues. This territory might well be explored using the concept of ecological karma. For example, intentional cruelty to animals is seen by some as immoral but what about intentional harm to plants as in forest clearing or farm field weeding? What are the eco-karma consequences of each action? Who is harmed? Who suffers and to what degree? In the realm of consumerism, nuanced ethical debate exists in some arenas (food choices, agricultural practices, energy sources), yet climate-related behaviours (driving, flying, heating, cooling) are barely considered to be ethical questions. The process of moralization can be ignited by powerful experiences that shift paradigms or make an unforgettable (and often painful) impression. Buddhist meditative practices may open a person to be more receptive to such experiences and thus to the ethical dilemmas they present.

Influences from and on Other Modern Streams of Environmental Ethics

Buddhist philosophy and ethics have been in the modern Western mix of ideas across the last century and have played a distinct role in influencing modern environmental ethics streams. Likewise, the efforts to define a Buddhist environmental ethic are influenced by a number of new Western ideas that challenge the dominant world views that have rationalized tremendous environmental harm. Here I briefly review these streams of thought to consider overlaps and intersections with Buddhist approaches as part of the evolving conversations in environmental ethics and philosophy.

Philosopher Arne Naess (1989) and sociologist Bill Devall (1985) first identified Buddhist thought as congruent with the philosophy of deep ecology, primarily because of the non-dualistic views of all sentient beings and the emphasis on self-realization through identifying beyond the self to the vast shared reality of infinite others. This is essentially the Buddhist liberation method to relieve delusional suffering from believing in a false, separate self. Several other philosophies also cultivate closeness with nature, reducing human–nature barriers through reverence for life (Schweitzer 1969), biophilia (Kellert 1993), and a sense of wonder (Carson 1968). Of these, a reverence for life aligns most with the Buddhist precept of not killing. Wonder and biophilia derive from a Western romantic orientation to nature and a sense of ecstatic spiritual union, something emphasized less in Buddhist practice and culture. Nonetheless, all three of these provide fertile ground for a version of Zen intimacy with other beings.

Several Western approaches draw directly on human relationships with the land or the planet itself as the place to start. Aldo Leopold's land ethic (1966) was among the first to offer a holistic ecological view of life communities, extending personal ethics to something much larger than individual relations. The bioregionalist movement drew on the land ethic as well as the principles of deep ecology to promote grounding in local land processes and land-based human cultures (see, for example, Snyder 1990). The new universe story, developed by 'geologian' Thomas Berry and physicist Brian Swimme, extended this sense of connection to the cosmos. The story was made into a popular film by Mary Evelyn Tucker and Swimme that has now been shown around the world in multiple languages to an enormous range of audiences. In these philosophies the primary point is to see human life as a *part* of the whole, not as the centre. Land ethic and bioregional philosophers see this in ecological terms, while the universe story emphasizes a Teilhardian evolution culminating in the modern human era. Though Buddhism per se has had little influence on these streams, the popularizing of each of these has created a generally receptive field for Buddhist environmental ideas and practices.

This is also the case for new environmental ethics arising out of the religion and ecology movement and academic field. With fresh interpretations of Christian and Jewish texts and ethical principles, Buddhist thinkers have been invited to participate in clarifying interreligious dialogues in forums such as the American Academy of Religion. Topics such as consumerism, population growth, and food practices have found common ground between Western and Asian religious perspectives (as in the Harvard Religion and Ecology conference volumes). Process theology, in particular, holds some important parallels with the Buddhist world view of life as dynamic, co-arising, and process rich. The scholarly arena of religion and ecology has been one of the most significant contexts for developing Buddhist environmental ethics. Arguably, this has been a more appreciative arena for such philosophical evolution than either the field of environmental philosophy or the field of Buddhist philosophy and ethics.

Several other streams of thought have been critical to the development of Western environmental ethics but have almost gone unnoticed in Buddhist environmental ethics. These are the principles underlying ecofeminism, ecojustice, and sustainability values such as the precautionary principle. The first two draw from the social liberation movements of feminism and civil rights, neither of which has been a major influence on Western Buddhism environmental thought, and vice versa. However, ecofeminist deconstruction of philosophical dualisms and implied power relations can also be supported by parallel Buddhist logic. The precautionary principle holds possibility for alignment with Buddhist ethics, as it is rooted in causing the least harm possible, a clear parallel to the precept of non-killing. Buddhist environmental ethics could reinforce this principle and its important, though controversial, role in public policy.

Buddhist Environmental Ethics and Consumerism

Two of the more challenging environmental concerns of the twenty-first century are escalating consumerism and rapid global climate change. In this part of the chapter, I take up each of these concerns as examples of a mode of analysis and application for Buddhist environmental ethics. I draw on Buddhist principles for analysis and offer a constructivist approach to individual and social ethics based on Buddhist sensibilities. I call for an emergent contextual approach to developing ethics based in responsive practice as described by Kasulis (2006).

Consumerism can generally be seen as the addictive need for material goods and services to meet emotional needs for identity, security, and acceptance, also sometimes promoted as an avenue to self-development and self-fulfilment. The environmental impacts of runaway consumer products and purchasing have been well documented, from plastics pollution in the ocean to pesticide poisoning of food and soils. A Buddhist analysis parallels other religious critiques, looking at moral imperatives on both personal and social levels, and calling for responsible and ethical action.

In earlier work (Kaza 2010) I identified three critiques based in Buddhist understanding. First, consumerism reinforces ego-based views of self through the core process of identity formation. Through attachment to material accumulation, people relate to material objects as real and permanent, reifying the personal self as similarly fixed in identity. This delusion prevents people from experiencing the world as interdependent and dynamically co-arising. Attachment to a false view of self as object can lead to greater and greater need for self-reinforcing possessions.

Second, consumerism promotes significant harm to living beings. Consumer products of all kinds create suffering for animal and plant life and harmful impacts on the people who produce consumer goods as well as those who consume them. The foundational principle behind all Buddhist ethics is non-harming or *ahimsa*; thus Buddhists are called morally to investigate the harms involved in consumer goods and mitigate those harms where possible.

Third, consumerism actively promotes craving, desire, and dissatisfaction, the very sources of suffering described in the teaching of the Four Noble Truths. Products are designed to relieve real and imagined suffering and replace unpleasant states of mind with pleasant states. Craving also includes aversion, in which one craves relief or escape from what is unpleasant or undesirable. Marketers take advantage of consumers' endless needs, offering a remarkable array of products designed to relieve almost any form of human suffering.

Buddhist philosophy is rich with antidotes and insights for addressing the debilitating nature of desire and dissatisfaction. Unhooking from the deep biological and psychological conditioning of desire is a core liberating path in Buddhist practice. An ethical Buddhist environmental position can be built on teachings that emphasize modesty, frugality, contentment, and non-harming. Practising with desire can be framed through in-depth study of the five *skandhas* as they are reinforced through consumerism. One can study personal hooks for or against 'stuff' as a way to moderate unsustainable or immoral levels of consumption. The Mahāyāna teaching on skilful means also supports an individual virtue ethic, helping people make pragmatic choices that aim towards ethical ideals along a middle path spectrum. An individualist environmental ethic derives fairly readily from Buddhist principles and can be seen in the virtue arguments for reduce, reuse, and recycle programmes, harm-reducing food ethics, and support for frugal lifestyles.

A Buddhist *social* ethic addressing consumerism requires a more broadly comprehensive systems analysis, examining the linked chains of impact and conditionality that drive social patterns of consumerism. This means looking at consumerism in social contexts such as family and peer settings, in social institutions such as schools, hospitals, and religious settings, and in political economic contexts such as trade agreements and product regulations. Such an analysis is extremely complex and daunting to religion and ethics scholars. It is far easier to affirm a Buddhist individual virtue ethic than to construct a plausible basis for a social environmental ethic. Nonetheless, it is inaccurate and incomplete to view individual ethical struggles related to consumerism distinct from the powerful driving forces shaping the context of individual choice-making. These choices are shaped by profit motives, brand promotion, market share, class identity, and legal acceptability, among others. A Buddhist social ethic calls for a different orientation to ethical decision-making, one that relies broadly on a systems understanding through the laws of karma and interdependence. In a systems context, individual actions will then be most effective if aligned with uniting and broadly inclusive social goals.

Two practice elements of such a social ethic are skilful means and compassion, both applied to the expanded social networks that contain and shape personal decisions. The practice of skilful means offers a helpful moderating pragmatism in the face of righteous pressures to achieve personal environmental ideals. It is simply not possible to do all the necessary research and reflection on consumer items in every aspect of one's existence to achieve a virtuous ideal. For example, a person may choose a vegetarian food ethic based on the principle of non-harming and could still fall far short of reducing environmental harm because of the chemical impacts of vegetable farming. One could then aim for organic vegetarian food choices but still not mitigate harm to farm workers on industrial scale organic farms. Even with thoughtful and well-researched food choices, a person may not be able to attain a similar level of virtuous action in transportation or energy use due to personal or system limitations. A skilful means approach encourages personal action where possible, with awareness of the sociopolitical system that may or may not be evolving to support environmental sustainability in the long run. The practice of compassion helps reduce frustration and cultivate patience with the aim of steady progress towards ethical goals related to reducing the impacts of consumerism.

In spite of all the highly motivated ethically concerned efforts of many people, Buddhists and non-Buddhists, we are a long way from the United Nations Millennium goals for well-being and sustainability. Today's environmental ethics must be emergent and contextual of necessity, working with extreme complexity across global bio-geopolitical systems. They cannot generate expectations of virtuous perfection but must instead support the flawed but hopeful efforts of all who take up whatever ethically helpful actions they can manage. Awareness in one arena of environmental ethics, such as consumerism, can lay a practice foundation for cultivating awareness in other challenging arenas. Perhaps the most challenging call at this moment in time is for climate ethics that can address threats to climate and sea level stability worldwide. With policy commitments lagging far behind scientific evidence, and climate justice issues impacting nation states in widely disparate ways, it is not clear what will yet emerge as ethical guidelines for international discussions. The last section of this chapter is an effort to contribute a Buddhist perspective to that emerging conversation.

Buddhist Environmental Ethics and Climate Change

Climate change as an environmental challenge raises moral and ethical issues in many dimensions, from present to future time, from distributional to intergenerational justice (Jamieson 2014). The physical consequences of climate change are well documented by climate scientists and summarized in the most recent report of the Intergovernmental Panel on Climate Change in 2014. They include accelerating melt rates of glaciers and ice shelves, thawing permafrost, ocean acidification, severe drought, hotter wildfires, and more extreme weather events. Climate models predict that climate-related disasters will become more common, with increasing impacts on human and ecological systems. In some areas, people already are suffering from widespread famine, in others, from emotional stress and social chaos due to displacement and loss. Even with significant efforts to reduce atmospheric levels of carbon dioxide and other potent greenhouse gases, human societies will still have to deal with the unfolding consequences of current loads of carbon.

Scientific forecasts have had limited success in generating motivation for significant global policy change. Political resistance has blocked carbon tax proposals, undercut carbon emission targets, and slowed mitigation planning for inevitable climate change impacts. It has become increasingly apparent that human behaviour and attitudes are determining the direction of planetary climate. Only recently have religious leaders and institutions added their voices to advocacy groups calling for a moral response to the unfolding climate crisis. Buddhist groups and thinkers have been a part of this conversation and, in some ways, may have fewer barriers than more divided denominations to developing a climate ethic. In recent years Buddhists have drawn attention to the rapidly melting glaciers of the 'Third Pole' of the Himalayan Mountain range, the source of almost all the major life and culture-giving river systems in Asia—the Ganges, Brahmaputra, Salween, Yangtze, Mekong, and Irawaddy rivers (Stanley et al. 2009). A Buddhist Declaration on Climate Change has been signed by twenty-six Buddhist leaders in seventeen countries. Buddhist temples have launched alternative energy projects in India, Japan, Canada, and Australia and climate resources for Buddhists have been posted at Ecobuddhism.org and OneEarthSangha.org. Even so, Buddhist leaders and organizations have had relatively limited influence in the global reach of climate change and there are few Buddhist environmental groups addressing this issue as a top priority.

In earlier work I proposed three avenues for engaging Buddhist thinking: exposing dualistic thinking, developing Buddhist climate ethics, and building capacity for resilience (Kaza 2014). Here I will focus on foundations for a Buddhist climate ethic, following the mode of analysis laid out above for consumerism. This Buddhist analysis parallels other religious critiques, such as the ground-breaking encyclical by Pope Francis, 'Laudato Si', in 2015. Such critiques address the scale of the planetary crisis and delineate moral imperatives at both the personal and social levels, calling for responsible ethical action. Not unlike other calls, a Buddhist perspective aims to relieve suffering through compassion and skilful means. With climate change as a practice field, a Buddhist moral call will reflect understanding of the laws of conditioned interdependence and karmic consequence. Buddhist teachings emphasizing intention and compassion can strengthen resolve to navigate the ethically complex challenges of climate change.

Buddhist tools may be most useful in deconstructing climate denial, a significant barrier to moral action. Norgaard's ethnographic study of Norwegian citizens (2011) attributes the persistence of denial to three common explanations: (1) people do not know enough to act effectively; (2) people can compartmentalize concerns and live with substantial cognitive dissonance; and (3) people have significant emotional blocks to dealing with climate change. Fear, anxiety, and insecurity are common as well as helplessness and guilt around the uneven impacts. For some people the strongest experience is a sense that the entire web of life is threatened, with only despair and enormous loss on the horizon. Norgaard found that climate attitudes are reinforced by emotional norms that favour maintaining personal locus of control. Typical responses to climate topics were to: (1) take a 'tough' attitude and not show any feelings of powerlessness and uncertainty; (2) 'stay cool' and not be too serious about anything, but especially not something as monumental as climate change; and (3) 'be smart' by showing you are informed and have answers for climate challenges. For their own mental health, people found it was important to focus only on what they could do to be effective and to otherwise keep a positive attitude towards life.

Norgaard observed that 'people occupying privileged social positions encounter "invisible paradoxes"—awkward, troubling moments they seek to avoid, pretend not to have experienced, and forget as quickly as possible once those moments have passed' (2011: 217). For example, people in privileged socioeconomic classes have almost no contact with today's extreme methods of energy extraction such as mountain top removal and fracking. These tend to take place in areas where local cultures have little or no say over the impoverishment of their homelands. For those with the privilege to do so, it is simpler to maintain a state of denial than to engage the moral complexities that arise in confronting climate change. I call this an *environmental privilege* for those who live comfortably in the developed world. Through the chosen convenience of ignorance, environmentally privileged people perpetuate the damaging energy and climate relations that support their lifestyles.

To address these challenges I look at elements of Buddhist philosophy that can support a climate ethic through individual actions. As with consumerism, such an ethic can be based on teachings that emphasize non-harming and frugality, with the goal of minimizing one's carbon footprint. In effect, a personal climate ethic can be framed as a way to moderate one's consumption in terms of carbon pollution. For example, commuting to work by walking, biking, or mass transit would be a more virtuous choice than commuting by car or plane because one would personally be contributing less carbon pollution (and therefore less harm) to the atmosphere. Practising mindfulness in relation to energy use or carbon intensive products can be a path to individual liberation. One can study one's personal hooks or triggers related to maintaining privileged climate-controlled homes or one's desires for high carbon footprint food choices such as red meat and imported fruits. For the person conditioned to climate privilege, it may be difficult to avoid common rationalizations tied up in even simple pragmatic choices. The Buddhist concept of skilful means may be helpful in evaluating moral choices and checking carefully for degrees of suffering and liberation in climate options at hand.

Working more directly with personal climate denial can be done through close study of the three basic types of desires in Buddhist psychology that contribute to climate-related suffering. These are: (1) greed, the desire for more of something (e.g. more of something that would generate a greater carbon impact); (2) aversion, the desire for less of something (e.g. less personal concern, fear, or grief related to climate losses or simply less engagement in difficult climate conversations); and (3) delusion, the desire for illusory options or self-made fantasies (e.g. false assurances that climate change is not really 'a problem' or a belief that technological fixes will solve all). This sort of personal practice is part of understanding the complexities of individual actions and belief systems that maintain currently unsustainable levels of carbon and other greenhouse gas emissions. However, as I argued with consumerism, the sum total of individual actions, no matter how ethical and thoughtful, will not be enough to make a significant difference in the timeframe needed to minimize disaster. To think otherwise is to promulgate another form of denial.

Thus it becomes evident that a Buddhist climate ethic must incorporate a *social* ethic to address the systems level drivers of climate change. Climate social ethics are currently motivating citizen campaigns to transition from fossil fuels to renewable energy sources and resist fossil fuel infrastructure developments. They are behind a broad global movement to divest financial portfolios from fossil fuels, particularly on college campuses, state and city budgets, and retirement pensions. They are informing urban transportation planning and building design, and they are raising difficult questions about climate justice. Climate activists across the globe have shifted their attention from the personal to systemic, sharing strategies that bridge cultures, geographies, and nation states.

The elements I propose for a Buddhist social ethic addressing climate are those I discussed for consumerism: non-harming, compassion, and skilful means. Non-harming aligns well with the *precautionary principle*, an important institutional policy approach that advises restraint where the degree of harm is unknown. This principle is well established in European Union law and is supported by a deep and thoughtful scholarly literature. Considerable climate harm could be reduced through consistent broad-based application of the precautionary principle to energy extraction, building design, and transportation efficiencies, for example. Another approach is to develop social, political, and economic indicators that measure well-being at the levels of city, state, region, or nation and use these guidelines to minimize climate harm. One effort to do this has been taken up by the Buddhist country of Bhutan through its innovative policy goal of Gross National Happiness, a direct challenge to the global economic standard of GNP, gross national product.

The practice of compassion is typically understood as a personal experience of opening to the suffering of others, in this case the suffering caused by climate change. But as part of a Buddhist social ethic, compassion would be an expression of understanding across geographies and cultures, perhaps shown through physical or social mitigation measures in anticipation of sea level rise or severe drought. Compassion between nation states is often made manifest through the generosity of support funds to accomplish necessary climate work. I believe compassion is the most direct route to breaking through first world climate denial and environmental privilege. The true magnitude of climate change impacts must be experienced to be believed; it is difficult to maintain denial in the face of massive flooding, dramatic wildfires, or staggering economic agricultural loss. Through direct experience, compassion is supported by wisdom insight born from glimpsing the true social and karmic complexity of climate change. The practice of compassion also provides a social context for living with grief and other emotional states generated by what will inevitably be irreversible harms (Moser 2012).

Skilful means as a Buddhist concept offers practical and multiple ways of approaching the many ethical challenges of climate change. Direct relief can be the skilful answer to climate disasters requiring major infrastructure response (refugee camps, water and food distribution, road and bridge repair). Emergency preparedness may be the skilful means for neighbourhoods to be ready for power outages, flooding, food shortages. These may reflect a Buddhist moral sensibility in maintaining social calm and equanimity before or during a crisis, though they are not uniquely Buddhist contributions to a climate ethic. Texts on skilful means indicate that the spiritual goal is liberating insight into the nature of suffering. Breaking the delusional grip of climate denial means exposing assumptions of climate privilege that are causing suffering. This will be challenging work in an emotional minefield that touches all aspects of human existence.

As with consumerism, I suggest here that both individual and social environmental ethics informed by Buddhism be seen as emergent and contextual. The fields of climate science, social science, and policy are changing rapidly, as is the climate itself. Climate ethics are now a product of mass actions, social media streams, global conferences, and utility negotiations. Leadership for best ethical practices is coming from cities and states, interfaith groups, and religious as well as political leaders. Even as ideas and principles evolve, people and governments must continue to act on the ground as members in a global conversation.

Related to a call for climate ethics is a call for resilience, in order to keep focused on the important work at hand. *Resilience* is the capacity to rebound socially, economically, politically, and psychologically from climate-related impacts. Buddhist mindfulness-based stress reduction techniques are now being taught in schools, hospices, prisons, and business places. Emergency workers could benefit from such resilience training for dealing with climate crises. To build capacity for resilience, I believe it is necessary to address—not suppress or resist—the troubling emotions associated with climate change. Such emotional self-knowledge cultivated through Buddhist awareness practice can build capacity for helping others break through denial and be able to act effectively.

Given the emergent nature of climate ethics, I suggest that a Buddhist climate ethic rest on the foundational laws of karma and interdependence and therefore a Buddhist sense of deep time. The Buddhist term *kalpa* refers to an unfathomable stretch of time before (and after) humans on earth with periods of history seen as many *kalpa*s long. A climate ethic could emphasize the long aeons of climate time, shifting perception away from a small scale self-centred perspective to a more appropriate scale for human endeavour. Such a long view of time can encompass the rapid climate changes we will need to address in the coming years. It will take many people over many decades, with Buddhist social ethics or other ethics, to achieve planetary climate stability. A climate ethic based in the practices of non-harming and compassion, using skilful means, and accepting a deep view of time is one that can serve for the long scope of what will be needed.

Conclusion

This chapter reflects my sense of possibility for a Buddhist environmental ethic that takes a wider view beyond the virtue ethics approach supported by others. It is informed by my practice training in Zen Buddhism and my academic training in environmental thought and values, and motivated by my very strong concern for the health of the planet. The value in developing a Buddhist environmental ethic is not theoretical for me; it is part of an evolving and much needed conversation about 'how shall we care' for this home planet. I come to this position from a sense of urgency and candour about the state of the earth's ecological systems. I see environmental ethics being worked out every day in legal decisions, household choices, and market strategies. This is a fruitful and dynamic arena, with activists, ministers, engineers, students, and lawmakers all helping to shape ethical change on the ground. Consumerism and climate change are two of the most engaging of these conversations; we can expect much will change in the next decade.

Using these two arenas, I have argued for complementary development of both individual virtue ethics and constructivist social ethics. While there is certainly merit in plumbing the breadth and depth of past Buddhist teachings for guidance on environmental thought, there is also a role for creative construction reflecting the calls of the times. An emergent ethic will take into consideration the nature of the dialogue, who is contributing, and how Buddhist voices may help shape the direction of human–environment relations across the globe. Buddhists in partnership with other earth-centred faith traditions as well as other advocacy communities can play an important role in the evolution of environmental ethics broadly speaking. Buddhist values such as non-harming, mindfulness, and compassion have already entered the mainstream of Western thought. Buddhist logic such as non-dualistic thinking can offer a critical perspective in challenging objectified views of nature and self.

The work of environmental ethics is broad and rich; the call for thoughtful relations with the natural world and earth's systems is compelling. In the midst of political conflict, energy challenges, and climate impacts, there is certainly room for Buddhist contributions. This chapter is one such contribution, with a call for many more responses to come. May the merit of this effort be dedicated to positive outcomes for the world's countless living beings and all the places they inhabit.

Works Cited

Abram, D. (1997) *The spell of the sensuous: perception and language in a more-than-human world*. New York: Vintage Books.

Aitken, R. (1984) *The mind of clover: essays in Zen Buddhist ethics*. San Francisco: North Point Press.

Barnhill, D. L. (2001) Relational holism: Hua-yen Buddhism and deep ecology. In: D. L. Barnhill and R. S. Gottlieb (eds), *Deep ecology and world religions*. Albany, NY: State University of New York Press, 77–106.

Batchelor, M., and Brown, K. (eds) (1992) *Buddhism and ecology*. London: Cassell Publishers.

Bays, J. C. B. (2009) *Mindful eating: a guide to rediscovering a healthy and joyful relationship with food*. Boston: Shambhala.

Callicott, J. B., and Ames, R. T. (eds) (1989) *Nature in Asian tradition of thought: essays in environmental philosophy*. Albany, NY: State University of New York Press.

Carson, R. (1968) *The sense of wonder*. New York: Harper Collins.

Chapple, C. K. (1993) *Nonviolence to animals, earth, and self in Asian traditions*. Albany, NY: State University of New York Press.

De Silva, P. (1998) *Environmental philosophy and ethics in Buddhism*. New York: St. Martin's Press.

Devall, B. (1985) *Deep ecology: living as if nature mattered*. Layton, UT: Gibbs Smith Publisher.

Gross, R. (1998) Buddhist values for overcoming pro-natalism and consumerism. In: *Soaring and settling: Buddhist perspectives on contemporary social and religious issues*. New York: Continuum, 108–124.

Harris, I. (2002) Buddhism and ecology. In: D. Keown (ed.), *Contemporary Buddhist ethics*. Richmond, UK: Curzon Press, 113–136.

Hunt-Badiner, A. (ed.) (1990) *Dharma Gaia: a harvest of essays in Buddhism and ecology*. Berkeley: Parallax Press.

Hunt-Badiner, A. (ed.) (2002) *Mindfulness in the marketplace: compassionate responses to consumerism*. Berkeley, CA: Parallax Press.

Ives, C. (2013) Resources for Buddhist environmental ethics. *Journal of Buddhist ethics*, 20, 541–571.

James, S. P. (2004) *Zen Buddhism and environmental ethics*. Burlington, VT: Ashgate.

Jamieson, D. (2014) *Reason in a dark time*. New York: Oxford University Press.

Kasulis, T. P. (2006) Zen as a social ethics of responsiveness. *Journal of Buddhist ethics*, 13, 1–12.

Kaza, S., and Kraft, K. (eds) (2000) *Dharma rain: sources of Buddhist environmentalism*. Boston: Shambhala.

Kaza, S. (2005a) Western Buddhist motivations for vegetarianism. *Worldviews: environment, culture, religion*, 9 (3), 385–411.

Kaza, S. (ed.) (2005b) *Hooked! Buddhist writings on greed, desire, and the urge to consume.* Boston: Shambhala.

Kaza, S. (2010) How much is enough? Buddhist perspectives on consumerism. In: R. K. Payne (ed.), *How much is enough? Buddhism, consumerism and the human environment.* Boston: Wisdom, 39–62.

Kaza, S. (2014) Buddhist contributions to climate response. *Journal of oriental studies,* 24, 73–92.

Kellert, S., and Wilson, E. O. (1993) *The biophilia hypothesis.* Washington: Island Press.

Keown, D. (2005) *Buddhist ethics: a very short introduction.* New York: Oxford University Press.

Kraft, K. (1997) Nuclear ecology and engaged Buddhism. In: M. E. Tucker and D. Williams (eds), *Buddhism and ecology: the interconnection of dharma and deeds.* Cambridge, MA: Harvard University Press, 269–290.

Leopold, A. (1966) *A Sand County almanac with other essays on conservation from Round River.* New York: Oxford University Press.

Loori, J. D. (1999) *Teachings of the insentient: Zen and the environment.* Mount Tremper, NY: Dharma Communications Press.

Loy, D. (2008) *Money, sex, war, karma: notes for a Buddhist revolution.* Boston: Wisdom.

Macy, J. (1991) *Mutual causality in Buddhism and general systems theory.* Albany: State University of New York Press.

Macy, J., and Brown, M. Y. (2014) *Coming back to life: the updated guide to the work that reconnects.* Gabriola Island, BC: New Society Publishers.

Moore, K. D., and Nelson, M. P. (2010) *Moral ground: ethical action for a planet in peril.* San Antonio: Trinity University Press.

Moser, S. C. (2012) Getting real about it: navigating the psychological and social demands of a world in distress. In: D. R. Gallagher, R. N. L. Andrews, and N. L. Christensen (eds), *Environmental leadership: a reference handbook.* Los Angeles: Sage, 432–440.

Naess, A. (1989) *Ecology, community, and lifestyle.* Cambridge: Cambridge University Press.

Nhat Hanh, T. (2008) *The world we have: a Buddhist approach to peace and ecology.* Berkeley: Parallax Press.

Norgaard, K. M. (2011) *Living in denial: climate change, emotions, and everyday life.* Cambridge, MA: MIT Press.

Sahni, P. (2007) *Environmental ethics in Buddhism: a virtues approach.* New York: Routledge.

Schimthausen, L. (1991) *Buddhism and nature.* Tokyo: The International Institute for Buddhist Studies.

Schweitzer, A. (1969) *Reverence for life.* New York: Harper and Row.

Sivaraksa, S. (ed.) (2001) Economic aspects of social and environmental violence from a Buddhist perspective. In: *Santi Pracha dhamma: essays in honor of the late Puey Ungphakorn.* Bangkok: Santi Pracha Dhamma Institute, 304–316.

Snyder, G. (1990) *The practice of the wild.* San Francisco: North Point Press.

Stanley, J., Loy, D. R., and Dorje, G. (eds) (2009) *A Buddhist response to the climate emergency.* Boston: Wisdom.

Tucker, M. E., and Williams, D. (eds) (1998) *Buddhism and ecology: the interconnection of dharma and deeds.* Cambridge, MA: Harvard University Press.

Weston, A. (1999) *An invitation to environmental philosophy.* New York: Oxford University Press.

Suggested Reading

Kaza, S. (ed.) (2005) *Hooked! Buddhist writings on greed, desire, and the urge to consume.* Boston: Shambhala.

Kaza, S., and Kraft, K. (eds) (2000) *Dharma rain: sources of Buddhist environmentalism.* Boston: Shambhala.

Loori, J. D. (1999) *Teachings of the insentient: Zen and the environment.* Mount Tremper, NY: Dharma Communications Press.

Macy, J. (1991) *Mutual causality in Buddhism and general systems theory.* Albany: State University of New York Press.

Nhat Hanh, T. (2008) *The world we have: a Buddhist approach to peace and ecology.* Berkeley, CA: Parallax Press.

Snyder, G. (1990) *The practice of the wild.* San Francisco: North Point Press.

Tucker, M. E., and Williams, D. (eds) (1997) *Buddhism and ecology: the interconnection of dharma and deeds.* Cambridge, MA: Harvard University Press.

CHAPTER 22

BUDDHISM, WAR, AND VIOLENCE

MICHAEL JERRYSON

INTRODUCTION

On 29 February 2016 at roughly 4 pm, an eighteen-year-old Tibetan monk, Kalsang Wangdu, set himself on fire. According to the Free Tibet movement, Kalsang had declared the Tibetan region needed complete independence (Wong 2016). In devotion to this cause, Kalsang self-immolated just outside his monastery, Retsokha Aryaling, in Kardze Prefecture, China.

Since 2009, over 140 Tibetan Buddhists have self-immolated in protest of the Chinese treatment of Tibetans and also for the political independence of Tibet. Beyond the stated justifications for self-immolation, these deaths raise ethical questions, namely the meaning of the self-immolations. Is self-immolation a form of suicide? If so, is it an act of violence? On 25 March 2013, the Fourteenth Dalai Lama addressed the nature of Tibetan self-immolations in an interview with the *Times of India*:

> Actually, suicide is basically [a] type of violence, but then questions of good or bad actually depend on the motivation and goal. I think [as far as the] goal is concerned, these people [are] not drunk; [they do] not [have] family problems. This [self-immolation] is for the *Buddhadharma*, for Tibetan national interest, but then I think the ultimate factor is their individual motivation. If motivation [consists of] too much anger, hatred, then it is negative, [but] if the motivation [is] more compassionate, [and with a] calm mind then such acts also can be positive. That is strictly speaking from a Buddhist view of point. Any action, whether violence or non-violence, is ultimately dependent on motivation. [transliterated from video footage, *Times Now* 2013]

The Dalai Lama's explanation underscores a Buddhist perspective on violence that does not view self-immolation as violence. Some may consider Kalsang Wangdu's self-immolation an act of violence, but a close examination of the Buddhist doctrine reveals that this is not necessarily the case. The Buddhist ethical violations that pertain to violence require evidence of harm or injury (*hiṃsā*). In this doctrinal vein, the Fourteenth Dalai Lama argues that when a person retains a positive and calm mind while committing a self-immolation, there is no violation.

There is an ample repository of examples in which Buddhists have deliberately caused harm or injury to others. With over 2,500 years of practice and a multitude of traditions, it should be no surprise that Buddhist traditions have adherents who go to war and engage in conflicts, torture, and other acts of violence. In countries such as Korea, Tibet, China, Japan, and Thailand, Buddhist monasteries served as military outposts, monks led revolts, and Buddhist principles served as war rhetoric for heads of state. Some of these acts of violence draw upon Buddhist scriptures; other acts involve Buddhist symbols and personas.

This chapter approaches the subject of Buddhist ethics not from the basis of scriptural analysis and the subsequent hermeneutical exercises. Instead, this chapter examines Buddhist ethics from the wider field of lived choices, and the doctrine that relates to those choices. Ethics pertains to the choices that people make. In the past, Buddhists have made choices to go to war and commit various acts of violence. It is important to explore their decisions and the relative material on which they based their decisions. This chapter reviews examples of Buddhist engagement with war, Buddhist perspectives on violence, and Buddhist responses to violence. Within this Handbook, suicide and euthanasia are discussed in separate chapters. Therefore, their discussion in this chapter will be brief to avoid unnecessary overlap.[1]

Buddhists and War

It would be a Herculean task to present Buddhist-inspired conflicts, wars, and the ethical debates and decisions surrounding them. Instead of a comprehensive list, this section provides a brief chronology of examples. This historiography is meant to show that the phenomena of Buddhist decisions to go to wars and engage in conflict are not anomalies, but part of a historical continuity.

A focus on war and Buddhism requires that we first examine statecraft. Since the third century BCE, Buddhist governments and groups chose to clash with opponents of different faiths, as Buddhists from different countries, and even Buddhists of different ordination lineages within the same country. On most occasions, the collusion of Buddhist

[1] See Martin Kovan's chapter, 'Being and its Other: Suicide in Buddhist Ethics', in this volume for a larger discussion of suicide and the Dalai Lama's interview. For an extended discussion of euthanasia, see Damien Keown's chapter on euthanasia in this volume.

authority and political power has provided a recipe for violence. Early scriptures are ambiguous about the relationship between Buddhist principles and sovereignty due in part to the crucial patronage of the Buddha by the North Indian monarchs of Magadha and Kosala in the fifth century BCE.

As states developed, Buddhist authority served to legitimize kings and rulers by granting them religio-political titles such as *Cakravartin* (universal rule; literally, 'one who turns the wheel'), *Dhammarāja* (ruler of the Buddhist doctrine), or in the case of Mongols and Tibetans, *Dalai Lama* (Ocean of Wisdom). Buddhist states use violence externally as well as internally. Early South Asian religious literature charged rulers with protecting their subjects from external forces, which involved warfare.

Buddhists have decided to go to war since the time of Aśoka in the third century BCE. These wars contain a myriad of causes and factors. However, they become sanctified to the participants by enlightened leaders, Buddhist rhetoric (*Dhamma*/*Dharma*), and Buddhist monks. Most Buddhist-inspired wars are either the result of a closely aligned monasticism and state, or a movement that contains millenarian elements.

In the first century CE Buddhist monks brought their traditions to China. Three hundred years later, there were Chinese Buddhist millenarian revolts and insurrections, often led by monks. Buddhist-inspired revolts also occurred within the Tabgatch Empire against the villainous Mara (402–517 CE), and messianic monks rebelled during the Sui and Tang dynasties (613–626). It was in the Tang Dynasty that Faqing led his soldier-monks in a revolt by asserting that ten deaths would enable them to complete their bodhisattva path (815). The White Lotus Society incorporated messianic elements into its Pure Land practices. By the thirteenth and fourteenth centuries, Buddhists had staged armed uprisings to establish their own states and to overthrow the Mongol Dynasty.

Mahāyāna Buddhist traditions were transported from China to Korea in the fourth century CE. Korea embraced Buddhist practices during the bloody Chinese interregnum (220–589 CE). This nascent Silla kingdom credited Buddhist protectors with causing the Chinese to make peace with them in 671 CE. Then Koreans brought Buddhist practices and beliefs to Japan in the sixth century CE. In Japan, powerful Buddhist monasteries gradually emerged, and armies were solicited to protect their landholdings. The close political ties between monasteries and state in the Heian period (794–1185 CE) drew monks into conflicts. During the twelfth century, Chinese and Korean monks fought in wars against the Jurchens, the Mongols, and the Japanese. In the next century, Japanese Shin adherents fought apocalyptic battles over Amita paradise.

Within the Theravāda traditions, Thai chronicles in the sixteenth century reveal monks as spies and conspirators. From 1699 until the mid-1950s, Lao and Thai holy men (*phumibun*) staged dozens of messianic revolts against Thailand. The leaders claimed to possess extraordinary powers and drew on the lore of Phra Si Ariya, the Thai version of Maitreya, the Buddha-to-be (Nartsupha 1984: 112). This claim of supernatural powers was not solely a phenomenon of revolts. The Thai king Taksin liberated his people from Burmese occupation in 1767 and declared himself a stream enterer—the first of four stages to sainthood in Theravāda Buddhism.

Buddhists and Buddhist monks directed their beliefs and practices into wars throughout Asia. Japanese peasants, inspired by Pure Land teachings, fought a battle of cosmic relevance to promote a Buddhist paradise during the Warring States period of the 1500s. Later, Japanese Zen monks fought as soldiers in the Russo-Japanese War of 1904 and 1905 (Victoria 2006). Within the Tibetan traditions there is a fraternity of fighter monks (*ldab ldob*). Although these monks are not soldiers, they equip themselves with at least one weapon. They are notable fighters and have served in special all-Tibetan frontier forces in the Indian Army of the Republic. More recently, Thai soldiers serve in covert operations as military monks (*thahān phra*). Unbeknownst to their abbots, these men fully ordain and retain their military status, guns, and monthly stipends (Jerryson 2011: 116–127).

In the colonial and postcolonial periods, Buddhists rebelled against the predominantly Christian colonialists, and reasserted their identities. Burmese monks such as U Ottama led anticolonial movements against the British in the 1930s. During the early 1940s, Korean monks equated the United States' growing military influence with 'Christian power' and sought to cleanse the world from demons and the evil of Mara (Tikhonov 2009: 8). Their sentiments were mirrored by Chinese Buddhists during the Korean War (1951–1953). Notable Chinese monks such as Ven. Juzan challenged Chinese Buddhists to fulfil their patriotic duty and assist North Korea by resisting the encroachment of US influence, which he saw as the same as subduing evils (Yu 2010: 142). However, Korean Buddhist movements against external forces turned internal in the 1950s. Korean Buddhist Chogye monks engaged in bloody conflicts with married monks over the issue of celibacy, claiming that monastic marriage practices were a by-product of Japanese colonialism.

After the fall of the Berlin Wall, the Buddhist world changed. Among the more costly sites of Buddhist conflict in contemporary times have been the Sri Lankan civil war against the LTTE (1983–2008), the current Tibetan uprisings in Chinese-controlled Tibet, and Buddhist and Muslim conflicts in Ladakh, India, Myanmar, and southern Thailand.

Buddhist War Ideologies

The examples provided in the preceding section display a myriad of justifications for Buddhists to go to war. Buddhists have had mundane reasons, such as the protection of land and property, and more abstract qualifications, such as millenarian and messianic aspirations. And there is evidence of a just war ideology within Buddhist traditions. This is visible in the more recent contemporary examples.

Moreover, in the contemporary period, Damien Keown notes, while the most authentically Buddhist candidate in the discourse of human rights is compassion (*karuṇā*), 'many modern states (even traditionally Buddhist ones such as Burma/Myanmar) seem to care little for their citizens, so it is not clear how compassion would move the authorities to agree to a framework of human rights in the first place' (2012: 224).

Often, Buddhists have invoked the need to bring civilization through war. One memorable example comes from the well-known Japanese Buddhist Rinzai monk Shaku Sōen. Sōen was the first Zen Buddhist monk to teach in the United States. Through his disciple, D. T. Suzuki, they helped establish a Western familiarity with Japanese Buddhist traditions. During the Russo-Japanese War (1904–1905), Soen framed the Japanese fight against Russia as an issue of justice and peace: 'In the present hostilities, into which Japan has entered with great reluctance, she pursues no egotistic purpose, but seeks the subjugation of evils hostile to civilization, peace and enlightenment' (Victoria 2006: 27).

The Russian novelist Leo Tolstoy, whose work on nonviolent resistance later influenced important figures such as Mohandas Gandhi and Martin Luther King Jr, wrote to Shaku Sōen. He had hoped to enlist Sōen in condemning the war between their two countries. In a letter back to Tolstoy, Sōen responded, once again, confirming a just war stance: 'Even though the Buddha forbade the taking of life, he also taught that until all sentient beings are united together through the exercise of infinite compassion, there will never be peace. Therefore, as a means of bringing into harmony those things which are incompatible, killing and war are necessary' (Victoria 2006: 29).

Another prominent example of Buddhist just war mentality is found in South Asia. In Sri Lanka, Buddhist monks became politically active and advocated strong forms of Buddhist nationalism. This was part of the growing ethnic and religious tension between Sinhalese Buddhists and the Tamil and Muslim minorities. M. A. Nuhman notes that extremist Buddhist groups emerged during this period, espousing a new ideology called *Jathika Chintanaya*. Literally meaning 'nationalist thought', the ideology sponsored an exclusivist vision of the country similar to the contemporary Talibanist Islamism in the Muslim world. Nuham writes, '*Jathika Chintanaya* justifies war and militarism within Buddhism, which is generally believed to be a religion of nonviolence and compassion' (2016: 38).

The *Jathika Chintanaya* ideology became part of the socialist-leading Janatha Vimukthi Peramuna (People's Liberation Front), which enlisted monks in an armed uprising during the 1980s. This ideology was expanded further in Sri Lankan Buddhist organizations that have expressed overt Buddhist nationalist sentiments. These include the Jathika Hela Urumaya (National Sinhala Heritage), the Sinhala Ravaya (Roar of the Sinhalese), Ravana Balaya (Ravana's Force), and the Bodu Bala Sena (the Army of Buddhist Power).

Buddhists and Violence: Harm/Injury

While war is embedded in statecraft and defined within these parameters, violence does not have a particular context to nuance its meanings. In the myriad of treatments of religion and violence, what often has been overlooked is the distinctive way in which a particular religion *understands* and *defines* violence.

From the very introduction of Buddhism to the Western world, Buddhist scholars have had to redress numerous misconceptions about Buddhism and Buddhists. Many of these mistakes are due to the false assumption that Western categories and terms are universal—and therefore applicable to Buddhism. In order to understand the relationship between Buddhism and violence, it is important to locate the way in which Buddhists and the Buddhist doctrine articulate violence. More often than not, when Western scholars discuss Buddhism and violence, they invoke the Buddhist precept of *ahiṃsā*. While scholars commonly translate *ahiṃsā* as 'non-violence', a more precise definition is 'non-harm' or 'non-injury'. As Stephen Jenkins, John Soboslai, and others argue, this nuance is significant when understanding Buddhist taxonomies of violence (see Jenkins 2010/2011: 311; Soboslai 2015).

As illustrated in the vignette at the beginning of this chapter, the Fourteenth Dalai Lama has argued that so long as the self-immolaters are sane and not expressing pain or anguish during their self-immolation, it is not a violation of *ahiṃsā* because there is no harm or injury. If *ahiṃsā* remains the means of understanding and articulating Buddhist views on violence, examples need to reflect this correct translation of *ahiṃsā*.

Scriptural Justifications for Murder

Similar to other religious traditions, Buddhist scriptures are awash with interdictions against harming sentient beings, and in expressing values such as generosity, compassion, and equanimity. However, there are Buddhist scriptures that either condone the use of violence or are hermeneutically ambiguous about the use of violence. According to Buddhist scriptures, a person accrues demerit through violent actions or even intentions to commit violence (injury/harm). The most severe of these actions is murder—an unwelcomed and illegal act of killing.

The esteemed Buddhist scholar Paul Demiéville argues that no other precept is so strictly followed by all Buddhists. He went so far as to say that not killing is a characteristic 'so anchored in Buddhism that it is practically considered a custom' (Demiéville 2010: 18). This custom is perhaps best understood as one of five moral precepts (Skt *pañcasīla*; Pali *pañcasīlāni*), which are to abstain from: killing sentient beings, stealing, lying, partaking of intoxicants that cloud the mind, and sexual misconduct. This practice is analogous to the five restraints (*yama*) in Hindu traditions, and underscores the social ethics of South Asian traditions. In addition to lay practices, there are canonical and commentarial sources throughout the different Buddhist schools that contain severe interdictions on violence. However, they also contain the exception to the rule.

Analogous to Carl Schmitt's notions of *Ausnahmezustand* (state of exception), Buddhist exceptions empower or legitimate kings and rulers.

These exceptions were not generated in a vacuum and did not remain simply 'exceptions'. The scriptures that condone or justify violence are connected to physical acts of violence. Either Buddhist authors try to rationalize the previous violence of Buddhist rulers—such as the early Magadha king Ajatashatru who killed his father, Bimbisara—or condone the current acts of a Buddhist state (often in defence of the religion), such as the Japanese imperial violence from the start of the Meiji period (1868) and onward.

Buddhist scholars have understood and analysed the ethical parameters of murder through three consistent variables:

(1) the intention of the person who commits the violence (e.g. is it accidental or deliberate, and if deliberate, is the mind clear of hatred and avarice?),
(2) the nature of the victim (e.g. human, animal, or supernatural), and
(3) the stature of the one who commits the violence (e.g. is the person a king, soldier, or a butcher?).

In order to treat the various ways in which Buddhist doctrine addresses the ethics of intention, victimhood, and the allowance for those to kill, the following examples are divided by traditional Western doctrinal categories: Theravāda, Mahāyāna, and Vajrayāna.

The 'Best' Intentions

Theravāda Doctrine

In Theravāda doctrine, monks are models for lay practice. As such, monastic rules and interdictions become the locus for understanding ethical concerns of murder. In the first book of the *Vinaya* is the 'Suttavibhanga' or 'The Analysis of the Rules'. It distinguishes the acts of manslaughter and attempted murder from the act of murder in numerous accounts. For example, in one particular instance an accidental death caused by pushing one's father yields no offence; the failed attempt to kill one's father by pushing him results in a grave offence. However, a death caused by the deliberate intention to kill results in expulsion (Horner 1992: 139). The same rationale is applied to issues of euthanasia and abortion. If a monk or nun advocates a quick death or techniques to abort a pregnancy and the advice leads to a death, the person would be expelled from the *Saṅgha*. Advice that was not heeded carries lesser penalties. Insanity also plays a role in assessing the act of murder. In a previous life as the Brahman Lomakassapa, the Buddha killed hundreds of creatures but was not in the correct state of mind. Lomakassapa was 'unhinged' with desire, and the text explains that a madman's crimes are pardonable (Horner 1963–1964: 14–17).

Mahāyāna Doctrine

Mahāyāna notions of skill-in-means (*upāya*) and emptiness provide justifications for violence, or in these instances murder. But within these rationalizations, the actors must not have ill thoughts or intentions when they perform the violence. Rather, their intentions should be compassionate and imbued with skill-in-means. In this vein, most exceptions require that the actor be a bodhisattva—an enlightened being. However, this is not always the case; in some cases the absence of any ill intent is sufficient to pardon an act of violence. In Chan Buddhism, the *Treatise of Absolute Contemplation* explains that murderous acts are analogous to brush fires. 'The man who renders his mind similar [to the forces of nature] is entitled to do equally as much' (Demiéville 2010: 56). Likewise, Japanese Zen interpretations of killing stress the vacuity of the act. Killing puts an end to the passions of a person's mind and fosters the Buddha-nature within (44).

Intentionality is a critical component in Mahāyāna ethics of violence. The issue is not simply whether a person engages in an accidental or deliberate action, but rather there are exceptions that allow for intentional violence.

One powerful intention is *upāya*, or skill-in-means. Skill-in-means is a method employed by awakened beings to help others awaken. Perhaps the most famous example of this comes from a section in chapter 3 of the *Lotus Sutra*, 'The Burning House'. The *Lotus Sutra* is one of the core scriptures in the Chinese Tiantai, Japanese Tendai, and Nichiren schools and is considered a sacred text. In the text, the Buddha tells a parable to his disciple Śāriputra about an old man and his children. The man attempts to rescue his children from a burning building, but they are enthralled by their games and do not heed his warnings. In order to get them to leave, he promises them three gifts; when they escape the building, they receive the greatest of these gifts. Śāriputra praises the Buddha and correctly interprets that the man should not be condemned for lying, even if he had not given the children any gifts. His action was just because he was trying to liberate the children from a very painful experience.

The *Lotus Sutra* provides not only the strategy of skill-in-means but also ambiguous excerpts on violence. In 1279 CE, Nichiren writes to his devoted samurai follower, Shijo Kingo, and explains that Shijo's faith in the *Lotus Sutra* helped saved him from a recent ambush. He enjoins Shijo to employ the strategy of the *Lotus Sutra* in his future work and quotes a section from chapter 23:

> 'All others who bear you enmity or malice will likewise be wiped out.' These golden words will never prove false. The heart of strategy and swordsmanship derives from the Mystic Law. Have profound faith. A coward cannot have any of his prayers answered. (Nichiren 2009: 1001)

The sentence quoted from the *Lotus Sutra* is generally regarded as metaphorical, but in this context Nichiren applies it literally in his address to a samurai about past and future acts of violence.

Perhaps the most extreme measure of skill-in-means to justify violence is found in the chapter 'Murder with Skill-in-Means: The Story of the Compassionate Ship's Captain' from the *Upāyakauśalya Sūtra*, or the *Skill-in-Means Sutra*. In one of his many previous births, the Buddha is the captain of a ship at sea and is told by water deities that a robber on board the ship intends to kill the five hundred passengers and the captain. Within a dream, the deities implore the captain to use skill-in-means to prevent this, since all five hundred men are future bodhisattvas and the murder of them would invoke on the robber immeasurable lifetimes in the darkest hells. The captain, who in this text is named Great Compassionate (Mahākarunika), wakes and contemplates the predicament for seven days. He eventually rationalizes:

> 'There is no means to prevent this man from slaying the merchants and going to the great hells but to kill him.' And he thought, 'If I were to report this to the merchants, they would kill and slay him with angry thoughts and all go to great hells themselves.' And he thought, 'If I were to kill this person, I would likewise burn in the great hells for one hundred-thousand eons because of it. Yet I can bear to experience the pains of the great hells, that this person not slay these five hundred merchants and develop so much evil *karma*. I will kill this person myself.' (Tatz 1994: 74)

The captain subsequently murders the robber, and the Buddha explains, 'For me, *saṃsāra* was curtailed for one hundred-thousand eons because of that skill in means and great compassion. And the robber died to be reborn in world of paradise' (74). Here, the skill-in-means is motivated by compassion, which ameliorated the karmic results of murder.

Vajrayāna Doctrine

Many of Vajrayāna's ethical foundations for justified violence are coterminous with those in Mahāyāna doctrine. One motif that justifies violence in Vajrayāna scriptures is defence—one of the most ubiquitous of reasons to commit violence. The questions arise though: What are the determinations of the aggression that necessitates the defence, and what does that defence entail? Within Vajrayāna scriptures, defence is mounted through rituals of sacrifice and cosmic battles.

Tantra texts range from ritual to practical and yogic purposes. Most germane to our discussion are the Tantric ritual goals, which involve the pacification of diseases, enemies, and emotions; augmentation of money, power, and merit; control of opponents, gods, and passions; and the killing of enemies, gods, sense of self, and so on (Davidson 2005: 35). Among the defensive rituals is the rite of fire sacrifice (*abhichara-homa*), which in the Indian *Mahāvairocana Abhisaṃbodhi Tantra* subdues hated foes. There are disparate but concerted commentaries on the fire sacrifice that expand on its transgressive and violent nature. The Indian Buddhist scholar-monk Bhavyakīrti writes on the *Cakrasaṃvara Tantra*:

> Then the destruction of all, arising from the vajra, is held [to be accomplished] with the great meat. It is the dreadful destroyer of all the cruel ones. Should one thus perform without hesitation the rites of eating, fire sacrifice (*homa*), and sacrificial

> offerings (*bali*) with the meats of dogs and pigs, and also [the meat of] those [chickens] that have copper [colored] crests, everything without exception will be achieved, and all kingdoms will be subdued. (Gray 2007: 252)

Whereas Bhavyakīrti's commentary invokes the violent sacrifice of animals for defensive purposes, other texts have more inclusive and aggressive positions. Vajrayāna doctrine differs considerably from Theravāda doctrine on the killing of animals, especially for dietary purposes. In Mongolian and Tibetan traditions, adherents are encouraged to eat larger animals instead of smaller ones. The death of one large animal such as a cow could feed many, whereas the death of one shrimp would not satisfy a person.

Defence does not pertain to simply threats to the state, but also includes preemptive attacks due to an imminent cosmic war. The most notable of these defensive positions is found in the Indian and Tibetan *Kālacakra Tantra*, referred to as the *Wheel of Time Tantra*. As mentioned by the Buddhologist Lambert Schmithausen, the text describes an eschatological war in which the army of the bodhisattva king of Shambhala finally conquers and annihilates the Muslim forces in order to destroy their barbarian religion and to reestablish Buddhism. One should note the historical context of this text. Scholars estimate that it was composed during the Muslim invasions of northern Indian in the eleventh century.

In some texts, the Mahāyāna principle of skill-in-means is applied to show violence as a redemptive act, which is often referred to as liberation killing. Such is the case of the Bodhisattva Vajrapāṇi, who kills the Hindu god Mahesvara, and revives Mahesvara as an enlightened follower of the Buddha. Similarly, Tibetan Buddhists from the Nyingma school have killing rituals that are meant to liberate their enemies (Mayer 1996: 108). The *Sarvadurgatipariśodhana Tantra*, translated as *The Purification of All Misfortunes*, advocates the killing of those 'who hate the Three Jewels, those who have a wrong attitude with regards to the Buddha's teachings or disparage the [Vajrayāna] masters' (Schmithausen 1999: 58). This position is partly justified through the notion of compassion, where killing an evil person prevents that person from committing further negative actions (karma).

One of the most famous examples of such compassionate killing comes from the Tibetan *Chos 'byung me tog snying po*, which details the Buddhist assassination of the Tibetan ruler Lang Darma in 841. At the time, the Tibetan king Lang Darma oversaw policies that reduced the power and control of monasteries and was viewed as anti-Buddhist. The author Nyang Nyi ma 'od relates that the Buddhist monk received a vision from a protective Buddhist deity, who directed him to kill the ruler. This killing both liberated the country from an anti-Buddhist ruler and also liberated the ruler—through his murder. The narrative of this liberation killing is part of the Tibetan collective memory, and the murder is recalled in ritual yearly in Tibetan monasteries in their dance—the *cham* (Meinert 2006: 100–101). This violent practice of liberation did not end in the ninth century, nor was it restricted to ignoble kings. The presence of Tibetan Buddhist

Tantric ritual killings and blood sacrifice was widespread enough for King Yeshe O (942–1024) to publicly oppose them and to argue hermeneutically for a distinction between the Tantric practices of liberation rites and sacrifice (Dalton 2011: 106–108).

The Weight of a Life: The Victim

Theravāda Doctrine

Regardless of intention, a monk's murder of a nonhuman does not result in expulsion. Monks who kill fearsome dryads (*yakkha*) and other nonhuman beings commit grave offences (*thullaccaya*), which require confessions (Horner 1992: 146–147). The monk Udayin's killing of crows (or of any other animal) also only merits a confession (Horner 1983: 1).

The commentaries offer similar interpretations of offences related to murder. The famous Indian scholar monk Buddhaghosa (fifth century CE) analysed the monastic laws on murder in his *Sumagala-vilasini* and claimed:

> In the case of living creatures without [moral] virtues, such as animals, [the act of killing] is less blameworthy when the creature has a small body, and more blameworthy when the being has a large body. Why? Because the greater effort [required] in killing a being with a large body; and even when the effort is the same, [the act of killing a large-bodied creature is still more blameworthy] because of its greater physical substance. In the case of beings that possess [moral] virtues, such as human beings, the act of killing is less blameworthy when the being is of little virtue and more blameworthy when the being is of great virtue. But when the body and virtue [of creatures] are equal, [the act of killing] is less blameworthy when the defilements and force of the effort are mild, more blameworthy when they are powerful. (Gethin 2004: 171–172)

The *Vinaya* rules and Buddhaghosa's accounts explain, among other things, Theravāda dietary habits. Thai, Lao, Burmese, and Sri Lankan lay Buddhists generally will eat chicken and pork and avoid beef, because the cow is a much larger animal. They also provide an area of ambiguity in regard to humanity and virtue. This distinction between human/nonhuman and virtuous/nonvirtuous humans has been raised in other Buddhist sources.

One of the more popular accounts comes from the Sinhalese mythohistorical chronicle, the *Mahāvaṃsa*. The Buddhist king Dutthagamani wages a just war against the Damil invaders led by King Elara. After a bloody and victorious battle, Dutthagamani laments for causing the slaughter of millions. Eight enlightened monks (*arahant*) comfort him with the explanation:

> From this deed arises no hindrance in thy way to heaven. Only one and a half human beings have been slain here by thee, O lord of men. The one had come unto

> the (three) refuges, the other had taken on himself the five precepts. Unbelievers and men of evil life were the rest, not more to be esteemed than beasts. But as for thee, thou wilt bring glory to the doctrine of the Buddha in manifold ways; therefore cast away from thy heart, O ruler of men! (Mhv XXV 109–111 [Geiger 1993: 178])

The monks' explanation includes the prerequisites discussed earlier for being a Buddhist. In this context, a Buddhist is one who takes the three refuges and follows the five moral precepts. By distinguishing Buddhists from non-Buddhists, the murders in this narrative are dismissed, since the non-Buddhists possess such little virtue they are on par with animals. Furthermore, the king has pure intentions with the desire to support and defend the Buddhist doctrine. The *Mahāvaṃsa*'s rationale and context was not overlooked by Sri Lankan Buddhists centuries later in their twenty-six-year civil war against the Liberation Tamil Tigers of Eelam (LTTE, 1983–2009) and has permeated Southeast Asia as a form of rhetoric, such as during the Cambodia anticommunist campaign in the 1970s.

A similar rationale was used by the prominent Thai Buddhist monk Kittiwuttho in the 1970s during the Thai campaign against communism. For Kittiwuttho, a communist was a bestial type of a person and not a complete person at that. More importantly, her or his death served to support the Buddhist doctrine (Keyes,1978: 153). Kittiwuttho drew on the *Anguttara Nikāya*, 'To Kesi, the Horse Trainer', to justify his stance on killing communists. Not widely used for this purpose, 'To Kesi the Horse Trainer' is about the Buddha's conversation with a horse trainer on the similarities between training people and horses. At one point, the Buddha explains that if a tamable person does not submit to any training, the untamable person is killed. However, shortly after this statement the Buddha explains that death is meant as the Buddha's abandonment of that person's needs, thus meaning the death of the person's ultimate potentiality (Thanissaro 1997).

Mahāyāna and Vajrayāna Doctrine

The School of Emptiness (*śunyavāda*) derives its teachings in part from the pan-Buddhist positions of no-self (Skt *anātman*) and of the two truths model: conventional truth and ultimate truth. Buddhists recognize that there is an eternal no-self (or, no-soul) and that everything we perceive in this world is impermanent and thus constitutes conventional truth. The philosopher Nāgārjuna is the most prominent and respected advocate of this principle and extends the idea of no-self to reality in its entirety, claiming that all phenomena are empty of essence. While emptiness serves to explain reality ontologically and epistemologically, it also provides a lens for valuing human life. This line of reasoning raises the query: If human life is empty of any true nature, what is destroyed in a murder?

One element that is commonly presented when justifying murder is the dehumanization of the intended victim(s). This dehumanization is present in Theravāda when monks consider communists or the followers of the Tamil king Elara less than human and thus meritoriously expendable. Within Mahāyāna doctrine, some humans are designated as *icchantika*s, those who are those barred from enlightenment.

Mahāyāna doctrine typically advocates proselytizing, with people undertaking the bodhisattva vows to work towards liberating all sentient beings (*bodhicitta*). This all-encompassing ethos has an exception with the *icchantika*. Considered the most vile and debased creatures, they have either committed the worst of deeds or repudiated the basic tenets of the doctrine; they are classified at a lower level than animals. Some texts, such as the Chinese version of the Mahāyāna *Mahāparinirvāṇa Sutra*, consider it more harmful to kill an ant than an *icchantika*. Within this text, the Buddha explains that no negative karma accrues from killing them:

> Just as no sinful *karma* [will be engendered] when one digs the ground, mows grass, fells trees, cuts corpses into pieces and scolds and whips them, the same is true when one kills an *icchantika*, for which deed [also] no sinful karma [will arise]. (Ming-Wood 1984: 68)

Perhaps the most extreme religious rhetoric of dehumanization occurs within Mahāyāna doctrine: If a person is empty of substance, what is being murdered? One scripture that offers an answer is the Chinese text called the *Susthitamati-Paripriccha*, which is often referred to as *How to Kill with the Sword of Wisdom*. Within the text, the fully enlightened being Mañjuśrī explains to the Buddha that, if one were to conceive of sentient beings as only names and thoughts, she or he should kill those names and thoughts. However, as long as a person clears the mind of holding a knife or killing, to kill the 'thoughts of a self and a sentient being is to kill sentient beings truly. [If you can do that,] I will give you permission to cultivate pure conduct [with me]' (Chang 1983: 65). Later in the text, Mañjuśrī attempts to assuage bodhisattvas of their guilt from committing violence and advances to kill the Buddha with his sword. The Buddha explains that there is neither killing nor killer. Hence, Mañjuśrī does not suffer any negative repercussions for attempting to kill the Buddha, since ultimately 'there is no sword and no karma and no retribution, who performs that karma and who will undergo the karmic retribution?' (Chang 1983: 69). The acts in this reality are empty of true existence; therefore violence is empty of any true repercussion. Another Chinese text, *The Catharsis of Ajātaśatru's Remorse*, justifies an act of matricide in a similar fashion. Mañjuśrī defends the criminal and explains that since the actor's thoughts were empty at the time of the deed, he should be exonerated (Demiéville 2010: 42).

A Licence to Kill

Theravāda Doctrine

Monastic ethics serve as exemplary rules for laypeople to model, but the 227 rules for Theravāda monks are not required for the laity. Different roles merit different ethics: the ethics for a monk is not the same as it is for a butcher or a soldier (although butchers were noted for having to spend many anguishing lifetimes to redress their negative karma). As for soldiers, Buddhist scriptures remain ambiguous in certain places as to the ramifications of their occupations. Some scriptures impose restrictions on monastic interactions with soldiers or declare that soldiers may not ordain while serving the state, but most do not directly condemn a soldier for following her or his duty. Instead, what is repeatedly emphasized in the ethics of this position is the soldier's state of mind.

One example of this comes from the fourth book and eighth chapter of the *Samyutta Nikāya*, '*Gamanisamyutta*' or the 'Connected Discourses to Headmen'. The Buddha counsels a headman, Yodhājīva, who is a mercenary, under the assumption that mercenaries who strive and exert themselves in battles will be reborn in the heavens. The Buddha explains that when a mercenary dies with the debased thoughts of slaughtering and killing other people, he is reborn in either the hell or animal realms (Bhikkhu Bodhi 2000: 1334–1335). In this scenario, Yodhājīva is cautioned to avoid debased thoughts at the time of death but not to avoid the act of killing. This warning against ill thoughts is relevant whether a person commits an act of aggression or even an act of self-defence. However, the ambiguity about the act itself is present and is found in contemporary contexts as well. In the recent civil war with the LTTE, Sri Lankan Buddhist monks preached to soldiers in order to suffuse their minds with mercy and compassion. Buddhist soldiers with 'cool heads' are less apt to make mistakes on the battlefield and harm civilians (Kent 2010: 172).

For kings and just rule there is a unique set of ethical parameters, which in the contemporary context apply to nation states. According to the commentaries (*atthakatha*), Theravāda's earliest model of a just ruler was the Mauryan emperor Aśoka. After a successful and bloody campaign against the Kalinga in which more than 100,000 died and 150,000 were enslaved, Aśoka repented and turned to the Buddhist doctrine. Typically, Aśoka's reign is praised after his turn to the Buddhist doctrine (and thus, after his conquests). However, Aśoka never disbanded his army after his Buddhist epiphany. He maintained the state policy of capital punishment and, according to literary records, killed more than 18,000 Jains and committed other atrocities well after his turn to righteous Buddhist kingship (Jenkins 2010: 63).

Early Buddhist scriptures tacitly support states. This may be due partly to the fact that the Buddha received most of his principal support in his early years from the kingdoms of Magadha and Kosala. The Buddha's relationship to the two kingdoms was stressed at times by their internecine conflict. As a moral and ethical liaison for both kingdoms, the Buddha responded on these occasions by condoning wars of defence over wars of aggression. This endorsement of defensive violence employs one of two modes on the ethics of state violence. According to Steven Collins, Theravāda scriptures present on occasion a categorical imperative to avoid violence. On other occasions, the doctrine offers an ethics of just war through reciprocity; the Buddha counsels kings to administer judgments and punishments, but with a clear and calm mind (Collins 1998: 420).

This latter mode is best evident in the 239th rebirth story of the Buddha, the *Harita-Mata Jātaka* ('Blue-Green Frog Birth Story'), in which the Buddha addresses a recent attack by the kingdom of Kosala on the kingdom of Magadha. As in other rebirth stories, the narrative serves as a didactic for the particular context as well as general readership. The story tells of a water snake that falls into a trap and is attacked by a throng of fish. Appealing to a blue-green frog for help, the frog, which is the Buddha-to-be, replies to the entrapped snake, 'If you eat fish that get into your demesne, the fish eat you when you get into theirs. In his own place, and district, and feeding ground, no one is weak.' Following the frog's explanation, the fish seize and kill the snake (Cowell 1990: 165).

Ethics of state violence are mentioned several times in the *The Questions of King Milinda*. Throughout the text, the Indo-Greek king Menander I questions the Buddhist monk Nāgasena about Buddhist principles. In the fourth book, called 'The Solving of Dilemmas', the king lists eight classes of men who kill living beings: lustful men, cruel men, dull men, proud men, avaricious men, needy men, foolish men, and kings in the way of punishment (Rhys Davids 1894: 17). As in the case of the other seven types of men, a king by his nature adjudicates punishments and kills living beings.

This aspect of rule is further described in a later conversation, when the king explains that if a man has committed a crime, the people would request that the criminal be deprived of goods, bound, tortured, put to death, or beheaded (Rhys Davids 1894: 239). In neither conversation does Nāgasena dispute the king's views on murder, and the presence of these duties in a book on Buddhist ethics is unmistakably notable. This approach to just rule is found in other canonical sources such as the twenty-sixth and twenty-seventh books of the *Digha Nikāya*. In 'The Sermon on the Knowledge of Beginnings', the king is entrusted with the moral responsibility to uphold the law and mete out punishments. The case is slightly different in 'The Lion's Roar at the Turning of the Wheel', in which the failure to fully uphold the Buddhist doctrine results in a need to implement punishments to maintain order.

Mahāyāna Doctrine

In some texts, killing or war is justified so long as it is done to defend the religion. In the Tibetan version of the Mahāyāna *Mahāparinirvāṇa Sutra*, Buddhists, especially kings, are expected to take up weapons and fight to defend their religion (Schmithausen 1999: 57–58). Similar to Theravāda doctrine, Mahāyāna doctrine contains different ethics for rulers than for lay practitioners. The Mongolian text *White History of the Tenfold Virtuous Dharma* instructs rulers to destroy those who are against the Buddhist teachings and to implement harsh measures when necessary (Wallace 2010: 93). The South Asian *Ārya-Bodhisattva-gocara-upāyaviṣaya-vikurvaṇa-nirdeśa Sūtra (Satyakaparivarta)*, which is loosely translated at *The Noble Teachings through Manifestations on the Subject of Skill-in-Means within the Bodhisattva's Field of Activity*, also provides instructions for rulers. It includes ways to administer Buddhist-sanctioned torture, capital punishment, and other forms of violence. In the text, the king is warned to avoid the exercise of *excessive* compassion and to imprison, terrorize, beat, bind, or harm 'uncivilized people' (Jenkins 2010: 64).

Mahāyāna doctrine provides a similar structure of exceptions for violence as Theravāda. However, the principles of emptiness and skill-in-means create a distinctive set of ethical considerations. These principles are shared in Vajrayāna doctrine, which is often said to have evolved out of Mahāyāna doctrine.

Vajrayāna Doctrine

Among the Vajrayāna foundational principles is the Mahāyāna conception of the bodhisattva, a being who is either enlightened or on the path to enlightenment. In some texts, these individuals, who are endowed with perfected compassion and wisdom, gain the benefits from an ethical double standard. As seen in the scriptures that address the Bodhisattva Mañjuśrī, ordinary people are bound by the provisional ethics; however, bodhisattvas may do anything, even commit murder. Fully enlightened beings are not hindered by the attachments of ill thoughts, so their actions are different from others. In addition, they use skill-in-means to liberate people and protect the religion.

Perhaps the most sacred person in Vajrayāna doctrine is the Dalai Lama. The lineage began with the Ngawang Lobsang Gyatso, who was named the Fifth Dalai Lama in the mid-seventeenth century. The Fifth Dalai Lama made use of his religious stature to commission killings. Johan Elverskog notes the ways in which the Fifth Dalai Lama Ngawang Lobsang Gyatso sought to consolidate his power in Tibet: 'He also needed soldiers willing to kill and maim in the name of the Dalai Lama. He found what he was looking for in the Upper Mongols, who in many ways became his fundamentalist Gelukpa death squad' (2010: 221). As he expanded the Gelukpa tradition and fought against the rival Buddhist schools, the Fifth Dalai Lama legitimated violence on his behalf. In the Tibetan *Song of the Queen Spring*, the Fifth Dalai Lama explains that advanced Buddhist yogis can commit just acts of violence because of their command over mental states and emotions (Maher 2010: 85). It is in this context that the Fifth Dalai Lama justifies violence committed by his school's protector, the Mongol ruler Gushri Khan. In addition to the fact that Gushri Khan was defending the *Dharma*, the Fifth Dalai Lama explains that the ruler was a bodhisattva (88).

State Violence

Balkrishna Gokhale (1968: 251) argues that early Buddhist thinkers had a Weberian conception of the state: 'For them the state is an organization of force or violence the possession of which is largely restricted to the king and his instruments.' The state had, and for many modern Buddhist governments still has, the duty to use violence to maintain order. There are various ways in which the state's implementation of Buddhist principles has harmed its citizens: laws on euthanasia and abortion, corporal punishment, and systemic policies that uphold discrimination.

Laws

One domain of state laws is euthanasia and abortion. These laws differ with each nation state and doctrinal grouping. The majority of Buddhist nation states do not support the use of euthanasia or abortion. Humans must endure the fruits of their negative actions; in this light, the dying persons expiate their past *kamma* through their suffering. And because Buddhist notions often pinpoint life at conception, the abortion of a foetus is the ending of a self. This stance has created problems in some countries such as Thailand, where abortion is prohibited but abortions are performed. Thai Buddhists believe that the foetuses' spirits must be appeased, and so aborted foetuses are brought to monasteries for cremation. Japanese Buddhists perform a foetus memorial service (*mizuko kuyō*) for stillborn, aborted, or miscarried foetuses. During these ceremonies, offerings are made to the Bodhisattva Jizō (*Mahāparinirvāṇa*), the guardian of children.[2]

Corporal Punishment

Throughout the many iterations of the state over the centuries, Buddhists have supported their government's right to adjudicate punishments in order to maintain the Buddhist ethos. In addition to the state's function of preserving the *Dharma*, some interpret corporal punishments as executions of the law of karma. For others, however, the system of punishment is itself an application of negative actions. As indicated earlier under doctrinal justifications, the majority of Buddhists condone corporal punishments, which includes torture as well as capital punishment.

The Buddhist position on punishments has changed over the centuries. In the sixteenth century, the Mongolian Khutukhtu Setsen Khung Taiji edited the *White History of the Tenfold Virtuous Dharma*, which advised measures such as blinding someone for stealing or cutting out a tongue for a lie (Wallace 2010: 93). Various punishments were carried out in Mongolia until the social revolution in 1921. Thailand does not maintain laws like those found in the *White History*, but it has been cited by nongovernmental organizations such as Amnesty International and Human Rights Watch for their torture techniques of suspects, sometimes on temple grounds (Jerryson 2011: 139).

The Sri Lankan Buddhist scholar Ananda Abeysekara reminds scholars to situate constantly evolving terms such as 'Buddhism' and 'violence' in a particular context. In his fieldwork, he notes that some torture techniques can carry a Buddhist connotation, such as the Sri Lankan *dhammacakke gahanava* (hitting the wheel of the *Dhamma*). For this torture, Buddhists—sometimes JVP Buddhist monks—were forced to contort their bodies into the shape of a wheel; their bodies were then spun and beaten until the person passed out or bled to death (Abeysekara 2002: 230–231).

[2] For a larger and more detailed discussion of abortion, see Michael Barnhart's chapter on abortion and reproduction in this volume.

There is a distinctive different between torture and self-inflictions, particularly in light of the Buddhist value of harm/injury. Instances such as the *dhammacakke gahanava* are done to a person as a means of causing harm. Buddhists have applied forms of self-mortification in order to gain merit, display filial piety, or express devotion. These practices are most frequently seen in Chinese traditions, wherein Buddhist monks wrote in blood, sliced off parts of their body, and engaged in extreme ritual exposures to the sun (Yu 2012). As mentioned earlier in this chapter, Buddhists can judge these acts, similar to self-immolations, as compassionate acts and not violations of *ahiṃsā*.

Some nation states are not supportive of the death penalty. For example, Sri Lanka has had a long history of opposition to the death penalty. In 1815, the British implemented the death penalty, but in 1978 it was revoked. Subsequently there have been periodic attempts to reinstate this policy.

While the conception of the state was taken for granted by early Buddhist thinkers, it became emboldened by modern Buddhist advocates and rulers. One example is the Sri Lankan government in its indiscriminate use of force against 'enemies of the state'. Another notable example is the Thai government's use of *lèse-majesté* to impose corporal punishment on those who disrespect the Buddhist monarchy.

Identity and Discriminatory Violence

The vast corpus of Western scholarship on religion and violence pertains largely to negative political and physical examples, i.e. war and conflict. Subjects such as alienation are relegated to Johan Galtung's descriptor 'structural violence' or left out entirely. The Buddhist focus on harm/injury as violence becomes especially relevant in the context of alienation, discrimination, and subjugation. No one appreciates being excluded from privileges; rather, people often say they are *harmed* by such exclusion.

Perhaps the lynchpin that connects Buddhist traditions to the realm of violence is a person's identification as a Buddhist. In her assessment of Abrahamic religions, Regina Schwartz argues that the origin of violence is a person's identity formation. She finds that 'imagining identity as an act of distinguishing and separating from others, of boundary making and line drawing, is the most frequent and fundamental act of violence we commit' (1997: 5). This tendency to separate and distinguish from others in Abrahamic traditions is also found in Buddhist traditions. In early South Asian societies, Buddhist traditions were aniconic and without strict identity markers. But as early as the first century CE, this changed. The crystallization of a Buddhist identity introduced adherents of the *Buddhadharma* (Buddhist teaching) to a new arena of politics and forms of alterity.

Ordinarily, a Buddhist identity is attached to other identifications, often ethnic and national markers. This is especially prominent in Southeast Asia: in Thailand, to be Thai is to be Buddhist (Jerryson 2011: 143–177); in Myanmar, to be Burmese is to be Buddhist (Bechert 1984). Part of this connection began in the late nineteenth and early twentieth century during the era of nation state building. As Anne Hansen writes in her work on colonial Cambodia, 'Put simply, the French wanted (for themselves and their Khmer colleagues) to be modern in their understanding of Buddhism; the Khmer wanted to be Buddhist in a modern world' (2007: 131). During these nation state operations, ethnic and religious hostilities flared in South and Southeast Asia. The most recent iteration of these hostilities comes under the umbrella of nationalism and its corollary national identities: thus, an attack on the nation becomes an attack on Buddhism. Research suggests that this phenomenon intensifies in diaspora; Eve L. Mullen notes that for Tibetans in the United States, 'What is deemed to be Tibetan is Buddhist and what is Buddhist is actively patriotic' (2006: 186).

In the era of nation states and nation-building, Buddhists such as Tibetan, Thai, Cambodian, and Burmese consider their nationality intimately connected with Buddhism. Due to this collusion of identities, an attack on the nation becomes an attack on Buddhism (and vice versa). In drawing the parameters for Buddhist traditions, it is clear that there is a high variance of cultural practices and beliefs.

In addition to the identification of *being* a Buddhist, there are identifications within Buddhism that offer privileges or lack thereof. Religious texts are suffused with gender and racial stereotypes. While there is not sufficient space in this chapter to devote to a thorough treatment of such stereotypes, it is important to provide a brief overview.

Gender distinctions in Buddhist traditions are so pronounced that Bernard Faure argues a consistent feminist critique could shatter Buddhism in its foundation (1998: 281). In the heterosexually dominated narrative, women are subservient to men—either in recollections of the Buddha and his past lives or in the pantheon of deities and bodhisattvas. Buddhist traditions were among the earliest to grant women ordination (along with Jains), but this was not without contest. The Buddha's favourite disciple Ānanda had to ask three times for their admittance, and after the Order of Nuns was created, the Buddha explained the life of the *Dharma* was cut short because women were included. There were early female Buddhist saints such as those found in the collection of female hagiographies (*Therīgāthā*), but South Asian Buddhist women have learned to identify themselves from the perspective of male heroes (Wilson 1996: 5).

Through the centuries most countries did not sustain their Order of Nuns; some, such as Thailand, never initiated it. In the alternative practices of Tantra, the division of sexual bodies and sacrality are not much different. Charlene Makley points out that the paradigmatically male bodies of Tibetan incarnate lamas (Tib *sprulsku*) act as crucial indexes of the local divine cosmos (2007: 25). There is much to say about a religion that focuses on overcoming attachment, and depicts women as seductresses in texts and images, such as Mara's daughters. Viewed from this perspective, it is not a coincidence that sex ranks higher than murder among the highest offences (*pārājika*).

Buddhist practices also have been used to sustain racial categories. The earliest of these dates back to the South Asian Brahmanical caste system, which was officially rebuked by the Buddha. However, the monastic guidelines contain a wealth of physical restrictions for those who wish to ordain, and the vast majority of his early Buddhist followers were of the higher castes (particularly of the merchant and priest castes). Within the early South Asian social system, racial divisions were physically mapped by skin tones; those people with darker skin pigmentations were designated as the lower castes.

The preference for lighter skin pigmentation is largely the result of labour conditions. Those of the lower castes worked outside in the sun, whereas the wealthy could afford to stay indoors. This early method of racializing bodies has changed, but is still evident within contemporary Buddhist societies of South and Southeast Asia and has been reinforced by global media and entertainment.

Sri Lankan society still maintains a caste system, and Thai society retains a preference for lighter skin tones as well. Within these nation states, it is generally the white tourists who visit the beaches to tan; whitening creams are commonly advertised. The preference for lighter skin pigmentation is mapped onto Buddhist images, with light skin tones for the Buddha and darker skin tones for his adversaries. In some accounts, Mara and his minions are depicted with darker skin tones, such as in Thai Buddhist murals. These features suggest a structural level of violence that integrates Buddhist lore and racialized subjects (for examples, see Jerryson 2011: 143–177).

Beyond identifications such as gender and race is the larger treatment of the Other. In South and Southeast Asia, Buddhist governments and communities have engaged in 'politics of belonging' through Islamophobic policies and practices. One of the more prominent examples is the 969 movement in Myanmar. The numerals 9-6-9 represent the Three Jewels: nine characteristics of the Buddha, six characteristics of the *Dharma*, and nine characteristics of the *Saṅgha*. Burmese Buddhist monks created the symbol in response to Muslim shopkeepers using the symbol 786 to indicate *halal* certifications. Nyi Nyi Kyaw points out that the movement uses this symbol 'because its leaders want to convey the message that it represents the Three Gems of Buddhism and, symbolically drawing on the qualities of the Holy Trinity, indicates to Buddhists that it is a noble endeavor' (2016: 1998). Members of the movement, and its affiliate Ma-Ba-Tha (The Patriotic Association of Myanmar), repeatedly have engaged in anti-Muslim rhetoric that seeks to alienate and ostracize minorities in Myanmar.

Buddhist Responses to Violence

As popularized in the West, there are many Buddhists who view peace as a quintessentially social endeavor. Christopher Queen speaks to this shift in his introduction to *Engaged Buddhism in the West*:

> For Buddhists and practitioners of the other world faiths, it is no longer possible to measure the quality of human life primarily in terms of an individual's observance of traditional rites, such as meditation, prayer, or temple ritual; or belief in dogmas such as 'the law of karma,' 'buddha-nature,' 'the will of God,' or 'the Tao.' (2000: 1)

For these Buddhists, it is not enough to engage in Buddhist meditation and participate in traditional rituals; one must concern oneself with the suffering of this world. In this way, as Buddhists have been involved in justifying, inflaming, and initiating political conflicts since their political beginnings, so too have they been involved in resolving them.

Thich Nhat Hanh, nominated by Martin Luther King Jr for the Nobel Peace Prize, makes use of this example in his work. In his collection of scriptural sources, Thich Nhat Hanh recounts a section in the *Dhammapada-Aṭṭhakathā* in which the Buddha intervenes in the Rohini River conflict between his family's clan and a neighbouring clan:

> He said, 'Your Majesties, which is more precious, water or human lives?' The kings agreed that human lives were infinitely more precious. The Buddha said, 'Your Majesties, the need for adequate irrigation water has caused this conflict. If pride and anger had not flared up, this conflict could have been resolved. There is no need for war! Examine your hearts. Do not waste the blood of your people because of pride and anger. Once pride and anger are released, the tensions that lead to war will disappear. Sit down and negotiate how the river water can be shared equally with both sides in this time of drought. Both sides must be assured of an equal amount of water.' (Nhat Hanh 1991: 339)

It was through the Buddha's careful review of the conflict that he was able to locate the seed that had germinated into open hostilities. Once he had located the problem, the Buddha pressed both sides to acknowledge the higher costs of the conflict, and to compromise on their mutual needs for the benefit of the two kingdoms. Using the Buddha as a model, many Buddhists and Buddhist monks have engaged in conflict resolution in similar ways.

One example of conflict resolution and peace-building comes from Japanese Buddhism. Nichiren argued for the use of Buddhist principles and the *Lotus Sutra* for military purposes in the thirteenth century. However, by the mid-twentieth century, Nichiren Buddhist monks advocated for an end to nuclear proliferation and conflict through Buddhist principles. One example comes from Fujii Nichidatsu, who founded an order within Nichiren Buddhism in 1917 called Nipponzan Myohoji. The order took a new direction in 1931, when Fujii met Mohandas Gandhi and became a strong supporter of Gandhi's *satyāgraha* (true-force) and nonviolence. After the bombings of Hiroshima and Nagasaki, Fujii oversaw the building of the order's first 'peace pagoda' (Skt *śānti stūpa*). Taking his inspiration from the *Lotus Sutra* (Chapter 11), Fujii saw the pagoda as a locus of Buddhist sacrality, as well as a vision of future universality:

> The appearing of a Pagoda touches the hearts and minds of all people. Those who venerate this Pagoda absolutely reject nuclear warfare and firmly believe that a peaceful world will be manifested. The vision of a Pagoda has the power to bring about a spiritual transformation. It illumines the dawn of a spiritual civilization. (cited in Green 2000: 139)

In the twenty-first century, the Nipponzan Myohoji continue their work to reduce nuclear weapons and to promote peace. Although small in numbers (roughly 1,500;

Kisala 2006: 463), they have nonetheless globalized their efforts. There are now over eighty of their peace pagodas worldwide.

Another example of Buddhist conflict resolution comes from one of the bloodiest conflicts of the twentieth century. Led by Pol Pot, the Khmer Rouge controlled Cambodia from 1975 to 1979. During those four years, they orchestrated the genocide of 1.7 million people, nearly 21 per cent of Cambodia's total population (Cambodian Genocide Program). In the aftermath, Cambodia has been riddled with political and social conflicts. One of the important building blocks in its reconciliation process has come from Cambodian Buddhist monks such as Maha Ghosananda, who have worked to heal societal tensions.

Maha Ghosananda is recognized as an important figure, not only for his work on peace-building, but for his transnational connections. He studied at the Buddhist University in Phnom Penh and then travelled to India to work on his doctorate at the Buddhist University of Nalanda. Ian Harris writes that it was in India that Maha Ghosananda 'seems to have come under the influence of Fujii Nichidatsu, who founded the Japanese peace-oriented Buddhist sect Nipponzan Myohoji and was himself involved with the work of Gandhi' (2005: 207).

Later, Maha Ghosananda served as a consultant to the United Nations Economic and Social Council and advocated the political need to address human suffering. For Buddhists like Maha Ghosananda, the Cambodian society needed to move forward through forgiveness. Similar to Thich Nhat Hanh's accounts of the Buddha's mediation, Maha Ghosananda has worked to bring Cambodians together in their efforts towards reconciliation: 'Reconciliation does not mean that we surrender rights and conditions, but rather that we use love in all our negotiations' (Coalition for Peace and Reconciliation 1997: 6).

Conclusion

This chapter has provided examples of Buddhist approaches to war and violence, but it is far from comprehensive. For the purposes of this discussion, it has avoided exegetical exercises and reviews of rich academic debates on Buddhist principles and their relevance. Instead, the chapter has delimited space to historical examples of Buddhist choices and justifications about war and violence.

The discourse on violence is continuing to expand, and there is ample work on subjects left unaddressed in this chapter. Such areas include the Buddhist challenges to accepting non-heterosexual identities, Spivakian discussions of 'epistemic violence', the violence in video games, and violence in virtual realities. New sub-fields on violence are also emerging, such as inquiries into the relationship between Buddhism and blasphemy.[3] One of the more notable absences, however, is the treatment of animals.

[3] See the special issue of the *Journal of Religion and Violence* (4 [2] 2016) on Buddhism and blasphemy.

Wherein various Buddhist traditions have different dietary restrictions, they also have differing ways in ethicizing the killing of animals.[4]

The larger lacuna in this chapter comes from the deliberate focus on agency and violence. The sections in this chapter cover the Buddhists who engage in war, their rationality, and their justifications to kill. However, it does not provide the corollary. There is a wealth of Buddhist perspectives on coping with and surviving extremely violent scenarios and wars. The discourse on Buddhists coping with violence is, in and of itself, voluminous. Unfortunately, it is beyond the purview of this chapter. Hopefully, future work in Buddhism, war, and violence will address Buddhist perspectives from both the aggressor and victim points of view.

Works Cited

Abeysekara, A. (2002) *The colors of the robe: religion, identity, and difference.* Columbia: University of South Carolina Press.

Bechert, H. (1984) 'To be Burmese is to be Buddhist': Buddhism in Burma. In: H. Bechert and R. Gombrich (eds), *The world of Buddhism: Buddhist monks and nuns in society and culture.* London: Thames & Hudson, 147–158.

Bhikkhu Bodhi (trans.) (2000) *The connected discourses of the Buddha: a translation of the Saṃyutta Nikāya.* Boston: Wisdom.

Chang, G. C. (ed.) (1983) How to kill with the sword of wisdom. In: *A treasury of Mahayana sūtras: selections from the Mahāratnakūṭa Sūtra.* University Park and London: Pennsylvania State University Press, 41–72.

Coalition for Peace and Reconciliation (1997) CPR update: a newsletter of the Dhammayietra Center. Phnom Penh: CPR.

Collins, S. (1998) *Nirvana and other Buddhist felicities: utopias of the Pali imaginaire.* Cambridge: Cambridge University Press.

Cowell, E. B. (ed.) (1990) *The Jātaka or stories of the Buddha's former births.* Reprint of 1895 edition. Delhi: Motilal Banarsidass Publishers.

Dalton, J. P. (2011) *Taming the demons: violence and liberation in Tibetan Buddhism.* Princeton: Yale University Press.

Davidson, R. M. (2005) *Tibetan renaissance: tantric Buddhism in the rebirth of Tibetan culture.* New York: Columbia University Press.

Demiéville, P. (2010) Buddhism and war. Translated by M. Kendall. In: M. Jerryson and M. Juergensmeyer (eds), *Buddhist warfare.* New York: Oxford University Press, 17–58.

Elverskog, J. (2010) *Buddhism and Islam on the Silk Road.* Philadelphia: University of Pennsylvania Press.

Faure, B. (1998) *The red thread: Buddhist approaches to sexuality.* Princeton: Princeton University Press.

Geiger, W. (trans.) (1993) *The Mahāvaṃsa or the great chronicle of Ceylon.* Reprint of 1912 edition. New Delhi and Madras: Asian Educational Services.

[4] For a rich analysis of Buddhist ethics on animals and violence, see Stewart (2014) and Keown (2012).

Gethin, R. (2004) Can killing a living being ever be an act of compassion? The analysis of the act of killing in the Abhidhamma and Pali commentaries. *Journal of Buddhist ethics*, 11, 167–202.

Gokhale, B. (1968) Dhamma as a political concept. *Journal of Indian history*, 44 (August), 249–261.

Gray, D. B. (2007) Compassionate violence? On the ethical implications of Tantric Buddhist ritual. *Journal of Buddhist ethics*, 14, 238–271.

Green, P. (2000) Walking for peace: Nipponzan Myohoji. In: C. Queen and S. King (eds), *Engaged Buddhism in the west*. Somerville, MA: Wisdom, 128–158.

Hansen, A. (2007) *How to behave: Buddhism and modernity in colonial Cambodia, 1860–1930*. Honolulu: University of Hawai'i Press.

Harris, I. (2005) *Cambodian Buddhism: history and practice*. Honolulu: University of Hawai'i Press.

Horner, I. B. (trans.) (1963–1964) *Milinda's questions*. London: Luzac and Company.

Horner, I. B. (trans.) (1983) *The book of the discipline (Vinaya-Pitaka): Volume III (Suttavibhanga)*. Reprint of 1942 edition. Oxford: Pali Text Society.

Horner, I. B. (trans.) (1992) *The book of the discipline (Vinaya-Pitaka): Volume I (Suttavibhanga)*. Reprint of 1938 edition. Oxford: Pali Text Society.

Jenkins, S. (2010) Making merit through warfare and torture according to the *Ārya-Bodhisattva-gocara-upāyaviṣaya-vikurvaṇa-nirdeśa Sūtra*. In: M. Jerryson and M. Juergensmeyer (eds), *Buddhist warfare*. New York: Oxford University Press, 59–76.

Jenkins, S. (2010/2011) On the auspiciousness of compassionate violence. *Journal of the International Association of Buddhist Studies*, 33 (1–2), 299–331.

Jerryson, M. (2011) *Buddhist fury: religion and violence in southern Thailand*. New York: Oxford University Press.

Kent, D. (2010) Onward Buddhist soldiers. In: M. Jerryson and M. Juergensmeyer (eds), *Buddhist warfare*. New York: Oxford University Press, 157–177.

Keown, D. (2012) Buddhist ethics: a critique. In: D. L. McMahan (ed.), *Buddhism in the modern world*. New York: Routledge, 215–232.

Keyes, C. (1978) Political crisis and militant Buddhism. In: B. L. Smith (ed.): *Religion and legitimation of power in Thailand, Laos, and Burma*. Chambersburg, PA: ANIMA, 147–164.

Kyaw, N. N. (2016) Islamophobia in Buddhist Myanmar: the 969 movement and anti-Muslim violence. In: M. Crouch (ed.), *Islam and the state in Myanmar: Muslim–Buddhist relations and the politics of belonging*. New Delhi: Oxford University Press, 183–210.

Maher, D. F. (2010) Sacralized warfare: the fifth Dalai Lama and the discourse of religious violence. In: M. Jerryson and M. Juergensmeyer (eds), *Buddhist warfare*. New York: Oxford University Press, 77–90.

Makley, C. E. (2007) *The violence of liberation: gender and Tibetan Buddhist revival in post-Mao China*. Berkeley: University of California Press.

Mayer, R. (1996) *A scripture of the ancient tantra collection, the Phur-pa bcu-gnyis*. Oxford: Kiscadale Publications.

Meinert, C. (2006) Between the profane and the sacred? On the context of the rite of 'liberation' (*sgrol ba*). In: M. Zimmermann (ed.), *Buddhism and violence*. Lumbini, Nepal: Lumbini International Research Institute, 99–130.

Ming-Wood, L. (1984) The problem of the *icchantika* in the Mahāyāna *Mahāparinirvāna Sūtra*. *Journal of the International Association of Buddhist Studies*, 7 (1), 57–81.

Mullen, E. (2006) Tibetan religious expression and identity: transformations in exile. In: E. Arweck and W. J. F. Keenan (eds), *Materializing religion: expression, performance and ritual.* Aldershot, UK: Ashgate, 175–189.

Nartsupha, C. (1984) The ideology of holy men revolts in north east Thailand. *Senri ethnological studies*, 13, 111–134.

Nhat Hanh, T. (1991) *Old path white clouds: walking in the footsteps of the Buddha*. Translated by M. Ho. Berkley: Parallax Press.

Nichiren (n.d.) The strategy of the *Lotus sutra*. Translated by Soka Gakkai International. In: *Writings of Nichiren Daishonin*. Soka Gakkai International, 1000–1001. Available from: www.nichirenlibrary.org [Accessed 17 January 2009].

Nuhman, M. A. (2016) Sinhala Buddhist nationalism and Muslim identity in Sri Lanka. In: J. C. Holt (ed.), *Buddhist extremists and Muslim minorities in Sri Lanka*. New York: Oxford University Press, 18–53.

Queen, C. (2000) Introduction: a new Buddhism. In: C. Queen and S. King (eds), *Engaged Buddhism in the West*. Somerville, MA: Wisdom, 1–34.

Rhys Davids, T. W. (1894) *Questions of King Milinda, part II*. Sacred Books of the East, volume 36. Oxford: Clarendon Press. Available from: http://www.sacred-texts.com/bud/sbe36/sbe3600.htm.

Schmithausen, L. (1999) Buddhist attitudes toward war. In: J. E. M. Houben and K. R. Van Kooji (eds), *Violence denied: violence, non-violence and the rationalization of violence in south Asian cultural history*. Leiden, Netherlands, and Boston: Brill, 39–67.

Schwartz, R. M. (1997) *The curse of Cain: the violent legacy of monotheism*. Chicago: University of Chicago Press.

Soboslai, J. (2015) Violently peaceful: Tibetan self-immolation and the problem of the non/violence binary. *Open Theology*, 1 (1), 146–159. Available from: https://www.degruyter.com/downloadpdf/j/opth.2014.1.issue-1/opth-2015-0004/opth-2015-0004.pdf [Accessed 3 June 2015].

Stewart, J. (2014) Violence and nonviolence in Buddhist animal ethics. *Journal of Buddhist ethics*, 21, 623–655.

Tatz, M. (trans.) (1994) Murder with skill in means: the story of the ship's captain. In: *The Skill in Means (Upāyakauśalya) Sutra*. New Delhi: Motilal Banarsidass, 73–74.

Thanissaro Bhikkhu (trans.) (1997) Kesi Sutta: to Kesi the horsetrainer. *Anguttara nikaya*. Available from: http://www.accesstoinsight.org/tipitaka/an/an04/an04.111.than.html [Accessed 25 July 2010].

Tikhonov, V. (2009) Violent Buddhism—Korean Buddhists and the Pacific War, 1937–1945. *Sai*, 7, 169–204.

Times Now (2013) Special: The Dalai Lama. 25 March 2013. Available from: https://www.youtube.com/watch?v=-XXZslT3mmE [Accessed 17 April 2013].

Victoria, B. (2006) *Zen at War*. Second edition. Lanham, MD: Rowman and Littlefield.

Wallace, V. (2010) Legalized violence: punitive measures of Buddhist Khans in Mongolia. In: M. Jerryson and M. Juergensmeyer (eds), *Buddhist warfare*. New York: Oxford University Press, 91–104.

Wilson, L. (1996) *Charming cadavers: horrific figurations of the feminine in Indian Buddhist hagiographic literature*. Chicago: University of Chicago Press.

Wong, E. (2016) Tibetan monk, 18, dies after self-immolation to protest Chinese rule. *The New York Times*, 3 March.

Yu, J. (2012) *Sanctity and self-inflected violence in Chinese religions, 1500–1700*. New York: Oxford University Press.

Yu, X. (2010) Buddhists in China during the Korean War (1951–1953). In: M. Jerryson and M. Juergensmeyer (eds), *Buddhist warfare*. New York: Oxford University Press, 131–156.

Suggested Reading

Bartholomeusz, T. J. (2002) *In defense of dharma: just-war ideology in Buddhist Sri Lanka*. New York: Routledge Curzon.

Baumann, M. (2001) Buddhism: developmental periods, regional histories, and a new analytical perspective. *Journal of global Buddhism*, 2, 1–43.

Broido, M. M. (1988) Killing, lying, stealing and adultery: a problem of interpretation in the tantras. In: D. S. Lopez, Jr (ed.), *Buddhist hermeneutics*. Honolulu: University of Hawai'i Press, 71–118.

Jerryson, M. (2010) Introduction. In: M. Jerryson and M. Juergensmeyer (eds), *Buddhist warfare*. New York: Oxford University Press, 1–16.

Keown, D. (1999). Attitudes to euthanasia in the *vinaya* and commentary. *Journal of Buddhist ethics*, 6, 260–270.

McGranahan, C., and Litzinger, R. (eds) (2012) Self-immolation as protest in Tibet. *Cultural anthropology* (special edition). Available from: http://www.culanth.org/?q=node/526.

Reuter, C. (2004) *My life is a weapon: a modern history of suicide bombing*. Princeton: Princeton University Press.

Ruth, R. A. (2011) *In Buddha's company: Thai soldiers in the Vietnam War*. Honolulu: University of Hawai'i Press.

Schober, J. (2010) *Modern Buddhist conjunctures in Myanmar: cultural narratives, colonial legacies, and civil society*. Honolulu: University of Hawai'i Press.

Skidmore, M. (2004) *Karaoke fascism: Burma and the politics of fear*. Philadelphia: University of Pennsylvania Press.

CHAPTER 23

THE ETHICS OF ENGAGED BUDDHISM IN ASIA

SALLIE B. KING

Introduction

This chapter examines the ethics of contemporary Engaged Buddhism, also known as Socially Engaged Buddhism. Engaged Buddhism is a contemporary form of Buddhism found throughout the Buddhist world (unless suppressed by government). It has no single founder or headquarters, but has arisen over time in multiple countries in response to the challenges facing those societies. Engaged Buddhism may be defined as those forms of Buddhism that intentionally and nonviolently engage with the social, political, economic, and environmental issues of society and the world on the basis of and as an expression of Buddhist beliefs, values, concepts, world view, and practices. It is neither a new Buddhist sect nor does it belong to any established sect; Buddhists of any sect may also be Engaged Buddhists. It is particularly the sustained intention of applying Buddhism to the problems of society in a nonviolent way that identifies Engaged Buddhism.[1]

Engaged Buddhism must carefully be distinguished from another form of activist Buddhism, contemporary Buddhist nationalism, as found in Sri Lanka and Myanmar in the late twentieth and early twenty-first centuries. Engaged Buddhism and Buddhist nationalism are two altogether different ideologies. Engaged Buddhism is nonviolent. Nationalist Buddhism is an implicitly violent stance inasmuch as it accords second-class status to non-Buddhists within the nation, sometimes denying minorities the right to be part of the nation; moreover, it frequently directly incites violence. Nationalist Buddhism is chauvinistic; its *raison d'être* is to support the group self in the

[1] The author thanks the University of Hawai'i Press for permission to reuse excerpts from her *Being Benevolence: The Social Ethics of Engaged Buddhism* (2005) and her *Socially Engaged Buddhism* (2009).

form of nation and Buddhism. It uses its majority power to oppress minorities. Engaged Buddhism is often non-partisan, seeking the good of all and often working to reconcile groups in conflict; sometimes it acts nonviolently on behalf of beleaguered groups such as the former untouchable class. Engaged Buddhism is in all cases solidly supportive of democracy; nationalist Buddhism is sometimes associated with demagoguery.

An initial description of Engaged Buddhism may perhaps best be sketched by briefly introducing some of its more important leaders and movements. Tenzin Gyatso, the Fourteenth Dalai Lama (b. 1935), is the spiritual leader of the Tibetan people and head of the Tibetan Liberation Movement, which struggles nonviolently for Tibetan self-determination. The Dalai Lama is famous throughout the world for championing non-violence, as well as a non-sectarian spirituality emphasizing kindness, compassion, and universal responsibility.

Thich Nhat Hanh (b. 1926), Vietnamese Zen monk and poet, coined the term 'Engaged Buddhism' and is arguably the most important ideologist of the movement. He came to international fame during the years of the Vietnam War, during which he was part of a movement that advocated a 'Third Way', siding with neither the North nor South Vietnamese side, but with life. After the war, Nhat Hanh took up residence in France, from where he has created and taught a form of Buddhist spirituality and social activism that has appealed to people all over the world.

A. T. Ariyaratne (b. 1931) founded Sarvodaya Shramadana, the largest nongovernment organization in Sri Lanka, as a Buddhist self-help movement to support rural Sri Lankans struggling with deep poverty, aiming to build a society in which all needs are met—economic, social, cultural, psychological, political, and spiritual. During Sri Lanka's civil war, Sarvodaya played a major role as a peacemaker.

Dr B. R. Ambedkar (1891–1956) led a mass conversion movement of India's ex-untouchable 'Dalits' ('oppressed') from Hinduism to Buddhism in order to claim freedom from the stigma of so-called 'untouchability' within the Hindu caste system, thus initiating a movement of Dalit conversion to Buddhism for reasons that are simultaneously social, political, psychological, and spiritual.

In Cambodia, Somdech Preah Maha Ghosananda (1929?–2007), sometimes called the Gandhi of Cambodia, was an important leader for peace and reconciliation in that country after the fall of the genocidal Khmer Rouge. He created the annual Dhammayatra, or Peace Walk, which accompanied refugees returning home from refugee camps and supported Cambodians during the first post-Khmer Rouge voting.

In Thailand, a number of 'development monks' have pioneered ways to help impoverished villagers, such as by providing loans for seed from donations made to the temples. 'Ecology monks' work throughout Southeast Asia to protect the highly endangered environment, with particular concern for protecting life, land, and fishing sites threatened by deforestation and dams.

In 1988 and again in 2007 (the 'Saffron Revolution'), the streets of Burma/Myanmar filled with people led by monks, nuns, and students to protest the actions of their government. Myanmar at the time was ruled by a brutal military regime and the people were demonstrating for democracy and human rights. Throughout the same years, the National League for Democracy, led by Aung San Suu Kyi, a self-professed adherent of

Engaged Buddhism, gave organized political structure to the wish of the people for a more humane and democratic government. Suu Kyi spent most of the years between 1989 and 2010 under house arrest. In 2015 her party won the national elections by a landslide and in 2016 she became de facto head of state. From 1988 until 2016, Aung San Suu Kyi was seen as a hero of nonviolence, both in Myanmar and globally; she was awarded the Nobel Peace Prize in 1991. In 2016, while Suu Kyi was de facto head of state, the Myanmar military began a series of catastrophic and systematic attacks on the Burmese Rohingya minority, attacks labeled as 'ethnic cleansing' by the United Nations and the United States. At the time of writing, Aung San Suu Kyi has taken no publicly visible action attempting to halt the attacks. The few statements she has made on the subject defend the military's action and minimize the harm done. Under these circumstances, she can no longer be considered an exemplar of Engaged Buddhism. On the contrary, a true Engaged Buddhist would have done everything in her power to stop these attacks and protect the innocent from harm.

Taiwan is the home of Tzu Chi ('Compassionate Relief'), a huge Buddhist charitable organization founded by the nun Venerable Cheng Yen (b. 1937). With over four million members and branches throughout the world, it is the world's largest Buddhist charitable organization and the largest charity in the Chinese-speaking world. Though led by a nun, Tzu Chi programmes consist almost entirely of actions by lay volunteers. Its major programmes are in the fields of health, international disaster relief, education, environmental protection, culture, and the promotion of volunteerism, vegetarianism, and compassionate values.

Other important Engaged Buddhist organizations in East Asia should be briefly mentioned. Dharma Drum Mountain (Fa Gu Shan) and Fo Guang Shan ('Buddha's Light Mountain') are very large Humanistic Buddhism organizations in Taiwan. In Japan, important Engaged Buddhist movements developed based on the teachings of Nichiren, viz. Sōka Gakkai (and its international branch, Sōka Gakkai International), Risshō Kōseikai, and Nipponzan Myōhōji, all working especially on behalf of global peace. In South Korea, a number of smaller organizations have recently developed, among them the Jungto Society led by the monk Pomnyum Sunim, which works in many areas such as environment, peace, and the eradication of poverty (Tedesco 2003). There are many other Engaged Buddhist movements and organizations throughout the Buddhist world.

While there are important characteristics that unite all Engaged Buddhists, there is clearly also diversity. It may be helpful heuristically to see these leaders and movements as falling into three major forms of Engaged Buddhism: (1) Nondualistic—this group is exemplified by Thich Nhat Hanh and the Dalai Lama. Its hallmarks are a non-judgmental and compassionate approach in speaking of those with whom they are in conflict and a non-adversarial approach to conflict resolution, aiming for reconciliation or a win-win outcome. (2) Prophetic—the exemplars of this form of Engaged Buddhism, such as B. R. Ambedkar, may use strongly dualistic, judgmental, and oppositional rhetoric and analysis with respect to those with whom they are in conflict. (3) Humanistic—this form of Engaged Buddhism derives most directly from the ideas of the twentieth-century reformer of Chinese Buddhism, Venerable Taixu. Today it is found in Taiwan where it plays a major role in the Buddhist Renaissance.

History

Scholars have argued over the question of whether or not Engaged Buddhism should be regarded as something new in the history of Buddhism. It is easy to see why. On the one hand, one can easily point to much sentiment among Buddhists past and present that Buddhism is solely about escaping from *saṃsāra*. The future Buddha leaves home in order to become a wanderer in search of an answer to the problems represented by old age, sickness, and death. After he has realized enlightenment and taught the *Dharma*, the Buddha achieves *parinirvāṇa*, leaving *saṃsāra* never to return. His teaching emphasizes the importance of detachment. To encourage this sentiment, the practices include meditation on a decomposing human body. *Saṃsāra* itself is characterized by intrinsic ignorance, suffering, and impermanence. The Buddhism that looks at things this way would have nothing to do with pointless efforts to cure the incurable ills of *saṃsāra*, society included. Moreover, a good deal of Buddhist practice, today and in the past, has been so-called merit-making or 'kammatic' Buddhism, i.e. the widespread form of Buddhist practice that consists primarily in efforts to avoid personally acquiring negative karma and in actions motivated by the desire to acquire positive karma, thereby earning a good rebirth. Merit-making Buddhism is concerned primarily with one's own good, one's own happiness and suffering, in the present and in future lives. This kind of Buddhism contrasts sharply with Engaged Buddhism.

On the other hand, when considering whether Engaged Buddhism should be regarded as something new in the history of Buddhism, it is necessary to recall that the Buddha himself taught on many occasions about secular matters, as recorded in the Pāli scriptures. The Buddha taught about proper and considerate behaviour within the family and with teachers, friends, and mendicants; he gave teachings on financial matters, such as how much money to save and how much to invest in business; he gave teachings on ethical and unethical ways of earning a livelihood; he personally advised rulers and taught that kings should not focus on punishing criminals but upon eliminating the causes of human evil, such as poverty. He intervened to try to stop a war; he personally nursed a sick disciple and urged his followers to learn the healing arts of the time.

Moreover, many instances could be named in which Buddhists have in the past engaged in significant ways with the needs of their societies. The great King Aśoka based his humanistic policies upon his conversion to Buddhist values. Throughout Southeast Asia in the premodern period, one typically found a Buddhist temple in every village of any size. The *bhikkhu*s of such a temple performed many secular functions—they taught children the rudiments of literacy and maths, attended to the villagers' medical needs, advised the village elders, and counselled individuals, in addition to their more purely religious functions. In the capital, *bhikkhu*s often served as advisers to the rulers.

In East Asia, monks also taught village children, healed the sick, and frequently advised rulers. In China, temples established hostels, medical treatment centres, dispensaries and orphanages. They provided relief grain during famines, built bridges, and planted shade trees alongside roads. In Japan, Kūkai (774–835) established the first school in Japan for the children of commoners, offering free meals along with education. The Tōkeiji and Mantokuji temples sheltered women who were desperate to escape their husbands, earning them both the nickname 'Divorce Temple'. Thus there is much engagement with society and its problems in the history of Buddhism. It should be noted, however, that not all social and political engagement by Buddhists of the past would likely be embraced by contemporary Engaged Buddhists as ancestral to their movement. For example, Zen masters training the Japanese samurai to be better warriors crosses the line into participation in a culture of chauvinistic loyalty and violence and thus cannot be seen as the same ideology as Engaged Buddhism.

Engaged Buddhism arose in the twentieth century largely in response to the multiple crises that hit Buddhist Asia in that century. Large parts of the Second World War, the Cold War, and the Vietnam War (which spread into neighbouring countries) were fought there, resulting in millions of deaths. There has been genocide in Cambodia and foreign invasion and cultural genocide in Tibet, again resulting in millions of deaths in both countries. Countries such as Sri Lanka have been impoverished and politically uprooted by colonial occupiers. Buddhist Asia has generated some extremely repressive governments, for example, the former military government in Myanmar. The ecological crisis has become quite acute in some areas, such as Thailand, where landslides caused by deforestation has caused extensive loss of life and seriously harmed some fishing and agricultural areas. Buddhist Asia has also seen some long-term social ills—namely, the repression of ex-untouchables in India and the repression of women throughout Asia—come to a head in the twentieth century, owing in part to the encounter with Western cultures. Finally, in the latter half of the twentieth century, Buddhist Asia was subjected to the forces of rapid modernization, Westernization, and globalization, transforming cultural patterns that have existed for centuries. Clearly, if Buddhism had no response to crises, challenges, and suffering of this magnitude, it would be consigning itself to increasing irrelevance in the lives of the people. Ultimately, in country after country, a generation of creative, charismatic, and courageous leaders did respond to these crises and challenges in ways that were new and yet resonant with tradition, sparking in many cases a widespread embrace of these new ways among both laity and the ordained *saṅgha*.

The crises and challenges of the twentieth century were thus the primary impetus that required Engaged Buddhism to arise when it did. In addition to this primary impetus, four secondary influences on Engaged Buddhism may briefly be named: Mahātma Gandhi (1869–1948), modernity, Chinese Buddhist reformers, and Western influence. As for Gandhi, many of the Engaged Buddhists have acknowledged being influenced by the great pioneer of spiritually based social activism, who demonstrated how to create powerful social activism that remained thoroughly nonviolent. (A prominent exception to this embrace of Gandhi is B. R. Ambedkar, who regarded Gandhi's handling of the caste system and Dalit community—formerly called 'untouchables'—as misguided and woefully inadequate.)

Modernity has strongly influenced Engaged Buddhism in three ways. First, the Engaged Buddhists are in all cases involved in bringing Buddhism into the modern world, developing a modern Buddhism that meets the needs of Buddhists and Buddhist societies today. Second, many of them import the disciplines and tools of modern social sciences, particularly sociology, economics, and political science, and apply them to the social issues with which they contend. Third, they generally embrace the idea of transforming society, that is, the very idea that individuals and groups can intervene in society in such a way as to change social institutions in a desired direction, e.g. changing government from military junta to democracy, or changing the economic system from capitalism to socialism. The embrace of this prototypically modern idea is key to what changes earlier Buddhist social engagement to Engaged Buddhism. For example, classically, compassion meant offering food to a beggar who passed by your door. Today, Engaged Buddhism, with modern awareness of the possibility of social transformation, is interested in eradicating hunger and its causes at its roots; consequently, Sarvodaya Shramadana has created a major institution aiming to eliminate Sri Lankan hunger and poverty by bringing roads, computers, and solar power to thousands of Sri Lankan villages, creating new cottage industries, a new banking system that gives micro-loans, and so on. To do all this requires a modern way of thinking that can imagine changing the fundamental institutions of society as a real possibility.

The Chinese Buddhist reformer Taixu (1890–1947) worked to revitalize the moribund Chinese Buddhism of his time, advocating that it turn away from its focus on funeral services and a fortunate rebirth here or in the Pure Land, and focus instead on this life and this world. He founded Renjian Fojiao, Buddhism for the Human World or Humanistic Buddhism, as a vehicle for a Buddhism that would serve the needs of human beings here and now. A number of refugees from the chaos of mid-twentieth-century mainland China brought the ideas of Humanistic Buddhism to Taiwan where they took root and developed. These refugees included the great scholar Venerable Yin Shun, who deepened and developed the ideas of Humanistic Buddhism, as well as Ven. Hsing Yun, founder of Fo Guang Shan (Buddha's Light Mountain) and Ven. Sheng Yen, founder of Dharma Drum Mountain, two of the three largest Humanistic Buddhism institutions in Taiwan.

Moreover, the work of Taixu, Yin Shun, and the Humanistic Buddhists was known to Vietnamese intellectuals including Thich Nhat Hanh, and played a role in his development of Engaged Buddhism (DeVido 2009), though the latter also cites the longstanding Vietnamese Buddhist activist tradition as another inspiration. It should be noted that both Taixu and Taiwanese Buddhism were influenced by Japanese Buddhism, in which Buddhist community service and an expectation of this-worldly benefits were common (Yao 2014).

Finally, although there is Western influence on the development of Engaged Buddhism, it is not what many people suppose. Engaged Buddhists are modern Buddhists who live in a globalized world where they regularly interact with people and ideas from all over the world, and in which Western thought certainly plays a dominant role. Some Engaged Buddhists have Western educations. Asian and Western Engaged Buddhists interact regularly in such Engaged Buddhist institutions as the International Network of Engaged Buddhists, Sakyadhita, and the Triratna Buddhist Community.

Despite this, Engaged Buddhism is not formed by Western ideas. Its leaders embrace those Western ideas that they find useful, such as human rights, and leave alone or criticize those Western ideas that they find problematic, such as the idea of political justice (King 2005: 202f.), judging these and other ideas always from a Buddhist point of view. The greatest Western influence on Engaged Buddhism, apart from the ideas of modernity discussed above, is the legacy and living presence of Christian charitable and social work throughout Asia. The countless schools, hospitals, and orphanages; the food and medicine provided; the work on behalf of women, low caste groups, the disabled, and the downtrodden; the example of all this and much more charitable work done by Christians all over Asia challenges Buddhists, who espouse love and compassion as much as Christians, to put that compassion into practice in a concrete way, to benefit humanity (and other beings) materially and not just spiritually.

Ethical Principles and Practice

The first part of this discussion considers ethical principles and practices that pertain to all instances of Engaged Buddhism. Subsequent sections then focus on the heuristically identified sub-categories of nondualistic, prophetic, and humanistic Engaged Buddhism.

Engaged Buddhism Generally

The Imperative to Act

Fundamentally, Engaged Buddhists stress the imperative to act, in three dimensions: (1) by requiring acts of commission, not only of omission, as the standard for Buddhist morality; (2) by engaging with the suffering not only of oneself, but of others as well; and (3) by engaging with the suffering of others here and now, whether one believes oneself to be 'ready' or not.

The first two of these qualities can be seen in Thich Nhat Hanh's transformation of the Five Lay Precepts. In its traditional form, the first precept invites the practitioner to live by the following affirmation: 'I undertake to observe the precept to abstain from the taking of life.' In Nhat Hanh's reformulation, the precept reads as follows:

> Aware of the suffering caused by the destruction of life, I vow to cultivate compassion and learn ways to protect the lives of people, animals, plants, and minerals. I am determined not to kill, not to let others kill, and not to condone any act of killing in the world, in my thinking, and in my way of life. (1993: 13)

First, the traditional precept might well be interpreted as implying an ethic in which it would be morally sufficient for one to avoid committing acts of killing. Nhat Hanh's version moves the frame of morality from passivity (refraining from wrong action) to activity (one must act and act rightly in order to fulfil the intention of the precept). Secondly, the precept is no longer entirely personal, but is now both personal and social: not only am I concerned about what I do, I must also be concerned about what others do; not only will I not kill, I must intervene in order to try to prevent others from killing and learn ways to protect lives. Here, it is not enough to try to keep one's own hands clean, thereby avoiding accruing negative karma, an attitude that usually encourages the belief that it will be (karmically) safer to remove oneself from the fray. Indeed, in Nhat Hanh's ethics one must wade deeply into the fray and take action in its midst. Moreover, the overall framework of one's thinking cannot be what one stands to gain and lose karmically. The framework now is one's global awareness of all the suffering of all beings; one's concern is for all of life.

One can see here, and indeed throughout Engaged Buddhism, that the arising of the latter does not represent a large *theoretical* step in the context of Buddhist ideas. One could interpret classic concepts in the Engaged Buddhist way very easily. One could, for example, make a case that the Engaged Buddhist interpretation is truer to the teachings of the Buddha, with his emphasis on selflessness and lack of desire, than is merit-making Buddhism, with its endorsement of the self-centred desire for a happy future life. Thus Engaged Buddhism is, among other things, a *reform* movement in the Buddhist world. However, due to the popularity of ideas like merit-making Buddhism, Engaged Buddhism often represents a significant change in *practice*.

Given its overarching concern with the welfare of all, one might wonder whether Engaged Buddhism represents a kind of triumph of Mahāyāna perspectives in the Buddhist world. But Engaged Buddhism represents a challenge to much traditional Mahāyāna as well as Theravāda. The third point above notes that Engaged Buddhism requires practitioners to engage with the suffering of others here and now, whether one believes oneself to be 'ready' or not. The widespread Mahāyāna belief being challenged here is that one should defer trying to help others until one has realized enlightenment, or advanced bodhisattvahood, oneself. Thus, the well-known 'Ten Oxherding Pictures' of the Zen tradition depict 'entering the marketplace with bliss-bestowing hands' as the ultimate stage of Zen practice, and this notion seems to be very much in harmony with the values of Engaged Buddhism. However, 'entering the marketplace' is depicted as the tenth of ten stages of practice, following nine stages in which the Zen practitioner is far beyond the reach of human society, either alone with the ox (representing Buddha-nature), alone in a rural hut, or vanished into the *ensō*, the Zen circle of vast empty space. In the Ten Oxherding Pictures, it is only after all this that the practitioner is ready to re-enter the world as a helping bodhisattva.

Thus, Chan Khong, Thich Nhat Hanh's closest associate, recalls that before she met Thich Nhat Hanh, she was discouraged by her previous monk teacher when she expressed her wish to be a nun who would engage in social work on behalf of the poor. The monk told her, 'You need to study scriptures more and work to become enlightened. After you are enlightened, you will be able to save countless beings' (Nhat Hanh 1993: 15f.). Of course, such deferral in most cases results in permanent deferral; with this very high bar of readiness, one never does arrive at the stage at which one is 'ready' to begin social engagement. In contrast to this kind of attitude, Engaged Buddhists do not see social engagement as something to be deferred, but as something to take up in the present, at any stage of practice. This leads to the next point.

The Oneness of Spirituality and Social Engagement

Not only *should* social engagement not be deferred, it *need* not be deferred. In Engaged Buddhism, social engagement is typically both a method of spiritual practice and an expression of the fruits of that practice. That is, spiritual practice is not defined as something that requires one to remove oneself from the fray of ordinary life, at least not all the time. Thich Nhat Hanh, for example, emphasizes the practice of mindfulness meditation. He teaches his followers to engage in such practice in a fairly traditional way as a daily meditation in a quiet and peaceful setting, but he also teaches it as a practice that one turns to in the midst of everyday life, or in a way that infuses all of everyday life:

> Meditation is not to get out of society, to escape from society, but to prepare for a re-entry into society. We call this 'engaged Buddhism.' When we go to a meditation center, we may have the impression that we leave everything behind—family, society, and all the complications involved in them—and come as an individual in order to practice and to search for peace. This is already an illusion, because in Buddhism there is no such thing as an individual. (Nhat Hanh 1987a: 45)

Because 'there is no such thing as an individual' (*anātman*), the individual and society 'inter-are', as Nhat Hanh puts it. Therefore, the very idea of an individualistic practice that one does by oneself for oneself makes no sense from the start. There are times, certainly, when one pulls away in order to practise focusing the mind and so forth, but such times apart are always held in the larger context of the all-inclusive whole. Nhat Hanh, as one who strongly emphasizes interconnectedness and Mahāyāna nondualism, consistently tears down the conceptual walls between individual and society, self, and other, 'spiritual' practice and 'mundane' life. If one pulls away briefly from society, whatever one does while apart is for the sake of re-entering society. In this way, the bodhisattva who 'enters the marketplace with bliss-bestowing hands' is not a being one will become in a distant, largely mythical, future, but the being who one is now, albeit very imperfectly. One practises always—while in society and while apart from it, while on the sitting cushion and while demonstrating in the street for regime change—every moment a training, a test, and an engagement. Spiritual practice, when held in this larger perspective, is seen as part of social engagement inasmuch as it helps the individual develop the selflessness, compassion, inner strength, and courage that one needs in social engagement. Social engagement is spiritual practice inasmuch as it provides endlessly varied challenges and reality tests of the selflessness and inner strength one thinks one has developed.

This kind of thinking is also found in Tzu Chi. The founder of the Tzu Chi movement, Venerable Cheng Yen, makes very clear that those who engage in social service are engaging in spiritual practice. Tzu Chi focuses on giving medical, material, and loving care to the sick, elderly, and victims of natural disasters. But this is only half of the giving in this movement. As Cheng Yen puts it, 'The poor and wretched receive help, the rich and fortunate activate their love, and thus both can be grateful to each other.' In her view, it is equally important for her followers to have the opportunity to 'activate their love' as for the needy to receive help; the movement is for the benefit of both the needy and the fortunate. The needy are seen as giving the fortunate something real and needed—the opportunity to develop their compassion, thereby developing their spirituality, inner peace, and joy. Cheng Yen advises her followers,

> Give whatever you can, whether a little or a lot. Strive persistently with equanimity and patience. You will soon reach the level at which, 'There is no giver, there is no receiver, there is no gift.' Giving and receiving will be nothing more than part of the natural order of things. (Shih 1999: 49, 51)

In short, by engaging in the practice of giving as consistently and energetically as some might engage in the practice of meditation, Cheng Yen claims that it is possible to achieve some of the lofty spiritual goals of Buddhism, i.e. to become selfless to the degree expressed in the *Diamond Sūtra*. Clearly, the volunteers' acts of service—whether accompanying the sick in hospitals, comforting the survivors of natural disasters, or sorting plastic bottles in a recycling centre—are conceived as much as spiritual trainings as they are aid to those in need.

Benevolence: Loving-kindness, Compassion, and the Bodhisattva

Benevolence in all its forms—typically referred to as *mettā* (loving-kindness) in Theravāda countries, *karuṇā* (compassion) in Mahāyāna countries, and even as 'love' when Western audiences are addressed—is clearly the most important foundation for Engaged Buddhist ethics in the area of values. This, of course, is a classic emphasis in Buddhism from the start, but Engaged Buddhism characteristically emphasizes that Buddhists must put their compassion, love, and kindliness into practical action. Thus, Macy reports, *mettā* 'is presented by the [Sarvodaya] Movement as the fundamental attitude that must be cultivated to develop motivation for service, capacity to work harmoniously with others, and, above all, the nonviolence that is a central premise of Sarvodaya'. Compassion, she continues, 'is seen by the Movement as the translation of *metta* [sic] into action on behalf of others. It includes the concepts of service and "self-offering" that have been central to Sarvodaya since its inception'. A Sarvodaya guideline states, 'Feeling sorry for people is not enough. Act to help them' (1985: 38–39).

The direct objects of benevolence in Engaged Buddhism range from the individual to the global level and frequently are directed at both, or all, sides of a conflict. Sarvodaya Shramadana engaged in extensive peacemaking work during the civil war in Sri Lanka. When a ceasefire was declared, Sarvodaya began to sponsor a series of massive, outdoor loving-kindness (*mettā*) meditations, some of them attracting over a half million participants, including people from both warring sides and all of Sri Lanka's ethnic and religious groups, with the aim of increasing the ceasefire's chances of success. Participants in the mass meditations pledged as follows.

> I am a participant in the mass meditational effort to bring about spiritual awakening within the country and across the entire planet. I make my contribution to unite people of all ethnic backgrounds, nationalities, religions, political views, without any difference whatsoever. Through this endeavor of mine, ours, may violence and war cease to exist. (Sarvodaya Shramadana 1999: 11)

With this intention, participants were taught *mettā* meditation, culminating in the cultivation of *mettā* for people of all ethnic backgrounds, nationalities, religions, and political views. At the end of the session, participants were directed to spend five minutes radiating their loving-kindness out to everyone. Participants pledged to challenge themselves to work for peace every day, to challenge those who endorsed violence or who made negative remarks about persons of other ethnicities or religions, and to challenge journalists who only publicize violence and not peacemaking. This practice accomplished several things at once: it publicly demonstrated that a great many Sri Lankans wanted an end to violence, thus reducing some of the psychological strength of those promoting violence; it helped to build a culture of peace in the midst of a culture of war; and it helped strengthen the resolve and dedication of participants.

Turning to the figure of the bodhisattva, traditionally in Chinese Buddhism, elite practitioners took bodhisattva vows, vowing to attain Buddhahood for the sake of all sentient beings, while the masses looked to the great celestial bodhisattvas with devotion and prayed to them for their help. Today, some new practices around bodhisattvahood have been developed by Engaged Buddhists. Tzu Chi, in particular, simultaneously encourages devotion towards Guanyin, the Bodhisattva of Compassion—as the great exemplar of compassion rather than as someone whose help practitioners are beseeching—and strongly encourages its volunteers to understand themselves to be the 'eyes and hands' of Guanyin, using their millions of eyes to see everyone who needs help and their millions of hands to give that help. In other words, rather than encouraging only its elite members to see themselves in the role of the bodhisattva, it encourages its millions of lay volunteers to be active, rather than passive, to give help, rather than seek it, to be engaged themselves in bodhisattva work. They understand 'bodhisattva work' as synonymous with the caring and helping work that they engage in—helping the poor, the sick, and disaster survivors; as well as the work of encouraging themselves and others to develop their loving-kindness and compassion. Venerable Cheng Yen assures them that 'anyone who really wants to can become a bodhisattva in this world' (Shih 1999: 51).

Using a different approach, the Fourteenth Dalai Lama works towards a similar end: the universalization and practicalization of the bodhisattva ideal. The Dalai Lama, in many of his public talks and writings, removes the specifically Buddhist language from the ideal and promotes a secularized version of altruism that he calls 'universal responsibility'. This universal responsibility is based upon classical Buddhist thought as found in traditional texts:

> if it is correct that, given the broadly interdependent nature of reality, our habitual distinction between self and other is in some sense an exaggeration, and if on the

> basis of this I am right in suggesting that our aim should be to extend our compassion toward all others, we cannot avoid the conclusion that compassion . . . belongs at the heart of all our actions, both individual and social. (1999: 173)

On the basis of this bodhisattva-like perspective, the Dalai Lama promotes for his global and mostly non-Buddhist audience a secularized version of bodhisattva action:

> I am convinced that it is essential that we cultivate a sense of what I call universal responsibility. . . . What is entailed . . . is . . . a reorientation of our heart and mind away from self and toward others . . . an attitude of mind whereby, when we see an opportunity to benefit others, we will take it in preference to merely looking after our own narrow interests. (1999: 162f.)

He makes it clear that this entails practical care and service here and now. 'A sense of responsibility toward all others also means that . . . we have a duty to care for each member of our society. . . . We need, therefore, to ensure that the sick and afflicted person never feels helpless, rejected, or unprotected' (1999: 169). Ultimately, the ideal towards which this practice aspires is the traditional Mahāyāna bodhisattva ideal of *mahākaruṇā*, great compassion (Tib. *nying je chen mo*):

> When we enhance our sensitivity toward others' suffering through deliberately opening ourselves up to it, it is believed that we can gradually extend our compassion to the point where the individual feels so moved by even the subtlest suffering of others that they come to have an overwhelming sense of responsibility toward those others. This causes the one who is compassionate to dedicate themselves entirely to helping others overcome both their suffering and the causes of their suffering. In Tibetan, this ultimate level of attainment is called *nying je chenmo*, literally 'great compassion'. (1999: 124)

However, in line with the 'imperative to act' principle of Engaged Buddhism that we have already seen, with its refusal to defer bodhisattva action until after enlightenment, the Dalai Lama makes clear that he is 'not suggesting that each individual must attain these advanced states of spiritual development in order to lead an ethically wholesome life', but rather is only pointing to the level of 'ultimate attainment' so that it can act as an inspiration to those living ordinary laypersons' lives in society, 'doing what [they] can' for others, as imperfect beings, here and now (1999: 124, 163).

Nonviolence

The primary reason for Engaged Buddhists' commitment to nonviolence is the all-embracing scope of their benevolence; the wish to harm anyone is inconsistent with universal compassion and loving-kindness. Nonviolence is also inherent in Engaged Buddhists' commitment to a unified Buddhist spiritual social activism. An example of this is Nhat Hanh's signature concept of 'being peace': 'Without being peace, we cannot do anything for peace. ... If we are not peaceful, then we cannot contribute to the peace movement' (1987a: 80). Of course, one cannot 'be peace' simply by wishing for it; it requires a certain kind of spiritual cultivation. That is, it requires cultivating universal benevolence, non-preferentialism, selflessness, inner peace, and so on. These qualities, in turn, undermine the development of qualities conducive to violence—fear, anger, and preference for one's own group. Thus, for Nhat Hanh, inner and outer peace are interdependent; one cultivates personal peacefulness in order to be able to engage nonviolently in social activism.

Another major root of Engaged Buddhists' nonviolence is their thinking in terms of karma and causality. For example, in Cambodia, as the genocidal Khmer Rouge gradually lost its hold on power, Maha Ghosananda advocated forgiveness by all to all: 'I do not question that loving one's oppressors—Cambodians loving the Khmer Rouge—may be the most difficult attitude to achieve. But it is a law of the universe that retaliation, hatred, and revenge only continue the cycle and never stop it' (1992: 69). To preach this message, Maha Ghosananda turned to a *Dhammapada* verse much quoted by Engaged Buddhists: 'In those who harbor thoughts of blame and vengeance toward others, hatred will never cease. In those who do not harbor blame and vengeance, hatred will surely cease. For hatred is never appeased by hatred. Hatred is appeased by love. This is an eternal law' (1992: 27). The 'eternal law' referenced here is the law of karma—intentional actions cause consequences of a like kind to befall the one who does the deed. Thus, because of karma, it is impossible to end suffering with the use of violence; suffering and violence will inevitably recur when violence is used. To overcome violent situations, Engaged Buddhists typically turn to thinking based upon causality: remove the fuel and the fire goes out; when you have a problem, remove the causes of the problem; to end a war, remove the causes of war. Thus, in its effort to end Sri Lanka's civil war, Sarvodaya identified poverty and ethnic hatred as the root causes of that war and developed many programmes intended to eliminate those causal factors.

The Use of Standard Buddhist Concepts, Values and Practices, Adapted so as to Be Applied to Engaging Society's Problems

Engaged Buddhists speak *as* Buddhists and typically justify their teachings on social engagement in terms of classical Buddhist concepts, values, and practices, both Theravāda and Mahāyāna. We have seen this already; one further example will have to suffice here: the use made by Sarvodaya Shramadana of the Four Noble Truths. In the classic version as presented in the Pāli texts, the Four Noble Truths are: (1) *duḥkha* (dis-satisfactoriness inherent in *samsāric* life); (2) the cause of *duḥkha*; (3) the cessation of *duḥkha*; and (4) the path leading to the cessation of *duḥkha*. The first Noble Truth states the problem (*duḥkha*), the second Noble Truth identifies the root cause(s) of the problem (ignorance and craving), the third Noble Truth instils hope and motivation by affirming that the problem can be resolved and gives an idea of what that resolved condition might be like (*nirvāṇa*), and the fourth Noble Truth details how to go about resolving the problem (the Noble Eightfold Path). This much is classical Buddhist thought.

Ariyaratne uses the Four Noble Truths as a template for the analysis of social problems and how to work with them. Focusing on his work with deeply impoverished Sri Lankan villages, the first Noble Truth (stating the problem) becomes: 'a decadent village', characterized as having poverty, conflict, and stagnation; the second Noble Truth, cause, identifies the causes of this 'ill' in such factors as ignorance, egoism, ill will, possessiveness, and disunity; the third Noble Truth, the 'hope', envisions a village characterized by sharing, cooperation, constructive activity, equality, love, and selflessness; finally, the fourth Noble Truth lays out Sarvodaya's ideas of how the village could rejuvenate itself, with economic development, health programmes, educational programmes, cultural development, and spiritual development (Macy 1985: 34). Sarvodaya then set about developing programmes in all the needed areas. In this way, the programmes are new, but the form of analysis and even much of the content of thinking is classical, albeit put to new use. For example, the ignorance, egoism, ill will, and possessiveness named as causes of the problematic 'decadent village' are the same factors named in traditional Theravāda as the causes of *duḥkha*. It naturally follows that the love and selflessness named as characteristics of the desired end state in a Sarvodaya village are the same as prominent factors in the classical nirvanic condition. It is no surprise, then, that, alongside economic development, spiritual development is an integral part of the Sarvodaya 'development' programme necessary for the eradication of poverty.

This is just one example of an Engaged Buddhist movement's creative use of a classic and central Buddhist tenet. Conceptually, all the Engaged Buddhists make frequent use of such classic Buddhist concepts as the Four Noble Truths, interdependence, causality, karma, *duḥkha, anātman*, human enlightenability, and Buddha-nature. In values, they emphasize nonviolence, compassion, loving-kindness (*mettā*), selflessness, and altruism. In spiritual practices (*bhāvanā*), they emphasize such practices as the lay precepts, giving (*dāna*), mindfulness, the bodhisattva ideal, and devotion to the Bodhisattva Guanyin (the Bodhisattva of Compassion). To be sure, as in the example of Sarvodaya's use of the Four Noble Truths, many of these are taken in new directions by the Engaged Buddhists. By the same token, however, what may be new or challenging to a traditional Buddhist can be, and frequently is, justified by the Engaged Buddhists as a new way of speaking of classic Buddhist concepts, values, and practices.

Nondualistic Engaged Buddhism

Nondualistic Engaged Buddhism is exemplified by the Dalai Lama and Thich Nhat Hanh, the two most popular Buddhist teachers in the non-Buddhist world; as such, it represents Engaged Buddhism to many in the West. Moreover, the distinctive features of nondualistic Engaged Buddhism, nonadversariality and nonjudgment, are little known and little understood among Western social activists. Thus, while conceiving and constructing a modern, socially activist form of Buddhism is probably Engaged Buddhism's greatest contribution to Buddhist Asia, expressing and acting on the idea of nondualistic social activism, necessarily entailing nonviolence, is probably its greatest contribution to ethical thought in the West.

Perhaps the most fundamental philosophical basis of the nonadversarial element in Engaged Buddhist ethics is the perception that 'self and 'other' are interdependent and therefore have common interests. The Dalai Lama writes,

> If the self had intrinsic identity, it would be possible to speak in terms of self-interest in isolation from that of others. But because this is not so, because self and others can only really be understood in terms of relationship, we see that self-interest and others' interest are closely interrelated. Indeed, within this picture of dependently originated reality, we see that there is no self-interest completely unrelated to others' interests. Due to the fundamental interconnectedness which lies at the heart of reality, your interest is also my interest. From this, it becomes clear that 'my' interest and 'your' interest are intimately connected. In a deep sense, they converge. (1999: 47)

That is, interdependence and *anātman* are the root logical foundations of the nonadversarial element in nondualistic Engaged Buddhist ethics. If self and other are not in reality separate from each other, it is logically impossible for their interests to be separate from each other. Thus, knowing that we are interconnected and that our interests are interconnected, when we are in a conflict situation, we ought, if we are skilful in our behaviour, to look for a win-win outcome that will fulfil the true interests of everyone involved.

The conceptual binding together of self and other entailed in Buddhist ideas of interdependence and *anātman* is experientially complemented, in the understanding of Engaged Buddhists, by feelings of empathy, explained by the Dalai Lama as the universal 'inability to bear the sight of another's suffering', and regarded by him as the foundation of all ethical behaviour, since it is 'the source of that most precious of all human qualities', compassion (1999: 64, 73). Theoretical interdependence of self and other combined with experiential empathy and compassion culminate in nondualist Engaged Buddhism in their characteristic ethical stance of nonadversariality, the shunning of personal hostility, antagonism, or ill will of any kind towards those with whom one is in conflict, and ultimately the nonrecognition of such a thing as an 'enemy' at all. Thus, Cambodian Engaged Buddhist Maha Ghosananda, in an affirmation showing the influence of Gandhi as well as the necessary connection between nonadversariality and nonviolence, states,

> How do we resolve a conflict, a battle, a power struggle? What does reconciliation really mean? Gandhi said that the essence of nonviolent action is that it seeks to put an end to antagonism, not the antagonists. This is important. The opponent has our respect. We implicitly trust his or her human nature and understand that ill will is caused by ignorance. (1992: 62)

For Maha Ghosananda, nonadversariality was primarily based in universal benevolence; it also necessarily entailed nonjudgmentalism:

> [L]ove embraces all beings, whether they are noble-minded or low-minded, good or evil. ... The unwholesome-minded must be included because they are the ones who need loving kindness the most. In many of them, the seed of goodness may have died because warmth was lacking for its growth. It perished from coldness in a world without compassion. (1992: 68)

In a way of thinking fundamentally shaped by awareness of causality—the universal law of cause and effect—and of *anātman* or non-self, nonjudgmentalism emerges quite naturally. In this view, there is no self or soul to 'be' good or evil in any unchanging or inherent way. What we are is the product of causes and conditions. Those who are 'unwholesome-minded' are so because of the unwholesome causes and conditions to which they have been exposed, not because that is inherently who they are. Moreover, as causes and conditions change, so can our behaviour and state of mind; there is no static 'being', only constantly changing patterns of thought and behaviour that do become self-reinforcing over time, but also may be changed at any time when new causes and conditions are introduced. This understanding points towards a compassionate response, rather than a judgmental one.

We see this constellation of causality and non-self in the famous poem by Thich Nhat Hanh, 'Please Call Me By My True Names'. In the poem, Nhat Hanh writes:

> I am the mayfly /and I am the bird that eats the mayfly; I am the frog/ and I am also the grass-snake who eats the frog; I am the 12-year old girl, refugee on a small boat,/ who throws herself into the ocean after being raped by a sea pirate,/ and I am the pirate, my heart not yet capable of seeing and loving. (1987a: 64)

Nhat Hanh's surprising 'I' language disturbs the reader, who by no means wants to identify with a rapist pirate. This, however, is exactly Nhat Hanh's point. In his commentary on the poem he writes,

> I saw that if I had been born in the village of the pirate and raised in the same conditions as he was, I am now the pirate. There is a great likelihood that I would become a pirate. I cannot condemn myself so easily. ... If you or I were born today in those fishing villages, we might become sea pirates in 25 years. (1987a: 62)

The perspective expressed in this poem and commentary is troubling for some, who see Nhat Hanh here as removing the basis for moral accountability. But this is not Nhat Hanh's intent. Rather, he aims to widen the reader's view to encompass all the factors converging on the tragedy:

> I saw that many babies are born along the Gulf of Siam, hundreds every day, and if we educators, social workers, politicians, and others do not do something about the situation, in 25 years a number of them will become sea pirates. That is certain. If you take a gun and shoot the pirate, you shoot all of us, because all of us are to some extent responsible for this state of affairs. (1987a: 62)

Nhat Hanh's point is to enlarge our understanding by helping us to perceive the broad picture of causation, and to enlarge our compassion by disallowing our urge to figuratively remove ourselves from the fray and sit in judgment upon 'others' whom we keep at arm's distance and take some relief in judging as 'evil'. Certainly he would advocate protecting children from pirates and the like; he also would advocate protecting would-be pirates from acting upon any impulses to harm others that they might have acquired; these needs, in fact, go hand in hand and acting upon them both maintains compassion for everyone involved. Finally, he also would advocate everyone engaging in the effort to remove the root causes of piracy and other ills in poverty, the global economic order, ignorance, hopelessness, and so on. The Dalai Lama sums up this perspective:

> This is not to say that people are not responsible for their actions. But let us remember that they may be acting largely out of ignorance. A child brought up in a violent environment may not know any other way to behave. As a result, the question of blame is rendered largely redundant. (1999: 107)

Crucial to the nonadversarial aspect of nondualistic Engaged Buddhism is a strongly expressed and consciously held intention of maintaining loving-kindness and compassion towards those with whom one is in conflict, even when they are committing acts of severe violence. During the Saffron Revolution in Myanmar, monks and nuns chanted the *Mettā Sutta* as they protested in the streets, invoking loving-kindness on behalf of the suffering people of Myanmar, but also on behalf of their oppressors, the military junta ruling Myanmar. In the case of the Tibet–China struggle, at the height of the violence inflicted by the PRC upon Tibet, the Dalai Lama wrote a prayer, 'A Prayer of Words of Truth', in which he implored all buddhas and bodhisattvas to send their compassion to Tibetans and Chinese alike. What could be the rationale for invoking compassion upon those acting violently? 'The violent oppressors are also worthy of compassion./ Crazed by demonic emotions, they do vicious deeds/ That bring total defeat to themselves as well as to others' (Gyatso 1992: 87). That is, the Dalai Lama's compassion extends to encompass the Chinese, even those directly attacking the Tibetans, because with their violent attacks on the Tibetans they are karmically harming themselves severely.

As a consequence of its nonadversariality and all-embracing benevolence, an effort to reconcile parties and find a win-win solution typically becomes the goal in nondualistic Engaged Buddhism. In Vietnam, Nhat Hanh and his colleagues advocated during the war years a 'Third Way', not on the side of the North or the South, but only on the side of life. Similarly, during the civil war in Sri Lanka that pitted religions and ethnic groups against each other, Sarvodaya did not blame the war on either the Tamil Hindu side or the Sinhalese Buddhist side, but on poverty and ethnic hatred, and advocated and worked for 'a sustainable, spiritually balanced island that works for all' (Sarvodaya n.d.).

Prophetic Engaged Buddhism

Prophetic Engaged Buddhism, exemplified by Dr B. R. Ambedkar, is distinguished by its practitioners adopting the prophetic voice. That is, unlike nondualistic Engaged Buddhism, which endeavours to reconcile or bring together conflicting parties and therefore avoids 'us' versus 'them' oppositional stances, prophetic Engaged Buddhism occupies the more familiar dualistic stance, in which one's own side in a conflict opposes the other side. In nondualistic Engaged Buddhism, compassionate concern for the other side is an integral part of thinking about a conflict. In prophetic Engaged Buddhism, the other side is the cause of the problem and simply needs to change; righteous anger, though certainly not violence, may play a role in its relationship with the other side. Nonetheless, prophetic Engaged Buddhism remains Engaged Buddhist inasmuch as it remains strictly nonviolent while struggling with the ills of society (in Ambedkarite Buddhism, casteism) on the basis of Buddhist values and beliefs (in Ambedkarite Buddhism, especially the belief in intrinsic human dignity and equality and the universal human potential to grow towards the highest spiritual goals).

Dr Ambedkar, born an untouchable, rose to become one of the most highly educated and important leaders of post-Raj India—he was post-Raj India's first Law Minister and the major author of its Constitution—but was still subjected to sometimes violent caste prejudice. After struggling for years to reform Hinduism and free it of the caste system, Ambedkar finally decided that it was impossible for Hinduism to reform itself in this respect and severed his relations with it, publicly burning a copy of the *Manusmṛti*, the *Book of Manu*, which justified and codified the caste system. After a multi-year search, he converted to Buddhism as a public act and example that he recommended as a way forward for the community of ex-untouchables. For both Ambedkar and the ex-untouchable community, the act of conversion to Buddhism is a social and political act as much as a spiritual act, and a decisive break with Hinduism as much as an embrace of Buddhism. An important element of conversion to Ambedkarite Buddhism is the taking of twenty-two vows composed by Ambedkar; eight of these explicitly express that the convert renounces Hinduism, does not believe in its gods and goddesses, and will not worship them.

It is clear why Ambedkar felt it necessary to take up an oppositional, adversarial stance vis-à-vis Hinduism. On the basis of a lifetime of experience, he had reached the conclusion that Hinduism had poisoned the souls of the 'untouchables', reducing them to such a deplorable, enervated condition that they could not even stir themselves to revolt against their oppressors. In his view, there was no possibility of them raising themselves without making a clean break with Hinduism and inspiriting themselves sufficiently to reject what held them down, the caste system itself. The oppositional stance that was necessary was above all psychological. The convert needed to renounce Hinduism and its negation of one's own self-worth while simultaneously embracing Buddhism and its affirmation of one's self-worth. Thus, in the conversion vows, one announces that one is 'having a rebirth'. The old, oppressed person is gone; a free person, equal to any, is born.

As in other forms of Engaged Buddhism, this newly reborn person affirms that s/he will practise compassion and loving-kindness towards all living beings.

Ambedkarite Buddhism is not the only example of prophetic Engaged Buddhism. Lay Engaged Buddhist Sulak Sivaraksa, Thailand's 'best known lay Buddhist intellectual and social critic', frequently speaks in a highly critical, prophetic voice, denouncing the Thai government for undemocratic acts, criticizing 'establishment Buddhism' for subservience to the state and inattention to the needs of the poor (Swearer 1996: 196f.) and calling upon Sri Lankan Buddhists to acknowledge the crimes they have committed against Sri Lankan Tamils. Another example shows that even a movement that is predominantly nondualistic may at times use a tactic that is oppositional and thus prophetic. Thus, during the Saffron Revolution in Myanmar, monks demonstrating in the streets turned their food bowls upside down, indicating that they would not accept food donations from members of the military regime or their supporters. This directly refused their opponents the favoured traditional method for earning merit and also publicly declared, without need of words, that the *saṅgha* judged the military regime to be morally bankrupt.

Humanistic Engaged Buddhism

The Humanistic Buddhism of Taiwan follows Venerable Taixu and Venerable Yinshun in turning the focus of Buddhism away from death and rebirth and towards life here and now. Consequently, Humanistic Buddhists typically make service to the living—humans at all stages of life, animals, and the environment—a cornerstone of their Buddhist life and practice. They typically promote environmentalism, vegetarianism, harmonious relationships, and human well-being through a Buddhist way of life and a host of practical, hands-on projects in which millions of laypeople volunteer. Projects include health care, elder care, orphan and child care, disaster and emergency relief at home and abroad, education, recycling, environmental protection, cultural development, inter-religious and inter-communal friendship, and more.

Humanistic Buddhism is like nondualistic Engaged Buddhism insofar as it expresses a very strong ethic of active benevolence and is unqualifiedly universalistic in its application. However, Humanistic Buddhism has a very different political stance as compared to nondualistic Engaged Buddhism, largely due to the particular history of Taiwan.

From 1949 to 1987, Taiwan was under strict martial law, the purpose of which was to suppress political opposition to the ruling Kuomintang party, which had fled the communist victory in mainland China. Many people were imprisoned, tortured, or executed at the slightest suspicion of communist sympathy or unsanctioned political activity. Buddhist monastics fleeing communism on the mainland were subject to a great deal of suspicion and threat (as possible communist spies) during this period and quickly learned to keep a low profile and certainly avoid all political activity.

The nondualistic Engaged Buddhism of South and Southeast Asia and Tibet largely came about in response to the crises of the twentieth century (war, colonialism, invasion, genocide) that forced Engaged Buddhists time and again into struggles with ruling powers. In Taiwan during the years of crisis (the years of martial law), Buddhism was far too weak for there to be any question of its confronting the government; a robust and reformed Taiwanese Buddhism did not develop until after the crisis was over. Thus, unlike nondualistic Engaged Buddhism, Humanistic Buddhism's political stance vis-à-vis the Taiwanese government is typically co-operative, constructive, and non-confrontational. Importantly, this makes it possible for it to manifest one version of what Engaged Buddhism can look like when it is not in crisis mode, but simply a part of ordinary life.

Among the Humanistic Buddhist movements, Tzu Chi has taken a particularly apolitical stance. Venerable Cheng Yen has, in fact, made the avoidance of confrontational politics a requirement for Tzu Chi members. Her followers are asked to observe the 'Tzu Chi Ten Precepts', the tenth of which forbids members to 'participate in politics or demonstrations' (Tzu Chi 2011). This stance has proven to be of significant use as it has made possible the entrée of large numbers of Tzu Chi volunteers to the People's Republic of China and even North Korea for the purpose of disaster relief at times of earthquake, flood, and food shortage. It is certain that without its strictly apolitical stance, Tzu Chi would never have been admitted to these countries. Moreover, beginning in the mid-1990s, Buddhist institutions in the PRC itself began to provide charitable and social services of a kind and in a way consistent with Taiwanese Humanistic Engaged Buddhism. Projects include disaster relief, elder care, maternity wards, medical clinics, and schools for needy children, and are found scattered throughout China (Laliberté 2011). This is a very significant development for mainland Chinese Buddhism and for Engaged Buddhism that, again, would not have been possible had Taiwanese Humanistic Buddhism exhibited a conflictual relationship with government.

Conclusion

Engaged Buddhism is an effort to apply the ideals of Buddhist ethics—selflessness, benevolence, and peacefulness—in practice in the world. It is very much an idealistic movement, with no desire to compromise those ethics in order to find a place in a world that is far from ideal; on the contrary, it aspires to bring the world up to the level of Buddhist ideals. As such, it is highly experimental, and a work in progress.

Works Cited

Chan Khong (Cao Ngoc Phuong) (1993) *Learning true love: how I learned and practiced social change in Vietnam*. Berkeley: Parallax Press.

Cheng Yen (1999). A new millennium of goodness, beauty and truth. In: D. W. Chappell (ed.), *Buddhist peacework: creating cultures of peace*. Boston: Wisdom, 47–52.

DeVido, E. A. (2009) The influence of Chinese Master Taixu on Buddhism in Vietnam. *Journal of global Buddhism*, 10, 413–458.
Ghosananda, Maha (1992). *Step by step: meditations on wisdom and compassion*. Berkeley: Parallax Press.
Gyatso, T., XIVth Dalai Lama (1992) *A prayer of words of truth*. Translated by R. A. F. Thurman in Tibet and the Monastic Army of Truth. In: K. Kraft (ed.), *Inner peace, world peace: essays on Buddhism and nonviolence*. Albany: State University Press of New York, 87–88.
Gyatso, T., XIVth Dalai Lama (1999) *Ethics for the new millennium*. New York: Riverhead Books.
King, S. B. (2005) *Being benevolence: the social ethics of engaged Buddhism*. Honolulu: University of Hawai'i Press.
Laliberté, A. (2011) Buddhist revival under state watch. *Journal of current Chinese affairs*, 40, (2), 107–134.
Macy, J. (1985) *Dharma and development: religion as resource in the Sarvodaya self-help movement*. Revised edition. West Hartford, CT: Kumarian Press.
Nhat Hanh, Thich (1987a) *Being peace*. Berkeley: Parallax Press.
Nhat Hanh, Thich (1993) *For a future to be possible: commentaries on the five wonderful precepts*. Berkeley: Parallax Press.
Sarvodaya Shramadana (1999) *Sarvodaya peace meditation programme: introduction and guide to participants*. Ratmalana, Sri Lanka: Sarvodaya Vishva Lekha.
Sarvodaya Shramadana (n.d.) The solution to continuing war: an overview of the Sarvodaya People's Peace Plan. Available from: http://www.sarodaya.org/PeaceInitiative/SarodayaPeoplesPeacePlan.htm [Accessed 9 February 2001].
Swearer, D. K. (1996) Sulak Sivaraksa's Buddhist vision for renewing society. In: C. S. Queen and S. B. King (eds.), *Engaged Buddhism: Buddhist liberation movements in Asia*. Albany: SUNY Press, 195–236.
Tedesco, F. (2003) Social engagement in South Korean Buddhism. In: C. Queen, C. Prebish, and D. Keown (eds), *Action dharma: new studies in engaged Buddhism*. London: RoutledgeCurzon, 154–182.
Tzu Chi Foundation (2011) The spirit of the ten Tzu Chi precepts. Available from: http://tw.tzuchi.org/en/index.php?option= com_content&view=article&id=837%3Athe-spirit-of-the-ten-tzu-chi-precepts&catid=116%3Atzu-chi-path&Itemid=324 [Accessed 18 February 2016].
Yao Y. (2014) Japanese influence on Buddhism in Taiwan. *Journal of the Oxford Centre for Buddhist Studies*, 6, 141–156. Available from: http://jocbs.org/index.php/jocbs/article/view/77/97 [Accessed 8 July 2016].

Suggested Reading

Gyatso, T., XIVth Dalai Lama (1999) *Ethics for the new millennium*. New York: Riverhead Books.
King, S. B. (2005) *Being benevolence: the social ethics of engaged Buddhism*. Honolulu: University of Hawai'i Press.
Macy, J. (1985) *Dharma and development: religion as resource in the Sarvodaya self-help movement*. Revised edition. West Hartford, CT: Kumarian Press.

Nhat Hanh, Thich (1987) *The miracle of mindfulness: a manual on meditation*. Revised edition. Boston: Beacon Press.

Nhat Hanh, Thich (1993) *For a future to be possible: commentaries on the five wonderful precepts*. Berkeley: Parallax Press.

Queen, C. S., and King, S. B. (eds) (1996) *Engaged Buddhism: Buddhist liberation movements in Asia*. Albany: SUNY Press.

CHAPTER 24

THE ETHICS OF ENGAGED BUDDHISM IN THE WEST

CHRISTOPHER QUEEN

What is Engaged Buddhism?

Socially engaged Buddhism came to international attention after the Second World War in Asia and the West. Social movements such as the Buddhist conversion of Dalit or low-caste citizens in India and the Sarvodaya Shramadana village development movement in Sri Lanka in the 1950s were followed by the Vietnamese anti-war movement and the Tibetan liberation movement in the 1960s and 1970s. The postwar period also saw the rise of Nichiren-inspired peace movements in Japan, Pure Land-inspired social service movements in Taiwan, and human rights and environment protection movements in Korea, Thailand, and Cambodia. In the West, since the 1960s, scores of civil society groups inspired by Buddhist ideas and practices were founded to address violence and war, poverty, environmental destruction, race relations, criminal justice, human services, and other issues. Global coalitions, such as the International Network of Engaged Buddhists (INEB) and the Sakyadhita International Association of Buddhist Women bridged distinctions between East and West (Queen and King 1996; Queen 2000; Queen, Prebish, and Keown 2003).

Engaged Buddhism has been studied by a generation of scholars. While some argue that Buddhism has always been socially engaged, finding precursors of social action in Buddhist texts offering advice to monarchs (*Cakkavatti-sīhanāda Sutta* or Nāgārjuna's *Precious Garland*), or in the public welfare projects of Buddhist kings such as Aśoka Maurya (third century BCE) or the Sui dynasts of China (581–618 CE), these examples do not fit the pattern of today's counter-cultural movements. Engaged Buddhism, the name Thich Nhat Hanh gave to the Vietnamese anti-war movement in the 1960s, is not a policy of enlightened Buddhist monarchs or governments. The anti-caste activism of the Dalit Buddhists, the anti-Chinese protests of Tibetan monastics, and the village-based development projects and peace demonstrations of the Sarvodaya movement are popular, non-government movements, inspired by ordained and lay leaders who publicly oppose the social, political, military, and corporate structures they believe to be the cause of widespread suffering and harm. Their social and political actions cannot be measured solely in terms of public benefit—governments and non-Buddhist groups may endorse similar goals—but rather in the ways in which Buddhist teachings and practices are interpreted and applied to mobilize peaceful, collective responses to society-wide challenges. The terms 'Engaged Buddhism' and 'socially engaged Buddhism' in these settings point to ethical distinctions that are useful to review.

Traditional Buddhist ethics were often expressed in threefold formulas. 'To avoid evil, to cultivate good, and to cleanse the mind' appears in the *Dhammapada*, the *Mahāpadānasutta*, and an early form of the *Patimokkha*, the monastic disciplinary code. The 'three trainings' of morality, concentration, and wisdom (*śila, samādhi, prajñā*) identify steps on the Eightfold Path, the fourth 'Noble Truth' in the Buddha's first sermon. Formal expressions of Mahāyāna Buddhist ethics, such as Asaṅga's chapter on ethics (India, fifth century CE), Atiśa's *Lamp of the Path to Enlightenment and its Explanation* (Tibet, eleventh century CE), and Gyōnen's *Risshū Kōyō* (Japan, thirteenth century CE), have been summed up as 'avoiding evil, cultivating good, and saving all beings' (Chappell 1996: 351).

These objectives of Buddhist ethics may be characterized as paths of *Discipline*, rules of avoidance and restraint, such as the five lay precepts (*pañcasīla*) and ancient monastic codes (*vinaya*), that define 'avoiding evil'; paths of *Virtue*, lists of sublime attitudes (*brahmavihāras*) and saintly perfections (*pāramitā*) that define 'doing good'; and paths of *Altruism* in which the bodhisattva's vow to 'save all beings', attested in most Mahāyāna scriptures, is illustrated in the *Upāsaka Precept Sūtra* by the superiority of laypersons, renouncers, and divine beings who demonstrate great compassion (*mahā karuṇā*) in their commitment to assist others (Queen 2000: 11–17).

In contrast to these paths of individual discipline, virtue, and altruism, the ethics of *Engagement* addresses social sources of suffering through collective actions. Unlike the morality (*śila*) of the Eightfold Path, recommending skilful modes of speech, conduct, and livelihood for individual actors, the idea of collective action or 'engagement' to address external threats to social existence may well be influenced by notions of 'social suffering' identified in the modern social sciences (Kleinman et al. 1996). For the post-war generation of Engaged Buddhists, social suffering is caused by such things as the caste system in India, the war in Vietnam, village poverty in Sri Lanka, and the conquest and political domination of Tibet by Chinese invaders. The list may easily be expanded to include structural racism in industrial societies, ethnic warfare in developing countries, global economic exploitation, transnational income inequality, and the climate crisis threatening ecologically fragile communities and ultimately all forms of life. In these situations, threats to the well-being of humans, animals, and ecosystems are caused by institutionalized, depersonalized forces that transcend the conduct of any one actor. In this sense the sufferers may be considered *victims*, a category of analysis not found in traditional Buddhist discourse.

The disjunction between the Buddhist ethics of individual discipline, virtue, and altruism, on one hand, and the ethic of social engagement, on the other, may be traced to foundational ideas. Early Buddhist soteriology, manifested in the Four Noble Truths, is grounded in the claim that suffering (*dukkha*)—a universal property of existence, along with impermanence (*anicca*) and insubstantiality (*anatta*)—is caused by mental habits of the sufferer that are referred to as poisons (Pāli *kilesa*, Skt *kleśa*). Enumerated as hatred, greed, and delusion (*dosa, lobha, moha*), or craving (Pāli *taṇhā*, Skt *tṛṣṇā*), they constitute the second Noble Truth introduced in the Buddha's first sermon.

The subject of this suffering is the individual sufferer, and the cause of suffering is his or her state of mind, preceded by the states that make up the evolving psycho-physical personality. The accumulated action (karma) of these states arose over many lifetimes in the past and will generate states of suffering or liberation in lifetimes to come. This round of rebirths, or cyclic existence (*samsāra*), is the metaphysical matrix of traditional Buddhist ethics (Harvey 2000: 8–20). In this context, the Buddhist practitioner works to relieve his or her own suffering by embracing efficacious beliefs, attitudes, and activities. This work may produce ripple effects 'for the good of the many, for the happiness of many, with compassion toward the world', as the Buddha described the intent of his disciples' missionary work.

On the other hand, the social effects of one sufferer's mental poisons may merge with those of others to create and amplify conditions of general suffering, such as poverty, lawlessness, or war. Here a righteous monarch (*dhammaraja*) may intervene with public works like hospitals, food banks, road building, conflict mediation, and animal shelters. Bodhisattvas may employ skilful means (*upāya kauśalya*) or transfer their vast merit to rescue those who suffer from collective calamities. In these scenarios, however, it is important to recognize the ethics of altruism that link those who help and those who are helped. Simple compassion and sympathy motivate the social action we find in these stories (Aronson 1980; Jenkins 2003). Missing is a recognition that social conditions such as poverty, lawlessness, and war have become institutionalized and depersonalized, and that all practitioners—not simply the righteous king or the virtuous saint—may be required to act in concert on behalf of the victims of social suffering, including themselves. This is what distinguishes Engaged Buddhism from its predecessors.

Studies of Engaged Buddhism have revealed a wide range of practices that target structures and institutions of social suffering. In addition to Dalit Buddhists and Vietnamese monks in Asia, examples in the West include the Zen Peacemakers' retreats at Auschwitz and on the streets of Manhattan, bearing witness to the Nazi holocaust and to urban homelessness, and the protest and service activities of groups like the Buddhist Peace Fellowship and the Prison Dharma Network. These Buddhist engagements target institutions that broker suffering or the relief of suffering, as well as the plight of the individual victims of these structures. Overall, the challenges are structural and the responses are collective. Buddhists who care for individual sufferers through chaplaincy and ministry programmes are frequently engaged in efforts to reform the structures in which they serve. These might be military, industrial, correctional, medical, or educational settings—often 'total institutions' of the kind Erving Goffman described in 1961.

Three emerging realities have shaped the practice of Engaged Buddhism in recent years. One is the new generation of Buddhists who are making their voices heard in print, social media, and on the Internet. With the publication of Sumi Loundon's *Blue Jean Buddha* (2001) and *Buddha's Apprentices* (2005), Brad Warner's *Dharma Punx* (2004) and *Against the Stream* (2007), and other works by writers under the age of forty, the views of so-called Gen X, Gen Y, and Millennial Buddhists have found a wide audience. The leadership of socially engaged organizations such as the Buddhist Peace Fellowship has passed to younger activists, and new online organizations such as Dharma Geeks and writers such as David Chapman offer podcasts and blogs on topics ranging from the commercialization of meditation to the nature of Buddhist ethics itself.

Another development is the breakdown of distinctions between Engaged Buddhism in Asia and the West. The flourishing of international organizations such as INEB, Sakyadhita, the Free Tibet movement, Soka Gakkai International, Nipponzan Myohoji, Tzu Chi, and many others has promoted common perspectives on the nature of social suffering and a range of challenges to global stability. Whether in Berkeley or Bangkok, Engaged Buddhists are unlikely to blame the victims of social and natural disasters for their 'collective bad karma', for example. Asian activists do not specialize in earthquake or poverty relief while Western activists protest institutional and official oppression; all these activities have been globalized. The rising challenges of technological innovation and the struggle for social justice are not limited to anglophone, Euro-American, or industrialized societies. They may be witnessed wherever citizens and groups are linked by global flows of information, goods, services, and travel.

Finally, we cannot consider the evolution of Buddhist practice in Asia and the West without acknowledging its advancing *modernity* and *secularity*, however these jumbo terms may be defined. Recent observers have treated Engaged Buddhism as both a product of Buddhist modernism and a needed counterweight to the commercialization of Buddhist thought and practice in the West and increasingly in Asia (McMahan 2008; Carrette and King 2005). This chapter is an attempt to contribute to current discussions of Buddhist modernism and what has rightly been called 'the selling of spirituality'.

In the next two sections, let us take a closer look at Engaged Buddhism in the West by (1) comparing the attitudes and careers of four influential Buddhists, and (2) visiting the debate over Buddhist-inspired mindfulness training programmes in secular settings: industry, the military, clinical practice, and education. These thumbnail case studies are offered to show how differences of intention, training, branding, and setting may help to define Engaged Buddhism. The implication that there must be an 'unengaged Buddhism' has disturbed practitioners who regard all Buddhism as engaged, as well as Buddhists who practise social service and activism but choose not to call it 'Engaged Buddhism'. We will regard these concerns as problems of definition and not substance. Likewise, our review of the debate over secular applications of mindfulness is not intended to impugn their efficacy for stress reduction, improved performance, and life satisfaction. Rather, it is intended to raise questions about their efficacy as avenues of morality and liberation, as understood by traditional Buddhists. Is the label 'Buddhist' rightly erased in these settings, and has something of human and social value been lost?

Four Buddhists: Engaged or Not?

In the final pages of *The Making of Buddhist Modernism* (2008), David L. McMahan describes two roads that Buddhism may travel in the coming years, one that serves 'to challenge, critique, augment, and offer alternatives to modern, [W]estern ideas, social practices and values', and the other, in which 'Buddhism fades into vague New Age spiritualities, self-help therapies, and purely personal paths of self-improvement'. In the first scenario,

> Buddhism's sophisticated techniques of meditation combined with its vigorous ethical reflection offer forms of psychological and spiritual self-cultivation that can transcend the self-absorption and social irrelevance that has beset some modern psychotherapies and New Age spiritualities. Engaged Buddhism, furthermore, brings a unique perspective and a new vocabulary to the discourses of human rights, war and peace, environmentalism, and other pressing social and political concerns, expanding their conceptual resources. (McMahan 2008: 260)

In the second scenario,

> Buddhism becomes a purely personalized mode of self-help with scant ethical ramifications to where it becomes a mere commercial trope ... accommodated so thoroughly to the values of [W]estern (and increasingly globalizing) popular culture and its consumerism and commercialism that its capacity to critique these elements of contemporary culture—for which Buddhist has such ample resources—is neutralized. (McMahan 2008: 261)

The latter road, which McMahan calls 'global folk Buddhism', may be littered with 'Zen popcorn, Zen tea, Buddha bikinis and Buddha bars', or it may find expression in the lives of practising Buddhists who miss or dismiss the potential for service and social critique represented by Engaged Buddhism. They may be *religious* in their embrace of traditional beliefs and practices—karma, rebirth, meditation, awakening—or they may claim to be *secular* in distancing themselves from some of these features. These practitioners may illustrate the paths of discipline, virtue, and altruism, but they may not regard engagement—social service or reform of society—as intrinsic or even appropriate to a spiritual path. In order to sharpen these distinctions, let us consider four well-known voices in contemporary Buddhism.

The advance of secularism has not prevented some Western converts from seeking the rigorous training leading to ordination as a Buddhist monk. Scholars of Buddhism, such as Robert Thurman (Columbia University), George Dreyfus (Williams College), and Robert Buswell (UCLA), and *Dharma* teachers, such as Jack Kornfield, Bernie Glassman, Karma Lekshe Tsomo, Lama Surya Das, and Pema Chödrön, have taken vows and worn the robes of Buddhist monastics. Among the countless numbers of less visible Westerners who have pursued monastic practices, some have embraced forms of activism and service associated with Engaged Buddhism and some have not.

Two Western-born, Theravāda monks illustrate the alternatives. Bhikkhu Bodhi (born Jeffrey Block in 1944) and Thānissaro Bhikkhu (born Geoffrey DeGraff in 1949) grew up in New York and received elite monastic educations in Asia. Thānissaro trained under the respected Thai forest monk Ajaan Fuang Jotiko, and Bodhi trained under the eminent Balangoda Ananda Maitreya Thero in Sri Lanka. Both have been recognized as translators and interpreters of Pāli scriptural and commentarial literature, with many publications to their credit. Thānissaro is abbot of the Metta Forest Monastery, near San Diego, which he co-founded in 1991, while Bodhi teaches at monasteries in New York and New Jersey and directs Buddhist Global Relief, which he founded in 2008.

Thānissaro Bhikkhu and Bhikkhu Bodhi have taken divergent positions with respect to Engaged Buddhism. In 1997 Thānissaro assumed editorship of the widely used textbook *The Buddhist Religion*, and contributed a chapter in which he questions the orthodoxy of certain adaptations of Buddhism in the West. 'In many cases the appropriation of Buddhist ideas has led to what might be called "extrapolated Buddhism", in that themes are taken out of their original framework and extrapolated to radically different contexts.' As examples, he cites the adoption of Zen teachings and techniques by Roman Catholic contemplatives; and Engaged Buddhism, 'which interprets Buddhist teachings on the interdependence of all things as a call to an activist approach to social and environmental reform'. He sees these adaptations as a dangerous imposition of Western values on Buddhist teachings, which have been subsequently exported back to Asia. These values include 'the climate of tolerance and eclecticism in which the [Western] study of Buddhism developed', cultural and ethical relativism, anti-clericalism, gender equality, the mixture of meditation with psychotherapy, and doubts about the doctrine of rebirth, 'one of the few common denominators among the various Asian traditions [of Buddhism]' (Robinson, Johnson, and Thānissaro 1997: 300–309).

On the other hand, Thānissaro's commitment to traditional Theravāda doctrines and institutions is reflected in his leadership of the Metta Forest Monastery, whose mission 'is to give men the opportunity to ordain as bhikkhus to practice in line with Dhamma and Vinaya (training rules) taught by the Buddha over 2,500 years ago' (Metta Forest Monastery 2016). This is not the global folk Buddhism that McMahan posed as an alternative to socially engaged Buddhism. Indeed, Thānissaro Bhikkhu's orthodoxy may be considered an epitome of the paths of discipline and virtue set forth in ancient Theravāda Buddhism. Rather, his insistence on traditional Buddhism has been consistently coupled with this rejection of Engaged Buddhism.

Bhikkhu Bodhi, in contrast, has become a vocal advocate of socially engaged Buddhism. Moved by the suffering inflicted by the Indian Ocean earthquake and tsunami in 2004, Bodhi raised $160,000 for relief projects but was alarmed to find that few

Buddhist organizations in the West were set up to dispense the gifts. In 2007 he issued 'A Challenge to Buddhists' in *Buddhadharma: The Practitioner's Quarterly*:

> It seems to me that we Western Buddhists tend to dwell in a cognitive space that defines the first noble truth [of suffering] largely against the background of our middle-class lifestyles: as the gnawing of discontent; the ennui of over-satiation; the pain of unfulfilling relationships; or, with a bow to Buddhist theory, as bondage to the round of rebirths... I know we engage in lofty meditations on kindness and compassion and espouse beautiful ideals of love and peace. But note that we pursue them largely as *inward, subjective experiences* geared toward personal transformation. Too seldom does this type of compassion roll up its sleeves and step into the field. Too rarely does it translate into pragmatic programs of effective action realistically designed to diminish the actual sufferings of those battered by natural calamities or societal deprivation. (Bodhi 2007)

Citing Christian Aid, World Vision, and American Jewish World Service as organizations that do not proselytize but provide relief and development aid while tackling the causes of poverty and injustice, Bodhi asks, 'Why doesn't Buddhism have anything like that? Surely we can find a supporting framework for this in Buddhist doctrine, ethical ideals, archetypes, legends, and historical precedents.'

In 2008 Bhikkhu Bodhi founded Buddhist Global Relief (BGR). In the United States and a dozen countries in Asia, Africa, and Latin America, BGR works 'to provide direct food aid to people afflicted by hunger and malnutrition, to promote ecologically sustainable agriculture, to support the education of girls and women, and to give women an opportunity to start right livelihood projects to support their families'. The registered charity raises funds through online appeals and annual Feed the Hungry walks and concerts, and partners with interfaith and secular organizations such as UNICEF, CARE, Direct Relief, Oxfam America, and the International Medical Corps. BGR sees its motivation as distinctively Buddhist. 'The Buddha taught that it is the government's duty to guard and protect all the residents of the land, eliminating poverty through state-sponsored deeds of charity', but we who live in relative affluence should—in the absence of government intervention—'broadly extend our range of concern to the entire global community'. This statement might stand as the epitome of the path of Buddhist social engagement, as it has evolved over recent decades (Buddhist Global Relief 2016).

Ordained Buddhists in the West have not been alone in considering social engagement as an integral part of their practice. Among lay Buddhists, we may contrast the careers of Stephen Batchelor, born in Dundee, Scotland in 1953, a writer, teacher, and former monk trained in the Vajrayāna, Theravāda, and Mahāyāna traditions, with that of Steve Jobs (1955–2011), born in San Francisco, founder of Apple Inc. and a lifelong student of Zen Buddhism. Both men have come to represent a secular face of contemporary Buddhism, Jobs expressing, like authors Jack Kerouac in *Dharma Bums* (1958) and Robert Persig in *Zen and the Art of Motorcycle Maintenance* (1974), an avid attraction to Western versions of Asian spirituality, and Batchelor expressing, in his career as a monk, lay *Dharma* teacher, and commentator on contemporary Buddhism, an intellectual encounter with the contradictions of modern Buddhist practice.

After youthful experiments with LSD and travels in India, Jobs settled into a lifelong practice of meditation, attending retreats at the Tassajara Zen Mountain Center in California and studying under Japanese Zen priest Kōbun Chino Otogawa. Like many of his generation, he was influenced by classics of Western Buddhism, such as Shinryū Suzuki's *Zen Mind, Beginner's Mind* (1970) and Chögyam Trungpa's *Cutting through Spiritual Materialism* (1973), and he adopted a quasi-monastic public image with his signature blue-jean-black-turtleneck uniform. He coined Zen-sounding slogans like 'the journey is the reward' for his first Mac computer design team, married in a Buddhist ceremony, and delivered a commencement address in which he exhorted graduates to live each day as if it were their last. To some, his willingness to address matters of life and death in the face of his own struggle with cancer was an indication of his sincere embrace of Buddhism (Silverman 2011).

For those who knew Steve Jobs personally as family members or employees, however, his practice of Zen Buddhism was paradoxical. He reportedly had little patience for those who did not measure up to his standards. He fought patrimony of his first child in court, claiming to be sterile before withdrawing his suit and marrying the mother. He terminated Apple's new philanthropic programmes in 1997 after an absence from the company and left no record of personal philanthropy from his $7 billion estate. Perhaps best known to those who expected Jobs to manifest Buddhist compassion was his seemingly nonchalant response to questions concerning work conditions at the Asian factories that supply parts for Apple products. When a rash of worker suicides was reported at the Foxconn industrial park in Shenzhen, China, Jobs asked, 'Weren't the suicide rates at the factory lower than those in the Chinese population at large?' In the end, it appeared that Engaged Buddhism, defined as philanthropic and activist responses to systemic human suffering, was not an ingredient of Steve Jobs's Zen practice.

Stephen Batchelor, author, teacher, and former monk, has reached a different audience than that of Steve Jobs. Batchelor's training and ordination under Tibetan lamas, his exposure to *vipāssana* meditation under S. N. Goenka in India, and his monastic Zen experience in Korea prepared the ground for an international career as meditation teacher and author of influential books and translations. These include surveys, such as *The Tibet Guide* (1987) and *The Awakening of the West: Encounters of Buddhism with Western Culture* (1994), with introductions by the Dalai Lama; translations of classical texts by Nāgārjuna and Śāntideva, and commentaries by his teacher, Geshé Rabten; and, most influentially, his own evolving reflections on the ways in which traditional teachings may or may not have meaning for modern Buddhists. These investigations, written in a confessional style with a minimum of academic references, include *Alone with Others: An Existential Approach to Buddhism* (1983), *The Faith to Doubt: Glimpses of Buddhist Uncertainty* (1990), *Buddhism without Beliefs: A Contemporary Guide to Awakening* (1997), *Confessions of a Buddhist Atheist* (2010), and *After Buddhism: Rethinking the Dharma for a Secular Age* (2015).

In these writings, Batchelor consistently holds that the Buddha and his greatest followers were agnostic with respect to metaphysical claims and diverse in their prescriptions for Buddhist practice. In *Alone with Others*, in which he employs concepts of existentialists Martin Heidegger and Paul Tillich, he explains that he has omitted discussion of certain 'standard traditional topics' such as the Four Noble Truths, karma, and rebirth, turning rather to 'certain points that I consider central to the Buddhist path ... without too many peripheral considerations' (Batchelor 1983: 21). Thirty-two years later, in *After Buddhism*, Batchelor is still treating karma and rebirth and other mythical and metaphysical features of the early tradition as peripheral to the four 'tasks' of ethical practice, as he now terms the Four Noble Truths. The secular vision of scientific environmentalism offers a more compelling motive for human responsibility for the past and future than the generalized speculations of karma theory, he argues.

> Biology, physics, ecology, psychology, and history provide boundless illustrations of conditioned arising made flesh, from the most intimate details of our own mental states to the most devastating accounts of melting polar ice caps. This vision is likewise able to awaken and fine-tune our moral sense. It brings the dharma firmly down to earth. Before our stunned gaze, the *dukkha* of which Gotama spoke is rendered more immediate, palpable, and extensive than ever before. (Batchelor 2015: 305)

Such an approach would seem to provide an opening for the expansion of Buddhist ethical practice to include socially engaged Buddhism. As Batchelor admits, 'Rather than concern ourselves with our own hypothetical rebirth, we are challenged to assume a heightened responsibility for this planet and the continued flourishing of its inhabitants, human, animal, and vegetable, as we live our lives now.' Yet, surprisingly, he follows with a caveat:

> This vision does not, however, constitute a plea for a 'socially engaged' Buddhism. It is a plea to recover what the dharma has always been about: embracing the suffering of the world, letting go of reactivity, and experiencing that still, clear center from which we respond to the world in ways no longer determined by self-interest. (Batchelor 2015: 305–306)

Here, Batchelor expresses a longstanding ambivalence about the claim that social action, reflected in organized programmes of service, philanthropy or protest, should occupy a central place in contemporary Buddhist practice.

In *Buddhism without Beliefs*, his most widely read book, Batchelor notes that political, social, and financial institutions contribute to the confusion and craving of modern life so that 'a socially engaged vision of dharma practice [must recognize] that each practitioner is obliged by an ethics of empathy to respond to the anguish of a globalized, interdependent world' (Batchelor 1997: 112). In *The Awakening of the West*, he cites the social activism of the Ambedkar Buddhists and Ven. Sangharakshita, their British champion, to end the oppression of the caste system (Batchelor 1994: 331–333). These citations clearly support the case for Engaged Buddhism. But when Batchelor lists social engagement in his Ten Theses of Secular Dharma, it occupies the last rung from the bottom: 'Practitioners seek to understand and diminish the structural violence of societies and institutions as well as the roots of violence that are present in themselves' (Batchelor 2015: 322). In the context of Batchelor's continuing project of finding contemporary expressions for traditional Buddhist spirituality, each of these mentions of social engagement appears either as an afterthought or a passing bow to the implications of collective suffering, which he acknowledges but seems hesitant to embrace.

In these four Buddhists, we see divergent responses to the challenges of secularism, modernity, and social engagement. The monks Thānissaro and Bodhi react in contrasting ways to a society driven by commerce and power politics, despite common Theravāda roots in Buddhist Asia. In his writings and at his monastery, Thānissaro disavows socially engaged Buddhism, insisting instead on traditional Thai forest training, away from the cacophony of places like Bangkok and LA. Meanwhile, Bhikkhu Bodhi finds warrant in the Pāli scriptures for a Buddhist response to the prevalence of hunger and starvation in many parts of the world. Steve Jobs's practice of Zen did not prompt him to end the oppressive work conditions in factories making Apple products, or to spend his or his company's wealth to relieve structural suffering in society at large. Finally, Stephen Batchelor has found ways to communicate Buddhist teachings to secular audiences, and, as a writer, teacher, and volunteer prison chaplain, to demonstrate his sincere humanity and concern for others. Yet he has not seen a compelling connection between the core tasks of Buddhist practice, centring on personal spirituality, and the institutional causes of suffering in society.

Is Mindfulness Training Socially Engaged?

Another avenue for consideration of the nature and place of Engaged Buddhism in the West is the rise of meditation and mindfulness training, sometimes offered by Buddhist organizations and teachers, but more often sponsored by secular organizations with trademarks unrelated to Buddhism. The most successful of these programmes is Mindfulness Based Stress Reduction (MBSR), developed in 1979 by MIT-trained scientist Jon Kabat-Zinn. Tested for many years in the pain clinic for cancer patients at the University of Massachusetts Medical Center, MBSR has been adapted for use in diverse clinical settings, public schools, employee training, military boot camps, and corporate boardrooms, and marketed to global audiences on the Internet. By 2014, there were more than a thousand MBSR instructors teaching meditation classes throughout the United States and thirty foreign countries (Pickert 2014).

Although Kabat-Zinn adapted the mindfulness techniques he learned on Buddhist retreats at the Insight Meditation Society in Massachusetts and elsewhere, he has consistently validated their effectiveness by reference to clinical studies rather than Buddhist texts or testimony, which are rarely mentioned in his promotional literature. Applications of MBSR have been developed for employees in Silicon Valley companies such as Apple, Facebook, eBay, Google, and Twitter, and major corporations such as Hughes Aircraft, General Mills, Abbot Laboratories, General Motors, Ford, AOL Time Warner, and Goldman Sachs. With $4.3 million in grants from the Department of Defense, Mindfulness Based Mind Fitness Training (MMFT) was developed to train US Marines and US Air Force drone pilots to 'improve resilience and mission effectiveness in high-stress environments'. Spin-offs of MBSR in clinical psychology and psychotherapy include Mindfulness Based Cognitive Therapy (MBCT), Acceptance and Commitment Therapy (ACT), Dialectical Behavior Therapy (DBT), Mindfulness Based Relapse Prevention (MBRP), Mindfulness Based Trauma Therapy (MBTT), and Mindfulness Based Eating Awareness Training (MB-EAT). Americans spent some $4 billion on mindfulness-related programmes by 2007, and the National Institutes of Health spent over $100 million on research into mindfulness applications by the end of 2014 (Pickert 2014; Wylie 2015).

Scores of commercial Internet sites have appeared to guide individuals in the mindfulness of daily life, offer interactive courses in meditation and mindfulness with teachers and classmates meeting in real-time via live-streaming technology, and create 'virtual sanghas', Buddhist communities with shared spiritual and social networking objectives. Two of the most successful online platforms are Headspace and Buddhist Geeks. Headspace, a smartphone application ('app') devoted to meditation, was founded in London in 2010 by Andy Puddicombe, a former Buddhist monk, and Rich Pierson, a former advertising executive. Marketed as a 'gym membership for the mind', Headspace sells mindfulness programmes to subscribers for $12.95 per month or $419.95 'forever'. By 2015, it had amassed over two million subscribers.

Buddhist Geeks, an 'online magazine' offering instructional podcasts, live conferences, and 'life retreats' (virtual meditation sessions), grew out of conversations in 2006 between Vincent Horn and Ryan Oelke, religion majors at Naropa University. Offering podcasts to 'tech-savvy Buddhists looking for a fresh perspective', the website attracted one million downloads in the first year and increased to 100,000 downloads per month in the second year. In a 2015 podcast, Vincent Horn projected the future of Buddhist Geeks in 'cloud-based sanghas', ever-new contemplative technologies ('technodelics') such as electroencephalography (EEG) headsets of the kind used to test Tibetan monks in neuroscience experiments, and finally, an accelerated 'unbundling' of mindfulness from traditional Buddhist ethics, meditation, and wisdom. While he admitted that this process has already elicited 'concerns regarding mindfulness losing its liberative potential or becoming subsumed by the more negative aspects of capitalist culture', Horn expects 'additional elements of Buddhism to become unbundled—such as compassion, concentration, and even meditative insight'. At the same time, he looks forward to 'a new kind of engaged perspective':

> What would an engaged, contemplative movement look like that's not organized around 20th century forms of activism and localized communities, but instead employs the incredible power of technology and the deep learning of the modern age in a way that has a global scope and impact? Those are the questions we're asking. Not that we have the answers. (*Tricycle* 2013)

Any multi-billion-dollar industry will attract close scrutiny, and the rise of secular mindfulness training—variously called a 'movement', 'revolution', 'business', or 'fad'—has had advocates and detractors, both inside and outside the worlds of Buddhist practice and studies. Perhaps the most widely cited critique of MBSR and its offshoots appeared on the Huffington Post website in 2013, titled 'Beyond McMindfulness', by Ron Purser, professor of management at San Francisco State University, and David Loy, Zen teacher and writer. The authors, both teachers of Buddhist meditation, begin by comparing the myriad book titles containing the words 'mindful' and 'mindfulness' with previous trends devoted to 'The Zen of . . .' and 'The Tao of . . .'. The authors argue that marketing savvy has overwhelmed verifiable results in many of the settings in which mindfulness training is now offered. While they choose not to question the physiological and psychological benefits reported by mindfulness trainers, practitioners, and researchers, they focus instead on what they consider the 'dark side' of the movement: the absence of the moral and ethical values in which mindfulness was originally embedded in traditional Buddhist precept and practice (Purser and Loy 2013).

The Eightfold Path consists of three divisions, as we have seen: morality, concentration, and wisdom. All the steps of the path are considered to be correlative and mutually reinforcing, but the critical connection that Purser and Loy wish to make is that mindfulness, one of the three kinds of concentration, cannot be considered in isolation from right speech, right action, and right livelihood, the three categories of morality. In its secular applications, they argue, mindfulness has been decoupled not only from religion in general and Buddhism in particular, but from morality itself. Moreover, invoking another formulation of the Buddhist *Dharma*, these applications have failed to address the institutional expressions of the mental poisons that cause suffering.

> Many corporate advocates [of mindfulness training] argue that transformational change starts with oneself: if one's mind can become more focused and peaceful, then social and organizational transformation will naturally follow. The problem with this formulation is that today the three unwholesome motivations that Buddhism highlights—greed, ill will, and delusion—are no longer confined to individual minds, but have become institutionalized into forces beyond personal control. (Purser and Loy 2013)

The result is that the equanimity and mental clarity resulting from the practice of mindfulness meditation, in the absence of morality training, may serve to distract practitioners from the effects that their speech, action, and livelihood, motivated by greed, ill will, and delusion, may have on others. Mindfulness training in the absence of morality may blind practitioners to the social, institutional, economic, and political conditions that have precipitated or exacerbated the stress and suffering they have turned to meditation to escape.

Let us look at four applications of mindfulness training that have received the most attention, namely, mindfulness programmes adapted for corporate, military, psychotherapeutic, and educational settings. In each case, we may ask whether mindfulness training addresses collective expressions of the poisons of greed, ill will, and delusion, such as corporate profit-taking, military violence, and psychotherapeutic and educational malpractice. Have contemporary applications of secular mindfulness training in industry, the military, clinics, and schools brought 'a unique perspective and a new vocabulary to the discourses of human rights, war and peace, environmentalism, and other pressing social and political concerns'—McMahan's account of Engaged Buddhism—or its opposite, 'a purely personalized mode of self-help with scant ethical ramifications'?

Corporate Mindfulness

Corporate mindfulness programmes, many based on Kabat-Zinn's MBSR, are now offered to employees at major companies around the world. One model is the in-house mindfulness training department, such as Google's Search Inside Yourself Leadership Institute (SIYLI), co-founded in 2013 by Chade-Meng Tan (known as 'Meng' and 'Jolly Good Fellow', his official company title); Marc Lesser, software engineer, public relations officer, and former director of Tassajara Zen Mountain Center; and Phillipe Goldin, director of the Clinically Applied Affective Neuroscience laboratory at Stanford University and former interpreter for Tibetan lamas in India and Nepal. Based on Meng's 2012 book, *Search inside Yourself: The Unexpected Path to Achieving Success, Happiness (and World Peace)*, the institute illustrates its motto, 'We Put Mindfulness to Work', with a parody:

> A zen teacher, an engineer and a Stanford neuroscientist walk into a room and ... they start a world-changing organization. This is the simplified story of our founders Marc Lesser, Meng and Philippe Goldin. Their combined expertise in mindfulness, business and science are at the core of what SIYLI offers. (Search Inside Yourself Leadership Institute 2016)

The courses offered by the institute to other corporations and to individuals throughout the country claim to 'enhance focus, increase resilience and adaptability in the face of challenges, reduce stress responses, improve access to creativity and innovative thinking, and create personal and professional alignment'. It is hard to find objectives in this list and others that would support the claims of Meng's book and the institute's website to 'change the world' or promote 'world peace'. Indeed, all of the benefits cited for Search

Inside Yourself programmes relate to individual well-being; none relate to community building in the workplace or service to the world outside of the corporation.

Another manifestation of mindfulness training in the corporate setting is the growth of the Wisdom 2.0 conferences founded by Soren Gordhamer in 2009 for employees of the technology industry, and increasingly, entrepreneurs and celebrities associated with spiritual teachings and practices. The 2016 conference, held at the Marriott Marquis in San Francisco, attracted three thousand registrants from twenty-four countries and featured sand-painting by Tibetan monks, yoga and meditation sessions, and speeches by Jon Kabat-Zinn and *Dharma* teachers Jack Kornfield, Sharon Salzberg, Joan Halifax, Trudy Goodman, and others. In publicity for its annual conference and regional workshops Wisdom 2.0 claims to have 'sparked an ardent conversation ... in communities around the globe of the value of mindfulness in our high-speed, interconnected age'. In offering tickets for the one-day LA conference, ranging in price from $300 to $2500, Wisdom 2.0 makes clear the connection between commerce and spirituality:

> Join us for an intimate gathering to explore the power and possibility of conscious entrepreneurship in the digital age. As more and more people long to not just make money, but to do so in a meaningful way that addresses real world problems, Wisdom 2.0 LA seeks to support this movement. (Wisdom 2.0 2016)

Among the intimate gatherings is a session titled 'Conversations with Money (CW$): Money as a radical business teacher', followed by a meditation session titled 'Peace of the Present'.

During the Wisdom 2.0 conference in San Francisco in 2014, activists entered a packed meeting of mindfulness instructors during a panel titled 'Three Steps to Corporate Mindfulness the Google Way'. The intruders unfurled a banner and began handing out leaflets reading 'Eviction-Free San Francisco' to protest the eviction of low-income renters near private bus stops where upper-income employees are transported to the Google campus and other Silicon Valley companies. In San Francisco, low-rent apartments are routinely 'flipped'—remodelled and re-rented or sold to Silicon Valley employees for a large profit. While security guards moved in to remove the protesters, a panelist provided voice-over on the sound system, inviting the audience to 'check in with your body [to] see what it's like to be around people who have heartfelt ideas that may be different from what we're thinking.... Take a minute to see what it's like.' To better 'see' these things the meditation instructors closed their eyes and practised mindfulness until guards removed the visitors. No discussion of local housing justice issues was introduced as the panel returned to 'corporate mindfulness the Google way' (Wylie 2015).

Military Mindfulness

In 2004, Elizabeth Stanley, an associate professor at Georgetown University and former US Army intelligence officer, and Amishi Jha, a neuroscientist at the University of Miami, developed a pilot study to test mindfulness training for the US Marines. The Pentagon was impressed with the results and awarded them $2 million to adapt MBSR to combat training for all the services. Called Mindfulness-Based Mind Fitness Training (MMFT, pronounced M-Fit), the eight-week programme 'employs mindfulness of breathing, meditation in various postures, concentrated attention, working with painful sensations, relaxing mind-body, reduction of stress and extended periods of silence'. The programme aims 'to build resilience and optimize individual and team performance'. Drone pilots are trained to overcome information overload from satellite and war-zone images, headphone noise, and other pilots' voices by focusing on their breath and bodily sensations as they sit in front of multiple screens at the command centre at Creech Air Force Base in Nevada. For combat troop training, Stanley writes, 'soldiers learning how to fire the M-16 rifle are taught to pay attention to their breath and synchronize the breathing process to trigger the finger's movement, squeezing off the round while exhaling'. Since the introduction of M-Fit programmes, the US Army has invested $125 million more on 'comprehensive soldier fitness' programmes, including $31 million to Professor Martin Seligman at the University of Pennsylvania to develop positive psychology training for 1.1 million troops (Purser 2014).

While it may seem obvious that the use of Buddhist-based mindfulness techniques to train more efficient killing flies in the face of fundamental Buddhist moral teachings, such as the promotion of Right Livelihood and the First Precept, 'I undertake the training to abstain from killing'—it is notable in this context that the ancient precepts are presented as ethical 'trainings' and not as moral absolutes or divine commandments—some Buddhist leaders have defended the M-Fit programme, or at least refused to denounce it. In the Buddhist journal *Enquiring Mind*, Jon Kabat-Zinn argued that 'woven into mindfulness is an orientation toward non-harming ... that invites seeing the interconnectedness between the seer and the seen. ... Even if your initial motivation is to cause harm, by the time you finish you may have a different motivation. I have to trust that.' In 2009 Dr Jha presented findings of the M-Fit programme to the Dalai Lama at the Mind and Life Institute, which studies the interface between neuroscience and Buddhist meditation. She expressed personal reservations about the application of Buddhist meditation to military training and asked for His Holiness's advice. After a pause to consult with his translator, the Dalai Lama reportedly said, 'Zero.' After another pause he added 'I appreciate your work. That's all.' Finally, Jack Kornfield, a pioneer in the introduction of Burmese mindfulness meditation to the United States in the 1970s, serves on the eight-member board of advisors for the M-Fit programme along with two Army generals and a congressman, implying his approval of the programme.

In a wide-ranging denunciation of Mindfulness-Based Mind Fitness Training, Christopher Titmuss, a Buddhist meditation teacher based in Britain, asks, 'Are Buddhist mindfulness practices used to support international war crimes?' Noting that Barbara Gates, while editing an issue of *Enquiring Mind* dedicated to the Buddhist ethics of war and peace, continued to express ambivalence over the MMFT programme—'In Buddhist circles, there is hot debate on the impact of doing mindfulness training with the military. As editor, I still don't know definitely where I stand on the issue'—Titmuss makes clear his own position:

> The Buddha never wavered from his determination to persuade human beings to abstain from killing and to negotiate resolution to major conflicts involving nation states, tribes and political organizations. He spoke up tirelessly for a non-violent view toward the dynamics of human existence, rather than a compromise through justifications used to support the killing fields of war. (Titmuss 2014)

Mindfulness Therapy and Teaching

We turn now to applications of secular mindfulness training in the fields of psychotherapy and education. As in the cases of employee and military training, we find that mindfulness-based programmes in clinical and school settings have their defenders and detractors. We suggested above that these mindfulness apps may be understood as institutional expressions of the three poisons of Buddhist psychology. The profits garnered by the multi-billion-dollar mindfulness industry in corporate and employee training suggests an institutionalization of the Buddhist poison of *lobha* or greed. The multi-million-dollar MMFT programmes deployed by the Pentagon to sharpen military performance for ground troops and drone pilots suggests an institutionalization of the Buddhist poison of *dosa* or ill will—not towards the trainees, of course, but towards their ultimate targets in the theatres of war. As we turn to the burgeoning programmes of mindfulness-based psychotherapy and educational technology, we ask if we will encounter some form of *moha*, ignorance or delusion, the third Buddhist poison.

By 2014, more than one thousand Mindfulness-Based Cognitive Therapy (MBCT) courses were being offered in the United Kingdom. Forty-three trusts (specialty areas) of the National Health Service offer and reimburse such courses, and major universities such as Oxford, Bangor, and Exeter help to train instructors for this burgeoning non-medical specialty. Studies have shown that MBCT may reduce relapses into depression by 44 per cent and facilitate the reduction or discontinuation of psychotropic medication for a range of patients suffering mental distress. At the same time, observers have identified two troubling trends that have accompanied the rapid growth of the practice. One is the increasingly frequent appearance of adverse side effects, such as 'depersonalization, where people feel like they are watching themselves in a film'. This may be related to another trend, the growth of untrained or underqualified instructors. According to Dr Florian Ruths, consultant psychiatrist at the Maudsley Hospital in South London,

> There is a lot of enthusiasm for mindfulness-based therapies and they are very powerful interventions. But they can also have side-effects. Mindfulness is delivered to potentially vulnerable people with mental illness, including depression and anxiety, so it needs to be taught by people who know the basics about those illnesses, and when to refer people for specialist help. (Booth 2014)

In the United States, according to a general survey by the National Institutes of Health, 20 million adult Americans tried meditating between 2006 and 2007—10 per cent of all respondents. With the meteoric rise of mindfulness programmes in the US, administered by practitioners of vastly different training, the incidence of adverse side effects has grown proportionately. A leader in the study and rescue of meditators who have entered a 'dark night of the soul' through misguided referral or instruction is Dr Willoughby Britton, assistant professor of psychiatry and human behaviour at Brown University Medical School. Comparing information about meditators who experienced psychiatric breakdowns during retreat programmes at leading Buddhist centres with that of breakdowns resulting from secular training programmes, Britton developed a database of case studies and founded a therapeutic facility to treat patients recovering from what might be called meditation illnesses. Through her research project, Varieties of Contemplative Experience, and her treatment facility, Cheetah House, Britton's team has discovered a fundamental mismatch between the objectives of traditional Buddhist meditation—to promote insight into the impermanence, insubstantiality, and dissatisfaction of life—and secular mindfulness training, which aims to reduce stress and enhance executive skills. The correlations between these divergent objectives and the kinds of illness reported in the Dark Night studies are ongoing. The great majority of mindfulness programme alumni report positive experiences with mindfulness, Britton says, 'but then I get another phone call and meet someone who's in distress, I see the devastation in their eyes, and I can't deny that this is happening'. Whether *moha* or Buddhist delusion is at issue in these cases remains to be seen (Rocha 2014).

The controversy over secularized mindfulness training in educational settings is based on different considerations. Like the explosion of mindfulness-based interventions in business, government, and medicine, mindfulness in the schools has taken off both nationally and internationally. One organization, Mindful Schools, founded in the California Bay Area in 2007 as a not-for-profit training organization with online and in-person courses, content, and trainers, is now active in fifty states and more than one hundred countries. Its programme, targeted to grade-school-age children, typically introduces short periods of meditation throughout the school day, focusing on bodily relaxation, non-judgmental awareness, mindful breathing, and mental projection of well-being to others—in short, a secularized form of Buddhist *satipaṭṭhāna* (non-judging awareness of body and thoughts), *ānāpānasati* (breathing awareness), and *metta bhāvana* (loving-kindness practice). Controlled studies of student outcomes in the programme have shown improved attention and focus, emotional regulation, empathy, social skills, and grades; and decreased stress, anxiety, and anti-social behaviours. Classroom teachers have reported feelings of improved efficacy and success in delivering the curriculum, better communication with students, reduced stress, and greater job satisfaction (Mindful Schools 2016).

Critics of educational mindfulness programmes do not question the results of these studies, but focus on the degree to which the programmes represent a covert introduction of religious teaching into public schools, in violation of the constitutional separation of church and state. A leading critic, Candy Gunther Brown, author of *Healing*

Gods (2013) and *Testing Prayer* (2012) and professor of religious studies at Indiana University, argues that secularizing Buddhist meditation amounts to little more than changing vocabulary. Instead of quoting Buddhist scriptures, mindfulness educators quote scientific studies touting the advantages of the practice. The words 'Buddhism' and 'meditation' are erased, but the trappings of religion remain: the posture and hand gestures of meditation and prayer, specific meditation instructions, and wishing others well in the language of intercessory prayer, lacking only reference to the Buddha or invocation of God. Brown points to advocates of school-based mindfulness who admit their own Buddhist training and commitment: Caverly Morgan, founder of Peace in Schools, the Portland, Oregon high-school for-credit mindfulness programme, trained in a Zen monastery for eight years; and Trudy Goodman, founder of Insight LA, who explained to Dharma Geeks founders Vincent and Emily Horn that mindfulness is a form of 'stealth Buddhism ... getting children to engage in the same practice of mindfulness that is taught in Buddhist classes ... "whether they want it or not"' (Brown 2016).

Tellingly, Brown's criticism of educational mindfulness programmes does not include the arguments against other secularized mindfulness interventions we have examined. While Mindful Schools, Peace in Schools, and similar programmes have found a willing market in the public sector for their services, they are resolutely not-for-profit like their clients, and therefore beyond charges of commercialism. Similarly, mindfulness-based education appears to promote the ethical values we associate with Buddhist practice: the cultivation of moral virtues, social harmony, self-reliance, psychological well-being, and, as a bonus, an increased sense of right livelihood among teachers who sometimes complain of work conditions and outcomes in the public schools. Even the criteria for assessing the social engagement of Buddhist practice—its capacity to promote collective and institutional transformation beyond its benefits to individuals—may seem to be met in the results reported by Mindful Schools and other vendors. As critic Candy Brown admits,

> There is a perceived crisis in U.S. public education. Religious disestablishment coincided with desegregation, new immigration, and accelerating urbanization—social developments that many observers blame for a seeming epidemic of poor academic performance, bullying, violence, stress, obesity, sex, and drugs. In the wake of Supreme Court rulings, schools cannot use Protestant religious practices such as prayer and Bible reading to inculcate moral and ethical character. Teachers and administrators welcome offers by Buddhist meditators to teach 'secularized' versions of practices that instill the same moral and ethical virtues as religion. (Brown 2015)

In other words, this instance of 'stealth Buddhism' in fact serves its practitioners and society in ways that are contested in the fields of industry, government, and medicine. Absent the failure of corporate mindfulness programmes to identify and address the institutional causes of workplace suffering; absent the failure of M-Fit trainers to question the morality of preparing combatants for more efficient killing; and absent the failure of medical and government authorities to set standards for mindfulness instructors and therapists and to prevent increased illness and suffering among vulnerable patients, it appears that mindfulness-in-the-schools has much to offer without the adverse side effects accompanying its cousins in the corporate and military worlds.

Yet the poison of *moha*, Buddhist delusion or ignorance, may remain as an ingredient of the accelerating spread of mindfulness-based programmes. While elements of Buddhist ethical teaching may be discernible in clinical, social, or educational applications—the virtues of loving-kindness, compassion, empathetic joy, and impartiality come to mind—the larger objective of Buddhist practice, within which mindfulness and other techniques are embedded, clearly transcends such results as stress reduction and job satisfaction. The profound personal and social transformations that may potentially follow awakening to the teachings of impermanence, insubstantiality, and spiritual suffering, for example, are not possible through simply following the breath and allowing thoughts and feelings to come and go.

Robert Sharf, professor of Buddhist studies at the University of California, Berkeley, has shown how twentieth-century Burmese reformers, such as Mahāsī Sayadaw (1904–1982), at whose feet some of the pioneers of Western insight and mindfulness meditation studied in the 1960s, created a meditation technique for laypersons by leaving most of its preliminaries behind.

> [T]he success of the modern *vipassanā* movements lies precisely in the way they operationalize *vipassanā* or 'liberating insight.' *Vipassanā* was traditionally understood as a kind of analytic discernment cultivated through memorizing, internalizing, and 'bearing in mind' (*sati*) key abhidharmic categories. This required, among other things, a serious grasp of Buddhist epistemology. Reformers like Mahāsī could jettison this by approaching *sati* as 'mindfulness' and treating *vipassanā* as the meditative experience of 'bare awareness.' Path and goal become one, and advanced stages of insight are available to anyone willing to follow a simple technique. (Sharf 2014)

In writing that the path and goal become one, and that insight is available to anyone who can following simple directions, Sharf is reporting the *claims* of modern Burmese reformers and their distant predecessors in medieval China, who invented Chan (Zen) Buddhism by means of a similar manoeuvre. He is not affirming that it is so. This is a long story, but its relevance to the contemporary rise of secular mindfulness-based programmes is clear. Jon Kabat-Zinn and his followers, who consciously decoupled the 'simple technique' of mindfulness for use in classrooms, clinics, hotel ballrooms, and the battlefield, knew that they were not offering Buddhism, and they have been right not to claim that they were. The *moha* here is not a deception of the public, but possibly a true delusion regarding the benefits of secular mindfulness training itself. When Kabat-Zinn, Kornfield, and other traditionally trained Buddhist teachers claim that the mindfulness training of corporate CEOs, combat troops, and drone pilots carries with it 'an orientation toward non-harming… that invites seeing the interconnectedness between the seer and the seen', they are either denying the neutrality of mindfulness with respect to institutional exploitation and violence, or they have been seduced by the thought that human goodness—Buddha-nature?—will shine through in the end.

The Ethics of Engaged Buddhism: New Directions

In a recent article titled 'Elements of Engaged Buddhist Ethical Theory', Sallie B. King finds a version of natural law in the traditional notions of *Dharma* and *paṭicca-samuppāda*, a progressive altruism implicit in the practice of the *pañcasīla* or ethical precepts, and a virtue-centred, principle-based ethics, as articulated by the modern Thai commentator Buddhadāsa. An adept of the Buddha's way is 'One whose mind is free of grasping at and clinging to a self or possession of self, is one whose bodily and verbal actions are truly and perfectly virtuous. Any other sort of ethics or morality is just an up-and-down affair.' King also enumerates characteristics that may be found in the Engaged Buddhist leaders she cites: non-adversariality, non-judgmentalism, pragmatism, nonviolence, and the imperative to act in the face of suffering. In the end, she argues that 'there is no single feature of engaged Buddhist ethics which cannot be found in more traditional Buddhist ethics. All the features of engaged Buddhist ethical theory cited here can be and are justified by the words of the Buddha, Mahāyāna scriptures, and other traditional teachings' (King 2009: 201).

I have argued that the essence of Engaged Buddhism, as it is manifested in leaders and movements in Asia and the West, is an awareness of the collective nature of suffering, as it is caused or mediated by social and environmental conditions, structures, and institutions—and that this emphasis has not found frequent expression in traditional Buddhist thought and practice. This does not negate the psychological experience of 'unsatisfactoriness' that constitutes the original meaning of the Buddhist *dukkha*, but it does recognize that individuals and groups of individuals who share common experiences—often dictated by racial, caste, or gender identities, work conditions, the presence of war or disease, or changes in the natural environment, to name but a few—suffer in ways that cannot rationally be blamed on their own states of mind or behaviour in the past or present. This notion of social suffering has emerged among practitioners who have resolutely identified themselves as Buddhist in recent times. And insofar as they have turned to address social and institutional causes of suffering, as it impinges on themselves and others, many have further identified themselves as Engaged Buddhists. The ways in which external, depersonalized causes of suffering are addressed vary widely with the circumstances, of course, and here the traditional idea of skilful means may be usefully applied.

Engaged Buddhism in its many forms poses a challenging question for modern observers: are current theories of Buddhist ethics adequate to account for the rise of leaders, organizations, and the millions of practitioners who address themselves to social suffering in the name of Buddhism? Is there a need for an Ethics of Engaged Buddhism? If Engaged Buddhism may be considered a fourth kind of ethical practice—or a fourth *yāna*, as I have proposed elsewhere—where might we look for analytical categories to account for its originality? (Queen 2000: 11–26).

Two Western approaches to philosophical ethics have been proposed in recent years to account for Buddhist ethics: the virtue ethics propounded by Aristotle, and the consequentialist (utilitarian, pragmatic) ethics associated with such nineteenth-century thinkers as Jeremy Bentham and J. S. Mill. Damian Keown argued in *The Nature of Buddhist Ethics* that the cultivation of personal virtue rests at the centre of the Buddha's teachings, as attested throughout the Pāli Canon (Keown 2001). More recently, Charles Goodman and Barbra Clayton have pointed to the strong consequentialist elements in the writings of Mahāyāna thinkers like Śāntideva. Their argument may be summarized by observing that the Theravāda ethics of the early period focus on self-purification through the practice of what I have called 'discipline' (observing lay and monastic precepts) and 'virtue' (cultivating benevolent attitudes and qualities), while Mahāyāna thinkers have focused on the possibility of universal salvation implied by the bodhisattva's vow to save all beings, however many lifetimes it may take—a shift in ethical focus I have called 'altruism'. Clayton illustrates the bodhisattva's commitment to both virtue and consequence when she distils Śāntideva's programme into three steps: guarding the self from acquiring unwholesome and harmful qualities and habits; purifying oneself of such qualities and habits; and cultivating one's merit or karmic fruitfulness in order to transfer or dedicate it for the benefit of others (Clayton 2009). Here again we see the familiar formula, 'Avoid harm, purify the mind, and do good to others' (discipline, virtue, altruism). Missing in these theories is an account of a path of engagement with social suffering.

One may admit that the Mahāyāna vow to save all beings appears to address a collective suffering, yet one is left with many questions. How often in traditional texts is the transfer or dedication of karmic fruitfulness to others described or acted out in real programmes of service? Is such social action—assuming it is real and not merely aspirational—considered a way to acquire merit and karmic fruitfulness or a way to 'spend' it on others in service of the original vow? Is social service or activism a true form of ethical practice for bodhisattvas, or a by-product of their success at self-purification? Some observers, such as Stephen Jenkins, have documented passages in Indian and Tibetan Buddhist literature in which social action—feeding the hungry, serving the poor—is recommended or carried out. But the objective in these cases is to remove material obstacles to the proper work of Buddhist practice, the avoidance of harmful habits, the cultivation of wholesome ones, and ultimately, the achievement of liberation from rebirths, the attainment of *nibbāna* (for Theravādins) or Buddhahood (for Mahāyānists). There is no indication in these texts that the 'numberless beings' may be victims of impersonal social systems, structures, institutions—or even natural calamities—that cause hunger, poverty, and war, and that may be subject to the skilful means of remedial social action (Jenkins 2003).

It is with these questions in mind that I propose two avenues of investigation in the quest for an ethics of socially engaged Buddhism. The first is prompted by the well-documented contribution of John Dewey's American pragmatism to the formulation of Engaged Buddhism by B. R. Ambedkar in the decades leading up to his conversion in 1956. As one of Ambedkar's mentors during his doctoral studies at Columbia University between 1913 and 1916, Dewey offered insights that help to explain Ambedkar's 'new vehicle' (*Navayana*) of social service and activism in the name of *Dharma*. Among these are a focus on the institutional grounding of social ideals such as liberty, equality, and fraternity, and the social nexus of religion itself, which Dewey termed a 'common faith' in his Terry Lectures at Yale in 1934. Dewey was not acquainted with Buddhist thought, but Ambedkar repeatedly demonstrates the congruence between Deweyan and Buddhist conceptions in his writings on caste, religion, and social transformation. It is in the politics of public institutions, deliberative bodies, and courts of law; the competition for commercial markets and consumer loyalties; and the battle for hearts and minds in the information media, scholarly discourse, and school and university classrooms that religious values and ethical norms evolve and come into conflict, according to Dewey and Ambedkar (Nanda 2002; Queen 2004, 2015; Straud 2016).

The second resource for understanding the sociological turn of contemporary Engaged Buddhism is the work that Joanna Rogers Macy first undertook in her 1978 doctoral dissertation at Syracuse University, titled 'Interdependence: Mutual Causality in Early Buddhist Teachings and General Systems Theory', and later published as *Mutual Causality in Buddhism and General Systems Theory: The Dharma of Natural Systems* (1991). As a leading voice of Engaged Buddhism in the West, who continues to fight for a wide range of social and environmental causes, Macy, now in her eighties, still writes on ethical theory with a sense of urgency. Her discovery of a congruence between ancient Buddhism and modern systems philosophy is both original and heuristic. Viewing the teaching of dependent origination ('mutual causality') side by side with the systems analysis of cybernetic feedback, self-organizing and regulating wholes, and the movement of information and energy among nested hierarchies (particularly self and society), Macy offers insights into cosmology ('impermanent, interdependent'), epistemology ('co-arising of knower and known'), psychology ('co-arising of body and mind'), ethical theory ('co-arising of doer and deed'), social psychology ('co-arising of self and society'), and social change ('mutual morality', 'the dialectics of personal and social transformation') (Macy 1991).

While is it not possible to develop these proposals here, we can identify points of connection and suggest avenues for further investigation. Calling the practice of Engaged Buddhism *a sociological turn* for Buddhist ethics is intended in two ways. Just as features of the Buddhist liberation movements of the late twentieth century, embodying universal principles of human rights, sweeping social critique, and spontaneous popular uprising, recall the late eighteenth-century revolutions of Europe and America (without the violence), so the analysis of such movements requires perspectives of the new social sciences that emerged in the nineteenth and early twentieth centuries, when thinkers like Marx, Freud, James, Durkheim, and Weber took religion seriously as an independent variable for personal and social change (Glock and Hammond 1973). The growing influence of the natural sciences on social thought, illustrated by Humboldt's interdisciplinary naturalism (Wulf 2015) and Darwin's science of evolution, along with the theoretical and technological advances in physics and information science in the twentieth century, help to account for the perspectives advanced by the American Dewey and Europeans

Ludwig von Bertalanffy and Ervin Laszlo, whom Macy cites in her systems analysis. Engaged Buddhism is a creature of the modern world and is best understood by philosophies of modernity that take religion into account.

Dewey was born in 1859, the year of Darwin's *Origin of Species*, and his philosophy is best regarded as organismic and evolutionary. The opening pages in his *Democracy and Education* (1916) set the stage for his account of social change:

> The most notable distinction between living and inanimate beings is that the former maintain themselves by renewal. . . . Life is a self-renewing process through action on the environment. . . . The continuity of any experience, through renewal of the social group, is a literal fact. Education in its broadest sense, is the means of this social continuity of life. (Dewey 1944: 1–5)

Ambedkar, who studied under Dewey when this book was in drafts and lecture notes, later marked these and similar passages with red pencil (Queen 2004). As Ambedkar shows in his most influential books, *The Annihilation of Caste* (1936) and *The Buddha and his Dhamma* (1957), the philosophies of education, history, and religion must be understood in settings of social flux, where intellectual inquiry, critical valuing, and the work of social reconstruction are aspects of the struggle for existence, 'the survival of the fittest'. The specific environments for this struggle are the institutions of society—governments, courts, schools, religious shrines, and commercial markets—which are subject to influence by thinkers, leaders, and groups. Ambedkar's second favourite European slogan, after 'Liberty, Equality, Fraternity', was the motto that playwright and Fabian Society leader George Bernard Shaw coined for the London School of Economics, where Ambedkar earned his second doctorate. 'Educate, Agitate, Organize' had already become the battle cry of his anti-caste irregulars in the years leading up to the massive Buddhist conversion, but now it appears on posters alongside images of the Buddha and Ambedkar himself.

Dewey was not a religious man in the conventional sense, but he concluded his Terry Lectures, titled *A Common Faith*, by nesting human action in the flow of nature and history:

> We who live now are parts of a humanity that extends into the remote past, a humanity that has interacted with nature. The things in civilization we most prize are not of ourselves. They exist by the doings and sufferings of the continuous human community in which we are a link. Ours is the responsibility of conserving, transmitting, rectifying and expanding the heritage of values we have received that those who come after us may receive it more solid and secure, more widely accessible and more generously shared that we have received it. Here are all the elements for a religious faith that shall not be confined to sect, class, or race. Such a faith has always been implicitly the common faith of mankind. It remains to make it explicit and militant. (Dewey 1934: 87)

Dewey touches here on many themes central to Engaged Buddhists and the social service and activism they practice: a vivid sense of the past as prologue to the present; selves nested in nature and a continuous human community that transcends individual personality. Responsibility for others is expressed in the doings and sufferings of those who seek to conserve and transmit the values of the past; to rectify and expand them for the benefit of those confined by sect, race, and class (and, we must add, caste, gender, and disability); and to make these latent elements of social consciousness explicit *and militant*. While this note of militancy is certainly not characteristic of all Engaged Buddhists, it has resonated with Ambedkar's followers for sixty years and may be witnessed in other Engaged Buddhists, East and West, who urgently yearn for social change in the face of perennial struggles.

Joanna Macy's discovery of systems theory during her graduate studies—reminiscent of Ambedkar's discovery of Deweyan pragmatism during his graduate studies—led to a highly original reading of Buddhist ethics which no one has attempted to elaborate in the intervening years. The general systems theory that had taken shape by the 1960s, like the pragmatism of Dewey, William James, and C. S. Peirce, reflected a movement to place the natural and social sciences alongside philosophy and the humanities and to identify common patterns of organization and interaction. Just as Darwinian theory accounted for biological emergence without reference to supernatural agency, so general systems theory finds emergent properties at each level of organization, from particulate to cultural levels, inclusive of physical energy, life forms, human consciousness, and systems of thought and culture. Augmented by cybernetic and information theories formulated with the use of computers in the 1940s, systems theorists offered dynamic models of interaction and transformation at all levels. Writing in the 1970s, Macy applied the systems principles of integration, adaptation, emergence, and hierarchy to specific problems of ethics in early Buddhist teaching (Queen 1986).

In this chapter, I have argued that Engaged Buddhism has expanded the ethical horizon of spiritual practice to encompass those who suffer from causes and conditions that transcend their own attitudes and behaviours—their own karma, to use the traditional term. Engaged Buddhists are typically concerned with social injustice and systemic oppression that may only be addressed by collective action. Service-oriented Buddhist practice, as much as social activism, is often prompted by an awareness of systemic conditions, such as the lack of compassionate hospice care for the dying or inhumane treatment of prisoners in correctional institutions. I have argued that the ethics of personal discipline and virtue and the consequentialism of altruistic aspiration and service in the traditional Buddhisms of Asia and the West fail to account for the collective nature of suffering and its remediation implied and exemplified by the liberation movements we have surveyed. It is here that the social theories of Dewey and Macy may be of service. Macy writes,

> General systems theory offers fresh ways of understanding and imagining [the] particular and participatory nature of personhood. Through the process termed feedback, the words and acts by which a person would modify her world shapes her in turn. Furthermore, her very existence is constituted by networks of biological and social relationships, in which she, like other open systems, is a 'holon'—both an integral whole and a part within a larger whole. As open systems interact, be they atom

> or organism, they form larger self-sustaining patterns, which in turn relate to build yet more inclusive and more varied forms. (Macy 1991: 185)

Macy goes on to illustrate the systems conception of the 'co-arising of self and society' with reference to the *Aggañña Sutta*, an early Buddhist account of the rise of social suffering and the potential roles of *Saṅgha* and state in mitigating it. But inasmuch as today's Engaged Buddhism did not exist in classical times, Macy's theory of Buddhist social action is more readily applicable to the movements we see at present—movements of the kind that she, Ambedkar, and many others have spearheaded.

In the final chapter of her study of mutual causality and social change, Macy shows how the memes of tree and flame—prominent in Buddhist imagery and contemporary systems theory—are paradigmatic for an ethic of socially engaged Buddhism:

> Significant to both general systems theory and early Buddhist teachings, these images serve to convey the interdependence of our lives and also the process by which transformation takes place. ... The holonic structure, reticulating into subsystems and merging in larger branches, is that of a tree, while the process by which it happens in the transformation of energy and information is like that of a flame.... As the Buddha's teachings attest, the realization of both transiency and relationship breaks down the walls of ego; freeing us from that anxious cell, it releases the heart to loving-kindness, the will to self-restraint and sharing. (Macy 1991: 219–220)

Here we glimpse the outlines of an ethics of Engaged Buddhism that is sufficient to account for the elements we have observed in principle and practice above. These are the grounding of spiritual and social transformation in substructures and superstructures of organization—symbolized by the organic roots and branches of a tree, but worked out in theoretical detail in the systems cybernetic analysis of Macy's text—and an account of the cultivation of virtues such as loving-kindness, self-restraint, and sharing that subjects these structures to the impermanence and relativity that lie at the heart of Buddhist ontology and the modern scientific paradigm. Similar formulations may readily be found in John Dewey's writings (McDermott 1981).

Insofar as some of the ethical implications of Dewey's philosophy and general systems theory have been discovered and applied in an introductory way by respected Buddhist thinkers in Asia and the West, it remains for scholars to subject these offerings to further consideration and critique. While such a project is worthwhile in and of itself as an exercise in constructive moral philosophy, we may also hope that such ruminations will be of value to those who practise Engaged Buddhism in the challenging times ahead.

Works Cited

Aronson, H. B. (1980) Motivations to social action in Theravada Buddhism: uses and misuses of traditional doctrines. In: A. K. Narain (ed.), *Studies in history of Buddhism*. Delhi: B. R. Publishing, 1–13.

Batchelor, S. (1983) *Alone with others: an existential approach to Buddhism*. New York: Grove Press.

Batchelor, S. (1994) *The awakening of the west: the encounter of Buddhism and western culture*. Berkeley: Parallax Press.

Batchelor, S. (1997) *Buddhism without beliefs: a contemporary guide to awakening*. New York: Riverhead.

Batchelor, S. (2015) *After Buddhism: rethinking the dharma for a secular age*. New Haven: Yale University Press.

Bodhi, Bhikkhu (2007) A challenge to Buddhists. *Lion's Roar* [formerly *Buddhadharma: The Practitioner's Quarterly*]. Available from: http://www.lionsroar.com/a-challenge-to-buddhists/> [Accessed 4 September 2016].

Booth, R. (2014) Mindfulness therapy comes at a high price for some, say experts. Available from: https://www.theguardian.com/society/2014/aug/25/mental-health-meditation [Accessed 6 November 2016].

Brown, C. G. (2015) Mindfulness meditation in public schools: side-stepping Supreme Court religion rulings. Available from http://www.huffingtonpost.com/candy-gunther-brown-phd/mindfulness-meditation-in_b_6276968.html [Accessed 6 November 2016].

Buddhist Global Relief (2016) Guideposts, core beliefs. Available from: https://buddhistglobal-relief.org/active/guideposts.html [Accessed 5 November 2016].

Carrette, J., and King, R. (2005) *Selling spirituality: the silent takeover of religion*. London: Routledge.

Chappell, D. W. (1996) Searching for a Mahayana social ethic. *Journal of religious ethics*, 24 (2), 351–375.

Clayton, B. R. (2009) Śāntideva, virtue, and consequentialism. In: J. Powers and C. Prebish (eds), *Destroying Mara forever: Buddhist ethics essays in honor of Damien Keown*. Ithaca, NY: Snow Lion, 15–30.

Dewey, J. (1934) *A common faith*. New Haven: Yale University Press.

Dewey, J. (1944) *Democracy and education*. New York: Macmillan.

Glock, C. Y., and Hammond, P. E. (eds) (1973) *Beyond the classics? essays in the scientific study of religion*. New York: Harper and Row.

Goffman, E. (1961) *Asylums: essays on the social situation of mental patients and other inmates*. New York: Anchor Books.

Harvey, P. (2000) *An introduction to Buddhist ethics*. Cambridge: Cambridge University Press.

Jenkins, S. (2003) Do bodhisattvas relieve poverty? In C. Queen, C. Prebish, and D. Keown (eds), *Action dharma: new studies in engaged Buddhism*. London: RoutledgeCurzon, 38–49.

Keown, D. (2001) *The nature of Buddhist ethics*. New York: Palgrave.

King, S. B. (2009) Elements of engaged Buddhist ethical theory. In: J. Powers and C. Prebish (eds), *Destroying Mara forever: Buddhist ethics essays in honor of Damien Keown*. Ithaca, NY: Snow Lion, 187–206.

Kleinman, A., Das, V., and Lock, M. (eds) (1996) *Social suffering*. Berkeley: University of California Press.

Macy, J. (1991) *Mutual causality in Buddhism and general systems theory*. Albany: State University of New York Press.

McDermott, J. J. (ed.) (1981) *The philosophy of John Dewey*. Chicago: University of Chicago Press.

McMahon, D. L. (2008) *The making of Buddhist modernism*. Oxford: Oxford University Press.

Metta Forest Monastery (2016) Welcome. Available from: http://www.watmetta.org/about.html [Accessed 3 September 2016].

Mindful Schools (2016) Mindful schools homepage. Available from: http://www.mindfulschools.org [Accessed 6 November 2016].

Nanda, M. (2002) *Breaking the spell of dharma and other essays.* New Delhi: Three Essays Press.

Pickert, K. (2014) The art of being mindful. *Time magazine*, 183 (4).

Purser, R. (2014) The militarization of mindfulness. Available from: http://www.inquiringmind.com/Articles/MilitarizationOfMindfulness.html [Accessed 6 November 2016].

Purser, R., and Loy, D. (2013) Beyond McMindfulness. Available from: http://www.huffingtonpost.com/ron-purser/beyond-mcmindfulness_b_3519289.htm [Accessed 6 November 2016].

Queen, C. S. (1986) *Systems theory in religious studies: a methodological critique.* PhD diss., Boston University.

Queen, C. S. (ed.) (2000) *Engaged Buddhism in the west.* Boston: Wisdom.

Queen, C. S. (2004) Ambedkar's dhamma: source and method in the construction of Engaged Buddhism. In S. Jondhale and J. Beltz (eds), *Reconstructing the world: B. R. Ambedkar and Buddhism in India.* New Delhi: Oxford University Press, 132–150.

Queen, C. S. (2015) A pedagogy of the dhamma: B. R. Ambedkar and John Dewey on education. *International journal of Buddhist thought and culture*, 24, 7–21.

Queen, C. S., and King, Sallie B. (eds) (1996) *Engaged Buddhism: Buddhist liberation movements in Asia.* Albany: State University of New York Press.

Queen, C. S., Prebish, C., and Keown, D. (eds) (2003) *Action dharma: new studies in engaged Buddhism.* London: RoutledgeCurzon.

Robinson, R. H., et al. (1997) *The Buddhist religion: a historical introduction.* Fourth edition. Belmont, CA: Wadsworth.

Rocha, T. (2014) The dark knight of the soul. Available from: http://www.theatlantic.com/health/archive/2014/06/the-dark-knight-of-the-souls/372766/ [Accessed 6 November 2016].

Search Inside Yourself Leadership Institute (2016) Available from: https://siyli.org/ [Accessed 6 November 2016].

Sharf, R. (2014) Mindfulness and mindlessness. *Philosophy east & west*, 64 (4), 952–953.

Silverman, S. (2011) What sort of Buddhist was Steve Jobs, really? Available from: http://blogs.plos.org/neurotribes/2015/10/26/what-kind-of-buddhist-was-steve-jobs-really [Accessed 6 November 2016].

Straud, S. R. (2016) Pragmatism and the pursuit of social justice in India: Bhimrao Ambedkar and the rhetoric of religious reorientation. *Rhetoric society quarterly*, 46 (1), 5–27.

Titmuss, C. (2014) Are Buddhist mindfulness practices used to support international war crimes? Available from: http://christophertitmussblog.org/are-buddhist-mindfulness-practices-used-to-support-international-war-crimes [Accessed 6 November 2016].

Tricycle (2013) The Buddhist geek: an interview with digital innovator Vincent Horn. Available from: http://tricycle.org/magazine/buddhist-geek/ [Accessed 6 November 2016].

Wisdom 2.0 (2016) Wisdom 2.0 homepage. Available from: http://www.wisdom2summit.com/ [Accessed 6 November 2016].

Wulf, A. (2015) *The invention of nature: Alexander von Humboldt's new world.* New York: Knopf.

Wylie, M. S. (2015) How the mindfulness movement went mainstream—and the backlash that came with it. Available from http://www.alternet.org/personal-health/how-mindfulness-movement-went-mainstream-and-backlash-came-it [Accessed 6 November 2016].

Suggested Reading

Batchelor, S. (2015) *After Buddhism: rethinking the dharma for a secular age*. New Haven: Yale University Press.

Bellah, R. (1970) The sociology of religion. In: *Beyond belief: essays on religion in a post-traditional world*. New York: Harper and Row, 3–19.

Macy, J. (1991) *Mutual causality in Buddhism and general systems theory*. Albany: State University of New York Press.

McDermott, J. J. (ed.) (1981) *The philosophy of John Dewey*. Chicago: University of Chicago Press.

McMahon, D. L. (2008) *The making of Buddhist modernism*. Oxford: Oxford University Press.

Queen, C. S. (ed.) (2000) Introduction: the shapes and sources of engaged Buddhism. In: *Engaged Buddhism in the west*. Boston: Wisdom, 1–44.

Queen, C. S. (2004) Ambedkar's dhamma: source and method in the construction of Engaged Buddhism. In S. Jondhale and J. Beltz (eds), *Reconstructing the world: B. R. Ambedkar and Buddhism in India*. New Delhi: Oxford University Press, 132–150.

PART V

CONTEMPORARY ISSUES

CHAPTER 25

HUMAN RIGHTS

DAMIEN KEOWN

INTRODUCTION

THE importance of human rights for Buddhism is evident from the attention the subject has received in recent decades. Leading Buddhists from many Asian countries, such as the Dalai Lama (Tibet), Aung San Suu Kyi (Myanmar), A. T. Ariyaratne (Sri Lanka), Maha Ghosananda (Cambodia), and Sulak Sivaraksa (Thailand), have expressed their concerns about social and political issues on numerous occasions using the language of human rights. Institutions have been established by Buddhists to defend and promote human rights. These include the Cambodian Institute of Human Rights, the Tibetan Centre for Human Rights and Democracy, and the Thai National Human Rights Commission. Several Asian countries with large Buddhist populations (Thailand, Myanmar, Lao, Cambodia, and Vietnam) are also members of the ASEAN Intergovernmental Commission on Human Rights (AICHR) founded in 2009.

The human rights record of Buddhism itself, however, is not unblemished. Human rights abuses were recorded on both sides in the Sri Lankan civil war, and although hostilities ceased in 2009, harassment, intimidation, torture, exploitation, and violence by Buddhists have continued, including attacks on Muslim and Christian minorities (Statement 2015). In Myanmar, Buddhist factions have mounted pogroms against Rohingya Muslims in Rakhine State (Suu Kyi has defended her failure to condemn such atrocities by claiming she is now a 'politician' rather than a human rights campaigner). In Japan and China, Buddhism has colluded with state institutions of repression and control (Shiotsu and Gebert 1999; Schmidt-Glintzer 2010: 123). One of the most prominent Buddhist campaigners for human rights, the current Dalai Lama, has himself been charged with denying religious freedom in the so-called 'Shugden controversy' (Mills 2003). Buddhism has also been accused of failing to protect the rights of women (Tsedroen 2010: 209; Satha-Anand 1999).

Documenting the Buddhist record on human rights, however, is not our main concern. Our focus instead will be on the concept of human rights and its relation to

Buddhist doctrine and ethics. Discussions of this kind often begin by describing a paradox, which Christopher Gowans formulates in the following terms: 'It is widely acknowledged that human rights were not explicitly recognized or endorsed in traditional Buddhist texts. ... And yet human rights are endorsed and advocated by most (although not all) engaged Buddhists today' (2015: 245). Taking this paradox as our starting point, our task is to survey the intellectual bridgework that must be put in place if human rights are to be given an authentic grounding in Buddhist doctrine. An important first step is to ask if the concept of 'rights' is intelligible in Buddhism, and, if so, whether appeals to human rights are consistent with Buddhist values. This will occupy us in the first part of the chapter. The second part will review possible foundations for human rights in Buddhist teachings.

Rights, Human Rights, and Buddhist Ethics

The intellectual history of human rights is complex, and cannot be explored here in any depth (see Ishay 2008; Donnelly 2013). We may simply note that the immediate antecedents of today's human rights were spoken of as 'natural' rights, in other words, rights that flow from human nature. From the seventeenth century onwards, philosophers and statesmen began to define these rights and enshrine them in constitutions, declarations, charters, and manifestos in a tradition that has continued into modern times. The most well known modern charter of human rights is The Universal Declaration of Human Rights (UDHR) proclaimed by the General Assembly of the United Nations in December 1948. Human rights thinking has continued to evolve since the publication of this document, and further covenants and declarations have followed. Two in particular are important, namely the International Covenant on Economic, Social, and Cultural Rights, and the International Covenant on Civil and Political Rights. Both were approved by the United Nations in 1966 and came into force a decade later. These three documents are often referred to collectively as the International Bill of Human Rights. Subsequent instruments have been enacted to address specific problems such as discrimination (for example, on grounds of race and gender) and to uphold the rights of particular groups (such as children, migrant workers, the disabled, and indigenous peoples). These various 'generations' of human rights initiatives (Montgomery 1986: 69f.) collectively secure a broad range of rights and freedoms, which while difficult to classify neatly may be thought of as falling into five main areas (Glendon 2001: 174): (1) rights of the person (e.g. life, liberty, and freedom of religion); (2) rights before the law (e.g. equality before the law and the right to a fair trial); (3) political rights (e.g. freedom of assembly and the right to vote); (4) economic and social rights (e.g. social security and employment rights); and (5) the rights of communities and groups (e.g. protection against genocide, and the rights of children). The Human Rights Council, a forty-seven-member body inaugurated in 2006 with its headquarters in Geneva, is charged, under the supervision of the UN High Commissioner for Human Rights, with reviewing the compliance of member states with their human rights obligations.

The nature, scope, and foundations of the rights just described are contested, but the main philosophical approaches may be identified briefly. *Naturalists* hold that human rights are an expansion of the 'natural rights' referred to earlier, and are said to be enjoyed by human beings 'as such' or 'simply in view of their humanity'. Naturalists identify 'objective foundations for human rights in morality and reason' (Freeman 1994: 512). On one version of this view, that of the premodern natural law tradition, rights are seen as rationally required for the promotion of the 'common good' (the flourishing of individuals and their communities). Naturalist conceptions have been termed *foundationalist* (Rorty 2010) since, as noted, they understand human rights as the expression of an underlying and independent order of moral values, in some sense innate in human nature. *Anti-foundationalists* by contrast, although supporting human rights, deny that any theoretical foundation for them exists. Instead, they seek to justify respect for human rights on a contextual basis emphasizing 'contingency, construction, and relativity' (Freeman 1994: 511) and attach particular importance to the role of the sentiments. *Sceptics*, for their part, attack belief in human rights in various ways. Some dismiss them as mere fictions like 'witches' and 'unicorns' (MacIntyre 1981: 69), while others claim they are vacuous on the grounds there is no agency or mechanism directly responsible for their enforcement. Sceptics who are *relativists* deny that human rights can be universal given the empirical diversity of cultures and moral values. Perhaps understandably in the face of these conflicting opinions, *agreement conceptions* of human rights have become popular. Here, diversity is acknowledged and philosophical differences bracketed in order to reach agreement on 'a set of important overlapping moral expectations to which different cultures hold themselves and others accountable' (Twiss 1998: 31). We shall meet examples of some of these positions in the second part of this chapter, but for now we consider what attitude Buddhism should adopt in general towards human rights and the institutions which seek to promote them as international norms. Some counsel caution, and raise objections of two kinds—cultural and conceptual—to Buddhism becoming too closely associated with the human rights movement.

Cultural Objections

An initial objection concerns the alien cultural and historical origins of both rights and human rights. It cannot be denied, as Peter Junger notes, that the label of 'human rights' is 'a product of the traditions of Western Europe and the parochial histories of that region' (1998: 56). As Sobisch and Brox observe, much scepticism towards documents such as the UDHR 'stems from the assumption that universalism equals imperialism, in the sense that societies are forced to conform to ethnocentric ideas, disregarding or even denying cultural differences' (Sobisch and Brox 2010: 161). In the 1990s, the political leaders of a number of Asian states (notably Malaysia, Indonesia, and Singapore, with strong backing from China) began to criticize the idea of human rights on grounds of its Western intellectual genealogy (Langlois 2001). According to them talk of human rights promotes individualism in contrast to 'Asian values' which are said to be more community-oriented (Narayan 1993). It was also claimed that human rights are a luxury that less developed countries cannot afford, and that economic development should remain the priority. In some cases, it was hard not to see this 'cultural critique' (Amartya Sen's term) as a smokescreen to conceal the poor human rights record of certain Asian and Middle Eastern countries. Sen has challenged the view that there is anything specifically 'Asian' about such values (1997), and the Dalai Lama has also repudiated the view that human rights 'cannot be applied to Asia and other parts of the Third World because of differences in culture and differences in social and economic development' (Keown et al. 1998: xviii).

As human rights evolved in the final decades of the twentieth century, cultural pluralism has been increasingly recognized and incorporated into transnational human rights thinking. Clapham notes how human rights have been claimed 'in the contexts of anti-colonialism, anti-imperialism, anti-slavery, anti-apartheid, anti-racism, and feminist and indigenous struggles everywhere', observing that in many cases 'the chanting on the ground' did not 'sing to the West's tune' (2007: 19). Sobisch and Brox point out that 'the globalization of a discourse on human rights does not simply equal Westernization' because 'traveling ideas like human rights are not unequivocally constructed, translated and manifested: there is always room for interpretation' (2010: 161). Simon Caney (2001) offers Theravāda Buddhism as an example of how non-Western ethical traditions can embrace human rights, while Harding comments with respect to Thailand, 'I see no reason to deny the validity of attempts by the state to explain human rights in Buddhist terms' (2007: 20). As Schmidt-Leukel points out, however, there remains the question of the appropriate balance between 'Asian values' and 'Western Liberalism' (2010: 59). Too much emphasis on collectivism can stunt the development of individuality, whereas a one-sided stress on individual rights may fail to nurture a sense of community and social responsibility. Clearly, a 'middle way' is desirable.

Conceptual Objections

In modern times the vocabulary of rights has become the *lingua franca* of political and ethical discourse. In contrast to the ubiquitous references to rights in today's globalized world, however, there appears to be no term in any canonical Buddhist language that conveys the idea of a right understood as a subjective entitlement. Masao Abe writes 'the exact equivalent of the phrase "human rights" in the Western sense cannot be found anywhere in Buddhist literature' (quoted in Trauer 1995: 9 n. 11). The absence of a specific reference to rights need not mean, however, that Buddhism opposes the idea. Sometimes the same conceptual ground can be covered semantically in different ways, for example by using a locution like 'ought' or 'due' to express what is owed between parties. Alan Gewirth has argued that 'persons might have and use the concept of a right without explicitly having a single word for it' (quoted in Dagger 1989: 286). Andrew Clapham suggests that 'Religious texts like the Bible and the Koran can be read as creating not only duties but rights', and believes that concerns with regard to 'self-fulfilment, respect for others, and the quest to contribute to others' well-being are evident in Confucian, Hindu and Buddhist traditions' (2007: 5).

It seems clear, at least, that Buddhism acknowledges the existence of reciprocal *duties*. With respect to social justice the Rev. Vajiragnana comments:

> Each one of us has a role to play in sustaining and promoting social justice and orderliness. The Buddha explained very clearly these roles as reciprocal duties existing between parents and children; teachers and pupils; husband and wife; friends, relatives and neighbors; employer and employee; clergy and laity. ... No one has been left out. The duties explained here are reciprocal and are considered as sacred duties, for—if observed—they can create a just, peaceful and harmonious society. (1992)

The author apparently has in mind here the *Sigalovāda Sutta* (DN 31) in which the Buddha describes a set of six reciprocal duties. It does not seem unreasonable when analysing these relationships from the beneficiary's perspective to employ the vocabulary of rights. Thus parents have duties to their children, and children have a right to support, nurture, education, and protection from their parents. On this basis the distinction between rights and duties amounts to little more than a heuristic shift of perspective. As Hesanmi notes, 'Rather than erecting a false dichotomy between "rights" and "duty" what seems more reasonable is to affirm their correlativeness and mutual entailment' (2008: 504). Paul Lauren recalls Gandhi's observation that 'The true source of rights is duty', adding that 'ideas about human duties, or what one is due to do, led quite naturally to ideas about human rights, or what is due to one' (2011: 11). On this basis it does not seem unreasonable to suggest that despite the limitations of the classical Buddhist lexicon rights can be accommodated in Buddhist teachings.

Not everyone, however, agrees with this conclusion. Craig Ihara gives the example of a ballet performance, and concludes it would be 'bizarre' to describe a poor or faulty performance by any of the dancers as a violation of another dancer's rights. This is because the individuals are 'participants in a larger project, and what they ought to do is not a function of, nor properly analyzed into, what is owed to others' (1998: 45). The same, he suggests, may apply in Buddhism: thus 'I maintain that the notion of Dharma may be a part of a vision of society in which human life is ideally a kind of dance with well-defined role-responsibilities' (1998: 47). This means that 'If... Dharma is the same kind of cooperative enterprise ... then it is impossible for rights to be introduced without changing Buddhist ethics in a very fundamental way' (1998: 49).

Ihara does not specify what model of a Dharmic society he has in mind, and the vision of human life as a dance sounds utopian. The best model we have of a Dharmic society would seem to be the *saṅgha*, so perhaps we can take the *saṅgha* as an example to illustrate how collaborative performances can coexist along with rights and duties in the same 'cooperative enterprise'. If a member of the *saṅgha* (say, monk A) refuses to wear the regulation robes, it would be indeed be unusual for monk B to claim that his rights had been infringed. However, this does not mean monk A does not have a duty to wear the right robes: it means only that his duty is not specifically to monk B. His duty is to the *saṅgha*, and it is perfectly reasonable to analyse monk A's obligation as a duty 'owed to others'. A breach of this duty is an injustice to the *saṅgha*. The *saṅgha*, in turn, has a right to expect monk A to dress in accordance with *Vinaya* regulations, since this is a condition of ordination. The *saṅgha* has the further right to impose disciplinary sanctions for ecclesiastical offences and even expel monks from the order, actions that cannot easily be characterized as 'cooperative activities' (Ihara 1998: 49). The *Vinaya*, in fact, devotes considerable time to defining rules of 'due process' for the settlement of disputes (*adhikaraṇa-samatha*) so as to protect the rights of all parties involved. We may note further that reciprocal duties exist between individual monks, for example between novices and preceptors. As Thānissaro notes, 'The *Mahāvagga* (I.25.6; 32.1) states that a pupil should regard his mentor as a father; and the mentor, the pupil as his son. It then goes on to delineate this relationship as a set of reciprocal duties' (2013 vol. 1: 36). Thus while members of the *saṅgha* certainly have performative group roles (like communal chanting of the *Pāṭimokkha*), they have in addition both: (1) general duties to the *saṅgha* (which correlate with rights possessed by the *saṅgha*); and (2) specific duties to individual colleagues (who possess corresponding correlative rights). It would seem, then, that the vocabulary of rights can be intelligibly employed in the paradigm case of a Buddhist 'cooperative enterprise' (the *saṅgha*) without 'changing Buddhist ethics' in any fundamental way.

The philosophical and jurisprudential dimensions of rights are complex (see, for example, Hohfeld 1964), and no pretence is made to have offered a comprehensive analysis here. The objective has been more limited, namely to show that a conceptual space for rights can plausibly be located in Buddhist teachings. This is necessary in order to avoid premature foreclosure of the discussion on the grounds that Buddhism cannot meaningfully participate in contemporary human rights discourse other, perhaps, than in some derivative way by regarding rights as a 'skilful means'. Even if a conceptual foundation exists, however, it does not follow that the adoption and promotion of the concept of rights is innately desirable. Indeed, in the view of some commentators, the very idea of rights is in conflict both with Buddhism's metaphysics and its soteriology.

Metaphysics

The concern here arises in relation to the doctrine of 'no-self' (*anātman*). If there is ultimately no self, the argument goes, then who or what is the bearer of the rights in question? Christopher Kelley describes this as 'the paradox of the inherent dignity of empty persons' (2015: 3). Human rights naturalists, as we saw earlier, seek to ground human dignity in some notion of an *a priori* human nature, but Kelley suggests such notions presuppose belief in inherent existence and hence are 'essentially incompatible with the most fundamental idea in Buddhism—the theory of no-self' (2015: 13). Sallie

King suggests that to invoke the teaching of no-self in this connection is a 'red herring' (2005: 128), pointing out quite correctly that Buddhist ethics functions perfectly well in many contexts without assuming the existence of a permanent self. The doctrine of no-self (*anātman*) only denies the existence of a *transcendental* self (*ātman*), not of a phenomenal, empirical self. It does not deny the existence of human individuals with unique self-shaped identities, and if such identities provide an ontological foundation stable enough for the attribution of duties, as the Buddha clearly believed, presumably they also do for rights.

As Lauren Leve points out in the context of Buddhism in Nepal, the doctrine of no-self does not seem to inhibit Buddhists who claim the *protection* of human rights. She notes 'when Buddhists insist that national Hinduism violates their human rights to religious equality, they represent themselves as particular types of persons and political subjects' (2007: 98). She mentions the example of a senior Theravāda meditation teacher, noting that 'neither he nor his many students seemed to have any problem combining an anti-essentialist understanding of the self with the call for secular human rights and its implied identity' (2007: 105). Buddhist nationalists in countries like Sri Lanka, Myanmar, and Tibet, furthermore, rely on an ethnicized Buddhist religious identity as the basis of their political demands. It would thus appear that many Buddhists do not see the no-self doctrine as incompatible with ontologies of agency and identity. We will return to this topic in the second part of the chapter when we consider specific anti-foundationalist proposals.

Soteriology

The soteriological objection claims that the individualism implicit in rights is detrimental to both spiritual progress and social stability because it strengthens the ego and encourages selfish attitudes. Payutto observes that Western notions of rights involve 'competition, mistrust and fear'. Human rights, he notes, 'must be obtained through demand' (quoted in Seeger 2010: 82f.). Saneh Chamarik, echoing Payutto's concerns, states 'what really obstructs the attainment of freedom is not so much the social and conventional "chains" or restrictions, as one's own ego and the three poisons: lust, hatred, and delusion' (quoted in Seeger 2010: 91). In response, it might be pointed out that injustice, repression, and discrimination also give rise to negative states of mind, and that by enabling recourse to justice, human rights provide a way of dispelling these mental defilements and removing the conditions that give rise to them.

Some critics suggest that the threat to society posed by the clamour for individual rights must be opposed through strong social control. The Thai Buddhist reformer Bhikkhu Buddhadāsa expressed the view that the individual must be firmly subordinated to the state and called for 'A Dictatorial Dhammic Socialism' in an article of the same title (1989). As Schmidt-Leukel notes, it is hard not to see the influence of Asian communism (perhaps linked to the notion of the authoritarian Dhammarāja) in the background to views of this kind (2010: 61). Fears that rights inevitably lead to social instability seem exaggerated, although it must be admitted that demands for increased rights may provoke an adversarial reaction from vested interests. Specific fears also attach to the ownership of property, a right enshrined in Article 17 of the UDHR. Some see this as authorizing consumerism and the selfish accumulation of wealth. Against this, there is nothing in Buddhist teachings to prohibit the ownership of property (the precept against stealing seems to presuppose it), and the *saṅgha* has traditionally depended on the generosity of lay patrons for its existence. Views expressed by the Dalai Lama form a striking contrast to those of Buddhadāsa. He has stated: 'It is natural and just for nations, peoples, and individuals to demand respect for their rights and freedoms and to struggle to end repression, racism, economic exploitation, military occupation, and various forms of colonialism and alien domination' (quoted in King 2005: 156).

While it is true that rights are sometimes claimed for selfish reasons, they can also protect common interests. The right to freedom of association (UDHR Article 20.i), for example, is hardly individualistic, and as King points out, when the Dalai Lama calls for respect for human rights, such as freedom of religion, he often does so in the name of the people of Tibet (2005: 136). Collective rights are also claimed by communities themselves. In 2005, villagers in Myanmar relied on human rights conventions against enforced slavery to win a settlement against the Unocal company. The settlement was used in part to develop programmes to improve living conditions and provide health care and education for the affected communities (Clapham 2007: 27f.; cf. Goodale and Merry 2007). Later generations of human rights, such as those proclaimed in The Declaration on the Rights of Indigenous Peoples, are by nature difficult to classify as 'individualistic'.

Contrasting with the critiques considered so far are more affirmative approaches of the kind to be considered in the rest of this chapter. The more ambitious of these claim that human rights doctrines are completely foreshadowed in Buddhist teachings, while others emphasize particular doctrines as possible bridgeheads between the *Dharma* and human rights.

Buddhist Foundations for Human Rights

The various human rights declarations rarely offer a detailed justification for the rights they proclaim. This leaves scope, as Sumner Twiss has observed, for a range of theoretical underpinnings (1998). Charles Taylor (1999) has spoken of an 'unforced consensus' on human rights, suggesting there are different paths to human rights norms, and others have made reference to 'structural equivalents' or 'multiple foundations' which allow consensus to be reached in the face of pluralist cultural and philosophical perspectives (Donnelly 2013). Drawing on the Thai experience, Andrew Harding endorses this approach, observing that in a 'postmodern, multi-culturalist world of international human rights', '*we do better to try to agree on the content of human rights rather than on the justification for their observance*' (2007: 21: original emphasis). The UDHR was an agreement of this kind, and sought to express common aspirations through the medium of Enlightenment values without at the same time professing theological or philosophical unanimity. As Jacques Maritain famously reported, it was an agreement about rights '*on condition that no-one asks us why*' (quoted in Beitz 2009: 21: original emphasis). In this sense declarations like the UDHR, given their wide and ambitious scope, can be seen as political manifestos or gestures of social responsibility on the part of world governments. The 'manifesto rights' (Feinberg 1973: 67) they proclaim, accordingly, express desiderata but do not create legal entitlements. Understood in this way, the objections mentioned previously to Buddhism endorsing 'rights' lose much of their force: the question becomes simply whether Buddhism can in good conscience sign up to the terms of the proposed manifesto.

The main attraction of agreement conceptions is that they acknowledge moral diversity and avoid the charge of paternalism. The main drawback is that they give up any claim to ground human rights in universal moral values (Beitz 2009: ch. 4; Schaefer 2005: 48–50). A problem here is that a consensus that circumvents deep philosophical differences may be superficial, and any agreement that can command universal assent is likely to be 'minimalist' and 'thin' (Ignatieff 2003: 56). As James Nickel notes, it is doubtful whether 'there is sufficient agreement worldwide to support anything like the full range of rights declared in contemporary manifestos' (quoted in Freeman 1994: 493). Some Buddhists, moreover, may find it difficult to participate in a consensus that simply specifies rights as axioms (as opposed to conclusions from moral premises) without compromising traditional beliefs. They may point out, for example, that when the mythical universal ruler (Cakkavatti) spreads the *Dharma* to the four quarters of the globe he does so not by first negotiating with local rulers as to which aspects of the *Dharma* are acceptable and compromising on those that are not. Rather, the local rulers accept the *Dharma* in its entirety because they recognize its validity as a universal norm (DN. iii.62). A consensus reached by compromising on basic principles may be difficult to reconcile with the traditional view that the values embodied in *Dharma* are universal and eternal in an objective sense.

The *Dharma* and Human Rights

One commentator finds the UDHR, at least, in harmony with early Buddhist teachings both in letter and in spirit. L. N. Perera, a Sri Lankan scholar, has helpfully provided a commentary on each of the thirty articles of the UDHR, aiming to demonstrate as much (on the human rights said to be derivable from Japanese Buddhist teachings, see Peek 1995). In his Foreword to the commentary Ananda Gurugé writes:

> Professor Perera demonstrates that every single Article of the Universal Declaration of Human Rights—even the labour rights to fair wages, leisure and welfare—has

> been adumbrated, cogently upheld and meaningfully incorporated in an overall view of life and society by the Buddha. (Perera 1991: xi)

Perera makes three suggestions as to possible foundations for human rights. The first is the 'fundamental consideration that all life has a desire to safeguard itself and to make itself comfortable and happy' (1991: 29). Basing rights on supposedly universal facts about human nature, however, raises difficult questions of philosophical anthropology, and the empirical evidence often yields inconvenient counterexamples (such as self-destructive individuals who seem to care little about their fate). The goal of being 'comfortable and happy' is also too vague to serve as a moral criterion: human traffickers may aspire to be 'comfortable and happy' by systematically abusing human rights. Finally, desire seems a questionable foundation for rights given its generally negative portrayal in Buddhist teachings. Perera's second suggestion makes a connection to human dignity. He writes: 'Buddhism posits, as Jean-Jacques Rousseau did much later, that the essence of human dignity lies in the assumption of man's responsibility for his own governance' (1991: 28). Again, it is unlikely that Buddhism would wish to link human dignity quite so closely to politics. While political institutions may well be created through the exercise of distinctively human capacities, it is unlikely that Buddhism would locate 'the essence of human dignity' in their creation. According to the *Aggañña Sutta* (DN 27), the evolution of political societies is the consequence of depravity and decline, which makes them a dubious testament to human dignity.

As his final suggestion, in his commentary on Article 1.52 of the UDHR ('All human beings are born free and equal in dignity and rights'), Perera identifies a more promising foundation for human rights. In discussing the first sentence of the article he comments that 'Buddhahood itself is within the reach of all human beings ... and if all could attain Buddhahood what greater equality in dignity and rights can there be?' He expands on this in a remark towards the end of his commentary on Article 1:

> It is from the point of view of its goal that Buddhism evaluates all action. Hence Buddhist thought is in accord with this and other Articles in the Universal Declaration of Human Rights to the extent to which they facilitate the advancement of human beings toward the Buddhist goal. (1991: 24)

The connection made here between Buddhahood, human dignity, and human rights, is also affirmed by others, as we shall now see.

Buddhist Precepts

Several commentators, including the present author (Keown 1998b), have suggested that the Buddhist precepts, especially those which prohibit causing harm to others, provide a connection to human rights on the basis of the reciprocal understanding of rights and duties discussed previously. Thus when the precepts are broken, someone's rights are infringed. Somparn Promta (1994) has argued that the Five Precepts protect human rights, and as such the First Precept can be seen as an expression of the right to life (or more specifically the right not to be killed). In the same way Micheline Ishay notes, 'With the exception of adultery, the gist of these injunctions is reflected in the very first clauses of the Universal Declaration of Human Rights, which praise the spirit of brotherhood and the right to life, liberty, and the security of one's person' (2008: 30). Sallie King reports that senior Cambodian monks have expressed the view that human rights are 'the same as *sel pram* [the Five Lay Precepts]' (King, 2005: 139). King herself has observed how:

> the precepts imply that that society will be Good in which its members do not harm each other, steal from each other, lie to each other, etc. This in turn implies that a member of a Good society should have a reasonable expectation not to be harmed, stolen from, etc. Now one may or may not want to call such a thing a 'right', but it is certainly closing in on that ground in a practical sense, if not in the full conceptual sense. (2005: 144)

Most societies have rules protecting human life, prohibiting theft and lying, and governing sexual relationships (Michael Walzer characterizes such negative duties as the 'moral minimum' [1994: 9f.]). It should come as no surprise, therefore, that Buddhist precepts coincide with the core concerns of human rights charters. Sevilla raises a familiar problem here (also discussed by Evans 2012: 530ff.) concerning the motivation for keeping the precepts: if it is to accumulate good karma, does this not amount to egoism rather than a concern for the rights of others? If so, he asks rhetorically, 'why must I respect another's rights for his or her sake?' (2010: 223). His answer is that the rights of others must be respected because compassion requires it, but this answer only pushes the problem back, for a person may also have egotistical motives for performing compassionate acts. An alternative response is to point out that in respecting the precepts one promotes the good of both self and others and thus acts for the benefit of society at large, which seems to coincide more closely with the goal of human rights. In fact, Sevilla provides an answer of a similar kind when he writes, 'we must participate in the realization of the Buddha-nature possessed not only by ourselves but shared with others, by upholding the rights of others' (2010: 249). On this basis the justification for keeping the precepts is deontological, and grounded in respect for the common good (for parallels between Buddhism and Kant on human rights see Likhitpreechakul 2013).

Dependent Origination

Kenneth Inada has proposed a specific foundation for human rights in Buddhist metaphysics. In a discussion entitled 'The Buddhist Perspective on Human Rights', Inada suggests 'there is an intimate and vital relationship of the Buddhist norm or Dhamma with that of human rights' (1982). He explains: 'The reason for assigning human nature the basic position is very simple. It is to give human relations a firm grounding in the truly existential nature of things: that is, the concrete and dynamic relational nature of persons in contact with each other' (1982: 70). Here Inada seems to suggest it is specifically in the *interrelatedness* of persons that the justification for human rights is to be found. This is confirmed when he observes, 'Consequently, the Buddhist concern is focused on the experiential process of each individual, a process technically known as relational origination (*paṭicca-samuppāda*).' 'It is on this basis', he adds, 'that we can speak of the rights of individuals' (1982: 70f.).

The assumption is often made that interdependency provides a ground for moral respect on the basis that once we understand the nature of our deep dependence on others, moral feelings will spontaneously arise. Demonstrations of this in Buddhist literature often seem persuasive because they cite examples of parents, relatives, friends, teachers, and loved ones who have shown kindness to us. But does the affection and respect we feel for such people arise solely because we share a metaphysical relationship with them? Perhaps not, since people do not feel the same way about every aspect of what Inada calls the 'mutually constituted existential realm' we inhabit. Children who are trafficked have an interdependent relationship with their traffickers, but the well-being of children in such situations depends on *severing* the interdependent relationship in question. Sevilla is therefore right to point out that interrelationship is important 'not on the level of ontology but on the level of soteriology. We are interrelated not merely in what we are, but in our struggle to become what we ought to be' (2010: 227; cf. Shiotsu 2001: 149–152). The bare fact of interdependency, therefore, is an unpromising basis for human rights. It seems a *moral* foundation is needed rather than a metaphysical one.

Compassion

Perhaps compassion can meet this requirement. The Buddhist virtue of compassion (*karuṇā*) encourages us to develop the human capacity for empathy to the point where we can identify fully with the suffering of others. Some texts, for example the eighth chapter of the *Bodhicāryāvatāra*, speak of 'exchanging self and other' and recommend a meditational practice in which we imaginatively place ourselves in the other's position. In the West, the view known as 'sentimentalism' has long emphasized the role of the emotions in moral judgments. From this perspective, the attribution of human rights is 'an expression of a deep human ability to recognize the other as like oneself; to experience empathy for the other's needs and sufferings; to consent to, support, and rejoice in the fulfillment of the other's human capacities and well-being' (Cahill 1999: 45). Maria Vanden Eynde (2004) has drawn on Martha Nussbaum's work to suggest that Buddhist compassion can resolve the polarization between ethical theories of care and justice, while Jay Garfield (1998) believes compassion can provide a moral grounding for the Dalai Lama's views on human rights (for an evaluation of Garfield's essay see Rice 2005). Garfield finds the influential liberal philosophy of rights unsatisfactory, and drawing on Hume's ethical theory and the work of contemporary neo-sentimentalists, proposes a form of virtue or character ethics in which 'the moral life is grounded in the cultivation and exercise of compassion' (1998: 111). On this understanding, compassion provides the moral bedrock on top of which 'an edifice of rights' is constructed 'as a device for extending the reach of natural compassion and for securing the goods that compassion enables to all persons in a society' (124). Rights thus become the 'tools with which each individual can protect him/herself and achieve his/her own flourishing'. 'These tools', Garfield adds, 'will be available even when our compassion or those [sic] of others fails, and can even be used as rhetorical vehicles to reawaken that compassion' (124).

Garfield takes aim specifically at the liberal conception of human rights that separates the public and private spheres, but there are alternative conceptions of rights where this separation does not occur. The natural law tradition provides an example (e.g. Finnis 2011; Oderberg 2013). On this understanding there is no need for the two-tier solution Garfield proposes (an edifice of rights resting on a foundation of compassion) since the moral virtues (of which compassion is one) are integral to the generic human goods that rights protect. A more practical problem with making compassion the foundation for rights is that feelings are rarely impartial and can often change. While buddhas and great bodhisattvas may feel equal compassion at all times for all sentient beings, most ordinary mortals do not and never will. Garfield believes that human rights will be available even in the event of 'compassion fatigue' because the legal superstructure of rights will remain in place (1998: 126), but any weakening of the motivating foundation would surely reduce commitment to the rights founded upon it. The human rights abuses that occurred in the civil war in Sri Lanka suggest that the limits of Buddhist compassion are soon tested. Perhaps compassion can periodically be 'reawakened', but it seems to go against the grain of human rights thinking to suggest that individual A should have to awaken compassion in B in order to secure her human rights. And if compassion *cannot* be reawakened, human rights will simply evaporate, along with the unconditional protection they are supposed to provide. On this understanding human rights clearly cannot be *inalienable*, as the UDHR proclaims in its Preamble and the Dalai Lama also appears to believe.

While he offers no classification of his position, Garfield's account is anti-foundationalist with respect to rights. This can be seen from his comment that 'in no case is it either necessary or helpful to take the rights to which appeal is made as constituting moral bedrock' (1998: 126). Instead, it is compassion that is regarded as 'foundational' and 'fundamental'. Perhaps, however, the relation of these elements needs to be reordered. If compassion supplies the motivation to construct an edifice of rights, and if rights function to secure the goods that constitute human flourishing, it would seem to be *human flourishing* that ultimately grounds them both. Rather than seeing rights as flowing from compassion, accordingly, it may be more accurate to see compassion as the affective *response* of a virtuous person to the perception that the condition of beings falls short of what their dignity requires. Thus compassion may be thought of as having a cognitive structure incorporating eudaimonistic evaluations (Nussbaum 2001). On this understanding, in the specific context of human rights, compassion is the appropriate Buddhist response to injustice when society fails to give each his due as *Dharma* requires. (Compassion may, of course, arise in response to suffering of any kind, but human rights are centrally concerned with issues of social justice.) Rights are then the juridical measures that reason (*prajñā*) determines are necessary to redress and prospectively forestall such injustice. If Garfield's argument is reconstructed along these lines, rights cease to be foundationless and enjoy a naturalist foundation in the capacity to attain the state of peak human flourishing known as 'supreme and perfect awakening', a state in which reason and compassion play mutually supportive roles.

The 'Two Truths'

An approach in some ways related to the previous one has been developed by Christopher Kelley in what appears to be the only full-length treatment of human rights from a Buddhist perspective, and one we cannot do full justice to here. In essence, Kelley seeks to reconcile the Dalai Lama's ethics, specifically his often-voiced support for the Enlightenment concepts of inherent dignity and inalienable rights, with Madhyamaka metaphysics. The Dalai Lama has frequently spoken of a common human nature as the foundation for his humanitarian ethics, and refers to 'fundamental principles that bind us all as members of the same human family' (Keown et al. 1998: xix). As Kelley notes, he 'clearly supports a moral universalism based on our "shared humanity" ' (2015: 91). This implies foundationalism, which Kelley believes is in conflict with the anti-essentialist metaphysics of the Dalai Lama's Madhyamaka philosophy. Kelley's objective is to resolve the paradox and reach an 'unforced consensus' between these two positions by drawing on the notion of the 'two truths'. 'I contend', he writes, 'that this account of the two truths is how we can make sense of the paradox of the inherent dignity of empty persons' (2015: 30). Kelley believes this strategy allows him to interpret the Dalai Lama's position on human rights in a manner 'consistent with the postmodern rejection of innate human rights and dignity espoused by contemporary "anti-foundationalist" thinkers like Richard Rorty' (2015: 2). On this anti-foundationalist interpretation, feelings of sympathy are thought to lead to an emotional identification or 'mirroring' which gives rise to moral concern, manifesting itself as respect for other individuals and their rights. 'Such empathetic feelings', says Kelley, 'invariably lead one to behave in a [way] that is congruent with the moral principles associated with the various human rights' (2015: 141). Thus while rights are devoid of intrinsic nature they can, Kelley suggests, be said to have 'meaning and significance' in terms of a 'particular veridical framework' (2015: 30) or 'symbolic system' (2015: 36) such as that of the UNDR. The metaphysics of Dialectical Centricism (Madhymaka) are thereby seen as supporting a form of moral particularism, where in any given case 'The morally right response would have to be relative to the individual agent's unique set of circumstances' (2015: 164).

As with our earlier discussion of the compatibility of rights with the doctrine of no-self, some may wonder whether 'the inherent dignity of empty persons' involves a genuine paradox. It seems a paradox would only arise if 'inherent dignity' is understood in the sense of 'inherently existing dignity', in other words a dignity that in Madhyamaka terms possesses 'own-being' (*svabhāva*) and exists 'from its own side'. Foundationalists, however, do not (and certainly need not) claim this. They assert only that inherent dignity (and inalienable rights) exists in the way other entities in the world exist, in other words as enjoying what Kelley describes as 'conventional intrinsic existence' (2015: 33). On this basis, the Dalai Lama's moral universalism seems compatible with human rights foundationalism, which, it might be thought, provides the most intuitive interpretation of his views. It can, of course, reasonably be argued, as Kelley does, that anti-foundationalism provides a better philosophical (and psychological) account of human rights overall, and Kelley's arguments to this effect are sophisticated and worthy of study. Here it may simply be noted that providing a foundationless justification for human rights is far from unproblematic. As Freeman points out, 'if no beliefs are securely founded, anti-foundationalist beliefs themselves are not securely founded' (1994: 496), and in practical terms 'rights without reasons are vulnerable to denial and abuse' (1994: 493). It has also been argued that anti-foundationalism, as advocated by writers like Rorty and Ignatieff, itself appeals to moral foundations in a covert manner (Schaefer 2005), as well as presupposing a meta-theory along the lines of 'we should always act according to our own convictions' (Freeman 1994: 501). Finally, it is not clear how anti-foundationalism is to be reconciled with belief in karma. According to orthodox Buddhist teachings, abuses of human rights like torture and killing will inevitably attract negative karmic consequences. This is because karma, as the law of moral causation (*kamma-niyāma*), is thought to have an ontological foundation in natural law (*dhammatā*), being likened to physical laws governing heat (*utu-niyāma*) and biological growth (*bīja-niyāma*) (DN-a II.431). The existence of an objective moral law of this kind, however, seems incompatible with anti-foundationalist claims that moral truth is established solely on the basis of local veridical frameworks.

Buddha-nature

An overtly foundationalist suggestion is that Buddha-nature can provide the required basis for human rights. Anton Sevilla has suggested 'the fact that all beings have a common essence of Buddha-nature brings an inescapable sense of solidarity to the ethical task of Mahāyāna Buddhism'. 'The ethical demand to realize Buddha-nature', furthermore, 'is something we do with and for the community of sentient beings as a whole' (2010: 227). The manifestation of Buddha-nature is not a once-and-for-all event so much as a dynamic unfolding through continuous practice. Dōgen calls this the doctrine of 'The Oneness of Practice and Attainment' (*shushō-ittō*). Sevilla notes that 'practice is the very condition that manifests and expresses our Buddha-nature and our fundamental human goodness' (2010: 234), and sums up the relevance of Dōgen's insights for ethics and human rights as follows:

> The traditional idea of Buddha-nature and its realization shows that this ethical path is one of solidarity and compassion with all sentient beings, where we see our

> struggle in saṃsāra as shared and our liberation through Buddha-nature as liberation for all. It was upon this idea that we grounded the need for rights and the importance of rights for both one's own emancipation and that of others. (2010: 248)

The rights that issue from this understanding are said to have two characteristics. First, they will be 'grounded in a genuine sense of solidarity with human beings on the deepest ground of our shared struggle'; and second, they will be based 'not on a presumed human nature on which other people may or may not agree but rather on a historical response to the actual suffering of people and in solidarity with their struggle' (2010: 248). Sevilla is perhaps wise to avoid basing human rights on a specific conception of human nature given the variety of inconsistent views about how it is to be defined. A better candidate is human good, a possibility adumbrated in the reference to suffering and struggle. What such struggle involves is overcoming the obstacles that stand in the way of well-being, and since there is general agreement on what the obstacles are (tyranny, injustice, discrimination, and other abuses catalogued in human rights charters) it should be easier to reach agreement on the core values that structure well-being. Toru Shiotsu suggests that 'From the doctrine of Buddha-nature we can derive much related to the concept of human dignity' (2001: 146). One ground of human dignity is the capacity for rational choice, not in the sense of bare autonomy (as liberal theories of rights assume), but as the choice of those goods that are truly constitutive of human well-being. Human dignity (a dignity already manifest in its most radical form through the achievement of a human rebirth) arises from the innate capacity to participate in these goods. Examples would include life and health (protected by Articles 3 and 25.1), knowledge and education (protected by Article 26), friendship and sociability (protected by Articles 3, 13, and 20), and religious belief (protected by Article 18).

Dōgen's conception of human good, as Sevilla explains it, has much in common with Aristotelian conceptions of human flourishing as the progressive unfolding of potential through the cultivation of virtues (cf. Nussbaum 1997), as well as Western natural law thinking about rights as a requirement of justice which facilitate and promote the common good. Thus 'realizing one's Buddha-nature requires that we possess the rights and liberties necessary for us to pursue spiritually meaningful lives' (2010: 249). Human rights are thus the legal means by which moral theory is translated into normative practice. As Sevilla comments, 'Rights can be seen as institutional means for upholding certain general forms of right conduct' (2010: 222), and 'the ethical demand to realize Buddha-nature is something we do with and for the community of sentient beings as a whole' (2010: 227). In contrast to anti-foundationalism, such rights are seen as innate entitlements having an ontological foundation in the radical capacity of all beings to attain Buddhahood.

Buddha-nature has many attractions as a foundation for human rights. It grounds rights in human good; it explains why rights are inalienable and universal; it provides a Buddhist equivalent for 'human dignity'; and it can also encompass non-human forms of life (since dignity is a rank of being rather than an absolute state, different forms of life will have rights appropriate to their natures). As a formal doctrine, however, it is sectarian, and is understood differently among Mahāyāna schools. Some, like the Madhyamaka, may even wish to challenge its essentialist presuppositions. The concept of 'Buddha-nature' is also unknown in early Buddhism, although having antecedents in the belief that all beings have the capacity to attain awakening, as noted by Perera.

Conclusion

The modern idea of human rights has a distinctive cultural origin, but its underlying preoccupation with human good is one Buddhism shares. Human rights can be seen as an explication of what is 'due' under *Dharma* and hence an authentic expression of Buddhist teachings. Each of the proposals discussed in the first part of this chapter finds a resonance between human rights and specific aspects of those teachings. In this sense perhaps we should speak of multiple foundations for human rights. Yet focusing on individual teachings may be unnecessarily exclusive: approaches that emphasize compassion, for example, have little to say about wisdom. It might be thought that a successful foundation for human rights should be comprehensive, as well as rooted in the core teachings of Buddhism accepted by all schools. It would thus seem desirable for any proposed foundation to meet the criteria formulated by Evans, namely: (1) simplicity: ordinary Buddhists must be able to understand the argument; (2) universality: it must be based on principles that all Buddhists accept; (3) authority or dignity: the theory must articulate the moral inviolability, or its equivalent, of the human person; and (4) it must integrate Buddhist 'resignation' (acceptance of the reality of suffering) with human rights advocacy (1998: 141).

Perhaps the most basic Buddhist doctrinal foundation of all—the Four Noble Truths—can meet these requirements. All Buddhist schools affirm the account of human nature and its fulfilment set out in the Four Noble Truths, and all of the approaches considered have their foundation in some aspect or other of this teaching. The precepts form part of the fourth Noble Truth (under the category of *śīla* or 'morality'), and the doctrine of dependent origination, especially in its soteriological form, is associated with the second. The innate capacity for awakening (or 'Buddha-nature') is affirmed in the third Noble Truth. Universal compassion arises from an unrestricted sensitivity to human suffering, described in the first Noble Truth, and is the virtue that motivated the Buddha to teach the four truths (SN VI.1). An interpretation along these lines seems to meet the conditions Evans describes regarding simplicity, universality, authority, and authenticity. On this basis, the rights proclaimed by the UDHR and similar documents can be understood as facilitating the liberation from suffering and the achievement of self-realization proclaimed in the Four Noble Truths.

Incorporating human rights more formally within Buddhism, however, will require some doctrinal expansion and reconfiguration. Buddhism has not provided much in the way of theoretical accounts of the relationship between the individual and society. Early Buddhism teaches a path to liberation though self-development, and offers the *saṅgha* as the community in which this task can be carried out. Mahāyāna Buddhism believes that bodhisattvas will take upon themselves the responsibility for universal liberation. Little is said in the classical sources, at least, about the responsibilities of the broader political community and the social structures required to facilitate the common good, a subject with which human rights are centrally concerned. Buddhism now faces the challenge of discovering 'resources for fresh elaboration' (Cohen 2004: 213) so that its political and social teachings can evolve in response to new circumstances while remaining faithful to doctrinal foundations.

Works Cited

Beitz, C. R. (2009) *The idea of human rights*. Oxford: Oxford University Press.

Buddhadāsa, Bhikku (1989) *Me and mine: selected essays of Bhikkhu Buddhadasa*. Albany: State University of New York Press.

Cahill, L. S. (1999) Rights as religious or secular: Why not both? *Journal of law and religion*, 14, 41–52.

Caney, S. (2001) Human rights, compatibility and diverse cultures. In: S. Caney and P. Jones (eds), *Human rights and global diversity*. London: Frank Cass, 51–72.

Clapham, A. (2007) *Human rights: a very short introduction*. Oxford: Oxford University Press.

Cohen, J. (2004) Minimalism about human rights: the most we can hope for? *The journal of political philosophy*, 12, 190–213.

Dagger, R. (1989) Rights. In: T. Ball (ed.), *Political innovation and conceptual change*. Cambridge: Cambridge University Press, 292–308.

Donnelly, J. (2013) *Universal human rights in theory and practice*. Third revised edition. Ithaca, NY: Cornell University Press.

Evans, S. S. (1998) Buddhist resignation and human rights. In: D. Keown, C. Prebish, and W. Husted (eds), *Buddhism and human rights*. Richmond, UK: Curzon Press, 141–154.

Evans, S. A. (2012) Ethical confusion: possible misunderstandings in Buddhist ethics. *Journal of Buddhist ethics*, 19, 513–544.

Eynde, M. V. (2004) Reflection on Martha Nussbaum's work on compassion from a Buddhist perspective. *Journal of Buddhist ethics*, 11, 45–72.

Feinberg, J. (1973) *Social philosophy*. Englewood Cliffs, NJ: Prentice-Hall.

Finnis, J. M. (2011) *Natural law and natural rights*. Oxford: Clarendon Press.

Freeman, M. (1994) The philosophical foundations of human rights. *Human rights quarterly*, 16, 491–514.

Garfield, J. L. (1998) Human rights and compassion. In D. Keown, C. Prebish, and W. Husted (eds), *Buddhism and human rights*. Richmond, UK: Curzon Press, 111–140.

Glendon, M. A. (2001) *A world made new: Eleanor Roosevelt and the Universal Declaration of Human Rights*. New York: Random House.

Goodale, M., and Merry, S. E. (2007) *The practice of human rights: tracking law between the global and the local*. Cambridge: Cambridge University Press.

Gowans, C. W. (2015) *Buddhist moral philosophy: an introduction*. New York: Taylor and Francis.

Harding, A. (2007) Buddhism, human rights and constitutional reform in Thailand. *Asian journal of comparative law*, 2, 1–25.

Hesanmi, S. O. (2008) Human rights. In: W. Schweiker (ed.), *The Blackwell companion to religious ethics*. Malden, MA: Wiley-Blackwell, 501–510.

Hohfeld, W. (1964) *Fundamental legal conceptions*. New Haven: Yale University Press.

Ignatieff, M., et al. (eds) (2003) *Human rights as politics and idolatry*. Princeton: Princeton University Press.

Ihara, C. (1998) Why there are no rights in Buddhism: a reply to Damien Keown. In: D. Keown, C. Prebish, and W. Husted (eds), *Buddhism and human rights*. Richmond, UK: Curzon Press, 43–51.

Inada, K. K. (1982) The Buddhist perspective on human rights. In: A. Swidler (ed.), *Human rights in religious traditions*. New York: Pilgrim Press, 66–76.

Ishay, M. R. (2008) *The history of human rights: from ancient times to the globalization era*. Berkeley: University of California Press.

Junger, P. (1998) Why the Buddha has no rights. In: D. Keown, C. Prebish, and W. Husted (eds), *Buddhism and human rights*. Richmond, UK: Curzon Press, 53–96.

Kelley, C. D. (2015) Towards a Buddhist philosophy and practice of human rights. PhD diss., Columbia University.

Keown, D. (1998) Are there 'human rights' in Buddhism? In: D. Keown, C. Prebish, and W. Husted (eds), *Buddhism and human rights*. Richmond, UK: Curzon Press, 15–42.

Keown, D., Prebish, C., and Husted, W. (eds) (1998) *Buddhism and human rights*. Richmond, UK: Curzon Press.

King, S. B. (2005) *Being benevolence: the social ethics of engaged Buddhism*. Honolulu: University of Hawai'i Press.

Langlois, A. J. (2001) *The politics of justice and human rights: southeast Asia and universalist theory*. Cambridge: Cambridge University Press.

Lauren, P. G. (2011) *The evolution of international human rights: visions seen*. Philadelphia: University of Pennsylvania Press.

Leve, L. (2007) 'Secularism is a human right!' Double-binds of Buddhism, democracy and identity in Nepal. In: M. Goodale and S. E. Merry (eds), *The practice of human rights: tracking law between the global and the local*. Cambridge: Cambridge University Press, 78–113.

Likhitpreechakul, P. (2013) The Kantian dhamma: Buddhism and human rights. *Journal of the Oxford Centre for Buddhist Studies*, 5, 161–169.

MacIntyre, A. (1981) *After virtue: a study in moral theory*. London: Duckworth.

Mills, M. A. (2003) This turbulent priest: contesting religious rights and the state in the Tibetan Shugden controversy. In: R. Wilson and J. P. Mitchell (eds), *Human rights in global perspective: anthropological studies of rights, claims and entitlements*. London: Routledge, 54–70.

Montgomery, J. W. (1986) *Human rights and human dignity*. Grand Rapids, MI: Zondervan.

Narayan, U. (1993) What do rights have to do with it? Reflections on what distinguishes 'traditional nonwestern' frameworks from contemporary rights-based systems. *Journal of social philosophy*, 24, 186–199.

Nussbaum, M. C. (1997) Human rights theory: capabilities and human rights. *Fordham law review*, 66, 273–300.

Nussbaum, M. C. (2001) *Upheavals of thought: the intelligence of emotions*. Cambridge: Cambridge University Press.

Oderberg, D. S. (2013) Natural law and rights theory. In: G. Gaus and F. D'Agostino (eds), *The Routledge companion to social and political philosophy*. Abingdon, UK and New York: Routledge, 375–386.

Peek, J. M. (1995) Buddhism, human rights and the Japanese state. *Human rights quarterly*, 17, 527–540.

Perera, L. N. (1991) *Buddhism and human rights: a Buddhist commentary on the Universal Declaration of Human Rights*. Colombo, Sri Lanka: Karunaratne and Sons.

Promta, S. (1994) Rights in Buddhism. *Journal of Buddhist studies*, 1, 44–64.

Rice, E. (2005) Buddhist compassion as a foundation for human rights. *Social philosophy today*, 21, 95–108.

Rorty, R. (2010) Human rights, rationality, and sentimentality. In: C. J. Voparil and R. J. Bernstein (eds), *The Rorty reader*. Malden, MA: Wiley-Blackwell, 351–365.

Satha-Anand, S. (1999) Looking to Buddhism to turn back prostitution in Thailand. In: J. R. Bauer and D. A. Bell (eds), *The east Asian challenge for human rights*. Cambridge: Cambridge University Press, 193–211.

Schaefer, B. (2005) Human rights: problems with the foundationless approach. *Social theory and practice*, 31, 27–50.

Schmidt-Glintzer, H. (2010) Is Mahayana Buddhism a humanism? Some remarks on Buddhism in China. In: C. Meinert and H.-B. Zöllner (eds), *Buddhist approaches to human rights*. Piscatawny, NJ: Transaction Publishers, 113–124.

Schmidt-Leukel, P. (2010) Buddhism and the idea of human rights: resonances and dissonances. In: C. Meinert and H.-B. Zöllner (eds), *Buddhist approaches to human rights*. Piscatawny, NJ: Transaction Publishers, 41–62.

Seeger, M. (2010) Theravada Buddhism and human rights: perspectives from Thai Buddhism. In: C. Meinert and H.-B. Zöllner (eds), *Buddhist approaches to human rights*. Piscatawny, NJ: Transaction Publishers, 63–92.

Sen, A. (1997) *Human rights and Asian values*. New York: Carnegie Council on Ethics and International Affairs.

Sevilla, A. L. (2010) Founding human rights within Buddhism: exploring buddha-nature as an ethical foundation. *Journal of Buddhist ethics*, 17, 212–252.

Shiotsu T. (2001) Mahayana Buddhism and human rights: focusing on methods of interpretation. *Journal of oriental studies*, 11, 141–155.

Shiotsu T., and Gebert, A. (1999) Buddhism and human rights: points of convergence. How can Buddhism clarify the modern view of human rights? *Journal of oriental studies*, 9, 58–77.

Sobisch, J.-U., and Brox, T. (2010) Translations of human rights, Tibetan contexts. In: C. Meinert and H.-B. Zöllner (eds), *Buddhist approaches to human rights*. Piscatawny, NJ: Transaction Publishers, 159–178.

Statement by UN High Commissioner for Human Rights Zeid Ra'ad Al Hussein via Videolink to the Human Rights Council (2015) Available from: www.ohchr.org, n.p.

Taylor, C. (1999) Conditions of an unforced consensus on human rights. In: D. Bell and J. Butler (eds), *The east Asian challenge for human rights*. Cambridge: Cambridge University Press, 124–146.

Thānissaro, Bhikkhu (trans.) (2013) *The Buddhist monastic code*, volume 1. Third revised edition. Available from: www.accesstoinsight.org.

Traer, R. (1995) Buddhist affirmations of human rights. *Journal of Buddhist ethics*, 2, 1–12.

Tsedroen, J., Meinert, C., and Zöllner, H.-B. (2010) Women's rights in the Vajrayana tradition. In: C. Meinert and H.-B. Zöllner (eds), *Buddhist approaches to human rights*. Piscatawny, NJ: Transaction Publishers, 195–210.

Twiss, S. B. (1998) A constructive framework for discussing Confucianism and human rights. In: W. T. de Bary (ed.), *Confucianism and human rights*. New York: Columbia University Press, 27–53.

Vajiragnana, V. (1992) Justice in Buddhism. *Vesak sirisara*. Available from: http://enlight.lib.ntu.edu.tw/FULLTEXT/JR-AN/an140924.pdf.

Walzer, M. (1994) *Thick and thin: moral argument at home and abroad*. Notre Dame: University of Notre Dame Press.

Suggested Reading

Gowans, C. W. (2015) *Buddhist moral philosophy: an introduction*. New York: Taylor and Francis.

Inada, K. K. (1982) The Buddhist perspective on human rights. In: A. Swidler (ed.), *Human rights in religious traditions*. New York: Pilgrim Press, 66–76.

Keown, D., Prebish, C., and Husted, W. (eds) (1998) *Buddhism and human rights*. Richmond, UK: Curzon Press.

King, S. B. (2005) *Being benevolence: the social ethics of engaged Buddhism*. Honolulu: University of Hawai'i Press.

Meinert, C., and Zöllner, H.-B. (2010) *Buddhist approaches to human rights*. Piscatawny, NJ: Transaction Publishers.

Perera, L. N. (1991) *Buddhism and human rights: a Buddhist commentary on the Universal Declaration of Human Rights*. Colombo, Sri Lanka: Karunaratne and Sons.

Sevilla, A. L. (2010) Founding human rights within Buddhism: exploring Buddha-nature as an ethical foundation. *Journal of Buddhist ethics*, 17, 212–252.

CHAPTER 26

BUDDHISM AND WOMEN

ALICE COLLETT

INTRODUCTION

A basic Buddhist ethical precept is *ahiṃsā*, non-harm. Discrimination against any living being in any way, shape, or form can be and often is harmful. Therefore, the central question, when discussing the subject of women in Buddhism, is this: how can a tradition that has *ahiṃsā* as one of its central ethical tenets justify discrimination against women? The problem with this question, one that has been carried through the history of the tradition, revolves around what constitutes discrimination. That is to say, if women are considered to be (naturally) inferior to men—less capable, less able, less adept, less intelligent—then it is only fair, rather than discriminatory, to deny them the same privileges and opportunities afforded men. The principle here can be summed up with an analogy: one does not give an elephant, a cow, or a domestic dog a hot meal every day because animals are by nature different from humans, so do not require the same treatment.

In this chapter I will argue that although the idea of the inferiority of women is one that is very much alive today in some Buddhist traditions, just as it has been historically, it is a doctrinally and ethically unsubstantiated view. I aim to demonstrate that the reasons posited for female inferiority are unfounded and that there is no doctrinal or ethical basis for it within tradition. In fact, the opposite is instead the case; the arguments made in favour of female inferiority in no way accord with core Buddhist doctrine and the central ethical tenets of the tradition. This is so much the case that an obvious conclusion to be drawn is that the ideas about female inferiority came into Buddhism through ingestion of norms and mores of traditional societies rather than as an integral part of Buddhist ontological or ideological principles.

I will divide the chapter into two parts, looking first at the so-called Theravāda tradition and then at the Mahāyāna tradition. As will become clear, many aspects of the issue are present in both Theravāda and Mahāyāna texts and traditions in the same or similar ways, but there are also some important differences, given the respective foci of the traditions. A comparison between the two serves to highlight gender themes and issues that run through the tradition as a whole (to the extent we can say it is a whole), and therefore could be called mainstays of the tradition. Comparing the two also illuminates situational, historical, and circumstantial changes and adaptations.

With regards to Theravāda tradition, which centralizes the teachings of the Pāli Canon, I will tender that the main arguments put forward as to why women are inferior are both unethical and undoctrinal according to the ethics and doctrine that underwrite the canon. The same doctrinal tenets continue in Mahāyāna, but are reshaped, and the question of how core doctrine sits with the issue of gender differentiation manifests in narrative accounts of the phenomenon of sexual transformation. In this section I will also look at the 'glass ceiling' in Buddhism, as well as arguments and evidence in relation to the question of whether women can attain to the highest goals of the tradition—to become an *arahantī* in Theravāda, a bodhisattva in Mahāyāna, or to attain to ultimate Buddhahood itself.

Theravāda Tradition

To even attempt to divide up this chapter along Theravāda and Mahāyāna lines, as I have done, immediately throws up problems. First, there is the question of what constitutes Theravāda, a question explored by Skilling et al.'s recent volume (2013), amongst others. Second, an integral part of that question is the matter of when what we call Theravāda began. Neither of these questions are especially relevant to the topic under discussion in this chapter. The texts of the Theravāda tradition are the Pāli Canon, commentaries (*aṭṭhakathās*), sub-commentaries (*ṭīkās*), and other supplemental works. In this section, I will concentrate on the Pāli Canon and commentaries, with some recourse to other Pāli works.

In the last century or so of Western scholarship, the Pāli Canon has been judged to be particularly negative about women, and the Mahāyāna conversely more positive (for a discussion of this see Nattier 2003: 100; Collett 2006). Although such appraisals continue to be endorsed by some (see, for example, Powers 2009: 74), over the last decade or so opinion has begun to shift to a more multi-layered and multifaceted standpoint. New research has revealed more positive attitudes to women in the Pāli Canon and commentaries and has challenged the evidence of the Pāli Canon and commentaries by making comparisons with parallel works, such as those in Chinese and Tibetan (on positive attitudes in the Pāli Canon see, for instance, Walters 1995 and 2013 and Collett 2011 and 2013a; on comparisons with Chinese and Tibetan see, for instance, Chung 1999, the many works of Anālayo, and Bingenheimer 2008 and 2011). Positive portrayals of women in other early texts have also received more attention (see, e.g., Schopen 2008, 2010, Collett 2009, Clarke 2013, Muldoon-Hules 2013). The evidence of epigraphy has also been highlighted, which often presents images that counter the textual evidence (see, e.g., Barnes 2000, Skilling 2001, Schopen 2008, 2010, Collett 2015), and early

Gandhārī manuscript fragments have been studied and examined for what they can tell us about women in other early Indian traditions (Strauch 2013; Lenz 2013).

The Pāli Canon itself is now considered to be a layered collection, written and produced by multiple authors over long periods of time. There is much in the canon that is positive about women; for instance, its portrayals of exemplary female teachers such as Dhammadinnā and Khemā (see Krey 2010; Collett 2013a, 2015a; Anālayo 2011), a list of outstanding nuns and one of laywomen, many biographical accounts, and poems about/by other exemplary women. On the other hand, there are negative passages about women that question their character or deny that they can attain the heights of religious experience. To demonstrate some of the positives and negatives, and to set them in context, I will discuss some sections of two texts of the Pāli Canon, the *Aṅguttara-nikāya*, considered to be part of the earliest strata of the canon, and the *Jātakatthavaṇṇanā*, a later work.

In the *Aṅguttara Nikāya* (II.82–83), Ānanda asks the Buddha why women do not sit on courts of justice, embark on business, or reach the essence of any deed. The Buddha replies by listing certain negative characteristics of women, such as that they are, by nature, weak in wisdom (*duppañño*), uncontrollable, greedy, and envious. However, this vignette sits between two others, which, when the three are taken together, appear contradictory. These are all part of the section on The Fours (the AN is a collection of numbered discourses, grouped according to number, with the first section as The Ones, the second The Twos, and so on). Prior to the exchange between Ānanda and the Buddha (AN II.9), there is a list of the four types of people who 'adorn the *saṅgha*', that is to say, who improve and increase the quality of the community by their presence within it. These four types of persons are said to be competent, disciplined, self-confident, learned, experts in *Dhamma*, and practising in accord with *Dhamma*. These four types are monks, nuns, laymen, and laywomen. Therefore, both laywomen and nuns are assets in the community and bring strength and vitality to it. Further on in the section on The Fours, we find a list of four things that make a person foolish, incompetent, and altogether bad (*asappuriso*) (AN II.230). The four things that make a person this way are that the person is without faith, immoral, lazy, and unwise (*duppañño*). These things are disadvantageous and will result in a person failing to prosper. How then, can the nuns and laywomen who 'adorn the *saṅgha*' from the moral good and strength of their being and their practice also all—simply by being women—belong to the category of 'bad' people who accrue demerit because they are weak in wisdom? The first and third of these judgments are fairly standard for any religious community. The message conveyed is that those in our community who are committed to our foundational ideals and practice accordingly are good people and will make good progress, and conversely those who are immoral (according to our ethical code) or ignorant fools (because they do not see our truth) will likely suffer. To present women in the middle section of these three in this way demonstrates a different agenda at work on the part of the compilers/redactors of this section, and given that it starkly juxtaposes with the religious agenda of the first and third sections, looks more like the ingestion of social norms and mores than anything else.

Some of the worst comments about women in Pāli literature can be found in the *Jātakatthavaṇṇanā*. In this Pāli text, women are maligned and vilified with blanket one-liners that revile the generic woman, or womankind overall. Some of the most salient of these are as follows:

> women are naturally wicked and ... plot evil against you. (Jat 6, I. 128)
> women are lustful, heedless, vile and debase ... (Jat 61, I.285)
> given the opportunity, all women become wicked. (Jat 62, I.289)
> women are ungrateful and deceitful ... (Jat 63, I.295)
> women are feckless and immoral ... (Jat 64, I.300)
> women are common to all [referring to sexual infidelity], this immorality defines them... (Jat 65, I.301–302)
> women have insatiable sexual appetites ... (Jat 120, I.440)

I have argued elsewhere that taking these comments out of context to some extent distorts their import, as stories in the *Jātakatthavaṇṇanā* can be equally negative about men (Collett 2016). Both the examples in the *Aṅguttara-nikāya* and *Jātakatthavaṇṇanā* relate back to the central question of this chapter, the question of how and why women are considered to be inferior. As can be seen from the *Jātakatthavaṇṇanā* examples, it is women's nature that appears to be the problem: women are, by nature, evil, wicked, and immoral. In the Theravāda tradition, the notion of female inferiority, to the extent that it is captured in the textual evidence, is shaped around conceptualizations like this, relating to an apparent innate/inherent defect of womankind that underpins their character. These statements (arguments, if we can call them that) are shaped around two—what I consider to be—contradictory views; first, that women are of low intelligence and weak in wisdom, and second, that they are manipulative and thereby wicked/evil and dangerous.[1]

In what follows, I will address the question of female nature as the basis for an argument in favour of female inferiority. I will do this in a number of ways. First, I will argue that these two claims are contradictory in nature by demonstrating that narratives about manipulative and deceptive women tend to portray them as successful manipulators of others, and that to succeed at manipulation takes a high level of intelligence. Second, I will tackle the proposition from the point of view of Buddhist ethics, pointing out that it is not action but rather intention that is at the heart of Buddhist ethical and moral analysis, and that manipulation can be done for good ends. Third, I will set the point within

[1] While it is possible to make generalizations about this depiction of female nature—i.e. as of low intelligence and duplicitous/manipulative—it is not the case that there is any standard way to represent this in the texts. That is, there is no consistent formula, phrasing, or words that are used repeatedly to classify these apparent attributes. For example, in the *Aṅguttara-nikāya* passage above *duppañño* is used to describe low intelligence, but this is not always the word used to describe it. In a well-known verse about the nun Somā, women are said to have two-fingered wisdom (*dvaṅgulapaññāya*), which appears to mean something similar, to be indicating a low level of intelligence, but the commentaries disagree as to the correct meaning of this (Collett 2009: 99).

the broader rubric of core early Buddhist doctrine, focusing on *paṭicca-samuppāda* and raising the question of how human nature (of which female nature is a part) can be the problem, and can hinder religious attainment, when all of Buddhist doctrine conveys the exact opposite—that human nature is instead the key to liberation because of the distinctly human potential for transformation.[2]

First, then, on the contradiction. The two charges—of being of low intelligence and weak in wisdom, combined with the allegation of manipulative nature—would be contradictory to one another if it is the case that, in narratives that tell us about how manipulative women are, the female protagonists in question proved themselves to be skilled in manipulative techniques, as skill in manipulation requires intelligence.

A typical narrative of this stripe is one of the most popular biographies of Uppalavaṇṇā, a nun considered by the tradition to have been a direct disciple of the Buddha. Stories and accounts of Uppalavaṇṇā are popular both within Pāli Buddhism and in other traditions. Accounts of her in Pāli literature vary, and the following a summary based on the *Therīgāthā* and *Aṅguttara-nikāya* commentaries. Whilst the summary is fairly long, I have included it to demonstrate the ways in which characterizations of female nature are embedded in the narratives of the texts.

> In her next birth she was born inside a lotus flower, on a lake at the foot of a mountain. An ascetic (*tāpaso*), going to the lake saw the lotus flower, picked it and it opened to reveal the baby girl. The ascetic took her in as his daughter (milk coming to his thumb to feed her), and once again, when the toddler began to run around, lotus flowers would spring up in her step. In this life, she was known as Padumavatī. When she was older, a forester saw her and did not imagine one so beautiful could be human. However, when he saw her preparing food for her 'father' the hermit he became convinced she was indeed human. The forester took some food with the ascetic, and then went to Vārāṇasī to inform the king of this 'jewel of a woman' (*itthiratanaṃ*) he had met. The king wanted her for himself and so persuaded the ascetic to let him take her as his chief queen. Once he was with her, he did not pay attention to his other wives. The wives became jealous of her, desiring to create disharmony between her and the king. They spoke to the king, asking how such a woman, who has lotus flowers appear where she walks, could be human. 'Surely she is a demon (*yakkinī*)' they said. When she was pregnant and near to giving birth, the king was called away to battle at the border. The jealous wives took this as an opportunity and formulated a plot against her. They bribed an attendant to take her child away when it was born. Although she only had one child, four hundred and ninety-nine more were born from the moisture of her womb.[3] At this, each of the jealous women, of whom there

[2] I am taking for granted in this chapter that female nature is part of human nature. I have never read a Buddhist text that seems to come close to explicitly saying, nor unerringly implying, that men are humans and women subhuman.

[3] Within the Pāli Canon, four different types of possible birth are listed, including this type—moisture-born (*saṃsedajā*) (see, e.g., MN I.73, DN III.230, Miln 128–129). However, moisture-born is often used as a description of the rise of (what we would call) bacterial growth from rotting substances, such as rotting food or flesh, rather than the way it is used here.

> were also conveniently 500, took a child away, whilst the attendant smeared a log of wood with blood and placed it near Padumavatī, who had not yet come round from the birth. When she did come round, the attendant scolded her, thrusting the log of wood in front of her and telling her this was what she had given birth to. Ashamed, she got the attendant to dispose of the log. Meanwhile, the 500 wives had a box made for each child and kept them quiet in the boxes. When the king returned they told him to question the attendant, and that his beloved had given birth to a log of wood. Hearing the account the jealous wives wanted him to hear of what has transpired, the king realised Padumavatī must be descended from non-humans and threw her out of the house.
>
> She was taken in by an old woman, and meanwhile the jealous wives carried on scheming to dispose of the bodies of the children. They requested the king take them to the Ganges to make an offering, and each was able to conceal their box containing one child under their garments. At the river, they went in and released the boxes. However, the boxes were caught in a net not far off and the king, emerging from the Ganges, saw them. He had them opened, and Sakka had caused an inscription to be written in one of the boxes so that the king would know these were his 500 sons, born of Padumavatī. Feeling remorseful at having not believed her, he sent out a search party, offering a thousand coins for anyone who knew where she was. She was found and the pair reunited. The king made the 500 women her slaves, but after it was made known they were her slaves, she had them released and each of them (except one) was given a son to rear. She kept her womb-born child for herself. (Collett 2016: 77–78)

Essentially then, in this account, the 500 wives easily manipulate the king. Other stories of similarly manipulative and deceptive women can be found in a range of Pāli texts. An example of a devious mother appears in the story of Kumbhaghosaka in the *Dhammapada* commentary, in which a scheming female servant uses her daughter—in a version of the folkloric 'bed trick'—for her own ends. In attempting to discover if Kumbhaghosaka has some hidden wealth, she damages his mattress such that it is no longer possible for him to sleep on it, then suggests that he share her daughter's bed, conniving for a marriage between the pair. In the *Jātakatthavaṇṇanā*, there is a story of a lazy brahmin's wife who appears to spend her nights with lovers and friends enjoying pleasures, whilst during the day she feigns illness so that her husband runs about and looks after her (Jat 130).

As can be seen in each case, the manipulation by the women is on the whole fairly successful. In the story of the 500 jealous wives, each part that they contrived and steered worked; they simply didn't know there was a net on the river that would foil their well-structured and detailed planning. The devious mother's attempts at manipulation were also very successful and the brahmin's wife, although treated with exceptional cruelty for her manipulation of her husband after he discovered her games, was not found out by him; it took a third party (the Buddha in a previous life) to see through her subterfuge.

Manipulation in these contexts is seen as a vice, not morally good, and so manipulators do not win out unless their manipulation is part of a subplot which in the end leads to good. Nonetheless, it is not the case that the types of manipulation displayed and enacted by the women are crude and gross forms that are easily identified and seen through by the (usually) men who are subjected to the stratagem. The manipulation is clever and successful. The overall plot might be foiled, but never by a man with sharper intellect, who sees through the women's/woman's ruse easily. Therefore, the manipulation in these stories shows an advanced ability to assess and understand a situation underpinned, as it must be, by intelligence and thereby, as I noted above, demonstrates the opposite of a low level of intellect.

Turning now to address the invective on female nature from an ethical standpoint. As mentioned at many points in this volume, Buddhist ethics are an ethics of intention; that is, it is the intention behind the action rather than the action itself that is deemed to be ethical or unethical. Therefore, to attempt to say that women are inferior to men because they are manipulative is nonsensical from the point of view of Buddhist ethics, because manipulation can be done with good intention. And, in fact, there are ready examples, from the Pāli Canon, that demonstrate this. Take, for example, the biography of Bhaddā Kuṇḍalakesā (Collett 2014b, 2016). In the most popular account of Bhaddā Kuṇḍalakesā's life, she becomes infatuated with a thief whom she first sees as he is being led off to execution. Her father arranges his release, and they marry, but the thief-husband contrives to rob her of her jewels. Bhaddā Kuṇḍalakesā, although in the throes of ardour, astutely perceives his intentions, turns the tables, and manipulates him, eventually throwing him to his death off a cliff, in an act of seeming self-defence. In another example, the Buddha himself employs manipulation, with good intention, when he alleviates a woman's suffering by providing her with a teaching on the impermanence of human life. In the biography of Kisā-gotamī, when her child dies she is wrought with grief, and the Buddha requests of her that she find a mustard seed for him, that must come from a house in which there has been no death. He requests this knowing full well that each household will have experienced death and that her (practical) quest will be in vain, but that in pursuing his task she will come to the realization that death is a natural part of things, which she does.[4]

A broader problem with the 'nature' argument—that women are inferior because of their nature—is that to suggest human nature is static and unchanging contravenes foundational Buddhist doctrine. A fundamental principle of Buddhism is the belief in the possibility for human transformation. Without that possibility, Buddhism could barely be what it is. And underlying this belief is one of the key Buddhist doctrines in early Indian Buddhism and Theravāda, the doctrine of *paṭicca-samuppāda*. The doctrine is based on the principle that nothing comes into being in the world without a cause. The principle can be described as: 'When this arises, that comes to be; with the arising of this, that arises. When this does not exist, that does not come to be; from the cessation of this, that ceases' (MN II.32).

[4] As well as this, there are examples of men engaging in acts of manipulation for their own selfish ends, such as, for example, in the origin story of the fourth *parājikā* in the *Vinaya*, in which monks manipulate villagers into providing them with food during a famine by boasting about their supernormal abilities. Further, in Mahāyāna, the notion of *upāya*, 'skill in means', can be seen as a form of positive manipulation.

According to the doctrine of *paṭicca-samuppāda*, everything comes into being and passes away, everything is in this constant state of motion, is part of the flux and flow. And the doctrine relates both to the entire phenomenal world that we experience and to ourselves. There is a particular application of the doctrine that concerns the coming into being and passing away of the human person. This is the circle of twelve links. Each aspect of the human person comes into being dependent upon something else. Consciousness, and thereby human nature, comes into being dependent on certain other conditions, and it ceases to be accordingly as well. Thus, human nature is not static and unchanging, quite the contrary. And the possibility of the transformation of human nature, into something that may be beyond our current level of comprehension, is a fundamental part of the foundations of the Buddhist tradition, without which Buddhism itself would not be possible. Thus, to judge a woman as inferior to a man because of her 'female nature' is undoctrinal, according to *paṭicca-samuppāda*. To describe women as inferior because of female nature is to deny that female nature is human nature. Human nature (unlike that of animals) makes awakening possible. Awakening is possible because transformation of human nature is possible. Transformation of human nature is possible because of *paṭicca-samuppāda* in early Indian Buddhism and Theravāda, and because *paṭicca-samuppāda* underlies similar principles in Mahāyāna (discussed in the next section). Change is possible because things are dependently originated; if we want to change ourselves, we can set up the conditions to bring that about. This notion that the transformation of human nature is possible underwrites all fundamental Buddhist doctrine, in all schools. Without the possibility of the transformation of human nature there would be no goal in Buddhism, and no Buddhism, as there would have been no Buddha to start it off! The first human nature to undergo transformation was that of Gotama Buddha. To say a woman is inferior to a man because of her (static and unchangeable) 'female nature' is therefore to deny the quintessence of Buddhism.

Given that the idea of women being inferior comes from the notion that female nature is the problem, and this is both undoctrinal and does not chime with Buddhist ethics nor the principles that underlie moral decision-making, this suggests that the negativity towards women and sporadic misogyny we come across in Pāli literature has likely found its way in via ingestion of the traditional (non-Buddhist) view of women found in ancient South Asian societies, rather than for a doctrinally motivated or ethically significant reason grounded in Buddhist principles or teaching.

Mahāyāna Tradition

When assessing Mahāyāna, it soon becomes clear that it is difficult to make observations about any overarching 'Mahāyāna position' on women when so many texts are yet to be studied, and when those that have come to represent a generalized view of Indian Mahāyāna are a somewhat 'skewed' collection (Nattier 2003: 4–7). When we turn our attention to Mahāyāna texts, here we can talk more about authorial intention, and situate texts more fully as suggestive of the views of the individual and/or collective authors than with the layered Pāli canonical works, or other similar works, such as the Mūlasarvāstivāda *Vinaya*. This is an issue I have addressed previously, in relation to the work of Aśvaghoṣa, which has been, in the past, interpreted as the 'early Buddhist view on women' rather than as Aśvaghoṣa's own view (Collett 2013b), and in relation to Pāli commentarial literature (Collett 2016). As with Theravāda and the Pāli texts, we do again find in some Mahāyāna texts the same sorts of blanket statements about women; that they are of low intellect, wicked, and dangerous, and so on. (And again, it is important to consider such comments in context; see Dayal [1932] 1970: 225 for a discussion of similar remarks made about men). The *Bodhisattvabhūmi* of Asaṅga is an example of this, stating categorically that women cannot become buddhas because of their (static) female nature:

> Completely perfected Buddhas are not women. And why? Precisely because a bodhisattva, from the time he has passed beyond the first incalculable age (of his career) has completely abandoned the state of womanhood. Ascending (thereafter) to the most excellent throne of enlightenment, he is never again reborn as a woman. All women are by nature full of defilement and of weak intelligence. And not by one who is full of defilement and of weak intelligence is completely perfected Buddhahood attained. (Dutt 1966: 66, translation Willis 1985: 69, with one change)

Above I have addressed this issue of female nature as a type of human nature that renders complete progress impossible. As with pre-Mahāyāna traditions, such statements as this are not the majority of what we find in relation to women in Mahāyāna texts—quite the contrary, in fact. Overall, women are portrayed as good practitioners who attain to high levels of religious experience. A clear example of this is the laywoman Gaṅgottarā in the *Mahāratnakuṭa-sūtra* (Chang 1983: 37–40). Gaṅgottarā is a lay practitioner from Śravāstī. She goes to see the Buddha and they have an exchange in which Gaṅgottarā demonstrates an advanced and sophisticated comprehension of the true nature of things. Other examples of religiously impressive women in Mahāyāna texts can be found in the *Gaṇḍavyūha Sūtra*. Osto discusses these 'good friends' (*kalyāṇamitra*), and highlights their attainments. In the *Gaṇḍavyūha Sūtra* there are stories of women such as Queen Āśā, a laywoman only visible to advanced bodhisattvas, and the nun Siṃhavijṛmbhitā, a powerful *Dharma* teacher, who 'commands an impressive portfolio of spiritual attainments' (2008: 95). Other stories of women with similar good qualities can be found in a broad spectrum of Mahāyāna sutras, from the friend of Sadāprarudita, the merchant's daughter who helps him attain liberation in the influential and early *Prajñāpāramitā* literature (see Paul 1985: 115–134), through to the more peripheral and later (seventh-century) Chinese text *Hongzan fahua zhuan* (Accounts in Dissemination and Praise of the Lotus [Sutra], Stevenson 1995: 427–451). This latter text recounts the lives of two sisters, both nuns, who demonstrated august devotion to their practice (434), and mentions other nuns, including one who lived near the Kunshan district of Suzhou and who engaged in constant recitation of the *Lotus Sūtra*, 'which she performed devotedly twice a day for some twenty-odd years' (443–444).

Although Mahāyāna texts contain numerous stories of illustrious women, conceptualizations and inferences in relation to the inferiority of women continue. For Mahāyāna tradition, there is the question of whether women can become bodhisattvas. The Mahāyāna texts studied to date do not all provide clear evidence in relation to the answer to this question. In some texts there appears to be an implicit sense that women cannot attain bodhisattva status, but for no real discernible reason. In others it is stated that there are certain levels that cannot be attained, as with the *Bodhisattvabhūmi* example above, but often no concrete reason is offered. However, in other texts, women can be and are bodhisattvas. An example of the first one of these three positions is the women discussed above in the *Gaṇḍavyūha Sūtra*. As Osto notes, these women attain to high levels of religious experience themselves, such that some of them can teach others, but, according to Osto, no woman in the *Gaṇḍavyūha Sūtra* is ever given the title of bodhisattva. This appears most odd in relation to the nun Siṃhavijṛmbhitā, who herself teaches many advanced bodhisattvas. In contrast, entire works in Tibetan and Chinese devoted to the female bodhisattvas Tārā (Beyer 1978: 10) and Kuanyin demonstrate that bodhisattvas can be depicted in female form, as do other, more casual, passing references to them, for example, as aids to a Tantric deity in his subduing of lands for Buddhist ends (Huber 1997: 128–129).

The question of whether a woman can be a bodhisattva does not come up as fully in Theravāda or other non-Mahāyāna forms of Buddhism because there is not the focus on the bodhisattva ideal as found in Mahāyāna, but related questions do arise, such as whether women can become *arahants*, or whether indeed there could be such a thing as a female Buddha. In pre-Mahāyāna traditions, bodhisattva is the title of the historical Buddha in previous lives, used most often in the *Jātakatthavaṇṇanā*. And with regards to this type of bodhisattva, there are a few examples of women in this role. Ohnuma discusses the character of Rūpāvatī, in a narrative (*jātaka*) story of a previous life of the Buddha that involves bodily sacrifice. Karen Derris (2008) brings to light a forgotten medieval Pāli text of a *jātaka*-like tale of the Buddha (as Bodhisatta) as a woman. Ching-mei Shyu (2008) draws our attention to the Chinese *jātaka* collection, the *Liu du ji jing*, which contains three stories in which the Buddha was a woman in past lives, and Anālayo (2015) has published on a Chinese narrative from the *Ekottarika-āgama* in which the Buddha was a princess in a previous life. Anālayo and I have recently published (Collett and Anālayo 2014) on the question of whether women can be *arahants* in the early tradition. We argue that, although the title *arahantī* is rarely used—a fact that Banks Findley (1999) uses to suggest women are denied this role—a) the male equivalent is not a popular term, b) it is not always used in relation to specific males, and c) women demonstrate attainments that suggest they have reached this level.

The question as to whether women can become buddhas is a more complex one. According to the Pāli texts, notably the *Bahudhātukasutta*, there are five things a woman cannot attain, one of these being the state of Buddhahood. Anālayo (2009) has studied the Pāli and parallel versions of this sutta and concludes that the advocacy of women's inability to attain to high or developed states may have been a later addition to the texts of the traditions (2009: 166). Although this question of the unattainable states crops up in Mahāyāna as well (see Schuster 1981: 27–29; Nattier 2003: 98 n. 40), there are counters to this notion within other literature of the Indian Buddhist tradition, such as an *avadāna* story of a young girl who is predicted to future Buddhahood. *Avadāna* number 2 in the *Avadānaśataka*, a text connected to the Mūlasarvāstivāda, tells the story of Yaśomatī, a young girl who becomes committed to following the teachings of the Buddha. Seeing her, the Buddha knows and understands the trajectory of her lives to come, and predicts she will become a (male) buddha in the future, named Ratnamati. This prediction (*vyakaraṇa*) is categorical; this is not a possibility but an actuality. And the reason for it is that Yaśomatī, while still a female, has done everything necessary to ensure Buddhahood is attained in the future. So, if it is possible while in a female body to do all that is necessary to ensure future Buddhahood, how and why is it the case that women cannot become buddhas? The only other potential answer to that question presented by Mahāyāna tradition seems to be about embodiment, that is to say, it is simple biology that is the problem; a buddha cannot have a female body.

Aside from the 'nature' argument as typified by the *Bodhisattvabhūmi* quoted above, the other popular argument in Mahāyāna concerns the female body. This appears to originate from the literature of the thirty-two marks of a great man (*mahāpuruṣa*), which states that one such physical characteristic that buddhas will possess concerns how the male penis is fashioned. This notion that buddhas must be endowed with male genitalia comes more to the fore in Mahāyāna. The adoption of the list of thirty-two marks cements the idea of the Buddha having a male body, and, perhaps as a corollary of this, the notion that women need to be reborn as men in order to make progress on the path has become a mainstay of Mahāyāna tradition and is upheld by many living Mahāyāna traditions today. The apparent textual justification for this concerns phenomena of sexual transformation that occur with some frequency in Mahāyāna literature. In these narrative episodes, women spontaneously transform into men, or vice versa.[5]

In relation to gender in Mahāyāna Buddhism, sexual transformation is the most discussed and studied topic by contemporary scholars (see Schuster 1981; Paul 1985; Gross 1993; Peach 2002; Young 2004). In some of the earliest works on this topic, Nancy Barnes and Diana Paul agreed that sexual transformation appears to be illustrating something of what could perhaps be called a feminist agenda, in that it demonstrates that the conceptual categories of sex and gender are, ultimately, empty, used as it is in these episodes to illuminate the key Mahāyāna concept of *śunyatā*. Subsequent published works, particularly that of Lucinda Joy Peach and Jan Nattier, disagree with these evaluations, arguing instead that the narrative episodes on sexual transformation are not underpinned by a desire on the part of the authors to illustrate something akin to gender equality (Peach 2002; Nattier 2003: 98 n. 42).

[5] Nattier (2003: 98 n. 42) notes only one example of male to female transformation in studied Mahāyāna texts. Interestingly, in Hindu tradition it is the opposite, with male to female transformations being the most common (Goldman 1993).

To better understand these Mahāyāna narratives the historical context needs to be taken into consideration. The notion of a spontaneous physical transformation of sex has its roots in Brahmanical tradition, in texts that prefigure the Mahāyāna incidents.[6] In a forthcoming article I discuss this context for the narrative trope and argue that the appearance of the phenomena of sexual transformation in Mahāyāna should be seen both as a partial adoption of and a rejection of Brahmanical world view. As such, the Mahāyāna authors who introduced the narrative trope did not do so with the intention of illustrating how key Buddhist doctrine supports the advocacy of gender equality, but rather made use of a pre-existing trope to demonstrate the key concept of emptiness (*śunyatā*). In so doing, these Mahāyāna authors have, rather incidentally and accidentally, demonstrated my above point with regards to Buddhist doctrine, that discrimination against women is undoctrinal. Above, I have argued this in relation to the doctrine of *paṭicca-samuppāda*. The notion that all things are empty of inherent existence can be seen as a Mahāyāna reconceptualization and reconfiguring of the notion of *paṭicca-samuppāda*, although to say this does rather oversimplify the complex notion of *śunyatā*. Nonetheless, the religio-philosophic emphasis on reflecting upon and coming to terms with the emptiness of all phenomena is key to Mahāyāna practice. And one such aspect of the phenomenal world that is 'empty' is gender categorization and classification. And while Mahāyāna authors may well not have been intending to make this point in their narrative accounts of sexual transformation, they rather inadvertently do so.

Conclusion

On the question of the inferiority of women, which, as stated in the introduction, would be the only basis of deserved discrimination against women, the schools and traditions of Buddhism present similar, equally unfounded, reasons to espouse this proposition. The main difference between Theravāda and Mahāyāna is that Mahāyāna texts (inadvertently) demonstrate that gender discrimination is unhelpful and will not lead the practitioner to their goal, although this promulgation of the emptiness of the categories of sex and gender does not carry into the treatment of women in modern Mahāyāna Buddhism. The main reasons given for adherence to the idea of female inferiority are undoctrinal and neither chime with Buddhist ethics nor the principles that underlie moral decision-making, and thus appear more as ingestion of socio-cultural norms and values than something propagated as a foundational Buddhist principle. However, despite this, women have been and are discriminated against in certain Buddhist traditions and Buddhist communities today, and continue to suffer discrimination and be denied equal opportunities to men. These negative views on women, having found their way

[6] There is the one incident of spontaneous change of sex in Pāli literature, which is in a commentary, and is not canonical, as Goldman notes (1993: 391 n. 9); thus this episode also would be later than the Brahmanical sources. For a discussion of this episode see Anālayo 2014 and Appleton 2011.

into canonical and other literature, often viewed as sacrosanct, can be and are used to devalue women, and this devaluation, although not global, has become, in some quarters, a mainstay of Buddhist tradition.

Works Cited

Anālayo (2009) The *Bahudhātuka-sutta* and its parallels on women's inabilities. *Journal of Buddhist ethics*, 16, 137–190.

Anālayo (2011) Chos sbyin gyi mdo, Bhikṣuṇī Dharmadinnā proves her wisdom. *Chung-Hwa Buddhist journal*, 24, 3–33.

Anālayo (2014) Karma and female rebirth. *Journal of Buddhist ethics*, 21, 108–151.

Anālayo (2015) The Buddha's past life as a princess in the *Ekottarika-āgama*. *Journal of Buddhist ethics*, 22, 95–137.

Appleton, N. (2011) In the footsteps of the Buddha? Women and the bodhisatta path in Theravāda Buddhism. *Journal of feminist studies in religion*, 27 (1), 33–51.

Banks Findly, E. (1999) Women and the *arahant* issue in early Pali literature. *Journal of feminist studies in religion*, 15 (1), 57–76.

Barnes, N. J. (2000) The nuns at the stūpa: inscriptional evidence for the lives and activities of early Buddhist nuns in India. In: E. Banks Findly (ed.), *Women's Buddhism, Buddhism's women: tradition, revival, renewal*. Somerville, MA: Wisdom, 17–38.

Beyer, S. (1978) *The cult of Tārā: magic and ritual in Tibet*, Volume 1. Berkeley and Los Angeles: University of California Press.

Bingenheimer, M. (2008) The *Bhikṣuṇī Saṃyukta* in the shorter Chinese *Saṃyukta Āgama*. *Buddhist studies review*, 25 (1), 5–26.

Bingenheimer, M. (2011) *Studies in Āgama literature, with special reference to the shorter Chinese Saṃyuktāgama*. Taiwan: Shi Weng Feng Print Company.

Chang G. C. C. (ed.) (1983) *A treasury of Mahāyāna sūtras: selections from the Mahāratnakuṭa sūtra*. University Park, PA and London: The Penn State University Press.

Ching-mei S. (2008) A few good women: a study of the Liu Du Ji Jing (A Scripture on the Collection of the Sex Perfections) from literary, artistic and gender perspectives. PhD diss., Cornell University.

Chung I. Y. (1999) A Buddhist view of women: a comparative study of the rules for *bhikṣuṇīs* and *bhikṣus* based on the Chinese *prātimokṣa*. *Journal of Buddhist ethics*, 6, 29–105.

Clarke, S. (2013) *Family matters in Indian Buddhist monasticisms*. Honolulu: University of Hawai'i Press.

Collett, A. (2006) Buddhism and gender, reframing and refocusing the debate. *Journal of feminist studies in religion*, 22 (2), 55–84.

Collett, A. (2009) Somā the learned brahmin. *Religions of south Asia*, 3 (1), 93–109.

Collett, A. (2011) The female past in early Indian Buddhism: the shared narrative of the seven sisters in the *Therī-Apadāna*. *Religions of south Asia*, 5 (1), 209–226.

Collett, A. (2013a) *Women in early Indian Buddhism: comparative textual studies*. New York: Oxford University Press.

Collett, A. (2013b) Beware the crocodile: female and male nature in Aśvaghoṣa's *Saundarananda*. In: F. Ferrari and T. Dähnhardt (eds), *Charming beauties and frightful beasts: non-human animals in south Asian myth, ritual and folklore*. Sheffield: Equinox Publishing, 49–63.

Collett, A. (2015) Women as teachers and pupils in early Buddhist communities: the evidence of epigraphy. *Religions of south Asia*, 9 (1), 29–43.
Collett, A. (2016) *Lives of early Buddhist nuns: biographies as history*. New Delhi: Oxford University Press.
Collett, A. (forthcoming) Brahmanical influences on the phenomena of sexual transformation in Indian Mahāyāna literature.
Collett, A., and Anālayo (2014) *Bhikkhave* and *bhikkhu* as gender-inclusive terminology in early Buddhist texts. *Journal of Buddhist ethics*, 21, 760–797.
Dayal, H. ([1932] 1970) *The bodhisattva doctrine in Buddhist Sanskrit literature*. Delhi: Motilal Banarsidass.
Derris, K. (2008) When the Buddha was a woman: reimagining tradition in the Theravāda. *Journal of feminist studies in religion*, 24 (2), 29–44.
Dutt, N. (ed.) (1966) *Bodhisattvabhumi*. Patna: KP Jayaswal Research Institute.
Goldman, R. P. (1993) Transsexualism, gender, and anxiety in traditional India. *Journal of the American Oriental Society*, 113 (3), 374–401.
Gross, R. (1993) *Buddhism after patriarchy: a feminist history, analysis, and reconstruction of Buddhism*. Albany: State University of New York Press.
Krey, G. (2010) On women as teachers in early Buddhism: Dhammadinnā and Khemā. *Buddhist studies review*, 27 (1), 17–40.
Lenz, T. (2013) The British Library Kharosthī fragments: behind the birch bark curtain. In: A. Collett (ed.), *Women in early Indian Buddhism: comparative textual studies*. Oxford and New York: Oxford University Press, 46–61.
Muldoon-Hules, K. (2013) *Avadānaśataka*: the role of brahmanical marriage in a Buddhist text. In: A. Collett (ed.), *Women in early Indian Buddhism: comparative textual studies*. Oxford and New York: Oxford University Press, 192–220.
Nattier, J. (2003) *A few good men: the bodhisattva path according to the Inquiry of Ugra (Ugraparipṛcchā): a study and translation*. Honolulu: University of Hawai'i Press.
Paul, D. Y., and Wilson, F. (1985) *Women in Buddhism: images of the feminine in Mahāyāna tradition*. Berkeley and Los Angeles: University of California Press.
Peach, L. J. (2002) Social responsibility, sex change, and salvation: gender justice in the Lotus Sutra. *Philosophy east and west*, 52 (1), 50–74.
Powers, J. (2009) *A bull of a man: images of masculinity, sex, and the body in Indian Buddhism*. Cambridge, MA: Harvard University Press.
Schopen, G. (2008) Separate but equal: property rights and the legal independence of Buddhist nuns and monks in early North India. *Journal of the American Oriental Society*, 128 (4), 625–640.
Schopen, G. (2010) On incompetent monks and able urban nuns in a Buddhist monastic code. *Journal of Indian philosophy*, 38 (2), 107–131.
Schuster, N. (1981) Changing the female body: wise women and the bodhisattva career in some Mahāratnakūṭasūtras. *Journal of the International Association of Buddhist Studies*, 4 (1), 24–69.
Skilling, P. (2001) Nuns, laywoman, donors, goddesses: female roles in early Indian Buddhism. *Journal of the International Association of Buddhist Studies*, 24 (2), 241–274.
Stevenson, D. B. (1995) Tales of the Lotus Sutra. In: D. S. Lopez (ed.), *Buddhism in practice*. Princeton: Princeton University Press, 311–338.
Strauch, I. (2013) The Bajaur collection of Kharoṣṭhī manuscripts: Maḥāprajāpatī Gautamī and the order of nuns in a Gandhāran version of the Dakṣiṇāvibhaṅgasūtra. In: A. Collett (ed.),

Women in early Indian Buddhism: comparative textual studies. Oxford and New York: Oxford University Press, 18–45.
Walters, J. S. (1995) Gotamī's story: introduction and translation. In: D. S. Lopez, Jr (ed.), *Buddhism in practice*. Princeton: Princeton University Press, 107–132.
Walters, J. S. (2013) Wives of the saints: marriage and kamma in the path to arahantship. In: A. Collett (ed.), *Women in early Indian Buddhism: comparative textual studies*. Oxford and New York: Oxford University Press, 160–191.
Willis, Janice D. (1985) Nuns and benefactresses: the roles of women in the development of Buddhism. In: Y. Yazbeck Haddad and E. Banks Findly (eds), *Women, religion and social change*. New York: State University of New York Press, 59–86.
Young, S. (2004) *Courtesans and tantric consorts: sexualities in Buddhist narrative, iconography, and ritual*. New York: Routledge.

Suggested Reading

Anālayo (2009) The Bahudhātuka-sutta and its parallels on women's inabilities. *Journal of Buddhist ethics*, 16, 137–190.
Analayo (2014) Karma and female birth. *Journal of Buddhist ethics*, 21, 109–154.
Blackstone, K. R. (2000) *Women in the footsteps of the Buddha: struggle for liberation on the Therīgāthā*. Delhi: Motilal Banarsiddass.
Collett, A. (ed.) (2013) *Women in early Indian Buddhism: comparative textual studies*. New York: Oxford University Press.
Collett, A. (2016) *Lives of early Buddhist nuns: biographies as history*. New Delhi: Oxford University Press.
Goodwin, A. A. (2012) Right view, red rust, and white bones: a re-examination of Buddhist teachings on female inferiority. *Journal of Buddhist ethics*, 19, 198–343.

CHAPTER 27

BUDDHISM AND SEXUALITY

AMY PARIS LANGENBERG

INTRODUCTION

BECAUSE celibate monasticism is at the centre of Buddhist life, one might assume the topic of Buddhist sexual ethics to be simple and dull.[1] Scholars and casual observers alike have often assumed Buddhism to be a sex-negative religion. For example, Roger Corless begins his exploration of the intersection of queer theory and the *Dharma* by asking (in response to the poet James Broughton's quip that 'The Buddha is very down on desire') 'why is Buddhism so *very* down on desire and, therefore, sex? Can it be at least a little bit up on sex and still be recognizable as Buddhism?' (2004: 229). Minamoto Junko begins her study of the historical construction of sexuality in Japan by observing that 'The dominant Japanese sexual culture over the years has been permeated by negativity. Buddhism has had a strong influence on this culture's negative view of sexuality' (Minamoto and Glassman 1993: 87). The situation surrounding sexuality in the Buddhist world can be more usefully understood, however, as being similar to the complex sexual culture of Victorian Europe as described by Michel Foucault in volume 1 of his *History of Sexuality* (1978). Foucault argues that sexual prohibitions do not straightforwardly produce disciplined and properly sexual (or asexual) individuals; they also create the conditions for a host of suppressed or transgressive sexualities to emerge. Without the medicalization and criminalization of homosexuality that took place in Victorian Europe, for instance, the modern homosexual would not exist as such, according to Foucault's analysis. With prohibition comes resistance and critique, out of which arise deviant, defiant, or antinomian forms of personhood.

Consider, for instance, the monk who took a monkey as a lover in *pārājika* I of the Pāli *Vinaya*, the lay bodhisattva, Vimalakīrti, who visits brothels in order to ripen beings,

[1] The author would like to express appreciation for Anālayo's careful reading of and astute comments on an early draft.

or the entwined yogic lovers that populate medieval Tantric texts. Moreover, even circumscribed sexualities—the buttoned-up masculinity of the refined British aristocrat or perhaps the celibacy of the Buddhist monk—are no less magnetic for being so. We have no trouble believing in Miss Bennett's smouldering attraction to Mr Darcy, nor perhaps should we be shocked when the Buddha or certain of his disciples are described in the classical texts as beautiful and magnetic men.

Although only a limited number of scholarly studies have appeared to date on the topic of Buddhism and sexuality, most concur, explicitly or implicitly, that teachings such as the 'Sermon on Burning' (*Ādittapariyāya-sutta*) from the *Saṃyutta-nikāya* (35.28) in which the Buddha warns his monks that sense perception is ablaze with the flames of desire (also with hatred and delusion, sorrow and lamentation, birth and death) can begin but should not be allowed to end scholarly discussion of the topic (Cabezón 1993; Faure 1998; Gyatso 2005; Perera 1993; Powers 2009; Wilson 2003). As Bernard Faure observes, Buddhism's major traditions 'offer such a degree of inner complexity that any generalization in this domain would be improper' (1998: 9). Moreover, the rationally grounded critique of sensory desire as one element of *dukkha* (suffering) found in Buddhist discourses such as the *Ādittapariyāya-sutta* cannot be assumed to uniformly produce chastity or asexuality.

Following Faure, this chapter will take a Foucauldian approach that holds Buddhist sexual norms and ideals to be an evolving discourse productive of a wide variety of sexual persons. In keeping with this approach, it focuses on the manner in which Buddhist sexual ethics seek to foster states of self conducive to personal thriving in specific historical and social contexts, rather then Buddhist ethics as a universally applicable set of moral obligations. It mainly examines the discursive landscape of ancient, classical, and medieval Indian Buddhist sexual ethics, a tradition and body of texts influential across the Buddhist world, leaving its cross-cultural dimensions (how this discourse of sexuality has been embodied, rebelled against, and reinterpreted in pan-Asian Buddhist communities up to the present day) for specialists in particular Buddhist traditions to describe.

The Theory of *Brahmacarya*

Brahmacarya (Pāli *brahmacariya*), translatable as 'pure conduct', is the word used in Buddhist texts to denote the permanent celibacy of monastics. *Brahmacarya* also refers to the temporary celibacy undertaken by pious lay people at *uposatha*. In Pāli sources, the *brahmacariya* of the sage Gotama and his disciples is accorded special respect and is sometimes contrasted with vulgar village practices (*gāmadhamma*). For instance, in a long section on discipline (also found elsewhere in the discourses), the *Brahmajāla-sutta* states, 'Abandoning unchastity, the ascetic Gotama lives far from it, aloof from the village-practice of sex' (Walshe 1987: 68). In the *Vinaya* and commentarial tradition, sex is further glossed as sinful practice (*asaddhamma*) and low behaviour (*vasaladhamma*)

(Perera 1993: 62). In his comprehensive survey of Buddhist ethics, Peter Harvey observes that 'The most obvious and central difference between a monk or nun and a layperson is the former's commitment to celibacy: total avoidance of sexual intercourse' (2000: 89). Indeed, the placement of a rule saying that monks and nuns shall be defeated (*pārājika*) should they engage in sexual intercourse, at the very top of the code of monastic conduct (*prātimokṣa*), suggests that celibacy is the Rubicon separating those who have fully committed themselves to the monastic way of practising the Buddha's teachings from those left behind in the village who have not made that commitment.

In Pāli sources, Buddhist recluses distinguish their own pure sexual conduct from the worldly sensuality of ordinary people, and also from the mistaken and corrupt practices of other ascetic orders, some of whom are said to indulge in sex (Perera 1993: 74; Wijayaratna 1990: 104–105). That celibacy is a non-negotiable prerequisite for the homeless life can be seen to logically follow from the connection between sensory pleasure and suffering drawn repeatedly in the discourses. The *Mūlapariyāya-sutta* from the *Majjhima-nikāya* (1) states, '[The Tathāgata] has understood that delight (*nandī*) is the root of suffering' (Ñāṇamoli and Bodhi 1995: 89). Here, *nandī* refers to delight in all of its forms, not only sexual enjoyment (which, in fact, the sutta does not specifically mention). For the Buddha and his disciples, relief from suffering lies beyond the sensory and thus attaining happiness (as opposed to mere sensory delight) requires a withdrawal from sensuality of all sorts, including sexuality.

Kāma, referring to both to sensory desire and the pleasure one feels in obtaining the object of desire, is another important term used frequently in these contexts. *Kāma* encompasses all types of material desire, including lust for fields and property and money, but also, and paradigmatically, for sexual contact. Using a series of metaphors, the *Kāma-sutta* from the *Sutta-nipāta* (4.1) succinctly states in six verses that dangers and sufferings inevitably result from pursing *kāma*. The pleasure addict who greedily pursues wealth and women is soon swamped by misery 'like water into a broken boat' but the one who masters the pull of pleasures through mindfulness is like someone who avoids treading on the head of a snake. Mastering *kāma*, 'he would cross over the flood like one who has gone to the far shore after bailing out his boat' (Norman 2001: 103).

The *Mahāmāluṅkya-sutta* from the *Majjhima-nikāya* (64) indicates that sexual desire is inherent in the human state and latently present even before we have the ability to conceptualize or act upon it: 'A young tender infant lying prone does not even have the notion "sensual pleasures", so how could sensual desire arise in him? Yet the underlying tendency to sensual lust lies within him' (Bodhi and Ñāṇamoli 1995: 538). This latent sexuality is activated through experiences, mental habits, and behaviours. According to the doctrine of dependent arising (Skt *pratītyasamutpāda*; Pāli *paticcasamuppāda*), grasping at pleasure is the product of craving (Skt *tṛṣṇā*; Pāli *taṇhā*), which is stimulated by sensation (Skt and Pāli *vedanā*), which is in turn stimulated by sense contact (Skt *sparśa*; Pāli *phassa*) (*Majjhima-nikāya* 38; *Dīgha-nikāya* 15). It follows that when certain forms of sense contact cease, certain varieties of grasping and craving are lessened. Sexual contact is a form of *sparśa/phassa* that leads to a cascade of sensation, craving, and grasping resulting in misery. Therefore, those wishing to cultivate wisdom and conquer attachment must avoid inappropriate types of sex contact, and understand and generate the correct attitude towards it if and when it does occur (Perera 1993: 37–38).

According to the Pāli discourses and its major commentator, Buddhaghosa, it is not just the sex act itself which leads to *kāma* and thus to misery. Other sexual behaviours, what Buddhaghosa in the *Visuddhimagga* (following a passage from the *Aṅguttara-nikāya*) lists as the 'seven bonds of sexuality', elicit a cascade of sensual response that pollute the celibate monk's state of purity. These include: receiving a massage from a woman, joking with a woman, gazing into the eyes of a woman, listening to women's voices, recalling pleasant social interactions with women from former times, closely observing the life of a householder as he indulges in the 'five cords of desire', or fantasizing about being born in heaven as a result of *brahmacariya* (Buddhaghosa 1976: 51; Bodhi 2012: 1037–1039). As the critique implicit in the final 'bond' indicates, ending suffering is the stated and express purpose of celibacy according to the early Buddhist tradition, not, as is attested in the *Rig-Veda* and elsewhere, the attainment of heaven. Celibacy for the purposes of heavenly rewards, as in the case of the Buddha's half-brother Nanda who undertook vows in order to enjoy the sexual charms of heavenly nymphs in his next life, is termed the '*brahmacariya* of the fool' (Perera 1993: 84).

The Pāli sources contain traces of ambivalence regarding sensual delight. For instance, the *Mahāgosiṅga-sutta* (MN 32) describes the arhants' delight in a romantically moonlit grove where 'the sāla trees are in blossom, and heavenly scents seem to be floating in the air' (Bodhi and Ñāṇamoli 2005: 308). Sometimes this ambivalence appears to encompass even sexual pleasure, perhaps in response to broader South Asian views regarding *kāma* and *nandī* not orthodox to the Buddhist teachings. Brahmin sources, for instance the *Bṛhadāraṇyaka-upaniṣad*, sometimes depict procreative sex as sacramental. Many actions of the sacrificer's wife in Vedic Hindu rites are charged with sexual symbolism, as when she symbolically copulates with the altar broom or performs a repeated ritual action called 'grasping from behind' (*anvārambhana*). And according to Brahmin householder law, *kāma* is one of the four principal aims of life.

These and other pan-Indic intuitions regarding the spiritual and moral benefits of sexuality would have circulated within and at the margins of the monastic community. *Saṅghādisesa* IV from the Pāli *Vinaya* relates the story of the monk Udāyin who visits a lovely young widow and gladdens her with a *Dharma* talk. She asks what offering she might make that would be useful to him. He replies that while robes, alms food, lodgings, or medicines are easy to come by for a monk, what is rare and difficult to come by is sexual intercourse. The lady complies readily, apparently not perplexed by this request (Collett 2014: 69–73; Horner 1938: 222). Although on one reading of this story Udāyin is cynically taking advantage of a vulnerable and gullible woman, in fact, he and the young widow may have been sincere in their belief that sex constitutes a rare and valued offering to the *saṅgha*. In his study of sexuality in the Pāli *Vinaya*, L. P. N. Perera identifies this idea of sex as the 'highest gift' (*aggadāna*) to be a recurring trope within the Pāli sources and cites a number of other examples (1993: 100–102; Horner 1938: 61). Indexing the Brahmin tradition generally and the *Bṛhadāraṇyaka-upaniṣad* in particular, Perera surmises that this theme 'strongly savour[s] of a primitive cultural survival during the Buddha's day' (1993: 102). The modifier 'primitive' is needlessly tendentious and temporally inaccurate (as Brahmin ascetic traditions and householder law were by no means a figment of the distant past at the time of the *Vinaya*'s compiling), and there is no clear reason to regard the Udāyin story as historically locatable in 'the Buddha's day', but Perera's point—that misguided lay patrons and even monks sometimes espoused positive views of sex that did not strictly comply with mainstream Buddhist doctrine—is well taken nonetheless.

Furthermore, in reading the Pāli discourse, one sometimes has the sense that the *Rig-Vedic* analogy between sexual continence and spiritual heat as well as the brahmanical sacralization of the sex act presented themselves as metaphors even to those articulating the Buddha *Dharma* from an entirely orthodox and mainstream point of view. In the *Sakkapañha-sutta* from the *Dīgha-nikāya* (21), a heavenly bard called Pañcasikkha sings a love song within earshot of the Buddha in which he compares his feelings for his lover to the arhants' experience of the *Dharma*. The Buddha comes out of his meditation to praise his song. The *Sāmaññaphala-sutta* from the *same collection* (DN 2) uses what might be characterized as a sort of orgasmic language to describe the one who has cleansed himself of the five hindrances (desire, malice, sloth, excitement, and doubt) and entered into the first level of meditative absorption (*jhāna*):

> ... detached from sense-desires, detached from unwholesome states, he enters and remains in the first *jhāna*, which is ... filled with delight and joy. And with this delight and joy born of detachment, he so suffuses, drenches, fills and irradiates his body that there is no spot in his entire body that is untouched by this delight and joy born of detachment. (Walshe 1987: 102)

The sutta follows this statement with a simile involving a skilled bathman kneading a ball of oleaginous soap so that it becomes suffused throughout with oil. In the same way, the body of the meditating renouncer becomes saturated throughout with joy and pleasure (*pītisukha*). The soap ball image with its reference to kneading seems to place in high relief the embodied nature the meditator's joy, which in turn introduces a note of ambivalence about pleasure in general and its role in Buddhist soteriology (Anālayo 2014). That physically lush bodily qualities and experiences might be integral to spiritual attainments is a theme picked up in Mahāyāna visions of the bodhisattva, as will be discussed later in this chapter.

Buddhist Antinatalism

Buddhism's deep-seated antinatalism must be regarded as fundamental to Buddhist sexual ethics. Whereas procreative sex is valorized by some religious systems through mythology, fertility cults, religious morality, and the sacralization of marriage, the texts and traditions that chartered monastic Buddhism in India deny human reproduction any moral and soteriological value and indicate that procreation—and the realities of birth in general—are obstructive for the Buddhist path. In a signature truth statement replicated throughout the discourses, for instance, the Buddha asserts that 'With birth as condition, aging-and-death, sorrow, lamentation, pain, displeasure, and despair come to be. Such is the origin of this whole mass of suffering' (Bodhi 2000: 533). *Pārājika* I establishes procreative sex at the top of the list of transgressions that will ruin a monk's career (Gyatso 2005: 280). Non-procreative sex, while proscribed, is not as problematic for monastics.

Classical Buddhist treatments of the birth process are particularly illustrative of Indian Buddhist antinatalism. An early first-millennium sutra text called the 'Descent of the Embryo Scripture' (*Garbhāvakrānti-sūtra*), for instance, provides an overwhelmingly negative account of the birth process, drawing fulsomely from Indian Buddhist stocks of imagery about the foulness of the body (Kritzer 2014). Even when healthy, the womb is said to be full of semen, blood, and pus and likened to a foetid swamp or an oozing wound. Even a newborn body, however smooth and perfect, is said to be immediately subject to decay. The *Garbhāvakrānti-sūtra* does not regard the womb as a warm, cosy, and comfortable cradle for the developing foetus. On the contrary, the foetus is said to experience almost constant pain and discomfort during its tenure there. Sometimes the foetus dies in the womb, in which case it is carved up by the midwife and extracted piece by piece. Just after birth, it also experiences a variety of tortures, according to the sutra. The contentments of a healthy pregnancy, the triumph of a successful childbirth, and the peace of a healthy nursing newborn go unmentioned. Rather, in this text, childbirth, and by association, procreative sex with a woman, are collapsed into death, rendering them inauspicious (Langenberg 2017).

Paying attention to classical Buddhist antinatalism illuminates a second set of fundamental concerns, additional to the problem of desire, and foundational to the classical Buddhist sexual ethic. The fetter of sexual desire leads to suffering, but sexuality is also problematic because it is the biological engine that turns the wheel of *saṃsāra*, fuelling the cycle of human rebirth. To participate in procreative sex is to engage in the cosmic mechanism that endlessly generates ignorance and misery. Several noted scholars have commented on Buddhism's antinatalism in its various manifestations across Asia. William Lafleur, known among other things for his study of Japanese abortion ritual, analyses the ethical implications of what he terms 'anti-fecundism' in Japanese Buddhism in a lesser known article (2003). Rita Gross, grounding herself in the Tibetan tradition, examines Buddhist antinatalism in the context of contemporary environmental concerns associated with population pressure (Gross 2000). Both authors illuminate how, as a result of its deep negativity regarding procreation, premodern Indian Buddhism gave rise to concepts and disciplinary practices structured by sexual concerns different than those that preoccupied, for instance, the Christian Victorians Foucault set out to understand. Both comment on the potentially liberative effects of breaking a morally necessary connection between reproduction and sexuality: Lafleur draws our attention to the comparatively liberal attitude towards homosexuality demonstrated in some Buddhist monastic contexts, while Gross evokes the image of soteriologically valid Tantric sex. Working from a similar insight, José Cabezón notes that sex in Indian Buddhist monasticism was disciplined primarily along lines that mark the boundary between celibacy and heterosexuality, monasticism and lay life, withdrawal from and participation in biological processes, rather than the line between correct (reproductive) and deviant (homosexual, wanton, or autosexual) sex (Cabezón 1993).

If the monastic Buddhism of premodern India disciplined sex with a major aim of making it non-reproductive, the best way to accomplish this for the majority of members was, of course, by requiring strict celibacy. Second best was tolerating (or sometimes even valorizing) homosexual sex or non-ejaculative sexuality over ordinary heterosexuality. We observe both approaches in premodern Indian Buddhist sources. In her study of *Vinaya* law Janet Gyatso finds that, despite the availability of same-sex partners in monastic settings, 'the human female is considered the gold standard for sex: the most likely partner of a monk, and the one with whom the monk's behaviour is most closely regulated' (Gyatso 2005: 280). Leonard Zwilling, author of an early article on homosexuality in classical Buddhism, notes that despite a pervasive prejudice against sex and gender nonconforming individuals in early Buddhist sources, one also detects a 'certain laxity' regarding same-sex relations, which reflects the fact that:

> homosexuality, not to speak of homoerotic friendship, is not entirely incompatible with the monastic life, in that it presents no temptation for the parties involved to forsake the order to which they are committed, nor does it lead to family encumbrances many must have joined the saṃgha to escape. (1992: 209)

John Garret Jones notes what he describes as the homoerotic intimacy of Ānanda's relationship with the Buddha throughout their previous lives together as depicted in the *Jātaka* collection (Jones 1979: 107–115; Cabezón 1993: 88–89). This theme is also picked up by John Powers, who observes that in the discourse collections and the *Vinaya*, male friendships can be homoerotically charged but 'there is no sense that the men might fall in love, develop jealousies, or experience the sorts of relationship issues common to heterosexual couples' (Powers 2009: 161). It is possible that Japan's tradition of male–male monastic love may draw on this ethical undercurrent in the classical tradition (Faure 1998: 233–278; Langenberg 2015).

In the medieval Tantric traditions of India and Tibet documented by David Gray and Janet Gyatso, insertive but non-ejaculative sex is theorized as a fast path to liberating realizations, one deemed superior to celibacy for qualified practitioners (Gray 2007; Gyatso 1998). These developments also support the idea that the sex problematic in ancient, classical, and medieval Buddhism had at least as much to do with female fertility and the production of children as with the dangers of errant desire.

Brahmacarya as Applied Sexual Ethic in Monastic Buddhism

The first rule entailing 'defeat' for monks or expulsion from the order (*pārājika* I) states that 'whatever monk should indulge in sexual intercourse is one who is defeated, he is no longer in communion' (Horner 1938: 38). The first rule entailing adjudication by means of a formal meeting of the community (*saṅghādisesa* I)—the second most serious category of offence after defeat—states that 'intentional emission of semen is a matter entailing a formal meeting of the Order' (Horner 1938: 195). Other sexually related offences, including physical contact with women, suggestive speech, and meeting alone with a woman, are scattered across the rulebook. The commentary (*vibhaṅga*) unpacks these rules, detailing each vital element and illustrating their application with a large number of possible scenarios. Isaline Blew Horner famously bowdlerized what she deemed prurient commentarial texts in her 1938 Pali Text Society translation. She explains her decision in the introduction, referencing modern peoples' embarrassment at the 'crudeness' and 'lack of restraint' of 'early peoples [who] are not so much afraid of plain speech as we are' (Horner 1938: xxxvii). In a recent issue of Horner's *Book of Discipline*, the expurgated passages have been translated by Petra Kiefer-Pülz and included as an appendix (2014: 349–373). Both Horner and L. P. N. Perera insist that the detailing of sexual situations in the *suttavibhaṅga* portion of the Pāli *Vinaya* should not be viewed as indecent or deliberately obscene since it was intended only for the monastic community and motivated by the urgent need to legislate sexual impurity within monastic ranks (Horner 1938: xxxvii; Perera 1993: 39). For Perera, sexually explicit texts in the *Vinaya* must be interpreted in the context of canonical statements about *kāma* and *phassa*, and their soteriological consequences. In her study, Janet Gyatso, on the other hand, finds it difficult to ignore the obvious humour, double entendre, and wry self-referentiality of these texts (Gyatso 2005: 271–272). Gyatso allows herself to query 'the vinaya's hyper-analysis of proscribed sex acts' with a greater degree of hermeneutical complexity than Perera and Horner, introducing the possibilities of humour, fantasy, scholastic fastidiousness, and ethical ambiguity, in her study (Gyatso 2005: 271).

Rules about sex in the Pāli *Vinaya*, which present themselves one after the other with luxurious abundance and probe seemingly every corner of human sexual impulse, perfectly illustrate Foucault's critique of the 'suppressive hypothesis'. Rather than shutting down sexuality, the prohibitive stance taken by Buddhist monastic law seems to release a viral proliferation of sexual behaviours, if not in historical reality, at least in the discursive space of the *Vinaya*. There, sex is quantified and measured and specified in all of its variety. Sexual intercourse proper is legally defined as 'whenever the male organ is made to enter the female ... even for the length of a fruit of the sesame plant' (Horner 1938: 47). Since a certain monk, having persuaded a female monkey with a reward, is said to have engaged in repeated sexual intercourse with her (Horner 1938: 38–40, 341; Kieffer-Pülz 2014: 350–351, 354), intercourse with an animal is also designated a terminal breach of *brahmacariya*. The commentary to *pārājika* I also narrates the story of a monk who is approached by a deer while urinating. The deer takes his penis in its mouth and 'drinks the urine'. The monk consents, and is defeated (Kieffer-Pülz 2014: 358–359). Various other possible partners and orifices are also enumerated. Partners include, in addition to female humans and animals: female non-humans; hermaphrodite humans, non-humans, and animals; what we might call gender-queer (*paṇḍaka*) humans, non-humans, and animals; and male humans, non-humans, and animals (Anālayo 2015: 439–443; Gyatso 2003; Gyatso 2005: 278; Kieffer-Pülz 2014: 351–352; Zwilling 1992). Orifices include: the anus, the 'path of urine' or 'path of fluid' (a term for the vagina that implies a serious misunderstanding of its function), and the mouth (Horner 1938: 341; Kieffer-Pülz 2014: 351). Penetration to the length of a sesame seed in all of the above orifices of all of the above partner types qualifies as sexual intercourse leading to defeat.

We also hear of sex acts involving a variety of costuming choices; penetration by thumb;[2] acrobatic autoeroticism; sex with various orifices found in corpses in various stages of decomposition; incest; sex with a wooden doll or plaster figure; hand stimulation by female patrons; sex with *nāgas*, *yakkhas*, and ghosts; rape of a nun by a man; rape of a monk by a woman; and a monk being forced into sex with a female probationer, a female novice, a prostitute, a *paṇḍaka*, a female householder, or another monk (Horner 1938: 46–64; Kieffer-Pülz 2014: 350–359). These enumerated sexual behaviours result in varying levels of disciplinary action, depending on circumstances and the mental attitude of the monk. For instance, if the monk is acrobatic enough to insert his penis in his own mouth, he is defeated, despite the fact that a separate partner is not involved. When a monk is forced by 'an opponent' to have sex with a partner of any description and in any state of consciousness (awake, asleep, intoxicated, crazy, dead) and he nonetheless agrees to any or all phases of the sexual act (application, penetration, dwelling inside, withdrawal), he is defeated. If at the time of the sexual act, however, he is ignorant of the rule, does not agree, is asleep, is not in control of his mental state, either permanently or temporarily, or is a beginner, there is no offence (Horner 1938: 49–51; Kieffer-Pülz 2014: 353–354). If a monk stimulates himself using a plaster statue or a wooden doll, it is merely an offence of wrongdoing (*dukkaṭa*) (Horner 1938: 55; Kieffer-Pülz 2014: 355). If the monk is raped when he is incapacitated, even though his body may have exhibited a sexual response and he ejaculates semen, there is no offence (Horner 1938: 58; Kieffer-Pülz 2014: 357–358). If a monk has the intention of performing a sexual act with a woman but is stricken with conscience when he touches her, he is subject to formal disciplinary action by the community (*saṅghādisesa*) but not defeated (Horner 1938: 58). If a monk merely dreams of having sex, there is no offence (Horner 1938: 60–61). If a monk is completely passive but submits to being masturbated by a pious laywoman giving the 'highest gift' of sexual pleasure, then he is subject to formal disciplinary action but not defeated (Horner 1938: 61).

[2] The *pārājika* I commentary includes a scenario in which a monk comes upon a young girl (*dārikā*) lying on her back. The monk becomes aroused and inserts his thumb in her vagina. The girl dies. Kieffer-Pülz proposes that what is being described here is the sexual abuse of an infant (2014: 354 n. 3).

As Gyatso points out, desire (*kāma*) does not seem to be the only or even the most important factor in adjudicating sexual offence (2005: 280). In one case, a monk whose faculties are impaired and cannot feel pleasure or pain in his genitals has sex, thinking that this means there will be no offence. The Buddha rules that he is defeated. In general, the degree of offence is not calibrated to the absence or presence of sexual pleasure. The monk who has sex with a wooden doll, and presumably experiences plenty of pleasure (in fact, he is described as 'inflamed'), has committed only an offence of wrongdoing.

Gyatso also notes that, while insertive intercourse with any of the enumerated partners in any of the enumerated orifices results in defeat, in rules belonging to less serious offence categories that govern other sexual fetters (touching, consorting, flirting), this 'partner parity' drops away. For instance, it is more serious for a monk to have physical contact with or rub up against a live woman than against a dead woman, or a man (Gyatso 1005: 280). In the case of fully ordained female monastics (*bhikṣuṇīs*), for whom there are eight instead of four faults entailing defeat, partner parity drops away even at the level of *pārājika* offences. The *prātimokṣa* for *bhikṣuṇīs* specifies that intentional lustful physical contact with a man such as touching between the collarbones and the knees or handholding is a *pārājika*, even if no intercourse occurs as a consequence. Meeting a man in seclusion because of sexual attraction, flirting, immodesty, or making suggestive gestures are also *pārājika*-level transgressions for nuns (Tsomo 1996: 28–29, 82–83; Wijayaratna 1990: 93–94; Wijayaratna 2010: 119–122). If a *bhikṣuṇī* fashions a dildo out of glue, uses a dildo, engages in mutual masturbation with another nun, masturbates herself, or inserts two fingers past the first joint in her own vagina, however, she commits only an offence requiring expiation, a comparatively minor level of transgression (Tsomo 1996: 50, 111; Wijayaratna 2010: 128–129).[3] Here we see, again, that sexual behaviour, no matter how pleasurable, is taken less seriously if it is not likely to result in potentially reproductive heterosexual intercourse.

Gyatso also explores the ambiguous and surprising role that intention or mental attitude has in adjudicating sexual offences in the *Vinaya*. Intention is generally understood to be the most important factor in determining the moral quality of actions (*karman*). In the practical management of sexual behaviours with monastic communities, however, it is only one of the several factors that determine the severity of consequences. Whether or not a monk agrees to a sexual act or intends an act to be sexual certainly is of primary importance in determining whether that act entails defeat, as we have seen. And yet, in the case of the paradigmatic monastic sex offender, the monk Sudinna, intent

[3] Variations on these rules are attested in the sectarian *bhikṣuṇī Vinayas*. For instance, the *Dharmaguptaka Vinaya* rules against nuns masturbating one another, while the *Mūlasarvāstivāda Vinaya* mentions only the case of a nun masturbating her own self. Similarly, the Dharmaguptaka tradition rules against nuns fashioning dildos but does not rule against their use. The Mūlasarvāstivāda tradition states the opposite position, ruling against using dildos but not against fashioning them. The Pāli *Vinaya* tradition likewise attests variability in these rules. For the sake of brevity (and because it doesn't significantly affect the larger point I am making) I have not distinguished between these various traditions here.

(and desire) to have sex is somewhat lacking. Although he obviously responds sexually since he impregnates her, initially Sudinna agrees to have sex with his former wife with the most extreme reluctance and only out of a sense of family duty and obligation. The intention for him to have sex belongs more to his determined mother than to himself.

Gyatso argues that these surprising features of *Vinaya* law stem from the fact that it 'is not about spiritual attainment or enlightenment' but rather 'serves to define a community' (2005: 281). In other words, the monastic community is defined against ordinary householding, which means that sex acts that may lead directly or indirectly to the birth of children, or sex acts that resemble procreative sex, are deemed more serious than those (like masturbation) that merely express and inflame sensual desire. Gyatso's assertion that sex with a [fertile young] woman is 'the gold standard for sex' (2005: 280) follows from these insights.

While this line of analysis is fruitful, and based on the discovery of startling lines of tension within these texts that previous scholars have failed to articulate, I hesitate to separate the world of the suttas from the world of the *Vinaya*—theory and practice, if you will—quite so starkly. The *Vinaya* certainly 'define[s] a community' against and within a particular socio-historical context, but it must operate simultaneously as a practical handbook for the performance of virtue, something undoubtedly linked to 'spiritual attainment or enlightenment'. While acknowledging the helpfulness of Gyatso's discoveries, I would nudge any argument on the tension between intention and act, pleasure and fertility, hetero versus non-hetero partners evident in *pārājika* I and its commentary (and elsewhere in the Pāli *Vinaya*) onto a different course. Preventing monks from having children with women is not purely a matter of safeguarding the integrity of the community, however vital that may be. It is also a dimension of a profound Buddhist antinatalism, which is a basic component of both Buddhist soteriology and practical articulations of the path. Thus, the fact that sex with a woman is the 'gold standard' for what a monk must avoid, and Gyatso gets this (and many other things) right, may be viewed as a basic feature of Buddhist applied ethics, and not only an element of Buddhist institutional theory.

Though they were generically concerned with regulating the normative and potentially reproductive sexuality exemplified by Sudinna, *Vinaya* lawgivers exhibit a humane and intimate understanding of human sexuality that goes well beyond the missionary position, so to speak. They frankly acknowledge and go about adjudicating gender diversity, homosexuality, fetishism, sexual aggression, non-insertive sexual behaviours, and autoeroticism. The monk compelled to father a child behaves differently from a monk who simply wants to have an orgasm and must be disciplined along a somewhat different axis. Similarly, a monk who receives a sexual proposition as an offering from a pious laywoman must be disciplined differently than an incapacitated monk raped by a lusty passerby, a monk masturbated by a laywoman differently than one who has sex with his cellmate, a monk who uses one of his own orifices for gratification differently from a monk who uses a plaster sex toy, and on and on.

Although the *Vinaya* is sometimes read in a simplistic fashion as a series of rules that shall not be broken, in fact, by my reading, *Vinaya* lawgivers do not counter human sexuality with a brutal wall of prohibition. Rather, they are exquisitely responsive to subtle differences in the various possible scenarios. Thus, I interpret the multiple intersecting axes along which monks' sexuality is disciplined in the *Vinaya* (intentional/unconscious or unwilling, active/passive, hetero/non-hetero, insertive/non-insertive, procreative/non-procreative, impassioned/dispassionate, living partner/dead or inanimate partner) as engagements with the complexity of sexual behaviours (imagined or observed), which themselves are not simply 'natural' or prior to Buddhism but rather emerge hundredfold from the matrix of Buddhist sexual discourse. Buddhist monastic discipline adopts an elaborated disciplinary logic because it is responsive to and constructive of a prohibitive Buddhist sex discourse that has at least two major foci—the soteriology of suffering and the critique of pronatalism—and that generates multiple pockets of micro-resistance and transgression, multiple subjectivities, all of which lawgivers must arrange in a branching taxonomy of offence.

The Buddha is Sexy and Other Late Classical, Medieval, and Early Modern Interpretations of *Brahmacarya*

In a 2000 article discussing Buddhist perspectives on population and consumption, the late feminist Buddhist theologian Rita Gross argues that despite the monastic ideal of celibacy, in decoupling reproduction and sexuality Buddhist antinatalism makes room for an openness towards diverse human sexualities that is unusual in religious contexts. Gross observes that whereas the pronatalism of, for instance, Roman Catholicism leads to moral condemnation of non-reproductive sexual behaviours such as masturbation or homoerotic activity, Buddhist devalorization of reproduction as a primary good allows collaterally for the possibility of diverse sexual expression. Gross also praises Vajrayāna (Tantric) Buddhist partner yogas and *yab-yum* imagery (deities depicted in sexual embrace) in which 'sexuality is openly portrayed as a symbol of the most profound religious truths and as contemplative exercise for developing one's innate enlightenment' (Gross 2000: 421–422).

Gross writes in a constructive mode, not as an historian. Still, her insights regarding the possibilities that emerge when sexuality and reproduction are uncoupled provide a helpful lens through which to view certain surprising late classical, medieval, and early modern Buddhist themes. As Buddhist thinking and practice develops in ancient India (and interacts with the cultures of Tibet and beyond), the Buddha emerges as a sex symbol of sorts, bodhisattvas are advised to use sex as a teaching tool when appropriate, and sexuality is eventually harnessed to the soteriological aims of Buddhism. Gross challenges us to consider the positive engagements of sex (and sexiness) that are possible in antinatalist traditions such as Buddhism, despite its negative assessment of desire.

Although she does not invoke Foucault's work on sexuality, her insights regarding the way in which Buddhist soteriology supports a decoupling of reproduction and sexuality complement his critique of the repressive hypothesis. Both argue that moral and metaphysical suspicions about certain sorts of sex, and human sexuality in general, support an increasingly creative and complex engagement with sexuality, not a dampening of sexual imagination and behaviour.

It turns out that such engagements are not always marginal, but often mainstream, hiding in plain sight, so to speak. In his work on Buddhist masculinity, which draws attention to frequent depictions in Sanskrit and Pāli texts from India of the Buddha and his disciples as manly, virile, and sexually magnetic, John Powers argues for a Buddhist sexiness abiding at the very heart of the tradition (2009). According to Powers, celibate males on the Buddhist path are not cool, remote, abstract, asexual, or intellectual in the literature and art of ancient Buddhist India. Rather their physical beauty and strength is much emphasized. As has already been noted, in *Vinaya* texts monks are propositioned and even sexually aggressed by women, who appear to find them irresistible. For a range of complicated historically specific reasons, Euro-American scholarship and popular discourse has foregrounded the image of the androgynous, sexually effete Buddhist monk to the point where a potent Buddhist masculinity seems a contradiction in terms and is thus occluded. Powers notes, however, how 'struck' he was at once by 'the pervasiveness of ultra-masculine images in Indian Buddhist texts' (some of which he had read many times before without noticing this) upon initiating his research on Buddhist masculinity. 'Once I began looking,' he comments, such images,

> seemed to leap from the pages and confront me with a completely new version of the Buddha, one who personified the ideals of the Indian warrior class (*kṣatriya*), who caused women to faint because of his physical beauty, and who converted people to his teachings through the perceptual impact of his extraordinary physique. (Powers 2009: 3)

Powers's larger point, and it has not gone unchallenged by critics (Ciurtin 2010–2011), is that when the Buddha is described as the 'ultimate man' (*puruṣottama*) or 'bull among men' (*puruṣarṣabha*) the epithet refers not just to his ultimacy as the embodiment of wisdom or importance as a leader but also to his ideal masculinity and should be understood as such. In Powers's view, when in the 'Discourse to Caṅkī' (*Majjhima-nikāya* 94) the Buddha is described as 'handsome, comely, and graceful, possessing supreme beauty of complexion' (Bodhi and Ñāṇamoli 1995: 776; quoted at Powers 2009: 3), and when artistic depictions of the Buddha from India glorify his ideal beauty, perfect proportionality, and physically remarkable body (Powers 2009: 56–62), the emphasis really is on the charismatic nature of the Buddha's embodied form, his attractiveness at the basic level of bodies, not on the virtue and extraordinary wisdom of which his beauty is considered an expression.

On this reading, some Indian Buddhist texts are even more to the point, highlighting the perfection and transformative qualities of the Buddha's genitals. One of the thirty-two major marks (*lakṣaṇa*) of a Great Man (*mahāpuruṣa*) displayed on the Buddha's body is a penis that is sheathed like that of a stallion, bull, or bull elephant (Mrozik 2007: 64; Powers 2009: 13). According to the *Lakkhaṇa-sutta* of the *Dīgha-nikāya* (30), this particular mark of greatness (described in Pāli as *kosohitta vatthaguhya*) indicates that should he choose to remain in the world, the *mahāpuruṣa* will be the father of many sons. Should he leave the world and become a spiritual teacher (as does Gotama), he will also be endowed with many children, those who follow his teachings (*puttā vacanānasārino*) (*Dīgha-nikāya* 3.162).[4] In several cases, the Buddha's special penis functions as a tool of persuasion and legitimizing mark. In the *Brahmāyu-sutta* from the *Majjhima-nikāya* (91), for instance, the Buddha persuades a young brahmin that he himself really is an 'Accomplished One, a Fully Enlightened One, who draws aside the veil in the world' by displaying his sheathed penis (Bodhi and Ñāṇamoli 1995: 744–745). In a Mahāyāna text extant only in Chinese entitled the 'Discourse of the Ocean-Like Meditation of Buddha Remembrance', the Buddha converts a group of disbelieving Jain ascetics by lying on his back and extruding his penis from its special sheath until it wraps three times around a magically conjured image of Mount Sumeru and extends upwards to heaven (Powers 2009: 14). It is true that in these instances his unusual penis seems to impress rather than seduce (though perhaps this is a distinction without a difference). It is also important to emphasize that, according to the Buddhist logic of embodiment, the Buddha is well built and well endowed as a direct result of chastity, not desire. In other words, he may be the object of lust, but he does not himself lust. Furthermore, as in the *Gaṇḍavyūha-sūtra*, the Buddha's perfect chastity is sometimes said to be an impediment to any feelings of sexual desire on the part of his followers (Powers 2009: 13). Still, such prohibitive views must be considered against the background of masculine depictions of the Buddha, which suggest that his perfect and pure continence is not austere but rather results in a special sort of manly vibrancy and charisma. Indeed, one might argue, in a Foucauldian mode, that the Buddha's chastity produces and accentuates his masculinity. This model is then available for emulation by monastics.

Susanne Mrozik's seminal work on the embodied dimensions of Indian Buddhist ethics, which takes as its focus an early medieval treatise by the Nālandā monk, Śāntideva, entitled the *Compendium of Training* (*Śikṣāsamuccaya*), elucidates a theoretical basis for the hypermasculine images Powers highlights that is emic, not etic. The *Compendium* advises bodhisattvas to always please and provide enjoyment for other beings. Why? As Mrozik explains, according to Śāntideva, bodhisattvas must:

> use everything they have to attract living beings to them and therefore to the Dharma. Unless bodhisattvas can attract living beings, they will not be able fully to liberate these beings from the suffering of saṃsāric existence. Attracting living

[4] I am grateful to Natalie Gummer for sharing her so-far unpublished work on connections made in Pāli materials between the Buddha's impressively large tongue, eloquent and productive speech, and sheathed male organ.

beings is so important that bodhisattvas can even violate lay and monastic precepts [in order to do so]. (Mrozik 2007: 26)

Sometimes pleasing beings takes the form of sexual or romantic gratification. For instance, the *Upāyakauśalya-sūtra* (quoted in the *Compendium*) relates the story of Jyotis who, despite maintaining celibacy for 42,000 years, marries the woman who propositions him in order to bring her to the *Dharma* (Mrozik 2007: 27). According to the *Compendium*, the Bodhisattva Pryaṃkara takes a powerful vow as a result of which any woman who looks upon him with desire will be reborn as a man. Other Mahāyāna sutra and *śāstra* texts also contain the trope of bodhisattvas using their sexuality to transform beings. The *Śūraṅgamasamādhi-sūtra* narrates the tale of the Bodhisattva Māragocarānulipta seducing two hundred of Māra's female attendants. 'Seeing the perfect beauty of that bodhisattva, they became enamoured of him. Each one declared separately: If that man makes love to us, we will all comply with his instructions' (Lamotte 2009: 177). The bodhisattva frolics with Māra's ladies and completely fulfils their sexual cravings, which then evaporate. Seduced and then converted, they manifest firm resolve to follow the *Dharma*, and, upon receiving religious instruction from the bodhisattva, conceive the mind of enlightenment (*bodhicitta*). According to the *Vimalakīrti-sūtra*, the lay bodhisattva Vimalakīrti also visits brothels in order to ripen beings (Thurman 1976: 21). In the 'Chapter on Ethics' from his *Bodhisattvabhūmi*, the third-century scholastic Asaṅga also defends uncelibacy (what he calls 'the dharma of sexual embrace') for lay bodhisattvas if it comprises the best means for generating wholesome attitudes in sentient beings. He cautions, however, that such *upāya* (expedients) are out of the question for monastic bodhisattvas (Asaṅga 2016: 280–281; Tatz 1986: 71). In his commentary, the fourteenth-century Tibetan scholar Tsongkhapa further finesses this view, arguing that, unlike killing, stealing, or lying, which do not result in defeat if undertaken to benefit another being and not for one's own benefit, consciously engaging in uncelibacy, even when done for another's sake, is by definition a 'laying aside of training' (Tatz 1986: 213). Therefore, a monastic bodhisattva in effect becomes a lay bodhisattva when he engages in uncelibacy.

Matters of monastic discipline and matters of karmic fruits are not conflated in these ethical discussions. A bodhisattva will, out of compassion, promote wholesome mental states in another being by means of sex, even if he must give back his vows in order to do so. And according to the *Upālipariprccha* (quoted in the *Compendium*), 'sins of lust' committed by bodhisattvas for the purpose of attracting beings are said to be minor compared to, for instance, sins of anger, even though they spell defeat for his monastic status (Mrozik 2007: 27). Furthermore, even though Mahāyāna texts like Śāntideva's repeatedly state that ordinary sensual desires lead only to misery and ruin, when a woman desires a bodhisattva, she generates merit, not sin (45).

Interestingly, the bodies of female bodhisattvas do not seem to function as merit factories in the same way as male bodhisattva bodies, a fact which is illustrated by the story of the Bodhisattva Candrottarā told in the *Compendium*. Despite her status as a highly attained being, Candrottarā's stunning beauty poses a spiritual distraction for men, a danger against which she vociferously warns them in a sermon about the negative karmic consequences of unfettered lust (Mrozik 2007: 57). At another place, however, Śāntideva, quoting the *Vimalakīrti-nirdeśa*, references courtesan bodhisattvas who establish men in the *Dharma* by 'luring them with the hook of lust' (Śāntideva 1971: 291).

The Tantric sexual yogas theorized and practised in medieval India and medieval and early modern Tibet, understood by European scholars until relatively recently to be marginal, deviant, and possibly tribal in origin, relate to and are the logical extension of Powers's sexy celibates and Mrozik's pleasing bodhisattva bodies. Tantric traditions go beyond the mainstream Mahāyāna sexuality described above, however, in reinterpreting the *Vinaya*-defined *brahmacarya* of bodhisattvas and realized beings. While the embodiment of masculine beauty, and in possession of an unusual but powerful male member, the Buddha is celibate in the early and classical Indic texts Powers interprets. In Tantric imagery the buddhas abide in sexual union. For instance, the *Hevajra Tantra* begins with the phrase 'thus have I heard' (the standard opening line of the discourses) followed by a description of the Lord dwelling in the sexual organs (*bhaga*) of his consort (Snellgrove 1959, 2: 2). Furthermore, while bodhisattvas engage in sexual intercourse only under certain special circumstances and only for the sake of spiritually ripening other beings in the Mahāyāna text Mrozik examines, some Tantric writings, specifically the non-dual Buddhist Tantras classified as Mahāyoga and Yoginī, advise bodhisattvas to engage in sexual union as an essential component of their own spiritual practices (*caryā*), undertaken to attain powers (*siddhi*) and the non-dual gnosis of the Buddhas. For instance, the *Hevajra* advises practitioners that 'Taking a girl of the vajra [clan]—with a pretty face, wide eyes, with the glow of youth, with a body dark like a blue lotus, self-initiated, and compassionate—employ her in the performance of the practices (*caryā*)' (Wedemeyer 2013: 140).

In theory, Buddhist Tantric sexual yogas utilize the powerful energies aroused during sexual contact to achieve special forms of mind that attain beyond dualistic conceptions and constructed categories. They involve a complicated visualization of the structures of the subtle body, which possesses a central channel reaching from perineum to crown intercepted by obstructive knots at genitals, navel, heart, throat, and head called *cakras*. During sex, the Tantric yogi (who is generically male) must refrain from ejaculation and instead force the powerful subtle 'winds' generated by sex into the central channel, whereby they travel upwards, piercing the obstructing *cakras* and producing an intense experience of bliss which he then cognizes as non-dual. This type of yoga can be practised without a partner, but practising with a partner is understood to facilitate and intensify the experience of bliss that aids the generation of non-dual gnosis (see, for instance, Gyatso 1998: 190–197). Some Indian texts describe a technique of 'reverse urethral suction' by which male practitioners ejaculate but then reabsorb the co-mingled sexual fluids (Gray 2007: 121), but most Buddhist sexual yogas with a consort are non-ejaculative (almost all available accounts of sexual yoga assume a male physiology and assume the male perspective) and so, in that sense, still faithful to the non-reproductive celibate ethos of early Buddhism.

In some cases this Tantric reinterpretation of *brahmacarya* is explicit. In his commentary on the *Cakrasaṃvara Tantra*, an important Tantra of the Yoginī class, Jayabhadra glosses the text's instruction to 'observe chastity (*brahmacarya*) in meditation' as 'at the time of the trickling of the ejaculate seminal essence, one should observe, i.e., practice, chastity' (Gray 2007: 123), in other words, retain the semen. The eighteenth-century Tibetan Tantrika Jigme Lingpa makes the counter-intuitional statement that sexual yoga is an effective way for a monk who has transgressed against *brahmacarya* to purify himself. In her study of Lingpa's autobiographical writings, Janet Gyatso proposes a logic for this claim: 'in fact fulfillment yoga of the sexual sort would involve the most rigorous type of vow of all: what more difficult renunciation is there than to stop at the brink of orgasm and try to reverse the flow of sexual fluids back up the central channel?' (Gyatso 1998: 195). Although Lingpa writes at a somewhat later time than the traditions that mostly concern us here, his view may reflect an old belief. Tsongkhapa, for instance, explicitly disagrees with that sort of position in his commentary to Asaṅga's 'Chapter on Ethics', criticizing those who say, 'We are bodhisattvas. We are Tantrics. Even should we "supersede" [the *prātimokṣa* precepts], the latter status will purify us' (Tatz 1986: 211).

It is important to note at this juncture that, in considering Buddhist forms of Tantric practice that include sexuality, we are entering into a specialized and highly circumscribed esoteric realm. In his important 2013 study of Tantric Buddhism, Wedemeyer makes two vital points regarding descriptions of sexual (and other antinomian ritual) practices in medieval esoteric Buddhist Tantric literature. First, he argues for an engagement with the connotative as well as denotative content of these texts. In other words, while the possibility of performance of such rites is essential to their semiotics, it cannot be flatly assumed that such rites are described because they were performed. Their description is also an act of discursive creativity—a linguistically based evocation of a Buddhist vision of human thriving that builds its meanings from the complex symbolic, social, and ritual vocabulary of medieval India. Second, according to the texts themselves, esoteric Tantric practice (*caryā* or *vrata* or *caryāvrata*) that includes sexuality is to be performed only by a highly qualified person, for a limited duration of time, and only in a highly circumscribed ritually specific environment. 'Nowhere is the *caryāvrata* characterized', Wedemeyer notes, 'as daily (*nitya*) or quotidian Tantric practice. … the *vrata* is set apart in time as well as in space' (Wedemeyer 2013: 152). Thus, the long historical journey traced here from the exoteric Buddhist critique of desire and reproductivity located in the Pāli discourses and the ethical regulation of sexuality found in the *Vinaya* through Mahāyāna visions of bodhisattva sexiness to the rarefied world of the non-dual Buddhist Tantras is also a movement from a practical Buddhist sexual ethics for the Everyman to the specialized sexual ethics appropriate to the Buddhist spiritual hero, and to some extent, from a relatively straightforward treatment of sex to an increasingly complex and imaginative Buddhist semiotics of the sexual.

Lay Sexual Ethics

It is a Foucauldian irony that, in early Indian Buddhism, the sexuality of monastics is fully elaborated and deeply theorized while sexual ethics for the Buddhists who are presumably having more sex, i.e. non-monastic Buddhists (usually called 'laypeople' in English-language scholarship), are considered in broad strokes only. Here I am treating ordinary lay people as distinct from the lay bodhisattvas and Tantrikas discussed above, as does the tradition itself. Sexual ethics for householder Buddhists are thinly described in the *Discourses* and do not enter at all into any of the *Vinaya*s, which deal only with monastic conduct, although, as is proposed below, monastic sexuality is always the implicit, and sometimes the explicit, ethical model for lay sexuality. Lay sexual misconduct is proscribed by the third precept (*śīla*) observed by pious laypeople (*upāsaka*) and is generally understood, as it is in the *Sigālovāda-sutta* from the *Dīgha-nikāya* (31), in terms of adultery (literally, 'going to the wife of another man') (Cabezón 2008; Collins 2007: 263; Harvey 2000: 71). Sexual wantonness, such as visiting prostitutes, also meets with disapproval and is associated with the influence of wine and the wrong sorts of friends.[5] According to Steven Collins's research on the third precept in Pāli sources, even unmarried women who are 'guarded' by family members are 'not to be gone to' without the permission of the guardian, while only those unmarried women who have been promised to a man are forbidden by the third precept to have sex with men (as the latter constitutes a form of theft) (Collins 2007: 263–268). The point of reference in sources and commentaries on the third precept is heterosexual, in contrast to the frank treatments of monastic homosexuality and other forms of non-heterosexuality that appear in the *Vinaya*.

In the fourth century, Vasubandhu expands somewhat, though not at length, on the subject of lay sexual misconduct. His advice is, again, aimed at married male householders. In order to avoid sexual misconduct, *upāsakas* must avoid: intercourse with a 'forbidden woman', that is, another's wife, or one's own close relative; intercourse through a forbidden orifice; intercourse in an inappropriate place, including a public place, a religious shrine, or a monastery; and intercourse at an inappropriate time, including when one's wife is nursing or pregnant, or when she has taken a temporary vow of celibacy (Vasubandhu 1988, 2: 604). The *Upāsakaśīla-sūtra* ('The Sūtra on the Lay Precepts'), an Indic text translated in China in the fifth century, also contains a discussion of the third precept. It repeats the injunction against adultery and forbids intercourse with monks, other laymen, animals, prisoners, fugitives, destroyed female corpses, a girl under the protection of her parents, and the teacher's wife. Like Vasubandhu's commentary, this text also forbids sex involving the wrong organs and sex in inappropriate places such as stupas and temples. Additionally, it specifically criticizes the man who has sex with his wife after she has wandered forth from the home due to hardship, and the man who has

[5] See, for instance, the *Sigālovāda-sutta* or the *Parābhava-sutta* from the *Sutta-nipāta*.

sex with his wife thinking she is someone else, or sex with another, thinking she is his wife. Like the virtuous *bhikṣu*, the virtuous *upāsaka* must strive for purity in both conscious intention *and* act. Finally, the text reminds the reader in a logical move reminiscent of *Vinaya* casuistry that some forms of sexual misconduct are more serious than others (Shih 1994: 173).[6]

Influenced by Indic traditions, several prominent medieval and early modern Tibetan scholars also expand on the subject of lay sexual misconduct. Tsongkhapa's comments in the *Lamrim Chenmo* are particularly authoritative. Indeed, it is on the basis of this text that the Fourteenth Dalai Lama publically put forth the view that homosexuality is not permitted within Buddhism. He subsequently clarified and softened his statements about homosexuality, stating that 'It is wrong for society to reject people on the basis of sexual orientation' at a 1997 meeting with a group of concerned gay and lesbian Buddhists in San Francisco (Cabezón 2008). Like his Indic predecessors, Tsongkhapa's view is heteronormative and androcentric, and he analyses sexual misconduct in terms of partner, body parts, place, and time. Men, for instance, should not have sex with other men, or with *paṇḍakas*. They should also not have sex with 'those held by another' (i.e. someone else's wife), close family members (i.e. mothers), 'those protected by family' (i.e. someone else's daughter), female renouncers, or anyone protected by the king. The latter, he further explains, includes 'anyone for whom a punitive law has been laid down', likely the fugitives and prisoners mentioned in the *Upāsakaśīla-sūtra*. He should not have sex with a prostitute whose fee someone else has paid, implying that he is permitted to have sex with a prostitute whose fee he has paid himself. Incorrect orifices are specified as 'body parts other than the vagina', meaning the mouth, anus, or pressed together legs. To the usual list of inappropriate places, Tsongkhapa considerately adds 'uneven or hard places that are harmful to the person with whom you are having intercourse' as well as 'the vicinity of an abbot, a preceptor, or one's parents'. To the list of inappropriate times, Tsongkhapa adds the wife's menstrual period and illnesses. He also mentions that the virtuous layperson should not have sex during the day and not more than five times in a night (2000: 220–224). Many of these principles are also found in writings by Gampopa (1079–1153) and Patrul Rinpoche (1808–1887). The comparatively brief treatment of sexual misconduct by the latter also specifically forbids masturbation and sex with a prepubescent child (but not, apparently, sex with a pubescent child) (Patrul Rinpoche 1998: 107; Harvey 2000: 73).

This quasi-systematic lay sexual ethic, articulated in scholastic texts starting loosely in the mid-first millennium CE, appears to have been partly patterned, as José Cabezón observes, on a monastic legal discourse structured in terms of partners and orifices (Cabezón 2008). This makes sense, since these systematizers were themselves monastics who tended to regard householding not as an intrinsically valid way to live and valuable in its own right, but rather as an inferior second alternative to monasticism.

6 Unfortunately, the BDK English translation of this text contains some significant errors. I wish to acknowledge Robert Kritzer for his assistance in interpreting this passage.

In general, canonical and commentarial literature defines the *upāsaka* not as a householder per se, but as someone who has taken refuge and pledged to practise the five precepts, again, an inferior version of monasticism (Agostini 2008). Vasubandhu surmises in his *Abhidharmakośabhāṣya* that, though it would be ideal, householders can abstain only from sexual misconduct, not from sexuality itself, 'because they are not capable of difficult things'. He also states that the virtuous layperson should refrain from sexual misconduct 'because the Āryans have obtained abstention from it', thus explicitly modelling lay ethics on the ethical ideals of the renouncer (1988, 2: 603–604).

Tsongkhapa also places the sexual ethics of laypeople, which he says is mainly concerned with avoiding nonhuman rebirth, on a moral ladder that culminates in the higher discipline of bodhisattvas and *siddhas*. When, however, it is assumed that the normative *upāsaka* is heterosexual and married, and heterosexual reproductive sex is explicitly permitted, as is the case in the teachings considered here, sex with non-heterosexual partners (e.g. male, *paṇḍaka*) or in the wrong orifice (e.g. anus, mouth), which tends to be more tolerated than reproductive heterosexual intercourse in monastic settings, becomes explicitly forbidden in Buddhist lay ethics (as was attested by the Dalai Lama in various public remarks). Thus, it could be argued that explicit prohibitions against homosexuality for (generically male) laypeople in Indo-Tibetan Buddhism is more of an accident of the ethical borrowing and reshuffling of *Vinaya* principles evident in scholastic texts on lay sexual ethics than the product of a deeply theorized abomination of male homosexuality. Interestingly, because the assumed subject of these ethical teachings for laypeople is a heterosexual married man, same-sex female sexual contact falls completely outside of their scope and is thus not explicitly prohibited.

Conclusion

Several issues vitally important to understanding Buddhist sexuality have not been broached in this short chapter. Perhaps the most egregious omission is a comprehensive discussion of sexual ethics for women in ancient, classical, and medieval Indian Buddhism. While some feminist Buddhist scholarship analyses *representations* of female sexuality from a male ascetic perspective (Gross 1993; Lang 1986; Shaw 1994; Wilson 1996; Young 2004), a relatively few studies (Collett 2014; Collins 2007) have focused on normative sexual ethics for women in classical Buddhism, and to date very few works have broached the embodied sexual ethics of female Buddhist practitioners. Sarah Jacoby's 2014 study of the female Tibetan Buddhist adept and Tantric practitioner Sera Khandro (1892–1940), whose views and experiences are intimately related to the Indo-Tibetan tradition examined here, is a notable exception. Two important topoi emerge in the work that is available in the area of embodied female sexual ethics in Buddhism: namely, an active Buddhist female sexuality expressed through sex work, yogic partnering, autoeroticism, and female–female sexual contact; and a female vulnerability to rape, harassment, and exploitation.

This chapter on Buddhist sexual ethics focused specifically on early, classical, and medieval Indo-Tibetan sources, but it has been called forth by and is highly relevant to several important contemporary conversations. For instance, the classical perspectives captured here pertain to debates about sexual ethics erupting in *Dharma* communities across North America and Europe in response to multiple instances of sexual abuse by Buddhist teachers. The most infamous of these involved Richard Baker, who resigned as abbot of the San Francisco Zen Center in 1984 after revelations of sexual relationships with his students, and Ösel Tendzin, Regent of Vajradhatu (the Tibetan Buddhist *saṅgha* established by Chogyam Trungpa), who conducted numerous sexual relationships with students despite his HIV-positive status (Butler 1990). Multiple other cases of sexual abuse in American Buddhist communities have surfaced since the Ösel Tendzin revelations of the early 1990s, including the Eido Shimano affair of the early 2010s and, more recently, the cases of Joshu Sasaki, which was covered by the *New York Times*, and Sogyal Rinpoche (Lion's Roar Staff 2014).

Ann Gleig, one of the few scholars working on this topic, has highlighted the importance of Western therapeutic models in American Buddhist *saṅghas*' responses to these crises. This importation of psychotherapeutic insights and methods into Buddhist communities' self-understanding and self-regulation has, in Gleig's words, 'produced new Buddhist discourse, practices, authorities, organizational structures, and even soteriological models' (Gleig 2015). For instance, Gleig has identified an emerging 'ethic of transparency' in response to the sex scandals that have rippled through American Buddhist life. This newly articulated ethic combines traditional Buddhist modes of disciplinary confession with modern democratic ideals of transparency and accountability, while simultaneously contrasting itself with the secrecy of Buddhist esotericism (Gleig 2015).

Buddhist teachers involve themselves in harmful sexual intimacy with students (or do not) for a range of psychological reasons, but, in doing so (or not doing so), they also express and exploit a Buddhist sexuality and particular views about suffering, the body, authority, skilful teaching methods (*upāya*), compassion, and gender that are directly or indirectly grounded in the traditions described here. For instance, Sasaki is known to have suggested that his sexual relationships with students helped them to detach from self, and Ösel Tendzin claimed to be free from the effects of karma. It is probably not enough to simply label Buddhist teachers who inappropriately sexualize their students as confused, immature, or narcissistic, however clinically supportable such descriptions might be. Their behaviour should also be understood in relationship to the Buddhist ideas and practices in which they (and their students) root themselves, especially since, as Gleig notes, psychotherapeutic, democratic, and dharmic discourses intertwine in American Buddhist *saṅghas*' efforts to seek a way forward.

Another vital conversation in contemporary Buddhism is fuelled by individuals expressing non-normative gender and sexual identities in Buddhist communities. American and European LGBTQI Buddhists have been reading traditional sources against their own visions of gender non-binary, non-gender conforming communities, and diverse sexual orientations and expressions. For instance, some queer Buddhists simply reject Buddhist rules against homosexuality as 'cultural Buddhism' and draw instead on the doctrines of no-self and emptiness to validate their queerness (Corless 2004; Cabezón 1993; Cabezón 2008; Gleig 2012; Hopkins 1997). Thus, queer Buddhists are placing themselves into conversation with the classical Buddhist traditions partially described here in order to accomplish this creative work of adapting, critiquing, and repurposing.

As Foucault would predict, the fundamentally negative Buddhist position on desire and fertility produces not sexual desolation but an intricate social and discursive landscape peopled by sexually innovative monastics, charismatic celibates, sexually continent Tantric yogis, and, in our contemporary milieu, queer practitioners and sexually exploitative gurus. This landscape should be enough to convince us that Buddhist sexual ethics is not best understood as a deontology. Better we appreciate it as an embodied mode of being that emerges in a historically complex dialectic from vivid Buddhist soteriologies and visions of community.

Works Cited

Agostini, G. (2008) Partial *upāsakas*. In: R. Gombrich and C. Scherrer-Schaub (eds), *Buddhist studies*. Delhi: Motilal Banarsidass, 1–34.

Anālayo (2014) Perspectives on the body in early Buddhist meditation. In: Chuang K. (ed.), *Buddhist meditative traditions: their origin and development*. Taipei: Shin Wen Feng, 21–49.

Anālayo (2015) The Cullavagga on bhikkhuni ordination. *Journal of Buddhist ethics*, 22, 401–448.

Asaṅga (2016) *The bodhisattva path to unsurpassed enlightenment: a complete translation of the Bodhisattvabhūmi*. Translated by A. B. Engle. Boulder: Snow Lion.

Bodhi, Bhikkhu (trans.) (2000) *The connected discourses of the Buddha: a new translation of the Saṃyutta Nikāya*. Boston: Wisdom.

Bodhi, Bhikkhu (2012) *The numerical discourses of the Buddha: a complete translation of the Aṅguttara Nikāya*. Boston: Wisdom.

Bodhi, Bhikkhu, and Ñāṇamoli, Bhikkhu (trans.) (2005) *The middle length discourses of the Buddha: a translation of the Majjhima Nikaya*. Boston: Wisdom Publications.

Buddhaghosa (1976) *The path of purification: Visuddhimagga*. Translated by Bhikkhu Ñāṇamoli. Berkeley: Shambhala Publications.

Butler, K. (1990) Encountering the shadow in Buddhist America. *Common boundary magazine*. Available from: http://www.katybutler.com [accessed 13 July 2016].

Cabeźon, J. I. (1993) Homosexuality and Buddhism. In: A. Swidler (ed.), *Homosexuality and world religions*. Valley Forge, PA: Trinity Press International, 81–101.

Cabeźon, J. I. (2008) Thinking through texts: towards a critical Buddhist theology of sex. Frederic P. Lenz Distinguished Lecture, Naropa University. Available from: info-buddhism.com/Buddhism-Sexuality-Cabezon.html [accessed 11 April 2016].

Collett, A. (2014) Pali vinaya: reconceptualizing female sexuality in early Buddhism. In: A. Collett (ed.), *Women in early Buddhism: comparative textual studies*. Oxford: Oxford University Press, 62–79.

Collins, S. (2007) Remarks on the third precept: adultery and prostitution in Pali texts. *Journal of the Pali Text Society*, 29, 263–284.

Corless, R. (2004) Towards a queer dharmology of sex. *Culture and religion*, 5 (2), 229–243.

Faure, B. (1998) *The red thread: Buddhist approaches to sexuality*. Princeton: Princeton University Press.

Foucault, M. (1978) *The history of sexuality*, volume 1. Translated by R. J. Hurley. New York: Vintage.

Gleig, A. (2012) Queering Buddhism or Buddhist de-queering? Reflecting on differences amongst western LGBTQI Buddhists and the limits of liberal convert Buddhism. *Theology & sexuality*, 18 (3), 198–214.

Gleig, A. (2015) The shadow of the roshi: sex, scandal, and secrecy in American Zen Buddhism. *Sweeping Zen*. Available from: http://sweepingzen.com/the-shadow-of-the-roshi-sex-scandal-and-secrecy-in-american-zen-buddhism/ [accessed 13 July 2016].

Gray, D. (2007) *The Cakrasamvara tantra: the discourse of Śrī Heruka (Śrīherukābhidhāna)*. New York: Columbia University Press.

Gross, R. M. (1993) *Buddhism after patriarchy: a feminist history, analysis, and reconstruction of Buddhism*. Albany: State University of New York Press.

Gross, R. M. (2000) Population, consumption, and the environment. In: S. Kaza and K. Kraft (eds), *Dharma rain: sources of Buddhist environmentalism*. Boston: Shambhala, 409–422.

Gyatso, J. (1998) *Apparitions of the self: the secret autobiographies of a Tibetan visionary*. Princeton: Princeton University Press.

Gyatso, J. (2003) One plus one makes three: Buddhist gender, monasticism, and the law of the non-excluded middle. *History of religions*, 43 (2), 89–115.

Gyatso, J. (2005) Sex. In: D. Lopez (ed.), *Critical terms for the study of Buddhism*. Chicago: University of Chicago Press, 271–290.

Harvey, P. (2000) *An introduction to Buddhist ethics: foundations, values and issues*. Cambridge: Cambridge University Press.

Hopkins, J. (1997) The compatibility of reason and orgasm in Tibetan Buddhism: reflections on sexual violence and homophobia. In: G. D. Comstock and S. E. Henking (eds), *Que(e)rying religion: a critical anthology*. New York: Continuum, 372–383.

Horner, I. B. (trans.) (1938) *The book of the discipline (Vinaya-pitaka), volume 1*. Bristol, UK: Pali Text Society.

Jacoby, S. (2014) *Love and liberation: autobiographical writings of the Tibetan Buddhist visionary Sera Khandro*. New York: Columbia University Press.

Jones, J. G. (1979) *Tales and teachings of the Buddha: the Jataka stories in relation to the Pali canon*. London: George Allen & Unwin.

Kieffer-Pülz, P. (2014) Pārājika I and Saṅghādisesa I: hitherto untranslated passages from the Vinayapiṭaka of the Theravādins. In *The book of discipline (Vinaya-piṭaka), volume 1*. Bristol, UK: Pali Text Society, 349–373.

Kritzer, R. (2014) *Garbhāvakrāntisūtra: the sūtra on entry into the womb*. Studia Philologica Buddhica, 31. Tokyo: International Institute for Buddhist Studies.

Lafleur, W. R. (2003) Sex, rhetoric, and ontology: fecundism as an ethical problem. In: S. Ellingson and M. C. Green (eds), *Religion and sexuality in cross-cultural perspective*. London: Routledge, 51–82.

Lamotte, É. (2009) *Śūraṃgamasamādhisūtra: the concentration of heroic progress*. Translated by S. Boin-Webb. Honolulu: University of Hawai'i Press.

Lang, K. (1986) Lord Death's snare: gender-related imagery in the Theragāthā and the Therīgāthā. *Journal of feminist studies in religion*, 2, 59–75.

Langenberg, A. P. (2015) Sex and sexuality in Buddhism: a tetralemma. *Religion compass*, 9 (9), 277–286.

Langenberg, A. P. (2017) *Birth in Buddhism: the suffering fetus and female freedom*. London: Routledge.

Lion's Roar Staff (2014) Confronting abuse of power. *Lion's roar: Buddhist wisdom for our time*, 20 November. Available from: http://www.lionsroar.com/confronting-abuse-power/ [accessed 13 July 2016].

Minamoto J. and Glassman, H. (1993) Buddhism and the historical construction of sexuality in Japan. *U.S.-Japan women's journal, English supplement*, 5, 87–115.

Mrozik, S. (2007) *Virtuous bodies: the physical dimensions of morality in Buddhist ethics*. New York: Oxford University Press.

Norman, K. R. (trans.) (2001) *The group of discourses (Sutta-Nipāta)*. Oxford: Pali Text Society.

Patrul Rinpoche (1998) *Words of my perfect teacher: a complete translation of a classic introduction to Tibetan Buddhism*. Revised edition. Translated by the Padmakara Translation Group. New York: Altamira Press.

Perera, L. P. N. (1993) *Sexuality in ancient India: a study based on the Pali Vinayapitaka*. Kelaniya, Sri Lanka: Postgraduate Institute of Pali and Buddhist Studies, University of Kelaniya.

Powers, J. (2009) *A bull of a man: images of masculinity, sex, and the body in Indian Buddhism*. Cambridge, MA: Harvard University Press.

Śāntideva (1971) *Śikṣā Samuccaya: a compendium of Buddhist doctrine*. Translated by C. Bendall and W. H. D. Rouse. Reprint. Delhi: Motilal Banarsidass.

Shaw, M. (1994) *Passionate enlightenment: women in tantric Buddhism*. Princeton: Princeton University Press.

Shih H.-C., Bhikṣuṇī (1994) *The sutra on upāsaka precepts*. Berkeley: Numata Center for Buddhist Translation and Research.

Snellgrove, D. L. (ed.) (1959) *The hevajra tantra: a critical study*. 2 volumes. Oxford: Oxford University Press.

Tatz, M. (trans.) (1986) *Asanga's chapter on ethics with the commentary of Tsong-Kha-Pa. The basic path to awakening. The complete bodhisattva*. Lewiston: The Edwin Mellen Press.

Thurman, R. A. F. (trans.) (1976) *The holy teaching of Vimalakīrti: a Mahāyāna scripture*. University Park, PA: The Pennsylvania State University Press.

Tsomo, K. L. (1996) *Sisters in solitude: two traditions of Buddhist monastic ethics for women*. Albany: State University of New York Press.

Tsongkhapa (2000) *The great treatise on the stages of the path to enlightenment, volume 1*. Edited by J. W. C. Cutler and G. Newland. Boston: Snow Lion.

Vasubandhu (1988) *Abhidharmakośabhāṣyam*. Translated by L. de la Vallée Poussin and L. M. Pruden. Berkeley: Asian Humanities Press.

Walshe, M. (trans.) (1987) *The long discourses of the Buddha: a translation of the Dīgha Nikāya*. Boston: Wisdom.

Wedemeyer, C. (2013) *Making sense of tantric Buddhism: history, semiology, and transgression in the Indian traditions*. New York: Columbia University Press.

Wijayaratna, M. (1990) *Buddhist monastic life: according to the texts of the Theravāda tradition*. Translated by C. Grangier and S. Collins. Cambridge: Cambridge University Press.

Wijayaratna, M. (2010) *Buddhist nuns: the birth and development of a women's monastic order*. Kandy, Sri Lanka: Buddhist Publication Society.

Wilson, L. (1996) *Charming cadavers: horrific figurations of the feminine in Indian Buddhist hagiographic literature*. Chicago: University of Chicago Press.

Wilson, L. (2003) Buddhist views on gender and desire. In: D. W. Machacek and M. M. Wilcox (eds), *Sexuality and the world's religions*. Oxford: ABC-CLIO, 133–174.

Young, S. (2004) *Courtesans and tantric consorts: sexualities in Buddhist narrative, iconography and ritual*. London: Routledge.

Zwilling, L. (1992) Homosexuality as seen in Indian Buddhist texts. In: J. Cabezón (ed.), *Buddhism, sexuality, and gender*. Albany: State University of New York Press, 203–214.

Suggested Reading

Cabeźon, J. I. (2017) *Sexuality in Classical South Asian Buddhism*. Somerville, MA: Wisdom Publications.

Faure, B. (1998) *The red thread: Buddhist approaches to sexuality*. Princeton: Princeton University Press.

Gleig, A. (2012) Queering Buddhism or Buddhist de-queering? Reflecting on differences amongst western LGBTQI Buddhists and the limits of liberal convert Buddhism. *Theology & sexuality* 18 (3), 198–214.

Gyatso, J. (2005) Sex. In: D. Lopez (ed.), *Critical terms for the study of Buddhism*. Chicago: University of Chicago Press, 271–290.

Jacoby, S. (2014) *Love and liberation: autobiographical writings of the Tibetan Buddhist visionary Sera Khandro*. New York: Columbia University Press.

Lafleur, W. R. (2003) Sex, rhetoric, and ontology: fecundism as an ethical problem. In: S. Ellingson and M. C. Green (eds), *Religion and sexuality in cross-cultural perspective*. London: Routledge, 51–82.

Langenberg, A. P. (2015) Sex and sexuality in Buddhism: a tetralemma. *Religion compass*, 9 (9), 277–286.

Wilson, L. (2003) Buddhist views on gender and desire. In: D. W. Machacek and M. M. Wilcox (eds), *Sexuality and the world's religions*. Oxford: ABC-CLIO, 133–174.

CHAPTER 28

BUDDHIST PERSPECTIVES ON ABORTION AND REPRODUCTION

MICHAEL G. BARNHART

Introduction

Few moral issues provide better cases of intractable disagreement than abortion. Even U.S. Supreme Court actions on several occasions, reaffirming a woman's right to choose the procedure, have failed to resolve the issue, and worldwide, though abortion is often available, it is generally regarded as at best a necessary evil.[1] The fundamental objection is, of course, that abortion destroys a living being, a distinctively human, living being. This fact inevitably puts advocates of the choice to abort on the moral defensive. Furthermore, it explains the linkage between abortion and controversies surrounding assisted reproduction such as IVF or stem-cell research conducted using foetal tissue. Here again, the fundamental problem generally revolves around the destruction of foetal tissue. There are other objections surrounding these issues too: that one is 'playing God', for example. But what unites objectors and puts practitioners on the defensive is the destructive element in all such practices.

Unsurprisingly, given its strong affirmation of the value of life for its own sake, Buddhism is often interpreted as hostile to abortion and foetally destructive reproductive practices. The 'First Precept', as it is often called, prohibits destroying life and affirms the importance of *ahimsa* or non-injury. Other values associated with Buddhism, *mettā* (loving kindness), *dāna* (giving), and *karuṇā* (compassion), favour sacrifice towards the welfare of others thus undermining reasons that might support a choice to abort.

[1] The Pew Research Center reports a median percentage value of 56 per cent disapproval worldwide in its recent sampling of global morality. See http://www.pewglobal.org/2014/04/15/global-morality.

Add to this the fact that, to the extent the practice comes up at all, Buddhist scripture either explicitly forbids it or portrays it negatively, and the prospects for a more liberal view diminish markedly. However, it is not as though abortions are unheard of in countries that have strong Buddhist traditions and large numbers of Buddhists. Though laws and practices vary, abortion does take place in Sri Lanka, Burma, Thailand, and most especially, Japan. And in Japan, Buddhist priests and temples have crafted a rite, *mizuko kuyō*, specifically aimed at mitigating whatever suffering and damage an abortion may cause (see LaFleur 1992, 1998). Certain Buddhist values can be harnessed in support of women seeking abortions to mitigate harmful impacts either on their own or on their potential children's lives. Additionally, some contemporary Buddhists, though mostly Westerners, make a case for tolerance and compassionate understanding of a woman's choice to abort. All of this suggests that there may be a more 'liberal' strain to Buddhist thinking on this and related issues than one might expect.

This is not, of course, an unfamiliar situation in other contexts as well. Although the Roman Catholic Church strongly condemns abortion and maintains a very conservative attitude towards the broad range of related reproductive issues, abortions are common in strongly Catholic countries and amongst practising Catholics. Thus, caution in regard to whether Buddhism possibly harbours a more liberal acceptance of abortion is probably in order. One should not assume that practice drives belief, but that there is a case to be made in favour of a more liberalized approach is exactly what this discussion will examine, as well as the degree to which this departs from Buddhist orthodoxy. To the extent that it may, the question whether this would be a morally desirable direction for Buddhism to move will also be addressed.

Abortion, IVF, Stem-cell Research: Moral Issues

Abortion, IVF, similar ARTs (assisted reproductive technologies, such as Intracytoplasmic sperm injection [ICSI], a form of in-vitro fertilization [IVF] where a single sperm is injected into an egg cell), and embryonic stem-cell research all raise similar kinds of moral objections. That these objections have a religious basis in many cases is clear. However, they can be restated in relatively neutral terms. The central objection is that each of these practices involves the killing of a living, human being, one deserving of moral status and protection. This is what, following Michael Tooley (1972), we could call the 'conservative objection'. The actual arguments come in a variety of forms. Don Marquis has made the case that abortion suffers the same objection as any other form of killing: it deprives the victim of a valuable future. That is what makes killing wrong in our case and hence makes killing any being with a future reasonably similar to ours equally wrong. Since foetuses have a future just like ours, killing them is equally wrong (Marquis 1989). Others object that any distinction between a foetus and an infant is fundamentally arbitrary and thus abortion no different from infanticide. A more common and more religiously inflected position regards foetuses as persons because they contain the unique genetic blueprint of an individual human being and thus mark the beginning of a person's life. There is the potentiality argument to the effect that foetuses, even at the most embryonic stage, because they possess the genotype of a specific human person, are at least potential people and thus deserving of the same moral status as actual persons.

Extending the conservative position beyond the issue of abortion, conservatives attack ARTs that involve the inevitable destruction of embryos. IVF typically requires the creation of a larger number of fertilized eggs than will actually be implanted in a mother's uterus thus leading to the destruction of those that are unused. Stem-cell research also involves making use of embryos in destructive ways—insofar as using the stem cells involves 'killing' the embryo. Similar objections apply to contraceptive techniques that prevent implantation, such as certain types of IUD or abortifacient drugs that induce evacuation of fertilized egg cells.

On the other side, what, following Tooley, we could call the 'liberal' defence of abortion comes in a variety of forms and arguments that follow two broad strategies. (1) Liberals argue that the distinction between foetuses and babies/infants is not arbitrary (or alternatively that it does not matter that the distinction is hard to make out, e.g. Tooley and Mary Anne Warren [1973]) and, for one reason or another, makes a moral difference. (2) Liberals argue that women or parents can have very good and morally defensible reasons—defence of the life or health of the mother, for example—for seeking to abort. There are, of course, plenty of variations. Judith Jarvis Thomson is famous (or infamous) for arguing that the status of the foetus is not the dominant moral concern (Thomson 1971). Pregnancy is a transactional relationship between mother and foetus, and the right of the foetus to the mother's womb is hardly absolute, ultimately depending on maternal consent.

Without appearing to unduly favour the liberal position on these issues, it seems appropriate to point out the variety of circumstances and reasons that lead women to seek abortions. There are, of course, the familiar ones: the mother's life is endangered by carrying the foetus to term; rape or incest; the mother's psychological health is at stake; the mother and/or parents are too young and a baby would jeopardize their life chances such as access to education; family planning reasons; avoidance of transmission of heritable diseases or disabling conditions. However, there are others that may be less familiar: legal restrictions on family size such as in China; sex selection or sex preference, usually of boys over girls—a familiar issue in developing nations in particular; foetal reduction—to eliminate the dangers of multiple births and increase the chances of a successful singleton birth; vengeance in the manner of Medea, hopefully uncommon.

Not all of the above constitute morally commendable reasons for seeking an abortion, though some certainly are, mostly on grounds of beneficence and compassion. The last would be a very bad reason, while some are mixed. (Steinbock 1999 has argued that while there can be bad reasons for aborting, most abortions are not, in fact, wrong.) That China places restrictions on family size is of debatable merit, but that a family would then abort in order not to violate the law would be a defensible reason. The avoidance of inflicting a future of suffering, however, is generally regarded as a commendable reason, the non-identity problem notwithstanding. (This is the problem that one cannot be harmed by a decision by virtue of which one exists, since there was no one to be harmed when the decision was made; see Parfit 1984, ch. 16.) Liberal defenders of abortion, or of the right to choice, favourably cite such concerns; even those who take a relatively negative view of abortion itself can argue that in certain circumstances it is a necessity whose evil is outweighed by the overall good that will be done. It is worth pointing out that this is a defensible position.

Buddhism and Abortion: Scriptural Sources and Traditional Views

The most notable aspect of abortion with respect to Buddhist scripture is how little the subject actually comes up. Abortion as an issue of significant concern seems largely a modern phenomenon. However, the practice is probably as old as humanity itself, and thus the relative silence of Buddhist sources, as is the case in most other religious literatures as well, suggests that any attempt to reconstruct traditional judgments and attitudes must be taken with a large dose of caution. That said, when it does come up, abortion is almost always portrayed in a strongly negative light. An example from the monastic literature that is much quoted states,

> An ordained monk should not intentionally deprive a living thing of life even if it is only an ant. A monk who deliberately deprives a human being of life, even to the extent of causing an abortion, is no longer a follower of the Buddha.[2]

A few other passages exist in the *Vinaya* that clarify the wrongness of abortion, again much quoted in discussions of the issue. For example, as Peter Harvey reports, any monk who accedes to a request for abortion is 'defeated' in the religious quest if: the child dies even if he is remorseful; the child lives but the mother dies; neither dies; both die; and even 'if he simply tells her how to cause an abortion' (2000: 314). Harvey notes that in the last case, if the woman uses a method different from what the monk advocated, then his offence is 'less serious'.

[2] Both Damien Keown (1995: 93) and Peter Harvey (2000: 313) quote this passage from the *Vinaya Piṭaka* in Horner (1938–1966, 1: 97).

Another Theravādin authority, the fifth-century Buddhaghosa, in his commentary on these texts explains,

> The individual being begins from this tiny substance [and] gradually grows old with a natural lifespan of up to one hundred and twenty years. Throughout all of this until death, such is a human being... *who should deprive it of life* means 'separating it from life' either at the stage of the embryo by scorching, crushing, or the use of medicine, or at any subsequent stage by some similar kind of assault. (Quoted in Keown 1995: 94)

All of this is considered a grave offence.

Keown also reports that there are seven cases of abortion recorded in the *Vinaya*. They range from a monk providing an abortive remedy to a married woman pregnant with her lover's child to cases of rivalry between co-wives where one seeks to induce abortion in another for reasons of household politics. Keown reports that '[i]n all of the cases where abortion brings about the death of the child as intended, the judicial decision was that the offence fell into the category of "depriving a human being of life" ' (1995: 95).

However, given the vastness of the early scriptural literature, whether Theravāda or Mahāyāna, it is remarkable how little is said about a practice that certainly existed and may have been widespread. Interestingly, in her informative book *Buddhism after Patriarchy*, Rita Gross does not mention the practice at all, though she has some interesting things to say on the typical and very negative characterization of the woman's uterus (1993: 83–84). Given Buddhism's focus on *nirvāṇa* and liberation, from suffering through personal transformation, none of this is surprising. Monks, whether male or female, should not be in a position to concern themselves with such rather worldly matters in the normal course of their lives.

Given what is said about abortion, Harvey and Keown are probably right to conclude that the early Buddhist sources negatively judge abortive acts. The reason is also fairly clear. As Harvey claims, 'human life, with all its potential for moral and spiritual development, is seen as a rare and precious opportunity in a being wandering in the round of rebirths' (2000: 314). A pregnancy represents, therefore, a unique opportunity for the enlightenment of a being who has struggled through presumably numerous earlier lives, sort of as though one were to trip up a runner on the verge of winning a race. This is not unlike the sort of reason Marquis gives, i.e. that the wrongness of abortion, like the wrongness of murder, deprives a person of a valuable future like ours.

It is worth pointing out, however, that there is some divergence on exactly how one should interpret the early sources and the degree to which they allow exceptions to complete prohibition. While Keown takes traditional sources to discourage abortion in all but those cases where the mother's life is endangered (Keown 1995: 186 n. 56), Harvey (2000: 326) argues otherwise in *An Introduction to Buddhist Ethics*, enumerating four situations that could render abortion a 'necessary evil':

1) where there is a real threat to the life of the mother
2) where there is a possible threat to the life of the mother

3) where there is rape causing great trauma
4) where the alternative is a mentally ill woman further traumatized by having to give up her child for adoption

Harvey's argument for following a more flexible approach is essentially that while killing a foetus is a moral offence, the gravity of the offence varies depending on, among other things, the 'age of the fetus' (318) and presumably therefore its stage of development. This is because of Buddhaghosa's claim in his commentary on the *Majjhima Nikāya* (Harvey 2000: 52, 316) that the moral offensiveness of a specific act of killing depends crucially on a variety of factors including size, complexity, and the presence or absence of good qualities. Applying these considerations to the case of abortion, Havey concludes that because a foetus falls midway between a fully developed human being and a chimpanzee on the size and complexity scale, it is reasonable to argue that the seriousness of killing each is quite different. Specifically, the gravity of killing a foetus would fall midway on the moral scale between infant human and chimpanzee, and killing a foetus, depending on the circumstances, might be more like killing one than the other. Let's say it is possible by killing a chimpanzee to extract a drug that could mitigate a woman's trauma from being raped. Such a sacrifice, involving a creature of less complexity than a human being, is plausibly the lesser evil on Buddhaghosa's scale, as also would be the abortion of a foetus conceived through an act of rape. Although we would not treat an infant similarly, given the circumstances of rape, the sacrifice of the foetus is more like the sacrifice of the chimpanzee and therefore a necessary evil. Each of the four exceptions above, therefore, represent circumstances where a Theravāda Buddhist, what I will call a traditional Buddhist, might assent to abortion on the grounds that while we would not sacrifice an infant to save a woman in each of these circumstances, we might well sacrifice a chimpanzee. And the proximity of foetuses to chimpanzees on the moral scale might justify such abortions.

Keown disagrees strenuously with this line of reasoning, arguing that size and complexity make no moral difference when it comes to the treatment of human beings. He notes that, strictly speaking, Buddhaghosa does not apply the size consideration to human beings. But Harvey points out that Buddhaghosa does differentiate human beings based on their good qualities: 'the action [of killing a human being—someone capable of good qualities] is of lesser fault when they [the victims] are of few good qualities, greater fault when they are of many good qualities' (Harvey 2000: 52). However, this rather complicates matters as it is not at all clear that the qualities exhibited by a foetus are in any way inferior to a more fully developed human being. In short there is little evidence to support the existence of a scale where foetuses would rank less than developed human beings. Rather, Harvey's interpretation looks more like an attempt to justify widespread contemporary attitudes towards abortion than a viable interpretation of fifth-century Buddhist teaching. In any case, the range of circumstances where abortion would be permissible based on early texts is small and notably more circumscribed than what is legal in much of the world today.

Buddhism and Abortion: Modern Sources, Contemporary Views, and Practice

Of course, much hinges on what counts as Buddhist 'scripture' and whether more contemporary pronouncements on the issue count towards informing what we regard as the 'Buddhist view'. If we count such sources, the picture is a bit more mixed. While many of the sources that Harvey cites (2000: 320–326) take a fairly negative view, Keown (1995: 101–103) considers a number of contemporary Buddhists, Philip Kapleau and Robert Aitken for example, who take a more permissive position. Kapleau and Aitken, while not exactly espousing abortion, do allow that a woman could, if 'free of fear and selfish concerns', choose to abort as the '"right" course of action'. Both also insist on compassion for the woman who is faced with the choice and an understanding that she can be choosing in a way that balances competing sufferings. However, other Western Buddhists and commentators have reached decidedly negative conclusions about the permissibility of abortion, again on grounds that it involves the taking of life and, like murder, is an obvious violation of Buddhism's First Precept.

Non-Western Buddhist opinion, though a shade less likely to regard abortion as ever beneficial, exhibits similar ambivalence. As Keown points out, the Dalai Lama and numerous others from the Tibetan tradition regard abortion negatively. However, many Buddhists or Buddhist sympathizers, especially in Japan, will defend abortion as necessary at times. In *Liquid Life*, William LaFleur quotes a newspaper correspondent who is also Buddhist, Ochiai Seiko, who typifies what he regards as the middle ground of pragmatism between what he calls a 'liberationist' position of unfettered choice and the 'neo-Shintoist' traditionalism that sees abortion as 'a deep affront to a set of religious values' (LaFleur 1992: 193).

> Of course we who are Buddhists will hold to the end that a fetus is 'life'. No matter what kinds of conditions make abortion necessary we cannot completely justify it. But to us it is not just fetuses; all forms of life deserve our respect. We may not turn them into our private possessions. Animals too. Even rice and wheat share in life's sanctity. Nevertheless as long as we are alive it is necessary for us to go on 'taking' the lives of various kinds of such beings. (LaFleur 1992: 170)

But such 'pragmatism' as Ochiai's still finds abortion morally problematic, again because of the loss of life.

Turning from what people say to what they do, at least nowadays, the picture is just as murky. Given the fact that abortion comes up at all in ancient sources, it seems reasonable to assume that it has always existed in Asian societies with large Buddhist populations.[3] It is now legal in Thailand, Sri Lanka, Burma, and Japan—all societies where

[3] Given the strictures in the *Vinaya*, monks must have assisted women in aborting on occasion. While some did so for venal reasons, it is certainly possible that some were motivated by the compassionate reasons articulated by Kapleau and Aitken.

Buddhism is heavily influential. However, it is often not freely available. In Sri Lanka, abortion is legal only to protect the life of the mother. It is similarly restricted in Thailand (to protect the woman's health or in the case of rape or incest), although non-legal abortions are very common; a 1993 study of abortions in Thai hospitals found only 8 per cent of over 2,000 abortions were actually legal (Harvey 2000: 331). Thai society in general is fairly disapproving of abortion in any but the direst circumstances, but attitudes are somewhat more forgiving amongst patients and medical professionals (Lerdmaleewong 1998). Furthermore, professionals, especially obstetricians, take the view that some liberalization of Thai abortion law is in order, mostly in regard to cases where the health of the resulting child is affected—cases of AIDS infection or German measles, for example. It is worth noting that despite such views, almost all Buddhist respondents to surveys regard abortion as 'against Buddhist teachings' (Lerdmaleewong 1998: 37).

,Japan permits abortion without the sorts of restrictions found in Sri Lanka or Thailand. Yet, the existence of *mizuko kuyō*, rites that are meant to memorialize the foetus and apologize for its return back to the amorphous condition from whence it came (the concept of a watery kind of world of formlessness), speaks to the sort of moral ambivalence that Ochiai's remarks suggest.

To sum up, whether Asian or non-Asian, Buddhists express considerable ambivalence on the topic of abortion. In Asian societies where Buddhism has been historically influential, the practice is more legally constrained than many non-Asian countries. Asian Buddhists tend to emphasize the fact that the foetus is 'life' and abortion is at best a necessary evil in the direst of circumstances and therefore requiring some sort of atonement such as the *mizuko kuyō* rite. Interestingly, the rite has found its way into American Buddhist practice, though instead of constituting an apology or placating the potentially angry spirit of the aborted foetus, it is often seen as a means of therapeutically responding to the grief an abortion may occasion (see Wilson 2009: e.g. 177).

By contrast, non-Asian Buddhists like Kapleau focus more exclusively on the woman's motive and whether it reflects sufficiently broad-minded reflection on the reasons for aborting. There appear to be few cases where the tone is outright condemnation of the act alone.

Buddhism and the Morality of Abortion and Related Practices: Traditional Arguments

Thus far we have seen pronounced ambivalence within both the scriptural sources and contemporary practice and attitudes. On the one hand is the hard line 'no abortions are morally permissible' position, the case that Keown makes. It is certainly consistent with ancient sources and well supported by Buddhist precepts and teachings. On the other is the 'pragmatic' approach—one that acknowledges the moral status of the foetus as life but also weighs the possibly competing interests of the mother or others. The problem for the nuanced approach to abortion is hypocrisy. To what extent can we balance competing concerns, especially ones that, except in the case of the mother's life, do not speak to Buddhism's First—and virtually sacrosanct—Precept: the prohibition on the intentional taking of sentient life?

The tradition-based case, that abortion and any other practice that potentially violates the First Precept is impermissible, is based upon accounts of when sentient life begins. Here Buddhist texts supply a fair amount to go on.[4] Traditional Buddhist embryology holds that three conditions occur at the moment of conception: the sexual union of the parents; that the mother is properly fertile—her 'proper season'; and the entrance or 'descent' of the 'intermediate being' (Keown 1995: 69). This last element requires interpretation. Keown regards it as 'the spirit of a being seeking rebirth' who in descending into the mother's womb when the other two elements are present (and on some accounts it may even be attracted by the presence of sexual activity) completes the act of conception and inaugurates the life of a new individual human being. 'Spirit' is Keown's conceptual translation of the Pāli term, *viññana*—usually rendered as 'consciousness'—which represents one of the principal *skandhas* or five basic elements of the individual.[5] This element is thought to enter the conceptus, which is formed from the first two conditions: the ovum and the sperm. With these elements conjoined, the psychophysical totality that comprises the life of an individual human being is complete, thus becoming, according to Keown, the 'legitimate basis for the attribution of moral status' (Keown 1995: 29). In other words, it becomes a life deserving of the sorts of protections explicit in the First Precept, and any act, such as abortion, that 'terminates' this life is therefore impermissible.

That Keown's interpretation is largely in line with traditional Theravāda is buttressed when considering some of Buddhaghosa's claims and a number of longstanding monastic rules. In the monastic rules, the term 'human being' is understood to span the first moment of full conception, where all three elements are present, to the point where death takes place. Buddhaghosa maintains that 'the phrase *should deprive a human being of life* refers to human nature from the very beginning onwards'. He also claims that should a pregnant woman and her foetus die, it 'counts as two breaches of the precept against taking life' (Keown 1995: 96).

To sum up, Keown's interpretation of the traditional view may be expressed as the following argument:

1. The life of a human being exists at the very moment of conception.
2. Abortion, even at the earliest stage of foetal life, involves ending the life of a human being.

[4] In what follows I rely heavily on the especially clear, well-informed, and persuasive case Keown makes in *Buddhism and Bioethics* (1995).

[5] Of course, given the Buddhist 'doctrine' of *anattā* or no-self, it is important to keep in mind that *viññana* represents something other than a 'person' in the usual sense. It is an element of a person with the understanding that elements do not add up to a whole in any metaphysical sense, a 'soul' for example. Of course, whether this amounts to a reductionist account of the person is controversial and is a point to which we will return later.

3. Killing a human being violates the First Precept and is therefore wrong.
4. Therefore, abortion is always wrong.

Of course, this argument does not address the issue of conflicting interests and obligations. Suppose the mother's life is at stake, as considered earlier? While Keown himself does not much consider this conflict, one could respond that the existence of conflicting interests or even obligations does not alter the wrongness of abortion. Thus, even though society and some Buddhists will often abort to save the life of the mother, this fact does not minimize the wrong done by an abortion. In fact, if 'allowing to die' is less evil than 'killing', one could argue that the wrong done by allowing the pregnant woman to die is less than the wrong done by killing the foetus via abortion.

However, one may certainly question whether the first premise, that 'life begins at conception', is the only viable interpretation of Buddhist sources (see Garrett 2008: 94, 97). How do traditionalists understand and defend the first premise? For Keown, it depends on the embryology discussed above. To recapitulate, there are three conditions that must be present for a woman to become pregnant, the crucial one being that an 'intermediate being' (*gandhabba*, henceforth, IB) appears. So begins the life of what Keown terms an 'ontological individual', meaning a distinct being that is neither the sum of its parts nor merely a part of a whole (Keown 1995: 47). Since the physical elements (*rūpa*—the father's sperm mingling with the mother's menstrual blood) plus IB represent the totality that is an ontological individual, it follows that at that moment a life with moral status is existent.

Of course, one might wonder what the IB is exactly and how it relates to the traditional *skandha* theory and doctrine of *anatta*. Some of the ways the IB is described, for example as seeking an opportunity for rebirth, might suggest that it is a sort of soul that transmigrates. Furthermore, Buddhists have historically argued over whether the IB transits directly from one life immediately into another or whether it exists for some period in a sort of limbo between lives. If it can exist independently and engage in an active 'seeking' for another existential opportunity, it seems very self- or soul-like.

Keown's answer to this dilemma is that this third embryological element is really one of the *skandha*s, specifically *viññana* (Keown 1995: 26). And *viññana* is not in any way a distinct ontological individual, though Keown does describe it as 'the carrier wave of a person's moral identity' or one's 'spiritual DNA'. If so, the intermediate being is not really a being at all, but an element of a being. As a mere element, it cannot qualify as a soul or, more relevantly, an *atman*.

If this is the right way to think about the intermediate being, then Buddhist embryology comes down to supposing that when the IB joins the fertilized ovum, all the elements ingredient to a human being are present and so begins the life of the distinct individual. If we think of the intermediate being simply as *viññana*, we can say that for Buddhists, morally significant life begins the moment that consciousness, our spiritual DNA, the carrier wave of our moral identity, or however we want to think about it, joins the rest of the elements, which must already inhere in the fertilized ovum or conceptus. This embryology would suggest that the feeling, thought, and disposition *skandhas* are physically instantiated elements, perhaps neurologically. What is clear is that the *viññana* element is a separate element from the others.

Keown admits that the conceptus can exist separately from the *gandhabba*: 'Buddhism is not committed to the view that every fertilized embryo is animated. Instead, fertilized ova may best be seen as opportunities for the intermediate being to take rebirth' (1995: 84). This leaves open the possibility that the conceptus could exist for a rather extended period of time without the presence of the IB, perhaps until obvious signs of actual foetal consciousness emerge, say at twenty-some weeks. Perhaps the IB 'descends' only at that point, and only then do we have a being that is endowed with moral identity.

Obviously, this possibility contradicts Buddhaghosa's claims that the elements all come together at the moment of conception, but nonetheless does not contradict the embryology. This interpretation accepts the basic claim that the essential elements come together to create the whole person endowed with moral status and that they come together in the womb. What it modifies is the timeline along which these events happen. The obvious point is that if personhood depends on all the elements coming together, and this can happen long after the non-*viññana* elements have conjoined to create the conceptus, then moral personhood, from a Buddhist point of view, may not exist until much later in pregnancy. Since the first premise would then be false, only abortions that happen later in pregnancy would be wrong on Buddhist grounds.

However, Keown rejects the timeline modification on the grounds that 'no new life has come into being, only the biological basis for one' (1995: 81). An unanimated embryo, lacking the presence of the intermediate being, would 'most probably develop abnormally and be lost in the course of the menstrual cycle'. In other words, the embryo is only normal and capable of development if the *gandhabba* is present, according to Buddhist embryology. Lacking that element, it is essentially stillborn, and there is no reason to think it will develop the sentience that we associate with a fully developed foetus.

Why a Buddhist has to think this, however, is very unclear. First of all, the logic of Keown's argument is decidedly circular. Why think an 'unanimated' embryo is abnormal? Because if it *was* animated, it would develop normally? And if lost it must therefore be unanimated? There are also plenty of empirical reasons to reject the claim. The biological basis for life, if that is what we have with an 'unanimated' embryo, seems to show all sorts of capability to develop when studied in a laboratory setting. It is interesting to note that Keown hedges his statement here, claiming only that such an embryo 'most probably' would not develop normally, which of course leaves open the possibility that the biological basis of life can get along with the business of developing quite nicely without the *gandhabba*, at least some of the time. Keown might reply that what is studied in the lab is equally an embryo in the full sense, that is, with the IB present. But how do we know? Because it is developing normally? But again, this is circular reasoning. One has to take it on faith that Buddhaghosa is correct and that the intermediate being is present at conception. (It also prejudices what some might argue should be an open question: whether to translate *viññana* strictly as consciousness, because on empirical grounds there seems little evidence of consciousness in embryos at inception.)

Another empirically based reason for rejecting the first premise emerges in Keown's discussion of twinning and recombination. 'The problem', Keown notes regarding twinning, is 'that one of these individuals was seen to come into being by emerging from the other after "fertilization"' (1995: 88) The exact opposite is the case with recombination—two supposedly distinct individuals, according to the Buddhaghosa theory, become one. 'This seems to cast doubt on the notion that "fertilization marks the beginning of individual life"', Keown remarks. But, he claims, this can be explained. In the case of twinning, this 'should be thought of as a process whereby the zygote produces a genetic duplicate of itself. In so doing, the original zygote retains its individuality, while creating another individual through mitotic cleavage' (1995: 89). In the case of recombination, 'the explanation for what has occurred must be that it [one embryo] died and the first embryo, as before, assimilated its cells' (1995: 91).

However, if it is within the potential of any fertilized ovum at some point in the gestational process to twin or recombine, does that not beg the question of whether we are dealing with two lives or one with regard to the original conceptus? If a conceptus can reproduce more than once, perhaps we are talking about multiple lives. If one is inclined to entertain doubts, as Keown seems to feel is reasonable, his answer does little to clear them up. It does not really help to insist that we are dealing with one life only but at the same time possibly the biological basis of others. Is it one life or more that are on the line when considering a single conceptus with or without an IB? One can also think up other explanatory scenarios as well. Could several IBs all contend for the same embryonic space? Could a few more embryos be created so that each is accommodated? In recombination, could it be that two distinct IBs decide they can get along together within the same embryo? (And would this explain multiple personality disorder later in life? Or schizophrenia?) We might imagine even more baroque possibilities. How do we choose between such explanations?

The fact that one zygote can spontaneously produce an identical zygote inspires doubt in the traditional embryology; why would insisting that these identical multiples are really distinct individuals clear up the question? The question cannot be answered empirically. Anything science may say about twinning, or recombination for that matter, will be in terms of the biochemical mechanics of cell division, and not by reference to intermediate or spiritual beings. By contrast, regarding fertilized eggs as mere biological basis and not as individual lives does not 'seem to cast doubt' in quite the same the way, Keown admits, as traditional embryology does. It does not go beyond what the available facts are or what science is likely to discover. If a conceptus is the mere biological basis of life, but not a life in its own right, because consciousness is not yet present, then there is no ethical need to explain the ontological status of a spontaneously generated or reabsorbed twin. To be fair, Keown—and perhaps Buddhaghosa as well—are not offering empirical reasons for their embryology (Garrett [2008] also points this out in regard to Tibetan Buddhism). Instead, they offer explanations of non-observable facts that do not contradict the observable facts. But if so, this is to accept that the embryology goes beyond the facts. However, if one translates *viññana* as 'consciousness' in some sense of the word and drops the timeline aspect of the traditional embryology, then the embryology is entirely correlated with the facts. There are no non-empirical facts that need explanation.

In other words, there is no empirical argument in favour of treating the embryo as more than just the biological basis of life that starts out lacking *viññana*. There is a meaningful empirical question about whether and when the conceptus manifests *viññana*, and there is no reason to think that point is at conception.

Furthermore, choosing a modified embryology, and therefore rejecting the premise that a distinctively individual human life begins at conception, does not contradict any obvious Buddhist principles, but only Buddhaghosa's embryology. But I also think there are good Buddhist reasons for choosing the modified view.

The first of these is the more empirically oriented aspect of the modified view. Throughout the Pāli Canon, the Buddha is portrayed as insisting on the authority of what is empirically evident as opposed to what is only supported on faith. Time and again, he rejects traditional teaching and doctrine on the grounds that there is no evidence for its claims, such as for an *ātman*, or for its effectiveness—that is, it fails the test of making a difference in the lives of its practitioners (see, e.g., the 'Discourse to the Kālāmas'; Holder 2006: 21). While it is true that Buddhaghosa-inspired embryology does not contradict what is experientially evident, it goes beyond what we can verify. By contrast, the modified view depends on what can be experientially verified: the conceptus exists because we can see it; it possesses *viññana* because it shows signs of consciousness at that point where we can see such signs. Admittedly, this last point is hard to verify empirically and would depend on somewhat inferential neurological evidence. Furthermore, there is uncertainty regarding the neurology of consciousness, and this will complicate the ascription of *viññana*. However, just because there is some uncertainty does not mean the judgment that the conceptus is conscious and possessed of *viññana* is not primarily empirical.

The second Buddhist reason for preferring the modified embryological timeline is that it takes *viññana* to be consciousness in its most rudimentary sense, and is therefore easy to square with the *anattā* understanding of the person. A person is not a 'self' or 'soul', but rather imputed to the five composite elements that find completion with the onset of *viññana* at some point later in pregnancy than conception or even implantation and early foetal development, probably in the twenty-some week range.[6] Of course, this position is somewhat hard to reconcile with the notion of the *gandhabba* as a being or a doctrine of rebirth, as nothing seems to be reborn exactly. Thus, it may be that adopting a modified (more modern?) view entails dropping these concepts as vestiges of a more

[6] When I say that the person is not a self, this does not mean I subscribe to some form of 'person reductionism' in the style of Parfit. To say a person is not a self is simply to say that a person is nothing beyond the five composite elements that constitute, as Keown maintains, its necessary and sufficient conditions. For example, one could think of the five elements as the supervenience base of the person.

superstitious past. However, with a little contortion, one can accommodate the IB and rebirth. The IB is simply the 'descent' of *viññana* with the onset of consciousness, and all of the *skandhas*, because they connect and reconnect in multifarious ways over time, represent the karmic continuity that rebirth promises. Rebirth is only the rebirth of elements, not of individuals.[7]

What Does a Liberal Buddhist View of Abortion and Reproduction Look Like?

To what kind of liberalism, with regard to abortion, does the modified view commit a Buddhist? As alluded to earlier, there are a range of positions on what kinds of abortion are permissible within a more liberal perspective. Moreover,the philosophical basis of each carries implications for the way one thinks about reproduction in general and the obligations that may exist between the woman and her foetus.

The 'liberal' position that appears most compatible with the modified Buddhist view is what is often called the 'interest view' and is very ably represented by Bonnie Steinbock (1992, 1999, 2006). She writes,

> My thesis is that killing fetuses is morally different from killing babies because fetuses are not, and babies are, sentient. By sentience, I mean the ability to experience pain and pleasure ... sentience is important because nonsentient beings, whether mere things ... or living things without nervous systems (e.g. plants) lack interests of their own. Therefore, nonsentient beings are not among those beings whose interests we are required to consider. (1999: 248)

At some point in pregnancy, of course, the foetus does become sentient—arguably with the onset of consciousness, around twenty to twenty-six weeks—at which point it has interests that must be taken into consideration. Once one has interests, one has what Steinbock calls 'moral status', which means that one's interests must be taken into account by others in any social interaction. Pre-sentient foetuses lack interests and therefore moral status; sentient foetuses have interests and therefore moral status. Of course, to say that one's interests need to be taken into account does not mean that they solely determine what is to be done. However, they must be considered along with the interests of any others that are involved. It is also important to note that

[7] This is most convincing if it is also true that individuals, in the sense of having a strong identity relation between life stages, do not exist either. This would be the case if Buddhist *skandha* theory were a form of person reductionism. The parts of the 'individual', so-called, are merely that, including *viññana* (the others being physical form, feeling, thought, and character or dispositions), and consciousness is more plausibly a mere part of an individual *if thought of as* consciousness rather than as an intermediate *being*. The *gandhabba* is a mere transitioning part, not a whole person or whole being.

lacking interests does not mean lacking any value whatsoever. A non-sentient being, for example a wilderness area or a work of art, can have value. However, it cannot suffer unlike sentient beings, which, because they can suffer, have 'a stake in their own existence'.

The interest that the newly sentient foetus has is the interest in not suffering. Once sentient it can feel pain and experience distress, negative experiences that everyone has an interest in avoiding. Beyond that it has very few interests, at least in the sense of that in which it can take an interest or have a stake. Of course, interests may extend beyond merely not suffering. A critic might argue that this way of construing interests leaves open the possibility that if I were temporarily unconscious I would lack interests, so that killing me would not violate my interests. Or, were I to become severely demented, I would lack interests.

However, this would be to misconceive what is meant by 'interest' on the interest view. I have interests even when temporarily unconscious, because I still have desires and beliefs. They may not be occurrent desires or beliefs, but their non-occurrence does not render them non-existent. They remain part of my dispositional pool, so to speak, by virtue of the fact that I formed such conscious desires, a point that a Buddhist should happily concede given that my dispositions constitute one of my composite elements. Because I have a desire for X, I have an interest in obtaining X, even if I'm not presently thinking of X or capable of thinking of X. Even after I have died, for example, interests in those directives are expressed in my last will and testament. Though it is unclear she would go that far, Steinbock's (2006) argument trends in this direction.

On the other hand, early stage embryos and first- through early second-trimester foetuses have never formed desires and lack consciousness; they are at best, pre-sentient. Hence they lack interests of which we must take account in deciding what to do.

The implications for abortion and the ways in which we think about reproduction are fairly clear. The life in which I can have a stake is the life that begins with the necessary conditions for conscious experience, at least enough conscious experience to suffer, as in the modified Buddhist view. To abort before the point at which this happens is not to harm my interests, because I simply do not have any. This is not to say that I lack value or that abortion is a trivial act. There may be other value-based reasons for discouraging an abortion. But there is no overall moral prohibition based on the interests of the foetus (or, according to Steinbock 1999: 250, the life of the foetus). Put in terms of the modified view, abortion of a pre-conscious, non-sentient conceptus is simply the ending of the development of the biological basis of a human life because the act represents intervention before the presence of *viññana* or the *gandhabba*/IB.

This position also aligns with the near universal Buddhist appraisal of the wrongness of suffering. Time and again in the early texts the Buddha announces that all he teaches he teaches for the relief of suffering. Indeed, the concept of *upāya* or expedient means can be interpreted as an extension of Buddha's concern with suffering: all doctrine and teaching must be measured against progress towards *nirvāṇa*, the final resolution of the problem of suffering. From the perspective of the interest view, of course, avoidance of suffering is only one of many interests that a person can have. But it is certainly one of the most basic and primal, and in the case of the foetus, arguably, the only interest it can have.

That is not to say there are no other considerations or reasons to value a pre-sentient foetus or that decisions on whether or not to abort are casual. Returning to the passage from LaFleur's book *Liquid Life*, where the Japanese journalist and Buddhist Ochiai Seiko was quoted noting the need to balance the sanctity of foetal life against the necessity of sometimes taking such life, we find echoes of the sorts of considerations that, for example, Margaret Olivia Little (2009) stresses:

> But the idea of respect for creation is also, if less frequently acknowledged, sometimes the reason why women are moved to *end* pregnancies ... decisions to abort often represent, not a decision to destroy, but a refusal to create. ... Some women decide to abort, that is, not because they do not *want* the resulting child—indeed they yearn for nothing more, and desperately wish the circumstances were otherwise—but because they do not think bringing a child into the world the right thing for them to do. (2009: 583)

One can choose to abort for the very same reasons one could choose to procreate: that there is a kind of rightness about the act; that the balance of interests and values make it admirable or commendable—life affirming. We create the children we do, at least when we are at our best, when we affirm a kind of respect for creation, but this can also be the reason we decide to end a pregnancy, out of concern for the life that is forming and its place in the panoply of creation. What the interest view adds to this is simply the understanding that the decision whether to continue a pregnancy becomes much more challenging once the interests of the foetus become entangled in what is already deep and complicated.[8]

Of course, to some on the liberal side of the abortion and reproduction issue, the interest view may appear too modest in its appreciation of the rights of the pregnant woman or insufficiently permissive with regard to later-term abortions. Though women clearly have a right to abort before sentience, the morality of that choice is much cloudier on the interest view once the foetus is conscious—at least to the point of sentience.

Some on the liberal side argue that the very limited interests of a foetus are of little moral relevance in regard to abortion. Both Michael Tooley and Mary Anne Warren argue that the conservatives are, in a sense, right: there is no morally relevant difference between a foetus at whatever stage and an infant. But whereas conservatives argue that if killing an infant is obviously wrong so is killing a foetus, Tooley and Warren argue that if abortion is not wrong, killing an infant is not obviously wrong either. Tooley and Warren maintain that there is a non-arbitrary and morally significant difference between beings deserving of moral status and those that are not, and it is whether the individual can

[8] A particularly salient and contemporary example would be termination to avoid complications of the Zika virus such as microencephaly. A Buddhist might easily feel that such a birth would be extremely 'unpropitious' and termination an act of kindness to a forming foetus.

entertain the idea of himself as an enduring entity. Since infants and foetuses clearly lack a self-concept, they cannot value such a thing or have a stake in its persistence. Hence, they cannot be said to have morally cognizable interests whereas the mother does, and her interests become the relevant default consideration in any abortion decision. Tooley and Warren, of course, draw the line at killing young children on the grounds that they possess a sense of themselves and a capacity for social interaction with others.

Steinbock's version of the interest view is also vulnerable on the following point. For Steinbock, the capacity to suffer, an experience that by its nature is unwanted (see Parfit 2011: 73–82), gives the sentient foetus interests. Of course, one could agree but add that it just gives the foetus an interest in avoiding suffering, not in continuing its life. All abortions, and perhaps infanticides, should be painless, thus mitigating potential suffering. It does not show, however, that the foetus has an interest in not being killed. This is not an attack on the interest view so much as a criticism of exactly what interest is at stake and whether it ever counts against any actual abortion.

Whether this presents an insurmountable problem for Steinbock is hard to say. She might reply that to be sentient is not only to enjoy the present moment but also to appreciate its continuation, at least its painless continuation—a point that a Tooley/Warren position also misses. If that is the case, then killing the foetus is contrary to something in which it has a stake. The broader question, however, is where the liberal Buddhist position fits in this constellation of views.

The important similarities between the interest view and a liberal Buddhism were first, the fact that moral status starts with the arrival of consciousness and the capacity to suffer. From the liberal Buddhist position, one is not violating the First Precept with an abortion before the twenty-to-twenty-six-week point simply because a full being does not exist. Secondly, the moral balancing of interests in any abortion decision that the interest view defends fits very well with the kinds of pragmatic attitudes exhibited by contemporary Buddhists generally. It is worth noting, however, that the interest view presumes such balancing when there are interests ascribable to the foetus. At the point where such interests exist, of course to terminate the pregnancy is a violation of the First Precept for any Buddhist. Thus, it is not clear that a liberal Buddhist can consistently subscribe to balancing interests after sentience. If so, the liberal Buddhist would draw a more conservative line between permissible and impermissible abortions than either Steinbock or certainly Tooley would commit to.

One final and noteworthy parallel between the interest view and Buddhist concerns is that on both views a decision to abort is open to moral criticism even when the foetus lacks sentience. As noted, foetuses may lack moral status but retain value, and this value becomes reflected in the moral appraisal we make of someone's reasons either to procreate or to end a pregnancy. Steinbock, in fact, argues there can be 'terrible reasons for having a child'. For example, 'quite a lot of young teenagers of 15 or 16 decide to keep their babies because of the status and prestige that comes with being a mother' (Steinbock 1999: 261). Equally, a vengeful abortion would count as a morally offensive act. It destroys something of value, a developing foetus, without the counterweight of any significant interest worth protecting on the mother's part. On the other hand, most reasons that women give for abortion, such as that birth control measures failed or even that their cultures place a premium on a particular sex, are eminently defensible. In cultures that practise selective abortion of girls, the 'social realities in which it may occur' include the possibility of mistreatment of the mother or the resulting child (Steinbock 1999: 262). To Buddhists of whatever stripe, these would be exactly the right sort of considerations, involving, as they do, compassionate concern for all those affected by an action, not merely self-regarding satisfaction.

Works Cited

Garrett, F. (2008) *Religion, medicine, and the human embryo in Tibet*. London and New York: Routledge.

Gross, R. (1993) *Buddhism after patriarchy: a feminist history, analysis, and reconstruction of Buddhism*. Albany: State University of New York Press.

Harvey, P. (2000) *An introduction to Buddhist ethics: foundations, values and issues*. Cambridge: Cambridge University Press.

Holder, J. J. (2006) *Early Buddhist discourses*. Indianapolis: Hackett.

Horner, I. B. (trans.) (1938–1966) *The book of discipline*. 6 volumes. London: Pali Text Society.

Keown, D. (1995) *Buddhism and bioethics*. New York: St. Martin's Press.

LaFleur, W. R. (1992) *Liquid life: abortion and Buddhism in Japan*. Princeton: Princeton University Press.

LaFleur, W. R. (1998) Abortion, ambiguity, and exorcism: a review essay based on Helen Hardacre's *Marketing the menacing foetus in Japan*. *Journal of Buddhist ethics*, 5, 384–400.

Lerdmaleewong, M. (1998) Abortion in Thailand: a feminist perspective. *Journal of Buddhist ethics*, 5, 22–48.

Little, M. O. (2009) The morality of abortion. In: B. Steinbock, J. D. Arras, and A. J. London (eds), *Ethical issues in modern medicine: contemporary readings in bioethics*. Seventh edition. Boston: McGraw Hill, 576–584.

Marquis, D. (1989) Why abortion is immoral. *Journal of philosophy*, 86, 183–202.

Parfit, D. (1984) *On reasons and persons*. Oxford: Oxford University Press.

Parfit, D. (2011) *On what matters*, Volume 1. Oxford: Oxford University Press.

Steinbock, B. (1992) *Life before birth: the moral and legal status of embryos and foetuses*. Oxford: Oxford University Press.

Steinbock, B. (1999) Why most abortions are not wrong. In: R. B. Edwards and E. E. Bittar (eds), *Advances in bioethics: bioethics for medical education*, Volume 5. Stamford, CT: JAI Press, 245–267.

Steinbock, B. (2006) The morality of killing human embryos. *Journal of law, medicine and ethics*, 34 (1), 26–34.

Thomson, J. J. (1971) A defense of abortion. *Philosophy and public affairs*, 1 (1), 47–66.

Tooley, M. (1972) Abortion and infanticide. *Philosophy and public affairs*, 2 (1), 37–65.

Warren, M. A. (1973) On the moral and legal status of abortion. *Monist*, 57, 43–61.

Wilson, J. (2009) *Mourning the unborn dead: a Buddhist ritual comes to America*. Oxford: Oxford University Press.

Suggested Reading

Barnhart, M. (1998) Buddhism and the morality of abortion. *Journal of Buddhist ethics*, 5, 276–297.

Florida, R. (1991) Buddhist approaches to abortion. *Asian philosophy*, 1, 39–50.

Jones, K. (1989) *The social face of Buddhism*. London: Wisdom.

Keown, D. (1999) Buddhism and abortion: is there a 'middle way'? In: D. Keown (ed.), *Buddhism and abortion*. Honolulu: University of Hawai'i Press, 199–218.

LaFleur, W. R. (1990) Contestation and consensus: the morality of abortion in Japan. *Philosophy east and west*, 40 (4), 529–542.

Lesco, P. A. (1986) A Buddhist view of abortion. *Journal of religion and health*, 26, 214–218.

Steinbock, B. (2007) Moral status, moral values, and human embryos: implications for stem cell research. In: B. Steinbock (ed.), *The Oxford handbook of bioethics*. Oxford: Oxford University Press, 416–440.

CHAPTER 29

EUTHANASIA

DAMIEN KEOWN

Introduction

A discussion of this kind raises methodological issues that due to constraints of space we can only mention briefly (for a fuller discussion see Keown 2001: 11–21). An initial problem concerns the nature of Buddhism itself. As is well known, Buddhism is made up of a collection of sects and schools, many of which evolved during a variety of historical periods in different cultures. While this may be thought to make consensus unlikely, the evidence suggests that a normative position on euthanasia can be discerned.

To help clarify this position we will draw on two main sources. The first is the corpus of religious texts that Buddhists regard as authoritative. Virtually all schools of Buddhism regard scripture—especially those canonical texts purporting to record the oral teachings of the Buddha—as authoritative on questions of doctrine and ethics. But here a problem presents itself: which textual sources should be used given that the major traditions of Buddhism each have their own canons of scripture, and each of these collections is extensive? Fortunately, there is a good deal of common ground in one section of the canon that is particularly relevant to our present enquiry, namely the Monastic Rule or *Vinaya*. As Paul Williams notes, 'What unifying element there is in Buddhism, Mahāyāna and non-Mahāyāna, is provided by the monks and their adherence to the monastic rule.' 'Thus', he concludes, 'in spite of the considerable diversity in Buddhism there is relative unity and stability in the moral code' (1989: 4–6). What is especially valuable about the *Vinaya* is that it records actual cases of euthanasia and assisted suicide on which the Buddha passes judgment, thus providing a precedent for contemporary practice. The *Vinaya* will therefore be the textual source to be consulted in the 'Textual Sources' section of the chapter.

The second source we will draw on is a short survey (inevitably limited but hopefully representative) of contemporary attitudes and practice in two Asian countries with large Buddhist populations, namely Japan and Thailand. It seems desirable to include this contemporary perspective in order to ensure that modern views are represented in the discussion. There are two reasons for choosing Japan and Thailand: first, there is more published information available on these countries, and second they provide examples of Mahāyāna and Theravāda perspectives. As mentioned, some reference will also be made in the course of the next section to the views of contemporary Tibetan Buddhist teachers, which will further broaden the evidence base.

Apart from the question of sources, a more general concern is whether the parameters of the Western debate on euthanasia can be taken as universal. In the West the issue is seen largely as one of individual rights (specifically the 'right to die'), whereas in Asia the issue is framed more in terms of family duties and obligations. Counterbalancing differences of this kind are features that facilitate cross-cultural dialogue. The globalization of Western medical training and technology means that issues in medical ethics cross cultural boundaries in a way that others do not. To some extent this is borne out by research comparing the attitudes of doctors in Thailand and the USA that suggests a 'substantial overlap in Thai and American doctors' vocabulary' when discussing medical ethics (Grol-Prokopczyk 2013: 92). This research also shows that epistemological problems of cross-cultural communication and understanding are not reducible simply to the existence of different ethical paradigms in Asia and the West. Doctors in Thailand also display diversity in their attitudes and a 'schism in ethical styles' in terms of which while 'some hew closely to the secular, deontological model, others embrace a virtue ethics that liberally cites Buddhist principles and emphasizes the role of doctors' good character' (Grol-Prokopczyk 2013: 92). Clearly there are various starting points from which to approach this issue, both in Asia and the West. The approach adopted here aims to reflect as far as possible the views of the mainstream tradition.

Defining Euthanasia

Suicide is the subject of a separate chapter in this work and so will not be mentioned below other than in passing. It should be noted, however, that conclusions reached about the ethics of suicide are not *ipso facto* applicable to euthanasia. There are additional medical and legal issues surrounding euthanasia that have social implications that an individual suicide does not. Chief among these is the fact that in euthanasia medical personnel licensed and often remunerated by the state act to terminate life with the state's approval. Society and the state are thus complicit in causing death in a way that is not the case in suicide (Somerville 2014: 210). The fact that suicide has been decriminalized in many jurisdictions, furthermore, does not mean that legislatures approve of the practice: it means only that criminalization is not seen as an appropriate means of addressing a complex social problem. The state still seeks to prevent suicide, which is why assisting suicide remains a crime in most jurisdictions. Nor will 'physician-assisted suicide' (PAS) feature much in the discussion for two reasons. First, much of what is said about euthanasia will apply *mutatis mutandis* to PAS; and second, there has been little specific discussion of PAS in relation to Buddhism.

As regards euthanasia, it is important to clarify how it will be understood in this chapter. An essential ingredient in all forms of euthanasia is the intentional shortening of life, and since this is usually contemplated in a medical context euthanasia will be understood here as *the intentional killing of a patient by act or omission as part of his medical care*. The qualification *intentional* is of importance, as will become clear below.

As to the forms of euthanasia, a distinction is often made in respect of its active and passive modes. *Active* euthanasia is the deliberate killing of a person by an act, as for example, by lethal injection. *Passive* euthanasia is the intentional causing of death by an omission, as for example, by not providing nutrition, hydration, or some other requisite for life. Contrary to some opinions, it is hard to see a significant moral distinction between these two modes of euthanasia given that they share the common aim of causing death, and for this reason our definition treats them as equivalent. Each of the two modes of euthanasia just described (active and passive) can take three forms: (1) voluntary, (2) non-voluntary, and (3) involuntary. *Voluntary* euthanasia involves a request by a legally competent patient that his life should be terminated. *Non-voluntary* euthanasia is the killing of a non-competent patient. *Involuntary* euthanasia is the intentional killing of a patient without his consent.

Euthanasia and the Withdrawal of Treatment

Confusion often arises from equating passive euthanasia with the refusal or withdrawal of medical treatment that incidentally leads to the patient's death. The classic case is turning off a life-support machine. To make a proper evaluation of this act we first need to classify its moral species. Is it an act of homicide, in other words an act ordered to the end of the patient's death? Or is it a therapeutic act, in other words, an act ordered to the patient's physical and mental well-being (to whatever degree this is achievable) within the normal parameters of his medical care?

We cannot reach a judgment on the matter simply by viewing the act 'from the outside' (a position sometimes known as 'physicalism'). Clearly, a doctor can perform the same act (such as administer an injection) with the intention either to kill or cure; yet these are acts of a very different moral species. We must therefore take into account the subjective dimension of the act, namely the doctor's intention (aim or purpose) in acting as she did. This means we need to know something of the doctor's deliberations, or the steps in the chain of reasoning that culminated in her act of turning off the machine. It may go something like this: the patient is suffering; death will end the patient's suffering; turning off the ventilator will cause the patient's death; therefore I will turn off the ventilator. In this case there is clearly a homicidal intent: turning off the ventilator is the means to cause the patient's death, which in turn is the means to relieve the patient's suffering. In this case there is euthanasia. The doctor's decision here finds its final justification in an implicit value judgment about the patient's life, namely that a life of such poor quality is no longer worth living and the patient would be 'better off dead'.

The doctor's chain of reasoning, however, may run along different lines, perhaps as follows: my obligation as a doctor is to restore the patient to health or mitigate his symptoms where possible; the treatment I am administering is doing neither and is simply prolonging the dying process; therefore I will (after due consultation with colleagues and any family members) withdraw the futile treatment and free the patient from the burden of this invasive medical intervention. The doctor is certainly aware that a consequence of turning off the ventilator will be the patient's almost immediate death, but her reasoning does not involve a homicidal intent, and so does not constitute a case of euthanasia. Here, *pace* Yu Kam Por (2007), no judgment is made about the value or otherwise of the patient's *life*, only about the efficacy or otherwise of the *treatment*.

Some may regard the above distinction as invalid or mere sophistry. Consequentialist philosophers in particular may be unimpressed. Given their prioritization of outcomes, they may regard issues of motivation and intent as of minor importance, or at best as having only instrumental value. However, this is not how the matter has been conventionally regarded by professional medical ethics and the law or, as I shall suggest, by Buddhist jurisprudence. Neither traditional medical ethics nor the law assume that a doctor who removes life support does so *as a means to kill the patient*. Just as a general may order his troops into battle foreseeing that many of them will die but without intending or wanting their deaths, the doctor in this case *foresees* the patient's death but does not *intend* it. That the foreseen shortening of life may be morally permissible is an implication of the ethical principle of 'double effect' (Cavanaugh 2006). In accordance with this principle, both medical ethics and the law acknowledge that a doctor who withdraws life support may properly do so provided her intention is not to shorten the patient's life, even if the patient's death is foreseen as a certain consequence (for the legal authorities see Jackson and Keown 2012: 107f.). For this reason the death certificate will not show the cause of death as 'withdrawal of ventilation by doctor', but some underlying morbidity such as cancer.

Dramatic cases such as withdrawal of ventilation are best considered against the background of ordinary medical practice where it is commonplace to discontinue disproportionate treatments (that is, futile or excessively burdensome treatments) even when life is shortened as a consequence. There is little point, for example, in treating pneumonia by administering antibiotics to a geriatric patient who has suffered several strokes and may have co-morbidities such as kidney failure. While life may be extended slightly by prescribing antibiotics to fight the infection, the treatment will not improve the patient's condition overall or change the underlying prognosis. The same might be said of 'Do Not Resuscitate' (DNR) protocols, where cardio-pulmonary resuscitation is withheld. No one would reasonably regard death in such circumstances as a case of intentional killing, even though the patient's life was shortened as a direct result of the doctor's decision and the doctor fully expected this outcome. Nor is the use of analgesics or other medication that may have the side effect of shortening life (in practice almost never the case) an example of euthanasia.

It brings clarity to the discussion and illuminates the salient moral features of the act if we classify as euthanasia only cases where a treatment is administered, withheld, or withdrawn with the *intention* of hastening the patient's death. The danger in conflating the withdrawal of treatment with passive euthanasia is that it makes it seem that euthanasia is already an accepted part of medical practice when (outside of a small number of jurisdictions where euthanasia is legal) it is not. And if *passive* euthanasia is accepted as a legitimate treatment option, it is hard to see what grounds there are to object to *active* euthanasia (Varelius 2016). Why force a patient to die a lingering death when a lethal injection will bring rapid closure?

This traditional Western view of matters seems to track the Buddhist emphasis on the role of intention as a key criterion of moral responsibility. In the absence of intention (*cetanā*) there is no good or bad karma (AN III.415). Theravāda commentaries make very clear, as Rupert Gethin notes, that 'whether or not we do things intentionally and with full consciousness is a crucial determinant of responsibility in the Buddhist view of things' (2004: 170). The same commentaries define an act of killing (an act contrary to the first precept) as follows: 'Killing a living creature is the intention to kill in one who perceives a living creature as such, when this occurs through the door of either the body or of speech and produces the exertion that cuts off the life-faculty [of that living being]' (Gethin 2004: 171).

Clearly, then, whether or not turning off a life-support machine breaks the first precept turns on the intention from which it is done and not, *pace* Kanjanaphitsarn, on whether one 'fully realized' what the result of the action would be (2013: 8). As Buddhaghosa makes clear, an act of culpable killing is not simply one done with the full realization (*sañjānanta*) 'I will take life': the act must also be done 'purposefully' (*cecca*), which is glossed as 'intending with the intention (*cetanā*) to kill, planning' (Heim 2013: 164). In other words, death must be integral to the plan, and will typically constitute an indispensable link in the causal chain that the agent postulates as necessary to achieve his end. With the proviso that intentional killing of this kind is always excluded, we might formulate the following criterion for use in Buddhist terminal care: if a treatment cannot produce an overall net improvement in a patient's condition and is simply prolonging the dying process, then it may be discontinued even when doing so hastens the patient's death. (It should be noted this will exclude patients in a persistent vegetative state [PVS] who although unconscious will not normally be dying or in receipt of artificial ventilation.)

Tibetan Buddhist Views

This criterion may be helpful when interpreting pronouncements from Tibetan Buddhist leaders that have sometimes been seen as offering support for euthanasia. The Dalai Lama, for example, has made a number of remarks on the subject including a much-quoted letter to *Asiaweek* in 1985 in which he said, 'In the event a person is definitely going to die and he is either in great pain or has virtually become a vegetable, and prolonging his existence is only going to cause difficulties and suffering for others, the termination of his life may be permitted according to Mahayana Buddhist ethics.'

Rather than condoning euthanasia here, the Dalai Lama may instead be expressing concern about artificial prolongation of the dying process. Unfortunately, the criteria mentioned here are not as clear as they might be: for instance, being a 'vegetable' is a crude term to use in a medical context. If this means that the patient is 'brain dead' then no moral issue arises, since by the standards of modern medicine (although perhaps not those of Tibetan Buddhism) the patient is already a corpse. It seems likely, then, that the Dalai Lama has in mind a case where the patient is not yet clinically dead but where death is imminent, and there is no possibility of a recovery. In such circumstances, the only relevant issue need be the timing of the withdrawal of life support, a matter usually resolved in discussion with the patient's family. While recognizing that the prognosis in individual cases will vary, there seems no reason why Buddhism should find a case of this kind morally problematic in principle. The aim of medicine, whether Western or Buddhist, has never been the prolongation of life by reference to some chronological measure.

The same conclusions might be drawn with respect to similar remarks by other high lamas. As Peter Harvey reports, 'Kalu Rinpoche has said that a terminal patient who himself chooses to be taken off a life-support system is doing an act which is karmically neither bad nor good' (2000: 302). If the act is karmically neutral this is presumably because it does not involve an intention to kill, and without an intention to kill there cannot be euthanasia as we understand it. The same may be said of comments made by Sogyal Rinpoche, also reported by Harvey:

> Life-support measures or resuscitation can be a cause of disturbance, annoyance, and distraction at the critical moment of death ... In general there is a danger that life-sustaining treatment that merely prolongs the dying process may only kindle unnecessary grasping, anger, and frustration in a dying person, especially if this was not his or her original wish. Relatives ... should reflect that if there is no real hope of recovery, the quality of the final days or hours of their loved one's life may be more important than simply keeping the person alive. (Harvey 2000: 301)

Once again, the comments refer to the discontinuation of futile treatment in order to allow the patient to die a natural death. This is something that has taken place uncontroversially in hospitals for centuries, including in Tibet. Perhaps the opinion of the learned lamas was informed by the teachings of the *rGyud bzhi*, an authoritative Tibetan medical text, according to which 'there was by no means an overarching charitable obligation for doctors working in the Buddhist tradition to protect or extend the patient's life at any cost. Instead, the guiding principle was to recognize the definitive signs of death that made further treatment pointless from a medical standpoint' (Schlieter 2016: 14). Although the advent of modern technology has meant that the interval between certain treatments being withdrawn and death taking place has dramatically shortened, the principle remains the same. The difference between this and euthanasia in practice is that if the patient does not die when the treatment is withdrawn the doctor will not follow up by administering a lethal injection.

Further comments made by the Dalai Lama in Canada in 1996 were reported as having 'boosted the spirits of supporters of legalized euthanasia' in view of his remark that 'mercy killing was permissible in certain exceptional circumstances' (WTNN 1996). The example he cited was 'the case of a person in a coma with no possibility of recovery', and elsewhere he has spoken of 'hopeless, irreversible cases' (Schlieter 2014: 324). More details would be needed to make a judgment, but if an expert diagnosis is made that there is no possibility of recovery (and doctors should always err on the side of caution), there is no point in continuing a treatment; and to discontinue a futile treatment (such as artificial ventilation) in such circumstances need be no more than the reluctant acceptance that the patient is beyond medical help. On the same occasion when asked for his views on euthanasia, the Dalai Lama responded, 'I think its better to avoid it', adding that Buddhists believed 'every life was precious and none more so than human life'. This was hardly the ringing endorsement of euthanasia some took it to be, and reinforces the need for caution in interpreting *ad hoc* comments on complex ethical issue of this kind. A more systematic analysis of Tibetan Buddhist views on euthanasia has been provided by Tsomo (2006), which reveals no support for euthanasia on the part of Tibetan lamas.

Moral Values

Autonomy

Discussion of euthanasia in the West has largely taken place in the context of the influential 'four principles' approach to medical ethics (Beauchamp and Childress 2013; Florida 1993). The four principles are autonomy, non-maleficence, beneficence, and justice. Of these, the principle of autonomy has assumed special importance in discussions of euthanasia and is often seen as a necessary corrective to paternalistic attitudes that have historically been prevalent in healthcare. In the context of terminal care this has often given rise to 'dysthanasia' (the opposite of 'euthanasia'), a form of overzealous therapy and obstinacy on the part of the attending physicians. Dysthanasia consists in delaying death as long as possible even when there is no hope of a cure and regardless of the additional suffering caused to the patient. Respect for patient autonomy, by contrast, shifts the balance in favour of the patient and is the basis for the 'informed consent' which governs treatment decisions in the doctor–patient relationship. As such, it places the physician under a *prima facie* obligation to respect the autonomous choice of the patient and is considered by many supporters of euthanasia to be the primary moral ground of the 'right to die'.

The involvement of the doctor, however, means the issue cannot be framed exclusively in terms of patient autonomy. The doctor is not simply an instrument of the patient's will, and must herself make a judgment, as with any medical intervention, as to whether or not the treatment is medically and ethically appropriate before administering it. This means that the critical judgment is in practice taken out of the patient's hands, giving rise to what some see as a logical 'slippery slope' from voluntary to non-voluntary euthanasia. The argument here is that if the physician's judgment that the patient would be 'better off dead' is valid in a case of voluntary euthanasia, it is hard to see why it is not also valid in a case of non-voluntary euthanasia. If the patient has not expressed a view to the contrary, his autonomy would arguably not be infringed, and beneficence alone may be thought sufficient to justify ending his suffering.

Autonomy, furthermore, is not a central value for Buddhism, and placing importance on it may be thought to strengthen belief in an independent 'self' (*ātman*), the existence of which Buddhism denies. What is emphasized in Buddhism is not autonomy but relational interdependency (*pratītya-samutpāda*). In terms of this teaching, individuals are not conceived of as autonomous moral legislators or ethical atoms but as nodes within a network of relationships in which each part is related to every other. As Chaicharoen and Ratanakul suggest,

> This concept affirms the interdependence of all beings. ... Suicide or assisted suicide as a 'right to die' cannot be absolute because people do not live alone but are members of communities who might be injured by their death or by a social policy that encourages such death. (1998: 39)

This view is echoed by Stonington, who notes, 'Interdependence means that doctors, patients and relatives must think about the emotions and interests of all parties involved in a medical decision' (2006: 1681; Fan 2015; Akabayashi and Hayashi 2014).

The Japanese in particular seem sceptical about the role of autonomy in end-of-life decisions. Hamano observes that '[u]nder certain circumstances the presence of choice may be an illusion' (2003: 17), and Nakamura Hajime comments, 'We do not forget that one's life has a social link and in broad meaning, a connection to universality. It is the condensation of inestimable lives' (quoted in Koike 2006: 31).

Japanese bioethicist Komatsu Yoshihiko coined the term 'reverberating death' to express a similar notion. He writes: 'I suggest that "death" reverberates. Both sides are affected: the dying and those who watch him or her die, the one who has died and those who have been deeply affected by it' (2007: 182). He notes how 'the 'right to die' rhetoric severs the connections between people, uproots the possibility of expanding such ties, and lures us gently towards death'. The danger with promoting autonomy as a solution to medical paternalism, he concludes, is that '[w]e shift the power from one side to the other but the basic *dualistic pattern* remains' (2008: 195, original emphasis).

This fact is increasingly recognized also by Western bioethicists such as Margaret Pabst Battin, a well-known advocate of rational suicide. A report in the *New York Times* explains how while caring for her quadriplegic husband she became more aware that '[w]e are social beings, and only the unluckiest of us live in a vacuum. ... Everyone's autonomy abuts someone else's' (Henig 2013). Buddhist psychology, too, seems to undermine belief in the existence of an autonomous will, and offers a more nuanced understanding of the psychological dynamics involved in motivation and choice (Heim 2013). Without going to the extreme of determinism, it seems clear there are powerful forces that shape and control the exercise of free will, suggesting that 'choice' in dying is often no more than an empty slogan.

Compassion

A second value often thought to support euthanasia is compassion. Compassion is of great importance in Buddhism, and is associated especially with the Mahāyāna ideal of the bodhisattva, someone who takes a vow to seek rebirth over countless aeons until all beings have been freed from suffering. A person who expresses a wish to die should naturally be treated with compassion and understanding, but in such a situation it is often not clear exactly what compassion requires. As Jens Schlieter points out, 'Even though the Buddhist idea of "compassion" is intimately tied to the aim of alleviating suffering, it has traditionally not been defined by certain "therapeutic" obligations in a practical manner' (2014: 328).

Compassion is a sentiment rather than a moral principle, and like any sentiment must always be expressed within ethical constraints. Under the Western 'four principles' approach, the virtue of compassion would be linked to the principle of beneficence. This imposes an obligation to restore the patient to health or, where this is not possible, to mitigate the symptoms of disease, control discomfort and pain, and provide basic nursing care. In a Buddhist reformulation of the 'four principles', Thai bioethicist Pinit Ratanakul regards compassion as a '*prima-facie* duty' (along with veracity, non-injury to life, and justice) (1988: 301f.). A duty to alleviate suffering, however, is not a duty to alleviate it at any price. As Chaicharoen and Ratanakul observe,

> … compassion is limited to giving drugs in sufficient quantities to relieve intense pain, as that experienced by cancer patients, as a last resort when no hope of recovery is possible and the patient is dying. This is the farthest that compassion can go. Beyond this point the precept against taking of life is violated. (1998: 38)

Ratanakul notes further how '[i]n some cases, compassion may mean permitting patients to meet the end naturally without futile prolongation of treatment. … However, it is clear that Buddhism is against euthanasia—the quick, supposedly merciful ending of life to relieve pain' (2009: 15).

A bodhisattva should aim to provide immediate relief from suffering where possible, but the deeper obligation is to be a friend and companion on the long and arduous path through many lifetimes until a final end to suffering is found in *nirvāṇa*. Euthanasia by itself cannot free beings from suffering, since according to the First Noble Truth suffering is inherent in existence.

In cases where suffering is due to karma, moreover, killing will only postpone the suffering to a later date. This is an argument the Dalai Lama has used against both euthanasia and assisted suicide (Delhey 2006: 54). Obviously this would not hold true for Buddhists who do not believe in rebirth, and such 'Buddhist modernists' might find the case for euthanasia more appealing. Even they, however, might believe that euthanasia expresses not a deeper solidarity with beings and a willingness to share their suffering but a severing of the relationship with the suffering patient.

Compassion can also express itself in more constructive ways through the provision of hospice care so that people do not die, or fear they will die, in distressing circumstances (Florida and Ratanakul 2012; Chaicharoen and Ratanakul 1998; Bruce 2012). As Ratanakul observes, 'The Buddhist objection to the experience of unbearable pain as the reason for euthanasia is justified. The hospice movement has shown that we already possess the means to control suffering and the knowledge to maintain people without severe pain' (2009: 15). It is interesting that experts in palliative care who assist patients to die naturally with dignity are (along with disability rights groups) among the strongest opponents of euthanasia. The justification for euthanasia in the last analysis rests not on compassion but on the reasons why it is thought to be in the patient's best interests to be killed rather than go on living. Taking compassion as the premise, therefore, does not mean that euthanasia must be the conclusion.

Textual Sources

The textual material most relevant to euthanasia is found in the division of the Buddhist canon known as the Monastic Rule (*Vinaya*). This is primarily a code of conduct for monks and nuns, but as Anālayo points out, 'The Buddhist monastic legislators did not operate from the perspective of a clear-cut divide between laity and monastics' (2014: 29). The decisions recorded in the *Vinaya* are based on jurisprudential principles that transcend monastic law, and in conjunction with the associated commentaries allow us to state with precision what constitutes culpable killing both by those who are ordained and those who are not.

The circumstances that gave rise to the promulgation of the monastic precept against taking human life (the third *pārājika*) have a direct bearing on euthanasia (Vin III.68ff.). The sources narrate an incident (recorded in all extant versions of the *Vinaya*) in which some monks became disgusted with their bodies and proceeded to kill themselves or lend assistance to one another in dying. Others engaged the services of a 'sham recluse' (*samaṇa-kuttaka*) who killed them in the belief he was helping them 'cross over' and attain *nirvāṇa* (Heim 2013: 161–165; Anālayo 2014). When the Buddha found out what had happened, he promulgated a precept against taking human life directly or providing anyone with a 'lethal instrument' (*satthahārakaṃ*) with which to commit suicide.[1] After this, in a separate incident (Vin III.71), a number

[1] On the meaning of *satthahārakaṃ* see the Addendum by Gombrich in Anālayo (2014: 43f.).

of monks encouraged a sick layman to commit suicide. The Buddha then extended the precept to exclude persuading or lending encouragement to anyone to end their life, as follows:

> Should any monk intentionally deprive a human being of life or look for some lethal instrument (*satthahārakaṃ*) [to assist him], or speak favourably of death, or incite [anyone] to death saying 'My good man, what need have you of this evil, difficult life? Death would be better for you than life', or who should deliberately and purposefully in various ways speak favourably of death or incite [anyone] to death: he is also one who is defeated, he is not in communion. (Vin III.72)

As Anālayo notes, the precept prohibits 'intentionally depriving a human being of life and assisting others in committing suicide, or inciting them to kill themselves' (2014: 25). Apart from euthanasia, this prohibition encompasses the kind of emotional blackmail that the vulnerable elderly in particular may experience at the hands of unsympathetic relatives or in uncaring medical institutions. It also includes the encouragement to die motivated by more benevolent sentiments, as the very next case reveals. According to the brief report: 'At that time a certain monk was ill. Out of compassion the other monks spoke favourably to him of death. The monk died' (Vin III.79). The commentary expands on this terse account:

> 'Out of compassion' means that those monks, seeing the great pain the monk was in from the illness, felt compassion and said to him: 'You are a virtuous man and have performed good deeds, why should you be afraid of dying? Indeed, heaven is assured for a virtuous man at the very instant of death'. Thus they made death their aim and ... spoke in favour of death. That monk, as a result of them speaking favourably of death, ceased to take food and died prematurely. It was because of this they committed an offence. (Vin-a II.464)

Here we see that it is wrong to make death one's aim even when motivated by the compassionate desire to ease suffering. A small selection of further cases confirming this principle can be mentioned in summary form. One (Vin III.85) concerns a monk who at the request of relatives assists in bringing about the death of a double amputee by prescribing a drink that will be fatal for him. The monk was expelled. A similar verdict was pronounced in the case of a nun who recommended a different concoction as a means of causing the death of another patient in the same condition (Vin III.86). In a third case, in order to spare a condemned criminal the mental distress of awaiting the appointed time of execution, a monk interceded with the executioner to carry out the sentence immediately, and this was duly done. Despite the compassionate motivation, and the fact that the prisoner's death was inevitable, the monk was judged guilty and expelled (Vin III.85).

The moral dilemmas that arise in end-of-life care were clearly as much of an issue for the early monastic community as they are today. We see this from a discussion in the Theravāda *Vinaya* commentary that helpfully distinguishes three sets of circumstances in which those close to death sometimes cease from taking food and medicine.

> 1) If someone is sick and, wishing to die (*maritukāmo*), ceases to eat even when medicine and attendants are available, this is an offence (*dukkaṭa*). 2) But if someone is very sick and suffering from a long illness, and the attending monks are wearied and dispirited thinking 'when will we ever cure him of this illness?' (Then) if he, (thinking) 'this body even being nursed will not survive, and the monks are wearied', stops eating and does not take medicine, it is acceptable (*vaṭṭati*). 3) If someone refrains from eating (thinking) 'this illness is intense, I am dying, and this special (meditative) attainment (*visesādhigamo*) of mine is close at hand', it is acceptable. (Vin A.2.467)

There is an important contrast here between the first case and the other two. The first case is distinguished by the patient's intention to die. His condition is not as grave as in the other two cases, but he rejects the medical resources on hand, not because they cannot improve or palliate his condition, but because he wishes to end his life. To deliberately seek death in such circumstances is said to be wrongful. The second case concerns a patient who is chronically ill and beyond medical help. This patient decides to discontinue medical support and refrain from eating. His reasoning is that the inconvenience of further treatment and life support both to himself and others can no longer be justified. Apart from finding the mechanics of eating and digestion onerous, terminal patients are often unable to metabolize food, so the attempt to nourish a dying body is in any event futile. In the third case, the dying patient comes to a similar conclusion but also has a desire to devote himself to spiritual practice without further distraction. In the second and third cases death is accepted as imminent and inevitable, but in contrast to the first case it is not intentionally chosen.

The circumstances of the Buddha's own death are relevant in this connection, and in some ways resemble the third option described above. In his eightieth year he suffered a 'dire sickness' in which 'sharp pains came upon him, even to death', but by a strong effort of will he resolved to fight the illness and keep his hold on life until he had addressed his disciples and taken leave of the Order. As he told his personal attendant Ānanda: 'just as a worn-out cart, Ānanda, can be kept going only with the help of thongs, so, methinks, the body of the Tathāgata can only be kept going by bandaging it up' (Rhys Davids 1910: 108). He added that the only time he felt at ease was when immersed in deep meditation. Later he announced that he had 'relinquished his life-faculty' (*ayusaṅkhāraṃ ossaji*) and predicted that his death would occur three months hence. Although some interpret this as 'a kind of suicide' (Delhey 2006: 36; cf. Anālayo 2014: 165ff.), it may be better understood as signifying the Buddha's acceptance that death was at hand and that efforts to extend his life would merely be a prolongation of the dying process with its attendant pain and suffering (hence dysthanasia). On this basis (and discounting hagiographical claims about the Buddha's ability to prolong his life for an aeon by means of supernatural powers) his death was no more suicide than that of the cancer patient who decides to forego another round of chemotherapy in order to enjoy a shorter but fuller life with her family in the time remaining.

Although the *Vinaya* cases discussed are ancient, the precedent they set for contemporary end-of-life care seems clear enough. The significance of these judgments is all the greater in light of the fact they were given at a time when the benefits of modern medicine and palliative care were not available. The cases reveal that the reasons for seeking euthanasia have not changed greatly, and the cases cover the main grounds on which euthanasia is commonly thought justifiable today, namely autonomy, compassion, and quality of life. The judgments demonstrate that it is wrong to take life directly, wrong to provide the means for others to kill themselves, wrong to incite someone to kill another, and wrong to emphasize the positive aspects of death and the negative aspects of life. The unifying principle underlying these judgments appears to be that any intention to cause death as a means to end suffering is immoral.

Euthanasia in Japan and Thailand

Japan

In this final section we consider empirical evidence from two parts of the Buddhist world. Euthanasia has not been legalized anywhere in Asia, although there is increasing debate on the issue in many countries.

In Japan, while there is no statutory regulation of end-of-life care, a series of court decisions from the mid-1990s onwards have provided judicial guidance (Kai 2009: 4ff.). In an attempt to further clarify the legal position, a document known as 'The Guideline on the Decision-Making-Process in Terminal Care' was issued in May 2007 by the Ministry of Health, Labour and Welfare (Kai 2009: 10). The Japanese Society for Death with Dignity (*songenshi*; formerly the Japan Euthanasia Society) has campaigned for the legalization of euthanasia since 1983 in a manner similar to Western organizations, although it is not clear to what extent it represents the views of Buddhists.

The Buddhist perspective has been investigated by Koike Kiyoyuki, who worked as a psychiatrist in Japan for forty years and has also translated an extensive selection of Buddhist texts relating to suicide and euthanasia. He concludes a lengthy review of the evidence with the comment, 'I think that most Japanese and a lot of Asian people are reluctant to accept the right to die in the depths of their minds' (2001 189). In Koike's view there is little demand for euthanasia in Japan. 'Almost without exception', he notes, 'family members and specialists care for patients with senile dementia, severe mental disorders and those in a vegetative state until their death. The lives of loved ones and patients are valued' (2006: 27). Other researchers have concluded that 'the Japanese society of modern times is more restrictive in its approach to the issue than many Western countries' (Hugaas 2006).

Evidence on religious attitudes can be found in a 1998 survey of 338 Japanese religious groups carried out by Tanida Noritoshi (2000). The survey, the first of its kind, included 157 Buddhist groups belonging to different Japanese sects. Tanida reports that '[a]ctive euthanasia was greeted unfavorably among the religionists in general, as it was among secular people', with less than 20 per cent of respondents indicating approval. The author also mentions 'Buddhism's tendency to deny futile treatments at the terminal setting', noting that 'Shinto and Buddhist organizations advocated "being natural" when medical treatment becomes futile in a terminal setting' (2000: 339). An earlier national survey in 1991 revealed that only 16 per cent of Japanese thought life should be sustained as long as possible while 78 per cent thought palliative care desirable even though it might shorten life (Kimura 1996). A survey of the views of Japanese doctors has been carried out by Macer, Hosaka, et al. (1996). Clearly, moral issues cannot be settled by opinion polls, but these results seem consistent with what we have described as the normative Buddhist position, namely a rejection of euthanasia in favour of a 'natural death'.

Japan has a distinctive and perhaps unique history with respect to both suicide and infanticide (*mabiki*), and some have seen such practices as evidence of Buddhist toleration of euthanasia (Becker 1990; Perrett 1996). Becker's comparison between the assisted suicide (*seppuku*) of the samurai warrior and a modern case of euthanasia, however, is strained, as is the parallel he draws between being 'cut down' by an enemy and 'cut down' by cancer. The two situations are far from 'the same' (Becker 1990: 551) for a number of reasons. Cancer is not a moral agent; the samurai will not be killed by a physician; he is not suffering from an illness; he is not in physical pain; and he does not make a truly autonomous choice since he is strongly obligated to seek death by his martial code of honour. It does not follow, moreover, that because Japanese samurai embraced Zen Buddhism their martial code must be seen as an authentic expression of Buddhist ethical values, any more than the warmongering of Japanese Zen masters in the Second World War (Victoria 1997, 2003) shows that Buddhism tolerates fanatical nationalism and ruthless slaughter. The disgraced samurai's feeling that death is his only option since he can no longer play a useful role in society, however, may find an echo in the feelings of uselessness and isolation experienced by many who seek euthanasia. Even so, this does not mean that death is an appropriate or justifiable remedy for such ills. As Peter Harvey notes, 'The central Buddhist response is one of aiding a person to continue to make the best of his or her 'precious human rebirth', even in very difficult circumstances', rather than prematurely ending his life (2000: 309).

Thailand

In Thailand, the topic of end-of-life care became a point of public controversy following the death of the renowned monk and teacher Buddhadasa in 1993 (Ratanakul 2000; Jackson 2003; Kanjanaphitsarn 2013: 2015). Following a stroke, he was rushed to Siriraj Hospital in a coma and spent just over a month in intensive care. Debate raged over whether the monk should have been allowed to die peacefully in his forest monastery, as he had specified in an advance directive, or whether efforts should have been made to prolong his life. Eventually, he was returned to his monastery by plane with respirator and feeding tubes in place, where he passed away less than an hour after arrival.

As Stonington notes, Buddhadasa's death 'spurred a critique of biomedicine', and led to his student Phra Paisal developing training programmes based on the premise that '[d]eath instead must become an *experience* and a *process* that can be faced, studied, and understood' (Stonington 2011: 120–121, original italics). Spurred by similar concerns, palliative care programmes began to take off (Wright 2010) inspired by the pioneering work of Dr Temsak Phungrassami, who had trained in palliative care in Australia. In July 2007, the work of various end-of-life organizations coalesced in a large conference in Bangkok entitled 'Culture, Death and the End of Life' (Stonington 2011: 130f.).

Despite the existence of a patients' 'bill of rights' (The Thai Medical Council 2000) authorizing patients to make decisions about their medical care, Thai physicians are reluctant to disconnect ventilators from terminal patients. While some physicians will allow a family member to remove breathing tubes, they will generally not do it themselves. Stonington and Ratanakul explain that Thai physicians 'have a complex array of reasons for declining to remove ventilator support, including their medical training, fear of litigation, and belief in the sanctity of life' (2006: 1680). A physician who performs such an action, it is thought, inevitably incurs spiritual demerit. There is also a common Thai belief that the last part of the body to die is the breath, and hence 'pulling out a patient's ventilator may feel like pulling out the patient's soul' (1680). Thai medical care focuses instead on encouraging the patient to let go of the mental attachments that are keeping him alive, hoping that when the patient is ready he will simply let go and die with the respirator still attached.

There are further distinctive aspects to the Thai situation. Children often feel they owe their parents a 'debt of life', and placing a parent in intensive care is their way of 'giving life' (*hai chīwit*) and paying back the debt of flesh (*neua*), blood (*leuat*), and breath (*lom haijai*), the basic elements of biological existence that their parents endowed them with (Stonington 2012: 840). The respirator is seen as a crucial tool in 'paying down' (*chai nī*) the debt of breath. Stonington reports how

> [o]ne family was so adamantly aggressive with medical care for their father that he underwent three rounds of cardiopulmonary resuscitation despite his constant pleas to go home and die. Eventually, after being resuscitated several times, the family took the old man home. (2012: 840)

The reason why the family eventually took the patient home is of interest. While hospitalization and intensive care is seen as a way of 'paying back' a debt to a parent, a hospital is also regarded as an inauspicious place to die. Hospitals are seen as places of metaphysical pollution haunted by evil spirits and the ghosts of people who have died. For this reason, the ceremonies that need to be performed are not thought to have the same spiritual potency, and so the merit the dying person can achieve is much less. The home, by contrast, is a much more auspicious place to die. As Stonington notes, 'The home is sacred and familiar. It is safe and warm. It has a long history of purity because it has been blessed by monks in many ceremonies, and it has been the site of a lifetime of good deeds and devoted love' (2012: 843). Once the patient is back home, the act of withdrawing an endotracheal breathing tube becomes ethical. As a nurse stated, 'It is unethical to withdraw the tubes in the hospital, but it is ethical to withdraw them at home' (Stonington 2012: 836). The rationale for this paradoxical judgment seems to be that once the debt of life has been paid in the hospital the patient can legitimately be assisted to die a good death by the removal of the respirator at home.

The reluctance to withdraw life support in hospital, however, has led to an accumulation of patients who are being kept alive by machines. Stonington describes one ward where 'half the patients were on mechanical ventilators. The air was sterile and filled with the beeps of machines. Nurses scuffled around with gloves, wheeling blood-pressure check units to the beds of almost corpse-like patients, strapped as modern cyborgs into the life-machines of medical innovation' (2012: 841). In view of the strain it places on resources, this is not a sustainable position. As Stonington and Ratanakul note, 'there is an urgent need for solutions to the 'ventilator problem'—both to patch the failing universal healthcare system and to help Thais make difficult decisions about intervention at the end-of-life' (2006: 1681). Cost is a reason offered by one Thai philosopher (Somparn Promta) for supporting euthanasia for disabled infants and incurable patients on life support (Kanjanaphitsarn 2013: 5).

As Chaicharoen and Ratanakul note, however, 'It is clear that active euthanasia including assisted suicide is against the Buddhist teaching' (1998: 37). They add that 'Thai lay Buddhists also are unwilling to see general policies adopted accepting passive euthanasia. As there are always risks and uncertainties, they would favor risking in favor of life and not against it' (1998: 38). In spite of this, they note public confusion in the face of cases such as that of 'a 94 year old woman, kept alive by artificial means for over a year' and 'an 11 year old girl in irreversible coma for years' (1998: 38). They report how when lay Buddhists were asked which factors should be important in end-of-life decision-making 'none could give a definite Buddhist answer. Some say yes and some no, but they could not find grounds in Buddhism to support their answers' (1998: 38).

Conclusion

Perhaps the preceding discussion will indicate the direction in which an answer might lie. To recap, it was suggested Buddhism rejects euthanasia but without imposing an obligation to preserve life at all costs. As Tibetan nun Karma Lekshe Tsomo sums up, 'From my examination of the debate and the responses of the Buddhist traditions on two core issues of the debate, I conclude that intractable pain does not justify euthanasia and that the principle to protect and nurture life does not necessitate extraordinary medical procedures' (2006: 174).

Much support for euthanasia arises from anxieties about the inappropriate use of medical science. There is understandable concern about patients being kept alive as 'prisoners of technology' when many feel the appropriate decision is to allow nature to take its course. The normative position identified here does not force dying patients to endure a living death hooked up to life-support machines, nor does it oblige doctors to subject terminal patients to piecemeal medical procedures when what they yearn for is a peaceful and dignified death in the company of their loved ones.

Neither doctor nor patient is under any obligation to prolong life purely as an end in itself. For Buddhists, death is not a final end but the doorway to rebirth and new life. As Chaicharoen and Ratanakul report, 'More and more elderly Buddhists, monks and lay people alike, express their wishes to be allowed to die in the last stage of their lives accepting death as a natural end simply because, they believe, this is the Buddhist way of facing the inevitable death' (1998: 40). The Buddha was fully aware of the problem of human suffering, and through both his words and example encouraged his followers to care for the sick and dying (de Silva 1994). As the record shows, however, he rejected euthanasia as an option in medical treatment. Buddhist physicians have followed his example for well over two thousand years (Keown 2014), and there is little evidence that Buddhists today see any compelling reason why this should change.

Works Cited

Akabayashi, A., and Hayashi Y. (2014) Informed consent revisited: a global perspective. In: A. Akabayashi (ed.). *The future of bioethics: international dialogues*. Oxford and New York: Oxford University Press, 735–749.

Anālayo, Bhikkhu (2012) Dabba's self-cremation in the *Saṃyukta-āgama*. *Buddhist studies review*, 29, 153–174.

Anālayo, Bhikkhu (2014) The mass suicide of monks in discourse and vinaya literature. *Journal of the Oxford Centre for Buddhist Studies*, 11–55.

Beauchamp, T. L., and Childress, J. F. (2013) *Principles of biomedical ethics*. Seventh edition. Oxford: Oxford University Press.

Becker, C. B. (1990) Buddhist views of suicide and euthanasia. *Philosophy east and west*, 40, 543–556.

Bruce, A. (2012) Welcoming an old friend: Buddhist perspectives on good death. In: H. Coward and K. I. Stajduhar (eds), *Religious understandings of a good death in hospital palliative care*. Albany: State University of New York Press, 51–76.

Cavanaugh, T. A. (2006) *Double-effect reasoning: doing good and avoiding evil*. Oxford and New York: Oxford University Press.

Chaicharoen, P., and Ratanakul, P. (1998) Letting-go or killing: Thai Buddhist perspectives on euthanasia. *Eubios journal of Asian and international bioethics*, 8, 37–40.

Delhey, M. (2006) Views on suicide in Buddhism: some remarks. In: M. Zimmerman (ed.), *Buddhism and violence*. Lumbini, Nepal: Reichert Verlag, 25–63.

de Silva, L. (1994) Ministering to the sick and the terminally ill. *Access to insight (legacy edition)*. Available from: www.accesstoinsight.org [accessed 30 December 2015].

Fan, R. (ed.) (2015) *Family-oriented informed consent: east Asian and American perspectives*. New York: Springer.

Florida, R. (1993) Buddhist approaches to euthanasia. *Studies in religion/sciences religieuses*, 22, 35–47.

Florida, R., and Ratanakul, P. (2012) Buddhist hospice care in Thailand. In: H. Coward and K. I. Stajduhar (eds), *Religious understandings of a good death in hospital palliative care*. Albany: State University of New York Press, 167–190.

Gethin, R. (2004) Can killing a living being ever be an act of compassion? The analysis of the act of killing in the Abhidhamma and Pāli commentaries. *Journal of Buddhist ethics*, 11, 166–202.

Grol-Prokopczyk, H. (2013) Thai and American doctors on medical ethics: religion, regulation, and moral reasoning across borders. *Social science & medicine*, 76, 92–100.

Hamano K. (2003) Should euthanasia be legalized in Japan? The importance of the attitude towards life. *The journal of the Literary Association of Kwansei Gakuin University*, 52, 15–27.

Harvey, P. (2000) *An introduction to Buddhist ethics: foundations, values and issues*. Cambridge: Cambridge University Press.

Heim, M. (2013) *The forerunner of all things: Buddhaghosa on mind, intention, and agency*. Oxford and New York: Oxford University Press.

Henig, R. M. (2013) A life-or-death situation. *New York Times magazine*, 17 July 2013.

Hugaas, J. V. (2006) Ethos, ethics, and end-of-life issues in Japan. PhD diss., University of Bergen.

Jackson, E., and Keown, J. (2012) *Debating euthanasia*. Oxford and Portland, OR: Hart Publishing.

Jackson, P. A. (2003) *Buddhadasa: Theravada Buddhism and modernist reform in Thailand*. Chiang Mai: Silkworm Books.

Kai K. (2009) Euthanasia and death with dignity in Japanese law. *Waseda bulletin of comparative law*, 26, 1–13.

Kanjanaphitsarn, S. (2013) An analytical study of euthanasia in Buddhism with special reference to the case of Buddhadāsa Bhikkhu's death. *International journal of Buddhist thought and culture*, 21, 141–154.

Kanjanaphitsarn, S. (2015) *Euthanasia in Buddhism: a case of Buddhadasa Bhikkhu's death*. Saarbrücken, Germany: Scholars' Press.

Keown, D. (2001) *Buddhism and bioethics*. London: Palgrave.

Keown, D. (2014) Buddhism and healthcare. *Japanese religions*, 36, 143–156.

Kimura R. (1996) Death and dying in Japan. *Kennedy Institute of Ethics journal*, 6, 374–378.

Koike K. (2001) Suicide and euthanasia from a Buddhist viewpoint: on Nikāya, Vinaya piṭaka and the Chinese canon. *Journal of Indian and Tibetan studies*, 5 (6), 144–190.

Koike K. (2006) The philosophical argument against the right to die, from a Buddhist viewpoint. *Journal of Philosophy and ethical health care and medicine*, 1, 27–42.

Komatsu Y. (2007) The age of a 'revolutionized human body' and the right to die. In: W. R. LaFleur, S. Shimazono, and G. Bohme (eds), *Dark medicine: rationalizing unethical medical research*. Bloomington, IN: Indiana University Press.

Macer, D., Hosaka T., Niimura Y., and Umeno T. (1996) Attitudes of university doctors to the use of advance directives and euthanasia in Japan. *Eubios journal of Asian and international bioethics*, 6, 63–69.

Perrett, R. W. (1996) Buddhism, euthanasia and the sanctity of life. *Journal of medical ethics*, 22, 309–313.

Ratanakul, P. (1988) Bioethics in Thailand: the struggle for Buddhist solutions. *Journal of medicine and philosophy*, 13, 301–312.

Ratanakul, P. (2000) To save or let go: Thai Buddhist perspectives on euthanasia. In: D. Keown (ed.), *Contemporary Buddhist ethics*. London: Curzon, 169–182.

Ratanakul, P. (2009) Compassion, health care, and Buddhist monks. *Dharma world* (April), 14–18.

Rhys Davids, T. W., and Rhys Davids, C. A. F. (trans.) (1910) *Dialogues of the Buddha*, Volume 2. London: Oxford University Press.

Schlieter, J. (2014) Endure, adapt, or overcome? The concept of 'suffering' in Buddhist bioethics. In: R. M. Green and N. J. Palpant (eds), *Suffering and bioethics*. Oxford and New York: Oxford University Press, 309–336.

Schlieter, J. (2016) Buddhist principles of Tibetan medicine? The Buddhist understanding of illness and healing and the medical ethics of the *rGyud-bzhi*. In: A. Weissenrieder and G. Etzelmüller (eds), *Religion and illness*. Eugene, OR: Wipf and Stock, 90–113.

Somerville, M. (2014) Exploring interactions between pain, suffering, and the law. In: R. M. Green and N. J. Palpant (eds), *Suffering and bioethics*. Oxford and New York: Oxford University Press, 201–230.

Stonington, S. (2011) Facing death, gazing inward: end-of-life and the transformation of clinical subjectivity in Thailand. *Culture, medicine, and psychiatry*, 113–133.

Stonington, S. (2012) On ethical locations: the good death in Thailand, where ethics sit in places. *Social science and medicine*, 75, 836–844.

Stonington, S., and Ratanakul, P. (2006) Is there a global bioethics? End-of-life in Thailand and the case for local difference. *PLoS medicine*, 3, 1679–1682.

Tanida, N. (2000) The view of religions toward euthanasia and extraordinary treatments in Japan. *Journal of religion and health*, 39, 339–354.

The Thai Medical Council (2000) The declaration of patient's rights. *The Thai Medical Council of Thailand bulletin*, 7, 2–3.

Tsomo, K. L. (2006) *Into the jaws of Yama, lord of death: Buddhism, bioethics, and death.* Albany: State University of New York Press.

Varelius, J. (2016) On the moral acceptability of physician-assisted dying for non-autonomous psychiatric patients. *Bioethics*, 30 (4), 227–233.

Victoria, B. D. (1997) *Zen at war*. New York: Weatherhill.

Victoria, B. D. (2003) *Zen war stories*. London: RoutledgeCurzon.

Williams, P. (1989) *Mahayana Buddhism: the doctrinal foundations*. London: Routledge.

World Tibet Network News (WTNN) (1996) Dalai Lama backs euthanasia in exceptional circumstances, 18 September. Available from: www.tibet.ca, n.p. [accessed 30 December 2015].

Wright, M. (2010) *Hospice and palliative care in southeast Asia: a review of developments and challenges in Malaysia, Thailand and the Philippines*. Oxford and New York: Oxford University Press.

Yu K. P. (2002) Terminating futile medical treatment and passive euthanasia: is there a difference? *Eubios journal of Asian and international bioethics*, 12, 137–138.

Suggested Reading

Harvey, P. (2000) *An introduction to Buddhist ethics: foundations, values and issues.* Cambridge: Cambridge University Press.

Jackson, E., and Keown, J. (2012) *Debating euthanasia*. Oxford and Portland, OR: Hart Publishing.

Kanjanaphitsarn, S. (2015) *Euthanasia in Buddhism: a case of Buddhadasa Bhikkhu's death.* Saarbrücken, Germany: Scholars' Press.

Keown, D. (1995) *Buddhism and bioethics*. London: Palgrave.

Nakasone, R. Y. (1990) *Ethics of enlightenment*. Fremont, CA: Dharma Cloud Publishers.

Ratanakul, P. (2004) *Bioethics and Buddhism*. Bangkok: College of Religious Studies, Mahidol University.

Tsomo, K. L. (2006) *Into the jaws of Yama, lord of death: Buddhism, bioethics, and death.* Albany: State University of New York Press.

CHAPTER 30

BEING AND ITS OTHER

Suicide in Buddhist Ethics

MARTIN KOVAN

Introduction

It is not surprising that ethical traditions across time and space have afforded suicide a unique philosophical status. Its psychological, ethical, and potentially soteriological nature make it one of the most obscure of acts to understand, and thence evaluate. It can be abject or awe-inspiring, depending on its context. It invokes logically and existentially transcendental categories of being and not-being. Uniquely of human acts it takes the mastery of one's death into one's own hands; it epitomizes an extreme of autonomy: an act of the self, by the self, for the self, that appears to glorify *and* repudiate that very self's existence.

The *summum bonum* of Buddhism is the extinguishment (as *nirvāṇa*) of the life of suffering we all know; it asserts we already, in one crucial sense, do not exist as the selves we take ourselves to be. It asks, in effect: on what basis can we either condemn, or condone, such an act when many of the presuppositions for our judgment are groundless? This chapter will elucidate those forms of Buddhist ethical thinking that attempt an answer to that question inasmuch as they make substantive judgment around the value of life and the possible value in its relinquishing, as evidenced in some pronounced instances of suicide in the Buddhist life-world.

Yet the status of suicide in Buddhism is at once contested and ambiguous, from the earliest Pāli record through to twentieth-century Mahāyāna praxes. Buddhist thought, rooted in a vision of ultimate freedom from embodied suffering, wrestles with these existential conundrums and introduces some more of its own.

The conditions for suicide are of course wide-ranging, and some limit circumscribing their discussion is necessary. The secondary literature on Buddhism and suicide is wide and increasingly deeply focused. This chapter draws on Kovan (2013; 2014), which situate contemporary cases of Tibetan Buddhist self-immolation in a synoptic account of Buddhist suicide.[1] My focus here is to draw conclusions from this various record relevant to a broader context of ethical and philosophical discussion. This chapter will focus on three main areas: (1) the defining canonical accounts of suicide in the extant Śrāvakayāna and Mahāyāna traditions; (2) their theorization in a Buddhist psychological and phenomenological understanding of suicide; and (3) the ramifications of that understanding for contemporary social and medical practice, namely in assisted suicide and autothanasia, and for recent Buddhist history, above all for evaluating the continuing phenomenon of Tibetan Buddhist self-immolation evident since 2009.

This chapter will not consider the wider anthropological, sociological, historical, and all recensional and post-canonical textual aspects of the understanding of suicide and its manifestations across millennia of traditional Buddhist monastic and lay society. It focuses instead on philosophical and psychological quandaries raised in general by the early Buddhist record, inasmuch as these inform the question of what suicide signifies for Buddhist normativity given its metaphysical and soteriological claims around the self (*attā*), selflessness (*anattā*), suffering (*dukkha*), and intention (*cetanā*). In seeking to clarify, if not resolve, that question, the chapter is concerned with the constitution and effects of suicide as objects of immediate ethical concern to a Buddhist world view.

Canonical and Orthodox Accounts of Suicide

Across the Buddhist textual spectrum suicide is regarded equivocally, tending to fall into two uneasily opposed camps. The textual discourse is complex and contested, and between the Śrāvakayāna and Mahāyāna canons, despite their theoretical continuity, even mutually undermining.

As long ago as the early 1920s Buddhist scholars such as de la Vallée Poussin and Woodward suggested that despite the canonical insistence on non-violence towards others codified in both the first precept and the third *pārājika* of the *Vinaya* proscribing homicide, the Buddhist tradition is equivocal about suicide. Despite texts that confirm, first, that suicide is not an ascetic act conducive to spiritual progress and, second, that no *arhat* or awakened being would ever commit suicide, Poussin in 1922 concluded 'we are confronted with a number of stories which prove beyond dispute that we are mistaken in these two important conclusions' (cited in Keown 1996: 10).

Since then a number of scholars have rehearsed Poussin's claim, notably Lamotte, who 'believed that Vakkali's case represented the normative position of early Buddhism

[1] Building on earlier work of Damien Keown, among others, the research which must be acknowledged as defining recent exegeses of Pāli, Sanskrit, and Chinese textual sources regarding Buddhist suicide is that of Anālayo and Martin Delhey, to whose work this account is gratefully indebted. There is also a growing body of Japanese-language research using Japanese and other Buddhist sources.

according to which an *arhat* may kill himself' (Delhey 2009: 72 n. 12). The putative Poussin-Lamotte 'transcendency hypothesis'—according to which 'a liberated person like an *arhat* can transcend moral rules, since he is "beyond good and evil"' (Delhey 2009: 72 n. 11)—made with regard to *arhat* suicide, and countered more recently by Keown and Harvey (2000: 291), could nevertheless be said to be echoed in a theoretically important statement of the 14th Dalai Lama, of March 2013. This statement was given in response to a question regarding self-immolation in a Buddhist context, but it also makes a general claim about the psychology, and ethical evaluation, of suicide:

> Suicide is basically a type of violence, but then [the] question of [its being] good or bad actually depend[s] on the motivation and goal. I think (as) [far as the] goal is concern[ed], [if] these people [self-immolators] (are) not drunk, (do) not (have) [a] family problem, this is for Buddha dharma, for [the] Tibetan National interest. But then I think the ultimate factor is their individual motivation. If [their] motivation [consists of] too much anger, hatred, then it is negative. [But] if the motivation [is] more compassionate, [and accompanied by a] calm mind, then such acts also can be positive. That is strictly speaking from the Buddhist viewpoint: [the ethical evaluation of] any action, whether violent or non-violent, is ultimately [a judgement which] depend[s] on motivation. (Gyatso 2013; edited for fluency)

As a 'type of violence', suicidal acts are very often driven by profound emotional distress, confusion, and mental affliction, and can only be regretted and, ideally, obviated. However, the Dalai Lama states that the essential arbiter for judging the value, meaning, and effect of suicide lies in the intention (*cetanā*) or motivation of the agent that informs it, being paradigmatically the deciding factor of any wholesome or skilful (*kusala*) action, whether toward self or other.[2] Should that intention involve the 'poisons' of desire (or greed) (*lobha*) or ignorance (*moha*), but especially aversion or hatred (*dosa*), in this case towards oneself and one's life, it is necessarily unwholesome or unskilful (*akusala*). It is very possibly true (as a commentator such as Keown suggests) that most suicidal acts can be so characterized.

However, Keown also consistently refutes this basis for normative reasoning as representative. For him, it implies a subjectivist metaethics that fails to account for what should objectively determine the culpability of any lethal act, including suicide (1996: 12). As we will see, his critique is important for any Buddhist discussion because in representing a principled theoretical resistance to that metaethics, it can be placed in the context of the specific question of whether suicide, as a lethal act (see Delhey 2009: 72 n. 11), should be more appropriately conceived as destructive or productive of value. Does the reflexive nature of suicide potentially modify its ethical status, as it does for the Dalai Lama? This question is especially germane in the canonical context of

[2] It is important to not read Buddhist ethics in this case as purely intentional*ist*. Nevertheless, a causal 'intentionalism' runs very deep in its discourse, and in the Tibetan Buddhist context includes the depth-psychological agency of dream-states and their dream-acts. Tsongkhapa follows Candrakīrti by including dream-conduct in the full spectrum of morality (*sīla*).

Buddhist adepts who appear to warrant antinomian exclusion from Buddhist teachings on *ahiṃsā* or nonviolence.

The Śrāvakayāna

The Theravāda *Vinaya* commentary on homicide (Vin III.68–86) with regard to inciting another to suicide, in which the commission of suicide itself is *not* a forbidden offence for inclusion among the third of the four *pārājika*, has been frequently noted and in some cases taken to support the permissibility of suicide for *arhat*s (notably by Lamotte 1987: 105). Inasmuch as a successful suicide would seem to make redundant any expulsion from the order, its absence from the rule is contrasted with three acts that, when successful, are equivalent to murder: instigating others to kill; consensual mutual killing; and coercing others to kill. But as Delhey notes, given the fact that 'non-fatal suicide as such is nowhere in the Theravāda *Vinaya* treated as an offence' (2009: 30–31), then death alone does not explain the absence of suicide from its rule.

Harvey reports two cases from the same *Vinaya* of a monk who attempts suicide by plunging from Vulture's Peak only to accidentally kill an innocent other in his fall. The response of the Buddha is that a monk is not allowed to 'throw himself off' (Vin III.82). Elsewhere, a group of monks throw a stone off the same site, with the same result: for the Buddha both events are 'not an offence entailing defeat, but something approximating to one, of which there are two grades: a grave offence [*thullaccaya*] and an offence of wrong-doing [*dukkaṭa*], the latter being less serious' (Harvey 2000: 289–290). For Harvey and Delhey (2006: 30 n. 12), this common judgment demonstrates that the culpable factor they share is the harm done to *another*, where 'in the first case, the offence did not reside in its being a case of attempted suicide' (Harvey 2000: 290).

However, it is significant that the Buddha's relevant rule (Vin III.82) is worded in literal terms of 'not casting oneself off' (*na … attānaṃ pātetabbaṃ*), a phrase which also figuratively means 'should not kill oneself'. If so, the attribution of the *dukkaṭa* offence to 'casting off', apparently exclusively due to the (lethal) harm caused to others, renders its suicidal dimension not wholly negligible—something the commentary to the rule (Vin A II.467), which explicitly appropriates suicide attempts to it, would corroborate. (Cf. also Miln 195–197; and non-Pāli recensional variations on this ruling, below.)

Yet the absence of any direct prohibition against suicide is also evident in the commentarial *Vinaya* literature. Mutual suicides or suicide attempts occur within the *saṅgha*; the Buddha responds (e.g. Vin III.71, 82) with a negative appraisal, again not because of self-harm, which in some cases proves minor, but because of the harm to innocent others which they have incidentally entailed (most critically causing accidental death). In sum, suicide is neither equivalent to, nor a form of, the offence of murder: yet suicide and murder are implicitly conflated, on the basis not of the intrinsic harm they engender, but on the effects they produce in an environment of significant others. Suicide appears as an indirect cause of disapprobation that itself eludes every explicit rule. Delhey claims of the textual recensions of the Śrāvakayāna schools as a whole that 'there seem to be marked differences in the views on suicide expressed in the heterogeneous source material' (2006: 28; also 2009: 71–72).

Moreover, the central function in all these cases of lethal intention, notably in its concomitant effect on others, is what appears to determine culpability. Although intended, suicide is self-directed, granted that it is also *prima facie* contrary to the first precept of non-violence. Yet even if suicide were explicitly included in the prohibition against lethal acts, expulsion from the order would not itself explain the root cause for its censure, but would merely punish it. We still seek explanation for that cause, not merely that it is so punishable. Considering those few detailed cases in which the Buddha appears to exonerate suicide might be the best means to attempt a positive explanation.

A Special Case: *Arhat* Suicide

The central, and oft-discussed, example of the three major suicide cases among the *saṅgha* found in the early Buddhist canon is in the *Channovāda Sutta* of the Theravāda *Majjhima Nikāya*. Channa is a severely ill monk, living in seclusion, and although faithful both to the Buddha and the *Dharma*, avows he will 'use a knife' to end his intolerable suffering. Despite receiving relevant teachings on forbearance from his two monastic visitors Sāriputta and Mahā-Cunda, Channa cuts his own throat. When told of the episode, the Buddha assures Sāriputta that Channa will not be reborn and is thereby blameless (*anupavajja*).

The Pāli commentaries on the sutta go to some lengths to justify the Buddha's response by claiming that Channa attains awakening in the very course of the act itself. Sudden enlightenment in the course of, or immediately following, the act of suicide is not uncommon throughout the Buddhist literature. The commentaries effectively reconcile the general disapprobation of any lethal act, but especially suicide by a normal *or arhat* monk alike, with the Buddha's reason for excusing it in this case.

Unlike much previous secondary commentary, Keown (1996) concludes that the Buddha's response is not a condoning of suicide by *arhats*. Rightly perceiving in this case, as elsewhere, the legal and ethical distinction between exoneration as a 'removal of the burden of guilt' in a specific circumstance and condonation as 'the approval of what is done' (18) as a class of action, Keown's reading is buttressed by the many assertions in the Pāli Canon repudiating any potential value in self-harm of any kind.

It also confirms the orthodox stance of the 14th Dalai Lama, above, if not the latter's metaethical reasoning. Keown voices the common-sense conclusion that:

> In the eyes of the commentary, Channa was an unenlightened person (*puthujjana*) who, afflicted by the pain and distress of a serious illness took his own life. Presented in this light, few ethical problems arise: suicides by the unenlightened are a sad but all too common affair. (28)

Yet, as Keown reports, despite the wealth of canonical reasons supporting it, 'no single underlying objection to suicide is articulated' (29–30).

The Pāli commentary states that Channa is a *samasīsin*, someone who dies and attains *nibbāna* simultaneously. He is thus far from ordinary in the usual sense of the unenlightened *puthujjana* except, apparently, at the moment he *initiates* his deed, according to Keown and the para-canonical commentary to which he appeals. However, Buddhist psychology theorizes that the profound virtue and insight constitutive of awakening does not emerge without contextual cause. Any proximal moments of a person's mental continuum giving *immediate* rise to the attainment of the Path of Seeing cannot be understood as normal or defiled in the manner that would otherwise be sufficient to obstruct that attainment.

Rather, powerful meritorious and cognitive-causal bases must abide in the immediately preceding continuum of the mind. It appears unwarrantable to assert that if Channa is really an *arhat* at the moment of his death, he is a benighted soul lost to his self-destructive defilements at the moment he initiates the deed just preceding it.[3] There is then still cause to consider what informs the Buddha's exceptionalist (and for Keown, unique) claim for Channa.

The other instances in the *Sutta-piṭaka* that concern suicide (mostly variations on the tale of Channa) as an apparently acceptable (*vaṭṭati*) act feature at least three main conditions: (1) they occur outside the monastic, but within a renunciate, context; (2) they involve presumed *arhats*; and (3) they are largely (but not exclusively) cases of autothanasia (two of the cases combine all three). (I am using the term 'autothanasia', as a distinct subset of suicide, to denote the self-willed termination of life, due to conditions of severe or terminal illness for which no cure or recovery can be reasonably expected.) Suicide in these latter canonical contexts is thus problematic by virtue of factors intrinsic to the distinct kinds of renunciate, awakened, and critically ill *self*, rather than the monastic other.

These three ascriptions should be considered in turn. First, at least two of the three individual cases concern critically ill monks living in isolated seclusion. This should be contrasted with the notorious mass-suicide of monks as recounted in the *Vinaya* (III.65) and *Saṃyuttanikāya* (V.320) where the Buddha's disappraisal of suicide is unequivocal inasmuch as the third *pārājika* rule prompted by it, initiated in and structured around a communal body, refers to moral and physical injury made to others (see Anālayo 2014 for the most thorough recent textual study of this episode).

The Buddha's response there is thus starkly unlike those brought to the monks acting in solitude, which condition frames suicide as a solipsistic rather than socially conditioned act. That condition renders their being acts which, Anālayo correctly concludes, 'simply do not belong to the category of *pārājika* rule' (2014: 25–26 n. 55): a legal

[3] See Delhey's (2009) survey of recensional variations justifying the Buddha's exoneration of Vakkali's suicide, and the canonical commentarial claims that see it as integral to spiritual praxis (85–86). Cf. also the Chinese *Ekottarikāgama* recension which offers a contrary account of this case (Delhey 2006: 36; 2009; Anālayo 2011), improbable, however, in light of this same causal claim, above.

conclusion that occludes an ethical one. It implies that any solitary monastic suicide, including that of non-*arhat*s, simply evades monastic jurisdiction if, as we have seen, both *pārājika* and *dukkaṭa* rulings do not apply to suicide. Yet suicide, as an intended act, is normatively implicated in the *pārājika* rule (at Vin III.73) and for some schools integral to its derivations (certainly for the Mahīśāsakas, among others, and the very influential Theravāda commentarial tradition): obviating others' suicide is what first prompted it from the Buddha (Vin III.71).

Second, the *arhat* is the exemplar who has realized *anattā*, dispelled illusion, and achieved affective purity, and is thus freed of the delusive self-construction true of the unrealized layperson and of the monk-in-training, both bound to the karmic causality of the illusory self. In evaluating the intentional bases of the act, it is thus significant that the question of whether suicidal *arhat*s are in fact already awakened, or only become so during or after the act, becomes of critical importance for the commentarial exegeses of the suttas concerning them. It is only an intention undefiled by cognitive and affective affliction that is free of that karmic structure, and hence of the general prohibition of harmful action.

Third, the critically ill (as Channa and Vakkali without question are) also may or may not be realized, and are it seems judged by the individual case. The Buddha's exoneration of Channa's suicide (which Keown accepts as the single exception that proves the canonical rule) is case-specific, and, for Delhey, so is that of Vakkali (Delhey 2009: 78)—and conceivably that of Godhika as well, whose *arhat*ship following his suicide is similarly confirmed by the Buddha. Hence, Delhey's claim that:

> it is impossible to detect a uniformly negative view on suicide in the canonical texts. Rather . . . different views on suicide . . . seem to differ not only according to the person and circumstances involved in each case but also according to the text passage or recension under consideration. (2006: 36)

This summary conclusion tends to confirm a particularist reading that endorses neither a purely permissive nor prohibitive account of suicide in early Buddhism, insofar as both features are evident in the textual record. Even as regards *arhat* suicide itself, Anālayo comes to the important conclusion that 'on consulting the early discourse versions one could have the impression that an arahant can commit suicide, whereas other texts see this as impossible' (2011: 167). As he suggests, alternate recensions of the canonical texts in Sanskrit and Chinese demonstrate still more variation on the patterns we have considered above.

Non-Pali Canonical Sources

Recent Buddhist Studies scholarship has focused on the Pāli, Sanskrit, and Chinese canonical and post-canonical recensions of material familiar from the Theravāda record, adding intriguing emphases of certain of the themes already encountered. We have seen that the Theravāda *Suttānta* records a general proscription of suicide, and that its *Vinaya* and commentaries do not explicitly forbid it, but what of other Śrāvakayāna schools?

Where the Sarvāstivāda *Vinaya* 'explicitly states ... that suicide is not an offence' (Anālayo 2010: 132), that of the Mahīśāsakas makes particular mention of such a rule. The Buddha's mention here of suicide as a 'grave offence' (*sthūlātyaya*) falling just short of *pārājika* status is significant not merely for its explicit legal claim regarding suicide, but for begging the question of why it does not qualify as an offence entailing full 'defeat'. For the Sarvāstivāda *Vinaya*, at the other extreme, Delhey notes (2006: 31) that suicide is specifically nominated as the form of killing which, when performed by a monk, similarly does not entail *pārājika* status.

Anecdotal report is also made of the Buddha failing to condemn an unsuccessful attempt of a sick monk that has resulted in the accidental death of a jackal, perhaps because its victim is non-human. However, the apparent Sarvāstivādan tolerance of suicide might also explain why the Buddha here fails to label this act an offence, which for other schools' *Vinaya* might sustain the *dukkaṭa* ruling, or (for especially the Dharmaguptaka, and perhaps the (Mūla)-Sarvāstivāda and Mahīśāsaka) even the grave offence also (Anālayo 2010: n. 36). What is important to note here is that there is no obviously uniform response to even attempted suicide across the Śrāvakayāna record.

Less equivocal from these findings is that they confirm that for these schools suicide is the more prohibitive where it entails harming another (human) being, and that where it does not do so, neither its commission nor its attempt are as full-fledged an offence as homicide. Where the Mahīśāsaka appears, with qualification, less tolerant of suicide,[4] the Sarvāstivāda more so, and the Theravāda to occupy a midpoint between them. What is also certain from these recensional variations is that suicide cannot be simply equated, ethically and legally, with homicide and so is conceived differently, especially in the case of the suicide of monastic high-adepts (such as Godhika), who might also be terminally ill (such as Channa and Vakkali) and/or enlightened *arhat*s, before, during, or following their acts, and who thereby represent the only kind of being able to commit suicide without demerit.

There are further clear lines of convergence between these schools and the Theravāda. The Mahīśāsaka *Vinaya* also raises the possibility of permissible suicide in the case of very ill monks who, thanks to their great virtue, could only expect a heavenly rebirth. But this line of thought is rejected on the grounds of a further appeal to the notion of merit, whereby the maintenance of virtuous life, whatever its quality, conduces to still more meritable activity and so karmic gain (*puṇya*). The same argument is applied to a

[4] A trend continued in the post-canonical Theravāda, again evident in the *Milindapañha*, which insists that even terminally ill *arhats* do not suicide because they are indifferent to both the pain of continued life and the putative pleasure of release from it in death (Miln 44–5). Buddhaghosa reiterates the same theme in contending that Channa's vulnerability to his suffering is proof of his not being an *arhat*.

lay context, in which suffering itself acts as the incentive to ameliorate its worst effects by cultivating the *Dharma* while one is still alive.

So too, in the *Pāyāsi Sutta* of the Pāli *Dīgha Nikāya*, in the course of a discussion concerning purported proofs for rebirth, the sceptical Prince Pāyāsi wonders why a virtuous ascetic would hesitate to commit suicide when surely he too would have a better rebirth. The response of the monk Kumāra-Kassapa is that a virtuous life is itself inherently meaningful, and so the ascetic would not prematurely end it:[5]

> Their life is profitable to those ascetics and Brahmins, for the longer such moral and well-conducted ascetics and Brahmins remain alive, the greater the merit that they create; they practice for the welfare of the many, for the happiness of the many, out of compassion for the world... (DN 23:13; Walshe 1987: 357–358)

Kumāra-Kassapa's claim is not exclusive to virtuous monks or ascetics; inasmuch as virtuous attainments of many kinds are available to all people, suicide militates against their cultivation. The Buddhist concern is that embodiment in the so-called *saṃsāric* world allows for the further accumulation of merit, in the forms of compassionate and wise action extended to other suffering sentient beings.

These reasons for rejecting suicide pertain to the Mahāyāna context as well, and form the exoteric bases for the bodhisattva's motivation for rebirth in the broad ethical nature of the so-called Greater Vehicle. Yet, as Buddhism historically evolves, suicide is also newly cast as a form of transcendental renunciation that hyperbolizes the same theme, under a quite different guise.

The Mahāyāna

The canonical Mahāyāna *Saddharmapuṇḍarīka (Lotus)* and *Samādhirāja Sūtras* famously register virtual paeans of praise for bodhisattva suicide by self-immolation: here it is an act of the greatest meritorious self-sacrifice to the buddhas and a demonstration of high wisdom realization. Moreover, for Nāgārjuna (by attribution) in the *Mahā-prajñā-pāramitā-śāstra*, the *Vinaya* itself indicates that suicide evades the karmic fault (*āpatti*) and merit (*puṇya*) that respectively ensue from wrongs done to others (*para-viheṭhana*) or benefit done them (*para-hita*) (Lamotte 1949: 740–742).

Chapter 11 of the same text explicitly describes the categories of *dāna* in which the Inner Offering (judged as more significant than the Outer) includes giving away one's head or marrow, or even one's whole body or life. For this canonical Mahāyāna text

[5] The paracanonical *Milindapañha* is noteworthy for its rejection of the legitimacy of *arhat* suicide, for the same reason of an aesthetic of sagacious timeliness, just as embodied life (as the *arhat* Śāriputra attests) is neither to be held onto nor pushed away. The realization of *anattā* implies, in these terms, a radical letting-be of the independently natural processes of life and death alike.

there would seem to be no greater act of selfless virtue. This attitude becomes epitomized especially in the Chinese transmissions of the *Samādhirāja* and *Lotus Sutra*s in which self-immolation receives its explicit discussion and endorsement, undergirding the known historical cases of medieval Chinese Buddhist self-immolations.

For the Mahāyāna, self-immolation also signifies the total sacrifice of that conventionally most cherished object—the human body—in a wisdom-purification of ignorance by fire. (A number of texts of the *Vinaya* qualify *arhat*s with the metaphor *aggikhandha*—'mass of fire').[6] Self-immolation either approaches, or fully epitomizes, the most conventionally radical 'total self-renunciation' (*ātmaparityāga*) in importantly non-nihilistic terms. Again, suicide entails karmic effect only insofar as it is motivated by delusion, attachment, or hatred—which returns to the psychological claim of the Dalai Lama quoted earlier.

Failing the negative psychological impetus of the three poisons, suicide is left, for the Pāli Buddhist sources, in some moral indetermination (Gethin 2004: 190), but for the Mahāyāna it is unequivocally an act, where these are absent, of moral-soteriological power. To what degree this reflects an ethical blamelessness is however unclear, inasmuch as other cases of religious suicide are not so valorized (by for example Śāntideva in the *Śikṣāsamuccaya*), especially when they are not committed by apparent holy beings.

Writing a decade after Keown, Michael Zimmerman (2006) echoes Delhey (2006: 57) and others in arguing that:

> against what seems to be the common scholarly view ... Buddhist thinkers treated suicide as something distinctly different from killing other sentient beings and that, in contrast to Western notions of human life as sacred, life does not have such a basic value in Buddhism. (Zimmerman 2006: 28)

Zimmerman's latter claim is only plausible if a typically Christian sacred or divinely sanctioned value is equated with the value that life indubitably, if instrumentally, does have for Buddhism. Yet, the Buddhist truism that proscribes all acts of violence, including suicide, remains in a still unresolved tension with the dichotomy Zimmerman identifies, and one that exerts considerable ambiguity right up to the response to the recent Tibetan Buddhist self-immolations. Mahāyāna Buddhist luminaries such as the 14th Dalai Lama and Thich Nhat Hanh continue to voice this normative schism with regard to suicide as a legitimate form of political and other Buddhist agency.

The early Buddhist attitude to suicide thus evolves towards overtly valorizing its religious forms, in the Mahāyāna vehicle. From the early implied in putative indifference to the sanctity of life claimed by Zimmerman, devotional suicide later appears to demonstrate the great virtue of its voluntary sacrifice—abundantly evident for example in the *Jātaka* tales, the fourth chapter of the *Abhisamayālaṃkāra*, the *Vyāghrīparivarta*, the *Suvarṇabhāsa*

[6] Anālayo (2012) offers a causal, if speculative, textual account of the origins for self-immolation in the fire imagery of the discourse on Dabba and his self-cremation, found in the Chinese Saṃyukta-āgama recension of parallel accounts in the Pāli *Udāna*.

Sūtra, and the *Lotus Sūtra*. Moreover, this virtue would appear to override an ethically autonomous value indirectly predicated of life as such. This shift of emphasis might be seen as indicating a soteriological development that recognizes, and legitimates, the differing capacities of those engaged on the Buddhist path, defined not by fixed doctrine but by the atemporal constitution of mind, and (non-)self, of each practitioner. This recognition could underpin not only the Mahāyāna but even the early Pāli records in their wide and otherwise causally obscure variations.[7]

The ethical distinction to be drawn thus lies between the understanding of suicide as an act of lethal self-harm or as something else, and whether its religious, political, or other utility is a meaningful one for Buddhist ethics. Given a broad understanding of lethality in which it enacts various forms of ideological value, suicide as a religious, and especially political, act entails a symbolic structure and intent. These latter forms of intentional act cannot be understood exhaustively in terms of the pathological self-annihilation signified in the category of *vibhavatṛṣṇā*, or the 'thirst for non-existence'. Rather, here there is a wide range of ethical nuance implied by the same act because 'suicide' as a single term covers and masks a wide variety of normative intentions.

As a willed act of the self, suicide is formally paradoxical: the mental continuum *qua* self in willing its own annihilation *asserts* itself. Perhaps to resolve that real ambiguity, the *Vinaya* identifies the harm it does to *others* as the objective basis for its (indirect) proscription. Where self-harm is not explicitly proscribed, it is also not clear whether the psychologically paradoxical structure of suicide, especially given the centrality of *anattā* to early Buddhist discourse, might inform the normative variations to which Delhey and Anālayo refer. Considering the psychological theory underpinning the foregoing normative claims might aid in understanding their heterogeneity.

Buddhist Psychology and the Phenomenology of Suicide: Mind, Motivation, and Ethical Causation

If, for Buddhism, there is ultimately no autonomous self, who or what agency appears to determine the ethical status of the act of self-annihilation? In the terms of Abhidhamma psychology, suicide is the effect of an extreme configuration of unwholesome intention (*akusala cetanā*) and volitional traits (*saṃskāras*). But if intention is ethically decisive, it also supervenes, whatever its conscious intention, on those latter determinants of afflictive motivation (*hetu*). At the same time, the object of intention is distinct from willed action directed to another person (and hence is objective only with

[7] Delhey (2009: 67–68) reads these shifts as historically determined (72). His admission however of wide variation even within certain contemporaraneous strands of textual stratification appears to imply criteria *internal* to broader exegetical trends as well.

reference to *the body* of the suicide). If we can only, at best, indirectly infer the qualitative intention of the agent, how can we evaluate suicidal action?

Gethin (2004) claims that, for the canonical Pāli texts, a potentially compassionate motivation informing *homicide* is, at least psychologically, untenable:

> ... that intentionally killing a living being is wrong is not in fact presented in Buddhist thought as an ethical principle at all; it is a claim about how the mind works, about the nature of certain mental states and the kinds of action they give rise to. It is a claim that when certain mental states (compassion) are in the mind it is simply impossible that one could act in certain ways (intentionally kill). (190)

We could call this the Abhidhammic-psychological 'internal argument'. Keown (1996) offers another, in a sense we could more familiarly identify as an 'external argument'. As we have seen, for Keown, if we have objective reasons for condemning the murder of sovereign others, these reasons cannot rely on the purely subjective mental states of the agent. Rather, they are grounded in the sovereign rights of the other as an autonomous person, where that sovereignty is threatened in deed (far more than word or thought).

For this reason, subjective motivation cannot be the final arbiter for the value, meaning, or effects of an act of killing *and/or* suicide, equivalently: 'In suicide, of course, there is no victim, but the comparison [between murder and suicide] illustrates that moral judgments typically pay attention to *what is done*, and not just the actor's state of mind' (Keown 1996: 12). For Keown killing qua suicide is unjustifiable in altruistic terms, though he bases his argument not on a prior Buddhist claim about suicide but on an ethical conceptualization of homicide. Conflating the two cases occludes constitutive differences between Western-ethical and Buddhist reasoning in this case, but suicide and homicide as well. (This difference is explicit in the presentation of self-immolation in the Mahāyāna where, as we have seen, transcendental claims for the praiseworthy ritual offering of the body undermine just the subject–object dualism to which Keown implicitly appeals.)

In summary, if (1) Buddhist normativity is determined not so much by public proscription as by inherent psychological conditions, including less conscious ones, on which such norms supervene, and (2) the status of killing turns finally on a question of the deepest levels of psychological intention and the volitional mind it informs, it seems likely that the normative substructure for suicide is no different. Thus, it would seem that Keown's equating of homicide and suicide is, at least psychologically, not misguided and the permissibility of the latter can (in Gethin's internal Abhidhammic terms) be determined with the same reasoning as the former.

As we have seen, Keown's external argument against the permissive view of Buddhist suicide relies on a claim for the ethical equivalence between suicide and homicide. For Keown, if subjectivism, as an argument for the permissibility of suicide in Buddhism, is used to justify homicide generally, it results in an absurd permissibility of killing sovereign others. As this is unacceptable, so too is the initial premise:

> The 'roots of evil' approach to moral assessment ... is subjectivist to the extent that it claims that the same action (suicide) can be either right or wrong depending on the state of mind of the person who suicides: the presence of desire (or fear) makes it wrong, and the absence of desire (or fear) makes it right ... In murder a grave injustice is done *to someone*, regardless of the murderer's state of mind. To locate the wrongness of murder solely in desire, is to miss this crucial moral feature of the act. (Keown 1996: 12)

An unstated premise of Keown's argument is that suicide is as much an instance of killing a sentient being as is homicide. This is surely generally true—a living (often young and healthy) body is taken from the sum of sentient lives, all of them alike embodying the high value of conscious sentience itself. The argument is valid, but are the premises sound?

Keown's argument can be reversed to support one that makes suicide categorically *not* equivalent to homicide because (as Nhat Hanh suggests) their intentional objects are psychologically as well as ontologically distinct. In suicide, first, it is not another's living body that is either neutralized (as in homicide) or symbolically value-exchanged (as in ritual sacrifice), but one's own. Second, we cannot conceive of a meaningful 'other' apart from the freedom of self-determination that (as Keown infers) the other as *person* embodies. Hence, Keown's argument implies that it is the *self-determination* of the other that is crucially at stake in determining the moral culpability of homicide.

However, these two factors—another's living body and autonomy—are just what is not at stake in suicide; rather, suicide puts one's own body and autonomy at stake by virtue of perhaps the most extreme self-determination possible. (Note, however, that this may still be fundamentally characterized by unwholesome motivation, which preserves Gethin's internal argument.) The ontological and psychological conditions of suicide do not thereby justify it, but nor do they implicate it in the sense Keown assumes with a claim for homicide–suicide equivalence.

An obvious objection might be that the value at issue is neither the body nor the constitutive will of personhood but the sheer 'life' it instantiates (as expressed in Keown 1998–1999: 18). To that the same refutation obtains: to conceive of human 'livingness' requires that sense in which it is always (in the first instance) a life *for* a subject (however minimal or compromised), for whom it is or always becomes a question what their being-alive signifies for them. Only secondary to subjective valorization can various responses to it by invested others (loved ones or society at large) be made at all. That understanding of personhood is what distinguishes intra-human behaviour from that involving the majority of non-human sentient creatures.

If the preservation of autonomy, just as much as the primary value of life, is what is decisive for Keown in the proscription of homicide and suicide alike, suicide must escape it: it expresses an unconditional assertion of embodied autonomy (and as against a possibly constraining other). This requires acknowledging it as a largely unobservable sequence of transactions between the afflicted volitions (*saṃskāras*), intention (*cetanā*), deeper mental motivation (*hetu*), and material form (*rūpa*) of the same autonomous living being, where his or her *own*, not another's, living sentience is at stake, and often for moral reasons as much as purely psychological ones.

It is just the nature and moral will of *the subject* that is being contested in suicide, and only secondarily that subject's relation to an observing (and perhaps even reciprocally invested) social world. Gethin's conclusion from the Abhidhamma remains in force (and despite, as we have seen, its lack of definitive *moral* articulation against suicide):

> Although the *Abhidhamma* model of the way in which the mind works can accommodate a set of circumstances where genuine compassion might play some part in an act of killing a living being, it does not allow that the decisive intention leading to the killing of a living [being] can ever be other than unwholesome and associated with some form of aversion (*dosa*). (2004: 189)

The Abhidhammic claim is fundamentally psychological; it is only secondarily ethical, and thence vulnerable to reified misrepresentation, such that what is really a (more or less misguided) psychological apprehension of the subject-self can become the 'objectively' fixed religious doctrine signified even in the comparative correctness of *sammā diṭṭhi* (or right view). That doctrinal view would misconstrue the original basis for what alone makes it right: that it is always the subject that apprehends those psychological-normative states that render benefit, or not. From this very point flows the phenomenological project of Buddhist ethics.

The foregoing, however, still does not justify suicide in the Buddhist context, and its aim is not by implication to endorse a permissive view of Buddhist suicide—whether personal, political, or religiously altruistic. It merely demonstrates that the problem of subjectivity with regard to apprehending the ethical nature of suicide appears stubbornly constitutive. While Buddhist psychology would suggest that suicide largely instantiates unwholesome (*akusala*) and afflictive mental-affective states and motivations, it appears that suicide, as a self-reflexive act, must also be considered in terms of its phenomenology: what it means, signifies, or instantiates *for* its agent. It may be a stated, inferred, or comparatively covert meaning, but it is always significant for Buddhist ethical evaluation.

Intention (*cetanā*) as the primary criterion of that ethical evaluation *is* this very meaning given normative status: the suicide acts as such just because he believes it is what *should* be done. In this sense it is not suicide per se that is at question, but the particular reasons informing its commission, and these will often vary even widely. Even an apparently abject act of self-annihilation is an expression of sense-giving meaning in its very rejection of life and its world, however misguided or gratuitous it may seem to observing others. However, at least in some cases, there may be compelling reason for, and some moral dignity in, the rejection of those worldly conditions.

SUICIDE AND TWENTY-FIRST CENTURY BUDDHISM

Political and Altruistic Suicide: Tibetan Buddhist Self-Immolation

These considerations become crucially relevant in recent cases of Tibetan Buddhist self-immolation, the most radical examples of Buddhist-inspired suicide, committed by monastics and lay faithful alike, since those in Vietnam in the 1960s. The Tibetan Buddhist self-immolations occurring largely from 2009 and inside Tibetan-Chinese territory, have been committed by men and women from the middle-aged to, very often, young people in their teens. At least 151 known cases up to mid-2017 have been documented; most, but not all, of these fatal (see Whalen-Bridge 2015 for a thorough recent survey).

Religious and political self-immolation operates in a global repertoire of contention. It is self-directed and, in that sense, not terroristic, and frequently regarded as an aberration of a particularly idealistic kind. Because altruistic suicidal protest intends avoiding harm to others, it is not as common, nor as 'effective', as protest that intends the large-scale killing of innocent others. The altruism in suicidal sacrifice, however, is that it appeals to those highest values at stake *for the living*, not merely for those who, in their religious or ideological sacrifice, renounce life. We can construe the nature of such sacrifice in a secular sense: for ethically commensurable reasons, parents will sacrifice their own bodies to save that of their child (even where the survival of both is theoretically possible) because they recognize the intrinsic value in preserving the hope of the best kind of survival for those who newly embody it.

Thus, the conventional value of giving one's life to a putative greater end is evident across a wide spectrum of ethical life, and I would suggest that Tibetan Buddhist self-immolation is of the same order of aspiration. By making such an absolute sacrifice, the Buddhist self-immolator unconditionally commits to transcending the needs and desires of the egoic self on behalf of the legitimate freedom of the oppressed other.

We have already observed the same impulse in the Mahāyānist who puts the alleviation of the other's suffering well before his own. This gesture of self-abnegation is the symbolic property of the act of self-immolation: an aspirational claim in which the self-immolator's body stands in for, or signifies, that value of freedom, which the act itself instantiates. (By contrast, a suicide bomber's sacrificed body may signify a very different value: the glory of fundamentalist supremacy, for example.) Does it instantiate that value negatively or positively? Is it *kusala* or its contrary? Any answer would seem to be determined by whatever interpretive framework is imputed of the intention of the act itself. In Mahāyāna terms it enacts an ethically immanent transcendence of the self (which for Buddhism remains ultimately illusory) and its otherwise insular domain.

However, the act is not the less real *qua* symbol, underwritten as it is with the highest cost any living being can pay: it ontologically relies on the value of life. Many non-Buddhist (but also Buddhist) and secular observers nonetheless dismiss or deny the symbolization of freedom in this way as fanciful wishful thinking. This is ironic considering the sense in which the same symbolic exchange of sacrifice to a more highly valued value via *consensual killing* (equivalent to mutual suicide) is conventionally recognized in the heroism of warfare. Arcane perhaps, but hardly fanciful when the same symbolic transfer thus underwrites conventionally justified, politically sanctioned, and even glorified lethality. The major distinction in the case of self-immolation is that only the agent himself is killed, instead of innumerable (and often innocent) others, for the putative greater cause. Yet that difference is also critical to what, as detailed above, makes homicide and suicide *ethically* incommensurable.

Where deontological ethics (central for example to human rights discourse) is grounded in a universally binding rational justification for individual action-guidance, transacted in a world of similarly guided others, the only legitimation personal or political suicide manifests is that given in a reflexive selfhood. By not being ethically bound to a wider world of rational-contractual others, the constitutive solipsism of suicide appears ineliminable. *Altruistic* suicide, however, radically revises solipsism as an ethical gesture, but not in terms of a would-be deontological, symmetrical obligation to the universal, abstract Other. Rather, it addresses an asymmetrically concrete *and* symbolic gift of appeal to others in their respective states of duress—here, obviously, the Tibetan oppressed, but (again in Mahāyānist terms) even their Chinese oppressors as well.

Altruistic self-immolation thus also signifies a difference between intellectual (or religious) argument, a moral 'thinking from the head' (an arguably culture-specific, conceptual reduction of values), and an ethical 'thinking from the soul' (an arguably universal-secular thinking in values per se). Hence, the self-immolator's claim transcends the kind of legitimation that could be made the object of rational ethical argument, even where it sustains inherent value (see Kovan 2014 for extended and detailed discussion). As *self*-empowered, it subverts a biopolitical status quo which emphasizes the political but not ethical impotence of subject bodies under state coercion.

As in Vietnam, now in Tibet, the solidarity and politicization of that same subject body (an ultimately collective Body) invests self-immolation with a gift of universal human appeal: in Buddhist terms a total proof against primordial 'grasping' (*upādāna*) at the ends of the mere self. Self-immolation then and now thus invokes empathy across cultural-political frontiers. Beyond reproach but also instrumentalization, its very altruism demands nothing in exchange, as such. It is in just that radically compassionate detachment that it can eloquently point to the gratuitous suffering of persons contingent on delusion, ill-will, and aversion, and leave the political imperative of its mitigation to the will of a collective conscience.

In what sense then is such ethical generosity properly political, if it does not blackmail its moral witness in the way other-directed terrorism does? While the very extremity of self-immolation provokes both empathy *and* alienation, and reconfigures conventional frames of political reference—as that of Thich Quang Duc in 1963 Vietnam succeeded in doing—it registers defiance of the contingent human causes of a historical circumstance of suffering: lacking that evident object, it would not (need to) occur, and recur. The power of Quang Duc's act was that it spoke unequivocally to an immediate historical-political injustice, the truth of which demanded its restitution.

Between ethics and politics, self-immolation thus demonstrates to what degree the moral force of the one can effectively determine the integrity of the other. If for Buddhist thought the truth-values of conventional morality are inherently revisable, so too is any response to the universal call such proof of commitment sends out to a wider world. It is on that hopeful possibility that the Buddhist-inspired self-immolators stake their claim in the absolute statement of their acts.

Assisted Suicide, Autothanasia, and the End of Life

What value can be identified regarding the agent who chooses to end his or her life for reasons of terminal illness or other incurable medical conditions? Here, death is sought as an end in itself, rather than a means to another, living end. Suicide is here a question of existential decision rather than symbolic intentionality, where dying is not meant to influence anyone else as the latter cases are intended to. As we saw above, the cases closest to these in the canonical record refer to gravely ill *arhat*s, seeking pragmatic release.

As Keown notes, these 'deaths occur in exceptional circumstances and all involve an extraordinary degree of saintliness or religious piety. They have little in common with the circumstances in which most suicides take place' (2001: 58). Moreover, inasmuch as the Buddha appears to exonerate the suicide of *arhat*s who are critically ill, it cannot be inferred from those cases that the suicide of ordinary terminally ill people (let alone that of the otherwise healthy) would be similarly exonerated in a normative Buddhist view. (The third canonical case of the Buddha's exoneration, of Godhika, a highly accomplished ascetic who is not—at least in the canonical sources—likewise ill, only confirms the same point.)

We can recall here the *Pāyāsi Sutta*, in which Kumāra-Kassapa argues against the ascetic's hurrying death by suicide because, being not yet realized, it would be as premature as an induced premature birth. Similarly, 'awaiting the maturity of the fruit is wiser than trying to shake it down before it is ready to drop' (D II.332). Likewise, the *arhat*, while beyond the constraint of forming the new karma relevant to rebirth in *saṃsāra*, embodies an example of the path that suicide would clearly compromise. This agrees also with the canonical dictum that the *arhat* is incapable of committing any lethal act.

Yet we have seen an exception in the Buddha's exoneration of cases of *arhat* autothanasia. Prohibition runs uneasily into justification, in this very specific context, which introduces further ambiguity. As a 'non-returner', the *arhat*'s social value reflects his function as an immanent ideal of the teachings for others, yet in this case his apparently permissible autothanasia does not appear to condone non-*arhat* cases of the same act.

However, we have also seen that the Mahāyāna conceives of the possibility of compassionately grounded suicide, and the ethically compelling cases of the Tibetan altruistic suicides just considered, committed by Buddhists of profound faith (if uncertain soteriological status), confirm the Mahāyāna claim as in no sense negligible. Yet, as the above discussion confirms, there is nothing prescriptive about altruistic suicide, even where registering profound a ethical statement when it occurs in the contexts that give that statement radical, context-dependent, meaning. Some normative middle ground between the exoneration and condemnation of suicide needs to be granted, if only because the record implies as much.

But there are crucial distinctions to be made in that task, and again the Pāli record perhaps offers the clearest cue. (Koike 2001 usefully summarizes distinctions made between suicide and the 'shortening' and 'abandoning' of life, and natural 'death with dignity' also evident in Sanskrit and Chinese sources.) I noted above that the cases of suicide apparently exonerated by the Buddha in the canon mainly involved incurable, severe sickness; hence these cases restrictively refer to what I have called autothanasia, to distinguish it from suicide as psychological pathology. While autothanasia remains a form of suicide, even in the case of the Buddha's own apparently willed death (Delhey 2006: 36), there is cause for agreeing with Keown that such self-willed death is, rather than suicidal, more a matter of allowing nature to take its imminent course.

There is a fine line between that non-resistance to death and active willingness towards its coming to pass, which remains possibly indeterminable (one which, for instance, otherwise healthy agents such as smokers, stuntmen, or soldiers might negotiate in their respective choices). Nevertheless, this distinction between wilful suicide and autothanasia, in any discussion of suicide in Buddhism, is perhaps the most important that must be made, just because it offers the only example of a transgression of the first precept that the Buddha appears to recognize as ethically salient: monks (and laypeople) are prohibited from any form of killing, yet autothanasia in very select cases appears permissible. We can focus on whether the permissibility of autothanasia for comparatively ordinary people, and by extension the assisted suicide of the terminally ill, can be inferred from the canonical cases of *arhat* suicide.[8]

Assisted suicide is the relatively simpler case in terms of its canonical treatment. Again, the textual record of the *Vinaya* (Vin III.68ff.) is unequivocal. Following the mass suicide of monks, the Buddha explicitly forbids the provision of the means for suicide, such as a lethal instrument, which can for present purposes be generalized to any modern form of technological mediation, such as lethal injection. The third *pārājika* encodes this prohibition, as well as a subsequent one (Vin III.71) prompted by the case of monks verbally aiding and abetting the autothanasia of an ill layman. Vin III.72 expressly prohibits the commission of lethal acts, the instrumental aiding of, and verbal encouragement or incitement to, the suicide or homicide of others as all equally culpable on pain of expulsion from the Buddhist order.

[8] Post-canonical Theravāda commentaries such as the *Samantapāsādikā* pre-empted such concerns in considering voluntary fasting to the death. While proscribed there, exceptions arise in the case of terminal illness, but also because ingesting food compromises the achievement of spiritual insight, here valorized over survival per se.

Can ancient case law for monastics be translated directly into the modern clinical setting, which as physician-assisted suicide is premised on facilitating a less painfully protracted death? Crucially, the prohibition extends to the incitement to death even with compassionate intent, and the *Vinaya* offers a prototypical range of cases which all indubitably render assisted suicide, even as a speech act, impossible to defend.

These cases concern people suffering debilitating illness (Vin III.79), disablement (Vin III.85–86), or an imminent threat of death by execution (Vin III.85), and they all conclude with a negative judgment of agents seeking to mitigate that suffering. Again, it appears that for the early Buddhist lifeworld the possibility of suicide's normativization, in the form of professional medical mediation, was itself deemed a form of unwholesome action.

Autothanasia, in some cases at least, is not so unambiguously represented. Here too the *Vinaya* commentary (Vin A.467) offers perhaps the clearest indication of an early, and so perhaps for that reason most fundamental, perspective. Two instances alone are given for potentially acceptable suicide, but only by self-starvation: where terminal illness is accompanied by the exhaustion of all medical treatment (including the effort of care) and natural death is imminent; and where the same circumstance is conducive, for yogic adepts, to concentrated meditative practice. But it is not clear that this is properly suicide, in terms of life being cut short, but rather a preparation for death.

In both cases the processes of natural death are prioritized and, possibly, esoterically engaged, to ensure an optimal passing from life rather than to hasten it unduly. While the commentary does not specify *arhat*s as the subject of these conditions, Gautama Buddha himself apparently took this latter course. It epitomizes Buddhist practice, which everywhere values the surest conscious self-direction in the processes of living and dying alike.

We have observed that despite its disapprobation, no legal prohibition against suicide among the laity or *saṅgha* (apart from its incitement in *others*) is evident in the early Buddhist sources. The Buddha appears to exonerate an exception: the autothanasia of terminally ill *arhat*s. This exceptionalist theme develops through the Mahāyāna, which newly *valorizes* self-sacrificial bodhisattva acts. This valorization of suicidal altruism is then carried through East Asian Buddhist religious history, then politically into the last century and, now, Tibetan Buddhism also.

Between the poles of proscription and a transcendental realization of the soteriological goals of the religion, the normative status of suicide in Buddhism traverses a full range, recognizing that people engage the act to express many and diverse values. None can be ethically evaluated independent of context and agency: a Buddhist ethics needs to respect, and seek to understand, each in turn.

Works Cited

Anālayo (2010) Channa's suicide in the Saṃyukta-āgama. *Buddhist studies review*, 27 (2), 125–137.

Anālayo (2011) Vakkali's suicide in the Chinese Āgamas. *Buddhist studies review*, 28 (2), 155–170.

Anālayo (2014) The mass suicide of monks in discourse and Vinaya literature. *JOCBS*, 7, 11–55.

Delhey, M. (2006) Views on suicide in Buddhism, some remarks. In: M. Zimmermann et al. (eds), *Buddhism and violence*. Lumbini, Nepal: Lumbini International Research Institute, 25–63.

Delhey, M. (2009) Vakkali: a new interpretation of his suicide. *Journal of the International College for Postgraduate Buddhist Studies*, 13, 67–107.

Gethin, R. (2004) Can killing a living being ever be an act of compassion? The analysis of the act of killing in the Abhidhamma and Pāli commentaries. *Journal of Buddhist ethics*, 11, 167–202.

Gyatso, T., the 14th Dalai Lama (2013) 'Times Now TV' India Interview; https://www.youtube.com/watch?v=-XXZslT3mmE.

Harvey, P. (2000) *An introduction to Buddhist ethics: foundations, values and issues*. Cambridge: Cambridge University Press.

Keown, D. (1996) Buddhism and suicide: the case of Channa. *Journal of Buddhist ethics*, 3, 8–31.

Keown, D. (1998–1999) Suicide, assisted suicide and euthanasia: a Buddhist perspective. *Journal of law and religion*, 13, 385–405.

Keown, D. (2001) *Buddhism and bioethics*. London and New York: Macmillan/St Martin's Press.

Kovan, M. (2013) Thresholds of transcendence: Buddhist self-immolation and Mahāyānist absolute altruism, part one. *Journal of Buddhist ethics*, 20, 775–812.

Kovan, M. (2014) Thresholds of transcendence: Buddhist self-immolation and Mahāyānist absolute altruism, part two. *Journal of Buddhist ethics*, 21, 385–430.

Lamotte, E. (1949) *Le traité de la grande vertu de sagesse de Nāgārjuna (Mahāprajñāpāramitāśāstra)*, Volume 2. Louvain: Bureaux du Muséon.

Walshe, M. (trans.) (1987) *The long discourses of the Buddha*. Boston: Wisdom.

Zimmerman, M. (ed.) (2006) *Buddhism and violence*. Lumbini, Nepal: Lumbini International Research Institute.

Suggested Reading

Anālayo (2012) Dabba's self-cremation in the Saṃyukta-āgama. *Buddhist studies review*, 29 (2), 153–174.

Koike K. (2001) Suicide and euthanasia from a Buddhist viewpoint: on nikāya, vinaya piṭaka and the Chinese canon. *Journal of Indian and Tibetan studies*, 5/6, 144–190.

Kovan, M. (2013) Thresholds of transcendence: Buddhist self-immolation and Mahāyānist absolute altruism, part one. *Journal of Buddhist ethics*, 20, 775–812.

Kovan, M. (2014) Thresholds of transcendence: Buddhist self-immolation and Mahāyānist absolute altruism, part two. *Journal of Buddhist ethics*, 21, 385–430.

Lamotte, E. (1987) Religious suicide in early Buddhism. *Buddhist studies review*, 4 (2), 105–118.

Shakya, T. (2012) Self-immolation: the changing language of protest in Tibet. *Revue d'études tibétaines*, 25, 19–39.

Whalen-Bridge, J. (2015) *Tibet on fire: Buddhism, protest, and the rhetoric of self-immolation*. New York: Palgrave Macmillan.

CHAPTER 31

BUDDHISM AND ANIMAL RIGHTS

PAUL WALDAU

INTRODUCTION

THE diverse intersection of human with nonhuman lives has long been an ethically fraught meeting place.[1] In many discussions around the world, the moral issues raised by the inevitable meeting of humans and nonhuman animals are subordinated to strictly human concerns because the issues raised by humans' encounters with nonhumans are deemed far less important than the issues generated by human-to-human encounters. Yet for Buddhists, some other religious traditions, a substantial number of small-scale societies around the world, and many individual citizens and animal protection organizations in industrialized societies, humans' inescapable interactions with nonhumans comprise a crucial subset of the moral issues raised when one living individual harms or extinguishes the life of another living being.

Even a superficial engagement with Buddhist ethical reflection reveals that Buddhists have prized humans' capacious abilities to care for living beings within *and* beyond the species line. A closer examination of Buddhist reflection on humans' relationship to other animals, however, permits one to see complex, multifaceted challenges that arise regularly for all humans who desire not only to protect, but also to notice and take seriously, the living beings outside our own species. In the first part of this chapter, Buddhist insights about the importance of *not* harming other living beings are examined in relationship to many familiar categories of human–nonhuman interactions, including food animals, companion animals, free-living or wild animals, and those nonhuman beings used solely for humans' benefit as work animals, sources of food and other materials,

[1] I first wrote an article under the title 'Buddhism and Animal Rights' as a chapter in *Contemporary Buddhist Ethics*, edited by Damien Keown (Richmond, UK: Curzon Press, 2000), 81–112.

entertainment, or mere research tools. In the second part, challenges that fall under the modern term 'animal rights' are addressed as they also provide illuminating perspectives on not only Buddhist attitudes towards nonhuman animals but also the very nature and extent of humans' ethical capacities to care about the individuals and communities that are the warp and weft of what a highly respected twentieth-century visionary referred to as Earth's 'larger community' (Berry 2006: 5).

Buddhists and Other Animals

Buddhists have long recognized, as do modern science and common sense in every culture, that humans are animals. But given that so many of the modern world's key domains (such as law, education, public policy, and economics, mentioned in the second part of the chapter) operate as if the dualism 'human versus animal' is a feature of the natural world rather than an artificial division that elevates humans through a denial of our obvious animality, it is worth exploring key features of Buddhist attitudes towards the most familiar nonhuman animals. To explore this topic well, one must consider two noteworthy but distinct diversities.

First, there is an extraordinary range of differences evident when one surveys the living beings in the grouping that modern sciences label 'nonhuman animals'. Today's dominant ways of talking have, however, conditioned most people to use the clearly anti-scientific habit of calling only nonhumans 'animals' in order to distinguish them from human animals. It is now accepted fact that our Earth is populated by countless different kinds of living beings. The number of different species is not at all well known—in fact, despite the extraordinary efforts made in the last century to count the number of Earth's species, scientists who offer their best guesses about the number of existing species acknowledge that such estimates may be off by a factor of ten. In other words, instead of there being, as present estimates surmise, eight to ten million species (only two million of which have been identified), there may in fact be 80–100 million *different* species. As noted in more detail in the second part of the chapter, the vast majority of the Earth's living beings are best described as 'micro animals' that our unaided senses cannot detect or relate to as discrete individuals. For example, the population of micro animals on and in any one human individual (or any other macro animal) is unfathomably large; as Kurokawa writes, 'In adults, the combined microbial populations exceed 100 trillion cells, about 10 times the total number of cells composing the human body' (2007: 169–170).

For obvious reasons, the forms of human ethics bequeathed to us by our human ancestors, including of course Buddhist ethics, focus only on the many 'macro' nonhumans that are easily visible to us. Our inherited ethical systems indicate that from time immemorial, humans have been concerned about our intersection with other macro animals. Further, as described in the second part of the chapter, in the past few decades many more specific details have been learned about nonhuman macro animals, making it far easier to assess the direct and immediate consequences of holding them captive, disrupting or destroying their habitat, or killing them for food and materials. The upshot of this great increase in knowledge is that every ethical tradition today faces new challenges to respond in caring, nuanced ways that take account of what today is demonstrably true of the more complex of our nonhuman neighbours. As noted below, the Buddhist tradition has affirmed in almost countless ways that humans are obliged to pay attention to those other living beings we are capable of noticing, and to take those beings seriously in an ethical sense. This robust affirmation (discussed later in this section) goes well beyond most forms of modern animal protection, which, as is discussed in the second part of the chapter, include only a few thousand species of the world's macro animals.

The extraordinary diversity and ubiquity of nonhuman lives, which pose a series of challenges to any ethically able observer, were met by the early Buddhists in intriguing, ethics-intensive ways that model well the central role that care for others plays in humans' daily lives and spiritual awareness. This is true despite the fact that humans' ethical abilities, so clearly rich and remarkable regarding ourselves and some familiar macro animals like elephants and dogs, are, as pointed out in the second part of the chapter, unquestionably limited in a number of profoundly important ways.

A second diversity is also noteworthy. This is the altogether different kind of diversity of sub-traditions found within Buddhism. It is common to encounter descriptions of the tradition as divided into Theravāda, Mahāyāna, and Vajrayāna or Tantrayāna—yet each of these major sub-traditions is, upon exploration, found to be comprised of many further subdivisions. Beyond the most familiar sub-traditions are more well-known forms of Buddhism such as Tibetan, Zen, and Pure Land Buddhism, and these are complemented today with many forms of what some scholars call 'New Buddhist Movements'. In actuality, the Buddhist tradition is, like all mature religious traditions, characterized by great internal diversity, which is why Richard Gombrich, one of the great scholars of Buddhism in the twentieth century, observed, 'About *all* Buddhists few valid generalizations are possible' (1988: 2). Nonetheless, it is revealing that '[o]n the complex and difficult issue of "other animals" ' it is possible to identify 'unanimity of a kind on the [ethical] significance which real, live individuals of other species have in the minds of Buddhists' (Waldau 2001: 153).

A Remarkable Foundation—The First Precept

One of humans' surpassing achievements in ethics appears in the Buddhist tradition's commitment to what is often described as 'the First Precept'. This moral vow or undertaking is stated in a variety of ways, as sometimes it is directed to *intentional killing* and at other times its focus is the more general problem of avoiding harm to other living beings (Waldau 2001: 146–149). At the very least, following the First Precept commits a Buddhist to a conscious effort to refrain from intentional killing any living being. As Lambert Schmithausen suggests, 'in the First Precept, and hence also for a Buddhist lay person, society is not to be taken in the narrow sense of human society, but in a broader sense of a community comprising all living or sentient beings' (1991a: 40; see also 1991b).

The First Precept is, most likely, not solely a Buddhist achievement, for this important commitment almost surely predates the Buddhist tradition. As Schmithausen suggests, a commitment to refrain from killing is 'the heritage of an earlier cultural stratum—a stratum in which killing animals (and even plants, earth and water) was, in a sense at least, as serious as killing people (not of course one's own ethnic group), because animals, too, were believed to take, if possible, revenge on the killer in the yonder world' (1991a: 38–39; see also McDermott 1989: 274). Snakes, for example, were thought to take offence that snake flesh was eaten, retaliating against the perpetrator. Other animals were thought to sense the odour of flesh eaten, this odour encouraging an attack by that kind of animal.

This key prohibition very likely has other roots as well. Particularly common, for example, are claims that connect the First Precept to early Buddhism's adoption of the belief in rebirth that was so characteristic of Indian subcontinent traditions—a belief that made possible the reasoning that the First Precept was important because every other being now living was in a prior life one's parent (either father or mother). Echoes of this sort of familial thinking can be found in the *Metta Sutta*: 'Just as a mother would protect with her life her own son, her only son, so one should cultivate an unbounded mind towards all beings, and loving kindness towards all the world' (Sn I.8; Norman 1984: 149–150). Damien Keown notes that although there is no definitive statement as to which forms of life are valued and why, Buddhists value forms of life that are 'karmic' or 'telic' (having a telos, or goal); the basis for this kind of valuing is possibly the assumption that other living beings have an 'intrinsic' value, that is, each living being is 'affirmatively valued for its own sake rather than as a means to something else (i.e., its value is not instrumental)' (1995: 36ff.).

Such multiple possibilities cited in connection with the First Precept explain why Horner suggests that 'no doubt a mixture of motives operated' in making the First Precept central to all sorts of Buddhists—notice how the following explanation of the First Precept's pre-eminence connects this undertaking to a wide range of human values and experiences:

> Such championship may have seen in non-harming a way to increase the moral welfare of the monks; it may have been part of a disinterested social reform movement; it may have been, as in the case of sacrifice, polemical in nature, anti-brahminical; and it may have been due to the presumption that animals have as much right to their lives, and to compassion, as have human beings. (Horner 1967: 27)

Whatever reason an individual Buddhist gives for his or her daily undertaking not to kill any living being, this commitment is a foundational ethical undertaking in several senses. It clearly broadens the range of beings about whom one should care; it is primary also in the sense that this commitment plays out in daily life; additionally, such a commitment requires one to notice, and then take seriously, one's nonhuman neighbours.

Thus, the *actual* lives in one's immediate environs—local elephants and tigers, neighbouring deer and dogs, and so many other macro animals, including humans—are deemed morally important. Such foundational features help account for why the First Precept was constantly foregrounded in Buddhist awareness in multiple ways, all with the effect of constantly reaffirming Buddhists' commitment to act in ways that protect animal lives. In a very real way, the constant reaffirmation honours the Buddhist insight that our human lives are lived within an overarching moral order, a principal feature of which is the sanctity of individual lives. The upshot is an engendering of animal protection and the positioning of daily compassion at the heart of the tradition.

This achievement has, it is true, been matched in a number of other religious traditions and cultures, of which the Jains are perhaps the best known. One can also find similar commitments in many small-scale societies, and a number of sub-traditions within the large and diverse Hindu, Sikh, Chinese, and Abrahamic traditions. The occurrence of such commitments in multiple places and different historical eras can be used to suggest that humans have recognized that each of us can, *if we choose*, live an encompassing ethical vision regarding both our local world and the larger community of living beings. With confidence, however, one can assert that few human communities, if any, have done so more impressively than have Buddhists, even though the tradition began at a time of limited awareness of the details of the lives of nonhuman neighbours who share ecological and geographical space with the human community.

Consider, then, an important consequence of the First Precept in light of the great diversity evident in nonhuman animals—many different kinds of animals, as already noted, come squarely within the First Precept's foundational concern for humans' interactions with living beings beyond the species line. The Buddha is reported, for example, to have observed that those who hold animals captive for entertainment purposes will suffer an awful fate (Rhys Davids 1922: 172). Today, there is much ferment around the world regarding the ethical propriety of exhibiting certain animals for entertainment, as happens in marine parks that promote performances by cetaceans (whales and dolphins) of one kind or another. Some countries have outlawed such exhibitions, and some proprietors have voluntarily agreed (in response to protests and heavy media-based criticism) to end breeding programmes of, for example, orcas and elephants.

The First Precept also applies, of course, to the much larger and more traditional area of human domination of nonhuman animals for food and materials. The historical Buddha is quoted repeatedly in Buddhist scriptures as observing that an awful fate awaits those who kill other animals, such as deer hunters, pig butchers, sheep butchers, and fowlers. In this particular area, the First Precept provides a basis for challenging the longstanding assumptions that dominate some of the most important ways modern humans talk about other animals, such as law-based and economics-based discourse that assumes any and all nonhuman animals can be mere resources rightfully owned by humans, but also killed at humans' whim, including for luxuries that are indisputably non-essential to a thriving human life. One can, therefore, argue that the historical Buddha laid out an approach that requires Buddhists to condemn unequivocally those who confine food animals in the manner of industrialized, 'factory' farming that produces most of the meat consumed today.

Similar reasoning can be applied to confinement and killing, and even harms short of death, that are part the annual killing of hundreds of millions of laboratory animals around the world in pursuit of research and product development that is a hallmark feature of modern economies. Justifications for such practices sometimes invoke utilitarian thinking (the good that flows to humans because of these practices is alleged to greatly outweigh the admitted harms to nonhumans). As or more often, however, the justification of the harms to and killing of nonhuman animals is, simply said, an outright denial of any value to the lives of the nonhuman experimental subjects. Such rationalizations of killing and other serious harms remain largely unquestioned today in mainline science, education, and government circles (Waldau 2001, 2006, 2011, 2013, and 2016).

Such attention to harms can also produce important insights about the most familiar of nonhuman beings today, namely, the 'domesticated animals' traditionally referred to as 'pets' and more recently as 'companion animals'. These animals—mostly dogs, cats, and horses, but also rabbits, birds, pigs, rats, mice, guinea pigs, and *dozens* of other species as well—are so familiar to their owners that they are often referred to as family members. This verbal habit is, of course, not accurate biology, but it nonetheless effectively signals to any listener that the speaker takes such beings seriously.

Owned companion animals in modern, industrialized societies are, to be sure, increasingly protected, although by no means fully so. Stray dogs, cats, horses, and on and on are not, however, well protected today, and the First Precept clearly has much to say about the intentional killing of so many unowned, unwanted, and 'feral' members of this 'companion animal' group. Consider dogs, for example—of the roughly one billion dogs alive today, only about one quarter fit into the common paradigm of an owned animal living with a human family (Coppinger and Coppinger 2016). The number killed intentionally each year around the world simply for want of a good home is unknown, although it surely reaches into the tens of millions.

The First Precept speaks not only to such intentional killing, but also to the intentional cruelties visited upon owned and unowned animals in this familiar category—the problem of intentional cruelty in contemporary societies is nominally addressed by anti-cruelty laws, but such laws are inconsistently enforced on owned animals and rarely apply to the hundreds and hundreds of millions of feral dogs, cats, and other nonhuman animals that roam the Earth today.

The First Precept has particular relevance to another major animal category that modern anti-cruelty laws do not focus on in *any* effective way at all, namely, the vast category of free-living individuals and communities that we traditionally group under the term 'wildlife'. In its proscription of killing, the First Precept is simply remarkable in its directness *and scope* regarding these animals. This is significant because the other categories—entertainment animals, food animals, research animals, and companion animals—are *constructed* categories integrally connected to human uses and needs. The question of nonhuman animals that live in their own communities and which are not integral parts of human uses and ownership is important for another reason—these free-living individuals and communities are in peril today. This group of animals has, as a category, suffered extraordinary devastation in the last few centuries, a fact which is poignantly captured not only by the current crisis of extinctions of nonhuman species but also by the comment of a respected Canadian naturalist regarding '[the] massive diminution of the entire body corporate of animate creation ... species that still survive as distinct life forms but have suffered horrendous diminishment' (Mowat 1996: 14).

The First Precept, then, prompts powerful questions about human choices that ignore fundamental moral issues involved in killing. It challenges the penchant today to use strictly utilitarian calculations to evaluate the use and abuse of nonhuman animals as resources that benefit humans rather than as fellow citizens of the larger community.

Animal Rights and Other Animals

It is hard to miss that the remarkable sensibilities toward nonhuman animals discussed above promote a way of living that is consonant with certain key features of modern animal protection sentiments. This worldwide movement is diverse in many ways, and goes under a variety of names other than 'animal protection' and 'animal rights', including 'animal welfare', 'anticruelty', and 'animal liberation' (Singer 1975). Animal protection in its modern forms is supported today by many academic disciplines such as animal law, animals and religion, animal studies, human–animal studies, anthrozoology, critical animal studies, and more (Waldau 2013). Yet, the focus of animal protection organizations around the world remains, relative to the First Precept, strikingly narrow. The target animals belong to perhaps several thousand species from the almost 5,000 species of mammals, 10,000 species of birds, and perhaps a thousand or fewer additional species drawn from amphibians, reptiles, fish, and insects. There are, to be sure, forms of ethics such as 'environmental ethics' or 'bioethics' that can, at times, go beyond macro animals and some of the most charismatic insects (such as monarch butterflies), but even these broad-minded efforts address only a small percentage of the Earth's millions and millions of species. In fact, much environmental protection is so pitched to human-level concerns that it would not be unusual if someone concluded that this large movement remains, on the whole, a human-centred enterprise.

'Animal rights' and its many synonyms, then, today carry multiple meanings developed over the last two centuries as modern humans have explored the ethically charged intersection of human and nonhuman lives (Waldau 2011). These meanings characteristically invoke moral values, but also call upon legal concepts and tools, such as specific legal rights for individuals and broader legislative prohibitions of certain acts considered, for example, to be cruel. 'Animal rights' (using this term as a generic description of all animal protection efforts), then, has had a noteworthy impact around the world since the 1970s, namely, increased awareness that, in turn, has prompted a constantly expanding series of discussions about how traditional and new ethical visions might respond to human impacts on non-human living beings. One option that has become well known because of Buddhists, Jains, small-scale/indigenous societies, and various secular movements is quite close to the spirit of the First Precept; namely, bringing certain nonhuman animals into the centre of ethical discussion, thereby moving away from an exclusive focus on humans. Another option has been to study the fact that some ancient cultures (and, yet again, in this matter the Buddhist tradition offers a paradigmatic example) have long insisted that the human–nonhuman intersection *necessarily* raises ethical concerns of the highest order.

While noteworthy results of the animal protection movement include the enactment within many societies of more protective laws and the emergence of forms of education that again take seriously humans' obligations to the more-than-human world, the impacts of today's increased awareness of problems at the human–nonhuman intersection go much further. There is today, for example, a renaissance in many of the ethical circles around the world, and this is particularly true within the Euro-American sphere that had for centuries featured radically human-centred accounts of the prized human abilities to care about 'others' that we name with terms like 'ethics' and 'morality'. Both an effect of this renaissance, but also a force pushing it further forward, has been engagement with the Buddhist tradition and, of course, the tradition's long-standing ethical inclusiveness regarding nonhuman animals. Such comparative and cross-cultural work, by which the extraordinary achievements of many different cultures and religious traditions are considered in relation to one another, has prospects of helping everyone see the different ways that extending ethics across the species line can produce valuable insights about the ethical challenges that humans face on a daily basis.

Consider whether animal rights (in the generic sense of animal protection) offers *additional* insights that, in turn, help the Buddhist tradition see further possibilities in its own profound commitment to the First Precept. A minor example opens this issue up nicely. One possible clarification of certain commitments not to kill another living being is recognition that in macro-to-macro animal encounters, harms to others may in some circumstances be a practical necessity, as in matters of self-defence or protection of one's extended family. Killing one's attacker in such cases may be the only way to stop the attack, and many have argued that killing as a last resort in such situations should not be completely proscribed for the moral being. Buddhists could answer, however, that in some cases when the Buddha in a past life was a nonhuman animal, he intentionally chose to sacrifice his life, although this was often for the sake of others rather than merely to stop an attack—similarly, Sutta 145 in the *Majjhima Nikaya* includes advice given by the Buddha to Punna that illustrates a similar nonviolent response to a threat of violence (Nanamoli and Bodhi 1995: 1117–1119).

This minor problem is overshadowed by profoundly more complex issues that arise because of fundamental limitations in our abilities to discern other living beings' individual and social realities. Humans struggle when considering such realities of their fellow species members, and all the more so regarding the actual realities of nonhuman animals who often have different sensory abilities and radically different modes of communication and perception. Further, consider another feature of the micro/macro problem. An unnoticed aspect of humans' finite ethical capacities is our inability to identify, let alone control, the trials and tribulations which our daily choices visit upon countless living beings invisible to humans. Aided by technology, such as microscopes, developed since the late seventeenth century, we know that our everyday world is populated by very small living beings whose lives are unimaginably different than those of the macro animals with which we are much more familiar. In daily life where a macro animal acts in ways that often kill micro animals on, in, and near the macro individual, there is no easy way to follow the First Precept. The First Precept remains powerful, of course, as a guide for humans' treatment of their fellow 'macro' animals. In this familiar domain, it offers a powerful critique of many intentional killings that occur in today's industrialized world. It is also directly relevant to the profound harms caused by holding other macro animals captive or disrupting or destroying the habitats of nonhuman communities. The upshot of such increased knowledge about the multiple ways that human choices create suffering and death for other living beings, both macro and micro, is that every ethical tradition today faces new challenges to respond in caring, nuanced ways that take account of what today is clearly known about the realities and abilities of humans' innumerable and often unseen nonhuman neighbours in local communities as well as those in our larger, shared Earth community.

Balances to Strike

Plumbing the implications of Buddhist views of nonhuman animals must go beyond the important step of lauding Buddhists' obvious concern for living beings outside the human species. In fact, as one encounters a justifiable excitement evident in scholars impressed by the deep commitment Buddhists asserted from the beginning of the tradition about the importance of refraining in daily life from killing other living beings, something akin to a balancing act is needed. A too heavy focus on the positive achievements, while understandable in today's world so starved of major ethical sources focusing on nonhuman animals, can obscure other, altogether relevant features of the tradition. For example, even a cursory review of Buddhist scriptures makes it clear that Buddhists at times acquiesced to harmful practices that fall short of death (discussed below regarding elephants), and thereby failed to notice serious harms that held centre stage in the societies in which the Buddhist tradition was born. As noted below, when attention is given to the non-lethal harms suffered by certain nonhuman animals as part of widespread, Buddhist-sanctioned practices, a full and fair evaluation of Buddhist attitudes towards nonhuman animals, especially in terms of ideas and values advanced by modern animal rights advocates, includes questions about whether Buddhist attitudes to certain non-lethal harms were consistent with the spirit and driving insights of the remarkable foregrounding of the First Precept's injunction to avoid intentional killing.

As we attempt such a balancing act, a crucial feature of the Buddhist tradition must be given due consideration, for it is strikingly different in spirit from that which drives a foundational value evident in contemporary animal rights discussions. Buddhists were not, as are today's animal protectionists, concerned to inventory the world. A listing of other animal species, a search for other animals' true abilities and realities, a dispassionate description of what humans can claim to *really* know about other animals—such familiar achievements are eminently those of a passionate, ethical disposition working hand in glove with the best of the dispassionate methods of the modern scientific search for truth. Because Buddhists were not motivated by a science-driven outlook or mentality, one risk to consider, then, is whether it is anachronistic to ask how an ancient religious tradition dealt with concerns framed in terms drawn from discussions developed millennia later.

Modern Animal Rights

A worldwide movement today replete with diverse ideas that rival the diversity evident across Buddhism's sub-traditions, the animal protection movement has fostered many important insights with impressive consequences that are different than the spirit and achievements of the First Precept. Yet because both movements are ethically charged, these two human achievements have some remarkably interesting overlaps. Neither movement exhausts the insights available to humans who recognize the importance of, first, noticing other animals and, second, then taking them seriously.

Contemporary animal protection efforts are, like the Buddhist tradition, surprisingly mixed on the issue of fundamental protections for nonhuman animals. It is true that modern animal protection includes approaches that propose *fundamental* limits on killing nonhuman animals—in this feature, the modern movement has some overlap with the Buddhist First Precept. The worldwide animal protection movement today features an extraordinary range of efforts to abolish or ameliorate a number of the harms done intentionally to certain animals used in research, food production, entertainment, or to wildlife living in or near human communities. Both movements, then, foreground protections that shield certain interests of individual nonhuman individuals in ways that imply such interests are more important than humans' interests in using the protected nonhumans as mere resources.

But 'animal rights' (in the generic sense of animal protection) is not a uniform set of ideas and values any more than Buddhism is. Indeed, upon closer examination, 'animal rights' functions as an umbrella term under which sit, so to speak, several distinguishable notions, of which four are listed here. 'Animal rights' includes, for example, both the notion of 'moral rights' for certain nonhuman animals and also the altogether distinct idea of '*legal* rights' for individual nonhumans of a small number of species (Dalal and Taylor 2014; Chapple 2014; Waldau 2011: 57–61; Keown et al. 1998). A third concept called 'animal welfare' must also be distinguished because, while it signals forms of animal protection that many people associate with the term 'animal rights', this term carries two dramatically different senses. There is a tepid sense of 'animal welfare', which is dissimilar from the kinds of animal protection associated with the First Precept or legal rights that shield a living being from serious harms. As I have written:

> [M]any people today use the idea of "animal welfare" to preserve human domination over certain animals. Some advocates of human superiority have rationalized

> humans' domination over other living beings by focusing on attempts to ameliorate in minor ways the terrible conditions that such domination creates for animals. Such rationalizations lead some to think that when we concede minor welfare improvements to farm animals or research animals, our domination of these animals is "gentler" or "less harsh", and thus ethically adequate. This version of "animal welfare" leads with the suggestion "let's improve their welfare" *but at the same time* maintains the right of humans to total domination as we do experiments on them or use them for food or resources. . . . When "animal welfare" comes to mean primarily that tough conditions for the animal are made better in some minor respect . . . the meaning of the word 'welfare' has been stretched so dramatically that is misleads . . . thus harming listeners' ability to make informed moral choices. (2011: 95–96)

Separating this tepid, weak sense of 'animal welfare' from the original, far more robust sense of 'animal welfare' helps immensely with the task of illuminating the sentiments expressed in the First Precept. I continued:

> The more substantial idea of welfare involves the animals' freedom from harms like captivity and pain, as well as the freedom to move around. When any of these important freedoms is violated, as it so often is when the minor sense of "animal welfare" prevails, there is very little true "welfare" that is being proposed . . . [as is the case when what prevails is] a more robust [animal welfare] concept along the lines of true moral protections for other animals because the latter matter in and of themselves. (2011: 95, 99)

There is significant overlap in a robust sense of 'animal welfare' and the Buddhist imperative so strongly stated in the First Precept. Modern animal protectionists who assert that killing other animals is morally problematic *and* also *live squarely within* the ethical spirit of such a commitment by conscientiously choosing forms of modern life that minimize harms to nonhuman animals (for example, ethical veganism) clearly have commitments that overlap with the commitments of Buddhists who work hard to live by the First Precept.

Comparing Animal Rights with Buddhist Views of Animal Protection

The modern animal rights movement has limits that can be used to reveal how powerful the insights are that undergird the First Precept. The modern movement does not, as a practical matter, offer all nonhuman animals protection. Characteristically, the nonhumans protected in early twenty-first-century animal protection efforts are either familiar animals (such as companion animals) or charismatic wildlife that is far away and not used in food or other economics-driven industries. In other words, the living beings focused on by major animal protection groups in the secular world comprise only a few hundred to a few thousand species of the millions upon millions of nonhuman animal species. The First Precept is not nearly so limited.

The narrowness of modern animal protection is in part explained by the youth of the modern, secular animal protection movement, which became a popular movement during the second half of the nineteenth century in certain western European countries. The early twenty-first-century version of this movement is considerably expanded, although its heavy concentration on owned companion animals *but far less often unowned or feral dogs and cats* reveals that many sectors of the modern animal protection movement remain an eminently human movement in the sense of protecting primarily the animals that humans have domesticated and still dominate. In an altogether different sense as well, the modern animal protection movement reflects 'human' features because it uses techniques of change developed in modern civil rights movements (such as efforts to secure law-based protections, and especially legal rights held by certain individuals but by no means all nonhuman animals, as a way to promote changes in social morality). Additionally, the secular animal protection movement faces many contemporary difficulties of the kind that arrive when the early stage of a revolution has to confront the challenges of sustaining initial successes—in this regard, the modern movement can be meaningfully contrasted with the maturity of Buddhist commitments evident in the First Precept.

Consider as well that many national versions of the modern animal protection movement foreground decidedly weak approaches, such as the human-centred form of 'animal welfare' described above that fails to protect nonhuman animals substantially from death or the great harms occasioned by confinement or loss of habitat. In this regard as well, modern animal protection can be *radically* different in tenor from the commitment driving the First Precept.

Finally, despite the emergence of committed individuals and organizations, to date no legal or national policy victories around the world have put in place protections matching either the absoluteness or the scope of the First Precept commitment.

Less Flattering Similarities and Comparisons

The comparisons above illuminate well the achievement that is the First Precept. But there are other features of Buddhist attitudes towards other animals that are not so impressive as the First Precept. Throughout the early Buddhist scriptures, there is a pronounced tendency to distinguish *and elevate* humans above nonhumans. This gambit at times gives Buddhist approaches to the human–nonhuman intersection features that are not unlike those of the human-centredness that drives the weak sense of animal welfare noted above—in effect, human-centredness in each case fosters separation and a sense of superiority and privilege that militate against recognition of the obvious shared features between humans and other animals.

It is, nonetheless, decidedly obvious that Buddhists' background assumptions about all living beings clearly entail awareness of continuity (all animals, human and nonhuman alike, are subject to birth, death, karma, and constant rebirth). Continuity also appears in the views that dominate the modern animal rights movement because the movement relies heavily on scientific views anchored in evolutionary insights. For this reason, the animal protection movement highlights the fact that many nonhuman animals feature traits, such as emotions, intelligence, sentience, and suffering, that are typical of humans. Yet, even though both Buddhists and the modern animal protection movement recognize that humans and nonhumans are rightfully understood to belong in one category, each at crucial strategic points distinguishes humans from other animals in ways that produce human advantage and nonhuman disadvantage, such as human-generated harms.

The origins and psychological anchors of such dualisms are, of course, quite different. In the modern movement, the weaker 'welfarist' forms of 'protection' discussed above can be characterized as in the service of human privilege because while they assuage guilt by offering minor protections to nonhuman animals, their overall effect is to maintain human domination and major harms for the nonhuman animals used in food and research. The dualism in the Buddhist tradition prevails for deep-seated, complex reasons related to cultural heritage, just as do certain gender-based explanations that appear in many Buddhist sub-traditions. Whatever one's conclusion about why the 'humans versus nonhumans' dualism prevails in each case, the results are sometimes implicit, sometimes explicit human-centrednesses that foster human privilege and domination.

But an important qualification must be made. In the case of Buddhism, the division is, in practical terms, far less exceptionalist than the hard and fast divisions that dominate so many of the modern world's key domains—examples include (1) modern legal systems dominated by the dualism between humans as 'legal persons' and nonhumans as 'legal things' (Waldau 2016: 21ff.); (2) education, in which the primary non-science field is call 'the humanities'; (3) the ideas and values of modern economics, which dominate public policy circles, such that modern economists often make statements that parallel Leon Walras's classic contention that 'Man alone is a person; minerals, plants and animals are things' (Walras 1954: 62); and (4) mainline religious traditions that promote exclusivist ideas in the spirit of this startling claim made by a leading late-nineteenth century Catholic theologian:

> Brutes are as *things* in our regard: so far as they are useful for us, they exist for us, not for themselves; and we do right in using them unsparingly for our need and convenience, though not for our wantonness. (Rickaby 1888: 250, with emphasis in the original)

Buddhist circles do not exhibit such crass dualisms often, but like so many human values, there are distortions when power is institutionalized. An example of this phenomenon in Buddhism appears in the advice that senior Buddhist monks gave to the Sri Lankan king Duttagāmani when he expressed remorse about the great loss of human life during war:

> That deed presents no obstacle on your path to heaven. You caused the deaths of just one and a half people, O king. One had taken the Refuges, the other the Five Precepts

as well. The rest were wicked men of wrong views who died like (or: are considered as) beasts. (Gombrich 1988: 141)

Notice how fully this advice from key Buddhists (the monk advisors) contravenes both the spirit and letter, as it were, of the First Precept. Counting as *only* 'a half people' the individual who had taken only the Three Refuges (that is, in the Buddha, the *Dharma*, and the *Saṃgha*) *but not* the Five Precepts reveals, ironically, that while the Five Precepts were considered by the monks a defining aspect of adherence to the tradition, these monks ignored the substance of the very first of these foundational precepts by dismissing the deaths of many humans. They also ignored that the First Precept *clearly* applies to 'beasts'.

The modern institutionalized side of animal protection is also a place where, as has happened in other social movements, some of the deepest values of the social movement get watered down. The reasons are diverse, of course, but one surely is that the very compromises that bring political advantage also bring dilution of both the message and commitment that are far more apparent at the grass roots level. The modern animal protection movement continues to diversify, which will in some instances, no doubt, mean the movement's key insights will be watered down in order to secure various changes in public policy guiding government and education or the operative private policies of businesses. The result can be altogether mild versions of 'animal protection' that in reality curtail very little of industrialized societies' most entrenched practices favouring human advantage at the expense of nonhuman animals' most basic interests.

Seminal Dissimilarity and Challenge for Buddhism—Other Animals' Realities

The question 'what *are* other animals' capabilities?' is one that has, in a wide range of contexts, more power than its answer. Evidence-based and critically thought out answers are hard to develop for many reasons. These include many other animals' penchant for avoiding humans, as well as a set of ethical problems (such as harms) that are occasioned by merely attempting to remain in certain nonhuman animals' presence. Perhaps most challengingly, though, are the inherent difficulties of discerning elusive phenomena like intelligence, feelings, and other kinds of awareness in any living being.

There are at least three factors that make attempts to discern other animals' realities so relevant. The first is the common-sense proposition that the harms one causes by one's own intentional and unintentional actions are relevant to any evaluation of the ethical features of one's actions. The second factor is another common-sense proposition, namely, that other animals have their own realities that are distinguishable from humans' (mis)construction of these realities. The third factor is a historical trend—many human groups have not exhibited a serious commitment to inquiring about other animals' realities. A salient consequence of this refusal has all too often been a facile dismissal of such realities. Absence of evidence about other animals has been, tragically (for other animals, but also for the human community), taken to be *evidence of the absence of important traits in other animals* that are similar to, perhaps even compete with, some of the special abilities characteristic of humans like intelligence, rich communication systems, complex social lives, tool-making, and emotions.

Evaluation of Buddhist attitudes towards and claims about other animals suffers from a particular disadvantage. As happened regularly with ancient traditions, writings given an honoured place had purposes entirely unrelated to inventory-like listings of other animals or reality-based descriptions of their lives. Such inventories are, to be sure, the stock and trade of sciences, not religious traditions—but as shown in my *The Specter of Speciesism: Buddhist and Christian Views of Animals*, Buddhists did in fact know some very important features about other animals' lives (Waldau 2001: chs 6 and 7). But as one of the most respected scholars of Buddhism, Edward Conze, observed, 'the statements of Buddhist writers are not meant to be descriptive propositions about features of reality, but advice on how to act, statements about modes of behaviour, and the experiences connected with them' (1975: 16). He adds, '*If* one ... isolates the Buddha's statements from the task they intend to perform, *then* they become quite meaningless, and lose all their force' (1975: 17, emphasis added). Such points have been made by many other scholars of Buddhism as well, as with the following metaphor about the non-inventory nature of such writings coming from Étienne Lamotte: 'The Word of the Buddha has only one flavour (*rasa*): that of deliverance' (1991: 46).

It is important when assessing Buddhist materials that mention other animals to note such features, for while references can be quite revealing 'between the lines', what one can learn about other animals and their environment is limited by the important features of Buddhism invoked by Gombrich when he asserts, 'Buddhism as such is not about this world. Such spheres of human activity as the arts and sciences are not part of its concerns' (1991: 10). Buddhist comments about other animals, then, often have at best an *indirect* relationship to the particulars of nonhuman lives that an interested human observer can, if she wishes, discover by empirical investigation. Far more often, such comments reflect *not* a principal purpose of description of the animals mentioned, but, instead, existing conventions of discourse about the 'deliverance' or soteriological preoccupations of the tradition's founder.

Hence, a challenge arises. Given that Buddhist comments mentioning other animals are not primarily concerned with evaluation of this world and the particulars of the beings mentioned, how might one assess what appears to be Buddhist acquiescence to harmful practices that fall short of death?

Clearly relevant, too, are *intentions*, which were the focus of the historical Buddha's revolutionary understanding that the goodness or badness of an act was not primarily a by-product of the sequence of actions done in the proper order and form (as was emphasized by the then contemporary brahmanical religion), but, instead, a matter of intention. As Gombrich frames this key point, the Buddha ethicized the notion of karma, focusing on intention over a slavish compliance in pursuit of ritual correctness (1988: 46).

In the end, an evaluation of how Buddhists engage the important issues of intention and the crucial existential issue of deliverance requires that one ask about what

Buddhists knew, or with specific effort might have known, about other animals' realities. Harms to other animals may, for example, be based on grievously ill-informed opinions, such that serious harms glossed over by well-intentioned and deliverance-seeking Buddhists are easily identified by an outsider who has more familiarity with the subject animals. In some cases, one may notice that serious but ignored harms are readily discerned by *anyone* who is inclined to inquire. In such cases, frankness and scholarly integrity require one to be fair to *both* Buddhists and nonhuman animals. It is argued here that not only does such a test matter ethically, but also that such questions are important enough to permit one to run the clear risk of anachronism when discussing Buddhist views of nonhuman animals, for doing so allows one to assess background features of Buddhist ethics and related attitudes towards nonhuman animals. The question asked here about whether or not the practice in question produced discernible, intentionally inflicted harms is as fully diagnostic as any test can be of the depth and breadth of an ethical claim. This kind of analysis bringing a number of modern concerns to bear in assessing Buddhist attitudes towards animals must stay in full contact with Buddhists' clarion call to practise the First Precept, for the latter is equally a key diagnostic tool needed when assessing the nature and scope of Buddhist ethics in the matter of nonhuman animals.

The Diagnostic Question of Non-Lethal Harms

Consider the following line of argument about what might be cast as Buddhist acquiescence to clearly harmful practices that fall short of death. This question is asked in the spirit of helping twenty-first-century readers concerned to do justice to both Buddhists and nonhuman animals discern what is arguably a gap in Buddhist claims about humans in relationship to other animals.

In an extended passage about traits that make monks worthy of offerings, the Buddha employed the prevailing instrumental use of elephants in war as a background metaphor.

> When a king's bull elephant has gone to battle, if it is pierced by one volley of arrows, or by two, three, four, or five volleys, it sinks, founders, does not brace itself, and cannot enter battle.... Possessing these ... factors, a king's bull elephant is not worthy of a king. (Bodhi 2012: 751)

This reference to undesirable traits in an elephant is matched by other passages (Bodhi 2012: 752, 756) that suggest elephants used in warfare should endure wounds—this is what makes them worthy of being owned by a king.

> When a king's bull elephant has entered the battle, it patiently endures being struck by spears, swords, arrows, and axes ... Possessing these ... factors, a king's bull elephant is worthy of a king. (Bodhi 2012: 756)

In an indirect way, the lesson, although about monks, normalizes not only uses of elephants as instruments of war, but also great harms to the elephants as a by-product of human-on-human warfare. The harms to elephants, which obviously can be very severe, are treated as a by-product of being 'worthy of a king' (Waldau 2001: 132ff.). The normalization of harms and violence in the service of a human interest continues in this characterization of what is worthy in an elephant.

> And how is a king's bull elephant one who destroys? Here, when a king's bull elephant has entered battle, it destroys elephants and elephant riders, horses and cavalry, chariots and charioteers, and infantry. It is in this way that a king's bull elephant is one who destroys. (Bodhi 2012: 755)

While there are many passages in the Buddhist scriptures that make it clear that elephants were deemed important by Buddhists, given individualized names and titles of honour, and understood to be presences or at least images to which a Buddha could be compared, there are at least as many, and very likely more, passages that normalize humans' instrumental uses of elephants, including ones like the above passages in which elephants were held to possess qualities that make them fit possessions of a human king. Such images, while clearly conveying respect, also prompt the question of whether elephants were valued primarily *not* for their individual selves, but as tools and property. The challenge here is that the 'valuing' of elephants as tools and property is not openly considered as a source of grave ethical problems.

There is, beyond this first issue, a second one, which can be summarized as the cultural belief that enjoyment of the benefits of instrumental use of elephants is a *reward* for acting in accord with the moral norm that the Buddhist tradition held to be the key to reality and an ethical life. This belief is evident in a passage where the Buddha is in a teaching mode and commenting upon fishermen who have caught fish and are selling them. Addressing monks, he asks, 'Have you ever seen or heard that a fish dealer, killing fish and selling them, might, by means of this work and livelihood, travel around by elephant or horse ... or enjoy wealth or live off a large accumulation of wealth?' (Bodhi 2012: 875). The Buddha is clearly condemning the killing of living things, and he does so by pointing out that there are negative karmic consequences to such acts. In the background, though, is again an implicit sanctioning of utilitarian uses of elephants (and horses)—the fisherman do not get the *reward* of 'going about on an elephant'. The lesson about the problems of fisherman killing fish (and similar lessons are taught regarding killing of deer or holding food animals captive for later slaughter) reveals that there were *not* negative consequences to riding around on a captive elephant, which is clearly a reward for *good* acts. The subtext, as it were, is an acceptance of the propriety of instrumental use of elephants.

What is possible to discern *if one chooses to notice elephants and take them seriously* is that domestication of elephants is ethically *very* problematic because it involves harms that are completely obvious to even the casual observer, as can be easily discerned in a description of contemporary Thais breaking a young wild elephant.

> After tying it to a tree, men would poke and prod and beat it with sticks for days on end ... until the youngster quit lashing out at its tormentors and stood dazed and exhausted and wholly subdued. Once the animal stopped reacting, the men would start touching it with their hands rather than sticks, and, rather quickly, the animal accepted their dominion and became receptive to their demands. If it did not, it might have wounds inflicted in its neck and salt rubbed into them, then a rattan collar with embedded thorns placed around the neck to make the animal more responsive. (Chadwick 1994: 378)

This modern example involves an ancient technique, for as can be seen in Gotama's comment, domestication of elephants, which has always required this kind of domination, was already an old, established tradition in India when the Buddhist scriptures were composed.

Another specific example conveys that the intentional infliction of pain and torment does not stop once dominion has been established. Significant injuries and harms continue, and although they fall for obvious reasons short of death, they would certainly have been noticed in both early and later Buddhist communities.

> Some of the traditional methods of handling elephants in India are extremely harsh. To restrain a newly captured, wilful, or musth animal, its leg may be clamped in an iron hoop with inward-pointing spikes. The harder the animal strains against the device, the deeper the points bite. A long pole, called a *valia kole*, is used to prod the giant in the sensitive ankle and wrist joint while the handler keeps out of reach of the trunk and tusks. (Chadwick 1994: 297)

Beyond recognizing the intentional choices made to inflict pain and other suffering so as to dominate the captive elephant, it is important to convey how easy it is for any observer to recognize that the interests of a large, trainable, intelligent mammal are abridged by captivity. This is, however, particularly evident when humans eliminate the multiple dimensions of an elephant's fuller life, namely, the dimensions available to elephants growing up in the intensely social reality that is elephant society (Waldau 2001: 75–80).

The serious harms caused by such deprivation, as well as a context in which an entire Buddhist society supported the willingness to go along with such harms, are evident in the following modern example from Chadwick.

> And he rocked, constantly, tugging on chains that bound his legs to the slightly raised platform on which he stood.... [T]his bull was never let out of the pavilion.... So for decades now, he had been here on his raised dais, rocking, straining, surging back and forth with unfathomable power.... Forever alone. Colossal. And very likely insane. That was the message in those eyes: madness. (1994: 352–353)

This elephant's name was Pra Barom Nakkot. An irony, of course, is that this individual was an honoured elephant, chained because he was considered a white elephant, that is, he had, from the human vantage point, a distinctive appearance. (Pra Barom Nakkot would not to the ordinary observer have seemed white, but only lighter in colour than most elephants. The key features are seven traditional marks that range from the lighter coloured skin to gait, carriage, and overall shape [1994: 348].)

In terms that might be drawn directly from early twenty-first-century animal protection discourse, Pra Barom Nakkot was, as a *direct* consequence of his status with the Buddhist humans who captured him, deprived of any chance at a normal life. He was not allowed in any way whatsoever to grow into his potential for developed interests of the kind that wild-living elephants natively possess. He could not interact in the complex social network that characterizes all young elephants' lives. He did not have the chance to develop alongside his mother who possessed a large brain, was a member of complex social systems, had the ability to teach Pra Barom Nakkot to communicate in rich ways, and lived amid a longstanding social group full of experienced individuals (her own matriarchs).

True, Pra Barom Nakkot was given many human-bestowed names and titles such as 'he who will progress much among the elephants', and it was even claimed that he 'outranked' most humans, for he was said to be 'like the highest of princes' (1994: 352). Such names do not mention, of course, that Pra Barom Nakkot was reduced to a mere symbol, for he was a prisoner of a traditional belief that his presence augmented the power and prospects of the Thai royal family.

From ancient times, it has been suggested that human ownership of an elephant makes that individual unsocial and a psychological misfit (1994: 311). Human intervention distorts any captive nonhuman's reality, but elephants provide a particularly good example, as can be seen in the impoverished life given Pra Barom Nakkot that stands in contrast to the full social envelope that he would have had if he been allowed to live his own life. In summary, this individual elephant was not noticed as individual, and clearly was not taken seriously *for who he was in reality*. He was dominated, instead, so that he could be made into a contemporary example of a longstanding reality in Buddhist-influenced cultures, namely, acceptance of the morality of those practices that had the direct effect of overriding the interests of creatures like Pra Barom Nakkot in favour of human interests.

An Animal Rights Challenge—Illuminating but Partial

An animal rights-based advocate can, of course, question any passive acceptance of such non-lethal harms. As a practical matter, however, and for the reasons advanced above about the power of the First Precept, such a challenge to Buddhist practices can, in one sense, be only partial, for in the background *and clearly nearby* are not only the life-affirming values driving the First Precept, but also values about (i) non-suffering as a basic good, and (ii) the great importance of a human developing compassion and kindness. All of these values clearly favour the challenges that animal rights advocates make to so many different modern practices. But critical thinking and frank evaluation of equivocations and ethical blindnesses regarding severe non-lethal harms require that the tensions in Buddhist views about nonhuman animals be laid out fully and fairly. Further, since Buddhism is a living tradition, not merely one that long ago was set in stone by its early history, the *present* state of the tradition is crucial to consider—Buddhists today so evidently value many forms of life beyond the species line that it can be said that the First Precept's spirit continues to guide contemporary Buddhism. For these reasons alone, one can ask if specific practices that entail harms to elephants and other creatures are consistent with, or in tension with, the spirit of the insights that inform the First Precept. To do so honours the tradition as a *living* tradition relevant to contemporary problems of the kind that the animal protection movement attempts to rectify. On this basis, it is possible to suggest that Buddhists' proscription on killing of other living beings carries a spirit that also leads to the conclusion that treatment of the kind 'lavished' on Pra Barom Nakkot and other elephants is immoral.

Reprise: Challenges of Diversity in a More-Than-Human World

Balance is a particularly important ingredient as one reads contemporary scholarship engaging the Buddhist tradition. Such scholarship is, like scholarship about all long-standing religious traditions, very diverse. On the one hand, one encounters a justifiable excitement evident in scholars impressed by the deep commitment Buddhists assert from the very beginning of their religious tradition to the importance of refraining in daily life from killing other animals. Against the background of the harms done to non-human animals in so many places around the world over the last few centuries, such a commitment marks the Buddhist tradition as astonishing in its concern for other animals. Excitement about this impressive feature of the Buddhist tradition, however, has led some scholars to make very positive claims along the lines of '*in Buddhist texts animals are always treated with great sympathy and understanding*' (Story 1964: 6–7). Such an evaluation obscures, however, important features of the tradition that, if examined critically, reveal that, like all human cultures, Buddhists in ways eminently relevant to ethical inquiry have failed to notice much about other animals. This is not a criticism of Buddhist achievements as much as it is an observation that takes into account the better collective understanding of how humans can, through humility and much cross-cultural sharing, better inquire into the different ways that other animals' lives invite humans to notice them, take them seriously, and then use our considerable moral abilities to refrain from intentional harms to them—indeed, this invitation is what led early Buddhists to constantly foreground the First Precept.

The possibilities humans have of creating a *modus vivendi* that does not require harm to other animal individuals and their communities have become more evident for many reasons in the early twenty-first century. One reason, of course, is the emergence of science-based findings produced by those who have taken other animals seriously—such science makes it clear that in the early twenty-first century it is possible to know much more about various nonhuman animals than ancient Buddhists could possibly have known, but which contemporary Buddhists and their living tradition can appreciate.

The Question of an Overall View

Given the attention to nonhuman animals that one easily finds in Buddhist materials of all kinds, it is natural to ask about the place of individual living beings outside our own species in this deep and moving tradition. We can ask, in fact, a very personal version of that question—'how should someone convinced of the wisdom of the Buddhist tradition treat individuals from other species that exist in the world at this present moment?' What might a Buddhist who seeks to be true to her own tradition say about the place of either the most complex *or* the simplest living individuals, or the surviving elephants and nonhuman great apes in Africa and Asia? What might other Buddhists say about the morality of placing certain nonhuman animals in zoos and experimental labs? What might yet others suggest about the ethical significance of helping or harming the cetaceans off any coast away from terrestrial humans?

Clearly, because the Buddhist tradition from its inception has expressed significant ethical concerns regarding treatment of nonhuman animals as fellow voyagers in *saṃsāra*, it must be said that the Buddhist tradition gives nonhuman animals a special place. At the same time, however, there is abundant evidence to support the view that the tradition at many different turns in its sacred writings promotes a *negative*, even dismissive, view of nonhuman animals' existence. Indeed, I have argued previously that because the Buddhist scriptures feature 'a constant disparagement or belittling of any biological being outside the humans species, and that this deprecation is closely allied with the coarse grouping of all other animals in a single category', living beings outside our own species are often portrayed less than positively for a variety of reasons in the Buddhist tradition (Waldau 2001: 153–155):

1. Buddhists held 'a negative view of the very fact of birth as any kind of animal other than a human animal'.
2. 'The product of bad conduct is existence as an(other) animal.' Relatedly, Buddhist scriptures also feature what appears, under modern standards, to be a disparagement of 'those humans who are non-"standard", that is, who are impoverished, ugly, or handicapped in some way'.
3. The Buddhist scriptures feature the view that there is 'a kind of culpability in (other) animality'.
4. Any and all nonhuman animals were seen as 'simple and easily understood by humans' and thereby grouped together in ways that 'potentially limits adherents' ability to notice the realities of the more complex nonhuman animals'.
5. 'Other animals are pests or not rightfully in competition with elevated humans' and even 'anti-human', 'inhuman', and 'low by human standards'.

Sustaining such views are the Buddhist tradition's acceptance of a hierarchical understanding of the life/death/rebirth cycle that prevailed throughout the Indian subcontinent.

Whatever the motivating factors, the simple fact is that Buddhist scriptures often contain descriptions of nonhuman animals that are, on the whole, decidedly negative. Such negativity supported development of the view that 'in a most fundamental way, (other) animals' existence must be unhappy, for the ... realm comprised of all nonhuman animals is one of the places of woe to the Buddhist mind' (Waldau 2001: 154).

For ancient Buddhists, then, membership in the human species is a most important paradigm, with an even more important paradigm established by the Buddha's teachings on how humans can liberate themselves from the suffering that necessarily is part of even the elevated human predicament. An upshot of such teachings was that the tradition has never emphasized seeing other animals in terms of *their* realities. Rather, the dominant claims about other animals tended to the ideological, that is, to biases about other animals' limited natures. The predictable results were negative prejudgments about nonhuman animals' possibilities that are, to some human eyes *today*, underdetermined by observable facts. The modern scientific era has been, of course, a two-edged sword, for many science-based practices have led to great harms. The scientific tradition, however, has also provided extraordinarily detailed information about some other animals' intelligence, emotions, and social abilities. Science, with its heritage of inquiry and humility in face of humanity's long past of extravagant claims about our own superiority and beauty, has thereby helped our species develop antidotes to such claims, namely, approaches that permit each of us to determine our own personal views by reference to other animals' observable capabilities.

One of the possible benefits of linking the powerful compassion driven by the First Precept to the insights of the modern animal rights movement, then, is the benefit of the latter's emphases on careful investigations of the day-to-day lives of other living beings. To claim such is in no way to repudiate the earlier caveat that risks of anachronism *always* lurk in such comparative observations. Finally, suspicion about loose generalizations, whether positive or negative, about Buddhist views of nonhuman animals remains in order, for as already mentioned, 'About *all* Buddhists few valid generalizations are possible.'

Conclusion

On the diverse and morally fraught issue of 'other animals', then, considerable care must be taken when claiming any kind of unanimity for Buddhists. With care, however, it can be argued that there is agreement of a kind on the significance that individuals of other species have in the minds of Buddhists, for even the casual observer quickly learns that this tradition promotes a profound commitment to the primacy of ethical reflection in human life, and thus *the lives of nonhumans matter to anyone who considers herself to be a moral being.*

Therefore, the Buddhist tradition offers a profoundly moving example of humans' remarkably alive and capacious abilities to care beyond the species line. At the same time, Buddhist reflections on humans' relationship to other animals represent the daunting complexities human face as they try to live an ethical life. Human abilities are limited, as every human knows; furthermore, we have inherited imperfect evaluations of other living beings, whose lives, even when we are at our best, are hard to discern. In facing the complex, multifaceted challenges that arise regularly when a human desires not only to protect, but also to notice and take seriously, the living beings outside our own species, Buddhists have not solved those problems but they have clearly achieved much that demands respect and admiration.

Works Cited

Berry, T. (2006) Loneliness and presence. In: P. Waldau and K. Patton (eds), *A communion of subjects: animals in religion, science, and ethics*. New York: Columbia University Press, 5–10.

Bodhi, Bhikku (2012) *The numerical discourses of the Buddha: a translation of the Anguttara Nikaya*. Somerville, MA: Wisdom Publications.

Chadwick, D. H. (1994) *The fate of the elephant*. San Francisco: Sierra Club.

Chapple, C. K. (2014) Nonhuman animals and the question of rights from an Asian perspective. In: N. Dalal and C. Taylor (eds), *Asian perspectives on animal ethics: rethinking the nonhuman*. New York: Routledge, 148–168.

Conze, E. (1975) *Buddhism: its essence and development*. New York: Harper and Row.

Coppinger, R., and Coppinger, L. (2016) *What is a dog?* Chicago: University of Chicago Press.

Dalal, N., and Taylor, C. (2014) *Asian perspectives on animal ethics: rethinking the nonhuman*. New York: Routledge.

Gombrich, R. (1988) *Theravada Buddhism: a social history from ancient Benares to modern Colombo*. London and New York: Routledge.

Gombrich, R. (1991) The Buddhist way. In: H. Bechert and R. Gombrich (eds), *The world of Buddhism: Buddhist monks and nuns in society and culture*. London: Thames and Hudson, 9–14.

Horner, I. B. (1967) *Early Buddhism and the taking of life*. The Wheel Publication, No. 104. Kandy, Ceylon: Buddhist Publication Society.

Keown, D. (1995) *Buddhism and bioethics*. London: Macmillan.

Keown, D., Prebish, C., and Husted, W. (1998) *Buddhism and human rights*. Surrey: Curzon.

Kurokawa, K., et al. (2007) Comparative metagenomics revealed commonly enriched gene sets in human gut microbiomes. *DNA Research*, 14 (4), 169–181.

Lamotte, E. (1991) The Buddha, his teachings and his saṅgha. In: H. Bechert and R. Gombrich (eds), *The world of Buddhism: Buddhist monks and nuns in society and culture*. London: Thames and Hudson, 41–58.

McDermott, J. P. (1989) Animals and humans in early Buddhism. *Indo-Iranian journal*, 32 (4), 269–280.

Mowat, F. (1996) *Sea of slaughter*. Shelburne, VT: Chapters Publishing.

Nanamoli, Bhikku, and Bodhi, Bhikkhu (1995) *The middle length discourses of the Buddha: a translation of the Majjhima Nikaya*. Boston, MA: Wisdom Publications.

Norman, K. R. (trans.) (1984) *Sutta Nipāta*. Oxford: Pali Text Society.

Rhys-Davids, Mrs (trans.) (1922) *The Book of the Kindred Sayings (Saṃyutta-Nikāya) or Grouped Suttas*. Pali Text Society's Translation Series No. 10. London: Oxford University Press.

Rickaby, J. (1988) *Moral philosophy*. London: Longmans, Green.

Schmithausen, L. (1991a) *Buddhism and nature: the lecture delivered on the occasion of the EXPO 1990—an enlarged version with notes*. Tokyo: The International Institute for Buddhist Studies.

Schmithausen, L. (1991b) *The problem of the sentience of plants in earliest Buddhism*. Tokyo: The International Institute for Buddhist Studies.

Singer, P. (1975) *Animal liberation: a new ethics for our treatment of animals*. New York: New York Review of Books/Random House.

Story, F. (1964) *The place of animals in Buddhism*. Kandy, Ceylon: Buddhist Publication Society.

Waldau, P. (2001) *The specter of speciesism: Buddhist and Christian views of animals*. New York: Oxford University Press.

Waldau, P. (2011) *Animal rights*. New York: Oxford University Press.

Waldau, P. (2013) *Animal studies—an introduction*. New York: Oxford University Press.

Waldau, P. (2016) Second wave animal law and the arrival of animal studies. In: D. Cao and S. White (eds), *Animal law and welfare—international perspectives*. New York: Springer, 11–43.

Waldau, P., and Patton, K. (eds) (2006) *A communion of subjects: animals in religion, science, and ethics*. New York: Columbia University Press.

Walras, L. (1954) *Elements of pure economics or the theory of social wealth*, trans. W. Jaffe from the 1883 edition of *Elements d'economie politique pure*. London: George Allen and Unwin.

Suggested Reading

Chapple, C. K. (2014) Nonhuman animals and the question of rights from an Asian perspective. In: N. Dalal and C. Taylor (eds), *Asian perspectives on animal ethics: rethinking the nonhuman*. New York: Routledge, 148–168.

Dalal, N., and Taylor, C. (2014) *Asian perspectives on animal ethics: rethinking the nonhuman*. New York: Routledge.

Keown, D., Prebish, C., and Husted, W. (1998) *Buddhism and human rights*. Surrey: Curzon.

Story, F. (1964) *The place of animals in Buddhism*. Kandy, Ceylon: Buddhist Publication Society.

Waldau, P. (2001) *The specter of speciesism: Buddhist and Christian views of animals*. New York: Oxford University Press.

Waldau, P., and Patton, K. (eds) (2006) *A communion of subjects: animals in religion, science, and ethics*. New York: Columbia University Press.

Index

969 movement 472

Abhidhamma/Abhidharma 10, 22, 51, 55, 163–164, 167, 171–173, 177, 179, 345, 367, 368, 375, 519, 640–641, 643
abortion 288–289, 403, 438, 459, 468–469, 572, 592–609
Ajita Kesakambalī 8, 65
Ājīvikas
Ambedkar, B. R. 137, 419, 428, 480, 481, 483, 496–497, 509, 521–523, 524, 525
anarchism 413, 418, 420, 422, 428
Angulimala Trust 401
Annen 30, 38, 39, 40, 44–46
Anscombe, Elizabeth 366
antinatalism, Buddhist 572–578
antinomianism 238, 252, 253–254, 567, 583, 633
Aquinas, Thomas 326
arahant 10, 14, 15, 24, 38, 56, 58, 61, 67–68, 78, 81, 83–85, 89–93, 135, 141, 143, 158, 332, 360, 463, 553, 561, 631–632, 633, 634–636, 637, 639, 646, 647
arhat. See *arahant*
Aristotle 317, 322, 324, 326, 330, 332, 373, 374, 407, 424, 521, 546
Ariyaratne, A. T. 480, 492, 531
Āryadeva 166, 391
Asaṅga 251, 337–338, 340, 350, 351, 352, 502, 560, 561, 562, 581, 583
Aśoka 124, 261, 392–393, 399, 402, 418, 455, 466, 482, 501
Aśvaghoṣa 251, 255, 257, 560
Atiśa 252, 256, 257, 502
Aung San Suu Kyi 395, 481, 484, 488, 531
Avadānas 84, 85, 88–89, 91
Avalokiteśvara bodhisattva 231, 296. *See also* Guanyin bodhisattva

Bankei 240
Bentham, Jeremy 521
Berry, Wendell 426–427, 428
Bhāvaviveka 164–165
Bhavideva 251, 255
Bhavyakirti 461–462
bodhisattva 17, 29–48, 81, 85–88, 135, 138–158, 162, 163, 167, 169, 171, 193, 206–207, 210–213, 215–220, 232, 248, 250, 256, 279, 280, 281–282, 286, 287, 323, 325, 329–331, 335–336, 339, 348, 393, 465, 467, 468, 486, 487, 489, 490, 502, 521, 543, 548, 561, 571, 578, 580–581, 583, 586
Boundless Qualities 337–355
Bourdieu, Pierre 416, 428
Brahmanism 7, 8, 60, 87, 253, 387, 396, 471, 563, 570, 571, 664. *See also* Hinduism
Bruno, Giordano 417, 422
Buddhadasa Bhikku 57, 266, 268, 418, 520, 537–538, 624–625
Buddhaghosa 9, 52, 54, 55, 70–71, 98, 127, 338–344, 346–347, 350, 351, 354–355, 463, 570, 596, 597, 600, 602–604, 615
Buddha-nature 38–39, 40, 48, 206, 219, 224–227, 235–236, 238, 281, 290, 325, 328, 394, 401, 439, 460, 472, 492, 519, 541, 545–547
Buddha's Light International Association 286, 287, 481
Buddhist Global Relief 440, 506, 507
Buddhist Peace Fellowship 240, 433, 440, 503, 504

Candrakīrti 164–165, 166, 167, 378, 391
capital punishment 398, 401, 402, 466, 467, 469, 470
capitalism 263, 268, 280, 286, 296, 387, 408–419, 420, 423, 425, 427–428, 484, 511

Cārvāka school 422
caste 24, 88–89, 387–388, 402, 471–472, 480, 483, 485, 486, 501, 502, 509, 520, 522, 523, 524
Chan. *See* Zen sects
Chekawa Yeshe Dorje 348
Cheng Yen 282, 285, 481, 487–488, 489, 498
Christian ethics 13–14, 151, 231, 238, 326, 417, 442, 447, 485, 507, 578, 593, 639, 664
communism 296, 387, 394, 408, 411, 419, 420, 423, 464, 497, 537. *See also* Marxism, socialism
Confucianism 221, 223, 234–235, 238, 240, 279, 280, 281, 282, 286, 287, 291, 535
consumerism 267, 275, 276, 286, 290, 418–419, 420, 421, 422, 424–425, 433, 438, 440, 442–448, 449, 505, 538
critical Buddhism 238, 420

Dalai Lama, Vth 468
Dalai Lama, XIVth 130, 137, 140, 149, 162, 298, 304, 309–310, 398–399, 453–454, 458, 468, 480, 481, 489–490, 492, 493, 495, 515, 531, 543, 544, 585, 586, 598, 615–616, 617, 619–620, 632, 639
Daochuo 190, 195, 199
Daoism 223, 279, 280, 281, 287, 291
Daojin 36–37
Daoxuan 33, 126
Darwin, Charles 522–524
Democritus 422
dependent origination 52, 53, 61, 66, 79, 145, 147, 164, 238, 255, 290, 328, 332, 348, 361, 375, 378, 433, 443, 493, 520, 522, 541–542, 547, 556, 558–559, 563, 569, 618
Descartes, René 362
Dewey, John 521–525
Dhammakāya movement 275
Dharma Drum Mountain 288, 481, 484
Dharma Geeks 504, 518
Dharmaguptaka school 33, 96, 116–132, 224, 228, 637
Dharmakīrti 361, 362, 365–375, 378–379
Dharmakṣema 34, 35, 36
Dharmarakṣita 348
Dōgen 221, 222, 223, 224–227, 228, 229, 230, 235, 236, 239, 242, 545–546
Drakpa Gyaltsen 256

Eightfold Path 1, 26, 51, 63, 81–84, 142, 228, 320, 321–323, 325, 388–389, 413, 424–425, 436, 491, 502, 512
Eisai 221, 227–230, 236, 239
emptiness 48, 146, 147, 154, 162–163, 166–174, 201, 216–217, 223, 226, 230, 254–256, 328, 377, 460, 464, 468, 562, 563
Engaged Buddhism 136–138, 149–158, 196, 212, 239–242, 266–270, 280, 284, 294, 387, 419, 433, 436, 440, 472–473, 479–498, 501–525, 532. *See also* Humanistic Buddhism
Engels, Friedrich 422
Epicureanism 417, 422
Epicurus 412, 417, 422, 425
euthanasia 459, 468–469, 611–627

Falungong 281
Faxian 126
Fazang 45
Five Precepts 1, 30–31, 56, 59, 79–80, 142, 221–223, 225, 231, 268, 273, 274–275, 280, 282, 287, 331, 332, 438, 515, 540–541, 547, 592, 600, 601, 615, 652–663, 668–669
Foucault, Michel 247, 250, 294, 295–296, 567, 568, 572, 574, 579, 584, 588
Four Boundless Qualities. *See* Boundless Qualities
Four Noble Truths 52, 54, 62, 64, 65, 66, 77, 79, 81–83, 84, 91, 92, 167–168, 177, 328, 332, 377, 425, 436, 443, 491–492, 502, 503, 507, 509, 547, 619
Francis, Pope 445
Free Tibet movement 504
Fujii Nichidatsu 473–474

Gadamer, Hans-Georg 319–320, 322
Gampopa 347–348, 585
Gandhi, Mahatma 157, 305–306, 418, 457, 473–474, 480, 483, 493, 535
Ganjin 37
Gelug school 178–179, 468
Gelukpa. *See* Gelug school
Goenka, S. N. 508
Gorampa 164, 257
Gross National Happiness 262, 433, 447
Guanyin bodhisattva 43, 206, 210–211, 218, 219, 230–231, 280, 281, 489, 492, 561. *See also* Avalokiteśvara

Guṇavarman 33, 34, 35, 125–126
Gyōki 34
Gyōnen 502

Hakuin 230, 234, 235–236
Hanshan 242
Heidegger, Martin 509
hierarchy 78, 90, 131, 232, 235, 271. *See also* caste
Hinduism 246, 253, 255, 388, 391, 399, 458, 462, 495, 496, 535, 537, 570, 654. *See also* Brahmanism
Hōkū 44
homosexuality 287–288, 567, 573, 575, 577, 578, 584–586, 587–588
Hōnen 185, 187, 193, 195
Hsing Yun 283, 287, 289–290, 484
Huayan sect 32, 45, 436, 437
Huisi 43
Humanistic Buddhism 280–281, 289–290, 481, 484, 497–498
Hume, David 173, 326, 327, 329, 353, 362, 376, 542
hungry ghosts 16, 19–20, 23, 41, 156, 188
Hye Ch'o 399

Ichikawa Hakugen 235–238
Imakita Kōsen 235
inequality 236, 284, 285–286, 352, 414, 502
intention 1, 8–10, 12, 14, 15, 25, 32, 42, 47, 55, 79, 83, 89–92, 142, 145, 152, 154, 157–158, 180, 197, 198, 200, 214–215, 231–232, 249, 272, 283, 288, 291, 330, 331, 332, 346, 366, 388, 417, 440, 446, 459, 460, 463, 464, 475, 491, 504, 555, 558, 574, 575, 576–578, 585, 591, 613–615, 616, 621–622, 631, 632, 634, 636, 640–641, 642, 643, 644, 646, 652, 655, 657, 658, 659, 663, 664–665, 667, 669
International Network of Engaged Buddhists 256, 433, 440, 484, 501, 504

Jainism 7, 8, 53, 60, 68, 78, 80, 119, 393, 466, 471, 580, 654, 657
Jamgön Kongtrül Lodrö Tayé 257
*Jātaka*s 81, 84–89, 141, 310, 335–336, 392, 398, 403, 432, 438, 554–555, 557, 561, 573, 639
Jewish ethics 442, 507
Jitsudō Ninkū 42, 43
Jizō bodhisattva 288, 469
Jobs, Steve 507–508, 510
Jōdo Shinshū. *See* Shin sect
Jungto Society 481

Kagyu sect 304
Kamalaśīla 165, 172, 343
Kannon. *See* Guanyin bodhisattva
Kant, Immanuel 231, 318, 353, 363–365, 367, 372–374, 541
Karmapa, XVIIth 130, 304, 309
Kerouac, Jack 507
Khenpo Jigmé Phuntsok 296, 299, 300, 307
Khenpo Ngawang Pelzang 338, 342
Khenpo Rigdzin Dargyé 295, 308–309
Khenpo Tsultrim Lodrö 297–298, 300–304, 307
Kierkegaard, Søren 231
killing 11, 12, 18, 25, 30, 31, 32, 34, 35, 38, 40–44, 47, 56, 201, 230, 231–232, 253, 254, 268, 284, 288, 289, 290, 298, 302, 329, 388, 395, 400, 402, 403, 441, 442, 457, 458–468, 475, 485–486, 515, 516, 518, 545, 581. *See also* abortion; capital punishment; euthanasia; suicide
King, Martin Luther, Jr. 148, 157, 457, 473
Kiyozawa Manshi 185, 202
*kōan*s 230–231
Kokan Shiren 229–230
Kuanyin. *See* Guanyin bodhisattva
Kūkai 482
Kumārajīva 35

Lalitavajra 257
Larung Buddhist Academy 293–295, 296, 297, 299–304, 307, 308, 310
Ledi Sayadaw 59, 62–63, 64
Lenin, V. I. 422
Leopold, Aldo 441
Lhakar movement 295, 304–306, 308, 310
Linji 237
Locke, John 323, 361
Lucretius 417, 422
Luxemburg, Rosa 414–415
Lyotard, Jean-François 325

Madhyamaka school 147, 162–180, 361, 368, 374–379, 544–545, 547. *See also* Prāsaṅgika school; Svātantrika school

Maha Ghosananda 474, 480, 491, 493, 531
Mahāsāṃghika school 96, 98, 101, 114
Mahāsī Sayadaw 519
Mahāvīra 53
Mahīśāsaka school 96, 118, 636, 637
Maitreya Buddha/bodhisattva 38, 200, 206, 210, 211, 279, 287, 337–338, 340, 350, 351, 352, 393, 455
Mañjuśrī bodhisattva 38, 210, 211, 465, 468
Mao Zedong 281, 295, 296, 304
Marx, Karl 407, 412, 413–414, 419, 421–423, 425, 426, 428
Marxism 238, 408, 411, 414–415, 419, 421–423
Menzan Zuihō 227
merit transfer 16–17, 147, 157–158, 198, 270, 274, 288, 503, 521
Metta Forest Monastery 506
Mill, John Stuart 412–413, 521
mindfulness 7, 10, 26, 52, 55, 57–67, 81–82, 142, 145, 151, 239, 241, 264, 346, 388, 417, 433, 446–447, 448, 449, 487, 492, 504, 510–519, 569
Mindfulness Based Stress Reduction 510–511, 512, 513, 515
Minling Lochen 257
Mipham Rinpoche 340
Moore, G. E. 326
Mūlasarvāstivāda school 96, 116, 117–123, 127–131, 560, 562, 637
Murdoch, Iris 350–351
Musō Soseki 236

Nāgārjuna 162, 163–164, 166, 361, 375–378, 396–397, 400, 464, 501, 508, 638
Ngari Panchen 257
Nhat Hanh, Thich 136, 137, 149, 154, 155, 212, 239–240, 241–242, 280, 387, 418, 433, 436, 437, 473, 474, 480, 481, 484, 485–487, 491, 492, 494–495, 501, 639, 642
Nichiren 216, 460, 473, 481
Nichiren sects 46, 212, 387, 428, 460, 473–474, 481, 501
Nipponzan Myōhōji 473–474, 481, 504
no self 79, 143, 146, 162, 163, 170, 176, 178–180, 323–324, 328, 329, 330, 332, 349, 359–362, 367, 375–379, 420, 424, 435, 443, 464, 487, 492–494, 536–537, 588, 601, 604, 631, 636, 640

Nyingma sect 257, 296, 304, 462

Order of Interbeing 149, 387
original awakening 224, 226

Patrul Rinpoche 148, 337, 339, 341, 342, 344, 346, 350, 351, 352, 585
poverty 136–137, 149, 150, 151–153, 156, 215, 236, 242, 265, 267, 285–286, 386–387, 395–396, 398, 419, 426, 433, 440, 480, 481, 482, 484, 488, 491–492, 495, 501, 502, 504, 507, 510, 521
Prāsaṅgika school 147, 164–169, 172–173, 175, 177
Prison Dharma Network 503
Pure Land(s) 17, 184, 187–192, 195, 199, 284, 289, 484
Pure Land sects 42, 46, 184–202, 285, 455, 501. *See also* Shin sect

realms of rebirth 7–9, 11, 15, 17, 19–21, 23–24, 30, 41, 42, 54, 55, 84–85, 143, 146, 156, 188, 201, 240, 280, 392, 398, 461, 463, 466, 570
Rennyo 201
Rinzai sect 227, 229–230, 232, 233, 240, 457
Risshō Kōseikai 210–211, 216–217, 481
Rongzom 256
Rorty, Richard 544, 545
Rousseau, Jean-Jacques 540
Ryōkan 242

Saffron Revolution 480, 495, 497
Saichō 38
Śaivism 253–254
Sakyadhita movement 484, 501, 504
Sakya sect 256
Sakya Pandita 256, 257
Samantabhadra bodhisattva 38, 210–211
Sangharakshita 509
Śaṅkarācārya 255
Śāntarakṣita 172
Santi Asoke movement 268–270, 272, 387
Śāntideva 17, 136, 137, 138–158, 162, 163, 169–180, 329, 341, 345–346, 347, 353, 354, 375, 508, 521, 542, 580–581, 582, 639
Sarvāstivāda school 10, 18, 19, 33, 35, 96, 101, 637

Sarvōdaya Śramadāna or Sarvodaya Shramadana movement 387, 480, 484, 488–489, 491, 492, 495, 501
Schumacher, E. F. 411–418, 423, 425, 426, 428
Se Chilbu Chokyi Gyaltsen 348
Sen, Amartya 412, 534
Seno'o Girō 425
Shaku Sōen 457
Shandao 190–196, 198, 199, 201
Sheng Yen 288–289, 290–291, 484
Shingon sects 37
Shinran 185–186, 187, 195–202
Shin sect 185–186, 196–198, 201–202, 455
Shinto 598, 624
Shōtoku 43–44
Sivaraksa, Sulak 212, 266, 387, 419, 428, 433, 497, 531
skilful means 143, 179, 207, 214–216, 230, 232, 239, 249, 251, 255, 282, 283, 287, 288, 329, 331–332, 335, 437, 438, 443, 444, 446, 447, 448, 449, 460, 462, 469, 503, 520, 521, 536, 581, 587
Smith, Adam 353
socialism 387, 413, 415–416, 418–419, 420, 457, 484, 523, 537. *See also* communism; Marxism
socially engaged Buddhism. *See* Engaged Buddhism
Socrates 320
Soga Ryōjin 202
Sōka Gakkai 281, 285, 387, 395, 481, 504
Sonshun 45
Sōtō sect 39, 224, 227, 229, 238, 240
Spinoza, Baruch 412, 417, 422, 425
Stoicism 326, 336
Sufficiency Economy 262–263
suicide 285, 309–310, 453–454, 458, 611, 612, 630–648. *See also* euthanasia
Suzuki, D. T. 229, 457
Suzuki Shōsan 231, 234, 235, 236, 240
Suzuki Shunryū 508
Svātantrika school 164–166, 172–173, 175, 177
systems theory 522–525

Taehyŏn 45
Taixu 280, 481, 484, 497
Takuan 234, 235, 239
Tanluan 190, 195
tantra 246–257, 461–463, 471, 561, 568, 573, 578, 582–583, 584, 586, 588, 652
Tārā bodhisattva 561
Tassajara Zen Mountain Center 508, 513
Teilhard de Chardin, Pierre 441
Tendai sect 29–30, 35–47, 212, 226, 228, 460
Ten Good Precepts 30, 31–32, 46, 142
Ten Oxherding Pictures 486
Thammayut Order 261
Thoreau, Henry David 422
Three Jewels 33, 35, 80, 84, 224, 225, 234, 248, 295, 333, 462, 472
Three Trainings 51, 52, 57, 67, 70, 502, 512
Tiantai sect. *See* Tendai sect
Tiep Hien movement. *See* Order of Interbeing
Tillich, Paul 509
Tolstoy, Leo 418, 457
Triratna Buddhist Community 484
Trungpa, Chögyam 148, 156, 508, 587
Tsongkhapa 164–166, 172, 178, 248, 257, 341, 343, 345, 346, 347, 348, 397, 581, 583, 585, 586
Tulku Tendzin Dargyé 302
two truths doctrine 164–166, 171–174, 367–368, 376–378, 544
Tzu Chi Association 282, 284–286, 290, 481, 487–488, 489, 498, 504

Universal Declaration of Human Rights 532, 538, 539–540, 543, 544, 547
U Ottama 456

Vajrapani bodhisattva 462
Vasubandhu 18, 32, 54–55, 345, 343, 346, 584, 586
vegetarianism 47, 286, 290, 297, 303, 304–305, 310, 432, 433, 444, 481, 497, 660
Vibhūticandra 256, 257

Wat Thammakai. *See* Dhammakāya movement
Weber, Max 260–261, 266, 269, 270–271, 274, 468, 522
White Lotus Society 455
Wisdom 2.0 Conference 514
Wittgenstein, Ludwig 325
Wuxue Zuyuan 239

Xuanzang 34, 35, 41
Xunzi 422

Yijing 33
Yin Shun 484, 497
Yogācāra school 23, 29, 30, 33, 34, 35, 41, 162, 172

Zen Peacemakers movement 503
Zen sects 39, 221–242, 285, 322, 325, 422, 432, 433, 437, 438, 439, 441, 449, 456, 457, 460, 480, 483, 486, 506, 507, 508, 510, 512, 513, 518, 519, 587, 624, 652. *See also* Rinzai sect; Sōtō sect
Zhanran 38
Zhiyi 39, 40, 41, 42, 43, 44, 45